PERFORMANCE

Satellit 1000 AM/FM/Shortwave

The Satellit 1000 has a distinct international flair, along with an elegant sense of design. Curious about what's happening in Great Britain or Greece? Shortwave radio is your way to tune in. And of course, you get the powerful sound and great reception that Grundig is known for. So whether you're tuning in to a station that broadcasts from around the corner or across the globe, you're assured of a clean, clear listening experience.

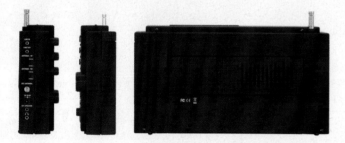

- Frequency Coverage: 100-30,000 KHz, includes shortwave, medium wave AM broadcast band and longwave; 76-90, 87-108 MHz FM broadcast band
- Digital Display: large 5.7 inch square, 240 x 320 pixel, dot matrix display. Shows all modes and selected functions
- Programmable Memories: 500 user programmable with alpha labeling plus 1200 user definable country memories, for a total of 1700
- Digital Phase Lock Loop (PLL) Synthesized Tuning with Direct Digital Synthesis (DDS) for drift-free frequency stability and finest tuning resolution
- Dual Conversion Superheterodyne Circuit: results in minimized interference through superior selectivity
- Excellent Sensitivity: yielding a true high-performance receiver

384.545302 PASSPOR 2008

Passport to world band radio

Receives AM Radio

Receives FM Radio

Receives Shortwave Radio

Alarm Clock

Headphone Jack

Grundig Radio Line By etón re_inventing radio www.etoncorp.com

2008 Passport to

TABLE OF CONTENTS

10

114

World Band Radio

TABLE OF CONTENTS

26

214

Cover: **"Rush Hour on Radio Road."** This is Gahan Wilson's 17th cover for IBS and 16th cover for PASSPORT TO WORLD BAND RADIO.

International Broadcasting Services, Ltd.

ISSN 0897-0157

OUR READER IS THE MOST IMPORTANT PERSON IN THE WORLD!

Editorial

Editor in Chief	Lawrence Magne
Editor	Tony Jones
Assistant Editor	Craig Tyson
Consulting Editor	John Campbell
Founder Emeritus	Don Jensen
PASSPORT REPORTS	Lawrence Magne, Dave Zantow; along with George Heidelman, George Zeller
WorldScan® Contributors	David Crystal (Israel), Alok Dasgupta (India), Graeme Dixon (New Zealand), Nicolás Eramo (Argentina), Paulo Roberto e Souza (Brazil), Alokesh Gupta (India), Jose Jacob (India), Anatoly Klepov (Russia), Célio Romais (Brazil), Nikolai Rudnev (Russia), David Walcutt (U.S.)
WorldScan® Software	Richard Mayell
Laboratory	J. Robert Sherwood
Artwork	Gahan Wilson, cover
Graphic Arts	Bad Cat Design; Mike Wright, layout
Printing	Transcontinental Printing

Administration

Publisher	Lawrence Magne
Associate Publisher	Jane Brinker
Offices	IBS North America, Box 300, Penn's Park PA 18943, USA; www.passband.com; Phone +1 (215) 598-9018; Fax +1 (215) 598 3794; mktg@passband.com
Advertising & Media Contact	Jock Elliott, IBS Ltd., Box 300, Penn's Park PA 18943, USA; Phone +1 (215) 598-9018; Fax +1 (215) 598 3794; media@passband.com

Bureaus

IBS Latin America	Tony Jones, Casilla 1844, Asunción, Paraguay; scheditor@passband.com
IBS Australia	Craig Tyson, Box 2145, Malaga WA 6062; addresses@passband.com
IBS Japan	Toshimichi Ohtake, 5-31-6 Tamanawa, Kamakura 247-0071; Fax +81 (467) 43 2167; ibsjapan@passband.com

Library of Congress Cataloging-in-Publication Data

Passport to World Band Radio.
1. Radio Stations, Shortwave—Directories. I. Magne, Lawrence
TK9956.P27   2007   384.54'5 07-22739
ISBN 978-0-914941-66-8

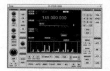

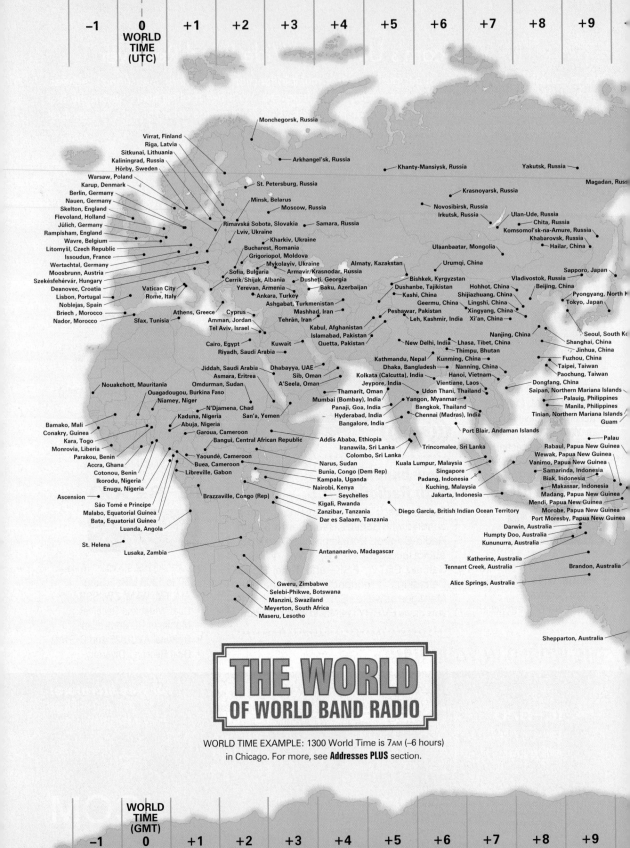

THE WORLD OF WORLD BAND RADIO

WORLD TIME EXAMPLE: 1300 World Time is 7AM (–6 hours) in Chicago. For more, see **Addresses PLUS** section.

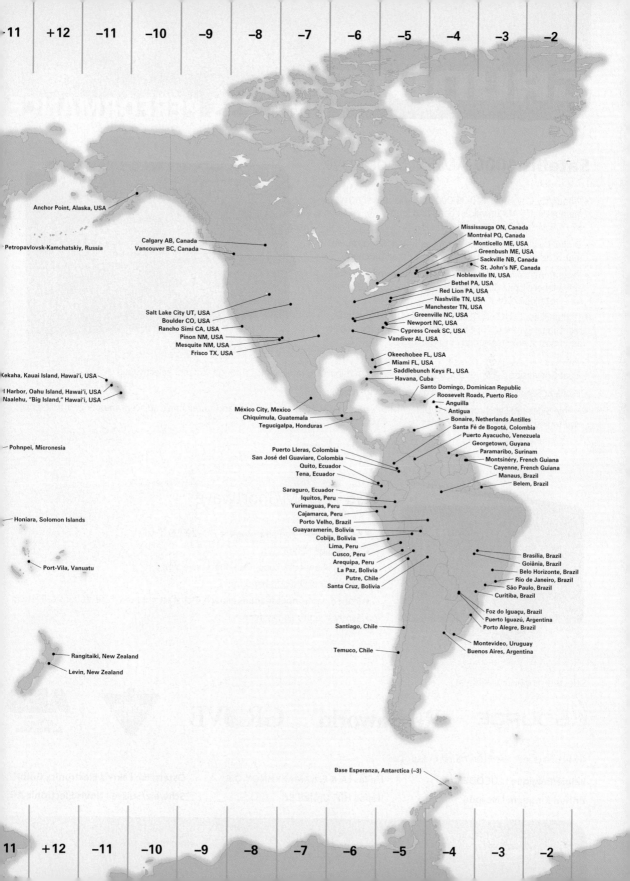

-11 +12 -11 -10 -9 -8 -7 -6 -5 -4 -3 -2

Anchor Point, Alaska, USA

Petropavlovsk-Kamchatskiy, Russia

Calgary AB, Canada
Vancouver BC, Canada

Mississauga ON, Canada
Montréal PQ, Canada
Monticello ME, USA
Greenbush ME, USA
Sackville NB, Canada
St. John's NF, Canada
Noblesville IN, USA
Bethel PA, USA
Red Lion PA, USA
Nashville TN, USA
Manchester TN, USA
Greenville NC, USA
Newport NC, USA
Cypress Creek SC, USA
Vandiver AL, USA

Salt Lake City UT, USA
Boulder CO, USA
Rancho Simi CA, USA
Pinon NM, USA
Mesquite NM, USA
Frisco TX, USA

Okeechobee FL, USA
Miami FL, USA
Saddlebunch Keys FL, USA
Havana, Cuba

Kekaha, Kauai Island, Hawai'i, USA
I Harbor, Oahu Island, Hawai'i, USA
Naalehu, "Big Island," Hawai'i, USA

Santo Domingo, Dominican Republic
Roosevelt Roads, Puerto Rico
Anguilla
Antigua
Bonaire, Netherlands Antilles
Santa Fé de Bogotá, Colombia
Puerto Ayacucho, Venezuela
Georgetown, Guyana
Paramaribo, Surinam
Montsinéry, French Guiana
Cayenne, French Guiana
Manaus, Brazil
Belem, Brazil

México City, Mexico
Chiquimula, Guatemala
Tegucigalpa, Honduras

Pohnpei, Micronesia

Puerto Lleras, Colombia
San José del Guaviare, Colombia
Quito, Ecuador
Tena, Ecuador

Saraguro, Ecuador
Iquitos, Peru
Yurimaguas, Peru
Cajamarca, Peru
Porto Velho, Brazil
Guayaramerín, Bolivia
Cobija, Bolivia
Lima, Peru
Cusco, Peru
Arequipa, Peru
La Paz, Bolivia
Putre, Chile
Santa Cruz, Bolivia

Honiara, Solomon Islands

Port-Vila, Vanuatu

Brasília, Brazil
Goiânia, Brazil
Belo Horizonte, Brazil
Rio de Janeiro, Brazil
São Paulo, Brazil
Curitiba, Brazil

Foz do Iguaçu, Brazil
Puerto Iguazú, Argentina
Porto Alegre, Brazil

Santiago, Chile

Montevideo, Uruguay
Buenos Aires, Argentina

Temuco, Chile

Rangitaiki, New Zealand

Levin, New Zealand

Base Esperanza, Antarctica (–3)

11 +12 -11 -10 -9 -8 -7 -6 -5 -4 -3 -2

Satellit 1000 AM/FM/Shortwave

- Frequency Coverage: 100-30,000 KHz, includes shortwave, medium wave AM broadcast band and longwave; 76-90, 87-108 MHz FM broadcast band
- Digital Display: large 5.7 inch square, 240 x 320 pixel, dot matrix display. Shows all modes and selected functions
- Programmable Memories: 500 user programmable with alpha labeling plus 1200 user definable country memories, for a total of 1700
- Digital Phase Lock Loop (PLL) Synthesized Tuning with Direct Digital Synthesis (DDS) for drift-free frequency stability and finest tuning resolution

- Dual Conversion Superheterodyne Circuit: results in minimized interference through superior selectivity
- Excellent Sensitivity: yielding a true high-performance receiver
- Single Sideband Synchronous AM Detector: selectable USB/LSB or double sideband to minimize adjacent frequency interference and fading distortion of AM signals

G5 AM/FM/Shortwave

- AM/FM-stereo and Shortwave (1711-29999 KHz)
- Single Side Band (SSB)
- Digital Phase Lock Loop (PLL) dual conversion
- Digital Display world-band radio
- Station name input features allow a 4-character input of the stations call letters
- Synthesized tuning system

Selected models available at:

Available under the Etón name in Europe:

België/Belgique I LUCODEX nv

United Kingdom I Nevada

Hellas I A. & E. ΔΑΜΑΣΚΗΝΟΥ Ο.Ε.

Italia I HiFi United Srl

Österreich I Novis Electronics GmbH

Schweiz/Suisse I Novis Electronic AG

GS350DL AM/FM/Shortwave

- AM (530-1710 KHz), FM (88-108 MHz) and Shortwave – continuous coverage from 3 to 28 MHz.
- Highly sensitive and selective analog tuner circuitry with AM/SW Frequency Lock
- Rotary volume control
- Main tuning knob and independent fine-tuning control knob
- Variable RF gain control

G1100 AM/FM/Shortwave

- AM/FM and 10 Shortwave bands (13, 16, 19, 22, 25, 31, 41, 49, 60, 75 meter)
- Analog tuning with digital frequency readout
- Digital display and clock with light
- Digital clock, selectable 12 or 24 hour clock display format, sleep function (5-120 minutes), alarm function selectable by either buzzer or radio, light and snooze function
- Input for AC adapter

GM300 AM/FM/Shortwave

- AM/FM-stereo and 7 Shortwave bands (49, 41, 31, 25, 22, 19 and 16 meters)
- Analog tuner with classic dial knob and digital display
- Rotary volume control
- Digital display shows frequency, time, sleep time and symbols for sleep timer and alarm activation
- Clock, sleep timer, alarm function

Suomi/Danmark | Intodesign

Sverige | Intodesign

Deutschland | MBA Marken-Vertriebs GmbH

España | ANMI Electronics

France | Elite Diffusion

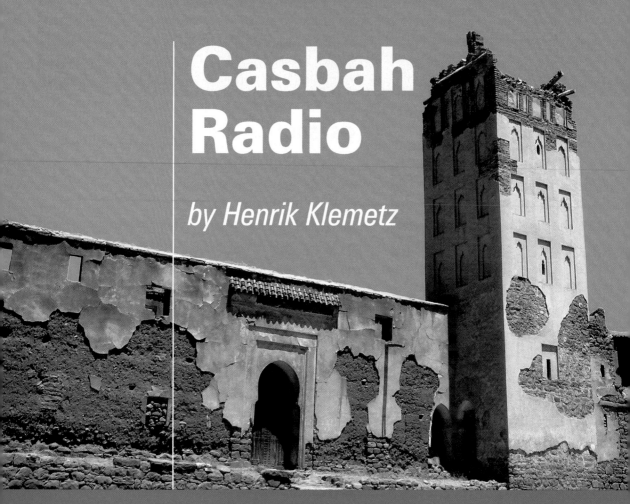

Casbah Radio

by Henrik Klemetz

Tangier lies on the southern shore of the Strait of Gibraltar, pincer of the Mediterranean. Founded by Phoenicians 500 years before Christ, its beauty and strategic siting have made it home to the legendary and the talented.

Hercules is said to have slept nearby before undertaking his labors, and Tangier was later an inspiration to Delacroix and Matisse. More recently it was first home to Islamic terrorist Jamal Zougam and second home to the Rolling Stones.

Favorable Location Entices Stations

Tangier is a Shangri-La for world band broadcasting. Lying below Eurasia, it is largely unaffected by solar storms that otherwise disrupt shortwave signals.

Even better, its location southwest of Russia and Eastern Europe gives it a degree of twilight immunity, a phenomenon which takes advantage of hour-to-hour shifts in ionospheric refraction to help overcome jamming. Twilight immunity was central to getting news and ideas to penetrate communist Europe's Iron Curtain.

Thus it was that a peaceful weapon emerged in Tangier to impact the Cold War: the Voice of America. The VOA's Tangier venture was a natural outcome, thanks to a long-standing special relationship between the United States and Morocco, the first country to recognize the fledgling American republic. The Treaty of Friendship between Morocco and the United States was signed in 1786 and is still in force.

Others have benefitted from this rapport. "Tangier was a good place for broadcasting," observed American wartime diplomat Fraser Wilkins in an interview for the Harry S. Truman library.[1] So, in 1946, RCA Communications set up an array of point-to-point transmitters for radio-telephone-telegraph service between the United States and Europe.

RCA shared the Tangier radiocommunication market with another American company: Mackay Radio & Telegraph, renowned during World War II for its telegraph services. Nonetheless, in 1949 "General" Sarnoff's RCA wound up as the sole contractor for building the Voice's relay facility in Tangier. Indeed, by September 1948 RCA was already relaying United Nations Radio on such fixed-service frequencies as 13470 and 15950 kHz.[2] Later, the VOA would relay UN Radio on in-band frequencies of 9700 and 7214 kHz.

The original VOA shortwave transmitter site was located some 22 miles (35 km) southwest of Tangier, near the border with French Morocco. It consisted of six 100 kW transmitters and one twin-50 kW transmitter sent to Tangier from Algiers, where they had been used by Allied Forces Headquarters since 1943.

Stamp issued in 1948 by the Spanish Post Office in Tangier.

Tangier is a Shangri-La for shortwave broadcasting, with twilight immunity from jamming.

Tangier's Casbah had ceased to be a cosmopolitan hideaway by 1970. Yet, it still managed to retain its architectural charm.

H. Klemetz

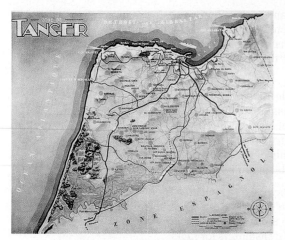

Tangier's International Zone as detailed in this period map.   Tangerjabibi

La Belle Époque

During its heyday, Tangier was a magnet for people from all over the globe—about half its 140,000 population consisted of Berbers, Jews, Spaniards and other non-Arabs.

Karl Åke Bergström, editor of the Swedish radio magazine *Nattugglan*, traveled to the International Zone of Tangier in 1952. "We never saw a place with such an amount of de luxe automobiles and such a variety of fancy merchandise for sale. In the Tangier stores you could find just anything," he marveled.

This *Belle Époque* was closely tied to Tangier's International Zone, created nearly a century ago. Because Great Britain needed free passage to and from the Mediterranean, it frowned on interest shown in Tangier by Spain, France and Germany. So, before World War I, the British called for an international conference to be held in Algeciras, Spain, opposite Gibraltar.

Its accords were finally implemented in 1923. A sizable area, including Tangier, became neutral, demilitarized and governed by an administrative body set up by the eight signatory states. France made the southern part of Morocco its protectorate, while Spain occupied the north.

A European quarter emerged next to the traditional Casbah, with its labyrinths of streets and alleys. Soon there was a rapid influx of post-war adventurers, millionaires, investors, smugglers, secret agents, merchants, prostitutes and drug addicts,[3] plus a potpourri of expats, refugees, artists and intellectuals.

With its three official languages Tangier had become one of the world's most exciting and cosmopolitan cities. Moslems worshiped on Fridays, Jews on Saturdays and Christians on Sundays.

To the delight of many, no taxes were levied. Instead, public expenditure was covered by import duties and a lottery. All currencies could be exchanged for gold, so in 1953 the telephone book listed no less than 85 banks and a similar number of hotels. But when the International Zone was eventually returned to Morocco, most money men left for juicier tax havens: Monte Carlo, Luxembourg, Andorra.

Radio's Leisurely Takeoff

In 1931 there were no radio stations in Tangier, reported the American writer Paul Bowles—hardly any radio receivers, either. But things changed fast. Only five years later Tangier hosted the 7th International Congress on Radio. Then, in 1937, the station that became Radio Africa was founded.

Even earlier, in 1935, a local station, Radio Tanger, had been founded by Tangier journalist André Pierre and a French lawyer named Hombourg. A year later the station was purchased by Charles Michelson and Louis-Jean Wolf, a Belgian businessman whose Brussels-based company, Pro-Radio, became the station's owner. Michelson planned to boost the station's power, then convert it into an affiliate of a global French network to be called Radio Impérial. Alas, the war thwarted these plans.

Fascist Era Enters, Exits

From 1940 and throughout the war years, Spain controlled the International Zone of

Tangier. Little is known about broadcasting during this period. Yet, there was reportedly a fascist station run by Spain's Falange Movement, as well as Radio Ibérica and a tiny station operated by Mussolini's Italian Consulate.[4]

Outside the International Zone, in Spanish Morocco, at least two or three other fascist stations were on world band during the Spanish civil war at the end of the 1930s. One was run by General Franco's Guardia Civil in the town of Alcázarquivir *(Ksar el-Kebir)*. The other, in the town of Melilla, was the brainchild of a ham sympathetic to Franco. Both were low-power, using amateur call signs and frequencies in the 40 meter ham segment.

Nine Lives of Jacques Trémoulet

The second entrepreneur to loom large in Tangier's broadcasting history was colorful French businessman Jacques Trémoulet. In 1947 his company CAPEC—Compagnie Africaine Publicitaire et Commerciale—purchased Radio Ibérica.[4] In turn, this company began operating Radio Africa/EA9AA, which two years later morphed into Radio Africa Tanger (RAT).

Radio Africa Maghreb (RAM), on mediumwave AM with 100 kW, was added to CAPEC's roster in July 1952. Its Arabic programs were simulcast on world band at certain hours of the day, while Radio Africa

Rue Shakespeare 39, now abandoned, was headquarters for Radio Africa Tanger during its initial years of activity on 41 meters.   Stig Hartvig Nielsen

Tanger used different hours. An additional mediumwave AM service, Radio Africa Gibraltar (RAG), aired a daily English half-hour for the British colonial fortress across the Strait.

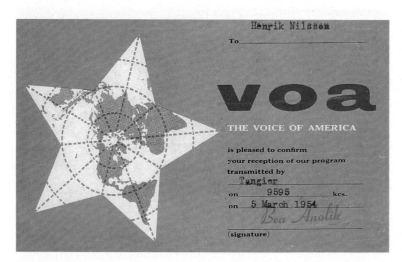

The Voice of America-Tangier's verification card from 1954. Today the VOA is Washington's redheaded stepchild, but it was decisive in winning the Cold War.   H. Klemetz

Trémoulet also fathered one of the oldest French broadcasting stations, Radio Toulouse, in 1924. He additionally owned two more commercial stations in southern France.

As France headed towards a state monopoly in broadcasting, Trémoulet needed to find extraterritorial commercial alternatives. Radio Luxembourg didn't pan out, so he founded Radio Andorra, which the French government eventually began jamming.

Worse, during the war Trémoulet completely misread the thrust of history. In 1942 he presided over SOFIRA, Société Financière de Radio, which used German and Italian capital to start construction of a new station—not just any new station, but rather a huge Nazi broadcasting complex in Monte Carlo, Monaco.

This was considered high treason by the postwar French government, which sentenced him to death. Yet, Trémoulet's charmed existence held fast and he was acquitted in 1949. He then hightailed it to Franco's Spain to help set up Radio Miramar de Badalona and Radio Intercontinental in Madrid.

The Madrid company planned to install a powerful 200 kW shortwave facility on the island of Fernando Poo, today's Bioko, which then belonged to Equatorial Guinea. This station was dubbed Radio Atlántica.

Atlántica would have put the Spanish on a level with the French and the Belgians, whose African shortwave transmitters in Brazzaville and Leopoldville were clearly heard in Europe. However, even though the station was listed in the 1949 *World Radio Handbook*, the project failed to take off.

Evangelism Thrives on Moslem Turf

Nevertheless, long-haul broadcasting was potentially viable because of monopolistic restrictions within Europe, including Sweden. In 1952 CAPEC leased airtime from Tangier, which it used for Sweden's commercial Dux Radio Stockholm-Tanger.

A NEW MISSIONARY VOICE

IBRA RADIO FROM RADIO AFRICA TANGIER

TO BRITAIN

Three years later CAPEC purchased two 10 kW shortwave transmitters, mainly for the Pentecostal IBRA Radio; outside IBRA's hours these frequencies were used by Radio Eurafrica and Radio Inter Africa. The usual Radio Africa-Tanger address, 9 rue de Russie, was announced for listeners' reception reports.

IBRA Radio remained in Tangier until 1959, when the International Zone was dismantled. At the end of the 1960s, Trémoulet offered IBRA a stake in Radio Trans Europa (RTE), a venture led by the German firm of Pro-Funk in concert with Deutsche Welle.

RTE's 250 kW Marconi transmitters targeted Eastern Europe from Sines, in Portugal. Other organizations eventually entering as partners were Adventist World Radio and Radio Canada International.

A 1944 book published in Switzerland mentions an existing Radio International in Tangier.[5] This would later merge with Radio Tanger, founded in 1946, which apparently was the city's first station to broadcast in Arabic in addition to the usual French and Spanish.

The founder of this amalgamated station, Radio Tanger-International, was historian Herbert R. Southworth. The American government had sent him to Rabat in French Morocco during the war to study fascist ideology, but he was reportedly also involved in editing Radio Rabat's Spanish-language news bulletins.

Southworth would pave the way for the Voice of Tangier, which later evolved into the worldwide Trans World Radio (see next article). In 1960 he moved to Paris, where he continued to organize his research on the Spanish Civil War.

Radio Tanger-International *(Mahattat iza´at al dawlía)* began leasing airtime as soon as it went on the air. At the end of the 1940's, "Bringing Christ to the Nations," by the Walter A. Maier Memorial Station, aired in English and other languages using Radio International on frequencies between 6100 and 6200 kHz. Power at the time was a mere 1 kW from a transmitter on the docks of Tangier.

Sweden's commercial Dux Radio was a huge success for Philips, its sponsor, and Radio Africa Tangier.

R. Fredriksson

In February 1954 Southworth offered American missionary Dr. Paul E. Freed airtime on 41 meters, using a surplus 2.5 kW transmitter. Tests from WIET, The Radio Voice of International Evangelism Tangier, were first reported in the "Sweden Calling DX-ers" weekly bulletin at the end of February.

This bulletin also reported another series of tests from Tangier. These took place an hour before and after WIET's tests, and included an hour-long commercial program in Danish. Produced in Copenhagen by Danmarks Reklame Radio (Denmark's Commercial Radio), these were most likely aired on Radio Tanger-International. Tests lasted for a couple of months, but failed to develop into a regular service.

Even at 90, John Handreck continues pursuing his lifelong interest in electronics. In 1954 he produced a short-lived Danish world band program from Tangier.

Erik Køie

DXer Erik Køie has met John Handreck, who produced the program in Denmark. Although now around 90 with impaired hearing, he still enjoys poking about his enormous collection of vintage electronics gear at Rosenørns Allé in Copenhagen.

WIET became WTAN, the Voice of Tangier, which by 1956 sported two Philips 10 kW transmitters in addition to surplus equipment used previously. Their transmitting site at Beni Makada, on the eastern outskirts of Tangier, was shared with Radio International's 50 kW mediumwave AM transmitter on 1233 kHz.

Radio Africa Tanger's former home at 9 rue de Russie, now occupied by the local police department.

Stig Hartvig Nielsen

Soon they were on the air in no less than 20 languages, including Norwegian. On December 30, 1956, Norwegian Lutherans began using WTAN for Norea Radio—Norea being the "Nordic Radio Evangelistic Association."

In his book *Towers to Eternity*, Dr. Freed recalls that Norwegian Lutheran laymen were most helpful. In particular, they aided with the $83,000 down payment for Monte Carlo's shortwave facilities after Tangier became reintegrated with Morocco. Monte Carlo thus became the starting point for the worldwide missionary organization Trans World Radio, and Norea Radio has continued to be heard in Norwegian and Swedish over TWR.

The 10 kW transmitter duo used by WTAN and Norea Radio belonged to Radio Tanger-International. One unit, manufactured by Philips, had been purchased by the Intercontinental Radio Company, S.A. (IRCO), whose intention was to revive the Dux Radio venture from 1952.

Using frequencies around the less-crowded range of 32 meters—9350-9490 kHz—tests in Danish, Finnish and Swedish created massive listener response. But times were changing. Television and FM were appearing in Scandinavia, so people started drifting away from shortwave.

IRCO and Dux were also hit by a royal decree ending the International Zone, which

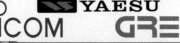

Radio Africa Tanger's five kilowatt shortwave transmitter was housed in the same hall as its mediumwave AM cousin.

Lars A. Rydén

meant their days were numbered. Only a few religious organizations held on until their host stations fled the Zone—notably Herbert W. Armstrong and his syndicated "The World Tomorrow."

Beni Makada, in Tangier's outskirts, housed shortwave transmitters for the Voice of Tangier. Also inside was a 50 kW mediumwave AM unit for Radio International.

Stig Hartvig Nielsen

Commercial Broadcasts Take Root

After World War II, contrary to what is generally believed, Tangier authorized only three commercial broadcasters to operate. This oligopoly remained intact, and no new broadcasting licenses were granted after 1949.

To get around this, two of the three authorized companies—Radio Africa and Radio Tanger-International—leased airtime to foreign organizations. The third, Pan American Radio (PAR) owned by the International Banking Corporation of Tangier, had other plans.

PAR had gone on the air in 1949 on popular 41 meters, where over 15 local stations in neighboring Spain were active after the war. PAR also briefly tested around 15050 kHz, but eventually settled on mediumwave AM instead.

PAR was originally on Boulevard Pasteur, the *"Champs-Élysées of Tangier,"* but soon moved to the top floor of the Stock and Currency Exchange Building on Delacroix Street. This allowed them to mount an antenna on the roof and transmit realtime currency rates several times a day.

Before long, the station was carrying programs in several languages, including Arabic and Hindi. News was relayed from Radio Nacional de España and the Voice

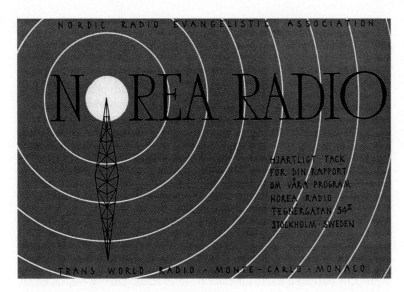

When the Voice of Tangier closed in 1959, Norea Radio helped found Trans World Radio in Monte Carlo. In return, TWR allowed Norea to use its facilities for decades thereafter.
Norea Radio

of America, plus the BBC in English and Spanish.

"This is the Pan American Radio, broadcasting from the International Zone of Tangier," they announced. But when the Moroccan Sultan claimed the Zone was to be reintegrated with Morocco, the station manager forbade all mention of the Zone.

A couple of years prior to the Moroccan takeover of the Zone, PAR had started a second multilingual service. Although called "Pan American Radio Intercontinental," it was intended only for local listeners. It aired evenings on 1594 kHz, which was shared with various low-power U.S. Navy and Air Force outlets in Morocco.[6]

According to one of his employees, PAR manager Jaime Surinyac expected to be granted a license to broadcast from Spanish soil. This didn't materialize, so PAR pulled the switch in September 1960.

Popular Station Targets Sweden

Even with the advent of television and FM, shortwave was able to satisfy musical and other tastes that domestic Swedish government stations had ignored.

Columns on shortwave listening were featured in popular newspapers and magazines, among them *Teknikens Värld*

Pan American was North Africa's pioneering equivalent to Bloomberg Radio. It aired realtime financial and other news from facilities smack atop Tangier's Stock and Currency Exchange Building.   H. Klemetz

Swedish pianist Charlie Norman, dressed up for the occasion, died in 2006. Norman was compère for shows transmitted to Sweden from Radio Africa Tanger.

Dux Radio

whose "radio club" had 15,000 members. In 1951, it organized a music contest using a 2.5 kW shortwave transmitter operated by Radio Africa Tanger on 7126 kHz. The response was overwhelming.

No wonder, then, that Dux Radio, a Philips subsidiary, felt their parent firm might sell more radios by sponsoring shows with broader listener appeal. So, in March 1952, they embarked on a twice-weekly entertainment feature in Swedish over Radio Africa Tanger. Programs were mailed to Tangier, then aired at the princely sum of eight dollars for half an hour.

The show's conductor was pianist and entertainer Charlie Norman, and the programs and prize winners were advertised every week in 160 newspapers throughout Sweden. Ads for local Philips vendors were placed alongside each Dux ad, which showed Charlie as a turbaned "Disk Sheikh" sporting a Moroccan dagger in his mouth. Dux also edited a manual and world map for shortwave listening; it sold 50,000 copies in just one year.

When CIA-parented Radio Liberation—later Radio Liberty—surfaced on March 1, 1953, most of 41 meters, including 7126 kHz, was disrupted by intense Soviet jamming. Thus, the first part of the Dux success story came to an end.

World Band Rescues Pentecostals

> The station's new site was originally a watchtower for swashbuckling buccaneers.

The Dux story may also have convinced the Swedish Pentecostal church to broadcast from Tangier in the mid-1950s. This came about because Swedish state radio allowed different Christian denominations to air Sunday services, but as of 1948 the Pentecostals were banished.

Pentecostal leader Lewi Pethrus, seeking to circumvent the ban, became aware of world band radio's potential while visiting the United States. So, in 1949, shortwave tests were aired over Radio Luxembourg, but reception was miserable.

Verification from Radio Tanger-International. The station was founded by American government researcher Herbert R. Southworth (photo, p. 14).

H. Klemetz

Verification Card

Radio Tanger — Radio International

34, Goya Street
Tangier, International Zone, Morocco

We acknowledge your listening report of *April 24/55*

RADIO INTERNATIONAL is a commercial radio station, broadcasting on medium waves (1232 kcs. 243.5 meters) and short waves (6110 kcs. 49 meters).

We broadcast from 7.00 hrs. to 8.15 hrs., from 12.00 hrs. to 16.00 hrs., and from 18.00 hrs. to 24.00 hrs. every day.

Programs in four languages: French, Spanish, Arabic and English.

Many thanks for your report.

RADIO TANGIER — RADIO INTERNATIONAL

Director.

HIERONYMUS BOSCH   Circa 1500

He then tried Radio Andorra, which boomed in on 5980 kHz, but the tapes never made it. It appears they were seized by French postal inspectors, as Radio Andorra, owned by the shadowy Trémoulet, was considered a *poste corsaire*—pirate—by the French government.

Pethrus then decided to broadcast from a ship anchored in the Stockholm archipelago. A vessel was purchased and converted, while a land-based studio was set up. The plan came to a halt when the church leader realized he might end up in court. Instead, in June 1954 he accepted a renewed offer by Trémoulet, who insisted Tangier was the perfect option.

The Swedish government wouldn't let the church transfer currency abroad to finance broadcasts, but paying organizational fees was allowed. So the church founded the International Broadcasting Association (IBRA), with headquarters in Tangier at 3 rue Henri Regnault.

"Fees" were sent to rue Henri Regnault by postal money order, much to the annoyance of the Tangier post office. In 1956, some 52,000 people coughed up the equivalent of four dollars, then in 1957 the fee rose by a dollar. These sums were decisive, as by that time airtime cost the equivalent of $120 an hour.

Tapes Traverse Desert Dunes

After successfully running tests, IBRA Radio fired up on July 29, 1955. The antennas, a pair of 40-meter towers, two new Brown Boveri 10 kW diesel-powered transmitters and a custom-built broadcasting house had been erected on a hill at Tahardaz, some 19 miles (30 km) southwest of Tangier along the Atlantic coast .

This hill had a certain notoriety, as in olden times it had been used as a watchtower by swashbuckling buccaneers. Sniffed one Swedish newspaper, "They are trying to teach us morals from Pirate Hill."

Most programs were recorded in Stockholm, then flown to Tangier. But there was no road to the transmitter site, so tapes had to be hauled over sun-scorched sand dunes until

The Swedish Pentecostal church planned to transmit in Swedish from Radio Andorra in the Pyrenees mountains. The plan failed when program tapes disappeared, presumably having been intercepted by French postal authorities.   R. Andorra via H. Klemetz

a microwave link with Tangier could be set up.

Signals went to Scandinavia through inexpensive rhombic antennas, which emit narrow but powerful low-angle beams. One

IBRA Radio does a field interview atop Phoenician ruins near Tangier. Pingstarkivet

Today's Ciné-Goya was home to Radio International in the early 1950s. The Tangier station went back even earlier, to at least 1944.   Stig Hartvig Nielsen

night, it occurred to a Swedish DXer to compare the field strengths of VOA-Tangier on 15210 kHz and IBRA-Tangier on 15205 kHz. "Little" IBRA won, hands down.

Initial programs in Swedish were soon followed by programs in Norwegian, Finnish, Danish, German, English, French and Dutch. Eventually, over 20 languages were aired before it all came to an end.

During the final evening of transmission, December 22, 1959, only one transmitter was on the air—even that was operating from

Present-day Radio Tanger is housed in a local building behind this street sign.   Stig Hartvig Nielsen

within a wooden crate so it could be spirited off to Barcelona later that night. Another, Radio Africa's high-power mediumwave AM unit, resurfaced after a couple of years on the Caribbean island of Montserrat.

Today, no world band station transmits from within the city. Although commercial Médi 1 (Radio Méditerranée Internationale), founded in 1980, has studios in Tangier, its transmitters are at Nador, 125 miles (200 km) to the east. Too, many organizations that once hired airtime in Tangier have disappeared, while others have moved.

However, thanks to the special relationship between Morocco and the United States, the VOA was able to remain on the air even after the International Zone was dismantled. Eventually the Voice moved to Briech, a new 1190-acre (4 sq km) site slightly farther south. It became operational on October 4, 1993.

Good Times Gone

There are few around today who can relate what life was like in Tangier during the brisk postwar years. One is Russian-born journalist Aleko Lilius, who authored *Turbulent Tangier* and *Lady Jaguar*.

Lady Jaguar includes a vivid description of the Canadian announcer Jim Davidson's first live transmission for PAR from Socco Chico square. That day, during "Meet The Bums," listeners' ears perked up as a nearby donkey got loose and ran amok, trashing stores and forcing diners to flee from café terraces.

Asunción "Tona" Pérez Pérez had her baptism in broadcasting at Radio Africa Tanger, then became program manager for PAR. She was reared in Tangier, where she went to school, worked, married and gave birth to two children.

In 1960, she had to pack up and leave for Barcelona, where she continues to reside to this day. "I was living on top of the world, without worrying about what was going on. I thought Tangier was just like any other town in the world and I did not realize that

WTAN, the Voice of Tangier, offered this verification card to listeners in 1956. WTAN was the precursor of today's Trans World Radio.

H. Klemetz

it was unique and, in addition to that, provisional."[7]

Italian-born Teresa Grecco Stodel also looks back with regret. She was fluent in Italian, French and Spanish, and did continuity announcing over PAR. She also participated in radio theater productions and sang commercial jingles in Spanish—a novelty at the time.

Grecco Stodel, who now lives in southern France, recently revisited Tangier. "It is appalling to see what they have done to the town," she mourned. "It is all a disaster."[7]

So it was that the curtain descended on Tangier's *Belle Époque* of great radio and greater living. In the early 1950s, nearly half of Tangier's 140,000 were émigrés, making it North Africa's cosmopolitan center. Today it is a Maghrebian metropolis of 600,000, but its vital international presence has faded to less than a thousand.

Exotic Tangier is no more.

PASSPORT *thanks Lars A. Rydén, Jari Savolainen, Erik Køie, Stig Hartvig Nielsen, Jos Strengholt, Carlos Hernández, Rolf Fredriksson and Åke Öhrvall, along with a tip of the hat to the several other helpful colleagues who were kind enough to share their knowledge and wisdom.*

[1]www.trumanlibrary.org/oralhist/wilkins.htm

[2]Information from Dr. Adrian Peterson, Adventist World Radio

[3]Tangier was "a place overrun with spies, mercenaries, and colonial agents," wrote Yunus Bahri, in his book *Berlin Radio*, Beiruth 1956. Bahri was an Arabic speaker on Radio Berlin 1939–1945 and was sent to Tangier to recruit Arabic speaking staff for the station.

[4]René Duval, *Histoire de la radio en France*, Paris 1979

[5]Arno Huth, *Radio—Heute und Morgen*, Zurich 1944

[6]Svend Martinsen lists the following stations on 1594 kHz, some heard as far as Scandinavia: WCOX-Sidi Slimane (April 1959), WBOS-Ben Guerir (1956), WIND-Nouasseur (1956), KFAD-Rabat (n/d).

[7]Personal interviews by the author, April 20 and 21, 2005

Studios for Médi 1 are about the only radio presence left in Tangier. Even then, its transmitters are located elsewhere. Stig Hartvig Nielsen

GRUNDIG
TIMELESS PERFORMANCE

Satellit 1000 AM/FM/Shortwave

- Frequency Coverage: 100-30,000 KHz, includes shortwave, medium wave AM broadcast band and longwave; 76-90, 87-108 MHz FM broadcast band
- Digital Display: large 5.7 inch square, 240 x 320 pixel, dot matrix display. Shows all modes and selected functions
- Programmable Memories: 500 user programmable with alpha labeling plus 1200 user definable country memories, for a total of 1700
- Digital Phase Lock Loop (PLL) Synthesized Tuning with Direct Digital Synthesis (DDS) for drift-free frequency stability and finest tuning resolution
- Dual Conversion Superheterodyne Circuit: results in minimized interference through superior selectivity
- Excellent Sensitivity: yielding a true high-performance receiver
- Single Sideband Synchronous AM Detector: selectable USB/LSB or double sideband to minimize adjacent frequency interference and fading distortion of AM signals

G5 AM/FM/Shortwave

- AM/FM-stereo and Shortwave (1711-29999 KHz)
- Single Side Band (SSB)
- Digital Phase Lock Loop (PLL) dual conversion
- Digital Display world-band radio
- Station name input features allow a 4-character input of the stations call letters
- Synthesized tuning system

Selected models available at:

RadioShack®

GS350DL AM/FM/Shortwave

- AM (530-1710 KHz), FM (88-108 MHz) and Shortwave – continuous coverage from 3 to 28 MHz.
- Highly sensitive and selective analog tuner circuitry with AM/SW Frequency Lock
- Rotary volume control
- Main tuning knob and independent fine-tuning control knob
- Variable RF gain control

G1100 AM/FM/Shortwave

- AM/FM and 10 Shortwave bands (13, 16, 19, 22, 25, 31, 41, 49, 60, 75 meter)
- Analog tuning with digital frequency readout
- Digital display and clock with light
- Digital clock, selectable 12 or 24 hour clock display format, sleep function (5-120 minutes), alarm function selectable by either buzzer or radio, light and snooze function
- Input for AC adapter

GM300 AM/FM/Shortwave

- AM/FM-stereo and 7 Shortwave bands (49, 41, 31, 25, 22, 19 and 16 meters)
- Analog tuner with classic dial knob and digital display
- Rotary volume control
- Digital display shows frequency, time, sleep time and symbols for sleep timer and alarm activation
- Clock, sleep timer, alarm function

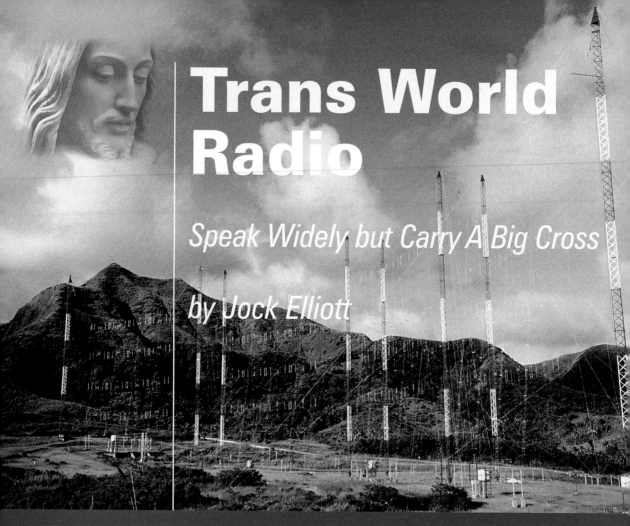

Trans World Radio

Speak Widely but Carry A Big Cross

by Jock Elliott

To David Tucker, Trans World Radio's president, it's simple: "Our mission is to reach the world for Christ through mass media. We take very seriously the command, 'Therefore go and make disciples of all nations.' "

This underpinning belies the complexity of what's become a legend in global religious radio. Tucker, a former 20-year executive for British Petroleum, explains, "Since our first transmitter—a 2,500 Watt surplus unit—went on the air in Tangier in February, 1954, our goal has been to try to reach as many people as possible who can't be reached by normal missionary means. The message is the most important thing for us, and the means has to blend with the accessibility."

"Whatever Works"

To do this requires research and a willingness to shift tactics. The effectiveness and availability of delivery options vary throughout the world, so TWR has adopted a "whatever works" attitude. In some areas of the world, almost every option is used. With others, only one is chosen.

Dr. David Tucker, president of Trans World Radio.
TWR

Technological and political changes are ongoing, so TWR keeps reinventing itself to reach its audience effectively. Case in point: For many years they broadcast into Russia by shortwave, as that was the only means available. But with the fall of the communist Iron Curtain in 1989, accessibility changed—for now, at any rate, they can broadcast through entire networks of local Russian stations. Nevertheless, they still use shortwave to reach Russian listeners who chose that medium years ago.

Delivery is tailored to each target area according to audience preferences. For example, youth might be interested in the Internet rather than shortwave. Tucker says, "Overarching all of this is that we need to get the Gospel to people as urgently as possible."

Guiding the commitment to using the best delivery mix is Bill Damick, who carries the olympian title of Knowledge Management Officer. His main job is to do contextual research about TWR's target areas, including communications trends—broadcast, Internet, cell phones—and demographic developments.

"We look at population growth issues around HIV/AIDS, political trends affecting the ability to broadcast in or to the country in question," Damick says, "and we also follow issues having to do with religious freedom and how Christians are being treated."

> Shortwave is the tool of choice where pavement and electric wires end.

From Monte Carlo, Kalman Dobos records a program in Hungarian.
TWR

Bonaire transmitter hall in 1966. At left is a 50 kW shortwave transmitter, while the mighty 500 kW mediumwave AM transmitter looms to the right. That beefy unit actually produced less than its rated 500 kW.   TWR

When to Use World Band

In the 1980s, TWR used 80 percent short-wave and 20 percent high-powered medi-umwave AM. Today, they broadcast 4,000 hours each week, but only about 20 percent is on shortwave. This is largely thanks to greater use of local placement: syndication over domestic FM and mediumwave AM outlets.

Nevertheless, world band is still critically important. "There are a large number of countries where you can't get permission to broadcast Christian content locally. You want to use whatever means you can to get through the door. In many places, short-wave is still that door," Damick explains.

He adds, "Some would argue that the Internet is the door, but the Internet has a gatekeeper and the gatekeeper can close that door, as the Saudis have, and other countries are threatening to do. In some areas, shortwave is the best way to go for access reasons; in other areas, shortwave is the best way for infrastructure reasons."

For example, a number of African govern-ments still broadcast domestically on short-wave. It's cheap, and there are lots of places where setting up a local station isn't easy.

In some parts of the continent over half the people own and use a world band radio. "Somebody described shortwave as the tool to use in Africa where the pavement and the electric wires end," Damick points out. So his colleagues are in the early stages of researching whether to install a shortwave transmitter in West Africa.

Shortwave is also the best medium to reach listeners in northern India, so airtime is leased from facilities in Russia. The Rus-sians view it not as a ministry, but rather as a simple business proposition.

Shortwave has also traditionally been the best way to reach India's large rural popula-

Bonaire studio operator Virgil Stanley cues an LP recording for airplay.   TWR

tion. Nevertheless, the ongoing population shift to cities means TWR's delivery mix is going to need tweaking.

That's India, but every country is different. In rural Afghanistan, for example, nearly all broadcasts are received off the world band airwaves.

Big Budget for Big Network

Trans World Radio's usable infrastructure is impressive. It includes 2,600 local FM and mediumwave AM stations; satellite distribution to Africa, Europe and Asia; and webcasts in a dozen languages. Additionally, they own or lease time from a number of international transmitting sites (*see* Sites Aplenty).

Considerable resources are needed for TWR to accomplish its mission. In 2005, expenses were $39.1 million: 84 percent for radio broadcasting, six percent for fundraising, ditto for management and the like, and four percent for "mission awareness."

All this has resulted in a worldwide organization of 469, including 160 supported missionaries. The rest are salaried staff in the United States, Guam, South Africa, Swaziland, Benin, Austria, Slovakia, Germany, Netherlands, Cambodia, the Middle East, Hong Kong, Singapore, Bonaire and Uruguay.

Power of Programs, Tower of Tongues

TWR's target demographics include children and adolescents, as well as women and those with health and other desperate needs. There is also a major focus on an obviously ripe potential listenership: the four billion who rely on oral communication. Finally, in key geographic areas niche programming caters to church leadership.

The late Paul E. Freed, founder of Trans World Radio, was formerly with British Petroleum. TWR

We use whatever gets through the door. In many places, shortwave is still that door.

Trans World Radio's Monte Carlo antenna farm. Each antenna is directed to a different target area—from the Iberian Peninsula to Eastern Europe and Russia. TWR

SITES APLENTY

Trans World Radio, like Sherwin-Williams paint, covers the globe. To accomplish this successfully calls for a vast network of transmitters strategically placed for long-distance reception. Here's the recent roster, but expect changes in the months to come.

Monaco/France TWR first operated from tiny Monaco on October 16, 1960, using studios and administrative facilities in Monte Carlo. However, the 100 kW transmitter was actually located in neighboring France.

Monaco's Monte Carlo quarter is home to Trans World Radio, which was incorporated in Monaco.

Shutterstock/Vladimir Melnik

Earlier this decade the Monte Carlo administrative operation in Monaco was moved to Vienna, although some staff remains in Monaco. In most cases studios have been relocated to the countries where the programs originate.

Leased-time transmissions from France today use 100 kW shortwave from Fontbonne and one Megawatt medium-wave AM from Roumoules. Programs in German were pulled from Monte Carlo, as TWR's German partner—ERF—had made significant cutbacks. Some TWR-sponsored German programs continue on mediumwave AM from Mainflingen, which ERF owns.

Albania During the Cold War, Radio Tirana's "Tirade Anna" was notorious for her over-the-top propaganda. Among other boasts was how churches and mosques were forced by Albania's Stalinist regime to close down, with defrocked ministers, priests and mullahs "being handed picks and shovels and made to do useful work."

No more. "Anna" is in retirement and Albania now welcomes those condemned by its former communist masters. This includes TWR, which fired up broadcasts on October 1, 1992 from Radio Tirana's mediumwave AM site at Fllaka and, later, shortwave facilities at Cerrik and Shijak. Cerrik is currently being used exclusively by China Radio International, while the three 100 kW transmitters at Shijak were split between Radio Tirana and TWR. TWR's mediumwave AM is on 1395 kHz (500 kW).

TWR ceased registering shortwave transmission from Albania as of autumn ("B") 2007.

Austria Österreichische Sender's Moosbrunn facility is used for transmissions to Russia and Belarus.

Germany TWR is aired over T-System International's shortwave facility at Jülich. Wertachtal is also being used, albeit at reduced power (100 kW), and Nauen is available should the need arise.

Moldova Since August 2, 1999, TWR has used a full Megawatt from Grigoriopol. This is still on 1548 kHz to the Balkans, as well as at 500 kW on 999 kHz to Russia and Ukraine.

Russia TWR first transmitted from here on June 1, 1993, using 250 kW shortwave. It currently airs from Russia to Europe and South Asia from various sites, with site usage being flexible.

Cyprus   TWR started on Cyprus May 1, 1974 from Cape Greco. Its 600 kW mediumwave AM transmitter is owned by Monte Carlo Radiodiffusion and is primarily for listeners in Arab countries.

United Arab Emirates   In a reprise of its experience in Morocco (see "Casbah Radio"), TWR successfully airs over world band from Dhabayya in this modern Moslem country.

Ascension Island   This isolated warhorse facility, long treasured by the BBC World Service, has been doing yeoman's duty for TWR since the summer of 2007. It offers superior world band coverage to West Africa.

Rwanda   TWR makes use of Deutsche Welle's Kigali's shortwave relay for 15 minutes twice weekly to East Africa.

South Africa   Since December 4, 1994 TWR has aired over SENTECH's 250/500 kW shortwave site at Meyerton.

Swaziland   TWR first broadcast from here on November 1, 1974. It now operates one 50 kW mediumwave AM and three 100 kW shortwave transmitters, although the latter often operate at lower power to save money. The original 50 kW shortwave unit remains on standby.

Armenia/Kyrgyzstan   On November 15, 1996, TWR began to lease airtime on a beefy Megawatt mediumwave AM transmitter in Gavar, Armenia.

For a time they also used a shortwave transmitter. Now, transmissions from Gavar are only on 864 and 1350 kHz, complemented by Bishkek, Kyrgyzstan, at 75 kW. Bishkek also targets west and central Asia on 6030 kHz with 100 kW.

Guam   Guam started on September 4, 1977 with four 100 kW shortwave units. Today there is a fifth such transmitter in regular use, along with six antennas for Asia and the Pacific.

Kazakhstan   An Almaty shortwave transmitter is used for broadcasts to India.

Sri Lanka   TWR commenced from what was then Ceylon on June 7, 1978. It still uses the same 400 kW mediumwave AM transmitter owned by the country's official SLBC.

Brazil   TWR-Brazil initially leased world band airtime from Rádio Nova Visão. Later, it purchased all three Nova Visão transmitters—on 5965 (7.5 kW), 9530 (10 kW) and 11735 kHz (50 kW).

Netherlands Antilles   TWR-Bonaire first broadcast to Central and South America on August 13, 1964. From the outset the nominally 500 kW mediumwave AM unit actually produced slightly lower power—even as the impish power meter registered "500 kW."

Today this is moot, as only 100 kW is used. Shortwave was also used for a number of years, but was dropped in 1996.

Uruguay   Service from here began on October 1, 1981 on mediumwave AM, and continues on Montevideo's Radio Rural, 610 kHz (50 kW).

Latin America—Local Placement   TWR locally places programs over a shrinking roster of regional world band transmitters. Today it is aired over the venerable HCJB, Ecuador, and Radio del Pacifico, Peru. However, the Peruvian transmitter is in deteriorated condition and could cease operation.

—TWR, Tony Jones and helpful colleagues.

The Bonaire transmitter building lies to the left, while the diesel generation plant is at the right. To the rear, a curtain antenna array towers above both structures.
TWR

Unlike official stations, TWR has to be effective or its support will wither away. Heading the roster of "musts" for success are to be audible and intelligible. To this end TWR broadcasts in an astounding number of languages, including regional variants—more than the BBC World Service, Voice of America, Deutsche Welle, Radio France Internationale and China Radio International—*combined*.

TWR defines and explains its potential for reaching audiences. Damick elaborates, "We have accountability to our donors, to our sponsors, those people who are giving every year, and we want to understand the environment we are broadcasting into. Every once in a while, we need to ask ourselves, 'Are we stuck in a traditional view? Do we need to expand or change?'

"We're not the only ones doing this. Every year, we sit down with other Christian broadcasters to parcel out responsibilities to the different organizations. For example, the Christian broadcasters decided to split up the big tribal languages. Currently about 98 percent have the potential to hear the Gospel in a language they understand . . . Now, whether they have the receiving device is the next question. That's why research is so important." They also discuss who has the most suitable site to broadcast and who has the best infrastructure to produce programs.

Another "must" is to respond promptly to changing sociopolitical conditions. This is why broadcasts have been expanded into Southeast Asia over the past five years as freedom has increased in Vietnam. Too, TWR is bringing a high-power mediumwave AM station online in Benin.

Oral Traditions Flourish

Just as important as how the physical message is delivered is its presentation. David Tucker states, "We are deliberately not political and are non-controversial. We preach as Jesus taught—giving the stories of the Bible, communicating them to people who

Bonaire studio manager Brad Swanson.
TWR

Shortwave transmitters are housed in this building in Monte Carlo built by Hitler during WWII. The Germans never used the building, whose transmitters are now used to broadcast the Gospel.
TWR.

don't have the Bible in their own language. We translate the story for them, trusting that the Spirit of God will use that and bring about a transformation in that person's life, in their town."

A trump card for TWR is catering to oral traditions that flourish throughout the world. According to the International Mission Board, 1.5 billion people have never been introduced to reading and writing in any form. Additionally, more than half the world's population prefers oral communication to pass on values and truths.

Damick explains, "Up to 40% of people in the world cannot or do not read. The United Nations says one in five cannot read. Another 20% purposefully lead non-literate lives.

"One of the countries where that is the case is Egypt, if you compare government literacy rates and newspaper readership rates. If you look at a media report on Egypt, you realize that some people may be called literate, but they do not read as a matter of course."

Oral traditions are particularly strong in other cultures, as well. UNESCO estimates that 52 percent of all oral communicators live in India and China, and that half speak in minority languages.

"In western culture, we tend to focus on words, but the rest of the world focuses

on relationships," Damick points out. "To communicate successfully, you have to find where the links are between where the audience is and what the Scripture teaches."

Reciting poetry is important in Arab oral culture, so broadcasting the Psalms is a natural door-opener. Another approach is to take Scripture and put it into the setting of a wise old village elder telling a story. As one report puts it, "The Bible reveals the power of oral communications. After all, Jesus never wrote a book."

Partnerships Foster Cultural Respect

"You need to exhibit respect for cultural forms," Damick explains. "Christ is both culturally and personally transforming. Sometimes you have to build credibility through pragmatic programming on health and hygiene."

Tucker, his colleague, elaborates, "It is important to realize that TWR is not merely foreigners sending western Christianity. National partner relationships exist with a number of groups, with their own Boards of Directors and ministry strategies.

"Most of TWR's studios are in the target areas. That helps to ensure that the programming is culturally adapted for them. Local nationals are committed to reaching their own people, and we make it a priority to be an assist to local churches with infrastructure, training, funding and sponsorship."

What's On Today?

Trans World Radio airs about 2,500 individual programs each week, using its own content and that provided by partners. Five broad categories take up varying percentages of airtime:

- Eighty-five percent goes to leadership development and teaching—basic Bible teaching, discipleship courses, devotional material and seminary-level programs.
- Six percent is for children and youth, including story-telling and discussions of issues important to teenagers. For example, programs have been aired on child abuse and witchcraft in Africa. Some use magazine format, others incorporate music.
- Between four and five percent is earmarked for programs targeted to societies with below-average literacy rates. These often take a story-telling approach to pass on Biblical principles. For instance, there's dramatized Bible reading with multiple voices, music and sound effects that's prepared in partnership with two other organizations: Bible Societies and Faith Comes by Hearing. Other programs in this category present the Bible chronologically, so it comes across as a continuous story.
- Two percent is dedicated to programs for women—health and hygiene, family relationships, child rearing and cottage industries.
- Finally, one percent goes to health and hygiene—HIV/AIDS, local health, food preparation, child-rearing and kindred topics.

Production varies by location, as well as the type and source of each program. If there's a desire to begin broadcasting in a new language—or to a new audience—an investigation is undertaken to determine the state of local churches and what types of programs can best support their activities.

These include overt Christian content, as well as socially focused material that's meaningful to the target audience. They also check with broadcast partners whose content may be useful, then decide whether to include it.

Once a basic concept is arrived at, creative teams are staffed with translators, editors, writers, announcers and technicians. When no nearby recording facilities are available, TWR often helps construct and equip simple studios.

While this is ramping up, they analyze available broadcast outlets: their own stations, leased-time facilities and, increasingly, local placement on independently owned stations. Simultaneously, they seek out funding from donors interested in a particular country, language group or program focus, as well as from partner organizations and foundations.

Most programs are produced months in advance to assure a steady flow and to fine-tune program quality. When possible, broadcasts are promoted by distributing schedules, notifying local churches, and advertising.

Government Hurdles

Program delivery can be a huge challenge. For starters, government broadcasting au-

Swaziland program producer Comfort Mbuza at the mic.
TWR

Trans World Radio's regional American offices are nestled in pleasant Cary, North Carolina.
TWR

thorities sometimes charge whopping sums to air private programs on their networks.

Too, available time slots, whether on official or independent stations, may be extremely brief. In part that's because some official agencies buy up or monopolize time to keep others off the air.

Personalized Outreach

Listeners are reached one-on-one, as well—by letter, telephone, SMS (text messages), email, correspondence and learning courses, plus through personal interaction during visits and listener gatherings. Specifics depend on cost, availability, safety and dependability of delivery options, as well as budget.

TWR also tries, whenever possible, to have Bibles available for distribution. In some instances, they provide recorded materials on tape or CD and via Internet download; at other times they provide tracts and excerpts of Scripture that are cheaper to mail.

In some languages, material is printed locally at lower cost through interaction with other ministries. In a few areas, radios are distributed to listener groups to encourage the establishment of local churches. Even simple booster antennas have sometimes been given away to improve reception.

Risks to Listeners and Staff

Listeners can face real difficulties. Fortunately, TWR, unlike some other broadcasters, isn't jammed by countries like China, North Korea, Iran or Cuba. However, in countries such as North Korea a person found with a world band radio runs the risk of being imprisoned.

When listeners convert to Christianity, potential risks abound. For example, in some countries it is illegal to convert from the religion of one's birth. Beyond that, freedom of religious choice is an alien and dangerous concept within many cultures.

Penalties can be severe—converts may be ostracized by their families or lose their jobs. In addition, local churches can be wary about taking these people in because they have been betrayed in the past. "We take the life-and-death risk extremely seriously, and try to sustain new converts with some sort of living and try to bring them within a community of Christians," Tucker says.

Listeners aren't the only ones at risk. TWR is intentionally vague about the location of its transmitters in potentially dangerous areas, even though researchers typically figure these out. That's because security is a problem for its workers in many regions—notably North Africa and the Middle East, as well as parts of Latin America and Asia.

Threats are common, but there is a reluctance to stir passions by publicizing past attacks. Nevertheless, a tower climber reveals to PASSPORT that he had "a gun stuck up my nose" by insurgents in South America. And in Southeast Asia the back window was shot out of a vehicle carrying TWR workers.

The Road Ahead

Looking toward the future, Damick predicts, "Shortwave will likely always be part of our mix. When it comes to new technologies, for us it's a waiting game.

"There doesn't seem to be any rapid upgrade to DRM. We are watching China closely—there is some talk that China will roll out some big changes and maybe will introduce DRM for domestic broadcasting."

Are TWR's efforts having meaningful impact? Tucker says definitely. In 1949, there were 750,000 Christians in China, but by 1979 Christianity had only survived and not grown. By 1999, however, the government was saying there were 14 million Christians in the country.

This didn't include "house church" Christians, so almost certainly there were millions more. Interestingly, TWR states that half reported that their first exposure to Christianity was through radio, mainly world band.

"Our great belief is that faith comes by hearing the Word of God," Tucker insists. "If you give truthful information and allow God to use it, it transforms people's lives."

DYNAMIC FEEDBACK

If signals aren't clean, crisp and reliable, listeners fall by the wayside.

Trans World Radio maintains high transmission standards by using remote monitoring systems (RMS) to keep tabs on its broadcasts to Asia, including India, and Europe/North Africa. Currently, there are RMS installations in six European countries and elsewhere that monitor reception and audio quality for world band and mediumwave AM broadcasts.

Asia

Systems are set up in four cities in northern India. Each uses a Ten-Tec RX320 or RX320D PC-controlled receiver, an antenna and a dedicated computer with Windows XP or 2000—along with UPS, broadband connection and monitoring software developed by Deutsche Welle. TWR Engineering can upload data or audio files, monitoring analyses, or both, then send them over the Internet to TWR-India or email recipients.

TWR also cooperates with other broadcasters—religious and non-religious—to host equipment and share remote monitoring data for India and other Asian locations.

Europe and North Africa

In Europe, TWR's engineers use a system based on a modified Lowe Electronics HF-225 receiver which stores monitoring data and is reached by normal telephone lines. Engineers access the receivers daily for field strength and modulation data, as well as 10–20 second audio clips.

TWR is also evaluating the use of RMS equipment in Africa, although there are no active installations yet.

	Receives AM Band	Receives FM Band	Receives Shortwave Band	Receives TV Band	Receives Weather Band	Crank Power	Cell Phone Charger
FR250	•	•	•			•	•
FR300	•	•		•		•	•
FR350	•	•	•			•	•
FR400	•	•		•	•	•	•
FR1000 Voice Link	•	•			•	•	•

Colors (varies by model): ● ● ● ● ● ● ○ ● ● ●

FR Series: Self-Powered Radio, including Cell Phone Charger and Flashlight

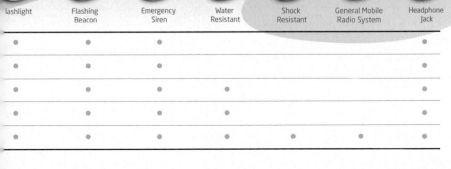

Flashlight

Flashing Beacon

Emergency Siren

Water Resistant

Shock Resistant

General Mobile Radio System

Headphone Jack

etón

re_inventing radio

www.etoncorp.com

✓ | Getting Started

World Band's Three Musts

World band isn't run-of-the-mill radio—it travels freely by skywave and needs special receivers. So here are three musts so you can master it right off.

Must #1: World Time and Day

World band schedules use a single time. World band is global, with programs aired around the clock from nearly every time zone.

Imagine the chaos if each station's schedule were given in its local time to listeners scattered all over the world.

Solution: World Time—one time zone for the entire planet.

World Time—officially called Coordinated Universal Time (UTC)—has replaced the virtually identical Greenwich Mean Time (GMT) as the global standard. It's in 24-hour format, so 2 PM is 14:00 ("fourteen hundred hours" or "fourteen hours"). Ideally, leading zeroes are shown; for example, 08:00, spoken as "oh-eight-hundred hours" or "eight hours," is more correct than 8:00. In the military, World Time (UTC) is often called Zulu or Zulu Time.

Don't forget to "wind your calendar," because at midnight a new *World Day* arrives. This can trip up even experienced listeners—sometimes radio stations, too. So if it is 9:00 PM EST Wednesday in New York, it is 02:00 hours World Time *Thursday*.

Bottom line for clocks: Purchase a radio with a 24-hour clock or buy a separate clock, then check out the sidebar "World Time: Setting Your Clock".

Specialty clock from PilotShopUSA.com gives an idea of regional times throughout the world.

Must #2: Finding Stations

PASSPORT **shows station schedules three ways: by country, time of day and frequency.** By-country is best for tuning to a given station. "What's On Tonight's" hour-by-hour format is like *TV Guide*, complete with program descriptions. The Blue Pages' quick-access grids show what you might be hearing when you're dialing around the bands.

World band frequencies are usually given in kilohertz (kHz), but some stations and radios use Megahertz (MHz). The only difference is three decimal places, so 6170 kHz is the same as 6.17 MHz, 6175 kHz equals 6.175 MHz, and so on.

FM and other stations keep the same spot on the dial, day and night— webcast URLs, too, sort of. But things are different on the international airwaves. World band radio is like a global bazaar where a variety of merchants come and go at various times of the day and night. So, where you once tuned in a French station, hours later you might find a Russian roosting on that same spot.

Or on a nearby perch. If you suddenly hear interference, it doesn't necessarily mean something is wrong with your radio—another station may have fired up on a nearby frequency. There are more stations on the air than available space, so sometimes they try to outshout each other.

> World Time— one time zone for one planet.

PASSPORT'S THREE-MINUTE START

Owner's manual a yawn? Try this:

1. Night time is the right time, so listen evenings when signals are strongest. In a concrete-and-steel building put your radio by a window or on a balcony.

2. Make sure your radio is plugged in or has fresh batteries. Extend its telescopic antenna fully and vertically. Set the DX/local switch, if there is one, to DX, but otherwise leave controls at the factory settings.

3. Turn on your radio after dark. Set it to 5900 kHz and begin tuning slowly toward 6200 kHz. You should hear stations from around the world.

Other times? Read the nearby sidebar, "Best Times and Frequencies for 2008."

This modish Parisian structure incorporates the offices of Radio France Internationale. RFI's broadcasts focus on the French language and Francophone culture, so relatively little is in English.   M. Wright

To cope with this, purchase a radio with superior adjacent-channel rejection—selectivity—and lean towards models with synchronous selectable sideband. PASSPORT REPORTS tests these and other features and tells you which models can hack it.

Because world band is full of surprises from one listening session to the next, experienced listeners like to stroll through the airwaves. Daytime, you'll find most stations above 11500 kHz; at night, below 10000 kHz, but there are interesting exceptions.

If a station can't be found or fades out, there is probably nothing wrong with your radio or the schedule. World band stations are located on *terra firma*, but because of the earth's curvature their signals eventually run into the sky-high ionosphere. When the ionosphere is suitably energized, it deflects these signals back down, after which they bounce off oceans or soil and sail back up to the ionosphere.

This bouncing up and down like a basketball continues until the signal arrives at your radio. However, if the ionosphere at any one "bounce point" isn't in a bouncing mood—it varies daily and seasonally, like the weather—the signal passes through the ionosphere and disappears into space. That's great for intergalactic travelers, but for the rest of us it's the main reason a scheduled signal might be audible one hour, gone the next.

No Censorship—War or Peace

World band stations cope with the ionosphere's changeability by operating within different frequency ranges, depending on the season and time of day—even the 11-year sunspot cycle. This changeability is part of the fun and lets you eavesdrop on juicy signals not intended for your part of the world.

The ionosphere is also why world band radio is free from regulation and snooping. Unlike on the Internet, nobody can know what you're hearing—world band signals don't rely on cables or satellites, just layers of heavenly gases. This makes world band the ultimate for not leaving tracks that could come back to haunt during states of national emergency, security-clearance investigations or employment checks.

The ionosphere also helps analog world band transmissions to be heard even when there's skywave jamming, the only type feasible outside urban areas. Daily jamming is currently limited to authoritarian regimes—Cuba, Iran and China, for example. Yet, even some democratic governments have infrastructures in place to disrupt communications during emergencies. As world band radio is largely beyond their control, it can inform even during the gravest of crises.

Bottom line: World band is almost always there, no matter what.

Must #3: The Right Radio

Choose carefully, but start affordably. If you just want to hear major stations, you'll do fine with one of the higher-rated moderately priced portables. If you want something better, a top-end portable can do surprisingly well with challenging signals and offer superior audio quality.

Tabletop supersets are aimed at experienced and demanding users. If that's you, go for it. Otherwise, pass until you're sure you want a Maserati instead of a Boxter.

Select a radio with digital frequency display. This makes digging out stations much easier—virtually all radios in PASSPORT REPORTS have this, but portables with analog display (slide-rule tuning) still abound. Some low-cost hybrids have analog tuning with digital frequency display, but most digital-display radios use synthesized tuning. These include such handy tuning aids as presets and keypads.

Also, get a radio that covers at least 4750–21850 kHz with no significant frequency gaps. Otherwise, it may miss some juicy stations.

An exotic outside antenna isn't a must unless you're using a tabletop model—portables are designed to work quite well with their built-in telescopic antennas. If you want to enhance a portable's weak-signal sensitivity, simply clip several yards or meters of insulated wire onto that antenna, or use one of the portable active antennas evaluated in PASSPORT REPORTS.

Bottom line: Avoid cheap models, especially with slide-rule tuning—they suffer from major defects. But don't break the bank.

_____

Prepared by Jock Elliott, Tony Jones and Lawrence Magne.

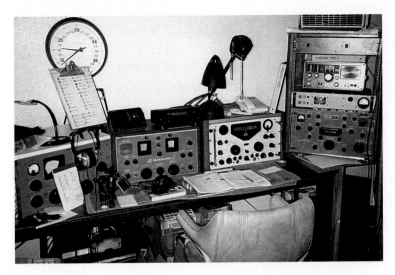

You don't need the latest in receivers to obtain first-class performance. Former Michigan state representative Rick Sitz is awash in top-end communications receivers. These feature audio quality, ergonomics and operational "feel" rarely found today at any price. R. Sitz

WORLD TIME: SETTING YOUR CLOCK

PASSPORT's "Addresses PLUS" lets you figure out local time in other countries by adding or subtracting from World Time. Use it to ascertain local time in a country you are hearing.

This sidebar shows the opposite: what to add or subtract from your local time to get World Time. For example, if you live near Chicago and it's 7:00 AM winter, the list below shows World Time as six hours later, or 13:00.

In the summer, with saving time in effect, World Time is only five hours later—noon, or 12:00. That's because World Time, unlike Chicago time, doesn't change with the seasons. So, once you've set your clock for World Time you won't have to fool with it again.

Many major international broadcasters announce World Time at the hour. On the Internet it's given at various sites, including time5.nrc.ca/webclock_e.shtml. For North America and vicinity, World Time is announced over official stations WWV in Colorado, WWVH in Hawaii and CHU in Ottawa. WWV and WWVH use world band frequencies of 5000, 10000 and 15000 kHz, with WWV also being on 2500 and 20000 kHz. CHU ticks away on 3330, 7335 and 14670 kHz.

Most world band radios now come with built-in 24-hour clocks. Separate clocks are also available from radio and other retailers. Watches, too.

WHERE YOU ARE	TO DETERMINE WORLD TIME
North America	
Newfoundland St. John's NF, St. Anthony NF	Add 3½ hours, 2½ summer
Atlantic St. John NB, Battle Harbour NF	Add 4 hours, 3 summer
Eastern New York, Miami, Toronto	Add 5 hours, 4 summer
Central Chicago, Mexico City, Nashville, Winnipeg	Add 6 hours, 5 summer
Mountain Denver, Salt Lake City, Calgary	Add 7 hours, 6 summer
Pacific San Francisco, Vancouver	Add 8 hours, 7 summer
Alaska	Add 9 hours, 8 summer
Hawaii	Add 10 hours
Central America & Caribbean	
Bermuda	Add 4 hours, 3 summer
Barbados, Puerto Rico, Virgin Islands	Add 4 hours
Bahamas	Add 5 hours, 4 summer
Cuba	Add 5 hours, 4 summer
Jamaica	Add 5 hours
Costa Rica	Add 6 hours

Europe

United Kingdom, Ireland, Portugal	Same time as World Time winter, subtract 1 hour summer
Continental Western Europe; parts of Central and Eastern Continental Europe	Subtract 1 hour, 2 hours summer
Elsewhere in Continental Europe: Belarus, Bulgaria, Cyprus, Estonia, Finland, Greece, Latvia, Lithuania, Moldova, Romania, Russia (Kaliningradskaya Oblast), Turkey, Ukraine	Subtract 2 hours, 3 summer
Moscow	Subtract 3 hours, 4 summer

Mideast & Africa

Côte d'Ivoire, Ghana, Guinea, Liberia, Mali, Morocco, Senegal, Sierra Leone	World Time exactly
Angola, Benin, Chad, Congo, Nigeria	Subtract 1 hour
Tunisia	Subtract 1 hour, 2 summer
Egypt, Israel, Jordan, Lebanon, Syria	Subtract 2 hours, 3 summer
South Africa, Zambia, Zimbabwe	Subtract 2 hours
Ethiopia, Kenya, Kuwait, Saudi Arabia, Tanzania, Uganda	Subtract 3 hours
Iran	Subtract 3½ hours

Asia & Australasia

Pakistan	Subtract 5 hours
India, Sri Lanka	Subtract 5½ hours
Bangladesh	Subtract 6 hours
Laos, Thailand, Vietnam	Subtract 7 hours
China (including Taiwan), Malaysia, Philippines, Singapore	Subtract 8 hours
Japan, Korea	Subtract 9 hours
Australia: *Victoria, New South Wales, Tasmania*	Subtract 11 hours local summer, 10 local winter (midyear)
Australia: *South Australia*	Subtract 10½ hours local summer, 9½ hours local winter (midyear)
Australia: *Queensland*	Subtract 10 hours
Australia: *Northern Territory*	Subtract 9½ hours
Australia: *Western Australia*	Subtract 9 hours local summer, 8 hours local winter (midyear)
New Zealand	Subtract 13 hours local summer, 12 hours local winter (midyear)

BEST TIMES AND FREQUENCIES FOR 2008

Dialing randomly within the full range of shortwave frequencies might get you nothing but dead air. That's because world band stations transmit on limited segments within the shortwave spectrum. Some of these are alive and kicking only by day, while others don't spring to life until night. Time of year also counts.

World band is always active, but many signals are strongest evenings because they're aimed your way. Still, lots of interesting stuff is heard outside prime time when, thanks to shortwave's scattering properties, signals beamed elsewhere are heard.

Experienced station hunters especially enjoy the hour or two on either side of dawn. Because propagation is different then, you may hear parts of the world that normally elude. Try after lunch, too—especially towards sunset. After midnight may also be interesting, especially winters.

Fine Print and Slippery Excuses: Treat this time and frequency guide like a good weather forecast: helpful, but not holy writ. Nature, as always, has a mind of its own, and world band is nature's radio.

This guide is most accurate if you're north of the African and South American continents. Even then, what you hear will vary depending on such things as your location, where the station transmits from, the time of year and your radio hardware.

☞ World band radio has fourteen official frequency segments. Nevertheless, broadcasters also operate "out of band" as legitimate secondary users, provided they don't cause harmful initial interference to such primary users as fixed-service utility stations.

☞ "Night" refers to your local hours of darkness, give or take.

Night—Very Limited Reception
Day—Local Reception Only

2 MHz (120 meters) **2300–2495 kHz**—used by a very few domestic stations, plus 2496–2504 kHz for time stations only.

Night—Limited Reception
Day—Local Reception Only

3 MHz (90 meters) **3200–3400 kHz**—overwhelmingly domestic broadcasters, but also some international stations.

Day and Night—Good-to-Fair in Europe and Asia except Summer Nights; Elsewhere, Limited Reception Night

4 MHz (75 meters) **3900–4050 kHz**—international and domestic stations, primarily not in or beamed to the Americas; 3900–3950 kHz mainly Asian and Pacific transmitters; 3950–4000 kHz also includes European transmitters; 4001–4050 kHz currently out-of-band.

World band is free from regulation and snooping.

Night—Fair Reception
Day—Regional Reception Only

5 MHz (60 meters) **4750–4995 kHz** and **5005–5100 kHz**—mostly domestic stations, plus 4996–5004 kHz for time stations only; 5061–5100 kHz currently out-of-band.

Night—Excellent Reception
Day—Regional Reception Only

6 MHz (49 meters) **5730–6300 kHz**—5730–5899 kHz and 6201–6300 kHz currently out-of-band.

Night—Good Reception
Day—Mainly Regional Reception

> Unlike on the Internet, nobody can know what you're hearing.

7 MHz (41 meters) **6890–6990 kHz** and **7100–7600 kHz**—6890–6990 kHz and 7351–7600 kHz currently out-of-band; 7100–7300 kHz no American-based transmitters and few transmissions targeted to the Americas. The 7100 kHz lower parameter for outside the Americas shifts to 7200 kHz in March of 2009.

Day—Fair Reception Winter; Regional Reception Summer
Night—Good Reception Summer

9 MHz (31 meters) **9250–9995 kHz**—9250–9399 kHz and 9901–9995 kHz currently out-of-band, plus 9996–10004 kHz for time stations only.

Day—Good Reception
Night—Variable Reception Summer

11 MHz (25 meters) **11500–12200 kHz**—11500–11599 kHz and 12101–12200 kHz currently out-of-band.

13 MHz (22 meters) **13570–13870 kHz**

15 MHz (19 meters) **15005–15825 kHz**—15005–15099 kHz and 15801–15825 kHz currently out-of-band, plus 14996–15004 kHz for time stations only.

Day—Good Reception
Night—Limited Reception Summer

17 MHz (16 meters) **17480–17900 kHz**

19 MHz (15 meters) **18900–19020 kHz**—few stations use this segment.

Day—Variable Reception
Night—Little Reception

21 MHz (13 meters) **21450–21850 kHz**

Day—Rare, if Any, Reception
Night—No Reception

25 MHz (11 meters) **25670–26100 kHz**

GRUNDIG

TIMELESS PERFORMANCE

Satellit 1000 AM/FM/Shortwave

- Frequency Coverage: 100-30,000 KHz, includes shortwave, medium wave AM broadcast band and longwave; 76-90, 87-108 MHz FM broadcast band
- Digital Display: large 5.7 inch square, 240 x 320 pixel, dot matrix display. Shows all modes and selected functions
- Programmable Memories: 500 user programmable with alpha labeling plus 1200 user definable country memories, for a total of 1700
- Digital Phase Lock Loop (PLL) Synthesized Tuning with Direct Digital Synthesis (DDS) for drift-free frequency stability and finest tuning resolution
- Dual Conversion Superheterodyne Circuit: results in minimized interference through superior selectivity
- Excellent Sensitivity: yielding a true high-performance receiver
- Single Sideband Synchronous AM Detector: selectable USB/LSB or double sideband to minimize adjacent frequency interference and fading distortion of AM signals

G5 AM/FM/Shortwave

- AM/FM-stereo and Shortwave (1711-29999 KHz)
- Single Side Band (SSB)
- Digital Phase Lock Loop (PLL) dual conversion
- Digital Display world-band radio
- Station name input features allow a 4-character input of the stations call letters
- Synthesized tuning system

Selected models
available at:

**Receives
AM Band**

**Receives
FM Band**

**Receives
Shortwave Band**

**Alarm
Clock**

**Headphone
Jack**

GS350DL AM/FM/Shortwave

- AM (530-1710 KHz), FM (88-108 MHz) and Shortwave – continuous coverage from 3 to 28 MHz.
- Highly sensitive and selective analog tuner circuitry with AM/SW Frequency Lock
- Rotary volume control
- Main tuning knob and independent fine-tuning control knob
- Variable RF gain control

G1100 AM/FM/Shortwave

- AM/FM and 10 Shortwave bands (13, 16, 19, 22, 25, 31, 41, 49, 60, 75 meter)
- Analog tuning with digital frequency readout
- Digital display and clock with light
- Digital clock, selectable 12 or 24 hour clock display format, sleep function (5-120 minutes), alarm function selectable by either buzzer or radio, light and snooze function
- Input for AC adapter

GM300 AM/FM/Shortwave

- AM/FM-stereo and 7 Shortwave bands (49, 41, 31, 25, 22, 19 and 16 meters)
- Analog tuner with classic dial knob and digital display
- Rotary volume control
- Digital display shows frequency, time, sleep time and symbols for sleep timer and alarm activation
- Clock, sleep timer, alarm function

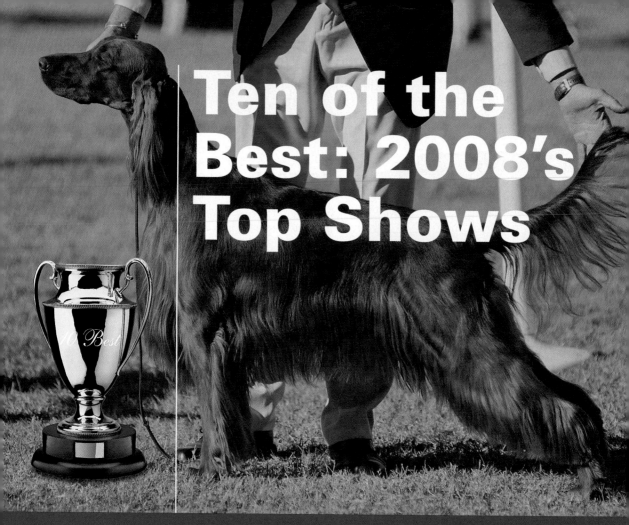

Ten of the Best: 2008's Top Shows

World band shows range from the weird to the wonderful, all "filtered through the shortwaves" as Ed Murrow once described it. Here are ten top choices so you can enjoy the very best.

Times and days are in World Time. "Winter" and "summer" refer to seasons in the Northern Hemisphere, where summer is in the middle of the calendar year.

"The State We're In"
Radio Netherlands

Program changes don't always please, but in 2007 Radio Netherlands came up with a surprise package: "The State We're In." Also known as "Human Rights, Human Wrongs," it is one of the best shows of any type to appear in recent years.

Human rights issues are the program's *raison d'être*, but are complemented by lighter fare—feline androids and vaginal embellishment, for starters. And it's all handled in context and with panache.

The full 50-minute version is aired weekends, local date in target areas, with a shorter 27-minute midweek edition for those preferring a compact format or who missed earlier broadcasts.

North America: (East) 1206 Saturday (one hour earlier in summer) on 11675 kHz, repeated at 2000 (and 1906 Sunday) winter on 15525 kHz, summer on 17735 kHz; and 0006 winter on 6165 kHz, summer on 9845 kHz; *(Central)* 2000 Saturday and 1906 Sunday on 15315 kHz, and 0106 Sunday (Saturday evening in the Americas) on 6165 kHz (summer on 9845 kHz). *(West)* 2000 Saturday and 1906 Sunday winter on 17725 kHz, summer on 17660 kHz; and 0506 Sunday (one hour earlier in summer) on 6165 kHz. The shortened midweek edition is at 1227 Tuesday (one hour earlier in summer) on 11675 kHz, and repeated Wednesday at 0027, 0127 and 0527 (one hour earlier in summer) on the same frequencies as the weekend broadcasts.

There's nothing for *Europe* or the *Middle East*, but two slots for *southern Africa* are 2000 Saturday and 1906 Sunday, winter on 7120 kHz and midyear on 5905 kHz. The midweek edition is at 1830 Tuesday on 6020 and (midyear) 7125 kHz, and 2000 Tuesday and 1900 Thursday on the same frequencies as the weekend broadcasts.

East and *Southeast Asia:* 1006 Saturday and 1027 Tuesday (midweek edition) on 6040 (winter), 9795 (winter), 12065, and (summer) 13710 and 13820 kHz. Some of these channels are also audible in parts of *Australasia*.

> **A show that has you saying, "I didn't know that!"**

"The State We're In" team: (front) Jonathan Groubert, Michèle Ernsting; (middle) Eric Beauchemin, Fiona Campbell, Marni Chesterton, Hélène Michaud; (rear) Bertine Krol, Dheedra Sujan, Tim Fisher, Marijke van der Meer.   RNW

"Christian Message from Moscow" program staff: Tatiana Shvetsova, author of the program; Vladimir Dyomin, director; Pavel Novichkov, narrator; and Elena Gashennikova, sound engineer. VoR

"Christian Message from Moscow"
Voice of Russia

The world's airwaves are increasingly home to predictable religious offerings and conspiracy politics masquerading as Christianity.

Not so the Voice of Russia's "Christian Message from Moscow," which focuses on Russian Orthodoxy. Here is a quality offering which weaves a web of spirituality from church music, spiritual prose by Russian authors, and historical accounts of the lives and work of monks and saints. The result is an emotive atmosphere rarely experienced on electronic media.

North America: Winter, 0231 Saturday (Friday evening local American date) on 6155, 6240, 7150, 7350, 13735 and 15425 kHz; summer, one hour earlier, it's 0131 Saturday on 7250, 9665 and 13775 kHz.

Europe: Winter, 2031 Saturday on 6145, 7105 and 7330 kHz; and 1931 Sunday on 6175, 7105 and 7290 kHz. Summer, 1931 Saturday on 7310, 9890 and 12070 (or 7195) kHz; and 1831 Sunday on 7370, 9890 and 11630 (or 9480) kHz.

Middle East: Winter, 1631 Saturday on 9470 kHz; summer, one hour earlier on 11985 kHz.

Southeast Asia: Winter, 0931 Saturday on 17495 and 17805 kHz; summer, 0831 Saturday on 17495 and 21790 kHz, and 1531 Saturday on 9660 kHz.

Australasia: Winter, 0631 Saturday on 17665 and 17805 kHz, and 0931 the same day on 17495 and 17665 kHz; midyear, times are one hour earlier, 0531 on 17635 and 21790 kHz, and 0831 on 17495, 17635 and 21790 kHz.

"Rear Vision"
ABC Radio National/Radio Australia

Radio Australia not only produces programs, it also carries material from the domestic Radio National. Among these double-duty delights is "Rear Vision," which as the name suggests dispenses with news reporting's usual short-term focus. Instead, it attempts to place contemporary people and events within a historical context. In so doing, it helps separate the genuinely important from glitz-of-the-day.

North America: Officially, Radio Australia only targets East and Southeast Asia and the Pacific, but it is also audible throughout North America for several hours a day—especially around local sunrise. "Rear Vision" is often best from coast to coast at 1330

Thursday on 6020, 9580 and 9590 kHz. Other continent-wide opportunities are 0230 Saturday, summer, on 15515 kHz; and 0800 Sunday winter on 9580 and 9590 kHz. In western North America there's also 1700 Thursday on 6020 and 11880 kHz.

East Asia: 0400 Wednesday on 21725 kHz. *Southeast Asia:* 0400 Wednesday on 17750 kHz, 1700 Thursday on 6080 and 9475 kHz, and 2000 Thursday on 9500 kHz.

"Inside Europe"
Deutsche Welle

Europe has more countries on world band than any other continent, so there is plenty of coverage of European events. Some of

"Inside Europe's" Barbara Gruber joined Deutsche Welle in 2001 after studying in Paris and New York. Co-host Helen Seeney is an Aussie transplant from Brisbane.

DW

the most interesting is on "Inside Europe," Deutsche Welle's weekly newsmagazine.

Background features, interviews and cultural reports emanate from throughout the Continent. Anecdotes are rarely in short supply, and often delight the intellectually curious by being associated with obscure topics: the history of rugby in southern France, for example.

Go figure—Deutsche Welle goes to the trouble of preparing outstanding programs, then pulls the plug on transmissions to Europe, North America and the Middle East. Thankfully, shortwave's scattering properties often come to the rescue, so try frequencies aimed elsewhere if you have a favorable receiving situation (see PASSPORT REPORTS).

Southern Africa: 0430 Friday, winter on 15445 kHz and summer on 12045 kHz. A repeat is at 2030 the same day, winter on 9410 and 13780 kHz, and midyear on 7130, 11795, 11865 and 15205 kHz. In *eastern and southern parts of the United States* try 0430, winter on 7225 kHz and summer on 7245 kHz—both aimed at Africa but heard well beyond.

Southeast Asia: 0030 Saturday, winter on 7265 and 9785 kHz, and summer on 7245 and 15595 kHz—also *northern and western Australia*.

"Newsline"
Radio Netherlands

Most stations can't match the newsgathering resources of major networks, and Radio Netherlands is no exception. Yet, its 27-minute "Newsline" tends to be more interesting and better produced than offerings from deep-pocketed competitors.

At most media organizations there is a predictable list of what subjects and countries should garner airtime. Not so at Radio Netherlands, where in-depth coverage is routinely given to worthy stories that typically get back-burner treatment elsewhere. Reporting is rock-solid, and as a bonus there's a roundup of Netherlands news and a review of Dutch newspapers.

Michel Walraven (foreground) and Richard Walker (on phone) preparing another edition of "Newsline" at Radio Netherlands.   RNW

All editions are aired Monday through Friday, local date in target areas.

North America: (East) 1200 (one hour earlier in summer) on 11675 kHz, repeated at 0000 on 6165 kHz (summer on 9845 kHz); *(Central)* 0127 on 6165 kHz (summer on 9845 kHz); *(West)* 0527 (one hour earlier in summer) on 6165 kHz.

There's nothing for *Europe* or the *Middle East*, but there are three slots for *southern Africa*: 1800 on 6020 and (midyear) 7125 kHz, and 1930 and 2030 winter on 7120 kHz, replaced midyear by 5905 kHz.

East and *Southeast Asia:* 1000 on 6040 (winter), 9795 (winter), 12065, and (summer) 13710 and 13820 kHz. Some of these channels are also heard in parts of *Australasia*.

"The Science Show"
ABC Radio National/Radio Australia

Of all science programs on world band, Radio Australia's "The Science Show" can be considered the most scientific. Presented by long-time host Robyn Williams, it's a flag-ship offering of the Australian Broadcasting Corporation's domestic Radio National.

Perforins and regenerative medicine share airtime with sleep disorders and jellyfish; biofuels and lunar eclipses with embryonic cells and the bee genome. It's hearty fare if you're serious about science.

Audible in *western North America* at 1600 Sunday on 6020 and 7240 kHz, and in *Southeast Asia* at 0400 Friday on 17750 kHz.

"Music and Musicians"
Voice of Russia

The Voice of Russia's musical lineup includes classical, jazz, folk and popular, but the star is the classical "Music and Musicians." A listener favorite going back decades, it remains as fresh as a spring flower.

Whether it be superb individual performances or sublime choral music, quality more than compensates for long-haul audio. Interviews and anecdotes are kept short, so that music occupies center stage. This is a 47-minute "must" for *les mélomanes*.

"Spectrum" host Rajiv Sharma proves that science can hold nearly anybody's attention when it is presented creatively.   DW

"Spectrum"
Deutsche Welle

World band has had its fair share of science and development programs, but few have stayed the course as commendably as Deutsche Welle's "Spectrum." Earthy subjects like soil erosion are complemented by such offbeat topics as invisibility cloaking devices. Using a worldwide team of reporters, "Spectrum" is tightly edited and never bores. It is science for everybody.

Deutsche Welle prepares great programs, but has ceased beaming them to Europe, North America and the Middle East. Nevertheless, thanks to shortwave's scattering properties you can try frequencies aimed elsewhere if you have a favorable receiving situation (see PASSPORT REPORTS).

Southern Africa: 0430 Tuesday, winter on 15445 kHz and summer on 12045 kHz. It repeats later the same day at 2030, winter on 9410 and 13780 kHz, and midyear on 7130, 11795, 11865 and 15205 kHz. In *eastern and southern parts of the United States* try 0430, winter on 7225 kHz and summer on 7245 kHz—both aimed at Africa but heard well beyond.

Southeast Asia: 0030 Wednesday, winter on 7265 and 9785 kHz, and summer on 7245 and 15595 kHz—also *northern and western Australia.*

North America: Winter, 0411 Sunday (Saturday evening local American date) on 6155, 7350, 9840, 12010, 12030, 12065, 13735 and 15425 kHz; summer, one hour earlier on 9435, 9515, 9665, 9860, 9880 (or 5900), 12065, 13775 and 15595 kHz.

Europe has three slots: Winter, 1811 Saturday and Sunday on 6055, 6175, 7105 and 7320 kHz; and 2111 Saturday on 7290 and 7330 kHz; summer, 1711 weekends on 7370, 9820, 9890 and 11675 (or 7320) kHz; and 2011 Saturday on 9890 and 12070 (or 7195) kHz.

Middle East: Winter, 1811 Saturday and Sunday on 7270 kHz; summer, one hour earlier on 11985 kHz. *Southern Africa* gets the same (one hour earlier in summer) on 11510 kHz.

Australasia: Winter, 0811 Monday on 17495, 17665 and 17805 kHz, midyear, one hour earlier on 17495, 17635 and 21790 kHz.

"Report from Austria—
The Week in Review"
Radio Austria International

For one reason or another worthy programs can sail under most listeners' radar.

So it appears to be with "Report from Austria—The Week in Review." Perhaps this is because Radio Austria International offers relatively little in English, even though its limited output is of superior quality.

"The Week in Review" selects the best from the weekday "Report from Austria." Most items are about Austria and Central Europe, plus there's Austrian perspective on major international events. Final minutes are given over to listener feedback.

All transmissions except to the Middle East are aired Saturday and Sunday, local days in target areas.

North America: (East) 0035 winter on 7325 kHz, and 0135 summer on 9870 kHz; *(West)* 1605 and 1635 winter on 13675 kHz, and summer one hour earlier on 13775 kHz. *Central America:* 0005 winter on 7325 kHz, and 0105 summer on 9870 kHz.

Europe: 1305 and 1335 winter (one hour earlier in summer) on 6155 and 13730 kHz. *Middle East:* Sunday only at 0605 and 0635 (one hour earlier in summer) on 17870 kHz.

South and *Southeast Asia* and *Australasia:* 1305 and 1335 winter on 17855 kHz, and summer one hour earlier on 17715 kHz.

Hecho en Cuba
encompasses a range of
Cuban musical types.
Shutterstock

"Hecho en Cuba"
Radio Rebelde

Every now and again, a show appears which defies definition.

Such is *"Hecho en Cuba,"* a showcase for the country's popular music. Originating from the domestic Radio Rebelde, it's a brew of Cuban ballads, rhythms and nostalgia. One moment there's *reggaetón* or Cristina Aguilera, the next it is one of yesteryear's great Cuban orchestras. It is all part of the love of life that attracts folks to Cuban culture and unites Cubans wherever they live.

"Hecho en Cuba" is aired at 1731 Monday through Friday (one hour earlier in summer) and is beamed to *North, South and Central America*. Frequencies tend to change, but try 11655, 13750, 15370, 17555 and 17735 kHz. Occasionally heard in *western Europe*.

**"Rear Vision"
ponders the
unfolding impact
of today's news.**

Prepared by the staff of Passport to World Band Radio.

Journalist Nina Haase
works on environmental
stories for Deutsche
Welle's "Spectrum."   DW

GRUNDIG
TIMELESS PERFORMANCE

G5 AM/FM/Shortwave
Winner of the Consumers Digest Best Buy Award 2007

- AM/FM-stereo and Shortwave (1711-29999 KHz)
- Single Side Band (SSB)
- Digital Phase Lock Loop (PLL) dual conversion
- Digital Display world-band radio
- Station name input features allow a 4-character input of the stations call letters
- Synthesized tuning system

Selected models available at:

 Radioworld® GROVE

Available under the Etón name in Europe:

België/Belgique I LUCODEX nv	Hellas I A. & E. ΔΑΜΑΣΚΗΝΟΥ Ο.Ε.	Österreich I Novis Electronics GmbH
United Kingdom I Nevada	Italia I HiFi United Srl	Schweiz/Suisse I Novis Electronic AG

GS350DL AM/FM/Shortwave

- AM (530-1710 KHz), FM (88-108 MHz) and Shortwave – continuous coverage from 3 to 28 MHz.
- Highly sensitive and selective analog tuner circuitry with AM/SW Frequency Lock
- Rotary volume control
- Main tuning knob and independent fine-tuning control knob
- Variable RF gain control

G1100 AM/FM/Shortwave

- AM/FM and 10 Shortwave bands (13, 16, 19, 22, 25, 31, 41, 49, 60, 75 meter)
- Analog tuning with digital frequency readout
- Digital display and clock with light
- Digital clock, selectable 12 or 24 hour clock display format, sleep function (5-120 minutes), alarm function selectable by either buzzer or radio, light and snooze function
- Input for AC adapter

GM300 AM/FM/Shortwave

- AM/FM-stereo and 7 Shortwave bands (49, 41, 31, 25, 22, 19 and 16 meters)
- Analog tuner with classic dial knob and digital display
- Rotary volume control
- Digital display shows frequency, time, sleep time and symbols for sleep timer and alarm activation
- Clock, sleep timer, alarm function

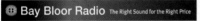

Suomi/Danmark | Intodesign

Sverige | Intodesign

Deutschland | MBA Marken-Vertriebs GmbH

España | ANMI Electronics

France | Elite Diffusion

Grundig Radio Line By etón re_inventing radio www.etoncorp.com

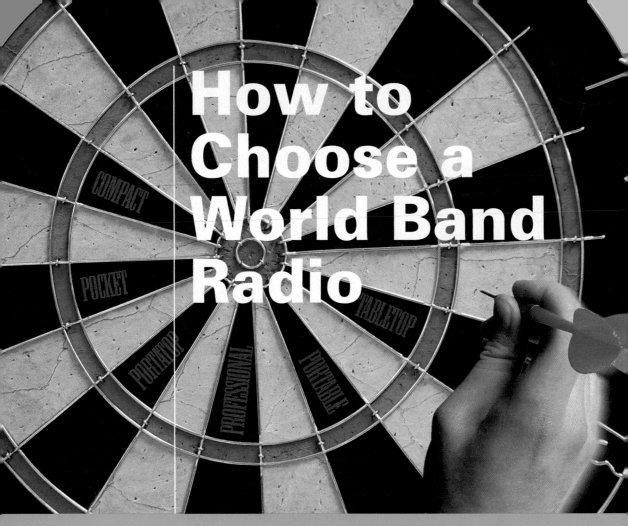

How to Choose a World Band Radio

Some electronic products are commodities. With a little common sense you can find something plenty good.

But not world band receivers, which can vary greatly from model to model. As usual money talks, but even that's a fickle barometer. Fortunately, many perform well and we rate them accordingly. Yet, even among models with comparable star ratings it helps to read the fine print.

Squeezed-in Stations

World band radio offers hundreds of channels, each shoehorned five kilohertz away from the other. That's more crowded than FM and around twice as crammed as mediumwave AM.

It gets worse: Global treks wear down signals, causing fading and reduced strength. To cope with these challenges, a world band radio has to perform electronic gymnastics. Some succeed, others don't.

This is why PASSPORT REPORTS was created. At International Broadcasting Services we've independently tested hundreds of world band radios, antennas and accessories since 1977. These evaluations include rigorous hands-on use by listeners, plus specialized lab tests developed over the years. These form the basis of PASSPORT REPORTS, and for the Full Monty on various popular premium receivers and antennas there are also Radio Database International White Papers®.

Four-Point Checklist

✔ **Price.** Want to hear major stations, or do you prefer gentler voices from exotic lands? Powerful evening signals, or weaker stations by day? Decide, then choose a radio that slightly surpasses your needs—this helps ensure against disappointment without spending too much.

Radio World's James Careless describes portables like the Etón Mini 300 as "cheap and cheerful."

Once the novelty of world band wears thin, most people give up on cheap radios—they're clumsy to tune, often receive poorly and can sound terrible. That's why we rarely cover analog-readout radios. Yet, even some models with digital frequency readout can disappoint.

Most find satisfaction with digital-readout portables selling for $50–150 in the United States or €50–130 in the United Kingdom, and having a rating of ✪✪¾ or more. If you're looking for elite performance, shoot for a costlier portable rated ✪✪✪¾ or better. If you want bragging rights, a five-star tabletop or a professional model is *numero uno*.

✔ **Location**. Signals are usually strongest around Europe, North Africa and the Near East; they're almost as good evenings in eastern North America. Otherwise, in the Americas—or in Hawaii, Australasia or the Middle East—spring for a receiver with superior sensitivity to weak signals. An accessory antenna helps, too.

✔ **Features.** Divide features between those for performance and those that impact operation (see sidebars), but regard them with a cynical eye. Radios with relatively few features sometimes outperform those tricked out with seductive goodies.

> A radio that slightly surpasses your needs helps avoid disappointment.

PASSPORT'S STANDARDS

At International Broadcasting Services we have been analyzing shortwave equipment since 1977. Our reviewers, and no one else, write and edit everything in PASSPORT REPORTS. Our lab tests are performed by an independent laboratory recognized as the world's leader. (For more on this, see the Radio Database International White Paper, *How to Interpret Receiver Lab Tests and Measurements*.)

The review process is completely separate from equipment advertising, which is not allowed within PASSPORT REPORTS. Our team members may not accept review fees from manufacturers, nor may they "permanently borrow" radios. International Broadcasting Services does not manufacture, sell or distribute world band radios or related hardware.

✔ **Where to buy?** Whether you buy in a store or from afar makes little difference. That's because world band receivers don't test well in stores except in the rare showroom with an outdoor antenna. Even then, long-term satisfaction is hard to gauge from a spot test, so check at different times.

One thing you can nail down in a store is ergonomics—how intuitive is the radio to operate? You can also get a thumbnail idea of world band fidelity by listening to mediumwave AM stations or a muscular world band station.

With Internet purchases from foreign countries, don't expect enforceable warranties. Too, AC voltages may be inappropriate, and packets are sometimes refused by customs because of trademark and other legal considerations.

CONVENIENCE FEATURES

To find stations quickly, look for *digital frequency readout*, found on virtually all models tested by PASSPORT REPORTS. Too, a *24-hour World Time clock* to know when to tune in; many receivers include them. The best allow time to be read while the frequency is being displayed.

If your radio doesn't include a World Time clock, there are standalone 24-hour clocks and watches. Seconds displayed numerically are a nice touch so you can be alert for station IDs.

Other handy features: direct-access tuning by *keypad* and station *presets* ("memories"); and any combination of a *tuning knob*, up/down *slewing controls* or *"signal-seek" scanning* to search for stations. A few models have handy *one-touch presets* buttons, like a classic car radio. Quick access to *world band segments* (meter bands) is another time saver.

Presets are important because world band stations don't stay on the same frequency all day. Being able to store a station's multiple frequencies makes the station easier to find. With sophisticated receivers, presets should be able to store not only frequency, but also such parameters as bandwidth, mode and AGC.

Useful but less important is an *on/off timer*. Also, look for an *illuminated display* and a good *signal-strength indicator*, either as an analog meter or a digital display.

Travelers prefer portables with *power-lock switches* or *recessed power buttons* so the radio won't go on by itself in luggage. ☞ Power locks on some Chinese portables don't disable display illumination.

If ergonomics stand out, bad or good, PASSPORT REPORTS says so. But few controls doesn't necessarily mean handier operation. Some receivers with many controls are easier to operate than comparable receivers with few controls—especially if operation involves complex software choices.

Icom's new IC-R9500 is tricked out with enough features for an Apache cockpit.

D. Zantow

PERFORMANCE FEATURES

A signal should sound pleasant, not just be audible. To help, some radios have features to ward off unwanted sounds or improve audio quality. Of course, just because a feature exists doesn't mean it functions properly, but PASSPORT REPORTS' team checks this out.

Reception "Musts"

Full world band coverage from 2300–26100 kHz is best, but 3200–21850 kHz is plenty good—even 5730–21850 kHz is usually okay. Less coverage? Look over "Best Times and Frequencies for 2008" elsewhere in PASSPORT to see what's missed.

Synchronous selectable sideband helps knock out adjacent-channel interference and reduce fading distortion. This advanced feature is found on a few portables, as well as most tabletop and professional models. PASSPORT REPORTS indicates which work well.

Especially if a receiver doesn't include synchronous selectable sideband, it benefits from having two or more *bandwidths* to reduce adjacent-channel interference. Some premium models have multiple bandwidths and synchronous selectable sideband—a killer combo.

Double (or multiple) conversion helps reject unwanted disturbances—images, unwanted growls, whistles and dih-dah sounds. Few cheaper models have it.

Spit and Polish

Tone controls are a plus, especially if continuous with separate bass and treble. For world band reception, *single-sideband* (SSB) isn't important, but is essential for utility or "ham" signals. SSB's main use for world band is to hear the American Forces Radio and Television Service.

Tabletop models flush out stubborn signals, but they're for veterans and are overkill for casual listening. Look for a tunable *notch filter* to zap howls; *passband offset* (also called *passband tuning* and *IF shift*) for superior adjacent-channel rejection and audio contouring, especially in conjunction with synchronous selectable sideband; and multiple *AGC* decay rates. At electrically noisy locations a *noise blanker* is essential, although performance varies greatly.

Some features count, some don't, and not all work well.

Digital signal processing (DSP) attempts to enhance reception quality. Until recently it has been much smoke, little fire, but it has been improving—slowly.

Digital Radio Mondiale (DRM), a form of digital transmission with good and bad points, is slowly being rolled out for world band. Thus far there have been far more DRM transmissions than models of DRM receivers, which to date have been like Elvis sightings. However, there are a few regular receivers that feed a 12 kHz IF to a personal computer to process DRM signals.

With portables an *AC adaptor* reduces operating costs and may improve weak-signal performance. Some are poorly made and cause hum or buzzing, but most are okay. With tabletop models an *inboard AC power supply* is preferable but not essential.

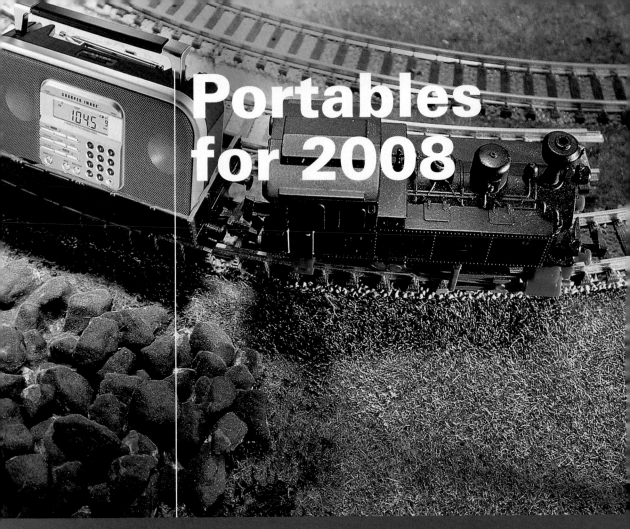

Portables
for 2008

Portables are world band's meat and potatoes. They are handy, affordable and usually do the trick whether at home or away.

Evening signals come in well throughout Europe and eastern North America, so there virtually any well-rated portable is okay. Elsewhere or daytime—when broadcasts tend to be more avail-able and interesting but weaker—a good portable can be boosted by an accessory antenna, covered in PASSPORT REPORTS.

DRM Digital Broadcasts

DRM-capable portables can pro-cess Digital Radio Mondiale (DRM) world band and other broadcasts. A trickle of these portables was sold in 2007 in Europe and Asia, and two car radios may be in the offing, but so far it's been more bun than beef.

For good reason. DRM, which has been around for years, is easy to jam and relatively ineffective with multi-hop transmissions, negating world band's two greatest virtues. Also, shortwave's characteristic fading causes DRM's digital signal to flop in and out. And DRM's wideband hash woefully disrupts conventional world band signals on adjacent, second-adjacent channels and beyond.

Nevertheless, at its best DRM provides audio quality that tops even the best analog world band audio. Whether this is worth myriad shortcomings in a medium dominated by news and talk is anybody's guess, but thus far the DRM world band receiver market has been anything but responsive.

This could do an about-face if China adopts DRM for domestic stations, as DRM holds much promise with groundwave signals. Only time will tell.

Find major updates to the 2008 PASSPORT REPORTS at www. passband.com.

Portables in Three Flavors

Think of pocket portables as being like cellphones, while compacts resemble Palm-type handhelds and large portables are similar to laptop PCs. You can't go wrong with a $150 compact rated at three or more stars, but lesser models can cut that in half or less.

Top end goes for the equivalent of five hundred dollars. That's for near-tabletop performance—more than you may need, but probably not more than you want.

Friendly skies? Pocket models are ideal, and their limited speaker audio can be overcome with earpieces. Yet, compact models, also relatively suitable for home, tend to perform better, sometimes sell for less, and are small and light enough for most.

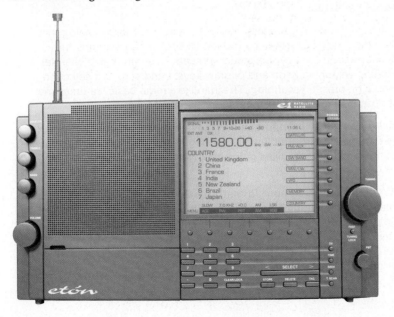

The Etón E1 is the top portable performer of all time. It also can be equipped to receive XM satellite broadcasts.

WHAT TO LOOK FOR

• **AC adaptor.** Those from by the manufacturer are usually best and should be free from significant hum and noise—those that aren't are cited under "Con." Some are multivoltage and operate almost anywhere in the world. Switching-type power supplies, legally required in some jurisdictions, may disrupt radio signals; PASSPORT REPORTS points these out.

• **Adjacent-channel rejection—I:** *selectivity, bandwidth.* World band stations are about twice as tightly packed as ordinary mediumwave AM stations. So, they tend to slop over and interfere with each other—DRM digital broadcasts are even worse. Radios with superior selectivity are better at rejecting interference, but at a price: better selectivity also means less high-end (treble) audio response and muddier sound. So, having more than one bandwidth allows you to choose between tighter selectivity (narrow bandwidth) when it is warranted, and more realistic audio (wide bandwidth) when it is not.

• **Adjacent-channel rejection—II:** *synchronous selectable sideband.* For tough catches, synchronous selectable sideband improves listening quality by minimizing selective-fading distortion and adjacent-channel interference. *Bonus:* Synchronous selectable sideband, as well as synchronous double sideband, greatly help reduce fading distortion with fringe mediumwave AM stations at twilight and even at night.

• **Ergonomics.** Some radios are a snap to use because they don't have complicated features. Yet, even sophisticated models can be designed to operate intuitively. Choose accordingly—there's no reason to take the square root and cube it just to hear a radio station.

• **Single-sideband demodulation.** If you are interested in hearing non-broadcast shortwave signals—hams and utility stations—single-sideband circuitry is *de rigueur.* Too, the popular low-powered American Forces Radio-Television Service requires this.

• **Speaker audio quality.** Unlike many portatop and tabletop models, few portables have rich, full audio through their speakers. However, some are much better than others, and with a model having line output you can connect amplified speakers for pleasant home listening; FM micro-transmitters, too.

• **Tuning features.** Models with digital frequency readout are so superior to analog that these are now the only radios normally tested by PASSPORT. Look for such handy tuning aids as direct-frequency access via keypad, station presets (programmable channel memories), up-down tuning via tuning knob and/or slew keys, band/segment selection, and signal-seek or other (e.g., presets) scanning. These make a radio easier to tune—no small point, given that dozens of channels may be audible at a time.

• **Weak-signal sensitivity.** Sensitivity is important if you live in a weak-signal location or tune exotic or daytime stations. Most portables have enough sensitivity to pull in major stations during prime time if you're in the likes of Europe, North Africa or eastern North America.

• **World Time clock.** World Time is in 24-hour format, so a 24-hour clock is a must. You can obtain one separately, but many radios have them built in; the best display time whether the radio is on or off. However, many portable radios' clocks tend to gain or lose time if not reset periodically. In North America and beyond, official shortwave time stations WWV on 2500, 5000, 10000, 15000 and 20000 kHz and CHU on 3330, 7335 and 14670 kHz are ideal for this; the Pacific is also served by WWVH in Hawaii on 2500, 5000, 10000 and 15000 kHz.

Longwave

The longwave band still includes domestic broadcasts in Europe, North Africa and Russia. If you live or travel in rural areas there, longwave coverage may be a plus. Otherwise, forget it.

Fix or Toss?

Portables aren't meant to be friends for life and are priced accordingly. The most robust models are usually not ready for the landfill until a decade or more of use, whereas pedestrian portables may give only a few years of regular service. Rarely are any except top-end models worth fixing outside warranty.

If you receive a DOA portable, insist upon an immediate exchange without a restocking fee—manufacturers' repair facilities tend to have a disappointing record. If out-of-warranty service is a priority, consider a tabletop model or the Etón E1/Grundig Satellit 1000 serviced by the renowned R.L. Drake Company.

Shelling Out

Street prices are cited, including European VAT where applicable. These vary plus or minus, so take them as the general guide they are meant to be. Shortwave specialty outlets and some other retailers usually have attractive prices, but duty-free shopping is not always the bargain you might expect.

eBay is no different for radios than anything else. On one hand, you may well get the lowest price, and in time you'll probably receive what you hoped for—indeed, eBay is usually the only global outlet for radios manufactured exclusively for the domestic Chinese market. On the other hand, based on our experience and reader reports, if you receive a problem or damaged radio you can usually forget making a successful claim, even if you paid extra for insurance.

eBay is also where hurt radios—especially costlier models—wind up being palmed off as "new in box." If you get stuck, don't expect the manufacturer to bail you out.

We try to stick to plain English, but specialized terms can be useful. If you come across something unclear, *see* Worldly Words.

What PASSPORT's Ratings Mean

Star ratings: ❂❂❂❂❂ is best. Stars reflect overall performance and meaningful features, plus to some extent ergonomics and perceived build quality. Price, appearance, country of manufacture and the like are not taken into account. To facilitate comparison, portable rating standards are very similar to those used for the portatop, tabletop and professional models reviewed elsewhere in this PASSPORT REPORTS.

A rating of at least ❂❂½ should please most who listen to major stations regularly during the evening. However, for casual use on trips virtually any small portable may suffice.

Passport's Choice. La crème de la crème. Our test team's personal picks of the litter—models we would buy or have bought for our personal use. Unlike star ratings, these choices are unapologetically subjective.

❂: A relative bargain, with decidedly more performance than the price would suggest.

Tips for Using This Section

Models are listed by size; and, within size, in order of world band listening suitability. Street selling prices are cited, including EU VAT where applicable.

Unless otherwise indicated, each model has:

- Keypad tuning, up/down slew keys, station presets and signal-seek tuning/scanning.
- Digital frequency readout to the nearest kilohertz or five kilohertz.
- Coverage of the shortwave spectrum, including world band, from at least 3200–26100 kHz.
- Coverage of the usual 87.5–108 MHz FM band, but not the Japanese and other FM bands below 87 MHz.

- Coverage of the mediumwave AM band in selectable 9 and 10 kHz channel increments from about 530–1705 kHz. No coverage of the 153–279 kHz longwave band.
- Adequate image rejection, almost invariably resulting from double-conversion circuitry.

Unless otherwise indicated, each model lacks:

- Single-sideband demodulation.
- Synchronous selectable sideband. However, when it is present the unwanted sideband is rejected approximately 25 dB by phase cancellation, not IF filtering.
- If 24-hour clock included, lacks tens-of-hours leading zero that properly should be displayed with World Time (UTC); also, clock does not show seconds numerically.

LAP PORTABLES

Pleasant for Home, Acceptable for Travel

A lap portable is for use primarily around the home and yard, car/RV trips, yachts and on the occasional flight. They are large enough to potentially perform well, usually sound better than compact models, yet are not too big to fit into a carry-on or briefcase. Most take 3–4 "D" (UM-1) or "C" (UM-2) cells, plus sometimes a couple of "AA" (UM-3) cells for memory backup.

These are typically just under a foot/30 cm wide and weigh in around 3–5 pounds/1.4–2.3 kg. For air travel, that's okay if you are a dedicated listener, but a bit much otherwise.

Proposed Version for 2008

❋❋❋❋⅜ 🗐 *Passport's Choice*

Etón E1, E1 Lextronix, Grundig Satellit 1000

Price: *Satellit 1000:* TBA in 2008. *E1:* $499.95 in the United States. CAD$499.00 in Canada. £399.95 in the United Kingdom. €598.00 in Germany. *AudioVox CNP2000 XM antenna with cable and required CNP2000H docking station:* $58.95 for both in the United States. *AudioVox CNP-EXT50 extension cord for XM antenna:* $17.95 in the United States. *KOK1-to-SO-239 aftermarket antenna jack adaptor:* $7.95 in the United States. *E1/Satellit 1000: KOK1 aftermarket male connector (for raw antenna cable):* $4.95 in the United States. *Universal Radio Large Portable Stand:* $16.95 in the United States. *Tenba Port Air 1114 padded carrying case:* $139.95 in the United States.

Pro: Incorporates virtually every tuning method available, including frequency/presets scanning, up/down slewing, keypad frequency selection, quick access to world band segments and a tuning knob. Tuning knob (*see* Con) features variable rate incremental tuning (VRIT); for many this makes bandscanning more convenient. 1,700 easy-to-use presets don't erase if batteries removed; 500 allow for user-written ID tags, while the remainder have factory-created country ID tags. Keypad frequency may be entered in kHz or MHz. Pleasant audio quality, aided by separate bass and treble controls (*see* Con). Overall receiver distortion unusually low (*see* Con). Full three-Watt (nominal) audio amplifier with AC adaptor; when batteries in use, amplifier output is automatically reduced so battery drain can be cut by half. Agreeable ergonomics, including keys with superior feel. Passband tuning (PBT, a/k/a IF shift), a first for a portable; performance excellent. Synchronous selectable sideband holds lock unusually well; adjacent-channel interference reduction and tonal response aided by passband tuning adjustment. Synchronous double sideband overcomes selective fading distortion and enhances fidelity during twilight and darkness (mixed skywave/groundwave) reception of fringe mediumwave AM stations "in the clear." Wide (20 kHz signal spacing) dynamic range good, IP3 excellent with preamp off, to the point that resistance to overloading, even with Beverage antennas, comparable to that of excellent tabletop supersets; wide DR/IP3 still tests as good with preamp on (*see* Con). Blocking good. Phase noise good, although still intrudes beyond 80 dB down. Sensitivity/noise floor good-to-excellent with preamp

Grundig's Satellit 1000 is scheduled for introduction in 2008. All indications are that it will be virtually identical to the existing Etón E1 except for color. Yet—name notwithstanding—it apparently won't receive satellite signals.

off, excellent-to-superb with 10 dB preamp on. Three well-chosen voice/music bandwidths (2.5, 5 and 8 kHz) with skirt selectivity and ultimate rejection that are excellent or better. Image rejection approaches professional caliber. Excellent first IF rejection. Tuning and display in 10 Hz steps, exceptionally precise for a portable; 100 Hz and 1 kHz tuning steps also selectable. On our current unit, frequency display came from factory absolutely accurate after lengthy warmup (*see* Con); frequency readout accuracy user-adjustable with a small flat-blade screwdriver through first vent slot just to right of "CE" sticker on back of cabinet. No chuffing or muting when tuning. Octave filters provide good front end selectivity by tabletop standards, which is exceptional for a portable. Single-sideband performance above average for a portable, aided by excellent frequency stability. Signal indicator, with 21 bars, uncommonly accurate from S3 through 60 dB over S9 even by professional standards. Audio line output jack (stereo on E1's FM/XM, Satellit 1000's FM) with proper level to feed external amplifier/speaker system, recorder or FM/AM microtransmitter; also, external speaker jack and separate jack for headphones or earpieces. Audio line input jack allows radio to be used as amp/speaker for CD players and the like. Useful battery-strength indicator. Selectable slow/fast AGC decay adjustment; a

third AGC option, "Auto," aids bandscanning by switching from slow to fast when radio tuned. Squelch. Telescopic antenna large and robust (*see* Con). Switches for internal/external antennas (if radio sounds "deaf," ensure these are in correct positions). Clock displays separately from frequency (*see* Con). Two-event timer with selectable on/off times. Snooze and sleep delay. FM above average with excellent sensitivity, aided by switchable FM preamp (17 dB). 0.1–30 MHz tuning range includes longwave broadcast band. Japanese FM. Three-level LCD illumination (*see* Con). Travel power lock. Elevation panel (*see* Con) helps tilt radio to handy operating angle. Well-written printed owner's manual; also on CD-ROM along with quick-start guide. *North America:* Excellent toll-free tech support. *E1, North America:* XM ready, easily implemented (*see* Con). Atomic-type clock automatically kept exceptionally accurate by signals on XM or world band WWV/WWVH (but not longwave WWVB in Colorado on 0.06 MHz) (*see* Con). XM module easily removable for future uses or modes. *Satellit 1000, North America:* Atomic-type clock automatically kept exceptionally accurate by signals on world band WWV/WWVH (but not longwave WWVB in Colorado on 0.06 MHz) (*see* Con). *Elsewhere, including EU:* New version under consideration would replace XM facility with one for DAB.

Con: No carrying handle or strap, nor is there any provision for one to be user-affixed—not even a pair of inconspicuous threaded screw holes; remedied by pricey aftermarket Tenba carrying case. When 2.5 kHz bandwidth used with BFO (or certain PBT settings with wider bandwidths), audio suffers from harshness resulting from high-order distortion products. Muted-sounding audio comes off as somewhat lifeless; needs to be crisper to reach fidelity potential. Narrow (5 kHz signal spacing) dynamic range/IP3 poor, although IP3 improves to fair with preamp off. Preamp, used by default with the telescopic antenna, generates mixing products in stressful reception situations; ironically, a major external antenna without the preamp tends to remedy the problem. Unlike that on the sibling Satellit 800

portatop, the E1's tuning knob shaft lacks ball bearings; it feels slightly grizzly when rotated and some units also have a minor degree of wobble. No rubber grip around tuning knob's circumference; no finger dimple, either (remediable, see fingerdimple.com). Front-mounted battery access door difficult to open. Telescopic antenna flops over when moved from full upright position. Dot-matrix LCD has limited useful viewing angle and lacks contrast in bright rooms or with illumination off; best contrast is found at angle provided by aftermarket Universal Radio stand, although built-in elevation panel also helps some. Reader reports—some confirmed, some not—indicate that streaks appear on the LCD on a scattering of units soon after purchase, requiring that the unit be exchanged under warranty. Non-

NUMBERS: TOP PORTABLE

	Etón E1/Grundig Satellit 1000[1]
Max. Sensitivity/Noise Floor	0.15 μV **S**/–132 dBm **E**[2]
Blocking	123 dB **G**
Bandwidths *(Shape Factors)*	8.0 *(1:1.45* **S***)*, 5.0 *(1:1.6* **E***)*, 2.5 (1.7, **E**)
Ultimate Rejection	80 dB **E**[3]
Front-End Selectivity	**G** [4]
Image Rejection	>90 dB **S**
First IF Rejection	75 dB **E**
Dynamic Range/IP3 (5 kHz)	55 dB **P**/–50 dBm **P**[5]
Dynamic Range/IP3 (20 kHz)	87 dB **G**/–2 dBm **G**[6]
Phase Noise	113 dBc **G**
AGC Threshold	0.3 μV **G**[7]
Overall Distortion, sync	2.6% **G**[8]

IBS Lab Ratings: **S** Superb   **E** Excellent   **G** Good   **F** Fair   **P** Poor

(1) E1 measured; forthcoming Satellit 1000 presumably will measure identically.
(2) Preamp on; 0.28 μV **E**/–126 **G** with preamp off.
(3) Phase noise prevents accurate measurement beyond 80 dB.
(4) Octave filters, unusually good for a portable.
(5) Preamp on; 57 dB **P**/–39 dBm **F** with preamp off.
(6) Preamp on; 88 dB **G**/+7 dBm **E** with preamp off.
(7) Preamp on; 0.9 μV **S** with preamp off.
(8) Harmonic distortion includes several high-order products.

standard connector for world band external antennas, and no adaptor or plug included. Variable-rate incremental tuning (VRIT), which some users don't care for, cannot be disabled. Mediumwave AM lacks directional reception, as it relies on the telescopic antenna in lieu of a customary horizontal ferrite-rod antenna. Included AC adaptor produces minor hum at headphone output. Lacks certain features, such as tunable notch and noise blanker, found on tabletop receivers. No PC interface. No attenuator or RF gain control, although neither needed. No dedicated buttons for presets. Frequency readout drifts very slightly until full warmup; our latest unit's readout was off by 30 Hz at cold start before settling to full accuracy after two hours. Clock display lacks numeric seconds; local time option in 24-hour format only. Line input jack requires above-average audio level to perform properly. Elevation panel flimsy. Paint on knobs, buttons and cabinet could eventually wear through. Four "D" cells not included. Like essentially all other world band portables, not designed to receive DRM digital broadcasts, nor is there a 12 kHz IF output to feed a DRM-configured PC. *Satellit 1000:* Cannot receive XM satellite broadcasts. *E1, North America:* XM reception requires purchase of separate outboard antenna and payment of monthly fee. XM reception not possible when traveling outside United States and Canada. Does not receive Sirius satellite signals. Significant current consumption when XM circuitry in use. Warranty honored only if radio purchased from authorized dealer, listed under each product at www.etoncorp.com. *United States:* Does not provide digital reception of HD Radio broadcasts.

☞ If you see this at bargain prices on eBay and the like, check first with Etón. The factory warranty applies only to units purchased from an authorized dealer.

☞ In January 2006 Etón recalled units s/n 3067–5462, as a defect allowed AC adaptor voltage to back up into internal batteries and cause swelling. The recall came off well. Yet, coincidentally or otherwise, virtually all reader complaints of unreliability and other issues have come from units—unusually re-

furbs—prior to s/n 5463 or units purchased on eBay. Few, if any, of these early-production are still on sale, but they should be avoided, whereas units manufactured after early 2006 and purchased from authorized dealers appear to be holding up normally or better.

Verdict: The Etón E1 is the best portable we've ever tested. It is scheduled to be joined in 2008 by the Grundig Satellit 1000, which appears to be identical except for no XM satellite option and a different color (black).

Either way, this receiver offers a killer combination of features and performance never before found in a portable. It completely dominates the performance end of the world band portable market, and even outperforms a number of costlier tabletop and PC-controlled models.

📄 An *RDI WHITE PAPER* is available.

New Versions for 2008
✪✪¾ ⊘ *Passport's Choice*
CCRadio-SW, Kaito KA-2100, Redsun RP2100, Roadstar TRA-2350P

Price: *CCRadio:* $149.95 including shipping in the United States. *Kaito KA-2100:* $129.95 in the United States. *Roadstar:* €69.95 in Germany. *Redsun export/English version:* $114.99 including global air shipping from China. *Redsun TG37 outboard single-sideband converter module/cable:* $32.99 including global air shipping from China. *CCRadio-SW protective case:* $29.95 in the United States.

Pro: Helpful tuning features include 50 station presets, of which 30 are for world band (*see* Con); two-speed (1/5 kHz) mute-free knob tuning knob with speed dimple (*see* Con); up/down slewing (*see* Con); signal-seek frequency scanning that works well; and meter key for quick access to world band segments (*see* Con). Worthy sensitivity to weak world band (*see* Con) signals. Superior sensitivity to mediumwave AM signals, thanks in part to the inboard Twin Coil Ferrite™ antenna (confirmed only on tested Redsun and CCRadio versions). Useful selec-

The CCRadio-SW is one variation of the Redsun RP2100. It is a pleasant performer for world band, and does especially well with long-distance mediumwave AM signals. Superior FM performance and audio, too.

tivity (adjacent-channel rejection), with two well-chosen bandwidths. Top-notch audio quality with separate and continuously variable bass and treble controls, beefy speaker magnet and superior audio electronics. Decent image rejection (see Con). Virtually no frequency drift. Travel power lock. Large LCD with good contrast; illumination of LCD (see Con) and keys, activated manually or when any knob turned or key pressed (see Con). Five-bar signal indicator (see Con). One-step attenuator. Continuous RF gain control (see Con). Selectable 9 kHz or 10 kHz mediumwave AM steps. Internal-external antenna switch for shortwave and FM. Separate mediumwave AM external antenna connection with spring-clip terminals (see Con). 455 kHz IF output jack for such ancillary devices as the Redsun TG37 outboard single-sideband module (see Con). Excellent FM performance, in stereo through headphones and line-output jack for recording. "Roger beep" for key pushes; can be switched off. Robust telescopic antenna swivels and rotates. Excellent carrying handle folds into top of cabinet. Three-bar battery indicator. Two clocks—World Time and local, 12 or 24 hour format (see Con). Sleep delay, up to 90 minutes. Two clock-radio/alarm timers with handy snooze bar. NiMH cells (see Con) can be recharged internally. May also be operated from—user's choice—four "D" or four "AA" batteries of any type. Optional protective case. *CCRadio:*

Improved tuning knob speed dimple. Included AC adaptor UL approved. 30-day money-back guarantee. *Kaito:* Powered by shielded internal AC transformer instead of customary outboard AC adaptor (see Con); nevertheless, may also be powered by an external 6–9V DC source, including AC adaptor. *Redsun (all versions):* Powered by shielded internal AC mains transformer (see Con) instead of customary outboard AC adaptor; nevertheless, may also be powered by an external 6–9V DC source, including AC adaptor. Outboard passive reel accessory antenna aids slightly in weak-signal reception. *Redsun Export/English version (information unverified):* Now nominally includes stereo earphones, NiMH rechargeable cells, and line-out cable and adaptor.

Con: No keypad, a major omission. Mediocre dynamic range ameliorated only slightly by attenuator or RF gain control. Poor front-end selectivity, so local mediumwave AM stations can "ghost" into shortwave spectrum and disrupt some world band reception. Although image rejection decent, smattering of weak images nonetheless appear 910 kHz down from fundamental frequencies of powerful signals. LCD unevenly illuminated. Illumination shifts from fulltime-on to timed-off when tuning knob turned. Shortwave spectrum divided into three "bands," complicating world band tuning and allowing only ten presets per "band." Carousel makes choosing presets a sequential chore. Volatile memory, including presets. Quick-access meter key for world band segments does not store last tuned frequency, although bandswitch does. Signal indicator overreads. Frequency display can be off by 1 kHz or so. Band-edge beep can't be turned off. Scanning and up/down slewing mute, hindering bandscanning. Faint, unobtrusive chuffing as tuning knob turned. Volume control has minor play. With stereo headphones, at lower volume the left ear a bit louder than the right. Pressing keys usually requires that radio be held in place with other hand. No elevation panel or tail bail. No rubber or similar protection for table. Clocks do not display independently of frequency readout. Sensitivity drops off above around 23 MHz, not an issue with world band. Single-sideband demodulation requires extra-cost Redsun TG37 module, powered by four separate "AA" batteries (not included) and available only from China. Antenna and IF output jacks not type normally found in much of the world; however, two antenna plugs provided with radio to help remedy this. Internal mediumwave AM antenna doesn't disconnect when outboard antenna connected, degrading directionality of outboard antenna. *Kaito:* Inboard power supply has no UL or CSA approval, although has CE approval for Europe. *Redsun:* No warranty or repair support outside China; our insured unit from eBay vendor arrived damaged, but "insurance" proved impossible to collect. Inboard power supply lacks UL or CSA approval. *Except Redsun export/English version:* Earpieces and required four "AA" or "D" batteries not included. NiMH rechargeable cells not included.

> In America $500 buys the best, but worthy offerings exist under $160.

Verdict: The North American CCRadio-SW and Kaito KA-2100, like their European and Asian stable mates, offer decent overall world band performance aided by a superior speaker and continuously variable bass and treble controls. As a result, audio quality is about as good as it gets. For pleasant and affordable listening to world band news and entertainment it is hard to beat, which accounts for the Passport's Choice.

Where this model—at least the tested CCRadio and Redsun versions—stands apart from other world band portables is in performance across all bands. Long-distance FM performs very nicely, indeed, but the real surprise is that faraway mediumwave AM stations come in so well—even though there's no synchronous selectable or double sideband to cope with selective fading distortion from fringe signals twilights and evenings.

Nevertheless, it craves better front-end selectivity and dynamic range, along with synchronous selectable sideband, inboard single-sideband demodulation and especially a keypad.

Evaluation of New Versions: China's Redsun was unknown just a handful of years back, but already their world band portables are appearing globally to a receptive audience. Its RP2100, in a growing roster of incarnations, sports an attractive black cabinet with large high-contrast LCD characters. The speaker grille is metal, not plastic, and knobs are generously spaced for large hands. Thanks to PLL tuning circuitry, there's no meaningful frequency drift.

Its carrying handle is long, tough, useful and folds flat across the cabinet top. The LCD and keys illuminate for about ten seconds when any key or knob is used, although LCD illumination is uneven.

Mediumwave AM tunes 520–1710 kHz in 10 kHz steps or 522–1620 kHz in 9 kHz steps, while FM covers the usual 87–108 MHz. Shortwave is 1711 to 29999 kHz, but broken up into three "bands" that complicate world band tuning: SW1 1711–10010 kHz, SW2 9990–20010 kHz and SW3 19990–29999 kHz.

Of the 50 station presets, ten are for each of the three shortwave "bands," ten for mediumwave AM and ten for FM. The channel preset is displayed, 1 through 10, on the LCD, but presets selection is serial via a single-direction carousel key; to go from, say, 1 to 8 you have to press that key fully eight times. The memory circuitry is volatile, but with power gone it takes a good day or two after the LCD fades away before data disappears.

There is no keypad for direct frequency entry—disappointing for a receiver with synthesized tuning—but with the archaic three "band" shortwave scheme its utility would be diminished, anyway.

Keys have good feel along with selectable "Roger beep." Yet, they are so stiff that you need to grip the cabinet with your other hand to keep the radio from sliding away, and there's no elevation panel, tilt bail or rubber feet to help avoid this. There is also slight hesitation before a key-press "takes," and at times even a second push is needed—apparently a minor software flaw.

Travel-Handy Features

All versions are very similar except for the AC power configuration. All but the CCRadio include a CE-approved single-voltage shielded inboard power supply, which is generally preferable to an AC adaptor but adds weight on trips. The CCRadio uses, instead, a UL-approved outboard AC adaptor; it also includes a deeper and more useful tuning knob speed dimple, a normally small point that assumes atypical usefulness because there's no keypad for tuning leaps.

Interestingly, battery operation is by either four "D" or four "AA" batteries; this allows weight-conscious travelers to use lightweight "AA" cells. Too, if they are NiMH cells they can be recharged inside the radio.

A quick-access meter key tunes to the edge of any chosen world band segment within the range of the shortwave "band" currently selected. Signal-seek scanning works very well, locking onto strong stations but, like the related slewing circuit, it mutes as it scans. Thankfully, the tuning knob does not suffer from muting—just faint, unobtrusive chuffing.

Treat for Ears

Two well-chosen bandwidths offer helpful fidelity-vs.-selectivity flexibility. When adjacent-channel interference isn't an issue, the wider filter in combination with the continuously tuned bass and treble controls makes for a real aural treat.

Sensitivity is quite respectable, although it drops off above around 23 MHz—not a problem for most, as the practical world band upper limit is 22 MHz. It's quiet too, with no hiss or digital buzz.

Dual conversion keeps images pretty much at bay, although a few appear 910 kHz below a powerful signal's fundamental frequency. More significant is poor front-end selectivity, which allows beefy local mediumwave AM signals to "repeat" at within the shortwave spectrum. These occasionally bother world band segments.

Dynamic range comes up short, as well, allowing overloading to annoy reception. This is especially noticeable at night around the 6 MHz world band segment, even with nothing more than the built-in telescopic antenna. Although there's a one-step attenuator and an RF gain control, neither helps much.

There's no synchronous selectable sideband, hardly surprising at this price. More peculiar is that there's no built in single-sideband demodulation—just a 455 kHz IF input/output that can be used for an optional external BFO available only from China.

A switch selects between the built-in short-wave/FM telescopic antenna and an external antenna. However, antenna and IF output jacks are unlike those customarily found on world band radios in many parts of the world. There's also a pair of spring clips for an outboard mediumwave AM antenna, but because the internal loopstick antenna cannot be disabled the all-important directionality of any outboard antenna is compromised.

FM is a delight. Sensitivity and selectivity are superior, and there's stereo output for headphones, as well as a line output for recording. Mediumwave AM also stands out, even if there is no synchronous detector to overcome fringe-zone selective fading distortion twilights and evenings.

Proposed Version for 2008

⭐⭐⅜ ⓒ

Etón S350DL, S350 Deluxe Lextronix, Grundig GS350DL, Tecsun BCL-3000

Price: *Etón S350DL:* $99.95 in the United States. CAD$129.00 in Canada. £69.95 in the United Kingdom. *S350 Deluxe Lextronix:* €98.00 in Germany. *Grundig GS350DL:* TBA in 2008. *PAL-to-F adaptor for external FM antenna:* $2.29 in the United States. *Franzus FR-22 120>220V AC transformer for BCL-3000:* $15–18 in the United States.

Pro: Speaker audio quality substantially above norm for world band portables. Separate bass and treble tone controls help shape audio frequency response. Reasonably powerful audio, helpful for where ambient noise is at least average. Two bandwidths, well-chosen, provide effective and flexible adjacent-channel rejection *vis-à-vis* audio fidelity. Sensitive to weak signals. No synthesizer, so exceptionally free from circuit noise ("hiss") and no chuffing while tuning. Relatively intuitive to operate, even for newcomers. World Time clock (*see* Con) with alarm, clock radio and sleep delay; may also be set to 12-hour format. Four-bar (eight bar) signal indicator. Battery-strength indicator (*see* Con). Low battery consumption, combined with four "D" cells, greatly reduces need for battery replacement. Most comfortable carrying handle of any world band radio tested; also, seconds as a shoulder strap. Easy-to-read LCD has large numbers, high contrast, is visible from a variety of angles and is brightly illuminated. LCD illumination may be left on fulltime or timed to turn off; illumination also comes on when tuning knob turned. FM reception quality slightly above average. FM in stereo through headphones. Sturdy, flexible telescopic antenna. RCA phono sockets provide stereo line output for recording, home FM transmitters and outboard audio systems. Mediumwave AM reception bet-

The Grundig GS350DL uses hybrid technology: analog tuning mated to a digital frequency counter. This means no keypad or presets, but audio is unusually pleasant.

ter than most. Battery cavity allows for four "AA" cells in addition to, or in lieu of, the usual four "D" cells; user-switchable between "AA" and "D," for example to select "AA" should "D" cells die. Available in red or black. *Etón:* Supplied outboard AC adaptor can be left behind on trips, making it lighter than BCL-3000. *North America:* Excellent toll-free tech support. *Tecsun:* Built-in 220V AC power supply eliminates need for outboard AC adaptor.

Con: Analog tuned with digital frequency counter, so tunable only by pair of concentric (fast/slow) knobs; thus, it lacks such helpful tuning aids as station presets, keypad and scanning. Unhandy MW/SW1/SW2/SW3 switch must be accessed often to tune mediumwave AM and within shortwave spectra; switch can be touchy, affecting frequency readings. Analog tuning uses string-pulley-gear hardware to turn variable capacitors, which results in frequency drift typically under 2 kHz on the DL version, along with some play and backlash—drift much improved over units produced before mid-2005. Single-conversion IF circuitry results in poor image rejection. No single sideband. Power button activates 90-minute

sleep delay; works as full-time "on" control only if held down three seconds. Some user-correctable nighttime overloading in strong-signal parts of the world. Does not tune relatively unused 2 MHz (120 meter) tropical world band segment. Clock not displayed independent of frequency, but button allows time to replace frequency for three seconds. Clock tends to be off slightly over time. Nominal 30 MHz low-pass filter has such high apparent insertion loss as to be useless except as a *de facto* attenuator. Battery-strength indicator gives little warning before radio becomes inoperative. Batteries (4 × "D") not included. AC adaptor less handy than built-in power supply. *Etón:* Warranty honored only if radio purchased from authorized dealer, listed under each product at www.etoncorp.com. *North America:* Minor but audible hum from speaker, headphones and line output with supplied 120V AC adaptor.

Verdict: The Etón S350DL—sold in China as the similar Tecsun BCL-3000—is full of welcome surprises as well as the other variety, and the forthcoming Grundig GS350DL is expected to be virtually identical. The big plus is sound, which is unmistakably above average. Flaws, too, are obvious and real: images, no single-sideband demodulation, a paucity of tuning aids and residual frequency drift. So, this analog-tuned model is not for DXing and can't demodulate most utility and ham signals.

But for world band listening it sounds terrific, is value priced and has superior customer support within North America and Europe.

Sharper Image's CT800 is inexpensive and includes an inboard power supply, something rarely found in a portable at any price. Otherwise, it's a dreary performer.

New for 2008

✪³⁄₈

Sharper Image CT800, Centrios 1219180

Price: *Sharper Image:* $39.95 in the United States. *Centrios:* CAD$99.99 in Canada.

Pro: Tuning aids include ten world band station presets (45 for all bands); keypad (*see* Con) in telephone format; up/down slewing; signal-seek scanning (*see* Con); and quick access to 13 world band segments (excludes 19 MHz). NTSC (U.S.) VHF-TV audio channels 2–13 (*see* Con); also, all seven 162 MHz NOAA (U.S.) weather frequencies. FM (*see* Con) in stereo through two aluminum cone speakers. Attractive, with illuminated blue display. Built-in 117V AC power supply uses beefy transformer. Dual clocks (*see* Con). Excellent large fold-down handle. Single-event clock radio/alarm. Telescopic antenna swivels and rotates (*see* Con). Programmable sleep timer (up to 90 minutes); nine-minute snooze. All buttons have good feel. Low battery indicator. Use of four "D" cells minimizes changing. Rubber feet protect table surface and reduce sliding.

Con: Poor world band sensitivity. Mediocre dynamic range. Poor image rejection. Annoying muting when slew tuning. Keypad requires entering leading zero with frequencies from 2 to 10 MHz. World band displays in nonstandard XX.XXx MHz format. Tunes world band only in 5 kHz steps. Both clocks solely in 12-hour format, not 24-hour/World Time. Clock doesn't display with radio on. Presets and clock backed up by battery, leaving only 45 seconds to change batteries before data erases. With AC power, world band signals sometimes mix with minor received hum; additionally, skosh of internal hum on all bands when audio turned down. No external antenna jack. Stereo and power LEDs excessively bright; translucent colored tape helps. Construction shortcomings on our unit include inoperative LCD dimmer, flimsy telescopic-antenna support and two vague bandswitch detents. No signal indicator. TV audio band becomes useless in the United States when HDTV replaces NTSC in 2009. Inferior FM/mediumwave AM performance. Mediumwave AM tunes only in 10 kHz steps, suitable solely for Western Hemisphere; 9 kHz, used elsewhere, not selectable. Scanner requires beefy signal to stop. Required four "D" batteries not included. *Sharper Image:* Warranty only 90 days.

Verdict: Useful for thrifty enjoyment of strong world band signals, and its inboard power transformer is exceptional for the price. Nevertheless, performance is uninspiring.

Evaluation of New Model: This bargain model is sold by the Sharper Image in the United States and in Canada by The Source. It is relatively heavy and large (12 × 7 × 3½ inches, or 305 × 78 × 89 mm), thanks to built-in stereo speakers and an internal 117V AC power transformer with AC cord—a desirable feature at any price.

World band coverage is complete from 2.0 to 26.1 MHz with no gaps or shortwave bandswitching. Mediumwave AM thankfully includes the X-band up to 1710 kHz.

Bonus Bands

There's more. In the early days of radio, when a manufacturer wanted to enhance sales appeal he'd instruct his engineers, "Add a band!" That spirit of inclusiveness is alive and well with this portable, which includes two bands not normally found on world band receivers: VHF-TV audio for NTSC (U.S.) channels 2–13 and all seven VHF channels of the U.S. National Weather Service (NOAA). Alas, those TV channels will go stone silent when HDTV takes over in 2009, and the weather feature lacks NOAA's All Hazards emergency alarm.

The keypad, which requires three steps to select a frequency, is in standard telephone layout and has keys with superior feel. However, the enter button is unhandy and a leading zero must be entered between 2–10 MHz. That's because the receiver's format for shortwave frequencies is in Megahertz (e.g., 09.810 MHz) rather than the usual kilohertz (9810 kHz). For that same reason the display shows as XX.XXx MHz, not XXXXX kHz.

The shortwave spectrum, including world band, is tuned only in 5 kHz steps—adequate for a simple portable. However, mediumwave AM tunes only in 10 kHz steps. This is fine for the Western Hemisphere, but elsewhere 9 kHz steps are needed. Less serious is the lone FM tuning rate of 200 kHz, which limits spot-on tuning outside the Americas.

Muting reduces digital chuffing with slew tuning, but the resulting silent moments are so intrusive as to make manual bandscanning virtually worthless. Most other world band radios handle this better.

Also bringing up the rear are lapses in quality, even when taking price into account. For example, the dimmer button doesn't function on our unit, which was purchased new. Too, the MW and FM bandswitch detents feel vague, while support for the telescopic antenna is flimsy. The illuminated blue display looks great, but the stereo and power LEDs are obnoxiously bright.

Bargain Performance

World band selectivity, although broad, is typical for an inexpensive portable. World band sensitivity, however, is uninspiring with the telescopic antenna, and there's no jack for an external antenna. Fudging this by clipping wire to the telescopic antenna results in little improvement unless the wire is fairly long, which in turn tends to generate overloading.

Single conversion results in poor image rejection. On shortwave this is manifested by "repeats" 910 kHz below each powerful fundamental signal.

When AC powers the radio, a skosh of hum piggybacks onto a number of world band signals. Additionally, there is a touch of hum at low volume.

Although FM is in stereo through slightly separated speakers, it lacks sensitivity, so weaker signals suffer from circuit noise. Mediumwave AM fares only slightly better, but profits from directional reception thanks to a relatively long ferrite rod antenna. Even the $500 Etón E1 lacks this.

Audio quality from the twin aluminum cone speakers is above average, albeit with a hollow "bonky" sound and uninspiring bass. There is a high-cut tone control—rare at this price—and plenty of punch for noisy environments.

In all, this eminently affordable portable is no barnburner. Yet, it is a passable performer for casual listening and a step in the right direction for Sharper Image.

COMPACT PORTABLES
Nice for Travel, Okay for Home

Compacts are hugely popular, and no wonder. They offer a value mix of affordable price, worthy performance, manageable size and acceptable speaker audio. They tip in at one to two pounds, under a kilogram, and are typically sized less than 8 × 5 × 1.5 inches/20 × 13 × 4 cm. Like pocket models, they almost always feed off "AA" (UM-3 penlite) batteries—but, usually, more of them. They travel almost as well as pocket models, but sound better through their larger speakers. They can also suffice for home use.

❂❂❂⅛ ☞ *Passport's Choice*
Sony ICF-SW7600GR

Price: *ICF-SW7600GR:* $159.95 in the United States. £124.00 in the United Kingdom. €169.95 in Germany. *MW-41-680 120V regulated AC adaptor (aftermarket, see below):* $19.95 in the United States. *Radio Shack 273-1758 120V adaptor with 273-1705 plug (aftermarket, see below):* $12.99 in the United States.

Pro: One of the great values in a meaningful world band radio. Far and away the least-costly model available with high-tech synchronous selectable sideband; this generally performs well, reducing adjacent-channel interference and selective-fading distortion on world band, longwave and mediumwave AM signals (*see* Con). Single bandwidth, especially when synchronous selectable sideband is used, exceptionally effective at adjacent-channel rejection. Robust, with superior quality of components and assembly for price class. Numerous helpful tuning features, including keypad, two-speed up/down slew, 100 station presets and "signal-seek, then resume" tuning. For those with limited hearing of high-frequency sounds, such as some men over the half-century mark, speaker audio quality may be preferable to that of Grundig G4000A/Yacht Boy 400PE (*see* Con). Single-sideband performance arguably the best of any portable; analog clarifier, combined with LSB/USB switch, allow single-side-

MAKE YOUR PORTABLE "HEAR" BETTER

Regardless of which portable you own, you can boost weak-signal sensitivity on the cheap. How cheap? Nothing, for starters.

Look for "sweet spots" to place your radio: near windows, appliances, telephones, building I-beams and the like. If your portable has an AC adaptor, try that, then batteries; sometimes the adaptor works better, sometimes batteries. Places to avoid are near computers and appliances with microprocessors; also, light dimmers, non-incandescent lighting and cable TV or telephone lines. Power lines and cords can be noisy, too.

> **Portables don't need separate antennas, but simple ones may help.**

Outdoor Antenna Optional

An outdoor antenna shouldn't be needed with a portable. Yet it can help, especially with models lacking in weak-signal sensitivity with their built-in telescopic antennas. With compact and pocket models, simplest is often best—sophisticated or big antennas can cause "overloading." Run several meters or yards of ordinary insulated wire to a tree, then clip one end to your set's telescopic antenna with an alligator or claw clip available from RadioShack and such. It's fast and cheap, yet effective.

If you are in a weak-signal location, such as central or western North America or Australia, and want signals to be more audible, even better is to erect an inverted-L (so-called "longwire") antenna. Also sometimes called random-length antennas, they are available at radio specialty outlets. Ordinary or substantial versions can be constructed from detailed instructions in the RDI White Paper, *PASSPORT Evaluation of Popular Outdoor Antennas*. Antenna length is not critical, but keep the lead-in wire reasonably short.

Use an outdoor antenna only when required—disconnect during thunder, snow or sand storms, and when the radio is off. And don't touch any connected antenna during dry weather, as discharged static electricity might flow through it and damage the radio.

Creative Indoor Solutions

All antennas work best outdoors, away from electrical noises inside the home. If your supplementary antenna has to be indoors, run it along the middle of a window with Velcro, tape or suction cups. In a reinforced-concrete building which absorbs radio signals, you can affix a telescopic car antenna so it sticks outdoors horizontally or partially erect, like a wall flagpole. These are all but invisible, but work because they reach away from the building.

Compact amplified ("active") antennas, reviewed in PASSPORT REPORTS, are handy but add to cost. Many are for tabletop models, but some are for portables.

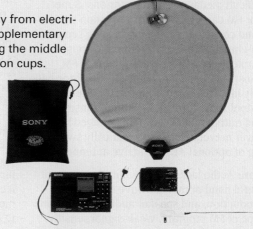

Best for portables is the travel-friendly Sony AN-LP1 antenna that folds up.   J. Brinker

Dollar for dollar, pound for pound, there's no better value in a world band radio than the Sony ICF-7600GR. Quality performance, quality construction.

band signals (e.g., AFRTS, utility, amateur) to be tuned with uncommon precision, and thus with superior carrier phasing and the resulting natural-sounding audio. Dual-zone 24-hour clock with single-zone readout, easy to set. Slightly smaller and lighter than most other compact models. Outboard reel passive wire antenna accessory aids slightly with weak-signal reception. Simple timer with sleep delay. Illuminated LCD has high contrast when read head-on or from below. Travel power lock. Superior reception of difficult mediumwave AM stations. Superior FM capture ratio aids reception when band congested, including helping separate co-channel stations. FM stereo through earpieces or headphones. Japanese FM (most versions) and longwave. Superior battery life. Weak-battery indicator. Stereo line output for recording, FM home transmitters and outboard audio systems. Hinged battery cover prevents loss. Automatically switching of optional AN-LP1 active antenna.

Con: Audio lacks tonal quality for pleasant world band or mediumwave AM music reproduction, and speaker audio tiring for any type of FM program. Weak-signal sensitivity, although respectable, not equal to that of the top handful of top-rated portables; helped considerably by extra-cost Sony AN-LP1 active antenna reviewed elsewhere

in this edition. Image rejection adequate, but not excellent. Three switches, including those for synchronous selectable sideband, located unhandily at the side of the cabinet. No tuning knob. Slow microprocessor lock time while slew tuning degrades band-scanning. No meaningful signal indicator. Synchronous selectable sideband holds lock decently, but less well on weak signals than in Sony's larger models; too, it tends to lose lock even more if batteries weak or if NiCd cells used. Synchronous selectable sideband alignment can vary with temperature, factory alignment and battery voltage, causing synchronous selectable sideband reception to be slightly more muffled in one sideband than the other. No AC adaptor included. In North America the optional Sony AC-E60A 120V AC "switching" adaptor causes serious interference to radio signals and, incredibly, is labeled "Not for use with radios"; to remedy this, Universal Radio offers its own MW 41-680 adaptor and Radio Shack has the 273-1758/273-1705 adaptor/plug combo. Reader reports indicate Sony's recommended 240V AC adaptor also causes serious interference to radio signals. Radio's adaptor socket is of an unusual size, making it difficult to find a suitable third-party AC adaptor. 1621–1705 kHz portion of American AM band and 1705–1735 kHz potential public-service segment are erroneously treated as shortwave, although this does not harm reception quality. Even though it has a relatively large LCD, same portion of display is used for clock and frequency digits; thus, clock doesn't display when frequency is shown, although pressing the EXE key allows time to replace frequency for nine seconds. No earphones or earpieces. No batteries (four "AA" needed).

Verdict: The robust Sony ICF-SW7600GR provides exceptional bang for the buck, even though it is manufactured in high-cost Japan. Its advanced-tech synchronous selectable sideband is a valuable feature that most other portable manufacturers have yet to engineer properly—even some professional models costing thousands of dollars still haven't got it right. To find this useful operating feature operating properly at this price is without parallel.

There's top drawer single-sideband reception for a portable, too, along with superior tough-signal FM and mediumwave AM reception—even if musical audio quality through the speaker is only *ordinaire*.

✪✪✪ *Passport's Choice*
Etón E5, E5 Lextronix, Grundig G5

Price: *E5/G5:* $149.95 in the United States. CAD$149.00 in Canada. £89.95 in the United Kingdom. €129.00 in Germany.

Etón's G5, also sold as the Grundig G5, includes a genuine tuning knob. Worthy overall performance and ergonomics, too, but there's no synchronous selectable sideband.

Pro: Much improved ergonomics over Degen/Kaito siblings, including dedicated volume controls and additional slewing buttons; main keypad and slewing buttons are nicely sized (*see* Con) with pleasant feel. Worthy tuning knob does not mute when turned (*see* Con). Very useful auto scanning circuit that on shortwave allows for two stop modes (scan, five-second pause, resume scan; scan, stop), with an FM-only mode for auto store to presets. 700 station presets store mode; each of 100 seven-presets "pages" can display a four-letter alphanumeric ID tag (*see* Con). Presets nonvolatile. Two ways to quick-access individual world band segments; returns to last-tuned frequency within each segment. Two bandwidths, well chosen. Superior sensitivity, low circuit noise. Dual conversion provides adequate image rejection (*see* Con). Superior dynamic range for a compact portable; thus, radio suitable for use with outdoor wire antennas. Above average single-sideband reception, thanks in part to analog fine-tuning thumbwheel (*see* Con) and freedom from excessive drift. Effective LED illumination (*see* Con) stays on for 15 seconds with battery power, continuously with AC adaptor. Audio quality slightly above average for compact portable, powerful enough to drive some external speakers (*see* Con). Clock displays separately from frequency (*see* Con). Four-event alarm. Sleep delay; once its 99-minute default is changed (i.e., to something between one and 98 minutes), new setting is retained. Four-bar battery indicator. Useful five-bar signal indicator. NiMH batteries recharge inside radio (*see* Con). Telescopic antenna rotates and

swivels. Travel power lock (*see* Con). Station presets and time not erased during battery charging or if batteries replaced quickly. Hinged battery cover prevents loss. Superior FM sensitivity. Excellent FM capture ratio aids reception when band congested, including helping separate co-channel stations. FM in stereo through earbuds, included (*see* Con). Simple tone control for FM (*see* Con). Stereo line output with proper audio level for recording, home FM transmitters and outboard audio systems. Japanese FM. Longwave. Indoor wire antenna and single-voltage AC adaptor/charger (*see* ☞). Vinyl carrying case has greater protection than case for the Degen DE1103/Kaito KA1103 (*see* Con). *North America:* Excellent toll-free telephone support.

Con: World band and mediumwave AM audio would profit from more crispness and a tone control (tone control works only on FM, and FM audio sounds better). Just as with the Degen DE1103/Kaito KA1103, volume blasts when radio initially turned on, although there's a way around this. Although some buttons nicely sized, most are small. LCD relatively difficult to read in low ambient light without illumination. Minor chuffing when tuning, although vastly preferable to the alternative of muted audio. Image rejection, although fairly good, not all it could be for a model with enough dynamic range to handle outboard antennas. Single sideband uses fine-tuning thumbwheel instead of USB/LSB selector; thumbwheel lacks center detent. Touchy fine-tuning thumbwheel makes manual ECSS reception impractical. AGC too fast in single-sideband mode, causing distortion; too, AGC swamped by exceptionally strong signals unless single-level attenuator used. Tuning knob has only 1 kHz step, although slewing buttons complement this nicely with 5 kHz step. Individual presets do not store bandwidth or ID tag. Signal indicator does not work on FM. Bandwidth chosen by hard-to-select slide switch on side of cabinet. No standard or rechargeable batteries (four "AA" needed). In principle, rubbery paint on cabinet might eventually wear through. Carrying case has creosote odor, remediable by thorough airing. Warranty honored only if radio purchased from authorized dealer, listed under each product at www.etoncorp.com.

Verdict: The Etón E5's and Grundig G5's worthy performance is similar to that of the Degen DE1103/Kaito KA1103. However, the Chinese-made E5/G5 clears up the '1103's seriously flawed ergonomics by, for example, including dedicated volume and slewing controls. On the other hand, the '1103 comes with rechargeable batteries, while the pricier E5/G5 doesn't.

Overall, the E5/G5 is one of the best compact portables around. What it lacks is synchronous selectable sideband, such as is found on Sony's similarly priced ICF-7600GR.

The Kaito KA1102 is an excellent value and relatively trouble-free. Also available in the Eastern Hemisphere under the Degen and Thieking brands.

★★★ *©* *Passport's Choice*
Degen DE1102, Kaito KA1102, Thieking DE1102

Price: *Kaito:* $79.95 in the United States. CAD$99.95 in Canada. *Thieking:* €89.00 in Germany.

Pro: Unusually small and light for a sophisticated compact model; only a skosh larger and one ounce (28 grams) heavier than its simpler sibling '1101. Two bandwidths, both well chosen. A number of helpful tuning features, including keypad, up/down slew (1 or 5 kHz steps for world band, 1 or 9/10 kHz for mediumwave AM), carousel selector for 49-16 meter segments, and signal-seek frequency scanning (*see* Con) and memory scanning; also, ten 19-preset "pages" provide a total of 190 station presets, of which 133 can be used for shortwave (*see* Con). Auto-store function automatically stores presets; works on all bands. Tunable BFO allows for precise signal phasing during single-sideband reception (*see* Con). No muting during manual shortwave bandscanning in 1 or 5 kHz steps, or mediumwave AM bandscanning in 1 kHz steps. PLL and BFO relatively free from drift during single-sideband operation (*see* Con). Above-average weak-signal sensitivity and image rejection. Little circuit "hiss." Superior speaker audio quality, intelligibility and loudness for size. Four-LED signal indicator for mediumwave AM and shortwave (*see* Con); three-bar signal indicator for FM (fourth LED becomes stereo indicator). World Time 24-hour clock displays seconds numerically when radio is off; when on, time (sans seconds) flashes on briefly when key is held down; user may choose 12-hour format, instead. Unusually appropriate for use in the dark, as display and keypad illuminated by pleasant blue light which works only in dark (*see* Con). Clicky keys have superior feel. LCD has excellent contrast when viewed from sides or below. Alarm with sleep delay (*see* Con). Travel power lock. Rechargeable NiMH batteries (3 × "AA"), included, can be charged within the radio; station presets and time not erased during charging. Switchable bass boost supplements high-low tone switch, significantly improves FM audio (*see* Con).

Low battery consumption except with FM bass boost. Battery-strength indicator. Hinged battery cover prevents loss. Superior FM weak- signal sensitivity. Excellent FM capture ratio aids reception when band congested, including helping separate co-channel stations. FM in stereo through earbuds, included (*see* Con). Japanese FM. Full coverage of mediumwave AM band. Includes short external wire antenna accessory, which in many locations is about the most that can be used without generating overloading. Available in black or aluminum colors. *Degen:* AC adaptor (220V). *Kaito:* AC adaptor (120V).

Con: Speaker audio, except FM, lacks low-frequency ("bass") response as compared to larger models. Bass-boost circuit, which could relieve this on world band, works only on FM. Dynamic range, although roughly average for a compact portable, not anywhere equal to that of the sibling '1101; overloads easily with a significant outdoor antenna, although much less often with the built-in antenna or a short outboard antenna. Not so straightforward to operate as some other portables; for example, single-sideband mode works only when presets "page 9" is selected (or SSB button is held in manually), even if no presets are to be chosen (in any event, presets don't store mode); otherwise, "ERR" is displayed; manufacturer says this is to prevent its Chinese consumers, who are unfamiliar with single sideband, from turning on the BFO accidentally and thus becoming confused. Slight warble in audio with ECSS reception, varies with how many signal LEDs are being illuminated; LEDs can't be turned off. Volume at earphone jack sometimes inadequate with weak or undermodulated signals; variable-level earphone jack misleadingly described as "line out." Power button activates a 99-minute sleep delay; to turn the radio on fulltime, a second key must be pressed immediately afterwards. No tuning knob. No LSB/USB switch. Displays in nonstandard XX.XX/XX.XXx MHz format. Signal indicator overreads. Little-used 2 MHz (120 meter) world band segment not covered. Degen's quality control, once well above average, appears to have become hit-or-miss. Clock doesn't

display when frequency is shown, although pushbutton allows time to replace frequency briefly. Always-on LCD/keypad illumination with AC adaptor, as described in owner's manual, did not function on test sample. LCD/keypad illumination dim and uneven. FM IF produces images 21+ MHz down.

Verdict: An exceptional price and performance winner from Degen—just don't expect much in the way of low-end audio.

✪✪✪ *Passport's Choice*
Grundig G4000A

Price: $149.95 in the United States. CAD$199.00 in Canada.

Pro: Speaker audio quality tops in size category for those with sharp hearing. Two bandwidths, both well-chosen. Ergonomically superior, a pleasure to operate. A number of helpful tuning features, including keypad, up/down slew, 40 station presets, signal-seek frequency scanning and scanning of station presets. Signal indicator. Dual-zone 24-hour clock, with one zone shown at all times; however, clock displays seconds only when radio is off. Illuminated display. Alarm with simple sleep delay. Tunable BFO allows for superior signal phasing during single-sideband reception (*see* Con). Outboard reel passive wire antenna accessory aids slightly with weak-signal reception. Generally superior FM performance,

The popular Grundig G4000A is a proven design with uncomplicated operation for pleasant world band listening.

especially in weak-signal locations. FM in stereo through earpieces. Longwave. AC adaptor. Excellent hardside leather travel case. *North America:* Excellent toll-free tech support.

Con: Circuit noise ("hiss") can be slightly intrusive with weak signals. No tuning knob. At many locations there can be break-through of powerful AM or FM stations into the world band spectrum. Keypad not in telephone format. No LSB/USB switch, and single-sideband reception is below par. Battery consumption slightly above norm. No batteries (six "AA" needed). Warranty honored only if radio purchased from autho-rized dealer, listed under each product at www.etoncorp.com.

Verdict: This popular Grundig digital-read-out portable offers superior audio quality, ease of use and a roster of other virtues. So it's hardly surprising that this Chinese-made receiver is unusually popular for enjoying world band programs, including music. Tough FM catches, too, although single-sideband isn't all it could be.

✪✪⅞ (see ☞)   **𝓒**
Degen DE1103, Kaito KA1103, Thieking DE1103

Price: *Kaito:* $89.95 in the United States. CAD$109.00 in Canada. *Thieking:* €119.00 in Germany.

Thieking's DE1103 is marketed within Europe. In North America it is available as the Kaito KA1103, in Asia as the Degen DE1103.

Pro: Two bandwidths, both well chosen (*see* Con). Helpful tuning features include tuning knob (*see* Con), keypad (*see* Con), world band segment up/down carousel, signal-seek (pause, resume) frequency scanning and presets scanning; also, sixteen "pages" holding 16 presets each provide 256 station presets, plus another dozen to quick-access world band segments (alternatively, "pages" may be bypassed for quick-access tuning, reducing available presets to 100). Presets store mode (*see* Con). Tuning knob not muted when tuned, facilitating bandscan-ning (*see* Con). Scanner works better than most. Radio can return to last-tuned fre-quency within ten world band segments, as well as FM and mediumwave AM. Superior dynamic range for a compact portable—bet-ter than that of DE1102/KA1102, and even approaching that of DE1101/KA1102. Tunable BFO (*see* Con) allows for precise signal phasing during single-sideband reception. Relatively free from drift during single-sideband operation. Above-average sensitivity aided by quiet circuitry. Using dual conversion, image rejection is above average (*see* Con). Speaker audio quality, although limited, fairly good except during single-sideband reception (*see* Con). Four-bar signal indicator (*see* Con). World Time 24-hour clock (*see* Con). Display and keypad illumination is about as good as it gets: Dur-ing battery operation, it can be switched not to go on; otherwise, it is automatically acti-vated by any of various controls, including those for tuning, and stays on for a full 15 seconds. Clicky keys with superior feel (*see* Con). Sleep delay. Two-event timer. NiMH batteries (4 × "AA"), included, slowly re-chargeable within radio. Travel power lock. Station presets and time not erased during battery charging or if batteries replaced quickly. Battery-strength indicator. Hinged battery cover prevents loss. Superior FM sensitivity. Excellent FM capture ratio aids reception when band congested, including helping separate co-channel stations. FM in stereo through earbuds, included (*see* Con). Stereo audio line output with appropriate level for recording, home FM transmitters and outboard audio systems. Japanese FM. Longwave (*see* Con) tunes down to 100 kHz. Elevation panel tilts radio to handy operating angle. Includes short external wire antenna accessory. Available in black or aluminum colors. *Degen:* AC adaptor (220V). *Kaito:* AC adaptor (120V).

Con: Hostile ergonomics include having to operate two controls to change volume; nonstandard single-row keypad; small keys; stiff slider controls; only one knob tuning rate (1 kHz, slow) for world band and mediumwave AM; and no center detent for fine-tuning (tunable BFO) thumbwheel. Pseudo-analog LCD "dial," a pointless gimmick that takes up space which could have been used to display useful information and provide proper keypad layout. No up/down slew controls. No tone control except "news-music" switch that works only on FM. No LSB/USB switch. Single-sideband has audible distortion, seemingly from AGC. Image rejection, although fairly good, not all that it could be for a model with enough dynamic range to handle some outboard antennas. Slight microprocessor noise when tuning knob turned—a small price to pay to avoid bandscan limitations brought about by muting. Even though dynamic range superior, AGC seemingly swamped by exceptionally powerful signals, causing lowered volume; switching attenuator to "LO" allows volume to return to normal level. Signal indicator overreads and does not operate on FM. Degen's quality control, once well above average, appears to have become hit-or-miss. Clock doesn't display when frequency is shown, although pushbutton allows time to replace frequency briefly. Presets do not store bandwidth. Longwave less convenient to access than other bands.

☞ The '1103 merits three stars for performance, but only two for ergonomics (*see* Evaluation).

☞ Unlike the sibling DE1101/KA1101 and DE1102/KA1102, the '1103's AC adaptor jack uses standard center-pin-positive polarity.

Verdict: Dreadful ergonomics and a wasted LCD make this a model to approach with caution. Yet, the Degen DE1103/Kaito KA1103 is a solid and versatile performer at a surprisingly low price. If you can endure its ergonomic shortcomings, the '1103 offers excellent performance value.

With its focus now on HD Radio, Sangean has stopped introducing world band radios. Still, its flagship **ATS 909** does nicely—especially with an external antenna.

✪✪⅞
Sangean ATS 909, Sangean ATS 909W, Roberts R861

Price: *ATS 909:* $259.95 in the United States. CAD$289.00 in Canada. £139.95 in the United Kingdom. *ATS 909W:* €165.00 in Germany. *AC adaptor:* Free with purchase in the United Kingdom. €9.95 in Germany. *R861:* £169.00 in the United Kingdom.

Pro: Exceptionally wide range of tuning facilities, including hundreds of world band station presets (one works with a single touch) and tuning knob. Tuning system uses 29 "pages" and alphanumeric station descriptors for world band. Two voice bandwidths. Tunes single-sideband signals in unusually precise 0.04 kHz increments without having to use a fine-tuning control, making this one of the handiest and most effective portables for listening to these signals (*see* Con). Shortwave dynamic range slightly above average for portable, allowing it to perform unusually well with an outboard antenna (*see* Con). Travel power lock. 24-hour clock shows at all times, and can display local time in various cities of the world (*see* Con). Excellent 1–10 digital signal indicator. Weak-battery indicator. Elevation panel tilts radio to handy operating angle (*see* Con). Clock radio feature offers three "on" times for three discrete frequencies.

Sleep delay. FM sensitive to weak signals (see Con) and performs well overall, has RDS feature, and is in stereo through earpieces, included. Illuminated display. Superior ergonomics, including tuning knob with detents. Longwave. *ATS 909W:* Japanese FM. *ATS 909 (North American units), ATS 909 "Super" and Roberts:* Superb, but relatively heavy, multivoltage AC adaptor with North American and European plugs. ANT-60 outboard reel passive wire antenna accessory aids slightly with weak-signal reception. Sangean service provided by Sangean America on models sold under its name. *ATS 909+mini-antenna (not tested):* includes accessory travel antenna. *ATS 909 "Super," available only from C. Crane Company:* According to C. Crane, includes enhanced tuning knob operation, elimination of muting between stations when bandscanning, improved filtering, enhanced LCD visibility and added bass response.

Con: Weak-signal sensitivity with built-in telescopic antenna not equal to that of comparable models; usually remediable with ANT-60 accessory antenna (provided) or other suitable external antenna. Tuning knob tends to mute stations during bandscanning; C. Crane Company offers a "Deluxe" modification to remedy this. Larger and heavier than most compact models. Signal-seek tuning, although flexible and relatively sophisticated, tends to stop on few active shortwave signals. Although scanner can operate out-of-band, reverts to default (in-band) parameters after one pass. When entering a new page, there is an initial two-second wait between when preset is keyed and station becomes audible. Although synthesizer tunes in 0.04 kHz increments, frequency readout only in 1 kHz increments. Software oddities; e.g., under certain conditions, alphanumeric station descriptor may stay on full time. Page tuning system enjoyed by some users, but cumbersome for others. Speaker audio quality only so-so, not aided by three-level treble-cut tone control. No carrying handle or strap. The 24-hour clock set up to display home time, not World Time, although this is easily overcome by not using world-cities-time feature or by creative setup of World/

Home display to London/Home. Clock does not compensate for daylight (summer) time in each displayed city. FM can overload in high-signal environments, causing false "repeat" signals to appear; capture ratio average. Heterodyne interference, possibly related to the digital display, sometimes interferes with reception of strong mediumwave AM signals. Battery consumption well above average. No batteries (four "AA" required). Elevation panel flimsy.

☞ Frequencies pre-programmed into "pages" vary by country of sale. It helps to keep a couple of empty pages to aid in editing, deleting or changing pre-programmed page information.

Verdict: While many models are similar to others being offered, this compact from Sangean marches to its own drummer. Relatively high battery consumption and insufficient weak-signal sensitivity lower its standing as a portable, and our star rating reflects this. Yet, when it is used as a *de facto* tabletop connected to household current and an outboard antenna, it becomes worthy of a three-star rating—even if not as a genuine portable. In part, this is because its circuitry is more capable than those of most other compact portables in handling the increased signal load from an outboard antenna.

As a result, this feature-laden model has a visible and enthusiastic following among radio aficionados for whom portability is not *de rigueur*. Like the tabletop Icom IC-R75, it is a favorite for tuning utility and ham signals, as it offers superior single-sideband performance at an attractive price. The '909 is also the only Sangean model still made exclusively in Taiwan.

✪✪✪⅛
Sangean PT-80, Grundig Yacht Boy 80

Price: *PT-80:* $159.95 in the United States. CAD$149.95 in Canada. *Yacht Boy 80:* €96.00 in Germany.

Pro: Excellent world band selectivity (*see* Con). Worthy sensitivity and image rejection. Numerous helpful tuning features, including tuning disc-type knob with raised dots (*see* Con); nicely located up/down slew-scan keys; 18 world band presets; 9 additional presets each for longwave, FM and mediumwave AM; "auto arrange" scanning of presets from low-to-high frequency; auto entry of presets (*see* Con); meter-segment selector; and selectable 5 kHz/1 kHz tuning steps on shortwave. For size, generally pleasant speaker audio in all bands (*see* Con). Single-sideband demodulation (*see* Con), with precise analog +/−1.5 kHz fine-tuning thumbwheel. No muting with tuning disc, aids bandscanning. Unusually attractive, sheathed in tan leather. Flip-open leather case excellent at protecting front, top and rear of the receiver (*see* Con). Leather case affixed to receiver with snaps and magnetic catches, so nearly impossible to misplace. Frequency easy to read, with decent-sized digits and good contrast. Illuminated LCD (*see* Con). Travel power lock (*see* Con). Tuning-disc lock. Superior mediumwave AM performance. On FM, superior capture ratio and worthy sensitivity. Dual-zone clock in 12 or 24 hour format (*see* Con). Alarm/clock radio with sleep delay. Rubber feet on bottom to prevent slipping. Stereo indicator (*see* Con). Hinged battery cover prevents loss. Keys have good feel (*see* Con). Weak-battery indicator. Outboard reel passive wire antenna accessory aids slightly with weak-signal reception. Longwave. Earbuds. *Sangean (North America):* 120V AC adaptor (*see* Con).

Con: During single-sideband reception, circuit "pulling" during strong modulation peaks causes annoying warbling in audio. Just enough drift at times to prompt occasional tweaking during single-sideband reception. World band and mediumwave AM audio slightly muffled; becomes clearer if station off-tuned by 1 kHz or so, which also can reduce adjacent-channel interference. Limited dynamic range; tends to overload with significant external antenna; attenuator helps, but also reduces signal considerably. (Better to skip attenuation and use the outboard reel antenna, letting out just enough wire to give good reception.) Attenuator doesn't work on mediumwave AM or longwave; however, in unusual circumstances this can be a convenience. Birdies.

Sangean's PT-80 is also sold as the Grundig Yacht Boy 80. It is the only Grundig-branded model available that's not from California's Etón Corporation.

Tuning disc has some "play," and raised dots can irritate finger during lengthy bandscanning sessions. Long-stroke keys need to be depressed fully to make contact. No meaningful signal indicator. Spurious signal rejection wanting; at one test location, and alone among several radios there, the PT-80 occasionally had a point-to-point voice transmission puffing away in the background throughout the entire shortwave spectrum. When radio on, displays either frequency or time, but not both at once. FM stereo indicator worked at some test locations, but not all. External antenna jack functions only on shortwave; however, this can also be a convenience. No audio line output for recording, home FM transmitters and outboard audio systems. Auto entry of presets does not function on world band. Leather case: 1) sags when used as an elevation panel; 2) has no holes for speaker on front, just on back, so audio is muffled when case closed; and 3) does not protect receiver's sides or bottom. Travel power lock does not deactivate LCD illumination key. No batteries (four "AA" required). *Sangean:* Country of origin, China, not shown on radio, manual or box. Instructions for setting clocks may confuse newcomers, as both clocks are referred to as being for "local time," not UTC, and the manual's mention of UTC mis-states it as "Universal Time Coordinated" instead of Coordinated Universal Time (however, the PT-50's manual gets it right). *Sangean (North*

America): 120V AC adaptor generates minor hum.

Verdict: This entry from Sangean is a pleasant performer on world band and superior on mediumwave AM and FM. Its main drawbacks: single-sideband reception with "warbling" audio, and no meaningful signal indicator.

With an external antenna, the sibling Sangean ATS 909 gets the nod, mainly for superior single-sideband performance, dual bandwidths, signal indicator and sophisticated presets. However, as a true portable for only occasional single-sideband listening the PT-80 holds its own, plus it doesn't mute during bandscanning and costs much less.

✪✪⅛ ⓒ *Passport's Choice*
Degen DE1101, Kaito KA1101

Price: *Kaito:* $59.95 in the United States. CAD$79.00 in Canada.

Pro: Exceptional dynamic range for a compact portable. Unusually small and light for a compact model. Two bandwidths, both well chosen. A number of helpful tuning features, including keypad, up/down slew and signal-seek frequency scanning (*see* Con); also, 50 station presets of which ten are for 3,000–10,000 kHz and ten for 10,000–26,100 kHz;

There are many inexpensive portables, but best is the Degen DE1101, sold in North America as the Kaito KA1101. It combines solid performance and robust construction for under $60.   D. Zantow

others are for FM, FML and mediumwave AM. Above-average weak-signal sensitivity and image rejection. Little circuit "hiss." Superior intelligibility and loudness for size. World Time 24-hour clock displays seconds numerically when radio is off; when on, time (sans seconds) flashes on briefly when key is held down. Illuminated display, works only in dark. Clicky keys have superior feel. LCD has excellent contrast when viewed from sides or below. Alarm with sleep delay (*see* Con). AC adaptor (120V Kaito, 220V Degen). Rechargeable NiMH batteries (3 × "AA"), included, can be charged within the radio; station presets and time not erased during charging. Low battery consumption. Battery-strength indicator. Hinged battery cover prevents loss. Travel power lock. Superior FM weak-signal sensitivity. Excellent FM capture ratio aids reception when band congested, including helping separate co-channel stations. FM in stereo through earbuds, included. "FML" covers Japanese FM. Line output socket (separate from earphone socket) for recording, FM home transmitters and outboard audio systems. Available in gray or aluminum colors. *Kaito:* Mediumwave AM 9/10 channel steps selectable, tunes up to 1710 kHz.

Con: Speaker audio quality lacks low-frequency ("bass") response as compared to larger models. Power button activates a 99-minute sleep delay; to turn the radio on fulltime, a second key must be pressed immediately afterwards. Station presets, slew and scanning require pressing bandswitch carousel button up to four times when tuning from below 10 MHz to above 10 MHz and *vice versa.* No tuning knob. Tunes world band only in 5 kHz steps and displays in nonstandard XX.XX/XX.XX₅ MHz format. Digital buzz under some circumstances, such as when antenna is touched. Spurious signals can appear when user's hand is pressed over back cover. With our unit, microprocessor locked up when batteries removed for over a day; resolved by pressing tiny reset button. No signal indicator (what appears to be an LED tuning indicator is actually an ambient-light sensor to disable LCD illumination except when it's dark). Degen's quality control, once well above average, appears to have become hit-or-miss. Clock doesn't display when frequency is shown, although pushbutton allows time to replace frequency briefly. Little-used 2 MHz (120 meter) world band segment not covered. On Degen unit tested, FM sounded best when tuned 50 kHz above nominal frequency on LCD; this would appear to be a sample-to-sample issue. *Degen:* Upper limit of mediumwave AM tuning is 1620 kHz, rather than the 1705 kHz band upper limit in the Americas, Australia and certain other areas. Mediumwave AM tunes only in 9 kHz steps, making it ill-suited for use in the Americas.

☞ The Kaito version comes with the proper 120V AC adaptor for North America, whereas the Degen version comes with a 220V AC adaptor suitable for most other parts of the world. Both are safe when used "as is," or with a Franzus or other recognized 120V-to-220V or 220V-to-120V AC converter. However, according to unconfirmed reports, the Degen version ordered by Americans from a vendor in Hong Kong comes with a 220-to-120V AC converter that appears to pose a fire hazard.

Verdict: Radio's Sixty-Buck Chuck. The Degen DE1101, sold in North America as the Kaito KA1101, is a knockout bargain. Engineered and manufactured in China, it is one of the smallest compact models tested, and has exceptional dynamic range. It comes with an enviable grab-bag of features and accessories, right down to inboard rechargeable batteries. But if you want music-quality audio, be prepared to use earpieces.

○○¾
Etón E10, Tecsun PL-350, Tecsun PL-550

Price: *Etón:* $129.95 in the United States. CAD$79.00 while supplies last in Canada. £69.95 in the United Kingdom.

Pro: Superior audio quality for size. Numerous helpful tuning features include 1/5 kHz knob, 5/100 kHz up/down slew, world band segment selector (covers all 14 segments), signal-seek frequency scanning, keypad and 550 station presets clustered within pages. Fully 500 presets are for general use (*see* Con), including world band; the other

The Etón E10, which carries a three-digit price tag, offers pleasant listening and loads of goodies. D. Zantow

50 are for the "Automatic Tuning System" (ATS), which installs strong FM and mediumwave AM stations (not world band) into presets, like when setting up a VCR. Presets pages programmable to hold 10, 20, 25 or 50 presets per page. Audio muting scarcely noticeable when tuning by knob. Respectable world band and mediumwave AM sensitivity, with low circuit noise. Overloading, which can appear with a substantial external antenna, controllable by two levels of attenuation via a three-position switch. Two bandwidths for program listening (*see* Con). Generally worthy ergonomics, including keys with positive-action feel (*see* Con). World Time clock (*see* Con) with alarm, clock radio (two on/off 30-minute timers), snooze and sleep delay (*see* Con); may also be set to 12-hour format. Clock reads out separately from frequency. Clock operates after batteries removed. LCD large and easy to read. Display illumination can either fade out in five seconds, be switched off before the five seconds have expired, or stay on fulltime when button held down more than five seconds. Five-bar signal indicator (*see* Con). External antenna jack for world band and FM. Novel 455/450 kHz IF control shifts images by 10 kHz (*see* Con). Elevation panel tilts radio to handy operating angle; rubber pads on bottom reduce sliding when panel in use. Worthy FM sensitivity for superior fringe reception. Japanese FM. Weak-battery indicator. Includes worthy travel pouch, stereo earbuds and outboard reel passive wire antenna. Numerous user-defined software

GETTING PAST AIRPORT ANNIE

Even in times of high alert, air travel with a world band radio is almost always trouble-free if common-sense steps are taken. To minimize the odds of delay at airport security, remember that their job is to be paranoid about you, so it's prudent to be paranoid about them.

• Answer all questions honestly, but don't volunteer information or joke around. Friendly banter can get you into the Dreaded Search corner. Equally, avoid rudeness and arguments.

• The nail that sticks out gets hammered first. Good security focuses on the unfamiliar or unusual, no matter how innocuous it may seem to you. Be gray.

• Bring a portable, not a portatop or tabletop—terrorists like big radios (they don't call them boom boxes for nothing). Best by far is a pocket or compact model.

• Stow your radio in a carry-on bag, not in checked luggage or on your person. Don't stuff it at the bottom, wrapped in clothing, like you're trying to hide something. Equally, it's usually best not to place it out in the open where it can be readily seen. However, if you decide to put a small radio into the manual inspection basket at the security portal, have it playing softly with earbuds or earphones attached, as though it were a Walkman you're listening to. Place any world band accessories, extra batteries, guides and instruction books in your checked luggage, or at least in a separate carry-on bag.

• Before entering the terminal, and certainly before entering the security area, preset the radio to a popular FM music station, then keep batteries inside the radio so you can demonstrate that it actually works. Don't mention world band or shortwave unless queried, as anything unfamiliar arouses suspicion.

• If asked what the radio is for, say it's for your own listening. If they persist, reply that you like to keep up with news and sports while away, and leave it at that. Don't volunteer information about alarm, snooze or other timer facilities, as timers can be components in bombs. If you're asked about stations, cite something that's usually safe, like the BBC in London, and avoid potentially "flagged" stations like Radio Pakistan or Radio Havana Cuba.

• If traveling in zones of war or civil unrest, or off the beaten path in parts of Africa or South America, take a radio you can afford to lose and which fits inconspicuously inside a pocket.

• If traveling to Bahrain, avoid taking a radio which has "receiver" visible on its cabinet. Security personnel may think you're a spy.

• When traveling to Malaysia, Bahrain or Saudi Arabia, don't take a model with single-sideband capability—or, at the very least, take steps to disguise this capability so it is not visually apparent. If things get dicey, point out that you listen to news and sports from the popular American AFRTS station, which transmits only in the upper-sideband mode. (PASSPORT can be used to verify this.)

Theft? Radios, cameras, binoculars, laptops and other glitzy goodies are almost always stolen to be resold. The more worn the item looks—affixing scuffed stickers helps—the less likely it is to be confiscated by corrupt inspectors or stolen by thieves.

Finally, if you're not traveling solo, ensure that at least one person watches your stuff when it's on the belt coming out of X-ray. If something is stolen there, it's all but guaranteed the security people will—or can—do little more than shrug.

functions, including page definitions for presets, FM frequency coverage and battery type (1.6V normal *vs.* 1.3V rechargeable). Travel power lock (*see* Con). *Etón:* 120V AC adaptor. Four "AA" NiMH cells that recharge inside radio. Stylish curved front panel, albeit silver colored. *North America:* Excellent toll-free tech support. *Tecsun (both):* Regulated 220V AC adaptor. *Tecsun PL-350:* Three "AA" NiMH cells that recharge inside radio. *Tecsun PL-550:* Four "AA" NiMH cells that recharge inside radio.

Con: Single-conversion circuitry allows for images, although these are weaker than usual even without the novel image-shifting control. Image-shifting control eliminates most image interference, but complicates operation. When image-shifting control adjusted from 455 kHz IF with wide bandwidth to the 450 kHz alternative to escape image interference, only the narrow bandwidth functions; too, when returning to the 455 kHz IF, the narrow bandwidth appears even if the wide bandwidth had originally been in use. Narrow bandwidth too broad for many DX situations. Signal indicator overreads somewhat. Antenna-tuning control seems pointless: does not work with external antenna; yet, with telescopic antenna appears to require only initial tweaking—no adjusting thereafter. No audio line output for recording, home FM transmitters and outboard audio systems. Signal-seek frequency scan rate is slow and stops only at strongest stations. Entering presets data unnecessarily complicated. Some keys relatively small for large fingers. Telescopic antenna, with fixed-height base, does not allow for full vertical positioning when radio laid flat; partially remedied by elevation panel. Travel power lock does not deactivate timers or LCD illumination key. Clock when in 24-hour format does not show leading tens-of-hours zero. Power switch needs to be held down for a second for radio to stay on fulltime; otherwise, sleep delay eventually turns off radio. FM frequency readout slightly off on one sample. *Etón:* Recessed keys not as easy as most to engage. Warranty honored only if radio purchased from authorized dealer, listed under each product at www.etoncorp.com. *Tecsun PL-350:* Simplified controls.

Verdict: The Etón E10 offers unusually pleasant program listening and is loaded with useful goodies, even if it does not demodulate single-sideband signals. There are some questionable features, but the good points are significant while negatives are mainly small potatoes.

✪✪¾

Sangean ATS 606AP, Sangean ATS 606S, Sangean ATS 606SP, Panasonic RF-B55, Roberts R876, Sanyo MB-60A

Price: *ATS 606AP:* $119.95 in the United States. CAD$169.00 in Canada. *ATS 606S:* €119.00 in Germany. *ATS 606SP:* €125.00 in Germany. *RF-B55:* £109.95 in the United Kingdom. *R876:* £129.99 or less in the United Kingdom. *MB-60A:* R1,000.00 in South Africa.

Pro: Relatively diminutive for a compact model. Single bandwidth reasonably effective at adjacent-channel rejection, while providing reasonable audio bandwidth. Speaker audio quality better than most for size (*see* Con). Weak-signal sensitivity at least average. Various helpful tuning features, including keypad, 54 station presets, slew, signal-seek tuning and meter band selection. Keys have superior feel. Easy to operate. Longwave. Dual-zone 24-hour clock. Illuminated LCD. Alarm. Sleep delay. Travel power

Sangean's veteran ATS 606 series is available worldwide under various names. Although compact-sized, it is small and handy enough for frequent flyers.

lock (*see* Con). Multi-bar battery strength indicator; also, weak-battery warning. Stereo FM through earphones or earbuds. Above-average FM weak-signal sensitivity and selectivity. Above-average capture ratio aids reception when band congested, including helping separate co-channel stations. Memory scan. Elevation panel tilts radio to handy operating angle; rubber feet reduce sliding while panel in use. *R876 and ATS 606AP:* UL-approved 120/230V AC adaptor, with American and European plugs, adjusts to proper AC voltage automatically. *ATS 606AP:* ANT-60 outboard reel passive wire antenna accessory aids slightly with weak-signal reception. In North America, service provided by Sangean America to models sold under its name. *RF-B55:* Cabinet and controls not painted, so should maintain their appearance unusually well. Made in Taiwan, and so indicated on radio and box.

Con: No tuning knob. Speaker audio quality lacks low-frequency ("bass") response as compared to larger models. Clock not readable while frequency displayed. No meaningful signal indicator. Keypad not in telephone format. Travel power lock doesn't disable LCD illumination button. No carrying strap or handle. No batteries (three "AA" needed). *ATS 606AP:* Country of manufacture (China) not specified on radio or box. *RF-B55:* No AC adaptor or outboard reel antenna included, although the owner's manual says that the radio is supposed to come with an "external antenna." Not available within the Americas.

Verdict: This classic continues to hold its own among travel-friendly compact models. Now, it is available in separate Chinese-made and Taiwanese-made versions.

New for 2008
✪✪⅝
Kchibo KK-S500

Price: $89.90 including global shipping from stores.ebay.com/v-com-collections.

Pro: Synchronous selectable sideband, heretofore unheard of near this price (*see* Con). Handy tuning features include tuning knob with 1/5 kHz tuning steps (0.1/1.0 MHz FM) and no muting, up/down slewing, keypad in standard telephone layout, quick access to world band segments, 1,000 non-volatile presets (600 shortwave, 200 mediumwave AM, 200 FM), signal-seek scanning, and presets scanning. Very good sensitivity on all bands. Excellent image rejection. Punchy audio (*see* Con). Single-step attenuator. Single-level tone control. Five-bar signal indicator (*see* Con). Excellent key feel. Superior LCD illumination (*see* Con). Travel power lock. Sturdy telescopic antenna swivels and rotates. External antenna jack for shortwave and FM (*see* Con). Selectable 9 kHz or 10 kHz mediumwave AM tuning steps (*see* Con). FM in stereo with headphones. Japanese FM. Clock displays separately from frequency and includes seconds; when off, also shows day, month and year. Two-event timer. Up to 90-minute sleep delay. Built-in battery recharging with selectable charging time. Includes three 2,300 mAh NiMH "AA" rechargeable cells, superior softside carrying case, regulated AC adaptor (*see* Con), earbuds and outboard passive reel accessory antenna.

Con: Not available outside China except through eBay, with no warranty or repair support. Synchronous selectable sideband performs poorly, losing lock and howling even on strong signals. No single-sideband demodulation, puzzling given the presence of synchronous selectable sideband circuitry. Tends to overload with external antenna; attenuator helps only to an extent. Somewhat muffled world band and mediumwave AM audio. Some synthesizer buzz when keys pressed. Power button must be pressed twice. Frequency display 1–2 kHz off on shortwave and mediumwave AM. Mediumwave AM tuning step would not change to 10 kHz on our unit; remained stuck at 9 kHz; fortunately, the available 1 kHz tuning step provides a workaround. Local mediumwave AM signals occasionally "ghost" into shortwave spectrum, annoying world band reception. Signal indicator overreads; also, shows ten bars when in reality there are only five. Some hum with included 110V AC adaptor. LCD icons too small. LCD illumination flickers slightly and can't be switched to stay continuously on with AC adaptor. No audio line output. Two of the three "AA" batteries hard to install and battery cover not hinged (both points moot if rechargeable cells used). Domestic model, so most panel markings in Chinese. No printed English manual, although one eBay vendor includes a simple PDF manual.

Verdict: Obviously, Kchibo did their homework when drawing up the engineering specifications for the KK-S500—on paper it has an incredible amount to offer at an exceptionally low price. Yet, our tests show that there is additional distance to go along the learning curve before hope turns fully into reality.

Case in point: the 'S500 has a powerful draw—synchronous selectable sideband at a breathtakingly low price. Alas, this is Kchibo's first try and it shows: the sync loses lock even with strong signals and has no auto-off while tuning.

Sensitivity, however, is above average and most other aspects of performance are quite decent. In all, this is a desirable new portable, even if it's not all that it was meant to be.

Evaluation of New Model: The KK-S500 appears to be solidly built for its class, right down to the telescopic antenna. It is unusually attractive, with a brushed aluminum insert that covers most of the plastic front cabinet. Also handily located on the front panel is the tuning knob.

The 'S500 is for the domestic China market, so most panel markings are in Chinese. There's no English owner's manual, either, although one eBay vendor provides a 21-page PDF version. However, it is simplistic and uses such broken English that it's sometimes impossible to follow. Fortunately, the radio is generally easy to use once you figure out which control does what.

To turn on the radio takes two taps of the power button—first to illuminate the LED, second to bring forth the juice. Fortunately, the power button isn't a "forced sleep timer" like those that afflict so many other Chinese portables. But keep the power button pressed down on the second tap, and the 10–90 minute sleep-delay timer pops right up.

Until now Kchibo has been known for low-end models. The new KK-S500 is its first foray into something more serious, but the attempt has been a mixed bag.

All buttons have good feel, but not the tuning knob—although it has detents for each step, it has enough rotational play to give it a sloppy feel. Too, it doesn't stick out enough to grab and the speed dimple is shallow, making it an ergonomic also-ran.

Presets? Nearly enough to satisfy the NSA, a thousand in all—600 for shortwave, 200 for mediumwave AM and 200 for FM—all scannable. There are ten presets per page, or 60 pages for shortwave, 20 for mediumwave AM, and 20 for FM. Alas, neither the 100 pages nor 1,000 presets can be tagged, which makes for some world class head-scratching when you're trying to figure out what preset is for which station.

Image rejection is excellent, and sensitivity is very good on all bands. Dynamic range is adequate, but there can be overloading with a significant external antenna—hardly needed, anyway, given the commendable sensitivity with the built-in telescopic antenna. Front-end selectivity is adequate, although with an outboard antenna there can be very limited ghosting of mediumwave AM signals into the shortwave spectrum.

Synchronous Selectable Sideband

There's only one bandwidth, but if the synchronous selectable sideband were to work properly it would have done the trick nicely. Alas, it loses lock and howls even with powerful stations, much less with weaker signals. Too, the sync does not automatically turn off as you tune, so you have to shut it off manually. Interestingly, given that the radio already has selectable-sideband circuitry, there is no provision for single-sideband signals.

Audio tends to be muffled except on FM. Too, although the included 110V AC adaptor uses an analog (non-switching) IC regulator, it lacks capacitors across the power diode rectifiers. This results in considerable hum with the telescopic antenna.

Signal-strength indicators are routinely sacrificed in low-cost portables, but not so the 'S500: Its indicator has five steps, even though it misleadingly shows ten bars. But no matter—it zooms to a full five bars with nearly every signal, making it virtually useless.

LCD illumination, green and attractive, stays on for ten seconds, although it flickers slightly can't be left on continuously with the AC adaptor in use. Most LCD characters are generously sized, but the itsy icons call for 20-15 eyesight.

Thankfully, the 24-hour clock displays separately from the frequency readout, and there's more: When the radio is off, it also shows day, month and year. A two-event timer includes programmable "on," with "off" always being after two hours.

Sangean's ATS505 series, also sold by Roberts, offers relatively little for the price.

The mediumwave AM band covers 522–1620 kHz, although 1630–1700 kHz is included within the shortwave band's tuning range. There are selectable 9 and 10 kHz tuning steps, but on our unit the 10 kHz setting refused to work; thankfully tuning can also be in 1 kHz steps, so the 10 kHz glitch is only an inconvenience. FM is in stereo through headphones and includes the Japanese FM band.

The battery cover is not hinged to prevent loss, and the lower two of the three "AA" batteries are frustratingly difficult to insert. Neither is an issue if the included NiMH rechargeable batteries and built in charger are used.

Finally, a robust softside carrying case offers good protection on trips. When new it smells like an old tire, so let it air out for a day or two.

✪✪⅝
Sangean ATS 505P, Sangean ATS 505, Roberts R9914

Price: *ATS 505P:* $129.95 in the United States. CAD$149.00 in Canada. £79.95 in the United Kingdom. €109.00 in Germany. *ATS 505:* €95.00 in Germany. *R9914:* £84.00 in the United Kingdom. AC adaptor: £16.95 in the United Kingdom.

Pro: Numerous helpful tuning features, including two-speed tuning knob, keypad, station presets (*see* Con), up/down slew, meter-band carousel selection, signal-seek tuning and scanning of presets (*see* Con). Automatic-sorting feature arranges station presets in frequency order. Analog clarifier with center detent and stable circuitry allows single-sideband signals to be tuned with uncommon precision and to stay properly tuned, thus allowing for superior audio phasing for a portable (*see* Con). Illuminated LCD. Dual-zone 24/12-hour clock. Alarm with sleep delay. Modest battery consumption. Nine-bar battery-strength indicator. Travel power lock (*see* Con). FM stereo through earbuds, included. Longwave. AC adaptor. *ATS 505P:* Tape measure antenna.

Con: Bandwidth slightly wider than appropriate for a single-bandwidth receiver. Large for a compact. Only 18 world band station presets, divided up between two "pages" with nine presets apiece. Tuning knob tends to mute stations during bandscanning by knob, especially when tuning rate is set to fine (1 kHz); muting with coarse (5 kHz) tuning is much less objectionable. Keys respond slowly, needing to be held down momentarily rather than simply tapped. Stop-listen-resume scanning of station presets wastes time. Pedestrian overall single-sideband reception because of excessively wide bandwidth and occasional distortion caused by AGC timing. Clock does not display independent of frequency. No meaningful signal indicator. No carrying handle or strap. Country of manufacture (China) not specified on radio or box. Travel power lock does not deactivate LCD illumination key. No batteries (four "AA" needed).

Verdict: An okay portable that demodulates single-sideband signals.

The Sony ICF-SW35 offers worthy reception, but tuning is dismal. It is best suited to occasional listening.

✪✪⅝
Sony ICF-SW35

Price: $89.95 in the United States. €99.00 in Germany.

Pro: Superior reception quality, with excellent adjacent-channel rejection (selectivity) and image rejection. Fifty world band station presets, which can be scanned within five "pages." Signal-seek-then-resume scanning works unusually well. Two-speed slew. Illuminated display. Dual-zone 24-hour clock. Dual-time alarm. Sleep delay. Travel power lock. FM stereo through earpieces, not included. Weak-battery indicator. Japanese FM (most versions) and longwave.

Con: No keypad or tuning knob. Synthesizer muting and poky slew degrade bandscanning. Speaker audio quality clear, but lacks low-frequency response ("bass"). Clock not displayed independent of frequency. LCD lacks contrast when viewed from above. No jacks for recording or outboard antenna. AC adaptor is extra and pricey. No batteries (three "AA" required).

Verdict: The Sony ICF-SW35 has superior rejection of images, which are the bane of most other under-$100 models. This Chinese-made compact lacks a keypad, which is partially overcome by a large number of station presets and effective scanning. Overall, a decent choice only if you listen to a predictable roster of stations.

✪✪½
Degen DE1105

Price: *via stores.ebay.com/v-com-collections:* $68.99 including global air shipping from China.

Pro: One thousand presets (*see* Con) within ten "pages" (*see* Con); presets do not erase if batteries removed or exhausted. Other handy tuning features include keypad, signal-seek frequency scanning, automatic tuning system (ATS) and up/down slewing. Also, a knurled wheel with un-muted variable-rate tuning shifts from slow (1 kHz) to fast (5 kHz) increments when rotated quickly (*see* Con). Worthy sensitivity and selectivity. Double conversion provides effective image rejection. Dynamic range resists overloading. Buttons have excellent feel (*see* Con). LCD and most buttons illuminate when touched or tuning wheel turned. Ten-bar signal indicator accurate and precise for price class. Internal automatic NiMH battery recharging virtually eliminates having to purchase batteries. Three-bar

The Degen DE1105 fares well against similarly priced models from other firms. However, certain other Degen models are slightly better for less money.   D. Zantow

battery-strength indicator, seconds as battery-charging indicator. Radio shuts down if batteries too low. Clock selectable between 12-hour and 24-hour formats; seconds displayed numerically (*see* Con). Worthwhile FM sensitivity and selectivity. FM in stereo with earpieces. Bass boost, albeit only on FM with earpieces. Japanese FM. Three alarms with sleep delay. Travel power lock. Hinged battery cover prevents loss. Includes soft carrying case, two "AA" NiMH batteries, earbuds, accessory wire antenna and 220V AC adaptor. Displays ambient (e.g., room) temperature (*see* Con).

Con: Not available outside China except via eBay with no warranty. Potentially confusing presets "page" system and user setup. Power button activates 99-minute sleep delay bypassed only by quickly pushing another button. World band coverage from 5800 to 26100 kHz, although reasonable, misses lesser 2, 3, 4 and 5 MHz (120, 90, 75 and 60 meter) segments and 5730–5795 kHz end of important 6 MHz (49 meter) segment. Because only one (narrow) bandwidth provided, world band and mediumwave AM audio quality only fair with earpieces and internal speaker. Except for frequency/clock, LCD information small and hard to see. Buttons undersized. Keypad not in

standard telephone format. Tuning wheel operates only in slow (1 kHz) increments within many "out-of-band" frequency zones. Degen's quality control, once well above average, appears to have become hit-or-miss. Clock shares display with frequency, so you can see one or the other but not both at once. Clock setting erases when batteries removed or exhausted. Mediumwave AM sensitivity only fair. No external antenna or audio line-out jacks. Temperature only in Celsius.

Verdict: The Chinese-made Degen DE1105 is a solid performer within its price class. Size and features make it especially welcome for use on trips, but for similar money there are better choices.

✪✪½
Etón E100, E100 Lextronix, Tecsun PL-200

Price: *Etón:* $99.95 in the United States. CAD$99.99 in Canada. £59.00 in the United Kingdom. *Lextronix:* €79.00 in Germany.

Pro: Handy size for travel. Very good weak-signal sensitivity. Above-average dynamic range. Superior audio for size, aided by hi/lo tone switch. Several handy tuning aids, including keypad; tuning knob in 1 kHz segments for world band/MW AM (*see* Con); 200 station presets, with eight pages where user selects how many presets per page; world band segment selector; and slew buttons (5 kHz world band increments, 9/10 kHz MW AM increments). Illuminated LCD, easy to read. World Time clock (*see* Con) with alarm, clock radio, snooze and sleep delay; may also be set to 12-hour format. Clock reads out separately from frequency. Signal-seek frequency scanning searches world band segments or preset channels (*see* Con). Five-bar signal/battery strength indicator, works well. Keys have positive-action feel (*see* Con). FM stereo with earbuds, included. Japanese FM. Travel power lock. Telescopic antenna swivels and rotates. Setting to allow for optimum performance from either regular or rechargeable batteries. Elevation panel tilts radio to handy operating angle. *Etón:* Excellent hardside leather travel case. Two "AA" alkaline batteries included. Stylish curved front panel, silver colored. *North America:* Excellent toll-free tech support. Owner's manual unusually helpful for newcomers. *Tecsun:* 220V AC adaptor/battery charger and rechargeable "AA" batteries included. Softside travel case protects better than most. Choice among three colors (red, gray, silver).

Con: Single-conversion IF circuitry results in mediocre image rejection. Signal-seek frequency scanning progresses slowly. Some muting when tuning by knob or slewing, slows down bandscanning. Tuning knob has no selectable 5 kHz step option. Power button activates 90-minute sleep delay; works as full-time "on" control only if held down for two seconds, a minor inconvenience; there is an additional three seconds to boot up, so basically it takes five seconds to turn on. World band frequencies on all Etón and Tecsun samples displayed 1 kHz high. Small, cramped keys. No jacks for line output or external antenna. *Etón:* No AC adaptor included. On our early sample the tuning knob rubbed the cabinet slightly. Warranty honored only if radio purchased from authorized dealer, listed under each product at www.etoncorp.com.

Verdict: A spit-and-polish offering for tuning major stations at home or away.

The Etón E100 is nicely sized for regular air travel. Images aside, it performs well.

○○⅜
Grundig YB 550PE, Tecsun PL-230

Price: *YB550PE (as available):* $59.99 in the United States.

Pro: Very good selectivity. Above-average dynamic range. Several handy tuning aids, including 200 station presets with eight pages where user selects how many presets per page; also, world band segment selector. For world band, slew buttons tune in 5 kHz increments, while a fine-tuning (encoder) thumbwheel tunes shortwave and mediumwave AM in 1 kHz increments. Illuminated LCD (*see* Con). World Time clock (*see* Con) with alarm, clock radio and sleep delay; may also be set to 12-hour format. Clock readout separate from frequency display, shows whether radio on or off. Signal-seek frequency scanning searches world

band segments or preset channels (*see* Con). Five-bar signal/battery strength indicator, works well. FM stereo with earbuds, included. Japanese FM. Travel power lock. Telescopic antenna swivels and rotates (*see* Con). Setting to allow for optimum performance from either regular or rechargeable batteries. *YB 550PE and PL-230:* Generally pleasant audio (*see* Con). Stylish. Removable elevation panel (*see* Con) tilts radio to handy operating angle. LCD easy to read. *PL-230:* AC adaptor/battery charger and rechargeable "AA" batteries included. *YB 550PE:* Three "AA" alkaline batteries included. *North America:* Excellent toll-free tech support.

Con: Weak-signal sensitivity only fair. Single-conversion IF circuitry results in mediocre image rejection. Signal-seek frequency scanning stops only on very strong signals. Power button activates 90-minute sleep delay; works as full-time "on" control only if held down for two seconds, a minor inconvenience. Takes an additional five seconds to fully turn on (or boot up). Small, cramped keys. *YB 550PE:* No AC adaptor included. *YB 550PE and PL-230:* Audio crispness on FM through earpieces not fully up to Grundig standard. Keypad has oddly placed zero key. Telescopic antenna placement on right side disallows tilting to left. Illumination dim. Snap-on elevation panel must be removed to replace batteries. Battery cover comes loose easily if elevation panel not attached. One of our two units displayed FM

Grundig's YB 550PE is priced to move, yet includes handy tuning aids. But performance is only okay.

50 Hz high, whereas world band frequencies on both samples were 1 kHz high. *Etón and Grundig:* Warranty honored only if radio purchased from authorized dealer, listed under each product at www.etoncorp.com.

☞ The Tecsun PL-230 is essentially identical to the YB 550PE except for color and the inclusion of rechargeable batteries and an AC adaptor/charger.

Verdict: Under-$100 radios used to look blah and often sounded that way, but no more. These stylish portables are straightforward to use and full of software conveniences. However, images and weak-signal

The Sangean ATS 404 is sensitive to weak signals, but overloads easily and suffers from images. Other models do better for less.

sensitivity keep them from reaching their full potential. There are signs that this model may be discontinued, so grab it while you can.

✪✪⅜
Sangean ATS 404, Sangean ATS 404P

Price: *ATS 404:* $79.95 in the United States. CAD$99.99 in Canada. €59.00 in Germany. *ATS 404P:* €65.00 in Germany. *ADP-808 120V AC adaptor:* $12.95 in the United States.

Pro: Superior weak-signal sensitivity. Several handy tuning features. Stereo FM through earpieces, included. Dual-zone 24/12-hour clock displays seconds numerically. Alarm with sleep delay. Travel power lock. Illuminated LCD. Battery-strength indicator. *ATS 404P:* Includes ANT 60 accessory antenna.

Con: Single-conversion IF circuitry results in poor image rejection. No tuning knob. Overloading, controllable by shortening telescopic antenna on world band and collapsing it on mediumwave AM band. Picks up some internal digital "buzz." Tunes only in 5 kHz increments. No signal indicator. Frequency and time cannot be displayed simultaneously. Travel power lock does not disable LCD illumination. No handle or carrying strap. AC adaptor extra. Country of manufacture (China) not specified on radio or box. No batteries (four "AA" needed).

Verdict: Better values can be found elsewhere.

Revived for 2008
✪✪⅜ **🖉**
Grundig Yacht Boy 300PE

Price: $49.99 in the United States.

Pro: Sensitive to weak world band and FM signals. Various helpful tuning features. World Time 24-hour clock with alarm, clock radio and 10–90 minute sleep delay (*see* Con). Illuminated LCD (*see* Con). 120V AC adaptor and supplementary antenna. Travel power lock (*see* Con). Stereo FM through earbuds, included. Excellent toll-free tech support.

Con: Mediocre image rejection. No tuning knob. Few station presets; e.g., only six for 2300–7800 kHz range. Tunes world band only in 5 kHz steps and displays in non-standard XX.XX MHz/XX.XX₅ MHz format. Keypad entry of even channels with all digits (e.g., 6 - 1 - 9 - 0, Enter) tunes radio 5 kHz higher (e.g., 6195); remedied by not entering trailing zero (e.g., 6 - 1 - 9, Enter). Unhandy carouseling "MW/SW1/SW2/FM" control required for tuning within 2300–7800 kHz *vs.* 9100–26100 kHz range or *vice versa*. Clock not displayed independent of frequency; button alters which one is visible. Nigh-useless signal-strength indicator. LCD illumination not disabled by travel power lock. No longwave. Does not tune unimportant 7805–9095 kHz range. Warranty honored only if radio purchased from authorized dealer, listed under each product at www.etoncorp.com.

Verdict: This model was dropped from Grundig's lineup in 2004, then revived at a lower price for North America in the late summer of 2007—there's no indication whether this is new old stock or revived production. Except for LCD illumination being enabled when the travel power lock is used, this Chinese-made model is bargain-priced and handy for air travel, especially where signals are weak.

New for 2008

✪✪
Degen DE1104

Price: *Export/English version via stores.ebay. com/radio-component:* $62.90 including global air shipping from China.

Pro: Generally excellent sensitivity, helpful for daytime listening (*see* Con). Pleasant, punchy audio with no audible hiss. Tone control with healthy bass boost. Dual conversion provides worthy image rejection. LCD easy to read, with excellent orange illumination and large characters; illumination can be switched on fulltime, even with battery power (*see* Con). Tuning knob (*see* Con) smooth, with minimal play. Buttons and switches have good feel. Electronic bandswitching for mediumwave AM/world

Revived for 2008 is the travel-oriented Grundig YB 300PE, now at a lower price.

band avoids mechanical pitfalls. Telescopic antenna swivels and rotates. Antenna jack for world band and FM (*see* Con). One-step attenuator (*see* Con). Four-bar signal indicator. Volume level shows in ten increments within little window. Travel power lock. Batteries recharge internally (*see* Con). Hinged battery cover prevents loss. Clock, in 12- or 24-hour format, displays separately from frequency. Sleep feature, up to 90 minutes. Two clock-radio "on" times include setting for day of week. Three-bar battery indicator. Three pages with 12 FM presets each. ATS (auto store) for FM, especially handy on trips. Signal-seek scanning on FM. Japanese FM. AC adaptor (*see* Con), thin cloth case, earbuds and indoor wire antenna (*see* Con).

Con: Not available outside China except via eBay with no warranty. World band

The DE1104 is a good example of why Degen's pioneering DE1101 and DE1102 are tough acts to follow.

D. Zantow

and mediumwave AM analog tuned with digital frequency counter, so tunable only by knob. Poor dynamic range causes overloading, especially evenings within 6 and 7 MHz (49 and 41 meter) segments, even with telescopic antenna; attenuator helps only slightly. Antenna jack meaningless, as wire antenna causes serious overloading. Some spurious variable-pitch whistles (not images). Lone bandwidth relatively broad. Sensitivity rolls off over upper 100 kHz of each world band segment; also, above 1300 kHz mediumwave AM. Annoying AC adaptor hum with telescopic antenna or included indoor wire antenna. World band coverage not continuous, omitting the little-used 2, 19 and 26 MHz (120, 15 and 11 meter) segments; also, 5730–5780, 7575–7600, 9250–9310, 9955–10000, 11500–11575, 15000–15030 and 15675–15825 kHz in other segments. Mediumwave AM tunes to roughly 1670 kHz, missing upper three X-band channels. World band displays 2 kHz high on our test unit, purchased new. LCD illumination not timed. FM presets, backed up by batteries, erase if more than one minute taken to change batteries. FM performance only fair. Tuning knob inoperative on FM. No line-audio output. Internal battery recharger has no timer. Required 4 × "AA" batteries not included.

Verdict: Worthy as a travel clock radio, although only FM has synthesized tuning. World band sensitivity and audio are superior, particularly for daytime listening, but dynamic range disappoints.

Evaluation of New Model: The Degen DE1104 uses modern synthesized tuning, but only on FM, which sports three pages of 12 station presets each. There's also ATS to auto-store FM stations—handy away from home—plus up/down slewing and signal-seek scanning. However, the tuning knob doesn't work on FM, and FM sensitivity and selectivity are pedestrian.

Meanwhile, world band and mediumwave AM make do with analog tuning complemented by a displayed digital frequency counter. Of course, analog tuning means non-FM stations can be accessed only by knob.

Analog tuning is in 12 "bands": one for mediumwave AM and 11 for major world band segments. Mediumwave AM misses the upper 35 kHz or so of the X-band, while world band omits the little-used 2, 19 and 26 MHz (120, 15 and 11 meter) segments. Also MIA are 5730–5780, 7575–7600, 9250–9310, 9955–10000, 11500–11575, 15000–15030 and 15675–15825 kHz in other segments.

Sensitive but Overloads

World band sensitivity is superior, but with a catch: It rolls off noticeably over the upper 100 kHz of each world band segment. Mediumwave AM, too, above 1300 kHz.

For daytime listening above 13.5 MHz, high sensitivity is a real plus. Alas, evenings this exceptional sensitivity combined with modest innards can cause overloading within lower segments, such as 6 and 7 MHz (49 and 41 meters)—even with the telescopic antenna. There's a single-step attenuator that is marginal for quelling overloading, but shortening the telescopic antenna helps. There is an external antenna jack, but an outboard antenna—even the little wire provided with the radio—only aggravates overloading.

Audio is superior—plenty of clean output, minimal hiss and a bass-boost switch. Selectivity, although relatively broad, is adequate for listening to most major signals. Double conversion reduces images, but varying-pitch image whistles sometimes appear anyway.

Time, in either 12- or 24-hour/World Time format, is displayed separately from frequency. There are two clock-radio settings, but no buzzer, and when the radio is off the first alarm's setting is displayed alongside current time. A nice touch is that not only the usual "on" time can be set, but also the day of the week. And for insomniacs there's a sleep timer—up to 90 minutes in ten-minute steps.

The LCD's characters—except for the four-bar signal indicator—are easy to read; excellent orange illumination switches on/off, but there's no timed setting. The handily located volume thumbwheel includes a

0–9 scale (and M for maximum) in a little window.

Alas, the included AC adaptor creates annoying hum with the telescopic antenna or an indoor outboard antenna. This disappears with an outdoor antenna, but that causes massive overloading. With a better, regulated non-switching (transformer) adaptor this problem disappears.

✪⅞ ℭ
Grundig G1100

Price: $49.95 in the United States.

Pro: Tunes by knob, not thumbwheel as did predecessor model (*see* Con). Slightly better world band coverage than predecessor model (*see* Con). Good world band and mediumwave AM sensitivity. Pleasant, vigorous audio (*see* Con). Easy-to-read LCD has large digits and good contrast. Clever, effective LCD illumination turns on and off by rotating tuning knob or pushing button. Travel power lock (*see* Con). Telescopic antenna swivels and rotates. Weak battery indicator. Elevation panel tilts radio to handy operating angle. World Time clock (*see* Con) with alarm, clock radio and snooze; may also be set to 12-hour format. Sleep delay up to two hours. FM in stereo through included earbuds; FM stereo indicator. Two "AA" batteries included. Superior carrying case. *North America:* Excellent toll-free tech support.

Con: Single conversion IF circuitry results in poor image rejection, with signals repeating at reduced strength 910 kHz down. Selectivity only okay. Analog tuned with digital frequency counter, so tunable only by stiff knob; thus, it lacks such helpful tuning aids as station presets, keypad and scanning. Analog tuning uses string and pulley configuration to turn variable capacitors; this results in play and makes it harder than usual to zero in on stations. Lacks coverage of little-used 2 and 25 MHz (120 and 11 meter) world band segments; also misses relatively unimportant 3 MHz (90 meter) segment and 5.73–5.9 MHz portion of important 6 MHz (49 meter) segment. Unhandy bandswitch must be accessed often to tune mediumwave AM and within shortwave spectra.

Grundig's G1100 has good sensitivity and a tuning knob. Images and selectivity aren't great, but the price is tempting.

Placing hand on or near cabinet rear causes frequency drift of up to 5 kHz. Placing hand or finger on LCD generates buzzing on mediumwave AM and lower world band frequencies. Audio has limited bass. FM hampered by overloading from strong local signals. Frequency reads out only in 5 kHz increments in XX.XX/XX.XX$_5$ MHz format. No signal indicator. Clock reads out only when radio off. Travel power lock does not disable LCD illumination. No AC adaptor (3V DC center-tip negative needed). Battery cover not hinged to prevent loss. Warranty honored only if radio purchased from authorized dealer, listed under each product at www.etoncorp.com.

Verdict: The G1100 has more spit and polish and better daytime frequency coverage than most cheaper alternatives. It's also backed up by a solid warranty and, in North America, a free help line.

It occupies a spot between "throwaway" models that are passable performers and sometimes not sold outside China, and more highly rated models that cost more.

✪¾ ℭ
Grundig G1000A, Tecsun DR-910

Price: *Grundig:* $49.95 in the United States.

Pro: Clock/timer with sleep delay (*see* Con). Illuminated LCD has bigger digits than most

The Grundig G1000A is priced identically to Grundig's newer G1100. The similar '1100 is a skosh better.

models of this size. Elevation panel tilts radio to handy operating angle. FM in stereo with earbuds, included. Two "AA" batteries included. Superior carrying case. *North America:* Excellent toll-free tech support.

Con: Analog tuned with digital frequency counter, so tunable only by thumbwheel, which is slightly touchy. Does not tune relatively unimportant 2, 3, 4, 5, 19 and 25 MHz (120, 90, 75, 60, 15 and 11 meter) segments; misses a small amount of expanded coverage of important 41 and 31 meter segments. Single-conversion IF circuitry results in poor image rejection. Audio lacks bass response. Frequency drift

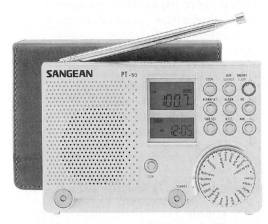

Among Sangean's newest offerings is the PT-50. It is more interesting as a multi-zone clock than as a radio.

with changes in temperature. Clock in 12-hour format, displays only when radio off. Displays in nonstandard XX.XX/XX.XX$_5$ MHz format. "Play" in bandswitch allows wiggling to slightly alter frequency readout. FM overloads in presence of strong signals, remediable by shorting antenna (which also reduces weak-signal sensitivity). On our units, FM frequency misread by 100 kHz (half a channel). If finger placed over LCD display, buzzing audible on mediumwave AM and lower world band frequencies. No AC adaptor. Warranty honored only if radio purchased from authorized dealer, listed under each product at www.etoncorp.com.

Verdict: More spit and polish, and better daytime frequency coverage, than truly cheaper alternatives. It's also backed up by a solid warranty from a reputable company. The G1000A occupies a spot between "throwaway" models that are passable performers, and more highly rated models that cost more.

✪¾
Sangean PT-50

Price: $79.95 in the United States. CAD$68.99 in Canada.

Pro: Unusually attractive, sheathed in tan leather. Flip-open leather case excellent at protecting front, top and rear of the receiver (*see* Con). Leather case affixed to receiver with snaps and magnetic catches, so nearly impossible to misplace. Two clocks, with separate display windows for home time and World Time. Changing home time to summer (savings) setting does not alter World Time. Handy disc to select time in any of 24 world zones (*see* Con). 24 or 12 hour clock format (*see* Con). Illuminated display. Reasonably clean, pleasant speaker audio for size (*see* Con). Travel power lock (*see* Con). FM in stereo through earpieces (*see* Con). Generally good mediumwave AM performance (*see* Con). Weak-battery indicator. Stereo indicator (*see* Con). Hinged battery cover prevents loss. Keys "clicky," with excellent feel. Alarm/clock radio with sleep delay and snooze. Rubber feet on bottom to prevent slipping.

Con: Analog tuned with digital frequency counter, so tunable only by thumbwheel, which is slightly touchy. Bandswitch must be adjusted when going from one world band segment to another, complicating operation. World band coverage omits 5730–5795 kHz portion of 49 meters; 6890–6990 and 7535–7600 kHz portions of 41 meters; 9250–9305 kHz portion of 31 meters; and all of 120, 90, 75, 60, 15, 13 and 11 meters. Frequency display nonstandard, being in Megahertz and reading out only to the nearest 10 kHz; thus, 6155 kHz shows as 6.15 and/or 6.16 MHz. Single-conversion IF circuitry results in poor image rejection. World band sensitivity and selectivity only fair. No external antenna socket. Speaker audio weak in bass. Audio amplifier lacks punch; stations with weak audio hard to hear, or break into distortion. Frequency drift with changes in temperature. Time-format selection applies to World and home displays alike, so 24 hours can't be used for World Time and 12 hours for home. Small LCDs with thin characters for size of radio. FM performance ordinaire, with mediocre capture ratio; in strong-signal situations there can be overloading. FM stereo indicator worked at some test locations, but not all. Pedestrian spurious-signal rejection on mediumwave AM. No meaningful signal indicator. Bandswitch designates world band segments as 1–7 rather than as MHz. No AC adaptor (needs 3-6V DC, center negative), batteries (two "AA" required) or earpieces. No audio line output for recording, home FM transmitters and outboard audio systems. Leather case: 1) collapses when used as elevation panel; 2) no perforations over speaker, so case has to be opened for listening; 3) does not protect receiver's sides or bottom; 4) when case closed, telescopic antenna can only be extended roughly horizontally, to the left; and 5) even when open, case blocks folded telescopic antenna and there is no cabinet detent for finger, so unfolding antenna is cumbersome (best is not to push antenna into the cabinet's snap-in antenna catch). Travel power lock does not deactivate LCD illumination key. Country of origin, China, not shown on radio, manual or box.

Tecsun's R9702 isn't a great performer and is available only from eBay. Yet, it is attractive for trips and is cheap enough to be lost without regret.

Verdict: Great clock, so-so radio. Unusually handy as a multi-zone timepiece and a class-act eyeful. Yet, by today's yardstick the PT-50's radio performance and features are inferior to various other models priced comparably or lower.

⭐¾
Tecsun R9702

Price: *via stores.ebay.com/v-com-collections:* $34.80 including global air shipping from China.

Pro: Dual conversion design provides worthy image rejection, exceptional at this price. Superior audio quality with decent bass and plenty of volume. Sensitive on world band. Large, easy-to-read LCD with good contrast and useful illumination. Mediumwave AM sensitivity above average for genre. FM in stereo through provided earbuds. Telescopic antenna rotates and swivels. Elevation panel tilts radio to handy operating angle. External power jack (3V DC, negative tip). Outboard wire antenna. Alarm (*see* Con) Superior travel case (*see* Con).

Con: Not available outside China except via eBay with no warranty and questionable shipment insurance. Analog tuned with digital frequency counter, so tunable only by stiff knob; thus, it lacks such helpful tuning aids as station presets, keypad and scanning. Frequency displays only to the nearest 10 kHz. World band coverage misses important 21 MHz (13 meter) segment and lesser 2, 3, 4, 5, 19 and 25 MHz (120, 90, 75, 60, 15 and 11 meter) segments. Shortwave spectrum divided into two "bands," complicating world band tuning. Selectivity only fair. Minor spurious signals. Clock, only in 12-hour format, doesn't display independent of frequency. No keyboard lock. No signal indicator. Mediumwave AM coverage omits 1645–1705 kHz. Battery cover not hinged to prevent loss. No clock radio; buzzer alarm unpleasant if volume turned up. No snooze or sleep timers. Required two "AA" batteries not included. Travel case has slight creosote odor that lessens with airing.

Verdict: Best of the truly cheap. With pleasant performance, display illumination, alarm and useful carrying case, this bargain is hard to beat for travel.

✪⅝
Anjan A-1004

Price: *via stores.ebay.com/v-com-collections:* $28.90 including global air shipping from China. As of presstime, not available from vendors outside China.

Pro: Appears to be solidly made; includes a beefy aluminum front panel in lieu of the customary plastic. Almost totally free from the digital buzzing that plagues many other analog-tuned models with digital frequency readout. Reasonable sensitivity for price

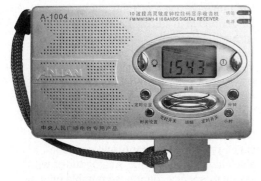

The Anjan A-1004 is yet another example that decent performance isn't found under $50. D. Zantow

class. LCD illumination, unusually effective (*see* Con). Pleasant room-filling audio for such a small package (*see* Con). In some respects, tuning wheel superior for price class (*see* Con). Telescopic antenna swivels. Clock/alarm function (*see* Con). Insertable elevation tab, attached to carrying strap, tilts radio to handy operating angle. Build quality appears to be above average for class.

Con: Not available outside China except via eBay with no warranty and questionable shipment insurance. Analog tuned with digital frequency counter, so tunable only by thumbwheel; this has some backlash and tends to be touchy. Single-conversion IF circuitry results in poor image rejection, particularly noticeable with a short outboard antenna. Audio lacks any trace of bass. World band coverage omits the 2, 3, 4, 5 and 25 MHz (120, 90, 75, 60 and 11 meter) world band segments. Always defaults to FM when first turned on. Frequency display nonstandard, being in Megahertz and reading out only to the nearest 10 kHz; thus, 6155 kHz shows as 6.15 and/or 6.16 MHz. Volume control touchy, especially on FM. Some batteries fit so tight as to be almost impossible to insert. Battery cover not hinged to prevent loss. Clock only in 12-hour format. Does not tune 1640–1710 kHz portion of the mediumwave AM band. Mediumwave AM sensitivity poor. FM sensitivity marginal. FM in mono only. No travel lock. Button must be kept depressed for LCD to be illuminated. Batteries (2 × "AA") and AC adaptor not included.

Verdict: The Anjan A-1004's metal front panel helps it stand apart from most portables. This classy touch appears to be characteristic of what seems to be above-average build quality within its price class. Audio, too, is okay, while overall performance is about as much as you'll find among cheap analog models with digital frequency readout.

Still, this is no breakthrough model. Image rejection and selectivity are lousy, there's overloading, tuning coverage isn't quite complete, frequency readout is imprecise and controls can be touchy. FM and mediumwave AM performance are both wanting, too.

New Version for 2008

✪½

Coby CX39, Tecsun R-333, Roadstar TRA-2415/N

Price: *Coby:* $14.99 in the United States. *Tecsun:* $44.90 including global air shipping from China. *Roadstar:* €18.95 in Germany.

Pro: Weak-signal sensitivity quite reasonable. Pleasant audio (*see* Con). Large, easy-to-read LCD with good contrast and timed illumination. Telescopic antenna swivels and rotates. Superior carrying handle. Clock radio (*see* Con). Batteries need changing less often than most (*see* Con). *Coby:* Built-in AC power supply.

Con: No warranty and questionable shipment insurance when purchased on eBay. Analog tuned with digital frequency counter, so tunable only by hit-and-miss thumbwheel that's only partially improved by fine-tuning control; also, can require extra step of choosing shortwave "band." Does not tune 2, 3, 19, 21 and 25 MHz (120, 90, 15, 13 and 11 meter) world band segments and 1650–1705 kHz portion of extended mediumwave AM band. Displays only to nearest 10 kHz (two world band channels) in nonstandard XX.XX MHz format. Poor selectivity. Single-conversion IF circuitry results in poor image rejection. Audio lacks bass response. FM mediocre and only in mono. Clock in 12-hour format, displays only when radio off. Clock radio has no snooze or sleep delay. No jack for AC adaptor, much less the adaptor itself. No travel power lock. Battery cover not hinged to prevent loss. Required three "D" batteries not included.

☞ The R-333 pushes the size envelope for a compact model—it's just over eight inches/21 cm wide—yet, is not quite large enough to be thought of as a laptop.

Verdict: Cheap nominal clock radio from China with superior illuminated LCD and good audio. There's little else to commend it, not even for certain customary clock-radio functions, but at $15 from Amazon the Coby is suitable as a throwaway or youngster's gift.

The Coby CX39 has sold for under $15. It's a performance bottom-feeder, but comes with inboard AC power. Tempting as a thrifty but unusual gift.

✪½

Lowe SRX-50

Price: £24.95 in the United Kingdom.

Pro: Five world band station presets, plus ten station presets for mediumwave AM and FM. Relatively simple to operate. Illuminated display. Alarm/snooze. FM stereo via earpieces, included. World Time clock. Longwave.

Con: Mediocre build quality. Does not tune important 5800–5895, 15505–15695,

Until 1999, U.K.'s Lowe Electronics offered a simple Chinese-made portable, the SRX-50. Apparently some new-old stock has surfaced, because it is once again available new.

17500–17900 and 21750–21850 kHz portions of 49, 19, 16 and 13 meters. No tuning knob; tunable only by presets and multi-speed up/down slewing/scanning in 5 kHz steps. Frequencies displayed in XX.XX/XX.XX₅ MHz format. Poor image rejection. Mediocre selectivity. Lacks bass response. Does not receive 1605–1705 kHz portion of mediumwave AM band. No signal indicator. No travel power lock. Clock not displayed independent of frequency. Mediumwave AM tuning increment only 9 kHz, not switchable, which makes for inexact tuning in the Americas where 10 kHz is the norm. Power switch shows no "off," although "auto radio" power-switch position performs comparable role.

Verdict: Although thoroughly outclassed by newer models, this "new old stock" has surfaced in the U.K. at Waters & Stanton (wsplc.com) as the "SRX-50."

✪½
jWIN JX-M14

Price: $14.95 as available in the United States.

Pro: Handy small size for travel. Clock with timer/alarm (*see* Con). Elevation panel tilts radio to handy operating angle. Earbuds included (in separate bubble pack).

The jWIN JX-M14, when you can find it, suffices as yet another stocking stuffer. Otherwise, forget it.   D. Zantow

Con: Increasingly hard to find. Mediocre weak-signal sensitivity; helps considerably to clip a few yards of wire to the built-in antenna. Mediocre selectivity. Analog tuned with digital frequency counter, so tunable only by thumbwheel, which is stiff. Does not tune 120, 75, 90, 60, 15, 13 or 11 meter segments; misses a small amount of expanded coverage of 49 and 41 meter segments. Single-conversion IF circuitry results in poor image rejection. Audio lacks bass response. Frequency counter completely omits last digit so, say, 9575 kHz appears as either 9.57 or 9.58 MHz. Clock in 12-hour format only, displays only when radio off. Display not illuminated. If hand is placed on rear of cabinet, world band drifts up to 10 kHz. Frequency drift with changes in temperature. LCD buzzes on mediumwave AM; if finger placed over LCD, buzz also audible on lower world band frequencies. Mediumwave weak-signal sensitivity uninspiring. FM overloads in strong-signal environments, remediable by shorting antenna (which also reduces weak-signal sensitivity). When first turned on, radio always reverts to FM band. FM in mono only. Two "AA" batteries not included. Warranty in the United States only 90 days and requires $12 advance payment for "return shipping"; add to that the owner's cost to ship, and warranty is of dubious value; best purchased from dealer who will swap if DOA.

Verdict: At almost a throwaway price, the Chinese-made jWIN JX-M14 is a passable portable for casual use on trips or as a stocking stuffer, provided a hank of wire is clipped on to give world band signals a boost. Usually in offbeat catalogs, but increasingly hard to find.

POCKET PORTABLES
Perfect for Travel, Marginal for Home

Pocket portables weigh around half a pound/0.2 kg and are between the size of an audio cassette jewel box and a handheld calculator. They operate off two to four "AA" (UM-3 penlite) batteries. These diminutive models are ideal to carry on your person, but listening to tiny speakers can be tiring.

If you plan to listen for long periods or to music, opt for using headphones or earpieces, or look into one of the better compact models.

Best by far is the Sony ICF-SW100 series, but it's been discontinued and is a challenge to find. There has been nothing else like it in the history of world band radio, nor may we ever see its likes again. So, if you want this Spook's Little Friend, grab it while you can.

✪✪✪⅛ (see ☞) *Passport's Choice*
Sony ICF-SW100E

Price: *ICF-SW100E:* £179.99 in the United Kingdom. €298.00 in Germany. *ACE-30HG 220V AC-to-3V DC adaptor:* £19.95 in the United Kingdom. *AC-E30A worldwide AC adaptor:* $13.95 in the United States.

Sony's incredible ICF-SW100E is the Aston Martin of minis. Don't leave Langley without it.

Pro: Tiny, easily the smallest tested, but with larger-radio performance and features. High-tech synchronous selectable sideband generally performs well, reducing adjacent-channel interference and selective-fading distortion on world band, longwave and mediumwave AM signals, while adding slightly to weak-signal sensitivity and audio crispness (*see* Con). Single bandwidth, especially when synchronous selectable sideband is used, exceptionally effective at adjacent-channel rejection. Relatively good audio, provided supplied earbuds or outboard audio are used (*see* Con). FM stereo through earbuds. Numerous helpful tuning features, including keypad, two-speed slew, signal-seek-then-resume scanning (*see* Con), five handy "pages" with ten station presets each. Station presets can display station name. Tunes in relatively precise 0.1 kHz increments. Good single-sideband performance (*see* Con). Good dynamic range. Worthy ergonomics for size and features. Illuminated display. Clock for many world cities, which can be made to work as a *de facto* World Time 24-hour clock (*see* Con). Timer and sleep delay. Travel power lock. Japanese FM (most versions) and longwave. Outboard passive reel accessory antenna aids slightly in weak-signal reception (*see* Con). Weak-battery indicator; about 16 hours from a set of batteries (*see* Con).

Con: Nigh impossible hard to find. Tiny speaker, although innovative, has mediocre sound, limited loudness and little tone shaping. Closing clamshell reduces speaker loudness and high-frequency response. Weak-signal sensitivity could be better, although included outboard active antenna helps. Expensive. No tuning knob. Clock not readable when station frequency displayed. As "London Time" is used by the clock for World Time, the summertime clock adjustment cannot be used if World Time is to be displayed accurately. Rejection of images, and 10 kHz "repeats" when synchronous selectable sideband off, could be better. In some urban locations, FM signals from 87.5 to 108 MHz can break through into world band segments with distorted sound, e.g. between 3200 and 3300 kHz. Synchronous selectable sideband tends to lose lock if batteries weak, or if NiCd cells are used. Synchronous selectable sideband alignment can vary with temperature, factory alignment and battery voltage, causing synchronous selectable sideband reception to be slightly more muffled in one sideband than the other. Batteries run down faster than usual when radio off. Tuning in 0.1 kHz increments means that non-synchronous single-sideband reception can be mis-tuned by up to 50 Hz, so audio quality varies. Signal-seek

ICOM'S IC-R20 HANDHELD

The popularity and frequency coverage of handheld scanners keep marching on. Some even cover world band, where they've traditionally performed poorly.

At around US$500/£300 the 'R20 is costlier than nearly any dedicated world band portable. Frequency coverage in the United States, where eavesdropping on cellular bands is *verboten*, is 150 kHz–822 MHz, 851–867 MHz and 896–3305 MHz. Elsewhere, or within the United States for government use, it's 150 kHz to 3305 MHz.

A neat tuning-related feature is "dual watch," which allows scanning aficionados to monitor two signals simultaneously. Alas, this multitasking goodie doesn't work with world band.

The large LCD is not easy to read except when illuminated. Keys have good feel; otherwise, ergonomics are only so-so because of limited "real estate" for controls. Tuning is by knob, keypad, up/down slewing and a thousand presets in increments of .01, .1, 5 , 6.25, 8.33, 9, 10, 12.5, 15, 20, 25, 30, 50 and 100 kHz.

The 'R20 has three bandwidths, each assigned by the received mode so none can be selected independent of mode. Unfortunately, the bandwidth for the AM mode, which includes world band, is a whopping 12 kHz. The single-sideband bandwidth, around 3 kHz, comes to the rescue by allowing for worthy ECSS reception of world band and mediumwave AM stations. It's a tiresome procedure but does the trick.

Alas, sensitivity disappoints—only powerful signals are suitably audible with the telescopic antenna. Another letdown is that the antenna tends to flop over when fully extended. The 'R20's dynamic range is significantly limited, too, so a serious outboard antenna tends to introduce overloading. Tweaking the RF gain control and single-step 30 dB attenuator can help, but not always. However, stability, as well as image and spurious-signal rejection, are commendable.

Speaker audio lacks punch, but otherwise is good considering the radio's size. There's also a built-in digital audio recorder. Its 65-minute "fine" setting is hardly high fidelity, but fares nicely for world band. There's a utility (homepage.ntlworld.com/tony.ling/radio/IC-R20/R20um23.htm, not tested) to convert the R20's .icw audio files to .wav. It's free, but takes some doing to install and make function, and requires Icom's CS-R20 software and cable package.

The Icom IC-R20 makes a tempting choice for scanning signals on VHF and above, and offers built-in recording. For certain niche applications, including low-profile field surveillance, these characteristics can come together to make it a best-of-breed choice.

For world band, though, the 'R20 is mainly an adjunct to scanning and for inboard recording.

Icom's IC-R20 underscores that handhelds aren't yet ready for prime time. Dedicated world band portables perform noticeably better for much less money, but the 'R20 succeeds with scanning aficionados who occasionally tune shortwave. It records, too.

frequency scanning sometimes stops 5 kHz before a strong "real" signal. No meaningful signal indicator. Mediumwave AM reception only fair. Mediumwave AM channel spacing adjusts peculiarly. Flimsy battery cover. No batteries (two "AA" required).

☞ The above star rating reflects audio quality through worthy earpieces. Speaker-audio rating is ✪✪✪.

☞ Herbert Thieking GmbH (thiecom.de), which exports, confirms that it has quantities of new 'SW100E units in stock as of presstime. Brits can also try Haydon Communications (haydon.info), while Waters & Stanton (wsplc.com) offers Sony's 220V AC adaptor. Sony's original 120V AC adaptor is history, but you can try their global adaptor (amazon.com).

☞ In early production samples, the cable connecting the two halves of the "clamshell" case tended to lose continuity with extended use because of a very tight radius and an unfinished edge; this was successfully resolved with a design change in 1997, and units since then have held up well. Sony offers a repair kit; so long as it continues to be available, tesp.com/sw100faq.htm offers installation and related tips.

Verdict: The ICF-SW100E is a benchmark in electronics development: For the first and only time, a serious shortwave receiver could be shoehorned into something smaller than a PC mouse.

Costly to manufacture with a price tag to match, almost certainly it won't be replicated in the future. Yet, with advanced-tech synchronous selectable sideband and features galore, this mighty mini outperforms even larger models.

New for 2008

✪✪✪⅜
Redsun RP300, CCRadio-SWP

Price: *CCRadio-SWP:* $49.95 including shipping in the United States. *Redsun RP300:* $42.99 including global air shipping from China. *SWPA 3V DC-to-120V AC adaptor:* $10.95 in the United States.

The inexpensive new CCRadio-SWP—Redsun SP300 in China—nicely enhances travel-portable options. Aside from the snazzy Sony ICF-SW100E, it is the best travel-sized portable on the market.

Pro: Good sensitivity on all bands, with no digital hash. Selectivity adequate. Handy tuning features include knob with mechanical encoder (*see* Con), keypad, up/down slewing, signal-seek scanning and presets scanning (*see* Con). 200 non-volatile EEPROM presets. Easy-to-read LCD with good contrast, proper (kHz) frequency format and ten-second illumination (*see* Con). Single-step attenuator for shortwave and FM. Clock in either 12- or 24-hour format. Up to 90-minute sleep delay. Tone switch helps ameliorate any shrillness. Beep alarm or single-event radio timer. Travel power lock. Punchy audio (*see* Con). Mediumwave AM performs nicely and tunes in 9 kHz or 10 kHz steps. FM stereo through earbuds, supplied. FM 70–108 MHz includes Japanese band. Elevation panel. Telescopic antenna rotates and swivels. Battery indicator. Superior softside carrying case. *CCRadio-SWP:* 30-day money-back guarantee. Optional AC adaptor, UL approved. *Redsun RP300:* Short wire antenna (*see* Con).

Con: Single conversion, so suboptimal image rejection. Keys, with only fair feel, sometimes sluggish to respond. Tuning knob's lone step, 1 kHz, sometimes ideal but can be annoyingly slow. Shortwave in two "bands," complicating tuning. Audio lacks bass. Misses 7500–9200 kHz. Clock and frequency share same display. Tuning knob lacks feel and rubs on case. On one sample, when turned fast the mechanical tuning encoder skips over frequencies; problem hasn't improved with use. No meaningful signal indicator. Volume controlled only by up/down keys, with earpiece volume being excessive while speaker volume is too loud at low settings. Marginal LCD illumination from only one side. FM fine for nearby reception, but not long distance. Battery cover not hinged. No antenna jack. No audio line output. AC adaptor and two "AA" batteries not included. *CCRadio-SWP:* Some shortwave hum with optional AC adaptor. *Redsun RP300:* Not available outside China except through eBay, with no warranty or service support. Annoying muting during bandscanning. Accessory short wire antenna sometimes causes overloading. Battery cover doesn't readily slide on. No optional AC adaptor offered as of presstime.

Verdict: Both versions of this "almost pocket" portable do nicely for travel and are attractively priced, but the 'SWP gets the nod because it doesn't mute during tuning. Too, one of our test units arrived with a tuning problem, which underscores the importance of customer support.

Evaluation of New Model: The Redsun RP300, although a bit much to stuff into a shirt pocket, is handy for travel and fits readily into coat pockets and purses.

Its LCD is large with good contrast, and there are tuning aids aplenty, including a real tuning knob. Shortwave coverage is quite adequate, but it is divided into two "bands," which complicates tuning. Too, keys lack crisp feel and tend not to respond instantly.

The tuning knob uses a mechanical encoder with tactile detents, but the knob feels spongy and rubs the case. It has only one speed—slow—which is fine at times, but annoying at others. Too, the Redsun version—but, thankfully, not the C. Crane version—mutes annoyingly with the tuning knob and up/down slewing. Worse, on one sample the encoder skips entire frequencies when turned fast, suggesting a QA glitch at the Redsun factory.

The 200 presets are not volatile, so your data, other than the clock/timer, remains safe no matter what. Volume is adjusted electronically by up/down keys, but even at low settings it's not close to zero. Indeed, with earpieces the entire level is set too high for comfort.

Sensitivity is good on shortwave, with no overloading unless the Redsun accessory antenna is used. Mediumwave AM sensitivity fares well, too—likely part of why it's offered by C. Crane, which over the years has become known for long-distance AM listening products. Mediumwave AM tuning steps are readily changed from 10 kHz (Americas) to 9 kHz (elsewhere) or vice versa, and coverage runs through 1710 kHz. FM is good, too, but won't win any DX contests.

Selectivity is typical for the price and excellent for mediumwave AM, but not up to tough adjacent-channel world band challenges. Single conversion results in suboptimal image rejection, but for its price class image rejection is pretty decent. Audio is clean and punchy, even if the one-step tone switch is needed to ameliorate minor shrillness.

No AC adaptor comes with either version. C. Crane offers an optional Condor D-6100-04 adaptor altered for proper plug and polarity. It works normally and has no buzz, but produces some hum with received signals.

New for 2008

✪✪

Degen DE11, Kaito KA11

Price: *KA11:* $49.95 in the United States.

Pro: Satisfactory world band sensitivity. Several handy tuning aids, including 1,000 non-volatile station presets within ten pages of 100 presets each; keypad (1 kHz increments for world band and mediumwave AM); up/down slewing (5 kHz increments for world band, 9/10 kHz for mediumwave AM); scanning (by-frequency and by-preset); presets for quick access to world band segments; and ATS (*see* glossary). Keypad in standard telephone format. No muting or chuffing on world band and FM (*see* Con). Above-average speaker audio and power for tiny radio. Buttons have good feel. LCD has good contrast and excellent timed illumination. Clock displays independent of frequency. Excellent ten-bar signal indicator. Four-bar battery indicator. Displays room temperature (*see* Con). Three on/off clock radio events; also, single-on alarm. Sleep timer, up to 99 minutes (*see* Con). Travel power lock also disables illumination. Telescopic antenna swivels and rotates (*see* Con). External antenna jack. Attenuator for world band and FM (*see* Con). FM in stereo with earpieces (provided) that provide worthy audio quality. Japanese FM (to 70 MHz). Elevation tab, albeit attached to carrying strap. Accessory wire antenna. Built-in recharging for two "AA" NiMH cells (*see* Con). *Degen DE11:* 220V AC adaptor (110V AC optional at some Chinese dealers). *Kaito KA11:* 117V AC adaptor. Mediumwave AM coverage to 1710 kHz.

Con: No world band coverage below 5800 kHz or above 18100 kHz, so misses 2, 3, 4, 5, 19, 21 and 25 MHz (120, 90, 75, 60, 15, 13 and 11 meter) world band segments and 5730–5795 kHz portion of 6 MHz (41 meter) segment. Power button activates 99-minute sleep delay; to turn radio on fulltime, a second ("exit") button must be pressed within two seconds. Poor image rejection. Poor selectivity from lone bandwidth. Microphonic or similar ringing audible with very strong world band signals. Modest dynamic range; attenuator does little to control resulting overloading. Volume control requires much rotation before any sound, then becomes unusually touchy. No tuning knob. No single sideband. LCD characters, other than for frequency, extremely small. Most buttons undersized. Fair-to-poor overall FM performance. Telescopic antenna exits from cabinet side, limiting tilt angle for optimum FM reception. On our unit, frequency display misreads by 50 kHz on FM. Digital buzz makes mediumwave AM DX all but impossible. Half-second muting pips when bandscanning mediumwave AM. No audio line output for recording. If AC adaptor unplugged then reinserted while radio on, microprocessor locks up; no reset control,

This year is notable for the appearance of two desirable travel portables, including this Kaito KA11 that's sold in China as the Degen DE11.

but lockup remediable by removing batteries for a minute or so. Required two "AA" batteries not included. No carrying case. Although our unit is satisfactory, Degen/Kaito QA has recently been spotty. Ambient temperature displays in Fahrenheit if clock in 12-hour format; displays only in Celsius if clock in 24-hour (World Time) format. *Degen DE11:* Mediumwave AM coverage only to 1620 kHz. *Kaito KA11:* AC adaptor has slight hum.

☞ Don't confuse with the very different Kaito KA011 emergency radio (see "Radios for Emergencies").

Verdict: The Degen DE11/Kaito KA11 includes a number of neat features. Yet, it offers little improvement over the earlier Degen DE105/Kaito KA105. World band coverage continues to be limited, image rejection and selectivity are poor, and there are unwelcome buzzing and ringing sounds. Even turning on the radio is a clunky procedure.

The kindred but slightly larger Degen DE1101/Kaito KA1101 covers all world band frequencies. It is also a vastly superior performer and goes for almost the same price.

Evaluation of New Model: The Degen DE11, sold in North America as the Kaito KA11, was introduced in October 2006. It is a travel-friendly 4¼" × 2¾" × 1" (110 × 71 × 23 mm) with limited but reasonable world band coverage of 5800–18000 kHz.

The '11 uses two "AA" batteries and includes inboard charging of NiMH cells, although no batteries of any sort are included. The KA11 does come with a 117V AC adaptor having a skosh of hum, while the DE11 comes standard with a 220V adaptor (some Chinese dealers offer 110V as a no-cost option).

Tuning Goodies

There are any number of helpful tuning aids, including fully a thousand non-volatile station presets. These are stored within ten pages of up to 100 channels each, but there's no alphanumeric tagging. No tuning knob, either.

Other tuning options include up/down slewing, scanning of either frequencies or station presets, presets for quick access to world band segments, and ATS (Auto Tuning Scan). ATS scanning automatically enters up to 100 active frequencies as presets within page 0; ATS scanning stops if it reaches the end of the segment before 100 presets are stored.

World band/mediumwave AM keypad tuning is in 1 kHz steps, while world band slewing is in 5 kHz steps; mediumwave AM slews in selectable 9 or 10 kHz increments. There is no chuffing or muting while surfing world band and FM frequencies, although there is minor muting on mediumwave AM.

To Turn On Radio, Press "Exit"

In some respects ergonomics are above par. For example, all keys have good tactile feel and the keypad is in standard telephone layout.

However, for some years, now, various Chinese portables have included power controls that turn off the radio after around an hour and a half. The '11, alas, is no exception. If you wish to turn on the radio for good, you have first to tap the power key, then within two seconds push the exit key.

Otherwise, 99 minutes later the radio goes silent.

The page system for station presets is equally counterintuitive. The manual helps, but its English reads like Borat of Kaitostan.

Speaker audio quality is superior for the radio's size and there is plenty of punch; indeed, with the included earpieces it sounds downright pleasant. However, the volume control requires too much rotation before anything is audible, then it becomes annoyingly touchy.

There is no line audio output for recording. However, to aid with weak-signal reception there's an external antenna jack for world band and FM. In principle, a single-step attenuator should help tame overloading that results from limited dynamic range; in practice, it has little positive effect.

Displays Time, Temperature

The LCD offers good contrast and includes an excellent ten-bar signal indicator and a four-bar battery indicator. The frequency, in XX.XXX MHz format, is easy to read, but otherwise deciphering the LCD characters tends to be a visual strain. The excellent orange timed illumination helps, but it can't be left on continuously even with the AC adaptor in use. However, the travel power lock acts on that illumination.

Three timers turn on the radio to chosen stations up to three times a day; each event lasts 1–99 minutes. For traditionalists, there's also a single "beep" alarm.

The 24/12-hour clock is thankfully displayed separately from the frequency readout, even if the time is small and hard to read. Also shown is ambient temperature, which becomes accurate only after the radio has been on for awhile. It reads in Fahrenheit when the clock is in 12-hour format, but only in Celsius with 24-hour (World Time) format—a textbook example of making something worse by trying to make it easier.

The microprocessor also has a glitch: Pull out the external power plug then reinsert it while the radio is on, and the receiver locks up. There is no reset control, but the radio can be revived by removing the batteries for a minute or so.

Performance Woes

World band sensitivity is adequate even with the short telescopic antenna. Unfortunately, performance goes downhill after that.

Selectivity with the lone bandwidth is uncomfortably wide for most world band reception. Image rejection is equally dismal, with fundamental signals repeating 900 kHz down at only slightly reduced strength. There's also microphonic-like ringing audible with very strong world band signals.

Other bands fare even worse. Digital buzz usually gets covered up on world band, but on mediumwave AM it grinds away except with powerful signals. This essentially rules out the '11 for even basic AM DXing. FM reception, too, is mediocre except with healthy local signals.

By now Degen should have gotten its act together. Eyebrows were raised a couple of years back when it introduced the high-value DE1101 and DE1102 models and their Kaito equivalents. Yet, since then they have stumbled their way through a string of models with design oddities, dubious QA and other shortcomings.

The '11, alas, is no exception.

⭐⭐ *Ⓒ*
Degen DE105, Kaito KA105

Price: *KA105:* $49.95 in the United States. CAD$59.00 in Canada.

Pro: Reasonably good selectivity from single bandwidth. Good voice-audio quality, with ample volume, for a small speaker (*see* Con). A number of helpful tuning features, including keypad (*see* Con), up/down slew (*see* Con) and signal-seek frequency scanning; also, 30 station presets, of which ten are for world band with others divided between FM and mediumwave AM. Above-average weak-signal sensitivity. Dual-zone

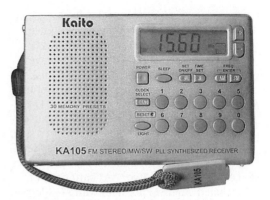

The Kaito KA105 may be inexpensive, but it comes with a genuine aluminum front panel.   D. Zantow

24-hour clock (*see* Con) with clock radio/alarm and sleep delay. Illuminated display via non-timed pushbutton. Clicky keys have superior feel. LCD has excellent contrast. Low battery consumption. Weak-battery indicator. Hinged battery cover prevents loss. Travel power lock (*see* Con). FM in stereo through earbuds, included (*see* Con). Telescopic antenna swivels and rotates (*see* Con). Insertable elevation tab, attached to carrying strap, tilts radio to handy operating angle. Includes short external wire antenna accessory. *Kaito:* Tough, attractive matte aluminum alloy face plate. 120V AC adaptor (*see* Con). Mediumwave AM 9/10 channel selectable steps. *Degen:* Available in either slate blue or silver.

Con: World band coverage of 5950–15600 kHz misses important 17 and 21 MHz (16 and 13 meter) segments, skips chunks of 6 and 15 MHz (49 and 19 meters), and omits lesser 2, 3, 4, 5, 19 and 25 MHz (120, 90, 75, 60, 15 and 11 meter) segments. Single-conversion IF circuitry results in poor image rejection. Speaker audio bereft of low-frequency ("bass") response. Audio through earbuds may be stronger in one channel at lower volume, whether in mono or stereo. No tuning knob. Keypad not in standard telephone format. Tunes world band only in 5 kHz steps and displays in nonstandard XX.XX/XX.XX₅ MHz format. Slow microprocessor lock time while slew tuning degrades bandscanning. Degen's quality control, once well above average, appears to have become hit-or-miss. No signal indicator. Clock doesn't display when frequency is shown. Mediumwave AM coverage of 520–1620 kHz omits 1625–1705 kHz. Mediumwave AM suffers slightly from LCD digital hash. FM has so-so sensitivity, mediocre capture ratio and some tendency to overload. FM audio distorted through earbuds. Because telescopic antenna exits from cabinet's side, it can't tilt to the right for optimum FM reception. Travel power lock does not disable LCD illumination. Two "AA" batteries not included. *Kaito:* Minor hum with AC adaptor.

Verdict: Except for the lack of single-sideband to hear the American Forces Radio and Television Service, this Chinese travel portable is a thrifty choice. Still, the larger Degen/Kaito siblings DE1101/KA1101 and DE1102/KA1102 cover more frequencies, perform significantly better and cost little more.

✪⅝ Ⓔ

Etón M300/Mini 300, Grundig GM300/M300/Mini 300, Tecsun R-919

Price: *Etón and Grundig:* $29.95 in the United States. €29.00 in Germany.

Etón's Mini 300 is no barnburner, but is tiny and hugely popular.

Pro: Weak-signal sensitivity quite reasonable. Pleasant room-filling audio for such a small package (*see* Con). Clock/alarm-timer with sleep delay (*see* Con). FM in stereo with earbuds, included. Low battery consumption. Available in five colors. Soft carrying case affixes to belt or purse strap. Two "AA" batteries included. *North America:* Excellent toll-free tech support.

Con: Analog tuned with digital frequency counter, so tunable only by thumbwheel, which is somewhat touchy. Does not tune 2, 3, 4, 5, 19, 21 and 25 MHz (120, 90, 75, 60, 15, 13 and 11 meter) segments; misses small bits of other world band segments. Single-conversion IF circuitry results in poor image rejection. Audio lacks bass response. Frequency drift with changes in temperature. Telescopic antenna does not rotate or swivel. Antenna's plastic base protrudes even when antenna collapsed. Displays in nonstandard $XX.XX/XX.XX_5$ MHz format. Display not illuminated. Minor drift when hand grasps back of cabinet. Frequency counter noise slightly audible when finger placed over LCD during mediumwave AM reception. Some FM overloading in strong-signal environments. Clock in 12-hour format, displays only when radio off. No jack for AC adaptor, much less the adaptor itself. *Etón and Grundig:* Warranty honored only if radio purchased from authorized dealer, listed under each product at www.etoncorp.com.

Verdict: Among the best of the really inexpensive portables, even though it comes up short on daytime frequency coverage, lacks display illumination and its clock isn't in World Time format. But thanks to true pocket size, nice weak-signal sensitivity and decent audio quality it is hard to resist for casual use on trips.

RECORDABLE PORTABLES

What happens if your favorite show comes on at an inconvenient time? Why, record it, of course, just like your favorite television show. This can be done using certain radios tied to separate recorders, but it's handier when everything is stuffed into one box.

New for 2008

✪✪⅛

Degen DE1121, Kaito KA1121, Thieking und Koch DE1121

Price (128 MB version): *Kaito:* $149.95 in the United States. *Thieking und Koch:* €219.00 in Germany.

Pro: Attached MP3 recorder/player with large LCD that's "information central" for recorder and radio. Records direct from radio or detaches for standalone use, whereupon separated radio makes do with small secondary LCD (*see* Con). Very good sensitivity. Dual conversion provides superior image rejection. Handy tuning methods include knob with 1/5 kHz world band steps—9/10 kHz for mediumwave AM, 50/100 kHz for FM, 1 kHz for longwave—with soft detent for each step; up/down slewing for world band in 5 kHz steps (9/10 kHz for mediumwave AM, 50 kHz for FM, 1 kHz for longwave); signal-seek scanning; keypad in customary telephone format; quick access to world band segments; 100 pages with up to four presets each for a total of 400 presets, and each page can display an eight-character alphanumeric tag (*see* Con). Little chuffing during bandscanning, and muting rarely intrudes (*see* Con). Two well-chosen bandwidths (*see* Con). Generally pleasant audio (*see* Con) with punch, superior bass and no hiss. Decent single-sideband performance (*see* Con) aided by good stability. Sleep function, up to 60 minutes (*see* Con). Automatic powering off after up to 120 minutes. Three-event on/off timer can also be used for unattended MP3 recordings (*see* Con). Main LCD's (*see* Con) worthy illumination can be timed or left on (*see* Con). External antenna jack for world band and FM (*see* Con). Mute button. Keys have good feel. Internal battery recharging with automatic shutoff for both radio and MP3 module, which charge separately. Telescopic antenna swivels and rotates. Clock, in 12- or 24-hour/World Time format (*see* Con), displays separately from frequency. Presets non-volatile; other data retained for one minute after batteries removed. MP3 player has fast forward/reverse, repeat,

New for 2008 is the Degen DE1121, sold in North America as the Kaito KA1121 and in Europe as the Thieking DE1121. Its detachable MP3 recorder is a world band first.   D. Zantow

shuffle and five equalization settings. Easy to program with computer, using standard text files; transferring MP3 or "memory" text files to and from computer via USB 2.0 is similarly easy. Firmware can be updated. Audio line input for MP3 recorder (*see* Con). Travel power lock and separate tuning-knob lock. Hinged battery cover. Two-level attenuator. Good FM performance. Japanese FM. Includes NiMH rechargeable batteries: 3 × "AA" for receiver, DF-6 NiMH (*see* Con) for MP3 module; also, thin cloth carrying bag, USB cable, line-input audio cable, indoor shortwave wire antenna, earbuds, Windows 98SE driver on CD, and AC adaptor. *Degen and Kaito:* Timer recording, fixed at low (32 kbps) bitrate, stores around 17 hours. *Kaito:* Firmware backup. *Thieking und Koch:* Timer recording fixed at quality-fidelity 128 kbps (*see* Con). Continuously tunes 50 kHz–29.999 MHz. Firmware can be updated, as available, by downloading. RoHS compliance signifies minimal use of undesirable substances during manufacture.

Con: Hostile ergonomics, with menus and sub-menus poorly labeled and/or illogical; skimpy Chinglish owners manual offers little assistance. Nigh-useless pseudo-analog "dial" on dot-matrix LCD forces miniaturization and preempts useful controls and displays; as a result, icons, some buttons and sub-LCD are undersized—also, no signal indicator. Rarely, microprocessor freezes up, displays strange characters or does not power radio off correctly; also, sometimes takes multiple presses for a key to act. Mediocre dynamic range limits use of accessory antennas. Substandard front-end selectivity, so strong local mediumwave and FM stations can bleed into shortwave spectrum. No audio line output. No tone control for mediumwave AM and world band. AGC decay too fast for single sideband, with clipping and distortion especially on stronger signals. AC adaptor causes minor hum with indoor antenna. Audible buzz with headphones, whether radio powered by batteries or AC adaptor. No separate LSB/USB switching; instead, uses fine-tuning control with no center detent. In mediumwave AM band, some muting during bandscanning with tuning knob and slewing. MP3 module uses nonstandard DF-6 NiMH rechargeable battery. Limited skirt selectivity allows powerful world band signals to splatter widely. 9/10 kHz mediumwave AM spacing, 12/24 hour clock format choices and page tagging done only via computer. Jack for AC adaptor/DC input requires nonstandard negative tip. Unpleasant "pop" when radio powered on or off. Frequency readout on sub-LCD uses nonstandard XX.XXx MHz layout, main LCD shows XX.XXX MHz. Sub-LCD not illuminated. Illumination toggle for main LCD squirreled within menu tree. Memory (256 MB) in MP3 player not ungradable to 512 MB. No pause control during recording, just playback. When radio section turned on, volume sometimes blasts briefly until preset volume level recognized. Line input requires high audio level. Three-event timer only daily; can't choose given day(s) of week. Power button activates 60-minute sleep delay; stays on fulltime only after left-arrow key pressed (does not have to be repeated unless batteries removed). Degen's quality control, once well above average, appears to have become hit-or-miss. *Degen and Kaito:* Omits little-used 2 MHz (120 meter) world band segment. Longwave coverage, unlike on Thieking und Koch version, starts at 140 kHz (Kaito)/150 kHz (Degen). *Kaito:* Overpriced at Kaito's website. *Thieking und Koch):* High bitrate limits recording time to around 4:20.

☞ Two levels of factory-installed internal memory are sometimes available: 256 MB or 512 MB, but the latter can't be upgraded. Tested firmware v1.1.

Verdict: The most exciting part of the DE/KA1121 is its detachable MP3 recorder, which provides up to 17 hours of off-the-air recording.

The radio suffers from hostile ergonomics and so-so receiver performance. Yet, its one-of-a-kind recorder is enough to put the '1121 on "must have" lists.

Evaluation of New Model: The new DE1121 grabs because it sports two separable modules: the radio, plus an MP3 recorder/player. The recorder includes an "information central" LCD for both the radio and the recorder. It can record from the radio or by itself, using a built-in microphone.

Although there's no alarm-buzzer, there are three on/off events for hands-off recording—even if it's tough to program and can't select days of the week. When the modules are decoupled the radio portion has to make do with a supplementary tiny, unilluminated LCD that shows frequency—in XX.XXx MHz format—and precious little else.

The main LCD's green illumination can be timed or toggled to stay on continuously. However, working the toggle is no walk in the park, as it is squirreled within a menu. Ditto the main LCD's contrast.

That LCD uses a dot-matrix configuration with tiny, hard-to-read icons; it lacks the casual readability of a normal LCD. Frequency is displayed in XX.XXX MHz format.

The radio uses three "AA" NiMH rechargeable batteries, while the recorder houses a nonstandard, hard-to-replace "Degen DF6" NiMH cell. Thankfully, all are included and are automatically recharged internally.

Versatile MP3 Recording

There are two recording choices: music (in stereo on FM) and voice. Music records at 32, 80 or 128 kbps. However, the only time the voice choice—32 kbps—appears is when the recorder is used with its built-in microphone. When undocked, the recorder can play computer-transferred 32–320 kbps MP3 and WMA files for up to 17 hours.

To record from the radio requires trudging through a counterintuitive menu to select one of the three quality (bitrate) settings, then it takes a good second to "take." The manual shows an instant-record shortcut at 32 kbps, but this works only with the microphone's voice mode or MP3 playback.

During playback you can pause the audio, but not during recording. Too, once the recorder is activated you can't adjust the radio except for volume and single-sideband fine tuning. The recording level is preset, too, so no adjustment is required or available.

The sparse owner's manual indicates that files (tracks) should be kept under one hour each, but actual testing has proven otherwise.

Overall, MP3 recording quality is excellent, and the bitrate is selectable during normal recording. During timer recording the Kaito and Degen incarnations automatically use the low-quality 32 kbps rate to allow for up to 17 hours of recording. However, the Thieking & Koch variant uses the wideband setting, 128 kbps, which drops recording time to under four and a half hours—still useful.

The player/recorder's format function is helpful when the '1121 is first being used and occasionally thereafter, like housecleaning, to "wipe the slate."

Many Roads to Rome

The Degen and Kaito versions cover 150–520 kHz longwave, 520–1710 kHz mediumwave AM, 3000–30000 kHz shortwave and 70–108 MHz FM. This encompasses the mediumwave AM "X" band, the Japanese FM band and all world band segments except little-used 2 MHz (120 meters).

In addition to the usual tuning features, there's quick access to eight world band segments and the AM/FM bands. Accessed world band segments are 5900–6400, 6900–7500, 9300–9900, 11500–12100, 13300–13900, 15100–15700, 17400–18000 and 21400–22000 kHz. Although during bandscanning these miss some potentially active frequencies, such as 5730–5895 kHz, the keypad accesses anywhere within 3000–30000 kHz.

When a new '1121 is initially turned on, it activates a timer that automatically turns off the radio after 60 minutes. Thankfully, this is readily and permanently defeated simply by pressing a key. There is another automatic power-off timer with a 60-minute default that can be tweaked by menu to as much as 120 minutes.

The numeric keypad is in telephone layout, with adequately sized keys. No illumination, but all have good feel and solid mechanical contact. Nevertheless, a processing bug sometimes keeps a command from "taking" until a key is pressed repeatedly. Indeed, on rare occasion this glitch also generates weird characters, errors on the screen, improper bootdown and unresponsive keys.

MAXIMUM MP3 RECORDING TIMES	
Quality Setting	**Time (MM:SS)**
32 kbps*	17:25
80 kbps	06:58
128 kbps	04:21

*"Voice" record setting, fixed at 32 kbps, has maximum record time of 16:56.

Times vary according to the number of tracks and other factors.

Degen DE1121 (256 MB memory). Timer recording quality varies by version.

Switching the power off, then back on banishes these gremlins.

The tuning knob has two user-selected rates for most bands, such as 1/5 kHz for world band; steps for other bands are appropriate for worldwide use. There is no play or wobble, and there's a helpful soft detent for each step. Even though muting is minimal, only minor chuffing appears during band-scanning except in the mediumwave AM band.

With 5 kHz—but not 1 kHz—steps the tuning knob jumps to the next world band segment once it reaches the end of a pre-defined segment. To get around this, use the slewing controls to tune past the segment parameter, then continue tuning normally; another trick is to enter a beyond-parameter frequency on the keypad.

Volume is controlled by modestly sized buttons complemented by a left-arrow key which mutes audio, but there are hiccups: when the radio is turned on, there's a slight "pop," after which the volume blasts away until the microprocessor recognizes the previous volume preset. That pop also appears when the radio is turned off. Too, the radio normally requires much higher volume than does the MP3 module, so remember to turn down the volume before switching over to the player.

Mixed Performance, Ergonomics

Sensitivity is commendable on all bands, so many available stations roll in. Although dynamic range is limited, this is not a problem with the telescopic antenna—or even the included short wire antenna.

Selectivity is aided by two well-chosen bandwidths, but both filters have mediocre ultimate selectivity. If a powerhouse signal is adjacent to—or even two channels away from—a much-weaker signal, the would-be DX catch tends to be swamped.

The '1121 receives single-sideband signals acceptably, in part because drift is virtually absent. However, there's no discrete LSB/USB switching, and AGC decay is fast enough to cause audible clipping and distortion.

The thumbwheel single-sideband clarifier is fairly easy to zero in, although there's no center detent. However, the single-sideband circuitry is nowhere equal to the rigorous demands of ECSS, and there's no synchronous selectable sideband.

Image rejection is as good as you could wish for. In light of that, it's surprising that front-end selectivity is substandard. Strong mediumwave AM signals, and even the occasional local FM station, can "ghost" into the shortwave spectrum to bother world band reception.

Audio is robust and generally pleasant, with decent bass and no hiss. There are no tone controls for the radio, but the player has five EQ settings. A stereo line input allows other devices to record in MP3, although a beefy level is needed to record properly.

A minor demerit except with FM and MP3 is buzzing with headphones, regardless of the type or whether AC or battery power is in use. There is also some hum on world band with the included 117V AC adaptor. An outdoor antenna resolves this but tends to generate overloading.

A selectable screen saver occupies about two thirds of the main LCD. This chews up resources while serving no useful purpose, so it's best left off.

There are 400 non-volatile station presets, with four presets per page. Presets can't be tagged, but each page can—although only by computer (ditto selecting mediumwave steps and clock format). Time is set within the radio's menu; although the manual indicates that time can be set more simply with the keypad, this did not work on our unit.

To program presets for normal tuning-around operation, choose menu>search> step. Use the up/down buttons to maneuver to the desired selection, then choose the menu book icon to enter the "step" mode.

The owner's manual is a masterpiece of Chinglish confusion. Accessing presets is convoluted enough, thanks to the '1121's dismal ergonomics, but the manual makes setting and accessing presets virtually a guessing game.

In plain English, there are two ways to access presets. Highlights:

1) From the menu screen, go to menu>search>memory, then choose a page by using the keypad (00 to 99) or up/down keys. Finally, use the two lower left-right buttons to select the desired frequency.

2) Choose menu>station>browser. This works the same as the preceding alternative, except that after you've had a peek at the frequency you need to enter it, which pretty much nullifies the convenience of a preset.

Easier, sort of, is to access presets by computer. With Windows XP, for example, it is pretty much plug-and-play, with no additional drivers needed—just drag and drop files.

The new '1121 in its various incarnations makes history by being the first world band receiver to provide useful on-board digital recording. That alone makes it worth considering in spite of its dubious ergonomics and mixed-bag performance.

The Sangean ATS-818ACS isn't cheap and uses sunset recording technology. Yet, this user-friendly classic is a proven performer.

★★½ ◎
Sangean ATS-818ACS

Price: $219.95 in the United States. CAD$212.99 in Canada. €165.00 in Germany.

Pro: Built-in cassette recorder. Price low relative to competition. Superior overall world band performance. Numerous tuning features, including 18 world band station presets. Two bandwidths for good fidelity/interference tradeoff. Analog clarifier with center detent and stable circuitry allows single-sideband signals to be tuned with uncommon precision, thus allowing for superior audio phasing for a portable (*see* Con). Illuminated display. Signal indicator. Dual-zone 24-hour clock, with one zone displayed separately from frequency. Alarm/timer with sleep delay. Travel power lock. Stereo through earpieces. Longwave. Built-in condenser mic. AC adaptor. *ATS818ACS "Deluxe," available only from C. Crane Company:* Eliminates muting between stations when bandscanning; also, RCA instead of mini jack for external antennas.

Con: Recorder has no multiple recording events, just one "on" time (quits when tape runs out). Tends to mute when tuning knob turned quickly, making bandscanning difficult (the C. Crane Company offers a $20.00/$29.95 modification to remedy this). Wide bandwidth a bit broad for world band reception without synchronous selectable sideband. Keypad not in telephone format. Touchy single-sideband clarifier. Recorder has no level indicator and no counter. Fast-forward and rewind controls installed facing backwards. No batteries (four "D" and three "AA" needed). Country of manufacture, China (formerly Taiwan), not specified on radio or box.

Verdict: A great buy, although recording is only single-event with no timed "off."

The PASSPORT portable-radio review team: David Zantow and Lawrence Magne; also, Tony Jones, with laboratory measurements performed independently by Rob Sherwood. Additional feedback from David Crystal and David Walcutt, with a tip of the hat to Lawrence Bulk.

Passport to Preparedness®

Trusted Information When Things Goes Wrong

When civilization's facade is stripped away, trusted information becomes the coin of the realm.

For this, world band delivers when others can't. It's invaluable in any crisis, but especially during warlike acts when domestic media may be unavailable or restrained.

Citizens of some countries already know this from painful experi-ence, but it applies anywhere. For example, according to solidly placed sources, should there be another event comparable to 9/11, Washington will shut down many communication channels and com-mandeer the rest. The goal would be to keep an enemy in the dark, but the civilian population would also be impacted. Imagine if the learned minds responsible for the Katrina recovery were your only source of information—whether through local broadcasts or NOAA All Hazards Radio.

World band has long been the gold standard for skirting official attempts at blocking information. That's because world band is nature's radio, soaring direct from faraway stations to listeners without wires or gate-keepers—no satellites, no cables, no local towers that can be switched off or manipulated. World band even resists deliberate jamming.

This has led to a brisk market in emergency radios, many with short-wave coverage. Most run from $40 to $100, and for cognoscenti there are even better solutions.

Must #1. Act in Advance

For example, do you already have a world band portable? Then spare batteries should allow it to serve nicely in a crisis, especially with something like the Sun Star solar battery charger from C. Crane, Universal Radio and others. The advantage: A quality battery-powered world band portable easily outperforms an ordinary emergency radio.

When a crisis comes, radios and batteries sell out quickly.

For regular portables, a large bubble pack of Energizer cells is all you need to weather even a massive event. Remember, it's the first few days—ten days, max—that count.

If you don't yet own a world band portable, consider getting one now—not after a crisis, when anything decent will have already flown off, or blown off, the shelf. Read through PASSPORT REPORTS' pages—the choice is vast.

Favor portables that handle single-sideband signals, explained in "Worldly Words." These can eavesdrop on ham radio and various aero-nautical and other utility communications; under the right conditions, even the low-powered American Forces Radio and Television Service. Also, avoid battery hogs and look for effectively illuminated LCDs, *de rigeur* for tuning in the dark—illuminated keypads help, too.

Terrorism gets the juicy headlines, but floods impact more people. Flooding can knock out local radio and television, along with phone service and electricity.

Shutterstock/Jerry Sharp

What to avoid? Cheap ordinary radios lacking digital frequency readout. Their imprecise dials make stations hard to find, they don't demodulate single-sideband signals and most are marginal performers. Windup radios have an obvious advantage in an emergency, but they perform crudely as radios and have limited long-term reliability. Best is to treat them as complimentary to a well-rated regular portable and cache of batteries.

Among windups only the Freeplay Summit, Kaito KA008 and KA011 meet PASSPORT's minimum testing requirements. However, we've bent the rules to include one series of analog-tuned portables because they outsell all others combined and have significant emergency features.

Must #2. Does It Work?

An emergency radio has to actually make useful noises during a crisis, so you need to check it out.

Pick a decent day, then step outdoors and tune to foreign stations that are weak but intelligible. Head to your safe room and compare how those same frequencies come in. If reception is similar, you're ready. If it's not, put up a simple outdoor wire inverted-L antenna—basically just a stretch of wire run

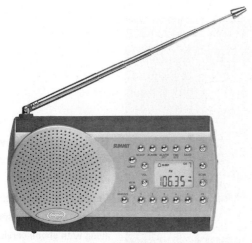

Freeplay's Summit is no barnburner, but remains as the best emergency radio.

outside. Cut it to a convenient length, then run the feedline into your room without nicking the insulation. If yard space is an issue, check out compact antennas reviewed in PASSPORT REPORTS; one model doesn't even require electricity.

Either way, keep PASSPORT nearby so you'll know what's on, when.

Must #3. What's Available

For battery powered radios look over "Portables for 2008." Dozens are tested, analyzed and rated.

For self-powered emergency portables, read on . . .

✪¼
Freeplay Summit

Price: $79.95 in the United States. CAD$89.99 in Canada. £49.95 in the United Kingdom. €119.95 in Germany.

Pro: Relatively technologically advanced for an emergency radio, including five world band presets and 25 more for other bands. Powered by rechargeable battery pack which, in turn, is juiced three ways: foolproof cranked alternator, solar energy and AC adaptor. NiMH battery pack replaceable, although nominally radio runs even if pack no longer takes a charge. Reasonably pleasant audio quality. Timed LCD illumination. Low-battery and crank-charge indicators. World Time 24-hour clock with alarm and sleep functions can also display in 12-hour format. Accessory reel antenna and AC adaptor. Travel power lock. Mediumwave AM tunes in 9/10 kHz steps. FM includes NTSC (North American) channel 6 TV audio. Longwave. More stylish than most. *Outside North America:* AC adaptor adjusts to line voltage (110–240V AC) anywhere in the world (*see* Con). Three types of power plugs for different countries; also, carrying pouch. *North America:* 120V AC adaptor works well.

Con: Slow battery recharge; full replenishment requires 24 hours with AC adaptor, 40 hours using sunlight, or 40 minutes of carpal-crunching cranking. Poor sensitivity on world band using built-in but under-sized telescopic antenna; reel-in accessory antenna, included, helps slightly. Lacks non-radio emergency features found on some other windup radios. Poor selectivity. Poor image rejection. Shortwave coverage of 5.95–15.6 MHz omits 2, 3, 4, 5, 17, 19, 21 and 25 MHz (120, 90, 75, 60, 16, 15, 13 and 11 meter) world band segments, along with lower end of 6 MHz (49 meters) and upper end of 15 MHz (19 meters). Inconvenient to tune, with no keypad, no tuning knob and "signal-seek" scanning that stops only at very powerful stations; this essentially leaves only single-speed (slow) up/down slewing and five world band presets to navigate the airwaves. No volume knob or slider; level adjustable only through up/down slew controls. Mutes for a second when-ever slew button pressed, an annoyance when bandscanning. Does not continuously display frequency—reverts back to clock after ten seconds. Tunes world band only in 5 kHz steps and displays in nonstandard XX.XX MHz/XX.XX5 MHz format. LCD hard to read in low light without illumination, which fades away after only four seconds. FM overloads in strong-signal environ-ments. One of the two units we purchased new was defective. No handle or carrying strap. *Outside North America:* Multivoltage AC adaptor disturbs reception with vigorous noise and hum; best is either to replace it with an aftermarket transformer or to keep it unplugged except to charge battery pack.

Verdict: Yes, its world band performance is mediocre. And, yes, it is bereft of most tun-ing aids and non-radio emergency features. Still, the Chinese-made Freeplay Summit is the most acceptable emergency radio we have come across. It performs reasonably on FM and mediumwave AM, too.

✪⅛
Kaito KA008

Price: $59.95 in the United States. CAD$49.95 in Canada.

Pro: Three ways to power the radio directly, as well as indirectly by charging a battery pack: 1) hand crank, 2) solar cells and 3) AC

The Kaito KA008 is nearly equal to the Freeplay Summit, but costs less.

adaptor. Can also conventionally be pow-ered by three ordinary "AA" batteries (*see* Con). Good world band sensitivity. Digital frequency readout (*see* Con). Generally wide coverage of shortwave spectrum for a radio of this type (*see* Con). Clock (*see* Con) with one-event alarm. Built in LED flashlight. LCD illuminated by LED (*see* Con). Loud, punchy audio (*see* Con). Telescopic antenna swivels and rotates. Unique LED battery status indicator. Includes 120V AC adaptor/charger, rechargeable battery pack, ear-buds, short outboard wire antenna (*see* Con) and waterproof carrying bag.

Con: Extremely sloppy tuning. Poor image and ultimate rejection. Poor FM perfor-mance. Frequency display/clock illumi-nation too dim to be of any real use, a significant drawback for an emergency radio. Quality control appears below par. Analog-tuned with digital frequency counter, so lacks such digital tuning aids as station presets and keypad. Frequency display reads out only to nearest 10 kHz in XX.XX MHz format. Audio distorts at high volume. Battery cover not hinged to prevent loss. World band coverage, in four "bands"—4000–9200, 8910–14300, 13850–19400 and 18680–26500 kHz—misses relatively unimportant 2 and 3 MHz segments. Band-switch must be adjusted when going from one world band segment range to another, complicating operation. Included wire antenna virtually worthless. FM in mono only. Clock only in 12-hour format, no option for 24-hour World Time. Three "AA" batteries not included for dry cell operation.

☞ The Kaito KA009 (around $45, not tested) is nominally similar, but adds coverage of the American weather band and VHF-TV audio.

Verdict: A marginal improvement over needle-and-dial emergency radios, the Kaito KA008 is inexpensive with flexible sources of power. Alas, performance is poor, tuning is extremely sloppy and quality control appears to be wanting. Worse, LCD illumination is virtually useless, making tuning a shot in the dark.

Overall, it suffices for rudimentary emergency situations—nothing more.

New for 2008
✪⅛
Kaito KA011

Price: $55.99 in the United States.

Pro: Three ways to power the radio directly, as well as indirectly by charging a battery pack: 1) hand crank, 2) solar cells and 3) AC adaptor. Can also be conventionally powered by three ordinary "AA" batteries (*see* Con). Good world band sensitivity. Digital frequency readout (*see* Con). Generally wide coverage of shortwave spectrum for a radio of this type (*see* Con). Clock (*see* Con) with one-event alarm. Built in LED flashlight. LCD illuminated by LED (*see* Con). Loud, punchy audio (*see* Con). Telescopic antenna swivels and rotates. Includes 120V AC adaptor/charger, rechargeable battery pack, earbuds and waterproof carrying bag.

Con: Sloppy tuning. Poor image and ultimate rejection. Poor FM performance. Frequency display/clock illumination too dim to be of any real use, a significant drawback for an emergency radio. Quality control appears below par. Analog-tuned with digital frequency counter, so lacks such digital tuning aids as station presets and keypad.

Frequency display reads out only to nearest 10 kHz in XX.XX MHz format; our sample reads slightly high. Audio distorts at high volume. Battery cover not hinged to prevent loss. World band coverage, in two "bands"— 3.04–7.98 and 8.65–20.96 MHz— misses 21 MHz segment and relatively unimportant 2 and 26 MHz segments. Bandswitch must be adjusted when going from one world band segment range to another, complicating operation. FM in mono only. Clock only in 12-hour format, no option for 24-hour World Time. Three "AA" batteries not included for dry cell operation.

Verdict: Similar to the Kaito KA008, preceding, but more costly with minor drawbacks and little in the way of pluses. Same poor performance, poor LCD illumination and dubious quality control, although the tuning knob is a skosh less sloppy.

Evaluation of New Model: The Kaito KA011, unlike most other emergency radios, sports digital frequency readout. That's nice, but it doesn't accomplish this through digitally synthesized tuning. Rather, it uses analog tuning tied into a frequency counter shared with the clock's IC. That simplified approach helps keep down costs, but also results in frequencies being shown only to the nearest 10 kHz (XX.XX MHz), while world band uses 5 kHz channels (XX,XXX kHz). Even then, our sample reads slightly high. Too, analog tuning precludes the use of station presets, keypad tuning and other modern conveniences found on radios with digitally synthesized tuning.

Flexible Power

A crank powers the radio either directly or by recharging the internal battery pack—an ideal arrangement. With a totally dead battery, two minutes of cranking provides more or less ten minutes of playing time: more if volume is low, less at the considerable but distorted full loudness. Alternatively, three ordinary (e.g., alkaline) "AA" batteries can be used, although the battery cover is not hinged to prevent loss.

There's also a solar panel on the rear that, like the crank, powers the set directly or by charging the battery pack. A splendid idea in principle, but it takes a healthy dose of sunlight to operate the set directly, and even then the audio is weaker than usual. Best is to stick to using the solar panel to charge batteries, but it's good to know that if they conk out there is a fallback—important for any emergency device.

Like the crank and solar cells, the included adaptor (120V AC in North America, presumably 220V AC in most other parts of the world) can also operate the radio directly or charge the battery pack. It works as it should, sparing you from wearisome cranking.

A 24-page owner's manual does a worthy job of explaining the radio. The included zip-style tote bag acts as a sealed waterproof pouch, too—a neat idea for an all-weather radio—but there's no room for the AC adaptor.

Kaito's KA011 is new for 2008, but hardly distinguishable from earlier models. Tuning is sloppy, while overall performance is little better except for world band sensitivity. Nevertheless, it is priced to move.

Good Coverage, Poor Performance

World band is divided into two "bands," roughly 3040–7980 and 8650–20960 kHz. This is reasonable coverage, even though it excludes the increasingly useful 21 MHz daytime segment and rarely used 2 and 26 MHz (120 and 11 meter) segments. Wouldn't, say, 9200–21900 kHz have made more sense as "band" parameters?

Mediumwave AM coverage is complete from 520 to 1770 kHz, while FM is 86.8 to 108.8 MHz. These parameters vary from sample to sample and with fluctuations in power.

World band sensitivity with the built-in telescopic antenna is quite good. However, an earmark of low-cost design is image-prone single conversion circuitry. On the '011 the result is so awful that image signals 910 kHz down in frequency are nearly as strong as the source signal; think of big aftershocks after an earthquake, and you'll get the idea. Also, the tuning knob has excessive play, which makes dialing stations a clumsy exercise.

Selectivity, although mediocre, is adequate for most world band signals. However, very

strong mediumwave AM signals completely swamp a wide frequency range. Otherwise, mediumwave AM performance is passable.

FM is another story—little sensitivity, so only the strongest stations are heard. Too, the capture ratio, like in some battlefields, is poor. Our unit also has intermittent FM reception because of a defective bandswitch or bad connection.

The cabinet's left side has a white LED flashlight—this ought to be *de rigueur* with all emergency radios, even though this one lacks a lens. However, the timed green LED that is supposed to illuminate the clock/frequency display is too dim to be of any real use. Given that in many emergencies there's no electricity, what's the point of digital frequency readout if it can't be seen in bad light?

The Kaito KA011 works adequately for simple emergencies. Nevertheless, it comes up short for regular world band listening and lacks important non-radio emergency features. Overall, the sibling KA008 is a touch preferable and costs less.

The PASSPORT emergency radio review team: David Zantow and Lawrence Magne.

McRADIOS: MILLIONS SOLD

Grundig FR-200, Etón FR-250, Tecsun Green-88

Price: *Grundig FR-200:* $39.95 in the United States. *Etón FR-200:* £24.95 in the United Kingdom. *Etón/Lextronix FR-200:* €39.95 in Germany. *Etón FR-250:* $49.95 in the United States. *AC adaptor (110–120V AC to 4.5V DC):* $9.95 in the United States. CAD$12.95 in Canada.

Standalone Dynamo

World band radios can be major sellers, but it takes understanding and focus that consumer electronics giants can rarely muster. For example, there have been millions of Grundig FR-200 and Etón FR-250 radios reportedly sold in North America in recent years. Also, a Tecsun version is offered in China and Etón now has a sales facility in Europe.

The '200/'250's sibling and related models succeed thanks to ubiquitous advertising, widespread availability and bargain pricing. They are powered not by ordinary batteries, but by a replaceable NiMH battery pack charged by crank-driven dynamo. Even if the battery pack dies the dynamo can power the radio.

Cellphone Recharge

A key non-radio emergency feature of the '250 is a cellphone recharger. It includes a short cable and adaptor plugs for popular phones.

The front panel sports a bright flashlight that could be as important as the radio during a blackout. The '200 uses a bulb, while the '250 goes one better with long-life but none-too-bright LEDs that second as a flashing red light. For hiking, traveling or bouncing around car trunks there's a rugged canvas bag with magnetic catch. The '250 also includes a siren loud enough to make neighborhood dogs bark.

Rudimentary Radio

The '200 has two shortwave "bands" of 3.2–7.6 MHz and 9.2–22 MHz. These include nearly all world band segments, which in an emergency could be the only source for credible news.

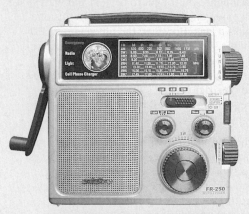

Etón/Grundig offers a variety of emergency portables. The FR-250 is priced smack in the middle.

Alas, the frequency readout crams hundreds of world band stations into a wee couple of inches—around five centimeters—of analog dial space, and the tuning knob has play. So global signals can be hunted down only by ear, and even then it's hard to tell whether you're hearing the station's real signal or its image 900 kHz or so down. However, there's a fine tuning control to make the process smoother.

Enter the FR-250. It has seven separate world band segments nicely spread out and augmented by a fine-tuning knob. Coverage omits the 3, 4, 5, 19 and 21 MHz (90, 75, 60, 15 and 13 meter) segments included on the '200, but it's a good tradeoff. As on the '200, the tuning knob has play.

Audio quality is pleasant with both models, but sensitivity to weak world band signals is marginal—ditto selectivity and image rejection. As to single-sideband signals, forget it.

FM, in mono only, includes NTSC (North American) channel 6 TV audio. FM overloads in strong-signal environments, but otherwise both it and mediumwave AM perform reasonably well.

The FR-200 and FR-250 don't send radio hearts aflutter. But they are eminently affordable, suffice for emergencies, are widely available and provide a number of non-radio emergency aids. Both come with a one-year warranty and superior product support.

Etón FR-350, American Red Cross ARC-350

Price: *FR-350 and ARC-350:* $59.95 in the United States. €69.00 in Germany.

The new Etón FR-350—no relation to the Etón S350—is the water resistant version of the FR-250. However, it's in a different package and has an additional daytime world band segment: 21 MHz.

Purchases Aid Red Cross . . . for Now

Perhaps more interestingly, like the rest of Etón's "FR" line it is also offered as part of the new ARC series. Except for appearance, these are identical except that a portion of their sales is donated to the American Red Cross.

This could change. In August 2007 Johnson & Johnson filed suit against the American Red Cross for allowing their shared red cross symbol to be licensed for commercial products— an activity that each year brings the charity nearly $10 million. Although the suit asks that all such licensed goods be destroyed, for now, at any rate, this activity is continuing.

The '350 tunes the important world band segments, skipping only 2, 3, 4 and 5 MHz used mainly by weak domestic stations in Latin America, Africa and Asia. The cabinet is slimmer than other FR models and includes a canvas carrying case and handy shoulder strap.

Rubber side panels and covered rear jacks help keep out water. To check this out we gave our '350 a vigorous dousing, and its innards emerged drier than a James Bond martini. This is an obvious plus not only for marine settings, but also for hurricanes, floods, tornadoes and tsunamis.

The power scheme is like what's on the larger, lower-cost '250. It comes with a replaceable NiMH battery pack that is charged internally by, among other things, a hand-cranked dynamo; an important backup is that the dynamo can also power the radio directly if the batteries are worn or missing. Three standard "AA" batteries (not included) can be used instead—say, if the dynamo fails—although it takes some doing to open the battery cavity.

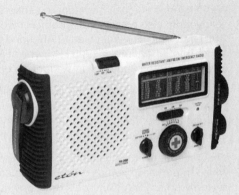

An AC adaptor/battery charger is included, a convenience over the '250 and '200. Although this accessory reduces tiresome cranking and resulting dynamo wear, as an adaptor it creates annoying hum at low volume.

Etón's ARC-350 includes a powerful siren, while its sales benefit the American Red Cross.

Useful Gizmos

Like on the '250, the '350's dynamo can recharge cellphones. Anyone who has heard 9/11 recordings where conversations were cut short by dying cellphone batteries will appreciate this. A short cable and adapter plugs are included for most phones.

The '350, like the '250, includes a flashlight with two white LEDs for modest illumination, along with a switchable flashing red LED for visual warning. LEDs generally have a much longer life than conventional filament bulbs, so the flashlight might outlast the radio. Flashlights use more juice than little radios, so having dynamo power means reliable lighting no matter how long an outage lasts. Claustrophobics trapped in dark places may appreciate this more than the radio itself.

There's also a LOUD siren, and it's no toy. As hurricane Katrina showed, when people are stranded in attics or trapped under rubble, an ear-blaster like this can make the difference between being overlooked and being rescued. Turn the crank occasionally and the siren wails nonstop.

No Digital Readout

The '350's frequency readout is analog, not digital, so finding a station is no stroll in the park: On our sample the dial is off by around 50 kHz, or fully ten world band channels. It spreads world band frequencies onto eight slide rule-type "bands," which allow for much easier fine tuning as opposed to the '200's "two 'bands' for everything."

On the '250 a concentric fine-tuning knob means you don't need safecracker's fingers. There is no such knob on the '350, although it is also is less needed because of the eight widely spread "bands." But the '350's string-and-pulley tuning has play, and on our unit the knob also rubs against the cabinet.

Same Performance, Different Features

The '350's world band performance and build quality are rudimentary and comparable to that of the '250 and '200: Single-conversion circuitry results in dismal image rejection. Too, sensitivity is marginal, selectivity isn't much better, and there's no single-sideband reception to receive hams, utilities or American Forces Radio. Audio, on the other hand, is surprisingly powerful and pleasant.

World band is uniquely resistant to censorship at the border. Yet, any worthwhile emergency radio also needs to do yeoman's work with local and regional stations. Here, the '350 fares well. Its mediumwave AM band tunes to the Western Hemisphere/Pacific's upper frequency limit of 1705 kHz, while FM covers 87.5 to 108 MHz and outputs to mono earpieces. Both bands pull in stations nicely in urban and rural environments alike.

The Etón FR-350 and ARC-350 are not radio's equivalent of a Lamborghini or even close. But they do what's important: provide you and your loved ones with valuable tools to pull through a crisis. They're affordable, widely distributed and have meaningful non-radio emergency features. Both include a one-year warranty and superior product support.

With reception virtually identical across Etón's and Grundig's FR and ARC product lines, which to purchase comes down to price and what features you want. Be careful, though, as some other FR/ARC models don't cover world band.

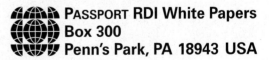

Tabletop Receivers for 2008

Tabletop receivers excel at flushing out faint stations swamped by other signals. That's why they are prized by radio aficionados known as DXers—telegraph shorthand for "long distance listeners."

But tabletop models aren't for everybody, and it shows. Even in prosperous North America and Europe, tabletop unit sales have been under competitive pressure from such portable street rods as the Etón E1.

Most tabletop models cost much more than portables; yet, they're far less expensive than professional supersets. For the price of a tabletop you tend to get not only excellent performance, but also worthy construction and ruggedness.

They are also relatively easy to service and tend to be supported by knowledgeable repair facilities.

What you rarely find in a tabletop is reception of the everyday 87.5–108 MHz FM band. For this, look to a portable.

When Going Gets Tough . . .

Not only DXers prefer tabletop sets. Like professional models and the very best portables, tabletops are ideally suited for where signals suffer from interference or tend to be weak—western and midwestern North America, for example, or Australia and New Zealand.

Even elsewhere, signals weaken when they pass over or near the magnetic North Pole, which periodically erupts into geomagnetic fury. To check, place a string on a globe—a conventional map won't do—between your location and the station's transmitter as shown in the Blue Pages. If the string passes near or above latitude 60 degrees north, beware.

> Tabletop receivers excel with weak, tough signals, including daytime broadcasts.

Superior Antennas Needed

One reason most tabletops do well is they accept outboard antennas without the side effects these can cause with everyday portables.

It's hard to overstate the benefit of a worthy accessory antenna properly placed outdoors or even on a balcony or window. Just as a sailboat needs a proper sail to catch the wind, a receiver benefits from an antenna that can grab more signals. Test results and ratings of antennas—small and large, indoor and out—are included in PASSPORT REPORTS.

Daytime Interesting but Weak

Daytime listening, notably during the afternoon, has grown in popularity, thanks to a wealth of interesting programs found outside prime time. These signals are usually beamed elsewhere, but the scattering properties of shortwave allow them to be audible far beyond their intended targets, albeit at reduced strength. So superior hardware helps: better receivers, worthy antennas.

But not always. Let's say you have a portable with a modest outdoor antenna, but reception is being disrupted by electrical noise—nearby dimmers, digital devices and whatnot. Reception may not improve with a tabletop model, as its superior circuitry boosts noises just as much as signals.

However, even here there may be an out. An active loop antenna (*see* Compact Antennas for 2008) may improve the signal-to-noise ratio because it can be aimed away from noise sources. So, you may profit from a good tabletop model even when there's local electrical noise—provided you have the right antenna, properly aimed.

Solutions for Apartments

If your antenna is inside a high-rise building, performance can disappoint—reinforced concrete soaks up signals. Too, in urban areas there can be intrusion from nearby broadcast, cellular and other transmitters.

Here, a good bet for tough stations is a superior receiver and antenna. Experiment with something like a homebrew insulated-wire antenna along, or just outside, a window or balcony. Or try an everyday telescopic car antenna angled out, like a wall flagpole, from a window or balcony ledge.

Or amplify your homebrew antenna with a good active preselector. Even simpler are factory-ready amplified (active) antennas with remote receiving elements, also rated in PASSPORT REPORTS.

If you don't live in an apartment, consider a passive (unamplified) outdoor wire antenna. Performance findings and installation tips are in the Radio Database International White Paper, *Popular Outdoor Antennas*, and are also summarized in "Wire Antennas for 2008."

Digital Ready?

Some "DRM Ready" tabletop models can receive experimental digital world band transmissions listed at www.drm.org/live-broadcast/livebroadcast.php.

However, DRM Ready isn't Plug and Play. Today's tabletops can reproduce DRM transmissions only when connected to a PC with separately purchased DRM software. For this combo to work properly, it's best to use an outboard antenna located for minimum pickup of noise from your computer hardware. Shielded cables help, too.

With a powerful DRM signal having a high bit rate and no interference, the result is virtually local-quality audio—to this extent, DRM lives up to its promise. However, shortcomings loom large: inferior long-distance (multi-hop) performance, including sporadic cutting out; susceptibility to disruption by noise and interference, including jamming; and wideband interference to analog stations on nearby frequencies.

After a number of years DRM has yet to catch on. Yet, it is a work in progress with powerful backers, especially in China, so results may improve over time. So, all other things being equal, it makes sense to favor a receiver with at least the potential to reproduce DRM.

Shortwave's Hidden Goodies

Although virtually all shortwave listeners enjoy shows over world band, some also seek out utility and ham signals nestled between world band segments. These have reception challenges and rewards of their own and, unlike world band, don't need receivers with quality audio. This allows some receivers with uninspiring audio to stand out: Icom's IC-R75, for example, and Japan Radio's NRD-545.

Other highly rated tabletop models perform solidly with world band and utility signals, alike.

Modern and Modular

Icom's IC-R1500 is actually the Icom IC-PCR1500 black box receiver mated to a control module so it can be operated without a PC. This is not a concept endearing to traditionalists, but it's creative and carves out a niche. Another niche: It's flexible enough for mobile use.

Complete Findings

Our unabridged laboratory and hands-on test results for each receiver are too exhaustive to reproduce here. However, they are available for selected current and classic models as PASSPORT's Radio Database International White Papers.

Tips for Using this Section

Receivers are listed in order of suitability for listening to difficult-to-hear world band stations; important secondary consideration is given to audio fidelity, ergonomics, perceived build quality and utility/ham reception. Street selling prices are cited, including

British VAT where applicable. Prices vary, so take them as the general guide they are meant to be. Haggling is rarely successful.

Accessories listed are known to be readily available. Those not normally found in your country sometimes can be special-ordered at the time of receiver purchase.

Unless otherwise stated, all tabletop models have the following characteristics. See "Worldly Words" for specialized terms.

- Digital frequency synthesis and display.
- Full coverage of at least the 155–29999 kHz longwave, mediumwave AM and shortwave spectra—including all world band frequencies—but no coverage of FM broadcasts (usually 87.5–108 MHz). Models designed for sale in certain countries have reduced shortwave tuning ranges; also, broadband models sold in the United States omit coverage of non-shortwave cellular frequencies.
- A wide variety of helpful tuning features.
- Synchronous selectable sideband via high-rejection IF filtering (not lower-rejection phase cancellation), advanced technology which helps reduce adjacent-channel interference and selective-fading distortion.

☞ ECSS: Many tabletop models can tune to the nearest 10 Hz or even 1 Hz, so its single-sideband circuitry can be used to manually phase the BFO (internally generated carrier) with the station's transmitted carrier. Called "ECSS" (exalted-carrier, selectable-sideband) tuning, this can be used in lieu of synchronous selectable sideband. However, it's inconvenient and—unlike synchronous selectable sideband which re-phases continually and perfectly—ECSS is always slightly out of phase. This can add a degree of harmonic distortion to music and speech; even tuning to the nearest Hertz may generate slow-sweep fading (for this reason, misphasing by two or three Hertz may provide better results). But beware: A few manufacturers incorrectly refer to synchronous selectable sideband as "ECSS."

- Proper demodulation of modes used by utility and ham signals, although in a few non-Western countries this is outlawed.

These modes include single sideband (LSB/USB) and CW ("Morse code"); also, with suitable ancillary devices, radioteletype (RTTY), frequency shift key (FSK) and radiofax (FAX).
- Meaningful signal-strength indication—either an analog meter or a digital indicator.
- Illuminated display.

What PASSPORT's Rating Symbols Mean

Star ratings: ✪✪✪✪✪ is best. Stars reflect overall performance and meaningful features, plus to some extent ergonomics and perceived build quality. Price, appearance, country of manufacture and the like are not taken into account. With tabletop models there is a slightly greater emphasis than on portables on the ability to flush out tough, hard-to-hear signals. Nevertheless, to facilitate comparison the tabletop rating standards are very similar to those used for professional and portable models reviewed elsewhere in this PASSPORT REPORTS.

Passport's Choice. La crème de la crème. Our test team's personal picks of the litter—models we would buy or have bought for our personal use. Unlike star ratings, these choices are unapologetically subjective.

☕: A relative bargain, with decidedly more performance than the price suggests. However, no tabletop receiver is cheap.

✪✪✪✪✪ 📖 *Passport's Choice*
AOR AR7030 PLUS, AOR AR7030

Price ('7030 receivers): *AR7030 PLUS:* $1,499.95 in the United States. £949.00 in the United Kingdom. €1,198.00 in Germany. *AR7030:* £799.00 in the United Kingdom. €1,039.00 in Germany.

Price (options—all '7030 models): *Optional MuRata ceramic bandwidth filters:* $59.95–79.95 each plus installation in the United States. £29.99–39.99 each including installation in the United Kingdom. €47.00–49.00 each plus installation in Germany.

The AOR AR7030 series gets the nod as the best tabletop performer. Excellent audio, too, although ergonomics are reminiscent of BMW's iDrive.

Optional Collins mechanical bandwidth filters: $99.95 each plus installation in the United States. £74.00 each including installation in the United Kingdom. €85.00–95.00 each plus installation in Germany. *FL124 daughter board for up to three crystal filters:* US$59.95 plus $25.00 installation in the United States. £24.99 including installation in the United Kingdom. €50.00 plus installation in Germany. *XTL2.4 crystal filter, 2.4 kHz bandwidth:* £79.00 including installation in the United Kingdom; special-order part from AOR Japan, so requires waiting period. *Aftermarket (Icom, Kenwood, JRC, Inrad, Kiwa et al.) 455 kHz crystal bandwidth filters:* equivalent of $150–300 each plus installation worldwide, depending on filter and vendor. *SM7030 service kit:* $89.95 in the United States. £39.95 in the United Kingdom. *BP123 inboard rechargeable battery with inboard recharger (nominally results in minor performance drop-off):* £99.99 in the United Kingdom. €99.95 in Germany.

Price (options—AR7030 PLUS):
UPNB7030 notch filter: $339.95 plus $25.00 installation in the United States. £163.00 including installation in the United Kingdom. €280.70 plus installation in Germany.

Price (options—AR7030): *NB7030 noise blanker & notch filter:* £198.00 including installation in the United Kingdom. €298.00 plus installation in Germany.

Pro: In terms of overall performance for program listening, as good a receiver as we've ever tested. With one exception (*see* Con), exceptionally quiet circuitry enhances DXing and weak-signal listening, alike. Superb world band and mediumwave AM audio quality when used with a first-rate outboard speaker or audio system. Synchronous selectable sideband performs exceptionally well at reducing distortion caused by selective fading, as well as at diminishing or eliminating adjacent-channel interference; also has synchronous double sideband. Superb dynamic range and third-order intercept point at both wide and narrow signal spacing. Superb image rejection. Superb first IF rejection. Superb AGC threshold with preamp on. Four voice bandwidths (AR7030 2.3, 7.0, 8.2 and 10.3 kHz), using cascaded ceramic filters; optional filters can raise total to six bandwidths—ceramic, mechanical or crystal (crystal filters require optional daughter board) (*see* Con). Bandwidths using ceramic filters have excellent shape factors and superb ultimate rejection. Sensitivity to weak signals excellent with preamp on (*see* Con: *AR7030*). Advanced tuning and operating features aplenty, including passband tuning. Optional tunable audio (AF) notch filter and noise blanker; notch extremely effective, with little loss of audio fidelity. Automatically self-aligns and centers bandwidth filters—whether ceramic, mechanical or crystal—for optimum performance, then displays measured bandwidth of each. Remote keypad (*see* Con). Accepts two antennas. IF output. World Time 24-hour clock displays seconds, calendar and timer/sleep-delay. Outstanding performance with local, distant and multipath twilight-fringe mediumwave AM signals. Superior service at U.K. factory and U.S. distributor (Universal Radio). Website (www.aoruk.com/7030bulletin.htm) provides technical updates and information. Owner's manuals available online (www.aoruk.com/manuals.htm). *AR7030 PLUS:* 400 scannable presets, instead of 100, with 14-character alphanumeric readout for station names (*see* Con). Bandwidth choices (2.3, 4.6, 6.6 and 9.8 kHz) preferable to those of AR7030. Optical tuning encoder inherently more reliable than mechanical encoder on AR7030 (*see* Con).

Con: Unusually convoluted ergonomics, including tree-logic operating scheme, especially in the PLUS version; once the initial glow of ownership has passed, some find this to be tiresome. No keypad on receiver; instead, it's part of an infrared wireless remote control which has to be aimed carefully at receiver's front or back. Although the remote can operate from across a room, LCD characters too small to be seen from such a distance. LCD omits certain useful information, such as signal strength, when radio in various status modes. Front end selectivity only fair. When four standard ceramic bandwidth filters are used with two optional mechanical filters, ultimate rejection, although superb with widest three bandwidths, cannot be measured beyond –80/–85 dB on narrowest three bandwidths because of phase noise; still, ultimate rejection is excellent or better with these configurations. Optional Collins filters measure as having poorer shape factors (1:1.8 to 1:2) than standard MuRata ceramic filters (1:1.5 to 1:1.7). LCD emits some digital electrical noise, a potential issue only if an amplified (active) antenna is used with its pickup element (e.g. telescopic rod) placed near receiver. 2.3 kHz bandwidth has some circuit noise (hiss) in single sideband or ECSS modes. Uses outboard AC adaptor instead of built-in power supply. *AR7030:* Unusual built-in preamplifier/attenuator design links both functions, so receiver noise rises slightly when preamplifier used in +10 dB position, or attenuator used at –10 dB setting. Lacks, and would profit from, a bandwidth of around 4 or 5 kHz; optional Collins mechanical bandwidth filter of 3.5 kHz (nominal at –3 dB, measures 4.17 kHz at –6 dB) thus worth considering. Only 100 presets and no alphanumeric readout. Mechanical tuning encoder occasionally skips frequency increments, notably if it has not been used for awhile. AGC decay somewhat slow in AM/sync modes. Not available from North American distributor. *AR7030 PLUS:* Tuning knob feel only fair.

Verdict: Engineered by John Thorpe and manufactured in England, the AR7030 is a smashing performer, with audio quality that can be a pleasure hour after hour. And it's even better and more robust in its PLUS incarnation.

But there is a catch. Like BMW's annoying iDrive, many functions are shoehorned into a tree-logic control scheme. The resulting ergonomics are uniquely hostile—especially in the PLUS version—even if operation ultimately is not that difficult to master. *Best bet:* Before buying, either lay hands on a '7030 or study the free online owner's manuals (www.aoruk.com/pdf/7030m.pdf and www.aoruk.com/pdf/fpu.pdf).

Ergonomics aside, for serious DXing the '7030 is today's top performer on the scotch side of a professional receiver, but there's more. With a suitable outboard speaker it is also one of the best sounding receivers at any price for hearing world band and mediumwave AM shows under a wide range of reception conditions.

⬚ An *RDI WHITE PAPER* is available for this model.

✪✪✪✪½
Japan Radio NRD-545

Price: $1,799.95 in the United States. CAD$1,999.00 in Canada. £1,399.95 in the United Kingdom. €1,598.00 in Germany. *NVA-319 external speaker:* $199.95 in the United States. €259.00 in Germany. *CGD-197 frequency stabilizer:* $99.95 in the United States. £89.95 in the United Kingdom. €149.00 in Germany.

Pro: Superior build quality, right down to the steel cabinet with machined screws. Easily upgraded by changing software ROMs if they ever became available. Fully 998 bandwidths provide unprecedented flexibility. Razor-sharp skirt selectivity, especially with voice bandwidths. Outstanding array of tuning aids, including 1,000 station presets (*see* Con). Wide array of reception aids, including passband offset, excellent manual/automatic tunable notch, and synchronous selectable sideband having good lock. Superb reception of single-sideband and other utility signals. Demodulates C-Quam AM stereo signals, which then need to be fed through an external audio amplifier, not provided (the headphone jack can't be used for this, as it is monaural). Highly adjustable AGC in all modes requiring BFO (*see* Con). Tunes in ultra-precise 1 Hz increments, although displays only in 10 Hz increments. Ergonomics, including the physical quality of the tuning knob and other controls, among the very best. Some useful audio shaping. Computer interface. Virtually no spurious radiation of digital "buzz." Hiss-free audio-out port for recording or feeding low-power FM transmitter to hear world band around the house. Internal AC power supply is quiet and generates little heat. Power cord detaches handily from receiver, like on a PC, making it easy to replace. Includes a "CARE package" of all needed metric plugs and connectors, along with a 12V DC power cord.

Con: Ultimate rejection only fair, although average ultimate rejection equivalent is 10–15 dB better; this unusual gap comes about from intermodulation (IMD) inside the digital signal processor, and results in audible "monkey chatter" under certain specific and uncommon reception conditions. Audio quality sometimes tough sledding in

NUMBERS: TOP TABLETOP RECEIVERS

	AOR AR7030 PLUS	Japan Radio NRD-545
Max. Sensitivity/Noise Floor	0.2 μV **E**/–131 dBm **E**[(1)]	0.2 μV **E**/–130 dBm **E**[(4)]
Blocking	>125 dB **E**	>127 dB **E**
Shape Factors, voice BWs	1:1.5–1:1.7 **E**	1:1.1 **S**
Ultimate Rejection	90 dB **S**	65 dB **G**
Front-End Selectivity	**F**	**E**
Image Rejection	102 dB **S**	>75 dB **E**
First IF Rejection	99 dB **S**	>90 dB **S**
Dynamic Range/IP3 (5 kHz)	82 dB **E**/–3 dBm **S**	66 dB **F**/–31 dBm **F**[(5)]
Dynamic Range/IP3 (20 kHz)	91 dB **E**/+11 dBm **S**	NA[(6,7)]
Phase Noise	129 dBc **E**	118 dBc **G**
AGC Threshold	0.7 μV **S**[(2)]	2 μV **G**
Overall Distortion, sync	0.5–3% **S**-**G**[(3)]	0.1–7% **S**-**P**[(3)]
Stability	2 Hz **S**	20 Hz **G**
Notch filter depth	55 dB **S**	37 dB **G**[(8)]

IBS Lab Ratings: **S** Superb   **E** Excellent   **G** Good   **F** Fair   **P** Poor

(1) Preamplifier on. With preamp off: 0.35 μV **E**/–126 dBm **G**.
(2) Preamplifier on. With preamp off: 2 μV **G**.
(3) Usually <1% **S**.
(4) NRD-545SE: 0.16 **S**/–133 dBm **E**.
(5) NRD-545SE: 73 dB **G**/–23 dBm **G**.
(6) Not measurable at 20 kHz separation. At 10 kHz: 80 dB **F G**/–10 dBm **F G**.
(7) NRD-545SE: 89 dB **G**/+1 dBm **E**.
(8) DSP notch tunes only 100–2,500 Hz.

the unvarnished AM mode—using synchronous selectable sideband helps greatly. No AGC adjustment in AM mode or with synchronous selectable sideband, and lone AGC decay rate too fast. Dynamic range only fair. Synchronous selectable sideband sometimes slow to kick in. Notch filter won't attenuate heterodynes (whistles) any higher in pitch than 2,500 Hz AF. Noise reduction circuit only marginally useful. Signal indicator overreads at higher levels. Frequency display misreads by up to 30 Hz, especially at higher tuned frequencies, and gets worse as the months pass. Station presets don't store synchronous-AM settings. Audio amplifier lacks oomph with some poorly modulated signals. No IF output, nor can one be retrofitted. World Time 24-hour clock doesn't show when frequency displayed. No tilt bail or feet. Anti-reflective paint on buttons and knobs becomes shiny with wear.

Verdict: In many ways Japan Radio's NRD-545 is a remarkable performer, especially for utility and world band DXing below 5.1 MHz. With its first-class ergonomics and the fine feel of superior construction, it is a pleasure to operate. In 2007 the Canadian price was significantly lowered, as well.

Yet, more is needed to make this the ultimate receiver it could be. By now Japan Radio should have issued a ROM upgrade to remedy at least some of these long-standing issues, but nothing appears to be in the offing.

Whether "monkey chatter" and other manifestations of DSP overload are an issue varies markedly from one listening situation to another—some hear it, others never do or feel it is insignificant. It depends on the specifics of the signal being received, what part of the world you are in and your own aural perceptions. Reader feedback suggests that most don't find it to be a significant drawback.

Digital signal processing (DSP) receivers don't have to be professional-grade or PC-controlled. Japan Radio's NRD-545 uses DSP technology to good effect in a conventional configuration.

★★★★½
Japan Radio "NRD-545SE"

Price: *NRD-545SE:* $1,899.00 in the United States. *Retrofit to change an existing receiver*

to "SE": $104.00 plus receiver shipping both ways.

Pro: Dynamic range, 5 kHz signal spacing, improves from 66 dB to 73 dB. Occasional enhancement of tough-signal reception.

Con: Not available outside North America. *With 8 kHz replacement filter:* Audio bandwidth reduced by 20 percent at the high end. *With 6 kHz replacement filter (not tested):* Audio bandwidth reduced by about 40 percent at the high end.

☞ For all except those who largely confine their listening to tough DX or utility catches, the 8 kHz filter is a preferable choice over the 6 kHz option.

Verdict: Sherwood Engineering, an American firm, replaces the stock DSP protection filter with one of two narrower filters of comparable quality. In principle, this should provide beaucoup decibels of audible improvement in the "monkey chatter" sometimes encountered on the '545 from adjacent-channel signals. Perhaps, but we couldn't hear the difference. What was noticed, instead, was an unwelcome reduction in audio crispness with world band signals—as well as, of course, with mediumwave AM reception.

The '545 is best suited to non-broadcast-listening applications, anyway, so for some DXers the Sherwood modification provides a slight but positive tradeoff. For these, the aural drawback of the Sherwood modification can be less important than its 7 dB improvement in dynamic range and occasional enhancement of tough-signal reception.

But if your main interest is in listening to world band programs, this modification is not the way to go.

New Version for 2008
★★★★⅜ ✪
Icom IC-R75

Price: *Receiver with UT-106 DSP accessory:* $599.95 in the United States. CAD$799.00 in Canada. *Icom Replacement Bandwidth Filters (e.g., FL-257 3.3 kHz):* $159.95 in the United States. CAD$340.00 in Canada. *SP-23 amplified audio-shaping speaker:* $169.95 in the United States. CAD$300.00 in Canada. *Pyramid PS-3KX aftermarket 120V AC 13.8V DC regulated power supply:* $22.95 in the United States.

Pro: Dual passband offset acts as variable bandwidth and a form of IF shift (*see* Con). Reception of faint signals alongside powerful competing ones aided by excellent ultimate selectivity and good blocking. Excellent front-end selectivity, with seven filters for the shortwave range and more for elsewhere. Two levels of preamplification, 10/20 dB, can be switched off. Excellent weak-signal sensitivity and good AGC threshold with 20 dB preamplification. Superior rejection of spurious signals, including images. Excellent stability, essential for unattended reception of RTTY and certain other types of utility transmis-

sions. Excels in reception of utility and ham signals, as well as world band signals tuned via ECSS. Ten tuning steps. Can tune and display in exacting 1Hz increments (*see* Con). Adjustable UT-106 DSP circuit with automatic variable notch filter helps to a degree in improving intelligibility, but not pleasantness, of some tough signals; also, it reduces heterodyne ("whistle") interference. Fairly good ergonomics, including smooth-turning weighted tuning knob; nice touch is spinning finger dimple, even if it doesn't spin very well. "Control Central" LCD easy to read and evenly illuminated by 24 LEDs with dimmer. Adjustable AGC—fast, slow, off. Tuning knob uses reliable optical encoder normally found only on professional receivers, rather than everyday mechanical variety. Low overall distortion. Pleasant and hiss-free audio with suitable outboard speaker; audio-shaping amplified Icom SP-23, although pricey, works well for a number of applications. 101 station presets. Two antenna inputs, switchable. Digital bar graph signal indicator, although not as desirable as an analog meter, is unusually linear above S-9 and can be set to hold a peak reading briefly. Audio-out port for recording or feeding low-power FM transmitter to hear world band around the house. World Time 24-hour clock, timer and sleep delay (*see* Con). Tunes to 60 MHz, including 6 meter VHF ham band. Tilt bail (*see* Con).

Con: Dual passband offset usually has little impact on received world band signals. DSP's automatic variable notch tends not to work with AM-mode signals not received via "ECSS" technique (tuning AM-mode signals as though they were single sideband). Mediocre audio through internal speaker, and no tone control to offset slightly bassy reproduction that originates prior to the audio stage; audio improves to pleasant with an appropriate external speaker, especially one that offsets the receiver's slight bassiness. Suboptimal audio recovery with weak AM-mode signals having heavy fading; largely remediable by ECSS and switching off AGC. Display misreads up to 20 Hz, somewhat negating the precise 1 Hz tuning. Keypad requires frequencies to be entered in MHz format with decimal or trailing zeroes, a

The most popular tabletop model is Icom's IC-R75, slightly altered for 2008.

pointless inconvenience. Some knobs small. Uses outboard AD-55 "floor brick" 120V AC adaptor in lieu of internal power supply; adaptor's emission field may be picked up by nearby indoor antennas or unshielded antenna lead-in wiring, which can cause minor hum on received signals (remediable by moving antenna or using shielded lead-in). AC adaptor puts out over 17.5V but the 'R75 is designed to run off 13.8V, so receiver runs hot and thus its voltage regulator's reliability suffers; dropping input voltage to 13–14V, such as with the Pyramid PS-3KX aftermarket regulated power supply, eliminates this shortcoming. Can read clock or presets' IDs or frequency, but no more than one at the same time. RF/AGC control operates peculiarly. Tilt bail lacks rubber protection for furniture surface. Keyboard beep heard at audio line output. No schematic provided. Sold only in North America; lacks CE approval, so not available within EU even from American dealers.

Verdict: The Japanese-made Icom IC-R75 is a tempting value—provided you live in the United States or Canada, the only countries where it is now available. The 'R75 is first-rate for unearthing tough utility and ham signals, as well as world band signals received via ECSS. For these applications nothing else equals it on the sunny side of a kilobuck.

It is less of an unqualified success for world band broadcasts. Its hopeless synchronous detector was removed in 2007—the old version's cartons are marked IC-R75-02, new ones IC-R75-12. Yes, Sherwood's SE-3 Mk IV accessory brings the 'R75's fidelity to life by adding top-notch synchronous selectable sideband and audio, but at $599 it costs as much as the receiver and complicates operation.

★★★★
Icom IC-R8500A

Price: *ICF-8500A:* $1,699.95 (government use/export only) in the United States. CAD$2,399.00 in Canada. £1,199.95 in the United Kingdom. €1,498.00 in Germany. *CR-293 frequency stabilizer:* $279.95 in the United States. CAD$540.00 in Canada.

American law prohibits receivers like the Icom IC-R8500, even though the rationale—overhearing analog cellphones—really no longer applies. Outside the United States the '8500 offers superior broadband reception.

£89.98 in the United Kingdom. €109.00 in Germany. *Aftermarket Sherwood SE-3 Mk IV:* $599.00 in the United States. *Aftermarket BHT DSP noise canceller (www.radio.bhinstrumentation.co.uk/index.html):* £69.96 in the United Kingdom.

Pro: Wide-spectrum multimode coverage from 0.1–2000 MHz includes longwave, mediumwave AM, shortwave and scanner frequencies. Physically very rugged, with professional-grade cast-aluminum chassis and impressive computer-type innards. Generally superior ergonomics, with generous front panel having large and well-spaced controls, plus outstanding tuning knob with numerous tuning steps. A thousand station presets and 100 auto-write presets have handy naming function. Superb weak-signal sensitivity. Pleasant, low-distortion audio aided by audio peak filter. Passband tuning ("IF shift"). Unusually readable LCD. Tunes and displays in precise 10 Hz increments. Three antenna connections. Clock-timer, combined with record output and recorder-activation jack, make for superior hands-off recording of favorite programs, as well as for feeding a low-power FM transmitter to hear world band around the house.

Con: No longer legally available to the public in the United States, as it receives cellular frequencies—even though digital cellphone traffic is virtually impossible to decipher with a receiver like this. No synchronous selectable sideband. Bandwidth choices for world band and other AM-mode signals leap from a very narrow 2.7 kHz to a broad 7.1 kHz with nothing between, where something is needed; third bandwidth is 13.7 kHz, too wide for world band, and there's no provision for a fourth bandwidth filter. Only one single-sideband bandwidth. Unhandy carousel-style bandwidth selection with no permanent indication of which bandwidth is in use. Poor dynamic range, surprising at this price point. Passband tuning ("IF shift") does not work in AM mode, which is used by world band and medium-wave AM-band stations. No tunable notch filter. Built-in speaker mediocre. Uses outboard AC adaptor instead of inboard power supply.

☞ Also tested with Sherwood SE-3 aftermarket accessory, which proved to be outstanding at adding selectable synchronous sideband. This combo also provides passband tuning in the AM mode which is used by nearly all world band stations. Adding the SE-3 and replacing the widest bandwidth with a 4 to 5 kHz bandwidth filter dramatically improve performance on shortwave, mediumwave AM and longwave.

Verdict: The large Icom IC-R8500 is a scanner that happens to cover world band, rather than *vice versa*. It is no longer available new in the United States.

As a standalone world band radio, this Japanese-made wideband receiver makes little sense. Yet, it is well worth considering if you want an all-in-one scanner that also serves as a shortwave receiver.

AOR's AR5000A +3 provides broadband coverage. Unlike Icom's IC-R8500, a version of the AOR is legal in the United States—although it is steeply priced.

✪✪✪✪
AOR AR5000A+3

Price: *AR5000A+3 (cellular-blocked version) receiver:* $2,499.95 in the United States. *AR5000A+3 (full-coverage version) receiver:* $2,599.95 (government use/export only) in the United States. CAD$3,299.00 in Canada. £1,799.00 in the United Kingdom. €1,979.00 in Germany. *Collins MF60 6 kHz mechanical filter (recommended):* $99.95 in the United States. £74.00 in the United Kingdom. €95.00 in Germany. *SDU-5600 spectrum display unit:* $1,449.95 in the United States. CAD$1,899.00 in Canada. £975.00 in the United Kingdom. €1,299.00 in Germany.

Pro: Ultra-wide-spectrum multimode coverage from 0.01–3,000 MHz includes longwave, mediumwave AM, shortwave and scanner frequencies. Helpful tuning features include 2,000 station presets in 20 banks of 100 presets each. Narrow bandwidth filter and optional Collins wide filter both have superb skirt selectivity (standard wide filter's skirt selectivity unmeasurable because of limited ultimate rejection). Synchronous selectable and double sideband (*see* Con). Front-end selectivity, image rejection, IF rejection, weak-signal sensitivity, AGC threshold and frequency stability are all superior. Exceptionally precise frequency readout to nearest Hertz. Most accurate displayed frequency measurement of any receiver tested to date. Superb circuit shielding results in virtually zero radiated digital "buzz." IF output (*see* Con). DRM modifiable; see www.aoruk.com/drm.htm#ar5000_drm or www.drmrx.org/receiver_mods.html. Automatic Frequency Control (AFC) works on AM-mode, as well as FM, signals. Owner's manual, important because of operating system, unusually helpful and available free at http://www.aoruk.com/manuals.htm.

Con: Synchronous detector loses lock easily, especially if selectable sideband feature in use, greatly detracting from the utility of this high-tech feature. Substandard rejection of unwanted sideband with selectable synchronous sideband. Overall distortion rises when synchronous detector used. Ultimate rejection of "narrow" 2.7

kHz bandwidth filter only 60 dB. Ultimate rejection mediocre (50 dB) with standard 7.6 kHz "wide" bandwidth filter, improves to an uninspiring 60 dB when replaced by optional 6 kHz "wide" Collins mechanical filter. Installation of optional Collins filter requires expertise, patience and special equipment. Poor dynamic range. Cumbersome ergonomics. No passband offset. No tunable notch filter. Needs good external speaker for good audio quality. World Time 24-hour clock does not show when frequency displayed. IF output frequency 10.7 MHz instead of more-useful 455 kHz.

Verdict: Unbeatable in some respects, inferior in others—it comes down to what you want. The optional 6 kHz Collins filter is strongly recommended, but it should be installed by the dealer at the time of purchase. Although some AOR receivers are engineered and manufactured in the United Kingdom, this model is strictly Made in Japan.

✪✪✪✪
Palstar R30CC/Sherwood

Price: *Sherwood SE-3 Mk IV:* $599.00 in the United States. *Palstar R30CC:* See below.

Pro: SE-3 provides nearly flawless synchronous selectable sideband, reducing adjacent-channel interference while enhancing audio fidelity. Foolproof installation; plugs right into the Palstar's existing IF output.

Con: Buzz occasionally heard during weak-signal reception. SE-3 costs roughly as much as a regular Palstar receiver.

Verdict: If you're going to spend $599 to upgrade a $659 receiver, you may as well spring for another model.

✪✪✪⅞ 🅒
Palstar R30CC

Price: $659.95 in the United States. CAN$859.00 in Canada. £469.95 in the United Kingdom. €649.00 in Germany. *SP30 speaker:* $58.95 in the United States. CAD$89.00 in Canada. €59.95 in Germany.

The American-made Palstar R30CC follows the KISS principle of practical simplicity. For 2008 this concept has been enhanced by reducing the number of available versions to one.   Universal Radio

Pro: Generally good dynamic range. Overall distortion averages 0.5 percent, superb, in single-sideband mode (in AM mode, averages 2.9 percent, good, at 60% modulation and 4.4 percent, fair, at 95% modulation) (*see* Con). Every other performance variable measures either good or excellent in PASSPORT's lab, and birdies are virtually absent. Excellent AGC performance with AM-mode and single-sideband signals. Robust physical construction of cabinet and related hardware. Microprocessor section well shielded to minimize radiation of digital "buzz." Features include selectable slow/fast AGC decay (*see* Con), 20–100 Hz/100–500 Hz VRIT (slow/fast variable-rate incremental tuning) knob, 0.5 MHz slew and 455 kHz IF output. One hundred non-volatile station presets, using a generally well-thought-out scheme (*see* Con); they store frequency, bandwidth, mode, AGC setting and attenuator setting; also, presets displayed by channel number or frequency. Excellent illuminated analog signal meter reads in useful S1–9/+60 dB standard and is reasonably accurate (*see* Con). LCD and signal-indicator illumination can be switched off. Also operates from ten firmly secured "AA" internal batteries (*see* Con). Lightweight and small (*see* Con). Good AM-mode sensitivity within longwave and mediumwave AM bands. Audio line output has suitable level and is properly located on back panel. Self-resetting circuit breaker for outboard power (e.g., AC adaptor); fuse used with internal batteries and comes with spare fuses. Tilt bail useful (*see* Con). Optional AA30A and AA30P active antennas, evaluated in PASSPORT REPORTS. Virtually superb skirt selectivity (1:1.4 wide and 1:1.5

narrow) and ultimate rejection (90 dB); bandwidths measure 6.3 kHz and 2.6 kHz, using Collins mechanical filters. Adjacent-channel 5 kHz heterodyne whistles largely absent with wide bandwidth. Audio quality pleasant with wide bandwidth (*see* Con).

Con: No keypad for direct frequency entry, not even as outboard mouse-type option; normally, only cheap portables don't have a keypad. No 5 kHz tuning step choice to aid in bandscanning. Lacks control to hop from one world band segment to another; instead, uses 0.5 MHz fast-slew increments. No synchronous selectable sideband without pricey Sherwood SE-3 Mk IV aftermarket accessory (see preceding review). ECSS tuning can be up to 10 Hz out of phase because of 20 Hz minimum tuning increment. Play in mechanical tuning encoder gives knob a sloppy feel, making precise ECSS tuning difficult. Lightweight plastic tuning knob lacks mass to provide good tuning feel. Lacks many features found in top-gun receivers, such as tunable notch filter, noise blanker, passband tuning and adjustable RF gain. Recovered audio fine with most signals, but with truly weak signals is not of the DX caliber found with top-gun receivers. No visual indication of which bandwidth is in use. No tone controls. Small identical front-panel buttons, including MEM button which, if accidentally pressed, can erase a preset. Station presets not as intuitive or easy to select as with various other models; lacks frequency information on existing presets during memory storage. No AGC off. No RF gain control. Uses AC adaptor instead of built-in power supply. High battery consumption. Batteries frustratingly difficult to install, requiring partial disassembly of the receiver and care not to damage speaker connections or confuse polarities. Receiver's light weight and tilt bail's lack of rubber sheathing allow it to slide around, especially when tuning knob pushed to change VRIT increments; the added weight of batteries helps slightly. Unsheathed tilt bail may mar desktop. Mono headphone jack produces output in only one ear of stereo 'phones; remedied by user-purchased mono-to-stereo adaptor. Signal meter illumination dims when volume turned high with AM-mode

signals; LCD illumination unaffected. Three bulbs used for illumination are soldered into place, making replacement difficult, although they should last a very long time. Intermittent microphonics in AM mode when using narrow bandwidth and internal speaker. Audio frequency response with wide filter results in slightly muffled audio; largely remedied by detuning 1–2 kHz, which unlike with some receivers doesn't significantly increase distortion.

☞ Works best when grounded.

Verdict: Although Ohio-made Palstar R30CC receiver is conspicuously lacking in tuning and performance features, what it sets out to do, it tends to do to a high standard. If you can abide the convoluted battery installation procedure and don't mind having to add an outboard antenna, it can also act as a field portable.

Nevertheless, Palstar's offering lacks a distinct identity. Although audio is fairly pleasant, especially in the original and now-discontinued basic version, there's no synchronous selectable sideband to make it a premium listening radio. Too, audio quality in the current version's narrow setting tends to be muffled.

The lack of operating features is especially disappointing—not even a keypad, something routinely found on portables costing a fraction as much. And the lack of signal-tweaking features, along with pedestrian weak-signal recovered audio, preclude serious DX use.

Yet, not everybody fits neatly into standard categories. One size doesn't fit all, and to that end the R30CC's straightforward concept and physical robustness make it a clear alternative.

✪✪✪⅝
Icom IC-R1500

Price: *IC-R1500 with control head and "black box" receiver:* $599.95 in the United States. CAD$599.00 in Canada. £419.95 in the United Kingdom. €625.00 in Germany. *UT-106 DSP unit:* $139.95 in the United

Icom's IC-R1500 comes with all kinds of goodies at a relatively affordable price.

States. CAD$250.00 in Canada. £79.95 in the United Kingdom. €99.00 in Germany. *OPC-1156 11½-foot/3.5-meter controller extension cable:* $21.95 in the United States. CAD$25.00 in Canada. £14.95 in the United Kingdom. €16.95 in Germany. *OPC-441 16½-foot/five-meter speaker extension cable:* $21.95 in the United States. £14.95 in the United Kingdom. €26.95 in Germany. *CP-12L 12V DC cigarette lighter power cable:* $27.95 in the United States. CAD$60.00 in Canada. £19.95 in the United Kingdom. *OPC-254L 12V DC fused power cord:* $12.95 in the United States. CAD$25.00 in Canada. £9.95 in the United Kingdom. *Aftermarket RF Systems DPX-30 antenna splitter for separate shortwave and scanner antennas:* $99.95 in the United States. €76.20 in Germany.

Pro: Generally excellent wired control head so '1500 can also be used as a standalone tabletop or, to a degree with the optional CP-12L power cord, a mobile receiver (*see* Con)—as well as a PC-controlled model *à la* sibling PC-R1500 (*see* PC Controlled Receivers chapter). Wideband frequency coverage in three versions: *(blocked U.S. version)* 0.01–810, 851–867, 896–1811, 1852–1868, 1897–2305.9, 2357–2812, 2853–2869, 2898–3109.8, 3136–3154.8, 3181–3300 MHz; *(blocked French version)* 0.01–30, 50.2–51.2, 87.5–108, 144–146, 430–440 and 1240–1300 MHz; *(unblocked version)* 0.01–3300 MHz; with all versions, specifications not guaranteed 0.01–0.5 and 3000–3300 MHz; BFO operation (single sideband and CW) up to 1300 MHz. Very good shortwave sensitivity. Tunes and displays in unusually

precise 1 Hz increments. Vast number of user-selectable tuning steps. Useful ECSS (*see* Con) aided by Gibraltar-class stability. Selectable fast/slow AGC decay (*see* Con). Three different user screens when PC controlled in lieu of control head. Excellent 'scope for up to a 1 MHz peek at radio spectrum in real time, 1–10 MHz in non-real time. Generally good IF shift (*see* Con). Operating software works well and can be flash-ROM updated online. Fully 2600 station presets clustered into 26 pages of 100 channels each. Generally pleasant audio quality (*see* Con). Audio available not only through the set's internal speaker (*see* Con) or an external speaker, but also via USB through the PC's audio system (*see* Con). Can record audio in .wav format onto hard drive (*see* Con). One-step (20 dB) attenuator (*see* Con). Optional UT-106 AF-DSP unit (not tested) for noise reduction and AF notch filtering.

Con: Poor dynamic range—no RF or IF gain control to help alleviate overloading, and attenuator has only one step. No synchronous selectable sideband; ECSS alternative sounds slightly out of phase even with 1 Hz tuning step. Control head provides most, but not all, operating functions available from PC control; for example, there's no keypad or spectrum 'scope, and presets simultaneously display only one frequency or alphanumeric tag. Control head has no stand or mounting bracket for desktop or mobile use, nor can it be attached to the body of the "black box." At one test location, some distortion encountered with single-sideband

This control head turns Icom's 'R1500 series into a combination standalone receiver and PC-controlled receiver. D. Zantow

signals through the 3 kHz bandwidth. Slight hiss. Audio only fair through black box's built-in speaker. Audio a bit weak through computer's USB port. No AGC off. IF shift operates only in single-sideband and CW modes. Mediumwave sensitivity only fair. Poor longwave sensitivity. Marginal noise blanker. No on/off multi-event timing for audio recording. Telescopic antenna and cable virtually useless on shortwave and not much better elsewhere within tuned frequency ranges. Software installation not always easy and only via computer's USB port (no serial connection). No schematic or block diagrams.

☞ Also, *see* Icom IC-R1500 within Receivers for PCs.

Verdict: The wideband Icom IC-R1500 is the more-or-less standalone version of the IC-PCR1500 computer-controlled black box receiver. It consists of the same basic box used by the 'PCR1500, along with an external wired control head that allows it to act independently as a real, if decidedly unusual, tabletop or, to a degree, mobile receiver. Thus, the 'R1500 can be operated by PC or, using the control head, by itself—but not both at the same time. The control head includes an illuminated LCD, tuning knob, volume, squelch and other controls. Nevertheless, operation is more flexible using a PC, as it includes keypad tuning and other pluses not found with the control head.

Icom IC-R2500

The Icom IC-R2500 (not tested) is priced about half-again over the '1500. It uses the same platform as the '1500, but adds diversity reception to help reduce fading effects (two widely spaced antennas—or, outside the shortwave spectrum, one horizontally and one vertically polarized—are required).

Additional extras are multi-channel monitoring/display, P25 (public service digital) board, D-Star and similar features oriented to VHF/UHF/SHF scanning.

✪✪✪ ✐
Yaesu VR-5000

Price: *VR-5000 Receiver, including single-voltage AC adaptor:* $599.95 in the United States. CAD$849.00 in Canada. £489.00 in the United Kingdom. €598.00 in Germany. *DSP-1 digital notch, bandpass and noise reduction unit:* $119.95 in the United States. CAD$199.00 in Canada. £94.95 in the United Kingdom. €85.00 in Germany. *DVS-4 16-second digital audio recorder:* $49.95 in the United States. CAD$80.00 in Canada. £29.95 in the United Kingdom. €28.50 in Germany. *Pyramid PS-3KX aftermarket 120V AC>13.8V DC regulated power supply:* $22.95 in the United States.

Pro: Unusually wide frequency coverage, 100 kHz through 2.6 GHz (U.S. version omits cellular frequencies 869–894 MHz). Two thousand alphanumeric-displayed station presets, which can be linked to any of up to 100 groupings of presets. Up to 50 programmable start/stop search ranges. Large and potentially useful "band scope" spectrum display (*see* Con). Bandwidths have superb skirt selectivity, with shape factors between 1:1.3 and 1:1.4. Wide AM bandwidth (17.2 kHz) allows local mediumwave AM stations to be received with superior fidelity (*see* Con). Flexible software settings provide a high degree of control over selected parameters. Sophisticated scanning choices (*see* Con). Dual-receive function, with sub-receiver circuitry feeding "band scope" spectrum display; when display not in use, two signals may be monitored simultaneously, provided they are within 20 MHz of each other. Sensitivity to weak signals excellent-to-superb within shortwave spectrum (*see* Con). Appears to be robustly constructed. External spectrum display, fed by receiver's 10.7 MHz IF output, can perform very well for narrow-parameter scans (*see* Con). Two 24-hour clocks, both of which are shown except when spectrum display mode is in use; one clock tied into an elementary map display and database of time in a wide choice of world cities. On-off timer allows for up to 48 automatic events. Sleep-delay/alarm timers. Lightweight and compact. Multi-level display dimmer. Optional DSP unit includes adjustable notch filtering, a bandpass feature and noise reduction (*see* Con). Tone control. Built-in "CAT" computer control interface (*see* Con). Control and memory backup/management software available from www.g4hfq.co.uk.

Con: Exceptionally poor dynamic range (49 dB at 5 kHz signal spacing, 64 dB at 20 kHz spacing) and IF/image rejection (as low as 30 dB) for a tabletop model; for listeners in such high-signal parts of the world as Europe, North Africa and eastern North America, this impacts reception of short-wave signals unless a very modest antenna is used; the degree to which VHF-UHF is degraded depends, among other things, on the presence of powerful transmissions in the receiver's vicinity. Sophisticated scanning choices of limited use, as false signals result from receiver's inadequate dynamic range. No synchronous selectable sideband, a major drawback for world band and mediumwave AM listening, but not for shortwave utility/ham, VHF or UHF reception. Has only one single-sideband bandwidth, a broad 4.0 kHz. Wide AM bandwidth (17.2 kHz) of no use for shortwave. For world band, the middle (8.7 kHz) AM bandwidth lets through adjacent-channel 5 kHz heterodyne, while the narrow bandwidth (consistently 3.9 kHz, not the 4.0 kHz of the SSB bandwidth) produces muffled audio. Line output level low. Audio distorts at higher volume settings. Limited bass response. Audio hissy, especially noticeable with a good outboard speaker. DSP-1 option a mediocre overall performer and adds distortion. Phase noise 94 dBc, poor. AGC threshold 11 microvolts, poor. No adjustment of AGC decay, and single-sideband AGC decay too slow.

Yaesu's VR-5000 features broadband coverage at relatively low cost. However, this results in performance compromises.

Most recent test unit's (firmware v1u.17) tuning encoder sometimes has rotational delay when shifting directions. Mediocre tuning-knob feel. Signal indicator has only five levels and overreads; an alternative software-selectable signal indicator—not easy to access or exit—has no markings other than a single reference level. Built-in spectrum display's dynamic range only 20 dB (–80 to –100 dBm), with very slow scan rate. Single-sideband frequency readout after warmup can be off by up to 100 Hz. Long learning curve: Thirty buttons often densely spaced, lilliputian and multifunction; along with carouseling mode/tune-step selection and a menu-driven command scheme, these combine to produce unintuitive ergonomics. Only one low-impedance antenna connector, inadequate for a wideband device that needs multiple antennas. Longwave sensitivity mediocre. Clocks don't display seconds numerically. Marginal display contrast. LED illumination uneven. AC adaptor instead of built-in power supply; adaptor and receiver both tend to run warm. Repeated microprocessor lockups, sometimes displayed as "*ERROR* LOW VOLTAGE," even though the receiver includes a 7.2V NiCd battery pack to help prevent this; unplugging set for ten minutes resolves problem until it occurs again; also helpful is to replace the receiver's AC adaptor with a properly bypassed and regulated non-switching AC adaptor/DC power supply of at least one ampere that produces no less than 13.5V DC—certainly no less than 13.2V DC—and no more than 13.8V DC, such as the Pyramid PS-3KX. Even with the aforementioned battery, clock has to be reset if power fails. Squelch doesn't function through audio line output (for recording, etc.). Line output gain low. Sub-receiver doesn't feed line output. Computer interface lacks viable command structure, limiting usefulness. Tilt feet have inadequate rise. Owner's manual doesn't cover all receiver functions, so user also has to learn by trial and error.

Verdict: With existing technology, so-called "DC-to-daylight" receivers that provide excellent shortwave performance are costly to produce and are priced accordingly.

The relatively affordable wideband Yaesu VR-5000 tries to overcome this. This Japanese-made model acts as a VHF/UHF scanner as well as a shortwave receiver, but falls woefully shy for world band in strong-signal parts of the world. Elsewhere, it fares better, especially if only a modest antenna is used.

✪✪✪
SI-TEX NAV-FAX 200

Price: $549.00 in the United States from www.si-tex.com. *SI-TEX ACNF 120V AC adaptor:* $15.95 in the United States. *NASA AA30 antenna for '200 receiver:* €49.00 in Germany.

Pro: Superior rejection of images. High third-order intercept point for superior strong-signal handling capability. Bandwidths have superb ultimate rejection. Comes with Mscan Meteo Pro Lite software

The drooping dollar has prompted a price increase for SI-TEX's NAV-FAX 200 maritime-oriented receiver.

(www.mscan.com) for WEFAX, RTTY and NAVTEX reception using a PC with Windows XP or older Windows OS, but not yet Vista. Comes with wire antenna and audio patch cable. Two-year warranty at repair facility in Florida.

Con: No keypad, and variable-rate tuning knob is difficult to control. Broad skirt selectivity. Single-sideband bandwidth relatively wide. Volume control fussy to adjust. Synthesizer tunes in relatively coarse 1 kHz increments, supplemented by an analog fine-tuning "clarifier" control. Only ten station presets. Single sideband requires both tuning controls to be adjusted. No synchronous selectable sideband, notch filter or passband tuning. Frequency readout off by 2 kHz in single-sideband mode. Uses AC adaptor instead of built-in power supply. No clock, timer or sleep-delay feature. This British-made model is available only through Si-Tek marine dealers in the United States and, on special order, Canada.

Verdict: Pleasant world band performance, although numerous features are absent and operation is more frustrating than on many other models. Logical for yachting at what was once an affordable price, but which in August 2007 was increased by $150 presumably because of the weakened dollar.

✪✪½
Realistic/Radio Shack DX-394

Price (as available): £249.99 in the United Kingdom.

Pro: Advanced tuning features include 160 tunable presets (*see* Con). Tunes in precise 10 Hz increments. Modest size, light weight and built-in telescopic antenna provide some portable capability. Bandwidths (*see* Con) have superior shape factors and ultimate rejection. Two 24-hour clocks, one shown independent of frequency display. Five programmable timers. 30/60 minute snooze feature. Noise blanker.

Con: Available at rising prices only as new old stock at one U.K. outlet. What appears to be four bandwidths turns out to be virtually one, which is too wide for optimum reception of many signals. Bandwidths, such as they are, not selectable independent of mode. No synchronous selectable sideband. Presets cumbersome to use. Poor dynamic range for a tabletop, especially in Europe and other strong-signal parts of the world when an external antenna is used. Overall distortion, although acceptable, higher than desirable.

Verdict: Discontinued years ago, but as of presstime is still being offered at www.haydon.info. Modest dimensions and performance.

The PASSPORT *tabletop-model review team consists of Lawrence Magne and David Zantow. Also, David Crystal, George Heidelman, Chuck Rippel, David Walcutt and George Zeller. Laboratory measurements by J. Robert Sherwood.*

Radio Shack dropped the DX-394 in 1999, but it is still available in the United Kingdom.

GHOST OF HEATHKITS PAST

Most shortwave kits are novelties or regenerative radios. But there is one exception: Ten-Tec's small 1254 world band radio, $195 or £169.00. Parts quality for this superheterodyne is excellent, and assembly runs a good 24 hours. It has 15 station presets, but otherwise is Zen-simple: no keypad, signal indicator, synchronous selectable sideband, tilt bail, LSB/USB settings or adjustable AGC. Tuning increments are 500 Hz for single sideband and 5 kHz for AM mode, plus there is an analog clarifier for tweaking between increments. It includes a 120V AC adaptor—oddly, even when purchased from AOR-UK, Ten-Tec's EU vendor.

Phase noise, front-end selectivity, and longwave and mediumwave AM sensitivity are poor. Bandwidth is a respectable 5.6 kHz, and there is worthy ultimate rejection, image rejection, world band sensitivity, blocking, AGC threshold and frequency stability. Dynamic range and first IF rejection are fair, while overall distortion is good—with an external speaker, audio is pleasant.

The Ten-Tec 1254 doesn't really compete with similarly priced portables. Yet, it is a fun weekend project, and the manufacturer's track record for hand-holding means that when you're through the radio should really work.

The smell of solder lives on with the Ten-Tec 1254 tabletop receiver. It is a genuine kit, just like Uncle Billy used to make as a kid, with hand-holding from Tennessee.

Professional Receivers for 2008

Field of Champions

Professional receivers usually operate in the shadows: low-profile intelligence surveillance, along with military and commercial communications. Although not many are optimized for shortwave/HF, the "proud and few" can't be beat for flushing out tough world band signals. They also eavesdrop with aplomb on military, civilian and espionage utility signals—homeland security in your home.

Compromises among today's consumer-grade tabletop receivers have prompted serious listeners and DXers to consider alternatives. Among these are professional receivers, which blend advanced digital technology with commercial-grade construction and service. All are costly, but one offers relatively attractive pricing and receives digital broadcasts.

New for 2008

Icom's ultra-pricey IC-R9500 thoroughly seduces us with all it can do, and how well—excellent ergonomics, too. At least in its early incarnation it also has hiccups, but even then it very nearly earns the top spot among receivers PASSPORT has tested. With a few tweaks this receiver could very nearly be in a league of its own.

Japan Radio's NRD-630 also debuts. Simpler and less exciting, it stands out by maintaining Japan Radio's legendary robustness.

Three Flavors

There are three types of professional receivers: easy for human operation, complex for human operation and no direct human operation.

The first is for personnel with minimal radio training. After all, if an AWACS radioman is disabled, uncomplicated operation allows buddies to take over. But operational simplicity also means performance compromises, so these receivers aren't covered here.

The second and smaller category goes to the other extreme, with no-holds-barred features and performance. These rarities are for skilled operators and are evaluated in PASSPORT REPORTS.

Simplest are "black box" professional receivers with virtually no on-unit controls. These operate remotely or from computers, often at official surveillance facilities. PASSPORT REPORTS doesn't test these as, aside from their stratospheric prices, some of the best are sold only to U.S. Federal agencies and NATO organizations. Indeed, some are so hush-hush that even manufacturers' names are aliases.

Nevertheless, there is a small but enthusiastic civilian market for consumer-grade black box receivers. These are evaluated and rated in "Receivers for PCs."

Find major updates to the 2008 PASSPORT REPORTS at www.passband.com.

Digital Reception

Alone among tested receivers, the Ten-Tec RX-340 is engineered to receive DRM digital world band broadcasts. While the Watkins-Johnson equivalent isn't DRM ready, this appears to be only because no user has as yet succeeded at creating what's needed.

DRM reception requires interfacing with a PC using separately purchased DRM software (www.drmrx.org).

Super Set, Super Skyhook

A top-rated, properly erected antenna is a must for any professional receiver. For test findings and installation tips, read the in-depth Radio Database International White Paper, *Evaluation of Popular Outdoor Antennas.* There are also antenna reviews in PASSPORT REPORTS.

Is reception being disrupted by nearby electrical noise, even with a good antenna? If so, a fancier receiver might be a waste of money. Before springing for a pricey new model, try eliminating the source of noise or reducing it by repositioning your antenna. If all else fails, consider a Wellbrook loop antenna—*see* "Compact Antennas for 2008."

No Zaps

Professional receivers are rugged and typically include MOV surge protection. Nevertheless, it helps to plug a serious radio into a serious non-MOV surge arrestor, such as Zero-Surge (www.zerosurge.com) or Brick Wall (www.brickwall.com). We've used probably a dozen ZeroSurges over the past two decades with nary a hiccup or need for replacement.

Any receiver's outdoor antenna should be fed through a static protector. This is especially so with the Watkins-Johnson WJ-8711A when it lacks the 8711/PRE option. Even better is to disconnect all outdoor antennas whenever you start to hear thunder.

Audio for Listening and DX

Most professional and a few consumer-grade receivers use DSP (digital signal processing) audio. In principle, there is no reason DSP audio quality can't equal that of conventional models, but in practice the tendency is for weak signals and static to sound harsh and tiring.

Helping offset this is recoverable audio, which with tough DX signals tends to be slightly better with DSP professional receivers. This is why these models are not strangers to "DXpeditions," where the most stubborn of radio signals are flushed out.

For world band, the Sherwood SE-3 fidelity-enhancing accessory has been exceptionally helpful with various current and discontinued professional receivers, and the new Mk IV version is scheduled to be available by the time you read this. While it doesn't fundamentally resolve the DSP audio issue, it helps significantly. It also provides exceptional-quality synchronous selectable sideband, a major plus.

Alas, it doesn't work with all receivers—notably the Icom IC-R9500. Other downsides are cost, operating complexity and a BFO that's less stable than those on most professional receivers. Nevertheless, with the WJ-8711A and RX-340 the SE-3 has become virtually a must-have accessory.

Which?

The top three professional receivers are remarkably similar in overall performance, ergonomics and toughness. Yet, there are differences.

Icom's new IC-R9500—German engineered, Japanese built—wins at stirring our collective juices. It's about as exciting as an F-16 and is priced accordingly, but has a couple of issues that should be dealt with.

Unless and until that happens, most will look to the other two. Among these, the Watkins-Johnson WA-8711A remains the valedictorian, although only by a bobbed nose. The remarkably similar Ten-Tec RX-340 costs less, is readily available, is DRM ready and is quickly and reliably serviced. It's the sensible choice in a field of champions.

Tips for Using this Section

Professional receivers are listed in order of suitability for listening to difficult-to-hear world band stations. Important secondary consideration is given to audio fidelity, ergonomics and reception of utility signals. Build quality is superior unless otherwise indicated. Selling prices, street, are as of when we go to press, and include European VAT where applicable.

Unless otherwise stated, all professional models have the following characteristics. *See* Worldly Words to understand specialized terms.

- Digital signal processing, including digital frequency synthesis and display.
- Full coverage of at least the 5–29999 kHz VLF/LF/MF/HF portions of the radio spectrum, encompassing all the longwave, mediumwave AM and shortwave portions—including all world band frequencies—but no coverage of the standard FM broadcast band (87.5–108 MHz).
- A wide variety of helpful tuning features, including tuning and frequency display in 1 Hz increments.
- Synchronous selectable sideband via high-rejection IF filtering (not lower-rejection phasing), which greatly reduces adjacent-channel interference and fading distortion. On some models this is referred to as "SAM" (synchronous AM).

☞ **ECSS:** Professional models tune to the nearest 1 Hz, allowing the user to use the receiver's single-sideband circuitry to manually phase its BFO (internally generated carrier) with the station's transmitted carrier. Called "ECSS" (exalted-carrier, selectable-sideband) tuning, this can be used with AM-mode signals in lieu of synchronous selectable sideband. However, in addition to the relative inconvenience of this technique, unlike synchronous detection, which rephases continually and essentially perfectly, ECSS is always slightly out of phase. This causes at least some degree of harmonic distortion to music and speech, while tuning to the nearest Hertz can generate slow-sweep fading (for this reason, high-pass audio filtering or mis-phasing by two or three Hertz may provide better results).

- Proper demodulation of modes used by non-world-band—utility and amateur—shortwave signals. These modes include single sideband (LSB/USB and sometimes ISB) and CW ("Morse code"); also, with suitable ancillary devices, radioteletype (RTTY), frequency shift key (FSK) and radiofax (FAX).
- Meaningful signal-strength indication.
- Illuminated display.
- Superior build quality, robustness and sample-to-sample consistency as compared to consumer-grade tabletop receivers.
- Audio output for recording, as well as low-power FM retransmission to hear world band around your domicile.

What PASSPORT's Rating Symbols Mean

Star ratings: ✪✪✪✪✪ is best. Stars reflect overall performance and meaningful features, plus to some extent ergonomics and perceived build quality. Price, appearance, country of manufacture and the like are not taken into account. With professional models there is a strong emphasis on the ability to flush out tough, hard-to-hear signals, as this is usually the main reason these sets are chosen by world band enthusiasts. Nevertheless, to facilitate comparison professional receiver rating standards are very similar to those used for the tabletop and portable models reviewed elsewhere in this PASSPORT REPORTS.

Passport's Choice. La crème de la crème. Our test team's personal picks of the litter—models we would buy or have bought for our personal use. Unlike star ratings, these choices are unapologetically subjective.

✪✪✪✪✪ *Passport's Choice*
Watkins-Johnson WJ-8711A

Price (receiver and factory options, FOB factory): *WJ-8711A:* $5,580.00 plus shipping worldwide. *871Y/SEU DSP Speech Enhancement Unit:* $1,200.00. *8711/PRE Sub-Octave Preselector:* $1,295.84. *871Y/DSO1 Digital*

Watkins-Johnson's
WJ-8711A. Valued by
government agencies,
tank tough and thoroughly
debugged.

Signal Output Unit: $1,150.00. *8711/SPK Internal Speaker:* $98.76 in the United States.

Price (aftermarket options): *Hammond RCBS1900517BK1 steel cabinet/wraparound and 1421A mounting screws and cup washers (as available):* $120–140 in the United States from manufacturer (www.hammondmfg.com/rackrcbs.htm) or Newark Electronics (www.newark.com). *Sherwood SE-3 MK IV accessory:* $599.00 plus shipping worldwide.

Pro: Proven robust. BITE (built-in test equipment) diagnostics and physical layout allows technically qualified users to make most repairs on-site. Users can upgrade receiver performance over time by EPROM replacement. Exceptional overall performance. Unsurpassed reception of feeble world band DX signals, especially when mated to Sherwood SE-3 synchronous selectable sideband device and WJ-871Y/SEU noise-reduction unit (*see* Con). Unusually effective "ECSS" reception, tuning AM-mode signals as though they were single sideband. Superb reception of non-AM mode "utility" stations. Generally superior audio quality when coupled to Sherwood SE-3 fidelity-enhancing accessory, the W-J speech enhancement unit and a worthy external speaker (*see* Con). Unparalleled bandwidth flexibility, with no less than 66 outstandingly high-quality bandwidths. Trimmer on back panel allows frequency readout to be user-aligned against a known frequency standard, such as WWV/WWVH or a laboratory device. Extraordinary operational flexibility—virtually every receiver parameter is adjustable. One hundred station presets. Synchronous detection ("SAM," for synchronous AM) reduces selective-fading distortion with world band, mediumwave AM and longwave signals, and works even on very narrow voice

bandwidths (*see* Con). Rock stable. Built-in preamplifier. Tunable notch filter. Effective noise blanking. Highly adjustable scanning of both frequency ranges and station presets. Easy-to-read displays. Large tuning knob. Unusually effective mediumwave AM performance. Can be fully and effectively computer and remote controlled. Passband shift (*see* Con). Numerous outputs for data collection from received signals, as well as ancillary hardware; includes properly configured 455 kHz IF output, which makes for instant installation of Sherwood SE-3 accessory and balanced line outputs (connect to balanced hookup to minimize radiation of digital "buzz"). Remote control and dial-up data collection; Windows control software available from manufacturer. Among the most likely of all world band receivers tested to be able to be retrofitted for eventual reception of digital world band broadcasts. Inboard AC power supply, which runs unusually cool, senses incoming current and automatically adjusts 90–264V AC, 47–440 Hz—a plus during brownouts or with line voltage or frequency swings. Superior-quality factory service (*see* Con). Comprehensive and well-written operating manual, packed with technical information and schematic diagrams. Hammond aftermarket cabinet/wraparound exceptionally robust.

Con: Static crashes and modulation-splash interference sound noticeably harsher than on analog receivers, although this has been improved in latest operating software. Synchronous detection not sideband-selectable, so it can't reduce adjacent-channel interference (remediable by Sherwood SE-3). Basic receiver has mediocre audio in straight AM mode; "ECSS" tuning or synchronous detection, especially with optional speech enhancement unit (W1 noise-reduction setting), alleviates this. Some clipping distortion in single-sideband mode. Complex to operate to full advantage. Circuitry puts out a high degree of digital buzz, relying for the most part on the panels for electrical shielding; one consequence is that various versions emanate digital buzz through the nonstandard rear-panel audio terminals, as well as through the signal meter and front-panel headphone jack—this problem lessened when Sherwood SE-3 used. Antennas with shielded (e.g., coaxial) feedlines less likely to pick up receiver-generated digital "buzz." Passband shift operates only in CW mode. Jekyll-and-Hyde ergonomics: sometimes wonderful, sometimes awful. Front-panel rack "ears" protrude, with the right one getting in the way of the tuning knob; fortunately, ears are easily removed. Mediocre front-end selectivity, remediable by 8711/PRE option (with insignificant 1.2 dB insertion loss); e.g. for those living near mediumwave AM transmitters. 871Y/SEU option reduces audio gain and is extremely difficult to install; best to have all options factory-installed. Signal indicator's gradations in dBm only. No DC power input. Keypad lettering wears off with use; replacement keys available at around $8 each, but minimum parts order is $100. Each receiver is built on order (David Shane at 1-800/954-3577), so it can take up to four months for delivery. Factory service can take as much as two months. Cabinet/wrap-

NUMBERS: TOP PROFESSIONAL RECEIVERS

	Watkins-Johnson WJ-8711A	Icom IC-R9500
Max. Sensitivity/Noise Floor	0.13 μV **S**/–136 dBm **E**	0.11 μV **S**/–136 dBm **E**[1]
Blocking	123 dB **G**	119 dB **G**
Shape Factors, voice BWs	1:1.21–1:1.26 **S**	1:1.52–1:1.63 **E**
Ultimate Rejection[5]	≤80 dB **E**	≤70–80 dB **E**
Front-End Selectivity	**F**/**E**[2]	**E**
Image Rejection	80 dB **E**	>100 dB **S**
First IF Rejection	—[3]	>100 dB **S**
Dynamic Range/IP3 (5 kHz)	74 dB **G**/–18 dBm **E**	100 dB **S**/+23 dBm **S**
Dynamic Range/IP3 (20 kHz)	99 dB **S**/+20 dBm **S**	110 dB **S**/+38 dBm **S**
Phase Noise	115 dBc **G**	134 dBc **S**
AGC Threshold	0.1 μV **P**[7]	0.16 μV **P**[4,7]
Overall Distortion, sync	8.2% **P**	0.4% **S**
Stability	5 Hz **S**	1 Hz **S**
Notch filter depth	58 dB **S**	55 dB **S**[6]

IBS Lab Ratings: **S** Superb **E** Excellent **G** Good **F** Fair **P** Poor

(1) Preamp 2 on. Preamp 1 on, 0.2 μV **E**/–130 dBm **E**. Preamp off, 0.7 μV, **F**/–120 dBm, **G**.

(2) **F** standard/**E** with optional preselector.

(3) Adequate, but could not measure precisely.

(4) Preamp 2 on. Preamp 1 on, 0.25 μV **P**. Preamp off, 1.1 μV, **E**.

(5) DSP measurements noise limited.

(6) Automatic notch (ANF). Manually tuned notches (two) 40–65 dB, **E**–**S**.

(7) **P** here not significant relative to overall audible performance.

around extra, available only on aftermarket from Hammond. Plastic feet have no front elevation and allow receiver to slide around. Available only through U.S. manufacturer, DRS Technologies (www.drs.com); receiver and factory options have been subjected to a number of price increases since 2000.

Verdict: The American-made WJ-8711A is, by a skosh, the ultimate machine for down-and-dirty world band DXing when money is no object.

Had there not been digital "buzz," inexcusable at this price—and had there been better audio quality, a tone control, passband shift and synchronous selectable sideband—the '8711A would have been audibly better for program listening. Fortunately, the Sherwood SE-3 accessory—a new version is scheduled for 2008—remedies virtually all these problems and improves DX reception, to boot; W-J's optional 871Y/SEU complements, rather than competes with, the SE-3 for improving recovered audio.

Overall, the WJ-8711A DSP, properly configured, is as good as it gets. It is exceptionally well suited to demanding connoisseurs with the appropriate financial wherewithal—provided they seek an extreme degree of manual receiver control.

New for 2008

✪✪✪✪✪ *Passport's Choice*
Icom IC-R9500

Price: *IC-R9500 receiver:* $13,500.00 in the United States. CAD$14,999.00 in Canada. £7,999.95 in the United Kingdom. €11,900 in Germany. *UT-122 digital voice decoder:*

$189.95 in the United States. CAD$390.00 in Canada. £149.95 in the United Kingdom. €215.00 in Germany. *SP-20 external speaker with four audio cutoff filters:* $219.95 in the United States. CAD$470.00 in Canada. £164.95 in the United Kingdom. €198.00 in Germany.

Pro: No-excuses 5 Hz–3.333 GHz broadband coverage on units sold outside the United States and France (*see* Con). Large seven-inch (18 cm) TFT color LCD offers numerous screen options and displays—even a screen saver; can also feed an external computer monitor. Versatile spectrum scope (*see* Con). Stellar dynamic range, image rejection and first-IF rejection—all as good as it gets. Preamplifier for below 30 MHz, plus a second preamp for all tuned frequencies. Exceptional dynamic range allows either preamplifier to be used virtually without introducing overloading (*see* Con). Excellent sensitivity with either preamp engaged (*see* Con). Excellent AGC threshold with both preamplifiers off (*see* Con). Top-drawer DSP bandwidths include three user-selectable pushbutton bandwidths per mode and four roofing filter choices. Gain equalized among roofing filters, with only an unavoidable 3 dB increase in noise floor with the narrowest filter. Bandwidth shape factor adjustable for single-sideband and CW modes. Twin passband tuning (PBT) works in all modes. Worthy AGC includes three adjustable presets that can be further tweaked by a front-panel knob. Excellent front-end selectivity, with half-octave filtering. Automatic notch filter (ANF), simple to use, simultaneously eliminates or greatly reduces several heterodynes. Dual manually tunable notch filters, although scarcely necessary with ANF, act on up to two more heterodynes.

Icom's new IC-R9500 is loads of fun for loads of money.   D. Zantow

Excellent recoverable audio, thanks in part to superb receiver phase noise. Generally excellent audio quality (*see* Con), with very low overall distortion on all audio frequencies and in all modes; also, excellent built-in speaker, aided by separate bass and treble controls with contours that can be quasi-permanently optimized for each reception mode; also, low-pass audio filter selectable for each mode. Synchronous selectable sideband aids in reducing adjacent-channel interference; also has synchronous double sideband (*see* Con). Tunes and displays in ultra-precise 1 Hz steps. Superior tuning knob includes moving spinner; also, "click" mode (*see* Con) for tuning steps. Two built-in recorders; primary has five audio-quality settings (*see* Con), using internal or external memory; secondary, with pleasant audio, useful for station IDs and addresses (*see* Con). Over 1,000 presets with alphanumeric tagging for each preset and each bank of presets. Easy-to-program presets store many variables, including selected antenna. Ten VFOs. Excellent ergonomics, including logical menu. Keys have superior tactile response, with feedback "Roger beep" adjustable for volume and pitch. Gibraltar stability, as good as it gets. Fan cooled (*see* Con). Superb signal indicator reads out in "S" units, dBμ, dBμ (EMF) and dBm; readings, extremely accurate except low-"S", remain constant regardless of changes in preamplification or attenuation; also, can output to an external analog signal meter. Separate discrimination indicator for FM and FM-wide. Five-step attenuator: 6, 12, 18, 24 and 30 dB. Speech synthesizer. FSK decoder. Ethernet for LAN and firmware updates. USB for external memory, keyboard and ancillary devices. Useful dual-mode noise blanker with adjustable depth and width. Three shortwave antenna inputs, front-panel selectable. Automatic center-tuning selectable for AM, SSB and CW signals; similarly, AFC selectable for FM and FM-wide. Dual clocks display discretely. Line output at appropriate level for audio recording; includes separate optical (TOSLINK) digital audio output (*see* Con). Five-event on/off timer stores day of week to enhance unattended recording and other turnkey operations. Sleep timer.

Excellent FM broadcast performance (*see* Con). Robust cabinet/wraparound and overall construction hint at trouble-free operation (*see* Con). Owner's manual includes schematics and block diagrams (*see* Con). *Outside United States:* Composite video can be fed to a television receiver.

Con: Synchronous selectable/double sideband loses lock readily and is mediocre at reducing selective-fading distortion. Lack of suitable IF output, so Sherwood SE-3 device cannot be added to enhance synchronous selectable/double sideband performance. ECSS in lieu of synchronous selectable sideband results in significant audio dropouts. High power consumption by AC mains or DC power. Runs warm-to-hot, even with fan that noisily cycles on and off; in principle, this could result in premature component failure. Neither the noise blanker nor DSP noise reduction particularly helpful. Optical (TOSLINK) digital audio output has distortion in single-sideband modes. Slight rotational delay when tuning knob using "click" option. Some DSP audio harshness with weak signals (S1–S5); also with static and impulse noises. AGC threshold becomes overly sensitive if either preamplifier on, although audible impact not significant. Public versions sold in the United States and France have blocked segments that limit tuning above 30 MHz. Keyboard requires all frequencies to be entered in MHz, complete with decimal. Only three of the primary recorder's five quality settings produce decent audio. Secondary recorder's 15-second limit too brief for most uses. Spectrum scope's circuit noise causes "grass" to appears along bottom of spectrum scope, covering up weak signal pips; this greatly diminishes scope's usefulness for DXing; remediable, if clunky, by having the 10.7 MHz IF output feed an external spectrum analyzer. At 44 pounds (20 kg), a challenge for one person to move and needs to be shipped carefully. No front elevation feet, which can make LCD hard to read; easily remediable by user or dealer. FM monaural only. Owner's manual lacks coverage of various operations, has no index and can be hard to follow.

☞ Once, after 12 hours of continuous operation, audio suddenly became "buzzy" and

The Icom IC-R9500's spectrum scope works nicely within active segments, such as 25 meters. Yet, faint signal pips tend to be lost under circuit-noise "grass."

D. Zantow

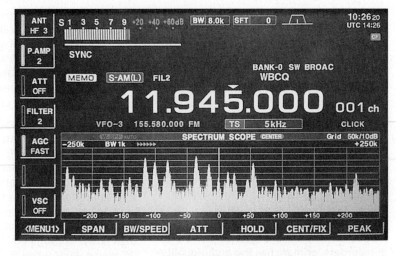

distorted in all modes. This was resolved by switching the set off then back on. It never occurred again.

☞ Firmware: v1.03; future upgrades could resolve some issues encountered during testing.

Verdict: The Icom IC-R9500, easily the costliest receiver tested to date, is in many ways the Mother of Supersets. For example, its dynamic range, image rejection, first IF rejection, stability and overall distortion are nearly off the charts—and most other indicators of performance are superior. Ergonomics are excellent for such a complex device, and robustness appears to be in the same league except for heat.

Yet, synchronous selectable sideband performance is mediocre, and there's not a suitable IF output for a Sherwood SE-3 to resolve it. Even ECSS—manually tuned selectable sideband—isn't an alternative, as that introduces audio dropouts. Were it not for this surprising triple whammy, along with scope limitations, the 'R9500 might well have ranked as PASSPORT's number one choice.

Evaluation of New Model: Nobody trying to lift Icom's new IC-R9500 is going to ask, "Where's the beef?" This electronic champ is built like Hercules and bends the scale at 44 pounds (20 kg).

Frequency coverage is serious—from 5 Hz to 3,335 MHz—so this is much more than just

a shortwave receiver. With lesser models this broadband approach invariably results in performance and operational compromises, but not so the '9500. It retains its considerable muscle and flexibility from nearly DC to daylight.

Well, almost. Thanks to exalted Congressional nabobs, the United States version for public sale lacks coverage around 800 MHz. This ensures that nobody can listen to analog cellphones which essentially don't exist anymore. The version for France has been neutered even more, albeit not under 30 MHz.

Superb Display

The 'R9500's seven-inch (18 cm) TFT color LCD is eye candy. It features a number of video and color controls, including a screen saver and nice two-level dimmer. Its output can also be viewed simultaneously on an external computer monitor, like one lying around from an old PC.

A composite video input/output connects to a standard television or from an external video source into the inboard display. This is disabled on the version sold in the United States, although creative types reportedly have come up with workarounds.

The LCD can display analog television signals of almost any type: NTSC, PAL or SECAM. Alas, this, too, is disabled on the United States version, and here, as well, solutions have quietly been devised. Nevertheless, this feature has a short shelf life, as it becomes moot once digital HDTV is mandated.

All LCDs have a limited viewing angle, and this is no exception. The lack of any elevation feet thus can make the LCD hard to read, so figure on doing a hillbilly foot job if the receiver isn't being rack-mounted.

Goodies Overfloweth

If you count all apples in the basket, the IC-R9500 has fully 1,220 presets. Of these, 1,000 are regular, while the remainder are to aid in scanning. Concentric knobs greatly simplify the quick selection of presets. Presets and banks of presets store all kinds of useful stuff and can be tagged alphanumerically.

The tuning knob is large, sensible and nicely weighted, with a rubber track around the gripping surface—and its spinner actually rotates. There's even a choice to have the knob click with each tuned step, although this introduces a skosh of rotational play. All other controls are equally top-drawer, with feel that varies from good to excellent. The keys' "Roger beep" feedback is even adjustable for volume and pitch.

Not sure if the receiver is tuned to a signal's exact middle? Try "auto tune," which acts comparably to automated magic eyes found on early wooden radios. It usually works well. Similarly, automatic frequency control (AFC) is selectable for FM and FM-wide signals.

The rear panel has just about every output and input imaginable: front-panel-selectable antenna inputs, including three for shortwave; DB-9 RS-232 connector; Icom's CI-V for CT-17 computer interface; output for external computer monitor; 10.7 MHz IF output; 10 MHz reference signal input/output; line output with excellent level, plus a second line output on the front.

There's also a SPDIF (TOSLINK) optical digital output jack. It works well for recording AM-mode signals. However, in our testing using a Sony MDS-JE480 Mini Disc recorder

deck's optical digital input, single-sideband audio was heavily distorted, clipped and even cut out regardless of receiver or recorder settings.

Voice "speech" output includes adjustable output level, and even the speed of the voice output is adjustable. There's also a broad range of connectivity options for PCs and ancillary digital devices: Ethernet, USB DB-9 and Icom's CI-V. Nonetheless, unlike on the Watkins-Johnson WJ-8711A and Ten-Tec RX-340, there is no 455 kHz IF output.

Power Piggy

The '9500 is no shortwave Prius. It slurps power like an Eisenhower-era refrigerator, generating heat that, in turn, causes air conditioning usage to rise. An internally mounted fan cycles on and off, but even for a high-CFM device it is noisy and doesn't do nearly enough to keep the receiver from getting hot. Gaming PCs have solved heat and noise issues, so here Icom has been asleep at the wheel.

The built-in AC power supply is nominally 100–120V and 220–240V, although swapping ranges requires that a different-value fuse be used. To power the receiver calls for the rear "sub" power switch to be switched on before the front power button is pressed. The front panel indicator glows orange once the power cord is attached and the rear switch is on.

Sterling Performance

Sensitivity is excellent when either of the two preamplifiers are used, and with some antennas they're needed for DXing.

With lesser receivers, preamplifiers tend to degrade dynamic range, but not so the '9500. Yet, there's a slight rub: AGC threshold, which is excellent with no preamps, becomes overly sensitive with either preamp; although in principle this drops AGC threshold performance to poor, in practice there is scant audible impact.

Dynamic range, like image and first IF rejection—stability, too—is nearly off the charts and accounts for much of the 'R9500's sky-high price tag. Front-end filtering and over-all distortion are also in an exalted league. No surprise, given the track record of the legendary German folks who engineered the '9500's hardware. (Firmware was developed in Japan.)

DSP bandwidths are excellent and include three user-preset quick-access bandwidths:

- AM mode bandwidths can be selected from 200 Hz to 10 kHz in 200 Hz incre-ments.
- Single-sideband and CW mode band-widths can be selected from 50 to 500 Hz in 50 Hz increments, and from 0.6 to 3.6 kHz in 100 Hz increments.

Also, four different roofing filters with bal-anced gain distribution can be selected for shortwave, and the shape factor can be tweaked in the single-sideband and CW modes.

The AGC works unusually well, and includes three AGC presets which store user-selected attack, hang and decay times; these can also be tweaked in real time by a front-panel knob.

Tunable notch filters, one automatic (ANF) and two manual, are impressively effective. By itself the ANF can nail several offending heterodynes at a time, so in practice the manual notch filters are unlikely to see much use. On the other hand, the noise blanker is merely satisfactory, while DSP noise reduction does little more than cut off high frequencies and add artifacts to the audio.

The bar-type signal indicator—useful and supremely accurate except for low-"S" readings—includes four readout scales: "S" units, dBµ, dBµ (EMF) and dBm. Remark-ably, the indicator doesn't change reading with changes in preamplifier or attenua-tor settings. There's even an output for an outboard analog signal meter, and an arrow along the bottom aids in using the squelch.

Sinking Sync

The provided synchronous selectable side-band helps somewhat in reducing adjacent-channel interference, but has little impact on selective fading. Additionally, it loses lock on weaker signals and during moder-ate-to-deep fades. There's also synchronous double sideband, but it, too, is only mini-mally effective at reducing selective fading distortion.

The '9500 is rock stable, which aids in reception of digital and other non-AM-mode signals. This stability should also help allow ECSS operation to be used when the syn-chronous selectable sideband isn't cutting the mustard. Unfortunately, there are nu-merous audio dropouts with ECSS, probably resulting from a firmware oversight.

Normally, the solution would be to attach a Sherwood SE-3 synchronous detector ac-cessory to the receiver's suitably configured 455 kHz IF output. This can be done on the Watkins-Johnson WJ-8711A and Ten-Tec RX-340 receivers, but not the 'R9500. This triple whammy of mediocre built-in sync, flawed ECSS and no ability to use aftermar-ket solutions keeps the 'R9500 from rising to the apex of our ratings heap.

Audio Generally Superior

Otherwise, audio quality is clearly supe-rior, with extremely low overall distortion in all modes. This is aided by effective bass and treble controls that come with a neat feature: the contour of each can be perma-nently set by the operator for each reception mode. DXers will also appreciate the '9500's excellent recovered audio.

Not enough? Even though there's no audible hiss, the receiver includes a high-cut (low-pass) audio filter that's selectable for each mode.

Most built-in speakers perform dismally, but not so the '9500's front-facing speaker that's an aural treat, especially for world band listening. Even better for DXing is Icom's SP-20 outboard speaker, which includes four audio cutoff filters.

So, is the '9500 ready for the McIntosh Audio Hall of Fame? Not quite. As with every other DSP receiver tested, there's more audio harshness than is found with analog circuitry, at least with weak signals. Static and impulse noise come through more harshly, too.

Scope Excellent, Except "Grass"

The spectrum scope's narrow mode covers various selectable ranges from plus or minus 2.5 kHz to plus or minus 5 MHz and functions while you're listening. The scope's filter width can be varied from 200 Hz to 20 kHz; the sweep speed can be changed, too, for whatever that's worth.

The scope's wide setting mutes the audio, but covers various selectable ranges from plus or minus 10 MHz to plus or minus 500 MHz. Wide or narrow, there's a 10/20/30 dB attenuator just for the spectrum scope that is useful within high-occupancy frequency segments. Various modes alter how the scope interacts with receiver tuning, while one setting highlights signal peaks.

Alas for DXing, the display is busy to watch even with few displayed signals, as scope circuit noise causes "grass" to show at the bottom of the screen unless the attenuator is used. This was never a problem with the predecessor IC-R9000, and makes it impossible to view weak signals.

The 10.7 MHz IF output can feed an external spectrum analyzer to complement the built-in LCD. We used an HP 3585A analyzer, which—grass begone!—completely resolved weak signal visibility. But it's a clunky and costly solution.

Flexible Recording

The '9500 has two built-in digital audio recorders. The primary, for long continuous recording, stores data using an internal "compact flash" 128 MB internal memory accessible through a rear trap door; it also outputs to the USB port for outboard storage. Internal memory gets chewed up pretty quickly, but changing over to a larger memory card requires pliers and running the menu-selectable CF format utility.

The five qualities of .wav recording are SQ1, SQ2, HQ1, HQ2 and SHQ, and audio tone controls act on recording but not playback. The best, SHQ, results in quality audio, and cutting back on treble helps with HQ2 and HQ1. But with either SQ level, distortion during fades can become irremediably harsh. Recording level is fully automatic.

A voice recorder screen displays the record file list, playback, deletes and so on. Each file includes the date of recording, quality and reception mode used. Fast forward and rewind buttons are here, as well.

The second internal recorder is instantly activated by pressing a key; it's useful for DXers checking on station IDs and addresses. It erases once power is removed, but the audio quality is good.

Given all that the '9500 does, it needs a thorough and organized manual. Alas, the printed owner's guide lacks an index and useful coverage of various topics. It can also be hard to follow—although it includes full

128 MB CF CARD TOTAL RECORDING TIMES	
Quality Setting	Time (HH:MM:SS)
*SHQ (48 kHz)	00:22:05
*HQ2 (24 kHz)	00:44:11
*HQ1 (16 kHz)	01:06:17
SQ2 (12 kHz)	01:28:22
SQ1 (8 kHz)	02:12:34

Actual recording times may vary slightly

*PASSPORT's recommend settings (see text)

schematics and block diagrams. There's no online or CD/DVD user's guide, either.

Overall, Icom's new IC-R9500 is a Ferrari in a box with many goodies and a few misfires. Should firmware and hardware tweaks eventually materialize, it could well become the gold standard for broadband receivers.

DRM Ready

❀❀❀❀❀ *Passport's Choice*
Ten-Tec RX-340

Price: $4,250.00 in the United States. £3,299.00 in the United Kingdom. *Hammond RCBS1900513GY2 or RCBS1900513BK1 13" deep cabinet/wraparound (www.hammondmfg.com/rackrcbs.htm), as available:* $99.95 in the United States. *Ten-Tec #307G (gray) external speaker:* $98.95 in the United States. *Ten-Tec #307B (black) external speaker:* £89.00 in the United Kingdom. *Sherwood SE-3 MK IV accessory:* $599.00 plus shipping worldwide.

Pro: Appears to be robust (*see* Con). BITE (built-in test equipment) diagnostics and physical layout allow technically qualified users to make most repairs on-site. Users can upgrade receiver performance over time by replacing one or another of three socketed EPROM chips (currently v1.10A). Superb overall performance, including unsurpassed readability of feeble world band DX signals, especially when mated to the Sherwood SE-3 device; in particular, superlative image and IF rejection, both >100 dB. Few birdies. Audio quality usually worthy when receiver coupled to Sherwood SE-3 accessory and a good external speaker. Average overall distortion in single-sideband mode a low 0.2 percent; in other modes, under 2.7 percent. Exceptional bandwidth flexibility, with no less than 57 outstandingly high-quality bandwidths having shape factors of 1:1.33 or better; bandwidth distribution exceptionally good for world band listening and DXing, along with other activities (*see* Con). Receives digital (DRM) world band broadcasts by connecting it to a PC using DRM software purchased separately; if nothing else, this helps protect your investment over the years to come. Tunes and displays accurately in ultra-precise 1 Hz increments. Extraordinary operational flexibility—virtually every receiver parameter is adjustable; e.g., the AGC's various time constants have 118 million possible combinations, plus pushbutton AGC "DUMP" to temporarily deactivate AGC (*see* Con). Worthy front-panel ergonomics, valuable given the exceptional degree of manual operation; includes easy-to-read displays (*see* Con). Also, large, properly weighted rubber-track tuning knob with fixed dimple and Oak Grigsby optical encoder provide superior tuning feel and reliability; tuning knob tension user-adjustable for personalized feel. Attractive front panel. Two hundred station presets, 201 including the scratchpad. Synchronous selectable sideband ("SAM," for synchronous AM), reduces selective-fading distortion, as well as diminishes or eliminates adjacent-channel interference, with world band, mediumwave AM and longwave signals; with earlier software, the lock was easily lost, but from v1.10A lock now holds

Ten-Tec's RX-340 has the best mix of price and performance. DRM ready, too.

acceptably (*see* Con). Built-in half-octave preselector comes standard. Built-in pream-plifier (*see* Con). Adjustable noise blanker, works well in most situations (*see* Con). Stable as Gibraltar. Tunable DSP notch filter with exceptional depth of 58 dB (*see* Con). Passband shift (passband tuning) works exceptionally well (*see* Con). Unusually ef-fective ECSS reception by tuning AM-mode signals as though they were single sideband. Superb reception of "utility" (non-AM mode) stations using a wide variety of modes and including fast filters for delay-critical digital modes. Highly adjustable scanning of both frequency ranges and station presets. Can be fully and effectively computer and remotely controlled (*see* Con). Numerous outputs for data collection and ancillary hardware, including properly configured 455 kHz IF output for instant hookup of Sher-wood SE-3 accessory. Remote control and dial-up data collection. Superb analog signal indicator (*see* Con). Inboard AC power sup-ply senses incoming current and automati-cally adjusts to anything from 90–264V AC, 48–440 Hz—a plus during brownouts or with line voltage or frequency swings. Superior control over fluorescent display dimming (*see* Con). Repair service at the Tennessee factory, $60 an hour, is reasonably priced by professional standards; although nominal repair turnaround is two to five weeks, in practice it is usually closer to two weeks. Comprehensive and well-written operating manual, packed with technical information and schematic diagrams.

Con: DSP microprocessor limitations result in poor dynamic range and fair IP3 at 5 kHz signal spacing. Blocking, phase noise and ultimate rejection pretty good but not of professional caliber. Complex to oper-ate to full advantage. Static crashes sound harsher than on analog receivers. Not all bandwidths available in all modes. Spuri-ous signals noted around 6 MHz segment (49 meters) at night at one test location equipped with superior antennas. When 9–10 dB preamplifier turned on, AGC acts on noise unless IF gain reduced by 10 dB. Notch filter does not work in AM, synchro-nous selectable sideband or ISB modes. Synchronous selectable sideband, although

improved over early production, loses lock easier than some other models; e.g., if listening to one sideband and there is a strong signal impacting the other sideband, lock can be momentarily lost; remediable by Sherwood SE-3 accessory. Passband shift tunes only plus or minus 2 kHz and does not work in ISB or synchronous selectable sideband modes; remediable with Sher-wood SE-3. Audio quality not all it could be; profits from Sherwood SE-3 accessory and an outboard speaker with quality fidelity. Occasional "popping" sound, notably when synchronous selectable sideband or ISB in use—may be from DSP overload. No AGC off except by holding down DUMP button. Noise blanker not effective at some test locations; for example, various other receivers work better at reducing certain noises. Audio power, especially through headphones, could be greater. With stereo headphones, one channel of headphone audio cuts out near full volume; also, at one position at lower volume. On our unit, occasional mi-nor buzz from internal speaker. Keypad not in telephone format; rather, uses computer numeric-keypad layout. Some ergonomic clumsiness when going back and forth between station presets and VFO tuning; too, "Aux Parameter" and "Memory Scan" knobs touchy to adjust. Signal indicator illuminated less than display. Digital "buzz" from fluorescent display emits from front of receiver, although not elsewhere. Standard serial cable does not work for computer control; instead, connector DB-25 pins have to be custom wired. No DC power input. Cabinet/wraparound extra, available only on aftermarket from Hammond.

Verdict: The Ten-Tec RX-340 is the value choice among professional-grade receivers. As it has been engineered to compete head-to-head with the Watkins-Johnson WJ8711A, it's hardly surprising that these two models are almost fraternal twins. However, the '340 is less costly, DRM ready, more readily available and more quickly serviced than the '8711A. When coupled to the Sherwood SE-3 fidelity-enhancing accessory—the new Mk IV version is scheduled for 2008—it is superb for rugged, no-compromise perfor-mance.

New for 2008 is Japan
Radio's NRD-630. No
performance screamer,
but tough and solid.

D. Zantow

New for 2008

✪✪✪✪¼
Japan Radio Co. NRD-630

Price: *NRD-630 receiver:* $8,999.95 by spe-
cial order in the United States. £6,995.95 as
available in the United Kingdom; £5,954.00
plus shipping for export from the United
Kingdom. *Cabinet/wraparound:* Not available (*see* ☞, below). *NDH-95 outboard 300-
channel memory scanning unit:* TBA in the
United States. *NVA-92L external speaker with
matching transformer:* $169.95 in the United
States.

Pro: Exceptionally robust, with superb
construction and parts, including an optical
tuning encoder; potentially long-lasting LED
displays and indicators throughout. Worthy
sensitivity (0.16 µV) and noise floor (–131
dBm) with low noise with selectable 13 dB
of preamplification (0.5 µV and –122 dBm,
respectively, with preamp off). Dual 32-bit
ICs. Excellent, pseudo-octave, front-end
selectivity. Superior dynamic range (95 dB
@ 20 kHz, 75 dB @ 5 kHz) and third-order
intercept points (+14 dBm @ 20 kHz, –16
dBm @ 5 kHz). Excellent blocking (129 dB).
Superb AGC threshold (0.8 µV) with preamplifier on (fair, 3.6 µV, with preamp off).
All bandwidths have superb shape factors
(1:1.2 to 1:1.4). Very good ergonomics,
with superior keys and other controls (*see*
Con). Handy tuning options include knob
with eight tuning steps, keypad, up/down
slewing with four steps, signal-seek scanning, and 300 tunable/scannable presets.
Selectable pulse rate for the tuning knob's
encoder. Weighted tuning knob, among the
best, has speed dimple. Tunes and displays
in ultra-precise 1 Hz increments. Receiver

Incremental Tuning (ΔF), tunes plus or
minus 200 Hz. Helpful four-step display/
panel dimmer. Stunning image rejection
of >110 dB; first IF rejection superb (96
dB). Limited digital hash. Two selectable
AGC decay settings, plus off, usually work
well (*see* Con). Passband tuning, performs
well. Two-step (10/20 dB) attenuator. Two
squelch modes. OCXO provides stability of
<5 Hz. Superb overall distortion in single-
sideband modes (≤0.5%) and in AM mode
(≤1%) above 400 Hz AF (*see* Con). Top-notch
analog signal indicator, also displays audio
level (*see* Con). Noise blanker, adequate for
most. ISB mode. BITE (built-in test equipment) diagnostics. Cool operation, with
quiet inboard switching power supply. Three
balanced isolated audio line outputs (line,
plus two for ISB). Button locks either tuning
knob or all controls. Separate RS-232 and
RS-423A computer ports. Can operate from
24V DC ship's power (*see* Con). Automatic
switchover from AC to/from DC (*see* Con).
Instruction manual includes full schematics
(*see* Con).

Con: Only six fixed DSP bandwidths, of
which three—measuring 2.5, 3 and 6
kHz—are for voice. No provision for adding
bandwidths. Ultimate rejection of 60 dB,
although noise limited, uninspiring. Harsh
audio quality, especially with static. Lacks
sophisticated adjustment of AGC attack,
hang and decay times. AGC attack distortion with some single-sideband signals. No
synchronous selectable sideband, although
ECSS works well. Single-function noise
blanker, no notch filtering, and generally
deficient in DSP adjustment of audio and
related variables. No motherboard or slide-
in daughterboards, unlike past JRC premium

models. No feet. Touchy controls. PBT control lacks center detent. DSP overloading occasionally causes artifacts with strong signals. Overall distortion in AM mode degrades to 10% below 400 Hz AF. Keyboard occasionally intermittent. Poor internal speaker (optional external speaker not tested). Signal indicator lacks illumination and proper markings. Nonstandard N-type antenna connector. Nonstandard AC and DC input jacks. Audio line outputs use DB-25 computer connector. No tension adjustment on tuning knob. Lacks safety certification from UL, CE or CSA, which limits availability in the EU and some other parts of the world. Does not operate from ~12V DC. Skimpy instruction manual lacks information on such relevant subjects as computer control and servicing.

☞ As of late 2007, no cabinet/wraparound was available. However, JRC is considering manufacturing one, and absent that there may be suitable aftermarket options.

☞ Tested firmware/software: 1.4 1.1

Verdict: Superbly constructed and tank-tough, Japan Radio's new NRD-630 is claimed to be a "marine training radio," according to the manufacturer. It boasts the sort of first-rate ergonomics and feel that's long been associated with Japan Radio, even though it lacks the preferred motherboard/daughterboards configuration. It is a pleasure simply to sit down and manipulate its controls, which bespeak quality from another and more fastidious era.

Nearly all characteristics of its radio performance are top-notch, and its built-in scanner is unusually flexible. The optional NDH-95 memory scanning unit, engineered years back for the NRD-93 receiver, gilds the lily.

However, DSP receivers tend to have audio that is relatively abrasive and fatiguing, especially with static. Even though the '630's DSP is powerful and new, its audio is harsher and more tiring, yet. DSP artifacts and intrusive bugs further detract.

The NRD-630 reflects Japan Radio's legendary obsession with hardware quality. But even though the circuit design is relatively advanced, its firmware and software have yet to take full advantage of the hardware's considerable potential.

Evaluation of New Model: As is traditional with Japan Radio products, the NRD-630 is magnificently constructed. Even long-life LEDs are used—no LCDs or fluorescent displays. Nevertheless, unlike with other professional JRC models, there is no motherboard with slide-in daughterboards.

Yet, even with tough parts, including the quiet inboard 100–240V AC switching power supply, the overall package is surprisingly light: under 13 pounds (6 kg). It's easily disassembled, too, and can be operated from 24V DC ship's power.

Great Ergonomics

Ergonomics are equally top-drawer. Direct frequency entry with the keyboard can be in MHz with decimal, or in kHz sans decimal. JRC always gets this right, and the NRD-630 is no exception.

The nicely weighted tuning knob activates a smooth, high-quality optical encoder that would have approached perfection if only it had included an adjustment for mechanical resistance. Eight user-selectable tuning steps—1, 10 and 100 Hz; and 1, 5, 9, 10 and 100 kHz—are supplemented by a user-selectable pulse rate for the encoder, a neat idea. Up/down slewing controls have only four tuning steps—1, 5, 9 and 10 kHz—but that's plenty.

A lock button helps prevent "oops" situations and disables either the tuning knob or all controls, as you prefer. Another nice touch is a dimmer with four well-chosen levels.

For nearly any application the internal 300 tunable/scannable presets are more than adequate. This makes the optional NDH-95, designed decades back for another receiver, almost superfluous. Programming is a snap, and presets are accessed by turning a large knob. Signal-seek or presets scanning works nicely.

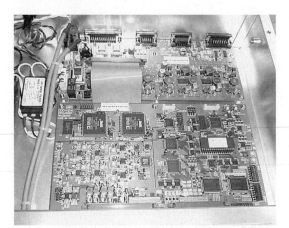

The Japan Radio NRD-630 dispenses with the motherboard/plug-in daughterboards found in prior JRC models. This makes on-the-spot repair more difficult for clients.   D. Zantow

Ergonomics aren't perfect, though. The passband tuning (PBT) control is touchy and lacks a center default dimple.

The '630's power supply is clean too, with no buzzing. No high-pitched display "whine," either, like that which has plagued other JRC professional models over the years. The entire receiver runs cool, too, which helps ensure long component life.

The included 117V AC power cord has only two wires, although there is wing nut to affix a ground wire—unusual, indeed, for the 21st century. Another clue that this receiver is not intended for the public is the absence of any safety certification: UL, CE or CSA. This could make the '630 virtually impossible for consumers to obtain within the EU.

The antenna connector is N-type, which is fine for VHF and UHF, but nonstandard for an HF/shortwave receiver. An adaptor is *de rigeur*.

Performance Essentials Excellent . . .

Sensitivity is excellent when the 13 dB preamplifier is engaged, and the related blocking measurement is also excellent. With some antennas sensitivity may be wanting for DXing if the preamp is off, but

interestingly the AGC threshold performs best—superbly, in fact—if the preamplifier is on. Another reason the preamplifier may be safely left on is the '630's superior dynamic range.

Skirt selectivity is superb, even though ultimate rejection reads only 60 dB—mainly because measurement is limited by noise. Front-end selectivity is excellent, too.

. . . but Opportunities Missed

All that having been said, bottom line is that the '630 fails to capitalize on its DSP design. For example, there are only three voice (nominally 2.7, 3.0 and 6.0 kHz) and three CW (0.3, 0.5 and 1.0 kHz) bandwidths, not the dozens or more which can easily be incorporated in a DSP receiver. No more can be added, either.

Also absent are the customary DSP controls over audio and related functions. Even the noise blanker is either on or off, with nary a diddle for the type of noise, although for common ignition and powerline pulse noises it works pretty well.

Ditto AGC adjustment. Whereas on serious professional receivers the attack, decay and hang times can be minutely tweaked, the '630 is an I Like Ike flashback to when AGC adjustments were fast, slow and off. Nevertheless, the "two speeds fit all" AGC performs well.

There is no tunable or automatic notch filter, a feature useful for amateurs, world band DXers and professional surveillance. Indeed, so vital is this feature that when David Tong first invented the automatic notch filter late in the Cold War, the British government immediately classified it.

The '630's excellent signal meter, although not illuminated, is linear, never pins and also can display audio level. Its calibration for audio is −10 to +5, but for signal strength is only 0–10—no "S" units or dBm.

We once tested a Rockwell-Collins professional receiver that radiated huge amounts of digital hash. According to the manufacturer, they saw no point is spending on shielding when their military clients invariably were using heavily shielded coaxial antenna lead-ins.

Here, the professional '630 acquits itself handsomely. Self-generated radiation is minimal on shortwave and almost as good on mediumwave AM.

During keyboard entries, immediately after pressing Enter the receiver very occasionally would become silent and the signal meter would rise to almost full scale. Key in another frequency, and the problem would disappear.

This points to the potential value of the '630's BITE—built-in test equipment—diagnostics. It's not handy, as the top cover has to be removed and the user's manual is clueless. But once the internal BITE button is pressed, a series of numbers is shown, followed by "good" if all is well.

Another internal button, reset, overcomes a microprocessor freeze. So far, we've never had to use it.

DSP Audio Issues

Two 32-bit Analog Devices ICs are used for DSP. Although these are relatively advanced, there are artifacts resulting from two DSP overloading issues.

First, at night with a good antenna—say, 49 meters—a pulsing-popping sound sometimes mixes with the desired signal. It doesn't pulse in concert with audio peaks, and even appears even on open carriers. Fortunately, the 10 dB attenuator resolves things, albeit at the expense of slightly reduced sensitivity, but it's not what you expect from a nine-kilobuck rig.

Second—only with huge mediumwave AM signals—clicking-popping noises may appear in concert with a signal's modulation peaks. Like the first anomaly, this isn't an issue with 10 dB attenuation . . . or if the preamplifier is off.

Professional receivers are not primarily intended for enjoying music. But they need to flush out useful modulation or data from faint signals, and to a degree this depends on audio quality.

DSP receivers inherently tend to produce audio that is just harsh enough, particularly with weak signals amidst static, that listening becomes unpleasant and ultimately tiring. The '630 is no exception, but with advanced processing it should be providing audio that's better than earlier DSP models.

Here, the '630 tends to disappoint. Yes, recoverable audio is excellent, so it passes muster for stringent professional and DX applications. And overall distortion is superb in single-sideband modes and worthy in the AM mode above 400 Hz. Yet, with weak signals and especially if there's static, DSP harshness makes listening more unpleasant and tiring than it should be.

The '630's pedestrian built-in speaker is not up to the fidelity potential of world band signals, either, so a good outboard speaker is a "must." Synchronous selectable sideband might have helped, but even though it's found on the $160 Sony ICF-7600GR it is not even an option on the '630. And the excellent Sherwood SE-3 synchronous accessory won't work with this receiver, either.

Single-sideband audio quality can be enhanced by carefully decreasing the RF gain control and/or by inserting the attenuator. It helps, too, if the AGC decay is slow.

Superb Hardware, Limited Firmware

The NRD-630 is an extremely well-constructed receiver for land and sea, with solid essential performance. However, Japan Radio, like most other receiver manufacturers, is rooted in a tradition of producing hardware, not firmware or software, and it shows. This is one superb piece of gear, but in today's market it's digital code that makes or breaks.

The PASSPORT *professional-model review team consists of David Walcutt, David Zantow and George Zeller, with Tony Jones, Lawrence Magne and Chuck Rippel. Laboratory measurements by J. Robert Sherwood.*

Receivers for PCs

Little Black Box, Do I Love Thee?

Most prefer to have knobs and keys to flush out signals, but not all. A dedicated core of radio enthusiasts and professionals prefer PC-controlled boxes.

Like a good marriage, mating a receiver with a PC adds new dimensions. For example, signals can be readily monitored from afar, using PC-controlled receivers in the field. Yet, this synergy can be offset by drawbacks, such as hardware complications, software glitches and instability—radio interference, too, from PC monitors, cables and so on. Professional receiving facilities are set up to overcome these challenges, but at home it's tougher.

Official surveillance organizations with deep pockets have traditionally been the chief market for PC-controlled receivers. However, they tend to favor commercial models priced beyond the means of ordinary mortals. So, models in PASSPORT REPORTS sell for under the equivalent of $1,200, although this year we've made an exception (sidebar) for something interesting.

Digital Broadcasts

DRM ready receivers can process Digital Radio Mondiale (DRM) world band and other broadcasts. These require separately purchased DRM software and, eventually, software updates.

Even handier are radios with *DRM reception*, where you can hear DRM with no additional software or hardware—just an everyday PC. A trickle of such portables was sold in 2007 in Europe and Asia, and a car radio may be in the offing, but so far that's been it.

Operating Systems

PASSPORT REPORTS' tests use Windows XP-Pro and XP-Home, which are widely supported by PC receivers. Some may work with Windows Vista, as well, but don't spring for this unless drivers are Certified for Windows Vista. Even then, our experience in 2007 suggests that, unless you love puzzles, Vista is best avoided until the final SP1 release in early 2008. If you're using Mac or Linux, check receiver manufacturers' websites for the growing roster of acceptable operating systems.

For long-term ownership, keep in mind that once a receiver becomes discontinued, it eventually may not work to full advantage—or at all—with new or revised computer operating systems. This can be overcome by retaining a legacy OS; for example, in a separate disk partition or on an old PC.

No matter how carefully a PC-controlled receiver is tested, its performance depends partly on your computer's configuration. To avoid an unwelcome surprise, it's best to purchase on a returnable basis—especially if either the receiver or your PC's OS has been in final release for less than a year.

> Like a good marriage, mating a receiver with a PC adds new dimensions.

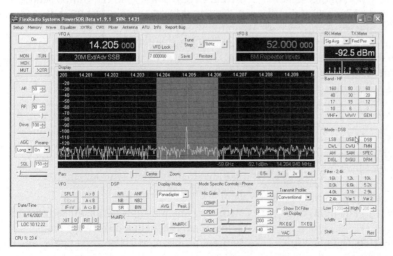

The new FLEX-5000A, scheduled to appear in receiver-only configuration, holds much promise (sidebar, p. 175). At an estimated $2,000 it will cost significantly less than a conventional professional receiver, yet variants of this model have earned praise from surveillance professionals.

Tips for Using this Section

Receivers are listed in order of suitability for listening to difficult-to-hear world band stations; important secondary consideration is given to audio fidelity, ergonomics and perceived build quality. Street selling prices are cited, including British VAT/GST where applicable. Prices vary, so take them as the general guide they are meant to be.

Unless otherwise stated, all PC-controlled models have the following characteristics. *See* Worldly Words for terminology.

- Digital frequency synthesis and display.
- Full coverage of at least the 155–29999 kHz longwave, mediumwave AM and shortwave spectra—including all world band frequencies—but no coverage of the dominant FM broadcast band (87.5–108 MHz). Models designed for sale in certain countries have reduced shortwave tuning ranges.
- A wide variety of helpful tuning features.
- No synchronous selectable sideband.

☞ ECSS: PC-controlled models typically tune to the nearest 10 Hz or even 1 Hz, allowing the operator to use the receiver's single-sideband circuitry to manually phase its BFO (internally generated carrier) with the station's transmitted carrier. Called "ECSS" (exalted-carrier, selectable-sideband) tuning, this can be used in lieu of synchronous selectable sideband. However, in addition to the relative inconvenience of this technique, unlike synchronous selectable sideband, which re-phases continually and perfectly, ECSS is always slightly out of phase. This causes at least some degree of harmonic distortion to music and speech, while tuning to the nearest Hertz can generate slow-sweep fading; for this reason, mis-phasing by two or three Hertz may provide better results.

- Proper demodulation of modes used by non-world-band shortwave signals. These modes include single sideband (LSB/USB) and CW ("Morse code"); also, with suitable ancillary devices, radioteletype (RTTY), frequency shift key (FSK) and radiofax (FAX).
- Meaningful signal-strength indication.

What PASSPORT's Rating Symbols Mean

Star ratings: ✪✪✪✪✪ is best. Stars reflect overall performance and meaningful features, plus to some extent ergonomics and perceived build quality. Price, appearance, country of manufacture and the like are not taken into account. To facilitate comparison, rating standards are similar to those used for tabletop, professional and portable models reviewed elsewhere in this PASSPORT REPORTS. PC receivers as a class have inherent hassles and bonuses; we don't attempt to judge whether this makes them "better" or "worse" than comparable conventional tabletop or professional receivers, so merely the fact they are PC-controlled is not reflected in the star ratings.

Passport's Choice. La crème de la crème. Our test team's personal picks of the litter—models we would buy or have bought for our personal use. Unlike star ratings, these choices are unapologetically subjective.

❷: A relative bargain, with decidedly more performance than the price would suggest. However, none of these receivers is cheap.

DRM Ready

✪✪✪✪¼ ❷ *Passport's Choice*
WiNRADiO G303i, WiNRADiO G303i-PD/P, WiNRADiO G303e, WiNRADiO G303e-PD/P

Price: *G303i:* $449.95 in the United States. CAD$549.97 in Canada. £319.95 in the United Kingdom. €629.00 in Germany. *G303i-PD/P:* $549.95 in the United States. CAD$678.97 in Canada. £369.95 in the United Kingdom. €698.00 in Germany. *G303e (external, not tested):* $549.95 in the United States. £379.95 in the United Kingdom. €659.00 in Germany *G303e-PD/P (external, not tested):* $699.95 in the United States. £439.95 in the United Kingdom. €759.00 in Germany. *DRM software:* $49.95 worldwide from www.winradio.com/home/download-drm.htm.

Pro: Plug and play aids setup. Once receiver is installed, the included software loads without problem; software uses open-source code, which allows for development of third-party software. With optional software, receives digital (DRM) world band and other broadcasts; DRM software distributed by WiNRADiO, so odds are good for successful installation and performance. Superb stability. Tunes and displays in ultra-precise 1 Hz increments. A thousand station presets, which can be clustered into any of 16 groups (see Con—Other). Excellent shape factors (1:1.6, 1:1.8) for 5.0 kHz and 3.2 kHz bandwidths aid selectivity/adjacent-channel rejection; 1.8 kHz bandwidth measures with good shape factor (1:2.3); many additional bandwidths available in the PD/P version, and perform similarly. Excellent shortwave sensitivity (0.21 µV)/noise floor (–130 dBm), good mediumwave AM and longwave sensitivity (0.4 µV)/noise floor (–125 dBm). Potentially excellent audio quality (see below). Excellent dynamic range (90 dB) and third-order intercept point (+5 dBm) at 20 kHz signal spacing (see Con—AGC/AVC). Phase noise excellent (see Con—AGC/AVC). Image rejection excellent. Spurious signals essentially absent. Screen, and operation in general, unusually pleasant and intuitive. Single-sideband performance generally excellent with strong signals (see Con—AGC/AVC). AGC fast, medium, slow and off. Spectrum display shows real-time signal activity, performs commendably and in particular provides signal strength readings to within plus or minus 3 dB. Spectrum scope sweeps between two user-chosen frequencies, displays the output while receiver mutes, then a mouse click can select a desired "peak"; it works quickly and well, and when the step size is small (e.g., 1 kHz) resolution is excellent and quite useful, resolving signals having as little as 350 Hz separation. Large signal indicator highly accurate, as good as we've ever tested; displays both as digitally and as a digitized "analog meter"; reads out in "S" units, dBm or microvolts. Two easy-to-read on-screen clocks for World Time and local time, display seconds numerically, as well as date. Superior, timely and free factory assistance via email, seemingly throughout the week. *G303i-PD/P (professional demodulation):* Continuously adjustable bandwidths from 1Hz to 15 kHz (single sideband/ECSS 1 Hz to 7.5 kHz), with

WiNRADiO's G303 series leads the pack in performance, yet at a relatively affordable price.

bandwidth presets, aid greatly in providing optimum tradeoff between audio fidelity and adjacent-channel interference rejection. AVC settings, limited to "on-off" in standard version, allow for control over decay and attack times. Improved audio quality in some test configurations. Demodulates ISB signals used by a small proportion of utility stations. SINAD and THD distortion indicators. AF squelch for FM mode. Operating software can be updated online, albeit with minor complication under limited circumstances.

Pro/Con—Sound: Outstanding freedom from distortion aids in providing good audio quality with appropriate sound cards/chips and speakers; sound quality and level can run the gamut from excellent to awful, depending on the PC's sound card or chipset, which needs to be full duplex. Sound Blaster 16 cards are recommended by manufacturer, but not all models work. During our tests the $130 Sound Blaster Audigy 2 performed with considerable distortion—it doesn't offer full duplex operation for the line input—whereas the $43 Sound Blaster PCI 512 worked splendidly. (ISA sound cards perform terribly; quite sensibly, these are not recommended by the manufacturer.) All input settings for the audio card need to be carefully set to match the settings within the receiver's software. If wrong, there may be no audio or it may be grossly distorted. Indeed, a sound card isn't always necessary, as some sound chipsets commonly found within PCs produce excellent audio with the G303i. Another reason the chipset may be preferable is that Sound Blaster manuals recommend that if there is an audio chipset on the motherboard, it first be disabled in the BIOS and all related software uninstalled—potentially a Maalox Moment. However, even with a suitable board or chipset installed, the user must carefully set the AGC and AVC (automatic volume control, termed "Audio AGC" on the G303i) for distortion-free audio. Powerful amplified speakers provide room-filling sound and allow the AVC to be kept off, thus reducing band noise that can be intrusive when it is on during weak-signal reception.

Con—AGC/AVC: Weak-signal reception can be compromised by the AGC, which "sees" 10–15 kHz of spectrum within the IF upon which to act. So, if an adjacent world band channel signal is 20 dB or more stronger than a desired weak signal, the AGC's action tends to cause the adjacent signal to mask the desired signal. Inadequate gain with the AVC ("Audio AGC") off, but the aggressive AVC adds listening strain with single-sideband signals, as it tends to increase band noise between words or other modulation peaks. Powerful outboard amplified speakers help reduce the need for the additional audio gain brought about by the AVC and thus are desirable, but be prepared for jumps in volume when you tune to strong stations. Reception sometimes further improves if the AGC is switched off and IF gain is manually decreased, but the operator then has to "ride" the volume control to smooth out major fluctuations. Manual ECSS tuning frequently helps, too. During moments of transient overload, the AVC can contribute to the creation of leading-edge "pops" with powerful signals (slightly more noticeable in the PD/P version). Single-sideband performance, particularly within crowded amateur bands, can be even more audibly compromised by the afore-mentioned out-of-passband AGC action. Dynamic range/IP3 at 5 kHz signal spacing couldn't be measured with AGC on, as test signals trigger the AGC and keep the receiver from going into overload; measurement with the AGC off resulted in exceptionally poor numbers (45 db/–62 dBm). Phase noise poor when measured close-in (5 kHz signal spacing) for the same reason.

Con—Other: No synchronous selectable sideband, and double-sideband "AMS" mode loses lock easily. First IF rejection only fair. Front-end selectivity, although adequate for most uses, could be better. Station presets ("memory channels") store only frequency and mode, not bandwidth, AGC or attenuation settings. No passband offset or tunable notch filter. Emits a "pop-screech" sound when first brought up or when switching from standard to professional demodulator. Uses only SMA antenna connection, typically found on handheld devices rather than tabletop receivers; an SMA-to-BNC adapter is included, but for the many shortwave antennas with neither type of plug a second adaptor or changed plug is needed. On our sample, country of manufacture not found on receiver, box or enclosed printed matter; however, website indicates manufacturing facility is in Melbourne, Australia. Erratum sheet suggests that a discone antenna be used; this is fine for reception above roughly 25 MHz; however, in our tests we confirmed that conventional shortwave antennas provide much broader frequency coverage with the G303i, just as they do with other shortwave receivers.

☞ Minimum of 1 GHz Pentium recommended by manufacturer, although in the process of checking this out we obtained acceptable results using vintage 400 MHz and 500 MHz Pentium II processors with Windows 2000. However, if your PC is multitasking, then 2 GHz or more helps keep the PC from bogging down. Primary testing was done using various desktop Pentium IV PCs at 1.5–2.4 GHz, 256–512 MHz RAM and Windows 2000, XP-Home and XP-Pro operating systems. WiNRADiO operating software used during tests were v1.07, v1.14, v1.25 and v1.26.

Verdict: The G303 is the best PC receiver tested, especially in the preferred Professional Demodulator version. It can also be configured for reception of DRM digital broadcast signals and is a pleasure to operate.

The G303 provides laboratory-quality spectrum displays and signal-strength indication. These spectrum-data functions are top drawer, regardless of price or type of receiver, and that's just the beginning of things done well. The few significant warts: AGC/AVC behavior, possible audio hassles during installation, and the absence of synchronous selectable sideband.

Nevertheless, with lower pricing for 2008, WiNRADiO's G303 is an attractive value. Although its costlier G313 sibling has certain advantages, for most the G303 is at least its equal for world band reception.

The WiNRADiO G313 series performs nicely, but costs twice as much as the sibling G303 series that's even better.

DRM Ready

✪✪✪✪
WiNRADiO G313i, WiNRADiO G313e

Price: *G313i:* $949.95 in the United States and worldwide. CAD$1,299.00 in Canada. £619.95 in the United Kingdom. €1,049 in Germany. *G313e (external, not tested):* $1,149.95 in the United States and worldwide. CAD$1,599.00 in Canada. £749.95 in the United Kingdom. €1,198.00 in Germany. *DRM software:* $49.95 worldwide from www.winradio.com/home/download-drm.htm. *Mini-Circuits BLP-30 BNC-to-BNC 30 MHz low-pass filter:* $32.95 in the United States.

Pro: Unlimited bandwidths—DSP bandwidths continuously variable in one Hertz increments from 1 Hz through 15 kHz (LSB/USB through 7.5 kHz). Bandwidth "presets" enhance ergonomics. Spectrum display either wideband (*see* Con) or narrowband; narrow allows for first-rate test and measurement of audio-frequency response of AM or single-sideband mode signals, spectra of data transmissions, frequency accuracy, amplitude modulation depth, frequency deviation, THD (total harmonic distortion) and SINAD (signal plus noise plus distortion to noise plus distortion ratio). Unlimited station presets—one thousand per file, each of which can be clustered into any of 16 groups; number of files limited only by hard disk capacity, so virtually no limit to presets. Station presets store frequency, IF shift, bandwidth and mode (*see* Con). Four VFOs. Large signal indicator as linear as any other tested to date. Signal indicator displays both digitally and as a

digitized "analog meter." Signal indicator reads out in "S" units, dBm or microvolts. Manufacturer's website, unusually helpful, includes downloadable calibration utility for signal indicator. Open source code allows for third-party development of software. Includes DSP electronics for audio, so sound card acts only as an optional audio amplifier (*see* Con) (*cf.* WiNRADiO G303), or 313's audio output can feed outboard audio system. Superb level of overall distortion (*see* Con: DSP audio). Notch filter, tunable 0–7500 Hz, has good (30 dB) rejection (*see* Con). Synchronous double sideband to help overcome selective fading distortion and enhance fidelity during twilight and darkness (mixed skywave/groundwave) reception of fringe mediumwave AM stations (*see* Con). Integrated audio recorder, a convenience for those without ReplayRadio or similar. Integrated IF recorder stores spectrum slice for subsequent analysis of received signals, and to "re-receive" the same swath of signals over and again experimenting with, for example, IF bandwidth, notch filter and noise blanker settings (*see* Con). Plug and play receiver software installed with no problems with XP Pro and XP Home. Does not overuse computer resources even while multitasking. Excellent shape factors at wider voice bandwidths (*see* Con). Excellent ultimate rejection. Excellent image rejection. Excellent phase noise as measured in lab (*see* Con). Spurious signals essentially nil. Screen, and operation in general, unusually pleasant and intuitive (*see* Con). Automatic frequency control (AFC) with FM and AM mode signals. With optional software, receives digital (DRM) world band and other broadcasts; DRM software distributed by WiNRADiO, so odds are good for successful installation and performance. Demodulates ISB signals used by some utility stations. Single-step (18 dB) attenuator. Receiver incremental tuning (RIT) aids with transceiving. Two easy-to-read clocks displayed on screen for World Time; also, second clock for local time (*see* Con); both show seconds numerically, as well as day and date. FM mode squelch. FM broadcasts receivable with extra-cost option. Operating software can be updated online. Excellent owner's manual. Superior, timely and free factory assistance via email, seemingly throughout the week.

Con: DSP audio causes static crashes and local noise to sound unusually harsh, potentially increasing listening fatigue. Synchronous detector lacks meaningful selectable sideband, IF shift notwithstanding. Poor AGC threshold contributes to reduced audibility of weak signals; improved by enabling switchable AVC at a low level, although this also increases pumping with single-sideband signals. AGC gain determined by all signals within the 15 kHz first IF filter, so background noise and audio can change in concert with on/off (e.g., CW) activity from adjacent carriers within the 15 kHz filter window; this can be an issue with utility and ham monitoring, but only rarely disturbs world band signals. Mediocre front-end selectivity, largely remediable by adding a Mini-Circuits BLP-30 or other outboard ~30 MHz low-pass filter. Poor close-in (5 kHz signal spacing) dynamic range/IP3. Bandwidth shape factors slip from excellent at wider bandwidths (e.g., 6 kHz) to fair at narrower voice bandwidths (e.g., 1.9 kHz). Phase noise or a kind of local oscillator noise keeps CW bandwidths (e.g., 0.5 kHz) from being measurable at –60 dB; consequently, CW shape factors also not measurable. Significant audible distortion if computer-screen volume turned up high; remediable if level not adjusted beyond "6"; sound card or outboard audio amplifier can provide additional volume if needed. Cyclical background sound, which doesn't vary

with carrier-BFO phasing, in manual ECSS mode. Mixed ergonomics—some functions a pleasure, others not. Tuning-steps in 5 kHz increments (world band channel spacing) impractical with mouse scroll wheel, as three keys have to be held down simultaneously; instead, up/down screen slew arrows can be used. Some screen icons small for typical PC displays/video cards. Real-time (always active) spectrum analyzer coverage width limited to 20 kHz (+/− 10 kHz), a pity given the exceptional resolution and analytical capabilities. IF recorder bandwidth also limited to 20 kHz. Tunable notch filter includes adjustable notch breadth, a creative but marginal option that complicates notch use. Notch filter takes unusually long to adjust properly using keypad, and small indicators make it prone to operating errors with GUI. First IF rejection only fair. Wideband spectrum analyzer not in real time, has disappointing resolution and thus of minor utility. SMA antenna connection; SMA-to-BNC adapter included, but for the many shortwave antennas with neither type of plug a second adaptor or changed plug is needed. Station presets don't store AGC or attenuator values. Noise blanker only marginally effective. Local-time (secondary) clock displays only in 24-hour format—no AM/PM.

☞ Also available with 9 kHz–180 MHz coverage in lieu of regular 9 kHz–30 MHz.

Verdict: With audio processing independent of the host PC—and heaps of additional goodies—the Australian WiNRADiO G313 is in many ways a solid improvement over the lower-cost WiNRADiO G303.

Alas, there's a hefty price to be paid for not using the PC sound card for audio processing: DSP harshness that aggravates static crashes and more. This limits its appeal, especially for tropical band and mediumwave AM DXing, but how much depends on your hearing and listening preferences.

The G313 is tempting for DRM, and it has excellent synchronous detection for alleviating selective fading distortion—a serious issue with dusk-to-dawn fringe analog mediumwave AM reception. But its selectable sideband capability is effectively nonexistent, and the "IF shift" doesn't help. This is a huge drawback in a kilobuck receiver, given that effective synchronous selectable sideband can be found on a $150 portable.

So, the G313's price/performance ratio is uninspiring for listening to broadcasts or monitoring utility/ham signals. But it excels with signal analysis and storage, thanks to a high-resolution spectrum analyzer with excellent test, measurement and recording capabilities. Add to that a highly linear and

adjustable signal indicator, and you can see why this model is spot-on for certain professional/surveillance applications. This also explains the kilobuck price, dirt cheap by professional standards.

Better for most world band listeners is the sibling WiNRADiO G303. How it sounds is partly a function of the host PC's sound card, but its audio is usually less tiring than that of the G313—particularly with static.

And it costs less than half as much.

NUMBERS: TOP PC RECEIVERS		
	WiNRADiO G303i (G313i)	Ten-Tec RX-320D
Sensitivity, World Band	0.21 μV 🅴 (0.3 μV 🅴)	0.31 to 0.7 μV 🅴-🅵(1)
Noise Floor, World Band	–130 dBm 🅴(–126 dBm 🅶)	–126 to –119 dBm 🅶-🅵(2)
Blocking	120 dB 🅶(116 dB 🅶)	>146 dB 🆂
Shape Factors, voice BWs	1:1.6 🅴-1:2.4 🅶 (1:1.7 🅴-1:2.4 🅶)	n/a(3)
Ultimate Rejection	70 dB 🅶(75 dB 🅴)	60 dB 🅶
Front-End Selectivity	🅶(🅵)	🅵
Image Rejection	85 dB 🅴(75 dB 🅴)	60 dB 🅶
First IF Rejection	52 dB 🅵(51 dB 🅵)	60 dB 🅶
Dynamic Range/IP3 (5 kHz)	45 dB 🅿/–62 dBm 🅿 (43 dB, 🅿/–62 dBm 🅿)	n/a(3)
Dynamic Range/IP3 (20 kHz)	90 dB 🅴/+5 dBm 🅴 (85 dB 🅶/+2 dBm 🅴)	n/a(3)
Phase Noise	124 dBc 🅴(4) (120 dBc 🅴)	106 dBc 🅵
AGC Threshold	2.7 to 8.0 μV 🅶-🅿(18 μV 🅿(5))	4.0 μV 🅵
Overall Distortion, voice	<1.0% 🆂(<1.0% 🆂(6))	<1% 🆂
Stability	5 Hz, 🆂(10 Hz 🅴)	80 Hz, 🅶
Notch filter depth	n/a (30 dB 🅶)	n/a

IBS Lab Ratings: 🆂 Superb   🅴 Excellent   🅶 Good   🅵 Fair   🅿 Poor

(1) Excellent 60 meters and up.

(2) Good 60 meters and up.

(3) Could not be measured accurately because of synthesizer noise and spurious signals, but appears to be very good.

(4) Worse at close-in measurement.

(5) 0.3 μV 🅶 with AVC enabled at –3 dB.

(6) See writeup, Con: DSP audio.

For sheer value among PC receivers, nothing quite equals the Ten-Tec RX-320D. Ready to receive Digital Radio Mondiale broadcasts, too.

DRM Ready

❶❶❶⅛ ⓒ *Passport's Choice*

Ten-Tec RX-320D

Price: *RX-320D:* $359.00 plus shipping worldwide. *DRM software:* $49.95 worldwide from www.winradio.com/home/download-drm.htm. *Third-party control software:* Varies from free to $99 worldwide.

Pro: The "D" version's 12 kHz IF output allows the receiver to receive digital (DRM) world band and other broadcasts by using DRM software purchased separately. Superior dynamic range. Apparently superb bandwidth shape factors (*see* Con). In addition to the supplied factory control software, third-party software is available, often for free, and may improve operation. Up to 34 bandwidths with third-party software. Tunes in extremely precise 1 Hz increments (10 Hz with tested factory software); displays to the nearest Hertz, and frequency readout is easily user-aligned. Large, easy-to-read digital frequency display and faux-analog frequency bar. For PCs with sound cards, outstanding freedom from distortion aids in providing good audio quality with most but not all cards and speakers. Fairly good audio, although with limited treble, avail-able via line output jack and speaker jack to feed PCs and/or an external speaker. Superb blocking performance helps maintain consistently good world band sensitivity. Passband offset (*see* Con). Spectrum display with wide variety of useful sweep widths (*see* Con). World Time on-screen clock (*see* Con). Adjustable AGC decay. Thousands of station presets, with first-rate memory configuration, access and sorting—including by station name and frequency. Only PC-controlled model tested which returns to last tuned frequency when PC turned off. Operating software can be updated online. Superior owner's manual. Generally superior factory help and repair support.

Con: No synchronous selectable sideband, although third-party software nominally automates retuning of drifty AM-mode signals received as ECSS. Some characteristic DSP roughness in the audio under certain reception conditions. Synthesizer phase noise measures only fair; among the consequences are that bandwidth shape factors cannot be measured exactly. Some tuning ergonomics only fair as compared with certain standalone receivers. No tunable notch filter. Passband offset doesn't function in AM mode. Signal indicator, calibrated 0–80, too sensitive, reading 20 with no antenna connected and 30 with only band noise being received. Mediocre front-end selectivity can allow powerful mediumwave AM stations to "ghost" into the shortwave spectrum, thus degrading reception of world band stations. Uses AC adaptor instead of built-in power supply. Spectrum display does not function with some third-party software and is only a so-so performer. Mediumwave AM reception below 1 MHz suffers from reduced sensitivity, and longwave sensitivity is atrocious. No internal speaker on outboard receiver module. World Time clock tied into computer's clock, which may not be accurate without periodic adjustment. Almost no retail sources outside the United States.

Verdict: The American-made Ten-Tec RX-320D is value priced and becomes even more attractive with aftermarket software. It performs very nicely and is well supported by the manufacturer.

SOON-TO-BE RECEIVER

With so much buzz surrounding the new PC-controlled Flex-5000A transceiver, we were pleased to find that the manufacturer plans to offer it as a receiver.

This receiver wasn't available in late 2007, but our tests found the '5000A transceiver to have exceptional overall reception performance. Commendable, too, is the manufacturer's eagerness to make improvements on the fly.

New for 2008   DRM Ready
✪✪✪✪¾
FLEX-5000A

Price: *FLEX-5000A HF Transceiver*: $2,799.00 in the United States. £1,695.00 in the United Kingdom. *Griffin PowerMate VFO Control Knob (not tested)*: $45.00 in the United States. £34.95 in the United Kingdom. *Astron RS-10A regulated power supply—105–125V AC in, 7.5 amp 13.8V DC out*: $69.99 in the United States.

Pro: DSP voice bandwidths have stellar shape factors of under 1:1.1; bandwidths selected by presets or two user-defined slider settings. Displays and tunes in ultra-precise 1 Hz increments. Superb third-order intercept points (+29 dBm at 5 kHz and 20 kHz separations). Superb-to-excellent dynamic range (96 dB at 5 kHz and 20 kHz separations) and ultimate rejection (86–98 dB). Excellent synchronous selectable/double sideband (*see* Con) with first-rate passband tuning (PBT). Includes DSP electronics for audio, so sound card acts only as optional audio amplifier. Generally top-grade audio (*see* Con), with overall distortion under 0.3 percent on all audio frequencies and in all modes. Three-band and ten-band graphic equalizer provide superior audio shaping/tone control (*see* Con). Excellent sensitivity (0.3 microvolts) and good noise floor (–127 dBm) with 16 dB preamplifier (*see* Con). Superb first IF/image rejection of 90 dB; before long, will be even better, states manufacturer. Front-end selectivity excellent-to-good above 0.5 MHz (*see* Con). Excellent phase noise (123 dBc). Good blocking (123 dB). AGC threshold excellent (0.5 microvolts) with preamplifier on, good (2.0 microvolts) when off. Rock-solid stability (1 Hz). Generally commendable screen ergonomics. AGC controlled by signals in the final DSP bandwidth; five AGC settings—one with user-adjustable attack, hang and decay times—plus off ("fixd"). Spectrum scope/Panadapter with up to 150 kHz peek at radio spectrum with above-average accuracy and resolution. Four antenna inputs (three SO239, one BNC) selectable from computer screen. DRM ready (*see* Con). Handy mute button. Two VFOs.

Two-zone clock, with discrete display, in 24-hour World Time format with date (*see* Con) and numeric seconds. Dual receive (second signal up to 150 kHz from fundamental). Worthy DSP noise reduction and automatic notch filtering with good (35 dB) depth. Presets limited only by available hard-disk space. Line audio output with auto level. Accurate, if small, signal indicator shows average peak level. Tuning by mouse, mouse wheel or keyboard; also, by standalone tabletop tuning knob accessory (*see* Con). Not difficult to set up. Manufacturer, aided by open-source code, appears to be unusually oriented to ongoing improvements. Thirty-day money-back guarantee. Two-year warranty.

The FLEX-5000A may look like a microwave oven, but don't be fooled. Inside is circuitry that outclasses most receivers—conventional or otherwise.

Con: Transceiver, not a dedicated receiver; using its 100 Watt transmitter requires government license. No internal speaker or audio amplifier; requires amplified speakers or headphones. Receive (only) current consumption 1.2–1.4 amps; power supply not included or even factory option, and H-P 1.5 amp supply inadequate; Astron RS-7A, which runs hot or, better, RS-10A or equivalent recommended. Requires fast computer with IEEE 1394A (FireWire) port. Keypad entry only in MHz, including decimal. Small time lag between tuning and action. Dual DSP noise blankers only okay. No auto-off for synchronous selectable/double sideband while tuning, causes squeal. Spectrum scope and dual-receive range varies with sample rate setting. No attenuator. Modicum of DSP audio harshness. Audio graphic equalizer preamp can add distortion. RF preamplifier does not operate below 2 MHz. No up/down frequency slewing. Band presets, for amateur bands, not optimum for world band, commercial, military or surveillance applications. Sensitivity only fair without preamplifier. Mediumwave AM signals ghost into longwave spectrum. Couldn't get DRM to function. Clock's second (local) time display only in 24-hour format. Owner's manual not available, at least as of presstime.

☞ Were the promised receiver to perform like the tested transceiver—but with band presets less specific to amateur applications, better front-end selectivity below 0.5 MHz and firmware/software improved in certain respects—it could receive five stars and might be designated as Passport's Choice. Transmitter not tested.

☞ Tested Software: PowerSDR v1.10.1 (single-sideband distortion), then v1.10.2 (distortion fixed). Firmware: v0.1.0.2. Test unit from very early production, so look for software, firmware and possibly even hardware enhancements in the months to come.

Verdict: The FLEX-5000A is a treat to the ears, with performance that's hard to beat. As a straight receiver, especially if under two kilobucks, the '5000A should become a value alternative to traditional professional receivers.

Evaluation of New Model: The FLEX-5000A amateur transceiver covers from 9 kHz to 65 MHz, with tuning resolution and steps down to 1 Hz.

Everything is operated from a PC, and on-screen ergonomics are excellent. Although there's slight tuning lag, frequencies are chosen by mouse pointer or computer keyboard, but only in MHz format with decimal. The mouse wheel acts as a *defacto* tuning knob, or better yet there's the optional Griffin PowerMate VFO Control Knob. Presets are limited only by available hard drive space.

The '5000A, which draws 1.2–1.4 amps, requires an external 13.8V DC power supply, not included. An H-P 1.5 amp power supply proved inadequate, but for North America a five-amp Astron RS-7A works fine, although it can get hot; the 7.5 amp RS-10A and 15 amp RS-20A run cooler. Transmitting requires more current, but thankfully there is a software setting to disable the transmitter.

Setup

The '5000A isn't for yesteryear's Dusty O'Dell. Instead, it requires a PC with high-speed single or dual core processing and a FireWire port (FireWire cable is included).

Uninstall any FireWire driver currently on your PC, then download the current PowerSDR program, the latest FireWire driver and owner's manual at flex-radio.com. Next, if your PC doesn't already have it, download Microsoft.NET framework—the elder v1.1.4322 is required, for whatever reason—from Microsoft.com. Install Flex-5000_driver, then reboot. Turn on the '5000A and, using "install the software automatically," allow the new hardware wizard to do its thing.

Next, configure the driver, hardware sampling rate, buffer size (try 2048 first) and operating mode, then install and configure the PowerSDR program. If you're not a licensed ham, disable the transmitter.

No audio amplifier is built-in, so amplified speakers and/or headphones are needed for direct audio. Otherwise, audio can be channeled into the PC's sound card using the VAC button.

Great Sync, Worthy Audio

Synchronous selectable/double sideband performs to a fare-thee-well, locking even on faint signals and whacking selective fading distortion. Sideband selection is by LSB/USB switching or, better, by cruising through the full signal with the superb passband tuning (PBT) control. Alas, during bandscanning the sync doesn't turn off automatically; if you don't turn it off manually, it squeals like a gored javelina.

Tone control is effective, using either a three-band or ten-band graphic equalizer. The end result is pleasant listening, along with superior recoverable audio. Yet, there is minor DSP audio harshness, along with distortion if the audio preamp is used.

Stellar Selectivity, Solid Performance

Selectivity choices are flexible and shape factors are astonishing—deep ultimate rejection, too. Selectivity just doesn't get any better than this except in textbooks.

With the preamplifier on, sensitivity and AGC threshold are excellent, while dynamic range remains robust. Front-end selectivity is superior, overall, except that mediumwave AM signals tend to ghost into the longwave spectrum. Some birdies, but the manufacturer is working on a "spur buster"—different from the existing Spur Reduction that has only minor impact on spurs, but reduces CPU load and thus tuning lag.

The AGC performs unusually well, as it is controlled by signals in the final DSP bandwidth. There are six factory AGC settings, one with user-adjustable attack, hang and decay times.

The scope has excellent resolution, with user-adjustable frequency slice—the largest, 192,000, displays up to 155 kHz. It is accurate and provides a whistle-clean look at signal quality, although it sweeps less spectrum than some other models.

The built-in audio recorder automatically controls level, but there's no timer. Its resulting .wav file format is peculiar and can only be played back within the FLEX-5000A program.

The noise reduction feature is relatively effective, although the two noise blankers are only about average. The automatic notch filter (ANF) works best with single-sideband and CW reception, but suffices with AM and SAM (synchronous) modes. The signal indicator is accurate and can show peak "average" readings.

DRM? Even with the latest Dream software we couldn't get it to decode, so no signals were audible. This should be easy to fix.

The FLEX-5000A can be equipped with a genuine tuning knob.

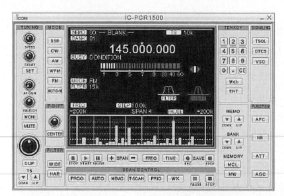

Icom's IC-PCR1500 combines reasonable price with broadband frequency coverage. This makes it attractive to world band listeners who also do VHF+ scanning or *vice versa*.

Icom IC-PCR2500, Icom IC-R2500

The $730 (£475) Icom IC-PCR2500 and $900 (£530) Icom IC-R2500 (both not tested) use the same platform as the '1500 series evaluated below. However, they add diversity reception to help reduce fading effects (accomplished with two widely spaced antennas—or, outside the shortwave spectrum, one horizontally and one vertically polarized). Synchronous selectable sideband also reduces the effects of AM-mode fading, but is unavailable on the '2500.

Additional extras are multi-channel monitoring/display, P25 (public service digital) board, D-Star (but not Icom's digital audio standard for PMR446) and other features oriented to VHF/UHF/SHF scanning.

✪✪✪⅝
Icom IC-PCR1500, Icom IC-R1500

Price: *IC-PCR1500 "black box" receiver:* $499.95 in the United States. CAD$499.00 in Canada. £369.95 in the United Kingdom. €529.00 in Germany. *IC-R1500 with control head and "black box" receiver:* $599.95 in the United States. CAD$599.00 in Canada. £419.95 in the United Kingdom. €625.00 in Germany. *UT-106 DSP unit:* $139.95 in the United States. CAD$250.00 in Canada. £79.95 in the United Kingdom. €99.00 in Germany. *OPC-1156 11½-foot/3.5-meter*

controller extension cable: $21.95 in the United States. CAD$25.00 in Canada. £14.95 in the United Kingdom. €16.95 in Germany. *OPC-441 16½-foot/five meter speaker extension cable:* $24.95 in the United States. £14.95 in the United Kingdom. €26.95 in Germany. *CP-12L 12V DC cigarette lighter power cable:* $27.95 in the United States. CAD$60.00 in Canada. £19.95 in the United Kingdom. €23.95 in Germany. *OPC-254L 12V DC fused power cord:* $12.95 in the United States. CAD$25.00 in Canada. £9.95 in the United Kingdom. €9.20 in Germany. *Aftermarket RF Systems DPX-30 antenna combiner (to 2000 MHz) for separate shortwave and scanner antennas:* $109.95 in the United States. €76.20 in Germany. *Aftermarket Diamond CX-210N two-position antenna switch (to 3000 MHz):* $69.95 in the United States. £56.95 in the United Kingdom. €69.95 in Germany. *Aftermarket Daiwa CS-201 GII two-position antenna switch (to 1300 MHz):* $39.95 in the United States. *Aftermarket Alpha Delta 4B/N four-position antenna switch (to 1300 MHz):* $94.95 in the United States.

Pro: Wideband frequency coverage in three versions: *(blocked U.S. version)* 0.01–810, 851–867, 896–1811, 1852–1868, 1897–2305.9, 2357–2812, 2853–2869, 2898–3109.8, 3136–3154.8, 3181–3300 MHz; *(blocked French version)* 0.01–30, 50.2–51.2, 87.5–108, 144–146, 430–440 and 1240–1300 MHz; *(unblocked version)* 0.01–3300 MHz; with all versions, specifications not guaranteed 0.01–0.5 and 3000–3300 MHz; BFO operation (single sideband and CW) up to 1300 MHz; includes FM broadcast reception. Fully 2600 station presets clustered into 26 pages of 100 channels each. Tunes and displays in unusually precise 1 Hz increments. Vast number of user-selectable tuning steps. Useful manual ECSS operation (*see* Con) aided by Gibraltar-class stability. Very good shortwave sensitivity. Selectable fast/slow AGC decay (*see* Con). Generally good IF shift (*see* Con). Operating software and firmware work well and can be updated online at www.icom.co.jp/world/download/index.htm. Plenty of IF gain and AGC acts in the final bandwidth, which help provide single-sideband performance that's significantly above average among PC-controlled models (*see* Con). Generally pleasant audio quality (*see* Con). Audio available not only through the set's internal speaker (*see* Con) or an external speaker, but also via USB through the PC's audio system (*see* Con). Can record audio in .wav format onto hard drive (*see* Con). One-step (20 dB) attenuator (*see* Con). Optional UT-106 AF-DSP unit (not tested). *IC-PCR1500 and IC-R1500 via PC:* Three different PC user screens. Excellent 'scope for up to a 1 MHz peek at radio spectrum in real time, 1–10 MHz in non-real time (see *Con*). Keypad tuning. Up to 22 alphanumeric tags and frequencies for presets display simultaneously. *IC-R1500:* Generally excellent wired control head so '1500 can also be used as a standalone tabletop receiver or, to a degree with the optional CP-12L power cord, a mobile receiver (*see* Con), as well as a PC-controlled model *à la* the IC-PCR1500.

Con: Few bandwidth choices. Poor dynamic range at 5 and 20 kHz separation points, although this improves considerably at wider spacing. No RF or IF gain control to help alleviate overloading, and attenuator has only one step. No synchronous selectable sideband; manual ECSS alternative sounds slightly out of phase even with 1 Hz tuning step. With one PC configuration, but not others, some distortion encountered with single-sideband signals through 3 kHz bandwidth. Slight hiss. Audio only fair through black box's built-in speaker. Audio a bit weak through computer's USB port. No AGC off. IF shift operates only in single-sideband and CW modes. Mediumwave sensitivity only fair. Poor longwave sensitivity. Marginal noise blanker. No on/off multi-event timing for audio recording. Telescopic antenna and cable virtually useless on shortwave and not much better elsewhere within tuned frequency ranges. Software installation not always easy. No schematic or block diagrams. *IC-R1500:* Control head provides most, but not all, operating functions available from PC control; for example, there's no keypad or spectrum 'scope, and presets simultaneously display only one frequency or alphanumeric tag. Control head has no stand or mounting bracket for desktop or mobile use, nor can it be attached to the body of the "black box."

> The primary market for PC receivers remains intelligence organizations.

Shutterstock/Pchemyan Georgiy

Verdict: Icom's '1500 series is a worthy step ahead of the discontinued IC-PCR1000. For starters, audio can be fed into a computer through its USB port and even recorded to hard disk. The '1500 series also uses an internal speaker or can feed an external speaker, and there's less audio hiss.

Frequency coverage is vast, and performance is generally worthy by broadband standards. Even though the '1500 series suffers from poor dynamic range at 5 and 20 kHz separation points, this improves dramatically at wider separation. However, a paucity of bandwidth choices and the lack of synchronous selectable sideband are distinct drawbacks. The excellent recording facility would have profited from multi-event timing, as well.

Icom's '1500 series receivers are especially attractive for broadband use with PCs to enhance performance and operation. In keeping with Icom tradition, they are also dramatically better than most other PC models for single-sideband reception of utility and amateur signals. Ergonomics are top-drawer, too, reflecting user-friendly software that's about as good as it gets. Between these pluses and pleasant audio quality, the '1500 lends itself to being enjoyed for hours on end.

DRM Reception

✪✪✪½
ELAD FDM77

Price: *FDM77, including DRM software:* $599.99 in the United States. £399.95 in the United Kingdom. €655.00 in Germany.

Pro: Receives world band and other DRM transmissions immediately after connection to a PC. Commendable ergonomics (*see* Con), with superior graphic interface and large icons. Handy tuning features include numeric selection directly above each digit, using keyboard arrows; MHz or kHz keypad entry, using PC keyboard or on-screen virtual keypad; up/down slewing, using on-screen or keyboard arrows; knob tuning, using mouse wheel or on-screen virtual tuning knob; 200 station presets per page, with as

many page files as PC's hard disk can hold; two VFOs; and auto bandscanning with real-time graphic spectrum display (*see* Con). 1 Hz frequency resolution (*see* Con) and tuning step. Large, accurate signal indicator using screen graphics that make it look like an analog "S" meter. Nineteen DSP bandwidths with shape factors that improve from good (1:2.1) to superb (1:1.4) as bandwidth narrows. Two variable notch filters with superb (50 dB) heterodyne (whistle) rejection. IF shift to aid in adjacent-channel interference rejection. Very good audio that includes a six-band graphic equalizer that can be bypassed by "flat" selection. Good sensitivity (0.5 µV) and noise floor (–125 dBm) with preamplifier on (*see* Con). Good image rejection (74 dB) and paucity of other spurious signals. AGC threshold good (3 µV) with preamplifier on (*see* Con). Overall distortion excellent-to-superb (2.2% to 0.1%), especially in single-sideband mode. Front-end selectivity good, thanks to octave filtering. Superb first IF rejection (93 dB). Drift under 100 Hz from near-cold start. Graphically displays 20 kHz of radio-spectrum, audio spectrum and oscilloscope. Selectable 10 dB preamp. Two antenna connectors: SO-239 for significant antennas; and BNC with an additional 20 dB of preamplification for use with whip and other short antennas. 15 dB attenuator. WAV recorder, with single-event timer, stores onto hard drive. World Time and local clocks (*see* Con). Operating software and firmware can be updated online from manufacturer's sometimes-poky server. Convenient mute button.

Con: No synchronous selectable sideband. Ergonomics, although usually superior, are compromised because bandwidth selection requires unnecessary screen shifting and the main screen doesn't show which bandwidth is in use; also, installation sometimes unforgiving (e.g., high-pitched audio can mix with received output if directions on CD and in owner's manual not followed precisely). Graphic equalizer can degrade audio quality in certain situations, requiring that the flat setting be substituted. AGC controlled by 455 kHz intermediate bandwidth of 7.5 kHz that's usually much wider than the PC sound card's DSP bandwidth; so, for example, when listening to a weak single-sideband signal and there's a stronger signal 5 kHz or less away on the opposite sideband, the weak signal can made impossible to copy because the AGC is controlled by the undesired signal. Phase noise (98 dBc) poor; prevents accurate assessment of blocking performance, which because of this measures as poor—even though it may actually be much better. AGC threshold drops to poor (8 µV) with preamplifier off. Sensitivity drops to only fair with preamplifier off. Measured dynamic range of 63 dB consistent at 50, 20 and 5 kHz separation points (translates to fair at 5 kHz separation, poor at 20 kHz separation); nevertheless, resisted overloading effectively during hands-on testing. Radio spectrum display shows only narrow 20 kHz slice—i.e., plus or minus 10 kHz on either side of the received signal. No noise blanker. Most front-panel LEDs are blue and excessively bright. Station presets store only frequency and mode, not such other variables as bandwidth. No external speaker jack, so audio must run through computer's sound card. Frequency display on our unit misreads by around 45 Hz. Runs warm; plastic end caps affixed with double-stick tape that loses stickiness as cabinet heats up. SO-239 antenna connector very loose on our unit; nevertheless, Universal Radio, Elad's North American Elad distributor and repair facility, indicates that to date there have no other FDM77 repair issues. Manual states USB 2.0 required; our tests underscore that this, as opposed to USB 1.0, is necessary to avoid jerky responses and locking up. Clock shows local time only in 24-hour format; although only 24-hour format shown, LCD inappropriately displays AM and PM. Owner's manual, although recently improved, not all it could be.

☞ Tested with v1.06 firmware and v1.15 and v3.06 operating software; all comments refer to results with the latter software.

Verdict: The Italian-made Elad FDM77 gets high marks for being the first to offer hassle-free DRM reception. It is also user friendly and performs nicely with conventional analog signals—even though it lacks synchronous selectable sideband.

Italy's **ELAD FDM77** is already a favorite among listeners to Digital Radio Mondiale transmissions.

DRM Ready
✪✪✪⅜
RFSPACE SDR-14

Price: *RFSPACE SDR-14:* $1,099.95 in the United States. *Comet HS-10 SMA-to-SO-239 antenna adaptor cable:* $16.95 in the United States. *DRM software:* $49.95 worldwide from www.winradio.com/home/download-drm.htm.

Pro: Excellent spectrum display shows, with audio ("demodulation"), up to a 150 kHz slice of radio spectrum; this can also be recorded to disk and played back in any mode or bandwidth (*see* Con). Worthy sensitivity. DSP bandwidth filtering feels razor sharp and performs beautifully. Relatively free from overloading. Stable. Tunes and displays down to 1 Hz increments. Passband tuning (*see* Con). Three-level attenuator, labeled as RF gain control. Adjustable AGC decay and hang times. Good quality, flexible USB cable. Receives 30–260 MHz minus front end filtering or amplification (*see* Con). Third-party software development supported. SpectraVue software nominally has Linux server support (not tested), in addition to Windows. With optional software, receives digital (DRM) world band and other broadcasts. World Time (UTC) clock shows date and day of the week. Operating software can be updated online from www.moetronix.com/spectravue.htm. Build quality appears solid. One year warranty. Fifteen day return privilege when ordered from the manufacturer. Helpful PDF operating manual (*see* Con).

The RFSPACE SDR-14's performance centers on specialty applications. It is priced accordingly.

A PC receiver is viable only so long as operating systems support it.

Con: AC adaptor's switching circuitry emits noise that disrupts reception even with outdoor antenna and shielded lead-in. Initial installation not always successful, necessitating troubleshooting with or without the assistance of the manufacturer; however, manufacturer's phone number and street address aren't published. SMA antenna connector, with no adaptor included for non-SMA antenna plugs; for most shortwave antennas an adaptor or new antenna plug is required. No synchronous selectable or double sideband, tunable notch filter, presets or scanning. Passband tuning operates only in LSB and USB modes and is complex to use. Noise blanker performs marginally, and no DSP noise reduction offered. Inadequate front end filtering, so mediumwave AM stations may bleed through slightly to impact world band listening. With demodulation, spectrum display limited to 150 kHz maximum bandwidth. Marginally useful 30–260 MHz reception, with an abundance of spurious signals that not even maximum attenuation can overcome. Requires a speedy computer with large disk capacity to use to full benefit; even then, heavy resource drain may impact multitasking. Harsh audio quality in AM mode. About a half-second lag when operating controls and when listening. No power switch, even though manufacturer recommends receiver be powered down when not in use. Operation manual, only on CD, not printed as a book.

☞ The included switching AC adaptor is electrically noisy and should be replaced with something quieter. Requirements are 12V DC output, one ampere minimum rating, center (tip) positive.

☞ Tested: software .014, SpectraVue 1.30.

Verdict: The RFSPACE SDR-14 is a niche device that does one thing very well: recording a slice of spectrum for later playback and analysis. Here, its advantage over the WiNRADiO G313 is that the slice may be up to 150 kHz, rather than 20 kHz.

However, this broader coverage comes at a price. The SDR-14, unlike the G313, requires a speedy processor and substantial disk space—especially in a multitasking environment. And it is nowhere as flexible outside its niche as the G313.

However appropriate the SDR-14 is for spectrum analysis, it is a dismal choice for world band listening or DXing.

Robert Sherwood and David Zantow, with Lawrence Magne.

WHERE TO FIND IT: INDEX TO TESTED RADIOS

PASSPORT REPORTS evaluates nearly every digitally tuned receiver on the market. Here is where each review is found, with those that are new, forthcoming, revised, rebranded or retested for 2008 in **bold**.

Comprehensive Radio Database International White Papers® are available for a number of popular new and classic premium receivers. Each RDI White Paper®—$6.95 in North America, $9.95 airmail elsewhere, including shipping—contains virtually all our panel's findings and comments during hands-on testing, as well as laboratory measurements and what these mean to you. These unabridged reports are available from key world band dealers, or order 24/7 from www.passband.com, autovoice +1 215/598-9018 or fax +1 215/598 3794—or write PASSPORT RDI White Papers, Box 300, Penn's Park, PA 18943 USA.

▤ *Radio Database International White Paper®* available.

Wire Antennas for 2008

Simple portables work nicely off their built-in telescopic antennas, and there are excellent compact antennas for tabletop and premium-portable models. Yet, outdoor wire antennas are still the best and thriftiest way to enhance a worthy receiver's world band reception.

First, three truths:

• *Location.* If you can't put a wire antenna outdoors, in the fresh air, consider a compact antenna (see next article). Erect safely and for best performance.

• *Apples and oranges.* Simple antennas for simple portables, sophisticated antennas for fancy models.

• *Signal-to-noise:* Boosting signals isn't enough. Success requires that signals be enhanced relative to electrical and receiver noise, and the best way to do this is to mount the antenna outdoors. The result—more signal, proportionately less noise—is decisive, as it upgrades the signal-to-noise ratio.

When Wire Antennas Help

No surprise—signals already booming in aren't going to profit from an El Supremo antenna. Your receiver's signal-strength indicator may read higher, but its automatic-gain control (AGC) ensures that what you hear isn't going to sound much different than before. In fact, it might sound worse.

With all portables except premium models, forget sophisticated antennas—outdoor or in, passive or active. Make do with the radio's built-in telescopic antenna, or for more oomph use an inverted-L wire antenna (see below) or one of the simpler compact antennas.

At the other extreme, a first-rate outdoor antenna is essential to elite receivers, which is why these rarely have built-in antennas.

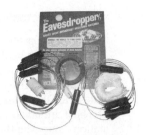

The ready-to-erect Eavesdropper Model T is PASSPORT's top value for above 3.9 MHz. It even includes static protection and 100 feet (30 m) of lead-in.

Volksantenne

Inverted-L antennas are simple, flexible and inexpensive. Inconspicuous, too, as they have no unsightly traps and, being end-fed, their feedlines are usually next to the house rather than dangling out in the open. For most radios they provide excellent results, and are even reasonable for omnidirectional mediumwave AM reception.

World band and specialty outlets usually stock inverted-L antennas, as well as such add-ons as baluns (see Worldly Words) and antenna tuners. These are made from superior materials and are priced accordingly; for example, for Brits it's only £25.95 for the Watson SWL-DX1. Other offerings are creative end-fed variants of the classic inverted-L.

Typical inverted-L antennas can be too long for many portables, causing overloading from hefty signals. Experiment, but usually the cheaper the portable, the shorter the inverted-L should be. Unlike most other antennas, the inverted-L performs similarly when shortened to avoid overloading or to fit into a yard.

> A choice antenna offers more signal, less noise.

Longwires Reduce Fading

Acres aplenty?

Lengthy inverted-L antennas, detailed in the RDI White Paper on outdoor antennas, can be over 200 feet/60 meters. These homebrew skyhooks are readily cobbled together from parts found at world band and amateur radio outlets and flea markets.

They qualify as genuine longwire antennas, thanks to their having one or more wavelengths (see Worldly Words). This helps reduce fading—something shorter antennas can't do—while improving the all important signal-to-noise ratio.

Lightning Protection

A good static protector is essential for an antenna during nearby thunderstorms, windy snowfalls and sandstorms. These generate inductive electrical charges that can seriously damage your radio. Some of the best are made by Alpha Delta Communications, but even these won't help against a direct lightning strike—for that, you need to disconnect the antenna and toss its feedline outdoors.

Pole-mounted utility lines are magnets for lightning. Worthy protection comes from a power-line surge arrestor, such as the advanced-tech ZeroSurge 2R7.5W, $129. That and backup power is provided by a double-conversion, full-sine-wave UPS, such as the excellent if noisy $370 Tripp-Lite Smart Online SU750XL. These double-conversion models are fundamentally superior as they are not line interactive.

Too, if you already have an emergency power plant, such as one of top performers from Kohler and Onan, it can be manually switched on during storms to decouple from utility power. This keeps most lightning surges from ever entering your home in the first place.

Erection Pitfalls

Most Americans don't encounter legal prohibitions on erecting world band antennas. However, covenants and deed restrictions, increasingly common in gated and other communities, can limit choices. Regardless, the Golden Rule of Aerials applies: Outdoor antennas should be neither unsightly nor particularly visible. If you want to annoy neighbors, put out pink plastic flamingos.

Most wire antennas are robustly constructed to withstand ice buildup during storms, but copper tends to stretch. Bungee straps or pulley counterweights help overcome this.

Antennas Breathe Fresh Air

Digital devices create so much RF pollution—electrical noise—that antenna location has become crucial. Indoors is usually the worst place.

You don't bathe in dirty water, so don't put your antenna where it is electrically "dirty." Instead, place it away from your house, power lines, cables and other potential noise sources. Once your antenna is hang-

IS BIGGER BETTER?

Accessory antennas come in two flavors: unamplified or "passive," usually outdoor—as well as amplified or "active," which can be indoor, outdoor or both. Unamplified antennas use a wire or rod receiving element to carry radio signals straight to the receiver. The wire antennas in this article are all unamplified and tend to be long.

Amplified or active antennas are electronically boosted to make up for their relatively short receiving elements. A few sought-after models even outperform big outdoor antennas, at least with staticky signals below 5 MHz. As yards shrink and restrictive covenants grow, limited-space amplified antennas are becoming more popular. Even landed homeowners sometimes prefer them because most are relatively inconspicuous and are easy to erect.

But bigger tends to be better, so amplified antennas have drawbacks. First, their short receiving elements usually don't provide the signal-to-noise enhancement of lengthier elements. Second, antenna amplifiers can generate noise of their own. Third, these amplifiers can overload, with results like when a receiver overloads: a mighty mumbling mishmash up and down the dial. Indeed, if antenna amplification is excessive it can overload the receiver, too.

Finally, amplified compact antennas often have mediocre front-end selectivity. This can allow jumbo mediumwave AM signals to get jumbled in with world band signals.

ing free in the breeze, you're likely to hear less "stuff" bothering stations.

Safe Installation

Safety is Rule One during installation. Avoid falls or making contact with potentially lethal electrical lines. If you want to be fried, go to the beach.

There's more to this than can be covered here, but it is detailed in the RADIO DATABASE INTERNATIONAL report, *Evaluation of Popular Outdoor Antennas*. Also, check out www. universal-radio.com/catalog/sw_ant/safeswl.html.

What's Best?

In that RDI White Paper are also test results for various popular outdoor wire antennas, three of which are touched on here. All are dipoles which rely on traps for frequency resonance, but a variety of mounting layouts are used:

* End-fed sloper, with the antenna about 30 degrees from horizontal.
* Center-fed tapered wing, with a tall (about 20 feet/6 meters) mounting amidships, plus two lower mountings.
* Center-fed horizontal, hung between two points of comparable height.

PASSPORT's star ratings mean the same thing regardless of whether an antenna is active or passive, big or little, indoor or out. This helps when you're trying to compare one type of antenna with another in PASSPORT REPORTS.

Nevertheless, passive antennas are more tricky than actives to evaluate properly. That's because their performance is partly dependent on such imponderables as local soil, moisture and bedrock formation. So, don't hold back from "rolling your own" or buying something that, tests be damned, you think might do well at your location. There are countless designs on the market and in how-to publications, and most wire antennas are frugal and forgiving.

Prices Up

Recent jumps in raw materials prices have resulted in significant price increases for most wire antennas. Eavesdropper, however, has gone up only modestly—especially considering that some versions include lead-in wire.

❶❶❶❶¾ *Passport's Choice*
Alpha Delta DX-Ultra

Price: $159.95 in the United States; coaxial cable $15–30 extra. CAD$199.95 in Canada; coaxial cable CAD$13–29 extra. €114.00 plus coaxial cable in the Netherlands (rys.nl).

Pro: Best overall performer of any antenna tested, passive or active. Little variation in performance from one world band segment to another. Rugged construction. Comes

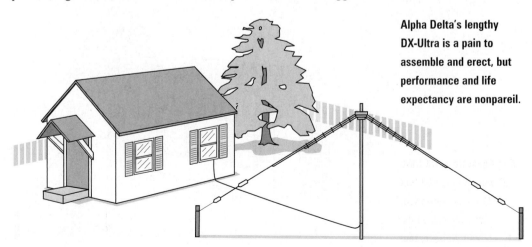

Alpha Delta's lengthy DX-Ultra is a pain to assemble and erect, but performance and life expectancy are nonpareil.

with built-in static protection. Wing design appropriate for certain yard layouts. Covers mediumwave AM band.

Con: Assembly a major undertaking, with stiff wire having to be bent and fed through spacer holes, then affixed. Unusually lengthy, 80 feet/25 meters. Coaxial cable lead-in not included. Relatively heavy, adding to erection effort. Warranty only six months.

Verdict: The Alpha Delta DX-Ultra rewards sweat equity—it is really more of a kit than a ready-to-go product. First, you have to purchase the needed lead-in cable and other hardware bits, then assemble, bend and stretch the many stiff wires, section by section.

Because the wire used should outlast the Pyramids, assembly is a trying and unforgiving exercise. Each wire needs to be rigorously and properly affixed, lest it slip loose and the erected antenna comes tumbling down, as it did at one of our test sites.

While all outdoor antennas require yard space, the Ultra is the longest manufactured antenna tested. It is also relatively heavy, making installation even more challenging than it already is. In ice-prone climates, ensure any trees or poles attached to the antenna are sturdy. And don't even think about using a chimney.

But if you have yard space and don't object to assembly and erection hurdles, you are rewarded with a mighty robust performer.

Properly mounted, is outmatched only by hugely long inverted-L aerials and costly professional-grade antennas.

✪✪✪✪½ *Passport's Choice*
Alpha Delta DX-SWL Sloper

Price: $119.95 in the United States; coaxial cable $15–30 extra, Transi-Trap static protector $30–60 extra. CAD$159.00 in Canada; coaxial cable CAD$13–29 extra, Transi-Trap static protector CAD$79–99 extra. €125.00 plus coaxial cable and static protector in the Netherlands (rys.nl).

Pro: Rugged construction. Sloper design uses traps to keep length down to 60 feet/18 meters, ideal for smaller yards. Covers mediumwave AM band.

Con: Requires assembly, a significant exercise. Does not include static protection or coaxial cable lead-in. Warranty only six months.

☞ A greatly shortened version of the Ultra, the 40-foot/12-meter DX-SWL-S (not tested), is available for $119.95, with coaxial cable and static protector extra. Its nominal coverage is 3.2–22 MHz, omitting the little-used 2 MHz (120 meter) world band segment. Although both Sloper versions nominally don't cover the scarcely used 25 MHz (11 meter) world band segment, our measurements of the full-length Sloper show excellent results at 25650–26100 kHz.

The Alpha Delta DX-SWL Sloper, at under 68 feet (21 m), is convenient for midsized yards. Rugged, too.

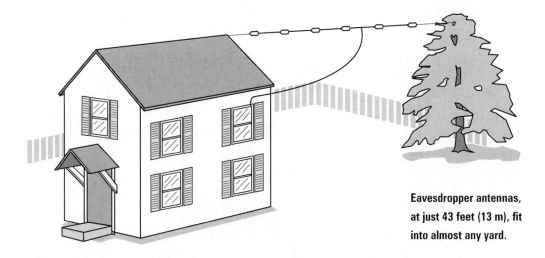

Eavesdropper antennas, at just 43 feet (13 m), fit into almost any yard.

Verdict: A robust performer for where space is limited, but a chore to assemble.

✪✪✪✪⅛ ❷ *Passport's Choice*
Eavesdropper Model T, Eavesdropper Model C

Price: *Model T:* $99.95, complete, in the United States. CAD$129.00 in Canada. *Model C:* $99.95 in the United States; coaxial cable $15–30 extra. CAD$129.00 in Canada; coaxial cable CAD$13–29 extra.

Pro: Unusually compact at 43 feet/13 meters, it fits into many yards. Comes with built-in static protection. Attractively priced. One-year warranty, after which repairs made "at nominal cost." Model T: Easiest to install of any Passport's Choice antenna—unpack, and it's ready to hang. Comes with ribbon lead-in wire, which tends to have less signal loss than coaxial cable. *Model C:* Easier than most to install, with virtually everything included and assembled except the coaxial cable lead-in.

Con: Some performance drop within the 2 MHz (120 meter) and 3 MHz (90 meter) tropical world band segments. *Model C:* Coaxial cable lead-in not included.

☞ Eavesdropper also makes the $99.95 sloper antenna (not tested), similar to Alpha Delta's DX-SWL Sloper. It comes with a static arrestor, but no coaxial cable lead-in.

Verdict: If your teeth gnash when you see "Some Assembly Required," take heart. The Eavesdropper T, unlike Alpha Delta alternatives, comes ready to go and is straightforward to erect. At most, you might want to get a pair of bungee straps to provide flexibility at the ends.

The size is user-friendly, too—the result of a compromise. There's no getting around the rule that the longer the antenna, the more likely it is to do well at low frequencies. Eavesdropper's designer, the late Jim Meadow, once told PASSPORT that he found few folks tuning below 4.7 MHz, but many people with limited yard space. So, he shrunk the Eavesdropper by focusing on performance above 4.7 MHz, yet allowed it to function decently lower down.

Our tests confirm this. The Eavesdropper horizontal trap dipoles perform quite nicely above 4.7 MHz, with a notch less gain than Alpha-Delta models in the 2 MHz and 3 MHz tropical world band segments.

In practice the ribbon lead-in wire used by the T version works surprisingly well, using phasing to help cancel out electrical noise. Too, it stands up to the elements and usually has less signal loss than coaxial cable used by its C sibling.

Prepared by Stephen Bohac, Jock Elliott, Tony Jones, Lawrence Magne, David Walcutt and George Zeller.

Compact Antennas for 2008

Do you tune world band by day, when signals are *sotto voce*, or seek out elusive stations? If so, put an accessory antenna near the top of your "must buy" list. Arguably the most interesting programs are found outside prime time, so a worthy antenna can literally open up new worlds.

Best are outdoor wire antennas that are unamplified—*passive*. Trouble is, they are lengthy, a pain to erect (think "big trees") and require yard space. So if you lack acreage, face community restrictions or are allergic to high-wire gymnastics, consider a compact antenna.

Amps Enhance

Compacts use a loop, small rod or short wire receiving element to grab signals. These don't provide much oomph, so an amplifier is added to make up the difference—the antenna then becomes *active*. Today, nearly all compact antennas are active and nearly all active antennas are compact.

Most are ideal for townhouses, apartments and travel. Some detached homes, too, as lawns shrink while houses balloon. Too, neighbors may sniff that wire antennas look like clotheslines.

Early amplified antennas were noisy, overloaded easily, generated harmonic "false" signals and deteriorated outdoors. They quickly earned a reputation for failing to deliver.

Now there are plenty of solid performers. While these still don't fully equal their outdoor wire cousins, the gap has narrowed considerably. Indeed, some occasionally outperform passive wire antennas on lower frequencies during high-static periods.

Proximate or Remote?

Compact antennas are either proximate or remote. A *proximate* model has its receiving element on or near an amplifier box by the receiver. A *remote* antenna, whether active or passive, allows the element to be mounted farther away—either indoors or, with some models, outdoors where reception tends to be superior.

Remote models are the way to go, as the receiving element can be put where electrical noise is weak yet radio signals are strong. Proximate models offer no such choice unless the receiver itself is where reception is best.

Most electrical noise comes from your house or the neighborhood, but not always. For example, some receivers emit electrical noise, usually from the front panel's digital display. With these, if you must use a proximate antenna put it towards the back or to one side.

> **Daytime stations sound better with a good antenna.**

Wellbrook's outdoor loop antennas profit from a rotor. Best is the Yaesu G-5500, which pirouettes on two axes. This is especially helpful with distant mediumwave AM stations.

Noise Droops with Loops

Cognoscenti gravitate to loop antennas because they tend to offer signals less disturbed by static and other noise. Too, they are relatively directional, so they can be pointed away from local electrical noise. All this improves the signal-to-noise ratio—especially within lower frequency segments.

Some government monitoring agencies even use costly banks of passive phased-array loops mounted near ground level. These outclass even massive rotatable beams, as they provide signals eerily devoid of noise.

Wellbrook loops stand out among affordable loops, as they use balanced feedlines and can roost outdoors. During high-static months their superior signal-to-noise ratios can make the difference between hearing static and understanding what's being said.

Most active antennas are designed for tabletop models, but not all. Degen's DE31, also sold with variations under the Kaito and Thieking brands, is a low-cost option for casual portable use. Sony's AN-LP1 is *el supremo* for portables, but it may have been discontinued—get it while you can!

No Juice, No Pollution

Often the first thing to go in a crisis is electricity. Batteries sometimes fill in, but nothing beats not needing electricity in the first place. Zero environmental impact, too.

The R.F. Systems GMDSS-1 is that most unusual of antennas: short, yet with no electronic amplification. And it is tough enough to withstand serious abuse without flinching.

Preselection *vs.* Broadband

Broadband amplifiers can cause all sorts of mischief. Some add noise and spurious signals, especially "ghosting" from the mediumwave AM band. Yet others have too much gain and overload receivers.

These shortcomings are palliated by tunable or switchable preselection, which limits the band of frequencies getting full amplification. Problem is, outboard preselectors almost always have controls that need manual tweaking.

There is a middle ground: A high-pass or band-rejection filter (e.g., from Kiwa Electronics or Par Electronics), which doesn't require as much operator intervention as a preselector. For example, a ~2 MHz high-pass filter is usually adequate to squash powerful mediumwave AM "ghosts."

How Much Oomph?

One way to judge an active antenna is simply by how much gain it provides. But that's like judging a car only by its horsepower.

An active antenna should provide signal levels comparable to those from a good passive wire antenna. Any less, and receiver circuit noise may become audible. Too much, and the receiver's circuitry—maybe the antenna's, too—might overload.

Like Smucker's, it needs to be just right.

When Your Antenna Arrives

Three tips so your antenna can reach its potential:

• Active antennas work best off batteries, which avoid hum and buzz caused by AC mains power. But if your antenna uses an AC adaptor, keep it and electrical cords away from the receiving element and feedline. If there's hum or buzz anyway, try substituting one of the better transformer-type AC adaptors from someplace like Jameco.com.

Electrically quiet AC adaptors are getting hard to come by, thanks to myopic, if well-intentioned, environmental legislation in California and beyond. These rules effectively mandate noisy switching-type power supplies by outlawing the inherently quiet transformer variety. Thankfully, mail order and the Internet offer transformer alternatives.

Regulated transformer-type AC adaptors are not inherently less prone to hum or buzz than non-regulated models. However, regulated adaptors are usually top-tier offerings, so the manufacturer is more likely to have spent additionally to reduce hum and buzz.

- Antenna performance is one third technology, another third geography and geology, and a third part installation. PASSPORT reports on the first and give tips on the third. Yet, much depends on the second: local conditions.

You can boost the odds by seeing how the receiving element performs at different spots—sometimes just moving it a few yards or meters can make a real difference. Jerry-rig the antenna until you're satisfied the best spot has been found, then mount it properly.

- Finally, if your radio has multiple antenna inputs, try each to see which works best.

Rocky Mountain high. Wellbrook's ALA100 makes an ideal aerial hoop for eagles and hawks. J.R. Sherwood

What Passport's Ratings Mean

Star ratings: ✪✪✪✪ is best for any type of antenna, but in reality even the best of compact antennas don't yet merit more than four stars when compared against long passive antennas. To help in deciding, star ratings for compact antennas can be compared directly against those for "lasso" antennas found elsewhere in this PASSPORT REPORTS. Stars reflect overall world band performance and meaningful features, plus to some extent ergonomics and build quality. Price, appearance, country of manufacture and the like are not taken into account.

Passport's Choice. La crème de la crème. Our test team's personal picks of the litter—models we would buy or have bought for our personal use. Unlike star ratings, these choices are unapologetically subjective.

✪: A relative bargain, with decidedly more performance than the price would suggest.

Active antennas are listed in descending order of merit. Unless otherwise indicated each has a one-year warranty.

✪✪✪✪½ *Passport's Choice*
Wellbrook ALA 100

Head amp and control unit; requires large homemade outdoor loop. Active, remote, broadband, 0.05–30 MHz

Price: £139.00 plus £5.00 shipping in the United Kingdom and Eire. £139.00 plus £15.00 shipping elsewhere.

Pro: With large (40-foot/12-meter) loop receiving element and relatively low-gain amplifier, has best signal-to-noise ratio, notably above 10 MHz, of any active model tested. Reduced pickup of thunderstorm static, especially below 8 MHz during local summer. Balanced loop design inherently helps reduce pickup of local electrical noise. Performance characteristics make it unusually complementary to passive outdoor wire antennas. Superior build quality. Supplied 117V AC adaptor (Stancor STA-300R) among best tested for not causing hum or buzzing. Although any large loop is inherently susceptible to inductive pickup of local thunderstorm static, during our tests the antenna's amplifier has not suffered static damage during storms; indeed, even nearby one kilowatt shortwave transmissions have not damaged it. Protected circuitry, using an easily replaced 315 mA fuse. Superior factory support. Easier to ship and less costly than other tested Wellbrook loops.

Con: Significant undertaking to install, as quasi-kit ALA 100 requires construction of 26–59 foot/8–18 meter homemade loop receiving element; however, the forthcoming ALA 100M's loop, scheduled for 2008, will need to be only half as large. As a practical matter receiving element should be mounted outdoors, another installation burden; too, if element's framework made from white PVC it can be an eyesore. Only moderate gain for reception within such modest-signal areas as Western Hemisphere, Asia and Australasia—a drawback only with receivers having relatively noisy circuitry. Impractical to rotate, thus inappropriate for nulling co-channel interference on mediumwave AM. BNC connector at the receiving element's base open to weather and thus needs to be user-sealed with Coax Seal, electrical putty or similar. Encapsulated amplifier makes repair impossible. Manufacturer cautions against allowing sunlight to damage head amplifier's plastic housing; yet, after three years of intense exposure at our high-UV main test site, Wellbrook's plastic seems no worse for the wear than any other outdoor antenna's plastic. No co-axial cable supplied. Available for purchase or export only two cumbersome ways: via Sterling cheque or International Money Order through the Welsh manufacturer (www. wellbrook.uk.com), or with credit card via an English dealer's unsecured email address (sales@shortwave.co.uk).

☞ The forthcoming ALA 100M, scheduled for 2008, will need a loop only half as large.

☞ Star rating is with relatively large pickup element of around 40-feet/12-meters in length. Performance drops at smaller lengths, such as near 25 feet/7.6 meters.

Verdict: Size matters, and this quasi-kit active antenna can get seriously big by compact antenna standards. Indeed, it almost occupies a "neither" world somewhere between truly compact active antennas and long passive wire antennas.

No plug-and-play, the plus-size ALA100 is a major slog to construct and install. Yet, the payoff for your toil, sweat and tears is exceptional quietness—a *sine qua non* for faint-signal reception.

If its installation, size, appearance and purchase hurdles don't deter you, you won't find a better active model than the British-made Wellbrook ALA 100. If you already use a passive outdoor wire antenna, this model's unique receiving characteristics should be unusually complementary.

WIRY ART OF DECEPTION

Listeners facing antenna restrictions have concocted a dog's breakfast of camouflaged and low-visibility outdoor wire antennas. Some, hidden in the open, look like clotheslines or are woven into volleyball nets. Yet others are tucked underneath awnings or canopies. Spooks-at-heart play to urban apathy by hanging varnished thin-wire antennas, then waiting to see what happens.

Modest passive stealth antennas can perform surprisingly well when mated to the MFJ-1020C, around $90. Just remove its telescopic antenna and—*voilà*—it becomes a tunable active preselector that outperforms comparably priced nominal preselectors.

Even regular active antennas can sometimes pass muster. One creative Australian even told a curious neighbor that his loop antenna was "art sculpture"—it worked!

Deep pockets? If you want something James Bondish, the SGC Stealth Antenna Kit (not tested) from wsplc.com is £299.95 in the United Kingdom, $495.24 plus shipping overseas. Stirred, of course, not shaken.

✪✪✪✪ *Passport's Choice*
Wellbrook ALA 330S

Outdoor-indoor loop. Active, remote, broadband, 2.3–30 MHz

Price: *ALA 330S:* £199.00 plus £10.00 shipping in the United Kingdom and Eire. £199.00 plus £30.00 shipping elsewhere. *Upgrade kit '330 to '330S:* £80.00 plus £10.00 shipping in the United Kingdom and Eire. £80.00 plus £15.00 shipping elsewhere. *TV or ham single-axis aftermarket rotor:* $70 and up in the United States.

Pro: Among the best signal-to-noise ratios, including at times reduced pickup of thunderstorm static, on all shortwave frequencies, of any active model tested; low-noise/low-static pickup characteristics most noticeable below 8 MHz, especially during local summer, when it sometimes outperforms sophisticated outdoor wire antennas. Higher shortwave gain (above 3 MHz) than sibling '1530/'1530+, which helps get signals into a better AGC range on most receivers. Balanced loop design inherently helps reduce pickup of local electrical noise; additionally, aluminum loop receiving element can be affixed to a low-cost TV or ham aftermarket rotor to improve reception by directionally nulling local electrical noise and, to a lesser degree, static. Rotatability also can slightly reduce co-channel shortwave interference below 4 or 5 MHz and even occasionally on higher frequencies. Superior build quality, including rigorous weatherproofing (*see* Con). Supplied 117V AC adaptor (Stancor STA-300R) among best tested for not causing hum or buzzing (*see* Con). Although any large loop is inherently susceptible to inductive pickup of local thunderstorm static, during our tests of the prior and current versions the antenna's amplifier has never suffered static damage during storms; indeed, even nearby one kilowatt shortwave transmissions have not damaged it. Protected circuitry, using an easily replaced 315 mA fuse. Threaded flange on "S" version improves mounting of loop receiving element (*see* Con). Superior factory support.

Wellbrook's ALA330S is top-rated for world band stations and shortwave utilities. It can be mounted almost anywhere, but usually works best higher up.

J.R. Sherwood

Con: Only moderate gain for reception within such modest-signal areas as Western Hemisphere, Asia and Australasia—a drawback only with receivers having relatively noisy circuitry. Slightly less gain than ALA 1530 within little-used 2.3–2.5 MHz (120 meter) tropical world band segment, a drawback only with receivers having relatively noisy circuitry. Mediumwave AM gain significantly inferior to that of the '1530. Flange for loop receiving element has metric pipe threading; most U.S. users will need to re-thread. Loop receiving element, about one meter across, is large and cumbersome to ship, although loop is slightly smaller than in the prior version. Mounting mast and optional aftermarket rotor add to cost and complexity. BNC connector at the receiving element's base is open to the weather and thus needs to be user-sealed with Coax Seal, electrical putty or similar. Encapsulated amplifier makes repair impossible. Manufacturer cautions against allowing high winds to stress mounting flange; however, one of our units survived 90+ mph (145 km/h) Rocky Mountain winds until the locally procured pipe coupling to which we had attached the antenna snapped. Manufacturer cautions against allowing sunlight to damage head amplifier's plastic housing; yet, after three years of intense exposure at a high-UV PASSPORT test site, Wellbrook's plastic seems no worse for the wear than any other outdoor antenna's plastic. Adaptor supplied for 117V AC runs very warm after being plugged in for a few hours, while amplifier tends to run slightly warm; nonetheless, after three years of use at PASSPORT test facility, neither has acted up. No coaxial cable supplied. Available for purchase or export only two cumbersome ways: via Sterling cheque or International Money Order through the Welsh manufacturer (www. wellbrook.uk.com), or with credit card via an English dealer's unsecured email address (sales@shortwave.co.uk).

☞ The manufacturer offers a kit to convert the earlier ALA 330 to the improved "S" version. Recommended.

Verdict: This excellent active antenna shines when it comes to reducing the impact of static and noise on weak signals below 8 MHz.

For limited-space situations, and even to complement passive wire antennas on large properties, the '330S is hard to equal. However, if your receiver tends to sound "hissy" with weak signals, then it probably needs an antenna which gives even more gain than the '330S so it can overcome internal receiver noise. Of course, with top-rated tabletop models this is not an issue.

For best reception the antenna should be mounted outdoors, away from the house and atop a rotor. However, this is more important with the ALA 1530 model (see below) when used for longwave and mediumwave AM reception. In the real world of limited options, reasonable results on shortwave are sometimes obtained even indoors sans rotor or with manual rotation, provided the usual caveats are followed for placement of the reception element. But there's no getting around the laws of physics: The Wellbrook loop is an antenna, and all antennas work much better when not shielded by absorptive materials or placed near sources of electrical interference.

What's not to like? An ordering procedure that's inconvenient and démodé. There are no dealers outside the United Kingdom, and there is still no secure way for those elsewhere to order by credit card on the Internet.

Overall, the '330S isn't in the same league as top-rated outdoor wire antennas. However, it can outperform even those antennas with some static-prone signals or when local electrical noise is a problem—provided it is erected properly.

Enhanced Version for 2008

❸❸❸⅛ *Passport's Choice*

Wellbrook ALA 1530+, Wellbrook ALA 1530, Wellbrook ALA 1530P

Outdoor-indoor loop. Active, remote, broadband, 0.15–30 MHz

Price: *ALA1530+:* £180.00 plus £10.00 shipping in the United Kingdom and Eire. £180.00 plus £30.00 shipping elsewhere. *ALA 1530:* £149.00 plus £10.00 shipping in the United Kingdom and Eire. £149.00 plus £30.00 shipping elsewhere. *ALA 1530P (not tested):* £159.00 plus £10.00 shipping in the United Kingdom and Eire. £159.00 plus £30.00 shipping elsewhere. *Yaesu G-5500/G-5500B twin-axis aftermarket rotor:* $639.95 in the United States. CAD$899.00 in Canada. £439.00 in the United Kingdom. €659.00 in Germany. *TV or ham single-axis aftermarket rotor:* $70+ in the United States.

Pro: Covers at comparable levels of performance not only shortwave, but also mediumwave AM and longwave (see Con). Mediumwave AM and longwave performance superb when coupled to a Yaesu

G-5500/G-5500B aftermarket rotor with twin-axis directionality, and is almost as good with cheaper single-axis TV or ham rotor; also, any rotor can slightly reduce co-channel shortwave interference below 4 or 5 MHz and even occasionally on higher frequencies. Very nearly the best signal-to-noise ratio among active models tested, including reduced pickup of thunderstorm static. Balanced loop design inherently helps reduce pickup of local electrical noise. Low-noise/low-static pickup characteristic most noticeable below 8 MHz during summer, when it sometimes outperforms sophisticated outdoor wire antennas. Slightly more gain than sibling ALA 330S within little-used 2.3–2.5 MHz (120 meter) tropical world band segment. Superior build quality, including rigorous weatherproofing (*see* Con). Supplied AC adaptor, properly bypassed and regulated, is among the best tested for not causing hum or buzzing (*see* Con). Although any large loop's amplifier is inherently susceptible to inductive pickup of local thunderstorm static, during our tests the antenna's amp never suffered static damage during storms; indeed, even nearby one kilowatt shortwave transmissions did no damage to the antenna amplifier. Protected circuitry, using an easily replaced 315 mA fuse. Superior factory support. *ALA 1530+:* Nominal full-spec operating frequency range of 50 kHz to 100 MHz. Nominal mediumwave AM IP3 improvement, resulting from nominal faint drop in mediumwave AM gain, although gain and IP3 are both scheduled to be enhanced slightly in 2008. *ALA 1530:* Nominal full-spec operating frequency range of 150 kHz (30 kHz with reduced sensitivity) to 30 MHz.

Con: Extended frequency range, as compared to the sibling '330S, can result in mediumwave AM signals surfacing within the shortwave spectrum, degrading reception—usually a more significant issue in urban and suburban North America than elsewhere (even the simplest rotor can help by turning the antenna perpendicular to an offending mediumwave AM signal's axis); this tends to be less of a problem at night because of reduced local transmitting powers, and is less of a problem in our latest

The Wellbrook ALA 1530 and 1530+ not only snare tough shortwave catches, but also mediumwave AM rarities.   J.R. Sherwood

unit. Prone to overloading some receivers in locations rich with strong mediumwave AM signals; this also tends to be less of a problem at night because of reduced local transmitting powers. Only moderate gain, slightly less than sibling ALA 330S, for reception within such modest-signal areas as Western Hemisphere, Asia and Australasia. Balanced loop receiving element, about one meter across, not easy to mount and is large and cumbersome to ship. Mounting mast and optional aftermarket rotor add to cost and complexity of erection. Flange for loop receiving element has metric pipe threading; most U.S. users will need to re-thread. BNC connector at the receiving element's base is open to the weather and thus needs to be user-sealed with Coax Seal, electrical putty or similar. Encapsulated amplifier makes repair impossible. Manufacturer cautions against allowing high winds to stress mounting flange; however, after three years of wind and sun at one outdoor test location, nothing untoward has materialized. Manufacturer cautions against allowing sunlight to damage head amplifier's plastic housing; yet, after three years of intense exposure at a high-UV PASSPORT test site, Wellbrook's plastic seems no worse for the wear than any other outdoor antenna's plastic. Adaptor supplied for 117V AC runs warm after being plugged in for a few hours, while amplifier tends to run slightly warm; nonetheless, after three years of use at PASSPORT test facility, neither has acted up. No coaxial cable supplied. Available for purchase or export only two cumbersome ways: via Sterling cheque or International Money Order through the Welsh manufacturer (www. wellbrook.uk.com), or with credit card via an English dealer's unsecured email address (sales@shortwave.co.uk).

☞ An antenna tuner may improve signal level by as much as 6 dB.

☞ Mediumwave AM and longwave performance directionality may suffer if the '1530 is not mounted well away from other antennas.

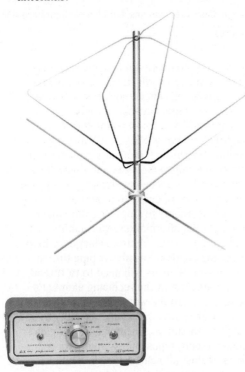

The Jolly Green Giant's eggbeater? No, it's the RF Systems DX-One Professional Mark II antenna, made in The Netherlands. J.R. Sherwood

☞ The '1530 is the sibling of the former ALA 330, not the newer ALA 330S.

☞ The "P" version, not tested, uses a semi-rigid plastic loop rather than aluminum and is for indoor use.

Verdict: Interested in distant broadcast goodies below the shortwave spectrum, as well as tuning world band? If so, the Wellbrook ALA 1530+ and ALA 1530 are hard to beat—so long as you don't live near local mediumwave AM transmission facilities. A rotor is *de rigeur* for nulling co-channel interference below 1.7 MHz, and also may help a skosh with tropical world band stations. As with all Wellbrook loop antennas the '1530+ and '1530 excel at rejecting noise and static, particularly below 8 MHz.

For multiband coverage, including mediumwave AM and longwave, the '1530+ and '1530 are both top-drawer choices. Both are comparably solid performers for world band, although not quite equal to siblings ALA 100 and ALA 330S.

Last year's unit or this year's, Plus or regular version, differences come down to how many angels can be put on the head of a pin. Wellbrook simply rules this segment of the antenna market.

●●●½ *Passport's Choice*
RF Systems DX-One Professional Mark II

Outdoor-indoor "eggbeater." Active, remote, broadband, 0.02–60 MHz.

Price: *DX-One Pro antenna:* $699.95 in the United States. £359.95 in the United Kingdom. €498.00 in Germany. €499.00 in the Netherlands.

Pro: Outstanding dynamic range. Very low noise. Outputs for two receivers. Comes standard with switchable band rejection filter to reduce the chances of mediumwave AM signals ghosting into the shortwave spectrum. Receiving element has outstanding build quality. Coaxial connector at head amplifier is completely shielded from the weather by a clever mechanical design. Superior low noise, high gain performance on mediumwave AM.

Con: Unbalanced design makes antenna susceptible to importing buzz at some locations; this is especially noticeable because of otherwise-excellent performance. AC power supply not bypassed as well as it could be, causing slight hum on some signals. More likely than most antennas to exacerbate fading, even though design nominally reduces fading effects. No coaxial cable supplied. Output position for 10 dB gain measures +6 dB. Warranty only six months.

Verdict: The pricey RF Systems DX-One Professional Mark II is a superior performer. As with any antenna having a small capture area and an unbalanced design, at some lo-cations it is prone to picking up local electrical noise. Made in the Netherlands.

✪✪✪½
DX Engineering DXE-ARAH2-1P

Outdoor-indoor dipole. Active, remote, broadband 0.06–30 MHz.

Price: *DXE-ARAH2-1P:* $289.00 in the United States. *Aftermarket coaxial cable and plugs (required):* Usually $15–45 in the United States.

Pro: Unusual capture length helps produce superior signal-to-noise ratio. Unlike with some other compact antennas, feedline

WHERE TO PLACE A REMOTE ANTENNA

When a remote compact antenna is installed properly it can perform very well. The bad news is that if you have room outdoors to mount it properly, you may also have room for a passive wire antenna that will perform better, yet. Maybe cheaper, too.

Here are three tips on placing remote models, but creativity rules:

- Outdoors, put the receiving element in the clear, away from objects. Metal degrades performance, so especially keep it away from metal and, if possible, use a nonconductive mast or capped PVC pipe. Optimum height from ground is usually around 10–25 feet/3–8 meters. Here, "ground" refers to the electrical ground—not only terra firma, but also reinforced concrete roofs and the like.

  Running a metal mast through a loop's receiving element can degrade performance. So, if you use a metal mast simply affix it to the mounting flange and stop there. In Wellbrook's case, its mounting flange is plenty tough, as evidenced by years of being exposed to blistery winds, ice and snow at our Rocky Mountain test cabin. The manufacturer states that the flange is good for winds up to 80 MPH (130 km/h), but our own experience suggests that it is even more robust.

  If a mast is impractical try a tree. Although sap is electrically conductive, this is a reasonable fallback, especially with hardwood deciduous varieties other than sugar maple. You may have to do some trimming to keep leaves away from the receiving element.

- When yard placement is impractical, put the receiving element outdoors as far as you dare. In a high rise consider using a balcony or someplace just outside a window. For example, if the receiving element is a rod, point it away from the building 70 degrees or so, like a wall flagpole. If you reside on the top floor, the roof may also be a good bet.

  If outdoor placement is out of the question, try the attic if the roof isn't foil-insulated or metal. With Wellbrook models this beats having it hog an entire room.

- If all else fails affix the receiving element against the inside-center of a large window. Radio signals, like light, sail right through glass.

DX Engineering's **DXE-ARAH2-1P** antenna performs nicely above 5 MHz. Rugged, too, once it's sealed.

J.R. Sherwood

does not act as involuntary antenna. Worthy gain above about 9 MHz, rising to peak at 27 MHz. Excellent freedom from mediumwave AM "ghosting" when internal jumper configured to roll off below 3 MHz. Very good mediumwave AM and longwave performance when 1) internal jumper configured for flat response, and 2) antenna located in relatively rural setting with no

The Dressler ARA 100 HDX will shortly vanish from dealer shelves, but the similar ATA 60 S is available and costs less.   J. R. Sherwood

nearby mediumwave AM stations. Excellent build quality. Circuit board not potted, facilitating repair.

Con: Uses two nine-foot/2.75-meter CB whips for pickup element, so takes up much more space than usual for a compact antenna. Eighteen-foot/5.5-meter wingspan limits mounting options if rotatability desired to null co-channel interference on mediumwave AM. If configured by jumper to receive mediumwave AM, overloading/intermodulation may occur at urban and suburban locations—especially with nearby stations below 1 MHz; according to the factory, single-whip version (DXE-ARAV-1P, $229 plus shipping) doesn't have this problem but requires grounding. Mediumwave AM and longwave gain drops sharply when jumper configured to avoid intermodulation within shortwave spectrum. Amplifier box not weatherproof without obtaining and applying sealant. No coaxial cables or printed owner's manual. Not widely available; when ordered from manufacturer, shipping charges not indicated until order nearly completed.

Verdict: A robustly constructed performer that is more active than compact. It acquits itself well from about 5 to 30 MHz, but similar performance can be had for less, while better performance isn't much costlier.

✪✪✪
Dressler ARA 100 HDX

Outdoor-indoor rod. Active, remote, broadband, 0.04–40 MHz.

Price (as available): $549.95 in the United States.

Pro: Superior build quality, with fiberglass whip and foam-encapsulated head amplifier to resist the weather (*see* Con). Very good gain below 20 MHz (*see* Con). Superior signal-to-noise ratio. Handy detachable "N" connector on bottom. AC adaptor with properly bypassed and regulated DC output is better than most. Suitable for packing diagonally in wide suitcase.

Con: Even though it has an amplifier with superior dynamic range, tends to overload in urban/suburban environments awash in powerful mediumwave AM signals unless antenna element mounted close to the ground; this tends to be less of a problem at night because of reduced local transmitting powers. Encapsulated design makes most repairs impossible. Above 20 MHz gain begins to fall off slightly. Body of antenna runs slightly warm. "N" connector at the head amplifier/receiving element exposed to weather, needs to be sealed with Coax Seal, electrical putty or similar by user. Gain control cumbersome to adjust; fortunately, in practice it is rarely needed. Reader reports suggest that ordering direct from the factory can be a frustrating experience.

☞ Star rating applies only when used where there is not significant ambient mediumwave RF, as the Dressler ARA 100 HDX, unless mounted close to the ground, is prone to overloading at locations rich with strong mediumwave AM signals or low-band VHF-TV stations. At some locations, even mounting antenna on the ground does not eliminate overloading. Mediumwave AM overloading seems exacerbated by pickup from coaxial cable lead-in, as it is not properly decoupled from antenna (unlike Wellbrook and DX Engineering models, which can be mounted high with long cables).

☞ Discontinued in 2006 and no longer stocked by most dealers. However, as of presstime Universal Radio in the United States still had a limited supply in stock.

Verdict: The robust Dressler ARA 100 HDX, made in Germany, is an excellent but costly low-noise antenna for locations not near one or more powerful mediumwave AM or low-band VHF-TV transmitters. Discontinued, but may still available new. Also, check out the similar Dressler ARA 60 S, below.

★★★ ⊘ *Passport's Choice*
MFJ-1020C (with short wire element)

Outdoor-indoor wire. Active, remote, manual preselection, 0.3–40 MHz.

Price: *MFJ-1020C (without antenna wire or insulators):* $99.95 in the United States. CAD$119.95 in Canada. £89.95 in the United Kingdom. €105.00 in Germany.

MFJ-1312D 120V AC adaptor: $15.95 in the United States. CAD$29.00 in Canada. *MFJ-1312DX 240V AC adaptor:* £15.95 in the United Kingdom.

Pro: Superior dynamic range, so functions effectively with an outboard wire receiving element, preferably mounted outdoors, in lieu of built-in telescopic antenna element. Sharp preselector peak unusually effective in preventing overloading. Works best off battery (*see* Con). Choice of PL-259 or RCA connections. Suitable for travel. 30-day money-back guarantee if purchased from manufacturer.

Con: Preselector complicates operation; tune control needs adjustment even with modest frequency changes, especially within the mediumwave AM band. Knobs small and touchy to adjust. High current draw (measures 30 mA), so battery runs down quickly. Removing sheet-metal screws often to change battery should eventually result in stripping unless great care is taken. AC adaptor, optional, causes significant hum on many received signals.

☞ The '1020C serves little or no useful purpose as a tunable preselector for reasonably long inverted-L antennas (anything above around 50–75 feet/15–20 meters) or resonant outdoor wire antennas. Additionally, the amplifier circuit is always present, so the '1020C cannot be used as an unamplified preselector targeted to improve front-end selectivity with significant wire antennas. Simply reducing amplification gain to improve front-end selectivity may or

The MFJ-1020C comes with a built-in telescopic antenna. Remove it, attach a random-length wire and—*voilà!*—you've got a superior active antenna that's surprisingly affordable. J.R. Sherwood

may not help to a degree, but it won't improve the signal-to-noise ratio or dynamic range. The reason is that the amplifier's gain potentiometer is merely an output pad (measured range of 40 dB).

☞ Two manufacturing flaws found on one of our "B" version units tested in the past, but the latest "C" unit had no defects. The owner's manual warns of possible "taking off" if the gain is set too high, but during our tests using a variety of receivers we encountered oscillation with only one model.

Verdict: The '1020C has a little secret: It's only okay the way the manufacturer sells it as a proximate active antenna, but as a preselector with an outdoor random-length wire antenna it is a worthy low-cost performer—better, in fact, than MFJ's designated shortwave preselector. Simply collapse (or, better, remove) the built-in telescopic antenna, then connect an outboard wire antenna to the '1020C's external antenna input.

Alas, the optional AC adaptor introduces hum much of the time, battery drain is considerable, and changing the built-in battery is inconvenient and relies on wear-prone sheet-metal screws. Best bet, unless you're into experimenting with power supplies: Skip the adaptor and use a large outboard rechargeable battery.

Peso for peso, the MFJ-1020C fed by a remote wire receiving element is the best buy among active antennas. The rub is that the use of several yards or meters of wire, preferably outdoors, makes it something of a hybrid requiring more space than other active antennas. But for many row houses, townhouses, ground-floor and rooftop apartments with a patch of outdoor space it can be a godsend. If visibility is an issue, use ultra-thin wire for the receiving element.

RF Systems GMDSS-1 antenna is tough and needs no juice, but other models are better for faint signals.   D. Zantow

✪✪✪
Dressler ARA 60 S

Outdoor-indoor rod. Active, remote, broadband, 0.04–60/100 MHz.

Price: $349.95 in the United States. £239.95 in the United Kingdom. €219.00 in Germany.

Pro: Superior build quality, with fiberglass whip and foam-encapsulated head amplifier to resist weather (*see* Con). Very good and consistent gain, even above 20 MHz. AC adaptor with properly bypassed and regulated DC output is better than most. Suitable for packing diagonally in wide suitcase.

Con: Encapsulated design makes most repairs impossible. RG-58 coaxial cable permanently attached on antenna end, making user replacement impossible. Gain control cumbersome to adjust; fortunately, in practice it is rarely needed. Reader reports suggest that ordering direct from the factory can be a frustrating experience.

☞ Star rating applies only when used where there is not significant ambient mediumwave RF, as the Dressler ARA 60 S, unless mounted close to the ground, appears to be prone to overloading at locations rich with strong mediumwave AM signals or low-band VHF-TV stations. At some locations, even mounting antenna on the ground may not eliminate overloading. Mediumwave AM overloading seems exacerbated by pickup from coaxial cable lead-in, as it does not appear to be properly decoupled from antenna (unlike Wellbrook and DX Engineering models, which can be mounted high with long cables).

Verdict: The robust Dressler ARA 60 S, made in Germany, is an excellent low-noise antenna for locations not near one or more powerful mediumwave AM or low-band VHF-TV transmitters.

✪✪⅞
RF Systems GMDSS-1

Outdoor vertical rod. Passive, remote, broadband, 0.1–25 MHz.

Price: *Antenna:* $259.95 in the United States. €150.00 in the Netherlands. *AK-1 mounting*

bracket kit: $22.95 in the United States. *AK-2 mounting bracket kit:* $34.95 in the United States. €32.00 in the Netherlands.

Pro: Superior signal-to-noise ratio for a compact antenna except within 21 MHz segment. Superior rejection of local electrical noise. Passive (unamplified) design avoids hum, buzz and other shortcomings often inherent with active antennas (*see* Con). No amplification required; yet, from about 9 MHz through 12 MHz this short antenna (6.5 feet/two meters) produces signals almost comparable to those from a lengthy outdoor wire antenna (*see* Con). Passive design allows it to function in emergency situations where electricity is not assured. Vertical configuration unusually appropriate for certain locations; can be further camouflaged with non-metallic paint. Superior build quality, using stainless steel and heavy UV resistant PVC; also, internal helical receiving element is rigorously sealed. No radials required, unusual for a vertical antenna. Worthy mediumwave AM reception for a nondirectional antenna.

Con: Except for approximately 9 MHz through 12 MHz, weak-signal performance varies from fair to poor, depending on the tuned frequency. A mounting kit is required and is extra. The AK-1 mounting bracket kit, sold in North America, not stainless. Connecting cable between antenna and radio not included.

☞ A slightly less costly ($199.95) variant of the GMDSS-1 is the RF Systems MTA-1, which nominally operates to full specification from 0.5–30 MHz.

Verdict: Although unamplified and scarcely taller than most men, the RF Systems GMDSS-1 vertical performs surprisingly well. However, pedestrian signal oomph in many world band segments limits its attraction except with a high-sensitivity receiver or an active preselector. Some portables also benefit from the modest signal input.

Made in the Netherlands, it is constructed like a tank. Between this and its complete independence from electricity, it is unusually appropriate for emergencies, civil disorders and hostile climates.

✪✪⅞
AOR LA380

Indoor loop. Active, essentially proximate, manual preselection 3–40 MHz/broadband 0.01–3 MHz & 40–500 MHz

Price: *LA380 antenna:* $379.95 in the United States. £189.00 in the United Kingdom. *BNC female-to-PL259 adaptor:* $4.95 in the United States.

Pro: Above-average gain. High-Q tunable preselector reduces the possibility of overload between 3 and 40 MHz (*see* Con). Rotatability nulls (reduces) local electrical noise and static below 10 MHz, to a lesser extent up to about 18 MHz. Rotatability can sometimes also slightly reduce co-channel shortwave interference; as is the norm with loop antennas, this modest nulling of co-channel skywave interference is best at frequencies below 5 MHz. Outstanding reception of time signals on 40 and 60

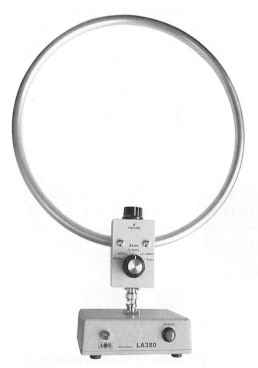

Wellbrook's loops shine, but they're large and available only from Wales. The AOR LA380 is smaller and more widely sold.   D. Zantow

kHz, which have preset tuning. Very easy to rotate and tune, with large knobs. Loop receiving element can be remotely mounted up to 16 feet/five meters away (*see* Con). Hum-free AC adaptor complemented by built-in voltage regulator in base unit. Knobs use set screws. Very solid metal lower box that has beefy non-stick-on rubber feet; uses machined, not self-tapping, cabinet/loop and BNC-connector screws. Three-foot/90-cm male-to-male BNC cable. Small footprint. One-foot/30-cm loop and small base module make antenna suitable for travel.

Con: Quasi-proximate model with preselector controls on receiving element; however, to be practical that element needs to be within user's grasp to adjust 3–40 MHz tunable preselector. High-"Q" preselection requires frequent tweaking when frequencies changed between 3–40 MHz. Tunable preselection, desirable, limited to 3–40 MHz; except for 40 and 60 kHz, which are specially peaked, other frequencies are broadband. Mediocre mediumwave AM performance. Male BNC connector on receiving element not snug, rocks slightly. Tuned by inexpensive plastic-cased tuning capacitor, underwhelming for price class. Receiving element

For handy travel use, nothing quite equals the Sony AN-LP1 foldaway loop antenna. The catch? It's now available only via a Japanese export vendor.

J.R. Sherwood

in plastic box; cover merely snaps on. Lacks 16-foot/five-meter male BNC/BNC cable for nominal remote mounting of receiving element. Lacks BNC female-to-PL259 adaptor for connection to many models of tabletop receivers.

Verdict: The nicely sized AOR LA380 is a decent performer—free from spurious signals, overloading and hum. Yet, its tunable preselector is part of the receiving element and needs frequent tweaking, so remote mounting isn't practical.

Where local electrical noise doesn't intrude, the '380's superior gain, handy size and ease of rotation make it an effective choice for indoor use. Made in Japan, generally well constructed and priced accordingly.

✪✪¾ ✐ *Passport's Choice*
Sony AN-LP1

Indoor-portable loop. Active, remote, manual preselection, 3.9–4.3/4.7–25 MHz.

Price (as available): $99.00 via stores. ebay.com/buyfromjapan; includes prompt express air shipping from Japan to the United States. ¥8,800 as available in Japan.

Pro: Excellent for use with portables. Very good overall performance, including generally superior gain (*see* Con), especially within world band segments—yet surprisingly free from side effects. Battery operation, so no internally caused hum or noise (*see* Con). Clever compact folding design for airline and other travel; also handy for institutional use where antenna must be stashed periodically. Can be used even with portables that have no antenna input jack (*see* Con). Plug-in filter to reduce local electrical noise (*see* Con). Low battery consumption (*see* Con).

Con: Seemingly discontinued, but in any event is now available only in and via Japan. Indoors only—can't be mounted outdoors during inclement weather. Functions acceptably on shortwave only 3.9–4.3 MHz and 4.7–25 MHz, with no mediumwave AM or longwave coverage. Gain varies markedly throughout the shortwave spectrum, in large part because the preselector's step-tuned resonances lack variable peaking. Preselector bandswitching complicates operation slightly. Operates only from batteries (two "AA," not included)—no AC adaptor provided, not even a socket for one. Consumer-grade plastic construction with no shielding. When clipped onto a telescopic antenna instead of fed through an antenna jack, the lack of a ground connection reduces performance. Plug-in noise filter unit reduces signal strength by several decibels.

☞ Sony recommends that the AN-LP1 not be used with the discontinued Sony ICF-SW77 receiver. However, our tests indicate that so long as the control box and loop receiving element are kept as far as possible from the radio, the antenna performs well.

☞ The Sony ICF-SW07 compact portable came with an AN-LP2 antenna. This is virtually identical in concept and performance to the AN-LP1, except that because it is designed solely for use with the 'SW07 it has automatic preselection to simplify operation. The AN-LP2 cannot be used with other radios, even those from Sony.

Verdict: This is the handiest model for travelers wanting superior world band reception on portables—and it is truly portable. It is often a worthy choice for portatop and tabletop models, as well, provided you don't mind battery-only operation. This Japanese-made device has generally excellent gain, low noise and few side effects. Priced right, too.

There is limited frequency coverage—90/120 meter DXers should look elsewhere—and the loop receiving element cannot be mounted permanently outdoors. Too, the lack of variable preselector peaking causes gain to vary greatly by frequency. Otherwise, the Sony AN-LP1 has been nothing short of a bargain.

The AN-LP1, seemingly discontinued in the first half of 2006, is no longer available in North America or Europe. Yet, it continues to be available from Japanese outlets. One—Buy from Japan—ships worldwide and has earned kudos from Passport readers for its prompt service.

★★½ ⊘
Ameco TPA

Indoor rod. Active, proximate, manual preselection, 0.22–30 MHz.

Price: *TPA:* $76.95 in the United States. CAD$98.00 in Canada.

Pro: Highest recovered signal with the longest supplied antenna of the four proximate models tested. Most pleasant unit to tune to proper frequency. Superior ergonomics, including easy-to-read front panel with good-sized metal knobs (*see* Con). Superior gain below 10 MHz. Suitable for travel.

Con: Proximate model, so receiving element has to be placed near receiver. Above 15 MHz gain slips to slightly below average. Overloads with external antenna; because gain potentiometer is in the first stage, decreasing gain may increase overloading as current drops through the FET. Preselector complicates operation, compromising otherwise-superior ergonomics. No rubber feet, slides around in use; user-remediable. Consumer-grade plastic construction with no shielding. Comes with no printed information on warranty; however, manufacturer states by telephone that it is the customary one year.

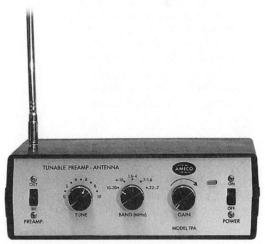

Radio graybeards wistfully recall when "Ameco" was known for gizmos like code-learning kits. Decades later the name soldiers on with the Ameco TPA.   J.R. Sherwood

Verdict: Back in the heyday of Hammarlund, Hallicrafters and National, there also was Ameco with its CW learning kits and the like. While most other American radio firms were crushed by the advance of technology, Ameco stayed light on its feet and survived. Well, sort of. Since 2004 Ameco has been associated with a new firm, Milestone Technologies of Colorado.

Ameco's TPA active antenna remains one of the best proximate models tested for bringing in usable signals with a telescopic antenna, and signal recovery is excellent. However, when connected to an external antenna it overloads badly, and reducing gain doesn't help.

★★½
McKay Dymek DA100E, McKay Dymek DA100EM, Stoner Dymek DA100E, Stoner Dymek DA100EM

Indoor-outdoor-marine rod. Active, remote, broadband, 0.05–30 MHz.

Price: *DA100E:* $199.95 in the United States. *DA100EM (marine version, not tested):* $219.95 in the United States.

Pro: Respectable gain and noise. Generally good build quality, with worthy coaxial cable and an effectively sealed receiving element; marine version (not tested) appears to be even better yet for resisting weather. Jack for second antenna when turned off. Minor gain rolloff at higher shortwave frequencies. Marginally suitable for travel. *DA100EM (not tested):*

All that remains of the late George McKay's line of world band components is the Dymek DA100E accessory antenna.   J.R. Sherwood

Weather-resistant fiberglass whip and brass fittings help ensure continued optimum performance.

Con: Slightly higher noise floor compared to other models. Some controls may confuse initially. Dynamic range among the lowest of any model tested; for many applications in the Americas this is adequate, but for use near local transmitters, or in Europe and other strong-signal parts of the world, the antenna is best purchased on a returnable basis. *DA100E:* Telescopic antenna allows moisture and avian waste penetration between segments, and thus potential resistance and/or spurious signals; user should seal these gaps with Coax Seal, electrical putty or similar. Telescopic antenna could, in principle, be de-telescoped by birds, ice and the like, although we did not actually encounter this. Warranty only 30 days.

Verdict: The DA100E is a proven "out of the box" choice, with generally excellent weatherproofing and coaxial cable. Because its dynamic range is relatively modest, it is more prone than some other models to overload, especially in an urban environment or other high-signal-strength location. In principle the extra twenty bucks for the marine version should be a good investment, provided its fiberglass whip is not too visible for your location.

★★¼
MFJ-1024

Indoor-outdoor rod. Active, remote, broadband, 0.05–30 MHz.

Price: $159.95 in the United States. CAD$219.00 in Canada. £139.95 in the United Kingdom. €172.00 in Germany. *MFJ-1312D 120V AC adaptor:* $15.95 in the United States. CAD$29.00 in Canada. *MFJ-1312DX 240V AC adaptor:* £15.95 in the United Kingdom.

Pro: Overall good gain and low noise. A/B selector for quick connection to another receiver. "Aux" input for passive antenna. Marginally suitable for travel. 30-day money-back guarantee if purchased from manufacturer.

Con: Significant hum with supplied AC adaptor; remedied when we substituted a suitable aftermarket adaptor. Non-standard power socket complicates substitution of AC adaptor; also, adaptor's sub-mini plug can spark when inserted while the adaptor is plugged in; adaptor should be unplugged beforehand. Dynamic range among the lowest of any model tested; for many applications in the Americas it is adequate, but for use near local transmitters, or in Europe and other strong-signal parts of the world, antenna is best purchased on a returnable basis. Slightly increased noise floor compared to other models. Telescopic antenna allows moisture and avian waste penetration between segments, and thus potential resistance and/or spurious signals; user should seal these gaps with Coax Seal, electrical putty or similar. Telescopic antenna could, in principle, be de-telescoped by birds, ice and the like after installation, although we did not actually encounter this. Control box/amplifier has no external weather sealing to protect from moisture, although the printed circuit board nominally comes with a water-resistant coating. Coaxial cable to receiver not provided. Mediocre coaxial cable provided between control box and receiving element. On our unit, a coaxial connector came poorly soldered from the factory.

Verdict: The MFJ-1024, made in America, performs almost identically to the Stoner Dymek DA100E, but sells for $40 less. However, that gap lessens if you factor in the cost of a worthy AC adaptor—assuming you can find or alter one to fit the unusual power jack—and the quality of the 1024's coaxial cable is not in Dymek's league.

✪✪¼
MFJ-1020C

Indoor rod. Active, proximate, manual preselection, 0.3–40 MHz.

Price: *MFJ-1020C:* $99.95 in the United States. CAD$119.95 in Canada. £89.95 in the United Kingdom. €105.00 in Germany. *MFJ-1312D 120V AC adaptor:* $15.95 in the United States. CAD$29.00 in Canada.

MFJ's compact 1024 isn't a top performer, but uses a remote element and is attractively priced. J.R. Sherwood

MFJ-1312DX 240V AC adaptor: £15.95 in the United Kingdom.

Pro: Rating rises to three stars if converted from a proximate to a remote model by connecting a wire to the external antenna input; see separate review, above. Superior dynamic range, and sharp preselector peak unusually effective in preventing overloading. Works best off battery (*see* Con). Choice of PL-259 or RCA connections. Suitable

The versatile MFJ-1020C has a removable telescopic element, as well as a connection for an outboard wire antenna. J.R. Sherwood

for travel. 30-day money-back guarantee if purchased from manufacturer.

Con: Proximate model, so receiving element has to be placed near receiver (can be converted, *see* Pro). Preselector complicates operation; tune control needs adjustment even with modest frequency changes, especially within the mediumwave AM band. Knobs small and touchy to adjust. High current draw (measures 30 mA), so battery runs down quickly. Removing sheet-metal screws often to change battery should eventually result in stripping unless great care is taken. AC adaptor, optional, causes significant hum on many received signals.

☞ Two manufacturing flaws found on one of our "B" version units tested in the past, but this year's "C" unit had no defects. The owner's manual warns of possible "taking off" if the gain is set too high, but during our tests using a variety of receivers we encountered oscillation with only one model.

Verdict: The MFJ-1020C, made in the United States, is okay as a proximate antenna with its own telescopic antenna. However, it works much better when coupled to a random-length wire in lieu of the built-in telescopic antenna; see the separate review earlier in this article.

Alas, the optional AC adaptor introduces hum much of the time, battery drain is considerable, and changing the built-in battery is inconvenient and relies on wear-prone sheet-metal screws. Best bet, unless you're into experimenting with power supplies: Skip the adaptor and use a large outboard rechargeable battery.

New for 2008
✪✪¼ (performance) ⊘ ✪ (practicality)
TG35

Indoor-portable loop (ferrite rod)/telescopic rod. Active, remote, broadband .03–3 MHz (ferrite rod)/3–30 MHz (telescopic rod).

Price: $73.90 including worldwide air shipping from stores.ebay.com/radio-component.

Pro: Good gain and low noise across full tuning range. Reasonably good dynamic range. Not prone to generate spurious signals. Long cable allows receiving element to be remotely mounted up to 16 feet/five meters away. Wide 0.3–30 MHz frequency coverage using two separate plugin receiving elements: a ferrite rod for mediumwave AM and 120 meters, and a telescopic rod for 3–30 MHz. Handy inductive coupler allows antenna to operate with receivers lacking external antenna jack. Suitable for travel. Mediumwave AM receiving element rotates to null co-channel interference and help reduce local-noise pickup (*see* Con). Telescopic receiving element swivels and rotates. Powered exclusively by NiMH rechargeable battery, so no internally caused hum or noise (*see* Con). Rechargeable by solar panels, provided (*see* Con); panels can offset battery depletion when idle over time. LED "on" indicator.

Con: No way to be powered by an AC adaptor or removable batteries, only by rechargeable internal battery similar to some found in cordless phones. Battery, being soldered into place, unusually difficult to replace. Battery charged primarily by connecting to a PC's USB port, but charging for 20 hours yields only 7.5 hours of operation. Battery's only other available means of charging is by provided solar cells; charging for fully three days in the sun yields merely 2.5 hours of operation. PC can charge battery only when computer not in hibernation or standby modes. Indoors only—can't be mounted outdoors during inclement weather. Mediocre build quality. Ferrite rod's small size—5½ inch/140 mm—limits potential to null co-channel mediumwave AM interference; placement some distance from the receiver also makes rotation inconvenient. No antenna adaptors included for receivers with PL-259 or BNC connection. Manufacturer and brand name unknown, although "DE35" appears on a circuit board, suggesting that the manufacturer may be Degen. No instructions included.

Verdict: There is such a thing as stealth antennas, but nothing else is quite so stealthy as the TG35 sold by a Chinese eBay vendor.

The new TG35 is as weird as a Gahan Wilson gnome. Yet, if you can live with its power oddities it can be mighty handy on trips. D. Zantow

After all, there is zero identification as to the manufacturer or brand name—just "TG35." Thank you, Mr. Bond.

This travel-friendly unit performs nicely with world band and mediumwave AM signals, alike. Alas, it is poorly made and operates only for relatively brief periods before requiring recharging. Most damning is that it can be charged only by Li Goldberg techniques requiring either days of sunlight or hours of tethering to a nearby PC.

Nevertheless, the antenna is affordable and reasonably portable, with good performance.

Evaluation of New Model: The new TG35 antenna is as weird as a Gahan Wilson gnome. Its main amplifier roosts near the receiving element within a large plastic box. For world band it is fed by a three-foot/one-meter plugin telescopic receiving element that covers 3–30 MHz. This element can be swapped out for a small ferrite rod which includes special electronics in its own little box; this element covers mediumwave .03 to 3 MHz, including the 520–1705 kHz AM band and the little-used 120 meter world band segment.

A 16-foot/five-meter length of UG-174 micro-coax runs from the main box at the receiving element to a small heart-shaped interface by the receiver. This interface, in turn, includes an on-off switch with LED indicator; it connects to the receiver by a 13-inch/33-cm cable.

There are no adaptors included for connection to, say, a tabletop or other receiver with BNC connector. However, a two-inch/five-cm inductive coupler allows the TG35 to connect to receivers lacking an antenna jack. It functions nicely.

Rube Goldberg Looks Down and Smiles

There is no way to power the TG35 from household current, even if you try an AC adaptor. Instead, the TG35 can be powered only by an internal 3.6V 600 mAh NiMH rechargeable cell. This is the same type of under-$20 battery used in a number of cordless phones, but with the TG35 it's soldered onto the main circuit board. So when it eventually gives out, likely in around five years, a replacement will first have to be located, then soldered in place—a silly and cumbersome procedure.

The battery can't be charged by conventional means, either. Rather, it has to be juiced by either a PC's USB port, using the included three-foot/90 cm cable, or solar cells which come affixed to the main box near the receiving element.

Brief Operation

In order to ensure the battery performed optimally, we totally cycled it a dozen times. Even then, a 20-hour charge from a PC resulted in only 7.5 hours of antenna operation. NiMH batteries tend to lose power over time even when not in use, so if they are charged in advance of a trip they'll provide even less operation time.

Adding to the inconvenience, the computer needs to be running; if it's in hibernation or standby, the USB port typically won't supply the needed 5V DC.

It gets worse when using the antenna's solar cells. In a sunny window for 75 hours, the cells mustered up a pitiful 2.5 hours of antenna operation. On the bright side, the solar feature provides enough juice to offset the battery's propensity to discharge when sitting idle.

Bargain Basement Board

The TG35's main circuit board is cheap, thin and on our sample is warped. The power LED is merely hot-glued into place.

Who Would've Thought It?

The TG35 comes across as marginal and peculiar. Yet, there's a surprise: It performs nicely. For starters, it has low noise and fairly good gain across its entire frequency range. Too, it isn't prone to generate spurious signals and doesn't need to be tuned when the received frequency is changed.

Another plus is that the ferrite rod receiving element, when properly aimed, helps null mediumwave AM co-channel interference and local electrical noise. Although the rod's short length limits nulling and remote placement makes turning inconvenient, this capability helps enhance signal-to-interference and signal-to-noise ratios.

Dynamic range is reasonable, so the antenna works well with the two provided receiving elements. But don't think of the TG35 as a low-cost amplifier, à la the MFJ 1020C, to Viagraize your favorite outdoor wire antenna. The TG35's dynamic range is good, but not hefty enough for that mission unless the wire is kept under, say, 15 feet/4.5 meters.

Weird, but It Works

Like B.C.'s mythical apteryx, a wingless bird with hairy feathers that can't fly, the TG35 is borderline useless. It can operate only after having been tethered for tens of hours to a PC which, by the way, can't be in hibernation mode—no small consideration, considering that before long all PCs probably will be required to hibernate. Yes, there's an included solar charger, but it doesn't cut the mustard.

Not weird enough? It uses a cordless phone battery. Firmly soldered into place.

But if you travel with a laptop or tablet PC having a spare USB port, the TG35 is small enough to stuff into a carry-on . . . if you don't mind explaining all those wires and boxes to Prunella the airport security lady.

New Versions for 2008
★★ ℰ
Degen DE31, Degen DE31MS, Kaito KA33, Thieking DE31-A, Thieking DE31-LM

Indoor-portable loop. Active, remote, manual preselection, 3.9–22 MHz

Price: *Degen DE31 (tested) via stores.ebay. com/radio-and-component:* $20.99 including air shipping from China to the United States. *Degen DE31MS via stores.ebay.com/radio-and-component:* $22.80 including air shipping from China to the United States. *Kaito KA33:* $39.95 in the United States. *Thieking DE31A:* €72.50 in Germany. *Thieking DE31-LM:* €72.00 in Germany.

Pro: Appropriate for use with portables. Meaningful gain, especially above 9 MHz. Very good dynamic range. Low noise and absence of spurious signals. Battery operation, so no internally caused hum or noise (*see* Con). Compact collapsible design for airline and other travel; also handy for institutional use where antenna must be stashed periodically. Long cable (*see* Con) allows loop to be placed relatively far from radio. Adaptor sometimes allows for connection to a receiver lacking 1/8-inch/4-mm antenna jack (*see* Con). Fairly low current draw (*see* Con). *DE31MS and KA33:* Also covers mediumwave AM 531–1602 kHz. *DE31-LM:* Also covers longwave and 531–1602 kHz mediumwave AM. *DE31A:* Coverage 1.8–22 MHz includes all tropical world band segments.

Con: Indoors only—can't be mounted outdoors during inclement weather. Touchy tuning control. Operates only from small batteries (two "AAA," not included) and has no AC adaptor or socket. Battery consumption, although low, nearly twice manufacturer's specification, so replacement rises accordingly. Consumer-grade plastic construction with no shielding. When clipped onto radio's telescopic antenna instead of fed through an antenna jack, the lack of a ground connection on the radio greatly reduces performance. Rotation for local-noise reduction impeded by limp-rope design. Small suction cup fails if it and glass surface not exceptionally clean; yet, when affixed, suction cup stubborn to remove. No carrying pouch to keep parts together. No reel to keep main cable from being tangled. *DE31, KA33 and DE31-LM:* Tunes shortwave only 3.9–22 MHz, so misses 2.3–2.5 and 3.2–3.4 MHz (120 and 90 meter) tropical world band segments. *DE31:* Likely to be unavailable shortly.

Verdict: Respectable performance, minimal investment.

The Kaito KA31/Degen DE31 and kindred models are eminently affordable and travel-friendly.

Con: Proximate model, so receiving element has to be placed near receiver. No AC power; although it accepts an AC adaptor, the lack of polarity markings complicates adaptor choice (it is center-pin positive).

⭐⭐

Vectronics AT-100

Indoor rod. Active, proximate, manual preselection, 0.3–30 MHz.

Price: $99.95 in the United States. CAD$109.00 in Canada. £79.95 in the United Kingdom.

Pro: Good—sometimes excellent—gain (*see* Con), especially in the mediumwave AM band. Good dynamic range. Most knobs are commendably large. Suitable for travel.

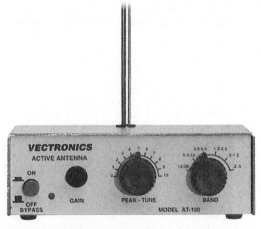

The proximate Vectronics AT-100 is an okay performer, but other models do better for less.   J.R. Sherwood

Preselector complicates operation, especially as it is stiff to tune and thus awkward to peak. Our unit oscillated badly with some receivers, limiting usable gain—although it was more stable with other receivers, and thus appears to be a function of the load presented by a given receiver.

Verdict: If ever there were a product that needs to be purchased on a returnable basis, this is it. With one receiver, this American-made model gives welcome gain and worthy performance; with another, it goes into oscillation nearly at the drop of a hat.

✪¾
Palstar AA30/AA30P

Indoor rod. Active, proximate, manual preselection, 0.3–30 MHz.

Price: $99.95 in the United States. £69.95 in the United Kingdom. €96.50 in Germany.

Pro: Moderate-to-good gain. Tuning control easily peaked. Can be powered directly by the Palstar R30/R30C and Lowe HF-350 tabletop receivers, an internal battery or an AC adaptor. Suitable for travel.

Con: Spurious oscillation throughout 14–30 MHz range. Overloads with external antenna. Proximate model, so receiving element has to be placed near receiver. Preselector complicates operation. No AC adaptor.

☞ Although the front panel is silk-screened AA30, the accompanying owner's manual refers to the AA30A. It is also promoted as

Palstar's AA30/AA30P offers little for the price. Look elsewhere.   J.R. Sherwood

the AA30P, although here, too, the front panel designation is AA30.

Verdict: Oscillation makes this a dubious choice except for reception below 14 MHz. Manufactured in the United States.

✪¾ ©
MFJ-1022

Indoor rod. Active, proximate, broadband, 0.3–200 MHz.

Price: *MFJ-1022:* $69.95 in the United States. CAD$69.00 in Canada. £59.95 in the United Kingdom. €62.00 in Germany. *MFJ-1312D 120V AC adaptor:* $15.95 in the United States. CAD$29.00 in Canada. *MFJ-1312DX 240V AC adaptor:* £15.95 in the United Kingdom.

Pro: Unusually broadband coverage reaches well into VHF spectrum. Considerable gain, peaking at 22.5 MHz, audibly helps signals that do not suffer from intermodulation. Idiot-proof to operate. Works best off battery (*see* Con). Suitable for travel. 30-day money-back guarantee if purchased from manufacturer.

Con: Proximate model, so receiving element has to be placed near receiver. Broadband design results in local mediumwave AM stations ghosting up to 2.7 MHz, and to a lesser degree up through the 3 MHz (90 meter) tropical world band segment at many locations; this often drops at night because of reduced local transmitting powers. Broadband design and high gain not infrequently results in intermodulation products/spurious signals and hiss between reasonable-level signals, and sometimes mixing with weaker signals. Within tropical world band segments, modest-level static from nearby thunderstorms, when coupled with overloading from local mediumwave AM signals, sometimes cause odd background sounds that are not heard with other antennas. High current draw (measures 35 mA), so battery runs down quickly. Removing sheet-metal screws often to change battery should eventually result in stripping unless great care is taken. AC adaptor, optional, causes significant hum on many received signals.

Verdict: Priced to move and offering broadband coverage, this compact antenna from MFJ couldn't be simpler to operate—one button, that's it. For helping to improve the listening quality of modest-strength international broadcasting signals, it works quite nicely. But don't expect to do much DXing, especially of the tropical world band segments unless you live well away from any mediumwave AM stations and maybe not even then. Forget the AC adaptor and stick to batteries.

Prepared by J. Robert Sherwood and David Zantow, with Lawrence Magne; also, a tip of the hat to George Heidelman and Chuck Rippel, as well as Lawrence Bulk.

MFJ's 1022 brings up the rear, even with unsurpassed simplicity of operation.   J.R. Sherwood

WHERE TO FIND IT: INDEX TO TESTED ANTENNAS

PASSPORT REPORTS evaluates the most relevant indoor and outdoor antennas on the market. Here's where to find each review, with models that are new, revised or retested for 2008 shown in **bold**. Passive—unamplified—antennas are in *italics*.

A comprehensive Radio Database International White Paper®, PASSPORT® *Evaluation of Popular Outdoor Antennas*, is available for $6.95 in North America, $9.95 airmail elsewhere, including shipping. It encompasses virtually all our panel's findings and comments during testing of passive wire antennas. Also included are details for proper and safe installation, along with instructions for inverted-L construction. This unabridged report is available from key world band dealers, or order 24/7 from www.passband.com, autovoice +1 215/598-9018 or fax +1 215/598 3794—or write PASSPORT RDI White Papers, Box 300, Penn's Park, PA 18943 USA.

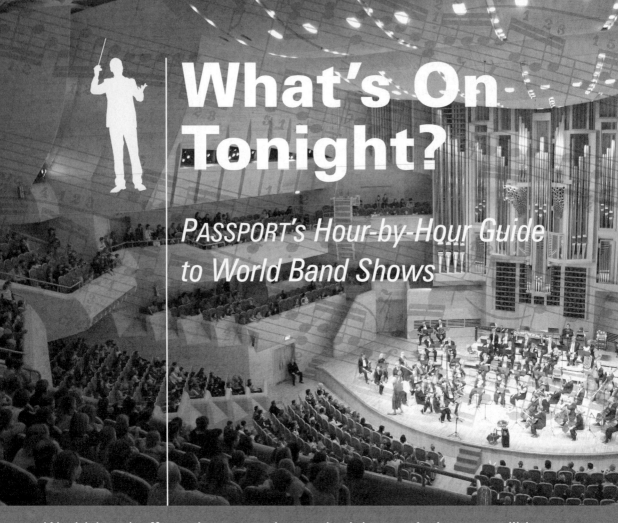

What's On Tonight?

PASSPORT's Hour-by-Hour Guide to World Band Shows

World band offers shows rarely found elsewhere, and they're unimpeded by gatekeepers. PASSPORT's "What's On" details the main English-language programs, with the best being tagged:

■ Station superior, with several excellent shows

● Show worth hearing

Some stations provide schedules, others don't. Yet, even official online schedules aren't always credible or complete. To resolve this, PASSPORT monitors stations around the world, firsthand, to detail and confirm schedule activity throughout the year. Additionally, to be as useful as possible, PASSPORT's schedules consist not just of observed activity, but also that which we have creatively opined will appear well into the year ahead. This predictive material is based on decades of experience, and is original from us. Although this is inherently less exact than confirmed real-time data, it has proven to be quite useful.

Primary frequencies are given for North America, western Europe, East Asia and Australasia, plus the Middle East, southern Africa and Southeast Asia. If you want secondary and seasonal channels, or frequencies for other parts of the world, check out "Worldwide Broadcasts in English" and the Blue Pages.

To eliminate confusion, World Time and World Day are used—both explained in "Getting Started" and "Worldly Words." Seasons are for the Northern Hemisphere (summer around July, winter around January).

Shutterstock/Margita Braze

00:00–05:59
North America—Evening Prime Time
Europe & Mideast—Early Morning
Australasia & East Asia—Midday and Afternoon

00:00

■**Radio Netherlands.** Tuesday through Saturday (weekday evenings in North America), ●*Newsline* (current events) is followed by a 30-minute feature. Tuesday, there's a look at all things Dutch; Wednesday, it's the midweek edition of ●*The State We're In*. Thursday's slot is *Radio Books*, replaced Friday by *Earth Beat* and Saturday by *Network Europe*. On the remaining days there's Sunday's ●*The State We're In* and Monday's *Amsterdam Forum* and *Reloaded* (highlights of the previous week's shows). Fifty-seven minutes to eastern North America winter on 6165 kHz, and summer on 9845 kHz.

■**Deutsche Welle,** Germany. Starts with five minutes of *News*, then ●*NewsLink*—commentary, interviews, background reports and analysis. On the half-hour there's *Sports Report* and *Radio D*, a German language course (Monday), *World in Progress* (Tuesday), ●*Spectrum* (science and technology, Wednesday) ●*Money Talks* (Thursday), *Living Planet* (Friday) and ●*Inside Europe* (Saturday). The Sunday features are *Sports Report* and *Inspired Minds*. Sixty minutes to East and Southeast Asia winter on 7265, 9785 and 15595 kHz, and summer on 7245 and 15595 kHz. Also heard in parts of Australia.

Radio Bulgaria. Winter only at this time. Tuesday through Saturday (weekday evenings in North America), *News* is followed by *Events and Developments*, replaced Sunday and Monday by *Views Behind the News*. The remaining time is taken up by regular programs such as *Keyword Bulgaria* and *Time Out for Music*, and weekly features like ●*Folk Studio* (Monday), *Sports* (Tuesday), *Magazine Economy* (Wednesday), *The Way We Live* (Thursday), *History Club* (Friday), *DX Programme* (Saturday) and *Answering Your Letters*, a listener-response show, on Sunday. Sixty minutes to eastern North America and Central America on 7400 and 9400 kHz. One hour earlier in summer.

Radio Canada International. Tuesday through Saturday, it's *The Link*, replaced Sunday by *Behind the Link* and Monday by *Maple Leaf Mailbag*. One hour to Southeast

00:00–00:30

Downtown Prague, where Radio Prague prepares news and Czech cultural reports for the world entire.

Shutterstock/Daniela Weinstein

Asia winter on 9880 kHz, and summer on 11700 kHz. Also winter only (one hour earlier in summer) to the central United States on 9755 kHz, and starts at 0005.

Radio Japan. Predominantly news programming at this hour. Twenty minutes to Europe on 5960 and/or 5920 kHz; to eastern North America on 6145 kHz; and to Southeast Asia on 13650 and 17810 kHz.

Radio Exterior de España ("Spanish National Radio"). Tuesday through Saturday (local weekday evenings in the Americas), there's Spanish and international *news*, commentary, Spanish pop music, a review of the Spanish press, and a general interest feature. Weekends, it's all features, including rebroadcasts of some of the weekday programs. Sixty minutes to eastern North America on 6055 kHz. Popular with many listeners.

China Radio International. *News* and reports fill the first half-hour, and are followed by a daily feature: *Front Line* (Monday), *Biz China* (Tuesday), *In the Spotlight* (Wednesday), ●*Voices from Other Lands* (Thursday), *Life in China* (Friday), *Listeners' Garden* (Saturday) and *China Horizons* (Sunday).

To Europe on 7130 kHz; to North America on 6020 and 9570 kHz; to East Asia winter on 9425 kHz, and summer on 13750 kHz; and to Southeast Asia winter on 11650 and 11885 kHz, and summer on 11885 and 15125 kHz. These days are World Time, so locally in North America it will be the previous evening.

Radio Ukraine International. Summer only at this time. Ample and interesting coverage of local issues, including news, sports, politics and culture. Recommended listening is ●*Music from Ukraine*, which fills most of the Monday (Sunday evening in the Americas) broadcast. Sixty minutes to eastern North America on 7440 (or 5820) kHz. One hour later in winter.

Voice of Greece. Monday and winter only at this time, and actually starts at 0005. Approximately 60 minutes of music in *Greek in Style*. To North America on 7475 and 9420 kHz; and to Central and South America on 12105 kHz. One hour earlier in summer. ☞ Monday World Time is Sunday evening in the Americas.

Radio Australia. Part of a 24-hour service to Asia and the Pacific. Begins with *World*

News, the Monday through Friday it's *The Breakfast Club*, a mix of talk and music for listeners in Asia and the Pacific. Winter Saturdays, there's *Asia Review*, *Asia Pacific Business* and *Talking Point*; and Sunday's feature is *The Spirit of Things*. In summer, Saturday features are *In the Loop (Rewind)* and *Australian Express*, replaced Sunday by *Background Briefing* (investigative journalism). On 9660, 12080, 13690, 15240, 15415 (from 0030), 17715, 17750, 17775 and 17795 kHz. In North America (best during summer) try 17715 and 17795 kHz. In East Asia tune to 13690 kHz, and for Southeast Asia there's 15415, 17750 and 17775 kHz.

Radio Prague, Czech Republic. Summer only at this time. *News*, then Tuesday through Saturday (weekday evenings in the Americas) there's *Current Affairs* and one or more features: *One on One* (Tuesday); *Talking Point* (Wednesday); *Czechs in History*, *Czechs Today* or *Spotlight* (Thursday); *Panorama* and *Czech Science* (Friday); and *Business Briefs* and *The Arts* on Saturday. The Sunday lineup is *Magazine*, *ABC of Czech* and *One on One*; replaced Monday by *Mailbox* and *Letter from Prague* followed by *Encore* (classical music), *Magic Carpet* (Czech world music) or *Czech Books*. Thirty minutes to North America and the Caribbean on 7345 and 9440 kHz. One hour later in winter.

Radio Austria International. Winter only at this time. Tuesday through Saturday (weekday evenings in the Americas), the 15-minute *Report from Austria* is aired at 0013. Sunday and Monday, it's ●*Report from Austria–The Week in Review* at 0005. The remainder of the broadcast is in German and (Tuesday through Saturday) Spanish. To Central America on 7325 kHz. One hour later in summer.

Radio Thailand. *Newshour*. Thirty minutes to eastern and southern Africa, winter on 9680 kHz and summer on 9570 kHz.

All India Radio. The final 45 minutes of a much larger block of programming targeted at East and Southeast Asia, and heard

well beyond. To East Asia on 9950, 11620, 11645 and 13605 kHz; and to Southeast Asia on 9705, 11620 and 13605 kHz.

Radio Cairo, Egypt. The final half-hour of a 90-minute broadcast to eastern North America. *Arabic by Radio* can be heard on the hour, and there's a daily *news* bulletin at 0015. See 2300 for more specifics. Winter on 9465 kHz, and summer on 9460 kHz.

Radio New Zealand International. A friendly package of *news* and features sometimes replaced by live sports commentary. Part of a 24-hour broadcast for the South Pacific, but also heard in parts of North America (especially during summer). On 15720 or 17675 kHz.

AFRTS Shortwave, USA. Network news, live sports, music and features in the *upper-sideband* mode from the American Forces Radio & Television Service. Transmitted from modestly powered U.S. Navy stations around the globe, so usually a tough catch. Try 4319, 5446.5, 5765, 6350, 7811, 10320, 12133.5, 12579 and 13362 kHz.

00:30

Radio Vilnius, Lithuania. Thirty minutes of news and background reports, mainly about Lithuania. Of broader appeal is *Mailbag*, aired every other Sunday (Saturday evenings local American date). For some Lithuanian music, try the next evening, towards the end of the broadcast. To eastern North America winter on 9875 kHz and summer on 11690 kHz.

Radio Austria International. Winter only at this time. Tuesday through Saturday (weekday evenings in the Americas), there's 15 minutes of *Report from Austria* at 0043. Sunday and Monday, it's ●*Report from Austria–The Week in Review* at 0033. The remainder of the broadcast is in German and (Tuesday through Saturday) Spanish. To eastern North America on 7325 kHz. One hour later in summer.

Radio Thailand. *Newshour*. Thirty minutes to central and eastern North America on 5890 (or 12095 kHz).

01:00–01:00

The Rijksmuseum Amsterdam, completed in 1885, is home to Dutch Masters paintings and other capstones of Dutch life and culture. Radio Netherlands excels in news and lifestyles from the Netherlands, bringing these direct to homes worldwide.   M. Wright

01:00

■**Radio Netherlands.** Repeat of the 0000 broadcast; see there for specifics. Fifty-seven minutes to central North America on 6165 kHz winter, and 9845 kHz summer.

Radio Austria International. Summer only at this time. Tuesday through Saturday (weekday evenings in the Americas), there's *Report from Austria* at 0113. Sunday and Monday, it's ●*Report from Austria–The Week in Review* at 0105. The remainder of the broadcast is in German and (Tuesday through Saturday) Spanish. To Central America on 9870 kHz. One hour earlier in winter.

Radio Prague, Czech Republic. *News,* then Tuesday through Saturday (weekday evenings in the Americas) there's the in-depth *Current Affairs* and a feature or two: *One on One* (Tuesday), *Talking Point* (Wednesday), *Czechs in History, Czechs Today* or *Spotlight* (Thursday), *Panorama* and *Czech Science* (Friday), and *Business Briefs* and *The Arts* on Saturday. The Sunday news is followed by *Magazine, ABC of Czech* and a repeat of

Wednesday's *One on One*; and Monday's lineup is *Mailbox* and *Letter from Prague* followed by *Encore* (classical music), *Magic Carpet* (Czech world music) or *Czech Books*. Thirty minutes to eastern and central North America and the Caribbean on 6200 and 7345 kHz.

Radio Slovakia International. *News* and features on Slovak life and culture. Monday (Sunday evening in North America), look for a listener-response program and a little Slovak music. Half an hour to eastern North America winter on 7230 kHz, and summer on 5930 kHz. Also year-round to South America on 9440 kHz.

China Radio International. Repeat of the 0000 broadcast, but with news updates. One hour to North America on 6005 (winter), 6020, 6080 (winter), 9570, 9580 and (summer) 9790 kHz, via CRI's Albanian, Cuban and Canadian relays. Also to Europe winter on 7130 kHz, and summer on 9470 kHz; and to Southeast Asia on 11650 (winter), 11885 and (summer) 15125 kHz.

Voice of Vietnam. A relay via the facilities of Radio Canada International. Begins with *news,* then there's *Commentary* or *Weekly Review,* followed by short features and some pleasant Vietnamese music (especially at weekends). A listener-response segment airs at 0115 Thursday (Wednesday evening local American date). Thirty minutes to eastern North America, with reception better to the south. On 6175 kHz. Repeated at 0230 and 0330 on the same channel.

Voice of Russia World Service. Summer only at this hour, and the start of a four-hour block of programming for North America. *News,* then Tuesday through Saturday (weekday evenings in North America), there's more news programming. This is replaced Sunday and Monday by *Moscow Mailbag.* Features fill the second half-hour: *Timelines* (Monday), *Kaleidoscope* (Tuesday and Friday), *Russian by Radio* (Wednesday), *The VOR Treasure Store* (Thursday), the evocative ●*Christian Message from Moscow* (Saturday) and *Our Homeland* on Sunday.

ATS-909

The **ATS-909** is the flagship of the Sangean line. It packs features and performance into a very compact and stylish package. Coverage includes all long wave, medium wave and shortwave frequencies. FM and FM stereo to the headphone jack is also available. Shortwave performance is enhanced with a wide-narrow bandwidth switch and excellent single side band performance. Five tuning methods are featured: keypad, auto scan, manual up-down, memory recall or tuning knob. The alphanumeric memory lets you store 306 presets. The three event clock-timer displays even when the radio is tuning and has 42 world city zones. The large backlit LCD also features a signal strength and battery bar graph. The ATS-909 will display RDS on PL, PS and CT for station name and clock time in areas where this service is available. Also features a record jack and tone switch. Includes AC adapter, carry case, stereo ear buds and Sangean ANT-60 roll-up antenna. 8½" x 5½" x 1½". Requires four AA cells (not supplied). #1909

ATS-606AP

The **ATS-606AP** covers *all* long wave, AM and shortwave frequencies (153 - 29995 kHz) plus FM stereo. It has digital readout, 1 kHz SW tuning, 54 memories & keypad entry. A dual digital clock-timer alarm shows local and UTC. With auto-scan, dial light, DX and lock switch. An excellent choice for shortwave broadcast listening (no SSB). With: case, earbuds and multilanguage manual. This enhanced "AP" version also includes the ANT-60 wind-up antenna and multi-voltage 110-230 VAC adapter. Requires 3 AA cells. 5¾"x3½"x1¼" 1 Lb. #3319

ATS-818ACS

Have you been waiting for a quality digital world band radio with a built-in cassette recorder? Now you have it in the exciting **Sangean ATS-818ACS**. This no-compromise receiver has full dual-conversion shortwave coverage (1.6 - 30 MHz) plus long wave, AM and FM (stereo to headphone jack). A BFO control is included for smooth SSB/CW reception. A big LCD display with dial lamp shows: frequency (1 kHz on SW), 24 hour time, battery indicator and signal strength. The receiver features an RF gain, tone control, wide-narrow selectivity, keypad entry, external antenna jack, manual tuning knob, plus 54 memories (18 for shortwave). The monaural recorder has a built-in mic and auto-shutoff. Includes AC power adapter. Requires 4 D cells and 3 AA cells (not supplied). 11¼" x 7" x 2½". #1069

PT-80

The Sangean PT-80 *Pro-Travel* is a compact digital radio with LW, AM, FM and continuous shortwave coverage. This dual conversion receiver features: 45 memories, single sideband, backlit LCD, dial lock plus dual world time clock with alarm, snooze and sleep. Tune by: keypad, autoscan, memory recall or rotary knob. Switches are provided for: Local-DX, dial lock and stereo-mono. With external antenna jack. Includes: AC adapter, earphones, wind-up antenna and butter-soft leather pouch. Requires 4 AA cells (not supplied). #1080

ATS-505P

The **Sangean ATS-505P** covers LW, AM, FM and all shortwave frequencies. The backlit display shows frequency or 12/24 time. Tune via the tuning knob, Up-Down buttons, auto tune, keypad or from the 45 memories. Other features include: SSB clarify knob, 9/10 kHz AM step, dial lock, stereo-mono switch, alarm by radio or buzzer, sleep-timer, tune LED, external antenna input and 6 VDC jack. With: AC adapter, ANT-60 wind-up antenna, case and earphones. Requires four AA cells (not supplied). 8.5" x 5.3" x 1.6" #3505

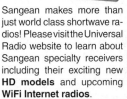

Sangean makes more than just world class shortwave radios! Please visit the Universal Radio website to learn about Sangean specialty receivers including their exciting new **HD models** and upcoming WiFi Internet radios.

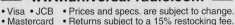

01:00–02:00

Best for eastern North America are 7250 and 9665 kHz. Farther west, use 13775 kHz.

Radio Habana Cuba. The start of a two-hour cyclical broadcast to North America. Tuesday through Sunday (Monday through Saturday evenings in North America), the first half-hour consists of international and Cuban *news* followed by *RHC's Viewpoint*. The next 30 minutes consist of a *news* bulletin and the sports-oriented *Time Out* (five minutes each) plus a feature: *Caribbean Outlook* (Tuesday and Friday), *DXers Unlimited* (Wednesday and Sunday), the *Mailbag Show* (Thursday) and *Weekly Review* (Saturday). Monday, the hour is split between *Weekly Review* and *Mailbag Show*. To eastern and central North America on 6000 and 6180 kHz.

Voice of Korea, North Korea. The dinosaur of world band and the last of the old-style communist stations. One hour to East Asia on 3560, 7140, 9345 and 9730 kHz; and to Central America on 11735, 13760 and 15180 kHz.

Radio Taiwan International. Ten minutes of *News*, followed by features: *The Occidental Tourist*, *Generation Why* and *Asia Review* (Monday); *Made in Taiwan* and *We've Got Mail* (Tuesday); *Strait Talk*, *Women Making Waves* and ●*Jade Bells and Bamboo Pipes* (Wednesday); *Trends*, *People*, *Instant Noodles* and *Chinese to Go* (Thursday); *Ilha Formosa*, *Mandopop* and *Taiwan Outlook* (Friday); *Walks of Life* and *Groove Zone* (Saturday); and *News Talk*, *Chinese to Go* (language lessons) *Stage, Screen and Studio* and *On the Line* (Sunday). One hour to the Philippines on 11875 kHz. Also heard in parts of Australia.

Radio Australia. Part of a 24-hour service to Asia and the Pacific, but which can also be heard at this time in parts of North America (better to the west). Begins with *World News*, then Monday through Friday it's the final hour of *The Breakfast Club*. Winter weekends, there's live sport in *Grandstand*. In summer, this is replaced by Saturday's *Pacific Review* and *Asia Pacific*

Business, and Sunday's *The Spirit of Things*. On 9660, 12080, 13690, 15240, 15415, 17715, 17750, 17775 (till 0130) and 17795 kHz. In North America (best during summer) try 17715 and 17795 kHz. In East Asia tune to 13690 kHz, and for Southeast Asia there's 15415, 17750 and 17775 kHz.

Radio Ukraine International. Winter only at this time; see 0000 for specifics. Sixty minutes of informative programming targeted at eastern North America. On 5820 (or 7440) kHz. One hour earlier in summer.

Radio New Zealand International. Continues with *news* and features sometimes replaced by live sports commentary. Continuous to the South Pacific, and also heard in parts of North America (especially during summer). On 15720 or 17675 kHz.

AFRTS Shortwave, USA. Network news, live sports, music and features in the *upper-sideband* mode from the American Forces Radio & Television Service. Transmitted from modestly powered U.S. Navy stations around the globe, so usually a tough catch. Try 4319, 5446.5, 5765, 6350, 7811, 10320, 12133.5, 12579 and 13362 kHz.

01:30

Radio Sweden. Summer only at this time. Tuesday through Saturday (weekday evenings in North America), it's a smorgasbord of *news* and features about Sweden. Sunday, there's a review of the main news stories of the previous week; and Monday it's *Network Europe*. Thirty minutes to South Asia on 11675 kHz, and to eastern North America on 6010 kHz. One hour later in winter.

Radio Austria International. Summer only at this time. Tuesday through Saturday (weekday evenings in the Americas), there's 15 minutes of *Report from Austria* at 0143. Sunday and Monday, it's ●*Report from Austria–The Week in Review* at 0135. The remainder of the broadcast is in German and (Tuesday through Saturday) Spanish. To eastern North America on 9870 kHz. One hour earlier in winter.

Voice of the Islamic Republic of Iran.
Unlike the broadcasts to other parts of the
world, the programs at this hour are from
the separate "Voice of Justice" service,
specially tailored to an American audience.
One hour to North America winter on 6120
and 7160 kHz, and summer on 7235 and
9495 kHz.

01:45

Radio Tirana, Albania. Tuesday through
Sunday (Monday through Saturday evenings in North America) and summer only
at this time. Approximately 15 minutes
of news and commentary from this small
Balkan country. To North America on 6110
(or 6115) and 7425 kHz. One hour later in
winter.

02:00

Radio Cairo, Egypt. The first hour of a
90-minute broadcast. A ten-minute news
bulletin is aired at 0215, with the remaining
time taken up by short features on Egypt,
the Middle East and Islam. For the intellectual listener there's *Literary Readings* at
0245 Monday, and *Modern Arabic Poetry* at
the same time Friday. More general fare is
available in *Listener's Mail* at 0225 Thursday
and Saturday. To North America on 7270
kHz.

Voice of Greece. Sunday and summer
only at this time. Sixty minutes of *Hellenes
Around the World* (also known as *Greeks
Everywhere*). To North America on 7475
and 9420 kHz, and to Australasia on 15650
kHz. For North America it's one hour later
in winter, and for Australasia it moves to
1400 Saturday. ☞ Sunday World Time is
Saturday evening in North America.

Radio Argentina al Exterior—RAE Tuesday through Saturday only (local weekday
evenings in the Americas). A freewheeling
presentation of news, press review, short
features and local Argentinean music. Not
the easiest station to tune, but popular with
many of those who can hear it. Fifty-five
minutes nominally to North America on

11710 kHz, but tends to be best heard in
the southern U.S. and the Caribbean. Sometimes pre-empted by live soccer commentary in Spanish.

Radio Bulgaria. Summer only at this time.
Starts with *News*, then Tuesday through
Saturday (weekday evenings in North
America) there's *Events and Developments*,
replaced Sunday and Monday by *Views
Behind the News*. The remaining time is split
between regular programs like *Keyword
Bulgaria* and *Time Out for Music*, and weekly
features like ●*Folk Studio* (Monday), *Sports*
(Tuesday), *Magazine Economy* (Wednesday),
The Way We Live (Thursday), *History Club*
(Friday), *DX Programme* (for radio enthusiasts, Saturday) and *Answering Your Letters*,
a listener- response show, on Sunday. Sixty
minutes to eastern North America and Central America on 9700 and 11700 kHz. One
hour later in winter.

Voice of Croatia. Summer only at this
time. Nominally 15 minutes of news, reports and interviews, but actual length varies. To North and South America on 9925
kHz. One hour later in winter.

**World band aficionado Simo Soininen feasts heartily
while celebrating ancient Finnish culture.**

S. Soininen

02:00–02:45

Radio Prague, Czech Republic. Winter only at this time. *News*, then Tuesday through Saturday (weekday evenings in the Americas) it's a combination of *Current Affairs* and one or more features: *One on One* (Tuesday), *Talking Point* (Wednesday), *Czechs in History*, *Czechs Today* or *Spotlight* (Thursday), *Panorama* and *Czech Science* (Friday), and *Business Briefs* and *The Arts* on Saturday. The Sunday lineup is *Magazine*, *ABC of Czech* and *One on One*; replaced Monday by *Mailbox* and *Letter from Prague* followed by *Encore* (classical music), *Magic Carpet* (Czech world music) or *Czech Books*. Half an hour to North America on 6200 and 7345 kHz. One hour earlier in summer.

Voice of Russia World Service. Winter, the start of a four-hour block of programming to North America; summer, it's the beginning of the second hour. *News*, features and music to suit all tastes. Winter fare includes *Russia and the World* (0211 Tuesday through Saturday), replaced Sunday and Monday by *Moscow Mailbag*. Features fill the second half-hour: *Timelines* (Monday), *Kaleidoscope* (Tuesday and Friday), *Russian by Radio* (Wednesday), *The VOR Treasure Store* (Thursday), ●*Christian Message from Moscow* (Saturday) and *Our Homeland* on Sunday. In summer, *News and Views* replaces *Russia and the World* and Sunday's *Moscow Mailbag*, with *Sunday Panorama* filling the Monday slot. There's a news summary on the half-hour, then *Russian by Radio* (Monday), ●*Folk Box* (Tuesday), *A Stroll Around the Kremlin* and *Musical Tales* (Wednesday and Saturday), *Our Homeland* (Thursday), ●*Jazz Show* (Friday) and *A Stroll Around the Kremlin* and ●*Songs from Russia* on Sunday. These days are World Time, so locally in North America it will be the previous evening. For eastern North America winter, tune to 6155, 6240 and 7250 kHz; summer, it's 9665 and 9860 kHz. Listeners in western states should go for 13735 and 15425 kHz in winter; and 13775 and 15595 kHz in summer.

Radio Habana Cuba. The second half of a two-hour broadcast to eastern and central North America. Tuesday through Sunday (Monday through Saturday evenings in North America), opens with 10 minutes of international *news*. Next comes *Spotlight on the Americas* (Tuesday through Saturday) or Sunday's *The World of Stamps*. The final 30 minutes consists of news-oriented programming. The Monday slots are *From Havana* and ●*The Jazz Place* or *Breakthrough* (science). On 6000 and 6180 kHz.

Radio Thailand. *News Magazine*. Thirty minutes to western North America on 15275 kHz.

KBS World Radio, South Korea. Opens with 10 minutes of *news*, then Tuesday through Saturday (weekday evenings in the Americas) there's a commentary and 30 minutes of *Seoul Calling* followed by a 15-minute feature: *Faces of Korea*, *Business Watch*, *Culture on the Move*, *Korea Today and Tomorrow* and *Seoul Report*, respectively. Sunday, the news is followed by *Worldwide Friendship* (a listener-response program), and Monday by *Korean Pop Interactive*. One hour to South America on 15575 kHz, and often heard in Japan, especially during summer. In North America, a shortened version of this broadcast can be heard at 0230; see there for specifics.

> China's CRI is filling a void left by tech-driven Western stations.

Radio Taiwan International. Ten minutes of *News,* followed by features: *The Occidental Tourist, Generation Why* and *Asia Review* (Monday); *Made in Taiwan* and *We've Got Mail* (Tuesday); *Strait Talk, Women Making Waves* and ●*Jade Bells and Bamboo Pipes* (Wednesday); *Trends, People, Instant Noodles* and *Chinese to Go* (Thursday); *Ilha Formosa, Mandopop* and *Taiwan Outlook* (Friday); *Walks of Life* and *Groove Zone* (Saturday); and *News Talk, Chinese to Go* (language lessons) *Stage, Screen and Studio* and *On the Line* (Sunday). These days are World Time, so locally in North America it will be the previous evening. One hour to eastern and central North America on 5950 and 9680 kHz.

Radio Australia. Continuous programming to Asia and the Pacific, but well heard in parts of North America (especially to the west). Begins with *World News,* then Monday through Friday it's *The World Today* (comprehensive coverage of world events). Winter weekends and summer Sundays, it's all sport in *Grandstand.* Summer Saturdays bring *Total Rugby* and *The Sports Factor* (Asia) or ●*Rear Vision* (Pacific). On 9660, 12080, 13690, 15240, 15415, 15515, 17750 and 21725 kHz. Best heard in North America (especially during summer) on 15515 kHz; in East Asia on 13690 and 21725 kHz (programming for the Pacific); and in Southeast Asia on 15415 and 17750 kHz.

Voice of Korea, North Korea. Repeat of the 0100 broadcast. One hour to South East Asia on 13650 and 15100 kHz. Also audible in parts of East Asia on 4405 kHz.

AFRTS Shortwave, USA. Network news, live sports, music and features in the *upper-sideband* mode from the American Forces Radio & Television Service. Transmitted from modestly powered U.S. Navy stations around the globe, so usually a tough catch. Try 4319, 5446.5, 5765, 6350, 7811, 10320, 12133.5, 12579 and 13362 kHz.

02:30

Radio Sweden. Tuesday through Saturday (weekday evenings in North America), it's

a smorgasbord of *news* and features about Sweden. Sunday, there's a review of the main news stories of the previous week; and Monday it's *Network Europe.* Thirty minutes to eastern North America winter and western North America summer on 6010 kHz, and to South Asia winter on 11550 kHz. For eastern North America and South Asia it's one hour earlier in summer, and for western North America it's one hour later in winter.

Radio Tirana, Albania. Tuesday through Sunday (Monday through Saturday evenings in North America) and summer only at this time. Thirty minutes of Balkan news and music to North America on 6110 (or 6115) and 7425 kHz. One hour later during winter.

Voice of Vietnam. Repeat of the 0100 broadcast; see there for specifics. A relay to eastern North America via the facilities of Radio Canada International on 6175 kHz. Reception is better to the south.

KBS World Radio, South Korea. Opens with 10 minutes of *news,* then Tuesday through Saturday (weekday evenings in North America) there's a commentary followed by a 15-minute feature: *Faces of Korea, Business Watch, Culture on the Move, Korea Today and Tomorrow* and *Seoul Report,* respectively. Sunday, the news is followed by *Worldwide Friendship* (a listener-response program), and Monday by *Korean Pop Interactive.* Thirty minutes to North America on 9560 kHz.

02:45

Radio Tirana, Albania. Tuesday through Sunday (Monday through Saturday local American date) and winter only at this time. Approximately 15 minutes of *news* and commentary from one of Europe's least known countries. To North America on 6110 and 7425 kHz. One hour earlier in summer.

Vatican Radio. Actually starts at 0250. Concentrates heavily, but not exclusively, on issues affecting Catholics around the world. Thirty minutes to eastern North America on 6040 or 6100 (summer), 6100 (winter) and 7305 kHz.

03:00

Radio Taiwan International. Repeat of the 0200 broadcast; see there for specifics. One hour to western North America on 5950 kHz, to South America on 15215 kHz, and to Southeast Asia on 15320 kHz.

China Radio International. *News* and reports fill the first half-hour, and are followed by a daily feature: *Front Line* (Monday), *Biz China* (Tuesday), *In the Spotlight* (Wednesday), ●*Voices from Other Lands* (Thursday), *Life in China* (Friday), *Listeners' Garden* (Saturday) and *China Horizons* (Sunday). One hour to North America on 9690 and 9790 kHz. Also available to East Asia winter on 9460, 13620 and 15120 kHz; and summer on 13750, 15120 and 15785 kHz. These days are World Time, so locally in North America it will be the previous evening.

Radio Ukraine International. Summer only at this time, and a repeat of the 0000 broadcast; see there for specifics. Sixty minutes to eastern North America on 7440 (or 5820) kHz. One hour later in winter.

Voice of Russia World Service. Continuous programming to North America at this hour. *News*, then winter it's *News and Views*—except Monday (Sunday evening in North America) when *Sunday Panorama* is aired instead. Features during the second half-hour include *Russian by Radio* (Monday), ●*Folk Box* (Tuesday), *A Stroll Around the Kremlin* and *Musical Tales* (Wednesday and Saturday), *Our Homeland* (Thursday), ●*Jazz Show* (Friday) and *A Stroll Around the Kremlin* and ●*Songs from Russia* on Sunday. In summer, the news is followed by a feature: *This is Russia* (Monday), *Encyclopedia "All Russia"* (Tuesday), *Moscow Mailbag* (Wednesday and Saturday), *Science Plus* (Thursday) and *Newmarket* (business) on Friday. More features follow a brief news summary on the half-hour and include *Our Homeland* (Monday), *Guest Speaker* (Tuesday through Saturday), *Spiritual Flowerbed*

(Tuesday), and Friday's ●*Russia–1,000 Years of Music*. Pride of place at this hour goes to Sunday's 47-minute ●*Music and Musicians* (classical music). In eastern North America, choose between 6155, 6240 and 7350 kHz in winter, and 9515, 9665, 9860 and 9880 (or 5900) kHz in summer. For western North America, there's 13735 and 15425 kHz in winter; and 9435, 12065, 13635 and 13775 kHz in summer.

Voice of Greece. Sunday and winter only at this time. Sixty minutes of *Hellenes Around the World* (also known as *Greeks Everywhere*). To North America on 7475 and 9420 kHz; and to Central and South America on 12105 kHz. One hour earlier in summer. ☞ Sunday World Time is Saturday evening in the Americas.

■**Deutsche Welle,** Germany. *News*, then Tuesday though Saturday it's ●*NewsLink Plus*—commentary, interviews, background reports and analysis. Sunday, there's *In-Box*, *Mission Europe* (German language lessons), *Sports Report* and *Inspired Minds*; and Monday, ●*Newsline* is followed by *Sports Report* and *Radio D* (German language lessons). Sixty minutes to South Asia winter on 9785 and 13790 kHz; and summer on 11695 and 13770 kHz. The frequencies 13770 and 13790 kHz are also audible in Southeast Asia.

Radio Australia. *World News*, then Monday through Friday there's *Regional Sport* followed by *In the Loop* (Pacific) or *Connect Asia* (Asia). Weekends, for all areas, there's live sports coverage in *Grandstand*. Continuous to Asia and the Pacific on 9660, 12080, 13690, 15240, 15415, 15515, 17750 and 21725 kHz. Also heard in North America (best in summer) on 15515 kHz. In East Asia, tune to 13690 and 21725 kHz, although these frequencies carry programming for the Pacific. For Southeast Asia, there's 15415 and 17750 kHz.

Radio Habana Cuba. Repeat of the 0100 broadcast. To eastern and central North America on 6000 and 6180 kHz.

Voice of Croatia. Winter only at this time. Nominally 15 minutes of news, reports and interviews, but actual length varies. To North and South America on 7285 kHz. One hour earlier in summer.

Radio Prague, Czech Republic. Summer only at this hour; see 0400 for program specifics. Half an hour to North America on 7345 and 9870 kHz. This is by far the best opportunity for listeners in western states. One hour later in winter.

Radio Cairo, Egypt. The final half-hour of a 90-minute broadcast to North America on 7270 kHz.

Radio Bulgaria. Winter only at this time, and a repeat of the 0000 broadcast; see there for specifics. A distinctly Bulgarian potpourri of news, commentary, features and music. Not to be missed is Monday's ●*Folk Studio* (Sunday evening local American date). Sixty minutes to eastern North America and Central America on 7400 and 9400 kHz. One hour earlier in summer.

Radio Romania International. Summer only at this time; see 0400 for specifics. Fifty-five minutes to western North America on 6150 and 9645 kHz, and to South Asia on 11895 and 15220 kHz. One hour later in winter.

Radio New Zealand International. Continues with *news* and features targeted at a regional audience. Part of a 24-hour transmission for the South Pacific, but also heard in parts of North America (especially during summer). On 15720 or 17675 kHz. Often carries commentaries of local sporting events. Popular with many listeners.

Voice of Korea, North Korea. Abysmal programs from the last of the old-style communist stations. Worth a listen just to hear how bad they are. One hour to East Asia on 3560, 7140, 9345 and 9730 kHz.

Voice of Turkey. Summer only at this time. *News,* followed by *Review of the Turkish*

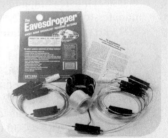

03:00–04:00

Lars and Marguerite Rydén tune in the world while visiting villages along Sweden's coast.

L. Rydén

Press and features (some of them exotic and unusual). Selections of Turkish popular and classical music complete the program. Fifty minutes to Europe and North America on 5975 kHz, and to the Mideast on 7270 kHz. One hour later during winter.

Voice of America. The start of four hours of continuous programming to Africa. Monday through Friday, *Daybreak Africa* fills the first half-hour, and is followed by *World News Now*. Weekends, 30 minutes of news are followed by Saturday's *Press Conference USA* or Sunday's *Issues in the News*. On 4930, 6035 (winter), 6080, 7340 (till 0330), 9885 and (summer) 12080 and 15580 kHz. Best for southern Africa are 4930 and 9885 kHz.

AFRTS Shortwave, USA. Network news, live sports, music and features in the *upper-sideband* mode from the American Forces Radio & Television Service. Transmitted from modestly powered U.S. Navy stations around the globe, so usually a tough catch. Try 4319, 5446.5, 5765, 6350, 7811, 10320, 12133.5, 12579 and 13362 kHz.

03:30

Radio Sweden. Tuesday through Saturday (weekday evenings in North America), it's a smorgasbord of *news* and features about Sweden. Sunday, there's a review of the main news stories of the previous week; and Monday it's *Network Europe*. Thirty minutes to western North America on 6010 kHz, and one hour earlier in summer.

Radio Prague, Czech Republic. Summer only at this time. See the 0400 winter broadcast for North America for program specifics. Thirty minutes to western North America on 6080 kHz, and to the Mideast and South Asia on 9445 and 11600 kHz. The broadcast to North America is 30 minutes later in winter, and for South Asia and the Mideast it's one hour later.

Kol Israel. Summer only at this time. *News* for 15 minutes from Israel Radio's domestic network. To Europe and eastern North America on 9345 and 11590 (or 7530) kHz, and to Australasia on 17600 kHz. One hour later in winter.

Voice of Vietnam. A relay via the facilities of Radio Canada International. Begins with *news*, then there's *Commentary* or *Weekly Review*, followed by short features and some pleasant Vietnamese music (particularly at weekends). Half an hour to eastern North America on 6175 kHz.

Radio Tirana, Albania. Tuesday through Monday (Monday through Saturday evenings local American date) and winter only at this time. *News*, features and Albanian music (especially Sunday). Thirty minutes to North America on 6110 and 7425 kHz. One hour earlier in summer.

04:00

■**Radio Netherlands.** Summer only at this time; see 0500 for specifics. Fifty-seven minutes to western North America on 6165 kHz, and one hour later in winter.

Radio Habana Cuba. Repeat of the 0200 broadcast. To eastern and central North America on 6000 and 6180 kHz.

Radio Prague, Czech Republic. Winter only at this time. *News*, then Tuesday through Saturday (weekday evenings in the Americas) there's the in-depth *Current Affairs* and a feature or two: *One on One* (Tuesday), *Talking Point* (Wednesday), *Czechs in History*, *Czechs Today* or *Spotlight* (Thursday), *Panorama* and *Czech Science* (Friday), and *Business Briefs* and *The Arts* on Saturday. The Sunday news is followed by *Magazine*, *ABC of Czech* and a repeat of Wednesday's *One on One*; and Monday's lineup is *Mailbox* and *Letter from Prague* followed by *Encore* (classical music), *Magic Carpet* (Czech world music) or *Czech Books*. Thirty minutes to North America on 5990, 6200 and 7345 kHz. By far the best opportunity for western states. One hour earlier in summer.

■**Radio France Internationale.** Weekdays only at this time. Starts with a bulletin of African *news* and an international newsflash. Next, there's a review of the French dailies, an in-depth look at events in Africa, the main news event of the day in France, and sports. Thirty information-packed minutes to East Africa on 7315 (winter), 9805 and (summer) 11995 kHz. Heard well beyond the intended target area.

Radio Ukraine International. Winter only at this time, and a repeat of the 0100 broadcast. Ample coverage of local issues, including news, sports, politics and culture. Well worth a listen is ●*Music from Ukraine*, which fills most of the Monday (Sunday evening in the Americas) broadcast. Sixty minutes to eastern North America on 5820 (or 7440) kHz. One hour earlier in summer.

Radio Australia. *World News*, then Monday through Friday, it's the final hour of *In the Loop* for listeners in the Pacific. Asia gets one or more features: *National Interest* (Monday), *Counterpoint* (Tuesday), ●*Rear Vision* and *Innovations* (Wednesday), *Background Briefing* (investigative journalism, Thursday), and ●*The Science Show* on Friday. Weekends, it's live sport in *Grandstand*. Continuous to Asia and the Pacific on 9660, 12080, 13690, 15240, 15415 (from 0430), 15515, 17750 and 21725 kHz. Should also be audible in parts of North America (best

during summer) on 15515 kHz. In East Asia, tune to 13690 or 21725 kHz, although these frequencies carry programming for the Pacific. For Southeast Asia there's 15415 and 17750 kHz.

■**Deutsche Welle,** Germany. *News*, followed Tuesday through Saturday by ●*NewsLink*—commentary, interviews, background reports and analysis. On the half-hour there's *Sports Report* and *World in Progress* (Monday), ●*Spectrum* (science and technology, Tuesday), ●*Money Talks* (Wednesday), *Living Planet* (Thursday), ●*Inside Europe* (Friday) and ●*Insight* (Saturday). Sunday, the news is followed by *In-Box*, *Mission Europe* (a German language course), *Sports Report* and *Inspired Minds*. Sixty minutes to Africa winter on 5905, 5945, 6180, 7225 and 15445 kHz; and summer on 7225, 7245, 12045 and 15445 kHz. Audible in southern Africa winter on 15445 kHz, and midyear on 12045 kHz.

Radio Romania International. Winter only at this time. Starts with *Radio Newsreel*, a combination of news, commentary and press review. Features on Romania complete the broadcast. Regular spots include Tuesday's *Pro Memoria*, *Romanian Hits* and *Sports Roundup*; Wednesday's *Business Club* and ●*The Skylark* (Romanian folk music); Thursday's *Society Today* and *Romanian Musicians*; and Friday's *Europa Express*. Saturday fare includes ●*The Folk Music Box* and *Sports Weekend*; and Sunday there's *The Week* and *World of Culture*. Monday's broadcast includes *Focus*. Fifty-five minutes to western North America on 6115 and 9515 kHz, and to South Asia on 9690 and 11895 kHz. These days are World Time, so locally in western North America it will be the previous evening. One hour earlier in summer.

Voice of Turkey. Winter only at this time. See 0300 for specifics. Fifty minutes to Europe and North America on 6020 kHz, and to the Mideast on 7240 kHz. One hour earlier in summer.

China Radio International. Repeat of the 0300 broadcast (see there for specifics);

04:00–05:00

one hour to North America winter on 6190 kHz, and summer on 6020 and 6080 kHz. Also to East Asia winter on 9460, 13620 and 15120 kHz; and summer on 13750, 15120 and 15785 kHz; and Central Asia on 17725 (winter), 17730 (summer) and 17855 kHz.

Radio New Zealand International. Continuous programming for the South Pacific. Part of a much longer broadcast, which is also heard in parts of North America (especially during summer). On 15720 or 17675 kHz. Sometimes carries commentaries of local sports events.

Voice of Russia World Service. Continues to North America at this hour. Opens with *News*, then a feature. Winter, there's *This is Russia* (Monday), *Encyclopedia "All Russia"* (Tuesday), *Moscow Mailbag* (Wednesday and Saturday), *Science Plus* (Thursday) and *Newmarket* (business) on Friday. More features follow a brief news summary on the half-hour and include *Our Homeland* (Monday), *Guest Speaker* (Tuesday through Saturday), *Spiritual Flowerbed* (Tuesday), and Friday's ●*Russia–1,000 Years of Music*. Not to be missed at this hour is Sunday's ●*Music and Musicians* (the best in classical music). The summer schedule has plenty of variety, and includes *Encyclopedia "All Russia"* and *The VOR Treasure Store* (Monday), *Moscow Mailbag*, ●*Music Around Us* and ●*Music at Your Request* (Tuesday), *Science Plus* and *Our Homeland* (Wednesday), the business-oriented *Newmarket* and ●*Folk Box* (Thursday), *Moscow Mailbag* and *The VOR Treasure Store* (Friday), *This is Russia* and *Timelines* (Saturday), and *Encyclopedia "All Russia"* and *Kaleidoscope* (Sunday). These days are World Time, so locally in North America it will be the previous evening. In eastern North America, choose from 6155, 7150 and 7350 kHz in winter, and 9665, 9860 and 9880 (or 5900) kHz in summer. Best winter bets for the West Coast are 9840, 12010, 12030 and 13735 kHz; and summer there's 9435, 13635 and 13775 kHz.

Voice of America. Continuous programming to Africa. Monday through Friday, *Daybreak Africa* fills the first half-hour, and

is followed by *World News Now*. Weekends, 30 minutes of news are followed by *On the Line*. On 4930, 4960, 6080 and 9575 kHz; also winter on 9775 kHz, and summer on 11835, 12080 and 15580 kHz. Best for southern Africa is 4930 kHz; and heard in North America on 9575 kHz.

AFRTS Shortwave, USA. Network news, live sports, music and features in the *upper-sideband* mode from the American Forces Radio & Television Service. Transmitted from modestly powered U.S. Navy stations around the globe, so usually a tough catch. Try 4319, 5446.5, 5765, 6350, 7811, 10320, 12133.5, 12579 and 13362 kHz.

04:30

Radio Prague, Czech Republic. Winter only at this time. See the 0400 broadcast to North America for program specifics. Thirty minutes to the Mideast and South Asia on 9890 kHz. One hour earlier in summer.

Kol Israel. Winter only at this time. *News* for 15 minutes from Israel Radio's domestic network. To Europe and eastern North America on 6280 (or 9345) and 7545 kHz, and to Australasia on 17600 kHz. One hour earlier in summer.

05:00

■**Radio Netherlands.** Tuesday through Saturday (weekday evenings in North America), ●*Newsline* (current events) is followed by a 30-minute feature. Tuesday, it's a look at all things Dutch; Wednesday, it's the midweek edition of ●*The State We're In*. Thursday's slot is *Radio Books*, replaced Friday by *Earth Beat* and Saturday by *Network Europe*. On the remaining days there's Sunday's ●*The State We're In* and Monday's *Amsterdam Forum* and *Reloaded* (highlights of the previous week's shows). Fifty-seven minutes to eastern North America on 6165 kHz, and one hour earlier in summer.

■**Deutsche Welle,** Germany. *News*, then Tuesday through Saturday it's ●*News-Link*—commentary, interviews, background

04:00–05:00

Radio France takes pride in reflecting French culture. Nevertheless, it is headquartered in a monument to generic architecture that would be equally unappealing in any other part of the world. M. Wright

reports and analysis. This is replaced Sunday by *Network Europe*, and Monday by a 10-minute edition of *NewsLink* followed by *Sports Report*. Thirty minutes to Africa, winter on 6180, 7285, 9755, 12045 and 15410 kHz; and summer on 5945, 9700 and 9825 kHz. Best for southern Africa are 12045 and 15410 kHz in winter (summer in the Southern Hemisphere) and 9825 kHz midyear.

■**Radio France Internationale.** Monday through Friday only at this time. Similar to the 0400 broadcast, but without the international newsflash. Thirty minutes to East Africa (and heard well beyond) on any two channels from 11995, 13680 and 15160 kHz.

Vatican Radio. Summer only at this time. Thirty minutes of programming oriented to Catholics. To Europe on 4005 and 7250 kHz. One hour later in winter.

Radio Ukraine International. Summer only at this time; see 0600 for specifics. Sixty minutes to western Europe on 9945 (or 7420) kHz. One hour later in winter.

Radio Japan. Ten minutes of *news*, then one or more features. Thirty minutes to Europe on 5975 kHz; to western North America on 6110 kHz; to Southeast Asia on 17810 kHz; to South Asia on 15325 kHz;

and to southern Africa on 9725 or 7215 kHz.

China Radio International. *News* and reports fill the first half-hour, and are followed by a daily feature: *Front Line* (Monday), *Biz China* (Tuesday), *In the Spotlight* (Wednesday), ●*Voices from Other Lands* (Thursday), *Life in China* (Friday), *Listeners' Garden* (Saturday) and *China Horizons* (Sunday). One hour to central and western North America on 5960 (winter), 6020 (summer) and 6190 kHz via CRI's Canadian relay. Also available to the Mideast and West Asia on 17505 kHz; and to Central Asia on 17725 (winter), 17730 (summer) and 17855 kHz. These days are World Time, so locally in North America it will be the previous evening.

Radio Habana Cuba. The start of a two-hour broadcast for North, Central and South America. Tuesday through Sunday (Monday through Saturday evenings in the Americas), the first half-hour consists of international and Cuban news followed by *RHC's Viewpoint*. The next 30 minutes consist of a news bulletin and the sports-oriented *Time Out* (five minutes each) plus a feature: *Caribbean Outlook* (Tuesday and Friday), *DXers Unlimited* (Wednesday and Sunday), the *Mailbag Show* (Thursday) and *Weekly Review* (Saturday). Monday, the hour is split

05:00–06:00

Cable car in Wellington, New Zealand, home to Radio New Zealand International.   Shutterstock/Albert H. Teich

between *Weekly Review* and *Mailbag Show*. On 6000, 6060, 9550 and 11760 kHz.

Radio Austria International. Summer Sundays only, and actually starts at 0505. See 0600 for more details. To the Mideast on 17870 kHz, and one hour later in winter.

Radio New Zealand International. Continues with regional programming for the South Pacific. Part of a 24-hour broadcast, which is also heard in parts of North America (especially during summer). On 9615 or 15720 kHz.

Radio Australia. *World News*, then Monday through Friday, continues with current events: *The World Today* for Asia, and *Pacific Beat* (including *On the Mat* and a sports bulletin) for listeners in the Pacific. Weekends, it's live sport in *Grandstand*. Continuous to Asia and the Pacific on 9660, 12080, 13690, 15160, 15240, 15415 (from 0530), 15515 and 17750 kHz. In North America (best during summer) try 15160 and 15515 kHz. In East Asia, tune to 13690 kHz, although it carries programming for the Pacific. For Southeast Asia there's 15415 and 17750 kHz.

Voice of Russia World Service. Winter, the final 60 minutes of a four-hour block of programming to North America; summer, the first of four hours to Australasia.

Opens with *News*, followed winter by features: *Encyclopedia "All Russia"* and *The VOR Treasure Store* (Monday), *Moscow Mailbag*, ●*Music Around Us* and ●*Music at Your Request* (Tuesday), *Science Plus* and *Our Homeland* (Wednesday), the business-oriented *Newmarket* and ●*Folk Box* (Thursday), *Moscow Mailbag* and *The VOR Treasure Store* (Friday), *This is Russia* and *Timelines* (Saturday), and *Encyclopedia "All Russia"* and *Kaleidoscope* (Sunday). These days are World Time, so locally in North America it will be the previous evening. Tuesday through Saturday summer, there's *Focus on Asia and the Pacific*, replaced Sunday by *This is Russia* and Monday by *Moscow Mailbag*. On the half-hour, look for *Russian by Radio* (Monday and Wednesday), *Kaleidoscope* (Tuesday), *Our Homeland* (Thursday), ●*Music Around Us* and ●*Music at Your Request* (Friday), ●*Christian Message from Moscow* (Saturday) and *The VOR Treasure Store* on Sunday. Winter only to eastern North America on 7150 and 7350 kHz, and to western parts on 9840, 13735 and 15425 kHz. Summer (winter in the Southern Hemisphere) to Australasia on 17635 and 21790 kHz.

AFRTS Shortwave, USA. Network news, live sports, music and features in the *upper-sideband* mode from the American Forces Radio & Television Service. Transmitted from modestly powered U.S. Navy stations around the globe, so usually a tough catch. Try 4319, 5446.5, 5765, 6350, 7811, 10320, 12133.5, 12579 and 13362 kHz.

05:30

Radio Thailand. Thirty minutes of *news* and short features relayed from one of the station's domestic services. To Europe winter on 11730 kHz, and summer on 17655 kHz.

Radio Romania International. Summer only at this time. *News* and commentary followed by short features on Romania. Twenty-five minutes to western Europe on 9655 and 11830 kHz. Also available to Australasia on 15435 and 17770 kHz. One hour later in winter.

06:00–11:59
Australasia & East Asia—Evening Prime Time
Western North America—Late Evening
Europe & Mideast—Morning and Midday

06:00

■**Deutsche Welle,** Germany. *News*, then Tuesday through Saturday it's ●*News-Link*—commentary, interviews, background reports and analysis. This is replaced Sunday by *In-Box* and *Mission Europe* (German language lessons), and Monday by a 10-minute edition of *NewsLink* followed by *Sports Report*. Thirty minutes to West and Central Africa and heard well beyond. Winter on 5945, 7240 and 12045 kHz; and summer on 7310 and 15275 kHz.

Radio Habana Cuba. The second half of a two-hour broadcast. Tuesday through Sunday (Monday through Saturday evenings in the Americas), opens with 10 minutes of international news. Next comes *Spotlight on the Americas* (Tuesday through Saturday) or Sunday's *The World of Stamps*. The final 30 minutes consists of news-oriented programming. The Monday slots are *From Havana* and ●*The Jazz Place* or *Breakthrough* (science). To North and Central America on 6000, 6060, 9550 and 11760 kHz.

China Radio International. Winter only at this time, and a repeat of the 0500 broadcast (see there for specifics). One hour to western North America on 6115 kHz, to the Mideast and West Asia on 11770 (winter), 11870 (summer), 15145 and 17505 kHz; and to Southeast Asia on 13645 (winter), 13660 (summer) and 17710 kHz.

Radio Austria International. Winter Sundays only. The 25-minute ●*Report from Austria–The Week in Review* is aired at 0605, and then repeated at 0635. The remainder of the one-hour broadcast is in German. To the Mideast on 17870 kHz, and one hour earlier in summer.

Radio Ukraine International. Winter only at this time. *News*, commentary, reports and interviews, providing ample coverage of Ukrainian life. Sixty minutes to western Europe on 7440 kHz. One hour earlier in summer.

■**Radio France Internationale.** Weekdays only at this time. Similar to the 0400 broadcast (see there for specifics), but includes a report on the day's main international story. Thirty minutes to East and West Africa winter on 7315 (or 9765), 11995 (or 15160) and 13680 kHz; and summer on 11725 (or 9765), 15160 and 17800 kHz. Heard well beyond the intended target area.

Radio Australia. Begins with *World News*, then Monday through Friday there's *Regional Sports* and *Talking Point*. Listeners in the Pacific then get a relay of Radio New Zealand International's *Dateline Pacific*. For Asia there's *Health Report* (Monday), *Law Report* (Tuesday), *Religion Report* (Wednesday), *Media Report* (Thursday), and *The Sports Factor* on Friday. These are replaced weekends by live sports coverage in *Grandstand*. Continuous to Asia and the Pacific on 9660, 12080, 13690, 15160, 15240, 15415, 15515 and 17750 kHz. Listeners in North America should try 15160 and 15515 kHz. In East Asia, tune to 13690 kHz, although the programming is for the Pacific. Southeast Asia has 15415 (from 0630 Monday through Friday) and 17750 kHz.

Radio New Zealand International. Continues with regional programming for the South Pacific, which is also heard in parts of North America (especially during summer). On 9615, 9765 or 9870 kHz.

Voice of Russia World Service. *News*, then winter it's *Focus on Asia and the Pacific* (Tuesday through Saturday), *This is Russia* (Sunday) and *Moscow Mailbag* (Monday). On the half-hour, look for *Russian by Radio* (Monday and Wednesday), *Kaleidoscope*

06:00–07:00

(Tuesday), *Our Homeland* (Thursday), ●*Music Around Us* and ●*Music at Your Request* (Friday), ●*Christian Message from Moscow* (Saturday) and *The VOR Treasure Store* on Sunday. In summer, the news is followed by *Science Plus* (Monday), *This is Russia* (Tuesday and Friday), the business-oriented *Newmarket* (Wednesday), *Encyclopedia "All Russia"* (Saturday) and *Moscow Mailbag* on the remaining days. The second half-hour offers plenty of variety: *Kaleidoscope* (Monday), *Russian by Radio* (Tuesday), ●*Jazz Show* (Wednesday), *The VOR Treasure Store* (Thursday), *Kaleidoscope* (Friday), ●*Folk Box* (Saturday) and *Timelines* on Sunday. Continuous programming to Australasia winter on 17665 and 17805 kHz, and summer on 17635 and 21790 kHz.

Vatican Radio. Winter only at this time. Thirty minutes with a heavy Catholic slant. To Europe on 4005 and 7250 kHz. One hour earlier in summer.

Voice of Malaysia. *News*, followed Monday, Wednesday, Friday and Sunday by a two-minute Malayan language lesson (replaced by a local pop hit on Tuesday). The next 33 minutes are given over to *Hits All the Way*. Saturday, it's the 35-minute *Mailbag*. The hour is rounded off with a feature: *New Horizon* (Monday), *ASEAN Focus* (Tuesday), *Malaysia in Perspective* (Wednesday), *Personality* (Thursday), *News and Views* (Friday), and *Weekly Roundup* and *Current Affairs* on the weekend. The first hour of a 150-minute broadcast to Southeast Asia and Australasia on 6175, 9750 and 15295 kHz.

AFRTS Shortwave, USA. Network news, live sports, music and features in the *upper-sideband* mode from the American Forces Radio & Television Service. Transmitted from modestly powered U.S. Navy stations around the globe, so usually a tough catch. Try 4319, 5446.5, 5765, 6350, 7811, 10320, 12133.5, 12579 and 13362 kHz.

06:30

Radio Bulgaria. Summer only at this time. *News*, followed by *Answering Your Letters* (Monday), ●*Folk Studio* (Tuesday) and *DX*

Programme (Sunday). Most of the remaining airtime is taken up by *Time Out for Music*. Thirty minutes to Europe on 9600 and 11600 kHz. One hour later in winter.

Radio Romania International. Winter only at this time. *News* and commentary followed by short features on Romania. Twenty-five minutes to western Europe on 7180 and 9690 kHz. Also available to Australasia on 15135 and 17780 kHz. One hour earlier in summer.

07:00

Radio Prague, Czech Republic. Summer only at this time. See 0800 for specifics. Thirty minutes to Europe on 9880 and 11600 kHz. One hour later in winter.

Radio Slovakia International. *News* and features on Slovak life and culture. Half an hour to Australasia winter on 13715 and 15460 kHz, and midyear on 9440 and 15460 kHz.

China Radio International. Weekdays, *News* is followed by *China Drive*, an upbeat "drive-time" show. Weekends there's *News and Reports*, *CRI Roundup* (Saturday), *Reports from Developing Countries* (Sunday) and *China Beat* (music). One hour to Europe on 11785 (winter), 13710 (summer) and 17490 kHz; and to Southeast Asia on 13645 (winter), 13660 (summer) and 17710 kHz.

Radio Ukraine International. Summer only at this time; see 0800 for specifics. Sixty minutes to western Europe on 9945 (or 7420) kHz. One hour later in winter.

■**Radio France Internationale.** Weekdays only at this time. Starts with a bulletin of African *news*. Next, there's a review of the French dailies, an in-depth look at events in Africa, the main news event of the day in France, and sports. Thirty information-packed minutes to West and Central Africa winter on 11725 kHz, and summer on 13675 kHz. Audible in southern Africa midyear.

Radio Australia. *World News*, then Monday through Friday, listeners in the Pacific get a repeat of *Pacific Beat*. For Asia there's

Life Matters. Winter weekends, there's a roundup of the latest sports action in *Grandstand Wrap*, then Saturday's *Rural Reporter* or Sunday's *Innovations*. These are replaced summer by the final hour of *Grandstand* (live sport). Continuous to Asia and the Pacific on 9660, 9710, 12080, 13630, 15160, 15240, 15415 and 17750 kHz. Listeners in North America can try 13630 kHz (West Coast) or 15160 kHz (best during summer). For East Asia there's 9715 kHz, but with programs for the Pacific. Southeast Asia has 15415 and 17750 kHz.

Voice of Malaysia. Starts weekdays with 45 minutes of *Fascinating Malaysia*, replaced Saturday by *Malaysia Rama* and *Malaysia in Perspective*, and Sunday by *ASEAN Melody* and *Destination Malaysia*. Not much doubt about where the broadcast originates! The hour ends with a 15-minute feature. Continuous to Southeast Asia and Australasia on 6175, 9750 and 15295 kHz.

Voice of Russia World Service. Continuous programming to Australasia. Winter, opens with *News*, then features: *Science Plus* (Monday), *This is Russia* (Tuesday and Friday), *Newmarket* (Wednesday), *Encyclopedia "All Russia"* (Saturday) and *Moscow Mailbag*, on the remaining days. For the second half-hour there's *Kaleidoscope* (Monday and Friday), *Russian by Radio* (Tuesday), ●*Jazz Show* (Wednesday), *The VOR Treasure Store* (Thursday), ●*Folk Box* (Saturday) and *Timelines* on Sunday. Summer, the news is followed by the informative *Russia and the World* on Tuesday, Thursday and Saturday. Other offerings include *This is Russia* (Wednesday), *Moscow Mailbag* (Friday) and *Newmarket* (Sunday). Class act of the week is Monday's masterpiece, ●*Music and Musicians*. On the half-hour there's a summary of the latest news, then more features: ●*Folk Box* (Tuesday), *Musical Tales* (Wednesday), ●*Jazz Show* (Thursday), *Our Homeland* (Friday), *Kaleidoscope* (Saturday) and *A Stroll Around the Kremlin* and ●*Songs from Russia* on Sunday. Winter (local summer) there's 17665 and 17805 kHz; and midyear, 17495, 17635 and 21790 kHz.

Radio New Zealand International. Continues with regional programming for the South Pacific, which is also heard in parts of North America (especially during summer). On 6095, 9765 or 9870 kHz.

Radio Taiwan International. Ten minutes of *News*, followed by features: *The Occidental Tourist*, *Generation Why* and *Asia Review* (Monday); *Made in Taiwan* and *We've Got Mail* (Tuesday); *Strait Talk*, *Women Making Waves* and ●*Jade Bells and Bamboo Pipes* (Wednesday); *Trends, People, Instant Noodles* and *Chinese to Go* (Thursday); *Ilha Formosa, Mandopop* and *Taiwan Outlook* (Friday); *Walks of Life* and *Groove Zone* (Saturday); and *News Talk, Chinese to Go* (language lessons) *Stage, Screen and Studio* and *On the Line* (Sunday). These days are World Time, so locally in North America it will be the previous evening. One hour to western North America on 5950 kHz.

AFRTS Shortwave, USA. Network news, live sports, music and features in the *upper-sideband* mode from the American Forces Radio & Television Service. Transmitted from modestly powered U.S. Navy stations around the globe, so usually a tough catch. Try 4319, 5446.5, 5765, 6350, 7811, 10320, 12133.5, 12579 and 13362 kHz.

"New Europe" broadcasts from several countries.

07:30–09:00

Should a tsunami strike Malaysian beaches, count on firsthand coverage by the Voice of Malaysia.

Shutterstock/Sean Lean Tung Pek

07:30

Radio Bulgaria. This time winter only. *News*, followed by *Answering Your Letters* (Monday), ●*Folk Studio* (Tuesday) and *DX Programme* (Sunday). Most of the remaining airtime is taken up by *Time Out for Music*. Thirty minutes to Europe on 7400 and 9400 kHz, and hour earlier in summer.

08:00

Radio Ukraine International. Winter only at this time. Interesting coverage of local issues, including news, sports, politics and culture. Sixty minutes to western Europe on 7440 kHz. One hour earlier in summer.

Voice of Malaysia. *News* and commentary, then *Golden Oldies*. The final half-hour of a much longer transmission targeted at Southeast Asia and Australasia on 6175, 9750 and 15295 kHz.

Radio Prague, Czech Republic. Winter only at this time. *News*, then Monday through Friday it's the in-depth *Current Affairs* and one or more features: *One on One* (Monday), *Talking Point* (Tuesday), *Czechs in History*, *Czechs Today* or *Spotlight* (Wednesday), *Panorama* and *Czech Science* (Thursday), and *Business Briefs* and *The Arts* (Friday).

Weekends, the news is followed by Saturday's *Insight Central Europe* or Sunday's *Mailbox* and *Letter from Prague* followed by *Encore* (classical music), *Magic Carpet* (Czech world music) or *Czech Books*. Thirty minutes to Europe on 7345 and 9860 kHz. One hour earlier in summer.

Radio Australia. Part of a 24-hour service to Asia and the Pacific, but which can also be heard at this time throughout much of North America. Begins with a bulletin of *World News*, then Monday through Friday there's an in-depth look at current events in *PM*. Winter weekends, there's *Asia Pacific Review* and *Jazz Notes* (Saturday), and *Correspondents Report* and ●*Rear Vision* (Sunday). These are replaced summer by *Grandstand Wrap* followed by Saturday's *Total Rugby* or Sunday's *Innovations*. On 5995, 9580, 9590, 9710, 12080, 13630, 15415 and 17750 kHz. Audible in parts of North America on 9580, 9590 and 13630 kHz. Best for East Asia is 9710 kHz, with 15415 and 17750 kHz the channels for Southeast Asia.

Voice of Russia World Service. Continuous programming to Australasia. Winter, *News* is followed by the informative *Russia and the World* on Tuesday, Thursday and Saturday. Other offerings include *This*

07:30–09:00

is Russia (Wednesday), *Moscow Mailbag* (Friday) and *Newmarket* (Sunday). Pick of the week is Monday's masterpiece, ●*Music and Musicians*. On the half-hour there's a summary of the latest news, then more features: ●*Folk Box* (Tuesday), *Musical Tales* (Wednesday), ●*Jazz Show* (Thursday), *Our Homeland* (Friday), *Kaleidoscope* (Saturday) and *A Stroll Around the Kremlin* and ●*Songs from Russia* on Sunday. In summer, the news is followed Tuesday through Saturday by *News and Views*, and Sunday and Monday by *This is Russia*. On the half-hour there's a summary of the latest news and a feature: *A Stroll Around the Kremlin* and *Musical Tales* (Monday), *Kaleidoscope* (Tuesday), *The VOR Treasure Store* (Wednesday), ●*Folk Box* (Thursday), ●*Jazz Show* (Friday), ●*Christian Message from Moscow* (Saturday) and *Timelines* on Sunday. Winter (local summer) there's 17665, 17805 and 17495 kHz; and midyear, 17495, 17635 and 21790 kHz.

Radio Taiwan International. Ten minutes of *News*, followed by features: *The Occidental Tourist*, *Generation Why* and *Asia Review* (Monday); *Made in Taiwan* and *We've Got Mail* (Tuesday); *Strait Talk*, *Women Making Waves* and ●*Jade Bells and Bamboo Pipes* (Wednesday); *Trends, People, Instant Noodles* and *Chinese to Go* (Thursday); *Ilha Formosa, Mandopop* and *Taiwan Outlook* (Friday); *Walks of Life* and *Groove Zone* (Saturday); and *News Talk, Chinese to Go* (language lessons) *Stage, Screen and Studio* and *On the Line* (Sunday). One hour to Australasia and Southeast Asia on 11715 (or 9610) kHz.

Radio New Zealand International. Continues with regional programming for the South Pacific. Part of a 24-hour broadcast which is also heard in parts of North America (especially during summer). On 6095, 9765 or 9870 kHz.

China Radio International. *News* and reports fill the first half-hour, and are followed by a daily feature: *Front Line* (Monday), *Biz China* (Tuesday), *In the Spotlight* (Wednesday), ●*Voices from Other Lands* (Thursday), *Life in China* (Friday), *Listeners' Garden* (Saturday) and *China Horizons* (Sunday). One

hour to Europe on 11785 (winter), 13710 (summer) and 17490 kHz; and to East Asia winter on 9415 kHz, and summer on 11620 kHz.

KBS World Radio, South Korea. Opens with 10 minutes of *news*, then Monday through Friday, a commentary. This is followed by 30 minutes of *Seoul Calling* and a 15-minute feature: *Faces of Korea, Business Watch, Culture on the Move, Korea Today and Tomorrow* and *Seoul Report*, respectively. Saturday's news is followed by *Worldwide Friendship* (a listener-response show), and Sunday by *Korean Pop Interactive*. Sixty minutes to Southeast Asia on 9570 kHz.

AFRTS Shortwave, USA. Network news, live sports, music and features in the *upper-sideband* mode from the American Forces Radio & Television Service. Transmitted from modestly powered U.S. Navy stations around the globe, so usually a tough catch. Try 4319, 5446.5, 5765, 6350, 7811, 10320, 12133.5, 12579 and 13362 kHz.

08:30

Radio Vilnius, Lithuania. Summer only at this time; see 0930 for specifics. To western Europe on 9710 kHz. One hour later in winter.

09:00

■**Deutsche Welle,** Germany. *News*, then Monday through Friday it's ●*NewsLink*—commentary, interviews, background reports and analysis. The second half-hour features *EuroVox* (Monday), *Hits in Germany* (Tuesday), ●*Arts on the Air* (Wednesday), *Cool* (a well produced youth show, Thursday) and *Dialogue* on Friday. Weekends, the news is followed by Saturday's *Network Europe* and ●*Insight*, and Sunday's *In-Box, Mission Europe* (German language lessons) and *World in Progress*. Sixty minutes to East Asia winter on 17710 and 21840 kHz, and summer on 15340 and 17705 kHz.

China Radio International. *News* and reports fill the first half-hour, and are followed

09:00–10:00

by a daily feature: *Front Line* (Monday), *Biz China* (Tuesday), *In the Spotlight* (Wednesday), ●*Voices from Other Lands* (Thursday), *Life in China* (Friday), *Listeners' Garden* (Saturday) and *China Horizons* (Sunday). One hour to Europe on 17490 kHz; to Australasia on 15210 and 17690 kHz; and to East Asia winter on 9415 kHz, and summer on 11620 kHz.

Voice of Greece. Sunday and summer only at this time, and actually starts at 0905. Fifty-five minutes of music in *Greek in Style*. To Europe on 9420 and 11645 kHz. Two hours later in winter.

Radio Japan. Ten minutes of *news*, then one or more features. Thirty minutes to Hawaii and South America on 9825 kHz; to South Asia on 15590 kHz; to Southeast Asia on 11815 kHz; and to Australasia on 11890 kHz (11845 or 12000 kHz may also be used).

Radio New Zealand International. Continuous programming for the islands of the South Pacific on 6095 or 9765 kHz. Audible in much of North America, especially in summer.

Voice of Russia World Service. Winter only at this time, and the last of four hours for Australasia. Tuesday through Sunday, *News* is followed by *News and Views*, replaced Monday by *This is Russia*. On the half-hour there's a news summary and a feature: *A Stroll Around the Kremlin* and *Musical Tales* (Monday), *Kaleidoscope* (Tuesday), *The VOR Treasure Store* (Wednesday), ●*Folk Box* (Thursday), ●*Jazz Show* (Friday), ●*Christian Message from Moscow* (Saturday) and *Timelines* on Sunday. On 17495 and 17665 kHz.

Radio Prague, Czech Republic. Summer only at this time. See 1000 for specifics. Thirty minutes to Europe on 9880 kHz, and to South Asia on 21745 kHz. One hour later in winter.

Radio Australia. *World News*, then Monday through Friday it's *Australia Talks* (a call-in show). Winter Saturdays there's *Margaret Throsby*, replaced summer by *Asia Review* and *Jazz Notes*. Sunday, it's *The Music Show*

Part I. Continuous to Asia and the Pacific on 9580, 9590, 11880 and 15415 kHz; and heard in North America on 9580 and 9590 kHz. For Southeast Asia there's 11880 and 15415 kHz.

AFRTS Shortwave, USA. Network news, live sports, music and features in the *upper-sideband* mode from the American Forces Radio & Television Service. Transmitted from modestly powered U.S. Navy stations around the globe, so usually a tough catch. Try 4319, 5446.5, 5765, 6350, 7811, 10320, 12133.5, 12579 and 13362 kHz.

09:30

Radio Vilnius, Lithuania. Winter only at this time. Thirty minutes of mostly *news* and background reports about events in Lithuania. A listener-response program, *Mailbag*, is aired every other Sunday. For a little Lithuanian music, try the second half of Monday's broadcast. To western Europe on 9710 kHz. One hour earlier in summer.

Kol Israel. Summer only at this time. *News* for 15 minutes from Israel Radio's domestic network. To Europe and eastern North America on 13855 and 15760 kHz. One hour later in winter.

10:00

■**Radio Netherlands.** Monday through Friday, ●*Newsline* (current events) is followed by a 30-minute feature. Monday, it's a look at all things Dutch, and Tuesday it's the midweek edition of ●*The State We're In*. Wednesday's slot is *Radio Books*, replaced Thursday by *Earth Beat* and Friday by *Network Europe*. Weekends, there's Saturday's ●*The State We're In* and Sunday's *Amsterdam Forum* and *Reloaded* (highlights of the previous week's shows). Fifty-seven minutes to East and Southeast Asia winter on 6040, 9795 and 12065 kHz; and summer on 12065, 13710 and 13820 kHz. Also widely heard in Australia.

Radio Australia. Monday through Friday, there's *World News*, *Asia Pacific* (regional current events) and a feature: *Health Report* (Monday), *Law Report* (Tuesday), *Religious Report* (Wednesday), *Media Report* (Thursday) and *Sports Factor* (Friday). The Saturday slots are taken by *Asia Pacific Business*, *Talking Point* and *Verbatim*; Sunday, it's the second part of *The Music Show*. Continuous to Asia and the Pacific on 9580, 9590, 11880 and 15415 kHz; and heard in North America on 9580 and 9590 kHz. Listeners in Southeast Asia have 11880 and 15415 kHz.

Radio Prague, Czech Republic. Winter only at this time. *News*, then Monday through Friday there's *Current Affairs* and a feature or two: *One on One* (Monday), *Talking Point* (Tuesday), *Czechs in History*, *Czechs Today* or *Spotlight* (Wednesday), *Panorama* and *Czech Science* (Thursday), and *Business Briefs* and *The Arts* (Friday). On Saturday the news is followed by *Magazine*, *ABC of Czech* and a repeat of Tuesday's *One on One*. Sunday's lineup is *Mailbox* and *Letter from Prague* followed by *Encore* (classical music), *Magic Carpet* (Czech world music) or *Czech Books*. Thirty minutes to South and Southeast Asia on 15700 kHz, and to West Africa on 21745 kHz. Audible well beyond. To Asia one hour earlier in summer, but the broadcast to Africa moves to 2100.

Voice of Mongolia. Original programming is aired on Monday, Wednesday and Friday, and is repeated on the following day. Starts with *News*, and then it's either a listener-response program (Monday) or reports and interviews. The entire Sunday broadcast is devoted to exotic Mongolian music. Thirty minutes to Southeast Asia and Australasia on 12085 kHz. Often well heard in parts of the United States during March and September.

China Radio International. Weekdays, *News* is followed by *China Drive*, an upbeat "drive-time" show. Weekends there's *News and Reports*, *CRI Roundup* (Saturday), *Reports from Developing Countries* (Sunday) and *China Beat*. Although mostly Chinese popular music, *China Beat* can sometimes surprise with jazz or Chinese versions of American folk and urban blues. One hour

Personnel from Asian stations confer on Digital Radio Mondiale at a workshop in New Delhi. Jose Jacob

to Europe on 17490 kHz; to Australasia on 15210 and 17690 kHz; to eastern North America summer on 6040 kHz; to Southeast Asia on 13590 and 13720 kHz; and to East Asia winter on 5955, 7135 and 7215 kHz; and summer on 11610, 11635 and 13620 kHz.

All India Radio. *News*, then a composite program of commentary, press review and features, interspersed with exotic Indian music. Look for a listener-response segment, *Faithfully Yours*, at 1030 Monday. One hour to East Asia on 13710 (or 13695), 15020, 15235 (or 15410) and 17800 kHz, and to Australasia on 13710 (or 13695), 17510 and 17895 kHz. Also beamed to Sri Lanka on 15260 kHz.

Voice of Korea, North Korea. Mind-numbing programs on themes such as the application of socialist thinking to steel production are basic fare for this world band curiosity. Worth the occasional listen just to hear how bad it is. One hour to Central America on 6285 (or 15180) and 9325 (or 11710) kHz; and to Southeast Asia on 6185 (or 11735) and 9850 (or 13650) kHz. Also audible in parts of East Asia on 3560 kHz.

Voice of Vietnam. Begins with *news*, then there's *Commentary* or *Weekly Review* followed by short features and pleasant Vietnamese music (especially at weekends).

10:00–11:00

Australia's Sydney Tower offers a birds-eye view of the city and its harbor landmarks.   Shutterstock/Graham Prentice

Half an hour to Southeast Asia on 9840 and 12020 kHz.

AFRTS Shortwave, USA. Network news, live sports, music and features in the *upper-sideband* mode from the American Forces Radio & Television Service. Transmitted from modestly powered U.S. Navy stations around the globe, so usually a tough catch. Try 4319, 5446.5, 5765, 6350, 7811, 10320, 12133.5, 12579 and 13362 kHz.

10:30

Radio Prague, Czech Republic. This time summer only. Repeat of the 0700 broadcast but with different programming on Saturday: *Magazine*, *ABC of Czech* and *One on One* replace *Insight Central Europe*. Thirty minutes to northern Europe on 9880 and 11665 kHz. One hour later during winter.

Kol Israel. Winter only at this time. *News* for 15 minutes from Israel Radio's domestic network. To Europe and eastern North America on 15760 and 17535 kHz. One hour earlier in summer.

Voice of the Islamic Republic of Iran. News, commentary and features, and a little Iranian music. Strongly reflects an Islamic point of view. One hour to South Asia, and widely heard elsewhere. On 15460 (winter), 15600 (summer) and 17660 kHz.

11:00

■**BBC World Service for the Caribbean.** The first 60 minutes of a two-hour broadcast. Weekdays, opens with *news*, then *Caribbean Report*, *Sport Caribbean*, *Caribbean Magazine*, *World Briefing*, *Analysis* and *Sports Roundup*. These are replaced weekends by *World Briefing* and Saturday's *Politics UK* (sometimes replaced by a documentary) or Sunday's ●*Heart and Soul*. Winter on 5875 and 9750 kHz, and summer on 6095 (or 9660) and 9465 kHz.

■**Radio Netherlands.** Summer only at this time; see 1200 for specifics. Fifty-seven minutes to eastern North America on 11675 kHz, and one hour later in winter.

China Radio International. Repeat of the 1000 broadcast, but with updated news. One hour to East Asia on 5955 kHz; to Southeast Asia on 13590 and 13720 kHz; to Europe on 13650 (summer), 13665 (winter) and 17490 kHz; and to North America winter on 5960 kHz, and summer on 6040 and 11750 kHz.

Radio Taiwan International. Ten minutes of *News*, followed by features: *Made in Taiwan*, *Generation Why* and *Asia Review* (Monday); *Strait Talk* and *We've Got Mail* (Tuesday); *Trends*, *Women Making Waves* and ●*Jade Bells and Bamboo Pipes* (Wednesday); *Ilha Formosa*, *People*, *Instant Noodles* and *Chinese to Go* (Thursday); *Walks of Life*, *Mandopop* and *Taiwan Outlook* (Friday); *News Talk* and *Groove Zone* (Saturday); and *The Occidental Tourist*, *Chinese to Go* (language lessons) *Stage, Screen and Studio* and *On the Line* (Sunday). Sixty minutes to Southeast Asia on 7445 kHz.

Radio Australia. *World News*, followed Monday through Friday by a bulletin of the

10:00–11:00

latest sports news and *PM* (current events). Weekends, there's Saturday's *Asia Review* and *All in the Mind*, replaced Sunday by *Sunday Profile* and *Speaking Out*. Continuous to East Asia and the Pacific on 5995, 6020, 9475, 9560, 9580, 9590, 11880 and 12080 kHz; and heard in much of North America on 6020, 9580 and 9590 kHz. Listeners in Southeast Asia should tune to 9475 and 11880 kHz. For East Asia there's 9560 kHz.

Radio Ukraine International. Summer only at this time. Sixty minutes of just about all things Ukrainian, including news, sports, politics and culture. A popular feature is ●*Music from Ukraine*, which fills most of the Sunday broadcast. To western Europe on 11550 (or 9950 or 15675) kHz. One hour later in winter.

Voice of Greece. Sunday and winter only at this time, and actually starts at 1105.

Fifty-five minutes of music in *Greek in Style*. To Europe on 9420 kHz, and to Australasia on 17525 kHz. For Europe it's two hours earlier in summer, and for Australasia it moves to 2305 Sunday

Voice of Vietnam. Repeat of the 1000 broadcast; see there for specifics. Half an hour to Southeast Asia on 7285 kHz.

Radio Singapore International. A three-hour package for Southeast Asia, and widely heard in Australasia. Starts with ten minutes of *news* (five at weekends), then Monday through Friday there's *Business and Market Report*, replaced Saturday by *Business Ideas*, and Sunday by *Connections*. These are followed by several mini-features, including a daily news and weather bulletin on the half-hour. Monday's lineup is *Undertones*, *Discovering Singapore*, *The Write Stuff* and *E-Z Beat*; and is replaced Tuesday by *A World of Our Own*, *Young Ex-*

11:00–12:00

Wenceslas Square honors Jan Palach, a student who opposed the 1968 Soviet invasion. Coverage of the Prague Spring and Czech resistence were among Radio Prague's finest hours.

Shutterstock/Pavol Kmeto

pressions, *The Business Feature*, *Assignment* and a shorter edition of *E-Z Beat*; Wednesday offers *Perspective*, *Traveller's Tales*, *Eco-Watch*, *The Business Feature* and *Classic Gold*; Thursday has *Frontiers, Eco-Watch*, *The Business Feature*, *Potluck* and *Love Songs*; and Friday brings *Asian Journal*, *Arts Arena*, *The Business Feature*, *Indonesian Media Watch* and *Classic Gold*. Saturday's list includes *Regional Press Review* and *Frontiers* and Sunday there's *Comment*, *Discovering Singapore* and *Science and Technology*. On 6080 and 6150 kHz.

AFRTS Shortwave, USA. Network news, live sports, music and features in the *upper-sideband* mode from the American Forces Radio & Television Service. Transmitted from modestly powered U.S. Navy stations around the globe, so usually a tough catch. Try 4319, 5446.5, 5765, 6350, 7811, 10320, 12133.5, 12579 and 13362 kHz.

11:30

Radio Bulgaria. Summer only at this time. *News*, followed by *DX Programme* (for radio enthusiasts, Sunday), *Answering Your Letters* (a listener-response show, Monday),

and ●*Folk Studio* (Bulgarian folk music, Tuesday). Most of the remaining airtime is taken up by *Time Out for Music*. Thirty minutes to Europe on 11700 and 15700 kHz, and one hour later in winter.

Radio Prague, Czech Republic. Winter only at this time. *News*, then Monday through Friday it's *Current Affairs* plus one or more features: *One on One* (Monday), *Talking Point* (Tuesday), *Czechs in History*, *Czechs Today* or *Spotlight* (Wednesday), *Panorama* and *Czech Science* (Thursday), and *Business Briefs* and *The Arts* on Friday. The Saturday news is followed by *Magazine*, *ABC of Czech* and a repeat of Tuesday's *One on One*. Sunday's lineup is *Mailbox* and *Letter from Prague* followed by *Encore* (classical music), *Magic Carpet* (Czech world music) or *Czech Books*. Thirty minutes to northern Europe on 11640 kHz, and to eastern and southern Africa on 17545 kHz. The European broadcast is one hour earlier in summer, but for Africa it moves to 1600.

Voice of Vietnam. *News*, then *Commentary* or *Weekly Review* followed by short features and pleasant Vietnamese music (especially at weekends). A listener-response segment airs at 1145 Wednesday. To East Asia on 9840 and 12020 kHz.

12:00–17:59
Western Australia & East Asia—Evening Prime Time
North America—Morning and Lunchtime
Europe & Mideast—Afternoon and Early Evening

12:00

■**BBC World Service for the Caribbean.**
The final 60 minutes of a two-hour broadcast. Weekdays, opens with *news*, then *Caribbean Business*, *Caribbean Report*, and *Caribbean Magazine*. The second half-hour features *Outlook* or news programming. These are replaced weekends by *Newshour*. Winter on 9660 and 9750 kHz, and summer on 9465 and 9660 kHz.

■**Radio Netherlands.** Monday through Friday, ●*Newsline* (current events) is followed by a 30-minute feature. Monday, it's a look at all things Dutch, and Tuesday it's the midweek edition of ●*The State We're In*. Wednesday's slot is *Radio Books*, replaced Thursday by *Earth Beat* and Friday by *Network Europe*. Weekends, there's Saturday's ●*The State We're In* and Sunday's *Amsterdam Forum* and *Reloaded* (highlights of the previous week's shows). Fifty-seven minutes to eastern North America on 11675 kHz, and one hour earlier in summer.

China Radio International. *News* and reports fill the first half-hour, and are followed by a daily feature: *Front Line* (Monday), *Biz China* (Tuesday), *In the Spotlight* (Wednesday), ●*Voices from Other Lands* (Thursday), *Life in China* (Friday), *Listeners' Garden* (Saturday) and *China Horizons* (Sunday). One hour to Europe on 13650 (summer), 13665 (winter), 13790 and 17490 kHz; to eastern North America winter on 9560 kHz; to East Asia on 5955 kHz; to Southeast Asia on 9730 and 11980 kHz, and to Australasia on 9760 and 11760 kHz.

Radio Japan. Ten minutes of *news*, then one or more features. Thirty minutes to Europe on 17585 or 17600 kHz; to eastern North America on 6120 kHz; to Southeast Asia on 13660 kHz; and to Australasia on 9625 kHz.

KBS World Radio, South Korea. Opens with 10 minutes of *news*, then Monday through Friday, a commentary. This is followed by 30 minutes of *Seoul Calling* and a 15-minute feature: *Faces of Korea*, *Business Watch*, *Culture on the Move*, *Korea Today and Tomorrow* and *Seoul Report*, respectively. Saturday's news is followed by *Worldwide Friendship* (a listener-response show), and Sunday by *Korean Pop Interactive*. Sixty minutes to eastern North America on 9650 kHz via their Canadian relay.

■**Radio France Internationale.** Opens with a *news* bulletin, then there's a 25-minute feature—*French Lesson*, *Crossroads*, *Voices*, *Rendez-Vous*, *World Tracks*, *Weekend* or *Club 9516* (a listener-response program). Thirty minutes to East Africa on 21620 (or 17800) kHz, and heard far beyond.

Polish Radio External Service. This time summer only. Sixty minutes of news, commentary, features and music—all with a Polish accent. Weekdays, starts with *News from Poland*—a potpourri of news, reports, interviews and press review. This is followed Monday by *Focus* (an arts program) and *Talking Jazz*; Tuesday by *A Day in the Life* (interviews) and *The Biz*; Wednesday by *Around Poland* and *Biz II*; Thursday by *Letter from Poland* and *Multimedia Show*; and Friday by *Weekly Commentary*, *Business Week* and *Offside*. The Saturday broadcast begins with a bulletin of *news*, and is followed by *Insight Central Europe* (a joint-production with other stations of the region), *A Look at the Weeklies*, and *Chart Show* (Polish popular music). The Sunday lineup includes *Europe East* (correspondents' reports) and *High Note*. To northern Europe on 9525 and 11850 kHz. One hour later in winter. 9525 kHz is sometimes heard in eastern North America.

One of the massive antenna arrays used by the Soviet "Woodpecker." This over-the-horizon radar's "tat-tat-tat" pulses disrupted world band during the closing years of the Cold War. Something similar reportedly was being heard in early autumn of 2007.   Pripyat

Radio Austria International. Summer only at this time. Weekdays, there's the 15-minute *Report from Austria* at 1205. Saturday and Sunday, ●*Report from Austria–The Week in Review* airs at 1205 and 1235. The remainder of the one-hour broadcast is in German. To Europe on 6155 and 13730 kHz, and to Asia and Australasia on 17715 kHz. One hour later in winter.

Radio Romania International. Summer only at this time; see 1300 for specifics. Fifty-five minutes to Europe on 11875 and 15220 kHz. One hour later in winter.

Radio Australia. *World News*, then Monday through Thursday it's *Late Night Live* (round-table discussion). On the remaining days there's *Classic Late Night Live* (Friday), ●*Saturday Night Country*, and *Sunday Night*. Continuous to Asia and the Pacific on 5995, 6020, 9475, 9560, 9580, 9590 and 11880

kHz; and well heard in much of North America on 6020, 9580 and 9590 kHz. Listeners in East Asia can tune to 9460 kHz; and in Southeast Asia to 9475 and 11880 kHz.

Radio Ukraine International. Winter only at this time. See 1100 for specifics. Sixty minutes to Europe on 9925 kHz. One hour earlier in summer.

Radio Singapore International. The second of three hours of continuous programming to Southeast Asia and beyond. Starts with five minutes of *news*, followed weekdays by *Newsline*. Most of the remaining time is devoted to short features. There's a weekday *Business and Market Report* on the half-hour, replaced weekends by a *news* bulletin. Monday's lineup includes *Perspective*, *Indonesian Media Watch*, *Frontiers*, *Eco-Watch* and *Young Expressions*; Tuesday, there's *Asian Journal*, *Undertones*, *Discovering Singapore* and *Film Talk*; replaced Wednesday by *Call from America*, *The Write Stuff*, *Snapshots* and *A World of Our Own*; Thursday offers, among others, *Connections*, *Comment*, *Assignment* and *Arts Arena*; and Friday has *Regional Press Review*, *Business Ideas* and *Limelight*. Saturday's *Connections*, *Perspective*, *Indonesian Media Watch*, *Young Expressions* and *Comment* are replaced Sunday by *Regional Press Review*, *Business Ideas*, *Call from America*, *Undertones* and *Potluck*. On 6080 and 6150 kHz.

Voice of America. *East Asia News Now*. Weekends, the second half-hour consists of Saturday's *Press Conference USA*, and Sunday's *Issues in the News*. The first hour of continuous programming to East and Southeast Asia; winter on 9640, 9760, 11705 and 11730 kHz; and summer on 6140, 9645, 9760 and 11860 kHz. For Australasia there's 9640/9645 kHz.

AFRTS Shortwave, USA. Network news, live sports, music and features in the *upper-sideband* mode from the American Forces Radio & Television Service. Transmitted from modestly powered U.S. Navy stations around the globe, so usually a tough catch. Try 4319, 5446.5, 5765, 6350, 7811, 10320, 12133.5, 12579 and 13362 kHz.

12:00–13:00

12:15

Radio Cairo, Egypt. The start of a 75-minute package of news, religion, culture and entertainment, much of it devoted to Arab and Islamic themes. The initial quarter hour consists of virtually anything, from quizzes to Islamic religious talks, then there's *news* and commentary, followed by political and cultural items. To South and Southeast Asia on 17835 kHz.

12:30

Radio Bulgaria. Winter only at this time. *News*, then *DX Programme* (for radio enthusiasts, Sunday), *Answering Your Letters* (a listener-response show, Monday), and ●*Folk Studio* (Bulgarian folk music, Tuesday). Most of the remaining airtime is taken up by *Time Out for Music*. Thirty minutes to Europe on 11700 and 15700 kHz and one hour earlier in summer.

Bangladesh Betar. *News*, followed by Islamic and general interest features and pleasant Bengali music. Thirty minutes to Southeast Asia, also heard in Europe, on 7250 kHz.

Voice of Vietnam. Repeat of the 1100 transmission; see there for specifics. Half an hour to Southeast Asia on 9840 and 12020 kHz. Frequencies may vary slightly.

Radio Thailand. Thirty minutes of *news* and short features to Southeast Asia and Australasia, winter on 9810 kHz and summer on 9835 kHz.

Voice of Turkey. This time summer only. Fifty-five minutes of *news*, features and Turkish music. To Europe on 15450 kHz, and to Southeast Asia and Australasia on 13685 kHz. One hour later in winter.

Radio Sweden. Summer only at this time. Monday through Friday, it's a smorgasbord of *news* and features about Sweden. Saturday, there is a review of the week's main news stories; and Sunday it's *Network Europe*. Thirty minutes to North America on 15240 kHz; and to Asia and Australasia on 13580 and 15735 kHz. One hour later in winter.

13:00

China Radio International. Repeat of the 1200 broadcast; see there for specifics. One hour to Europe on 13610 and 13790 kHz; to North America winter on 9570, 11885 and 15230 kHz, and summer on 9570, 9650 and 15260 kHz; to East Asia on 5955 kHz;

China Radio International's English Service staff in Shanghai for live coverage of the Ninth APEC Leaders Meeting. CRI

13:00–13:30

to Southeast Asia on 9730, 9870 and 11980 kHz; and to Australasia on 11760 and 11900 kHz.

Polish Radio External Service. This time winter only. *News*, commentary, music and a variety of features. See 1200 for specifics. Sixty minutes to Europe on 9525 and 11850 kHz. One hour earlier in summer.

Radio Prague, Czech Republic. Summer only at this hour. *News*, then Monday through Friday it's *Current Affairs* plus one or more features: *One on One* (Monday), *Talking Point* (Tuesday), *Czechs in History*, *Czechs Today* or *Spotlight* (Wednesday), *Panorama* and *Czech Science* (Thursday), and *Business Briefs* and *The Arts* on Friday. The Saturday news is followed by *Insight Central Europe*, and Sunday's lineup is *Mailbox* and *Letter from Prague* followed by *Encore* (classical music), *Magic Carpet* (Czech world music) or *Czech Books*. Thirty minutes to northern Europe on 13580 kHz, and to South Asia on 17540 kHz.

Radio Tirana, Albania. Tuesday through Sunday, and summer only at this time. A repeat of the previous day's broadcast. To eastern North America on 13750 kHz. Two hours later in winter.

Radio Romania International. Winter only at this time. Starts with *Radio Newsreel*, a combination of news, commentary and press review. Features on Romania complete the broadcast. Regular spots include Monday's *Pro Memoria*, *Romanian Hits* and *Sports Roundup*; Tuesday's *Business Club* and ●*The Skylark* (Romanian folk music); Wednesday's *Society Today* and *Romanian Musicians*; Thursday's *Europa Express*; and Friday's ●*The Folk Music Box* and *Sports Weekend*. Saturday there's *The Week* and *World of Culture*, and Sunday's broadcast includes *Focus*. Fifty-five minutes to Europe on 15105 and 17745 kHz. One hour earlier in summer.

Radio Jordan. Summer only at this time. The first hour of a partial relay of the station's domestic broadcasts, beamed to Europe on 11690 kHz. Continuous till 1630 (1730 in winter).

KBS World Radio, South Korea. Opens with 10 minutes of *news*, then Monday through Friday, a commentary. This is followed by 30 minutes of *Seoul Calling* and a 15-minute feature: *Faces of Korea, Business Culture on the Move, Korea Today and Tomorrow* and *Seoul Report*, respectively. Saturday's news is followed by *Worldwide Friendship* (a listener-response show), and Sunday by *Korean Pop Interactive*. Sixty minutes to Southeast Asia on 9570 and 9770 kHz.

Radio Austria International. Winter only at this time. Weekdays, there's 15 minutes of *Report from Austria* at 1205. Saturday and Sunday, ●*Report from Austria–The Week in Review* airs at 1205 and 1235. The remainder of the one-hour broadcast is in German. To Europe on 6155 and 13730 kHz, and to Asia and Australasia on 17855 kHz. One hour earlier in summer.

Radio Cairo: Nile polish, but audio often suffers.

Radio Cairo, Egypt. The final half-hour of the 1215 broadcast, consisting of listener participation programs, Arabic language lessons and a summary of the latest news. To South and Southeast Asia on 17835 kHz.

Radio Australia. Monday through Friday, *News* is followed by *Asia Pacific* and a feature: *Innovations* (Monday), *Australian Express* (Tuesday), *Rural Reporter* (Wednesday), ●*Rear Vision* (Thursday) and *All in the Mind* (Friday). Weekends, it's the second hour of ●*Saturday Night Country* and *Sunday Night*. Continuous programming to Asia and the Pacific on 5995, 6020, 9560, 9580 and 9590 kHz; and easily audible in much of North America on 6020 (West Coast), 9580 and 9590 kHz. In East Asia, try 9560 kHz.

Radio Singapore International. The third and final hour of a daily broadcast to Southeast Asia and beyond. Starts with a five-minute bulletin of the latest *news*, then most days it's music: *Singapop* (local talent, Monday and Thursday); *Rhythm in the Sun* (Latin sounds, Tuesday and Sunday); *Spin the Globe* (world music, Wednesday and Saturday); and *Hot Trax* (new releases, Friday). There's another news bulletin on the half-hour, then a short feature. Monday's offering is *Traveller's Tales*, replaced Tuesday by *The Write Stuff*. Wednesday's feature is *Potluck*; Thursday has *Call from America*; and Friday it's *Snapshots*. These are followed by the 15-minute *Newsline*. Weekend fare is made up of Saturday's *Assignment*, *Film Talk* and *Arts Arena*; and Sunday's *A World of Our Own* and *Limelight*. The broadcast ends with yet another five-minute news update. On 6080 and 6150 kHz.

Voice of Korea, North Korea. Abysmal programs from the last of the old-time communist stations. Socialist thinking shares airtime with choral tributes to the Great Leader. One hour to Europe on 7570 (or 13760) and 12015 (or 15245) kHz; and to North America on 9335 and 11710 kHz. Also heard in parts of East Asia on 4405 kHz.

Voice of America. Continuous programming to East and Southeast Asia. The weekday *East Asia News Now* is replaced weekends by *Jazz America*. Continuous programming to East and Southeast Asia winter on 9640, 9760 and 11705 kHz; and summer on 9645 and 9760 kHz. In Australasia tune to 9640/9645 kHz.

U.S. Navy's Blue Angels are hugely popular, as is the American Forces Radio & Television Service. World band coverage is global, but requires a superior radio.
Shutterstock/Jeremy R. Smith Sr.

AFRTS Shortwave, USA. Network news, live sports, music and features in the *upper-sideband* mode from the American Forces Radio & Television Service. Transmitted from modestly powered U.S. Navy stations around the globe, so usually a tough catch. Try 4319, 5446.5, 5765, 6350, 7811, 10320, 12133.5, 12579 and 13362 kHz.

13:10

Radio Japan. Ten minutes of *news*, then one or more features. Thirty minutes to South Asia on 11985 and/or 9875 kHz. Heard well beyond the target area, especially in East Asia.

13:30

Voice of Turkey. This time winter only. *News*, then *Review of the Turkish Press* and some unusual features with a strong local flavor. Selections of Turkish popular and classical music complete the program. Fifty-five minutes to Europe on 12035 kHz, and to South and Southeast Asia and Australasia on 11735 kHz. One hour earlier in summer.

Radio Sweden. See 1230 for program details. Thirty minutes to North America winter on 15240 kHz; to Central and East Asia winter on 7420 kHz; and to Southeast Asia and Australasia summer on 15735 kHz.

13:30–15:00

Voice of Vietnam. *News*, then *Commentary* or *Weekly Review* followed by short features and pleasant Vietnamese music (especially at weekends). A listener-response segment airs at 1345 Wednesday. To East Asia on 9840 and 12020 kHz.

All India Radio. The first half-hour of a 90-minute block of regional and international *news*, commentary, exotic Indian music, and a variety of talks and features of general interest. To Southeast Asia and beyond on 9690, 11620 and 13710 kHz.

14:00

Radio Japan. Ten minutes of *news*, then one or more features. Thirty minutes to northern Europe winter on 11780 kHz, and summer on 13630 kHz; to eastern North America and Central America on 11705 kHz; to Central and East Africa on 17580 kHz; to South Asia on 11985 or 9875 kHz; and to Southeast Asia on 7200 kHz.

Voice of Greece. Saturday and summer only at this time. Sixty minutes of *Hellenes Around the World* (also known as *Greeks Everywhere*). To Europe on 9420 and 15630 kHz, and also heard in parts of North America. One hour later in winter. Sometimes pre-empted by live sports commentary in Greek.

Voice of Russia World Service. Summer only at this time. Eleven minutes of *News*, followed Monday through Saturday by much of the same in *News and Views*. Completing the lineup are *Sunday Panorama* and *A Stroll Around the Kremlin*. A short summary of news on the half-hour is followed by features: *Our Homeland* (Monday and Friday), ●*Kaleidoscope* (Tuesday), *Russian by Radio* (Wednesday), *The VOR Treasure Store* (Thursday), *Timelines* (Saturday) and ●*Folk Box* on Sunday. To Southeast Asia on 6045, 7165, 15605 and 15660 kHz. One hour later in winter.

■**Radio Netherlands.** The first 60 minutes of an approximately two-hour broadcast targeted at South Asia. Monday through Friday, ●*Newsline* (current events) is fol-lowed by a 30-minute feature. Monday, it's a look at all things Dutch, and Tuesday it's the midweek edition of ●*The State We're In*. Wednesday's slot is *Radio Books*, replaced Thursday by *Earth Beat* and Friday by *Network Europe*. Weekends, there's Saturday's ●*The State We're In* and Sunday's *Amsterdam Forum* and *Reloaded* (highlights of the previous week's shows). Winter on 9345, 12080 and 15595 kHz; and summer on 9345, 9890 and 11835 kHz. Heard well beyond the target area.

Radio Australia. Weekdays, *World News* is followed by one or two features: *Big Ideas* (Monday), *Awaye* (Tuesday), *All in the Mind* and *Philosopher's Stone* (Wednesday), *Hindsight* (Thursday), and *Movietime* and *Arts on RA* on Friday. Weekends, it's the third hour of ●*Saturday Night Country* and *Sunday Night*. Continuous to Asia and the Pacific on 5995, 6080, 7240, 9475 (from 1430), 9590 and (from 1430) 11660 kHz (5995, 7240 and 9590 kHz are audible in North America, especially to the west). In Southeast Asia, use 6080, 9475 and 11660 kHz.

Radio Prague, Czech Republic. Winter only at this time. *News*, then Monday through Friday it's *Current Affairs* plus one or more features: *One on One* (Monday), *Talking Point* (Tuesday), *Czechs in History*, *Czechs Today* or *Spotlight* (Wednesday), *Panorama* and *Czech Science* (Thursday), and *Business Briefs* and *The Arts* on Friday. The Saturday news is followed by *Insight Central Europe*, and Sunday's lineup is *Mailbox* and *Letter from Prague* followed by *Encore* (classical music), *Magic Carpet* (Czech world music) or *Czech Books*. A friendly half-hour to eastern North America on 13580 kHz, and to South Asia on 11600 kHz.

Radio Taiwan International. Ten minutes of *News*, followed by features: *Made in Taiwan*, *Generation Why* and *Asia Review* (Monday); *Strait Talk* and *We've Got Mail* (Tuesday); *Trends*, *Women Making Waves* and ●*Jade Bells and Bamboo Pipes* (Wednesday); *Ilha Formosa*, *People*, *Instant Noodles* and *Chinese to Go* (Thursday); *Walks of Life*, *Mandopop* and *Taiwan Outlook* (Friday); *News Talk* and *Groove Zone* (Saturday);

and *The Occidental Tourist, Chinese to Go* (language lessons) *Stage, Screen and Studio* and *On the Line* (Sunday). Sixty minutes to Southeast Asia on 15265 kHz.

China Radio International. *News* and reports fill the first half-hour, and are followed by a daily feature: *Front Line* (Monday), *Biz China* (Tuesday), *In the Spotlight* (Wednesday), ●*Voices from Other Lands* (Thursday), *Life in China* (Friday), *Listeners' Garden* (Saturday) and *China Horizons* (Sunday). One hour to Europe winter on 9700 and 9795 kHz; and summer on 13710 and 13790 kHz; to North America winter on 13675, 13740 and 15230 kHz; and summer on 13740 kHz; to East Asia on 5955 kHz; to Southeast Asia on 9870 kHz; and to eastern and southern Africa on 13685 and 17630 kHz.

Voice of Africa, Libya. The first 60 minutes of a two-hour broadcast. Includes some lively African music. Look for a bulletin of *news* on the half-hour, and readings from "The Green Book" a little later. To Central and East Africa winter on 17725 and 21695 kHz, and summer on 17725 (or 21695) and 17870 kHz. Sometimes heard in North America, especially in summer.

All India Radio. The final hour of a 90-minute composite program of commentary, press review, features and exotic Indian music. To Southeast Asia and beyond on 9690, 11620 and 13710 kHz.

Radio Jordan. Winter, starts at this time; summer, it's the second hour of a partial relay of the station's domestic broadcasts, and continuous till 1630 (1730 in winter). Aimed at European listeners but also audible in parts of eastern North America, especially during winter. On 11690 kHz.

Radio Thailand. Thirty minutes of tourist features for Southeast Asia and Australasia. Winter on 9725 kHz, and summer on 9805 kHz.

AFRTS Shortwave, USA. Network news, live sports, music and features in the *upper-sideband* mode from the American Forces Radio & Television Service. Transmitted from modestly powered U.S. Navy stations around the globe, so usually a tough catch. Try 4319, 5446.5, 5765, 6350, 7811, 10320, 12133.5, 12579 and 13362 kHz.

14:30

Radio Sweden. Monday through Friday, it's a smorgasbord of *news* and features about Sweden. Saturday, there is a review of the week's main news stories; and Sunday it's *Network Europe*. Thirty minutes winter to Southeast Asia on 11550 kHz, and to western North America summer on 15240 kHz.

15:00

China Radio International. See 1400 for program details. One hour to Europe winter on 9435 and 9525 kHz, and summer on 11965 and 13640 kHz; to western North

This card confirms reception of Dux Radio's inaugural broadcast from Radio Africa Tanger (see p. 10). L. Rydén

15:00–16:00

Niharika Acharya produces Hindi programs for the Voice of America to India.   VoA

America on 13740 kHz; to East Asia on 5955 kHz; to Southeast Asia on 7325 and 9870 kHz; and to eastern and southern Africa on 6100, 13685 and 17630 kHz.

Radio Tirana, Albania. Tuesday through Sunday and winter only. A repeat of the previous day's broadcast. To eastern North America on 13640 kHz. Two hours earlier in summer.

Radio Austria International. Summer only at this time. Monday, the 15-minute *Report from Austria* airs at 1505 and 1545; Tuesday through Friday, the times are 1515 and 1545. Saturday and Sunday, there's ●*News from Austria–The Week in Review* at 1505 and 1535. The remainder of the broadcast is in German. To western North America on 13775 kHz, and one hour later in winter.

■**Radio Netherlands.** The final 57 minutes of an approximately two-hour broadcast targeted at South Asia. Monday through Friday, starts with a feature and ends with ●*Newsline* (current events); weekends, it's all features. The features are repeats of programs aired during the previous six days, and merit a second hearing. Winter on 9345, 12080 and 15595 kHz; and summer on 9345, 9890 and 11835 kHz. Heard well beyond the target area.

Voice of Greece. Saturday and winter only at this time. Sixty minutes of *Hellenes Around the World* (also known as *Greeks Everywhere*). To Europe (and heard in parts of North America) on 9420 kHz, and to Australasia on 17525 kHz. For Europe it's one hour earlier in summer, and for Australasia it moves to 0200 Monday. Sometimes pre-empted by live sports commentary in Greek.

Radio Australia. *World News*, then weekdays there's *Asia Pacific* and a feature on the half-hour: *Health Report* (Monday), *Law Report* (Tuesday), *Religion Report* (Wednesday), *Media Report* (Thursday) and *The Sports Factor* on Friday. These are replaced weekends by the final hour of ●*Saturday Night Country* and *Sunday Night*. Continuous programming to the Pacific (and well heard in western North America) on 5995, 7240 and 9590 kHz. Additionally available to Southeast Asia on 6080, 9475 and 11660 kHz.

Voice of Africa, Libya. The final 60 minutes of a two-hour broadcast. Look for a bulletin of *news* on the half-hour. To Central and East Africa winter on 17725 and 21695 kHz, and summer on 17725 (or 21695) and 17870 kHz. Sometimes heard in North America, especially in summer.

Voice of America. Continuous programming for East and Southeast Asia. The weekday lineup is five minutes of *news* followed by 55 minutes of music in *Border Crossings*. Weekends, there's Half an hour of news fare followed by Saturday's *Our World* or Sunday's *On the Line*, and an editorial. Winter on 13735 and 15460 kHz; and summer on 9760 and 15185 kHz. For Australasia, there's 15460 kHz in winter, and 15185 kHz midyear.

Radio Canada International. Monday through Friday, it's *The Link*, replaced Saturday by *Behind the Link* and Sunday by *Maple Leaf Mailbag*. Sixty minutes to South Asia winter on 9635 and 11975 kHz; and summer on 11675 and 17720 kHz. Heard well beyond the intended target area, especially to the west. Also to the northeastern United States (starts at 1505), winter on 9610 kHz, and summer on 9515 kHz.

Voice of Russia World Service. Winter, *News* is followed Monday through Saturday by much of the same in *News and Views*. Completing the lineup are *Sunday Panorama* and *A Stroll Around the Kremlin*. A short summary of news on the half-hour is followed by features: *Our Homeland* (Monday and Friday), ●*Kaleidoscope* (Tuesday), *Russian by Radio* (Wednesday), *The VOR Treasure Store* (Thursday), *Timelines* (Saturday) and ●*Folk Box* on Sunday. Summer weekdays, the news is followed by *Focus on Asia and the Pacific*, replaced Saturday by *This is Russia* and Sunday by *Moscow Mailbag*. The features that follow include some of the station's best: ●*Jazz Show* (Sunday and Monday), ●*Music Around Us* and ●*Music at Your Request* (Tuesday and Thursday), ●*Folk Box* (Wednesday), *A Stroll Around the Kremlin* and ●*Songs from Russia* (Friday) and ●*Christian Message from Moscow* on Saturday. To Southeast Asia winter on 7260 and 9660 kHz; and summer on 9660 kHz. Also available summer to Europe on 12040 (or 9810) kHz; and to the Mideast on 11985 kHz.

Radio Jordan. A partial relay of the station's domestic broadcasts, beamed to Europe on 11690 kHz. Continuous till 1630 (1730 in winter). Audible in parts of eastern North America, especially during winter.

Voice of Korea, North Korea. Repeat of the 1300 broadcast. One hour to Europe on 7570 (or 13760) and 12015 (or 15245) kHz; and to North America on 9335 and 11710 kHz. Also heard in parts of East Asia on 4405 kHz.

Voice of Vietnam. Repeat of the 1100 transmission; see there for specifics. Half an hour to Southeast Asia on 7285, 9840 and 12020 kHz. Frequencies may vary slightly.

AFRTS Shortwave, USA. Network news, live sports, music and features in the *upper-sideband* mode from the American Forces Radio & Television Service. Transmitted from modestly powered U.S. Navy stations around the globe, so usually a tough catch. Try 4319, 5446.5, 5765, 6350, 7811, 10320, 12133.5, 12579 and 13362 kHz.

15:30

Radio Sweden. Winter only at this time. Monday through Friday, it's a smorgasbord of *news* and features about Sweden. Saturday, there is a review of the week's main news stories; and Sunday it's *Network Europe*. Thirty minutes to western North America on 15240 kHz. One hour earlier in summer.

Voice of the Islamic Republic of Iran. News, commentary and features, strongly reflecting an Islamic point of view. One hour to South and Southeast Asia (also heard in parts of Australasia), winter on 6160 and 7330 kHz, and summer on 7370 and 9635 kHz.

16:00

■**Radio France Internationale.** *News* and reports from across Africa, international newsflashes and news about France. Next is a 25-minute feature—*French Lesson, Crossroads, Voices, Rendez-Vous, World Tracks, Weekend* or *Club 9516* (a listener-response program). A fast-moving hour to Africa winter on 11615 (or 15605) and 15160 kHz; and summer on 15160, 15605 and 17605 kHz. Often heard in parts of North America on 15160 kHz.

Radio Austria International. Winter only at this time. Monday, the 15-minute *Report from Austria* airs at 1605 and 1645; Tuesday through Friday, the times are 1615 and 1645. Saturday and Sunday, there's ●*News from Austria-The Week in Review* at 1605 and 1635. The remainder of the broadcast is in German To western North America on 13675 kHz, and one hour earlier in summer.

■**Deutsche Welle,** Germany. *News*, then the daily ●*NewsLink*—commentary, interviews, background reports and analysis.

16:00–16:00

Egypt's River Nile runs past Zamalek Island with its Cairo Tower.

Shutterstock/Adrian Lindley

The final 30 minutes consist of *World in Progress* (Monday), ● *Spectrum* (science and technology, Tuesday), ●*Money Talks* (Wednesday), *Living Planet* (Thursday), ●*Inside Europe* (Friday), *Dialogue* (Saturday), and ●*Insight* on Sunday. Sixty minutes to South Asia winter on 6170 and 9795 kHz; and summer on 6170, 9485 and 15640 kHz. The summer frequency 15640 kHz is well heard in Southeast Asia.

KBS World Radio, South Korea. Opens with 10 minutes of *news*, then Monday through Friday, a commentary. This is followed by 30 minutes of *Seoul Calling* and a 15-minute feature: *Faces of Korea, Business Watch, Culture on the Move, Korea Today and Tomorrow* and *Seoul Report*, respectively. Saturday's news is followed by *Worldwide Friendship* (a listener-response show), and Sunday by *Korean Pop Interactive*. One hour to Europe on 9515 kHz.

Radio Taiwan International. Ten minutes of *News*, followed by features: *Made in Taiwan, Generation Why* and *Asia Review* (Monday); *Strait Talk* and *We've Got Mail* (Tuesday); *Trends, Women Making Waves* and ●*Jade Bells and Bamboo Pipes* (Wednesday); *Ilha Formosa, People, Instant Noodles* and *Chinese to Go* (Thursday); *Walks of Life,*

Mandopop and *Taiwan Outlook* (Friday); *News Talk* and *Groove Zone* (Saturday); and *The Occidental Tourist, Chinese to Go* (language lessons) *Stage, Screen and Studio* and *On the Line* (Sunday). Sixty minutes to South Asia and southern China on 11550 kHz; and to South and Southeast Asia winter on 9785 or 11995 kHz, and summer on 11600 or 15515 kHz.

Voice of Korea, North Korea. Not quite the old-time communist station it was, but the "Beloved Leader" and "Unrivaled Great Man" continue to feature prominently, as does socialist thinking. One hour to the Mideast and Africa on 9990 and 11545 kHz. Also audible in parts of East Asia on 3560 kHz.

Radio Prague, Czech Republic. Summer only at this time. *News*, then Monday through Friday it's *Current Affairs* plus one or more features: *One on One* (Monday), *Talking Point* (Tuesday), *Czechs in History, Czechs Today* or *Spotlight* (Wednesday), *Panorama* and *Czech Science* (Thursday), and *Business Briefs* and *The Arts* on Friday. The Saturday news is followed by *Magazine, ABC of Czech* and a repeat of Tuesday's *One on One.* Sunday's lineup is *Mailbox* and *Letter from Prague* followed by *Encore* (classical music), *Magic Carpet* (Czech world music) or *Czech Books*. Half an hour to Europe on 5930 kHz, and to East Africa on 17485 kHz. The transmission for Europe is one hour later in winter, but the one for East Africa moves to 1130.

Voice of Vietnam. *News*, then *Commentary* or *Weekly Review* followed by short features and pleasant Vietnamese music (especially at weekends). A listener-response segment airs at 1615 Wednesday. Half an hour to Europe on 7280 and 9730 kHz. Also available to West and Central Africa on 7220 and 9550 kHz.

Radio Australia. Continuous programming to Asia and the Pacific. Monday through Friday, *World News* is followed by *Australia Talks*, and weekends by *Margaret Throsby* (Saturday) and ●*The Science Show* (Sunday). Beamed to the Pacific on 5995, 7240 and 9710 kHz; and to Southeast Asia on 6080, 9475 and 11660 kHz. Also well heard in western North America on 5995 and 7240 kHz.

Radio Ethiopia. An hour-long broadcast divided into two parts by the 1630 *news* bulletin. Regular weekday features include *Kaleidoscope* and *Women's Forum* (Monday), *Press Review* and *Africa in Focus* (Tuesday), *Guest of the Week* and *Ethiopia Today* (Wednesday), *Ethiopian Music* and *Spotlight* (Thursday) and *Press Review* and *Introducing Ethiopia* on Friday. For weekend listening, there's *Contact* and *Ethiopia This Week* (Saturday), or Sunday's *Listeners' Choice* and *Commentary*. Best heard in parts of Africa and the Mideast, but sometimes audible in Europe. On 7165 and 9560 kHz.

Radio Jordan. A partial relay of the station's domestic broadcasts, beamed to Europe on 11690 kHz. The final half-hour in summer, but a full 60 minutes in winter. Sometimes audible in parts of eastern North America, especially during winter.

Voice of Russia World Service. Continuous programming to Europe and beyond. *News*, then very much a mixed bag, depending on the day and season. Winter weekdays, the news is followed by *Focus on Asia*

and the *Pacific*, replaced Saturday by *This is Russia* and Sunday by *Moscow Mailbag*. The features that follow include some of the station's best: ●*Jazz Show* (Sunday and Monday), ●*Music Around Us* and ●*Music at Your Request* (Tuesday and Thursday), ●*Folk Box* (Wednesday), *A Stroll Around the Kremlin* and ●*Songs from Russia* (Friday) and ●*Christian Message from Moscow* on Saturday. Summer, the news is followed by *Science Plus* (Monday and Wednesday), *Moscow Mailbag* (Tuesday and Friday), the business-oriented *Newmarket* (Thursday), *Encyclopedia "All Russia"* (Saturday) and *This is Russia* on Sunday. More features follow a news summary on the half-hour, including *Spiritual Flowerbed* (Monday and Wednesday), *Guest Speaker* (Monday through Friday), ●*Russia–1,000 Years of Music* (Thursday), *The VOR Treasure Store* (Saturday) and *Timelines* on Sunday. To Europe winter on 6130 and 7320 kHz, and summer on 9890 kHz; and to the Mideast winter on 9470 kHz, and summer on 11985 kHz.

China Radio International. *News* and reports fill the first half-hour, and are followed by a daily feature: *Front Line* (Monday), *Biz China* (Tuesday), *In the Spotlight* (Wednesday), ●*Voices from Other Lands* (Thursday), *Life in China* (Friday), *Listeners' Garden* (Saturday) and *China Horizons* (Sunday). One hour to Europe winter on 7255, 9435 and 9525 kHz; and summer on 11940, 11965 and 13760 kHz. Also to southern Africa on 6100, 7150 (winter), 9570 and (midyear) 11900 kHz.

Radio Cairo, Egypt. The first 60 minutes of a two-hour broadcast of Arab music and features on Egyptian and Islamic themes, with *news*, commentary, quizzes, mailbag shows, and answers to listeners' questions. To southern Africa on 11740 kHz.

AFRTS Shortwave, USA. Network news, live sports, music and features in the *upper-sideband* mode from the American Forces Radio & Television Service. Transmitted from modestly powered U.S. Navy stations around the globe, so usually a tough catch. Try 4319, 5446.5, 5765, 6350, 7811, 10320, 12133.5, 12579 and 13362 kHz.

16:30–17:45

PASSPORT's Toshimichi Ohtake checks out global radio facilities when visiting Moscow.   T. Ohtake

16:30

Radio Slovakia International. Summer only at this time. *News* and features on Slovak life and culture. Sunday, look for a listener-response program and a little Slovak music. Half an hour to western Europe on 5920 and 6055 kHz. One hour later in winter.

Xizang [Tibet] People's Broadcasting Station, China. *Holy Tibet*, a 30-minute package of information and local (mostly popular) music. Sometimes acknowledges listeners' reception reports during the program. Well heard in East Asia, and sometimes provides fair reception in Europe. On 4905, 4920, 5240, 6110, 6130, 6200 and 7385 kHz.

17:00

Radio Prague, Czech Republic. See 1800 for program specifics. Thirty minutes winter to West and Central Africa on 15710 kHz, and summer on 17485 kHz. Also year round to Europe on 5930 kHz. Listeners in southern Africa should try 15710 kHz.

Radio Australia. Continuous programming to Asia and the Pacific. Starts with *World News*, then a feature: *Innovations* (Monday), *Australian Express* (Tuesday), *Rural Reporter* (Wednesday), ●*Rear Vision* (Thursday),

and *Big Ideas* on Friday. Monday through Thursday, *In the Loop (Rewind)* completes the hour. *Classic Late Night Live* fills the Saturday slot, and Sunday there's *In the Loop (Rewind)* and winter's *The Sports Factor* or summer's *Total Rugby*. Beamed to the Pacific on 5995, 9580, 9710 and 11880 kHz; and to Southeast Asia on 6080 and 9475 kHz. Also audible in parts of western North America on 5995 and 11880 kHz.

Polish Radio External Service. This time summer only. Monday through Friday, opens with *News from Poland*—a compendium of news, reports and interviews. A couple of features complete the broadcast. Monday's combo is *Around Poland* and *Talking Jazz*; Tuesday, it's *Letter from Poland* and *The Biz*; Wednesday, *A Day in the Life* (interviews) and *Multimedia Show*; Thursday, *Focus* (the arts in Poland) and *High Note*; and Friday, *Business Week* and *In Touch*, a listener-response show. The Saturday broadcast begins with *Europe East* (correspondents' reports), and is followed by *A Look at the Weeklies* and *Offside*. Sundays, it's five minutes of *news* followed by *Insight Central Europe* (a joint-production with other stations of the region), *The Kids* and *Chart Show*. Sixty minutes to northern Europe on 7140 and 7265 kHz. One hour later in winter.

Radio Ukraine International. Summer only at this time. A potpourri of things Ukrainian, with the Sunday broadcast often featuring some excellent music. Sixty minutes to Europe and beyond on 7490 (or 5830) kHz. One hour earlier in summer.

Radio Jordan. Winter only at this time. The final 30 minutes of a partial relay of the station's domestic broadcasts. To Europe on 11690 kHz.

Radio Romania International. Summer only at this time; see 1800 for specifics. Fifty-five minutes to Europe on 9535 and 11735 kHz. One hour later in winter.

Voice of Russia World Service. Continuous programming to Europe and beyond. Winter, *News* is followed by *Science Plus* (Monday and Wednesday), *Moscow Mailbag*

(Tuesday and Friday), the business-oriented *Newmarket* (Thursday), *Encyclopedia "All Russia"* (Saturday) and *This is Russia* on Sunday. More features follow a news summary on the half-hour, including *Spiritual Flowerbed* (Monday and Wednesday), *Guest Speaker* (Monday through Friday), ●*Russia–1,000 Years of Music* (Thursday), *The VOR Treasure Store* (Saturday) and *Timelines* on Sunday. In summer, the news is followed by *Moscow Mailbag* (Monday and Thursday), *Newmarket* (Tuesday), and *This is Russia* (Wednesday and Friday). Weekends, it's the excellent ●*Music and Musicians*. On the half-hour, the lineup includes *Kaleidoscope* (Monday), ●*Music Around Us* and ●*Music at Your Request* (Tuesday), *A Stroll Around the Kremlin* and *Musical Tales* (Wednesday), *Our Homeland* (Thursday) and ●*Folk Box* on Friday. To Europe winter on 7320 kHz, and summer on 9890 and (weekends) 9820 and 11675 (or 7320) kHz. For the Mideast, tune to 7270 or 9470 kHz in winter, and 11985 kHz in summer. In Southern Africa, try 11510 kHz midyear.

Radio Taiwan International. Ten minutes of *News*, followed by features: *Made in Taiwan*, *Generation Why* and *Asia Review* (Monday); *Strait Talk* and *We've Got Mail* (Tuesday); *Trends*, *Women Making Waves* and ●*Jade Bells and Bamboo Pipes* (Wednesday); *Ilha Formosa*, *People*, *Instant Noodles* and *Chinese to Go* (Thursday); *Walks of Life*, *Mandopop* and *Taiwan Outlook* (Friday); *News Talk* and *Groove Zone* (Saturday); and *The Occidental Tourist*, *Chinese to Go* (language lessons) *Stage, Screen and Studio* and *On the Line* (Sunday). Sixty minutes to central and southern Africa winter on 11850 kHz, and summer on 15690 kHz.

China Radio International. Weekdays, *News* is followed by *China Drive*, an upbeat "drive-time" show. Weekends there's *News and Reports*, *CRI Roundup* (Saturday), *Reports from Developing Countries* (Sunday) and *China Beat* (music). One hour to Europe winter on 7205 and 7255 kHz, and summer on 9695, 11940 and 13760 kHz; and to eastern and southern Africa on 6100, 7150 (winter), 9570 and (midyear) 11900 kHz.

Voice of Vietnam. Summer only at this time. Thirty minutes to western Europe via an Austrian relay on 9725 kHz. See 1800 for specifics. One hour later in winter.

Radio Cairo, Egypt. See 1600 for specifics. Continues with a broadcast to southern Africa on 11740 kHz.

AFRTS Shortwave, USA. Network news, live sports, music and features in the *upper-sideband* mode from the American Forces Radio & Television Service. Transmitted from modestly powered U.S. Navy stations around the globe, so usually a tough catch. Try 4319, 5446.5, 5765, 6350, 7811, 10320, 12133.5, 12579 and 13362 kHz.

17:30

Radio Bulgaria. Summer only at this time. *News*, followed weekdays by *Events and Developments*, and Saturday and Sunday by *Views Behind the News*. Thirty minutes to Europe on 5900 and 11600 kHz, and one hour later in winter.

Radio Slovakia International. Winter only at this time; see 1630 for specifics. Half an hour to western Europe on 5915 and 6055 kHz. One hour earlier during summer.

Kol Israel. Summer only at this time. *News* for 15 minutes from Israel Radio's domestic network. To Europe and eastern North America on 9345, 11590 and 13675 kHz. One hour later in winter.

17:45

All India Radio. The first 15 minutes of a two-hour broadcast to Europe, Africa and the Mideast, consisting of regional and international *news*, commentary, a variety of talks and features, press review and exotic Indian music. Continuous till 1945. To Europe on 7410, 9950 and 11620 kHz; to West Africa on 9445, 13605 and 15155 kHz; and to East Africa on 11935, 15075 and 17670 kHz.

Bangladesh Betar. *Voice of Islam*, a 30-minute broadcast focusing on Islamic themes. To Europe on 7250 and 9550 kHz.

18:00–18:00

18:00–23:59
Europe & Mideast—Evening Prime Time
East Asia—Early Morning
Australasia—Morning
Eastern North America—Afternoon and Suppertime
Western North America—Midday

18:00

■**Radio Netherlands.** The first 60 minutes of an approximately three-hour broadcast targeted at Africa, and heard well beyond. Monday through Friday, ●*Newsline* (current events) is followed by a 30-minute feature. Monday, it's a look at all things Dutch, and Tuesday it's the midweek edition of ●*The State We're In*. Wednesday's slot is *Radio Books*, replaced Thursday by *Earth Beat* and Friday by *Network Europe*. Weekends, there's Saturday's ●*The State We're In* and Sunday's *Amsterdam Forum* and *Reloaded* (highlights of the previous week's shows). On 6020, 7125 (summer), 11655 and (winter) 12050 kHz. Best for southern Africa is 6020 kHz.

Voice of Vietnam. Begins with *news*, which is followed by *Commentary* or *Weekly Review*, short features and some pleasant Vietnamese music (especially at weekends). Half an hour to Europe on 5955 kHz. Via an Austrian relay, and should provide good reception. One hour earlier in summer.

All India Radio. Continuation of the transmission to Europe, Africa and the Mideast (see 1745). *News* and commentary, followed by programming of a more general nature. Look for a listener-response segment, *Faithfully Yours*, at 1830 Monday. To Europe on 7410, 9950 and 11620 kHz; to West Africa on 9445, 13605 and 15155 kHz; and to East Africa on 11935, 15075 and 17670 kHz.

Voice of Korea, North Korea. The dinosaur of world band and the last of the old-style communist stations. One hour to Europe on 7570 (or 13760) and 12015 (or 15245) kHz. Heard in parts of East Asia on 4405 kHz.

Radio Prague, Czech Republic. Winter only at this time. *News*, then Monday through Friday there's *Current Affairs* and one or more features: *One on One* (Monday), *Talking Point* (Tuesday), *Czechs in History*, *Czechs Today* or *Spotlight* (Wednesday), *Panorama* and *Czech Science* (Thursday), and *Business Briefs* and *The Arts* (Friday). On Saturday the news is followed by *Insight Central Europe*, and Sunday fare is *Mailbox* and *Letter from Prague* followed by *Encore* (classical music), *Magic Carpet* (Czech world music) or *Czech Books*. Thirty minutes to Europe on 5930 kHz, and to Australasia on 9400 kHz. Europe's broadcast is one hour earlier in summer, but for Australasia it's two hours later.

Radio Kuwait. The first 60 minutes of a three-hour partial relay of the station's domestic broadcasts. At this hour it's a mix of western popular music and features on Islam and Kuwait. A news summary is aired on the half-hour. To western Europe and eastern North America on 11990 kHz.

Radio Ukraine International. Winter only at this time; see 1700 for specifics. Sixty minutes to Europe and beyond on 5840 kHz. One hour earlier in summer.

Radio Romania International. Winter only at this time. Starts with *Radio Newsreel*, a combination of news, commentary and press review. Features on Romania complete the broadcast. Regular spots include Monday's *Pro Memoria*, *Romanian Hits* and *Sports Roundup*; Tuesday's *Business Club* and ●*The Skylark* (Romanian folk music); Wednesday's *Society Today* and *Romanian Musicians*; Thursday's *Europa Express*; and Friday's ●*The Folk Music Box* and *Sports Weekend*. Saturday there's *The Week* and *World of Culture*, and Sunday's broadcast includes *Focus*. Fifty-five minutes to Europe on 7215 and 9640 kHz. One hour earlier in summer.

Radio Slovakia International. Summer only at this time. *News* and features on Slovak life and culture. Sunday, look for a listener-response program and a little Slovak music. Half an hour to western Europe on 5920 and 6055 kHz. One hour later in winter.

KBS World Radio, South Korea. Opens with 10 minutes of *news*, then Monday through Friday, a commentary. This is followed by 30 minutes of *Seoul Calling* and a 15-minute feature: *Faces of Korea*, *Business Watch*, *Culture on the Move*, *Korea Today and Tomorrow* and *Seoul Report*, respectively. Saturday's news is followed by *Worldwide Friendship* (a listener-response show), and Sunday by *Korean Pop Interactive*. One hour to Europe on 7275 kHz.

> **Korea's KBS World Radio is now a major broadcaster.**

Radio Australia. Sunday through Thursday, *World News* is followed by *Pacific Beat* (news and current events). The Friday slots are *Pacific Review* and *Australian Express*. Winter Saturdays there's *Correspondents Report* and the first half-hour of *Australia All Over*, replaced summer by *In the Loop (Rewind)* and ●*Australian Country Style*. Part of a continuous 24-hour service, and at this hour beamed to the Pacific on 6080, 7240, 9580, 9710 and 11880 kHz. Heard in East Asia on 6080 kHz. In western North America, try 11880 kHz. Sunday through Thursday there's separate programming for Southeast Asia on 9475 kHz: *The Music Show* (Sunday), *Big Ideas* (Monday), *Awaye* (Tuesday), *All in the Mind* and *Philosopher's Stone* (Wednesday), and *Hindsight* on Thursday. Friday and Saturday, the programming is the same as that for the Pacific.

Polish Radio External Service. This time winter only. See 1700 for program specifics. *News*, features and music reflecting Polish life and culture. Sixty minutes to Europe on 6015 and 7130 kHz. One hour earlier in summer. 6015 kHz is sometimes heard in eastern North America.

Voice of Russia World Service. Continuous programming to Europe and beyond. Predominantly news-related fare during the initial half-hour in summer, but the winter schedule offers a more varied diet. Winter, *News* is followed by *Moscow Mailbag* (Monday and Thursday), *Newmarket* (Tuesday), and *This is Russia* (Wednesday and Friday). Weekends, it's the excellent ●*Music and Musicians*. On the half-hour the lineup includes *Kaleidoscope* (Monday), ●*Music Around Us* and ●*Music at Your Request* (Tuesday), *A Stroll Around the Kremlin* and *Musical Tales* (Wednesday), *Our Homeland* (Thursday) and ●*Folk Box* on Friday. Summer weekdays, the first half-hour consists of *news* followed by *Russia and the World*. The Saturday slot is filled by *Newmarket*, replaced Sunday by *Encyclopedia "All Russia."* More features complete the hour, and include *Spiritual Flowerbed* (Monday and Wednesday), *Guest Speaker* (Monday through Friday), ●*Russia–1,000 Years of Music* (Thursday), *Kaleidoscope* (Saturday) and ●*Christian Message from Moscow* on Sunday. To Europe winter on 7105, 7320 and (weekends) 6055 and 6175 kHz; and summer on 9890 and 11630 (or

18:00–19:00

The Voice of America's Asha Aden specializes in Somali programs and issues.   VoA

9480) kHz. Also available winter only to the Mideast on 7270 kHz. In southern Africa, tune to 11510 and (midyear) 9850 kHz.

Radio Argentina al Exterior—R.A.E. Monday through Friday only. *News*, press review and short features on Argentina, plus folk music and tangos. Fifty-five minutes to Europe on 15345 kHz. May also use 9690 kHz.

Voice of America. Continuous programming to Africa. Monday through Friday, there's *Africa News Tonight* (shortened on Wednesday, when there's *Straight Talk Africa*). Weekends, it's *Nightline Africa*. Winter on 4930 (from 1830), 11975, 13710, 15580 and 17895 kHz; and summer on 4930 (from 1830), 6080, 15410, 15580 and 17895 kHz. Best for southern Africa is 4930 kHz.

China Radio International. *News* and reports fill the first half-hour, and are followed by a daily feature: *Front Line* (Monday), *Biz China* (Tuesday), *In the Spotlight* (Wednesday), ●*Voices from Other Lands* (Thursday), *Life in China* (Friday), *Listeners' Garden* (Saturday) and *China Horizons* (Sunday). To Europe winter on 6100 and 7110 kHz; and summer on 9600 and 13760 kHz.

Radio Taiwan International. Ten minutes of *News*, followed by features: *Made in Taiwan*, *Generation Why* and *Asia Review* (Monday); *Strait Talk* and *We've Got Mail* (Tuesday); *Trends*, *Women Making Waves* and ●*Jade Bells and Bamboo Pipes* (Wednesday); *Ilha Formosa*, *People*, *Instant Noodles* and *Chinese to Go* (Thursday); *Walks of Life*, *Mandopop* and *Taiwan Outlook* (Friday); *News Talk* and *Groove Zone* (Saturday); and *The Occidental Tourist*, *Chinese to Go* (language lessons) *Stage, Screen and Studio* and *On the Line* (Sunday). One hour to western Europe on 3965 kHz.

Radio Canada International. Monday through Friday, it's *The Link*, replaced Saturday by *Behind the Link* and Sunday by *Maple Leaf Mailbag*. One hour to Africa winter on 7185, 11875, 13650, 15365 and 17740 kHz, and summer on 9530, 11765, 15235 and 17810 kHz. Best for southern Africa are 15365 and 17740 kHz in winter (summer in the Southern Hemisphere), and 17810 kHz midyear. Heard well beyond the African continent.

AFRTS Shortwave, USA. Network news, live sports, music and features in the *upper-sideband* mode from the American Forces Radio & Television Service. Transmitted from modestly powered U.S. Navy stations around the globe, so usually a tough catch. Try 4319, 5446.5, 5765, 6350, 7811, 10320, 12133.5, 12579 and 13362 kHz.

18:15

Bangladesh Betar. *News*, followed by Islamic and general interest features; some nice Bengali music, too. Thirty minutes to Europe on 7250 and 9550 kHz.

18:30

Radio Bulgaria. This time winter only. *News*, then *Events and Developments* (weekdays) or *Views Behind the News* (Saturday and Sunday). Thirty minutes to Europe on 7400 and 9400 kHz, and one hour earlier in summer.

Voice of Turkey. This time summer only. *News*, then *Review of the Turkish Press*

followed by features on Turkish history, culture and international relations. Some enjoyable Turkish music, too. Fifty minutes to western Europe on 9785 kHz. One hour later in winter.

Kol Israel. Winter only at this time. *News* for 15 minutes from Israel Radio's domestic network. To Europe and eastern North America on 6985, 7545 and 9345 kHz. One hour earlier in summer.

18:45

Radio Tirana, Albania. Monday through Saturday, and summer only at this time. Approximately 15 minutes of *news* and commentary from this small Balkan country. To Europe on 6035 and 7465 kHz. One hour later in winter.

19:00

■**Radio Netherlands.** The second hour of an approximately three-hour block of programming for Africa. Monday through Friday, starts with a feature and ends with ●*Newsline* (current events); weekends, it's all features. The features are repeats of programs aired during the previous six days, and are worthy of a second hearing. On 5905 (summer), 7115 (summer), 7120 (winter), 11655, 12050 (winter) and 17810 kHz. In southern Africa, tune to 7115 or 7120 kHz, depending on the season. The weekend broadcasts are also available to North America, winter on 15315 and 15525 kHz; and summer on 15315, 17660 and 17735 kHz. On other days, listeners in the United States should try 17810 kHz, which is via a relay in the Netherlands Antilles.

Radio Australia. Begins with *World News*, then Sunday through Thursday it's the second hour of *Pacific Beat* (in-depth reporting on the region). Friday's slots go to *Asia Review* and ●*Rural Reporter*. Winter Saturdays, it's a continuation of *Australia All Over*; in summer, there's *Correspondents Report* and the first half-hour of *Australia All Over*. Part of a continuous 24-hour service, and at this hour beamed to the Pacific on

6080, 7240, 9500, 9580, 9710 and 11880 kHz. Listeners in western North America should try 11880 kHz, and best for East Asia is 6080 kHz. Sunday through Thursday there's separate programming for Southeast Asia on 9500 kHz: Sunday, it's the second hour of *The Music Show*, and Monday through Thursday there's *Asia Pacific* and a feature. Monday has *Health Report*, replaced Tuesday by *Law Report*, Wednesday by *Religion Report* and Thursday by *Media Report*. Friday and Saturday, the programming is the same as that for the Pacific.

All India Radio. The final 45 minutes of a two-hour broadcast to Europe, Africa and the Mideast (see 1745). Starts with *news*, then continues with a mixed bag of features and Indian music. To Europe on 7410, 9950 and 11620 kHz; to West Africa on 9445, 13605 and 15155 kHz; and to East Africa on 11935, 15075 and 17670 kHz.

Radio Kuwait. The second of three hours of a partial relay of the station's domestic broadcasts. At this hour it's a mix of western pop music and features on Kuwait. To western Europe and eastern North America on 11990 kHz.

■**Deutsche Welle,** Germany. *News*, then the daily ●*NewsLink*—commentary, interviews, background reports and analysis. Thirty minutes to Central, East and southern Africa winter on 9735, 11690, 13780 and 15275 kHz; and summer on 9895, 11795 and 17820 kHz. Best for southern Africa is 13780 kHz in winter, and 9895 kHz midyear.

Voice of Russia World Service. Continuous programming to Europe at this hour. Winter weekdays, the first half-hour consists of *news* followed by *Russia and the World*. This is replaced Saturday by *Newmarket*, and Sunday by *Encyclopedia "All Russia."* More features complete the hour, and include *Spiritual Flowerbed* (Monday and Wednesday), *Guest Speaker* (Monday through Friday), ●*Russia–1,000 Years of Music* (Thursday), *Kaleidoscope* (Saturday) and ●*Christian Message from Moscow* (Sunday). Monday through Saturday summer, it's

19:00–20:00

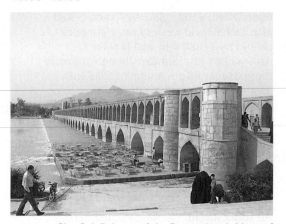

Si-o-Seh Pol, one of the five ancient bridges of Isfahan, Iran. L. Rydén

News and Views, with *Sunday Panorama* and *A Stroll Around the Kremlin* on the remaining day. On the half-hour, a news summary is followed by features: *Our Homeland* (Sunday and Monday), *Russian by Radio* (Tuesday), ●*Jazz Show* (Wednesday), *VOR Treasure Store* (Thursday), *A Stroll Around the Kremlin* and *Musical Tales* (Friday) and ●*Christian Message from Moscow* on Saturday. On 6175, 7105 and 7290 kHz in winter; and 7310, 9890 and 12070 (or 7195) kHz in summer.

China Radio International. *News* and reports fill the first half-hour, and are followed by a daily feature: *Front Line* (Monday), *Biz China* (Tuesday), *In the Spotlight* (Wednesday), ●*Voices from Other Lands* (Thursday), *Life in China* (Friday), *Listeners' Garden* (Saturday) and *China Horizons* (Sunday). One hour to the Mideast and North Africa on 7295 and 9435 (or 9440) kHz.

Radio Station Belarus. Summer only at this time. See 2000 for specifics. The first of two hours to Europe on 7105, 7390 and 7440 kHz. One hour later in winter.

Radio Slovakia International. Winter only at this time. *News* and features on Slovak life and culture. Sunday, look for a listener-response program and a little Slovak music. Half an hour to western Europe on 5915 and 7345 kHz. One hour earlier in summer.

Radio Thailand. A 60-minute package of *news*, features and (if you're lucky) enjoyable Thai music. To Northern Europe winter on 9805 kHz, and summer on 7155 kHz.

Voice of Korea, North Korea. For now, of curiosity value only. An hour of old-style communist programming to the Mideast on 9975 and 11535 kHz; and to southern Africa on 7100 and 11910 kHz. Also heard in parts of East Asia on 4405 kHz.

Voice of Vietnam. Repeat of the 1800 transmission (see there for specifics). Half an hour to Europe on 7280 and 9730 kHz.

Voice of America. Continuous programming for Africa. Opens with 30 minutes of news, with programs in Special (slow speed) English completing the hour. Winter on 4930, 4940, 11975, 13710, 15580 and 17895 kHz; and summer on 4930, 4940, 6080, 15410, 15445, 15580 and 17895 kHz. Best for southern Africa is 4930 kHz. In North America, try 11975 kHz in winter and 15445 kHz in summer.

AFRTS Shortwave, USA. Network news, live sports, music and features in the *upper-sideband* mode from the American Forces Radio & Television Service. Transmitted from modestly powered U.S. Navy stations around the globe, so usually a tough catch. Try 4319, 5446.5, 5765, 6350, 7811, 10320, 12133.5, 12579 and 13362 kHz.

19:30

Voice of Turkey. Winter only at this time. See 1830 for program details. Some unusual programs and friendly presentation make for entertaining listening. Fifty minutes to western Europe on 6055 kHz. One hour earlier in summer.

Voice of the Islamic Republic of Iran. A one-hour broadcast of news, commentary and features reflecting Islamic values. To Europe winter on 6010, 6255 and 7320 kHz, and summer on 6205, 6255 and 7205 kHz. Also available to southern Africa winter on 9855 and 11695 kHz, and midyear on 9800 and 9925 kHz.

19:45

Radio Tirana, Albania. Monday through Saturday, and winter only at this time. Approximately 15 minutes of *news* and commentary from this small Balkan country. To Europe on 6135 and 7465 kHz. One hour earlier in summer.

Vatican Radio. Summer only at this time, and actually starts at 1950. Thirty minutes of programming oriented to Catholics. To Europe on 4005, 5885 and 7250 kHz. One hour later in winter.

20:00

■**Deutsche Welle,** Germany. *News*, then the in-depth ●*NewsLink*. The second half-hour consists of features: *World in Progress* (Monday), ●*Spectrum* (science and technology, Tuesday), ●*Money Talks* (Wednesday), *Living Planet* (Thursday), ●*Inside Europe* (Friday), *Dialogue* (Saturday) and *Cool* (a

youth show) on Sunday. One hour to East, Central and southern Africa, winter on 9410, 9735 and 13780 kHz; and summer on 7130, 11795, 11865 and 15205 kHz. Best for southern Africa are 9410 and 13780 kHz in winter, and 7130, 11795 and 15205 kHz midyear.

Radio Canada International. Summer only at this time. Monday through Friday, it's *The Link*, replaced Saturday by *Behind the Link* and Sunday by *Maple Leaf Mailbag*. Sixty minutes to Europe, North Africa and the Mideast on 5850, 7235 and 15325 kHz. One hour later during winter.

■**Radio Netherlands.** The final 57 minutes of an approximately three-hour broadcast targeted at Africa. Monday through Friday, starts with a 30-minute feature. Monday, it's a look at all things Dutch, and Tuesday it's the midweek edition of ●*The State We're In*. Wednesday's slot is *Radio Books*, replaced Thursday by *Earth Beat* and Friday by *Network Europe*. The broadcast ends

20:00–20:30

VoA's Luna Shadzi hosts a pop-culture television show beamed into Iran. It originates from studios in the United States.   VoA

with ●*Newsline* (current events). Weekends, there's Saturday's ●*The State We're In* and Sunday's *Amsterdam Forum* and *Reloaded* (highlights of the previous week's shows). On 5905 (summer), 7115 (summer), 7120 (winter), 11655 (winter) and 17810 kHz. Best for southern Africa is 7115 or 7120 kHz, depending on the season. The weekend broadcasts are also available to North America, winter on 15315 and 15525 kHz; and summer on 15315, 17660 and 17735 kHz. On other days, listeners in the United States can try 17810 kHz, which is via a relay in the Netherlands Antilles.

Radio Kuwait. The final 60 minutes of a three-hour partial relay of the station's domestic broadcasts. At this hour it's mostly western popular music, with a short bulletin of news at 2050. To western Europe and eastern North America on 11990 kHz.

Radio Damascus, Syria. Actually starts at 2005. *News*, a daily press review, and different features for each day of the week. These can be heard at approximately 2030 and 2045, and include a mix of political commentary, Islamic philosophy and Arab and Syrian culture. Most of the transmission, however, is given over to Syrian and some western popular music. One hour to Europe, occasionally audible in eastern North America, on 9330 and/or 12085 kHz. Low audio level is often a problem.

Radio Australia. Starts with *World News*, then Sunday through Thursday it's the final hour of *Pacific Beat* (in-depth reporting). Winter, the Friday slots are *Saturday AM* and *Saturday Extra*; and summer, *Pacific Review* and ●*Australian Country Style*. Saturday, it's a continuation of *Australia All Over* (a popular show from the domestic ABC Local Radio network). Continuous programming to the Pacific on 6080 and 7240 (Friday and Saturday only), 9580, 11650, 11660, 11880 and 12080 kHz. In western North America, try 11650, 11660 and 11880 kHz. Sunday through Thursday there's separate programming for Southeast Asia on 9500 kHz: ●*The Science Show* (Sunday), and a feature followed by *In the Loop (Rewind)* on the remaining days. Monday's *Innovations* is replaced Tuesday by *Australian Express*, Wednesday by *Rural Reporter*, and Thursday by ●*Rear Vision*. Friday and Saturday, the programming is the same as that for the Pacific.

Voice of Russia World Service. Continuous programming to Europe at this hour. Starts with *News*, followed Monday through Saturday winter by *News and Views*. Sunday *Panorama* and *A Stroll Around the Kremlin* fill the Sunday slots. On the half-hour, a news summary is followed by features: *Our Homeland* (Sunday and Monday), *Russian by Radio* (Tuesday), ●*Jazz Show* (Wednesday), *VOR Treasure Store* (Thursday), *A Stroll Around the Kremlin* and *Musical Tales* (Friday) and ●*Christian Message from Moscow* on Saturday. Monday through Saturday summer, *News* is followed by features: *Science Plus* (Monday), *Moscow Mailbag* (Tuesday and Friday), *Newmarket* (Wednesday), *This is Russia* (Thursday) and *Encyclopedia "All Russia"* on Saturday. There's a summary of news on the half-hour, then features: *A Stroll Around the Kremlin* (Monday and Wednesday), ●*Songs from Russia* (Monday),

●*Music Around Us* and ●*Music at Your Request* (Tuesday), *Musical Tales* (Wednesday), ●*Folk Box* (Thursday), ●*Jazz Show* (Friday) and *Russian by Radio* on Saturday. Highlight of the week is ●*Music and Musicians* which follows the news on Sunday. Winter on 6145, 7105 and 7330 kHz; and summer on 9890 and 12070 (or 7195) kHz. Some channels are audible in eastern North America.

Radio Exterior de España ("Spanish National Radio"). Weekdays only at this time. Spanish and international *news*, commentary, Spanish pop music, a review of the Spanish press, and a general interest feature. Sixty minutes to Europe winter on 9680 kHz, and summer on 9665 kHz; and to West Africa year-round on 11625 kHz.

China Radio International. *News* and reports fill the first half-hour, and are followed by a daily feature: *Front Line* (Monday), *Biz China* (Tuesday), *In the Spotlight* (Wednesday), ●*Voices from Other Lands* (Thursday), *Life in China* (Friday), *Listeners' Garden* (Saturday) and *China Horizons* (Sunday). One hour to Europe on 5960, 7190, 7285 and 9600 kHz; to the Mideast and North Africa on 7295 and 9440 kHz; and to eastern and southern Africa on 11640 and 13630 kHz.

Radio Tirana, Albania. Monday through Saturday, summer only at this time. *News*, short features and some lively Albanian music (especially Saturday). Thirty minutes to Europe on 7465 kHz. Also to eastern North America Tuesday through Sunday on 13720 kHz with a repeat of the previous day's broadcast. One hour later in winter.

Radio Station Belarus. Winter, the start of a two-hour broadcast; summer, the final 60 minutes. Starts with 20 minutes of *News*, then it's a potpourri of local issues, including news, sports, politics and culture, depending on the season and day of the week. Most days summer, the final 20 minutes are given over to music. To Europe winter on 7360, 7390 and 7420 kHz; and summer on 7105, 7390 and 7440 kHz.

Radio Prague, Czech Republic. Summer only at this time. *News*, then Monday through Friday it's *Current Affairs* plus one or more features: *One on One* (Monday), *Talking Point* (Tuesday), *Czechs in History*, *Czechs Today* or *Spotlight* (Wednesday), *Panorama* and *Czech Science* (Thursday) and *Business Briefs* and *The Arts* on Friday. The Saturday news is followed by *Magazine*, *ABC of Czech* and a repeat of Tuesday's *One on One*. Sunday's lineup is *Mailbox* and *Letter from Prague* followed by *Encore* (classical music), *Magic Carpet* (Czech world music) or *Czech Books*. Thirty minutes to western Europe on 5930 kHz, and to Southeast Asia and Australasia on 11600 kHz. One hour later in winter.

Voice of America. Continuous programming for Africa. Monday through Friday, it's *Africa Beat* (modern African music, guest DJ spots, interviews), replaced weekends by ●*Music Time in Africa*. On 4930, 4940, 11975 (winter), 13710 (winter), 15445 (summer) and 15580 kHz. Best for southern Africa is 4930 kHz.

AFRTS Shortwave, USA. Network news, live sports, music and features in the *upper-sideband* mode from the American Forces Radio & Television Service. Transmitted from modestly powered U.S. Navy stations around the globe, so usually a tough catch. Try 4319, 5446.5, 5765, 6350, 7811, 10320, 12133.5, 12579 and 13362 kHz.

20:30

Radio Sweden. Winter only at this time. Monday through Friday, it's a smorgasbord of *news* and features about Sweden. Saturday, there is a review of the week's main news stories; and Sunday it's *Network Europe*. Thirty minutes to Australasia (one hour later in summer) on 7420 kHz.

Radio Thailand. Fifteen minutes of *news* targeted at Europe. Winter on 9535 kHz, and summer on 9680 kHz.

Radio Romania International. Summer only at this time. *News* and commentary followed by short features on Romania. Twenty-five minutes to Europe on 9515 and 11810 kHz, and to eastern North America on 11940 and 15465 kHz. One hour later in winter.

20:30–21:00

Voice of Turkey. This time summer only. *News*, followed by *Review of the Turkish Press* and features with a strong local flavor. Selections of Turkish popular and classical music complete the program. Fifty minutes to Southeast Asia and Australasia on 7170 kHz. One hour later during winter.

Radio Habana Cuba. The first half of a 60-minute broadcast. Monday through Saturday, there is international and Cuban news followed by *RHC's Viewpoint*. This is replaced Sunday by *Weekly Review*. To the Caribbean on 9505 kHz, and to eastern North America on 11760 kHz.

Voice of Vietnam. *News*, then it's either *Commentary* or *Weekly Review*, which in turn is followed by short features. Look for some pleasant Vietnamese music, especially at weekends. Half an hour to Europe on 7280 and 9730 kHz, and to West and Central Africa on 7220 and 9550 kHz.

20:45

All India Radio. The first 15 minutes of a much longer broadcast, consisting of a press review, Indian music, regional and international *news*, commentary, and a variety of talks and features of general interest. Continuous till 2230. To Western Europe on 7410, 9445, 9950 and 11620 kHz; and to Australasia on 9910, 11620 and 11715 kHz. Early risers in Southeast Asia can try the channels for Australasia.

Vatican Radio. Winter only at this time, and actually starts at 2050. Twenty minutes of predominantly Catholic fare. To Europe on 4005, 5885 and 7250 kHz. One hour earlier in summer.

21:00

■BBC World Service for the Caribbean. The first 60 minutes of a two-hour broadcast. Weekdays, opens with *news*, then there's *Sports Roundup*, *Caribbean Report*, *Business Daily* and another edition of *Sports Roundup*. Weekend fare consists of *World Briefing*, *Sports Roundup* and either Satur-

day's *Discovery* (science) or Sunday's ●*The Instant Guide* and *Over To You*. On 9525 (winter), 11675 and (summer) 13640 kHz.

Radio Exterior de España ("Spanish National Radio"). Summer weekends only at this time. Features, including rebroadcasts of programs aired earlier in the week. One hour to Europe on 9840 kHz, and to West Africa on 11625 kHz. Sometimes preempted by live sports in Spanish, and may start around 2135, or not at all. One hour later in winter.

Radio Ukraine International. Summer only at this time. *News*, commentary, reports and interviews, providing ample coverage of Ukrainian life. A listener-response program is aired Saturday, and most of Sunday's broadcast is a showpiece for Ukrainian music. Sixty minutes to western Europe on 7510 (or 5830) kHz. One hour later in winter.

Radio Canada International. Winter only at this time. See 2000 for program specifics. Sixty minutes to western Europe and North Africa on 5850 and 9770 kHz. One hour earlier in summer.

Radio Prague, Czech Republic. Winter only at this time. See 2000 for program details. *News* and features on Czech life and culture. Half an hour to western Europe (and easily audible in parts of eastern North America) on 5930 kHz, and to Australasia on 9430 kHz. One hour earlier in summer.

Radio Bulgaria. This time summer only. Starts with *News*, then Monday through Friday there's *Events and Developments*, replaced weekends by *Views Behind the News*. The remaining time is taken up by regular programs such as *Keyword Bulgaria* and *Time Out for Music*, and weekly features like *Sports* (Monday), *Magazine Economy* (Tuesday), *The Way We Live* (Wednesday), *History Club* (Thursday), *DX Programme* (for radio enthusiasts, Friday) and *Answering Your Letters* (a listener-response show, Saturday). The week's highlight is Sunday's ●*Folk Studio* (Bulgarian folk music). Sixty minutes to Europe on 5900 and 9700 kHz. One hour later during winter.

20:30–21:00

Radio Station Belarus. Winter only at this time; see 2000 for more details. Starts with 20 minutes of *News*, and ends most days with a music feature. To Europe on 7360, 7390 and 7420 kHz.

China Radio International. Repeat of the 2000 transmission; see there for specifics. One hour to Europe on 5960, 7190, 7285 and 9600 kHz. A 30-minute shortened version is also available for eastern and southern Africa on 11640 and 13630 kHz.

Voice of Russia World Service. Winter only at this time. *News*, then *Science Plus* (Monday), *Moscow Mailbag* (Tuesday and Friday), *Newmarket* (Wednesday), *This is Russia* (Thursday), *Encyclopedia "All Russia"* (Saturday) and the excellent ●*Music and Musicians* on Sunday. A news summary on the half-hour is followed by features: *A Stroll Around the Kremlin* (Monday and Wednesday), ●*Songs from Russia* (Monday), ●*Music Around Us* and ●*Music at Your Request* (Tuesday), *Musical Tales* (Wednesday), ●*Folk Box* (Thursday), ●*Jazz Show* (Friday) and *Russian by Radio* on Saturday. One hour

earlier in summer. To Europe on 7290 and 7330 kHz. Also audible in parts of eastern North America.

Voice of America. The final 60 minutes of seven hours of continuous programming for Africa. Opens with *news*, then it's music: *American Gold* (Monday), *Roots and Branches* (Tuesday), *Classic Rock* (Wednesday), *Top Twenty* (Thursday), *Hip Hop Connection* (Friday and Saturday), and *Fusion* (jazz) on Sunday. On 6080 and 15580 kHz.

Radio Australia. *World News*, then Sunday through Thursday there's a look at current events in *AM*, followed by *The Breakfast Club*. Winter Fridays, it's the final hour of *Saturday Extra*; summer, there's *Saturday AM* and the first half-hour of *Saturday Extra*. On the remaining day, it's Saturday's *Australia All Over*. Continuous to the Pacific on 9660, 11650, 11660, 12080, 13630 and 15515 kHz; and to Southeast Asia on 9500 and 11695 kHz. Listeners in western North America should try 11650 and 11660 kHz.

■**Deutsche Welle,** Germany. *News*, and then the daily ●*NewsLink*—commentary,

21:00–22:00

interviews, background reports and analysis. On the half-hour the weekday lineup is *EuroVox* (Monday), *Hits in Germany* (Tuesday), ●*Arts on the Air* (Wednesday), *Cool* (a youth show, Thursday), and *Dialogue* on Friday. Weekends, *Sports Report* is followed by *Radio D* (German language lessons, Saturday) and *Inspired Minds* (Sunday). One hour to West Africa, and audible in much of eastern and southern North America and the Caribbean. Winter on 7280, 9545 and 11690 kHz; and summer on 9735, 11865 and 15205 kHz. In North America, try 11690 kHz in winter, and 11865 and 15205 kHz in summer.

KBS World Radio, South Korea. Summer only at this time. Opens with 10 minutes of *news*, then Monday through Friday, a commentary. This is followed by a 15-minute feature: *Faces of Korea*, *Business Watch*, *Culture on the Move*, *Korea Today and Tomorrow* and *Seoul Report*, respectively. Saturday's news is followed by *Worldwide Friendship* (a listener-response show), and Sunday by *Korean Pop Interactive*. Thirty minutes to Europe on 3955 kHz. One hour later in winter.

Radio Tirana, Albania. Monday through Saturday, winter only at this time. Thirty minutes of news, short features and Albanian music. To Europe on 7430 kHz. Also to eastern North America Tuesday through Sunday on 9915 kHz with a repeat of the previous day's broadcast. One hour earlier in summer

Voice of Korea, North Korea. Repeat of the 1800 broadcast. The last of the old-time communist stations. One hour to Europe on 7570 (or 13760) and 12015 (or 15245) kHz. Also heard in parts of East Asia on 4405 kHz.

Radio Habana Cuba. The final 30 minutes of a one-hour broadcast. Monday through Saturday, there is a *news* bulletin and the sports-oriented *Time Out* (five minutes each), then a feature: *Caribbean Outlook* (Monday and Thursday), *DXers Unlimited* (Tuesday and Saturday), the *Mailbag Show* (Wednesday) and *Weekly Review* (Friday). These are replaced Sunday by a longer edition of *Mailbag Show*. To the Caribbean on

9505 kHz, and to eastern North America on 11760 kHz.

All India Radio. Continues to Western Europe on 7410, 9445, 9950 and 11620 kHz; and to Australasia on 9910, 11620 and 11715 kHz. Look for a listener-response segment, *Faithfully Yours*, at 2120 Monday. European frequencies are audible in parts of eastern North America, while those for Australasia are also heard in Southeast Asia.

21:15

Radio Damascus, Syria. Actually starts at 2110. *News*, a daily press review, and different features for each day of the week. These include a mix of political commentary, Islamic themes and Arab and Syrian culture. The transmission also contains Syrian and some western popular music. Sixty minutes to North America and Australasia on 9330 and/or 12085 kHz. Audio level is often very low.

Radio Cairo, Egypt. The start of a 90-minute broadcast focusing on Arab and Egyptian themes. The initial quarter-hour of general programming is followed by *news*, commentary and political items. This in turn is followed by a cultural program until 2215, when the station again reverts to more general fare. A big signal to Europe on 6250 or 9990 kHz.

AFRTS Shortwave, USA. Network news, live sports, music and features in the *upper-sideband* mode from the American Forces Radio & Television Service. Transmitted from modestly powered U.S. Navy stations around the globe, so usually a tough catch. Try 4319, 5446.5, 5765, 6350, 7811, 10320, 12133.5, 12579 and 13362 kHz.

21:30

Radio Romania International. Winter only at this time. *News* and commentary followed by short features on Romania. Twenty-five minutes to Europe on 6055 and 7145 kHz, and to eastern North America on 6115 and 9755 kHz. One hour earlier in summer.

Radio Prague, Czech Republic. Summer only at this time; see 2230 for program specifics. Thirty minutes to North America on 11600 kHz, and to West Africa on 9410 kHz. One hour later in winter.

Voice of Turkey. This time winter only. *News,* followed by *Review of the Turkish Press* and features, some of them unusual. Exotic Turkish music, too. Fifty minutes to Southeast Asia and Australasia on 7180 kHz. One hour earlier in summer.

Radio Sweden. Summer only at this time; see 2230 for specifics. Thirty minutes of news and features about Sweden. To Europe (one hour later in winter) on 6065 kHz, and to Australasia (one hour earlier in winter) on 7420 kHz.

22:00

■**BBC World Service for the Caribbean.** The final 60 minutes of a two-hour broadcast. Starts with *news,* then weekdays there's *World Briefing, World Business Report* and a feature: *Health Check* (Monday), *Digital Planet* (Tuesday), *Discovery* (science, Wednesday), ●*One Planet* (Thursday) and *Science in Action* (Friday). These are replaced Saturday by *From Our Own Correspondent* and ●*World Business Review,* and Sunday by a documentary and ●*Heart and Soul.* Winter on 5975 and 9525 kHz, and summer on 5975 and 13640 kHz.

Radio Bulgaria. This time winter only. See 2100 for specifics. News and features from the Balkans—don't miss Sunday's ●*Folk Studio* (Bulgarian folk music). Sixty minutes to Europe, also heard in parts of eastern North America, on 7400 and 9400 kHz. One hour earlier in summer.

Radio Romania International. Summer only at this time; see 2300 for specifics. Fifty-five minutes to western Europe on 7185 and 9675 kHz, and to eastern North America on 9790 and 11940 kHz. One hour later in winter.

Voice of Turkey. Summer only at this time. *News,* then *Review of the Turkish Press* and features on Turkish history and culture.

Traditional costume in a village museum in Dalecarlia, Sweden. L. Rydén

Selections of Turkish popular and classical music complete the program. Fifty minutes to western Europe and eastern North America on 6195 kHz. One hour later during winter.

Radio Cairo, Egypt. The second half of a 90-minute broadcast to Europe on 6250 or 9990 kHz; see 2115 for program details.

Radio Exterior de España ("Spanish National Radio"). Winter weekends only at this time. Features, including repeats of programs aired earlier in the week. One hour to Europe on 6125 kHz, and to West Africa on 11625 kHz. Sometimes pre-empted by live sports in Spanish, and may start around 2235, or not at all. One hour earlier in summer.

China Radio International. Weekdays, *News* is followed by *China Drive,* an upbeat "drive-time" show. Weekends there's *News and Reports, CRI Roundup* (Saturday), *Reports from Developing Countries* (Sunday)

22:00–23:00

and *China Beat* (music). One hour to Europe winter on 7170 kHz, and summer on 7175 kHz, via CRI's Moscow relay; and to East Asia winter on 5915 kHz, replaced summer by 9590 kHz.

KBS World Radio, South Korea. Winter only at this time. Opens with 10 minutes of *news*, then Monday through Friday, a commentary. This is followed by a 15-minute feature: *Faces of Korea, Business Watch, Culture on the Move, Korea Today and Tomorrow* and *Seoul Report*, respectively. Saturday's news is followed by *Worldwide Friendship* (a listener-response show), and Sunday by *Korean Pop Interactive*. Thirty minutes to Europe on 3955 kHz. One hour earlier in summer.

Voice of America. The first of two hours to East and Southeast Asia and the Pacific. Predominantly news fare at this hour. To East and Southeast Asia winter on 7120, 9490 and 11725 kHz; and summer on 7120, 9415, 11725 and 15185 kHz. For Australasia there's 9490 and 11725 kHz in winter, and 9415 kHz midyear.

Radio Australia. *News*, followed Sunday through Thursday by *AM* (current events) and, from 2240, *The Breakfast Club*. Winter Fridays, there's *In the Loop (Rewind)* and *Talking Point*, replaced summer by the final hour of *Saturday Extra*. Saturday, winter's *Correspondents Report* and *Innovations* are replaced summer by the final segment of *Australia All Over*. Continuous programming to the Pacific on 13630, 15230, 15515 and 17785 kHz; and to Southeast Asia on 15240 kHz. In North America, try 17785 kHz, especially during summer.

Radio Japan. Predominantly news programming at this hour. Twenty minutes to Australasia on 13640 kHz.

Radio Taiwan International. Ten minutes of *News*, followed by features: *Made in Taiwan, Generation Why* and *Asia Review* (Monday); *Strait Talk* and *We've Got Mail* (Tuesday); *Trends, Women Making Waves* and ●*Jade Bells and Bamboo Pipes* (Wednesday); *Ilha Formosa, People, Instant Noodles* and *Chinese to Go* (Thursday); *Walks of Life,*

Mandopop and *Taiwan Outlook* (Friday); *News Talk* and *Groove Zone* (Saturday); and *The Occidental Tourist, Chinese to Go* (language lessons) *Stage, Screen and Studio* and *On the Line* (Sunday). One hour to Europe via RTI's North American relay, winter on 9355 kHz, and summer on 15600 kHz.

Radio Ukraine International. Winter only at this time. A potpourri of things Ukrainian, with the Sunday broadcast often featuring some excellent music. Sixty minutes to Europe and beyond on 5840 kHz. One hour earlier in summer.

All India Radio. The final half-hour of a transmission to Western Europe and Australasia, consisting mainly of news-related fare. To Western Europe on 7410, 9445, 9950 and 11620 kHz; and to Australasia on 9910, 11620 and 11715 kHz. Frequencies for Europe are audible in parts of eastern North America, while those for Australasia are also heard in Southeast Asia.

AFRTS Shortwave, USA. Network news, live sports, music and features in the *upper-sideband* mode from the American Forces Radio & Television Service. Transmitted from modestly powered U.S. Navy stations around the globe, so usually a tough catch. Try 4319, 5446.5, 5765, 6350, 7811, 10320, 12133.5, 12579 and 13362 kHz.

22:15

Voice of Croatia. Summer only at this time. Nominally 15 minutes of news, reports and interviews, but actual length varies. To eastern North America and South America on 9925 kHz. One hour later in winter.

22:30

Radio Sweden. Winter only at this time. Monday through Friday, it's a smorgasbord of *news* and features about Sweden. Saturday, there is a review of the week's main news stories; and Sunday it's *Network Europe*. Thirty minutes to Europe on 6065 kHz, and one hour earlier in summer.

22:00–23:00

Radio Prague, Czech Republic. *News*, then Monday through Friday there's *Current Affairs* followed by a feature or two. Monday's *One on One* is replaced Tuesday by *Talking Point* (interviews); Wednesday's slot is *Czechs in History*; *Czechs Today* or *Spotlight*; Thursday's features are *Panorama* and *Czech Science*; and Friday brings *Business Briefs* and *The Arts*. Saturday's *Insight Central Europe* is replaced Sunday by *Mailbox* and *Letter from Prague* followed by *Encore* (classical music), *Magic Carpet* (Czech world music) or *Czech Books*. Half an hour to eastern North America winter on 5930 kHz, and summer on 7345 and 9415 kHz; also to West and Central Africa winter on 9435 kHz.

22:45

All India Radio. The first 15 minutes of a much longer broadcast, consisting of Indian music, regional and international *news*, commentary, and a variety of talks and features of general interest. Continuous till 0045. To East Asia on 9950, 11620, 11645 and 13605 kHz; and to Southeast Asia on 9705, 11620 and 13605 kHz.

23:00

Radio Canada International. Monday through Friday, it's *The Link*, replaced Saturday by *Behind the Link* and Sunday by *Maple Leaf Mailbag*. Winter only to Central America on 9580 kHz, and summer (starts at 2305, and one hour later in winter) to the central United States on 6100 kHz.

Voice of Turkey. Winter only at this hour; see 2200 for specifics. Fifty minutes to western Europe and eastern North America on 5960 kHz. One hour earlier in summer.

Radio Habana Cuba. Monday through Saturday, there is international and Cuban news followed by *RHC's Viewpoint*. On the half-hour there's a *news* bulletin and the sports-oriented *Time Out* (five minutes each), then a feature: *Caribbean Outlook* (Monday and Thursday), *DXers Unlimited* (Tuesday and Saturday), the *Mailbag Show* (Wednesday) and *Weekly Review* (Friday).

Sunday fare includes *Weekly Review* and a longer edition of *Mailbag Show*. One hour to South America on 9550 kHz, and also heard in parts of the United States.

Radio Australia. *World News*, followed Sunday through Thursday by *Connect Asia* (news, commentary and analysis), and Friday by *Asia Review* and *Talking Point.* Winter Saturdays, there's *Background Briefing* and *Perspective*, replaced summer by *Correspondents Report* and *Innovations*. Continuous to the Pacific on 9660, 12080, 13690, 15230, 17785 and 17795 kHz; and to Southeast Asia on 15240 (till 2330), 15415 and 17750 kHz. Listeners in North America should try 17785 and 17795 kHz, especially during summer.

China Radio International. *News* and reports fill the first half-hour, and are followed by a daily feature: *Front Line* (Monday), *Biz China* (Tuesday), *In the Spotlight* (Wednesday), ●*Voices from Other Lands* (Thursday), *Life in China* (Friday), *Listeners' Garden* (Saturday) and *China Horizons* (Sunday). One hour to the United States and Caribbean via CRI's Cuban and Canadian relays, winter on 5990, 6040 and 11970 kHz; and summer on 5990, 6145 and 11840 (or 13680) kHz. Also available to East Asia winter on 5915 kHz, and summer on 11690 kHz.

Voice of Greece. Sunday and summer only at this time. Actually starts at 2305. Approximately 60 minutes of music in *Greek in Style*. To North America on 7475 and 9420 kHz; and to Australasia on 15650 kHz. For North America it's one hour later in winter, and for Australasia it moves to 1105 Sunday. ☞ Monday World Time is Sunday evening in North America.

Radio Cairo, Egypt. The first hour of a 90-minute broadcast to eastern North America. A ten-minute *news* bulletin is aired at 2315, with the remaining time taken up by short features on Egypt, the Middle East and Islam. For the intellectual listener there's *Literary Readings* at 2345 Monday, and *Modern Arabic Poetry* at the same time Friday. More general fare is available in *Listener's Mail* at 2325 Thursday and Saturday. Winter on 9465 kHz, and summer on 9460 kHz.

23:00–23:30

Radio Romania International. Winter only at this time. Starts with *Radio Newsreel*, a combination of news, commentary and press review. Features on Romania complete the broadcast. Regular spots include Monday's *Pro Memoria*, *Romanian Hits* and *Sports Roundup*; Tuesday's *Business Club* and ●*The Skylark* (Romanian folk music); Wednesday's *Society Today* and *Romanian Musicians*; Thursday's *Europa Express*; and Friday's ●*The Folk Music Box* and *Sports Weekend*. Saturday there's *The Week* and *World of Culture*, and Sunday's broadcast includes *Focus*. Fifty-five minutes to western Europe on 6015 and 7105 kHz, and to eastern North America on 6115 and 9610 kHz. One hour earlier in summer.

Radio Bulgaria. Summer only at this time. Starts with *News*, then Monday through Friday there's *Events and Developments*, replaced weekends by *Views Behind the News*. The remaining time is taken up by regular programs such as *Keyword Bulgaria* and *Time Out for Music*, and weekly features like *Sports* (Monday), *Magazine Economy* (Tuesday), *The Way We Live* (Wednesday), *History Club* (Thursday), *DX Programme* (for radio enthusiasts, Friday) and *Answering Your Letters* (a listener-response show, Saturday). The week's highlight is Sunday's ●*Folk Studio* (Bulgarian folk music). Sixty minutes to eastern North America on 9700 and 11700 kHz. One hour later during winter.

All India Radio. Continuous programming to East and Southeast Asia. A potpourri of *news*, commentary, features and exotic Indian music. To East Asia on 9950, 11620, 11645 and 13605 kHz; and to Southeast Asia on 9705, 11620 and 13605 kHz.

Voice of America. The second and final hour of news-oriented programming to East and Southeast Asia and the Pacific. To East and Southeast Asia winter on 7120, 9490, 11725 and 15185 kHz; and summer on 7120, 9415, 11725 and 15185 kHz. For Australasia there's 9490 and 11705 kHz in winter, and 9415 kHz midyear.

AFRTS Shortwave, USA. Network news, live sports, music and features in the *upper-sideband* mode from the American Forces Radio & Television Service. Transmitted from modestly powered U.S. Navy stations around the globe, so usually a tough catch. Try 4319, 5446.5, 5765, 6350, 7811, 10320, 12133.5, 12579 and 13362 kHz.

23:15

Voice of Croatia. Winter only at this time. Nominally 15 minutes of news, reports and interviews, but actual length varies. To eastern North America and South America on 7285 kHz. One hour earlier in summer.

23:30

Radio Prague, Czech Republic. Winter only at this time. *News*, then Monday through Friday there's *Current Affairs* and one or more features: *One on One* (Monday), *Talking Point* (Tuesday), *Czechs in History*, *Czechs Today* or *Spotlight* (Wednesday), *Panorama* and *Czech Science* (Thursday), and *Business Briefs* and *The Arts* (Friday). On Saturday the news is followed by *Insight Central Europe*, and Sunday's lineup is *Mailbox* and *Letter from Prague* followed by *Encore* (classical music), *Magic Carpet* (Czech world music) or *Czech Books*. Thirty minutes to eastern North America on 5930 and 7345 kHz, and one hour earlier in summer.

Radio Vilnius, Lithuania. Thirty minutes of mostly *news* and background reports about events in Lithuania. Of broader appeal is *Mailbag*, aired every other Saturday. For some Lithuanian music, try the second half of Sunday's broadcast. To eastern North America winter on 7325 kHz, and summer on 9875 kHz.

Voice of Vietnam. *News*, then *Commentary* or *Weekly Review*. These are followed by short features and some pleasant Vietnamese music (especially weekends). Half an hour to Southeast Asia on 9840 and 12020 kHz. Frequencies may vary slightly.

Prepared by Tony Jones and the staff of PASSPORT TO WORLD BAND RADIO.

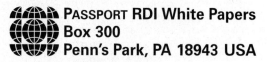

Addresses PLUS—2007

Station Postal and Email Addresses . . . PLUS Webcasts, Websites, Who's Who, Phones, Faxes, Bureaus, Future Plans, Items for Sale, Giveaways . . . PLUS Summer and Winter Times in Each Country!

PASSPORT shows how stations reach out to you, but Addresses PLUS also explains how you can reach out to stations. Here you'll find soup-to-nuts details, country by country, about how broadcasters go beyond world band radio to keep in touch, inform and entertain.

Making Contact

When broadcasting was in its infancy, listeners sent in "applause" cards to let stations how well they were being received. Stations would reply with a letter or illustrated card verifying ("QSLing" in Morse code) that the station the listener heard was, in fact, theirs. While they were at it, some stations threw in a free souvenir—station calendar, magazine, pennant or sticker.

The tradition continues, although obtaining QSLs is now more challenging—look under "Verification" in PASSPORT's "Worldly Words." Some stations also sell small items, while others air letters over audience feedback programs.

Postal Reimbursement

Most broadcasters reply to listener correspondence—even email—through the postal system. That way, they can send out printed schedules, verification cards and other "hands-on" souvenirs. Major stations usually do this for free, but smaller operations may seek postage reimbursement.

Best with Latin American and Indonesian stations is to enclose unused (mint) stamps from the station's country. These are available from two excellent sources: Plum's Airmail Postage, 12 Glenn Road, Flemington NJ 08822-3322 USA, plumdx@msn.com, phone +1 (908) 788-1020, fax +1 (908) 782 2612; as well as James E. Mackey, P.O. Box 270569, West Hartford CT 06127-0569 USA, phone +1 (860) 521-7254, http://users.net1plus.com/ryoung/OrderForm.htm. One way to help ensure your stamps are used to reply to you is to stick them onto a pre-addressed return airmail envelope—what's called a self-addressed stamped envelope, or SASE.

You can also prompt reluctant stations by donating a U.S. dollar or two, preferably hidden from prying eyes by something like a piece of reflective-lined plastic film from packaging. Registration often helps, as cash tends to get stolen. In some countries, though, registered mail attracts dishonest postal employees, especially in parts of Latin America. International Reply Coupons (IRCs), which recipients may exchange locally for air or surface stamps, are available at a number of post offices worldwide, particularly in large cities; in the United States, this is explained at http://pe.usps.gov/text/pub51/pub51_015.html#NL508_24. Thing is, they're increasingly hard to find, relatively costly, not fully effective, and aren't accepted by postal authorities in some countries.

> **Stations interact with listeners by mail, Internet and over the air.**

Stamp Out Crime

Mail theft is still a problem in some countries, although the overall situation is improving. Addresses PLUS identifies problem areas and offer proven countermeasures, but start by using common sense. For example, some postal employees are stamp collectors and steal mail with unusual stamps, so use everyday stamps. A postal meter, PC-generated postage or an aerogram are other options.

M. Wright

¿Que Hora Es?

World Time, explained in "Setting Your World Time Clock," is essential if you want to find out when your favorite station is on. But if you want to know what time it is in any given country, World Time and "Addresses PLUS" come together to provide the answer.

Here's how. So that you don't have to wrestle with seasonal changes in your own time, "Addresses PLUS" gives local times for each country in terms of hours' difference from World Time (it stays constant year-round). For example, if you look below under "Albania," you'll see that country is World Time +1; that is, one hour ahead of World Time. So, if World Time is 12:00, the local time in Albania is 13:00 (1:00 PM). On the other hand, México City is World Time –6; that is, six hours behind World Time. If World Time is 12:00, in México City it's 6:00 AM.

Local times shown in parentheses are for the middle of the calendar year—roughly April–October; specific seasonal changeover dates for individual countries are at www.timeanddate.com/worldclock.

Spotted Something New?

Something changed since we went to press? Please let us know! Your update information, especially copies of material received from stations, is highly valued. Contact the IBS Editorial Office, Box 300, Penn's Park, PA 18943 USA, fax +1 (215) 598 3794, addresses@passband.com.

Muchas gracias to the kindly folks and helpful organizations mentioned at the end of this chapter for their tireless cooperation in the preparation of this section. Without you, none of this would have been possible.

Using PASSPORT's Addresses PLUS Section

Stations included: All stations are listed if known to reply, however erratically. Also, new stations which possibly may reply to correspondence from listeners.

Leased-time programs: Private organizations/NGOs that lease program time, but which possess no world band transmitters of their own, are usually not listed. However, they can usually be reached via the stations over which they are heard.

Postal addresses are given. These sometimes differ from transmitter locations in the Blue Pages.

Phone and fax numbers. To help avoid confusion, telephone numbers have hyphens, fax numbers don't. All are configured for international dialing once you add your country's International access code (011 in the United States and Canada, 010 in the United Kingdom, and so on). For domestic dialing within countries outside the United States, Canada and most of the Caribbean, replace the country code (1–3 digits preceded by a "+") by a zero.

Giveaways. If you want freebies, say so politely in your correspondence. These are usually available until supplies run out.

Webcasting. World band stations which use streaming audio to simulcast and/or offer archived programming over the Internet are indicated by ☞.

Unless otherwise indicated, stations:

- Reply regularly within six months or so to most listeners' correspondence in English.
- Provide, upon request, free station schedules and verification ("QSL") postcards or letters (*see* Verification in "Worldly Words"). When other items are available for free or for purchase, it is specified.
- Do not require compensation for postage costs incurred in replying to you. Where compensation is appropriate, details are provided.

Local times. These are given in difference from World Time. For example, "World Time –5" means that if you subtract five hours from World Time, you'll get the local time in that country. So, if it were 11:00 World Time, it would be 06:00 local time in that country. Times in (parentheses) are for the middle of the year—roughly April–October. For exact changeover dates, see the explanatory paragraph, above, under "¿Que Hora Es?"

AFGHANISTAN   World Time +4:30

Radio Afghanistan (when activated), Afghan Radio & TV, P.O. Box 544, Ansari Wat, Kabul, Afghanistan. Contact: Foreign Relations Department.

ALBANIA   World Time +1 (+2 midyear)

Radio Tirana, External Service, Rruga Ismail Qemali Nr. 11, Tirana, Albania. Phone/Fax: +355 (4) 223-650. Fax: (technical directorate) +355 (4) 226 203. Email: (English Section) radiotirana-english@hotmail.com; (reception reports) dcico@abcom-al.com. Web: http://rtsh.com.al/radiotirana/index.php. Contact: Ms. Mira Bregu, Director of External Services; Adriana Bislea, English Department; Clara Ruci, Journalist/Translator/Broadcaster; Marjeta Thoma; Pandi Skaka, Producer; Diana Koci; (technical directorate) Arben Mehilli, Technical Director ARTV; (frequency management) Mrs. Drita Cico, Head of RTV Monitoring Center. May send free stickers and postcards. Email reports welcome.

ALGERIA   World Time +1

☛**Radio Algérienne (ENRS)**, 21 Boulevard des Martyrs, Algiers, Algeria. Phone: (Direction Générale) +213 (2) 148-3790. Fax: (Direction Générale) +213 (2) 123 0823. Email: (Direction Générale) dg@algerian-radio.dz; (International Relations) relex@algerian-radio.dz; (Direction Technique) technique@algerian-radio.dz. Web: (includes on-demand and streaming audio) www.algerian-radio.dz. Replies iregularly. French or Arabic preferred, but English accepted. Return postage helpful. Formerly transmitted direct from Algeria, but currently broadcasts via transmitters in the United Kingdom.

ANGOLA   World Time +1

☛**Rádio Nacional de Angola**, Caixa Postal 1329, Luanda, Angola. Fax: +244 (2) 391 234. Email: (general, including reception reports) diop@rna.ao; (Canzuela Magalhães) josela30@hotmail.com; (Fernandes) alefernandes@rna.ao; (Diatezwa) fdiatezwa@rna.ao; (reception reports only) departamento133@hotmail.com. Web: (includes streaming audio) www.rna.ao; if the audio link doesn't work, try www.netangola.com/p/default.htm. Contact: Dr. Júlio Mendonça, Director do Departamento de Intercâmbio e Opinião Pública; [Ms.] Josefa Canzuela Magalhães, Departamento de Intercâmbio e Opinião Pública; Dr. Eduardo Magalhães, Director Geral; (technical) Alé Fernandes, Director Técnico; Eng. Filipe Diatezwa, Director de Rede Emissoras. Replies irregularly. Best is to correspond in Portuguese and include $1, return postage or 2 IRCs.

ANTARCTICA   World Time –3 Base Antárctica Esperanza

Radio Nacional Arcángel San Gabriel—LRA36, Base Esperanza, V9411XAD Antártida Argentina, Argentina. Phone/Fax: +54 (2964) 421 519. Email: lra36esperanza@yahoo.com.ar, lra36@infovia.com.ar. Return postage required. Replies to correspondence in Spanish, and sometimes to correspondence in English or French, depending on who is at the station (the staff changes each year, usually around February).

ANGUILLA   World Time –4

Caribbean Beacon, Box 690, Anguilla, British West Indies. Phone: +1 (264) 497- 4340. Fax: +1 (264) 497 4311. Email: beacon@anguillanet.com. Contact: Monsell Hazell, Chief Engineer; Doris Lussington. $2 or return postage helpful. Relays University Network—*see* USA.

ARGENTINA   World Time –3

Radio Baluarte (when operating), Casilla de Correo 45, 3370 Puerto Iguazú, Provincia de Misiones, Argentina. Phone: +54 (3737) 422-557. Email: contatoarmoniafm@hotmail.com. Contact: Pastor Paulo Lima. Free tourist literature. Return postage helpful. The same programs are aired on 100.7 MHz (Radio Armonia), and both outlets are believed to be unlicensed. However, given the current radio licensing situation in the country, this is not unusual.

Radiodifusión Argentina al Exterior—RAE, Casilla de Correos 555, C1000WBC Buenos Aires, Argentina. Phone/Fax: +54 (11) 4325-6368; (technical) +54 (11) 4325-5270. Email: (general) rae@radionacional.gov.ar; (technical) operativa@radionacional.gov.ar; (Marcela Campos) camposrae@fibertel.com.ar (this address is to be phased out); (German Section) raedeutsch@yahoo.com.ar. Web: www.radionacional.gov.ar/rae/rae.asp. Contact: (general) John Anthony Middleton, Head of English Team; María Dolores López, Spanish Team; (administration) Marcela G. R. Campos, Directora; (technical) Gabriel Iván Barrera, DX Editor. Return postage (3 IRCs) appreciated. The station asks listeners not to send currency notes, as it's a breach of local postal regulations. Reports covering at least 20-30 minutes of reception are appreciated.

☛**Radio Nacional Buenos Aires**, Maipú 555, C1006ACE Buenos Aires, Argentina. Phone: +54 (11) 4325-9100. Fax: (management—Gerencia General) +54 (11) 4325 9433; (Director) +54 (11) 4325-4590, +54 (11) 4322-4313; (technical—Gerencia Operativa) +54 (11) 4325-5270. Email: (general) info@radionacional.gov.ar, buenosaires@radionacional.gov.ar; (director) direccion@radionacional.gov.ar; (technical) operativa@radionacional.gov.ar. Web: (includes streaming audio) www.radionacional.gov.ar. Contact: Eduardo García Caffi, Director. Return postage (3 IRCs) helpful. Prefers correspondence in Spanish, and usually replies via RAE (*see*, above).

ARMENIA   World Time +4 (+5 midyear)

☛**Public Radio of Armenia/Voice of Armenia**, Radio Agency, Alex Manoukyan Street 5, 375025 Yerevan, Armenia. Phone: +374 1055-1143. Fax: +374 1055 4600. Email: (general director) president@mediaconcern.am; (Amiryan) aa@arradio.am; (foreign broadcasts department, reception reports and comments on programs) pr@armradio.am. Contact: Armen Amiryan, Executive Director. Web: (includes on-demand and streaming audio) www.armradio.am. Free postcards and stamps. Requests 2 IRCs for postal reply. Replies slowly.

ASCENSION   World Time exactly

BBC World Service—Atlantic Relay Station, English Bay, Ascension (South Atlantic Ocean). Fax: +247 6117. Contact: (technical) Mrs. Nicola Nicholls, Transmitter Engineer. Nontechnical correspondence should be sent to the BBC World Service in London (see).

AUSTRALIA   World Time +11 (+10 midyear) Victoria (VIC), New South Wales (NSW), Australian Capital Territory (ACT) and Tasmania (TAS); +10:30 (+9:30 midyear) South Australia (SA); +10 Queensland (QLD); +9:30 Northern Territory (NT); +9 (+8 midyear) Western Australia (WA)

Australian Broadcasting Corporation Northern Territory HF Service—ABC Radio 8DDD Darwin, Administrative Center for the Northern Territory Shortwave Service, ABC, Box 9994, GPO Darwin NT 0801, Australia; (street address) 1 Cavenagh Street, Darwin NT 0800, Australia. Phone: +61 (8) 8943-3222; (engineering) +61 (8) 8943-3209. Fax: +61 (8) 8943 3235, +61 (8) 8943 3208. Contact: (general) Tony Bowden, Branch Manager; (administration) Barbra Lilliebridge, Administration Officer; Kathryn Ainsworth, Administration Officer, Business Service; (technical) Peter Camilleri; Yvonne Corby. Free stickers and postcards. "Traveller's Guide to ABC Radio" for $1. T-shirts US$20. Three IRCs or return postage helpful.

BBC World Service via Radio Australia—For verification direct from the Australian transmitters, contact John Westland, Director of English Programs at Radio Australia (see). Nontechnical correspondence should be sent to the BBC World Service in London (see).

📻**Christian Vision Communications (CVC)**, P.O. Box 6361, Maroochydore, QLD 4558, Australia. Phone: + 61-7-5477-1555. Fax: + 61-7-5477-1727. Email: (technical and nontechnical) enquiry@cvc.tv; (reception reports) dxer@cvc.tv, dxer@voice.com.au; ("Mailbag" program) mailbag@cvc.tv. Web: (includes on-demand and streaming audio) www.cvc.tv. Contact: (general) Mike Edmiston, Director; Raymond Moti, Station Manager; Richard Daniel, Corporate Relations Manager. May send T-shirt, baseball cap, key ring or other small gifts. Formerly Voice International Limited, and before that, Christian Voice International Australia.

HONG KONG ADDRESS (CHINESE SERVICE): Liu Sheng, Flat 1b, 67 Ha Heung Road, Kowloon, Hong Kong, China.

INDIA ADDRESS (HINDI SERVICE): CVC, P.O. Box 1, Kangra, Pin Code 176001, Himachal, India. Email: mail@thevoiceasia.com.

INDONESIA ADDRESS (INDONESIAN SERVICE): CVC, P.O. Box 2634, Jakarta Pusat, 10026 Indonesia. Phone: +62 (21) 390-0039.

INTERNATIONAL TOLL-FREE NUMBERS: (Indonesia only) 001-803-61-555; (India only) 000-800-610-1019.

TRANSMITTER SITE: CVC, PMB 5777, Darwin NT 0801, Australia. Phone: (general) +61 (8) 8981-6591, (operations manager) +61 (8) 8981-8822. Fax: +61 (8) 8981 2846. Contact: Mrs. Lorna Manning, Site Administrator; Robert Egoroff, Operations Manager.

📻**Community Development Radio Service—CDRS**, ARDS, Box 1671, Nhulunbuy NT 0881, Australia; (street address) 19 Pera Circuit, Nhulunbuy NT 0880, Australia. Phone: +61 (8) 8987-3910. Fax: +61 (8) 8987 3912. Email: (general) nhulun@ards.com.au, mediaservices@ards.com.au; (technical) dale@ards.com.au. Web: (includes on-demand audio) http://www.ards.com.au/broadcast.

htm. Contact: Dale Chesson, Radio Service Manager. Free station literature. Verifies reception reports.

CVC—see Christian Vision Communications, above.

EDXP News Report, 404 Mont Albert Road, Mont Albert, Victoria 3127, Australia. Phone/Fax: +61 (3) 9898-2906. Email: info@edxp.org. Web: http://edxp.org. Contact: Bob Padula. " EDXP News Report" is compiled by the "Electronic DX Press" and airs over several world band stations. Focuses on shortwave broadcasters beaming to, or located in Asia and the Pacific. Currently heard on Adventist World Radio, HCJB-Australia, WINB, WWCR, and World Harvest Radio. Verifies postal reports with full-detail "EDXP" QSL cards showing Australian fauna, flora, and scenery. Return postage required; four 50c stamps within Australia, and one IRC or US dollar elsewhere. Email reports welcome, and are confirmed with animated Web-delivered QSLs. Does not verify reports on Internet broadcasts.

HCJB Australia, P.O. Box 291, Kilsyth VIC 3137, Australia. Phone: +61 (3) 9761-4844. Fax: +61 (3) 9761 4061. Email: office@hcjb.org.au. Contact: Derek Kickbush, Director of Broadcasting; Dennis Adams; Ken Lingwood, Frequency Manager.

VERIFICATION OF RECEPTION REPORTS: Voice of the Great Southland, GPO Box 691, Melbourne VIC 3001, Australia. Email: english@hcjb.org.au. One IRC required for postal reply. Listeners to the Japanese broadcasts can send their reception reports to: HCJB Section, Yodobashi Church, Hyakunincho 1-17-8, Shinjuku-ku, Tokyo 169-0073, Japan. Return postage (stamps) required within Japan.

NEW DELHI OFFICE: Radio GMTA, P.O. Box 4960, New Delhi 110 029 India.

📻**Radio Australia**, GPO Box 428G, Melbourne VIC 3001, Australia. Phone: ("Openline" voice mail for listeners' messages and requests) +61 (3) 9626-1825; (switchboard) +61 (3) 9626-1800; (English programs) +61 (3) 9626-1922; (marketing manager) +61 (3) 9626 1723. Fax: (general) +61 (3) 9626 1899. Email: (general) english@ra.abc.net.au; (marketing manager) marketing@radioaustralia.net.au. (Web: (includes on-demand and streaming audio) www.radioaustralia.net.au. Contact: (general) Brendon Telfer, Head of English Language Programming; Mark Hemetsberger, Marketing & Communications Manager; Hanh Tran, Chief Executive; (technical) Nigel Holmes, Chief Engineer, Transmission Management Unit. All reception reports received by Radio Australia are forwarded to the Australian Radio DX Club for assessment and checking. ARDXC will forward completed QSLs to Radio Australia for mailing. For further information, contact Brendon Telfer, Director of English Programs at Radio Australia (Email: telfer.brendon@abc.net.au).

SAN FRANCISCO OFFICE, SCHEDULES: 2654 17th Avenue, San Francisco CA 94116 USA. Phone: +1 (415) 564-9968. Email: GPoppin@aol.com. Contact: George Poppin. This address, a volunteer office, only provides Radio Australia schedules to listeners (return postage not required). All other correspondence should be sent directly to the main office in Melbourne.

Yolngu Radio—see Community Development Radio Service, above.

AUSTRIA   World Time +1 (+2 midyear)

📻**Radio Austria International**, Listener Service, Argentinierstrasse 30a, A-1040 Vienna, Austria. Phone: +43 (1)

50101-16060. Fax: +43 (1) 50101 16066. Email: (frequency schedules, comments, reception reports) roi.service@orf. at. Web: (includes online reception report form) http:// oe1.orf.at/service/international_en; (on-demand and streaming audio from ÖE1, which makes up most of Radio Austria International's European service) http://oe1.orf. at. Contact: (general) Vera Bock, Listener Service; (English Department) David Ward.

FREQUENCY MANAGEMENT: ORF Sendetechnik, Attn. Ernst Vranka, Würzburggasse 30, A-1136 Vienna, Austria. Phone: +43 (1) 87878-12629. Fax: +43 (1) 87878 12773. Email: ernst.vranka@orf.at. Contact: Ing. Ernst Vranka, Frequency Manager.

Trans World Radio—*see* USA

AZERBAIJAN   World Time +4 (+5 midyear)

Voice of Azerbaijan, Medhi Hüseyin küçäsi 1, 370011 Baku, Azerbaijan. Free postcards, and occasionally, books. $1 or return postage helpful. Replies irregularly to correspondence in English.

BAHRAIN   World Time +3

Coalition Maritime Forces (CMF) Radio One—*see* INTERNATIONAL WATERS
Radio Bahrain, Broadcasting and Television, Ministry of Information, P.O. Box 194, Al Manāmah, Bahrain (if this fails, try P.O. Box 1075). Phone: (general) +973 1768-6000; (Arabic Service) +973 1778-1888; (English Service) +973 1762-9085. Fax: (Arabic Service) +973 1768 1544; (English Service) +973 1778 0911. Email: brtcnews@batelco.com. bh. Contact: A. Suliman (for Director of Broadcasting). $1 or IRC required. Replies irregularly.

BANGLADESH   World Time +6

Bangladesh Betar
NONTECHNICAL: External Services, Bangladesh Betar, Shah Bagh Post Box No. 2204, Dhaka-1000, Bangladesh; (street address, all services) 121 Kazi Nazrul Islam Avenue, Shah Bagh, Dhaka-1000, Bangladesh. Phone: (director general) +880 (2) 861-5294; (external service +880 (2) 861-8119; (external services) +880 (2) 8618-119. Fax: (director general) +880 (2) 861 2021. Email: (director general) dgbetar@bd.drik.net, dgbetar@bttb.net.bd. Web: (includes on-demand audio) www.betar.org.bd. Contact: Setub Uddin Ahmed, Director - External Services.
TECHNICAL: Research and Receiving Centre, National Broadcasting Authority, 121 Kazi Nazrul Islam Avenue, Shah Bagh, Dhaka-1000, Bangladesh. Phone: +880 (2) 862-5538, +880 (2) 862-5904. Fax: +880 (2) 861 2021. Email: rrc@dhaka.net. Contact: Mahesh Chandra Roy, Senior Engineer. Sometimes verifies reception reports.

BELARUS   World Time +2 (+3 midyear)

Belarusian Radio—*see* Radio Station Belarus for details.
Radio Grodno—*see* Radio Hrodna
Radio Hrodna, ul. Horhaha 85, Hrodna 230015, Belarus. Correspondence should be addressed to the attention of Mr. Alexander Bakurskiy. Verifies reception reports in Russian, Belarusian or English.

Radio Mahiliou, Mahiliou, Belarus. Email: radiomogilev@tut.by. Contact: Yury Kurpatin. Verifies reception reports in Russian or Belarusian. May also respond to reports in English or German. Return postage helpful.
Radio Moghilev—*see* Radio Mahiliou
Radio Station Belarus, 4 Krasnaya St., Minsk 220807, Belarus. Phone: (director) +375 (17) 284-4277; (foreign languages department) +375 (17) 284-5758. Email: (domestic Belarusian Radio) tvr@tvr.by; (external services) radio-minsk@tvr.by. Web: (includes on-demand and streaming audio) www.radiobelarus.tvr.by. Contact: Naum Galperovich, Director; Viacheslav Laktjushin, Head of Foreign Languages Service; Larisa Suarez, Listener Correspondence. Free stickers, Belarusian stamps and other small souvenirs.

BELGIUM   World Time +1 (+2 midyear)

RTBF-International, Bd. Auguste Reyers 52, boîte 16, B-1044 Brussels, Belgium. Phone: +32 (2) 737-4014. Fax: +32 (2) 737 3032. Email: rtbfi@rtbf.be. Web: (includes on-demand and streaming audio) www.rtbf.be. Contact: Philippe Caufriez, Directeur des Relations Internationales (or "Head, International Service" if writing in English). Broadcasts are essentially a relay of programs from the domestic services "La Première" and "Vivacité" of RTBF (Radio-Télévision Belge de la Communauté Française) via a transmitter in Wavre. Two specific programs on Africa: "Afri K'hebdo," african news and "Afri K'danse,", african culture and music. Return postage not required. Accepts email reception reports.
Radio Traumland, P.O. Box 15, B-4730 Raeren, Belgium. Phone: +31 87 301-722. Email: radiotraumland@skynet. be. Email reports can only be confirmed with electronic QSLs; for a postal reply include 1 IRC, $1, 1 Euro or mint Belgian/German stamps. Transmits via T-Systems International facilities in Germany (see).
Radio Vlaanderen Internationaal (RVI), B-1043 Brussels, Belgium. Phone: +32 (2) 741-5611, +32 (2) 741-3806/7, +32 (2) 741-3802. Fax: +32 (2) 741-4689. Email: info@rvi.be. Web: (includes on-demand and streaming audio) www.rvi.be. Contact: (station manager) Wim Jansen; (listener mail) Tine De Bruycker; Rita Penne.
Transmitter Documentation Project (TDP), P.O. Box 1, B-2310 Rijkevorsel, Belgium. Phone: +32 (3) 314-7800. Fax: +32 (3) 314 1212. Email: info@transmitter.org. Web: www.broadcast.be; (shortwave schedule) www.airtime. be/schedule.html. Contact: Ludo Maes, Managing Director. A free online publication by Belgian Dxer Ludo Maes. TDP lists current and past shortwave transmitters used worldwide in country order with station name, transmitter site & geographical coordinates, transmitter type, power and year of installation etc. Also brokers leased airtime over world band transmitters.

BENIN   World Time +1

Office de Radiodiffusion et Télévision du Benin (when operating), Boîte Postale 366, Cotonou, Benin. Phone/Fax: +229 302-184. Contact: Fidèle Ayikoue, Directeur Generale; (technical) Anastase Adjoko, Chef du Service Technique. Return postage, $1 or IRC required. Replies irregularly and slowly to correspondence in French.
PARAKOU REGIONAL STATION: ORTB-Parakou, Boîte

Postale 128, Parakou, Benin. Phone: +229 610-773, +229 611-096, +229 611080. Fax: +229 610 881. Contact: Eric Biokou, Ingénieur Chef. Return postage required. Replies tend to be extremely irregular, and a safer option is to send correspondence to the Cotonou address.

BHUTAN   World Time +6

📻**Bhutan Broadcasting Service**, Department of Information and Broadcasting, Ministry of Communications, P.O. Box 101, Thimphu, Bhutan. Phone: +975 (2) 323-071/72. Fax: +975 (2) 323 073. Email: thiny@druknet.bt (email service is irregular and messages may bounce). Web: (includes on-demand songs) www.bbs.com.bt. Contact: (general) [Ms.] Pema Choden, Managing Director; (technical) Dorji Thinley, Station Engineer. Three IRCs, return postage or $2 required. Replies irregularly.

BOLIVIA   World Time –4

NOTE ON STATION IDENTIFICATIONS: Many Bolivian stations listed as "Radio . . ." may also announce as "Radio Emisora . . ." or "Radiodifusora . . ."

Paitití Radiodifusión—*see* Radio Paitití, below.

Radio Amor de Dios (when operating), Iglesia Evangélica Amor de Dios, Calle Noaviri 2105, El Alto, La Paz, Bolivia.

Radio Camargo—*see* Radio Emisoras Camargo, below.

Radio Chicha, Tocla, Provincia Nor-Chichas, Departamento de Potosí, Bolivia.

Radio Eco

MAIN ADDRESS: Correo Central, Reyes, Ballivián, Beni, Bolivia. Contact: Gonzalo Espinoza Cortés, Director. Free station literature. $1 or return postage required. Replies to correspondence in Spanish.

ALTERNATIVE ADDRESS: Rolmán Medina Méndez, Correo Central, Reyes, Ballivián, Bolivia.

Radio Emisoras Ballivián (when operating), Correo Central, San Borja, Beni, Bolivia. Replies to correspondence in Spanish, and sometimes sends pennant.

Radio Emisoras Camargo, Casilla Postal 9, Camargo, Provincia Nor-Cinti, Chuquisaca, Bolivia. Email: jlgarpas@hotmail.com. Contact: Pablo García B., Gerente Propietario; José Luís García. Return postage or $1 required. Replies slowly to correspondence in Spanish.

Radio Estacion Frontera (when operating), Casilla de Correo 179, Cobija, Departamento de Pando, Bolivia.

Radio Estambul, Avenida Primero de Mayo esq. Loreto, Guayaramerín, Beni, Bolivia. Phone: +591 (3) 855-4145. Email: ninafelima@hotmail.com Contact: Sra. Felima Bruno de Yamal, Propietaria, who welcomes postcards, pennants or small flags from foreign listeners.

📻**Radio Fides**, Casilla 9143, La Paz, Bolivia. Fax: +591 (2) 237 9030. Email: rafides@fidesbolivia.com (if that fails, try: sistemas@radiofides.com). Web: (includes on-demand and streaming audio) http://fidesbolivia.com. Contact: R.P. Eduardo Pérez Iribarne, S.J., Director. Replies occasionally to correspondence in Spanish.

Radio Guanay (when operating), calle Boston de Guanay 123, Guanay, La Paz, Bolivia; or Casilla de Correo 15012, La Paz, Bolivia. Replies irregularly to correspondence in Spanish.

📻**Radio Illimani**, Av. Camacho 1485, Edificio La Urbana - 6to Piso, La Paz, Bolivia. Phone: +591 (2) 220-

0473, +591 (2) 220-0390, +591 (2) 220-0282. Email: illimani@comunica.gov.bo. Web: (includes streaming audio) www.comunica.gov.bo (click on "Radio Illimani"). Contact: Iván Maldonado, Director. $1 required, and registered mail recommended. Replies irregularly to friendly correspondence in Spanish.

Radio Juan XXIII [Veintitrés], Avenida Santa Cruz al frente de la plaza principal, San Ignacio de Velasco, Santa Cruz, Bolivia. Phone: +591 (3962) 2087. Phone/Fax: +591 (3962) 2188. Contact: Pbro. Elías Cortezón, Director; María Elffy Gutiérrez Méndez, Encargada de la Discoteca. Return postage or $1 required. Replies occasionally to correspondence in Spanish.

Radio La Voz del Campesino (when operating), Sipe Sipe, Provincia de Quillacollo, Departamento de Cochabamba, Bolivia. No known replies, but try using the good offices of DXer Rogildo Fontenelle Aragão: rogfara@yahoo.com.br, rogfara@bolivia.com (correspond in Spanish or Portuguese).

Radio Logos

U.S. BRANCH OFFICE: LATCOM, 1218 Croton Avenue, New Castle PA 16101 USA. Phone: +1 (412) 652-0101. Fax: +1 (412) 652 4654. Contact: Hope Cummins.

Radio Mallku, Casilla No. 16, Uyuni, Provincia Antonio Quijarro, Departamento de Potosí, Bolivia. Phone: +591 (2693) 2145. Email: (Olazo) max_nelson_t@hotmail.com; (FRUTCAS parent organization) frutcas@hotmail.es. Contact: Max Nelson Olazo. Spanish preferred. Return postage in the form of two U.S. dollars appreciated, as the station depends on donations for its existence. Station owned by La Federación Unica de Trabajadores Campesinos del Altiplano Sud (FRUTCAS) and formerly known as Radio A.N.D.E.S.

Radio Minería—*see* Radiodifusoras Minería

Radio Mosoj Chaski, Casilla 4493, Cochabamba, Bolivia; (street address) Calle Abaroa 254, Cochabamba, Bolivia. Phone: +591 (4) 422-0641, +591 (4) 422-0644. Fax: +591 (4) 425 1041. Email: chaski@bo.net. Contact: Paul G. Pittman, Administrator; Ann Matthews, Director. Replies to correspondence in Spanish or English. Return postage helpful.

NORTH AMERICAN OFFICE: Quechuan Radio, c/o SIM USA, P.O. Box 7900, Charlotte NC 28241 USA.

Radio Norteña (when operating), Caranavi, Departamento de La Paz, Bolivia.

Radio Nacional de Huanuni, Casilla 681, Oruro, Bolivia. Phone: +591 (2552) 0421. Email: fstmb@hotmail.com. Web: http://es.geocities.com/primeradelpais. Contact: Rafael Lineo Morales, Director General. Return postage or $1 required. Replies irregularly to correspondence in Spanish.

Radio Nueva Esperanza (when operating), Raúl Salmón 92 entre calles 4 y 5, Zona 12 de Octubre, El Alto, La Paz, Bolivia.

Radio Paitití, Casilla 172, Guayaramerín, Beni, Bolivia. Contact: Armando Mollinedo Bacarreza, Director; Luis Carlos Santa Cruz Cuéllar, Director Gerente; Ancir Vaca Cuéllar, Gerente-Propietario. Free pennants. Return postage or $3 required. Replies irregularly to correspondence in Spanish.

📻**Radio Panamericana**, Casilla 5263, La Paz, Bolivia; (street address) Av. 16 de Julio, Edif. 16 de Julio, Of. 902, El Prado, La Paz, Bolivia. Phone: +591 (2) 231-2644, +591 (2) 231-1383, +591 (2) 231-3980. Fax: +591 (2) 233-4271. Email: pana@panamericanabolivia.com. Web:

(includes streaming audio) www.panamericanabolivia. com. Contact: Daniel Sánchez Rocha, Director. Replies irregularly, with correspondence in Spanish preferred. $1 or 2 IRCs helpful.

Radio Perla del Acre (if reactivated), Casilla 7, Cobija, Departamento de Pando, Bolivia. Return postage or $1 required. Replies irregularly to correspondence in Spanish.

Radio Pío XII [Doce], Casilla 434, Oruro, Bolivia. Phone: +591 (258) 20-250. Fax: +591 (258) 20 544. Email: rpiodoce@entelnet.bo. Web: www.radiopio12.org. Contact: Pbro. Roberto Durette, OMI, Director General; José Blanco Villanueva. Return postage necessary.

Radio San Gabriel, Casilla 4792, La Paz, Bolivia. Phone: +591 (2) 241-4371. Phone/Fax: +591 (2) 241-1174. Email: rsg@fundayni.rds.org.bo; (technical, including reception reports) remoc@entelnet.bo. Contact: (general) Hno. [Brother] José Canut Saurat, Director General; Sra. Martha Portugal, Dpto. de Publicidad; (technical) Rómulo Copaja Alcón, Director Técnico. $1 or return postage helpful. Free book on station, Aymara calendars and *La Voz del Pueblo Aymara* magazine. Replies fairly regularly to correspondence in Spanish. Station of the Hermanos de la Salle Catholic religious order.

Radio San Miguel, Casilla 102, Riberalta, Beni, Bolivia.

TIPS FOR WINNING CORRESPONDENCE

Golden Rule: Write unto others as you would have them write unto you. The milk of human kindness is mighty skim these days, so a considerate message stands out.

Be interesting and helpful from the recipient's point of view, yet friendly without being chummy. Comments on specific programs are almost always appreciated, even if you are sending what is basically a technical report.

Incorporate language courtesies. Using the broadcaster's tongue is always best—Addresses PLUS indicates when it is a requirement—but English is usually the next-best bet. When writing in any language to Spanish-speaking countries, remember that what Anglos think of as the "last name" is actually written as the penultimate name. Thus, Juan Antonio Vargas García, which can also be written as Juan Antonio Vargas G., refers to Sr. Vargas; so your salutation should read, *Estimado Sr. Vargas*.

What's that "García" doing there, then? That's *mamita's* father's family name. Latinos more or less solved the problem of gender fairness in names long ago.

But, wait—what about Portuguese, used by all those stations in Brazil? Same concept, but in reverse. *Mamá's* father's family name is penultimate, and the "real" last name is where English-speakers are used to it, at the end.

In Chinese, the "last" name comes first. However, when writing in English, Chinese names are often reversed for the benefit of *weiguoren*—foreigners. For example, "Li" is a common Chinese last name, so if you see "Li Dan," it's "Mr. Li." But if it's "Dan Li"—and certainly if it's been Westernized into "Dan Lee"—he's already a step or two ahead of you, and it's still "Mr. Li" (or Lee). Less widely known is that the same can also occur in Hungarian. For example, "Bartók Béla" for Béla Bartók.

If in doubt, fall back on the ever-safe "Dear Sir" or "Dear Madam"—"Hi" is still not appropriate with most letters, although "Hello" usually does the trick. Or use email, where salutations are not expected but "Hi" is increasingly but not universally accepted. Avoid first names, too, especially for recipients outside the United States. However, if you know the recipient is an amateur radio operator ("ham")—and especially if you're a fellow ham—you can use the first name if you also include ham call letters in the address; e.g. Norman Gorman, WA3CRN, Station Engineer.

Be patient, as replies by post take weeks, sometimes months. Slow responders, those that tend to take many months to reply, are cited in Addresses PLUS. Erratic repliers, too.

Phone: +591 (385) 8268, +591 (385) 8363. Fax: +591 (385) 8268. Email: radiosanmiguel_riberalta@yahoo.es, radiosanmiguel_riberalta@hotmail.com. Contact: David Terrazas Irina, Director. Free stickers and pennants; has a different pennant each year. Return postage or $1 required. Replies irregularly to correspondence in Spanish.

Radio Santa Ana, Calle Sucre No. 250, Santa Ana de Yacuma, Beni, Bolivia. Contact: Mario Roberto Suárez, Director; Mariano Verdugo. Return postage or $1 required. Replies irregularly to correspondence in Spanish.

Radio Santa Cruz, Emisora del Instituto Radiofónico Fé y Alegría (IRFA), Casilla 672, Santa Cruz, Bolivia; (street address) Calle Mario Flores esq. Guendá Nº 20, Santa Cruz de la Sierra, Bolivia. Phone: +591 (3) 353-1817. Fax: +591 (3) 353 2257. Email: irfacruz@entelnet.bo. Contact: José Velasco, Director; Srta. María Yolanda Marcó Escobar, Secretaria de Dirección. Free pamphlets, stickers and pennants. Welcomes correspondence in English, French and Spanish, but return postage required for a reply.

Radio Tacana, Tumupasa, Provincia Iturralde, Departamento de La Paz, Bolivia.

Radio Universitaria (when operating), Campus Universitario, Av. Las Palmas, Cobija, Pando, Bolivia. Phone: +591 (384) 22-141. Email: radiouap@hotmail.com.

Radio Virgen de los Remedios, Casilla 198, Tupiza, Departamento de Potosí, Bolivia; (street address) Parroquia Nuestra Señora de la Candelaria, Tupiza, Departamento de Potosí, Bolivia. Phone: +591 (269) 44-662. Email: radiovirgenderemedios@hotmail.com. Contact: Padre Kazimierz Strzepek, Director General.

Radio Yura (La Voz de los Ayllus), Casilla 326, Yura, Provincia Quijarro, Departamento de Potosí, Bolivia; (street address) Calle Sucre 86 entre Bolívar y Omiste, Municipio Tomave-Ayllu, Yura, Provincia Quijarro, Departamento de Potosí, Bolivia. Phone: +591 (281) 36-216. Email: radioyura@hotmail.com, canal18@cedro.pts.entelnet.bo. Contact: Omar Flores. Free pennant, Bolivian stamps and stickers. Replies slowly to correspondence in Spanish.

Radiodifusoras Minería (if reactivated), Casilla de Correo 247, Oruro, Bolivia. Phone: +591 (252) 77-736. Contact: Dr. José Carlos Gómez Espinoza, Gerente Propietario. Free pennants. Replies to correspondence in Spanish.

Radiodifusoras Trópico, Casilla 60, Trinidad, Beni, Bolivia. Contact: Eduardo Avila Alberdi, Director. Replies slowly to correspondence in Spanish. Return postage required for reply.

BOTSWANA   World Time +2

IBB Botswana Transmitting Station
TRANSMITTER SITE: International Broadcasting Bureau, Botswana Relay Station, Moepeng Hill, Selebi-Phikwe, Botswana; (postal address) International Broadcasting Bureau, Botswana Transmitting Station, Private Bag 0038, Selebi-Phikwe, Botswana. Phone: +267 810-932. Fax: +267 261 0185. Email: manager_botswana@bot.ibb.gov. Contact: Station Manager or Transmitting Plant Supervisor. This address for specialized technical correspondence only, although reception reports may occasionally be verified. All other correspondence should be directed to the regular VOA or IBB addresses (*see* USA).

Radio Botswana, (if reactivated) Private Bag 0060, Gaborone, Botswana. Phone: +267 352-541, +267 352-861.

Fax: +267 357 138. Contact: (general) Ted Makgekgenene, Director; (technical) Kingsley Reetsang, Principal Broadcasting Engineer. Free stickers, pennants and pins. Return postage, $1 or 2 IRCs required. Replies slowly and irregularly.

BRAZIL   World Time −1 (−2 midyear) Atlantic Islands; −2 (−3 midyear) Eastern, including Brasília and Rio de Janeiro; −3 (−4 midyear) Western; −4 Northwestern; −5 Acre. There are often slight variations from one year to the next. Information regarding Daylight Saving Time can be found at http://pcdsh01.on.br.

NOTE: Postal authorities recommend that, because of the level of theft in the Brazilian postal system, correspondence to Brazil be sent only via registered mail.

CBN Anhanguera—*see* Rádio Anhanguera (Goiânia)

Rádio 8 de Setembro (if reactivated), Rua José Bonifacio 765, Centro, 13690-970 Descalvado SP, Brazil. Email: (Scapin) rscapin@gmail.com. Contact: Rafael Scapin. Replies to correspondence in Portuguese or English.

Rádio Alvorada (Londrina) (when operating), Rua Dom Bosco 145, Jardim Dom Bosco, 86060-340 Londrina PR, Brazil. Phone: +55 (43) 3347-0606. Fax: +55 (43) 3347 0303. Email: alvorada@radioalvorada.am.br; (Buranello) alburanello@sercomtel.com.br. Web: www.radioalvorada.am.br. Contact: Padre Silvio Andrei, Diretor; Alcindo Buranello, Gerente Administrativo. $1 or return postage helpful. Replies to correspondence in Portuguese.

Rádio Alvorada (Parintins), Rua Governador Leopoldo Neves 516, 69151-460 Parintins AM, Brazil. Phone: +55 (92) 3533-2002, +55 (92) 3533-3097. Fax: +55 (92) 3533 2004. Email: radio-alvorada@uol.com.br, sistemaalvorada@jurupari.com.br. Contact: Raimunda Ribeiro da Silva, Diretora. Return postage required. Replies occasionally to correspondence in Portuguese.

Rádio Alvorada (Rio Branco), Avenida Ceará 2150, Jardim Nazle, 69900-460 Rio Branco AC, Brazil. Phone: +55 (68) 3226-2301. Email: seve@jornalatribuna.com.br. Contact: José Severiano, Diretor. Occasionally replies to correspondence in Portuguese.

Rádio Araguaia—FM sister-station to Rádio Anhanguera (*see* next entry) and sometimes relayed via the latter's shortwave outlet. Usually identifies as "Araguaia FM."

Rádio Anhanguera (Araguaína), BR-157 Km. 1103, Zona Rural, 77804-970 Araguaína TO, Brazil. Return postage required. Occasionally replies to correspondence in Portuguese. Sometimes airs programming from sister-station Rádio Araguaia, 97.1 FM (*see* previous item).

Rádio Anhanguera (Goiânia), Rua Thomas Edison, Quadra 7, Setor Serrinha, 74835-130 Goiânia GO, Brazil; or Caixa Postal 13, 74823-000 Goiânia GO, Brazil. Email: anhanguera@radioexecutiva.com.br. Web: (streaming audio only) http://goiasnet.globo.com/tv_radio. Contact: Fábio de Campos Roriz, Diretor; Eng. Domingo Vicente Tinoco. Return postage required. Replies to correspondence in Portuguese, often slowly. Although—like its namesake in Araguaína (*see*, above)—a member of the Sistema de Rádio da Organização Jaime Câmara, this station is also an affiliate of the CBN network and often identifies as "CBN Anhanguera," especially when airing news programming.

Rádio Aparecida, Avenida Getúlio Vargas 185, Centro, 12570-000 Aparecida SP, Brazil; or Caixa Postal 2,

12570-970 Aparecida SP, Brazil. Phone/Fax: +55 (12) 3104-4400. Fax: +55 (12) 3104-4427. Email: (nontechnical) radioaparecida@radioaparecida.com.br; (Macedo) cassianomac@yahoo.com. Web: www.radioaparecida.com.br. Contact: Padre Inácio Medeiros, Diretor; Savio Trevisan, Departamento Técnico; José Moura; Cassiano Alves Macedo, Producer, "Encontro DX" (aired 2200 Saturday; one hour earlier when Brazil on DST). Return postage or $1 required. Replies to correspondence in Portuguese.

Rádio Bandeirantes, Rua Radiantes 13, Bairro Morumbi, 05699-900 São Paulo SP, Brazil. Phone: +55 (11) 3745-7552; (listener feedback) +55 (11) 3743-8040. Fax: +55 (11) 3745 8065. Email: (general) rbradio@band.com.br, rbnoar@band.com.br; (Huertas) ahuertas@band.com.br. Web: (includes streaming audio) www.radiobandeirantes.com.br. Contact: Augusto Huertas, Técnico Rádios. Free stickers, pennants and canceled Brazilian stamps. $1 or return postage required.

Rádio Boa Vontade, Av. São Paulo 722 - 3° andar, Bairro São Geraldo, 90230-160 Porto Alegre RS, Brazil. Phone: +55 (51) 3325-7019, +55 (51) 3374-0203. Email: rbv1300@yahoo.com.br, rbv1300am@hotmail.com. Web: (includes streaming audio) www.redeboavontade.com.br. Contact: José Joaquim Martins Rodrigues, Gerente da Rádio. Replies to correspondence in Portuguese.

Rádio Brasil, Av. Benjamin Constant, 1214, 5° andar, 13010-141 Campinas SP, Brazil. Email: radio@brasilcampinas.com. Web: www.brasilcampinas.com. Contact: Adilson Gasparini, Diretor Comercial e Artístico. Email reports accepted. Free stickers. Replies to correspondence in Portuguese.

Rádio Brasil Central, Caixa Postal 330, 74001-970 Goiânia GO, Brazil; (street address) Rua SC-1 No. 299, Parque Santa Cruz, 74860-270 Goiânia GO, Brazil. Phone: +55 (62) 201-7600. Email: rbc@agecom.go.gov.br. Web: www.agecom.go.gov.br/AM. Contact: Sílvio José da Silva, Gerente Executivo; Oscar Simões da Costa, Gerente Administrativo. Free stickers. $1 or return postage required. Replies to correspondence in Portuguese, and sometimes to correspondence in English.

Rádio Cacique (when operating), Rua Saldanha da Gama 168, Centro, 18010-060, Sorocaba SP, Brazil. Phone: +55 (15) 3234-3444, +55 (15) 231-3712. Email: radioc@radioc.com.br. Web: www.radiocacique.com.br. Contact: Edir Correa.

Rádio Caiari, Rua das Crianças 4646, Bairro Areal da Floresta, 78912-210 Porto Velho RO, Brazil. Phone: (studio) +55 (69) 3227-2277, +55 (69) 3216-0707; Phone/Fax: (Commercial Dept.) +55 (69) 3210-3621. Email: comercialcaiari@gmail.com, or online form. Web: www.radiocaiari.com.br. Contact: José Maria Gonzáles, Diretor; Alisângela Lima, Gerente Operacional. Free stickers. Return postage helpful. Replies irregularly to correspondence in Portuguese.

Rádio Canção Nova, Caixa Postal 57, 12630-000 Cachoeira Paulista SP, Brazil; (street address) Rua João Paulo II s/n, Alto da Bela Vista, 12630-000 Cachoeira Paulista SP, Brazil. Phone: (studio) +55 (12) 3186-2046. Fax: (general) +55 (12) 3186 2022 Email: (general) online form (radio@cancaonova.com.br may also work); (reception reports) dx@cancaonova.com. Web: (includes streaming audio) www.cancaonova.com/portal/canais/radio. Free stickers, pennants and station brochure sometimes sent on request. May send magazines. $1 helpful.

Rádio Capixaba, Caixa Postal 509, 29000-000 Vitória ES, Brazil; (street address) Av. Santo Antônio 366, 29025-000 Vitória ES, Brazil. Email: radiocap@terra.com.br. Contact: Jairo Gouvea Maia, Diretor; Sr. Sardinha, Técnico. Replies occasionally to correspondence in Portuguese.

Rádio Clube de Varginha (when operating), Caixa Postal 102, 37000-000 Varginha MG, Brazil. Email: sistemaclube@varginha.com.br. Contact: Mariela Silva Gómez. Return postage required. Replies to correspondence in Spanish and Portuguese.

Rádio Clube do Pará, Av. Almirante Barroso 2190 - 3° andar, Marco, 66095-020 Belém PA, Brazil. Phone/Fax: +55 (91) 3084-0100/111/112. Email: clubedamanha@radioclubedopara.com.br. Web: (includes streaming audio) www.radioclubedopara.com.br. Contact: Nonato Cavalcante, Diretor. Replies to correspondence in Portuguese or English, and verifies reception reports. Free stickers, postcards and occasional T-shirt.

Radio Clube Paranaense, Rua Rockefeller 1311, Prado Velho, 80230-130 Curitiba PR, Brazil. Phone: +55 (41) 332-2772. Fax: +55 (41) 332-2398. Email: (commercial department) clubcoml@rla13.pucpr.br, comercial @grupolumen.com.br. Web: (includes streaming audio) www.clubeb2.com.br. Contact: Toni Casagrande, Diretor; Vicente Mickosz, Superintendente.

Rádio Congonhas, Praça da Basílica 130, 36404-000 Congonhas MG, Brazil. Replies to correspondence in Portuguese. Free stickers.

Rádio Cultura Araraquara, Avenida Bento de Abreu 789, Bairro Fonte Luminosa, 14802-396 Araraquara SP, Brazil. Phone: +55 (16) 3303-7799. Fax: +55 (16) 3303 7792. Email: (administration) cultura@radiocultura.net; (listener feedback) ouvintes@radiocultura.net; (Wagner Luiz) wagner@radiocultura.net. Web: (includes streaming audio) www.radiocultura.net. Contact: Wagner Luiz, Diretor Artístico. Return postage required. Replies slowly to correspondence in Portuguese.

Rádio Cultura Filadélfia, Avenida Brasil 531, Sala 74, 85851-000 Foz do Iguaçu PR, Brazil. Phone: +55 (45) 523-2930. Replies irregularly to correspondence in Portuguese.

Rádio Cultura Ondas Tropicais, Rua Barcelos s/n, Praça 14 de Janeiro, 69020-200 Manaus AM, Brazil. Phone: +55 (92) 2101-4967, +55 (92) 2101-4953. Fax: +55 (92) 2101 4950. Email: radiocultura@hotmail.com. Contact: Maria Jerusalem dos Santos (also known as Jerusa Santos), Diretora. Replies to correspondence in Portuguese. Return postage appreciated. Station is part of the FUNTEC (Fundação Televisão e Rádio Cultura do Amazonas) network.

Rádio Cultura São Paulo, Rua Vladimir Herzog 75, Água Branca, 05036-900 São Paulo SP, Brazil; or Caixa Postal 11544, 05049-970 São Paulo SP, Brazil. Phone: (general) +55 (11) 3874-3122; (Cultura AM) +55 (11) 3874-3081; (Cultura FM) +55 (11) 3874-3092. Fax: +55 (11) 3611 2014. Email: (Cultura AM, relayed on 9615 and 17815 kHz) falecom@radiocultura.am; (Cultura FM, relayed on 6170 kHz) falecom@radioculturasp.fm.br. Web: (includes streaming audio) www.tvcultura.com.br. Contact: Eduardo Weber, Coordenador de Produção Cultura AM. $1 or return postage required. Replies slowly to postal correspondence in Portuguese.

Rádio Difusora Acreana, Rua Benjamin Constant 1232, Centro, 69900-161 Rio Branco AC, Brazil. Phone: +55 (68) 3223-9696. Fax: +55 (68) 3223 8610. Email:

comercialdifusora@ac.gov.br. Web: (streaming audio) www.ac.gov.br. Contact: Antônio Washington de Aquino Sobrinho, Diretor. Replies irregularly to correspondence in Portuguese.

Rádio Difusora Cáceres, Caixa Postal 297, 78200-000 Cáceres MT, Brazil; (street address) Rua Tiradentes 979, Centro, 78200-000 Cáceres MT, Brazil. Phone: +55 (65) 223-3830. Fax: +55 (65) 223-5986. Contact: Sra. Maridalva Amaral Vignard. $1 or return postage required. Replies occasionally to correspondence in Portuguese.

Rádio Difusora de Londrina, Caixa Postal 916, 86000-000 Londrina PR, Brazil; (street address) Rua Sergipe, 843 - Sala 05, 86010-360 Londrina PR, Brazil. Phone: +55 (43) 3322-1105; Phone/fax: +55 (43) 3324-7369. Email: radiodifusora690@aol.com, online form. Web: (includes streaming audio) www.radiodifusoradelondrina.com.br. Contact: Oscar Simões, Diretor. Free tourist brochure, which sometimes seconds as a verification. $1 or return postage helpful. Replies irregularly to correspondence in Portuguese.

Rádio Difusora de Macapá, Rua Cândido Mendes 525, Centro, 68900-100 Macapá AP, Brazil. Phone: +55 (96) 3212-1123. Fax: +55 (96) 3212 1111. Email: difusoramcp@yahoo.com.br. Contact: Carlos Luiz Pereira Marques, Diretor. $1 or return postage required. Replies irregularly to correspondence in Portuguese or English. Sometimes sends stickers, key rings and—on rare occasions—T-shirts.

Rádio Difusora de Poços de Caldas (if reactivated), Rua Rio Grande do Sul 631- 1º andar, Centro, 37701-001 Poços de Caldas MG, Brazil. Phone/Fax: +55 (35) 3722-1530. Email: difusora@difusorapocos.com.br, comercial@difusorapocos.com.br. Web: (includes streaming audio) www.difusorapocos.com.br. Contact: (general) Orlando Cioffi, Diretor Geral; (technical) Ronaldo Cioffi, Diretor Técnico. $1 or return postage required. Replies to correspondence in Portuguese.

Rádio Difusora do Amazonas, Av. Eduardo Ribeiro 639 - 20º andar, Centro, 69010-001 Manaus AM, Brazil. Phone: +55 (92) 3633-1001. Fax: +55 (92) 3234 3750. Email: fesinha@uol.com.br. Web: (includes streaming audio) www.difusoramanaus.com.br. Contact: Josué Filho, Diretor; Fesinha de Souza Anzoatégui. Replies to correspondence in Portuguese. $1 or return postage helpful.

Rádio Difusora Roraima, Avenida Capitão Ene Garcez 860, São Francisco, 69301-160 Boa Vista RR, Brazil. Phone/Fax: +55 (95) 3224-3101. Email: i-rico@hotmail.com. Web: (includes streaming audio) www.radiororaima.com.br. Contact: Barbosa Júnior, Diretor. Return postage required. Replies occasionally to correspondence in Portuguese.

Rádio Difusora Taubaté (if reactivated), Rua Dr. Sousa Alves 960, 12020-030 Taubaté SP, Brazil. Contact: Emilio Amadei Beringhs Neto, Diretor Superintendente. May send free stickers, pens, keychains and T-shirts. Return postage or $1 helpful.

Rádio Educação Rural de Coari, Praça São Sebastião 228, 69460-000 Coari AM, Brazil. Phone: +55 (97) 3561-2474. Fax: +55 (97) 3561 2633. Email: radiocoari@hotmail.com. Contact: Cícero Marques. $1 or return postage helpful. Replies irregularly to correspondence in Portuguese.

Rádio Educação Rural de Tefé, Caixa Postal 21, 69470-000 Tefé AM, Brazil. Phone: +55 (97) 3343-3017. Fax: +55 (97) 3343-2663. Email: rert@osite.com.br,

fjoaquim@mandic.com.br. Contact: Thomas Schwamborn, Diretor Administrativo. Verifies reception reports.

Rádio Educadora 6 de Agosto, Rua Coronel Brandão s/n, Bairro Aeroporto, 69930-000 Xapuri AC, Brazil. +55 (68) 3542-2975. Email: raimari.cardoso@hotmail.com. Contact: Raimari Sombra Cardoso, Coordenador. Replies to correspondence in Portuguese.

Rádio Educativa 6 de Agosto—*see* Rádio Educadora 6 de Agosto, above.

Rádio Educadora (Bragança), Praça das Bandeiras s/n, 68600-000 Bragança PA, Brazil. Phone: +55 (91) 3425-1295. Fax: +55 (91) 3425 1702. Email: fundacaoeducadora@uol.com.br. Contact: Padre Maurício de Souza, Diretor. $1 or return postage required. Replies to correspondence in Portuguese.

Rádio Educadora (Guajará Mirim), Praça Mário Corrêa No.90, 78957-000 Guajará Mirim RO, Brazil. Phone/Fax: +55 (69) 3541-6333. Email: radioeducadora@uol.com.br. Web: www.brasilcatolico.com.br/cursos/radiohome2.htm. Contact: José Hélio, Diretor. Return postage helpful. Replies to correspondence in Portuguese.

Rádio Educadora (Limeira), Caixa Postal 105, 13480-970 Limeira SP, Brazil; (street address) Rua Prof. Maria Aparecida Martinelli Faveri 988, Jardim Elisa Fumagalli, 13485-316 Limeira SP, Brazil. Email: (Bortolan) bab@zaz.com.br. Web: (streaming audio only) www.educadoram.com.br. Contact: Bruno Arcaro Bortolan, Gerente; Rosemary Ap. Giratto, Secretária Administrativa. Free stickers.

Rádio Gaúcha, Avenida Ipiranga 1075 - 3º andar, Bairro Azenha, 90169-900 Porto Alegre RS, Brazil. Phone: +55 (51) 3218-6600. Fax: +55 (51) 3218 6680. Email: (listener feedback) reportagem@rdgaucha.com.br, online form; (technical) gaucha@rdgaucha.com.br; (Klein) caio.klein@rdgaucha.com.br. Web: (includes streaming audio) www.rdgaucha.com.br. Contact: Caio Klein, Gerente Técnico. Replies irregularly to correspondence, preferably in Portuguese. Reception reports should be sent to the attention of "Eng. Caio Klein" at the station address above.

Rádio Gazeta, Avenida Paulista 900 -3º andar, Bairro Bela Vista, 01310-940 São Paulo SP, Brazil. Phone: +55 (11) 3170-5858. Fax: +55 (11) 3170 5828. Email: fuba@radiogazeta.com.br, comercial@radiogazeta.com.br. Web: www.radiogazeta.com.br. Contact: Benedito Leite da Costa, Supervisor de Operações. Free stickers. $1 or return postage necessary. Replies to correspondence in Portuguese.

Rádio Globo (Rio de Janeiro), Rua do Russel 434, Glória, 22210-210 Rio de Janeiro RJ, Brazil. Phone: +55 (21) 2555-8282. Fax: +55 (21) 2558 6385. Email: (administration) gerenciaamrio@radioglobo.com.br; (technical, Küssler) gilberto.kussler@sgr.com.br. Web: (includes streaming audio) http://radioclick.globo.com/globobrasil. Contact: Gilberto Küssler, Gerente Técnico. Rarely replies to correspondence, but try sending reception reports, in Portuguese, to Gilberto Küssler. Return postage helpful.

Rádio Globo (São Paulo), Rua das Palmeiras 315, Santa Cecilia, 01226-901 São Paulo SP, Brazil. Phone: +55 (11) 3824-3217. Fax: +55 (11) 3824 3210. Web: (includes streaming audio) http://radioclick.globo.com/globobrasil. Contact: (nontechnical) Paulo Novis, Diretor Geral; (technical) Roberto Cidade, Gerente Técnico. Replies occasionally to correspondence in Portuguese.

Rádio Globo Manaus, Av. Tefé 3025, Japiim, 69078-000 Manaus AM, Brazil. Phone: +55 (92) 2101-5500. Email:

adm@radiobare.com.br, manhadaglobo@radiobare.com.
br. Web: www.radioglobomanaus.com.br. Contact: Kátia
Cilene. Replies to correspondence in Portuguese. Formerly
known as Rádio Baré.

📻**Rádio Globo Santos**, Rua José Vaz Porto 175, Vila
Santa Rosa, 11431-190 Guarujá SP, Brazil. Phone: +55 (13)
3386-6092; (listener feedback) +55 (13) 3386-6965. Email:
atendimento@radioguarujaam.com.br. Web: (includes
streaming audio) www.radioguarujaam.com.br. Formerly
Rádio Guarujá Paulista.

📻**Rádio Guaíba**, Rua Caldas Júnior 219 - 2º Andar, 90019-
900 Porto Alegre RS, Brazil. Phone: +55 (51) 3215-6222.
Email: (administration) diretor@radioguaiba.com.br;
(technical) centraltecnica@radioguaiba.com.br; (Nagel)
nagel@radioguaiba.com.br. Web: (includes streaming
audio) www.radioguaiba.com.br. Contact: Ademar J. Dal-
lanora, Gerente Administrativo; Luciano Nagel, Produtor
Executivo. Reception reports are best sent to the attention
of Luciano Nagel. Return postage helpful. Free stickers.

Rádio Guarujá (if reactivated), Caixa Postal 45, 88000-
000 Florianópolis SC, Brazil. Email: guaruja@radioguaruja.
com.br. Contact: Mario Silva, Diretor; Joana Sempre Bom
Braz, Assessora de Marketing e Comunicação; Rosa
Michels de Souza. Return postage required. Replies irregularly to correspondence in Portuguese.
NEW YORK OFFICE: 45 West 46 Street, 5th Floor, Manhat-
tan, NY 10036 USA.

Rádio Imaculada Conceição, Avenida Mato Grosso 530,
Centro, 79002-906 Campo Grande MS, Brazil. Phone: +55
(67) 384-3164, +55 (67) 382-2238, +55 (67) 384-3345. $1
or return postage required. Replies to correspondence in
Portuguese. Formerly Rádio Educação Rural.

📻**Rádio Inconfidência**, Avenida Raja Gabáglia 1666, Lux-
emburgo, 30350-540 Belo Horizonte MG, Brazil. Phone:
+55 (31) 3297-7344, +55 (31) 3297-5803; (transmitter site)
+55 (31) 3394-1388. Fax: +55 (31) 3297 7348. Phone/
Fax: (Commercial Dept.) +55 (31) 3297-7343. Email:
(general) inconfidencia@inconfidencia.com.br; (technical)
engenharia@inconfidencia.com.br. Web: (includes streaming audio) www.inconfidencia.com.br. Contact: Isaias
Lansky, Diretor; Manuel Emilio de Lima Torres, Diretor
Superintendente; Jairo Antolio Lima, Diretor Artístico;
Eugenio Silva. Free stickers and postcards. May send CD
of Brazilian music. $1 or return postage helpful.

Rádio Integração (if reactivated), Rua de Alagoas 270,
Colégio, 69980-000 Cruzeiro do Sul AC, Brazil. Phone:
+55 (68) 3322-4637. Fax: +55 (68) 3322 6511. Email:
jornalintegracaoczs@hotmail.com. Contact: Albelia Be-
zerra da Cunha, Diretora. Return postage helpful.

📻**Rádio Itatiaia**, Rua Itatiaia 117, 31210-170 Belo
Horizonte MG, Brazil. Fax: +55 (31) 446 2900. Email:
itatiaia@itatiaia.com.br. Web: (includes on-demand and
streaming audio) www.itatiaia.com.br/am/index.html.
Contact: Lúcia Araújo Bessa, Assistente da Diretória;
Claudio Carneiro.

Rádio Jornal "A Crítica" (if reactivated), Av. André Araujo
1024A, Aleixo, 69060-001 Manaus AM, Brazil. Phone:
+55 (92) 2123-1039. Email: walteryallas@acritica.com.br.
Contact: Walter Yallas.

Rádio Marumby—see Rádio Novas de Paz

📻**Rádio Meteorologia Paulista**, Rua Capitão João
Marques 89, Jardim Centenário, 14940-000 Ibitinga, São
Paulo SP, Brazil; or Caixa Postal 91, 14940-000 Ibitinga
SP, Brazil. Phone: +55 (16) 242-6378/79/80. Fax: +55

(16) 242 5056. Email: radio.ibitinga@ibinet.com.br. Web:
(includes streaming audio from sister-station Ternura
FM, partly relayed by Rádio Meteorologia Paulista) www.
radioibitinga.com.br/meteorologia. Contact: Roque de
Rosa, Diretor. Replies to correspondence in Portuguese.
$1 or return postage required.

Rádio Missões da Amazônia, Travessa Dr. Lauro Sodré
299, 68250-000 Óbidos PA, Brazil. Phone/Fax: +55 (93)
3547-1699. Web: www.kaleb.hpg.ig.com.br. Contact:
Ronald Santos, Diretor. Return postage required. Replies
occasionally to correspondence in Portuguese.

📻**Rádio Mundial**, Av. Paulista 2198-Térreo, Cerqueira
César, 01310-300 São Paulo SP, Brazil. Phone: +55 (11)
3016 5999. Email: (general) radiomundial@radiomundial.
com; (administration) administrativo@radiomundial.com.
br. Web: (includes streaming audio) www.radiomundial.
com.br. Contact: (nontechnical) Luci Rothschild de Abreu,
Diretora Presidente.
REDE CBS PARENT ORGANIZATION: Rede CBS, Av. Paulista, 2200 - 14º andar, Cerqueira César, 01310-300 São
Paulo SP, Brazil. Phone: +55 (11) 3016 5999. Fax: +55
(11) 3016 5980. Email: comercial@redecbs.com.br. Web:
www.redecbs.com.br.

Rádio Municipal, Avenida Álvaro Maia s/n, 69750-000
São Gabriel da Cachoeira AM, Brazil. Phone/Fax: +55
(97) 3471-1768. Email: rmunicipalsgc@yahoo.com.br.
Contact: Rosane da Conceição Rodrigues Neto, Diretora.
Return postage necessary. Replies to correspondence in
Portuguese. Formerly Rádio Nacional de São Gabriel da
Cachoeira, prior to the station's transfer from Radiobrás
to the local municipality.

Rádio Nacional da Amazônia, Caixa Postal 258, 70359-970 Brasília-DF, Brazil; or SCRN 702/703 - Edif. Radiobrás - Subsolo, 70710-750 Brasília-DF, Brazil. Phone: +55 (61) 327-1981. Email: nacionaloc@radiobras.gov.br. Web: (includes streaming audio) www.radiobras.gov.br (click on "Rádio Nacional"). Contact: (technical) Taís Ladeira de Madeiros, Chefe da Divisão de Ondas Curtas da Radiobrás. Free stickers. Will occasionally verify reception reports if a prepared card is included.

Rádio Novas de Paz, Avenida Paraná 1896, 82510-000 Curitiba PR, Brazil; or Caixa Postal 22, 80000-000 Curitiba PR, Brazil. Phone: +55 (41) 257-4109. Contact: João Falavinha Ienzen, Gerente. $1 or return postage required. Replies irregularly to correspondence in Portuguese.

Rádio Novo Tempo, Caixa Postal 146, 79002-970 Campo Grande MS, Brazil; (street address) Rua Amando de Oliveira 135, Bairro Amambaí, 79005-370 Campo Grande MS, Brazil. Email: novotempo.ms@usb.org.br; (Ramos) ellen.ramos@usb.org.br. Web: www.asm.org.br (click on "Rádio Novo Tempo"). Contact: Ellen Ramos, Jornalista e Locutora; Pastor Paulo Melo. Return postage required. Replies to correspondence in Portuguese and verifies reception reports. Free stickers. A station of the Seventh Day Adventists.

Rádio Oito de Setembro—*see* Rádio 8 de Setembro

Rádio Pioneira de Teresina, Rua 24 de Janeiro 150 sul, 64001-230 Teresina PI, Brazil. Phone: +55 (86) 3221-8121. Fax: +55 (86) 3221 8122. Email: (general) pioneira@radiopioneira.am.br; (management) gerencia@radiopioneira.am.br; (comments on programs) programacao@radiopioneira.am.br; (director) rosemiro@radiopioneira.am.br. Web: www.radiopioneira.am.br. Contact: Rosemiro Robinson da Costa. $1 or return postage required. Replies slowly to correspondence in Portuguese.

Rádio Record, Caixa Postal 7920, 04084-002 São Paulo SP, Brazil. Email: radiorecord@rederecord.com.br. Web: (includes streaming audio) www.rederecord.com.br/radiorecord. Contact: Mário Luíz Catto, Diretor Geral; Antonio Carlos Miranda. Free stickers. Return postage or $1 required. Replies occasionally to correspondence in Portuguese.

Rádio Relógio (when operating), Rua Paramopama 131, Ribeira, Ilha do Governador, 21930-110 Rio de Janeiro RJ, Brazil. Phone: +55 (21) 2467-0201. Fax: +55 (21) 2467 4656. Email: radiorelogio@ig.com.br. Contact: Olindo Coutinho, Diretor Geral; Renato Castro. Replies occasionally to correspondence in Portuguese.

Rádio Rio Mar, Rua José Clemente 500, Centro, 69010-070 Manaus AM, Brazil. Phone: +55 (92) 3633-2295. Fax: +55 (92) 3232 7763. Email: decom@click21.com.br. Contact: Martin James Lauman, Superintendente. Replies to correspondence in Portuguese. $1 or return postage helpful.

Rádio Roraima—*see* Rádio Difusora Roraima

Rádio Rural (Petrolina), Caixa Postal 8, 56300-000 Petrolina PE, Brazil. Phone: +55 (87) 3861-2874, +55 (87) 3862-1522. Email: emissorarural@silcons.com.br. Contact: Padre Bianchi, Gerente; Maria Letecia de Andrade Nunes. Return postage necessary. Replies to correspondence in Portuguese.

Rádio Rural (Santarém), Avenida São Sebastião 622 - Bloco A, 68005-090 Santarém PA, Brazil. Phone: +55 (93) 3523-1006. Fax: +55 (93) 3523 2685. Email: edilrural@gmail.com.br. Web: www.viamazonica.com/radiorural. Contact: Padre Edilberto Moura Sena, Coordenador. Replies slowly to correspondence in Portuguese. Free stickers. Return postage or $1 required.

Rádio Senado, Caixa Postal 070-747, 70359-970 Brasília DF, Brazil; (physical address) Praça dos Três Poderes, Anexo II - Bloco B - Térreo, 70165-900 Brasília DF, Brazil. Phone: (general) +55 (61) 311-4691, +55 (61) 311-1257; (technical) +55 (61) 311-1285; (shortwave department) +55 (61) 311-1238. Fax: (general) +55 (61) 311 4238. Email: radio@senado.gov.br; (Fabiano) max@senado.gov.br. Web: www.senado.gov.br/radio/ondascurtas.asp; (streaming audio from FM Service, partly relayed on shortwave) mms://bombadil.senado.gov.br/wmtencoder/radio.wmv. Contact: Max Fabiano, Diretor; (technical) José Carlos Sigmaringa Seixas, Coordenador do Núcleo de Ondas Curtas.

Rádio Trans Mundial, Caixa Postal 18300, 04626-970 São Paulo SP, Brazil; (street address) Rua Épiro 110, 04635-030 São Paulo SP, Brazil. Phone/Fax: +55 (11) 5031-3533. Email: (general) rtm@transmundial.com.br; (technical) tecnica@transmundial.com.br; ("Amigos do Rádio" DX-program) amigosdoradio@transmundial.com.br. Web: (includes streaming audio) www.transmundial.com.br. Contact: José Carlos de Santos, Diretor; Samuel Matos, Diretor Técnico; Rudolf Grimm, programa "Amigos do Rádio." Free stickers, postcards, bookmarkers or other small gifts. Sells religious books and CDs of religious music (from hymns to bossa nova). Prices, in local currency, can be found at the Website (click on "Publicações"). Programming comes from São Paulo, but transmitter site is located in Santa Maria, Rio Grande do Sul.

Rádio Tupi, Rua João Negrão 595, Centro, 80010-200, Curitiba PR, Brazil. Phone: +55 (41) 323-1353. Contact: (technical) Eng. Latuf Aurani (who is based in São Paulo). Relays "Voz de Libertação" (*see*). Rarely replies, and only to correspondence in Portuguese.

Rádio Vale do Xingu, Rua Primeira de Janeiro 1359, Catedral, 68371-020 Altamira PA, Brazil. Phone/Fax: +55 (93) 3515-1182, +55 (93) 3515-4899, +55 (93) 3515-4411. Email: producao@valedoxingu.com.br. Contact: Ana Claudia Barros, Diretora.

Rádio Verdes Florestas, Fundação Verdes Florestas, Rua Mário Lobão 81, 69980-000 Cruzeiro do Sul AC, Brazil; (transmitter location) Estrado do Aeroporto, km 02, Bairro Nossa Senhora das Graças, Cruzeiro do Sul AC, Brazil. Phone/Fax: +55 (68) 3322-3309, +55 (68) 3322-2634. Email: verdesflorestas@yahoo.com.br. Contact: José Graci Soares Rezende. Return postage required. Replies occasionally to correspondence in Portuguese.

Rádio Voz do Coração Imaculado (when operating), Caixa Postal 354, 75001-970 Anápolis GO, Brazil; (street address) Rua Barão de Cotegipe s/n, Centro, 75001-970 Anápolis GO, Brazil. Email: radioimaculada@immacolata.com. Web: (includes streaming audio) www.immacolata.com/radiovoz. Contact: Padre Domingos M. Esposito. Operation tends to be irregular, as the station is funded entirely from religious donations.

Super Rádio Alvorada —*see* Rádio Alvorada (Rio Branco)

Voz de Libertação. Ubiquitous programming originating from the "Deus é Amor" Pentecostal church's Rádio Universo (1300 kHz) in São Bernardo do Campo, São Paulo, and aired over several shortwave stations, especially Rádio

Tupi, Curitiba (*see*). Streaming audio is available at the "Deus é Amor" Website, www.ipda.org.br.

Voz do Coração Imaculado—*see* Rádio Voz do Coração Imaculado

📻**Voz Misionária**, Caixa Postal 296, 88010-970 Florianópolis SC, Brazil; (street address) Rua Angelo Laporta 841, 88020-600 Florianópolis SC, Brazil. Email: dafaie@pop.com.br. Web: (includes streaming audio) www.gmuh.com.br/radio/radioma.htm. Contact: Davi Campos, Diretor Artístico; Dr. Cesino Bernardino, Presidente, GMUH; Jair Albano, Diretor. $1 or return postage required. Free diploma and stickers. Replies to correspondence in Portuguese. Relays mediumwave AM station Rádio Marumby.

GMUH MISSIONARY PARENT ORGANIZATION: Gideões Missionários da Última Hora—GMUH, Rua Joaquim Nunes 244, 88340-000 Camboriú SC, Brazil; (postal address) Caixa Postal 2004, 88340-000 Camboriú SC, Brazil. Phone: +55 (47) 261-3232. Email: gmuh@gmuh.com.br. Web: www.gmuh.com.br.

BRITISH INDIAN OCEAN TERRITORY   World Time +6

AFRTS-American Forces Radio and Television Service (Shortwave), Naval Media Center, PSC 466 Box 14, FPO AP 96595-0014 USA. Phone: +246 370-3680. Fax: +246 370 3681. Replies irregularly.

BULGARIA   World Time +2 (+3 midyear)

📻**Radio Bulgaria**

NONTECHNICAL AND TECHNICAL: P.O. Box 900, 1000 Sofia, Bulgaria; or (street address) 4 Dragan Tsankov Blvd., 1040 Sofia, Bulgaria. Phone: (general) +359 (2) 985-241; (Managing Director) +359 (2) 854-604; (Nedyalkov) *359 (2) 933 6733. Fax: (general, usually weekdays only) +359 (2) 871 060, +359 (2) 871 061, +359 (2) 650 560; (Managing Director) +359 (2) 946 1576; +359 (2) 988 5103; (Nedyalkov) +359 (2) 865 0560. Email: (English program and schedule information) english@bnr.bg (same format for other languages, e.g. french@ . . .; spanish@ . . .). (Nedyalkov) nedyalkov@bnr.bg. Web: (includes on-demand audio, plus streaming audio from domestice services not aired on shortwave) www.bnr.bg. Contact: (general) Mrs. Iva Delcheva, English Section; Svilen Stoicheff, Head of English Section; Ludmila Petra, Spanish Section; (administration and technical) Anguel H. Nedyalkov, Director; (technical) Atanas Tzenov, Director. Replies regularly, but sometimes slowly. Return postage helpful but IRCs may no longer be accepted. Verifies email reports with QSL cards. For concerns about frequency usage, contact BTC, below, with copies to Messrs. Nedyalkov and Tzenov of Radio Bulgaria.

FREQUENCY MANAGEMENT AND TRANSMISSION OPERATIONS: Bulgarian Telecommunications Company (BTC), Ltd., 8 Totleben Blvd., 1606 Sofia, Bulgaria. Phone: +359 (2) 88-00-75. Fax: +359 (2) 87 58 85, +359 (2) 80 25 80. Contact: Roumen Petkov, Frequency Manager; Mrs. Margarita Krasteva, Radio Regulatory Department.

📻**Radio Varna**, 22 Primorski blvd, 9000 Varna, Bulgaria. Phone: +359 (52) 602-802. Fax: +359 (52) 664 411. Email: bnr@radiovarna.com. Web: (includes streaming audio from the domestic service, not aired on shortwave) www.

radiovarna.com. Contact: (technical) Kostadin Kovachev, Chief Engineer.

BURKINA FASO   World Time exactly

📻**Radiodiffusion du Burkina**, 03 BP 7029, Ouagadougou 03, Burkina Faso. Phone: +226 5032-4302/03, +226 5032-4398. Fax: +226 5031 0441. Email: radio@rtb.bf; (Goba) nadowo2002@yahoo.fr. Web: (includes streaming audio). www.radio.bf. Contact: Pascal Goba, Chef des Programmes. Replies to correspondence in French. IRC or return postage helpful.

BURMA—*see* MYANMAR.

CANADA   World Time –3:30 (–2:30 midyear) Newfoundland; –4 (–3 midyear) Atlantic; –5 (–4 midyear) Eastern, including Québec and Ontario; –6 (–5 midyear) Central; except Saskatchewan; –6 Saskatchewan; –7 (–6 midyear) Mountain; –8 (–7 midyear) Pacific, including Yukon.

📻**Canadian Broadcasting Corporation (CBC)—English Programs**, P.O. Box 500, Station A, Toronto, Ontario, M5W 1E6, Canada. Phone: (toll-free, Canada only) +1 (866) 306-4636; (Audience Relations) +1 (416) 205-3700. Email: cbcinput@toronto.cbc.ca. Web: (includes on-demand and streaming audio) www.radio.cbc.ca.

LONDON NEWS BUREAU: CBC, 43-51 Great Titchfield Street, London W1P 8DD, United Kingdom. Phone: +44 (20) 7412-9200. Fax: +44 (20) 7631 3095.

PARIS NEWS BUREAU: CBC, 17 avenue Matignon, F-75008 Paris, France. Phone: +33 (1) 4421-1515. Fax: +33 (1) 4421 1514.

WASHINGTON NEWS BUREAU: CBC, National Press Building, Suite 500, 529 14th Street NW, Washington DC 20045 USA. Phone: +1 (202) 383-2900.

📻**Canadian Broadcasting Corporation (CBC)—French Programs**, Société Radio-Canada, C.P. 6000, succ. centre-ville, Montréal, Québec, H3C 3A8, Canada. Phone: (Audience Relations) +1 (514) 597-6000. Web: (includes on-demand and streaming audio) www.radio-canada.ca. Welcomes correspondence, but may not reply due to shortage of staff.

CBC Northern Québec Shortwave Service—*see* Radio Canada International, below.

📻**CFRX-CFRB** (when operating)

MAIN ADDRESS: 2 St. Clair Avenue West, Toronto, Ontario, M4V 1L6, Canada. Phone:(main switchboard) +1 (416) 924-5711; (talk shows switchboard) +1 (416) 872-1010; (news centre) +1 (416) 924-6717. Fax: (main fax line) +1 (416) 872 8683; (CFRB news fax line) +1 (416) 323 6816. Email: (comments on programs) cfrbcomments@cfrb.com; (News Director) news@cfrb.com; (general, nontechnical) info@cfrb.com; opsmngr@cfrb.com. Web: (includes on-demand and streaming audio) www.cfrb.com. Contact: (nontechnical) Carlo Massaro, Information Officer; Steve Kowch, Operations Manager; (technical) Ian Sharp, Engineer. Reception reports should be sent to the verification address, below.

VERIFICATION ADDRESS: Ontario DX Association, 155 Main St. N., Apt. 313, Newmarket, Ontario, L3Y 8C2, Canada. Email: odxa@rogers.com. Web: www.odxa.on.ca. Contact: Steve Canney, VA3SC.

CFVP-CKMX, AM 1060, Standard Broadcasting, P.O. Box 2750, Station 'M', Calgary, Alberta, T2P 4P8, Canada.

Radio Canada International is housed within Montreal's *Maison*. The logo is affectionately known by staffers as "the exploding pizza."

M. Wright

Phone: (general) +1 (403) 240-5800; (news) +1 (403) 240-5844; (technical) +1 (403) 240-5867. Fax: (general and technical) +1 (403) 240 5801; (news) +1 (403) 246 7099. Contact: (general) Gary Russell, General Manager; Beverley Van Tighem, Executive Assistant; (technical) Ken Pasolli, Technical Director.

CHU. Radio Station CHU, National Research Council of Canada, Bldg M-36, Room 1026, 1200 Montreal Road, Ottawa, Ontario, K1A 0R6, Canada. Phone: +1 (613) 993-3430. Fax: +1 (613) 952 1394. Email: radio.chu@nrc. ca, radiochu@nrc-cnrc.gc.ca, radio.chu.inms@nrc-cnrc. gc.ca; (Pelletier) raymond.pelletier@nrc.cnrc.gc.ca. Web: http://inms-ienm.nrc-cnrc.gc.ca/time_services/short-wave_broadcasts_e.html. Contact: Dr. Rob Douglas; Dr. Jean-Simon Boulanger, Group Leader; Raymond Pelletier, Technical Officer. Official standard frequency and World Time station for Canada on 3330, 7335 and 14670 kHz. Brochure available upon request. Those with a personal computer, Bell 103 compatible modem and appropriate software can get the exact time, from CHU's cesium clock, via the telephone; details available upon request, or direct from the Website. Verifies reception reports (including those sent via email) with a QSL card.

CKZN, CBC Newfoundland and Labrador, P.O. Box 12010, Station 'A', St. John's, Newfoundland, A1B 3T8, Canada. Phone: +1 (709) 576-5155. Fax: +1 (709) 576 5099. Email: (engineer) keith_durnford@cbc.ca. Web: (includes on-demand audio) www.stjohns.cbc.ca; (streaming audio) www.cbc.ca/listen/index.html# (click on "St. John's"). Contact: (general) Heather Elliott, Communications Officer; (technical) Shawn R. Williams, Manager, Transmission and Distribution; Keith Durnford, Supervisor, Transmission Operations; Terry Brett, Transmitter Department; Rosemary Sampson. Free CBC sticker and verification card with the history of Newfoundland included. Don't enclose money, stamps or IRCs with correspondence, as they will only have to be returned. Relays CBN (St. John's, 640 kHz) except at 1000–1330 World Time (one hour earlier in summer) when programming comes from CFGB Goose Bay.

CFGB ADDRESS: CBC Radio, Box 1029 Station C, Happy Valley, Goose Bay, Labrador, Newfoundland A0P 1C0, Canada. Email: (program relayed via CKZN) labmorns@cbc.ca.

CKZU-CBU, CBC, P.O. Box 4600, Vancouver, British Columbia, V6B 4A2, Canada—for verification of reception reports, mark the envelope, "Attention: Engineering." Phone: (general) +1 (604) 662-6000; (toll-free, U.S. and Canada only) 1-800-961-6161; (engineering) +1 (604) 662-6060. Fax: +1 (604) 662 6350. Email: (general) webmaster@vancouver. cbc.ca; (Newbury) newburyd@vancouver.cbc.ca. Web: (includes on-demand audio) www.vancouver.cbc.ca; (streaming audio) www.cbc.ca/listen/index.html# (click on "Vancouver"). Contact: (general) Public Relations; (technical) Dave Newbury, Transmission Engineer.

Église du Christ, C.P. 2026, Jonquière, Québec, G7X 7XC, Canada. Phone: +1 (514) 387-6163. Fax: +1 (514) 387-1153. E-mail: egliseduchrist@videotron.ca. Web: www3. sympatico.ca/micdan. Contact: Jean Grenier. Broadcasts via a transmitter in the United Kingdom.

High Adventure Gospel Communication Ministries— *see* Bible Voice Broadcasting, United Kingdom.

Radio Canada International

NOTE: (CBC Northern Québec Service) The following P. O Box 6000 postal address and street address are also valid for the Northern Québec Service, provided that you mention the name of the service and "17th Floor" on the envelope. RCI does not issue technical verifications for Northern Québec Service transmissions. Contact: Nathalie Chamberland.

MAIN OFFICE: P.O. Box 6000, Montréal, Québec, H3C 3A8, Canada; or (street address) 1400 boulevard René-Lévesque Est, Montréal, Québec, H2L 2M2, Canada. Phone: (general) +1 (514) 597-7500; (Audience Relations, Bill Westenhaver) +1 (514) 597-5899; (Listener Response phone number, English/French) +1 (514) 528-8821 (collect calls not accepted). Fax: (Audience Relations) +1 (514) 597 7760. Email: info@rcinet.ca. Web: (includes online reception report form and on-demand and streaming audio) www. rcinet.ca. Contact: (general and technical verifications) Bill Westenhaver, Audience Relations; (administration) Jean

Larin, Director. Free stickers, antenna booklet and lapel pins on request. May send other small gifts.

TRANSMISSION OFFICE, INTERNATIONAL SERVICES, CBC TRANSMISSION: Room B52-70, 1400 boulevard René-Lévesque Est, Montréal, Québec, H2L 2M2, Canada. Phone: +1 (514) 597-7618/19. Fax: +1 (514) 284 2052. Email: master_control@moncton.radio-canada.ca; (Théorêt) gerald_theoret@radio-canada.ca; (Bouliane) jacques_bouliane@radio-canada.ca. Contact: (general) Gérald Théorêt, Frequency Manager, CBC Transmission Management; Ms. Nicole Vincent, Frequency Management; (administration) Jacques Bouliane, Senior Manager, International Services. This office only for informing about transmitter-related problems (interference, modulation quality, etc.), especially by fax or email. Verifications are not given out at this office; requests for verification should be sent to the main office, above.

TRANSMITTER SITE: CBC, P.O. Box 6131, Sackville New Brunswick, E4L 1G6, Canada. Phone: +1 (506) 536-2690/1. Fax: +1 (506) 536 2342. Contact: Raymond Bristol, Sackville Plant Manager, CBC Transmission; Suzanne Gaudet, Sackville Master Control. All correspondence not concerned with transmitting equipment should be directed to the appropriate address in Montréal, above. Free tours given during normal working hours.

MONITORING STATION: P.O. Box 460, Station Main Stittsville, Ontario, K2S 1A6, Canada. Phone: +1 (613) 831-4802. Fax: +1 (613) 831 0343. Email: derek.williams@cbc.ca. Contact: Derek Williams, Manager of Monitoring.

Shortwave Classroom, R. Tait McKenzie Public School, 175 Paterson Street, Almonte, Ontario, K0A 1A0, Canada. Phone: +1 (613) 256-8248. Fax: +1 (613) 256 4791. Contact: Neil Carleton, VE3NCE, Editor & Publisher. *The Shortwave Classroom* newsletter was published three times per year as a nonprofit volunteer project for teachers around the world that use shortwave listening in the classroom, or as a club activity, to teach about global perspectives, media studies, world geography, languages, social studies and other subjects. Although no longer published, a set of back issues with articles and classroom tips from teachers around the globe is available for $10.

CENTRAL AFRICAN REPUBLIC   World Time +1

Radio Centrafrique, Radiodiffusion-Télévision Centrafricaine, B.P. 940, Bangui, Central African Republic. Contact: (technical) Directeur des Services Techniques. Replies on rare occasions to correspondence in French. Return postage required.

Radio ICDI, B.P 362, Bangui, Central African Republic. Phone: +236 508 622. Email: radioicdi@gmail.com; (Mbami) jmbami@icdinternational.org. Web: www.icdinternational.org/radio.html. Contact: Josue Mbami, Directeur. Station is run by Integrated Community Development International (ICDI).

ICDI HEAD OFFICE: ICDI, 3792 N. Oakwood Dr., Warsaw IN 46582 USA. Phone: +1 (574) 527-8920. Fax: +1 (360) 248 2990. Email: (Hocking) jimhocking@icdinternational.org. Contact: Jim Hocking, General Director.

☎Radio Ndeke Luka (if reactivated on shortwave), PNUD, B.P. 872, Bangui, Central African Republic; (street address) PNUD, Av. de l'Indépendance, Bangui, Central African Republic. Email: (including reception reports) ndekeluka@hotmail.com. Replies to correspondence in

French, and may reply in French to correspondence in English. The station is managed by the Fondation Hirondelle, based in Switzerland, and operates under the aegis of the United Nations, in partnership with the UNDP (United Nations Development Programme). The main studio is located in Bangui. Currently broadcasts domestically on FM, but hopes to return to shortwave.

*FONDATION HIRONDELLE:*Avenue du Temple 19C, CH 1012-Lausanne, Switzerland. Phone: +41 (21) 654-2020. Fax: +41 (21) 654 2021. Email info@hirondelle.org. Web: (includes on-demand news bulletins from Radio Ndeke Luka) www.hirondelle.org. Verifies reception reports.

CHAD   World Time +1

Radiodiffusion Nationale Tchadienne—N'djamena, B.P. 892, N'Djamena, Chad. Contact: Djimadoum Ngoka Kilamian; Ousmane Mahamat. Two IRCs or return postage required. Replies slowly to correspondence in French.

CHILE   World Time –3 (–4 midyear)

☎CVC—La Voz (formerly Radio Voz Cristiana)

TRANSMISSION FACILITIES: Casilla 395, Talagante, Santiago, Chile. Phone: (engineering) +56 (2) 855-7046. Fax: +56 (2) 855 7053. Email: (project engineer) antonio@cvclavoz.cl; (operations manager) gisela@cvclavoz.cl. Web: (includes streaming audio) www.cvclavoz.com. Contact: Antonio Reyes B., Project Engineer; Mathias Svensson, Transmission Engineer; Ms. Gisela Vergara, Operations Manager. Free program and frequency schedules. Sometimes verifies reception reports.

PROGRAM PRODUCTION: P.O. Box 2889, Miami FL 33144 USA; (street address) 15485 Eagle Nest Lane, Suite 220, Miami Lakes FL 33014 USA. Phone: +1 (305) 231-7704; (Portuguese Service) +1 (305) 231-7742. Email: (Gallardo) info@vozcristiana.com; (listener feedback) comentarios@vozcristiana.com. Web: (includes streaming audio) www.vozcristiana.com. Contact: (administration) Juan Mark Gallardo, Gerente de Programación.

ENGINEERING DEPARTMENT: Ryder Street, West Bromwich, West Midlands B70 0EJ, United Kingdom. Phone: +44 (121) 522-6087. Fax: +44 (121) 522 6083. Email: andrewflynn@christianvision.com. Contact: Andrew Flynn, Director of International Broadcasting.

VERIFICATIONS, PORTUGUESE DX PROGRAM: "Rádio DX," Caixa Postal 51, 90001-970 Porto Alegre RS, Brazil. Email: radiodx@radiocvc.com. Contact: Célio Romais.

Radio Esperanza

OFFICE: Casilla 830, Temuco, Chile. Phone: +56 (45) 213-790. Phone/Fax: +56 (45) 367-070. Email: esperanza@telsur.cl. Contact: (general) Juanita Cárcamo, Departamento de Programación; Eleazar Jara, Dpto. de Programación; Ramón P. Woerner K., Publicidad; Alberto Higueras Martínez, Locutor; (verifications) Rodolfo Campos, Director; (technical) Juan Luis Puentes, Dpto. Técnico. Free pennants, stickers, bookmarks and tourist information. Two IRCs, $1 or 2 U.S. stamps appreciated. Replies, often slowly, to correspondence in Spanish or English.

STUDIO: Calle Luis Durand 3057, Temuco, Chile. Phone/Fax: +56 (45) 240-161.

Radio Parinacota, Casilla 82, Arica, Chile. Phone: +56 (58) 245-889. Phone/Fax: +56 (58) 245 986. Email: rparinacota@latinmail.com. Contact: Tomislav Simunovich Gran, Director.

CHINA   World Time +8; still nominally +6 ("Urümqi Time") in the Xinjiang Uighur Autonomous Region, but in practice +8 is observed there, as well.

NOTE: If a Chinese regional station does not respond to your correspondence within four months, send your reception reports to China Radio International (*see*) which will verify them. CRI apparently no longer forwards correspondence to regional stations, as it sometimes did in the past.

📻**Central People's Broadcasting Station (CPBS)—China National Radio** (Zhongyang Renmin Guangbo Diantai), P.O. Box 4501, Beijing 100866, China. Phone: +86 (10) 6851-2435, +86 (10) 6851-5522. Fax: +86 (10) 6851 6630. Email: (services for Taiwan) cnrtw@cnrtw.com. Web: (includes on-demand and streaming audio) www.cnradio.com; (services for Taiwan) www.nihaotw.com. Contact: Wang Changquan, Audience Department, China National Radio. Tape recordings of music and news $5 plus postage. CPBS T-shirts $10 plus postage; also sells ties and other items with CPBS logo. No credit cards. Free stickers, pennants and other small souvenirs. Return postage helpful. Responds regularly to correspondence in English or Standard Chinese (Mandarin). Although in recent years this station has officially been called "China National Radio" in English-language documents, all on-air identifications in Standard Chinese continue to be "Zhongyang Renmin Guangbo Diantai" (Central People's Broadcasting Station). To quote from the Website of China's State Administration of Radio, Film and TV: "The station moved to Beijing on March 25, 1949. It was renamed the Central People's Broadcasting Station (it [sic] English name was changed to China National Radio later on) . . ."

China Business Radio. The Second Program of Central People's Broadcasting Station—China National Radio (*see*).

China Huayi Broadcasting Company—*see* China Huayi Broadcasting Corporation, below.

📻**China Huayi Broadcasting Corporation**, P.O. Box 251, Fuzhou, Fujian 350001, China. Email: (station) hanyu@chbcnews.com; (Yuan Jia) chrisyuanjia@sohu.com; Web: (includes streaming audio) www.chbcnews.com. Contact: Lin Hai Chun, Announcer; Yuan Jia, Program Manager. Replies to correspondence in English or Chinese. Although the station refers to itself in English as China Huayi Broadcasting Company, the correct translation of the Chinese name is China Huayi Broadcasting Corporation.

VERIFICATION OF RECEPTION REPORTS: Although verifications are sometimes received direct from the station, reception reports are best sent to the QSL Manager: Qiao Xiaoli, Fen Jin Xing Cun 3-4-304, Changshu, Jiangsu 215500, China. Recordings accepted, and return postage (IRC or $1US required for a QSL card, 2 IRCs or $2US for a QSL folder). Email: 2883752@163.com.

China National Radio—*see* Central People's Broadcasting Station (CPBS), above.

📻**China Radio International**, 16A Shijingshan Street, Beijing 100040, China; (English Service) P.O. Box 4216, CRI-2, Beijing 100040 China (other language sections also use this address, but with a different CRI number; for example, it's CRI-38 for the Spanish Service and CRI-39 for the Portuguese Service). Phone: (Director's office) +86 (10) 6889-1625; (Audience Relations.) +86 (10) 6889-1617, +86 (10) 6889-1652; (English newsroom/current affairs) +86 (10) 6889-1619; (Technical Director) +86 (10) 6609-

2577. Fax: (Director's office) +86 (10) 6889 1582; (English Service) +86 (10) 6889 1378, +86 (10) 6889 1379; (audience relations) +86 (10) 6889 3175; (administration) +86 (10) 6851 3174; (German Service) +86 (10) 6889 2053; (Spanish Service) +86 (10) 6889 1909. Email: (English) crieng@cri.com.cn, yinglian@cri.com.cn, garden@cri.com.cn; (Listener's Liason) gaohuiying@crifm.com; (English, technical, including reception reports) crieng@crifm.com; (Chinese) chn@cri.com.cn; (French) crifra@cri.com.cn; (German) ger@cri.com.cn (*see* also the entry for the Berlin Bureau, below); (Japanese) jap@cri.com.cn; (Portuguese) cripor@cri.com.cn; (Spanish) spa@cri.com.cn. Web: (includes on-demand and streaming audio) www.chinabroadcast.cn. Contact: Yang Lei, Director, English Service; Peichun Li, Deputy Director, English Service; Ms. Wang Anjing, Director of Audience Relations, English Service; Ying Lian, English Service; Gao Huiying, Editor, Listener's Liason; Shang Chunyan, "Listener's Garden"; Yu Meng, Editor; (administration) Li Dan, President, China Radio International; Xia Jixuan, Vice President; Wang Gengnian Director General; Xia Jixuan, Chen Minyi, Chao Tieqi and Wang Dongmei, Deputy Directors, China Radio International; Xin Liancai, Director International Relations, China Radio International. Pennants, stickers, desk calendars, pins, handmade papercuts and free bi-monthly *Messenger* newsletter for loyal listeners. Every year, China Radio International holds contests and quizzes, with the overall winner getting a free trip to China. T-shirts for $8. Two-volume, 820-page set of *Day-to-Day Chinese* language-lesson books $15, including postage worldwide; a 155-page book, *Learn to Speak Chinese: Sentence by Sentence*, plus two cassettes for $15. Two Chinese music tapes for $15. Various other books (on arts, medicine, Chinese idioms etc.) in English available from Audience Relations Department, English Service, China Radio International, 100040 Beijing, China. Payment by postal money order to Mr. Li Yi. Every year, the Audience Relations Department will renew the mailing list of the *Messenger* newsletter. CRI is also relayed via shortwave transmitters in Canada, Chile, Cuba, France, French Guiana, Mali, Russia and Spain.

SAN FRANCISCO OFFICE, SCHEDULES: 2654 17th Avenue, San Francisco CA 94116 USA. Phone: +1 (415) 564-9968. Email: GPoppin@aol.com. Contact: George Poppin. This address, a volunteer office, only provides CRI schedules to listeners (return postage not required). All other correspondence should be sent directly to the main office in Beijing.

📻**Fujian People's Broadcasting Station**, 2 Gutian Lu, Fuzhou, Fujian 350001, China. $1 or IRC helpful. Web: (includes on-demand audio) www.66163.com/fjbs. Contact: Audience Relations Section. Replies irregularly and usually slowly. Prefers correspondence in Chinese.

Gannan People's Broadcasting Station, 49 Renmin Xije, Hezuo Zhen, Xiahe, Gian Su 747000, China. Verifies reception reports written in Chinese or English. Return postage not required.

📻**Guangxi Foreign Broadcasting Station**, 12 Min Zu Avenue, Nanning, Guangxi 530022, China. Phone: +86 (771) 585-4403, +86 (771) 587-4745. Email: service@gxradio.com. Web: (includes on-demand and streaming audio) www.gxradio.com/foreignradio/index.asp. Free stickers and handmade papercuts. IRC helpful. Replies irregularly. Broadcasts in Vietnamese and Cantonese to listeners in Vietnam.

Hulunbuir People's Broadcasting Station, 11 Shengli Dajie, Hailar, Hulun Buir, Nei Menggu 021008, China. Phone: +86 (825) 6100-2065. Fax: +86 (825) 6100 2054. Replies in Chinese to correspondence in Chinese or English, and verifies reception reports.

☞**Hunan People's Broadcasting Station**, 167 Yuhua Lu, Changsha, Hunan 410007, China. Phone: +86 (731) 554-7202. Fax: +86 (731) 554 7220. Email: hnradio@163.com; (news channel, relayed on shortwave) hnradio@public.cs.hn.cn. Web: (includes on-demand and streaming audio) www.hnradio.com; (news channel, relayed on shortwave) www.hnradio.com/hnradio/weixing/weixing.htm; (streaming audio) www.hnradio.com/ssst/index.htm. Rarely replies.

☞**Nei Menggu (Inner Mongolia) People's Broadcasting Station**, 19 Xinhua Dajie, Hohhot, Nei Menggu 010058, China. Email: nmrb@nmrb.com.cn. Web: (includes streaming audio) www.nmrb.cn. Replies irregularly, mainly to correspondence in Chinese.

☞**Qinghai People's Broadcasting Station**, 96 Kunlun Lu, Xining, Qinghai 810001, China. Email: qhradio@sina.com. Web: (includes streaming audio) www.qhradio.com. Contact: Technical Department. Verifies reception reports in Chinese or English. $1 helpful.

Radio Television Hong Kong, C.P.O Box 70200, Kowloon, Hong Kong, China. Provides weather reports for the South China Sea Yacht Race (*see* www.rhkyc.org.hk./chinacoastraceweek.htm) on 3940 kHz.

CAPE D'AGUILAR HF STATION: P.O. Box 9896, GPO Hong Kong, China. Phone: +852 2888-1128; (station manager) +852 2888-1122; (assistant engineer) +852 2888-1130. Fax: +852 2809 2434. Contact: K.C. Liu, Station Manager; (technical) Lam Chi Keung, Assistant Engineer. Provides transmission facilities for weather reports to the South China Sea Yacht Race (*see*, above).

☞**Shaanxi People's Broadcasting Station**, 336 Chang'an Nanlu, Xi'an, Shaanxi 710061, China. Web: (includes streaming audio) www.sxradio.com.cn. Replies irregularly to correspondence in Chinese.

Sichuan People's Broadcasting Station, 119-1 Hongxing Zhonglu, Chengdu, Sichuan 610017, China. Replies occasionally.

Voice of China (Zhonghua zhi Sheng). The First Program of Central People's Broadcasting Station—China National Radio (*see*).

☞**Voice of Jinling** (Jinling zhi Sheng), P.O. Box 268, Nanjing, Jiangsu 210002, China; (street address) 8 Si Tze-Tang Lane, Nanjing, Jiangsu 210002, China. Phone: +86 (25) 8465-2900, +86 (25) 8465-2905. Fax: +86 (25) 8441 3235. Email: vojl@163.com; (Liu) liuruoy@hotmail.com. Web: www.vojradio.com; (streaming audio) mms://vod.jsgd.com.cn/audio0. Contact: [Ms.] Ruoyi Liu, Announcer/Reporter. Free stickers and calendars, plus Chinese-language color station brochure. Replies to correspondence in Chinese or English. Voice of Jinling is the Taiwan Service of Jiangsu People's Broadcasting Station.

Voice of Pujiang (Pujiang zhi Sheng), P.O. Box 3064, Shanghai 200002, China. Phone: +86 (21) 6208-2797. Fax: +86 (21) 6208 2850. Replies irregularly to correspondence in Chinese or English.

☞**Voice of the Strait** (Haixia zhi Sheng), P.O. Box 187, Fuzhou, Fujian 350012, China. Email: (English) vos@am666.net. Web: (includes streaming audio) www.vos.com.cn. Replies irregularly to correspondence in Chinese or English.

☞**Xinjiang People's Broadcasting Station**, 84 Tuanjie Lu, Urümqi, Xinjiang 830044, China. Phone: +86 (991) 256-0089. Email: mw738@21cn.com. Web: (includes on-demand and streaming audio) www.xjbs.com.cn. Contact: Editorial Office. Free tourist booklet, postcards and used Chinese stamps. Replies in Chinese to correspondence in Chinese or English. Verifies reception reports. $1 or 1 IRC helpful.

Xizang People's Broadcasting Station, 180 Beijing Zhonglu, Lhasa, Xizang 850000, China. Phone: (director) +86 (891) 681-9516; (technical division) +86 (891) 681-9521; (technical manager) +86 (891) 681-9525; (chief engineer) +86 (891) 681-9529. Phone/Fax: (general) +86 (891) 682-7910. Email: xzzbs2003@yahoo.com.cn. Web: www.tibetradio.cn. Contact: Mo Shu-ji, Director; (technical) Tuo Bao-shen, Technical Manager; Wang Yong (Chief Engineer). Chinese or Tibetan preferred, since correspondence in English is processed by freelance translators hired only when accumulated mail reaches a critical mass. Return postage required. Sometimes announces itself in English as "China Tibet Broadcasting Company" or "Tibet China Broadcasting Station."

"HOLY TIBET" ENGLISH PROGRAM: Foreign Affairs Office, China Tibet People's Broadcasting Company, 41 Beijing Middle Road, Lhasa, Xizang 850000, China. Phone: +86 (891) 681-9541. Contact: Ms.Tse Ring Dekye, Producer/Announcer. Two IRCs requested. Verifies reception reports.

☞**Yunnan People's Broadcasting Station**, 73 Renmin Xilu, Central Building of Broadcasting and TV, Kunming, 650031 Yunnan, China. Phone: +86 (871) 531-0270. Fax: +86 (871) 531 0360. Web: (includes streaming audio from music channel, not available on shortwave) www.ynradio.com.cn. Contact: Sheng Hongpeng or F.K. Fan. Free Chinese-language brochure on Yunnan Province, but no QSL cards. $1 or return postage helpful. Replies irregularly to correspondence in Chinese, and sometimes English.

CHINA (TAIWAN)   World Time +8

China Radio, 53 Min Chuan West Road 9th Floor, Taipei 10418, Taiwan, Republic of China. Phone: +886 (2) 2598-1009. Fax: +886 (2) 2598 8348. Email: readams@usa.net. Contact: Richard E. Adams, Station Director. Verifies reception reports. A religious broadcaster, sometimes referred to as "True Light Station," transmitting via leased facilities in Petropavlovsk-Kamchatskiy, Russia.

☞**Fu Hsing Broadcasting Station**, 5 Lane 280, Section 5, Chungshan North Road, Taipei 111, Taiwan, Republic of China. Email: fushinge@ms63.hinet.net. Web: (includes streaming audio) www.fhbs.com.tw. Contact: Xieyi Zhao, Station Manager. Free key rings and other small souvenirs. Replies to correspondence in Chinese or English and verifies reception reports. Return postage not required.

☞**Radio Taiwan International (RTI)**, P.O. Box 123-199, Taipei 11199, Taiwan, Republic of China; (street address) 55 Pei-An Road, Taipei 104, Taiwan, Republic of China. Phone: +886 (2) 2885-6168, X-752 or 753; (English) X-385 or 387; (French) X-386; (German) X-382; (Japanese) X-328; (Spanish) X-384. Fax: +886 (2) 2885 0023; (European languages) +886 (2) 2886 7088; (Japanese) +886 (2) 2885 2254. Email: (general) rti@rti.org.tw; (English) prog@rti.org.tw; (French) fren@rti.org.tw; (German) deutsch@rti.org.tw; (Japanese) jpn@rti.org.tw. Web: (includes on-demand

and streaming audio) www.rti.org.tw. Contact: (general) Wayne Wang Tao-Fang, Chief of International Affairs Section; (administration) Lin Feng-Jeng, Chairman; (technical) Peter Lee, Manager, Engineering Department. Free stickers. May send publications and an occasional surprise gift. Broadcasts to the Americas are relayed via WYFR's Okeechobee site in the USA. Also uses relay facilities in France, Germany and the United Kingdom.

BANGKOK OFFICE: P.O. Box 44 PorNorFor Trairat Bangkhen Bangkok 10223 Thailand.

BERLIN OFFICE: Postfach 309243, D-10760 Berlin, Germany.

DAKAR OFFICE: B.P. 6867, Dakar, Senegal.

HANOI OFFICE: G.P.O. Box 104 Hanoi, Vietnam.

MOSCOW OFFICE: 24/2Tverskaya St., Korpus 1, gate 4, 3rd Fl, 103050 Moscow, Russia. Contact: Chang Yu-tang.

NEW DELHI OFFICE: P.O. Box 4914, Safdarjung Enclave, New Delhi, 110 029 India.

SURABAYA OFFICE: P.O. Box 1024, Surabaya, 60008 Indonesia.

Trans World Broadcasting Ministry, 467 Chih Sien 1st Road 7/F, Kaohsiung 800, Taiwan, Republic of China. Phone: +886 (7) 235-9223/4. Fax: +886 (7) 235 9220. Email: letter@twbm.org.tw. Web: (includes on-demand audio) www.twbm.org.tw. Contact: Naishang Kuo, Manager; Daosheng Yao, Recording Engineer. Broadcasts via facilities of Radio Taiwan International (*see*).

NORTH AMERICAN OFFICE: 1 Spruce Street, Millbrae CA 94030 USA. Phone: +1 (925) 283-0210; (toll-free outside San Francisco Bay area) 1-866-235-224. Fax: +1 (650) 794 0172. Email: contact@twbm.com.

Voice of Han, B Building 5F, 3 Hsin-Yi Road, Sec.1, Taipei, Taiwan, Republic of China. Phone: +886 (2) 2321-5053. Fax: +886 (2) 2393 0970. Email: tony257@ms55.hinet.net. Web: (includes streaming audio) www.voh.com.tw. Contact: Tony Tu.

Voice of Kuanghua—the Mainland Service of Voice of Han (*see*).

CLANDESTINE

Clandestine broadcasts are often subject to abrupt change or termination. Being operated by anti-establishment political and/or military organizations, these groups tend to be suspicious of outsiders' motives. Thus, they are more likely to reply to contacts from those who communicate in the station's native tongue, and who are perceived to be at least somewhat favorably disposed to their cause. Most will provide, upon request, printed matter on their cause, though not necessarily in English. For detailed information on clandestine stations, refer to one of the following Internet sites:

ClandestineRadio.com (www.ClandestineRadio.com) specializes in background information on these stations and is organized by region and target country.

Clandestine Radio Watch (www.schoechi.de) contains clandestine radio information plus a twice monthly report on the latest news and developments affecting the study of clandestine radio.

"Andenet LeDemocracy Radio," Andenet Voice, C/O KNA Vice Chairman Office, P.O. Box 94509, Pasadena CA 91109-4509 USA. Email: andenetadmin@andenet.com. Web: (includes on-demand audio) www.andenet.com. Produced by the United States support group of Ethiopia's KINIJIT opposition party.

"Al Mustaqbal"—*see* USA

"Coalition Maritime Forces (CMF) Radio One"—*see* INTERNATIONAL WATERS

"Degar Radio," Montagnard Foundation, Inc., P.O. Box 171114, Spartanburg SC 29301 USA. Phone: +1 (864) 576-0698. Fax: +1 (864) 595 1940. Email: ksorpo@yahoo.com. Web: (Montagnard Foundation parent organization) www.montagnard-foundation.org. Contact: Kok Sor, President, Montagnard Foundation. Mint stamps or $1 helpful.

"Dejen Radio" (when operating), Liberty Bell Communications, Inc., P.O. Box 792, Indianapolis IN 46206-0792 USA. Email: dejen@ethiopiancommentator.com. Web: (on-demand audio) www.ethiopiancommentator.com/dejenradio. Contact: Hailemariam Adebe, President, Liberty Bell Communications, Inc. Replies irregularly.

"Democratic Voice of Burma" ("Democratic Myanmar a-Than"), P.O. Box 6720, St. Olavs Plass, N-0130 Oslo, Norway. Phone: (Director/Chief Editor) +47 (22) 868-486; (Aministration) +47 (22) 868-472. Email: (general) comment@dvb.no; (Director) director@dvb.no; (technical problems) comments@dvb.no. Web: (includes on-demand audio) www.dvb.no. Contact: (general) Dr. Anng Kin, Listener Liaison; Aye Chan Naing, Daily Editor; (administration) Harn Yawnghwe, Director; Daw Khin Pyone, Manager; (technical) Saw Neslon Ku, Studio Technician; Petter Bernsten; or Technical Dept. Norwegian kroner requested for a reply, but presumably Norwegian mint stamps would also suffice. Programs produced by Burmese democratic movements, as well as professional and independent radio journalists, to provide informational and educational services for the democracy movement inside and outside Burma. Opposes the current Myanmar government. Transmitted originally via facilities in Norway, but more recently has broadcast from sites in Germany, Madagascar and Central Asia.

"Freedom Broadcast for North Korea"—*see* Radio Free North Korea

"Furusato no Kaze"—*see* JAPAN

"Information Radio" (when operating), 193rd Special Operations Wing, 81 Constellation Court, Middletown PA 17057 USA. Email: (Public Affairs Officer) pa.193sow@paharr.ang.af.mil. Web: (193rd Special Operation Wing parent organization) www.paharr.ang.af.mil. Contact: Public Affairs Officer. Psy-ops station operated by the 193rd Special Operations Wing of the Pennsylvania Air National Guard.

"Minghui Radio." Web: (includes on-demand audio) www.mhradio.org. Via leased facilities in Taiwan, and supports the Falun Dafa organization.

"Minivan Radio" (when operating), 64 Milford Street, Salisbury SP1 2BP, United Kingdom. Phone: +94 77757-1409, +960 777-7037. Email: info@minivanradio.net. Web: (includes on-demand audio) www.minivanradio.net. Contact: Monica Michie. Return postage helpful. Promotes human rights in the Maldives and is opposed to the present government. Via Germany's T-Systems Media & Broadcast (*see*).

"Moj Them Radio" (Hmoob Moj Them), P.O. Box 75666, Saint Paul MN 55175-0666 USA. Phone: +1 (952) 885-3274. Email: hmoob@mojthem.com, info@mojthem.com. Web: (includes on-demand audio) www.mojthem.com. Via Taiwan.

"National Radio of the Democratic Saharan Arab Republic"—*see* Radio Nacional de la República Arabe Saharaui Democrática, Western Sahara.

"Nihon no Kaze"—see JAPAN

"North Korea Mission Radio." Phone: +82 (2) 796-8846. Fax: +82 (2) 792 7567. Email: main@cornerstone.or.kr. Web: www.cornerstone.or.kr.

NORTH AMERICAN OFFICE: Cornerstone Ministries International, P.O. Box 4002, Tustin CA 92781 USA. Phone: +1 (714) 569-0042. Fax: +1 (714) 569-0043. Email: info@cornerstoneusa.org. Web: (under construction) www.cornerstoneusa.org.

"Quê Huong Radio"—see USA

☞**"Open Radio for North Korea,"** ("Yollin Pukhan Pangsong"), 3901 Fair Ridge Drive, Fairfax VA 22033 USA. Phone: +1 (202) 246-2571; (South Korea) +82 (10) 7151-2765. Email: nkradio@nkradio.com. Web: (includes on-demand audio) www.nkradio.com. Contact: Tae Keung Ha, Executive Director.

☞**"Radio Anternacional,"** BM Box 1499, London WC1N 3XX, United Kingdom. Phone: +44 (20) 8962-2707. Fax: +44 (20) 8346 2203. Email: radio7520@yahoo.com; (Majedi) azarmajedi@yahoo.com. Web: (includes on-demand audio) www.radio-international.org. Contact: Ms. Azar Majedi. Broadcasts via a transmitter in Moldova. Has ties to the Worker-Communist Party of Iran.

☞**"Radio Democracy Shorayee."** Email: info@radioshora.org. Web: (includes on-demand audio) www.radioshora.org. Verifies reception reports. Opposes the government of Iran.

"Radio Free Afghanistan"—see USA

☞**"Radio Free Chosun."** Web: (includes archived audio of most recent broadcast) http://rfchosun.org, (English) http://rfchosun.org/eng.

"Radio Free North Korea" ("Jayu Pukhan Pangsong"), Room 502, Sinjeong Building, Sinjeong 7 dong 210-16, Yengcheong-gu, Seoul, Republic of Korea. Phone: +82 (2) 2652-8350, +82 (2) 2699-0977. Fax: +82 (2) 2652 8349, +82 (2) 2699 0978. Web: www.freenk.net.

"Radio Freedom, Voice of the Ogadeni People"—see "Radio Xoriyo"

☞**"Radio Insurgente."** Email: online form. Web: (includes on-demand audio) www.radioinsurgente.org. Station of the Mexican "Ejército Zapatista de Liberación National."

"Radio International"—see "Radio Anternacional"

"Radio Nacional de la República Arabe Saharaui Democrática"—see WESTERN SAHARA

☞**"Radio Payam-e Dost"** (Bahá'í Radio International), P.O. Box 765, Great Falls VA 22066 USA. Phone: +1 (703) 671-8888. Fax: +1 (301) 292 6947. Email: payam@bahairadio.org. Web: (includes on-demand audio) www.bahairadio.org. Does not verify reception reports.

"Radio Racja"—see POLAND

☞**"Radio República,"** P.O. Box 110235, Hialeah FL 33011 USA. Email: info@radiorepublica.org. Web: (includes streaming audio) www.radiorepublica.org. Broadcasts are produced by the Florida-based "Directorio Democrático Cubano," and are partly funded by the U.S. government. Via WRMI (see USA) and transmitters in Germany and the United Kingdom.

"Radio Voice of the People"—see ZIMBABWE

"Radio VOP"—see ZIMBABWE

☞**"Radio Xoriyo,"** ("Halkani wa Radio Xoriyo, Codkii Ummadda Odageniya"). Email: ogaden@yahoo.com (some verifications received from these addresses). If these fail, try webmaster@ogaden.com. Web: (archived audio of most recent broadcast; click on "Radio Xoriyo") www.ogaden.com. Broadcasts are supportive of the Ogadenia National Liberation Front, and hostile to the Ethiopian government. Via Germany's T-Systems Media & Broadcast (see).

"Radio Waaberi" (if reactivated), 5529 Walnut Blossom Dr. #5, San Jose CA 95123 USA. Email: (Ali Gulaid) alimardhal@yahoo.com. Web: (includes on-demand audio) www.radiowaaberi.org. Contact: Ali Gulaid, President. A Somali broadcast to East Africa via Germany's T-Systems Media & Broadcast (see).

☞**"Radio Zamaneh,"** P.O. Box 92027, 1090 AA Amsterdam, Netherlands; (street address) Linnaeusstraat 35-F, 1093 EE Amsterdam, Netherlands. Email: contact@radiozamaneh.com, info@radiozamaneh.com. Web: (includes streaming audio) www.radiozamaneh.com. Contact: Medhi Jami, Director. Verifies reception reports (including those sent by email) with a QSL card.

"Shiokaze"—see JAPAN

☞**"Sound of Hope"**

TAIWAN OFFICE: Sound of Hope Radio Network, 42 Xingda Road, South District, Taichung 402, Taiwan, Republic of China. Contact: Yue Chen, Listeners' Service Department.

NORTH AMERICAN OFFICE: Sound of Hope Radio Network, 2520 Wyandotte Street - Suite A, Mountain View CA 94043 USA. Phone: +1 (866) 432-7764. Fax: +1 (415) 276 5861. Email: contact@soundofhope.org. Web: (includes on-demand audio) www.soundofhope.org.

Via leased facilities in Taiwan, and supports the Falun Dafa organization.

"Sudan Radio Service"—see USA

☞**"SW Radio Africa,"** P.O. Box 243, Borehamwood, Herts., WD6 4WA, United Kingdom. Phone: +44 (20) 8387-1441. Email: (technical, including reception reports) tech@swradioafrica.com; (Jackson) gerry@swradioafrica.com. Web: (includes on-demand and streaming audio) www.swradioafrica.com. Contact: [Ms.] Gerry Jackson, Station Manager; (technical) Keith Farquharson, Technical Manager. Return postage helpful. Run by exiled Zimbabweans in the United Kingdom, and opposes the Mugabe government.

☞**"Tensae Ethiopia Voice of Unity,"** P.O.Box 2945, Washington DC 20013 USA. Phone/Fax: +1 (206) 339 9297. Email: tensae.ethiopia@gmail.com. Web: (includes on-demand audio) www.tensae.net. Broadcasts via a transmitter in western Russia.

☞**"Voice of Biafra International,"** 1629 K Street NW, Suite 300, Washington DC 20036 USA. Phone: +1 (202) 508-3795. Fax: +1 (202) 508 3759. Email: biafrafoundation@yahoo.com; (Nkwocha) oguchi@mbay.net. Web: (includes on-demand audio) www.biafraland.com/vobi.htm. Contact: Oguchi Nkwocha, M.D. A project of the Biafra Foundation and the Biafra Actualization Forum. Formerly via South Africa's Sentech facilities, but in summer 2007 switched to a transmitter of World Harvest Radio (see) in the United States.

"Voice of China" ("Zhongguo zhi Yin"), P.O. Box 273538, Concord CA 94527 USA; or (street address) 2261 Morello Avenue - Suite A, Pleasant Hill, California 94523 USA. Web: www.china21century.org/default.asp?menu=xu (click on "VOC"). Financial support from the Foundation for China in the 21st Century. Transmits via facilities in Taiwan.

SPONSORING ORGANIZATION: Foundation for China in the 21st Century, P.O. Box 11696, Berkeley CA 94701 USA. Email: info@china21century.org.

"Voice of China Reborn." Email: china@vocr.org.

"Voice of Meselna Delina" ("Dimtsi Meselna Delina"), Tesfa Delina Foundation, Inc., 17326 Edwards Road, Suite A-230, Cerritos CA 90703 USA. Email: info@delina.org. Web: http://vodm.asmarino.com; (Tesfa Delina Foundation parent organization) www.delina.org. Opposed to the current Eritrean government.

☎**"Voice of Democratic Eritrea International"** ("Sawt Eritrea al-Dimuqratiya-Sawtu Jabhat al-Tahrir al-Eritrea"), Postfach 1946, D-65409 Rüsselsheim, Germany. If this fails, try the ELF-RC office, below. Phone: +49 (228) 356-181. Web: (on-demand audio) www.nharnet.com/Radio/radiopage.htm. Contact: Seyoum O. Michael, Member of Executive Committee, ELF-RC; Neguse Tseggon. Station of the Eritrean Liberation Front-Revolutionary Council, hostile to the government of Eritrea. Via T-Systems Media & Broadcast (see), in Germany.

ELF-RC PARENT ORGANIZATION: ELF-RC Office, Neue-Mainzer Str. 24, D-60311 Frankfurt am Main, Germany. Phone: +49 (69) 2424-8583. Phone/Fax: +49 (69) 2424-8637. Web: www.nharnet.com.

"Voice of Ethiopian Unity"—see "Voice of the Democratic Path of Ethiopian Unity

"Voice of Iranian Kurdistan"—see "Voice of Kurdistan"

"Voice of Iraqi Kurdistan"—see IRAQ

"Voice of Jammu Kashmir Freedom" ("Sadai Hurriyati Jammu Kashmir"), P.O. Box 102, Muzaffarabad, Azad Kashmir, via Pakistan. Contact: Programme Manager. Pro-Moslem and favors Azad Kashmiri independence from India. Believed to transmit via facilities of Radio Pakistan. Return postage not required, and replies to correspondence in English.

☎**"Voice of Komala"** (when operating), c/o Representation of Komala Abroad, Postfach 800272, D-51002 Köln, Germany; Phone/Fax: (North America) +1 (561) 760 5814. Email: komala_radio@hotmail.com. Web: (includes on-demand audio) http://radio.komala.org. Replies to correspondence in English.

☎**"Voice of Kurdistan"** (formerly "Voice of Iranian Kurdistan"). Fax: +1 (717) 326 7615. Email: info@radiokurdistan.net. Web: (includes on-demand audio) www.radiokurdistan.net. For further contact, try one of the PDKI (Democratic Party of Iranian Kurdistan parent organization) offices, below.

PDKI INTERNATIONAL BUREAU: AFK, Boîte Postale 102, F-75623 Paris Cedex 13, France. Phone: +33 (1) 4585-6431. Fax: +33 (1) 4585 2093. Email: pdkiran@club-internet.fr. Web: www.pdk-iran.org. Contact: Khosrow Abdollahi. Replies to correspondence in English.

PDKI CANADA BUREAU: P.O. Box 29010, London, Ontario N6K 4L9, Canada. Phone/Fax: +1 (519) 680-7784. Email: pdkicanada@pdki.org. Web: www.pdki.org.

"Voice of Mesopotamia" ("Dengê Mezopotamya") Phone: +32 (53) 648-827/29. Fax: +32 (53) 680 779. Email: info@denge-mezopotamya.com. Web: www.denge-mezopotamya.com. Contact: Ahmed Dicle, Director.

KURDISTAN WORKERS PARTY (PKK, also known as Kongra-Gel, KGK) SPONSORING ORGANIZATION: Web: www.kongra-gel.com.

"Voice of Oromia Independence." Email: rswo2006@gmail.com, or online form. Web: (includes on-demand audio) www.awofio.com/Radio-rswo.htm. Broadcast of the Front for Independence of Oromia (Adda Walabummaa Oromiyaa) via a transmitter in western Russia.

☎**"Voice of Oromo Liberation"** ("Sagalee Bilisummaa Oromoo"), Postfach 510610, D-13366 Berlin, Germany; (street address) SBO, Prinzenallee 81, D-13357 Berlin, Germany. Phone/Fax: +49 (30) 494 3372. Email: sbo13366@aol.com. Web: (includes on-demand audio) www.oromoliberationfront.org/sbo.html. Contact: Taye Teferah, European Coordinator. Occasionally replies to correspondence in English or German. Return postage required. Station of the Oromo Liberation Front of Ethiopia, an Oromo nationalist organization. Via Germany's T-Systems Media & Broadcast (see).

☎**"Voice of Patriots"** ("Ye-Arbegna Dimts"). Web: (EPPF parent organization; includes on-demand audio) www.eppf.info. Broadcast of the Ethiopian People's Patriotic Front.

"Voice of the Communist Party of Iran" ("Seda-ye Hezb-e Komunist-e Iran")

COMMUNIST PARTY OF IRAN SPONSORING ORGANIZATION: C.D.C.R.I., Box 704 45, S-107 25 Stockholm, Sweden. Phone/Fax: +46 (8) 786-8054. Email: cpi@cpiran.org. Web: www.cpiran.org.

"Voice of the Democratic Alliance"
Web: (Eritrean Democratic Alliance parent organization) www.erit-alliance.org. Airs via the facilities of Radio Ethiopia, and is opposed to the Eritrean government.

☎**"Voice of the Democratic Path of Ethiopian Unity,"** Finote Democracy, P.O. Box 88675, Los Angeles CA 90009 USA; or Finote Democracy, P.O. Box 73337, Washington DC 20056 USA. Fax: (Washington) +1 (202) 291 7645. Email: efdpu@aol.com. Web: (includes on-demand audio) www.finote.org. Via Germany's T-Systems Media & Broadcast (see).

"Voice of the Kurdistan People"—see IRAQ

"Voice of the Iranian Revolution"—same contact details as "Voice of the Communist Party of Iran" (see).

"Voice of the Worker" ("Seda-ye Kargar") (when operating)

WORKER-COMMUNIST PARTY OF IRAN (WPI) PARENT ORGANIZATION: Web: www.wpiran.org.

WPI INTERNATIONAL OFFICE: WPI, Office of International Relations, Suite 730, 28 Old Brompton Road, South Kensington, London SW7 3SS, United Kingdom. Phone: +44 (77) 7989-8968. Fax: +44 (87) 0136 2182. Email: wpi.international.office@ukonline.co.uk, markazi@ukonline.co.uk.

☎**"Voice of Tibet"**

ADMINISTRATIVE OFFICE: Voice of Tibet Foundation, St. Olavsgate 24, N-0166 Oslo, Norway. Phone: (administration) +47 2211-2700. Fax: +47 2211 5474. Email: voti@online.no; (Norbu) votibet@online.no. Web: (includes on-demand audio) www.vot.org. Contact: Øystein Alme, Project Manager [sometimes referred to as "Director"]; Chophel Norbu, Project Coordinator.

MAIN EDITORIAL OFFICE: Voice of Tibet, Narthang Building, Gangchen Kyishong, Dharamsala-176 215 H.P., India. Phone: +91 (1892) 228-179/222, +91 (1892) 222 384. Fax: +91 (1892) 224 957. Email: (editor-in-chief) voteditor@yahoo.com. Contact: Karma Yeshi Nazee, Editor-in-Chief; Tenzin Peldon, Assistant Editor.

A joint venture of the Norwegian Human Rights House, Norwegian Tibet Committee and World-View International. Programs focus on Tibetan culture, education, human rights and news from Tibet. Opposed to Chinese control of Tibet. A colorful QSL card is issued from the office in Dharamsala. Return postage helpful. Broadcasts via transmitters in Madagascar and Tajikistan.

"Voz de la Resistencia" (when operating)
Email: (FARC-EP parent organization) elbarcino@laneta.
apc.org (updated transmission schedules and QSLs
available from this address, but correspond in Spanish).
Contact: Olga Lucía Marín, Comisión Internacional de las
FARC-EP. Station of the Fuerzas Armadas Revolucionarias
de Colombia - Ejercito del Pueblo.
◎"Zena Tewahedo," EOTC Holy Synod, P.O. Box 7097,
Los Angeles CA 90007 USA. Email: eotcholysynod@eotc
holysynod.org. Web: (includes on-demand audio) www.
eotcholysynod.org/Radio.html. Broadcast of theHoly
Synod of the Ethiopian Orthodox Tewahedo Church
(EOTC) in Exile.

COLOMBIA   World Time –5

NOTE: Colombia, the country, is always spelled with two
o's. It should never be written as "Columbia."
Alcaravan Radio—*see* La Voz de Tu Conciencia
La Voz de Tu Conciencia, a/c Colombia para Cristo,
Calle 44 No. 13-67, Bogotá, D.C., Colombia. Phone:
+57 (1) 338-4716. Email: contacto@fuerzadepaz.com,
libreria@fuerzadepaz.com; (Stendal, specialized technical correspondence only) martinstendal@etb.net.co. Web:
www.fuerzadepaz.com/emisoras.asp. Contact: Russel
Martín Stendal, Administrador; Rafael Rodríguez R., QSL
Manager. Station is actually located in Puerto Lleras, in
the guerrilla "combat zone." Sometimes carries program-
ming from sister stations Alcaravan Radio (1530 kHz) or
Marfil Estéreo (88.8 MHz). Replies to correspondence in
English or Spanish. Return postage helpful. Free stickers
and paper pennant.
La Voz del Guaviare, Carrera 22 con Calle 9, San José
del Guaviare, Colombia. Phone: +57 (986) 840-153/4. Fax:
+57 (986) 840 102. Email: mercorio@col3.telecom.com.co.
Contact: Luis Fernando Román Robayo, Director General.
Replies slowly to correspondence in Spanish.
Marfil Estéreo—*see* La Voz de Tu Conciencia
Radio Líder (when operating), Calle 45 No. 13-70, Bo-
gotá, Colombia. Phone: +57 (1) 323-1500. Fax: +57 (1)
288 4020. Email: radiolider@cadenamelodia.com. Web:
www.cadenamelodia.com. Rarely replies. A station of the
Cadena Melodía network.

CONGO (DEMOCRATIC REPUBLIC)   World
Time +1 Western, including Kinshasa; +2 Eastern

Radio Bukavu (when operating), B.P. 475, Bukavu, Demo-
cratic Republic of the Congo. $1 or return postage required.
Replies slowly. Correspondence in French preferred.
Radio CANDIP, B.P. 373, Bunia, Democratic Republic of
Congo. Letters should preferably be sent via registered
mail. $1 or return postage required. Correspondence in
French preferred.
Radio Kahuzi. Email: radiokahuzi@kivu-online.com. Web:
www.besi.org. Contact: Richard & Kathy McDonald. Veri-
fies reception reports by email.
HOME OFFICE: Believers Express Service, Inc. (BESI),
P.O. Box 115, San Marcos CA 92079 USA. Phone/Fax:
+1 (760) 598-1190. Email: radiokahuzi@sbcglobal.net.
Contact: Barbara Smith, Home Office Secretary. Verifies
reception reports.
◎Radio Okapi, 12 Av. des Aviateurs, Kinshasa, Gombe,
Democratic Republic of the Congo. Email: online form.

Web: (includes on-demand and streaming audio) www.
radiookapi.net. A joint project involving the United Nations
Mission in the Democratic Republic of the Congo (MONUC)
and the Swiss-based Fondation Hirondelle.
MONUC:
(USA) P.O. Box 4653, Grand Central Station, New York NY
10163-4653 USA. Phone: +1 (212) 963-0103. Fax: +1 (212)
963 0205. Email: info@monuc.org. Web: www.monuc.org.
Verifies reception reports.
(Congo) 12 Av. des Aviateurs, Kinshasa, Gombe, Democratic
Republic of the Congo; or B.P. 8811, Kinshasa 1, Democratic
Republic of the Congo. Phone: +243 81- 890-6747. Fax:
+243 890 56208. Contact: Georges Schleger, VE2EK, Communications Officer & Head of Technical Services.
FONDATION HIRONDELLE: Avenue du Temple 19C, CH
1012-Lausanne, Switzerland. Phone: +41 (21) 654-2020.
Fax: +41 (21) 654 2021. Email: info@hirondelle.org. Web:
www.hirondelle.org. Contact: Dennis Roshier, Administrator. Verifies reception reports.

CONGO (REPUBLIC)   World Time +1

Radiodiffusion Nationale Congolaise (also announces
as "Radio Nationale" or "Radio Congo"), Tèlèdiffusion du
Congo, B.P. 2912, Brazzaville, Congo. Contact: Félix Los-
sombo, Le Directeur Administratif et Financier; Gaspard
Bemba, Le Directeur de l'Inspection Technique des Réseaux
et de la Qualité des Services; Jean Médard Bokatola. Return
postage required, but smallest denomination currency
notes (e.g. $1US or 1 euro) reportedly cannot be changed
into local currency. Replies irregularly to letters in French
(and sometimes, English) sent via registered mail.

COSTA RICA   World Time –6

◎Faro del Caribe—TIFC (when operating), Apartado
2710, 1000 San José, Costa Rica. Phone: +506 226-4358,
+506 227-5048, +506 286-1755. Fax: +506 227-1725.
Email: radio@farodelcaribe.org, 1080@farodelcaribe.org;
(technical) tecnico@farodelcaribe.org. Web: (includes
streaming audio) www.farodelcaribe.org. Contact: Lic.
Ronald Ortiz R., Administrador; (technical) Salvador López,
Ingeniero. Free stickers, pennants, books and bibles. $1
or IRCs helpful. Verifies reception reports in Spanish or
English.
U.S. OFFICE, NONTECHNICAL: Misión Latinoamericana,
P.O. Box 620485, Orlando FL 32862 USA.
Radio Exterior de España—Cariari Relay Station, Cari-
ari de Pococí, Costa Rica. Phone: +506 767-7308, +506
767-7311. Fax: +506 225 2938.
Radio Universidad de Costa Rica (when operating),
Apartado 1-06, 2060 Universidad de Costa Rica, San Pedro
de Montes de Oca, San José, Costa Rica. Phone: (general)
+506 207-4727; (studio) +506 225-3936. Fax: +506 207
5459. Email: radioucr@cariari.ucr.ac.cr. Web: http://cari-
ari.ucr.ac.cr/~radioucr/radioucr. Contact: Marco González
Muñoz; Henry Jones, Locutor de Planta; Nora Garita B.,
Directora. Marco González is a radio amateur, call-sign
TI3AGM. Free postcards, station brochure and stickers.
Replies slowly to correspondence in Spanish or English.
$1 or return postage required.
University Network—*see* USA

Dubrovnik, a recognized historic community within Croatia. Voice of Croatia reaches out daily in English to the Americas, as well as to countrymen in Europe, Australasia, the Americas and the high seas.

Shutterstock/Marina Ljubanovic

CROATIA   World Time +1 (+2 midyear)

Glas Hrvatske (Voice of Croatia), Phone: +385 (1) 634-2601; (Editor-in-Chief) +385 (1) 634-2602. Email: (Croatian) glas.hrvatske@hrt.hr; (English) voiceofcroatia@hrt.hr; (Spanish) vozdecroacia@hrt.hr; (Zlatko Kuretić) zlatko.kuretic@hrt.hr. Web: (includes streaming audio) www.hrt.hr/hr (click on station name) or (direct) www.hrt.hr/hr/glashrvatske/gh.php; (on-demand audio in English and Spanish) www.hrt.hr/audio_clip (choose "Glas Hrvatske" from menu at top left). Contact: Zlatko Kuretić, Editor-in-Chief. Glas Hrvatske is the external service of Croatian Radio.
TRANSMISSION COMPANY: Odašiljači i Veze d.o.o (Transmitters & Communications Ltd)., Ulica grada Vukovara 269d, HR-10000 Zagreb, Croatia. Phone: +385 (1) 6186-000. Fax: +385 (1) 6186 100. Email: nikola.percin@oiv.hr. Web: www.oiv.hr. Contact: Nikola Perčin, Managing Director. This independent state-owned company replaces the former Transmitters and Communications Department of HRT.
SHORTWAVE COORDINATION: Email: mladen.golubic@oiv.hr. Contact: Mladen Golubić.
TRANSMITTING STATION DEANOVEC: P.O. Box 3, HR-10313 Graberje Ivanićko, Croatia. Phone: +385 (1) 2830-533. Fax: +385 (1) 2830 534. Email: dane.pavlic@oiv.hr. Contact: Dane Pavlić, Head of Station. Glas Hrvatske transmits from Deanovec shortwave station for listeners in Europe and the Mediterranean; and via Germany's T-Systems Media & Broadcast (*see*) to Australasia and the Americas.

CUBA   World Time –5 (–4 midyear)

Radio Habana Cuba, Apartado Postal 6240, 10600 La Habana, Cuba. Phone: (general) +53 (7) 878-4954; (English Department) +53 (7) 877-6628. Fax: +53 (7) 870 5810. Email: radiohc@enet.cu; (Arnie Coro) arnie@rhc.cu, coro@enet.cu. Web: (includes on-demand and streaming audio) www.radiohc.cu; (streaming audio) http://multimedia-radio.cubasi.cu. Contact: (general) Lourdes López, Head of Correspondence Department; Isabel García, Director of English Department; (administration) Luis López López, General Director; (technical) Arnaldo Coro Antich, ("Arnie Coro"), Producer, "DXers Unlimited"; Arturo González, Head of Technical Department. Free pennants, stickers, keychains, pins and other small souvenirs. DX Listeners' Club. Free sample *Granma International* newspaper. Contests with various prizes, including trips to Cuba.
Radio Rebelde, Departamento de Relaciones Públicas, Apartado Postal 6277, 10600 La Habana 6, Cuba; (street address) Calle 23 n° 258 entre L y M, El Vedado, 10600 La Habana, Cuba. For technical correspondence (including reception reports), substitute "Servicio de Onda Corta" in place of "Departamento de Relaciones Públicas." Reception reports can also be emailed to Radio Habana Cuba's Arnie Coro (arnie@radiohc.cu) for forwarding to Radio Rebelde. Phone: +53 (7) 831-3514. Fax: +53 (7) 334 270. Web (includes on-demand and streaming audio): www.radiorebelde.com.cu; (streaming audio) http://multimedia-radio.cubasi.cu. Contact: Jorge Luis Martín Cuevas, Jefe de Relaciones Públicas. Replies slowly, with correspondence in Spanish preferred.

CYPRUS   World Time +2 (+3 midyear)

Bayrak Radio International (when operating), BRTK Campus, Dr. Fazil Küçük Boulevard, P.O. Box 417, Lefkosa - T.R.N.C., via Mersin 10, Turkey. Phone: +90 (392) 225-5555. Fax: (general) +90 (392) 225 4581. Email: (general) brt@cc.emu.edu.tr; (technical, including reception reports) tosun@cc.emu.edu.tr. Web: (includes streaming audio) www.brt.gov.nc.tr. Contact: Mustafa Tosun, Head of Transmission Department; Halil Balbaz, Transmitter Manager; Ülfet Kortmaz, Head of Bayrak International; Bertil Wedin, Producer of "Magazine North."
BBC World Service—East Mediterranean Relay Station, P.O. Box 209, Limassol, Cyprus. Contact: Steve Welch. This address for technical matters only. Other correspondence should be sent to the BBC World Service in London (*see*).
Cyprus Broadcasting Corporation, Broadcasting House, P.O. Box 4824, Nicosia 1397, Cyprus; (street address) RIK Street, Athalassa, Nicosia 2120, Cyprus. Phone: +357 (2) 286-2000. Fax: +357 (2) 231 4050. Email: rik@cybc.com.cy. Web: (includes streaming audio from domestic services not on shortwave) www.cybc.com.cy. Contact: (general) Pavlos Soteriades, Director General; Evangella Gregoriou, Head of Public and International Relations; (technical) Andreas Michaelides, Director of Technical Services. Free stickers. Replies irregularly, sometimes slowly. IRC or $1 helpful.

CZECH REPUBLIC   World Time +1 (+2 midyear)

Radio Prague, Czech Radio, Vinohradská 12, 12099 Prague 2, Czech Republic. Phone: +420 (2) 2155-2900; (Czech Department) +420 (2) 2155-2922; (English Department) +420 (2) 2155-2930; (German Department) +420 (2) 2155-2941; (French Department) +420 (2) 2155-2911; (Spanish Department) +420 (2) 2155-2950; (Russian Department) +420 (2) 2155-2964. Phone/Fax: (Oldrich Cip, technical) +420 (2) 2271-5005. Fax: (all languages)

ADDRESSES PLUS 293

+420 (2) 2155 2903. Email: (general) cr@radio.cz; (English Department) english@radio.cz; (German Department) deutsch@radio.cz; (French Department) francais@radio.cz; (Spanish Department) espanol@radio.cz; (Russian Department) rusky@radio.cz; (Program Director) Gerald.Schubert@radio.cz; (Internet Department) cr@radio.cz; (free news texts) robot@radio.cz, writing "Subscribe English" (or other desired language) within the subject line; (technical, chief engineer) cip@radio.cz. Web: (includes on-demand and streaming audio) www.radio.cz. Contact: (general) Marie Pittnerova; Gerald Schubert, Editor-in-Chief; (administration) Miroslav Krupička, Director; (technical) Oldrich Čip, Chief Engineer. Free stickers; also key chains, pens, bookmarks, mouse pads and other souvenirs when available.
RFE-RL—see USA

DIEGO GARCIA—see BRITISH INDIAN OCEAN TERRITORY

DJIBOUTI World Time +3
🔲**Radio Télévision de Djibouti**, Boîte Postale 97, Djibouti, Djibouti; (street address) Avenue Saint Laurent du Var, Djibouti, Djibouti. Phone: +253 352-294. Fax: +253 356 502. Email: (general) rtd@intnet.dj; (technical) rtdtech@intnet.dj. Web: (includes on-demand audio) www.rtd.dj. Contact: (general) Abdi Atteyeh Abdi, Directeur Général; (technical) Yahya Moussed, Chef du Service Technique. Verifies reception reports. Transmission facilities are located at Dorale, about 10 km west of Djibouti City.

DOMINICAN REPUBLIC World Time –4
🔲**Radio Amanecer Internacional**, Apartado Postal 1500, Santo Domingo, Dominican Republic; (street address) Juan Sánchez Ramírez #40, Santo Domingo, Dominican Republic. Phone: +1 (809) 688-5600, +1 (809) 688-5609. Fax: +1 (809) 227 1869. Email: cabina@radioamanecer.org, or online form. Web: (includes streaming audio) www.radioamanecer.org. Contact: (general) Lic. Germán Lorenzo, Director; (technical) Ing. Sócrates Domínguez. $1 or return postage required. Replies slowly to correspondence in Spanish.
Radio Barahona (if reactivated), Apartado 201, Barahona, Dominican Republic; or (street address) Gustavo Mejía Ricart No. 293, Apto. 2-B, Ensanche Quisqueya, Santo Domingo, Dominican Republic. Phone: +1 (809) 524-4040. Fax: +1 (809) 524 5461. Contact: (general) Rodolfo Z. Lama Jaar, Administrador; (technical) Ing. Roberto Lama Sajour, Administrador General. Free stickers. Letters should be sent via registered mail. $1 or return postage helpful. Replies to correspondence in Spanish.
EMPRESAS RADIOFÓNICAS PARENT ORGANIZATION: Empresas Radiofónicas S.A., Apartado Postal 20339, Santo Domingo, Dominican Republic. Phone: +1 (809) 567-9698. Fax: +1 (809) 472-3313. Web: www.suprafm.com.
Radio Cima Cien (if reactivated), Apartado 804, Santo Domingo, Dominican Republic. Fax: +1 (809) 541 1088. Contact: Roberto Vargas, Director. Free pennants, postcards, coins and taped music. Roberto likes collecting stamps and coins.
Radio Cristal Internacional (when operating), Apartado Postal 894, Santo Domingo, Dominican Republic; or

(street address) Calle Pepillo Salcedo No. 18, Altos, Santo Domingo, Dominican Republic. Phone: +1 (809) 565-1460, +1 (809) 566-5411. Fax: +1 (809) 567 9107. Contact: (general) Fernando Hermón Gross, Director de Programas; Margarita Reyes, Secretaria; (administration) Darío Badía, Director General; or Héctor Badía, Director de Administración. Seeks reception reports. Return postage of $2 appreciated.

ECUADOR World Time –5 (–4 sometimes, in times of drought); –6 Galapagos
NOTE: IRCs are exchangeable only in the cities of Quito and Guayaquil, so enclosing $2 for return postage may be helpful when writing to stations in other locations.
🔲**HCJB Global Voice, The Voice of the Andes**
STATION: Casilla 17-17-691, Quito, Ecuador. Phone: (general) +593 (2) 226-6808; (frequency management) +593 (2) 226-6808 (X-4627). Fax: (general) +593 (2) 226 7263; (frequency manager) +593 (2) 226 3267. Email: (general) info@hcjb.org.ec; (Graham) agraham@hcjb.org.ec; (frequency management) irops@hcjb.org.ec; (language sections) format is language@hcjb.org.ec; so to reach, say, the Spanish Department, it would be spanish@hcjb.org.ec. Web: (English, includes on-demand audio and online reception report form) www.hcjbglobal.org; (Spanish, includes on-demand and streaming audio) www.vozandes.org. Contact: (general) Spanish [or other language] Department; (administration) Jim Estes, HCJB Regional Director; Doug Weber, Radio Director; Allen Graham, Frequency Manager. Free religious brochures, calendars, stickers and pennants. IRC or $1 required.
INTERNATIONAL HEADQUARTERS: HCJB Global, P.O. Box 39800, Colorado Springs CO 80949-9800 USA; (street address) 1065 Garden of the Gods Rd., Colorado Springs CO 80907 USA. Phone: +1 (719) 590-9800. Fax: +1 (719) 590 9801. Email: info@hcjbglobal.org; (Hirst) jhirst@hcjbglobal.org. Web: www.hcjbglobal.org. Contact: Jon Hirst, Communications Director; Andrew Braio, Public Information; (administration) Richard D. Jacquin, Director, International Operations. Various items sold via U.S. address—catalog available. This address is not a mail drop, so listeners' correspondence, except those concerned with purchasing HCJB items, should be directed to the usual Quito address.
ENGINEERING CENTER: HCJB Global Technology Center, 2830 South 17th Street, Elkhart IN 46517-4008 USA. Phone: +1 (574) 970 4252. Fax: +1 (574) 293 9910. Email: info@hcjbtech.org. Web: www.hcjbtech.org. Contact: Dave Pasechnik, Project Manager; Bob Moore, Engineering. This address only for those professionally concerned with the design and manufacture of transmitter and antenna equipment. Listeners' correspondence should be directed to the usual Quito address.
REGIONAL OFFICES: Although HCJB has over 20 regional offices throughout the world, the station wishes that all listener correspondence be directed to the station in Quito, as the regional offices do not serve as mail drops for the station.
HD2IOA, Instituto Oceanográfico de la Armada (INOCAR), Avenida de la Marina, Vía Puerto Marítimo, Código Postal 5940, Guayaquil, Ecuador. HD2IOA is a time signal station operated by Ecuador's Naval Oceanographic Institute. Replies to correspondence in Spanish (and sometimes, English) and verifies reception reports.

INSTITUTO OCEANOGRÁFICO DE LA ARMADA PARENT ORGANIZATION:
Phone: +593 (4) 248-1300. Fax: +593 (4) 248 5166. Email: inocar@inocar.mil.ec. Web: www.inocar.mil.ec.

La Voz de Saquisilí—Radio Libertador (when operating), Calle 24 de Mayo, Saquisilí, Cotopaxi, Ecuador. Phone: +593 (3) 721-035. Contact: Arturo Mena Herrera, Gerente-Propietario. Reception reports actively solicited. Return postage, in the form of $2 or mint Ecuadorian stamps, appreciated; IRCs difficult to exchange. Spanish strongly preferred.

La Voz del Napo, Misión Josefina, Juan Montalvo s/n, Tena, Napo, Ecuador. Phone: +593 (6) 886-356. Email: coljav20@yahoo.es, lavozdelnapo@yahoo.es. Contact: Padre Humberto Dorigatti, Director. Free pennants and stickers. $2 or return postage required. Replies irregularly to correspondence in Spanish or Italian.

La Voz del Upano
STATION: Vicariato Apostólico de Méndez, Misión Salesiana, 10 de Agosto s/n, Macas, Provincia de Morona Santiago, Ecuador. Phone: +593 (7) 505-247. Email: radioupano@easynet.net.ec. Contact: Sra. Leonor Guzmán, Directora. Free pennants and calendars. On one occasion, not necessarily to be repeated, sent tape of Ecuadorian folk music for $2. Otherwise, $2 required. Replies to correspondence in Spanish.
QUITO OFFICE: Procura Salesiana, Equinoccio 623 y Queseras del Medio, Quito, Ecuador. Phone: +593 (2) 255-1012.

Radio Buen Pastor—*see* Radio El Buen Pastor

Radio Chaskis, Jirón Roldos Aguilera y Panamericana Norte, Otavalo, Imbabura, Ecuador; (offices) Calle Bolívar 805 y Juan Montalvo, Otavalo, Imbabura, Ecuador. Phone: +593 (62) 920-922, +593 (62) 920-256. Email: radiochaskis@hotmail.com. Contact: Luis Enrique Cachiguango Cotacachi, Propietario. Welcomes correspondence in Spanish, but replies are irregular because of limited resources.

Radiodifusora Cultural Católica La Voz del Upano—*see* La Voz del Upano, above.

Radiodifusora Cultural, La Voz del Napo—*see* La Voz del Napo, above.

Radio El Buen Pastor, Asociación Cristiana de Indígenas Saraguros (ACIS), Reino de Quito y Azuay, Correo Central, Saraguro, Loja, Ecuador. Phone: +593 (2) 00-146. Contact: (general) Dean Pablo Davis, Sub-director; Segundo Poma, Director; Mark Vogan, OMS Missionary; Mike Schrode, OMS Ecuador Field Director; Juana Guamán, Secretaria; Zoila Vacacela, Secretaria; (technical) Miguel Kelly. $2 or return postage in the form of mint Ecuadorian stamps required, as IRCs are difficult to exchange in Ecuador. Station is keen to receive reception reports; may respond to English, but correspondence in Spanish preferred. $10 required for QSL card and pennant.

Radio Federación Shuar, Casilla 17-01-1422, Quito, Ecuador. Phone/Fax: +593 (2) 250-4264. Contact: Manuel Jesús Vinza Chacucuy, Director; Yurank Tsapak Rubén Gerardo, Director; Prof. Albino M. Utitiaj P., Director de Medios. Return postage or $2 required. Replies irregularly to correspondence in Spanish.

☛**Radio María**, Baquerizo Moreno 281 y Leonidas Plaza, Quito, Ecuador. Phone: +593 (2) 256-4714. Web: (includes streaming audio) www.radiomariaecuador.org. A Catholic radio network currently leasing airtime over La Voz del Napo (*see*), but which is looking into the possiblity of setting up its own shortwave station.

Radio Oriental, Casilla 260, Tena, Napo, Ecuador. Phone: +593 (6) 886-033, +593 (6) 886-388. Contact: Luis Enrique Espín Espinosa, Gerente General. $2 or return postage helpful. Reception reports welcome.

☛**Radio Quito** (when operating), Casilla 17-21-1971, Quito, Ecuador. Phone/Fax: +593 (2) 250 8301. Email: radioquito@ecuadoradio.com. Web: (includes streaming audio) www.elcomercio.com/secciones.asp?seid=329. Contact: Xavier Almeida, Gerente General; José Almeida, Subgerente. Free stickers. Return postage normally required, but occasionally verifies email reports. Replies slowly, but regularly.

EGYPT   World Time +2 (+3 midyear)

WARNING: MAIL THEFT. Feedback from PASSPORT readership indicates that money is sometimes stolen from envelopes sent to Radio Cairo.

Egyptian Radio, P.O. Box 1186, 11511 Cairo, Egypt. Email: ertu@ertu.gov.eg. Web: (under construction) www.ertu.gov.eg; (streaming audio) http://live.sis.gov.eg/live. For additional details, *see* Radio Cairo, below.

Radio Cairo
NONTECHNICAL: P.O. Box 566, Cairo 11511, Egypt. Phone: +20 (2) 677-8945. Fax: +20 (2) 575 9553. Email: (English Service) egyptianoverseas_english@hotmail.com; (Spanish Service) radioelcairoespa@yahoo.com; (Brazilian Service) brazilian_prog@egyptradio.tv. Web: (English Service) www.freewebs.com/overseas-radio; (French Service) http://listen.to/overseas-radio-fra; (Russian Service) http://listen.to/overseas-radio-russia. Contact: Mrs. Amal Badr, Head of English Programme; Mrs. Sahar Kalil, Director of English Service to North America and Producer, "Questions and Answers"; Marwan Khattab; Mrs. Magda Hamman, Secretary. Free stickers, postcards, stamps, maps, papyrus souvenirs, calendars and *External Services of Radio Cairo* book. Free booklet and individually tutored Arabic-language lessons with loaned textbooks from Kamila Abdullah, Director General, Arabic by Radio, Radio Cairo, P.O. Box 325, Cairo, Egypt. Arabic-language religious, cultural and language-learning audio and video tapes from the Egyptian Radio and Television Union sold via Sono Cairo Audio-Video, P.O. Box 2017, Cairo, Egypt; when ordering video tapes, inquire to ensure they function on the television standard (NTSC, PAL or SECAM) in your country. Once replied regularly, if slowly, but recently replies have been increasingly scarce. Comments welcomed about audio quality—*see* TECHNICAL, below. Avoid enclosing money (*see* WARNING, above).

TECHNICAL: Egyptian Radio and Television Union, Broadcast Engineering Sector, Maspero TV Building, P.O. Box 1186, 11511 Cairo, Egypt. Phone/Fax: +20 (2) 2574-6840. Email: (general) freqmeg@yahoo.com; (Lawrence) niveenl@hotmail.com. Contact: Hamdy Emara, Chairman of Engineering Sector; Hamdy Moneer, Head of Engineering & Training; Mrs. Niveen W. Lawrence, Director of Monitoring & Frequency Management. Comments and suggestions on audio quality and level especially welcomed. One PASSPORT reader reported that his letter to this address was returned by the Egyptian postal authorities, but we have not received any other reports of returned mail.

EL SALVADOR   World Time –6

Radio Imperial (when operating), Apartado 56, Sonsonante, El Salvador. Fax: +503 450-0189. Contact: (general) Nubia Ericka García, Directora; Pastor Pedro Mendoza López; (technical) Moisés B. Cruz G., Ingeniero. Replies to correspondence in English or Spanish, and verifies reception reports by fax, if number provided. $1 helpful.

ENGLAND—*see* UNITED KINGDOM

EQUATORIAL GUINEA   World Time +1

Radio Africa, P.O. Box 851, Malabo, Equatorial Guinea. Email: radioafrica@myway.com.
U.S. ADDRESS FOR CORRESPONDENCE AND VERIFICATIONS: Pan American Broadcasting, 2021 The Alameda, Suite 240, San Jose CA 95126-1145 USA. Phone: +1 (408) 996-2033; (toll-free, U.S. only) 1-800-726-2620. Fax: +1 (408) 252 6855. Email: info@panambc.com; (Bernald) gbernald@panambc.com; (Jung) cjung@panambc.com. Web: www.panamericanbroadcasting.com. Contact: (listener correspondence) Elaine Lingard; (general) Mher Sousanian, Office and Sales Administrator; Gene Bernald, President. $1, mint U.S. stamps or 2 IRCs required for a reply.
Radio East Africa—same details as "Radio Africa," above.
Radio Nacional de Guinea Ecuatorial—Bata ("Radio Bata"), Apartado 749, Bata, Río Muni, Equatorial Guinea. Phone: +240 (8) 2592. Fax: +240 (8) 2093. Contact: José Mba Obama, Director; Julián Esono Ela, Programa "Cartas del Oyente". Replies irregularly to correspondence in Spanish.
Radio Nacional de Guinea Ecuatorial—Malabo ("Radio Malabo") (when operating), Apartado 195, Malabo, Isla Bioko, Equatorial Guinea. Phone: +240 (9) 2260. Fax: (general) +240 (9) 2097; (technical) +240 (9) 3122. Contact: (general) Román Manuel Mané-Abaga, Jefe de Programación; Ciprano Somon Suakin; Manuel Sobede, Inspector de Servicios de Radio y TV; (technical) Hermenegildo Moliko Chele, Jefe Servicios Técnicos de Radio y Televisión. $1 or return postage required. Replies irregularly to correspondence in Spanish.

ERITREA   World Time +3

Radio Bana, Adult Education and Media, Ministry of Education, P.O.Box 609, Asmara, Eritrea. Phone: +291 (1) 125-546. Contact: Saada Ahmedin, English Panel. Verifies reception reports.
Radio UNMEE—*see* UNITED NATIONS
⬛Voice of the Broad Masses of Eritrea (Dimtsi Hafash), Ministry of Information, Radio Division, P.O. Box 872, Asmara, Eritrea; or Ministry of Information, Technical Branch, P.O. Box 242, Asmara, Eritrea. Phone: +291 (1) 116-084, +291 (1) 120-497. Fax: +291 (1) 126 747. Email: nesredin@tse.com.er. Web: (includes on-demand audio) www.shabait.com (click on "Dimtsi Hafash"). Contact: Ghebreab Ghebremedhin; Berhane Gerzgiher, Director, Engineering Division. Return postage or $1 helpful. Free information on history of the station and about Eritrea.

ETHIOPIA   World Time +3

Radio Ethiopia: (external service) P.O. Box 654; (domestic service) P.O. Box 1020—both in Addis Ababa, Ethiopia (address your correspondence to "Audience Relations"). Phone: (main office) +251 (1) 116-427, +251 (1) 551-011; (engineering) +251 (1) 200-948. Fax: +251 (1) 552 263. Web: www.angelfire.com/biz/radioethiopia. Contact: (external service, general) Kahsai Tewoldemedhin, Program Director; Ms. Woinshet Woldeyes, Secretary, Audience Relations; Ms. Ellene Mocria, Head of Audience Relations; Yohaness Ruphael, Producer, "Contact"; (administration) Kasa Miliko, Head of Station; (technical) Terefe Ghebre Medhin; Zegeye Solomon. Free stickers and tourist brochures. Poor replier.
⬛Radio Fana (Radio Torch), P.O. Box 30702, Addis Ababa, Ethiopia. Phone: +251 (1) 516-777. Fax: +251 (1) 515 039. Email: rfana@telecom.net.et. Web: (includes on-demand audio) www.radiofana.com. Contact: Woldu Yemessel, General Manager; Mesfin Alemayehu, Head, External Relations; Girma Lema, Head, Planning and Research Department. Station is autonomous and receives its income from non-governmental educational sponsorship.
⬛Voice of the Tigray Revolution (Dimtsi Woyane Tigray), P.O. Box 450, Mekelle, Tigray, Ethiopia. Phone: +251 (34) 441-0545, +251 (34) 441-0544. Web: (includes on-demand audio) www.dimtsiwoyane.com. Contact: Fre Tesfamichael, Director. $1 helpful.

FINLAND   World Time +2 (+3 midyear)

Scandinavian Weekend Radio, P.O. Box 99, FI-34801, Virrat, Finland. Phone: (live when on air, and SMS service) +358 (400) 995-559. Email: (general) info@swradio.net; (technical) esa.saunamaki@swradio.net; (reception reports) online report form. Web: www.swradio.net. Contact: Alpo Heinonen; Esa Saunamäki, Chief Editor; Teemu Lehtimäki, QSL Manager. Two IRCs, $2 or 2 euros required for verification via mail. Web reports verified via the Internet. Free stickers.

FRANCE   World Time +1 (+2 midyear)

⬛Radio France Internationale (RFI)
MAIN OFFICE: B.P. 9516, F-75016 Paris Cedex 16, France; (street address) 116, avenue du président Kennedy, F-75016 Paris, France. Phone: (general) +33 (1) 5640-1212; (International Affairs and Program Placement) +33 (1) 4430-8932, +33 (1) 4430-8949; (Service de la communication) +33 (1) 4230-2951; (Audience Relations) +33 (1) 4430-8969/70/71; (Media Relations) +33 (1) 4230-2985; (Développement et de la communication) +33 (1) 4430-8921; *(Fréquence Monde)* +33 (1) 4230-1086; (English Service) +33 (1) 5640-3062; (Spanish Department) +33 (1) 4230-3048. Fax: (general) +33 (1) 5640 4759; (International Affairs and Program Placement) +33 (1) 4430 8920; (Audience Relations) +33 (1) 4430 8999; (other nontechnical) +33 (1) 4230 4481; (English Service) +33 (1) 5640 2674; (Spanish Department) +33 (1) 4230 4669. Email: (Audience Relations) courrier.auditeurs@rfi.fr; (English Service) english.service@rfi.fr; (Maguire) john.maguire@rfi.fr; (Spanish Service) america.latina@rfi.fr. Web: (includes on-demand and streaming audio) www.rfi.fr. Contact: John Maguire, Editor, English Language Service; J.P. Charbonnier, Producer, "Lettres des Audit-

eurs"; Joël Amar, International Affairs/Program Placement Department; Arnaud Littardi, Directeur du développement et de la communication; Nicolas Levkov, Rédactions en Langues Etrangères; Daniel Franco, Rédaction en français; Mme. Anne Toulouse, Rédacteur en chef du Service Mondiale en français; Christine Berbudeau, Rédacteur en chef, *Fréquence* **Monde**; Marc Verney, Attaché de Presse; (administration) Jean-Paul Cluzel, Président-Directeur Général; (technical) M. Raymond Pincon, Producer, "Le Courrier Technique." Free *Fréquence* **Monde** bi-monthly magazine in French upon request. Free souvenir keychains, pins, lighters, pencils, T-shirts and stickers have been received by some—especially when visiting the headquarters at 116 avenue du Président Kennedy, in the 16th Arrondissement. Can provide supplementary materials for "Dites-moi tout" French-language course; write to the attention of Mme. Chantal de Grandpre, "Dites-moi tout." "Le Club des Auditeurs" French-language listener's club ("Club 9516" for English-language listeners); applicants must provide name, address and two passport-type photos, whereupon they will receive a membership card and the club bulletin. RFI exists primarily to defend and promote Francophone culture, but also provides meaningful information and cultural perspectives in non-French languages.

TRANSMISSION OFFICE, TECHNICAL: TéléDiffusion de France, Direction de la Production et des Méthodes, Service ondes courtes, 10 rue d'Oradour sur Glane, 75732 Paris Cedex 15, France. Phone: (Gruson) +33 (1) 5595-1553; (Meunier) +33 (1) 5595-1161. Fax: +33 (1) 5595 2137. Email: (Gruson) jacques.gruson@tdf.fr; (Penneroux) michel.penneroux@tdf.fr. Contact: Jacques Gruson; Alain Meunier; Michel Penneroux, Business Development Manager AM-HF; Mme Annick Daronian or Mme Sylvie Greuillet (short wave service). This office is for informing about transmitter-related problems (interference, modulation quality), and also for reception reports and verifications.

UNITED STATES PROMOTIONAL, SCHOOL LIAISON, PROGRAM PLACEMENT AND CULTURAL EXCHANGE OFFICES:

NEW ORLEANS: Services Culturels, Suite 2105, Ambassade de France, 300 Poydras Street, New Orleans LA 70130 USA. Phone: +1 (504) 523-5394. Phone/Fax: +1 (504) 529-7502. Contact: Adam-Anthony Steg, Attaché Audiovisuel. This office promotes RFI, especially to language teachers and others in the educational community within the southern United States, and arranges for bi-national cultural exchanges. It also sets up RFI feeds to local radio stations within the southern United States.

NEW YORK: Audiovisual Bureau, Radio France Internationale, 972 Fifth Avenue, New York NY 10021 USA. Phone: +1 (212) 439-1452. Fax: +1 (212) 439 1455. Contact: Gérard Blondel or Julien Vin. This office promotes RFI, especially to language teachers and others within the educational community outside the southern United States, and arranges for bi-national cultural exchanges. It also sets up RFI feeds to local radio stations within much of the United States.

NEW YORK NEWS BUREAU: 1290 Avenue of the Americas, New York NY 10019 USA. Phone: +1 (212) 581-1771. Fax: +1 (212) 541 4309. Contact: Ms. Auberi Edler, Reporter; Bruno Albin, Reporter.

WASHINGTON NEWS BUREAU: 529 14th Street NW, Suite 1126, Washington DC 20045 USA. Phone: +1 (202) 879-6706. Contact: Pierre J. Cayrol.

SAN FRANCISCO OFFICE, SCHEDULES: 2654 17th Avenue, San Francisco CA 94116 USA. Phone: +1 (415) 564-9968. Email: GPoppin@aol.com. Contact: George Poppin. This address, a volunteer office, only provides RFI schedules to listeners (return postage not required). All other correspondence should be sent directly to the main office in Paris.

Voice of Orthodoxy—*see* Voix de l'Orthodoxie, below.

Voix de l'Orthodoxie, B.P. 416-08, F-75366 Paris Cedex 08, France. Phone: +33 (1) 4977-0366. Fax: +33 (1) 4353 4066. Email: voix.orthodoxie@wanadoo.fr. Web: www.russie.net/orthodoxie/vo. Contact: Michel Solovieff, General Secretary. Broadcasts religious programming to Russia via a shortwave transmitter in Kazakstan. Verifies reception reports, including those written in English.

ADDRESS IN RUSSIA: Golos Pravoslavia, 39 Nab. Leyt. Schmidta, 199034 St. Petersburg, Russia. Phone/Fax: +7 (812) 323-2867.

FRENCH GUIANA   World Time −3

Radio France Internationale Guyane Relay Station, Télédiffusion de France S.A., Délégation Territoriale de Guyane, B.P. 7024, 97307 Cayenne Cedex, French Guiana. Phone: Tel: +594 350-550. Fax: +594 350 555. Contact: (technical) Le Responsable pour Groupe Maintenance. All correspondence concerning nontechnical matters should be sent directly to the main addresses (*see*) for Radio France Internationale in France. Can consider replies only to technical correspondence in French. Sometimes verifies reception reports.

GABON   World Time +1

☎**Afrique Numéro Un**, B.P. 1, Libreville, Gabon. Fax: +241 742 133. Email: online form. Web: (includes streaming audio) www.africa1.com. Contact: Hermann Madiba. Free calendars and bumper stickers. $1, 2 IRCs or return postage helpful. Replies very slowly.

RTV Gabonaise, B.P. 10150, Libreville, Gabon. Contact: André Ranaud-Renombo, Le Directeur Technique, Adjoint Radio. Free stickers. $1 required. Replies occasionally, but slowly, to correspondence in French.

PASSPORT's Mike Wright catches the Metro near the Latin Quarter of Paris.   C. George

GEORGIA   World Time +4

Republic of Abkhazia Radio, Abkhaz State Radio and TV Co., Aidgylara Street 34, Sukhum 384900, Abkhazia, via Russia; or Zvanba Street 8, Sukhum 384900, Abkhazia, via Russia. If these fail, try the following address: c/oNational Library of Abkhazia, Krasnodar District, P.O. Box 964, 354000 Sochi, Russia. Phone: +995 (881) 24-867, +995 (881) 25-321. Fax: +995 (881) 21 144. Contact: Zurab Argun, Director.

GERMANY   World Time +1 (+2 midyear)

Der Herold der Christlichen Wissenschaft, Michael Seek, Chefredakteur, Postfach 370427, D-14134 Berlin, Germany. Email: redaktion@csherold.de. Replies to correspondence in German. Return postage helpful. Via T-Systems Media & Broadcast (see).
ALTERNATIVE ADDRESSES:
Radiosendungen CW, Postfach 7330, D-22832 Norderstedt, Germany. Contact: Ms. Erika Bethmann (reception reports, etc.).
Radiosendungen CW, Steindamm 97, D-20099 Hamburg, Germany.
SCHEDULES AND RELIGIOUS PUBLICATIONS: Der Herold der Christlichen Wissenschaft,
One Norway Street C04-10, Boston MA 02115-3195 USA. Email: herold@csps.com. Web: www.heroldcw.com/herold/radio.jhtml.
Christlichen Wissenschaft—see Der Herold der Christlichen Wissenschaft, above.
☞**Deutsche Welle**
MAIN OFFICE: Kurt-Schumacher-Str. 3, D-53113 Bonn, Germany; or (postal address) Deutsche Welle, D-53110 Bonn, Germany. Phone: (English Service) +49 (228) 429-164142. Fax: +49 (228) 429 154000. Email: info@dw-world.de; (English Service) english@dw-world.de. To reach specific individuals by email at Deutsche Welle the format is: firstname.lastname@dw-world.de. For language courses: bildung@dw-world.de. Web: (includes on-demand and streaming audio) www.dw-world.de. Contact: Erik Bettermann, Director General; Marco Vollmar, Head of English and German Services. Broadcasts via transmitters in Ascension, Kazakhstan, Netherlands Antilles, Portugal, Russia, Rwanda, Singapore, South Africa, Sri Lanka, United Arab Emirates and United Kingdom.
CUSTOMER SERVICE: Phone: +49 (228) 429-4000. Fax: +49 (228) 429 154000. Email: info@dw-world.de. All technical mail and reception reports should be sent to the Customer Service.
☞**Deutschlandfunk**, Raderberggürtel 40, D-50968 Köln, Germany. Phone: +49 (221) 345-0. Fax: +49 (221) 345 4802. Email: (program information) hoererservice@dradio.de. Web: (includes on-demand and streaming audio) www.dradio.de/dlf. Verifies reception reports in German or English.
☞**DeutschlandRadio-Berlin** (if reactivated), Hans-Rosenthal-Platz, D-10825 Berlin Schönberg, Germany. Phone: +49 (30) 8503-0. Fax: +49 (30) 8503 6168. Email: (program information) dkultur@dradio.de. Web: (includes on-demand and streaming audio) www.dradio.de/dkultur. Contact: Dr. Karl-Heinz Stamm; Ulrich Reuter. Verifies reception reports in German or English. Sometimes sends stickers, pens, magazines and other souvenirs. The station's shortwave transmitter was damaged in July 2007.

☞**Freie Volksmission Krefeld** (Free People's Mission Krefeld), Postfach 100707, D-47707 Krefeld, Germany; (street address) Freie Volksmission, Am Herbertzhof 15, D-47809 Krefeld, Germany; (English correspondence) Mission Center, P.O. Box 100707, D-47707 Krefeld, Germany. Phone: +49 (2151) 545-151. Email: postmaster@freie-volksmission.de; (reception reports) peter.vitsek@freie-volksmission.de. Web: (includes on-demand and streaming audio) www.freie-volksmission.de. Contact: Peter Vitsek, Technical Department. Replies to correspondence in English or German and verifies reception reports. Formerly broadcast via T-Systems Media & Broadcast (see), and currently airs programs over WWCR, USA (see).
Hamburger Lokalradio
STUDIO ADDRESS: Kulturzentrum Lola, Lohbrügger, Landstrasse 8, D-21031 Hamburg, Germany. Phone: +49 (40) 7269-2422. Fax: +49 (40) 7269 2423. Web: www.hamburger-lokalradio.de, www.hhlr.de.
EDITORIAL ADDRESS: Michael Kittner, Hamburger Lokalradio, Max-Eichholz-Ring 18, D-21031 Hamburg, Germany. Phone/Fax: +49 (40) 738-2417. Email: m.kittner@freenet.de. Contact: Michael Kittner.
Broadcasts regularly on FM and cable, and intermittently on world band via T-Systems Media & Broadcast (see) and a Latvian transmitter. Replies to correspondence in German or English. Return postage required for postal reply.
Missionswerk Friedensstimme, Postfach 100638, D-51606 Gummersbach, Germany; (street address) Gimborner Str. 20, D-51709 Marienheide, Germany. Phone: +49 (2261) 24717. Fax: +49 (2261) 60170. Contact. N. Berg. Replies to correspondence and verifies reception reports in German or Russian. Broadcasts to Russia via T-Systems Media & Broadcast (see).
☞**Missionswerk Werner Heukelbach**, D-51700 Bergneustadt 2, Germany. Email: info@missionswerk-heukelbach.de. Web: (includes on-demand audio) www.missionswerk-heukelbach.de. Contact: Manfred Paul. Religious broadcaster heard via the Voice of Russia, and formerly via T-Systems Media & Broadcast (see). Replies to correspondence in German or English and verifies reception reports.
MV Baltic Radio, R&R Medienservice, Roland Rohde, Seestrasse 17, D-19089 Göhren, Germany. Phone: +49 (3861) 301-380, +49 (178) 895-3872. Fax: +49 (3861) 302 9720. Email: info@rrms.de, info@mvbalticradio.de. Web: www.mvbalticradio.de. Contact: Roland Rohde. Replies to correspondence in German or English, and verifies reception reports. IRC or $1 required for postal reply. A monthly broadcast produced in Göhren (Mecklenburg-Vorpommern) and aired via facilities of T-Systems Media & Broadcast (see).
Radio Gloria International, c/o Coloradio, Jordanstrasse 2, D-01099 Dresden, Germany. Email: radiogloria@aol.com. Verifies email reports via the Internet; $2 or 2 euros required for verification by mail. Broadcasts irregularly via T-Systems Media & Broadcast (see).
☞**Radio Santec**, Marienstrasse 1, D-97070 Würzburg, Germany. Phone: (0800-1600 Central European Time, Monday through Friday) +49 (931) 3903-264. Fax: +49 (931) 3903 195. Email: info@radio-santec.com. Web: (includes on-demand and streaming audio) www.radio-santec.com. Contact: Janett Wood. Reception reports verified with QSL cards only if requested. Radio Santec is the radio branch of Universelles Leben (Universal Life).
☞**Radio Zusa**. Email: online form. Web: (includes streaming audio) www.zusa.de. A community radio station nor-

mally on FM only, but which also broadcasts irregularly via T-Systems Media & Broadcast (*see*). Has studios in three different towns—*see* Website for details.

Stimme des Evangeliums, Evangelische Missions-Gemeinden, Jahnstrasse 9, D-89182 Bernstadt, Germany. Phone: +49 (7348) 948-026. Fax: +49 (7348) 948-027. Contact: Pastor Albert Giessler. Verifies reception reports in German or English. A broadcast of the Evangelical Missions Congregations in Germany, and aired via T-Systems Media & Broadcast (*see*).

T-Systems Business Services GmbH, Media & Broadcast, Business Unit Hoerfunk, Bastionstrasse 11-19, D-52428 Jülich, Germany. Phone: (Brodowsky, Sales & Marketing) +49 (2461) 937-164; (Horst Tobias, Frequency Manager) +49 (2461) 340-451. Fax: (sales office) +49 (2461) 937 165; (frequency management office) +49 (2461) 340 452. Email: walter.brodowsky@t-systems.com. Contact: Walter Brodowsky, Sales & Marketing Manager for Shortwave Broadcasts; Horst Tobias, Frequency Manager. Reception reports accepted by mail or fax, and should be clearly marked to the attention of Walter Brodowsky. T-Systems Media & Broadcast operates transmitters at Jülich, Nauen and Wertachtal, which are leased to various international world band stations.
NOTE: Despite the sale of the Jülich transmitting site to CVC, media arm of the United Kingdom's Christian Vision, the contract allows T-Systems Media & Broadcast to continue using the site for its customers. For more information on CVC, *see* Australia.

T-Systems Media & Broadcast—*see* T-Systems Business Services GmbH, Media & Broadcast, above.

GHANA   World Time exactly

WARNING—CONFIDENCE ARTISTS: Attempted correspondence with Radio Ghana may result in requests, perhaps resulting from mail theft, from skilled confidence artists for money, free electronic or other products, publications or immigration sponsorship. To help avoid this, correspondence to Radio Ghana should be sent via registered mail.

Ghana Broadcasting Corporation—Radio Ghana (when operating), P.O. Box 1633, Accra, Ghana; (street address) Broadcasting House, Ring Road Central, Kanda, Accra, Ghana. Phone/Fax: +233 (21) 768-975, +233 (21) 221-161, +233 (21) 786-561. Email: online form. Web: www.gbcghana.com. Contact: (general) Director of Corporate Affairs; (administration) Director of Radio; (technical) Director of Engineering, or Propagation Department. Replies tend to be erratic, and reception reports are best sent to the attention of the Propagation Engineer, GBC Monitoring Station. Enclosing an IRC, return postage or $1 and registering your letter should improve the chances of a reply.

GREECE   World Time +2 (+3 midyear)

⬛Foni tis Helladas (Voice of Greece)
NONTECHNICAL: ERA-5, The Voice of Greece, 432 Mesogion, Aghia Paraskevi, 15342 Athens, Greece. Phone: +30 210-606-6895/96, +30 210-606-6297/98, +30 210-606-6398. Fax: +30 210 606 6309. Email: (including reception reports) era5@ert.gr. Web: (includes streaming audio) www.voiceofgreece.gr. Contact: Angeliki Barka, Head of Programmes; Gina Vogiatzoglou, Managing Director. Free tourist literature.

TECHNICAL: ERA-5, General Technical Directorate, Mesogion 432, 15342 Athens, Greece. Phone: (Charalambopoulos) +30 210-606-5585. Fax: +30 210 606 6264. Email: (reception reports) era5@ert.gr; apodimos_era5@ert.gr; (technical information, schedules, Charalambopoulos) bcharalabopoulos@ert.gr. Contact: Babis Charalambopoulos, Planning Engineer. Technical reception reports may be sent via mail, fax or email.

⬛Radiophonikos Stathmos Makedonias, Angelaki 14, 54636 Thessaloniki, Greece. Phone: +30 2310-299-400. Fax: +30 2310 299 550. Email: eupro@ert3.gr. Web: (includes streaming audio) www.ert3.gr. Contact: (general) Mrs. Tatiana Tsioli, Program Director; Lefty Kongalides, Head of International Relations; (technical) Dimitrios Keramidas, Engineer. Free booklets, stickers and other small souvenirs.

GREENLAND   World Time exactly Northeast; –1 (World Time midyear) Eastern; –3 (–2 midyear) Central; –4 Western

Kalaalit Nunaata Radioa (KNR), Postbok 1007, DK-3900 Nuuk, Greenland; (street address) Vandsøvej 15, DK-3900 Nuuk, Greenland. Phone: +299 361-500. Fax: +299 361 502. Email: info@knr.gl. Web: www.knr.gl. Does not operate on shortwave, but relays part of its programming to fishermen on 3815 kHz via a 100-watt USB transmitter of the Ammassalik Radio coastal station in Tasiilaq (*see*, below). Replies to correspondence in English, and verifies reception reports.

OZL Ammassalik Radio, Silasiorpimmut B920, DK-3913 Tasiilaq, Greenland. Email: ozl@tele.gl. Replies to correspondence in English, and verifies reception reports.

GUAM   World Time +10

Adventist World Radio—KSDA
OPERATIONS AND ENGINEERING: P.O. Box 8990, Agat, GU 96928 USA. Phone: +1 (671) 565-2289. Fax: +1 (671) 565 2983. Email: brook@awr.org. Contact: Brook Powers. This address for specialized technical correspondence only. For further information, *see* AWR listing under USA.

Trans World Radio—KTWR
MAIN OFFICE, ENGINEERING INQUIRIES & FREQUENCY COORDINATION ONLY: P.O. Box 8780, Agat, GU 96928 USA. Phone: +1 (671) 828-8637. Fax: +1 (671) 828 8636. Email: (Ross) ktwrfcd@guam.twr.org. Contact: George Ross, Frequency Coordination Manager. This office will also verify email reports with a QSL card. Requests reports covering 15-30 minutes of programming. All English listener mail of a nontechnical nature should be sent to the Australian office (*see* next entry). Addresses for listener mail in other languages are given in the broadcasts. Also, *see* Trans World Radio, USA.
ENGLISH LISTENER MAIL, NONTECHNICAL: Trans World Radio, P.O. Box 390, Box Hill, Victoria 3128, Australia. Phone: +61 (3) 9899 3800. Fax: +61 (3) 9899 3900. Email: infoaus@twr.org. Web: http://twraustralia.org. Contact: John Reeder, National Director.

GUATEMALA   World Time –6

Radio Amistad (if reactivated), Iglesia Bautista Getsemani, San Pedro La Laguna, Solola, Guatemala.
ADDRESS FOR RECEPTION REPORTS: David Daniell, Asesor

de Comunicaciones, Apartado Postal 25, Bulevares MX, 53140 Mexico. Phone/Fax: +52 (55) 5572-9633. Email: dpdaniell@aol.com. Replies to correspondence in English or Spanish.

Radio Buenas Nuevas, San Sebastián 13020, Huehuetenango, Guatemala. Contact: Israel G. Rodas Mérida, Gerente. $1 or return postage helpful. Free religious and station information in Spanish. Sometimes includes a small pennant. Replies to correspondence in Spanish.

Radio Coatán—*see* Radio Cultural Coatán

☞**Radio Cultural—TGNA** (when operating), Apartado 601, 01901 Guatemala City, Guatemala; (studios) 4Av. 30-09 Zona 3, Guatemala City, Guatemala. Phone: +502 2472-1745, +502 2471-4378, +502 2440-0260. Fax: +502 2440-0260. Email: tgn@radiocultural.com; tgna@guate.net. Web: (includes streaming audio) www.radiocultural.com. Contact: Wayne Berger, Chief Engineer; Heidy Chávez; [Ms.] Yojhana Ajsivinac, Secretary. Free religious printed matter, tourist information and pennant (when available). Return postage or $1 appreciated.

Radio Cultural Coatán—TGCT, San Sebastián Coatán 13035, Huehuetenango, Guatemala. Phone: +502 7758-3491, +502 7758-5494. Email: radiocoatan@hotmail.com. Contact: Sebastián Pablo, Director. $1 or return postage required. Often announces as just "Radio Coatán."

Radio K'ekchi—TGVC (if reactivated), 3ra Calle 7-15, Zona 1, 16015 Fray Bartolomé de las Casas, Alta Verapaz, Guatemala; (Media Consultant) David Daniell, Asesor de Comunicaciones, Apartado Postal 25, Bulevares MX, 53140 Mexico. Phone: (station) +502 7950-0299; (Daniell, Phone/Fax) +52 (55) 5572-9633. Fax: (station) +502 7950 0398. Email: dpdaniell@aol.com. Contact: (general) Gilberto Sun Xicol, Gerente; Ancelmo Cuc Chub, Director; Mateo Botzoc, Director de Programas; (technical) Larry Baysinger, Ingeniero Jefe. Free paper pennant. $1 or return postage required. Replies to correspondence in Spanish.

☞**Radio Verdad**, Apartado Postal 5, Chiquimula, Guatemala. Phone: +502 7942-5689. Phone/Fax: +502 7942-0362. Email: radioverdad@intelnett.com; radioverdad5@yahoo.com. Web: (includes streaming audio) www.radioverdad.org. Contact: Dr. Édgar Amílcar Madrid Morales, Gerente. May send free pennants or calendars. Replies to correspondence in Spanish or English. Return postage appreciated. An evangelical and educational station.

GUINEA   World Time exactly

Radiodiffusion-Télévision Guinéenne, B.P. 391, Conakry, Guinea. If no reply is forthcoming from this address, try sending your letter to: D.G.R./P.T.T., B.P. 3322, Conakry, Guinea. Phone/Fax: +224 451-408. Email: (Issa Conde, Directeur) issaconde@yahoo.fr. Contact: (general) Yaoussou Diaby, Journaliste Sportif; Boubacar Yacine Diallo, Directeur Général/ORTG; Issa Conde, Directeur; Seny Camara; (administration) Momo Toure, Chef Services Administratifs; (technical, studio) Mbaye Gagne, Chef de Studio; (technical, overall) Direction des Services Techniques. Return postage or $1 required. Replies very irregularly to correspondence in French.

GUYANA   World Time –3

☞**Voice of Guyana** (when operating), Homestretch Avenue, Georgetown, Guyana. Phone: +592 223- 5162. Fax:

+592 223 5163. Email: vog560am@homeviewguyana.com. Contact: (general) Mrs. Jasminee Sahoye, Programme Manager; (technical) Roy Marshall, Senior Technician; Shiroxley Goodman, Chief Engineer. $1 or IRC helpful. Sending a spare sticker from another station helps assure a reply. Note that when the station's mediumwave AM transmitter is down because of a component fault, parts of the shortwave unit are sometimes 'borrowed' until spares become available. As a result, the station is sometimes off shortwave for several weeks at a time.

HOLLAND—*see* NETHERLANDS

HONDURAS   World Time –6

☞**La Voz Evangélica—HRVC** (when operating)
MAIN OFFICE: Apartado Postal 3252, Tegucigalpa, M.D.C., Honduras. Phone: +504 234-3468/69/70. Fax: +504 233 3933. Email: programas@hrvc.org. Web (includes streaming audio): www.hrvc.org. Contact: (general) Srta. Orfa Esther Durón Mendoza, Secretaria; Tereso Ramos, Director de Programación; Alan Maradiaga; Modesto Palma, Jefe, Depto. Tráfico; (technical) Carlos Paguada, Director del Dpto. Técnico; (administration) Venancio Mejía, Gerente; Nelson Perdomo, Director. Free calendars. Three IRCs or $1 required. Replies to correspondence in English, Spanish, Portuguese or German.
REGIONAL OFFICE, SAN PEDRO SULA: Apartado 2336, San Pedro Sula, Honduras. Phone: +504 557-5030. Contact: Hernán Miranda, Director.
REGIONAL OFFICE, LA CEIBA: Apartado 164, La Ceiba, Honduras. Phone: +504 443-2390. Contact: José Banegas, Director.

Radio HRMI, Radio Misiones Internacionales
STATION: Apartado Postal 20583, Comayagüela, M.D.C., Honduras. Phone: +504 233-9029, +504 238-4933. Contact: Wayne Downs, Director. $1 or return postage helpful.
U.S. OFFICE: IMF World Missions, P.O. Box 6321, San Bernardino CA 92412, USA. Phone +1 (909) 466-5793. Fax: +1 (909) 370 4862. Email: jkpimf@msn.com. Contact: Dr. James K. Planck, President; Gustavo Roa, Coordinator.

Radio Luz y Vida—HRPC, Apartado 303, San Pedro Sula, Honduras; (reception reports in English) HRPC Radio, P. O. Box 303, San Pedro Sula, Honduras. Phone: +504 654-1221. Fax: +504 557 0394. Email: efmhonduras@globalnet.hn. Contact: Donald R. Moore, Station Director; or, to have your letter read over the air, "English Friendship Program." Return postage or $1 appreciated.

HUNGARY   World Time +1 (+2 midyear)

☞**Kossuth Rádió**, Bródy Sándor utca 5-7, H-1800 Budapest, Hungary. Phone: +36 (1) 328-7945. Web: (includes streaming audio) www.mr1-kossuth.hu; (on-demand audio) http://real1.radio.hu.

Radio Budapest, Hungarian Radio, International Relations Department, Bródy Sándor utca 5-7, H-1800 Budapest, Hungary. Phone: +36 (1) 328-8108. Fax: +36 (1) 328 7004. Email: nki@radio.hu. Does not verify reception reports.

INDIA   World Time +5:30

WARNING—MAIL THEFT: PASSPORT readers report that letters to India containing IRCs and other valuables have disappeared en route when not registered. Best is either to register your letter or to send correspondence in an unsealed envelope, and without enclosures.

VERIFICATION OF REGIONAL STATIONS: All Indian regional stations can be verified via New Delhi (*see* All India Radio—External Services Division for contact details), but some listeners prefer contacting each station individually, in the hope of receiving a direct QSL. Well-known Indian DXer Jose Jacob makes the following suggestions: address your report to the station engineer of the respective station; specify the time of reception in both World Time (UTC) and Indian Standard Time (IST); instead of using the SINPO code, write a brief summary of reception quality; and if possible, report on local programs rather than relays of national programming from New Delhi. Jose adds that reports should be written in English, and return postage is not required. Enclosing currency notes is against the law.

Akashvani—All India Radio

ADMINISTRATION/ENGINEERING: Directorate General of All India Radio, Akashvani Bhawan, 1 Sansad Marg, New Delhi-110 001, India. Phone: (Director General) +91 (11) 2371-0300 Ext. 102; (Engineer-in-Chief) +91 (11) 2342-1058; (Phone/Fax) +91 (11) 2342-1459; (Director, Spectrum Management) +91 (11) 2342-1062, +91 (11) 2342-1145. Fax: +91 (11) 2371 11956; (Director General) +91 (11) 2342 1956. Email: airlive@air.org.in; (Director General) dgair@air.org.in; (Engineer-in-Chief) einc@air.org.in; (Director, Spectrum Management) spectrum-manager@air.org.in; (Singh, Engineer-in-Chief) hrsingh@air.org.in. Web: www.allindiaradio.gov.in. Contact: (technical) H.R. Singh, Engineer-in-Chief; V.P. Singh, Director, Spectrum Management & Synergy; B.K Obrai, Deputy Director, Spectrum Management & Synergy.

AUDIENCE RESEARCH: Audience Research Unit, All India Radio, Press Trust of India Building, 2nd floor, Sansad Marg, New Delhi-110 001, India. Phone: (general) +91 (11) 2371-0033, +91 (11) 2371-9215; (Director) +91 (11) 2338-6506. Contact: Ramesh Chandra, Director.

CENTRAL MONITORING STATION: All India Radio, Ayanagar, New Delhi-110 047, India. Phone: +91 (11) 2650-2955, +91 (11) 2650 1763.

COMMERCIAL SERVICE: Vividh Bharati Service, AIR, P.O. Box 11497, 101 M.K. Road, Mumbai-400 020, India. Phone: +91 (22) 2203-7193.

INTERNATIONAL MONITORING STATION—MAIN OFFICE: International Monitoring Station, All India Radio, Dr. K.S. Krishnan Road, Todapur, New Delhi-110 097, India. Phone: +91 (11) 2584-2939. Contact: B.L. Kasturiya, Deputy Director; D.P. Chhabra or R.K. Malviya, Assistant Research Engineers—Frequency Planning.

NATIONAL CHANNEL: AIR, Gate 22, Jawaharlal Nehru Stadium, Lodhi Road, New Delhi-110 003. Phone: +91 (11) 2584-3825; (station engineer) +91 (11) 2584-3207. Contact: J.K. Das, Director; V.D. Sharma, Station Engineer.

NEWS SERVICE DIVISION: News Service Division, Broadcasting House, 1 Sansad Marg, New Delhi-110 001, India. Phone: (general, newsroom) +91 (11) 2342-1100, +91 (11) 2342-1101; (Special Director General—News) +91 (11) 2342-1218; (News on phone in English) +91 (11) 2332-4343/1259; (News on phone in Hindi) +91 (11) 2332-4242/1258. Fax: +91 (11) 2371 1196. Email: (general, newsroom) nbhnews@air.org.in; (Director General) dgn@air.org.in. Web: www.newsonair.com. Contact: P.K. Bandopadhyay, Director General—News.

PROGRAMMING: Broadcasting House, 1 Sansad Marg, New Delhi-110 001 India. Phone: (general) +91 (11) 2371-5411.

RESEARCH AND DEVELOPMENT: Office of the Chief Engineer R&D, All India Radio, 14-B Ring Road, Indraprastha Estate, New Delhi-110 002, India. Phone: (general) +91 (11) 2337-8211/12; (Chief Engineer) +91 (11) 2337 9255, +91 (11) 2337-9329. Fax: +91 (11) 2337 9329, +91 (11) 2337 9674. Email: rdair@nda.vsnl.net.in. Contact: A.K. Bhatnagar, Chief Engineer.

TRANSCRIPTION AND PROGRAM EXCHANGE SERVICES: Akashvani Bhawan, 1 Sansad Marg, New Delhi-110 001, India. Phone: (Director, Transcription & Program Exchange Services: V.A. Magazine) +91 (11) 2342-1927. Contact: D.P. Jadav, Director.

All India Radio—Aizawl, Radio Tila, Tuikhuahtlang, Aizawl-796 001, Mizoram, India. Phone: (engineering) +91 (389) 2322-415. Fax: +91 (389) 2322 114. Email: aizawl@air.org.in. Contact: (technical) S. Nellai Nayagam, Station Engineer.

All India Radio—Aligarh, Anoopshahar Road, Aligarh-202 001, Uttar Pradesh, India. Phone: (engineering) +91 (571) 2700-972. Email: aligarh@air.org.in. Contact: S.K. Agarwal, Station Engineer.

All India Radio—Bengaluru [Bangalore] Shortwave Transmitting Centre

HEADQUARTERS: see All India Radio—External Services Division.

AIR OFFICE NEAR TRANSMITTERS: Superintending Engineer, Super Power Transmitters, All India Radio, Yelahanka New Town, Bengaluru-560 065, Karnataka, India. Phone: +91 (80) 2226-1243. Email: bangalore.spt@air.org.in (may change to bengaluru.spt@air.org.in). Contact: (technical) L.M. Ambhast, Superintending Engineer; T. Rajendran, Station Engineer.

All India Radio—Bhopal, Akashvani Bhawan, Shyamla Hills, Bhopal-462 002, Madhya Pradesh, India. Phone: (engineering) +91 (755) 2661-241. Email: bhopal@air.org.in. Contact: (technical) Sudhir Sodhia, Station Engineer.

All India Radio—Chennai

EXTERNAL SERVICES: see All India Radio—External Services Division.

DOMESTIC SERVICE: Avadi, Chennai-600 002, Tamil Nadu, India. Phone: (engineering) +91 (44) 2638-3204. Email: chennai.avadi@air.org.in.

All India Radio—External Services Division

MAIN ADDRESS: Broadcasting House, 1 Sansad Marg, P.O. Box 500, Parliament Street, New Delhi-110 001, India. Fax: +91 (11) 2371 0057. Contact: (general) P.P. Setia, Director of External Services; S.C. Panda, Audience Relations Officer; "Faithfully Yours" program. Email: esd@air.org.in. Web: (includes online reception report form) www.allindiaradio.gov.in. Contact: (DX Program, Tamil External Service) Thanka Jaisakthivel, Producer & Presenter. QSL cards for this DX program are available from: Vanoli Ulagam (Radio World), Thiraikadal Adaivaram Thamiizh Naatham, All India Radio, Kamarajar Salai, Chennai-600004, Tamil Nadu, India. Replies can be somewhat erratic from External Services Division.

VERIFICATION ADDRESS: Spectrum Management, All India Radio, Room 204, Akashani Bhavan, New Delhi-110 001, India; or P.O. Box 500, New Delhi-110 001, India. Fax: +91 (11) 2342 1062, +91 (11) 2342 1145. Email: spectrum-manager@air.org.in, or online form (www.allindiaradio. gov.in/recepfdk.html). Contact: V. P. Singh, Director, Spectrum Management & Synergy. Audio files accepted.

All India Radio—Gangtok, Old M.L.A. Hostel, Gangtok-737 101, Sikkim, India. Phone: (engineering) +91 (3592) 202-636. Email: gangtok@air.org.in. Contact: (general) Y.P. Yolmo, Station Director; (technical) A.K. Sarkar, Assistant Engineer.

All India Radio—Gorakhpur

NEPALESE EXTERNAL SERVICE: see All India Radio—External Services Division.

DOMESTIC SERVICE: Town Hall, Post Bag 26, Gorakhpur-273 001, Uttar Pradesh, India. Phone/Fax: (engineering) +91 (551) 2337-401. Email: gorakhpur@air.org.in. Contact: (technical) Dr. S.M. Pradhan, Superintending Engineer; P.P. Shukle, Station Engineer.

All India Radio—Guwahati

EXTERNAL SERVICES: see All India Radio—External Services Division.

DOMESTIC SERVICE: P.O. Box 28, Chandmari, Guwahati-781 003, Assam, India. Phone: (engineering) +91 (361) 2660-235. Email: guwahati@air.org.in. Contact: (technical) P.C. Sanghi, Superintending Engineer; H.S. Dhillon, Station Engineer.

All India Radio—Hyderabad, Rocklands, Saifabad, Hyderabad-500 004, Andhra Pradesh, India. Phone: (engineering) +91 (40) 2323-4904. Fax: +91 (40) 2323 2239, +91 (40) 2323 4282. Email: hyderabad@air.org.in. Contact: (technical) S.S. Reddy, Superintending Engineer; P.S. Nagabhushanam, Station Engineer.

All India Radio—Imphal, Palau Road, Imphal-795 001, Manipur, India. Phone: (engineering) +91 (385) 220-534. Email: imphal@air.org.in. Contact: (technical) M. Jayaraman, Superintending Engineer.

All India Radio—Itanagar, Naharlagun, Itanagar-791 111, Arunachal Pradesh, India. Phone: (engineering) +91 (360) 2212-881. Fax: +91 (360) 2213 008, +91 (360) 2212 933. Email: itanagar@air.org.in. Contact: J.T. Jirdoh, Station Director; P.K. Bez Baruah, Assistant Station Engineer; P. Sanghi, Superintending Engineer. Verifications direct from station are difficult, as engineering is done by staff visiting from the Regional Engineering Headquarters at AIR—Guwahati (*see*); that address might be worth contacting if all else fails.

All India Radio—Jaipur, 5 Park House, Mirza Ismail Road, Jaipur-302 001, Rajasthan, India. Phone: +91 (141) 2366-263. Fax: +91 (141) 2363 196. Email: jaipur@air.org.in. Contact: (technical) S.C. Sharma, Station Engineer; C.L. Goel, Assistant Station Engineer.

All India Radio—Jammu—*see* Radio Kashmir—Jammu.

All India Radio—Jeypore, Jeypore-764 005, Orissa, India. Phone: (engineering) +91 (6854) 232-524. Email: jeypore@air.org.in. Contact: K. Naryan Das, Assistant Station Engineer.

All India Radio—Kohima, P.O. Box 42, Kohima-797 001, Nagaland, India. Phone: (engineering) +91 (370) 2245-556. Email: kohima@air.org.in. Contact: (technical) M. Tyagi, Superintending Engineer; K.K Jose, Assistant Engineer; K. Morang, Assistant Station Engineer. Return postage, $1 or IRC helpful.

Asian Broadcasting Union attendees at All India Radio's DRM conference. Here, they check out a digital test broadcast. Alokesh Gupta

All India Radio—Kolkata, G.P.O. Box 696, Kolkata—700 001, West Bengal, India. Phone: (engineering) +91 (33) 2248-1705. Email: kolkata@air.org.in. Contact: (technical) S.K. Pal, Superintending Engineer.

All India Radio—Kurseong, Mehta Club Building, Kurseong-734 203, Darjeeling District, West Bengal, India. Phone: (engineering) +91 (354) 2344-350. Email: kurseong@air.org.in. Contact: (general) George Kuruvilla, Assistant Director; (technical) R.K. Sinha, Chief Engineer; B.K. Behara, Station Engineer.

All India Radio—Leh, Leh-194 101, Ladakh District, Jammu and Kashmir, India. Phone: (engineering) +91 (1982) 252-080. Email: leh@air.org.in; (station engineer) seairleh@rediffmail.com. Contact: (technical) V.S. Nagar, Station Engineer.

All India Radio—Lucknow, 18 Vidhan Sabha Marg, Lucknow-226 001, Uttar Pradesh, India. Phone: (engineering) +91 (522) 2237-601. Email: lucknow@air.org.in. Contact: Dr. S.M. Pradhan, Superintending Engineer. This station now appears to be replying via the External Services Division, New Delhi.

All India Radio—Mumbai

EXTERNAL SERVICES: see All India Radio—External Services Division.

COMMERCIAL SERVICE (VIVIDH BHARATI): All India Radio, P.O. Box 19705, 101 M K Road, Mumbai-400 091, Maharashtra, India. Phone: (director) +91 (22) 2869-2698; (engineering) +91 (22) 2868-7351. Email: vbs@vsnl.com. Contact: Vijayalakshmi Sinha, Director; (technical) Superintending Engineer.

DOMESTIC SERVICE: Broadcasting House, Backbay Reclamation, Mumbai-400 020, Maharashtra, India. Phone: (engineering) +91 (22) 2202-9853. Email: mumbai. malad@air.org.in.

All India Radio—New Delhi, Broadcasting House, New Delhi-110 011, India. Phone: (engineering) +91 (11) 2371 0113. Email: delhi.bh@air.org.in. Contact: (technical) V. Chaudhry, Superintending Engineer.

HIGH POWER TRANSMITTERS (250 kW), KHAMPUR: New Delhi-110036, India. Phone: +91 (11) 2720-2158; (Station

Engineer) +91 (11) 2720-3560. Email: delhi.khampur@air.
org.in. Contact: V.K. Baleja, Station Engineer.
HIGH POWER TRANSMITTERS (50 & 100 kW), KINGSWAY:
New Delhi-110009, India. Phone: +91 (11) 2743-6661.
Email: hptkingsway@yahoo.com.
All India Radio—Panaji Shortwave Transmitting
Centre
HEADQUARTERS: see All India Radio—External Services
Division, above.
HIGH POWER TRANSMITTERS, AIR: Goa University PO, Goa-
403206, India. Phone: (engineering) +91 (832) 2230-696.
Email: panaji.spt@air.org.in; airtrgoa@sancharnet.in. Con-
tact: (technical) S. Jayaraman, Superintending Engineer.
All India Radio—Port Blair, Haddo Post, Dilanipur, Port
Blair-744 102, South Andaman, Andaman and Nicobar
Islands, Union Territory, India. Phone: (engineering)
+91 (3192) 230-682. Fax: +91 (3192) 230 260. Email:
portblair@air.org.in. Contact: V.M. Ratnaprasad, Station
Engineer. Registering letters appears to be useful.
All India Radio—Ranchi, 6 Ratu Road, Ranchi-834 001,
Jharkhand, India. Phone: (engineering) +91 (651) 2283-
310. Email: ranchi@air.org.in. Contact: (technical) H.K.
Sinha, Superintending Engineer.
All India Radio—Shillong, P.O. Box 14, Shillong-793 001,
Meghalaya, India. Phone: (engineering) +91 (364) 2222-
272. Email: shillong.nes@air.org.in. Contact: (general)
C. Lalsaronga, Director NEIS; (technical) R. Venugopal,
Superintending Engineer; H. Diengdoh, Station Engineer.
Free booklet on station's history. Replies tend to be rare,
due to a shortage of staff.
All India Radio—Shimla, Choura Maidan, Shimla-171
004, Himachal Pradesh, India. Phone: (engineering) +91
(177) 2811-355. Email: shimla@air.org.in. Contact: (tech-
nical) V.K. Upadhayay, Superintending Engineer; Krishna
Murari, Assistant Engineer. Return postage helpful.
All India Radio—Srinagar—see Radio Kashmir—Srinagar.
All India Radio—Thiruvananthapuram, P.O. Box 403,
Bhakti Vilas, Vazuthacaud, Thiruvananthapuram-695 014,
Kerala, India. Phone: (engineering) +91 (471) 2325-009.
Phone/Fax: (station director) +91 (471) 2324-406. Email:
thiruvananthapuram@air.org.in; (comments on programs)
pm@airtvm.com; (comments on reception) mail@airtvm.
com. Web: www.airtvm.com. Contact: K.A. Muraleed-
haran, Station Director; (technical) K.V. Ramachandran,
Station Engineer.
Radio Kashmir—Jammu, Palace Road, Jammu-188 001,
Jammu and Kashmir, India. Phone: (engineering) +91 (191)
2544-411. Email: jammu@air.org.in.
Radio Kashmir—Srinagar, Sherwani Road, Srinagar-190
001, Jammu and Kashmir, India. Phone: (engineering) +91
(194) 2452-100/177. Email: srinagar@air.org.in. Contact:
G.H. Zia, Station Director.
☎**Trans World Radio—India**, L-15 Green Park, New Delhi -
110 016, India. Phone (11) 2651-5790. Email: info@twr.
in; (Devadoss) ddevadoss@in.twrsa.org. Web: (includes
on-demand and streaming audio) www.radiovv.org, www.
radio882.com. Verifies reception reports by email. Contact:
E. Daniel Devadoss; Shakti Verma, Technical Director.

INDONESIA   World Time +7 Western: Waktu Indonesia

Bagian Barat (Jawa, Sumatera); +8 Central: Waktu Indonesia
Bagian Tengal (Bali, Kalimantan, Sulawesi, Nusa Tenggara);
+9 Eastern: Waktu Indonesia Bagian Timur (Papua,
Maluku)

NOTE: Except where otherwise indicated, Indonesian
stations, especially those of the Radio Republik Indonesia
(RRI) network, will reply to at least some correspondence
in English. However, correspondence in Indonesian is more
likely to ensure a reply.
Kang Guru Radio English, Indonesia Australia Language Foundation, P.O. Box 3095, Denpasar 80030, Bali,
Indonesia. Phone: +62 (361) 225-243. Fax: +62 (361) 263
509. Email: kangguru@ialf.edu. Web: www.kangguru.org.
Contact: Kevin Dalton, Kang Guru Project Manager; Ra-
chel Pearson, ELT Media and Training Specialist; Ms. Ogi
Yutarini, Project Coordinating Officer. Free "Kang Guru"
magazine. This program is aired over various RRI outlets,
including Jakarta and Sorong.
Radio Pemerintah Daerah Kabupaten TK II—RPDK
Manggarai, Ruteng, Flores, Nusa Tenggara Timur, Indone-
sia. Contact: Simon Saleh, B.A. Return postage required.
Radio Pemerintah Daerah Kabupaten Daerah TK
II—RSPK Ngada, Jalan Soekarno-Hatta, Bjawa, Flores,
Nusa Tenggara Tengah, Indonesia. Phone: +62 (384) 21-
142. Contact: Drs. Petrus Tena, Kepala Studio.
Radio Republik Indonesia—RRI Ambon (when operat-
ing), Jalan Jendral Akhmad Yani 1, Ambon 97124, Maluku,
Indonesia. Phone: +62 (911) 52-740, +62 (911) 53-261, +62
(911) 53-263. Fax: +62 (911) 53 262. Contact: Drs. H. Ali
Amran; Pirla C. Noija, Kepala Seksi Siaran. A very poor
replier to correspondence in recent years. Correspondence
in Indonesian and return postage essential.
Radio Republik Indonesia—RRI Banda Aceh (when
operating), Kotak Pos 112, Banda Aceh 23243, Aceh, Indonesia. Phone: +62 (651) 22-116/156. Contact: Parmono
Prawira, Technical Director; Ahmad Prambahan, Head;
S.H. Rosa Kim. Return postage helpful.
Radio Republik Indonesia—Bandar Lampung, see RRI
Tanjung Karang listing below.
Radio Republik Indonesia—RRI Bandung (when operating), Stasiun Regional 1, Kotak Pos 1055, Bandung
40122, Jawa Barat, Indonesia. Email: rribandung@yahoo.
com. Web: www.kangguru.org/rristationprofiles.htm.
Contact: Drs. Idrus Alkaf, Kepala Stasiun; Mrs. Ati Kus-
miati; Eem Suhaemi, Kepala Seksi Siaran. Return postage
or IRC helpful.
Radio Republik Indonesia—RRI Banjarmasin (when
operating), Stasiun Nusantara 111, Kotak Pos 117, Banjarmasin 70234, Kalimantan Selatan, Indonesia. Phone:
+62 (511) 268-601, +62 (511) 261-562. Fax: +62 (511) 252
238. Contact: Jul Chaidir, Stasiun Kepala; Harmyn Husein.
Free stickers. Return postage or IRCs helpful.
Radio Republik Indonesia—RRI Bengkulu, Stasiun Regional 1, Kotak Pos 13 Kawat, Kotamadya Bengkulu 38227,
Indonesia. Phone: +62 (736) 350-811. Fax: +62 (736) 350
927. Contact: Drs. Drs. Jasran Abubakar, Kepala Stasiun.
Free picture postcards, decals and tourist literature. Return
postage or 2 IRCs helpful.
Radio Republik Indonesia—RRI Biak (when operating),
Kotak Pos 505, Biak 98117, Papua, Indonesia. Phone:
+62 (981) 21-211, +62 (981) 21-197. Fax: +62 (981) 21
905. Contact: Butje Latuperissa, Kepala Seksi Siaran;
Drs. D.A. Siahainenia, Kepala Stasiun. Correspondence
in Indonesian preferred.
Radio Republik Indonesia—RRI Bukittinggi (when
operating), Stasiun Regional 1 Bukittinggi, Jalan Prof.
Muhammad Yamin 199, Aurkuning, Bukittinggi 26131,
Propinsi Sumatera Barat, Indonesia. Phone: +62 (752) 21-

319, +62 (752) 21-320. Fax: +62 (752) 367 132. Contact: Mr. Effendi, Sekretaris; Zul Arifin Mukhtar, SH; Samirwan Sarjana Hukum, Producer, "Phone in Program." Replies to correspondence in Indonesian or English. Return postage helpful.

Radio Republik Indonesia—RRI Denpasar (when operating), Kotak Pos 3031, Denpasar 80233, Bali, Indonesia. Phone: +62 (361) 222-161, +62 (361) 223-087. Fax: +62 (361) 227 312. Contact: I Gusti Ngurah Oka, Kepala Stasiun. Replies slowly to correspondence in Indonesian. Return postage or IRCs helpful.

Radio Republik Indonesia—RRI Dili (when operating), Stasiun Regional 1 Dili, Jalan Kaikoli, Kotak Pos 103, Dili 88000, Timor-Timur, Indonesia. Contact: Harry A. Silalahi, Kepala Stasiun; Arnoldus Klau; Paul J. Amalo, BA. Return postage or $1 helpful. Replies occasionally to correspondence in Indonesian.

Radio Republik Indonesia—RRI Fak Fak, Jalan Kapten P. Tendean, Kotak Pos 54, Fak-Fak 98612, Papua, Indonesia. Phone: +62 (956) 22-519, +62 (956) 22-521. Contact: Bahrun Siregar, Kepala Stasiun; Aloys Ngotra, Kepala Seksi Siaran; Drs. Tukiran Erlantoko; Richart Tan, Kepala Sub Seksi Siaran Kata. Station plans to upgrade its transmitting facilities with the help of the Japanese government. Return postage required. Replies occasionally.

Radio Republik Indonesia—RRI Gorontalo, Jalan Jendral Sudirman 30, Gorontalo 96115, Sulawesi Utara, Indonesia. Fax: +62 (435) 821 590/91. Contact: Drs. Bagus Edi Asmoro; Drs. Muhammad. Assad, Kepala Stasiun; Saleh S. Thalib, Technical Manager. Return postage helpful. Replies occasionally, preferably to correspondence in Indonesian.

☞Radio Republik Indonesia—RRI Jakarta

STATION: Stasiun Nasional Jakarta, Kotak Pos 356, Jakarta 10110, Daerah Khusus Jakarta Raya, Indonesia; or (street address) Jalan Medan Merdeka Barat 4-5, Jakarta 10110, Indonesia. Phone: +62 (21) 345-9091, +62 (21) 384-6817. Fax: +62 (21) 345 7132, +62 (21) 345 7134. Email: rri@rri-online.com. Web: (includes on-demand audio) www.rri-online.com. Contact: Drs. Beni Koesbani, Kepala Stasiun; Drs. Nuryudi, MM. Return postage helpful. Replies irregularly.

"DATELINE" ENGLISH PROGRAM: see Kang Guru Radio English.

TRANSMITTERS DIVISION: Jalan Merdeka Barat 4-5, Jakarta 10110 Indonesia. Phone/Fax: +62 (21) 385-7831. Email: sruslan@yahoo.com, sruslan@msn.com. Contact: Sunarya Ruslan, Head of Transmitters Division.

Radio Republik Indonesia—RRI Jambi (when operating), Jalan Jendral A. Yani 5, Telanaipura, Jambi 36122, Propinsi Jambi, Indonesia. Contact: Kepala Siaran; H. Asmuni Lubis, BA. Return postage helpful.

Radio Republik Indonesia—RRI Jayapura, Kotak Pos 1077, Jayapura 99200, Papua, Indonesia. Phone: +62 (967) 33-339. Fax: +62 (967) 33 439. Contact: Harry Liborang, Direktorat Radio; Hartono, Bidang Teknik; Dr. David Alex Siahainenia, Kepala. Return postage of $1 helpful. Replies to correspondence in Indonesian or English.

Radio Republik Indonesia—RRI Kendari, Kotak Pos 7, Kendari 93111, Sulawesi Tenggara, Indonesia. Phone: +62 (401) 21-464. Fax: +62 (401) 21 730. Contact: Drs. M. Hazir Kasrah, Manajer Seksi Siaran. Return postage required. Replies slowly to correspondence in Indonesian.

Radio Republik Indonesia—RRI Kupang (Regional I) (when operating), Jalan Tompello 8, Kupang 85225, Timor,

Indonesia. Phone: +62 (380) 821-437, +62 (380) 825-444. Fax: +62 (380) 833 149. Contact: Drs. P.M. Tisera, Kepala Stasiun; Qustigap Bagang, Kepala Seksi Siaran; Said Rasyid, Kepala Studio. Return postage helpful. Correspondence in Indonesian preferred. Replies occasionally.

Radio Republik Indonesia—RRI Madiun (when operating), Jalan Mayjend Panjaitan 10, Madiun 63133, Jawa Timur, Indonesia. Phone: +62 (351) 464-419, +62 (351) 459-198, +62 (351) 462-726, +62 (351) 459-495. Fax: +62 (351) 464 964. Web: www.kangguru.org/rristationprofiles. htm. Contact: Sri Lestari, SS; Imam Soeprapto, Kepala Seksi Siaran. Replies to correspondence in Indonesian or English. Return postage helpful.

Radio Republik Indonesia—RRI Makassar, Jalan Riburane 3, Makassar, 90111, Sulawesi Selatan, Indonesia. Phone: +62 (411) 321-853. Contact: H. La Sirama, S. Sos., Senior Manager of Broadcasting Division. Replies irregularly to correspondence in Indonesian or English. Return postage, $1 or IRCs helpful.

Radio Republik Indonesia—RRI Malang (when operating), Kotak Pos 78, Malang 65140, Jawa Timur, Indonesia; or (street address) Jalan Candi Panggung No. 58, Mojolangu, Malang 65142, Indonesia. Email: makobu@mlg. globalxtrem.net. Contact: Drs.Tjutju Tjuar Na Adikorya, Kepala Stasiun; Ml. Mawahib, Kepala Seksi Siaran; Dra Hartati Soekemi, Mengetahui. Return postage required. Free history and other booklets. Replies irregularly to correspondence in Indonesian.

Radio Republik Indonesia—RRI Manado (when operating), Kotak Pos 1110, Manado 95124 Propinsi Sulawesi Utara, Indonesia. Phone: +62 (431) 863-392. Fax: +62 (431) 863 492. Contact: Costher H. Gulton, Kepala Stasiun; Untung Santoso, Kepala Seksi Teknik. Free stickers and postcards. Return postage or $1 required. Replies occasionally to correspondence in Indonesian.

Radio Republik Indonesia—RRI Manokwari (when operating), Regional II, Jalan Merdeka 68, Manokwari 98311, Papua, Indonesia. Phone: +62 (962) 21-343. Contact: Eddy Kusbandi, Manager; Nurdin Mokogintu. Return postage helpful.

Radio Republik Indonesia—RRI Mataram (when operating), Stasiun Regional I Mataram, Jalan Langko 83 Ampenan, Mataram 83114, Nusa Tenggara Barat, Indonesia. Phone: +62 (370) 23-713, +62 (370) 21-355. Contact: Drs. Hamid Djasman, Kepala; Bochri Rachman, Ketua Dewan Pimpinan Harian. Free stickers. Return postage required. With sufficient return postage or small token gift, sometimes sends tourist information and Batik print. Replies to correspondence in Indonesian.

Radio Republik Indonesia—RRI Medan (when operating), Jalan Letkol Martinus Lubis 5, Medan 20232, Sumatera, Indonesia. Phone: +62 (61) 324-222/441. Fax: +62 (61) 512 161. Contact: Kepala Stasiun, Ujamalul Abidin Ass; Drs. S. Parlin Tobing, SH, Produsennya, "Kontak Pendengar"; Drs. H. Suryanta Saleh. Free stickers. Return postage required. Replies to correspondence in Indonesian.

Radio Republik Indonesia—RRI Merauke, Stasiun Regional 1, Kotak Pos 11, Merauke 99611, Papua, Indonesia. Phone: +62 (971) 21-396, +62 (971) 21-376. Contact: (general) Drs. Buang Akhir, Direktur; Achmad Ruskaya B.A., Kepala Stasiun, Drs.Tuanakotta Semuel, Kepala Seksi Siaran; John Manuputty, Kepala Subseksi Pemancar; (technical) Daf'an Kubangun, Kepala Seksi Tehnik. Return postage helpful.

Radio Republik Indonesia—RRI Nabire, Kotak Pos 110, Jalan Merdeka 74 Nabire 98811, Papua, Indonesia. Phone: +62 (984) 21-013. Contact: Muchtar Yushaputra, Kepala Stasiun. Free stickers and occasional free picture postcards. Return postage or IRCs helpful.

Radio Republik Indonesia—RRI Padang, Kotak Pos 77, Padang 25111, Sumatera Barat, Indonesia. Phone: +61 (751) 28-363, +62 (751) 21-030, +62 (751) 27-482. Contact: H. Hutabarat, Kepala Stasiun; Amir Hasan, Kepala Seksi Siaran. Return postage helpful.

Radio Republik Indonesia—RRI Palangkaraya (when operating), Jalan M. Husni Thamrin 1, Palangkaraya 73111, Kalimantan Tengah, Indonesia. Phone: +62 (536) 21-779. Fax: +62 (536) 21 778. Contact: Andy Sunandar; Drs.Amiruddin; S. Polin; A.F. Herry Purwanto; Meyiwati SH; Supardal Djojosubrojo, Sarjana Hukum; Dr. S. Parlin Tobing, Station Manager; Murniaty Oesin, Transmission Department Engineer; Gumer Kamis; Ricky D. Wader, Kepala Stasiun. Return postage helpful. Will respond to correspondence in Indonesian or English.

Radio Republik Indonesia—RRI Palembang (when operating), Jalan Radio 2, Km. 4, Palembang 30128, Sumatera Selatan, Indonesia. Phone: +62 (711) 350-811, +62 (711) 309-977, +62 (711) 350-927. Contact: Drs. H. Mursjid Noor, Kepala Stasiun; H.Ahmad Syukri Ahkab, Kepala Seksi Siaran; H.Iskandar Suradilaga. Return postage helpful. Replies slowly and occasionally.

Radio Republik Indonesia—RRI Palu, Jalan R.A. Kartini 39, Palu 94112, Sulawesi Tengah, Indonesia. Phone: +62 (451) 21-621, +62 (451) 94-112. Contact: Akson Boole; Nyonyah Netty Ch. Soriton, Kepala Seksi Siaran; Gugun Santoso; Untung Santoso, Kepala Seksi Teknik; M. Hasjim, Head of Programming. Return postage required. Replies slowly to correspondence in Indonesian.

Radio Republik Indonesia—RRI Pekanbaru (when operating), Kotak Pos 51, Pekanbaru 28113, Kepulauan Riau, Indonesia. Phone: +62 (761) 22-081, +62 (761) 23-606, +62 (761) 25-111. Fax: +62 (761) 23 605. Contact: (general) Hendri Yunis, ST, Kepala Stasiun, Ketua DPH; Arisun Agus, Kepala Seksi Siaran; Drs. H. Syamsidi, Kepala Supag Tata Usaha; Zainal Abbas. Return postage helpful.

Radio Republik Indonesia—RRI Pontianak, Kotak Pos 1005, Pontianak 78117, Kalimantan Barat, Indonesia. Phone: +62 (561) 734-987. Fax: +62 (561) 734 659. Contact: Ruddy Banding, Kepala Seksi Siaran; Achmad Ruskaya, BA; Drs. Effendi Afati, Producer, "Dalam Acara Kantong Surat"; Subagio, Kepala Sub Bagian Tata Usaha; Augustwus Campek; Rahayu Widati; Suryadharma, Kepala Sub Seksi Programa; Muchlis Marzuki B.A. Return postage or $1 helpful. Replies some of the time to correspondence in Indonesian (preferred) or English.

Radio Republik Indonesia—RRI Samarinda, Kotak Pos 45, Samarinda, Kalimantan Timur 75110, Indonesia. Phone: +62 (541) 743-495. Fax: +62 (541) 741 693. Contact: Siti Thomah, Kepala Seksi Siaran; Tyranus Lenjau, English Announcer; S. Yati; Marthin Tapparan; Sunendra, Kepala Stasiun. May send tourist brochures and maps. Return postage helpful. Replies to correspondence in Indonesian.

Radio Republik Indonesia—RRI Semarang (when operating), Kotak Pos 1073, Semarang 50241, Jawa Tengah, Indonesia. Phone: +62 (24) 831-6686, +62 (24) 831-6661, +62 (24) 831-6330. (Phone/Fax, marketing) +62 (24) 831-6330. Web: www.kangguru.org/rristationprofiles.htm. Contact: Djarwanto, SH; Drs. Sabeni, Doktorandus;

Drs. Purwadi, Program Director; Dra. Endang Widiastuti, Kepala Sub Seksi Periklanan Jasa dan Hak Cipta; H. Sutakno, Kepala Stasiun; Mardanon, Kepala Teknik. Return postage helpful.

Radio Republik Indonesia—RRI Serui, Jalan Pattimura Kotak Pos 19, Serui 98213, Papua, Indonesia. Phone: +62 (983) 31-150, +62 (983) 31-121. Contact: M. Yawandare, Manager Siaran. Replies occasionally to correspondence in Indonesian, although Mr. Yawandare also understands English. IRC or return postage helpful.

Radio Republik Indonesia—RRI Sibolga (when operating), Jalan Ade Irma Suryani, Nasution No. 11, Sibolga 22513, Sumatera Utara, Indonesia. Phone: +61 (631) 21-183, +62 (631) 22-506, +62 (631) 22-947. Contact: Mrs. Laiya; Mrs. S. Sitoupul; B.A. Tanjung. Return postage required. Replies occasionally to correspondence in Indonesian.

Radio Republik Indonesia—RRI Sorong
STATION: Kotak Pos 146, Sorong 98414, Papua, Indonesia. Phone: +62 (951) 21-003, +62 (951) 22-111, +62 (951) 22-611. Contact: Drs. Sallomo Hamid; Tetty Rumbay S., Kasubsi Siaran Kata; Mrs. Tien Widarsanto, Resa Kasi Siaran; Ressa Molle; Mughpar Yushaputra, Kepala Stasiun; Umar Solle, Station Manager; Linda Rumbay. Return postage helpful. Replies to correspondence in English.
"DATELINE" ENGLISH PROGRAM: See Kang Guru Radio English.

Radio Republik Indonesia—RRI Sumenep (when operating), Jalan Urip Sumoharjo 26, Sumenep 69411, Madura, Jawa Timur, Indonesia. Phone: +62 (328) 62-317, +62 (328) 21-811, +62 (328) 21-317, +62 (328) 66-768. Contact: Dian Irianto, Kepala Stasiun. Return postage helpful.

Radio Republik Indonesia—RRI Surabaya, (when operating) Stasiun Regional 1, Kotak Pos 239, Surabaya 60271, Jawa Timur, Indonesia. Phone: +62 (31) 534-1327, +62 (31) 534-2327, +62 (31) 534-1327, +62 (31) 534-5474, +62 (31) 534-0478, +62 (31) 547-3610. Fax: +62 (31) 534 2351. Contact: Zainal Abbas, Kepala Stasiun; Usmany Johozua, Kepala Seksi Siaran; Drs. E. Agus Widjaja, MM, Kasi Siaran; Pardjingat, Kepala Seksi Teknik; Ny Koen Tarjadi. Return postage or IRCs helpful.

Radio Republik Indonesia—RRI Surakarta (when operating), Kotak Pos 40, Surakarta 57133, Jawa Tengah, Indonesia. Phone: +62 (271) 634-004/05, +62 (271) 638-145, +62 (271) 654-399, +62 (271) 641-178. Fax: +62 (271) 642 208. Contact: H. Tomo, B.A., Head of Broadcasting; Titiek Sudartik, S.H., Kepala. Return postage helpful.

Radio Republik Indonesia—RRI Tanjungkarang, Kotak Pos 24, Bandar Lampung 35213, Indonesia. Phone: +62 (721) 555-2280, +62 (721) 569-720. Fax: +62 (721) 562 767. Contact: M. Nasir Agun, Kepala Stasiun; Hi Hanafie Umar; Djarot Nursinggih, Tech. Transmission; Drs. Doewadji, Kepala Seksi Siaran; Drs. Zulhaqqi Hafiz, Kepala Sub Seksi Periklanan; Asmara Haidar Manaf. Return postage helpful. Also identifies as RRI Bandar Lampung. Replies in Indonesian to correspondence in Indonesian or English.

Radio Republik Indonesia—RRI Tanjungpinang, Stasiun RRI Regional II Tanjungpinang, Kotak Pos 8, Tanjungpinang 29123, Kepulauan Riau, Indonesia. Phone: +62 (771) 21-278, +62 (771) 21-540, +62 (771) 21-916, +62 (771) 29-123. Contact: M. Yazid, Kepala Stasiun; Wan Suhardi, Produsennya, "Siaran Bahasa Melayu"; Rosakim, Sarjana Hukum. Return postage helpful. Replies occasionally to correspondence in Indonesian or English.

Radio Republik Indonesia—RRI Ternate (when operating), Jalan Sultan Khairun, Kedaton, Ternate 97720 (Ternate), Maluku Utara, Indonesia. Phone: +62 (921) 21-582, +62 (921) 21-762, +62 (921) 25-525. Contact: (general) Abd. Latief Kamarudin, Kepala Stasiun; (technical) Rusdy Bachmid, Head of Engineering; Abubakar Alhadar. Return postage helpful.

Radio Republik Indonesia Tual (when operating), Watden, Pulau Kai, Tual 97661 Maluku, Indonesia.

Radio Republik Indonesia—RRI Wamena (when operating), RRI Regional II, Kotak Pos 10, Wamena, Papua 99511, Indonesia. Phone: +62 (969) 31-380. Fax: +62 (969) 31 299. Contact: Yoswa Kumurawak, Penjab Subseksi Pemancar. Return postage helpful.

Radio Republik Indonesia—RRI Yogyakarta (when operating), Jalan Amat Jazuli 4, Kotak Pos 18, Yogyakarta 55224, Jawa Tengah, Indonesia. Fax: +62 (274) 2784. Phone: +62 (274) 512-783/85, +62 (274) 580-333. Email: rri-yk@yogya.wasantara.net.id. Contact: Phoenix Sudomo Sudaryo; Tris Mulyanti, Seksi Programa Siaran; Martono, ub. Kabid Penyelenggaraan Siaran; Mr. Kadis, Technical Department; Drs. H. Hamdan Sjahbeni, Kepala Stasiun. IRC, return postage or $1 helpful. Replies occasionally to correspondence in Indonesian or English.

Radio Siaran Pemerintah Daerah TK II—RSPD Halmahera Tengah, Soasio, Jalan A. Malawat, Soasio, Maluku Tengah 97812, Indonesia. Contact: Drs. S. Chalid A. Latif, Kepala Badan Pengelola.

Voice of Indonesia, Kotak Pos 1157, Jakarta 10001, Daerah Khusus Jakarta Raya, Indonesia; (street address) Jalan Medan Merdeka Barat No. 4-5, Jakarta 10110 Indonesia. Phone: +62 (21) 345-6811. Fax: +62 (21) 350 0990. Email: voi@rri-online.com. Web: www.rri-online.com. Contact: Anastasia Yasmine, Head of Foreign Affairs Section; Amy Aisha, Presenter, "Listeners Mailbag." Free stickers and calendars. Correspondence is best addressed to the individual language sections. Be careful when addressing your letters to the station as mail sent to the Voice of Indonesia, Japanese Section, has sometimes been incorrectly delivered to NHK's Jakarta Bureau. Very slow in replying but enclosing 4 IRCs may help speed things up.

INTERNATIONAL WATERS

Coalition Maritime Forces (CMF) Radio One (when operating), MARLO Bahrain, PSC 451 Box 330, FPO AE 09834-2800, USA. Email: (including reception reports) marlo.bahrain@marlobahrain.org. Web: (MARLO Bahrain parent organization) www.marlobahrain.org. Station of the Maritime Liaison Office (MARLO) of the United States Navy. Broadcasts via low power transmitters on ships in the Persian Gulf and nearby waters. Verifies reception reports.

IRAN World Time +3:30 (+4:30 midyear)

Voice of the Islamic Republic of Iran
MAIN OFFICE: IRIB External Services, P.O. Box 19395-6767, Tehran, Iran. Phone: +98 (21) 204-2808; (English Service) +98 (21) 201-3720, +98 (21) 216-2895, +98 (21) 216-2734. Fax: +98 (21) 205 1635, +98 (21) 204 1097, + 98 (21) 291 095; (English Service) +98 (21) 201 3770; (technical) +98 (21) 654 841. Email: (all technical matters other than reception reports) sw@irib.ir, tech@irib.

ir; (English Service) englishradio@irib.ir (same format for German, Spanish and Italian, e.g. spanishradio@irib.ir); (French Service) radio_fr@irib.ir. Web: (includes streaming audio) www.irib.ir/worldservice. Contact: Mohammad B. Khoshnevisan, IRIB English Radio. Free books on Islam, magazines, calendars, bookmarkers, tourist literature and postcards. Verifications require a minimum of two days' reception data on two or more separate broadcasts; return postage appreciated. Is currently asking listeners to send their telephone numbers so that they can be called by the station. You can send your phone number to the postal address above, or fax it to: + 98 (21) 205 1635.
SIRJAN TRANSMITTING STATION: P.O. Box 369, Sirjan, Iran. Contact: Aliasghar Shakoori Moghaddam, Head of Sirjan Station.

Mashhad Regional Radio, P.O. Box 555, Mashhad Center, Jomhoriye Eslame, Iran. Contact: J. Ghanbari, General Director.

IRAQ World Time +3 (+4 midyear)

Voice of Iraqi Kurdistan ("Aira dangi Kurdestana Iraqiyah"). Web: (includes streaming audio) http://kdp.nu (click on "KDP's Media," then on "KDP info"). Station of the Kurdistan Democratic Party-Iraq (KDP), led by Masoud Barzani. Broadcasts from its own transmitting facilities, located in the Kurdish section of Iraq. To contact the station or to obtain verification of reception reports, try going via one of the following KDP offices:
KDP INTERNATIONAL RELATIONS BUREAU (U.K.): Phone: +44 (207) 498-2664. Fax: +44 (207) 498 2531.
KDP REPRESENTATION IN WASHINGTON: 17115 Leesburg Pike #110, Falls Church VA 22043 USA. Phone: +1 (703) 533-5882. Fax: +1 (703) 599 5886. Email: pdk7usa@aol.com.
KDP-SWEDEN OFFICE: Email: party@kdp.se. Web: (includes streaming audio) www.kdp.se. Contact: Alex Atroushi. Reception reports to this address have sometimes been verified by email.

IRELAND World Time exactly (+1 midyear)

Radio Telefís Éireann (when operating on shortwave), Donnybrook, Dublin 4, Ireland. Phone: +353 (1) 208-3111. Fax: +353 (1) 208 3080. Email: (Pope) bernie.pope@rte.ie. Web: (includes on-demand and streaming audio) www.rte.ie/radio. Contact: Mrs. Bernie Pope, Network Support, who will verify reception reports, including those sent by email. Broadcasts irregularly, mainly for sports or election coverage.

ISRAEL World Time +2 (+3 midyear)

Bezeq—Israel Telecommunication Corp. Ltd., Engineering and Planning Division, Radio and T.V. Broadcasting Section, P.O. Box 62081, Tel-Aviv 61620, Israel. Phone: +972 (3) 626-4562, +972 (3) 626-4500. Fax: +972 (3) 626 4559. Email: (Oren) mosheor@bezeq.com; or rms2@bezeqint.net. Web: www.bezeq.co.il. Contact: Moshe Oren, Frequency Manager. Bezeq is responsible for transmitting the programs of the Israel Broadcasting Authority (IBA), which *inter alia* parents Kol Israel. This address only for pointing out transmitter-related problems (interference, modulation quality, network mixups, etc.), especially by fax, of transmitters based in Israel. Does not verify reception reports.

📻**Galei Zahal (Israel Defence Forces Radio)**, Zahal, Military Mail No. 01005, Israel. Phone: +972 (3) 512-6666. Fax: +972 (3) 512 6760. Email: glz@galatz.co.il. Web: (includes on-demand and streaming audio) www. glz.msn.co.il.

📻**Kol Israel**, P.O. Box 1082, Jerusalem 91010, Israel. Phone: (general) +972 (2) 530-2222; (Engineering Dept.) +972 (2) 501-3453; (Hebrew voice mail for Reshet Bet program "The Israel Connection") +972 (3) 765-1929. Fax: (English Service) +972 (2) 530 2424. Email: (English Service) englishradio@iba.org.il; (correspondence relating to reception problems, only) engineering@israelradio.org; (Reshet Bet program for Israelis abroad) kesherisraeli@yahoo.com. Web: (includes on-demand and streaming audio) www. israelradio.org; (on-demand and streaming audio) www. iba.org.il. Contact: Edmond Sehayeq, Head of Programming, Persian broadcasts; Yishai Eldar, Reporter, English News Department; Steve Linde, Head of English News Department; Sara Gabbai, Head of Western Broadcasting Department; (administration) Yonni Ben-Menachem, Director of External Broadcasting; (technical, frequency management) Raphael Kochanowski, Director of Liaison and Coordination, Engineering Dept. No verifications or freebies, due to limited budget.

SAN FRANCISCO OFFICE, SCHEDULES: 2654 17th Avenue, San Francisco CA 94116 USA. Phone: +1 (415) 564-9968. Email: GPoppin@aol.com. Contact: George Poppin. This address, a volunteer office, only provides Kol Israel schedules to listeners (return postage not required). All other correspondence should be sent directly to the main office in Jerusalem.

ITALY   World Time +1 (+2 midyear)

📻**Italian Radio Relay Service**, IRRS-Shortwave, Nexus-IBA, P.O. Box 11028, 20110 Milano, Italy; (reception reports) P.O. Box 10980, 20110 Milano, Italy. Phone: +39 (02) 266-6971. Fax: +39 (02) 7063 8151. Email: (general) info@nexus.org; (reception reports) reports@nexus.org; (Cotroneo) alfredo@nexus.org; (Norton) ron@nexus.org. Web: www.nexus.org/radio.htm; (streaming audio) http://mp3.nexus.org; (International Public Access Radio) www. nexus.org/IPAR; (European Gospel Radio) www.egradio.

org. Contact: (general) Vanessa Dickinson; Anna S. Boschetti, President; Alfredo E. Cotroneo, CEO; (technical) Ron Norton, Verification Manager. Correspondence and reception reports by email are answered promptly and at no charge, but for budget reasons the station may be unable to reply to all postal correspondence. Two IRCs or $1 helpful.

JAPAN   World Time +9

📻**Furusato no Kaze** (Wind of the Homeland), Headquarters for the Abduction Issue, 1-6-1 Nagata-cho, Chiyoda-ku, Tokyo 100-8968, Japan. Phone: +81 (3) 3522-2300. Email: info@rachi.go.jp. Web: (includes on-demand audio) www.kantei.go.jp/jp/singi/rati/radio/radio.html. Replies to correspondence in Japanese or English, but does not verify reception reports.

PROGRAM PRODUCTION: Japan Center for Intercultural Communications, 2-7-7 Hirakawa-cho, Chiyoda-ku, Tokyo 102-0093, Japan. Web: http://home.jcic.or.jp.

📻**Nihon no Kaze** (Ilbone Baram, Wind of Japan), Korean-language sister-station to Furusato no Kaze (*see*), with same contact details. Web: (includes on-demand audio) www.kantei.go.jp/jp/singi/rati/radio/radio_k.html.

📻Radio Japan/NHK World

MAIN OFFICE: NHK World, Nippon Hoso Kyokai, Tokyo 150-8001, Japan. Phone: +81 (3) 3465-1111. Fax: (general) +81 (3) 3481 1350; (" from Tokyo" and Production Center) +81 (3) 3465 0966. Email: (general) nhkworld@nhk.jp; (Spanish Section) rj-espa@intl.nhk.or.jp. Web: (English, includes on-demand and streaming audio) www.nhk.or.jp/english; (Japanese, includes on-demand and streaming audio) www.nhk.or.jp/nhkworld. Contact: (administration) Saburo Eguchi, Deputy Director General; Shuichiro Sunohara, Deputy Director International Planning & Programming; Tadao Sakomizu, Director, English Service; Ms. Kyoko Hirotani, Planning & Programming Division.

ENGINEERING ADMINISTRATION DEPARTMENT: Nippon Hoso Kyokai, Tokyo 150-8001, Japan. Phone: +81 (3) 5455-5395, +81 (3) 5455-5384, +81 (3) 5455-5376, +81 (3) 5455-2288. Fax: +81 (3) 3485 0952, + 81 (3) 3481 4985. Email: (general) rj-freq@eng.nhk.or.jp; yoshimi@eng.nhk. or.jp, kurasima@eng.nhk.or.jp. Contact: Fujimoto Hiroki, Frequency Manager; Akira Mizuguchi, Transmissions Manager; Tetsuya Itsuk; Toshiki Kurashima.

MONITORING DIVISION: NHK World/Radio Japan. Fax: +81 (3) 3481 1877. Email: info@intl.nhk.or.jp.

HONG KONG BUREAU: Phone: +852 2509-0238.

EUROPEAN (LONDON) BUREAU: Phone: +44 (20) 7393-8100.

LOS ANGELES OFFICE: Phone: +1 (310) 586-1600.

USA (NEW YORK) BUREAU: Phone: +1 (212) 704-9898.

📻**Radio Nikkei**, Nikkei Radio Broadcasting Corporation, 9-15 Akasaka 1-chome, Minato-ku, Tokyo 107-8373, Japan. Fax: +81 (3) 3583 9062. Web: (includes on-demand and streaming audio) www.radionikkei.jp. Contact: H. Nagao, Public Relations; M. Teshima; Ms. Terumi Onoda; H. Ono. Sending a reception report may help with a reply. Free stickers and Japanese stamps. $1 or 2 IRCs helpful.

📻**Shiokaze** (Sea Breeze), 3-8-401 Koraku 2-chome, Bunkyo-ku, Tokyo 112-0004, Japan. Phone: +81 (3) 5684-5058. Fax: +81 (3) 5684 5059. Email: chosakai@circus.ocn.ne.jp. Web: www.chosa-kai.jp. Broadcast of the Investigation Commission on Missing Japanese Probably Related to

North Korea (COMJAM). Verifies reception reports with a QSL card, including those sent by email.

JORDAN   World Time +2 (+3 midyear)

📻**Radio Jordan**, P.O. Box 909, Amman, Jordan; or P.O. Box 1041, Amman, Jordan. Phone: (general) +962 (6) 477-4111; (International Relations) +962 (6) 477-8578; (English Service) +962 (6) 475-7410, +962 (6) 477-3111; (Arabic Service) +962 (6) 463-6454; (Saleh) +962 (6) 474-8048; (Al-Arini) +962 (6) 474-9161. Fax: (general) +962 (6) 478 8115; (English Service) +962 (6) 420 7862; (Al-Arini) +962 (6) 474 9190. Email: (general) online form; (programs) rj@jrtv.gov.jo; (Director of Radio TV Engineering) arini@jrtv.gov.jo. Web: (includes streaming audio) www.jrtv.jo/rj. Contact: (general) Jawad Zada, Director of Foreign Service; Mrs. Firyal Zamakhshari, Director of Arabic Programs; Qasral Mushatta; (administrative) Abdul Hamid Al Majali, Director of Radio; Mrs. Fatima Massri, Director of International Relations; Muwaffaq al-Rahayifah, Director of Shortwave Services; (technical) Youssef Al-Arini, Director of Radio TV Engineering. Free stickers. Replies irregularly and slowly. Enclosing $1 helps.

KENYA   World Time

Kenya Broadcasting Corporation, P.O. Box 30456, Harry Thuku Road, 00100 Nairobi, Kenya. Phone: +254 (20) 334-567. Fax: +254 (20) 220 675. Email: (general) kbc@swiftkenya.com; (management) mdkbc@swiftkenya.com; (technical services) kbctechnical@swiftkenya.com. Web: www.kbc.co.ke. Contact: (general) Henry Makokha, Liaison Office; (administration) Joe Matano Khamisi, Managing Director; (technical) Nathan Lamu, Senior Principal Technical Officer; Augustine Kenyanjier Gochui; Lawrence Holnati, Engineering Division; Daniel Githua, Assistant Manager Technical Services (Radio). IRC required. Replies irregularly. If all you want is verfication of your reception report(s), you may have better luck sending your letter to: Engineer in Charge, Maralal Radio Station, P.O. Box 38, Maralal, Kenya.

KOREA (DPR)   World Time +9

Korean Central Broadcasting Station, Chongsung-dong, Moranbong District, Pyongyang, Democratic People's Republic of Korea. If you don't speak Korean, try sending your correspondence via the Voice of Korea (see).
Regional KCBS stations—Not known to reply, but a long-shot possibility is to try corresponding in Korean to the Pyongyang address, above.
Pyongyang Broadcasting Station—Correspondence should be sent to the Voice of Korea (see next item), which sometimes verifies reception reports on PBS broadcasts.
Voice of Korea, External Service, Radio-Television Broadcasting Committee of the DPRK, Pyongyang, Democratic People's Republic of Korea (*not* "North Korea"). Phone: +850 (2) 381-6035. Fax: +850 (2) 381 4416. Phone and fax numbers valid only in those countries with direct telephone service to North Korea. Free publications, pennants, calendars, newspapers, artistic prints and pins. Do not include dutiable items in your envelope. Replies can sometimes be irregular, especially to countries not having diplomatic relations with North Korea. Mail from

these countries is sent via circuitous routes and apparently does not always arrive. One way around the problem is to add "VIA BEIJING, CHINA" to the address, but replies via this route tend to be slow in coming. An alternative route is to send your letters via the English Section of China Radio International. Place your correspondence in a separate envelope addressed to the Voice of Korea, and ask CRI to forward your letter to Pyongyang. Explain the mail situation to the people in Beijing and you may have success. Another gambit is to send your correspondence to an associate in a country—such as China, Ukraine or India—having reasonable relations with North Korea, and ask that it be forwarded. Send correspondence in a sealed envelope without any address on the back. That should be sent inside another envelope. Include 3 IRCs to cover the cost of forwarding.

KOREA (REPUBLIC)   World Time +9.

📻**KBS World Radio**
MAIN OFFICE, INTERNATIONAL BROADCASTING DEPARTMENT: KBS World Radio, Global Center, Korean Broadcasting System, Yoido-dong 18, Youngdeungpo-gu, Seoul, Republic of Korea 150-790. Phone: (general) +82 (2) 781-3650/60/70; (English Section) +82 (2) 781-3674/5/6; (Korean Section) +82 (2) 781-3669/71/72/73; (German Section) +82 (2) 781-3682/3/9; (Japanese Section) +82 (2) 781-3654/5/6 (Spanish Section) +82 (2) 781-3679/81/97. Fax: (general) +82 (2) 781 3694/5/6. Email: (English) english@kbs.co.kr; (German) german@kbs.co.kr; (Japanese) japanese@kbs.co.kr; (Spanish) spanish@kbs.co.kr; (other language sections use the same format, except for Vietnamese: vietnam@kbs.co.kr); (Executive Director) hheejoo@kbs.co.kr. Web: (includes streaming audio) http://world.kbs.co.kr. Contact: Ms. Hee Joo Han, Executive Director, KBS World-External Radio & TV; Park Young-seok, Chief; (administration) Sang Myung Kim; (English Section) Chae Hong-Pyo, Manager; Ms. Seung Joo ("Sophia") Hong, Producer; Mr. Chun Hye-Jin, DX Editor, *Seoul Calling*; (Korean Section) Hae Ok Lee, Producer; (Japanese Section) Ms. Hye Young Kim, Producer; (Spanish Section) Ms. Sujin Cho, Producer; (German Section) Chung Soon Wan, Manager; Lee Bum Suk, Producer; Sabastian Ratzer, Journalist. Free stickers, calendars, *Let's Learn Korean* book and a wide variety of other small souvenirs. *History of Korea* is available on CD-ROM (upon request) and via the station's Website.
ADDRESS IN ARGENTINA: KBS World Radio, Casilla de Correo 950, S2000WAJ Rosario, Argentina.
ENGINEERING DEPARTMENT: IBC, Center, Korean Broadcasting System, Yoido-dong 18, Youngdeungpo-Gu, Seoul, Republic of Korea 150-790. Phone: (general) +82 (2) 781-5141/5137; (Radio Transmission Division) +82 (2) 781-5663. Fax: +82 (2) 781 5159. Email: (Radio Transmission Division) poeto@hanmail.net; (Frequency Manager) kdhy@kbs.co.kr; (Planning Engineer) pulo5@kbs.co.kr. Contact: Mr. Oh Daesik, Radio Transmission Division; Mr. Dae-hyun Kim, Frequency Manager; Mr. Chun-soo Lee, Planning Engineer.

📻**Korean Broadcasting System (KBS)**, 18 Yoido-dong, Youngdeungpo-gu, Seoul, Republic of Korea 150-790. Phone: +82 (2) 781-1000; (duty officer) +82 (2) 781-1711/1792; (news desk) +82 (2) 781-4444; (overseas assistance) +82 (2) 781-1473/1497. Fax: +82 (2) 781

1698, +82 (2) 781 2399. Web: (includes streaming audio) http://kbs.co.kr.

KUWAIT   World Time +3

IBB Kuwait Transmitting Station, c/o American Embassy-Bayan, P.O.Box 77, Safat, 13001 Kuwait, Kuwait. Contact: Transmitter Plant Supervisor. This address for specialized technical correspondence only, although reception reports may occasionally be verified. All other correspondence should be directed to the regular VOA or IBB addresses (see USA).

Radio Kuwait, P.O. Box 397, 13004 Safat, Kuwait; (technical) Department of Frequency Management, P.O. Box 967, 13010 Safat, Kuwait. Phone: (general) +965 242-3774; (technical) +965 241-5301. Fax: (general) +965 245 6660; (technical) +965 241 5946. Email: info@media.gov. kw. Web: (streaming audio) www.media.gov.kw. Contact: (general) Manager, External Service; (technical) Wessam Najaf. Sometimes gives away stickers, desk calendars, pens or key chains.
TRANSMISSION AND FREQUENCY MANAGEMENT OFFICE: Ministry of Information, P.O. Box 967 13010 Safat, Kuwait. Phone: +965 241-3590, +965 243-6193. Fax: +965 241 7830. Email: kwtfreq@media.gov.kw. Contact: Ahmed J. Alawdhi, Head of Frequency Section.

KYRGYZSTAN   World Time +6

Kyrgyz National Radio, Kyrgyz TV and Radio Center, 59 Jash Gvardiya Boulevard, 720010 Bishkek, Kyrgyzstan. Phone: (general) +996 (312) 253-404, +996 (312) 255-741; (Director) +996 (312) 255-700, +996 (312) 255-709; (Assemov) +996 (312) 650-7341, +996 (312) 255-703; (technical) +996 (312) 257-771. Fax: +996 (312) 257 952. Email: ntrk@ktr.kg. Web: (includes streaming audio) www. ktr.kg; (English) www.ktr.kg/tv/en. Contact: (administration) Myrsakul Mambetaliev, Director; (general) Talant Assemov, Editor - Kyrgyz/Russian/German news; Gulnara Abdulaeva, Announcer - Kyrgyz/Russian/German news; (technical) Mirbek Uursabekov, Technical Director. Kyrgyz and Russian preferred, but correspondence in English or German can also be processed. For quick processing of reception reports, use email in German to Talant Assemov.
TRANSMISSION FACILITIES: Ministry of Transport and Communications, 42 Issanova Street, 720000 Bishkek, Kyrgyzstan. Phone: +996 (312) 216-672. Fax: +996 (312) 213 667. Contact: Jantoro Satybaldiyev, Minister. The shortwave transmitting station is located at Krasnaya-Rechka (Red River), a military encampment in the Issk-Ata region, about 40 km south of Bishkek.
Radio Maranatha, Kulatov Street 8/1, Room 411, Bishkek, Kyrgyzstan. Phone: +996 (312) 273-845.
Hit Shortwave—music programming aired over Radio Maranatha (see, above).

LAO PEOPLE'S DEMOCRATIC REPUBLIC   World Time +7

NOTE: Although universally known as Laos, the official name of the country is "Lao People's Democratic Republic." English has now replaced French as the preferred foreign language.

Houa Phanh Provincial Radio Station, Sam Neua, Houa Phanh Province, Lao P.D.R. Phone: +856 (64) 312-008. Fax: +856 (21) 312 017. Contact: Mr. Veeyang, Hmong Announcer, and the only person who speaks English at the station; Ms. Nouan Thong, Lao Announcer; Mr. Vilaphone Bounsouvanh, Director; Mr. Khong Kam, Engineer.
Lao National Radio
PROGRAM OFFICE AND NATIONAL STUDIOS: Lao National Radio, Phaynam Road, Vientiane, Lao P.D.R; (postal address) P.O. Box 310, Vientiane, Lao P.D.R. Phone: +856 (21) 212-097/428/429/431/432; (Head of English service & External Relations) +856 (21) 252-863. Fax: +856 (21) 212 430. Email: laonatradio@lnr.org.la. (Head of English Service) inpanhs@hotmail.com. Web: (includes on-demand audio in Lao and English) www.lnr.org.la. Contact: Mr. Bounthan Inthaxay, Director General; Mr. Inpanh Satchaphansy, Head of English Service & External relations; Mr. Vorasak Pravongviengkham, Head of French Service; Ms. Mativarn Simanithone, Deputy Head, English Section; Ms Chanthery Vichitsavanh, Announcer, English Section. Sometimes includes a program schedule and Laotian stamps when replying.
HF TRANSMITTER SITE: Transmitting Station KM6, Phone Tong Road, Ban Chommany Neuk, Vientiane Province, Lao P.D.R. Phone: +856 (21) 710-181. Contact: Mr. Sysamone Phommaxay, Station Engineer.
TECHNICAL OFFICE: Mass Media Department, Ministry of Information & Culture, 01000 Thanon Setthathirath, Vientiane, Lao P.D.R; or P.O. Box 122, Vientiane, Lao P.D.R. Phone/Fax: +856 (21) 212-424. Contact: Mr. Dy Sisombath, Deputy Director General & Manager, Technical Network Expansion Planning.

LATVIA   World Time +2 (+3 midyear)

RNI Radio, c/o Raimonds Kreicbergs, P.O. Box 371, LV-1010 Riga, Latvia. Phone: +371 2922-4105. Email: kreicbergs@parks.lv. A shortwave relay service.

LEBANON   World Time +2 (+3 midyear)

Radio Voice of Charity, Rue Fouad Chéhab, Jounieh, Lebanon; or B.P. 850, Jounieh, Lebanon. Phone: +961 (9) 918-090, +961 (9) 917-917, +961 (9) 636-344. Fax: +961 (9) 930 272. Email: mahaba@radiocharity.org.lb. Web: (includes streaming audio from domestic service) www. radiocharity.org. Contact: Father Fadi Tabet, General Director. Operates domestically on FM, and airs a 30-minute daily Arabic broadcast via the shortwave facilities of Vatican Radio. Replies to correspondence in English, French or Arabic, and verifies reception reports. Return postage helpful.

LESOTHO   World Time +2

Radio Lesotho (if reactivated), P.O. Box 552, Maseru 100, Lesotho. Phone/Fax: +266 323-371. Email: online form. Web: (includes streaming audio) www.radioles.co.ls. Contact: (administration) Ms. Mpine Tente, Principal Secretary, Ministry of Information and Broadcasting; (technical) Motlatsi Monyane, Chief Engineer. Return postage necessary, but do not include currency notes—local currency exchange laws are very strict.

LIBERIA World Time exactly

Radio ELWA, Box 192, Monrovia, Liberia. Phone: +231 (6) 515-511. Email: radio.staff@elwaministries.org; (Nyantee) moses.nyantee@elwaministries.org. Web: www.elwaministries.org (click on "Radio Station"). Contact: Moses T. Nyantee, Station Manager.

Radio Veritas, P.O. Box 3569, Monrovia, Liberia. Phone: +231 221-658. Email: radioveritas@hotmail.com. Contact: Ledgerhood Rennie, Station Manager.

Star Radio, P.O. Box 3081, 1000 Monrovia 10, Liberia; (street address) 12 Broad Street, Snapper Hill, Monrovia, Liberia. Phone: +231 (77) 104-411. Email: starradio_liberia@yahoo.com. Web: www.starradio.org.lr. Contact: James Morlu, Station Manager. An independent station supported by the Swiss-based Fondation Hirondelle. Transmits round the clock on 104 FM in Monrovia, and airs a morning broadcast on world band via a leased transmitter operated by VT Communications (see United Kingdom). *FONDATION HIRONDELLE:* Avenue du Temple 19C, CH 1012-Lausanne, Switzerland. Phone: +41 (21) 654-2020. Fax: +41 (21) 654 2021. Email: info@hirondelle.org. Web: www.hirondelle.org. Contact: Darcy Christen, Star Radio Program Officer. Verifies reception reports.

LIBYA World Time +2

🔊**Libyan Jamahiriyah Broadcasting Corporation**, P.O. Box 9333, Tripoli, Libya. Phone: +218 (21) 361-4508. Fax: +218 (21) 489 4240. Web: (includes streaming audio) www.ljbc.net. Contact: Youssef Aimoujrab.

Voice of Africa, P.O. Box 4677, Soug al Jama, Tripoli, Libya (P.O.B. 2009 and P.O.B. 4396 should also work). Phone: +218 (21) 444-0112, +218 (21) 444-9106. Fax: +218 (21) 444 9875. Email: (English) info@en.ljbc.net, info@voiceofafrica.com.ly. Web: (under construction) www.voiceofafrica.com.ly. The external service of the Libyan Jamahiriyah Broadcasting Corporation. Replies slowly and irregularly.

LITHUANIA World Time +2 (+3 midyear)

🔊**Radio Vilnius**, Lietuvos Radijas, Konarskio 49, LT-2600 Vilnius, Lithuania. Phone: +370 (5) 236-3079. Email: radiovilnius@lrt.lt. Web: (includes on-demand audio) www.lrt.lt (click on "English"). Contact: Ms. Ilona Rukiene, Head of English Department. Free stickers, pennants, Lithuanian stamps and other souvenirs.

MADAGASCAR World Time +3

Radio Feon'ny Filazantsara, 165 Route Circulaire, Ankorahotra, Madagascar. Phone: +261 2022-30364. Email: info@filazantsara.org, mm.flm@wanadoo.mg. Web: www.filazantsara.org. A broadcast produced by the Lutheran Church of Madagascar (Fiangonana Loterana Malagasy) and aired via the Madagascar relay of Radio Nederland (see). *LUTHERAN CHURCH OF MADAGASCAR PARENT ORGANIZATION:* Fiangonana Loterana Malagasy. P.O. Box 741, 101 Antananarivo, Madagascar. Phone: +261 321-2107, +261 2022-21001. Fax: +261 2022 33767. Email: flm@wanadoo.mg.

Radio Madagasikara, B.P. 442 - Anosy, 101 Antananarivo, Madagascar. Phone: +261 2022-21745. Fax: +261 2022 32715. Email: (Webmaster) radmad@dts.mg. Web: http://takelaka.dts.mg/radmad. Contact: Mlle. Rakotonirina Soa Herimanitia, Secrétaire de Direction, a young lady who collects stamps; Mamy Rafenomanantsoa, Directeur; J.J. Rakotonirina, who has been known to request hi-fi catalogs. $1 required, and enclosing used stamps from various countries may help. Tape recordings accepted. Replies slowly and somewhat irregularly, usually to correspondence in French.

Radio Nederland Wereldomroep—Madagascar Relay, B.P. 404, Antananarivo, Madagascar. Contact: (technical) Rahamefy Eddy, Technische Dienst; J.A. Ratobimiarana, Chief Engineer.Verifies reception reports. Nontechnical correspondence should be sent to Radio Nederland Wereldomreop in the Netherlands (see).

MALAYSIA World Time +8

Asia-Pacific Broadcasting Union (ABU), P.O. Box 1164, 59700 Kuala Lumpur, Malaysia; (street address) 2nd Floor, Bangunan IPTAR, Angkasapuri, 50614 Kuala Lumpur, Malaysia. Phone: (general) +60 (3) 2282-3592; (Programme Department)+60 (3) 2282-2480; (Technical Department) +60 (3) 2282-3108. Fax: +60 (3) 2282 5292. Email: (Programme Department) prog@abu.org.my; (Technical Department) tech@abu.org.my. Web: www.abu.org.my. Contact: (administration) David Astley, Secretary-General; (technical) Sharad Sadhu and Rukmin Wijemanne, Senior Engineers, Technical Department.

🔊**Radio Malaysia, Kuala Lumpur**
MAIN OFFICE: RTM, Angkasapuri, Bukit Putra, 50614 Kuala Lumpur, Malaysia; (postal address) RTM, P.O. Box 11272, 50740 Kuala Lumpur, Malaysia. Phone: +60 (3) 2282-5333, +60 (3) 2282-4976. Email: (programs) programradio@rtm.net.my; (technical) teknikalradio@rtm.net.my. Web: (includes streaming audio) www.rtm.net.my. Contact: (general) Madzhi Johari, Director of Radio; (technical) Ms. Aminah Din, Deputy Director Engineering (Radio); Abdullah Bin Shahadan, Engineer, Transmission and Monitoring; Ong Poh, Chief Engineer. May sell T-shirts and key chains. Return postage required.
ENGINEERING DIVISION: 3rd Floor, Angkasapum, 50616 Kuala Lumpur, Malaysia. Phone: +60 (3) 2285-7544. Fax: +60 (3) 2283 2446. Email: zulrahim@rtm.net.my. Contact: Zulkifli Ab Rahim.
TRANSMISSION OFFICE: Controller of Engineering, Department of Broadcasting (RTM), 43000 Kajang, Selangor Darul Ehsan, Malaysia. Phone: +60 (3) 8736-1530, +60 (3) 8736-1530/1863. Fax: +60 (3) 8736 1226/7. Email: rtmkjg@rtm.net.my. Contact: Jeffrey Looi; Ab Wahid Bin Hamid, Supervisor, Transmission Engineering.

Radio Malaysia Sarawak (Kuching), RTM Sarawak, Jalan Satok, 93614 Kuching, Sarawak, Malaysia. Phone: +60 (82) 248-422. Fax: +60 (82) 241 914. Email: rtmkuc@rtm.net.my. Contact: (general) Yusof Ally, Director of Broadcasting; Mohd. Hulman Abdollah; Wilson Eddie Gaong, Head of Secretariat for Director of Broadcasting; (technical, but also nontechnical) Colin A. Minoi, Technical Correspondence; (technical) Kho Kwang Khoon, Deputy Director of Engineering. Return postage helpful.

Radio Malaysia Sarawak (Miri), RTM Miri, Bangunan Penyiaran, 98000 Miri, Sarawak, Malaysia. Phone: +60 (85) 423-645. Fax: +60 (85) 411 430. Email: rtmmiri@rtm.net.my. $1 or return postage helpful.

Radio Malaysia Sarawak (Sibu), RTM Sibu, Bangunan Penyiaran, 96009 Sibu, Sarawak, Malaysia. Phone: +60 (84) 323-566. Fax: +60 (84) 321 717. Email: rtmsibu@rtm. net.my. $1 or return postage required. Replies irregularly and slowly.

Voice of Islam—Program of the Voice of Malaysia (*see*, below).

📻**Voice of Malaysia**, Suara Malaysia, Wisma Radio Angkasapuri, P.O. Box 11272, 50740 Kuala Lumpur, Malaysia. Phone: (general) +60 (3) 2288-7824; (English Service) +60 (3) 2282-7826. Fax: +60 (3) 2284 7594. Email: vom@rtm. net.my. Web: http://202.190.233.9/vom/utama.htm; (streaming audio) www.rtm.net.my. Contact: (general) Mrs. Mahani bte Ujang, Supervisor, English Service; Hajjah Wan Chuk Othman, English Service; (administration) Santokh Singh Gill, Director; Mrs. Adilan bte Omar, Assistant Director; (technical) Lin Chew, Director of Engineering; (Kajang transmitter site) Kok Yoon Yeen, Technical Assistant. Free calendars, stickers or other small souvenirs. Two IRCs or return postage helpful. Replies slowly and irregularly.

MALI   World Time exactly

Office de Radiodiffusion Télévision du Mali, B.P. 171, Bamako, Mali. Phone: +223 212-019, +223 212-474. Fax: +223 214 205. Email: (general) ortm@ortm.net; (Traore) cotraore@sotelma.ml. Web: www.ortm.net. Contact: Karamoko Issiaka Daman, Directeur des Programmes; (administration) Abdoulaye Sidibe, Directeur General; (Technical) Nouhoum Traore. $1 or IRC helpful. Replies slowly and irregularly to correspondence in French (preferred) or English.

MAURITANIA   World Time exactly

📻**Radio Mauritanie**, B.P. 200, Nouakchott, Mauritania. Phone: +222 525-2101. Fax: +222 525 1264. Email: rm@mauritania.mr. Web: (includes streaming audio) www.radiomauritanie.com. Contact: Madame Amir Feu; Lemrabott Boukhary; Madame Fatimetou Fall Dite Ami, Secretaire de Direction; Mr. El Hadj Diagne; Mr. Hane Abou. Return postage or $1 required. Rarely replies.

MEXICO   World Time –6 (–5 midyear) Central, South and Eastern, including D.F.; –7 (–6 midyear) Mountain; –7 Sonora; –8 (–7 midyear) Pacific

📻**Radio Educación Onda Corta—XEPPM**, Angel Urraza No. 622, Col. del Valle, 03100- México, D.F., Mexico. Phone: (switchboard) +52 (55) 1500-1050; (director's office) +52 (55) 1500-1051; (engineering department) +52 (55) 1500-1087; (transmission plant) +52 (55) 5745-7282. Fax: (general) +52 (55) 1500 1097. Email: (general) rmoreno@radioeducacion. edu.mx; (Virginia Bello) direccion@radioeducacion.edu.mx; (Jesús Alvarez) ingenieria@radioeducacion.edu.mx; (Nicolás Hernández) nhem@radioeducacion.edu.mx. Web: (includes on-demand and streaming audio) www.radioeducacion. edu.mx. Contact: (administration) Virginia Bello Méndez, Directora General; (technical) Ing. Jesús Alvarez Tapia, Jefe Técnico; Nicolás Hernández Menchaca, Jefe del Departamento de Planta Transmisora. Free stickers, calendars and station photo. Return postage or $1 required. Replies, sometimes slowly, to correspondence in English, Spanish, Italian or French.

📻**Radio Mil Onda Corta—XEOI**, Prol. Paseo de la Reforma No. 115, Col. Paseo de las Lomas, 01330-México, D.F., Mexico; or Apartado Postal 21-1000, 04021-México, D.F., Mexico (this address for reception reports and listeners' correspondence on the station's shortwave broadcasts, and mark the envelope to the attention of Dr. Julián Santiago Díez de Bonilla). Phone: (studios) +52 (55) 5258-1351; (NRM Comunicaciones parent organization) +52 (55) 5258-1200. Email: online form; (reception reports) ingenieria@nrm.com.mx. Web: (includes streaming audio) www.radiomil.com.mx. Contact: (administration) Lic. Gustavo Alvite Martínez, Director de Radio Mil; Edilberto Huesca P., Vicepresidente Ejecutivo de NRM Comunicaciones; (technical) Juan Iturria, Ingeniero Jefe; (shortwave service) Dr. Julián Santiago Díez de Bonilla. Free stickers. $1 or return postage required.

📻**Radio Transcontinental de América—XERTA**, Apartado Postal 207-033, 06078-México, D.F., Mexico; (street address) Calle López 157-Despacho 4, Col. Centro, 06070-México, D.F., Mexico. Phone: +52 (55) 5512-8853, +52 (55) 1163-5979, +52 (55) 2789-7629. Email: info@xertaradio.com; (Carrillo) davidcar230@yahoo.com. mx. Web: (includes streaming audio) www.xertaradio.com. Contact: Rubén Castañeda Espíndola, Director General; David Carrillo.

📻**Radio UNAM [Universidad Nacional Autónoma de México]—XEYU** (when operating), Adolfo Prieto 133, Colonia del Valle, 03100-México, D.F., Mexico. Phone: +52 (55) 5623-3250/51; (Huerta) +52 (55) 5623-3270. Fax: +52 (55) 5687 3989. Email: (general) contacto@www. unam.mx; (Huerta) teohm@servidor.unam.mx; (Mejía) emejiay@servidor.unam.mx. Web: (includes on-demand and streaming audio) www.radiounam.unam.mx. Contact: Mtro. Fernando Alvarez del Castillo A., Director General; (technical) Lic. Teófilo Huerta Moreno, Jefe del Departamento de Planeación; Ing. Eusebio Mejía Yerves, Encargado Técnico. Free tourist literature and stickers. $1 or return postage required. Replies irregularly to correspondence in Spanish.

Radio Universidad—XEXQ Onda Corta, Apartado Postal 456, 78001-San Luis Potosí, SLP, Mexico; (street address) Gral. Mariano Arista 245, Centro Histórico, 78000-San Luis Potosí, SLP, Mexico. Phone: +52 (444) 826-1345; (studio) +52 (444) 826-1347. Fax: +52 (444) 826 1388. Contact: Lic. Leticia Zavala Pérez, Coordinadora; Lizbeth Deyanira Tapia Hernández, Radio Operadora.

MICRONESIA   World Time +11

Pacific Missionary Aviation (PMA) Radio Station (when operating), P.O. Box 517, Pohnpei FM 96941, Federated States of Micronesia. Phone: +1 (691) 320-1122, +1 (691) 320-2496. Fax: +1 (691) 320 2592. Email: radio@pmapacific.org, pmapohnpei@mail.fm. Web: www. radio.pmapacific.org. Contact: Roland Weibel; Norbert Kalau.

MOLDOVA   World Time +2 (+3 midyear)

Radio DMR, ul. Rozy Lyuksemburg 10, MD-3300 Tiraspol, Moldova. Email: (general) radiopmr@inbox.ru; (English Service) irpmr@mail.ru. Web: www.president-pmr.org. Contact: Arkady D Shablienko, Director; Ms. Antonina N. Voronkova, Editor-in-Chief; Ernest A. Vardanean, Editor and Translator; Vadim A. Rudomiotov, Announcer; Vlad Butuk, Technician Engineer. Replies to correspondence in Russian or English. Return postage helpful. Broadcasts from the separatist, pro-Russian, "Dniester Moldavian Republic" (also known as "Trans-Dniester Moldavian Republic").

Radio PMR (Radio Pridnestrovskaya Moldavskaya Respublika)—*see* Radio DMR, above.

MONGOLIA   World Time +8

Mongolian Radio—same postal and email addresses as Voice of Mongolia, below. Phone: (administration) +976 (11) 323-520, +976 (11) 328-978; (editorial) +976 (11) 329-766; (MRTV parent organization) +976 (11) 326-663. Fax: +976 (11) 327 234. Contact: A. Buidakhmet, Director.
Voice of Mongolia, C.P.O. Box 365, Ulaanbaatar 13, Mongolia. Phone: +976 (1) 321-624; (English Section) +976 (11) 327-900. Fax: +976 (11) 323 096; (English Section) +976 (11) 327 234. Email: mr@mongol.net; (Densmaa) densmaa9@yahoo.com. Contact: (general) Mrs. Narantuya, Chief of Foreign Service; Mrs. Zorigt Densmaa, Mail Editor; Mrs. Oyunchimeg Alagsai, Head of English Department; Ms. Tsegmid Burmaa, Japanese Department; (administration) Ch. Surenjav, Director; (technical) Ing. Ganhuu, Chief of Technical Department. Correpondence should be directed to the relevant language section and 2 IRCs or 1$ appreciated. Sometimes very slow in replying. Accepts reception reports with recordings, preferably containing five-minute excerpts of the broadcast(s) reported, but cassettes or CDs cannot be returned. Free pennants, postcards, newspapers, Mongolian stamps, and occasionally, CDs of Mongolian music.
TECHNICAL DEPARTMENT: C.P.O Box 1126, Ulaanbaatar Mongolia. Phone: +976 (11) 363-584. Fax: +976 (11) 327 900. Contact: Mr. Tumurbaatar Gantumur, Director of Technical Department; Ms. Buyanbaatar Unur, Engineer, Technical Center of Transmission System.

MOROCCO   World Time exactly

IBB Morocco Transmitting Station, Briech, c/o US Embassy, 2 Avenue Mohammed El Fassi, 10000 Rabat, Morocco. Phone: (office) +212 (3) 993-2481. Fax: +212 (3) 993 5571. Email: manager_morocco@mor.ibb.gov. Contact: Station Manager. Does not welcome direct communication from the public; *see* USA for acceptable VOA and IBB Washington addresses and related information.
☞**Radio Medi Un**
MAIN OFFICE: B.P. 2055, Tanger, Morocco; (street address) 3, rue Emsallah, 90000 Tanger, Morocco. Phone: +212 3993-6363. Fax: +212 3993 5755. Email: (general) medi1@medi1.com; (technical) technique@medi1.com; or multi-contact online form. Web: (includes on-demand and streaming audio) www.medi1.com (or www.medi1.co.ma). Contact: J. Dryk, Responsable Haute Fréquence. Two IRCs helpful. Free stickers. Correspondence in French preferred.
PARIS BUREAU, NONTECHNICAL: 78 Avenue Raymond Poincaré, F-75016 Paris, France. Phone: +33 (1) 45-01-53-30. Correspondence in French preferred.
Radio Mediterranée Internationale—*see* Radio Medi Un, above.

☞**Radiodiffusion-Télévision Marocaine**, 1 rue El Brihi, Rabat, Morocco. Phone: (general) +212 (3) 776-6880; (technical) +212 (3) 770-1740, +212 (3) 720-1404. Fax: (general) +212 (3) 776 6888; (technical) +212 (3) 770 3208. Email: (general) rtm@rtm.gov.ma, or online form; (technical) hammouda@rtm.gov.ma. Web: (includes on-demand audio) www.snrt.ma. Contact: (administration) Mme. Latifa Akharbach, Dir. de la Radio Marocaine; (technical) Mohammed Hammouda, Ingénieur. Correspondence welcomed in English, French, Arabic or Berber, but rarely replies.

MYANMAR (BURMA)   World Time +6:30

Defense Forces Broadcasting Unit, Taunggi, Shan State, Myanmar. Email: sny@mandalay.net.mm. Occasionally replies to correspondence in English.
☞**Myanma Radio**, GPO Box 1432, Yangon-11181, Myanmar; or (street address) 426, Pyay Road, Yangon-11041, Myanmar. Phone: +95 (1) 531-850. Fax: +95 (1) 525 428. Email: mrtv@mptmail.net.mm. Web: (includes streaming audio) www.myanmar.com/RADIO_TV.HTM. Contact: Ko Ko Htway, Director (Broadcasting).

NAGORNO-KARABAGH   World Time +4 (+5 midyear)

Voice of Justice, Tigranmetz Street 23a, Stepanakert, Nagorno-Karabagh. Contact: Mikael Hajyan, Station Manager. Replies to correspondence in Armenian, Azeri, Russian or German.

NAMIBIA   World Time +2 (+1 midyear)

Radio Namibia/Namibian Broadcasting Corporation (if reactivated on shortwave), P.O. Box 321, Windhoek 9000, Namibia. Phone: (general) +264 (61) 291-3111; (National Radio—English Service) +264 (61) 291-2440; (German Service) +264 (61) 291-2330; (Schachtschneider) +264 (61) 291-2188. Fax: (general) +264 (61) 217 760; (German Service) +264 (61) 291 2291; (Duwe, technical) +264 (61) 231 881. Email: (German Service) gssecretary@nbc.com.na. To contact individuals, the format is initiallastname@nbc.com.na; so to reach, say, Peter Schachtschneider, it would be pschachtschneider@nbc.com.na. Web: www.nbc.com.na. Contact: (general) Corry Tjaveondja, Manager, National Radio; (technical) Peter Schachtschneider, Manager, Transmitter Maintenance; Joe Duwe, Chief Technician. Free stickers.

NEPAL   World Time +5:45

☞**Radio Nepal**, G.P.O. Box 634, Singha Durbar, Kathmandu, Nepal. Phone: (general) +977 (1) 424-3569, +977 (1) 423-1803/4; (executive director) +977 (1) 422-3910; (programme section) +977 (1) 424-2569; (engineering) +977 (1) 424-1923; (chief engineer) +977 (1) 422-5467. Fax: (executive director) +977 (1) 422 1952; (news division) +977 (1) 422 8652. Email: (director) radio@rne.wlink.com.np; (technical) radio@engg.wlink.com.np. Web: (includes on-demand and streaming audio) www.radionepal.org. Contact: (general) Tapanath Shukla, Executive Director; Ram Sharan Karki, Deputy Executive Director; P. Shivakoti, Director; Pandav Sunuwar, Chief of Programme Section; (technical) Ramesh Jung Kharkee, Chief Engineer - Transmission; Bishnu Prasad Shivakoti, Chief Engineer - Studios

TWR Bonaire transmitter in 1970, when just-installed Continental transmitters were being checked out. Church Roswell is at the 250 kW shortwave transmitter, while Arthur Thompson takes meter readings. Meanwhile, Joe Good mans the 500 kW mediumwave AM transmitter's control console.   TWR

and Planning. 3 IRCs necessary, but station urges that neither mint stamps nor cash be enclosed, as this invites theft by Nepalese postal employees. Replies irregularly. *KHUMALTAR SHORTWAVE STATION:* Phone: +977 1 552-1221, +977 (1) 554-3480. Fax: +977 1 554 3481. Email: radio@txs.wlink.com.np. Contact: Padma Jyoti Dhakhwa, Chief Technical Officer; Madhu Sudan Thapa, Deputy Chief Technical Officer.

NETHERLANDS   World Time +1 (+2 midyear)

KBC Radio, Argonstraat 6, 6718 WT Ede, Netherlands. Phone: +31 (318) 552-491. Fax: +31 (318) 437 801. Email: kbc@planet.nl, info@k-po.com. Web: www.kbcradio.eu. Contact: Tom de Wit. Verifies reception reports (including those sent by email) with a QSL card. A former pirate broadcaster now legally airing via transmitters in Lithuania.

Radio Nederland Wereldomroep (Radio Netherlands)
MAIN OFFICE: P.O. Box 222, 1200 JG Hilversum, Netherlands. Phone: (general) +31 (35) 672-4211; (English Language Service) +31 (35) 672-4242; (24-hour listener Answerline) +31 (35) 672-4222. Fax: (general) +31 (35) 672 4207, but indicate destination department on fax cover sheet; (English Language Service) +31 (35) 672 4239. Email: (English Service) letters@rnw.nl; (Spanish Service): cartas@rnw.nl; ("Media Network") medianetwork@rnw.nl. Web: (includes on-demand and streaming audio) www.radionetherlands.nl. Contact: (management) Jan Hoek, Director-General; Joop Dalmeijer, Editor-in-Chief; Andy Clark, Head of English Language Service. The Radio Netherlands Music Department produces concerts heard on many NPR stations in North America, as well as a line of CDs, mainly of classical, jazz, world music and the Euro Hit 40. Most of the productions are only for rebroadcasting on other stations, but recordings on the NM Classics label are for sale. More details available at www.rnmusic.nl. Visitors welcome, but must call in advance.
PROGRAMME DISTRIBUTION, NETWORK AND FREQUENCY PLANNING: P.O. Box 222, 1200 JG Hilversum, The Netherlands. Phone: +31 (35) 672-4422. Fax: +31 (35) 672 4429. Contact: Leo van der Woude, Frequency Manager; Jan Willem Drexhage, Head of Programme Distribution.

NETHERLANDS ANTILLES   World Time –4

Radio Nederland Wereldomroep—Bonaire Relay, P.O. Box 45, Kralendijk, Netherlands Antilles. This address for specialized technical correspondence only. All other correspondence should be sent to Radio Nederland Wereldomroep in the Netherlands (*see*).

NEW ZEALAND   World Time +13 (+12 midyear)

Radio New Zealand International (Te Reo Irirangi O Aotearoa, O Te Moana-nui-a-kiwa), P.O. Box 123, Wellington, New Zealand. Phone: +64 (4) 474-1437. Fax: +64 (4) 474 1433, +64 (4) 474 1886. Email: info@rnzi.com. Web: (includes on-demand and streaming audio and online reception report form) www.rnzi.com. Contact: Florence de Ruiter, Listener Mail; Myra Oh, Producer, "Mailbox"; (administration) Ms. Linden Clark, Manager; (technical) Adrian Sainsbury, Technical Manager. Free stickers, schedule/flyer about station, map of New Zealand and tourist literature available. English/Maori T-shirts for US$20; sweatshirts $40; interesting variety of CDs, as well as music cassettes and spoken programs, in Domestic "Replay Radio" catalog (VISA/MC). Two IRCs or $2 for QSL card, one IRC for schedule/catalog. Email reports verified by email only.
Radio Reading Service—ZLXA, P.O. Box 360, Levin 5500, New Zealand. Phone: (general) +64 (6) 368-2229; (engi-

neering) +64 (25) 985-360. Fax: +64 (6) 368 7290. Email: (general, including reception reports) info@radioreading.org. Web: www.radioreading.org. Contact: (general) Ash Bell, Manager/Station Director; (technical, including reception reports) Brian Stokoe. Operated by volunteers 24 hours a day, seven days a week. Station is owned by the "New Zealand Radio for the Print Disabled Inc." Free brochure, postcards and stickers. $1, return postage or 3 IRCs appreciated.

NIGER   World Time +1

▣La Voix du Sahel, O.R.T.N., B.P. 361, Niamey, Niger. Phone: (director) +227 7022-2208, +227 9697-9241; (technical director) +227 2072-2747, +227 9392-8014. Fax: +227 2072 2548. Email: (director) maigaric@yahoo.fr; (technical director) maraka_laouali@yahoo.fr. Web: (includes on-demand audio) www.ortn-niger.com. Contact: (administration) Mahaman Chamsou Maïgari, Directeur; (technical) Laouali Maraka, Directeur technique ORTN. $1 helpful. Correspondence in French preferred.

NIGERIA   World Time +1

WARNING—MAIL THEFT: For the time being, correspondence from abroad to Nigerian addresses has a relatively high probability of being stolen.
WARNING—CONFIDENCE ARTISTS: For years, now, correspondence with Nigerian stations has sometimes resulted in letters from highly skilled "pen pal" confidence artists. These typically offer to send you large sums of money, if you will provide details of your bank account or similar information (after which they clean out your account). Other scams are disguised as tempting business proposals; or requests for money, free electronic or other products, publications or immigration sponsorship. Persons thus approached should contact their country's diplomatic offices. For example, Americans should contact the Diplomatic Security Section of the Department of State [phone +1 (202) 647-4000], or an American embassy or consulate.
Radio Nigeria—Abuja, Broadcasting House, P.M.B. 71, Gark1, Abuja, Federal Capital Territory, Nigeria. Phone: +234 (9) 882-1065. Fax: +234 (9) 882 1341. Contact: Ben Obeta. Two IRCs, return postage or $1 required. Replies slowly.
Radio Nigeria—Enugu (if reactivated), P.M.B. 1051, Enugu, Enugu State, Nigeria. Phone: +234 (42) 254-400. Fax: +234 (42) 254 173. Two IRCs, return postage or $1 required. Replies slowly.
Radio Nigeria—Ibadan (when operating), Broadcasting House, P.M.B. 5003, Ibadan, Oyo State, Nigeria. Phone: +234 (22) 241-4093, +234 (22) 241-4106. Fax: +234 (22) 241 3930. $1 or return postage required. Replies slowly.
Radio Nigeria—Kaduna, P.O. Box 250, Kaduna (Kaduna), Nigeria. Contact: Shehu Muhammad, Chief Technical Officer. $1 or return postage required. Replies slowly.
Radio Nigeria—Lagos (if reactivated), Broadcasting House, P.M.B. 12504, Ikoyi, Lagos, Nigeria. Phone: +234 (1) 269-0301. Fax: +234 (1) 269 0073. Two IRCs or return postage helpful. Replies slowly and irregularly.
Voice of Nigeria
ABUJA OFFICE: 6th Floor, Radio House Herbert Macaulay, Garki, Abuja, Federal Capital Territory, Nigeria. Phone: +234 (9) 234-6973, +234 (9) 234-4017. Fax: +234 (9) 234

6970. Email: (general) vonabuja@rosecom.net; (English Service) englishvon@yahoo.com; (Idowu) tidowu@yahoo.com. Web: www.voiceofnigeria.org. Contact: Ayodele Suleiman, Director of Programming; Tope Idowu, Editor *"Voice Of Nigeria Airwaves"* program magazine & Special Assistant to the Director General; Frank Iloye, Station Manager; (technical) Timothy Gyang, Deputy Director, Engineering.
LAGOS OFFICE: P.M.B. 40003, Falomo, Lagos, Nigeria. Phone: +234 (1) 269-3075, +234 (1) 269-3078. Fax: +234 (1) 269 3078, +234 (9) 269 1944. Email: vonlagos@nigol.net.ng.
Replies from the station tend to be erratic, but continue to generate unsolicited correspondence from supposed "pen pals" (*see WARNING—CONFIDENCE ARTISTS,* above); faxes, which are much less likely to be intercepted, may be more fruitful. Two IRCs or return postage helpful.

NORTHERN MARIANA ISLANDS   World Time +10

Far East Broadcasting Company—Radio Station KFBS, P.O. Box 500209, Saipan, Mariana Islands MP 96950 USA. Phone: +1 (670) 322-3841. Fax: +1 (670) 322 3060. Email: saipan@febc.org; (programs) kfbsprog@febc.org. Web: www.febi.org. Contact: Robert Springer, Director; Irene Gabbie, FEBC Programming. Replies sometimes take months. Also, *see* FEBC Radio International, USA.

OMAN   World Time +4

BBC World Service—A'Seela Relay Station
Resident Engineer, VT Communications, BBC Relay Station, P.O. Box 40, Al Ashkarah, Post Code 422, Oman. Email: rebers@omantel.net.com. Contact: Dave Battey, Resident Engineer; Afrah Al Orimi. Nontechnical correspondence should be sent to the BBC World Service in London (*see*).
▣Radio Sultanate of Oman, Ministry of Information, P.O. Box 600, Muscat, Post Code 113, Sultanate of Oman. Phone: +968 2460-2127, +968 2460-4577, +968 2460-3222, +968 2460-3888; (frequency managment) +968 2460-2494; (engineering) +968 2460-1538. Fax: (general) +968 2469 3770; (frequency management) +968 2460 4629, +968 2460 7239. Email: abulukman@hotmail.com. Web: (includes streaming audio) www.oman-radio.gov.om. Contact: (Directorate General of Technical Affairs) Mohamed Al Marhoubi, Director General of Engineering; Salim Al-Nomani, Director of Frequency Management. Verifies reception reports. $1, mint stamps or 3 IRCs helpful.

PAKISTAN   World Time +5 (+6 midyear)

▣Pakistan Broadcasting Corporation—same address, fax and contact details as Radio Pakistan, below. Web: (includes on-demand and streaming audio) www.radio.gov.pk.
Radio Pakistan, P.O. Box 1393, Islamabad 44000, Pakistan; (street address) Broadcasting House, Constitution Avenue, Islamabad 44000, Pakistan. Phone: +2 (51) 921-6942, +92 (51) 921-7321. Fax: +92 (51) 920 1861, +92 (51) 920 1118, +92 (51) 922 3877. Email: (general) cnoradio@isb.comsats.net.pk, info@radio.gov.pk. Web: www.radio.gov.pk/ext_svc.htm. Contact: S. Waheed. Free stickers, pennants and *Pakistan Calling* magazine. May

also send pocket calendar. Replies irregularly to postal correspondence; better is to use email if you can. Plans to replace two 50 kW transmitters with 500 kW units if and when funding is forthcoming.
VERIFICATION OF RECEPTION REPORTS: Frequency Management Cell, 303 Peshawar Road, Rawalpindi, Pakistan. Email: cfmpbchq@isb.comsats.net.pk (reception reports to this address have been verified with QSL cards). Contact: (technical) Ahmed Nawaz, Senior Broadcast Engineer, Room No. 324, Frequency Management Cell; Iftikhar Hussain Malik, Engineering Manager, Frequency Management Cell.

PALAU   World Time +9

Radio Station T8BZ (formerly KHBN and name still used), P.O. Box 66, Koror, Palau PW 96940. Phone: +680 488-2162, +680 544-1050. Fax: (main office) +680 488 2163; (engineering) +680 544 1008. Email: (general) hamadmin@palaunet.com; (technical) highadventure@fastmail.fm. Contact: (technical) Bentley Chan, Chief Engineer & Engineering Manager. IRC requested.

PAPUA NEW GUINEA   World Time +10

NOTE: Regional stations are sometimes off the air due to financial or technical problems which can take weeks or months to resolve. IRCs are reportedly not exchangeable in the country, and some provincial stations prefer mint stamps to US currency notes.
Catholic Radio Network—*see* Radio St. Gabriel
National Broadcasting Corporation of Papua New Guinea, P.O. Box 1359, Boroko 111, NCD, Papua New Guinea. Phone: +675 325-5233, + 675 325-5949, +675 325-6779. Fax: +675 323 0404, +675 325 0796, +675 325 6296. Email: pom@nbc.com.pg. Web: (under construction) www.nbc.com.pg. Contact: (general) Joseph Ealedona, Managing Director; Ephraim Tammy, Director, Radio Services; (technical) Bob Kabewa, Sr. Technical Officer; F. Maredey, Chief Engineer. Return postage helpful. Replies irregularly.
Radio Bougainville, P.O. Box 35, Buka, NSP, Papua New Guinea. Contact: Ivo Tsika, Station Manager; Aloysius Rumina, Provincial Programme Manager; Ms. Christine Talei, Assistant Provincial Manager; Aloysius Laukai, Senior Programme Officer. Replies irregularly.
Radio Central (when operating), P.O. Box 1359, Boroko, NCD, Papua New Guinea. Contact: Steven Gamini, Station Manager; Lahui Lovai, Provincial Programme Manager; Amos Langit, Technician. Return postage (mint stamps) helpful. Replies irregularly.
Radio Eastern Highlands (when operating), P.O. Box 311, Goroka, EHP, Papua New Guinea. Phone: +675 732-1533, +675 732-1733. Contact: Tony Mill, Station Manager; Tonko Nonao, Program Manager; Ignas Yanam, Technical Officer; Kiri Nige, Engineering Division. $1 or return postage required. Replies irregularly.
Radio East New Britain (when operating), P.O. Box 393, Rabaul, ENBP, Papua New Guinea. Contact: Esekia Mael, Station Manager; Oemas Kumaina, Provincial Program Manager. Return postage required. Replies slowly.
Radio East Sepik, P.O. Box 65, Wewak, ESP, Papua New Guinea. Contact: Elias Albert, Assistant Provincial Program Manager; Luke Umbo, Station Manager.

Radio Enga (when operating), P.O. Box 300, Wabag, Enga Province, Papua New Guinea. Phone: +675 547-1213. Contact: (general) John Lyein Kur, Station Manager; Robert Papuvo, (technical) Gabriel Paiao, Station Technician.
Radio Gulf (when operating), P.O. Box 36, Kerema, Gulf, Papua New Guinea. Contact: Tmothy Akia, Station Manager; Timothy Akia, Provincial Program Manager.
Radio Madang, P.O. Box 2138, Madang, Papua New Guinea. Phone: +675 852-2415. Fax: +675 852 2360. Email: (Gedabing) geo@daltron.com.pg. Contact: Geo Gedabing, Provincial Programme Manager; Michael Samuga, Assistant Manager. Return postage helpful.
Radio Manus, P.O. Box 505, Lorengau, Manus, Papua New Guinea. Phone: +675 470-9029. Fax: +675 470 9079. Contact: (technical and nontechnical) John P. Mandrakamu, Provincial Program Manager. Station is seeking the help of DXers and broadcasting professionals in obtaining a second hand, but still usable broadcasting quality CD player that could be donated to Radio Manus. Replies regularly. Return postage appreciated.
Radio Milne Bay (when operating), P.O. Box 111, Alotau, Milne Bay, Papua New Guinea. Contact: (general) Trevor Webumo, Assistant Manager; Simon Muraga, Station Manager; Raka Petuely, Program Officer; (technical) Philip Maik, Technician. Return postage in the form of mint stamps helpful.
Radio Morobe (when operating), P.O. Box 1262, Lae, Morobe, Papua New Guinea. Fax: +675 472 6423. Contact: Henry Tamarus, Provincial Director; Ken L. Tropu, Assistant Program Manager; Peter W. Manua, Program Manager; Aloysius R. Nase, Station Manager.
Radio New Ireland (when operating), P.O. Box 140, Kavieng, New Ireland, Papua New Guinea. Contact:Tonko Nanao, Provincial Director; Otto A. Malatana, Station Manager; Ruben Bale, Provincial Program Manager. Currently off air due to a shortage of transmitter spares. Return postage or $1 helpful.
Radio Northern (when operating), Voice of Oro, P.O. Box 137, Popondetta, Oro, Papua New Guinea. Contact: Roma Tererembo, Assistant Provincial Programme Manager; Misael Pendaia, Station Manager. Return postage required.
Radio Sandaun, P.O. Box 37, Vanimo, Sandaun Province, Papua New Guinea. Contact: (nontechnical) Gabriel Deckwalen, Station Manager; Celina Korei, Station Journalist; Elias Rathley, Provincial Programme Manager; Mrs. Maria Nauot, Secretary; (technical) Paia Ottawa, Technician. $1 helpful.
Radio Simbu, P.O. Box 228, Kundiawa, Chimbu, Papua New Guinea. Phone: +675 735-1038, +675 735-1082. Fax: +675 735 1012. Contact: (general) Jack Wera, Manager; Tony Mill Waine, Provincial Programme Manager; Felix Tsiki; Thomas Ghiyandiule, Producer, "Pasikam Long ol Pipel." Cassette recordings $5. Free two-Kina banknotes.
Radio Southern Highlands (when operating), P.O. Box 104, Mendi, SHP, Papua New Guinea. Contact: (general) Andrew Meles, Director Provincial Radio; Miriam Piapo, Programme Officer; Benard Kagaro, Programme Officer; Lucy Aluy, Programme Officer; Jacob Mambi, Shift Officer; Nicholas Sambu, Producer, "Questions and Answers"; (technical) Ronald Helori, Station Technician. $1 or return postage helpful; or donate a wall poster of a rock band, singer or American landscape.
Radio St. Gabriel, P.O. Box 7671, Boroko, NCD, Papua New Guinea. Web: www.catholicpng.org.pg. Contact:

Fr. Zdzislaw Mlak, Station Manager. Replies irregularly. Formerly known as Catholic Radio Network.
RECEPTION REPORTS: Email: wwilson@tepng.com. Contact: Wayne Wilson, Construction Manager, TE(PNG).

Radio Western, P.O. Box 23, Daru, Western Province, Papua New Guinea. Contact: Robin Wainetti, Manager; (technical) Samson Tobel, Technician. $1 or return postage required. Replies irregularly.

Radio Western Highlands (when operating), P.O. Box 311, Mount Hagen, WHP, Papua New Guinea. Contact: (general) Anna Pundia, Station Manager; (technical) Esau Okole, Technician. $1 or return postage helpful. Replies occasionally. Often off the air because of theft, armed robbery or inadequate security for the station's staff.

Radio West New Britain, P.O. Box 412, Kimbe, WNBP, Papua New Guinea. Fax: +675 983 5600. Contact: Valuka Lowa, Provincial Station Manager; Darius Gilime, Provincial Program Manager; Lemeck Kuam, Producer, "Questions and Answers"; Esekial Mael. Return postage required.

Wantok Radio Light, P.O. Box 1273, Port Moresby, NCD, Papua New Guinea. Fax: +675 321 4465. Email: online form; (Olson, technical) david@heart-to-serve.com. Web: www.wantokradio.net. Contact: (general) Sarah Good; (technical) David Olson, Chief Engineer. Return postage required for postal reply. Verifies reception reports. Wantok Radio Light is the shortwave station of the PNG Christian Broadcasting Network, and is a joint project involving Life Radio Ministries, HCJB Global Radio and others.

PARAGUAY   World Time –3 (–4 midyear)

Radio Nacional del Paraguay (if reactivated), Blas Garay 241 entre Yegros e Iturbe, Asunción, Paraguay. Phone: +595 (21) 390-375. Fax: +595 (21) 390 376. Email: info@rnpy.com. Web: www.rnpy.com. $1 or return postage required. Replies, sometimes slowly, to correspondence in Spanish. Currently off the air, as the transmitter needs a new component costing several thousand dollars.

PERU   World Time–5

NOTE: Obtaining replies from Peruvian stations calls for creativity, tact, patience—and the proper use of Spanish, not form letters and the like.

Frecuencia Líder (Radio Bambamarca), Jirón Jorge Chávez 416, Bambamarca, Hualgayoc, Cajamarca, Peru. Phone: (office) +51 (74) 713-260; (studio) +51 (74) 713-249. Contact: (general) Valentín Peralta Díaz, Gerente; Irma Peralta Rojas; Carlos Antonio Peralta Rojas; (technical) Oscar Lino Peralta Rojas. Free station photos. *La Historia de Bambamarca* book for 5 Soles; cassettes of Peruvian and Latin American folk music for 4 Soles each; T-shirts for 10 Soles each (sending US$1 per Sol should suffice and cover foreign postage costs, as well). Replies occasionally to correspondence in Spanish. Considering replacing their transmitter to improve reception.

Frecuencia San Ignacio (when operating), Jirón Villanueva Pinillos 330, San Ignacio, Cajamarca, Peru. Contact: Franklin R. Hoyos Cóndor, Director Gerente; Ignacio Gómez Torres, Técnico de Sonido. Replies to correspondence in Spanish. $1 or return postage necessary.

Frecuencia VH—*see* Radio Frecuencia VH

La Voz de la Selva—*see* Radio La Voz de la Selva

La Voz del Campesino—*see* Radio La Voz del Campesino

Ondas del Suroriente—*see* Radio Ondas del Suroriente

Radio Altura, Casilla de Correo 140, Cerro de Pasco, Pasco, Peru. Phone: +51 (63) 721-875, +51 (63) 722-398. Contact: Oswaldo de la Cruz Vásquez, Gerente General. Replies to correspondence in Spanish.

Radio Ancash, Casilla de Correo 221, Huaraz, Ancash, Peru; (street address) Jr. Francisco Araos 114 independencia, Huaraz, Ancash, Peru. Phone: +51 (43) 421-359, +51 (43) 421-381. Fax: +51 (43) 422 992. Email: online form. Web: (includes streaming audio) www.radioancash.org. Contact: Armando Moreno Romero, Gerente General. Replies to correspondence in Spanish.

Radio Atlántida (when operating)
STATION: Jirón Arica 441, Iquitos, Loreto, Peru. Phone: +51 (94) 234-452, +51 (94) 234-962. Contact: Pablo Rojas Bardales. $1 or return postage required. Replies irregularly to correspondence in Spanish.

Radio Bambamarca—*see* Frecuencia Líder, above.

Radio Bethel—*see* Radio Bethel Arequipa, below.

Radio Bethel Arequipa (if reactivated), Avenida Unión 215 - 3er piso, Distrito Miraflores, Arequipa, Peru. Contact: Josué Ascarruz Pacheco. Usually announces as "Radio Bethel" and belongs to the "Movimiento Misionero Mundial" evengelistic organization.

RADIO BETHEL PARENT STATION IN LIMA: Avenida 28 de Julio 1781, La Victoria, Lima, Peru. Phone: +51 (1) 613-1717, +51 (1) 613-1725. Fax: +51 (1) 613 1726. Email: webmaster@bethelradio.com.pe. Web: (includes on-demand and streaming audio) www.bethelradio.com.pe. Provides some of the programming for its namesake in Arequipa.

Radio Cajamarca, Jirón La Mar 675, Cajamarca, Peru. Phone: +51 (44) 921-014. Contact: Porfirio Cruz Potosí.

Radio Centinela del Norte (when operating), Distrito de Cortegano, Provincia de Celendín, Dpeartamento de Cajamarca, Peru.

Radio Chincheros, Jirón Apurímac s/n, Chincheros, Departamento de Apurímac, Peru.

Radio Chota, Jirón Anaximandro Vega 690, Apartado Postal 3, Chota, Cajamarca, Peru. Phone: +51 (76) 351-240. Contact: Aladino Gavidia Huamán, Administrador. $1 or return postage required. Replies slowly to correspondence in Spanish.

Radio Cultural Amauta, Apartado Postal 24, Huanta, Ayacucho, Peru; (street address) Jr. Cahuide 278, Huanta, Ayacucho, Peru. Phone/Fax: +51 (66) 322-153. Email: radioamauta@hotmail.com; radioamauta60@yahoo.es. Web: (includes streaming audio) www.rca.es.vg. Contact: Pelagio Ñaupa Gálvez, Administrador.

Radio Cusco, Apartado Postal 251, Cusco, Peru. Phone: (general)+51 (84) 225-851; (management) +51 (84) 232-457. Fax: +51 (84) 223 308. Contact: Sra. Juana Huamán Yépez, Administradora; Raúl Siú Almonte, Gerente General; (technical) Benjamín Yábar Alvarez. Free pennants, postcards and key rings. Audio cassettes of Peruvian music $10 plus postage. $1 or return postage required. Replies irregularly to correspondence in Spanish or English. Station is looking for folk music recordings from around the world to use in their programs.

Radio del Pacífico, Apartado Postal 4236, Lima 1, Peru; (street address) Av. Guzmán Blanco 465 - 7° piso, Lima, Peru. Phone: +51 (1) 433-7879. Fax: +51 (1) 433 3276. Email: informes@grupopacifico.org. Web: (includes streaming audio) www.grupopacifico.org/radio.html. Contact: Doris Manco Flores. $1 or return postage required. Replies occasionally to correspondence in Spanish.

Radio El Sol de los Andes (when operating), Jirón 2 de Mayo 257, Juliaca, Peru. Phone: +51 (54) 321-115. Fax: +51 (54) 322 981. Contact: Armando Alarcón Velarde.

Radio Espacial, Jirón Bolívar N° 130, Otuzco, Peru. Phone: +51 (44) 436-236.

Radio Frecuencia VH ("La Voz de Celendín"), Jirón Arica, cuadra 5, Celendín, Cajamarca, Peru. Contact: Eleuterio Vásquez Castro, Director Gerente.

Radio Frecuencia San Ignacio—*see* Frecuencia San Ignacio

Radio Horizonte, Apartado Postal 69 (or Santo Domingo 639), Chachapoyas, Amazonas, Peru. Phone: +51 (41) 477-793. Contact: Sra. Rocío García Rubio, Ing. Electrónico, Directora; Percy Chuquizuta Alvarado, Locutor; María Montaldo Echaiz, Locutora; Marcelo Mozambite Chavarry, Locutor; Ing. María Dolores Gutiérrez Atienza, Administradora; Juan Nancy Ruíz de Valdez, Secretaria; Yoel Toro Morales, Técnico de Transmisión; María Soledad Sánchez Castro, Administradora. Replies to correspondence in English, French, German and Spanish. $1 required.

Radio Huanta 2000, Jirón Gervacio Santillana 455, Huanta, Peru. Phone/Fax: +51 (66) 332-105. Contact: Ronaldo Sapaico Maravi, Departmento Técnico; or Sra.

Lucila Orellana de Paz, Administradora. Free photo of staff. Return postage or $1 appreciated. Replies to correspondence in Spanish.

Radio Huarmaca (when operating), Av. Grau 454 (detrás de Inversiones La Loretana), Distrito de Huarmaca, Provincia de Huancabamba, Región Grau, Peru. Contact: Simón Zavaleta Pérez. Return postage helpful.

Radio Ilucán (when operating), Jirón Lima 290, Cutervo, Región Nororiental del Marañón, Peru. Phone: +51 (44) 737-010, +51 (44) 737-231. Email: radioilucan@hotmail.com. Contact: José Gálvez Salazar, Gerente Administrativo. $1 required. Replies occasionally to correspondence in Spanish.

Radio La Hora, Av. Garcilaso 180, Cusco, Peru. Phone: +51 (84) 225-615, +51 (84) 231-371. Contact: (general) Edmundo Montesinos Gallo, Gerente General; (reception reports) Carlos Gamarra Moscoso, who is also a DXer. Free stickers, pins, pennants and postcards of Cusco. Return postage required. Replies to correspondence in Spanish. Reception reports are best sent direct to Carlos Gamarra's home address: Av. Garcilaso 411, Wanchaq, Cusco, Peru.

Radio La Voz, Andahuaylas, Apurímac, Peru. Contact: Lucio Fuentes, Director Gerente.

Radio La Voz de Bolívar, Jirón Cáceres s/n, Bolívar, Provincia de Bolívar, Departamento de La Libertad, Peru. Phone: +51 4423-0277 Contact: Julio Dávila Echevarría, Gerente. May send free pennant. Return postage helpful.

Radio La Voz de Chiriaco (when operating), Jirón Ricardo Palma s/n, Chiriaco, Distrito de Imaza, Provincia de Bagua, Departamento de Amazonas, Peru. Contact: Hildebrando López Pintado, Director; Santos Castañeda Cubas, Director Gerente; Fidel Huamuro Curinambe, Técnico de Mantenimiento. $1 or return postage helpful.

Radio La Voz de la Selva, Jirón Abtao 255, Casilla de Correo 207, Iquitos, Loreto, Peru. Phone: +51 (94) 265-245. Fax: +51 (94) 264 531. Email: lvsradio@terra.com.pe. Contact: Julia Jáuregui Rengifo, Directora; Marcelino Esteban Benito, Director; Pedro Sandoval Guzmán, Announcer; Mery Blas Rojas. Replies to correspondence in Spanish.

Radio La Voz de las Huarinjas, Barrio El Altillo s/n, Huancabamba, Piura, Peru. Phone: +51 (74) 473-126, +51 (74) 473-259. Contact: Alfonso García Silva, Gerente Director (also the owner of the station); Bill Yeltsin, Administrador. Replies to correspondence in Spanish.

Radio La Voz del Campesino, Av. Ramón Castilla s/n en la salida a Chiclayo, Huarmaca, Provincia de Huancabamba, Piura, Peru. Contact: Fermín Santos. Replies slowly and irregularly to correspondence in Spanish.

Radio Libertad de Junín, Cerro de Pasco 528, Apartado Postal 2, Junín, Peru. Phone: +51 (64) 344-026. Contact: Mauro Chaccha G., Director Gerente. Replies slowly to correspondence in Spanish. Return postage necessary.

Radio Luz y Sonido, Apartado Postal 280, Huánuco, Peru; or (street address) Jirón Dos de Mayo 1286, Oficina 205, Huánuco, Peru. Phone: +51 (62) 512-394, +51 (62) 518-500. Fax: +51 (62) 511 985. Contact: (technical) Jorge Benavides Moreno; (nontechnical) Pedro Martínez Tineo, Director Ejecutivo; Lic. Orlando Bravo Jesús; Seydel Saavedra Cabrera, Operador/Locutor. Return postage or $2 required. Replies to correspondence in Spanish, Italian and Portuguese. Sells video cassettes of local folk dances and religious and tourist themes.

Radio Madre de Dios, Apartado Postal 37, Puerto Maldonado, Madre de Dios, Peru; (street address) Daniel

Alcides Carrión 385, Puerto Maldonado, Madre de Dios, Peru. Phone: +51 (82) 571-050. Fax: +51 (82) 571 018, +51 (82) 573 542. Contact: (administration) Padre Rufino Lobo Alonso, Director; (general) Alcides Arguedas Márquez, Director del programa "Un Festival de Música Internacional," heard Mondays 0100 to 0200 World Time. Sr. Arguedas is interested in feedback for this letterbox program. Replies to correspondence in Spanish. $1 or return postage appreciated.

Radio Marañón, Apartado Postal 50, Jaén, Cajamarca, Peru; or (street address) Francisco de Orellana 343, Jaén, Cajamarca, Peru. Phone: +51 (44) 731-147, +51 (44) 732-168. Fax: +51 (44) 732 580. Email: (general) correo@radiomaranon. org.pe; (director) pmaguiro@radiomaranon.org.pe. Web: www.radiomaranon.org.pe. Contact: Francisco Muguiro Ibarra S.J., Director. Return postage necessary. May send free pennant. Replies slowly to correspondence in Spanish and (sometimes) English.

Radio Melodía, San Camilo 501-A, Cercado, Arequipa, Peru. Phone: +51 (54) 205-811, +51 (54) 223-661. Fax: +51 (54) 204 420. Contact: Elba Alvarez Delgado, Gerente. Replies to correspondence in Spanish.

Radio Municipal, Jirón Tacna 385, Panao, Pachitea, Huánuco, Peru. Email: dalsmop1@hotmail.com. Contact: Pablo Alfredo Albornoz Rojas, Gerente Técnico, who collects station stickers and pennants. Replies to correspondence in Spanish.

Radio Naylamp (if reactivated), Avenida Andrés Avelino Cáceres 800, Lambayeque, Peru. Phone: +51 (74) 283-353. Contact: Dr. Juan José Grández Vargas, Director Gerente. Free stickers, pennants and calendars. Return postage necessary.

Radio Ondas del Huallaga, Jirón Leoncio Prado 723, Apartado Postal 343, Huánuco, Peru. Phone: +51 (62) 511-525, +51 (62) 512-428. Contact: Flaviano Llanos Malpartida, Representante Legal. $1 or return postage required. Replies to correspondence in Spanish.

Radio Ondas del Suroriente, Jirón Ricardo Palma 510, Quillabamba, La Convención, Cusco, Peru.

📻**Radio Oriente**, Vicariato Apostólico, Calle Progreso 112-114, Yurimaguas, Alta Amazonas, Loreto, Peru. Phone: +51 (65) 352-156, +51 (65) 351-611. Fax: +51 (94) 352 128. Email: (general) info@radiooriente.org; (director) rovay@qnet.co.pe, geovanni@radiooriente.org. Web: (includes streaming audio) www.radiooriente.org. Contact: (general) Sra. Elisa Cancino Hidalgo; Juan Antonio López-Manzanares M., Director; (technical) Pedro Capo Moragues, Gerente Técnico. $1 or return postage required. Replies occasionally to correspondence in English, French, Spanish and Catalan.

Radio Paucartambo, Plaza de Armas 124, Paucartambo, Departamento de Cusco, Peru. Contact: Roberto Villasante, Administrador.

Radio Quillabamba, Jirón Ricardo Palma 442, Apartado Postal 76, Quillabamba, La Convención, Cusco, Peru. Phone: +51 (84) 281-002. Fax: +51 (84) 281 771. Contact: Padre Francisco Javier Panera, Director. Replies very irregularly to correspondence in Spanish.

Radio Reina de la Selva, Jirón Ayacucho 944, Plaza de Armas, Chachapoyas, Región Nor Oriental del Marañón, Peru. Phone: +51 (74) 757-203. Contact: José David Reina Noriega, Gerente General; Jorge Oscar Reina Noriega, Director General. Replies irregularly to correspondence in Spanish. Return postage necessary.

Radio San Andrés, La Municipalidad, Distrito de San Andrés, Provincia de Cuturvo, Departamento de Cajamarca, Peru. Email: (Meza): leoncio_meza@hotmail.com. Contact: Leoncio Samane Meza.

Radio San Antonio (Callalli), Parroquia San Antonio de Padua, Plaza Principal s/n, Callalli, Departamento de Arequipa, Peru. Contact: Hermano [Brother] Rolando.

Radio San Antonio (Villa Atalaya), Jirón Iquitos s/n, Villa Atalaya, Departamento de Ucayali, Peru. Email: (Zerdin) zerdin@terra.com.pe. Contact: Gerardo Zerdin.

Radio San Miguel, Av. Huayna Cápac 146, Huánchac, Cusco, Peru. Contact: Sra. Catalina Pérez de Alencastre, Gerente General; Margarita Mercado. Replies to correspondence in Spanish.

Radio San Miguel de El Faique (if reactivated), Distrito de El Faique, Provincia de Huancabamba, Departamento de Piura, Peru.

Radio San Nicolás, Jirón Amazonas 114, Rodríguez de Mendoza, Peru. Contact: Juan José Grández Santillán, Gerente; Violeta Grández Vargas, Administradora. Return postage necessary.

Radio Santa Ana, Av. San Martín 636, Santa Ana, Provincia La Convención, Cusco, Peru.

Radio Santa Mónica (when operating), Urbanización Marcavalle P-20, Cusco, Peru. Phone:+ 51 (84) 225-357. Contact: Nicolás Córdoba Orozco, Gerente General. Replies irregularly to correspondence in Spanish. Return postage or $1 required.

Radio Santa Rosa, Jirón Camaná 170, Casilla 4451, Lima 01, Peru. Phone: +51 (1) 427-7488. Fax: +51 (1) 426 9219. Email: radiosantarosa@terra.com.pe. Web: http://barrioperu.terra.com.pe/radiosantarosa. Contact: Padre Juan Sokolich Alvarado, Director; Lucy Palma Barreda. Free stickers and pennants. $1 or return postage necessary. Replies to correspondence in Spanish or English.

Radio Sicuani, Jirón 2 de Mayo 212, Sicuani, Canchis, Cusco, Peru; or Apartado Postal 45, Sicuani, Peru. Phone: +51 (84) 351-136, +51 (84) 351-698. Fax: +51 (84) 351 697. Email: cecosda@mail.cosapidata.com.pe. Contact: Doris Ochoa Vargas, Directora.

Radio Tacna (when operating), Aniceto Ibarra 436, Casilla de Correo 370, Tacna, Peru. Phone: +51 (52) 714-871. Fax: +51 (52) 723 745. Email: scaceres@viabcp.com. Contact: (nontechnical and technical) Ing. Alfonso Cáceres Contreras, Gerente de Operaciones; (administration) Yolanda Vda. de Cáceres C., Directora Gerente. Free stickers and samples of *Correo* local newspaper. $1 or return postage helpful. Audio cassettes of Peruvian and other music $2 plus postage. Replies irregularly to correspondence in Spanish or English.

Radio Tawantinsuyo, Av. Sol Nº 806, Cusco, Peru. Phone: +51 (84) 226-955, +51 (84) 228-411. Contact: Iván Montesinos, Gerente; Teresa López, Administradora. Replies occasionally to correspondence in Spanish. If no reply is forthcoming, try using the good offices of Carlos Gamarra Moscoso of Radio La Hora (*see*). Return postage required.

Radio Tarma, Jirón Molino del Amo 167, Apartado Postal 167, Tarma, Peru. Phone/Fax: +51 (64) 321-167, +51 (64) 321-510. Contact: Mario Monteverde Pomareda, Gerente General. Sometimes sends 100 Inti banknote in return when $1 enclosed. Free stickers. $1 or return postage required. Replies irregularly to correspondence in Spanish.

📻**Radio Unión**, Av. José Pardo 138, Miraflores, Lima 27, Peru. Phone: +51 (1) 712-0145. Email: admin@unionlaradio. com. Web: (includes streaming audio) www.unionlaradio.

com. Contact: Raúl Rubbeck Jiménez, Director Gerente; Juan Zubiaga Santiváñez, Gerente; Natividad Albizuri Salinas, Secretaria; Juan Carlos Sologuren, Dpto. de Administración, who collects stamps. Free satin pennants and stickers. IRC required, and enclosing used or new stamps from various countries is especially appreciated. Replies irregularly to correspondence and tape recordings, with Spanish preferred.

📻**Radio Universal**, Jr. José Santos Chocano G-11, Urbanización Santa Mónica, Cusco, Peru. Phone: +51 (84) 226-765, +51 (84) 238-822. Fax: +51 (84) 234 494. Email: webmaster@radiouniversalcusco.com. Web: (includes streaming audio) www.radiouniversalcusco.com. Contact: Luis Villasante Colpaer, Gerente.

📻**Radio Victoria**, Jr.Reynel 320, Mirones Bajo, Lima 1, Peru. Phone: +51 (1) 336-5448. Fax: +51 (1) 427 1195. Email: (Ramos) silvioramos777@hotmail.com. Web: (streaming audio) www.ipda.com.pe. Contact: Henrique Silvio Ramos, Administrador. Replies to correspondence in Spanish. Free stickers. Station owned by the Brazilian-run Pentecostal Church "Dios Es Amor," with local headquarters at Av. Arica 248, Lima; Phone: +51 (1) 330-8023. Their program "La Voz de la Liberación" is produced locally and aired over numerous Peruvian shortwave stations.

📻**Radio Virgen del Carmen ("RVC")**, Plaza Bolognesi Nº 142, Cercado, Huancavelica, Peru. Fax: +51 (67) 451-257. Email: (López Alvarado) jlopez_alvarado@hotmail.com. Web: (includes sreaming audio) www.radiovirgendelcarmen.com. Contact: José Santos López Alvarado, Director General. Replies irregularly to correspondence in Spanish. Return postage helpful.

Radio Visión, Jr. Juan Fanning, Urbanización San Juan, Chiclayo, Departamento de Lambayeque, Peru. Email: consultas@iplacosecha.org; (Pastor Córdova) iplacosecha13@yahoo.es. Contact: Jorge Tessen; Pastor Francisco Córdova Rodríguez. Replies to correspondence in Spanish. Return postage helpful for postal reply. Station owned by Iglesia Pentecostal "La Cosecha."

Radiodifusora La Voz del Rondero, Calle Unión 409, Huancabamba, Piura, Peru. Phone: +51 (74) 473-233. Contact: Federico Ibáñez Maticorena, Director.

PHILIPPINES   World Time +8

Far East Broadcasting Company—FEBC Radio International (External Service)
MAIN OFFICE: P.O. Box 1, Valenzuela, Metro Manila, Philippines 0560. Phone: (general) +63 (2) 292-5603, +63 (2) 292-9403, +63 (2) 292-5790; (International Broadcast Manager) +63 (2) 292-5603 ext. 158. Fax: +63 (2) 292 9430, +63 (2) 292-5603, +63 (2) 291 4982; (International Broadcast Manager) +63 (2) 292 9724, but lacks funds to fax replies. Email: info@febcintl.org; info@febc.org.ph (reception reports to this address are sometimes verified with a QSL card); (Peter McIntyre) pm@febc.jfm.org.ph. Web: www.febcintl. org. Contact: (general) Peter McIntyre, Manager, International Operations Division; (administration) Carlos Peña, Managing Director; (engineering) Ing. Renato Valentin, Frequency Manager; Larry Podmore, IBG Chief Engineer; (listener correspondence) Menchie Marcos. Free stickers and calendar cards. Three IRCs appreciated for airmail reply. Plans to add a new 100 kW shortwave transmitter.
INTERNATIONAL SCHEDULING OFFICE: FEBC International, 291 Serangoon Road, #04-00 Serangoon Building, Singa-

pore 21807, Singapore. Phone: +65 6392-3154. Fax: +65 6392 3156. Email: freqmgr@febcintl.org. Contact: Chris Cooper, Information Systems Manager.
NEW DELHI BUREAU, NONTECHNICAL: c/o FEBC, Box 6, New Delhi-110 001, India.

IBB Philippines Transmitting Station
MAIN ADDRESS: International Broadcasting Bureau, Philippines Transmitting Station, c/o US Embassy, 1201 Roxas Boulevard, Ermita 1000, Manila, Philippines.
ALTERNATIVE ADDRESS: IBB/PTS, PSC 500 Box 28, FPO AP 96515-1000.
These addresses for specialized technical correspondence only, although reception reports may occasionally be verified. All other correspondence should be directed to the regular VOA or IBB addresses (*see* USA).

📻**Philippine Broadcasting Service—DUR2** (when operating), Bureau of Broadcasting Services, Media Center, Bohol Avenue, Quezon City, Philippines. Relays DZRB Radio ng Bayan and DZRM Radio Manila. Web: (Radio ng Bayan streaming audio) www.pbs.gov.ph.

Radyo Pilipinas, the Voice of Democracy, Philippine Broadcasting Service, 4th Floor, PIA Building, Visayas Avenue, Quezon City 1100, Metro Manila, Philippines. Phone: (general) +63 (2) 924-2620, +63 (2) 920-3963, +63 (2) 924-2548; (engineering, Phone/Fax) +63 (2) 924-2268. Email: (general) radyo_pilipinas_overseas@yahoo.com (if this fails, try: pbs.pao@pbs.gov.ph); Web: www.pbs. gov.ph/DZRP_page.htm. Contact: (nontechnical) Evelyn Salvador Agato, Officer-in-Charge; Tanny V. Rodriguez, Station Manager; Joy Montero; (technical) Danilo Alberto, Supervisor; Miguelito ("Mike") Pangilinan, Chief Engineer. Free postcards and stickers. Verifies reception reports.

📻**Radio Veritas Asia**
STUDIOS AND ADMINISTRATIVE HEADQUARTERS: P.O. Box 2642, Quezon City, 1166 Philippines. Phone: +63 (2) 939-0011 to 14, +63 (2) 939-4692; (technical director) +63 (2) 938-1940. Fax: (general) +63 (2) 938 1940; (frequency manager) +63 (2) 939 7556. Email: (general) rveritas-asia@rveritas-asia.org, or online form; (program department) rvaprogram@rveritas-asia.org; (audience research) rva-ars@rveritas-asia.org; (technical) technical@rveritas-asia.org. Web: (includes on-demand and streaming audio) www.rveritas-asia.org. Contact: (administration) Ms. Erlinda G. So, Manager; (general) Ms. Cleofe R. Labindao, Audience Relations Officer; Ms. Shiela Hermida, Audience Relations Section; Mrs. Regie de Juan Galindez; Msgr. Pietro Nguyen Van Tai, Program Director; (technical) Honorio L. Llavore, Technical Director; Alex M. Movilla, Assistant Technical Director; Alfonso L. Macaranas, Frequency and Monitoring. Free caps, T-shirts, stickers, pennants, rulers, pens, postcards and calendars. Free bi-monthly newsletter *UPLINK*. Return postage appreciated.
TRANSMITTER SITE: Radio Veritas Asia, Palauig, Zambales, Philippines. Contact: Fr. Hugo Delbaere, CICM, Technical Consultant.
BRUSSELS BUREAUS AND MAIL DROPS: Catholic Radio and Television Network, 32-34 Rue de l' Association, B-1000 Brussels, Belgium; or UNDA, 12 Rue de l'Orme, B-1040 Brussels, Belgium.

PIRATE

Pirate radio stations are usually one-person operations airing home-brew entertainment and/or iconoclastic viewpoints. In order to avoid detection by the authorities, they tend to appear irregularly, with little concern for the niceties of conventional program scheduling. Most are found in Europe chiefly on weekends and holidays, often just above 6200 and 7375 kHz; and in North America mainly during evenings, just below 7000 kHz (usually 6925 plus or minus 10 kHz) or around 6855 kHz. These *sub rosa* stations and their addresses are subject to unusually abrupt change or termination, sometimes as a result of forays by radio authorities.

A popular Internet source of information is the Free Radio Network (www.frn.net). Too, the Website of The Association of Clandestine Radio Enthusiasts (www.theaceonline.com) archives the excellent "Free Radio Weekly" pirate newsletter. For Europirate DX news, try:

Swedish Report Service: SRS, Ostra Porten 29, SE-442 54 Ytterby, Sweden. Web: www.srs.pp.se.

Free Radio Service Holland: FRSH, P.O. Box 2727, NL-6049 ZG Herten, Netherlands. Email: freak55@gironet.nl, peter.verbruggen@tip.nl. Web: www.frsholland.nl.

FRC-Finland, P.O. Box 82, FIN-40101 Jyvaskyla, Finland. A good list of pirate links can be found at: www.alfalima.net/links-links.htm.

For up-to-date listener discussions and other pirate-radio information on the Internet, the usenet URLs are: alt.radio.pirate and rec.radio.pirate.

POLAND   World Time +1 (+2 midyear)

☞**Polish Radio External Service** (Polskie Radio dla Zagranicy), P.O. Box 46, PL-00-977 Warsaw, Poland; (street address) al. Niepodległości 77/85, 00-977 Warsaw, Poland. Phone: (general) +48 (22) 645-9305; (English Section) +48 (22) 645-9262; (German Section) +48 (22) 645-9333. Fax: +48 (22) 645 3952. Email: (Polish Section) zagranica@polskieradio.pl; (English Section) english.section@radio.com.pl; (German Section) deutsche.redaktion@polskieradio.pl. Web: (includes on-demand and streaming audio) www.polskieradio.pl/zagranica. Contact: Aleksander Kropiwnicki, Editor, English Service. On-air Polish language course with free printed material. Free stickers, pens, key rings, stamps and sometimes T-shirts, depending on resources.

Radio Racja, ul. Ciapla 1/7, PL-15-472 Bialystok, Poland. Phone: +48 (85) 654-5193. Email: radioracja@wp.pl. Web: www.racyja.com. Broadcasts in Belarusian and is opposed to President Lukashenko.

PORTUGAL   World Time exactly (+1 midyear); Azores World Time –1 (World Time midyear)

Deutsche Welle—Relay Station Sines, Pro-Funk GmbH, Monte Mudo, P-7520-065 Sines, Portugal. Phone: +351 (269) 870-280. Fax: +351 (269) 870 290. Email: profunk@mail.telepac.pt. This address for specialised technical correspondence only. All other correspondence (including reception reports) should be directed to the main offices in Bonn, Germany *(see)*. Also used by RDP Internacional *(see next entry)*.

☞**RDP Internacional—Rádio Portugal**, Av. Marechal Gomes da Costa 37, 1849-030 Lisboa, Portugal. Phone: (general) +351 (21) 382-0000. Fax: (general) +351 (21) 382 0165. Web: (includes streaming audio and bilingual English-Portuguese online reception report form) http://programas.rtp.pt/EPG/radio. Contact: Isabel Saraiva, Listeners' Service Department; Christiane Haupt. Verifies reception reports. Return postage not required. Free stickers and other small gifts. May also send literature from the Portuguese National Tourist Office.

ENGINEERING (INCLUDING FREQUENCY MANAGEMENT): Direcção Engenharia e Tecnologias, Rádio e Televisão de Portugal, Av. Marechal Gomes da Costa 37, Bloco B-2º, 1849-030 Lisboa, Portugal. Phone: +351 (21) 382-0228. Fax: +351 (21) 794 7670. Contact: Mrs. Teresa Beatriz Abreu, Frequency Manager; or Ms. Paula Carvalho.

ROMANIA   World Time +2 (+3 midyear)

☞**Radio România International**, 60-62 Berthelot St., RO-70747 Bucharest, Romania; or P.O. Box 111, RO-70756 Bucharest, Romania. Phone: (general) +40 (21) 222-2556, +40 (21) 303-1172, +40 (21) 303-1488, +40 (21) 312-3645; (English Department) +40 (21) 303-1357, +40 (21) 303-1465; (engineering) +40 (21) 303-1193. Fax: (English Service) +40 (21) 319 0562; (Engineering Services) +40 (21) 312 1056/7, +40 (21) 615 6992. Email: (general) rri@rri.ro; (English Service) engl@rri.ro; (Spanish Service) span@rri.ro. Web: (includes streaming audio) www.rri.ro; (on-demand audio) www.wrn.org/listeners/stations/station.php?StationID=106. Contact: Ioana Masariu, Head of the English Service; Daniel Bilt, Editor "DX Mailbag;" Victoria Sepciu, Spanish Service. Replies slowly. Concerns about frequency management should be directed to the PTT *(see, below)*, with copies to the Romanian Autonomous Company *(see farther below)* and to a suitable official at RRI.

TRANSMISSION AND FREQUENCY MANAGEMENT, PTT: General Directorate of Regulations, Ministry of Communications, 14a Al. Libertatii, R-70060 Bucharest, Romania. Phone: +40 (21) 400-1312, +40 (21) 400-177. Fax: +40 (21) 400 1230. Contact: Mrs. Elena Danila, Head of Frequency Management Department.

TRANSMISSION AND FREQUENCY MANAGEMENT, AUTONOMOUS COMPANY: Romanian Autonomous Company for Radio Communications, 14a Al. Libertatii, R-70060 Bucharest, Romania. Phone: +40 (21) 400-1072. Fax: +40 (21) 400 1228, +40 (1) 335 5965. Email: marian@snr.ro. Contact: Mr. Marian Ionitá, Executive Director of Operations.

RUSSIA   (Times given for republics, oblasts and krays):

• World Time +2 (+3 midyear) Kaliningradskaya;

• World Time +3 (+4 midyear) Adygeya, Arkhangelskaya, Astrakhanskaya, Belgorodskaya, Bryanskaya, Chechnya, Chuvashiya, Dagestan, Ingushetiya, Kabardino-Balkariya, Kalmykiya, Kaluzhskaya, Karachayevo-Cherkesiya, Ivanovskaya, Karelia, Kirovskaya, Komi, Kostromskaya, Krasnodarskiy, Kurskaya, Leningradskaya (including St. Petersburg), Lipetskaya, Mariy-El, Mordoviya, Moskovskaya (including the capital, Moscow), Murmanskaya, Nenetskiy, Nizhegorodskaya, Novgorodskaya, Severnaya Osetiya, Orlovskaya, Penzenskaya, Pskovskaya, Rostovskaya, Ryazanskaya, Saratovskaya, Smolenskaya, Stavropolskiy, Tambovskaya, Tatarstan, Tulskaya, Tverskaya, Ulyanovskaya, Vladimirskaya, Volgogradskaya, Vologodskaya, Voronezhskaya, Yaroslavskaya;

- World Time +4 (+5 midyear) Samarskaya, Udmurtiya;
- World Time +5 (+6 midyear) Bashkortostan, Chelyabinskaya, Khanty-Mansiyskiy, Komi-Permyatskiy, Kurganskaya, Orenburgskaya, Permskaya, Sverdlovskaya, Tyumenskaya, Yamalo-Nenetskiy;
- World Time +6 (+7 midyear) Altayskiy, Novosibirskaya, Omskaya, Tomskaya;
- World Time +7 (+8 midyear) Evenkiyskiy, Kemerovskaya, Khakasiya, Krasnoyarskiy, Taymyrskiy, Tyva;
- World Time +8 (+9 midyear) Buryatiya, Irkutskaya, Ust-Ordynskiy;
- World Time +9 (+10 midyear) Aginskiy-Buryatskiy, Amurskaya, Chitinskaya, Sakha;
- World Time +10 (+11 midyear) Khabarovskiy, Primorskiy, Yevreyskaya;
- World Time +11 (+12 midyear) Magadanskaya, Sakhalinskaya;
- World Time +12 (+13 midyear) Chukotskiy, Kamchatskaya, Koryakskiy.

VERIFICATION OF STATIONS USING TRANSMITTERS IN ST. PETERSBURG: Transmissions of certain world band stations—such as Radio Vlaanderen International or China Radio International—when emanating from transmitters in St. Petersburg, may be verified directly from: Mikhail Timofeyev, SPbRC Technical Department, St. Petersburg Regional Center, ul. Akademika Pavlova 3, 197022 St. Petersburg, Russia. The current schedule can be viewed at http://spb.rtrn.ru/info.asp?view=1553. Free stickers and paper pennants. $1 or IRC required.

Adygey Radio—*see* Maykop Radio

Amur Radio—*see* Blagoveschensk Radio

Arkhangel'sk Radio, GTRK "Pomorye," ul. Popova 2, 163061 Arkhangel'sk, Arkhangel'skaya Oblast, Russia; or U1PR, Valentin G. Kalasnikov, ul. Suvorov 2, kv. 16, Arkhangel'sk, Arkhangel'skaya Oblast, Russia. Replies irregularly to correspondence in Russian.

Blagoveschensk Radio, GTRK "Amur," per Svyatitelya Innokentiya 15, 675000 Blagoveschensk, Russia. Contact: V.I. Kal'chenko, Chief Engineer.

Buryat Radio—*see* Ulan-Ude Radio

Kabardino-Balkar Radio—*see* Nalchik Radio

Kamchatka Rybatskaya—a special service for fishermen off the coasts of China, Japan and western North America; *see* Petropavlovsk-Kamchatskiy Radio for contact details.

Khanty-Mansiysk Radio, GTRK "Yugoriya," ul. Mira 7, 626200 Khanty-Mansiysk, Russia. Contact: (technical) Vladimir Sokolov, Engineer.

Krasnoyarsk Radio, Krasnoyarskaya GTRK, "Tsentr Rossii," ul. Mechnikova 44A, 660028 Krasnoyarsk, Krasnoyarsky Kray, Russia. Email: postmaster@telegid.krasnoyarsk. su. Contact: Valeriy Korotchenko; Anatoliy A. Potehin, RAØAKE. Free local information booklets in English/Russian. Replies in Russian to correspondence in Russian or English. Return postage helpful.

Kyzyl Radio, GTRK "Tyva," ul. Gornaya 31, 667003 Kyzyl, Respublika Tyva, Russia. Email: tv@tuva.ru. Replies to correspondence in Russian.

Magadan Radio, GTRK "Magadan," ul. Kommuny 8/12, 685024 Magadan, Magadanskaya Oblast, Russia. Phone: +7 (41322) 22-935. Fax: +7 (41322) 24 977. Email:

center@magtrk.ru. Web: www.magtrk.ru. Contact: Viktor Loktionov, V.G. Kuznetsov. Return postage helpful. Occasionally replies to correspondence in Russian.

Mariy Radio—*see* Yoshkar-Ola Radio

Mayak—*see* Radiostantsiya Mayak

Maykop Radio, GTRK "Adygeya," ul. Zhukovskogo 24, 385000 Maykop, Republic of Adygeya, Russia. Contact: A.T. Kerashev, Chairman. English accepted but Russian preferred. Return postage helpful.

Murmansk Radio, GTRK "Murman," per. Rusanova 7, 183032 Murmansk, Murmanskaya Oblast, Russia. Phone: +7 (8152) 472-327. Email: radio@tvmurman.com. Web: http://sampo.ru/~tvmurman/index_ie.html. Contact: D. Perederi (chairman).

Nalchik Radio, GTRK "Kabbalk Teleradio," pr. Lenina 3, 360000 Nalchik, Republic of Kabardino-Balkariya, Russia. Contact: Kamal Makitov, Vice-Chairman. Replies to correspondence in Russian.

Perm Radio, Permskaya GTRK "T-7," ul. Tekhnicheskaya 7, 614070 Perm, Permskaya Oblast, Russia. Contact: M. Levin, Senior Editor; A. Losev, Acting Chief Editor.

Petropavlovsk-Kamchatskiy Radio, GTRK "Kamchatka," ul. Sovetskaya 62, 683000 Petropavlovsk-Kamchatskiy, Kamchatskaya Oblast, Russia. Contact: A.F. Borodin, Head of GTRK "Kamchatka." Email: gtrkbuh@mail.iks. ru. $1 required for postal reply. Replies in Russian to correspondence in Russian or English. Currently inactive on shortwave, apart from a special program for fishermen—*see* Kamchatka Rybatskaya.

Radio Gardarika (when operating), Radio Studio Dom Radio, Ligovsky Prospekt 174, 197002 St. Petersburg, Russia. Email: studiosw@metroclub.ru. Contact: Suvorov Alexey, Shortwave Project Manager. Replies to correspondence in Russian or English. Return postage helpful.

Radio Nalchik—*see* Nalchik Radio, above.

Radio Radonezh—*see* Radiostantsiya Radonezh

🔊**Radio Rossii** (Russia's Radio), GRK "Radio Rossii," Yamskogo Polya 5-YA ul. 19/21, 125040 Moscow, Russia. Phone: +7 (495) 213-1054, +7 (495) 250-0511, +7 (495) 251-4050. Fax: +7 (495) 250 0105, +7 (495) 233 6449, +7 (495) 214 4767. Email: direction@radiorus.ru Web: (includes on-demand and streaming audio) www.radiorus. ru. Contact: Sergei Yerofeyev, Director of International Operations [sic]; Sergei Davidov, Director. Free English-language information sheet.

Radio Studio—*see* Radio Gardarika

🔊**Radiostantsiya Radonezh** (when operating), ul. Pyatnitskaya 25, Moscow 115326, Russia. Phone/Fax: +7 (495) 950-6356. Email: radonezh@radonezh.ru. Web: (includes on-demand and streaming audio) www.radonezh.ru/radio. Replies to correspondence in Russian or English.

🔊**Radiostantsiya Tikhiy Okean** ("Radio Station Pacific Ocean"), GTRK "Vladivostok," ul. Uborevicha 20-A, 690091 Vladivostok, Primorskiy Kray, Russia. Phone: +7 (4232) 223-454. Email: ptr@ptr-vlad.ru. Web: (includes streaming audio) www.ptr-vlad.ru/tv&radio; (unofficial, includes schedule) http://oceandx.narod.ru. Contact: (technical) Alexey Giryuk, Engineer, Technical Department. $2 return postage helpful. Replies to correspondence in Russian or English, and verifies reception reports. A program for mariners produced by Primorye Radio and aired on 810 kHz mediumwave AM and shortwave.

Russian International Radio (Russkoye Mezhdunarodnoye Radio)—a service of the Voice of Russia (*see*) in cooperation with the domestic Russkoye Radio. Email: rir@ruvr.ru.

Sakhalin Radio, GTRK "Sakhalin," ul. Komsomolskaya 209, 693000 Yuzhno-Sakhalinsk, Sakhalinskaya Oblast, Russia. Phone: (Director of Radio) +7 (42422) 729-349. Phone/Fax: (GTRK parent company) +7 (42422) 35286. Email: (Romanov) romanov@gtrk.sakhalin.su. Web: www.gtrk.ru/Company/o_radio.html. Contact: S. Romanov, Director of Radio.

Tatarstan Wave ("Tatarstan Dulkynda"), GTRK "Tatarstan," ul. Gor'kogo 15, 420015 Kazan, Tatarstan, Russia. Phone: (general) +7 (8432) 384-846; (editorial) +7 (8432) 367-493. Fax: +7 (8432) 361 283. Contact: Hania Hazipovna Galinova. Formerly known as Voice of Tatarstan. *ADDRESS FOR RECEPTION REPORTS:* QSL Manager, P.O. Box 134, 420136 Kazan, Tatarstan, Russia. Contact: Ildus Ibatullin, QSL Manager. Offers an honorary diploma in return for 12 correct reports in a given year. The diploma costs 2 IRCs for Russia and 4 IRCs elsewhere. Accepts reports in Russian or English. Return postage helpful.

Ulan-Ude Radio, Buryatskaya GTRK, ul. Erbanova 7, 670000 Ulan-Ude, Republic of Buryatia, Russia. Contact: Z.A. Telin; Mrs. M.V. Urbaeva, 1st Vice-Chairman; L.S. Shikhanova.

🕭**Voice of Russia**, FGU RGRK "Golos Rossii," ul. Pyatnitskaya 25, 115326 Moscow, Russia. Phone: (Chairman) +7 (495) 950-6331; (International Relations Department) +7 (495) 950-6440; (Technical Department) +7 (495) 950-6115. Fax: (Chairman) +7 (495) 230 2828; (Letters Department, World Service in English) +7 (495) 951 9552; (Zhamkin, Editor-in-Chief) +7 (495) 951 9532. Email: (Letters Department, World Service in English) world@ruvr.ru; (for all language services) letters@ruvr.ru; (Spanish) cartas@ruvr.ru; (German) post-de@ruvr.ru. Web: (includes on-demand and streaming audio) www.ruvr.ru. Contact: (Letters Department, World Service in English) Elena Osipova or Elena Frolovskaya; (Chairman) Armen Oganesyan; (International Relations Department) Victor Kopytin, Director; (Technical Department) Mrs. Rachel Staviskaya, Director; (World Service in English) Vladimir L. Zhamkin, Editor-in-Chief. For language services other than English contact the International Relations Department. *SAN FRANCISCO OFFICE, SCHEDULES:* 2654 17th Avenue, San Francisco CA 94116 USA. Phone: +1 (415) 564-9968. Email: GPoppin@aol.com. Contact: George Poppin. This address, a volunteer office, only provides Voice of Russia schedules to listeners (return postage not required). All other correspondence should be directed to the Voice of Russia in Moscow.

Yakutsk Radio, NVK "Sakha," ul. Ordzhonikidze 48, 677007 Yakutsk, Respublika Sakha, Russia. Contact: (general) Alexandra Borisova; Lia Sharoborina, Advertising Editor; Albina Danilova, Producer, "Your Letters"; (technical) Sergei Bobnev, Technical Director. Russian books $15; audio cassettes $10. Free station stickers and original Yakutian souvenirs. Replies to correspondence in English.

RWANDA   World Time +2

Deutsche Welle—Relay Station Kigali. Correspondence should be directed to the main offices in Bonn, Germany *(see)*.

🕭**Radio Rwanda**, B.P. 83, Kigali, Rwanda. Phone: +250 76180. Fax: +250 76185. Email: radiorwanda@yahoo. com. Web: (streaming audio) www.orinfor.gov.rw/radiorwanda.eng.html. Contact: Marcel Singirankabo. $1 required. Occasionally replies, with correspondence in French preferred.

SAO TOME E PRINCIPE   World Time exactly

Voice of America/IBB—São Tomé Relay Station, P.O. Box 522, São Tomé, São Tomé e Príncipe. Contact: Transmitting Station Manager. This address for specialized technical correspondence only. All other correspondence, including reception reports, should be sent to the usual VOA or IBB addresses in Washington *(see USA)*.

SAUDI ARABIA   World Time +3

🕭**Broadcasting Service of the Kingdom of Saudi Arabia**, P.O. Box 61718, Riyadh-11575, Saudi Arabia. Phone: (general) +966 (1) 404-2795; (administration) +966 (1) 442-5493; (engineering) +966 (1) 442-5170; (frequency management) +966 (1) 442-5127. Fax: (general) +966 (1) 402 8177; (engineering and frequency management) +966 (1) 404 1692. Email: (Al-Samnan) alsamnan@yahoo. com. Web: (streaming audio) www.saudiradio.net. Contact: (general) Mutlaq A. Albegami; (technical) Suleiman Al-Samnan, Director of Engineering; Youssef Dhim, Frequency Management. Free travel information and book on Saudi history.

SENEGAL   World Time exactly

🕭**West Africa Democracy Radio (WADR)**, P.O. Box 16650, Dakar-Fann, Senegal; (street address) Sacré-Coeur 1, Villa N 8408, Dakar, Senegal. Phone: +221 869-1569. Fax: +221 864 7009. Email: wadr@wadr.org; (Abdou Lô) abdoulo@wadr.org, abdoulo@hotmail.fr. Web: (includes on-demand audio) www.wadr.org. Contact: Abdou Lô, Bilingual Researcher. Verifies reception reports. Correspondence in French preferred. One IRC or $1 requested for postal reply. Broadcasts via leased facilities in the United Kingdom.

SERBIA   World Time +1 (+2 midyear)

🕭**International Radio Serbia**, Hilendarska 2, P.O. Box 200, 11000 Beograd, Serbia. Phone: +381 (11) 324-4455. Fax: +381 (11) 323 2014. Email: radioyu@bitsyu.net, radioju@sbb.co.yu. Web: (includes on-demand audio) www.radioyu.org. Replies irregularly. $1 helpful.

Radio Beograd—a service of Radio-Televizija Srbije *(see, below)*.

🕭**Radio-Televizija Srbije** (when operating), Takovska 10, 11000 Beograd, Serbia. Phone: +381 (11) 321-2000. Email: rtstv@rts.co.yu. Web: (includes streaming audio) www.rts.co.yu. Broadcasts irregularly via the transmitters of International Radio Serbia *(see)*.

SEYCHELLES   World Time +4

BBC World Service—Indian Ocean Relay Station, P.O. Box 448, Victoria, Mahé, Seychelles. Phone: +248 78-496. Fax: +248 78 500. Contact: (technical) Albert Quatre, Senior Engineer. Nontechnical correspondence should be sent to the BBC World Service in London *(see)*.

SIERRA LEONE   World Time exactly

🔊 **Cotton Tree News (CTN)**, Fourah Bay College, Mount Aureol, P.O. Box 766, Freetown, Sierra Leone. Phone: (Bennett) +232 (76) 536-394. Email: (Bennett) abennett@hirondelle.org. Web: (includes on-demand audio) www.cottontreenews.org. Contact: Anne Bennett, Project Coordinator in Sierra Leone. Reception reports can be emailed to Anne Bennett for verification. Cotton Tree News is an independent radio production directed by Fondation Hirondelle and funded by DFID, the European Commission, Irish Aid and the Swiss Agency for Development and Cooperation. Transmits on 107.3 MHz FM in Freetown, and airs a morning broadcast on world band via a leased transmitter operated by VT Communications (*see* UNITED KINGDOM).

FONDATION HIRONDELLE: Avenue du Temple 19C, CH 1012-Lausanne, Switzerland. Phone: +41 (21) 654-2020. Fax: +41 (21) 654 2021. Email: info@hirondelle.org. Web: www.hirondelle.org. Verifies reception reports.

SINGAPORE   World Time +8

BBC World Service—Far Eastern Relay Station, VT Communications, 51 Turut Track, Singapore 718930, Singapore. Phone: + 65 6793-7511/3. Fax: +65 6793 7834. Email: (Wui Pin Yong) wuipin@singnet.com.sg. Contact: (technical) Mr. Wui Pin Yong, Operations Manager; or Far East Resident Engineer. Nontechnical correspondence should be sent to the BBC World Service in London (*see*).

🔊 **MediaCorp Radio**, Farrer Road, P.O. Box 968, Singapore 912899, Singapore; (street address) Caldecott Broadcast Centre, Caldecott Hill, Andrew Road, Singapore 299939, Singapore. Phone: (general) +65 6333-3888; (transmitting station) +65 6793-7651. Fax: +65 6251 5628. Web: (includes streaming audio) www.mediacorpradio.com.sg. Free regular and Post-It stickers, pens, umbrellas, mugs, towels, wallets and lapel pins. Do not include currency in envelope. Successor to the former Radio Corporation of Singapore.

🔊 **Radio Singapore International**, Farrer Road, P.O. Box 5300, Singapore 912899, Singapore; (street address) Caldecott Broadcast Centre, Annex Building Level 1, Andrew Road, Singapore 299939, Singapore. Phone: (general) + 65 6359-7663; (English Service) + 65 6359-7671. Fax: (general) +65 6259 1357. Email: info@rsi.sg; (English Service) english@rsi.sg (if these don't work, try the online email form). Web: (includes on-demand audio) www.rsi.sg. Contact: (general) Sakuntala Gupta, Programme Director, English Service; Augustine Anthuvan, Assistant Programme Director, English Service; (technical) Lim Wing Kee, RSI Engineering. Free souvenir T-shirts and key chains to selected listeners. Do not include currency in envelope.

SLOVAKIA   World Time +1 (+2 midyear)

🔊 **Radio Slovakia International**, Mýtna 1, P.O. Box 55, 817 55 Bratislava 15, Slovakia. Phone: +421 (2) 5727-3734, +421 (2) 5727-3731; (Editor-in-Chief) +421 (2) 5727-3730; (English Service) +421 (2) 5727-3736 or +421 (2) 5727-2737; (technical) +421 (2) 5727-3251. Fax: +421 (2) 5249 6282 or +421 (2) 5249 8247; (technical) +421 (2) 5249 7659. Email: (general) rsi@slovakradio.sk; (English Section) englishsection@slovakradio.sk; for other language sections, the format is rsi_language@slovakradio.sk, where the language is written in English (e.g. rsi_spanish@slovakradio.sk); (Miller) miller@slovakradio.sk. Web: (includes on-demand audio and online reception report form) www.slovakradio.sk/inetportal/rsi/index.php (www.rsi.sk may also work). Contact: Pete Miller, English Section (who will send worldwide stamps on request).

SOLOMON ISLANDS   World Time +11

Solomon Islands Broadcasting Corporation (Radio Happy Isles), P.O. Box 654, Honiara, Solomon Islands. Phone: +677 20051. Fax: +677 23159, +677 25652. Web: www.sibconline.com.sb. Contact: (general) David Palapu, Manager Broadcast Operations; Julian Maka'a, Producer, "Listeners From Far Away"; Walter Nalangu, News & Current Affairs; Rachel Rahi'i, Commercial/Advertising; Bart Basi, Programmes; (administration) Grace Ngatulu; (technical) Cornelius Rathamana, Chief Engineer. IRC or $1 helpful. Problems with the domestic mail system may cause delays.

SOMALIA   World Time +3

Radio Galkayo (when operating), 2 Griffith Avenue, Roseville NSW 2069, Australia. Phone/Fax: +61 (2) 9417-1066. Email: svoron@hotmail.com. Contact: Sam Voron, VK2BVS, 6OOA, Australian Director. Replies to email correspondence at no charge, but $5, AUS$5 or 5 IRCs required for postal replies. A community radio station in the Mudug region, Puntland State, northern Somalia and supported by local and overseas volunteers. Seeks volunteers, donations of radio equipment and airline tickets, and is setting up a Radio Galkayo Amateur Radio Club station.

Radio Hargeysa—*see* SOMALILAND.

🔊 **Radio Shabelle** (when operating), Global Building, 3rd Floor, Mogadishu, Somalia. Phone: +252 (1) 659-699, +252 (1) 227-733, +252 (5) 933-111. Fax: +252 (1) 659 699. Email: info@shabelle.net; (Malik) maalik@shabelle.net. Web: (includes on-demand audio) www.shabelle.net. Contact:Abdi Malik Yusuf Mohamud, Chairman.

SOMALILAND   World Time +3

NOTE: "Somaliland," claimed as an independent nation, is diplomatically recognized only as part of Somalia.

Radio Hargeysa (when operating), P.O. Box 14, Hargeysa, Somaliland, Somalia. Email: radiohargeysa@yahoo.com. Contact: Muhammad Said Muhummad, Manager.

ADDRESS IN GERMANY: c/o Konsularische Vertretung Somaliland, Baldur Drobnica, Zedernweg 6, D-50127 Bergheim, Germany. Contact: Baldur Drobnica. Verifies reception reports (including those in English). Return postage required ($1 for Europe, $3 elsewhere). Baldur Drobnica is a radio amateur, call-sign DJ6SI.

SOUTH AFRICA   World Time +2

BBC World Service via South Africa—For verification direct from the South African transmitters, contact Sentech (*see*, below). Nontechnical correspondence should be sent to the BBC World Service in London (*see*).

🔊 **Channel Africa**, P.O. Box 91313, Auckland Park 2006, South Africa. Phone: (executive editor) +27 (11)

714-2255; (technical) +27 (11) 714-2537. Fax: (executive editor) + 27 (11) 714 2537; (technical) +27 (11) 714 2072. Email: (general) africancan@channelafrica.org; (Ntenteni) ntentenit@sabc.co.za; (Moloto) molotod@sabc.co.za; (Mate, technical) matemm@channelafrica.org. Web: (includes on-demand and streaming audio) www.channelafrica.org. Contact: (general) Thami Ntenteni, Executive Editor; David Moloto, Content Senior Manager; (technical) Maurice M. Mate, Web & Technical Senior Manager. Reception reports are best directed to Sentech (see), which operates the transmission facilities.

📻**Radiosondergrense (Radio Without Boundaries)**, P.O. Box 91312, Auckland Park 2006, South Africa. Phone: +27 (11) 714-2702. Fax: +27 (11) 714 3472. Email: info@rsg.co.za. Web: (includes streaming audio) www.rsg.co.za. Reception reports are best directed to Sentech (see, below), which operates the shortwave transmission facilities. RSG (Radiosondergrense) is a modern, progressive Afrikaans public broadcasting service of the South African Broadcasting Corporation. RSG provides up-to-date news, information and entertainment to people who speak and understand Afrikaans. The shortwave operation is scheduled to be eventually replaced by a satellite and FM network.

Sentech Ltd., Transmission Planning, Private Bag X06, Honeydew 2040, South Africa. Phone: (general) +27 (11) 471-4400, +27 (11) 691-7000; (shortwave) +27 (11) 471-4658. Fax: (shortwave) +27 (11) 471 4754. Email: (Kathy Otto) ottok@sentech.co.za. Web: (schedules & frequencies) www.sentech.co.za. Contact: Kathy Otto, HF Coverage Planner. Sentech verifies reception reports on transmissions from the Meyerton shortwave facilities.

📻**South African Radio League—Amateur Radio Mirror International**, P.O. Box 90438, Garsfontein 0042, South Africa. Email: armi@sarl.org.za. Web: www.sarl.org.za/public/ARMI/ARMI.asp; (on-demand and streaming audio) www.amsatsa.org.za. Contact: Hans van deGroenedaal. Accepts email reception reports. Amateur Radio Mirror International is a weekly broadcast aired via Sentech's Meyerton facilities.

Trans World Radio Africa
NONTECHNICAL CORRESPONDENCE: Trans World Radio Africa, P.O. Box 4232, Kempton Park 1620, South Africa. Phone: +27 (11) 974-2886. Fax: +27 (11) 974 9960. Email: online form. Web: www.twrafrica.org.
TECHNICAL CORRESPONDENCE: Reception reports and other technical correspondence are best directed to Sentech (see, above) or to TWR's Swaziland office (see). Also, see USA.

SPAIN   World Time +1 (+2 midyear)

📻**Radio Exterior de España (Spanish National Radio, World Service)**
MAIN OFFICE: Apartado de Correos 156.202, E-28080 Madrid, Spain. Phone: (general) +34 (91) 346-1081/1083; (Audience Relations) +34 (91) 346-1149. Fax: +34 (91) 346 1815. Email: (Director) dir_ree.rne@rtve.es. Web: (includes on-demand and streaming audio) www.ree.rne.es. Contact: (Audience Relations) Pilar Salvador M.; (Assistant Director) Pedro Fernández Céspedes; (Director) Francisco Fernández Oria. Free stickers and tourist information. Verification of reception reports is temporarily suspended due to "staffing and budget constraints." Listeners are requested not to send cash or IRCs, since the limited services which still exist are free. An alternative, for those who understand Spanish, is to send a reception report on the program "Españoles en la Mar" which is produced in the Canary Islands by Mary Cortés. Times and frequencies can be found at the REE Website. Reports should be sent to: Programa "Españoles en la Mar," Apartado Postal 1233, Santa Cruz de Tenerife, Islas Canarias, Spain. Magazines and small souvenirs are sometimes included with verifications from this address. Correspondence in Spanish preferred, but English also accepted.
TRANSCRIPTION SERVICE: Radio Nacional de España, Servicio de Transcripciones, Apartado 156.200, Casa de la Radio (Prado del Rey), E-28223 Madrid, Spain.
HF FREQUENCY PLANNING OFFICE: Prado del Rey. Pozuelo de Alarcom, E-28223 Madrid, Spain. Phone: (Huerta) +34 (91) 346-1276; (Arlanzón) +34 (91) 346-1639; (Almarza) +34 (91) 346-1978. Fax: (Huerta & Almarza) +34 (91) 346 1402; (Alanzón) +34 (91) 346 1275. Email: (Almarza) planif_red2.rne@rtve.es; (Huerta & Arlanzón) plan_red.rne@rtve.es. Contact: Fernando Almarza, Frequency Planning; Salvador Arlanzón, HF Frequency Manager; José Maria Huerta, Technical Director.
NOBLEJAS TRANSMITTER SITE: Centro Emisor de RNE en Onda Corta, Ctra. Dos Barrios s/n, E-45350 Noblejas-Toledo, Spain.
COSTA RICA RELAY FACILITY—see Costa Rica.

SRI LANKA   World Time +5:30

Deutsche Welle—Relay Station Sri Lanka, 92/1 D.S. Senanayake Mawatha, Colombo 08, Sri Lanka. Phone: +94 (11) 2464-483. Fax: +94 (11) 2699 450. Contact: R. Groschkus, Resident Engineer. This address for specialized technical correspondence only. All other correspondence should be sent to Deutsche Welle in Germany (see).

Radio Japan/NHK—All correspondence should be sent to the Radio Japan address in Tokyo (see Japan).

📻**Sri Lanka Broadcasting Corporation** (also announces as "Radio Sri Lanka" in the external service), P.O. Box 574, Independence Square, Colombo 7, Sri Lanka. Phone: +94 (11) 2697-491. Fax: (general) +94 (11) 2691 568; (Director General) +94 (11) 2695 488. Web: (includes streaming audio) www.slbc.lk.

Voice of America/IBB—Iranawila Relay Station.
ADDRESS: Station Manager, IBB Sri Lanka Transmitting Station, c/o U.S. Embassy, 210 Galle Road, Colombo 3, Sri Lanka. Contact: Walter Patterson, Station Manager. This address for specialized technical correspondence only, although some reception reports may be verified, depending on who is at the site. All other correspondence should be directed to the regular VOA or IBB addresses (see USA).

ST. HELENA   World Time exactly

Radio St. Helena (when operating), Pounceys, St. Helena, South Atlantic Ocean. Phone/Fax: +290 4542. Email: station.manager@helanta.sh. Contact: Miss Laura Lawrence, Station Manager. Verifies reception reports if 3 IRCs included. Does not verify email reports. Aired on world band once each year—usually late October or early November, but may test irregularly at other times.

Broadcasting House, Stockholm, Sweden. Programs are prepared here, then transmitted from a myriad of remote sites.   L. Rydén

SUDAN   World Time +3

Radio Peace
ADDRESS FOR RECEPTION REPORTS: pete@edmedia.org. Contact: Peter Stover, who requests that audio attachments not be sent with reception reports.
Sudan Radio and TV Corporation (SRTC), P.O.Box 1094, Mulazmin, Omdurman, Sudan. Phone:+249 (87) 572-956, +249 (87) 574-187. Fax:+249 (87) 556 006, +249 (87) 572 956. Email: info@srtc.gov.sd. Web: www.srtc. gov.sd; (streaming audio) www.sudanradio.info. Replies irregularly. Return postage necessary.

SURINAME   World Time −3

Radio Apintie, Postbus 595, Paramaribo, Suriname; (street address) verl. Gemenelandsweg 37, Paramaribo, Suriname. Phone: (studio) +597 400-500, (office) +597 400-450. Fax: +597 400 684. Email: apintie@sr.net. Web: (includes streaming audio) www.apintie.sr. Contact: Charles E. Vervuurt, Director. Free pennant. Return postage or $1 required. Email reception reports preferred, since local mail service is unreliable.

SWAZILAND   World Time +2

Trans World Radio, P.O. Box 64, Manzini, Swaziland. Phone: +268 505-2781/2/3. Fax: +268 505 5333. Email: (Chief Engineer) sstavrop@twr.org; (Mrs. Stavropoulos) lstavrop@twr.org. Web: (transmission schedule) www. twrafrica.org/programmes/index.asp. Contact: (general) J.M Blosser, Station Director; (technical) Mrs. L. Stavropoulos, DX Secretary. Free stickers, postcards and calendars. A free Bible Study course is available. May swap canceled stamps. $1, return postage or 3 IRCs appreciated. Also, *see* USA.

SWEDEN   World Time +1 (+2 midyear)

IBRA Radio, SE-141 99 Stockholm, Sweden. Phone: +46 (8) 608-9680. Fax: +46 (8) 608 9650. Email: ibra@ibra. se. Web: (Swedish) www.ibra.se; (English) www.ibra.org.

Contact: Mikael Stjernberg, Public Relations Manager; Helene Hasslof. Free pennants and stickers. IBRA Radio's programs are aired over various world band stations, including Trans World Radio and FEBA Radio; and also broadcast independently via transmitters in Germany and Russia. Accepts email reception reports.
Radio Sweden, SE-105 10 Stockholm, Sweden. Phone: (general) +46 (8) 784-7288 or +46 (8) 784-7207; (listener voice mail) +46 (8) 784-7238; (technical department) +46 (8) 784-7282/6. Fax: (general) +46 (8) 667 6283; (listener service) +46 8 660 2990. Email: (general) radiosweden@sr. se; (English Service) mark.cummins@sr.se; george. wood@sr.se; (PR & Information) victoria.padin@sr.se, frida. sjolander@sr.se; (technical) anders.backlin@sr.se. Web: (includes on-demand and streaming audio) www.sr.se/rs or (shortcut to the English web page) www.radiosweden. org. Contact: (administration) Anne Sseruwagi, Director General, SR International; Gundula Adolfsson, Head of Radio Sweden; (English Service) Mark Cummins, Head of English Service; Gabby Katz, Producer; Bill Schiller, Producer; George Wood, Webmaster; (public relations and information) Victoria Padin, or Frida Sjolander; (technical department) Anders Backlin.
TRANSMISSION AUTHORITY: TERACOM, Svensk Rundradio AB, P.O. Box 17666, SE-118 92 Stockholm, Sweden. Phone: (general) +46 (8) 555-420-00; (Wiberg) +46 (8) 555-420-66. Fax: (general) +46 (8) 555 420 01; (Wiberg) +46 (8) 555 20 60. Email: (general) info@teracom.se; (Wiberg) magnus.wiberg@teracom.se. Web: www.teracom.se. Contact: (Frequency Planning Dept.—Head Office): Magnus Wiberg; (Engineering) Hakan Widenstedt, Chief Engineer. Free stickers; sometimes free T-shirts to those monitoring during special test transmissions. Seeks monitoring feedback for new frequency usages.

SWITZERLAND   World Time +1 (+2 midyear)

European Broadcasting Union, 17A Ancienne Route, CH-1218 Grand-Saconnex, Geneva, Switzerland; or Case Postal 67, CH-1218 Grand-Saconnex, Geneva, Switzerland. Phone: +41 (22) 717-2111. Fax: +41 (22) 747 2010. Email: ebu@ebu.ch. Web: www.ebu.ch. Contact: Mr. Jean Réveillon, Secretary-General. Umbrella organization for broadcasters in 49 European and Mediterranean countries.
International Telecommunication Union, Place des Nations, CH-1211 Geneva 20, Switzerland. Phone: (switchboard) +41 (22) 730-5111; (Broadcasting Services Division) +41 (22) 730-5933, +41 (22) 730-6136; (Terrestrial Services Department) +41 (22) 730-5514. Fax: (general) +41 (22) 733 7256; (Broadcasting Services Division) +41 (22) 730 5785. Email: (general) itumail@itu.int; (schedules and reference tables) brmail@itu.int. The ITU is the world's official regulatory body for all telecommunication activities, including world band radio. Offers a wide range of official multilingual telecommunication publications in print and/or digital formats.
Radio Réveil, Paroles, Les Chapons 4, CH-2022 Bevaix, Switzerland. Phone: +41 (32) 846-1655. Fax: +41 (32) 846 2547. Email: contact@paroles.ch. Web (includes on-demand audio): www.paroles.ch. An evangelical radio ministry, part of the larger Radio Réveil Paroles de Vie organization, which apart from broadcasting to much of Europe on longwave, mediumwave AM and FM, also targets an African audience via the shortwave facilities of Germany's T-Systems Media

& Broadcast (see). Replies to correspondence in French or English, and verifies reception reports.

Stimme des Trostes, Missionswerk Arche, CH-9642 Ebnat-Kappel, Switzerland. Contact: Herbert Skutzik, Secretary. Replies to correspondence in German or English, and verifies reception reports. Return postage helpful. Via Germany's T-Systems Media & Broadcast (see).

SYRIA   World Time +2 (+3 midyear)

Radio Damascus, Syrian Radio and Television, P.O. Box 4702, Damascus, Syria. Fax: +963 (11) 223 4336. Email: (English Section) mmhrez@shuf.com; (Riad Sharaf Al-Din, Spanish Section) riadsharafaldin@yahoo.com; (Marian Galindo, comments and reception reports in Spanish) radiodamasco@yahoo.com. Web: (Spanish Department) http://cobaq10.iespana.es/damasco. Contact: Adnan Salhab; Farid Shalash; Mohamed Hamida; (Spanish Section) Riad Sharaf Al-Din, Supervisor de Programas; Marian Galindo, Locutora; (technical) Mazen Al-Achhab, Head of Frequency Department. Free stickers, pennants and occasionally books and newspapers. Replies can be highly erratic, and sometimes slow. Members of the Spanish Section have suggested listeners use email, because of letters going astray.

TAIWAN—see CHINA (TAIWAN)

TAJIKISTAN   World Time +5

Radio Tajikistan, kuchai Chapaeva 31, 734025 Dushanbe, Tajikistan.

Voice of Tajik (Ovoji Tajik), Chapaev Street 31, 734025 Dushanbe, Tajikistan. Fax: +992 (372) 211 198. Return postage (IRCs) helpful.

TANZANIA   World Time +3

Radio Tanzania, Nyerere Road, P.O. Box 9191, Dar es Salaam, Tanzania. Phone: +255 (51) 860-760. Fax: +255 (51) 865 577. Email: radiotanzania@raha.com; (reception reports) nyamwocha@yahoo.com. Contact: (general) Abdul Ngarawa, Director of Broadcasting; Mrs. Edda Sanga, Controller of Programs; Ndaro Nyamwocha; Ms. Penzi Nyamungumi, Head of English Service and International Relations Unit; (technical) Taha Usi, Chief Engineer; Emmanuel Mangula, Deputy Chief Engineer. Replies to correspondence in English. Reports should go directly to Mr. Nyamwocha listed above. $1 return postage helpful.

Voice of Tanzania—Zanzibar, Department of Broadcasting, Radio Tanzania Zanzibar, P.O. Box 1178, Zanzibar, Tanzania—if this address brings no reply, try P.O. Box 2503. Phone: +255 (54) 231-088. Fax: + 255 (54) 257 207. Contact: Yusuf Omar Sunda, Director-General. $1 return postage helpful.

THAILAND   World Time +7

BBC World Service—Asia Relay Station, P.O. Box 20, Muang, Nakhon Sawan 60000, Thailand; (physical address) Mu 1, Tambon Ban Kaeng, Muang District, Nakhon Sawan 6000, Thailand. Phone: +66 5622-7275/6. Fax: +66 (56) 227 277. Contact: Ms. Jaruwan Meesaurtong, Executive Secretary; Ms. Sukontha Saisaengthong, Senior Engineer.

Nontechnical correspondence should be sent to the BBC World Service in London (see UNITED KINGDOM).

IBB Thailand Transmitting Station, P.O. Box 99, Ampur Muang, Udon Thani 41000, Thailand. Email: thai@voa.gov. This address for specialized technical correspondence only, although some reception reports may be verified. All other correspondence should be directed to the regular VOA or IBB addresses (see USA).

Radio Thailand World Service, 236 Vibhavadi Rangsit Road, Huai Khwang, Bangkok 10320, Thailand. Phone: + 66 (2) 277-4022. Fax: +66 (2) 274 9298/9, +66 (2) 277 1840. Web: www.hsk9.com. Contact: Mrs. Chantima Choeysanguan, Executive Director; Ms. Porntip Utogapach, Director; Ms. Suweraya Lohavicharn, Producer; (technical) Mr. Boontharm Ratanasang, Director; Mr. Weerasac Cherngchow, Assistant Director. Free pennants. Replies irregularly, especially to those who persist.

TRANSMITTER SITE: Rang-sit, Tumbol Klong haa, Amphur Klong laung, Pathumthani Province 12120, Thailand. Phone: +62 (30) 27-523. Contact: Mano Tamkal, Technician.

TOGO   World Time exactly

☞**Radio Lomé** (when operating), B.P. 434, Lomé, Togo. Phone: +228 221-2492/3. Fax: +228 221 3673. E-mail: radiolome@radiolome.tg. Web: (includes on-demand and streaming audio) www.radiolome.tg. Return postage, $1 or 2 IRCs helpful. French preferred, but English accepted.

TUNISIA   World Time +1 (+2 midyear)

Arab States Broadcasting Union, 6, rue des Enterpreneurs, Z.I. Ariana Cedex, TN-1080 Tunis, Tunisia. Phone: +216 (70) 838-855. Fax: +216 (70) 838 531, +216 (70) 838 203. Email: a.suleiman@asbu.intl.tn. Contact: Abdelrahim Suleiman, Director, Technical Department; Bassil Ahmad Zoubi, Head of Transmission Department.

☞**Radiodiffusion Télévision Tunisienne**, 71 Avenue de la Liberté, TN-1070 Tunis, Tunisia. Phone: +216 (71) 801-177. Fax: +216 (71) 781 927. Email: info@radiotunis.com. Web: (includes on-demand and streaming audio) www.radiotunis.com/news.html. Contact: Mongai Caffai, Director General; Mohamed Abdelkafi, Director; Kamel Cherif, Directeur; Masmoudi Mahmoud; Mr. Bechir Betteib, Director of Operations; Smaoui Sadok, Le Sous-Directeur Technique. Replies irregularly and slowly to correspondence in French or Arabic. $1 helpful. For reception reports try: Le Chef de Service de la Récepcion de l'Office National de la Télédiffusion, O.N.T, Cité Ennassim I, Bourjel, 1002 Tunis, Tunisia; or B.P. 399, 1080 Tunis, Tunisia. Phone: +216 (71) 801-177. Fax: +216 (71) 781 927. Email: ont.@ati.tn. Contact: Abdesselem Slim.

TURKEY   World Time +2 (+3 midyear)

☞**Voice of Turkey** (Turkish Radio-Television Corporation External Service)

MAIN OFFICE, NONTECHNICAL: TRT External Services Department, TRT Sitesi, Turan Güneş Blv., Or-An Çankaya, 06450 Ankara, Turkey; or P.K. 333, Yenisehir, 06443 Ankara, Turkey. Phone: (general) +90 (312) 490-9800/9801; (English desk) +90 (312) 490-9842. Fax: (English desk) +90 (312) 490 9846. Email: (English desk) englishdesk@trt.net.

tr; (French Service) francais@trt,net,tr; (German Service) deutsch@trt.net.tr; (Spanish Service) espanol@trt.net.tr. Web: (includes streaming audio) www.trt.net.tr. Contact: (English and non-technical) Mr. Osman Erkan, Chief, English desk. Technical correspondence, such as on reception quality should be directed to: Ms. Sedef Somaltin *(see* next entry below). On-air language courses offered in Arabic and German, but no printed course material. Free pennants, and tourist literature.
MAIN OFFICE, TECHNICAL (FOR EMIRLER AND ÇAKIRLAR TRANSMITTER SITES AND FOR FREQUENCY MANAGEMENT): TRT Teknik Yardimcilik, TRT Sitesi, C Blok No:525, ORAN, 06109 Ankara, Turkey. Phone: +90 (312) 490-1732. Fax: +90 (312) 490 1733. Email: sedef.somaltin@trt.net.tr, kiymet.erdal@trt.net.tr. Contact: Mr. Haluk Buran, TRT Deputy Director General (Head of Engineering); Ms. Sedef Somaltin, Engineer & Frequency Manager; Ms. Kiymet Erdal, Engineer & Frequency Manager. The HFBC seasonal schedules can be reached directly from: www.trt.net.tr/duyurufiles/vot.htm.
SAN FRANCISCO OFFICE, SCHEDULES: 2654 17th Avenue, San Francisco CA 94116 USA. Phone: +1 (415) 564-9968. Email: GPoppin@aol.com. Contact: George Poppin. This address, a volunteer office, only provides TRT schedules to listeners (return postage not required). All other correspondence should be sent directly to Ankara.

TURKMENISTAN   World Time +5

Radio Turkmenistan, National TV and Radio Broadcasting Company, Mollanepes St. 3, 744000 Ashgabat, Turkmenistan. Phone: +993 (12) 251-515. Fax: +993 (12) 251 421. This country is currently under strict censorship and media people are closely watched. A lot of foreign mail addressed to a particular person may attract the attention of the security services. Best is not to address your mail to particular individuals, but to the station itself.

UGANDA   World Time +3

Dunamis Shortwave, High AdventureGospel Communications Ministries (HAGCM), P.O. Box 425, Station E, Toronto, Ontario M6H 4E3, Canada. Email: (reception reports) dunamis4.750@hotmail.com.
UBC Radio (formerly Radio Uganda)
GENERAL OFFICE: P.O. Box 7142, Kampala, Uganda. Phone: +256 (41) 257-256. Fax: +256 (41) 257 252. Web: www.ubc.ug. Contact: (general) Charles Byekwaso, Controller of Programmes; Mrs. Florence Sewanyana, Head of Public Relations. $1 or return postage required. Replies infrequently and slowly. Correspondence to this address has sometimes been returned with the annotation "storage period overdue"—presumably because the mail is not collected on a regular basis.
ENGINEERING DIVISION: P.O. Box 2038, Kampala, Uganda. Phone: +256 (41) 256-647. Contact: Leopold B. Lubega, Principal Broadcasting Engineer; Rachel Nakibuuka, Secretary. Four IRCs or $2 required. Enclosing a self addressed envelope may also help to get a reply.

UKRAINE   World Time +2 (+3 midyear)

Radio Ukraine International, Kreshchatyk Str. 26, 01001 Kyiv, Ukraine. Phone: (Ukrainian Service) +380 (44) 279-1757; (English Service) + 380 (44) 279-5484; (German Service) +380 (44) 279-3134. Fax: (Ukrainian Service) +380 (44) 279 7894; (English Service) +380 (44) 278 2534; (Technical Department) +380 (44) 239 6029. Email: (Ukrainian Service) marinenko@nrcu.gov.ua; (English Service) vsru@nrcu.gov.ua; (German Service) rui@nrcu.gov.ua; (technical, including reception reports) egorov@nrcu.gov.ua. Web: (includes on-demand and streaming audio) www.nrcu.gov.ua; (streaming audio) http://media.wnet.ua/lists/rui2.m3u. Contact: Olexander Dykyi, Director; Zhanna Mescherska, Deputy-Director; Mykola Marynenko, Editor-in-Chief, Ukrainian Section; Volodymyr Perpadia, Editor-in-Chief, German Section; Zhanna Mescherska, Editor-in-Chief, English Section; (technical) Alexander Egorov, Head of Technical Department. Free stickers, calendars and Ukrainian stamps.

UNITED KINGDOM   World Time exactly (+1 midyear)

BBC Monitoring, Caversham Park, Reading, Berkshire RG4 8TZ, United Kingdom. Phone: (Commercial) +44 (118) 948-6289. Fax: (Commercial) +44 (118) 946 3823. Email: marketing@mon.bbc.co.uk. Web: www.monitor.bbc.co.uk. Media information is a vital tool for broadcast news organisations, modern governments, analysts and journalists alike. BBC Monitoring focuses on providing hard news including international affairs, major domestic and regional developments, political and military conflict, disasters and crime. As well as reporting news from the media, BBC Monitoring has a team of media specialists which reports news about the media in individual countries as well as trends in the media industry, regionally and globally.
Items are based on their own research as well as reports monitored from the mass media. Reports can be delivered by email or retrieved from their database. Contact the Commercial Department for subscription prices and information on their other products.
☞BBC World Service
MAIN OFFICE, NONTECHNICAL: Bush House, Strand, London WC2B 4PH, United Kingdom. Phone: (general) +44 (20) 7240-3456; (Press Office) +44 (20) 7557-2947/1; (International Marketing) +44 (20) 7557-1143. Fax: (Audience Relations) +44 (20) 7557 1258; ("Write On" listeners' letters program) +44 (20) 7436 2800; (Audience and Market Research) +44 (20) 7557 1254; (International Marketing) +44 (20) 7557 1254. Email: (general listener correspondence) worldservice@bbc.co.uk; ("Write On") writeon@bbc.co.uk. Web: (includes on-demand and streaming audio) www.bbc.co.uk/worldservice. Also, *see* Ascension, Oman, Seychelles, Singapore and Thailand. Does not verify reception reports due to budget limitations.
SAN FRANCISCO OFFICE, SCHEDULES: 2654 17th Avenue, San Francisco CA 94116 USA. Phone: +1 (415) 564-9968. Email: GPoppin@aol.com. Contact: George Poppin. This address, a volunteer office, only provides BBC World Service schedules to listeners (return postage not required). All other correspondence should be sent directly to the main office in London.
TECHNICAL: See VT Communications.
☞BFBS—British Forces Broadcasting Service (when operating), Services Sound and Vision, Chalfont Grove, Narcot Lane, Chalfont St. Peter, Gerrards Cross, Buckinghamshire SL9 8TN, United Kingdom; or BFBS Worldwide,

World Radio Network's central London Network Operations Centre handles incoming and outgoing feeds and transmission services for over 50 international television and radio clients. WRN

P.O. Box 903, Gerrards Cross, Buckinghamshire SL9 8TN, United Kingdom. Email: (general) adminofficer@bfbs.com. Web: (includes on-demand and streaming audio) www. ssvc.com/bfbs. Normally only on satellite and FM, but hires additional shortwave facilities when British troops are fighting overseas.

Bible Voice Broadcasting
EUROPEAN OFFICE: P. O. Box 220, Leeds LS26 0WW, United Kingdom. Phone: +44 (1900) 827-355. Email: mail@biblevoice.org; (schedules) reception@biblevoice. org. Web: www.biblevoice.org. Contact: Martin and Liz Thompson.
NORTH AMERICAN OFFICE: High Adventure Gospel Communication Ministries, P.O. Box 425, Station E, Toronto, Ontario M6H 4E3, Canada. Phone: +1 (905) 898-5447; (toll-free, U.S. and Canada only) 1-800-550-4670. Email: highadventure@sympatico.ca. Contact: Mrs. Marty McLaughlin.
Bible Voice Broadcasting is a partnership between Bible Voice (U.K.) and High Adventure Gospel Communication Ministries (Canada).

Commonwealth Broadcasting Association, CBA Secretariat, 17 Fleet Street, London EC4Y 1AA, United Kingdom. Phone: +44 (20) 7583-5550. Fax: +44 (20) 7583 5549. Email: cba@cba.org.uk. Web: www.cba.org.uk. Publishes the annual *Commonwealth Broadcaster Directory* and the quarterly *Commonwealth Broadcaster* (online subscription form available).

European Music Radio, c/o A. Taylor, 32 Shearing Drive, Carshalton, Surrey, SM5 1BL, United Kingdom. Phone: +44 (77) 4315-2908. Email: studio@emr.org.uk. Web (includes streaming audio) www.emr.org.uk. An Internet station which also airs intermittently on world band via Germany's T-Systems Media & Broadcast (*see*) and a transmitter in Latvia.

FEBA Radio, Ivy Arch Road, Worthing, West Sussex BN14 8BX, United Kingdom. Phone: +44 (1903) 237-281. Fax: +44 (1903) 205 294. Email: (general) info@feba.org.uk; (Whittington) rwhittington@feba.org.uk. Web: www.feba. org.uk. Contact: (nontechnical) Angela Brooke, Supporter Relations; (technical) Richard Whittington, Schedule Engi-

neer. Does not verify reception reports. Try sending reports to individual program producers (addresses are usually given over the air).
IBC-Tamil, 3 College Fields, Prince George's Road, Colliers Wood, London SW19 2PT, United Kingdom. Phone: +44 (20) 8100-0012. Fax: +44 (20) 8100 0003. Email: radio@ibctamil.co.uk. Web: (includes on-demand and streaming audio) www.ibctamil.co.uk. Contact: A.C. Tarcisius, Managing Director; S. Shivaranjith, Manager; K. Pillai; or Public Relations Officer. Replies irregularly.
VT Communications, 20 Lincoln's Inn Fields, London WC2A 3ED, United Kingdom. Phone: +44 (20) 7969-0000. Fax: +44 (20) 7396 6223. Email: marketing@merlincomm unications.com. Web: www.vtplc.com/communications. Contact: Fiona Lowry, Chief Executive; Rory Maclachlan, Director of International Communications & Digital Services; Ciaran Fitzgerald, Head of Engineering & Operations; Richard Hurd, Head of Transmission Sales; Laura Jelf, Marketing Manager; Kirsty Love, Marketing Coordinator. Formerly known as Merlin Communications International. Does not verify reception reports.
WRN (formerly World Radio Network), P.O. Box 1212, London SW8 2ZF, United Kingdom. Phone: +44 (20) 7896-9000. Fax: + 44 (20) 7896 9007. Email: (general) contactus@wrn.org. Web: (includes on-demand and streaming audio) www.wrn.org. Contact: Tim Ayris, Marketing Manager. Provides Webcasts and program placements for international broadcasters.

UNITED NATIONS World Time –5 (–4 midyear)

Radio UNMEE
Web: (includes on-demand audio) www.un.org/Depts/ dpko/unmee/radio.htm.
NEW YORK OFFICE: Same contact details as United Nations Radio, below.
ERITREA OFFICE: P.O. Box 5805, Asmara, Eritrea. Phone: +291 (1) 151-908. Email: kellyb@un.org.
ETHIOPIA OFFICE: ECA Building, P.O. Box 3001, Addis Ababa, Ethiopia. Phone: +251 (1) 443-396.

Radio service of the United Nations Mission in Eritrea and Ethiopia (UNMEE). Aired via facilities in the United Arab Emirates, and also relayed over Eritrea's national radio, Voice of the Broad Masses of Eritrea.

☞**United Nations Radio** (when operating), Secretariat Building, Room S-850A, United Nations, New York NY 10017 USA; or write to the station over which UN Radio was heard. Phone: +1 (917) 367-5007. Fax: +1 (212) 963 6869. Email: (general, comments on programmes) unradio@un.org; (reception reports) audio-visual@un. org. Web: (includes on-demand audio) http://radio. un.org. Contact: (general) Susan Farkas, Chief, Radio and Television Service; Ransford Cline-Thomas, Chief, Radio Section; or Department of Public information. Reception reports (including those sent by email) are verified with a QSL card.

URUGUAY   World Time −2 (−3 midyear)

☞**Emisora Ciudad de Montevideo** (when operating), Arenal Grande 2093, 11800 Montevideo, Uruguay. Phone: +598 (2) 924-1312. Email: online form. Web: (includes streaming audio) www.emisoraciudaddemontevideo.com. uy. Contact: Aramazd Yizmeyian, Director General. Free stickers. Return postage helpful.

Radiodifusion Nacional—*see* SODRE

☞**Radio Universo** (when activated on shortwave), Ferrer 1265, 27000 Castillos, Dpto. de Rocha, Uruguay. Email: am1480@adinet.com.uy. Web: (includes streaming audio) www.universoam.com. Contact: Juan Héber Brañas, Propietario. Currently only on 1480 kHz mediumwave AM, but has been granted a license to operate on shortwave.

☞**SODRE**, Radiodifusión Nacional, Casilla 1412, 11000 Montevideo, Uruguay. Phone: +598 (2) 916-1933; (technical) +598 (2) 915-7865. Email: (director) direccionradios@sodre. gub.uy; (technical) organizacion@sodre.gub.uy. Web: (includes streaming audio) www.sodre.gub.uy. Contact: (management) Sergio Sacomani, Director de Radiodifusión Nacional; (technical) José Cuello, División Técnica Radio; Pedro Ramela, Jefe Dpto. Plantas.

USA   World Time −4 Atlantic, including Puerto Rico and Virgin Islands; −5 (−4 midyear) Eastern, −6 (−5 midyear) Central, including northwest and southwest Indiana; −7 (−6 midyear) Mountain, except Arizona; −7 Arizona; −8 (−7 midyear) Pacific; −9 (−8 midyear) Alaska, except Aleutian Islands; −10 (−9 midyear) Aleutian Islands; −10 Hawaii; −11 Samoa

☞**Adventist World Radio**
HEADQUARTERS: 12501 Old Columbia Pike, Silver Spring MD 20904 USA. Phone: +1 (301) 680-6304; (toll-free, U.S. only) 1-800-337-4297. Fax: +1 (301) 680 6303. Email: info@awr.org. Web: (includes on-demand audio) www. awr.org.
NONTECHNICAL LISTENER CORRESPONDENCE: E-mail: letters@awr.org.
RECEPTION REPORTS AND LISTENER QUERIES (BY REGION):
AFRICA, AMERICAS AND EUROPE: P.O. Box 29235, Indianapolis IN 46229 USA. Phone/Fax: +1 (317) 891-8540. Email: adrian@awr.org. Contact: Dr. Adrian M. Peterson. Provides technical information, processes reception reports and issues verifications.

ASIA AND THE PACIFIC: Listener Relations, Adventist World Radio—Asia/Pacific, 798 Thompson Road, Singapore 298186, Singapore. Email: radio@awr.org. Contact: Rhoen Catolico, Asst. Program Director/Listener Relations.
AWR EUROPE FREQUENCY MANAGEMENT OFFICE: Postfach 100252, D-64202 Darmstadt, Germany. Phone: (Dedio) +49 (6151) 953-151; (Crillo) +49 (6151) 953-153. Fax: +61 (6151) 953 152. Email: (Dedio) dedio@awr.org; (Cirillo) pino@awr.org. Contact: Claudius Dedio, Frequency Coordinator; Giuseppe Cirillo, Monitoring Engineer.

Al Mustaqbal (when operating), EDC, 1000 Potomac Street NW - Suite 350, Washington DC 20007 USA. Phone: +1 (202) 572-3700. Fax: +1 (202) 223-4059. Email: (Houssein) ahoussein@edc.org. Contact: Abdoulkhader Houssein. A project of Education Development Center, Inc., funded by the U.S. Agency for International Development (USAID), and targeted at Somali-speaking children in Ethiopia. Broadcast via a transmitter in the United Arab Emirates. Off the air during school vacations.

☞**AFRTS-American Forces Radio and Television Service (Shortwave)**, Naval Media Center, NDW Anacostia Annex, 2713 Mitscher Road SW, Washington DC 20373-5819 USA. Web:http://myafn.dodmedia.osd.mil/ radio/shortwave; (AFRTS parent organization) www.afrts. osd.mil; (2-minute on-demand audio news clips): www. defenselink.mil/news/radio; (Naval Media Center) www. mediacen.navy.mil. The Naval Media Center is responsible for all AFRTS broadcasts aired on shortwave.
VERIFICATION OF RECEPTION REPORTS: Department of Defense, Naval Media Center Detachment, AFRTS-DMC, 23755 Z Street, Bldg. 2730, Riverside CA 92518-2017 USA (mark the envelope, "Attn: Officer in Charge"). Email: qsl@dodmedia.osd.mil. Replies irregularly.
FLORIDA ADDRESS: NCTS-Jacksonville-Detachment Key West, Building A 1004, Naval Air Station Boca Chica, Key West, FL 33040 USA.
Also, *see* BRITISH INDIAN OCEAN AUTHORITY.

Aurora Communications (under construction), Mile 129, Sterling Highway, Ninilchik, Alaska, USA. Plans to commence broadcasts to Russia when circumstances allow.

Broadcasting Board of Governors (BBG), 330 Independence Avenue SW, Room 3360, Washington DC 20237 USA. Phone: +1 (202) 619-2538. Fax: +1 (202) 619 1241. Email: pubaff@ibb.gov. Web: www.bbg.gov. Contact: Kathleen Harrington, Public Relations. The BBG, created in 1994 and headed by nine members nominated by the President, is the overseeing agency for all official non-military United States international broadcasting operations, including the VOA, RFE-RL, Radio Martí and Radio Free Asia.

☞**Eternal Good News**, International Radio Broadcasts, Wilshire Church of Christ, Oklahoma City OK USA; or P.O.Box 5333, Edmond OK 73083, USA. Phone: +1 (405) 359-1235, +1 (405) 340-0877. Email: eternalgoodnews @sbcglobal.net. Web: (includes on-demand audio) www. oldpaths.net/Works/Radio/Wilshire/index.html. Contact: Germaine Charles Lockwood, Evangelist; Sandra Lockwood, Secretary; George Bryan. Programs are aired via world band transmitters in Germany, Russia and United Arab Emirates, as well as U.S. station World Harvest Radio.

☞**Family Radio Worldwide**
NONTECHNICAL: Family Stations, Inc., 290 Hegenberger Road, Oakland CA 94621-1436 USA. Phone: (general) +1 (510) 568-6200; (toll-free, U.S. only) 1-800-543-1495; (engineering) +1 (510) 568-6200 ext. 242. Fax: (main of-

fice) +1 (510) 568 6200. Email: (international department, shortwave program schedules) international@familyradio. com. Web: (includes streaming audio and online email form) www.familyradio.com. Contact: (general) Harold Camping, General Manager; David Hoff, Manager of International Department. Free gospel tracts (50 languages), books, booklets, quarterly *Family Radio News* magazine and frequency schedule. Free CD containing domestic and international program schedules plus audio lessons in MP 3 format and bible study materials. 2 IRCs helpful.

TECHNICAL: WYFR—Family Radio, 10400 NW 240th Street, Okeechobee FL 34972 USA. Phone: +1 (863) 763-0281. Fax: +1 (863) 763 8867. Email: (technical) fsiyfr@okeechobee. com; (frequency schedule) wyfr@okeechobee.com. Contact: Dan Elyea, Engineering Manager; Edward F. Dearborn, Chief Operator; (frequency schedule) Evelyn Marcy.

FEBC Radio International
INTERNATIONAL HEADQUARTERS: Far East Broadcasting Company, Inc., P.O. Box 1, La Mirada CA 90637 USA. Phone: +1 (310) 947-4651. Fax: +1 (310) 943 0160. Email: febc@febc.org. Web: www.febi.org. Operates world band stations in the Philippines and Northern Mariana Islands (*see*). Does not verify reception reports from this address.

Federal Communications Commission, 445 12th Street SW, Washington DC 20554 USA. Phone: +1 (202) 418-0190; (toll-free, U.S. only) 1-888-225-5322. Fax: +1 (202) 418 0232. Email: tpolzin@fcc.gov. Web: (general) www.fcc. gov; (high frequency operating schedules) http://ftp.fcc. gov/ib/sand/neg/hf_web/seasons.html. Contact: (International Bureau, technical) Thomas E. Polzin.

⟲Fundamental Broadcasting Network, Grace Missionary Baptist Church, 520 Roberts Road, Newport NC 28570 USA. Phone: +1 (252) 223-6088; (toll-free, U.S. only) 1-800-245-9685; (Robinson) +1 (252) 223-4600. Email: fbn@fbnradio.com. Web: (includes streaming audio) www. fbnradio.com. Contact: Pastor Clyde Eborn; A. Robinson; (technical) David Gernoske, Chief Engineer. Verifies reception reports. IRC or (within the USA) SASE appreciated. Accepts email reports. Free stickers. A religious and educational non-commercial broadcasting network which operates sister stations WBOH and WTJC.

Gospel for Asia, 1800 Golden Trail Court, Carrollton TX 75010 USA. Phone: +1 (972) 300-7777; (toll-free, U.S. only) 1-800-946-2742. Email: info@gfa.org. Web: www.gfa.org. Contact: Michele Alexander, Radio Department. Transmits via facilities in Germany and U.A.E.

CALIFORNIA OFFICE: P.O. Box 1210, Somis, CA 93066 USA. Email: gfaradio@mygfa.org. Contact: Rhonda Penland, Coordinator.

CANADIAN OFFICE: 245 King Street E., Stoney Creek, Ontario L8G 1L9, Canada. Phone: +1 (905) 662-2101. Email: infocanada@gfa.org.

UNITED KINGDOM OFFICE: P.O. Box 166, York YO10 5WA, United Kingdom. Phone: +44 (1904) 643-233. Email: infouk@gfa.org.

International Broadcasting Bureau (IBB)—Reports to the Broadcasting Board of Governors (*see*), and includes, among others, the Voice of America, RFE-RL, Radio Martí and Radio Free Asia. IBB Engineering (Office of Engineering and Technical Operations) provides broadcast services for these stations. Contact: (administration) Brian Conniff, Director; Joseph O'Connell, Director of External Affairs. Web: www.ibb.gov/ibbpage.html.

FREQUENCY AND MONITORING OFFICE, TECHNICAL: IBB/EOF: Spectrum Management Division, International Broadcasting Bureau (IBB), Room 4611 Cohen Bldg., 330 Independence Avenue SW, Washington DC 20237 USA. Phone: +1 (202) 619-1669. Fax: +1 (202) 619 1680. Email: (scheduling) dferguson@ibb.gov; (monitoring) bw@his.com. Web: (general) http://monitor.ibb.gov; (email reception report form) http://monitor.ibb.gov/now_you_try_it.html. Contact: Bill Whitacre (bw@his.com).

KAIJ
STUDIOS AND ADMINISTRATION OFFICE: 1784 W. Northfield Blvd. - Suite 305, Murfreesboro TN 37129-1702 USA. Phone: +1 (615) 469-0702. Email: (general) studio@kaij. us; (marketing) tedrandall@kaij.us. Web: www.kaij.us. Contact: George McClintock, General Manager; John McClintock, Program Director; Ted Randall, Director of Marketing.

TRANSMITTER SITE: RR#3 Box 120, Frisco TX 75034 USA; or Highway 380 West, Prosper TX 75078 USA (physical location: Highway 380, 3.6 miles west of State Rt. 289, near Denton TX; transmitters and antennas located on Belt Line Road along the lake in Coppell TX). Phone: +1 (972) 346-2758. Contact: Walt Green or Fred Bithell.

KJES—King Jesus Eternal Savior
STATION: The Lord's Ranch, 230 High Valley Road, Vado NM 88072-7221 USA. Phone: +1 (505) 233-2090. Fax: +1 (505) 233 3019. Email: kjes@family.net. Contact: Michael Reuter, Manager. $1 or return postage appreciated.

SPONSORING ORGANIZATION: Our Lady's Youth Center, P.O. Box 1422, El Paso TX 79948 USA. Phone: +1 (915) 533-9122.

⟲KNLS—New Life Station
OPERATIONS CENTER: World Christian Broadcasting, 605 Bradley Ct., Franklin TN 37067 USA (letters sent to the Alaska transmitter site are usually forwarded to Franklin). Phone: +1 (615) 371-8707 ext.140. Fax: +1 (615) 371 8791. Email: knls@aol.com. Web: (includes on-demand audio of sample programs) www.knls.org. Contact: (general) Dale R. Ward, Executive Producer; L. Wesley Jones, Director of Follow-Up Teaching; Rob Scobey, Senior Producer, English Language Service; (technical) F.M. Perry, Frequency Coordinator. Free *Alaska Calling!* newsletter and station pennants. Free spiritual literature and bibles in Russian, Mandarin or English. Free Alaska books, tapes, postcards and cloth patches. Two free DX books for beginners. Special, individually numbered, limited edition, verification cards issued for each new transmission period to the first 200 listeners providing confirmed reception reports. Stamp and postcard exchange. Return postage appreciated.

TRANSMITTER SITE: P.O. Box 473, Anchor Point AK 99556 USA. Phone: +1 (907) 235-8262. Fax: +1 (907) 235 2326. Contact: (technical) Kevin Chambers, Chief Engineer.

⟲KTBN—Trinity Broadcasting Network:
GENERAL CORRESPONDENCE: P.O. Box A, Santa Ana CA 92711 USA. Phone: +1 (714) 832-2950. Fax: +1 (714) 730 0661. Email: comments@tbn.org. Web: (Trinity Broadcasting Network, includes streaming audio) www.tbn.org; (shortwave) www.tbn.org/index.php/2/21.html. Contact: Dr. Paul F. Crouch, Managing Director. Monthly TBN newsletter. Free booklets, stickers and small souvenirs sometimes available.

TECHNICAL CORRESPONDENCE: Engineering/QSL Department, 2442 Michelle Drive, Tustin CA 92780-7015 USA. Phone: +1 (714) 665-2145. Fax: +1 (714) 730 0661. Email:

(Gilroy) cgilroy@tbn.org. Contact: Cheryl Gilroy, QSL Manager; Ben Miller, Vice President, Engineering. Reception reports should be sent to: Trinity Broadcasting Network, Attention: Superpower KTBN Radio QSL Manager Cheryl Gilroy, 2442 Michelle Drive, Tustin CA 92780 USA. Return postage (IRC or SASE) appreciated. Although a California operation, KTBN's shortwave transmitter is located at Salt Lake City, Utah.

KTMI—Transformation Media International (under construction), 240 2nd Avenue SW, Albany OR 97321 USA. Phone: +1 (541) 259-5900. Fax: +1 (541) 812 7611. Email: (Brosnan) mbrosnan03@yahoo.com; (Lund) bob@lund.com. Contact: Ms. Michele Brosnan, Director of Operations; Robert Lund, Chief Engineer.

KVOH—La Voz de Restauración, 4409 W. Adams Blvd., Los Angeles CA 90016 USA. Phone: +1 (323) 766-2454. Fax: +1 (323) 766-2458. Email: kvoh@restauracion.com. Web: (includes streaming audio) www.restauracion.com/pgs/radio.htm.

KWHR-World Harvest Radio:
ADMINISTRATION OFFICE: See World Harvest Radio.
TRANSMITTER: Although located 6 1/2 miles southwest of Naalehu, 8 miles north of South Cape, and 2000 feet west of South Point (Ka La) Road (the antennas are easily visible from this road) on Big Island, Hawaii, the operators of this rural transmitter site maintain no post office box in or near Naalehu, and their telephone number is unlisted. Best bet is to contact them via their administration office (*see* World Harvest Radio), or to drive in unannounced (it's just off South Point Road) the next time you vacation on Big Island.

Leading The Way, P.O. Box 20100, Atlanta GA 30325 USA. Phone: +1 (404) 841-0100. Email: (Wattenbarger) adam@leadingtheway.org; (reception reports) qsl@leadingtheway.org. Web: www.leadingtheway.org; (includes on-demand audio) www.oneplace.com/ministries/leading_the_way. Contact: Adam Wattenbarger, Senior Producer for Radio. Airs via U.K. facilities of VT Communications (*see*) and various world band religious broadcasters.

Leinwoll (Stanley)—Telecommunication Consultant, 305 E. 86th Street, Suite 21S-W, New York NY 10028 USA. Phone: +1 (212) 987-0456. Fax: +1 (212) 987 3532. Email: stanl00011@aol.com. Contact: Stanley Leinwoll, President. This firm provides frequency management and other engineering services for some private U.S. world band stations, but does not correspond with the general public.

Little Saigon Radio, 15781 Brookhurst St. - Suite 101, Westminster CA 92683 USA. Phone: +1 (714) 918-4444. Web: (includes streaming audio from domestic service) www.littlesaigonradio.com. Contact: Joe Dinh, Technical Director. A Californian mediumwave AM station which airs a special broadcast for Vietnam via leased facilities in Taiwan.

National Association of Shortwave Broadcasters, 10400 NW 240th Street, Okeechobee, FL 34972 USA. Phone: +1 (863) 763-0281. Fax: +1 (863) 763 8867. Email: nasbmem@rocketmail.com. Web: www.shortwave.org. Contact: Dan Elyea, Secretary-Treasurer. Association of most private U.S. world band stations, as well as a group of other international broadcasters, equipment manufacturers and organizations related to shortwave broadcasting. Includes committees on various subjects, such as digital shortwave radio. Interfaces with the Federal Communications Commission's International Bureau and other broadcasting-related organizations to advance the interests of its members. Publishes *NASB Newsletter* for members and associates and is available for free via their website. Annual one-day convention held early each spring; non-members wishing to attend should contact the Secretary-Treasurer in advance; convention fee typically $50 per person.

Overcomer Ministry ("Voice of the Last Day Prophet of God"), P.O. Box 691, Walterboro SC 29488 USA. Phone: (voicemail) +1 (843) 538-6689. Fax: +1 (843) 538 6689. Email: brotherstair@overcomerministry.org; (technical) brothermark@overcomerministry.org. Web: (includes on-demand and streaming audio) www.overcomerministry.org. Contact: Brother R.G. Stair. Sample "Overcomer" newsletter and various pamphlets free upon request. Via Germany's T-Systems Media & Broadcast (*see*) and various U.S. stations.

Pan American Broadcasting, 2021 The Alameda, Suite 240, San Jose CA 95126-1145 USA. Phone: +1 (408) 996-2033; (toll-free, U.S. only) 1-800-726-2620. Fax: +1 (408) 252 6855. Email: info@panambc.com; (Bernald) gbernald@panambc.com; (Jung) cjung@panambc.com. Web: www.panambc.com. Contact: (listener correspondence) Terry Kraemer; (general) Carmen Jung, Office and Sales Administrator; Gene Bernald, President. $1, mint U.S. stamps or 2 IRCs required for reply. Operates transmitters in Equatorial Guinea (*see*) and hires airtime over a number of world band stations, plus T-Systems Media & Broadcast facilities in Germany.

Quê Huong Radio, 2670 South White Road, Suite 165, San Jose CA 95148 USA. Phone: +1 (408) 223-3130. Fax: +1 (408) 223 3131. Web: (includes on-demand audio) www.quehuongmedia.com. Contact: Nguyen Khoi, Manager. A Californian Vietnamese station operating on mediumwave AM, and which broadcasts to Vietnam via a transmitter in Central Asia.

Radio Farda—a joint venture between Radio Free Europe-Radio Liberty (*see*) and the Voice of America (*see*). Email: radiofarda@rferl.com. Web: (includes on-demand and streaming audio) www.radiofarda.com. Broadcasts a mix of news, information and popular Iranian and western music to younger audiences in Iran. Reception reports are best sent to Radio Free Europe-Radio Liberty (*see*).

Radio Free Afghanistan—the Afghan service of Radio Free Europe-Radio Liberty (*see*). Web: (includes on-demand and streaming audio) www.azadiradio.org.

Radio Free Asia, Suite 300, 2025 M Street NW, Washington DC 20036 USA (for reports on reception, add "Reception Reports" before "Radio Free Asia"). You can also submit reception reports at: www.techweb.rfa.org (click on the QSL REPORTS link) or send them via email to: QSL@rfa.org. Phone: (general) +1 (202) 530-4900; (president) +1 (202) 457-4902;(vice president of editorial) +1 (202) 530-4907; (vice-president of administration) +1 (202) 530-4906; (chief technology officer) +1 (202) 530-4958; (director of production support) +1 (202) 530-4943. Fax: +1 (202) 721 7468. Email: (individuals) the format is lastnameinitial@rfa.org; so to reach, say the CTO, David Baden, it would be badend@rfa.org; (language sections) the format is language@rfa.org; so to contact, say, the Vietnamese section, address your message to vietnamese@rfa.org; (general) communications@rfa.org; (reception reports) qsl@rfa.org. Web: (includes on-demand audio) www.rfa.org; (automated reception report system) www.techweb.rfa.org. Contact: (administration) Libby Liu, President; Daniel Southerland, Vice President of Editorial; (technical) David M. Baden, Chief Technology Officer; A. J. Janitschek, Director of Production Support; Sam Stevens, Director of Technical Support. RFA, originally created in 1996 as the Asia Pacific Network, is funded as a private nonprofit U.S. corporation by a grant from the US Congress to the Broadcasting Board of Governors (see).

HONG KONG OFFICE: Room 904, Mass Mutal Tower, 38 Gloucester Road, Wanchai, Hong Kong, China.

THAILAND OFFICE: Maxim House, 112 Witthayu Road, Pathomwan, Bangkok 10330, Thailand.

Radio Free Europe-Radio Liberty (RFE-RL)

PRAGUE HEADQUARTERS: Vinohradská 1, 110 00 Prague 1, Czech Republic. Phone: +420 (2) 2112-1111; (outreach coordinator) +420 (2) 2112-2407; (president) +420 (2) 2112-3000; (news desk) +420 (2) 2112-3629; (public relations) +420 (2) 2112-3012; (technical operations) +420 (2) 2112-3700; (broadcast operations) +420 (2) 2112-3550; (affiliate relations). +420 (2) 2112-2539. Fax: +420 (2) 2112 3013; (president) +420 (2) 2112 3002; (news desk) +420 (2) 2112 3613; (public relations) +420 (2) 2112 2995; (technical operations) +420 (2) 2112 3702; (broadcast operations) +420 (2) 2112 3540; (affiliate operations) +420 (2) 2112 4563. Email: the format is lastnameinitial@rferl.org; so to reach, say, Luke Springer, it would be springerl@rferl. org; (reception reports) siskovaa@rferl.org. Web: (includes on-demand and streaming audio) www.rferl.org. Contact: Kestutis Girnius, Managing Editor, News and Current Affairs; Jeffrey Gedmin, President; Luke Springer, Deputy Director, Technology; Jana Horakova, Public Relations Coordinator; Uldis Grava, Marketing Director; Christopher Carzoli, Broadcast Operations Director; Anna Siskova, Outreach Coordinator.

WASHINGTON OFFICE: 1201 Connecticut Avenue NW, Washington DC 20036 USA. Phone: +1 (202) 457-6900; (Director of Communications) +1 (202) 457-6947; (newsdesk) +1 (202) 457-6950; (technical) +1 (202) 457-6963. Fax: +1 (202) 457 6992; (news desk) +1 (202) 457 6997; (technical) +1 (202) 457 6913. Email: (Jensen) jensend@rferl. org. Web: *see*, above. Contact: Don Jensen, Director of Communications.

A private non-profit corporation funded by a grant from the Broadcasting Board of Governors, RFE/RL broadcasts in 14 languages (but not English) from transmission facilities now part of the International Broadcasting Bureau (IBB), *see*.

Radio Martí, Office of Cuba Broadcasting, 4201 N.W. 77th Avenue, Miami FL 33166 USA. Phone: +1 (305) 437-7000; (Director) +1 (305) 437-7117; (Technical Operations) +1 (305) 437-7051. Fax: +1 (305) 437 7016. Email: infomarti@ocb.ibb.gov; (Ray de Arenas) mraydearenas @ ocb.ibb.gov. Web: (includes on-demand and streaming audio) www.martinoticias.com/radio.asp. Contact: (technical) Michael Pallone, Director, Engineering and Technical Operations; Tom Warden, Chief of Radio Operations; Margaret Ray de Arenas, Assistant to the Director, Engineering and Technical Operations.

Smyrna Radio International (projected), c/o Smyrna Baptist Church, 7000 Pensacola Blvd., Pensacola FL 32505 USA. Phone: +1 (850) 477-0998.

Southern Sudan Interactive Radio Instruction (sSIRI) (when operating)—a project of the Education Development Center (*see* Sudan Radio Service, below, for contact information). Broadcasts are via transmitters brokered by

VT Communications (*see* United Kingdom). Is off the air during school holidays in southern Sudan.

PRODUCTION STUDIOS, KENYA: 28 Mugumo Road, P.O. Box 25010, 00603 Lavington, Nairobi, Kenya.

Suab Xaa Moo Zoo, Hmong District, 12287 Pennsylvania Street, Thornton CO 80241-3113 USA. Phone: +1 (303) 252-1793; (toll-free, U.S. only) +1 (877) 521-7814. Fax: +1 (303) 252 7911. Email: hkm@hmongdistrict.org. Web: (includes on-demand audio) www.hmongdistrict. org/communication.htm.

ALTERNATIVE ADDRESS: Christian and Missionary Alliance, P.O. Box 35000, Colorado Springs CO 80935-3500 USA. Phone: +1 (719) 599-5999. Email: webmaster@cmalliance. org.

A Hmong religious broadcast to Southeast Asia via leased facilities in Taiwan.

Sudan Radio Service, Education Development Center, 1000 Potomac Street NW, Suite 350, Washington DC 20007 USA. Phone: +1 (202) 572-3700. Fax: +1 (202) 223 4059. Email: srs@edc.org; (Groce) jgroce@edc.org, jgroce@sudanradio.org. (Laflin) mlaflin@edc.org. Web: (includes on-demand audio) www.sudanradio.org; (EDC parent organization) www.edc.org. Contact: Jeremy Groce, Radio Programming Advisor, EDC; Mike Laflin, Director, EDC.

PRODUCTION STUDIOS, KENYA: c/o EDC, P.O. Box 4392, 00100 Nairobi, Kenya. Phone: +254 (20) 570-906, +254 (20) 572-269. Fax: +254 (20) 576 520. Email: srs@sudanradio. org; (Renzi) mtamburo@sudanradio.org. Contact: Tamburo Michael Renzi, SRS Marketing Coordinator.

Trans World Radio

INTERNATIONAL HEADQUARTERS: P.O. Box 8700, Cary NC 27512 USA. Phone: +1 (919) 460-3700; (toll-free, U.S. only) 1-800-456-7897. Fax: +1 (919) 460 3702. Email: online form. Web: (includes on-demand audio) www.twr. org. Contact: (general) Jon Vaught, Public Relations; Richard Greene, Director, Public Relations; Joe Fort, Director, Broadcaster Relations; Bill Danick; (technical) Glenn W. Sink, Assistant Vice President, International Operations. Free "Towers to Eternity" publication for those living in the U.S. This address for nontechnical correspondence only.

TRANS WORLD RADIO EUROPE (TECHNICAL): Trans World Radio, Postfach 141, A-1235 Vienna, Austria. Phone: +43 (1) 863-120. Fax: +43 (1) 863 1220, +43 (1) 862 1257. Email: eurofreq@twr-europe.at. Web: www.twreurope.org. Contact: Rudolf Baertschi, Technical Director; Bernhard Schraut, Deputy Technical Director; Jeremy Mullin, Frequency Coordinator. Verifies reception reports.

TRANS WORLD RADIO EUROPE (NONTECHNICAL): Trans World Radio Europe, Communications Department, P.O. Box 12, 820 02 Bratislava 22, Slovakia. Fax: +421 (2) 4329 3729. Web: www.twreurope.org.

Also, *see* GUAM, INDIA, SOUTH AFRICA and SWAZILAND.

Truth for the World, P.O. Box 5048, Duluth GA 30096-0065 USA. Email: tftworld@aol.com; (Grubb) jmgrubb@tftw. org. Web: www.tftw.org. Contact: Don Blackwell, Director of Broadcasting. Airs programs via world band stations in Equatorial Guinea, Sri Lanka, U.S.A. and elsewhere.

University Network, P.O. Box 1, Los Angeles CA 90053 USA. Phone: +1 (818) 240-8151; (toll-free, U.S. and Canada only) 1-800-338-3030. Web: (includes streaming audio) www.drgenescott.com. Transmits over WWCR (USA); Caribbean Beacon (Anguilla, West Indies) and the former

WEWN's Jesuit Father
Mitch Pacwa hosts
"EWTN Live" and
"The Holy Rosary in
the Holy Land."   WEWN

AWR facilities in Cahuita, Costa Rica. Does not verify reception reports.

📻Voice of America—All Transmitter Locations
(Main Office) 330 Independence Avenue SW, Washington DC 20237 USA; (listener feedback) Voice of America, Audience Mail, Room 4409, 330 Independence Ave SW, Washington DC 20237 USA. If contacting the VOA directly is impractical, write c/o the American Embassy in your country. Phone: (Office of Public Affairs) +1 (202) 401-7000; (Audience Mail Division) +1 (202) 619-2770; (Africa Division) +1 (202) 619-1666, +1 (202) 619-2879; (Office of Research) +1 (202) 619-4965; (administration) +1 (202) 619-1088. Fax: (Office of Public Affairs) +1 (202) 619 1241; (Africa Division) +1 (202) 619 1664; (Audience Mail Division and Office of Research) +1 (202) 619 0211. Email: (general business) publicaffairs@voa.gov; (reception reports and schedule requests) letters@voa.gov; (listener feedback) letters@voanews.com; (VOA Special English) special@voanews.com. Web: (includes on-demand and streaming audio) www.voa.gov. Contact: Mrs. Betty Lacy Thompson, Chief, Audience Mail Division, B/K. G759A Cohen; Larry James, Director, English Programs Division; Joe O'Connell, Director, Office of Public Affairs; (reception reports) QSL Desk, Audience Mail Division, Room G-759-C. May send free stickers, fridge magnets pens and calendars. Also, see Botswana, Greece, Morocco, Philippines, São Tomé e Príncipe, Sri Lanka and Thailand.

VOA ASIA NEWS CENTER: 17th Floor Asia Orient Tower, 33 Lockhart Road, Wanchai, Hong Kong, China. Phone: +852 2526-9809. Fax: +852 2877 8805. Email: jenjano@voanews.com. Contact: Jennifer A. Janin, Director.

Voice of America/IBB—Greenville Relay Station, P.O. Box 1826, Greenville NC 27834 USA. Phone: (site A) +1 (252) 752-7115 or (site B) +1 (252) 752-7181. Fax: (site A) +1 (252) 758 8742 or (site B) +1 (252) 752 5959. Contact: (technical) Bruce Hunter, Manager; Glenn Ruckleson. Nontechnical correspondence should be sent to the VOA address in Washington.

Voice of Joy (when operating), Box 610411, Dallas, TX 75261 USA. Email: voiceofjoy@comcast.net. Web: www.voiceofjoy.net. Contact: Dean Phillips. Broadcasts ir-

regularly via transmitters in various countries. Verifies reception reports.

📻WBCQ—"The Planet," 274 Britton Road, Monticello ME 04760 3110 USA. Phone: +1 (207) 985-7547; (transmitter site, urgent technical matters only) +1 (207) 538-9180. Email: wbcq@wbcq.com. Web: (includes on-demand audio) www.wbcq.com. Contact: Allan H. Weiner, Owner; Elayne Star, Assistant Manager. Verifies reception reports if 1 IRC or (within USA) an SASE is included. Does not verify email reports.

WBOH—*see* Fundamental Broadcasting Network

📻WEWN—EWTN Global Catholic Radio, 5817 Old Leeds Rd., Birmingham AL 35210 USA. Phone: +1 (205) 271-2900. Fax: +1 (205) 271 2926. Email: (general) wewn@ewtn.com; (technical) radio@ewtn.com; (Spanish) rcm@ewtn.com. To contact individuals, the format is initiallastname@ewtn.com; so to reach, say, Thom Price, it would be tprice@ewtn.com. Web: (includes on-demand and streaming audio and online reception report form) www.ewtn.com/radio. Contact: (general) Thom Price, Director of English Programming; Doug Archer, Director of Spanish Programming; (marketing) John Pepe, Radio Marketing Manager; (administration) Michael Warsaw, President; Doug Keck, Sr. Vice-President, Programming & Production; Scott Hults, Vice President, Communications; Frank Leurck, Station Manager; (technical) Terry Borders, Vice President Engineering; Glen Tapley, Frequency Manager. Listener correspondence welcome. IRC or return postage appreciated for correspondence. Although a Catholic entity, WEWN is not an official station of the Vatican, which operates its own Vatican Radio (see).

📻WHRA-World Harvest Radio:
ADMINISTRATION OFFICE: See World Harvest Radio.
TRANSMITTERS: Located in Greenbush, Maine. Technical and other correspondence should be sent to the main office of World Harvest Radio (see).

📻WHRI-World Harvest Radio:
ADMINISTRATION OFFICE: See World Harvest Radio.
TRANSMITTERS: Located in Cypress Creek, South Carolina. Technical and other correspondence should be sent to the main office of World Harvest Radio (see).

WINB—World International Broadcasters, 2900 Windsor Road, P.O. Box 88, Red Lion PA 17356 USA. Phone: (all departments) +1 (717) 244-5360. Fax: +1 (717) 246 0363. Email: (reception reports) winb40th@yahoo.com. Web: www.winb.com. Contact: (general) Mrs. Sally Spyker, Manager; (Sales & Frequency Manager) Hans Johnson; (technical) Fred W. Wise, Technical Director; John H. Norris, Owner. Return postage helpful outside United States. No giveaways or items for sale.

WJIE Shortwave (if reactivated), P.O. Box 197309, Louisville KY 40259 USA. Phone: +1 (502) 968-1220. Fax: +1 (502) 964 3304. Email: (Rumsey) doug@wjie.org (put "WJIE International Shortwave" in the Subject line); (Freeman, technical) morgan@wjie.org. Web: (includes streaming audio) www.wjiesw.com. Contact: Morgan Freeman; Doug Rumsey.

WMLK—Assemblies of Yahweh, 190 Frantz Road, P.O. Box C, Bethel PA 19507 USA. Phone: +1 (717) 933-4518, +1 (717) 933-4880; (toll-free, U.S. only) 1-800-523-3827. Email: (general) aoy@wmlkradio.net; (technical) technician@wmlkradio.net; (Elder Meyer) jacobmeyer@wmlkradio.net; (McAvin) garymcavin@wmlkradio.net. Web: (includes streaming audio) www.wmlkradio.net. Contact: (general) Elder Jacob O. Meyer, Manager and Producer of "The Open Door to the Living World"; (technical) Gary McAvin, Operating Engineer. Free stickers, *The Sacred Name Broadcaster* monthly magazine, and other religious material. Bibles, audio and video (VHS) tapes and religious paperback books offered. Enclosing return postage ($1 or IRCs) helps speed things up.

World Harvest Radio, LeSEA Broadcasting, 61300 Ironwood Road, South Bend IN 46614 USA; or P.O. Box 12, South Bend IN 46624 USA. Phone: +1 (219) 291-8200. Fax: +1 (219) 291 9043. Email: (general) whr@lesea.com; (Sarkisian) lsarkisian@lesea.com. Web: (includes streaming audio and online reception report form) www.whr.org; (LeSEA Broadcasting parent organization, includes streaming audio) www.lesea.com. Contact: (technical) Lori Sarkisian. World Harvest Radio T-shirts available. Return postage appreciated.

ENGINEERING DEPARTMENT: P.O. Box 50450, Indianapolis, IN 46250 USA.

WRMI—Radio Miami International, 175 Fontainebleau Blvd., Suite 1N4, Miami FL 33172 USA. Phone: +1 (305) 559-9764. Fax: +1 (305) 559 8186. Email: info@wrmi.net. Web: (includes streaming audio) www.wrmi.net. Contact: (technical and nontechnical) Jeff White, General Manager/Sales Manager. Free station stickers and tourist brochures. Sells "public access" airtime to nearly anyone to say virtually anything for $1 per minute.

WRNO WORLDWIDE (if reactivated), c/o Good News World Outreach, P.O. Box 895, Fort Worth TX 76101 USA. Phone: +1 (817) 850-9990. Fax: +1 (817) 850 9994. Web: www.wrnoworldwide.org. Contact: Dr. Robert Mawire; Janet Mawire.

TRANSMITTER SITE: 4539 I-10 Service Road North, Metairie LA 70006 USA.

WTJC—*see* Fundamental Broadcasting Network

WWBS (if reactivated), P.O. Box 18174. Macon GA 31209 USA. Phone: +1 (912) 477-3433. Email: wwbsradio@aol.com. Contact: Joanne Josey. Return postage required for postal reply.

WWCR—World Wide Christian Radio, F.W. Robbert Broadcasting Co., 1300 WWCR Avenue, Nashville TN 37218 USA. Phone: (general) +1 (615) 255-1300. Fax: +1 (615) 255 1311. Email: wwcr@wwcr.com. Web: (includes streaming audio) www.wwcr.com. Contact: (nontechnical) Cathy Soares, Program Director; (technical) Zach Harper, Operations Manager; Jason Cooper, Chief Engineer. Free program guides, updated monthly. Return postage helpful. For items sold on the air and tapes of programs, contact the producers of the programs, and *not* WWCR. Replies as time permits. Carries programs from various political organizations, which may be contacted directly.

WWRB—World Wide Religious Broadcasters, Airline Transport Communications, Listener Services, Box 7, Manchester TN 37349 USA. Phone: (8:00 PM - 2:00 AM Eastern Time) +1 (931) 728-6087. Email: (general) online form; (Dave Frantz) dfrantz@tennessee.com. Web: www.wwrb.org. Contact: Dave Frantz, Chief Engineer; Angela Frantz. Verifies reception reports with a large certificate and automatic membership of the WWRB Shortwave Listener's Club. Does not accept email reports.

WWV/WWVB (official time and frequency stations): NIST Radio Station WWV, 2000 East County Road #58, Ft. Collins CO 80524 USA. Phone: +1 (303) 497-3914. Fax: +1 (303) 497 4063. Email: (general) nist.radio@boulder.nist.gov; (Deutch) deutch@boulder.nist.gov. Web: http://tf.nist.gov/timefreq/stations/wwv.html. Contact: Matthew J. ("Matt") Deutch, Engineer-in-Charge. Along with branch sister station WWVH in Hawaii (*see*, below), WWV and WWVB are the official time and frequency stations of the United States, operating over longwave (WWVB) on 60 kHz, and over shortwave (WWV) on 2500, 5000, 10000, 15000 and 20000 kHz.

PARENT ORGANIZATION: National Institute of Standards and Technology, Time and Frequency Division, 325 Broadway, Boulder CO 80305-3328 USA. Phone: +1 (303) 497-5453. Fax: +1 303-497-6461. Email: (Lowe) lowe@boulder.nist.gov. Contact: John P. Lowe, Group Leader.

WWVH (official time and frequency station): NIST Radio Station WWVH, P.O. Box 417, Kekaha, Kauai HI 96752 USA. Phone: +1 (808) 335-4361; (streaming audio) +1 (808) 335-4363; (Automated Computer Time Service) +1 (808) 335 4721. Fax: +1 (808) 335 4747. Email: (general) wwvh@boulder.nist.gov; (Okayama) okayama@boulder.nist.gov. Web: http://tf.nist.gov/stations/wwvh.htm. Contact: Dean T. Okayama, Engineer-in-Charge. Along with sister stations WWV and WWVB (*see* preceding), WWVH is the official time and frequency station of the United States, operating on 2500, 5000, 10000 and 15000 kHz.

WYFR—Family Radio—*see* Family Radio Worldwide

VANUATU   World Time +11

Radio Vanuatu, Information and Public Relations, Private Mail Bag 049, Port Vila, Vanuatu. Phone: +678 22999, +678 23026. Fax: +678 22026. Contact: Jean-Gabriel Manguy, Head; Maxwell E. Maltok, General Manager; Ambong Thompson, Head of Programmes; (technical) K.J. Page, Principal Engineer; Willie Daniel, Technician.

VATICAN CITY STATE   World Time +1 (+2 midyear)

Radio Vaticana (Vatican Radio)

MAIN AND PROMOTION OFFICES: 00120 Città del Vaticano, Vatican City State. Phone: (general) +39 (06) 6988-3551; (Director General) +39 (06) 6988-3945; (Programme Director) +39 (06) 6988-3996; (Publicity and

VoA's broadcasts to Africa reach significant audiences, including those hearing this newscast oriented to Zimbabweans. VoA

Promotion Department) +39 (06) 6988-3045; (technical, general) +39 (06) 6988-4897; (frequency management) +39 (06) 6988-5258. Fax: (general) +39 (06) 6988 4565; (frequency management) +39 (06) 6988 5062. Email: sedoc@vatiradio.va; (Director General) dirgen@vatiradio.va; (frequency management) gestfreq@vatiradio.va (sometimes verifies reception reports); (technical direction, general) sectec@vatiradio.va; (Programme Director) dirpro@vatiradio.va; (Publicity and Promotion Department) promo@vatiradio.va; (French Section) magfra@vatiradio.va; (German Section) deutsch@vatiradio.va. Web: (includes on-demand and streaming audio) www.vatican.va/news_services/radio; (includes on-demand and streaming audio) www.vaticanradio.org. Contact: (general) Elisabetta Vitalini Sacconi, Promotion Office and schedules; Carol Ganbardella, Secretary, English Service; Eileen O'Neill, Head of Program Development, English Service; Fr. Lech Rynkiewicz S.J., Head of Promotion Office; Fr. Andrzej Koprowski S.J., Program Director; Dr. Giacomo Ghisani, Head of International Relations; Sean Patrick Lovett, Head of English Service; Veronica Scarisbrick, Producer, "On the Air;" (administration) Fr. Federico Lombardi S.J., Director General; (technical) Sergio Salvatori, Frequency Manager, Direzione Tecnica; Dr. Alberto Gasbarri, Technical Director; Giovanni Serra, Frequency Management Department. Correspondence sought on religious and programming matters, rather than the technical minutiae of radio, but does verify reception reports. Free station stickers and paper pennants.
INDIA OFFICE: Loyola College, P.B. No 3301, Chennai-600 03, India. Fax: +91 (44) 2825 7340. Email: (Tamil) tamil@vatiradio.va; (Hindi) hindi@vatiradio.va; (English) india@vatiradio.va.

REGIONAL OFFICE, INDIA: Pastoral Orientation Centre, P.B. No 2251, Palarivattom, India. Fax: +91 (484) 2336 227. Email: (Malayalam) malayalam@vatiradio.va.
JAPAN OFFICE: 2-10-10 Shiomi, Koto-ku, Tokyo 135, Japan. Fax: +81 (3) 5632 4457.

VENEZUELA   World Time –4:30

Observatorio Cagigal—YVTO (when operating), Apartado 6745, Armada 84-DHN, Caracas 103, Venezuela. Phone: +58 (212) 481-2266. Email: armdhn@ven.net, shlv@dhn.mil.ve. Contact: Luis Ojeda Pérez, Director; Jesús Alberto Escalona, Director Técnico. $1 or return postage helpful.
Radio Amazonas (when operating), Av. Simón Bolívar 4, Puerto Ayacucho 7101, Amazonas, Venezuela. Contact: Angel María Pérez, Propietario.
ADDRESS FOR RECEPTION REPORTS: Sr. Jorge García Rangel, Radio Amazonas QSL Manager, Calle Roma, Qta: Costa Rica No. A-16, Urbanización Alto Barinas, Barinas 5201, Venezuela. Two IRC's or $2 required.
🔊**Radio Nacional de Venezuela - Antena Internacional,** Final Calle Las Marías, entre Chapellín y Country Club La Florida, 1050 Caracas, Venezuela. Phone: +58 (212) 730-6022, +58 (212) 730-6666. Fax: +58 (212) 731 1457 Email: ondacortavenezuela@hotmail.com. Web: (includes streaming audio from domestic services not on shortwave) www.rnv.gov.ve. Contact: Ali Méndez Martínez, periodista y representativo de onda corta; Freddy R. Santos. Currently broadcasts via the transmission facilities of Radio Habana Cuba. "Antena Internacional" is also aired at 0600-0700 World Time (subject to change) on mediumwave AM via Radio Nacional's domestic "Canal Informativo," available in streaming audio at the RNV Website.

VIETNAM   World Time +7

NOTE: Reception reports on Vietnamese regional stations should be sent to the Voice of Vietnam Overseas Service (*see*).
Voice of Vietnam—Domestic Service (Đài Tiêng Nói Viêt Nam, TNVN)—Addresses and contact numbers as for all sections of Voice of Vietnam—Overseas Service, below. Contact: Phan Quang, Director General.
🔊**Voice of Vietnam—Overseas Service**
(MAIN ADDRESS FOR NONTECHNICAL CORRESPONDENCE AND GENERAL VERIFICATIONS): 58 Quán Sú, Hànôi, Vietnam. Phone: +84 (4) 934-4231. Fax: +84 (4) 934 4230. Email: (Vietnamese) vovnews@hn.vnn.vn; (English) english@vovnews.vn. Web: (includes on-demand and streaming audio) www.vov.org.vn. Contact: Ms. Hoang Minh Nguyet, Director of International Relations.
STUDIOS (NONTECHNICAL CORRESPONDENCE AND GENERAL VERIFICATIONS): 45 Ba Trieu Street, Hànôi, Vietnam. Phone: (director) +84 (4) 825-7870; (English service) +84 (4) 934-2456, +84 (4) 825-4482; (newsroom) +84 (4) 825-5761, +84 (4) 825-5862. Fax: (English service) +84 (4) 826 6707. Email: btdn.vov@hn.vnn.vn; (English) englishsection@vov.org.vn (Spanish Service contact) tiengnoi_vietnam2004@yahoo.es. Contact: Ms. Nguyen Thi Hue, Director, Overseas Service. Voice of Vietnam Overseas Service broadcasts in 11 foreign languages, namely English, French, Japanese, Russian, Spanish, Mandarin, Cantonese, Indonesian, Lao, Thai, Khmer and Vietnamese for overseas Vietnamese.

TECHNICAL CORRESPONDENCE: Office of Radio Reception Quality, Central Department of Radio and Television Broadcast Engineering, Vietnam General Corporation of Posts and Telecommunications, Hànôi, Vietnam.

WESTERN SAHARA World Time exactly

📻**Radio Nacional de la República Arabe Saharaui Democrática** (when operating). Email: rasdradio@yahoo.es. Web: (streaming audio) http://web.jet.es/rasd/radio-nacional.htm. Pro-Polisario Front, and supported by the Algerian government. Operates from Rabuni, near Tindouf, on the Algerian side of the border with Western Sahara.

YEMEN World Time +3

📻**Republic of Yemen Radio**, Technical Department, P. O. Box 2371, Sana'a, Yemen. Phone: +967 (1) 282-060. Fax: +967 (1) 282 053. Email: (Tashi) ali_tashy@yahoo.com. Web: (includes on-demand audio): www.yradio.gov.ye. Contact: Eng. Ali Ahmed Tashi, Technical Department Director. Verifies reception reports. Return postage appreciated.

ZAMBIA World Time +2

📻**The Voice - Africa**
STATION: Radio Christian Voice, Private Bag E606, Lusaka, Zambia. Phone: +260 (1) 273-191. Fax: +260 (1) 279 183. Email: voicefm@zamnet.zm. Web: (includes streaming audio) www.voiceafrica.net. Contact: Philip Haggar, Station Manager; Lenganji Nanyangwe, Assistant to Station Manager; Beatrice Phiri. Free calendars and stickers; pens, as available. Free religious books and items under selected circumstances. Sells T-shirts and sundry other items. $1 or 2 IRCs appreciated for reply. Verifies reception reports. Broadcasts Christian teachings and music, as well as news and programs on farming, sport, education, health, business and children's affairs. Formerly known as Radio Christian Voice.
U. K. OFFICE: The Voice, P.O. Box 3040, West Bromwich, West Midlands, B70 0EJ, United Kingdom. Phone:+44 (121) 224-1614. Fax: +44 (121) 224 1613. Email: feedback@voiceafrica.net; (Joynes) sandra@voiceafrica.net. Contact: Sandra Joynes, Office Administrator.
Radio Zambia, Mass Media Complex, Alick Nkhata Road, P.O. Box 50015, Lusaka 10101, Zambia. Phone: (general) +260 (1) 254-989, +260 (1) 253-301, +260 (1) 252-005; (Public Relations) +260 (1) 254-989, X-216; (engineering) +260 (1) 250-380. Fax: +260 (1) 254 317, +260 (1) 254 013. Web: www.znbc.co.zm; (streaming audio) www.coppernet.zm/home.html. Contact: (general) Keith M. Nalumango, Director of Programmes; Lawson Chishimba, Public Relations Manager; (administration) Duncan H. Mbazima, Director-General; (technical) James M. Phiri, Director of Engineering. Free *Zamwaves* newsletter. Sometimes gives away stickers, postcards and small publications. $1 required, and postal correspondence should be sent via registered mail. Tours of the station given Tuesdays to Fridays between 9:00 AM and noon local time; inquire in advance. Used to reply slowly and irregularly, but seems to be better now.

ZIMBABWE World Time +2

Radio Voice of the People, P.O. Box 5750, Harare, Zimbabwe. Email: voxpopzim@yahoo.co.uk, voxpop@ecoweb.co.zw. Web: www.vopradio.co.zw. Contact: John Masuku, Executive Director. Airs via Radio Nederland facilities in Madagascar.
Radio VOP—*see* Radio Voice of the People, above.
📻**Zimbabwe Broadcasting Corporation**, Broadcasting Center, Pockets Hill, P.O. Box HG444, Highlands, Harare, Zimbabwe. Phone: +263 (4) 498-610, +263 (4) 498-630; (Guinea Fowl Shortwave Transmitting Station) +263 (54) 22-104. Fax: +263 (4) 498 613. Email: zbc@zbc.co.zw; (general enquiries) pr@zbc.co.zw; (engineering) hbt@zbc.co.zw. Web: (includes streaming audio) www.zbc.co.zw. Contact: (general) Rugare Sangomoyo; Lydia Muzenda; (administration) Alum Mpofu, Chief Executive Officer; (news details) Munyaradzi Hwengwere; (Broadcasting Technology, Engineering) Craig Matambo. $1 helpful.

Prepared by Craig Tyson (Australia), editor, with Tony Jones (Paraguay). Special thanks to David Crystal (Israel), Graeme Dixon (New Zealand), Jose Jacob (India), Fotios Padazopulos (USA), George Poppin (USA), Célio Romais (Brazil), Paulo Roberto e Souza (Brazil) and George Zeller (USA); also, the following organizations for their support and cooperation: Conexión Digital and RUS-DX/Anatoly Klepov (Russia).

Worldwide Broadcasts in English— 2008

Country-by-Country Guide to Best-Heard Stations

Dozens of countries reach out in English, and this is where you'll find their times and frequencies. For what shows are on, hour-by-hour, see "What's On Tonight."

• **Top Times**: "Best Times and Frequencies," earlier in PASSPORT, pinpoints where each world band segment is found and offers helpful tuning tips. Focus on late afternoon and evening, when most programs are beamed your way—although around dawn and early afternoon can be productive, as well.

☞ Dusk and evening, tune segments between 5730 and 10000 kHz in winter, 5730 and 15800 kHz in summer. Daytime it's 9250–21850 kHz winter, 11500–21850 kHz summer. Around dawn explore 5730–17900 kHz year-round for fewer but intriguing catches.

Times and days of the week are in World Time (UTC), explained in "Setting Your World Time Clock" and "Worldly Words"; for local times in each country see "Addresses PLUS." Midyear, typically April through October, some stations are an hour earlier (⬛) or later (⬛) because of Daylight Saving/Summer Time. Stations may also extend their hours for holidays, emergencies or sports events.

Frequencies used only seasonally are labeled **S** for summer (midyear) and **W** for winter.

• **Strongest frequencies:** Frequencies in *italics* tend to be best, as they are from relay transmitters that may be near you. Some signals not beamed your way may also be heard, especially when targeted to nearby parts of the world. Frequencies with no target zones are typically for domestic coverage, so they're unlikely to be heard unless you're in or near that country.

> **While the VoA cuts back English, others expand its use.**

Indigenous Music

Programs not in English? Turn to "Voices from Home" or the Blue Pages. Stations for diaspora sometimes carry delightful native music that's enjoyable listening, regardless of language.

Schedules for Entire Year

To be as useful as possible over the months to come, PASSPORT's schedules consist not just of observed activity, but also that which we have creatively opined will take place during the forthcoming year. This predictive material is based on decades of experience and is original from us. Although inherently not as exact as real-time data, over the years it's been of tangible value to PASSPORT readers.

Shutterstock/Yare Marketing

ALBANIA

RADIO TIRANA

0245-0300 &		
0330-0400 ▣	Tu-Su 6110/6115 & Tu-Su 7425 (E North Am)	
1300-1330	⑤ Tu-Su 13750 (E North Am)	
1500-1530	⑩ Tu-Su 13640 (E North Am)	
1945-2000 ▣	M-Sa 7465 (W Europe)	
1945-2000	⑩ M-Sa 6135 (Europe)	
2000-2030	⑤ M-Sa 7465 (Europe), ⑤ Tu-Su 13720 (E North Am)	
2100-2130	⑩ M-Sa 7430 (Europe), ⑩ Tu-Su 9915 (E North Am)	

ARGENTINA

RADIO ARGENTINA AL EXTERIOR-RAE

0200-0300	Tu-Sa 11710 (Americas)
1800-1900	M-F 15345 (Europe)

AUSTRALIA

RADIO AUSTRALIA

0000-0130	17775 (SE Asia)
0000-0200	17715 (Pacific & N America), 17795 (Pacific & W North Am)
0000-0700	13690 (Pacific & E Asia)
0000-0800	9660 & 15240 (Pacific)
0000-0900	12080 (S Pacific), 17750 (SE Asia)
0030-0400	15415 (SE Asia)
0200-0500	21725 (E Asia)
0200-0700	15515 (Pacific & N America)
0430-0500	15415 (SE Asia)
0500-0800	15160 (Pacific & N America)
0530-0600	15415 (SE Asia)
0600-0630	⑩ Sa/Su 11970, Sa/Su 15290, Sa/Su 15415 & ⑤ Sa/Su 17585 (SE Asia)
0630-1100	15415 (SE Asia)
0700-0900	9710 (Pacific), 13630 (Pacific & W North Am)
0800-0900	5995 (Pacific)
0800-1400	9580 (Pacific & N America)
0800-1600	9590 (Pacific & W North Am)
0900-1300	11880 (SE Asia)
1100-1200	12080 (S Pacific)
1100-1300	9475 (SE Asia)
1100-1400	5995 (Pacific), 6020 (Pacific & W North Am), 9560 (E Asia & Pacific)
1400-1700	7240 (Pacific & W North Am)
1400-1800	5995 (Pacific & W North Am), 6080 (SE Asia)
1430-1700	11660 (SE Asia)
1430-1900	9475 (SE Asia)
1600-2000	9710 (Pacific)
1700-2100	9580 (Pacific), 11880 (Pacific & W North Am)
1800-2000	6080 (Pacific & E Asia), 7240 (Pacific)
1900-2200	9500 (SE Asia)
2000-2100	F/Sa 6080 & F/Sa 7240 (Pacific), F/Sa 12080 (S Pacific)
2000-2200	11650 & 11660 (Pacific)
2100-2200	9660 (Pacific), 11695 (SE Asia), 12080 (S Pacific)
2100-2300	13630 & 15515 (Pacific)
2200-2330	*15240* (SE Asia)
2200-2400	⑩ 12010 & 13620 (SE Asia), 15230 (Pacific), 17785 (Pacific & N America)
2300-2400	9660 (Pacific), 12080 (S Pacific), 13690 (Pacific & E Asia), 17795 (Pacific & W North Am)
2330-2400	15415 & 17750 (SE Asia)

AUSTRIA

RADIO AUSTRIA INTERNATIONAL

0005-0015	⑩ Su/M 7325 (C America)
0015-0030	⑩ 7325 (C America)
0035-0045	⑩ Su/M 7325 (E North Am)
0045-0100	⑩ 7325 (E North Am)
0105-0115	⑤ Su/M 9870 (C America)
0115-0130	⑤ 9870 (C America)
0135-0145	⑤ Su/M 9870 (E North Am)
0145-0200	⑤ 9870 (E North Am)
0605-0630 &	
0635-0700 ▣	Su 17870 (Mideast)
1205-1220	⑤ M 17715 (SE Asia & Australasia)
1205-1230	⑤ Sa/Su 17715 (SE Asia & Australasia)
1215-1230	⑤ Tu-F 17715 (SE Asia & Australasia)

1235-1300	**S** Sa/Su 17715 (SE Asia & Australasia)
1245-1300	**S** M-F 17715 (SE Asia & Australasia)
1305-1320 ⬅	M 6155 & M 13730 (Europe)
1305-1320	**W** M 17855 (SE Asia & Australasia)
1305-1330 ⬅	Sa/Su 6155 & Sa/Su 13730 (Europe)
1315-1330	**W** Tu-F 17855 (SE Asia & Australasia)
1335-1345	**W** Sa/Su 17855 (SE Asia & Australasia)
1335-1400 ⬅	Sa/Su 6155 & Sa/Su 13730 (Europe)
1345-1400 ⬅	Tu-F 6155 & Tu-F 13730 (Europe)
1345-1400	**W** 17855 (SE Asia & Australasia)
1505-1520	**S** M *13775* (W North Am)
1505-1530	**S** Sa/Su *13775* (W North Am)
1515-1530	**S** Tu-F *13775* (W North Am)
1535-1600	**S** Sa/Su *13775* (W North Am)
1545-1600	**S** M-F *13775* (W North Am)
1605-1620	**W** M *13675* (W North Am)
1605-1630	**W** Sa/Su *13675* (W North Am)
1615-1630	**W** Tu-F *13675* (W North Am)
1635-1700	**W** Sa/Su *13675* (W North Am)
1645-1700	**W** M-F *13675* (W North Am)
2335-2345 ➡	Sa/Su 9870 (S America)
2345-2400	9870 (S America)

BANGLADESH

BANGLADESH BETAR

1230-1300	7250 (SE Asia)
1745-1900	7250 & 9550 (Europe)

BELARUS

RADIO STATION BELARUS—(Europe)

2000-2200	**S** 7105 & **S** 7440
2100-2300 ⬅	7390
2100-2300	**W** 7360 & **W** 7420

BULGARIA

RADIO BULGARIA

0000-0100	**W** 7400 & **W** 9400 (E North Am)

0200-0300	**S** 9700 & **S** 11700 (E North Am)
0300-0400	**W** 7400 & **W** 9400 (E North Am)
0630-0700	**S** 9600 & **S** 11600 (W Europe)
0730-0800	**W** 7400 & **W** 9400 (W Europe)
1230-1300 ⬅	11700 & 15700 (W Europe)
1730-1800	**S** 5900 & **S** 9600 (W Europe)
1830-1900	**W** 7400 & **W** 9400 (W Europe)
2100-2200	**S** 5900 & **S** 9700 (W Europe)
2200-2300	**W** 7400 & **W** 9400 (W Europe)
2300-2400	**S** 9700 & **S** 11700 (E North Am)

CANADA

CANADIAN BROADCASTING CORP—(E North Am)

0000-0300 ⬅		Su 9625
0200-0300 ⬅		Tu-Sa 9625
0300-0310 & 0330-0609 ⬅		M 9625
0400-0609 ⬅		Su 9625
0500-0609 ⬅		Tu-Sa 9625
1200-1255 ⬅		M-F 9625
1200-1505 ⬅		Sa 9625
1200-1700 ⬅		Su 9625
1600-1615 & 1700-1805 ⬅		Sa 9625
1800-2400 ⬅		Su 9625
1945-2015, 2200-2225 & 2240-2330 ⬅		M-F 9625

CFRX-CFRB—(E North Am)

24 Hr	6070 (Irr)

CFVP-CKMX—(W North Am)

24 Hr	6030

CKZN—(E North Am)

24 Hr	6160

CKZU-CBU—(W North Am)

24 Hr	6160

RADIO CANADA INTERNATIONAL

0000-0005	**S** 6100 (N America)
0000-0100	**W** *9880* & **S** *11700* (SE Asia)

0005-0105 ◾S Tu-Sa 6100 & ◾W 9755 (N America)
0100-0200 ◾W *5840* & ◾W *7255* (S Asia)
0105-0205 ◾W Tu-Sa 9755 (N America)
1500-1600 ◾W *9635*, ◾S *11675*, ◾W *11975* & ◾S *17720* (S Asia)
1505-1605 ◾S 9515 & ◾W 9610 (N America)
1605-1705 ◾S 9515 (N America)
1705-1905 ◾W 9610 (N America)
1800-1900 ◾S *9530* (E Africa), ◾S *11765* (C Africa), ◾W *11875* (C Africa & E Africa), ◾W 13650 (N Africa & W Africa), ◾S 15235 (W Africa), ◾W 15365, ◾W 17740 & ◾S *17810* (W Africa & C Africa)
2000-2100 ◾S *7235* (W Europe & N Africa), ◾S 15325 (W Europe)
2100-2200 ◾◄ *5850* (W Europe)
2100-2200 ◾W 9770 (W Europe)
2300-2330 ◾W *6160* (E Asia)
2300-2400 ◾W 9580 (N America & C America)
2305-2400 ◾S 6100 (N America)

CHINA

CHINA RADIO INTERNATIONAL

0000-0100 6075 (S Asia), 7130 (Europe), 7180 (S Asia), ◾W 9425 (E Asia), 11885 (SE Asia), ◾S 13750 (E Asia)
0000-0200 *6020* & *9570* (N America), ◾W 11650 & ◾S 15125 (SE Asia)
0100-0200 ◾W *6005* (N America), ◾W 6075 (S Asia), ◾W *6080* (E North Am), ◾W 7130 (Europe), ◾W 7180 (S Asia), ◾S 9470 (Europe), ◾S 9535 (S Asia), *9580* (E North Am), ◾S *9790* (W North Am), ◾S *9800* (E North Am), ◾S 11870 (S Asia), ◾W 11885 & ◾S 15785 (SE Asia)
0200-0300 13640 (S Asia)
0200-0400 11770 (S Asia)
0300-0400 *9690* (N America & C America), *9790* (W North Am), 15110 (S Asia)

0300-0500 ◾W 9460, ◾W 13620 & ◾S 13750 (E Asia), 15120 (C Asia & E Asia), ◾S 15785 (E Asia)
0400-0500 ◾S *6080* (N America), ◾W *6190* (W North Am)
0400-0600 ◾S *6020* (W North Am), 17725/17730 & 17855 (C Asia)
0500-0600 ◾W *5960* (N America), *6190* (W North Am), ◾W *7220* (N Africa)
0500-0700 ◾S *11710* (N Africa), 17505 (N Africa & W Africa)
0500-0900 11880, 15465 & 17540 (S Asia)
0500-1100 15350 (S Asia)
0600-0700 ◾W *6115* (W North Am), ◾W *11750* (N Africa), ◾W 11770 (Mideast), ◾S 11870 (Mideast & W Asia), 15145 (Mideast)
0600-0800 ◾W 13645, ◾S 13660 & 17710 (SE Asia)
0700-0900 ◾W *11785* & *13710* (W Europe)
0700-1300 17490 (Europe)
0800-1000 ◾W 9415 & ◾S 11620 (E Asia)
0900-1000 17750 (S Asia)
0900-1100 15210 & 17690 (Australasia)
1000-1100 ◾W 5955 (E Asia), ◾W 7135, ◾W 7215, ◾S 11610 & ◾S 11635 (C Asia & E Asia), ◾S 13620 (E Asia), 15190 (S Asia)
1000-1200 ◾S *6040* (E North Am), 13590 & 13720 (SE Asia)
1100-1200 ◾W *5960* (E North Am), ◾W 9570 (S Asia), ◾S *11750* (W North Am), 11795 & 13645 (S Asia)
1100-1300 11650 (S Asia), ◾S *13650* & ◾W *13665* (W Europe)
1100-1400 ◾S 11660 (S Asia)
1100-1500 5955 (E Asia)
1200-1300 ◾W 7250 & 9460 (S Asia), 9760 (Australasia), 11690 (C Asia), ◾W 12080, ◾S 13610 & ◾S 13645 (S Asia)
1200-1400 9730 (SE Asia), 11760 (Australasia), 11980 (SE Asia), 13790 (Europe)

1300-1400	*9570* (E North Am), **S** *9650* (E North Am & C America), **S** 9760 (Australasia), **W** *11885* (W North Am), **W** 11900 (Australasia), 13610 (Europe), **S** 13755 (S Asia), **S** *15260* (W North Am), **W** *15540* & **S** *17625* (S America)
1300-1500	**W** 7300 (S Asia), 9765 (C Asia), **W** *15230* (E North Am & C America)
1300-1600	9870 (SE Asia)
1400-1500	**W** 9460 (S Asia), **W** 9700 & **W** 9795 (Europe), 11675 & **S** 11765 (S Asia), **W** *13675* (W North Am), **S** 13710 & **S** 13790 (Europe)
1400-1600	*13685* (E Africa), *13740* (W North Am), *17630* (C Africa)
1500-1600	5955 (E Asia), 7160 (S Asia), 7325 (SE Asia), **W** 9785 & **S** 9800 (S Asia), **S** 13640 (Europe)
1500-1700	**W** 9435, **W** 9525 & **S** 11965 (Europe)
1500-1800	*6100* (S Africa)
1600-1800	**W** 7150 (E Africa & S Africa), **W** 7255 (Europe), **S** 9570 (E Africa & S Africa), **S** 11900 (S Africa), **S** 11940 (Europe)
1600-1900	**S** 13760 (Europe)
1700-1800	**W** 6100 & **S** 9695 (Europe)
1800-1900	**W** 6100, **W** 7110 & **S** 9600 (Europe)
1900-2000	9440/9435 (Mideast, W Africa & C Africa)
1900-2100	7295 (Mideast & N Africa)
2000-2100	9440 (Mideast, W Africa & C Africa)
2000-2130	*11640* (E Africa & S Africa), *13630* (E Africa)
2000-2200	*5960* (W Europe), 7190 (Europe), *7285* (W Europe), 9600 (Europe)
2200-2300	**W** 5915 (E Asia), **W** *7170* & **S** *7175* (N Europe), **S** 9590 (E Asia)
2300-2400	**S** 5915 (S Asia), *5990* (C America), **W** *6040* (E North Am), **W** 6145 (E Asia),

Taipei's World Trade Center, hub for much of Taiwan's vast export activity.   Shutterstock

S *6145* (E North Am), 7180 (S Asia), **S** 11685 (E Asia), **S** *11840* & **W** *11970* (W North Am)

CHINA (TAIWAN)
RADIO TAIWAN INTERNATIONAL

0200-0300	*5950* (E North Am), *9680* (N America), 11875 (SE Asia)
0300-0400	*5950* (W North Am), *15215* (S America), 15320 (SE Asia)
0700-0800	*5950* (W North Am)
0800-0900	9610 (SE Asia & Australasia)
1100-1200	7445 (SE Asia)
1400-1500	15265 (SE Asia)
1600-1700	**W** *9785/11995* (S Asia & SE Asia), 11550 (E Asia & S Asia), **S** *15515/11600* (S Asia & SE Asia)
1700-1800	**W** *11850* (C Africa), **S** *15690* (C Africa & S Africa)
1800-1900	*3965* (W Europe)
2200-2300	**W** 9355 & **S** *15600* (Europe)

CROATIA

VOICE OF CROATIA
0200-0215	⑤ *9925* (N America & S America)
0300-0315	ⓦ *7285* (N America & S America)
2215-2230	⑤ *9925* (S America)
2315-2330	ⓦ *7285* (S America)

CUBA

RADIO HABANA CUBA
0100-0500	6000 (E North Am), 6180 (N America)
0500-0700	6000 (W North Am), 6060 (E North Am), 6180 (North Am), 11760 (Americas)
2030-2130	9505 (C America), 11760 (E North America)
2300-2400	9550 (S America)

CZECH REPUBLIC

RADIO PRAGUE
0000-0030	⑤ 7345 (E North Am & C America), ⑤ 9440 (N America & C America)
0100-0130	6200 & 7345 (N America & C America)
0200-0230	ⓦ 6200 & ⓦ 7345 (N America & C America)
0300-0330	⑤ 7345 (N America & C America), ⑤ 9870 (W North Am & C America)
0330-0400	⑤ *6080* (W North Am), ⑤ 9445 (Mideast & E Africa), ⑤ 11600 (Mideast & S Asia)
0400-0430	ⓦ *5990* (Irr) (W North Am), ⓦ 6200 (W North Am & C America), ⓦ 7345 (N America & C America)
0430-0500	ⓦ 9890 (Mideast, E Africa & S Asia)
0700-0730	⑤ 9880 & ⑤ 11600 (W Europe)
0800-0830	ⓦ 7345 & ⓦ 9860 (W Europe)
0900-0930	⑤ 9880 (W Europe), ⑤ 21745 (S Asia)
1000-1030	ⓦ 15700 (S Asia), ⓦ 21745 (W Africa)
1030-1100	⑤ 9880 & ⑤ 11665 (N Europe)
1130-1200	ⓦ 11640 (N Europe), ⓦ 17545 (C Africa & E Africa)
1300-1330	⑤ 13580 (W Europe), ⑤ 17540 (S Asia)
1400-1430	ⓦ 11600 (S Asia), ⓦ 13580 (N America)
1600-1630	⑤ 17485 (E Africa)
1700-1730	▣ 5930 (W Europe)
1700-1730	ⓦ 15710 (W Africa & C Africa), ⑤ 17485 (C Africa)
1800-1830	▣ 5930 (W Europe)
1800-1830	ⓦ 9400 (Asia & Australasia)
2000-2030	⑤ 11600 (SE Asia & Australasia)
2100-2130	▣ 5930 (W Europe)
2100-2130	ⓦ 9430 (SE Asia & Australasia)
2130-2200	⑤ 9410 (W Africa & C Africa), ⑤ 11600 (N America)
2230-2300	ⓦ 5930 (N America), ⑤ 7345 (E North Am & C America), ⑤ 9415 (N America), ⓦ 9435 (W Africa & C Africa)
2330-2400	ⓦ 5930 (N America), ⓦ 7345 (N America & C America)

EGYPT

RADIO CAIRO
0000-0030	9460/9465 (E North Am)
0200-0330	7270 (N America)
1215-1330	17835 (S Asia & SE Asia)
1600-1800	11740 (C Africa & S Africa)
1900-2030	15375 (W Africa)
2115-2245	6250/9990 (Europe)
2300-2400	9460/9465 (E North Am)

FRANCE

RADIO FRANCE INTERNATIONALE
0400-0430	ⓦ 7315 & M-F 9805 (E Africa)
0500-0530	ⓦ M-F 9805/13680, ⓦ M-F 11995, ⑤ M-F 13680 & ⑤ M-F 15160/11995 (E Africa)

0600-0630   W M-F 7315 & S M-F 11725/9765 (W Africa & C Africa), W M-F 11995/15160, W M-F 13680, S M-F 15160 & S M-F 17800 (E Africa)

0700-0730   W 11725/15605 & S 13675 (W Africa & C Africa)

1200-1230   S 17800/21620 & W 21620 (E Africa)

1600-1700   W 11615/15605 (C Africa & E Africa), 15160 (W Africa & C Africa), S 15605 (C Africa & S Africa), S 17605 (E Africa)

GERMANY

DEUTSCHE WELLE

0000-0100   S 7245, W 7265 & W 9785 (SE Asia), 15595 (E Asia)

0100-0200   W 9850 (S Asia)

0300-0400   W 9785 & S 11695 (S Asia), S 13770 (S Asia & SE Asia), W 13790 (S Asia)

0400-0500   W 5905 (W Africa), W 6180 (C Africa & E Africa), S 7225 (W Africa), W 7225 (C Africa & E Africa), S 7245 (W Africa & C Africa), S 12045 (E Africa & S Africa), S 15445 (C Africa & E Africa), W 15445 (C Africa & S Africa)

0500-0530   S 5945 (W Africa), W 6180 (C Africa & E Africa), W 7285 (W Africa), S 9700 (C Africa & S Africa), W 9755 (W Africa), W 12045 (S Africa), W 15410 (E Africa, C Africa & S Africa)

0600-0630   W 5945 (W Africa & C Africa), W 7240 & S 7310 (W Africa), W 12045 & S 15275 (W Africa & C Africa)

0900-1000   S 15340, S 17705, W 17710 & S 17770 (E Asia), W 21840 (E Asia & SE Asia)

1600-1700   W 5925, 6170, S 9485 & W 9795 (S Asia), S 15640 (S Asia & SE Asia)

1900-1930   S 9565 & W 9735 (E Africa & S Africa), S 9895 (S Africa), W 11690 (C Africa & E Africa), S 11795 (E Africa), W 13780 (E Africa & S Africa), W 15275 (C Africa, E Africa & S Africa)

2000-2100   S 7130 (S Africa), W 9410 (C Africa & S Africa), W 9735 (C Africa, E Africa & S Africa), S 11795 (E Africa & S Africa), S 11865 (C Africa & S Africa), W 13780 (W Africa, C Africa & S Africa), S 15205 (C Africa, E Africa & S Africa)

2100-2200   W 7280 (W Africa), S 9735 (C Africa & E Africa), W 11690 & S 11865 (W Africa), W 13780 (W Africa & C Africa), S 15205 (W Africa)

INDIA

ALL INDIA RADIO

0000-0045   9705 (E Asia & SE Asia), 9950 (E Asia), 11620 (SE Asia), 11645 (E Asia), 13605 (E Asia & SE Asia)

1000-1100   13695/13710 (E Asia & Australasia), 15020 (E Asia), 15260 (S Asia), 15410/15135 (E Asia), 17510 (Australasia), 17800 (E Asia), 17895 (Australasia)

1330-1500   9690, 11620 & 13710 (SE Asia)

1745-1945   7410 (Europe), 9445 (W Africa), 9950 & 11620 (Europe), 11935 (E Africa), 13605 (W Africa), 15075 (E Africa), 15155 (W Africa), 17670 (E Africa)

2045-2230   7410 & 9445 (Europe), 9910 (Australasia), 9950 (Europe), 11620 & 11715 (Australasia)

2245-2400   9705 (E Asia & SE Asia), 9950 (E Asia), 11620 (SE Asia), 11645 (E Asia), 13605 (E Asia & SE Asia)

The European DX Council's annual conference, which took place in St. Petersburg, Russia.   T. Ohtake

IRAN

VOICE OF THE ISLAMIC REPUBLIC

0130-0230	🆆 6120, 🆆 7160, 🆂 7235 & 🆂 9495 (N America)
1030-1130	🆆 15460, 🆂 15600 & 17660 (S Asia)
1530-1630	🆆 6160, 🆆 7330, 🆂 7370 & 🆂 9635 (S Asia & SE Asia)
1930-2030	🆆 6010 & 🆂 6205 (Europe), 🆆 *6250/6255* (W Europe), 🆂 *7205* & 🆆 7320 (Europe), 🆂 *7540* (W Europe), 🆂 9800, 🆆 9855, 🆂 9925 & 🆆 11695 (S Africa)

ISRAEL

KOL ISRAEL

0330-0345	🆂 11590/9345 & 🆂 13720/7530 (W Europe & E North Am), 🆂 17600 (Australasia)
0430-0445	🆆 6280/9345 & 🆆 7545 (W Europe & E North Am), 🆆 17600/15640 (Australasia)
0930-0945	🆂 13680 & 🆂 15760 (W Europe & E North Am)
1030-1045	🆆 15640 (W Europe & E North Am), 🆆 17535 (W Europe & N America)
1730-1745	🆂 9345 (W Europe), 🆂 13675 (W Europe & E North Am)

1830-1845 🔲	11590 (W Europe & E North Am)
1830-1845	🆆 7545 (W Europe), 🆆 9345 (W Europe & E North Am)

JAPAN

RADIO JAPAN

0000-0020	*5960/5920* (W Europe), *6145* (E North Am & C America), 13650 & 17810 (SE Asia)
0500-0530	*5975* (W Europe), *6110* (W North Am), 🆂 *7215* & 🆆 *9725* (S Africa), 15325 (S Asia), 17810 (SE Asia)
0900-0930	9825 (Pacific & S America), 11815 (SE Asia), 🆆 11845, 11890 & 🆆 12000 (Australasia), 15590 (S Asia)
1200-1230	*6120* (E North Am & C America), 9625 (Australasia), *17600/17585* (Europe)
1310-1340	🆆 9875 & 🆂 11985 (S Asia)
1400-1430	🆆 9875 (S Asia), *11705* (E North Am), 🆆 *11780* (N Europe), 🆂 11985 (S Asia), 🆂 *13630* (N Europe), 17580 (C Africa & E Africa)
2200-2220	13640 (Australasia)

JORDAN

RADIO JORDAN—(W Europe & E North Am)

1400-1730 ⇦	11690

KOREA (DPR)

VOICE OF KOREA

0100-0200	3560, 7140, 9345 & 9730 (E Asia), 11735, 13760 & 15180 (C America)
0200-0300	4405 (E Asia), 13650 & 15100 (SE Asia)
0300-0400	3560, 7140, 9345 & 9730 (E Asia)
1000-1100	3560 (E Asia), [W] 6185 (SE Asia), [W] 6285 & [W] 9335 (C America), [W] 9850 (SE Asia), [S] 11710 (C America), [S] 11735 & [S] 13650 (SE Asia), [S] 15180 (C America)
1300-1400 & 1500-1600	4405 (E Asia), [W] 7570 (W Europe), 9335 & 11710 (N America), [W] 12015, [S] 13760 & [S] 15245 (W Europe)
1600-1700	3560 (E Asia), 9990 & 11545 (Mideast & N Africa)
1800-1900	4405 (E Asia), [W] 7570, [W] 12015, [S] 13760 & [S] 15245 (W Europe)
1900-2000	3560 (E Asia), 7100 (S Africa), 9975 (Mideast & N Africa), 11910 (S Africa)
2100-2200	4405 (E Asia), [W] 7570, [W] 12015, [S] 13760 & [S] 15245 (W Europe)

KOREA (REPUBLIC)

KBS WORLD RADIO

0200-0300	15575 (S America)
0230-0300	*9560* (W North Am)
0800-0900	9570 (SE Asia)
1200-1300	*9650* (N America)
1300-1400	9570 & 9770 (SE Asia)
1600-1700	9515 (Europe)
1800-1900	7275 (Europe)
2200-2230 ⇦	*3955* (W Europe)

KUWAIT

RADIO KUWAIT

0500-0800	15110 (S Asia)
1800-2100	11990 (Europe & E North Am)

LIBYA

RADIO JAMAHIRIYA

1200-1400	[S] 17870 (E Africa)
1400-1600	17725 (C Africa), [W] 21695 (E Africa)

LITHUANIA

RADIO VILNIUS

0030-0100 ⇦	9875 (E North Am)
0030-0100	[S] 11690 (E North Am)
0130-0200	[W] 7325 (E North Am)
0930-1000 ⇦	9710 (W Europe)
2330-2400	[W] 7325 (E North Am)

MALAYSIA

VOICE OF MALAYSIA

0300-0600 & 0600-0825	6175 & 9750 (SE Asia), 15295 (Australasia)

MOLDOVA

RADIO DMR—(Europe)

1600-1620	[S] M-F 5965
1620-1640	[W] F 5965
1700-1720	[W] M-F 6235
1720-1740	[W] F 6235

MONGOLIA

VOICE OF MONGOLIA—(E Asia, SE Asia & Australasia)

1000-1030	12085

NETHERLANDS

RADIO NETHERLANDS

0000-0100	[W] *6165* & [S] *9845* (E North Am)
0100-0200	[W] *6165* & [S] *9845* (N America)
0400-0500	[S] *6165* (W North Am)
0500-0600	[W] *6165* (W North Am)
1000-1100	[W] *6040* (E Asia), [W] *9795* (E Asia & SE Asia), [S] *12065*

(E Asia & Australasia),
🆆 *12065* (E Asia, SE Asia &
Australasia), 🆂 *13710* &
🆂 *13820* (E Asia & SE Asia)

1200-1300 ▱	*11675* (E North Am)
1400-1600	*9345*, 🆂 *9890*, 🆂 *11835*, 🆆 *12080* & 🆆 *15595* (S Asia)
1800-1900	*6020* (S Africa), 🆂 *7125* (C Africa & S Africa), 🆂 11655 (E Africa)
1800-2000	🆆 *11655* (C Africa & E Africa), 🆆 *12050* (E Africa)
1900-2000	🆂 11655 (W Africa & C Africa), 🆆 *11805* (E Africa)
1900-2100	🆂 *5905* (E Africa), 🆂 *7115* & 🆆 *7120* (C Africa & S Africa), Sa/Su *15315* (W North Am), 🆆 Sa/Su *15525* (E North Am), 🆂 Sa/Su *17660* (W North Am), 🆂 Sa/Su *17735* (E North Am), *17810* (W Africa)
2000-2100	🆆 *11655* (W Africa & C Africa)

NEW ZEALAND

RADIO NEW ZEALAND
INTERNATIONAL—(Pacific)

0000-0400	15720/17675
0400-0500	🆆 15720
0500-0700	9615/15720
0700-1100	7145/9885
1100-1300	🆆 9870/13840
1300-1750	🆂 6095/7145
1751-1850	🆆 6095 & 🆂 9845/9630
1851-2050	🆂 11725/9630
2051-2400	15720/17675

OMAN

RADIO SULTANATE OF OMAN
| 0300-0400 | 15355 (E Africa) |
| 1400-1500 | 15140 (Europe & Mideast) |

PHILIPPINES

RADYO PILIPINAS—(S Asia & Mideast)
| 0200-0330 | 🆂 11880, 🆆 12025, 15285, 🆂 15510 & 🆆 17770 |

ROMANIA

RADIO ROMANIA INTERNATIONAL
0100-0200	🆆 6150, 🆆 9515, 🆂 9690 & 🆂 11825 (E North Am)
0400-0500	🆆 6115 & 🆆 9515 (W North Am), 🆆 9690 (S Asia), 🆂 9780 & 🆂 11795 (W North Am), 🆆 11895, 🆂 15110 & 🆂 17870 (S Asia)
0630-0700	🆆 7180, 🆂 9655, 🆆 9690 & 🆂 11830 (W Europe), 🆆 15135, 🆂 15440, 🆂 17770 & 🆆 17780 (Australasia)
1300-1400	🆂 11845, 15105 & 🆆 17745 (W Europe)
1800-1900	🆆 7120, 🆂 9635, 🆆 9640 & 🆂 11730 (W Europe)
2130-2200	🆆 6055 (W Europe), 🆆 6115 (E North Am), 🆆 7145, 🆂 7210 & 🆂 9535 (W Europe), 🆆 9755, 🆂 11940 & 🆂 15465 (E North Am)
2300-2400	🆆 6015 (W Europe), 🆆 6115 (E North Am), 🆂 6140, 🆆 7105 & 🆂 7265 (W Europe), 🆆 9610, 🆂 9645 & 🆂 11940 (E North Am)

RUSSIA

VOICE OF RUSSIA
0100-0400	🆂 *9665* (E North Am)
0100-0500	🆂 13775 (W North Am)
0200-0300 ▱	*7250* (E North Am)
0200-0400	🆆 *6240* (E North Am), 🆆 15425 (W North Am)
0200-0500	🆂 *9860* (E North Am), 🆂 13635 (W North Am)
0200-0600	🆆 12040 & 🆆 13735 (W North Am)
0300-0400	🆂 12065 (W North Am)
0300-0500	🆆 *6155* (E North Am), 🆂 9435 (W North Am), 🆂 *9515* & 🆂 9880/5900 (E North Am)
0300-0600	🆆 *7350* (E North Am)
0400-0500	🆆 12010 & 🆆 12030 (W North Am)

0400-0600	▥ 7150 (E North Am), ▥ 9840 (W North Am)
0500-0900	◪ 17635 & ◪ 21790 (Australasia)
0600-0900	▥ 17805 (Australasia)
0600-1000	▥ 17665 (Australasia)
0800-1000 ▭	*17495* (SE Asia & Australasia)
0800-1000	▥ 15195 (S Asia)
1400-1500	◪ 6045 & ◪ 7165 (E Asia & SE Asia), ◪ 9745, ◪ *11755* & ◪ 15605 (S Asia), ◪ 15660 (SE Asia)
1500-1600	◪ 9625 (S Asia), *9660* (SE Asia), ◪ 12040/9810 (Europe)
1500-1700	▥ 7260 (E Asia & SE Asia)
1500-1800	◪ 11985 (Mideast & E Africa)
1600-1700 ▭	*4965* & *4975* (W Asia & S Asia)
1600-1700	◪ 6070 (S Asia), ▥ 6130 (Europe), ▥ 7305 (S Asia), ◪ 12055 (W Asia & S Asia), ◪ *12115* (S Asia), ◪ 15540 (Mideast)
1600-1800	◪ 7350 (S Asia & SE Asia), ◪ 9405 (S Asia), ▥ 9470 (Mideast & E Africa)
1600-1900	▥ 7320 (Europe)
1600-2100	◪ 9890 (Europe)
1700-1800	◪ Sa/Su 9820 & ◪ Sa/Su 11675/7320 (N Europe)
1700-1900	▥ 5910 (S Asia), ▥ 7125 (SE Asia), ▥ 7270 (Mideast)
1800-1900	▥ Sa/Su 6055 & ▥ Sa/Su 6175 (N Europe), ▥ 7295 (E Africa & S Africa), ◪ 9850 (E Africa), ◪ 11630/9480 (N Europe)
1800-2000 ▭	*11510* (E Africa & S Africa)
1800-2100	▥ 7105 (N Europe)
1900-2000	▥ 6175 & ▥ 7290 (N Europe), ◪ 7310 (Europe), ▥ 7335 (E Africa & S Africa)
1900-2100	◪ 12070/7195 (Europe, N Africa & W Africa)
2000-2100	▥ 6145 (Europe)
2000-2200	▥ 7330 (Europe)
2100-2200	▥ 7290 (N Europe)
2200-2400	▥ 5955 (E Asia)

SERBIA

INTERNATIONAL RADIO SERBIA—

(Europe)

1400-1430 &	
1930-2000 ▭	6100/7240

SINGAPORE

MEDIACORP RADIO

1400-1600 &	
2300-1100	6150

RADIO SINGAPORE INTERNATIONAL—

(SE Asia)

1100-1400	6080 & 6150

SLOVAKIA

RADIO SLOVAKIA INTERNATIONAL

0100-0130	◪ 5930 & ▥ 7230 (N America), 9440 (S America)
0700-0730	◪ 9440, ▥ 13715 & ▥ 15460 (Australasia)
1630-1700	◪ 5920 (W Europe)
1730-1800 ▭	6055 (W Europe)
1730-1800	▥ 5915 (W Europe)
1830-1900	◪ 5920 & ◪ 6055 (W Europe)
1930-2000	▥ 5915 & ▥ 7345 (W Europe)

SOUTH AFRICA

CHANNEL AFRICA

0300-0355	◪ 5960 & ▥ 7390 (E Africa)
0300-0500	3345 (S Africa)
0500-0555	9685 (W Africa & C Africa)
0500-0700	7230/7240 (S Africa)
0600-0655	15255 (W Africa & C Africa)
0700-0800	◪ 7240 & ▥ 9620 (S Africa)
1000-1200 &	
1400-1600	9620/9625 (S Africa)
1500-1555	17770 (E Africa)
1700-1755	15235 (W Africa & C Africa)
2000-2200	3345 (S Africa)

SPAIN

RADIO EXTERIOR DE ESPAÑA

0000-0100	6055 (N America)
2000-2100	◪ M-F 9665 (Europe),

W M-F 9680 (W Europe),
M-F 11625 (W Africa)

2100-2200   S Sa/Su 11625 (W Africa),
S Sa/Su 9840 (Europe)

2200-2300   W Sa/Su 6125 (W Europe),
W Sa/Su 11625 (N Africa &
W Africa)

SWEDEN

RADIO SWEDEN

0130-0200   S *11675* (S Asia)
0230-0300 ▣ *6010* (E North Am)
0230-0300   W *11550* (S Asia)
0330-0400 ▣ *6010* (W North Am)
1230-1300   S 13580 (E Asia &
Australasia)
1330-1400 ▣ 15240 (E North Am & C
America)
1330-1400   W 7420 (E Asia), S 15735
(SE Asia & Australasia)
1430-1500   W 11550 (SE Asia)
1530-1600 ▣ 15240 (W North Am)
1530-1600   W Sa/Su 7440 (Mideast)
1830-1900 ▣ W-F 6065 (E Europe)
2030-2100 ▣ *7420* (SE Asia &
Australasia)
2130-2200   *7120* (C Africa)
2230-2300 ▣ 6065 (Europe)

Listener reply card from the Voice of Turkey. Its
broadcasts have assumed added importance since
Turkey applied for EU membership.   VoT

SYRIA

RADIO DAMASCUS

2005-2105   9330 (Europe), 12085 (W
Europe)
2110-2210   9330 (Australasia), 12085
(N America)

THAILAND

RADIO THAILAND

0000-0030   S 9570 & W 9680 (E Africa
& S Africa)
0030-0100   *5890* (E North Am)
0200-0230   15275 (W North Am)
0530-0600   W 11730 & S 17655
(Europe)
1230-1300   W 9810 & S 9835 (SE Asia
& Australasia)
1400-1430   W 9725 & S 9805 (SE Asia
& Australasia)
1900-2000   S 7155 & W 9805 (N
Europe)
2030-2045   W 9535 & S 9680 (Europe)

TURKEY

VOICE OF TURKEY

0300-0350   S 5975 (Europe & N
America), S 7270 (Mideast)
0400-0450   W 6020 (Europe & N
America), W 7240 (Mideast)
1230-1325   S 13685 (S Asia, SE Asia &
Australasia), S 15450 (W
Europe)
1330-1425   W 11735 (S Asia, SE Asia &
Australasia), W 12035 (W
Europe)
1830-1920   S 9785 (W Europe)
1930-2020   W 6055 (W Europe)
2030-2120   S 7170 (S Asia, SE Asia &
Australasia)
2130-2220   W 7180 (S Asia, SE Asia &
Australasia)
2200-2250   S 6195 (W Europe & E
North Am)
2300-2350   W 5960 (W Europe & E
North Am)

UKRAINE

RADIO UKRAINE INTERNATIONAL

0100-0200 &
0400-0500 ▣   7440/5820 (E North Am)

0500-0600	Ⓢ 9945/7420 (W Europe)
0600-0700	Ⓦ 7440 (W Europe)
0700-0800	Ⓢ 9945/7420 (W Europe)
0800-0900	Ⓦ 7440 (W Europe)
1100-1200	Ⓢ 11550/9950 (W Europe)
1200-1300	Ⓦ 9925 (W Europe)
2100-2200	Ⓢ 7510/5830 (W Europe)
2200-2300	Ⓦ 5840 (W Europe)

UNITED KINGDOM

BBC WORLD SERVICE

0000-0030	*3915* (SE Asia), Ⓦ *7340, 11945 & 17615* (E Asia)
0000-0100	*5970* (S Asia), Ⓢ *7105* (E Asia), Ⓦ *7105* (W Asia), *9740* (SE Asia), Ⓦ *11955* & Ⓢ *15310* (S Asia)
0000-0200	*6195* (SE Asia), Ⓦ *9410* (S Asia)
0000-0300	*15360* (SE Asia)
0100-0200	Ⓦ *5970* (S Asia), Ⓢ *9580* (W Asia), 11955 (S Asia)
0100-0300	Ⓦ *7320* (W Asia), *11750, 15310* & Ⓢ *17790* (S Asia)
0100-0400	Ⓢ *9410* (W Asia)
0200-0300	*6030* (E Africa), Ⓦ *9410* & *11955* (S Asia), Ⓦ *17760* (E Asia)
0200-0400	Ⓦ *6195* (W Asia)
0300-0400	6005 (W Africa), Ⓢ 6030 & Ⓦ 6145 (S Africa), Ⓦ 7130 (E Africa), Ⓦ 9410 (E Europe), *9750* (E Africa), Ⓦ *11760* (C Asia)
0300-0500	Ⓢ *12035* (E Africa), Ⓢ *15360* (SE Asia & Australasia), Ⓦ *15360* (E Asia, SE Asia & Australasia), *17760* (E Asia)
0300-0600	3255 (S Africa), 7160 (W Africa & C Africa), 15310 (S Asia)
0300-0700	*17790* (S Asia)
0300-1030	*21660* (E Asia)
0300-2200	*6190* (S Africa)
0330-0600	Ⓦ *11665* & Ⓢ *15420* (E Africa)
0400-0500	*7120* (W Africa), Ⓦ *12095* (E Africa)
0400-0600	Ⓦ *9410* (W Asia), Ⓢ 12095 (E Europe), *15575* (W Asia & C Asia)

0400-0700	Ⓢ 9410 (Europe), Ⓢ *11760* (W Asia)
0400-0708	*6005* (W Africa)
0500-0530	Ⓦ *15420* & Ⓢ *17885* (E Africa)
0500-0600	11955 (SE Asia & Australasia), Ⓢ *15565* (S Asia), *17640* (E Africa)
0500-0700	Ⓦ 5875 (E Europe), Ⓢ 9410 (N Africa), *11765* (W Africa), Ⓦ *12095* (E Europe)
0500-0800	Ⓦ 6195 (Europe), *11695* (S Asia), *15360* (SE Asia & Australasia)
0500-1000	Ⓢ *17760* & Ⓦ *17760* (E Asia & SE Asia)
0530-0600	Ⓦ M-F *15420* & Ⓢ M-F *17885* (E Africa)
0600-0700 ◨	6195 (N Africa)
0600-0700	Ⓦ 7160, Ⓦ 9410 & Ⓦ 9825 (N Africa), *11955* (SE Asia & Australasia), 17640 (E Africa)
0600-0730	*15575* (W Asia)
0600-0800	Ⓢ *3255/9860* (S Africa), Ⓢ 12095 (N Africa), Ⓦ Sa/Su *15420* & Ⓢ Sa/Su *17885* (E Africa)
0600-1200	*15310* (S Asia)
0600-1600	Ⓦ *11940* (S Africa)
0630-0700	Ⓢ *11990* (W Africa & C Africa)
0700-0800	Ⓦ 9410 & Ⓦ 11765 (N Africa), Ⓢ *11765* (W Africa), 11955 (SE Asia & Australasia), Ⓦ *12095* & Ⓦ 13820 (N Africa), Ⓢ 17830 (W Europe & N Africa)
0700-0900	Ⓢ 15485 (W Europe & N Africa)
0700-1000	*15400* (W Africa), Ⓢ 17640 (Europe)
0700-1200	*17790* (S Asia)
0700-1400	*11760* (Mideast)
0730-0900	Sa/Su *15575* (W Asia)
0800-0900	*6195* (SE Asia)
0800-1000	*17830* (W Africa & C Africa)
0800-1030	Ⓦ *15285* (SE Asia), Ⓢ *15360* (E Asia)
0800-1300	*21470* (S Africa)
0800-1400	*17885* (E Africa)

0800-1600	9740 (SE Asia & Australasia), ⬛S 9860 (S Africa)	1600-2200	3255 (S Africa)
0900-1100	6195 (SE Asia)	1615-1700	⬛S Sa/Su 9695, Sa/Su 11860, Sa/Su 15420 & ⬛W Sa/Su 17885 (E Africa)
0900-1400	15575 (W Asia)	1700-1745	6005 & 9630 (E Africa)
0900-1500	⬛W 11895 (E Asia), 15485 (W Europe & N Africa)	1700-1830	11955 (S Asia)
1000-1100	Sa/Su 17830 (W Africa & C Africa)	1700-1900	⬛S 6195 (Europe), ⬛S 7380 (E Africa), ⬛S 9410 (E Europe & N Africa), ⬛W 11755 (E Africa), ⬛S 12095 (E Europe)
1000-1130	Sa/Su 15400 (W Africa)		
1000-1300	⬛S 17760 (E Asia)	1700-2100	⬛W 12095 (N Africa)
1000-1400	17640 (Europe)	1700-2200	⬛W 6195 (N Africa)
1030-1100	9605, ⬛W 11750, ⬛S 11945, 15285, ⬛W 15545 & ⬛S 21660 (E Asia)	1800-1830	⬛S 5975 & ⬛W 9740 (S Asia)
		1800-2000	⬛W 5875 (E Europe & N Africa), ⬛W 5955 & ⬛S 5995 (C Asia), ⬛W 6195 (E Europe), ⬛W 9480 (S Asia), ⬛S 17795 (W Europe & N Africa)
1100-1200	⬛W 5875 & ⬛S 9660 (C America)		
1100-1300	⬛S 9465 & ⬛W 9750 (C America)		
1100-1700	6195 (SE Asia)	1800-2300	⬛W 9410 (N Africa)
1100-2100	17830 (W Africa & C Africa)	1830-2000	⬛S 9485 (W Asia)
1200-1300	9660 (C America)	1830-2100	6005 & 9630 (E Africa)
1200-1400	⬛S 11750 (E Asia), ⬛W 17790 (S Asia)	1900-2100	⬛S 9410 (N Africa), ⬛S 9455 (E Africa)
1200-1500	⬛W 5975 (E Asia), ⬛W 15310 (S Asia)	2100-2200	3915 (S Asia & SE Asia), 6005 (S Africa), ⬛W 6125 (E Asia), 6195 (SE Asia), 11675 (C America & S America), ⬛S 11945 (E Asia)
1200-1600	⬛S 15310 & ⬛S 17790 (S Asia)		
1300-1400	15420 (E Africa)		
1300-1900	21470 (S Africa)	2100-2300	⬛W 9525 (C America), ⬛S 12095 (N Africa), ⬛S 13640 (C America)
1400-1500	⬛W 11760 & ⬛S 15575 (W Asia), ⬛W 17885 (E Africa)		
1400-1600	⬛S 5980 (E Asia), ⬛W 9410 & 11920 (S Asia), ⬛S 17640 (Europe)	2100-2400	5965 (E Asia)
		2200-2300	⬛W 5935 & ⬛S 5955 (SE Asia), ⬛W 5955 (E Asia), 5975 (C America), ⬛S 7110 (S Asia), 9660 (SE Asia), ⬛S 11995 & ⬛S 12010 (E Asia), 12080 (S Pacific)
1400-1700	⬛W Sa 9410 (Europe), ⬛S Sa 12095 (N Africa), ⬛S 21660 (E Africa)		
1500-1530	⬛S 9695, 11860, 15420 & ⬛W 17885 (E Africa)		
1500-1600	5975 & ⬛S 5975 (S Asia), ⬛W 6040 (SE Asia)	2200-2400	6195 & 9740 (SE Asia)
		2300-2400	3915 (SE Asia), ⬛W 5985, ⬛W 7340 & 11945 (E Asia), 11955 (SE Asia & Australasia)
1500-1700	⬛S 11760 (W Asia), ⬛W 12095 (Europe), ⬛W 15105 (E Africa), ⬛S 15485 (W Europe & N Africa)		
1500-2300	15400 (W Africa)	2330-2400	⬛W 6170 & ⬛S 9580 (E Asia)
1600-1700	⬛S 11920 (S Asia), ⬛S 17790 (Europe)		
1600-1800	3915 (S Asia & SE Asia), 5975 (S Asia), ⬛W 9410 (N Africa), ⬛S 9510 & ⬛W 9740 (S Asia), ⬛W 11665 (N Africa)		

USA

AFRTS-AMERICAN FORCES RADIO & TV SERVICE

24 Hr	4319/12579 USB (S Asia), 5447 USB (C America), 5765/13362 USB &

6350/10320 USB (Pacific), 7811 USB & 12134 USB (Americas)

FAMILY RADIO

0000-0045	[W] 9715 (W North Am), [S] 17805 (S America)
0000-0100	[S] 6065 & [W] 6085 (E North Am), [W] 11720 (S America), [S] 11835 (W North Am)
0000-0445	9505 (N America)
0100-0200	*15195 (S Asia)*
0100-0445	6065 (E North Am)
0200-0245	[S] 11835 (W North Am)
0200-0300	5985 (C America), [W] 9525 (W North Am), 11855 (C America)
0300-0400	[W] 9985 (S America), 11740 (C America), [S] 15255 (S America)
0400-0445	6855 (E North Am)
0400-0500	7780 (Europe), 9715 (W North Am)
0445-0500	[W] 6855 (E North Am)
0500-0600	6855 (E North Am), [W] 7520 & [S] 9355 (Europe)
0600-0700	6000 (C America), 9680 (N America), [S] 11530 (C Africa & S Africa), [W] 11530 & [S] 11580 (Europe), [W] 11580 (W Africa & C Africa)
0600-0745	7780 (Europe)
0700-0800	[W] 9495 & [S] 9505 (C America), 9715 (W North Am)
0700-0845	[S] 9930 & [W] 9985 (W Africa)
0700-1045	[W] 7455 (N America)
0700-1100	6855 (E North Am)
0700-1245	[S] 5985 (N America)
0800-0845	5950 (W North Am)
0845-1145	[W] 5950 (W North Am)
0900-1100	*9450 (E Asia)*
0900-1145	[S] 9755 (W North Am)
1000-1245	[S] 5950 & [W] 6890 (E North Am)
1100-1145	[W] 6000 & [S] 9550 (S America)
1100-1200	[S] 7780 (C America), [S] 9625 (S America), [W] 11725 (C America), [W] 11830 (S America)
1100-1345	[W] 7780 (N America)
1200-1300	[W] 11530 & [S] 17555 (S America)
1200-1345	[W] 11970 (W North Am)
1200-1645	[S] 17750 (W North Am)
1300-1400	[W] *7240 (SE Asia)*, 11830 & [S] 11865 (N America), [S] *11895 (SE Asia)*
1300-1500	[W] *7155*, [S] *9415* & *11560 (S Asia)*
1300-1600	[W] 11855 & [S] 11910 (E North Am)
1400-1500	[W] *7535* & [S] *11640 (E Asia)*, 13695 (E North Am)
1400-1600	[S] 11830 (N America)
1400-1645	[W] 11565 (N America), [W] 17760 (W North Am)
1500-1545	[W] 15210 & [S] 15770 (S America)
1500-1600	*6280* & [W] *12015 (S Asia)*, [W] *13660 (E Africa)*, [S] *15520 (S Asia)*, [S] *15750 (E Africa)*
1600-1645	11830 & [S] 11865 (N America), 13695 (E North Am)
1600-1700	6085 (C America), [S] *11850* & [W] *12010 (S Asia)*, [W] 17690 (W Africa), [S] 21525 (C Africa & S Africa)
1600-1800	21455 (Europe)
1600-1945	18980 (Europe)
1645-1945	[W] 13695 (E North Am)
1700-1800 ➡	*3955 (W Europe)*
1700-1800	*21680 (E Africa)*
1700-2000	[S] 13690 (E North Am)
1700-2145	[W] 17555 & [S] 17795 (W North Am)
1800-1845	[S] 17535 (W Africa)
1800-1900	[S] *7240 (Mideast)*, [W] *7240 (Mideast & W Asia)*, [W] *7345 (Mideast)*, *7395* & [W] *13660 (E Africa)*, [S] *13780 (Mideast)*, [S] *15750 (E Africa)*
1800-2100	[W] 15115 (W Africa)
1800-2145	[S] 13800 & [W] 17535 (N America)
1900-1945	6085 (C America), [W] 15565 (Europe)
1900-2000	[S] *7370* & [W] *7395 (E Africa)*, [S] 18930 (Europe)

Voice of America's Andriy Godovanec broadcasts to Ukraine. VoA

1900-2100	*3230* (S Africa), *6020* (E Africa)
1900-2200	**S** 17845 (W Africa)
1945-2145	**S** 18980 (Europe)
2000-2045	**S** 17750 (Europe)
2000-2100	**W** 17575 (S America)
2000-2200	**W** 5745 & **W** 6855 (Europe), **S** *7360* (W Europe), *15195* (E Africa), **S** 17725 (S America)
2100-2200	**W** *5955* & **S** *6045* (S Africa), **S** 11565 (Europe), **W** 15565 (W Africa)
2115-2315	*11875* (C Africa)
2200-2245	**S** 15770 (C Africa & S Africa), **W** 21525 (W Africa & C Africa)
2200-2345	11740 (N America)
2300-2400	**W** 15170, **S** 15255, **W** 15400 & **S** 17750 (S America)

KJES
0200-0300 ▭	7555 (W North Am)
0300-0330 ▭	7555 (N America)
1400-1500 ▭	11715 (E North Am)
1500-1600 ▭	11715 (W North Am)
1900-2000 ▭	15385 (Australasia)

KNLS-NEW LIFE STATION—(E Asia)
0800-0900	**W** 9615 & **S** 11870
1000-1100	**W** 6150 & **S** 9795
1200-1300	**W** 6150, **W** 6915, **S** 9615 & **S** 9780
1400-1500	**W** 6150 & **S** 9795

KTBN—(E North Am)
0000-0100	**W** 7505 & **S** 15590
0100-1500	7505
1500-1600	**W** 7505 & **S** 15590
1600-2400	15590

UNIVERSITY NETWORK
0000-0200	*13750* (C America)
0000-1200	*5030* (C America), *6150* (C America & S America), *7375* (S America)
24 Hr	*9725* (N America)
1200-2400	*11870* (S America)
1800-2400	*13750* (C America)

VOA-VOICE OF AMERICA
0000-0030	**S** *7555* (W Asia & S Asia)
0030-0100	**W** *7130*, **W** *9620*, **S** *9715* & **S** *9780* (SE Asia), **W** *11695* (S Asia & SE Asia), *11725* (E Asia), 11805 (SE Asia), **W** *12005* (E Asia), *15185* (SE Asia & S Pacific), *15205* (SE Asia), **S** *15290* (E Asia), **S** *15560* (SE Asia), **S** *17820* (E Asia)
0100-0200	**W** *7200*, 11705, **S** *11725*, **W** *11820* & **W** *12005* (S Asia)
0130-0200	**W** Tu-Sa 5960 & Tu-Sa 7405 (C America), **S** Tu-Sa 13740 (C America & S America)
0300-0330	**S** *7340* (E Africa & S Africa)
0300-0430	*9885* (C Africa)
0300-0500	**W** *15580* (W Africa & C Africa)
0300-0600	*4930* (S Africa), *6080* (C Africa & S Africa)
0300-0700	**S** *12080* (C Africa & E Africa), **S** *15580* (C Africa)
0400-0430	**S** *11835* (C Africa)
0400-0500	*4960* & **S** 9575 (W Africa & C Africa)
0430-0500	**S** *11835* (C Africa)
0430-0700	**W** *9885* (W Africa & C Africa)
0500-0630	**W** *6105* (W Africa & C Africa)
0500-0700	**S** *6180* (W Africa), **W** *15580* (C Africa & E Africa)
0530-0630	**S** M-F *13710* (Africa)
0600-0700	*6080* (W Africa), **W** *11835* (C Africa & S Africa)

1200-1300	**S** *6160* (SE Asia), **W** *11730* (S Asia & SE Asia), **S** *11750* (SE Asia), **W** *15190* (E Asia)
1200-1400	*9645* (SE Asia & Australasia), **W** *11705* (E Asia)
1200-1500	*9760* (E Asia, S Asia & SE Asia)
1400-1500	**W** *9695* & **W** *11655* (S Asia), **W** *11885* (SE Asia & S Pacific), **W** *12150* (S Asia), **S** *13795* (C Africa), **S** *15185* (SE Asia & S Pacific), **S** *15490* (S Asia), **S** *17685* (C Africa & S Africa), **S** *17730* (C Africa & E Africa), **W** *17895* (C Africa)
1400-1530	**W** *6080* (C Africa & S Africa)
1400-1600	*7125* (S Asia), **W** *15205* (S Asia & C Asia), **W** *15580* & *17715* (C Africa & E Africa)
1400-2100	**S** *15580* (C Africa)
1400-2200	**S** *6080* (C Africa & S Africa)
1500-1600	**W** *6110* & **S** *6160* (S Asia & SE Asia), **W** *7175* (E Asia), **S** *9590* (S Asia & SE Asia), **W** *9645* (S Asia), **S** *9760* (S Asia & SE Asia), **W** *9760* (E Asia, S Asia & SE Asia), **W** *11890* (S Asia), **S** *12040* (E Asia), **W** *12150* & *13735* (E Asia & SE Asia), **S** *13795* (C Africa & E Africa), **W** *13865* (E Africa), **S** *15105* & **S** *15195* (S Asia), **S** *15445* (W Asia & S Asia), **W** *15460* & **S** *15550* (SE Asia & Australasia), *17895* (C Africa)
1530-1800	**W** *6080* (C Africa)
1600-1700	**S** *12080* (C Africa), **S** *13600* (SE Asia & Australasia), **W** *13600* (C Africa & S Africa), **W** *15445* (C Africa & E Africa), **W** *17640* (E Africa), **W** *17715* (C Africa & E Africa), **S** *17895* (C Africa & S Africa), **W** *17895* (C Africa)
1600-1730	*4930* (S Africa)
1600-2100	**W** *15580* (Africa)
1700-1730	**W** M-F *11815*, **W** M-F *13755* & M-F *17730* (S Africa)
1700-1800	**W** *15445* (C Africa & E Africa)
1700-2000	**W** *13710* (E Africa & S Africa)
1700-2200	**S** *15410* (Africa)
1730-1830	Sa/Su *4930* (S Africa)
1800-1830	*17730* (S Africa)
1800-2000	**W** *11975* (W Africa & C Africa), **S** *17895* (C Africa & S Africa), **W** *17895* (C Africa)
1800-2200	**W** *6080* (W Africa)
1830-2100	*4930* (S Africa)
1900-2000	**S** *7395*, **S** *9670*, **W** *9785* & **W** *12015* (Mideast)
1900-2030	*4940* (W Africa & C Africa)
1900-2100	**W** *15240* & **S** *15445* (W Africa & C Africa)
2000-2100	**W** *11975* & **W** *13710* (C Africa)
2030-2100	Sa/Su *4940* (W Africa & C Africa)
2030-2130	**W** *7595* (W Asia & S Asia)
2030-2400	**S** *7555* (W Asia & S Asia)
2100-2200	**W** *15580* (W Africa & C Africa), **S** *15580* (C Africa, E Africa & S Africa)
2130-2400	**W** *7405* (W Asia & S Asia)
2200-2400	**W** *7120* & **S** *7215* (SE Asia), *11725* (E Asia & S Pacific), *15185* (SE Asia & S Pacific), *15290* (E Asia)
2230-2300	**W** *7230*, **W** *9780* & *13755* (E Asia)
2230-2400	**S** *9570* & **S** *15145* (E Asia)
2300-2400	**W** *6180*, **W** *7205*, **S** *13755* & **W** *15150* (E Asia)
2330-2400	**S** *7260* (SE Asia), **W** *11655* (E Asia), **W** *13640* & **S** *13725* (SE Asia)

WBCQ-"THE PLANET"—(N America)

0000-0100	5105
0000-0230	9330/13610 LSB
0000-0530	7415
0100-0500	M/Sa 5105
0230-0500	Tu-Su 9330/13610 LSB
0530-0600	Su/M 7415
0600-0800	Su 7415
1700-2030	M-F 17495/18910

1945-2100 ◫	M-F 7415 & M-F 9330/13610 LSB
2030-2200 ◫	M-Sa 17495/18910
2100-2200 ◫	M-Sa 7415
2100-2400 ◫	M-F 5105 & 9330/13610 LSB
2200-2400 ◫	7415 & M-F 17495/18910

WBOH—(C America)

0200-1105 &	
1200-0100 ◫	5920

WEWN

0000-0500	5810 (N America)
0500-0800	5610/7570 (Europe)
0500-1300	5850 (N America)
1300-1400	⑤ 5850 & Ⓦ 9955 (N America)
1400-1600	9955 (N America)
1600-1900	Ⓦ 15785 (Europe)
1600-2200	Ⓦ 9450 & ⑤ 13615 (N America)
1700-2000	⑤ 15220 (Europe)
2000-2200	⑤ 15220 & Ⓦ 17595 (W Africa)
2200-2400	Ⓦ 7560 (Europe), 9975 (N America), ⑤ 15745 (Europe)

WMLK—(Europe & N America)

1600-2100	Su-F

WRMI-RADIO MIAMI INTERNATIONAL

0000-0500 ◫	Tu-Sa 7385 (N America)
0500-1000 ◫	7385 (N America)
1000-1045 ◫	Su-F 9955 (C America)
1045-1100 ◫	9955 (C America)
1100-1200 ◫	Su 9955 (C America)
1200-1230 ◫	Sa 9955 (C America)
1230-1300 ◫	Sa/Su 9955 (C America)
1300-1400 ◫	9955 (C America)
1400-1700 &	
2100-2300 ◫	7385 (N America)
2300-2400 ◫	M-F 7385 (N America)

WTJC—(E North Am)

0400-0300 ◫	9370

WWCR

0000-0100	⑤ 3210/7465 & Ⓦ 3210 (E North Am)
0000-0200	5935/13845 & Ⓦ 7465 (E North Am)
0000-1200	5070 (E North Am)
0100-0300	5790/7465 (E North Am)
0100-0900	3210 (E North Am)
0200-1200	5935 (E North Am)

0300-1100	5790 (E North Am)
0900-1000	3210/9985 (E North Am)
1000-1100	Ⓦ 9985 & ⑤ Su-F 15825 (E North Am)
1100-1130	⑤ Sa/Su 15825 (E North Am)
1100-1200	Ⓦ Su-F 15825 (E North Am)
1100-1400	5790/7465 (E North Am)
1130-1200	⑤ 15825 (E North Am)
1200-1230	⑤ 15825 & Ⓦ Sa/Su 15825 (E North Am)
1200-1300	Ⓦ 5070 (E North Am)
1200-1400	5935/13845 (E North Am)
1230-2100	15825 (E North Am)
1400-1600	7465/9985 (E North Am), 12160 (Irr) (E North Am & Europe)
1400-2400	13845 (E North Am)
1600-1800	9985 (E North Am)
1600-2200	12160 (E North Am & Europe)
1800-1900	⑤ 9975 & Ⓦ 9985 (E North Am)
1900-2200	9975 (E North Am)
2100-2145	⑤ Sa/Su 15825 (E North Am)
2100-2200	Ⓦ 15825/7465 (Irr) (E North Am)
2145-2200	⑤ 15825 (E North Am)
2200-2245	Ⓦ Sa/Su 9985 (E North Am)
2200-2400	5070/12160 (E North Am & Europe), Ⓦ 7465 (E North Am)
2300-2400	Ⓦ 3210/9985 (E North Am)

WWRB

0000-0500 ◫	5085 (E North Am)
0000-0530 ◫	5745 (N America)
0000-0600 ◫	5050 (N America), 6890/3185 (E North Am)
0500-1300 ◫	5085 (Pacific)
1300-2300 ◫	9320 (E North Am)
1600-2300 ◫	11920 (E North Am & Europe)
1700-2300 ◫	15250 (Africa)
2300-2400 ◫	Sa/Su 5085 & 6890/3185 (E North Am)

VATICAN STATE

VATICAN RADIO

0140-0200	Ⓦ 5915, Ⓦ 7335, Ⓦ 9650 & ⑤ 12055/7335 (S Asia)

0250-0320	*6100/6040* (E North Am & C America), 7305 (E North Am)
0300-0330	◪ 7360 (E Africa), ◪ 9660 (C Africa & E Africa), ◪ *12070* & ◪ *15560* (S Asia)
0500-0530	◪ 7360, 9660 & 11625 (C Africa & S Africa), ◪ 13765 (E Africa)
0600-0630 ◁	4005 (Europe), 7250 (W Europe)
0630-0645	◪ M-Sa 6185 (W Europe), ◪ M-Sa 9645 (Europe)
0630-0700	◪ 7360, ◪ 9660 & ◪ 11625 (W Africa), ◪ 11625 (C Africa & S Africa), ◪ 13765 (W Africa), ◪ 15570 (C Africa & S Africa)
0730-0745 ◁	M-Sa 4005 (Europe), M-Sa 7250 (W Europe), M-Sa 11740 (W Europe & N Africa), M-Sa 15595 (Mideast)
0730-0745	◪ M-Sa 6185 (E Europe), ◪ M-Sa 9645 (N Africa)
1130-1200	F 15595, ◪ F 17515 & ◪ F 17765 (Mideast)
1530-1600	◪ *9310*, ◪ 11850, ◪ *12065*, 13765 & ◪ 15235 (S Asia)
1615-1630	◪ 15595 (Mideast)
1715-1730 ◁	4005 (Europe), 7250 & 9645 (W Europe)
1715-1730	◪ 9635 (Mideast)
1730-1800	◪ 9755 & 11625 (E Africa), 13765 & ◪ 15570 (C Africa & S Africa)
1950-2020	◪ 9645 (W Europe)
2000-2030	◪ 7365, ◪ 9755 & ◪ 11625 (W Africa), ◪ 11625 (C Africa & S Africa), ◪ 13765 (W Africa)
2050-2120 ◁	4005 & 5885 (Europe), 7250 (W Europe)

VIETNAM

VOICE OF VIETNAM

0100-0130, 0230-0300 & 0330-0400	*6175* (E North Am & C America)

Alabama's WEWN is a global multilingual outlet for ETWN Radio, ultimately led by the purposeful Mother Angelica. Thom Price hosts its contemporary music program, "Catholic Jukebox."   WEWN

1000-1030	9840 & 12020 (SE Asia)
1100-1130	7285 (SE Asia)
1130-1200	9840 & 12020 (E Asia)
1230-1300	9840 & 12020 (SE Asia)
1330-1400	9840 & 12020 (E Asia)
1500-1530	7285, 9840 & 12020 (SE Asia)
1600-1630	7220 (W Africa & C Africa), 7280 (Europe), 9550 (W Africa & C Africa), 9730 (Europe)
1700-1730	◪ *9725* (W Europe)
1800-1830	◪ *5955* (W Europe)
1900-1930	7280 & 9730 (Europe)
2030-2100	7220 (W Africa & C Africa), 7280 (Europe), 9550 (W Africa & C Africa), 9730 (Europe)
2330-2400	9840 & 12020 (SE Asia)

YEMEN

REPUBLIC OF YEMEN RADIO—(Mideast)

1800-1900	9780

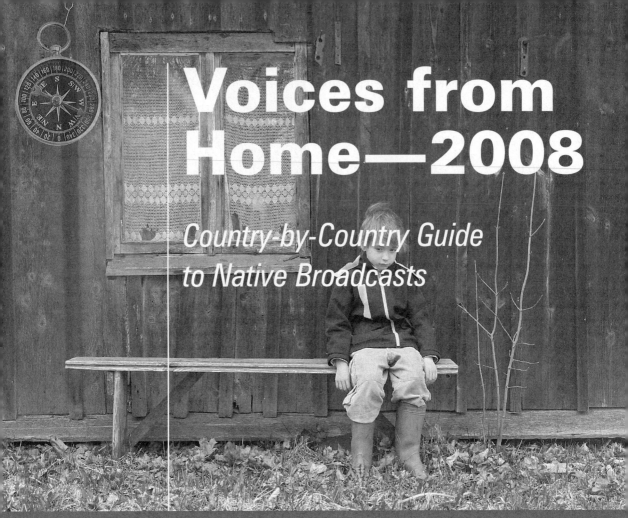

Voices from Home—2008

Country-by-Country Guide to Native Broadcasts

For some, English offerings are merely icing on the cake. Their real interest is in eavesdropping on broadcasts for *nativos*—the home folks. These can be enjoyable regardless of language, especially when they offer traditional music.

Some you'll hear, many you won't, sometimes because they're gone for political or economic reasons. Keep in mind that most native-language broadcasts are weaker than those in English, so you'll need patience, an electrically quiet location and superior hardware. PASSPORT REPORTS shows which radios and antennas work best.

When to Listen

Some broadcasts come in daytime between 9300 and 21850 kHz. However, signals from Latin America and sub-Saharan Africa peek through near twilight or during darkness, especially from 4700 to 5100 kHz. See "Best Times and Frequencies" for specifics.

Times and days of the week are in World Time (UTC), explained in "Setting Your World Time Clock" and "Worldly Words"; for local times in each country see "Addresses PLUS." Midyear, typically April through October, some stations are an hour earlier (◁) or later (▷) because of Daylight Saving/Summer Time. Stations may also extend their hours for holidays, emergencies or sports events.

Frequencies used only seasonally are labeled **S** for summer (midyear) and **W** for winter. Frequencies in *italics* may be best, as they come from relay transmitters that may be near you. Signals not aimed your way may also be heard, especially when beamed to nearby regions. Frequencies with no target zones are usually for domestic coverage, so they're unlikely to be heard unless you're in or near that country.

> **It helps to have patience, a good location and superior hardware.**

Schedules for Entire Year

To be as useful as possible over the months to come, PASSPORT's schedules consist not just of observed activity, but also that which we have creatively opined will take place during the forthcoming year. This predictive material is based on decades of experience and is original from us. Although inherently not as exact as real-time data, over the years it's been of tangible value to PASSPORT readers.

Vysoké Tatry, Slovakia. Radio Slovakia International maintains contact with countrymen throughout much of North America, Australasia, Europe and the high seas.

Shutterstock/Radovan

ALBANIA—Albanian
RADIO TIRANA
0000-0030	S 9410 (E North Am)
0000-0130	W 6110 & W 7425 (E North Am)
0730-1000 ⬅	7105 (Europe)
2030-2200	S 7465 & S 9390 (Europe)
2130-2300	W 6005 (Europe), W 7430 (W Europe)
2300-2400	S 9410 (E North Am)

ARGENTINA—Spanish
RADIO ARGENTINA AL EXTERIOR-RAE
1200-1400	M-F 11710 (S America)
2200-2400	M-F 6060 (C America & S America), M-F 11710 (Europe & N Africa), M-F 15345 (Europe)

AUSTRIA—German
RADIO AUSTRIA INTERNATIONAL
0005-0015	W Tu-Sa 7325 (C America)
0035-0045	W Tu-Sa 7325 (E North Am)
0105-0115	S Tu-Sa 9870 (C America)
0135-0145	S Tu-Sa 9870 (E North Am)
0500-1305 ⬅	6155 & 13730 (Europe)
0600-0700 ⬅	M-Sa 17870 (Mideast)
1200-1215	S Tu-F 17715 (SE Asia & Australasia)
1220-1300	S M 17715 (SE Asia & Australasia)
1230-1245	S M-F 17715 (SE Asia & Australasia)
1300-1315	W Tu-F 17855 (SE Asia & Australasia)
1305-1345 ⬅	Tu-F 6155 & Tu-F 13730 (Europe)
1320-1400 ⬅	M 6155 & M 13730 (Europe)
1320-1400	W M 17855 (SE Asia & Australasia)
1330-1345	W M-F 17855 (SE Asia & Australasia)
1400-1830 ⬅	13730 (Europe)
1400-2308 ⬅	6155 (Europe)
1500-1515	S Tu-F *13775* (W North Am)
1520-1530	S M *13775* (W North Am)
1530-1545	S M-F *13775* (W North Am)
1600-1615	W Tu-F *13675* (W North Am)
1620-1630	W M *13675* (W North Am)
1630-1645	W M-F *13675* (W North Am)

1830-2308 ⬅	5945 (Europe, N Africa & Mideast)
2335-2345 ➡	M-F 9870 (S America)

BANGLADESH—Bangla
BANGLADESH BETAR
1630-1730	7250 & 9550 (Mideast)
1915-2000	7250 & 9550 (Europe)

BRAZIL—Portuguese
RADIO BANDEIRANTES
24 Hr	6090, 9645, 11925

RADIO BRASIL CENTRAL
0000-0330 ➡	4985, 11815
0330-0600 ➡	4985 (Irr), 11815 (Irr)
0600-2400 ➡	4985, 11815

RADIO CULTURA
0000-0200 ➡	6170, 9615, 17815
0700-2400 ➡	9615, 17815
0800-2400 ➡	6170

RADIO GUAIBA
0700-0300 ➡	6000, 11785

RADIO NACIONAL DA AMAZONIA
0000-0050	6180
0000-0230 ➡	11780
0230-0650 ➡	Su 11780
0650-2400 ➡	11780
0655-0750	W 6180
0750-2400	6180

BULGARIA—Bulgarian
RADIO BULGARIA
0000-0100	S 7400 (S America), S 9700 & S 11700 (E North Am)
0100-0200	W 7300 (S America), W 7400 & W 9400 (E North Am), W 9500 (S America)
0400-0430	S Sa/Su 7200 (E Europe), S Sa/Su 7400 (S Europe), S Sa/Su 9600 & S Sa/Su 11600 (W Europe)
0430-0500	S 7200 (E Europe), S 7400 (S Europe), S 9600 & S 11600 (W Europe)
0500-0530 ⬅	Sa/Su 9400 (E Europe)
0500-0530	W Sa/Su 5900 (S Europe), W Sa/Su 7400 (E Europe), W Sa/Su 7400 & W Sa/Su 9400 (W Europe)

0530-0600 ▣ 9400 (E Europe)
0530-0600 ▥ 5900 (S Europe), 7400 (E Europe), ▥ 7400 & ▥ 9400 (W Europe)
1000-1030 ▤ 7400 (S Europe)
1100-1130 ▣ 11600 (E Europe), 11700 (W Europe), 13600 (E Europe), 15700 (W Europe)
1100-1130 ▥ 5900 (S Europe)
1200-1400 ▤ 9400 (W Europe)
1300-1500 ▣ 11700 & 15700 (W Europe)
1500-1600 ▤ 5900 (E Europe), ▤ 7400 (S Europe), ▤ 11600 (Mideast), ▤ 15800 (S Africa)
1500-1700 ▥ 9400 (Mideast)
1600-1700 ▣ 9400 (E Europe)
1600-1700 ▥ 5900 (S Europe), ▥ 7200 (E Europe), ▥ 17500 (S Africa)
1800-1900 ▤ 7400 (S Europe)
1800-2000 ▤ 9800 (Mideast), ▤ 11800 (W Europe)
1900-2000 ▥ 5900 (S Europe)
1900-2100 ▥ 9700 (W Europe & Mideast)

RADIO VARNA
0000-0300 ▤ M 9900 (Europe & Mideast)
0000-0400 ▥ M 6000 (Europe)
2100-2400 ▤ Su 9900 (Europe & Mideast)
2230-2400 ▥ Su 6000 (Europe)

CANADA—French
CANADIAN BROADCASTING CORP—(E North Am)
0100-0300 ▣ M 9625
0300-0400 ▣ Su 9625 & Tu-Sa 9625
1300-1310 &
1500-1555 ▣ M-F 9625
1700-1715 ▣ Su 9625
1900-1945 ▣ M-F 9625
1900-2310 ▣ Sa 9625

RADIO CANADA INTERNATIONAL
1705-1905 ▤ 9515 (N America)
1900-2000 ▤ 7235 (W Europe & N Africa), ▥ 9670 (C Africa), ▥ 9770 & ▤ 11765 (E Africa), ▥ 11845 & ▥ 13650 (N Africa & W Africa), ▤ 13730 (C Africa & E Africa), ▤ 15235 (W Africa), ▤ 15325 (W Europe), ▥ 15365 (W Africa & C Africa)
1905-2005 ▥ 9610 (N America)
2000-2100 ▣ 5850 (W Europe)
2005-2105 ▤ 9515 (N America)
2100-2200 ▥ 7235 & ▤ 7370 (N Africa), ▤ 9690 (W Africa), ▥ 9805, ▥ 11845 & ▤ 15325 (N Africa)
2105-2205 ▥ 6100 (N America)
2300-2330 ▤ 9525 (E Asia & SE Asia)

CHINA
CENTRAL PEOPLE'S BROADCASTING STATION
Chinese
0000-0005 5925, 7620, 9665
0000-0030 ▥ 6040, ▥ 7275, 7335, 11710, ▤ 11800, ▤ 11835, ▤ 15380
0000-0100 ▥ 4460, 5945, ▥ 6080, 6090, 6125, 7150, ▥ 7245, 7315, 9480, ▤ 9620, ▤ 9630, ▤ 9645, ▥ 9820, 9830, 9845, 11740, ▤ 11845
0000-0105 6165, 9170
0000-0130 ▥ 7290, ▤ 17890
0000-0200 ▥ 6155, 9755, 9775, ▥ 11925, ▤ 15500, ▤ 17580
0000-0400 9530, 11685
0000-0600 4750, 4800, 6030, 7140, 7230, 9500, 9675, 9720, 11610, 11670, 11720, 11750, 11760, 11835, 11960, 12045, 13610, 15550, 17625
0030-0130 ▥ 11710, ▤ 17605
0030-0600 11800, 11915, 15380
0055-0613 9685/15710, 11620, 11935
0100-0300 ▥ 6090, ▤ 9570
0100-0400 15570
0100-0600 9620, 9630, 9645, 9810, 11660, 11845, 15370, 15480, 15540, 17550, 17565, 17595
0130-0600 17605, 17890

Don Van den Akker taking meter readings on the 50 kW shortwave transmitter at TWR's facility in Bonaire.

TWR

0200-0500	11630, 12055, 13700, 15390	0730-0850	W-M 9830, S W-M 17595, W W-M 17845
0200-0600	12080, 15270, 15500, 17580	0800-0850	W W-M 7305, W W-M 7345, S W-M 11750, S W-M 15550
0300-0600	9570		
0355-0900	11905	0800-0900	W Th-Tu 9820, S Th-Tu 11845
0355-1100	15880		
0500-0600	9530, 11685, 15570	0830-0850	W W-M 4460, S W-M 9645
0600-0730	W-M 17565, W-M 17595	0850-0900	11630, 11960, 12055, 13700, 15390
0600-0800	Th-Tu 9530, Th-Tu 11685, W-M 11750, Th-Tu 11845, W-M 15550, Th-Tu 15570	0850-1000	W 7305, 9675, S 11750, 15480, 17580, 17605, W 17845, 17890
0600-0830	W-M 9645	0850-1030	17550
0600-0850	W-M 4750, W-M 4800, W-M 6030, W-M 7230, W-M 9500, W-M 9630, W-M 9675, W-M 11720, W-M 11760, W-M 11960, W-M 12045, W-M 13610, W-M 15370, W-M 15380, W-M 15480, W-M 17550, W-M 17580, W-M 17605, W-M 17890	0850-1100	W 4460, W 7345, S 9645, 11720, 12045, 15370, 15380, S 15550, S 17595
		0850-1200	9630, 11760
		0850-1300	13610
		0850-1733	4750, W-M 4800, 6030, 7230, 9500, 9830
		0855-1000	17625
0600-0855	Th-Tu 17625	0900-1000	9570, 9720, 11915, 12080, 15500
0600-0900	Th-Tu 7140, Th-Tu 9570, Th-Tu 9620, Th-Tu 9720, Th-Tu 9810, Th-Tu 11610, Th-M 11660, Th-Tu 11670, Th-Tu 11800, Th-Tu 11835, Th-Tu 11915, Th-Tu 12080, Th-Tu 15270, Th-Tu 15500, Th-Tu 15540	0900-1030	9530, 11800
		0900-1100	W 7315, W 9820, 11610, S 11660, S 11845, 15540
		0900-1200	W 6165, 11670, S 11905
		0900-1230	9810
		0900-1300	W 3985, S 7140, W 7245, W 7350, 9480, S 9620, S 11685
0600-1100	11835	0900-1601	9775
0700-0850	W-M 11630, W-M 12055, W-M 13700, W-M 15390	0900-1733	6175
		0955-2200	9410

0955-2400	5925, 7620
1000-1100	W 6125, 11630, 12055, 13700, 15390
1000-1200	W 9515, W 11925, S 17580, S 17625, S 17890
1000-1300	W 5945, W 7335, S 11915, S 15480
1000-1601	6090, 6155, 9755
1000-1733	5030, 7305, 11710
1030-1200	W 7375, S 11800
1030-1300	W 6010, S 9530
1030-1733	9845
1100-1200	W 9860, S 12045
1100-1300	W 7130, W 7140, S 11610, S 11835
1100-1601	7315, 9820, 11740
1100-1733	4460, 6125, 7275, 7345, 9710
1100-1804	9170
1200-1400	W 6180, 9420, 9630, W 9890, S 11630, S 13700
1200-1601	6065, 7375, 9515
1200-1733	6080, 7110, 7290, 9860, 11925
1200-1804	6165
1230-1601	7150
1300-1601	3985, 7130, 7140, 7245, 7335
1300-1733	5945, 9810
1400-1601	6010, 7350, 9480
2000-2200	7305
2000-2300	5030, 6080, 7275, 9810, 9890, 9900
2000-2330	4460, 9710, 11925
2000-2400	4750, 4800, 5945, 6030, 6125, 6175, W 6180, 6950, 7230, 7290, 7345, 9455, 9500, 9655, 9830, 9845, S 11630, 11710
2055-2400	6165, 9170
2100-2200	6040
2100-2300	6010, 6155, 6190, 7140, 7245, 7360, 9480, 9820
2100-2330	6065, 7130
2100-2400	6090, 7150, 7315, 7335, 9515, 9755, 9775, 11740
2200-2400	W 6040, 9665, 11750, S 11800
2300-2400	W 6080, W 6155, W 6190, S 7140, W 7140, W 7245, W 7275, S 9620, S 9630, 9675, W 9820, W 9890,

	W 9900, S 11610, S 11845, S 12045, 13610, S 13700, S 15380, S 15500
2330-2400	W 4460, W 7130, S 9645, 11670, 11720, S 11835, W 11925, S 17580

CHINA RADIO INTERNATIONAL
Chinese

0000-0100	S *5960* (E North Am), W *6005* (N America), W *6040* (E North Am), 11780 (E Asia), W 11845 (SE Asia), 11900 (E Asia), S *11930* (W North Am), S 12035 & 13580 (SE Asia)
0000-0300	13655 (E Asia)
0100-0200	W 7250, W 7300 & S 11640 (S Asia), W 11640 (SE Asia), S 11650 (S Asia), 13580 & S 15140 (SE Asia)
0100-0400	15160 (E Asia)
0200-0300	W 7330 (S America), *9580* (E North Am), *9690* (N America & C America), S 9815 (Mideast, N Africa & S America), 11695 (S America)
0200-0400	*6020* & *9570* (N America)
0300-0400	9450 (S Asia), W 13655 (E Asia), S 13690 (Europe), S 15230 (E Asia), 17540 (S Asia)
0300-0600	15130 (E Asia)
0400-0500	13640 & 15170 (S Asia)
0500-0700	W 13620 & W 13655 (E Asia), 15120 (C Asia & E Asia), 15170, S 15230 & S 15785 (E Asia)
0600-0800	W 13750, S 17615 & 17740 (SE Asia)
0600-0900	17650 (Europe)
0700-0900	S *11785* & W *11855* (W Europe)
0800-0900	W 7180, 11640, W 13610 & S 15230 (E Asia)
0800-1000	15565 & 17560 (W Asia & C Asia)
0800-1100	S 9880 (E Asia)
0900-1000	7190, W 9440 & S 13620 (E Asia), W 13850 (SE Asia), 15440 (Australasia), 17500

	(S Asia), [S] 17540 (SE Asia), 17670 (Australasia)
0900-1100	[W] 5965 (E Asia), 11980, 15250 & [W] 15340 (SE Asia), 15525 (S Asia), [S] 17530 (SE Asia)
1000-1100	[W] 6020 (C Asia), [W] 7255 & [S] 9890 (C Asia & E Asia), 13850 (SE Asia), [S] 17540 (C Asia & E Asia)
1000-1200	17650 (Europe)
1100-1200	7160 & [W] 7200 (E Asia), [W] 11620 (Australasia), [S] 11750 (E Asia), [W] 11980 (S Asia), [W] 15440 & [S] 15460 (Australasia)
1100-1300	[S] 13755 (S Asia)
1200-1300	[W] 7205 (S Asia), 9570 (E North Am), 15110 (Mideast), [W] 15540 & [S] 17625 (S America)
1200-1400	7160 & 9855 (SE Asia)
1300-1400	7205 (E Asia), 13650 (Mideast)
1400-1500	7210 (E Asia), [S] 9730 (S Asia)
1400-1600	[S] 15220 (W North Am)
1500-1600	5910 (SE Asia), 7150 (E Asia), 7265 & 9560 (S Asia), [W] 9700 & [W] 9740 (Europe), [W] 13675 (W North Am), [S] 13680 & [S] 13710 (Europe)
1600-1700	[W] 17735 (W North Am)
1730-1830	[W] 7120 (Europe), 7160, 7315, [W] 9695 & [S] 9745 (Mideast), [S] 11660 (Europe)
1800-1900	6100 (S Africa)
2000-2100	7120 (Europe), 7245 (Mideast & N Africa), 7335 (Europe), 9865 (Mideast)
2200-2300	5975 (Mideast), [W] 6100, 6140 & [W] 7125 (SE Asia), 7190 (E Africa & S Africa), [S] 7215 & [W] 7220 (SE Asia), 7265 (Mideast & W Asia), [W] 7305 (E Asia), 7325, [S] 9460 & [S] 9470 (SE Asia), [W] 9555 & [S] 9675 (E Asia)
2230-2300	15505 (W Africa, C Africa & E Africa)
2230-2400	11975 (N Africa)
2300-2400	7170 (W Africa), [S] 11900 (E Asia)

Cantonese

0000-0100	11820 & 17495 (SE Asia)
0400-0500	9790 (W North Am), [W] 13655, 15160 & [S] 15230 (E Asia)
0700-0800	11640, [W] 13610 & [S] 15230 (E Asia)
1000-1100	15440 & 17670 (Australasia)
1100-1200	9540 (Australasia), 9590 & 9645 (SE Asia), 13580 (Australasia)
1200-1300	[W] 9560 & [S] 11855 (E North Am & C America)
1700-1800	[W] 7220 (E Africa & S Africa), [S] 9435 (E Africa)
1900-2000	[S] 7140, [W] 7215, [W] 9770 & [S] 11895 (Europe)
2300-2400	6140, 7325, [W] 9425, 9460, [S] 11650, 11945/11935 & [S] 15100 (SE Asia)

CHINA (TAIWAN)

RADIO TAIWAN INTERNATIONAL
Amoy

0000-0100	11875 (SE Asia), 15440 (W North Am)
0500-0600	15580 (SE Asia)
1000-1100	11605 (E Asia)
1200-1300	11715 (SE Asia)
1300-1400	11635 & 15465 (SE Asia)
2100-2200	[W] 5950 & [S] 13690 (E North Am)

Chinese

0000-0300	9660 (E Asia)
0000-0400	15245 (E Asia)
0000-0500	11640 & 11885 (E Asia)
0100-0200	[W] 11825, 15215 & [S] 17845 (S America)
0200-0500	15290 (SE Asia)
0400-0500	5950 (W North Am), 9680 (N America), 15320 (SE Asia)
0400-0600	15270 (SE Asia)
0500-0600	[W] 9495 & [S] 9505 (C America)
0900-1000	11520 (SE Asia), 11605 (E Asia), 11635 (SE Asia), 11715 (Australasia), 15525 (SE Asia)

0900-1100	9415 (E Asia)
0900-1400	6150 (E Asia)
0900-1500	6085 (E Asia)
0900-1600	11665 (E Asia)
0900-1800	7185 (E Asia)
1000-1400	9780 (E Asia)
1100-1200	11715 (Australasia)
1100-1300	11710 (E Asia)
1100-1800	9680 (E Asia)
1200-1300	11605 (E Asia), 15465 (SE Asia)
1300-1400	15265 (SE Asia)
1300-1500	7445 (SE Asia)
1400-1500	**W** *9720* (E Asia)
1400-1800	6145 & 7130 (E Asia)
1600-1800	7365 (E Asia)
1900-2000	9955, **S** *17750* & **W** *17760* (Europe)
2200-2300	*3965* (W Europe)
2200-2400	*5950* (E North Am), 6105 & 6150 (E Asia), 11635 (SE Asia), 11710 & 11885 (E Asia), *15440* (W North Am)
2300-2400	9660 & 15245 (E Asia)

Cantonese

0100-0200	*5950* (E North Am), 15290 (SE Asia), *15440* (W North Am)
0200-0300	15610 (SE Asia)
0500-0600	*5950* (W North Am), *9680* (N America), 15320 (SE Asia)
1000-1100	11635 (SE Asia), 11715 (Australasia), 15270 & 15525 (SE Asia)
1200-1300	6105 (E Asia), 11915 (SE Asia)
2200-2300	**W** *5745* & **S** *11565* (Europe)

CROATIA—Croatian
VOICE OF CROATIA

0000-0100	**S** *9925* (E North Am & S America)
0000-0200	**S** 6165 (Europe), **W** *7285* (E North Am & S America)
0100-0200	**S** *9925* (N America & S America)
0200-0300	**W** *7285* (N America & S America)
0215-0230	**S** 6165 (Europe), **S** *9925* (N America & S America)
0250-0300	**S** *9925* (N America & S America)

0250-0500	**S** 6165 (Europe)
0300-0500	**S** *9925* (W North Am)
0315-0330 &	
0350-0400	**W** *7285* (N America & S America)
0400-0600	**W** *7285* (W North Am)
0500-0600	**W** 6165 (Europe)
0500-0800 ▭	*9470* (Australasia)
0600-1000	**S** *13820/11610* & **W** *13820/11690* (Australasia)
0600-2300 ▭	6165 (Europe)
2200-2215 &	
2250-2300	**S** *9925* (S America)
2300-2315 ▭	6165 (Europe)
2300-2315	**W** *7285* (S America)
2300-2400	**S** 6165 (Europe), **S** *9925* (E North Am & S America)
2350-2400 ▭	6165 (Europe)
2350-2400	**W** *7285* (S America)

CUBA—Spanish
RADIO HABANA CUBA

0000-0100	Tu-Sa 6000 (E North Am), Tu-Sa 6180/9820 (N America)
0000-0500	5965 (C America), 6060 (E North Am), 6140 (C America), 9600 & 11705 (S America), 11760 (Americas), 11875 (S America)
0200-0500	9550 (S America)
1100-1300	6180 (E North Am), 9600 (N America)
1100-1400	6000 (C America)
1100-1500	9550 (C America & S America), 11805 (S America), 12000 (E North Am), 15190 (S America)
1300-1500	13680 (N America), 15370 (E North Am)
2100-2300	9550 (C America & S America), 11705 (S America), 11800 (C America)
2300-2400	M-F 6000 (E North Am), M-F 6180/9820 (N America)

RADIO REBELDE

24 Hr	5025
0300-0400	6120 (C America)

1100-1500 ◧	9505 & 11655 (C America)
1700-1830 ◧	M-Sa 11655 & M-Sa 13750 (Irr) (C America), M-Sa 15370 (S America), M-Sa 15570 (C America), M-Sa 17555 & M-Sa 17735 (S America)
1830-1900 ◧	M-Sa 11655 (Irr) (C America), M-Sa 15370 (Irr) (S America), M-Sa 15570 (Irr) (C America), M-Sa 17555 (Irr) & M-Sa 17735 (Irr) (S America)

CZECH REPUBLIC—Czech

RADIO PRAGUE

0030-0100	▥ 5930 (S America), ▥ 7345 (N America & C America)
0130-0200	▤ 6200 (N America & C America), ▤ 7345 (S America)
0230-0300	▥ 6200 & ▤ 7345 (N America & C America), ▥ 7345 (S America), ▤ 9870 (W North Am & C America)
0330-0400	▥ 6200 (W North Am & C America), ▥ 7345 (N America & C America)
0830-0900	▤ 15710 (E Africa & Mideast)
0930-1000 ◧	11600 (W Europe)
0930-1000	▤ 9880 (W Europe), ▤ 21745 (S Asia), ▥ 21745 (C Africa & E Africa)
1030-1100	▥ 15700 (S Asia), ▥ 21745 (W Africa)
1100-1130	▤ 11665 (N Europe), ▤ 15710 (S Asia)
1200-1230	▥ 11640 (N Europe), ▥ 17545 (S Asia, SE Asia & Australasia)
1330-1400 ◧	6055 (Europe), 7345 (W Europe)
1430-1500	▥ 11600 (S Asia), ▥ 13580 (N America)
1530-1600	▤ 17485 (E Africa)
1630-1700 ◧	5930 (W Europe)
1630-1700	▥ 15710 (W Africa & C Africa)
1730-1800	▤ 5930 (E Europe & Asia),

	▤ 17485 (C Africa)
1830-1900	▥ 5930 (W Europe), ▥ 9400 (Asia & Australasia)
1930-2000	▤ 11600 (SE Asia & Australasia)
2030-2100 ◧	5930 (W Europe)
2030-2100	▥ 9430 (SE Asia & Australasia)
2100-2130	▤ 9410 (W Africa & C Africa), ▤ 11600 (W Europe)
2200-2230	▥ 5930 (W Europe), ▥ 9435 (W Europe & S America)
2330-2400	▤ 7345 (S America), ▤ 9440 (N America & C America)

EGYPT—Arabic

EGYPTIAN RADIO

0000-0030	▤ 11665 (E Africa)
0000-0300	▤ 12050 (Europe & E North Am)
0000-0400	▥ 6290 (Europe & E North Am)
0700-1100 ◧	15115 (W Africa)
1100-2300	▤ 12050 (Europe & E North Am)
1200-2400	▥ 6290 (Europe & E North Am)
1800-2330	▥ 9960 (E Africa)
1900-2400	▤ 11665 (E Africa)
2300-2400	▤ 12050 (Europe & E North Am)

RADIO CAIRO

0000-0045	9360 (C America & S America), 9735 (S America)
0030-0430	▤ 9460 & ▥ 9465 (E North Am)
1015-1215	15170 (Mideast)
1300-1600	15365/15285 (W Africa & C Africa)
2000-2200	7210/7325 (Australasia)
2330-2400	9360 (C America & S America), 9735 (S America)

FRANCE—French

RADIO FRANCE INTERNATIONALE

0400-0430	Sa/Su 9805 (E Africa)
0400-0500	▥ 5925 & 7135 (C Africa),

W 9780/11995 (E Africa),
S 9790 (C Africa & S Africa)

0500-0530 W Sa/Su 9805/13680, W Sa/Su 11995, S Sa/Su 13680 & S Sa/Su 15160/11995 (E Africa)

0500-0600 ◄ 11700 (E Africa)

0500-0600 W 5925 (N Africa & W Africa), W 7135 & S 9790 (W Africa), W 9790 (C Africa & S Africa), S 11700/7135 (N Africa & W Africa), S 15300 (C Africa & S Africa)

0500-0700 W 7135 (N Africa & W Africa)

0600-0630 W Sa/Su 7315 & S Sa/Su 9765/11725 (W Africa & C Africa), W Sa/Su 11995/15160, W Sa/Su 13680, S Sa/Su 15160 & S Sa/Su 17800 (E Africa)

0600-0700 ◄ 11700 (C Africa & S Africa)

0600-0700 W 5925 (W Africa), S 7135/13695, 9790 & S 11700 (N Africa & W Africa), 13695 & S 15300 (C Africa & S Africa)

0700-0800 W 9790, 11700 & 13695 (N Africa & W Africa), W 13695 (C Africa & S Africa), 15170 (C Africa), 15300 (W Africa, C Africa & S Africa)

0700-0900 17850 (C Africa & S Africa)

0800-0830 Sa/Su 11830 (C Africa)

0800-1000 13675 & 17620 (W Africa)

0800-1600 15300 (N Africa & W Africa)

0900-1400 S 17850 (C Africa & S Africa)

1000-1500 W 13675 (W Africa)

1100-1130 S 15365/17800 (C America)

1100-1200 17525 (C Africa)

1130-1200 6175 (W Europe & Atlantic), 13640 & W 17610 (C America)

1200-1400 15160 (C Africa), 17620 (W Africa), W 21580 (C Africa & S Africa)

View atop Notre Dame looking toward Montmartre. During World War II the Resistance communicated by shortwave from graveyards. M. Wright

1200-1500 W 21685 (W Africa)

1230-1300 W 21620 (E Africa)

1500-1600 W 17620 (W Africa)

1500-1700 13675 (W Africa)

1600-1700 S 15300 (W Africa), W 15300 (Africa), 17620 (W Africa), 17850 (C Africa & S Africa)

1700-1800 W 11705 (C Africa & S Africa), S 13695 (N Africa & W Africa), W 13695 (Africa), S 17850 (C Africa & S Africa)

1700-1900 S 15300 (Africa)

1700-2000 11995 (W Africa)

1800-1900 W 9790 (E Africa, C Africa & S Africa)

1800-2000 S 11705 (C Africa & S Africa), 13695 (N Africa & W Africa)

1900-2000 W 6175 & W 7315 (W Africa), 9790 (W Africa, C Africa & S Africa), S 15300 (W Africa)

2000-2100 W 9790 & S 11995 (W Africa), S 13695 (N Africa & W Africa)

2000-2200 W 6175 (W Africa), 7160 (C Africa), 7315 (N Africa & W Africa)

GABON—French

AFRIQUE NUMERO UN

0500-2315	9580 (C Africa)
0700-0800	17630 (Irr) (W Africa)
0800-1600	17630 (W Africa)
1600-1900	15475 (W Africa & E North Am)

GERMANY—German

DEUTSCHE WELLE

0000-0200	Ⓦ 7120 (W Asia), Ⓦ 7285 (C Asia), Ⓢ 9430 (C America), Ⓢ 9545 (S America), Ⓦ 9545, Ⓢ 9640 & Ⓦ 9655 (C America), Ⓦ 11690 (S America)
24 Hr	6075 (Europe)
0200-0400	Ⓦ 6075 & Ⓢ 7310 (Mideast), Ⓢ 9825 (Mideast & W Asia)
0400-0600	Ⓢ 9480 (C Africa & E Africa), Ⓢ 9620 (S Africa), Ⓦ 9735 (C Africa & E Africa), Ⓦ 13780 (E Africa), Ⓢ 15605 (C Africa & E Africa), Ⓦ 17800 (E Africa & S Africa)
0600-0700	Ⓦ 6130 (W Africa)
0600-0800	Ⓦ 7210 (N Europe), Ⓦ 11865 (Mideast), Ⓦ 12005 (S Africa), Ⓦ 12025 (E Europe & W Asia), Ⓢ 12045 (S Africa), Ⓢ 13780 (Mideast), Ⓦ 15410 (W Africa & C Africa), Ⓢ 15605 (C Africa & S Africa), Ⓢ 17860 (W Africa)
0600-1000	Ⓢ 9480 (N Europe)
0600-1800	Ⓦ 9545 (S Europe & Atlantic)
0700-0800	Ⓢ 15275 (W Africa & S Africa)
0800-1000	Ⓦ 9785 & Ⓢ 9855 (Australasia), Ⓢ 15605 & Ⓦ 17520 (SE Asia & Australasia)
0800-1600	13780 (Mideast)
1000-1100	Ⓦ 9865 (S America)
1000-1200	5905 (C America), Ⓦ 5910, Ⓦ 7265 & Ⓢ 7350 (E Asia), Ⓢ 9900 (SE Asia & Australasia), Ⓦ 15430 (SE Asia), Ⓢ 15595 (S America), Ⓦ 15610 (SE Asia & Australasia), Ⓢ 17635 & Ⓢ 17845 (E Asia & SE Asia), Ⓢ 21840 (S America)
1100-1200	Ⓦ 17770 (S America)
1200-1400	Ⓢ 9565 (C Asia), Ⓦ 15610 (S Asia & C Asia), Ⓦ 17630 & Ⓢ 17845 (S Asia & SE Asia)

While Americans languish at airports, travelers to and from Frankfurt am Main use a vast network of swift, hassle-free trains to get around.

Shutterstock/Joerg Humpe

1400-1600	**S** *9655* & *15275* (Mideast), **W** *15335* (S Europe, Mideast & W Asia)
1600-1800	**W** *7255* (E Africa & S Africa), **W** *12055* (C Africa & E Africa), **W** *12070* (Mideast), **S** *13780* (E Africa), **W** *13780*, **S** *15275* & **S** *17650* (C Africa & E Africa)
1600-2000	**S** *6150* (C Africa & E Africa)
1800-1900	**W** *13780* (N Africa)
1800-2000	**S** *9735* (N Africa), **W** *11725* (W Africa), **W** *12070* (C Africa & S Africa), **S** *15275* (W Africa), **W** *15440* (S Africa), **S** *17610* (C Africa & S Africa)
1800-2200	**S** *9545* (Europe)
2000-2100	**W** *9545* (S Europe & Atlantic), **W** *11935* (Australasia)
2000-2200	**S** *7330* (Australasia), **S** *9545* (Atlantic & S America), **S** *9875* (Australasia)
2100-2200	**W** *9545* (W Africa & C Africa), **W** *11935* (Australasia)
2200-2400	**W** *5875* (SE Asia), **W** *5900* (E Asia), **S** *7420* (E Asia & SE Asia), *9545* (S America), **S** *9775* (C America & S America), **W** *11690* & *11865* (S America), **S** *11965* (SE Asia), **S** *15640* (E Asia)
2300-2400	**W** *6050* (SE Asia)

GREECE—Greek

FONI TIS HELLADAS

0000-0005	**W** *7475* (Europe), **W** *12105* (W Africa, Atlantic & S America), **S** M-Sa *15650* (Mideast & Australasia)
0000-0200	**S** *15650* (Mideast & Australasia)
0005-0105 **◧**	Tu-Su *7475* & Tu-Su *9420* (Europe & N America)
0005-0105	**W** Tu-Su *12105* (W Africa, Atlantic & S America)
0105-0300 **◧**	*7475* (Europe & N America), *9420* (Europe & Americas)
0105-0300	**W** *12105* (W Africa, Atlantic & S America)
0200-0300	**S** M-Sa *15650* (Mideast & Australasia)
0300-0355	**S** *15650* (Mideast & Australasia)
0300-0400 **◧**	M-Sa *7475* (Europe & N America)
0300-0400	**W** M-Sa *9420* (Europe & N America), **W** M-Sa *12105* (W Africa, Atlantic & S America)
0400-0555 **◧**	*7475* (Europe & N America)
0400-0600 **◧**	*9420* (Europe & N America)
0400-0700	**W** *12105* (W Africa, Atlantic & S America)
0600-1000 **◧**	*9420* (Europe)
0700-1000	**W** *12105* (W Africa)
0905-1000	**S** M-Sa *9420* (Europe)
1100-1200	**W** M-Sa *9420* (Europe), **W** M-Sa *17525* (Mideast & Australasia)
1100-1300	**S** *15630* (W Europe & Atlantic)
1200-1400 **◧**	*9420* (Europe)
1200-1400	**W** *17525* (Mideast & Australasia)
1300-1400	**S** Su-F *15630* (W Europe & Atlantic)
1400-1500 **◧**	Su-F *9420* (Europe)
1400-1500	**S** *15630* (W Europe & Atlantic), **W** Su-F *17525* (Mideast & Australasia)
1500-1555	**W** *17525* (Mideast & Australasia)
1500-2400 **◧**	*9420* (Europe)
1600-2000 **◧**	*15630* (W Europe & Atlantic)
1900-2255	**S** *15630* (W Europe, Atlantic & N America)
2000-2400	**W** *7475* (Europe)
2300-2400	**W** *12105* (W Africa, Atlantic & S America), **S** M-Sa *15650* (Mideast & Australasia)
2305-2400	**S** *15650* (Mideast & Australasia)

RS MAKEDONIAS—(Europe)

1100-1655	9935
1700-2255	7450

HUNGARY—Hungarian

RADIO BUDAPEST

0000-0100	**S**	6195 (N America)
0100-0200	**W**	5980 (N America)
0130-0230	**S**	6140 (N America)
0200-0300	**W**	6145 (N America)
1100-1200	**S**	21590 (Australasia)
1200-1300	**W**	17690 (Australasia)
1800-1900	**S**	11795 (Australasia)
1900-2000	**W**	9845 (Australasia)
1900-2300	**◻**	3975 & 6025 (Europe)
2000-2100	**S**	11695 (N America)
2100-2200	**W**	5970 (N America)
2200-2300	**W**	5980 (Europe)
2300-2400	**◻**	Sa/Su 6025 (Europe), 9665 (S America)

RADIO KOSSUTH—(Europe)

0300-0700	**S**	M-Sa 3975
0400-0730	**S**	5995
0400-1900	**◻**	6025
0500-0830	**◻**	Su 3975
0500-0830	**W**	Su 6145
1100-1200 &		
1500-1800	**◻**	3975

INDIA—Hindi

ALL INDIA RADIO

0315-0415	11840 & 13695 (Mideast & W Asia), 15075 (Mideast & E Africa), 15185 & 17715 (E Africa)
0430-0530	15075, 15185 & 17715 (E Africa)
1615-1730	7410 (Mideast & W Asia), 9950 (E Africa), 12025 & 13770 (Mideast & W Asia), 15075 & 17670 (E Africa)
1945-2045	7410 & 9950 (Europe)
2300-2400	9910, 11740 & 13795 (SE Asia)

ISRAEL

GALEI ZAHAL—(Europe)
Hebrew

24 Hr	6973 & 15785

KOL ISRAEL
Hebrew

0000-0330	**S**	11590/9345 (W Europe & E North Am)
0000-0430	**W**	7545 (W Europe & E North Am)
0400-0500	**S**	11590/9345 (W Europe & E North Am)
0500-0600	**W**	7545 (W Europe & E North Am)
0600-0800	**◻**	15760 (W Europe & E North Am)
0700-0930	**S**	15760 (W Europe & E North Am)
0800-1030 &		
1130-1455	**W**	17535 (W Europe & N America)
1800-1900	**S**	13675 (W Europe & E North Am)
1900-1945	**W**	7545 (W Europe)
2000-2300	**S**	9400/11585 (W Europe & E North Am)
2100-2215	**◻**	15640/15615 (S America)
2100-2400	**W**	7545 (W Europe & E North Am)
2300-2400	**S**	11590/9345 (W Europe & E North Am)

Yiddish

1600-1625	**S**	9345 (W Europe)
1700-1725	**◻**	11590 (Europe), 15760 (W Europe & E North Am)
1700-1725	**W**	9345 (Europe)

JAPAN—Japanese

RADIO JAPAN

0100-0500		17560 (Mideast), 17810 (SE Asia)
0200-0300	**S** *11780* & **W** *11860* (SE Asia)	
0200-0400		*11935* (S America)
0200-0500		*5960* (E North Am), 15325 (S Asia)
0200-0800		15195 (E Asia)
0530-0600		17810 (SE Asia)
0530-0900		17585 (SE Asia)
0700-0730		15220 (W Africa), **W** *17685* (Mideast)
0700-0800		6145 & 6165 (E Asia)
0700-0900		17860 (SE Asia)
0800-0900		9825 (Pacific & S America)
0800-1000		*11740* (SE Asia), *17650* (W Africa)
0800-1700		9750 (E Asia)
0900-1000		*6195* (S America)
0930-1700		11815 (SE Asia)
1500-1700		9535 (W North Am & C America), *12045* (S Asia), *21630* (C Africa)

1700-1900	6035 (E Asia), 7200 (SE Asia), ☑ 9575 (Mideast & N Africa), 9835 (Pacific & S America), ⬛ 13740 (Mideast & N Africa), 15355 (S Africa)
1900-2200	☑ 7225 (SE Asia)
2000-2100	6165 (E Asia)
2000-2200	6085 (E Asia), 11665 (SE Asia), 13640 (Australasia)
2000-2400	11910 (E Asia), ⬛ 13680 (SE Asia)
2100-2200	9560 (E Asia)
2200-2300	☑ 7115 & ⬛ 9650 (Mideast), ⬛ 11955 & ☑ 15220 (S America)
2200-2400	☑ 11665 (SE Asia), ⬛ 15265 & ☑ 17605 (S America)

RADIO NIKKEI

0000-0730	3945, 6115, 9760
0000-0800	3925
0000-1200	6055, 9595
0730-0800	Sa/Su 3945, Sa/Su 6115, Sa/Su 9760
0800-0900	Sa/Su 3945 (Irr), Sa/Su 6115 (Irr), Sa/Su 9760 (Irr)
0800-1200	3925
1200-1330	M-Sa 3925, M-Sa 6055, M-Sa 9595
1330-1500	M-Sa 3925 (Irr), M-Sa 6055 (Irr), M-Sa 9595 (Irr)
2045-2300	3925
2045-2400	6055, 9595
2300-2400	3925, 3945, 6115, 9760

JORDAN—Arabic

RADIO JORDAN

0500-0810 ▭	11810 (Mideast, S Asia & Australasia)
0600-0815 ▭	11960 (E Europe)
1130-1300 ▭	15290 (N Africa & C America)
1200-1600 ▭	11810 (Mideast, S Asia & Australasia)
1745-2200	⬛ 11810 (Mideast, S Asia & Australasia)
1845-2100 ▭	9830 (W Europe)
1845-2300	☑ 6105 (Mideast, S Asia & Australasia)

KOREA (DPR)—Korean

KOREAN CENTRAL BROADCATING STATION

0000-0630	6100
0000-1800	2850, 9665, 11680
0900-0950	4405, 7140 & 9345 (E Asia)
1200-1250	3560 (E Asia), ☑ 6185 (SE Asia), ☑ 6285 & ☑ 9335 (C America), ☑ 9850 (SE Asia), ⬛ 11710 (C America), ⬛ 11735, ⬛ 13650 & ⬛ 15180 (SE Asia)
1330-1800	6100
1400-1450	3560 (E Asia), ☑ 6185, ☑ 9850, ⬛ 11735 & ⬛ 13650 (SE Asia)
1700-1750	4405 (E Asia), ☑ 7570 (W Europe), 9335 & 11710 (N America), ☑ 12015, ⬛ 13760 & ⬛ 15245 (W Europe)
2000-2050	3560 (E Asia), ☑ 6285 (Europe), 7100 (S Africa), 9325 (Europe), 9975 & 11535 (Mideast & N Africa), 11910 (S Africa), ⬛ 12015 (Europe)
2000-2400	2850, 6100, 9665, 11680
2300-2350	3560, 4405 & 7140/7180 (E Asia), ☑ 7570 (W Europe), 9345, 9975 & 11535 (E Asia), ☑ 12015, ⬛ 13760 & ⬛ 15245 (W Europe)

PYONGYANG BROADCASTING STATION

0000-0050	3560, 7140, 9345 & 9730 (E Asia)
0000-0925	6248 (E Asia)
0000-1800	6398 (E Asia)
0000-1900	3320 (E Asia)
0200-0630	3250 (E Asia)
0700-0750	4405, 7140 & 9345 (E Asia)
0900-0950	3560, 9975 & 11735 (E Asia), 13760 & 15245 (E Europe)
1000-1050 & 1200-1250	4405, 7140 & 9345 (E Asia)

1300-1350	▥ 6285, 9325 & ▨ 12015 (Europe)
1500-1900	6248 (E Asia)
1500-2030	3250 (E Asia)
2100-2400	3320, 6248 & 6398 (E Asia)

KOREA (REPUBLIC)—Korean

KBS WORLD RADIO

0300-0400	11810 (S America)
0700-0800	*9870 (Europe)*
0900-1000	15210 (Mideast)
0900-1100	7275 (E Asia), 9570 (SE Asia)
1200-1300	7275 (E Asia)
1400-1500	*9650 (N America)*
1600-1800	7275 (Europe), 9730 (Mideast & Africa)
1700-1900	9515 (Europe)

KUWAIT—Arabic

RADIO KUWAIT

0200-0500	6055 (Mideast & W Asia)
0200-0700	11675 (W North Am)
0200-1305	15495 (N Africa)
0400-0740	15505 (E Europe & W Asia)
0800-0925	15110 (S Asia)
0900-1305	6055 (Mideast & W Asia)
1015-1740	15505 (W Africa & C Africa)
1200-1505	17885 (E Asia & Australasia)
1315-1600	15110 (S Asia)
1315-1605	13620/11990 (Europe & E North Am)
1615-1800	11990 (Europe & E North Am)
1730-2130	9880 (N Africa)
1745-2130	15505 (Europe & E North Am)
1800-2400	15495 (W Africa & C Africa)
1815-2400	9855 (Europe & E North Am)

LITHUANIA—Lithuanian

RADIO VILNIUS

0000-0030 ▱	9875 (E North Am)
0000-0030	▨ 11690 (E North Am)
0100-0130	▥ 7325 (E North Am)

0900-0930 ▱	9710 (W Europe)
2300-2330	▥ 7325 (E North Am)

MOROCCO

RADIO MEDI UN—(Europe & N Africa)
Arabic & French

0500-0400	9575

RTV MAROCAINE
Arabic

0000-0500	▥ 5980 & ▨ 11920 (N Africa & Mideast)
0900-2200	15345/15340 (N Africa & Mideast)
1100-1500	15335 (Europe)
2200-2400	7135 (Europe)

NETHERLANDS—Dutch

RADIO NEDERLAND

0300-0400	▨ *6190 (W North Am)*
0400-0500	*5975 (C America),* ▥ *6165 (N America)*
0500-0600	▨ *6165 (W North Am),* ▨ *7310 (Europe)*
0500-0700	▨ *6015 (S Europe)*
0600-0700	▥ *6120 (S Europe),* ▥ *6165 (W North Am),* ▥ *7305 (Europe),* ▨ *11655 (N Europe)*
0600-0800	*9625 (Australasia)*
0600-0900 ▱	9895 (S Europe)
0600-1800 ▱	5955 (W Europe)
0700-0800	▥ *7220 (Europe),* ▨ *9610 (N Europe),* ▨ *11935 (S Europe),* ▥ *11935 (W Europe)*
0800-0900	▨ *6035 &* ▥ *11895 (Europe),* ▥ *11935 (S Europe & Atlantic),* ▥ *13700 (Europe)*
0800-1500	▨ Sa/Su 13700 (S Europe & N Africa)
0900-1000	*6035 (Europe)*
0900-1100	▥ *6120 &* ▥ Sa *13700 (S Europe)*
0900-1600 ▱	Sa/Su 9895 (S Europe)
0930-1015	M-Sa 6020 (C America)
1000-1200	▥ *6035 (Europe)*
1100-1200	*21560 (SE Asia)*
1200-1300	▨ *17745 (E Asia),* ▥ *21480 (SE Asia)*

Mozart once played
this organ at St. Bavo's
Church, Haarlem, The
Netherlands.

M. Wright

1300-1400	*5910* (E Asia & SE Asia), **S** *13735* (SE Asia), **W** *17580* & **S** *17585* (S Asia & SE Asia), **W** *17810* (SE Asia)
1500-1700	**S** 13700 (S Europe & N Africa)
1600-1700 ◀	9895 (S Europe)
1600-1700	**W** *9750* (S Europe), **S** 9895 (S Europe & N Africa), **W** *11655* (E Africa), *13840* (Mideast), **S** *15335* (Europe, Mideast & N Africa)
1700-1800	**W** 6010 (S Europe & Atlantic), *6020* (S Africa), **S** *9895* (C Africa), **W** *9895* (E Africa & Europe), **S** *11655* (E Africa), **W** *11655* (C Africa)
2100-2200	**W** *11655* (W Africa & C Africa), **S** *15315* (Atlantic & W Africa), **W** *15315* (S America), *17810* (W Africa), **S** *17895* (S America)
2100-2300 ◀	6040 (W Europe)
2100-2300	**W** *9895* (N Africa & E Africa)
2200-2300	**W** *11730* (Atlantic & S America), *15315* & **S** *15540* (S America)
2300-2400	**W** *6165* (E North Am), **W** *9520* & **S** *9525* (C America & S America), **S** *11970* (E North Am)

OMAN—Arabic

RADIO SULTANATE OF OMAN

0000-0200	9760 (Europe & Mideast)
0200-0300	15355 (E Africa)
0200-0400	**S** 6085/6000 & **W** 6085/7175 (Mideast)
0400-0600	9515 (Mideast), 17590 (E Africa)
0600-0800	17630/17660 (Europe & Mideast)
0600-1400	13640 (Mideast)
0800-1000	17630 (Europe & Mideast)
1400-1800	15375 (E Africa)
1500-2200	15140 (Europe & Mideast)
1800-2000	6190 & 15355 (E Africa)
2000-2200	6085 (E Africa), 13640 (Europe & Mideast)
2200-2400	15355 (Europe & Mideast)
2300-2400	9760 (Europe & Mideast)

PORTUGAL—Portuguese

RDP INTERNATIONAL

0000-0200	**S** Tu-Sa 15295 (S America)
0000-0300 ◀	Tu-Sa 9715 (E North Am), Tu-Sa 13700 (C America)
0000-0300	**W** Tu-Sa 11980 (S America)
0500-0800	**S** M-F 7240 (Europe)
0600-1300	**W** M-F 9815 (Europe)
0645-0800	**S** M-F 11850 (Europe)
0700-0800	**S** Sa/Su 12020 (Europe)
0700-1000	**S** Sa/Su 12000 (W Africa & S America), **S** Sa/Su 15160 (E Africa & S Africa)

0745-0900	◩ M-F 11660 (Europe)
0800-1055	◩ Sa/Su 17710 (W Africa & S America)
0800-1100	◩ Sa/Su 21830 (E Africa & S Africa)
0800-1200	◪ 12020 (Europe)
0800-1455	◩ Sa/Su 11875 (Europe)
0830-1000	◪ Sa/Su 11955 (Europe)
0930-1100	◩ Sa/Su 9815 (Europe)
1000-1200	◪ M-F 15575 (W Africa & S America)
1100-1300 ◀	21830 (E Africa & S Africa)
1100-1300	◩ M-F 21655 (W Africa & S America)
1100-1700 ◀	Sa/Su 21655 (W Africa & S America)
1200-1300	◪ M-F 15560 (Irr) (E North Am)
1200-1355	◪ Sa/Su 12020 (Europe)
1200-2000	◪ Sa/Su/Holidays 15560 (E North Am)
1300-1500	◪ M-F 15770 (Mideast & S Asia)
1300-1655 ◀	Sa/Su 21830 (E Africa & S Africa)
1300-1700	◩ Sa/Su/Holidays 15575 (E North Am)
1400-1600	◪ Sa/Su 15555 (Europe), ◩ M-F 15690 (Mideast & S Asia)
1500-1800	◩ Sa/Su 11960 (Europe)
1600-1900	◪ 15555 (Europe)
1700-1900	◩ Sa/Su/Holidays 17825 & ◩ M-F 17825 (Irr) (E North Am)
1700-2000 ◀	M-F 17680 (E Africa & S Africa), 21655 (W Africa & S America)
1700-2000	◩ M-F 11630 (Europe), Sa/Su 17680 (E Africa & S Africa)
1800-2100	◩ Sa/Su 11630 (Europe)
1900-2000	◪ Sa/Su 15555 (Europe)
1900-2100	◩ Sa/Su 15540 & ◩ M-F 15540 (Irr) (E North Am)
1900-2300	◪ 9820 (Irr) (Europe), ◪ 11945 (Irr) (S Africa)
2000-2100 ◀	Sa/Su 21655 (W Africa & S America)
2000-2100	◩ Sa/Su 17680 (E Africa & S Africa)
2000-2300	◪ M-F 15295 (Irr) (S America), ◪ Sa/Su/

	Holidays 15560 (Irr) (E North Am)
2000-2400	◩ 9460 (Irr) (Europe), ◩ 11825 (Irr) (E Africa & S Africa), ◩ 15555 (Irr) (W Africa & S America)
2100-2400	◩ 15540 (Irr) (E North Am)
2300-2400	◪ M-F 15295 (S America)

ROMANIA—Romanian
RADIO ROMANIA

0800-0900	◩ Su 11730 & ◪ Su 11970 (Mideast), ◪ Su 15270 (W Asia & S Asia), Su 15370 (Mideast), ◩ Su 15430, ◩ Su 17775 & ◪ Su 17805 (W Asia & S Asia)
0900-1000	◪ Su 11875 (N Africa & Mideast), ◪ Su 11945 (Mideast), ◩ Su 15380 (N Africa & Mideast), Su 15430 (Mideast), ◪ Su 15450 & ◩ Su 17745 (N Africa & Mideast), ◩ Su 17775 (Mideast)
1000-1100	◪ Su 11830 (W Europe), ◪ Su 11990 (N Africa), ◪ Su 15250 & ◩ Su 15260 (W Europe), Su 15380 & ◩ Su 17735 (N Africa), ◩ Su 17825 (W Europe)

RADIO ROMANIA INTERNATIONAL

0100-0200	◩ 6040 & ◩ 9640 (E North Am)
0100-0300	◪ 9525 (E North Am)
0200-0300	◩ 6040, ◩ 9640 & ◪ 11970 (E North Am)
1200-1300	◪ 7155, ◪ 11920 & ◪ 15195 (W Europe)
1300-1400	◩ 9610 (Europe), ◩ 11795 & ◩ 15170 (W Europe)
1400-1500	◪ 9760 & ◪ 11965 (W Europe)
1500-1600	◩ 9595 & ◩ 11970 (W Europe)
1600-1700	◪ 7195 & ◪ 9690 (Mideast)
1700-1800	◩ 6110 & ◩ 7220 (Mideast), ◪ 9625 & ◪ 11865 (W Europe)
1800-1900	◪ 9625 & ◪ 11765 (W Europe)
2000-2100	◪ 9630 & ◪ 11810 (W Europe)

The Moscow International House of Music is a delightful venue for performances eventually heard over the Voice of Russia.

Shutterstock

RUSSIA—Russian

RADIO ROSSII
0000-1800 ◄	*4050* (C Asia)
0400-0800	**S** 12070 (Europe)
0500-0800	**W** 9840 (Europe)
0825-1300	**W** 12075 & **S** 13665 (Europe)
1325-1600	**W** 7310 (Europe)
1325-2100	**S** 7120 (Europe)
1625-2200	**W** 5905 (Europe)
2200-2400 ◄	*4050* (C Asia)

RUSSIAN INTERNATIONAL RADIO
0000-0600 ◄	*7125* (E North Am)
0100-0300	**S** *5945* (Mideast)
0300-0400 ◄	*7250* (E North Am)
1000-1200	**S** 11750 (W Asia & C Asia)
1400-1500	**S** 15540 (Mideast)
1500-1600	**W** 12025 (W Asia & C Asia)
1500-1700	**S** 13855 (Mideast)
1500-1800	**W** 5945 (W Asia & C Asia), **W** 5985 (Mideast)
1600-1800	**S** 5925 (Mideast & W Asia)
1600-2100	**S** 5940 (Europe)
1700-1800	**S** 9825 (Mideast & W Asia)
1800-2000	**S** 9795 (Europe)
1800-2100	**W** 7310 (Europe)
1900-2100	**S** *5985* (Mideast & W Asia), **S** *9825* (Mideast)
2000-2100	**S** *7155* (Mideast)
2000-2200	**W** *5975* (Mideast)

VOICE OF RUSSIA
0100-0200	**S** *9860* (E North Am)
0100-0300	**S** 5900/6180 (S America), **S** 9880/5900 (E North Am), **S** 15425 (W North Am)
0200-0300	**W** 6155 (E North Am), **W** 6195 (S America), **W** 7350 & **S** *9515* (E North Am), **S** 12065 (W North Am)
0200-0400 ◄	7260 (C America & S America)
0200-0400	**W** 7150 & **W** 7240/6250 (E North Am), **W** 12010 & **W** 12030 (W North Am)
0300-0400 ◄	7330 (S America)
1200-1300	**S** 9640 (E Asia)
1200-1400	**S** 7165 (E Asia & SE Asia), **S** 9745 (S Asia), **S** 12030 (SE Asia & Australasia)
1200-1500	**S** 9555 (C Asia & S Asia), **S** 9875 (C Asia)
1300-1400	**W** 12025 (S Asia), **S** 15540 (Mideast), **S** 15660 (SE Asia)
1300-1500	**W** 6170 (E Asia), **W** 7260 (E Asia & SE Asia), **W** 9800 (SE Asia & Australasia), **W** *9885* (S Asia), **W** 11630/15460 (S Asia & SE Asia)
1300-1600	**W** 7135 (C Asia)
1300-1700	**W** 6185 (C Asia)
1400-1500	**W** 5940 (E Asia), **W** 5945 (W Asia & C Asia), **W** 7110

(S Asia), ▣ 12055 (S Asia & SE Asia), ▣ 13855 & ▣ *15430* (Mideast)

1400-1700	▣ 11830 (Mideast)
1400-1800	▣ 9800 (C Asia)
1400-1900	▣ 9480/7285 (Europe)
1500-1600	▣ *9555* (Mideast), ▣ 12055 (W Asia & S Asia), ▣ 13650/7130 (Mideast & W Asia), ▣ *13755* (Mideast)
1500-1700	▣ 6045 (Europe), ▣ 9865 (C Asia)
1500-1900	▣ 5995 (C Asia)
1500-2200	▣ 7285 (Mideast & W Asia)
1600-1700	▣ 6005 (Mideast), ▣ 7110 & ▣ *9885* (S Asia)
1700-1800	▣ 11630/9480 (N Europe), ▣ 13855 & ▣ 15540 (Mideast)
1700-2100	▣ 12055/7165 (Mideast & W Asia)
1800-1900	▣ 5985 (Mideast), ▣ 7290 (N Europe)
1900-2000	▣ 11630/9480 (N Europe)
1900-2100	▣ 5940 (Europe)
2000-2100	▣ 7230 (Europe & N Africa), ▣ 7290 (N Europe), ▣ 9795 (Europe)

SAUDI ARABIA—Arabic

BROADCASTING SERVICE OF THE KINGDOM

0300-0600	9580 (Mideast & E Africa), 15170 (E Europe & W Asia)
0300-0800	17895 (C Asia & E Asia)
0300-0900	9675 (Mideast)
0600-0900	15380 (Mideast), 17730 (N Africa), 17740 (W Europe)
0600-1700	11855 (Mideast & E Africa)
0900-1200	11935 (Mideast), 17615 (S Asia & SE Asia), 17805 (N Africa), 21495 (E Asia & SE Asia), 21705 (W Europe)
0900-1600	9675 (Mideast)
1200-1400	15380 (Mideast), 21600 (SE Asia)
1200-1500	17895 & 21505 (N Africa), 21640 (W Europe)
1300-1600	21460 (E Africa)
1500-1800	13710 & 15315 (N Africa), 15435 (W Europe)

1600-1800	15205 (W Europe), 17560 (C Africa & W Africa)
1700-2200	9580 (Mideast & E Africa)
1800-2300	9555 (N Africa), 9870 (W Europe), 11740 (C Africa & W Africa), 11820 (W Europe), 11915 (N Africa)

SINGAPORE—Chinese

MEDIACORP RADIO

1400-1600 & 2300-1100	6000

RADIO SINGAPORE INTERNATIONAL— (SE Asia)

1100-1400	6000 & 6185

SLOVAKIA—Slovak

RADIO SLOVAKIA INTERNATIONAL

0130-0200	5930 (N America), 9440 (S America)
0730-0800	▣ 9440 (Australasia)
1530-1600	▣ 5920 (W Europe)
1630-1700 ◀	6055 (W Europe)
1630-1700	▣ 5915 (W Europe)
1900-1930	▣ 5920 & ▣ 6055 (W Europe)
2000-2030	▣ 5915 & ▣ 7345 (W Europe)

SPAIN

RADIO EXTERIOR DE ESPAÑA
Galician, Catalan & Basque

1240-1255	▣ M-F *9765* (C America), ▣ M-F *11815* (C America & S America), ▣ M-F 13720 (W Europe), ▣ M-F *15170* (W North Am), ▣ M-F 15585 (Europe), ▣ M-F 21540 (C Africa & S Africa), ▣ M-F 21570 (S America), ▣ M-F 21610 (Mideast), ▣ M-F 21700 (N America & C America)
1340-1355	▣ M-F *15170* (W North Am), ▣ M-F 15585 (Europe), ▣ M-F 17595 (N America), ▣ M-F 21540 (C Africa & S Africa), ▣ M-F 21570 (S America), ▣ M-F 21610 (Mideast)

Spanish

0000-0200 ⒮ 11680 & ⒲ 11945 (S America)

0000-0400 ⒮ *6020* & ⒲ *11815* (C America & S America)

0000-0500 ⒲ 6125 (S America), 9535 (N America & C America), 9620 (S America), 15160 (C America & S America)

0100-0600 6055 (N America)

0200-0600 ⒮ *3350* & ⒲ *6040* (C America), ⒮ *6125* & ⒲ *11880* (N America)

0400-0800 *5965* (S America)

0500-0600 ⒮ 12035 (Europe)

0500-0700 11890 (Mideast)

0600-0700 ⒲ 13720 (W Europe)

0600-0800 ⊂⊃ 9710 (Europe)

0600-0800 ⒲ Sa/Su 11920 (W Europe)

0600-0900 12035 (Europe)

0700-0900 17770 & Sa/Su 21610 (Australasia)

0700-1240 13720 (W Europe)

0800-1000 M-F 21570 (S America)

0900-1240 15585 (Europe), 21540 (C Africa & S Africa), 21610 (Mideast)

1000-1200 M-F *11815* (C America & S America)

1000-1240 21570 (S America), ⒮ M-F 21700 (N America & C America)

1000-1300 ⒲ M-F 17595 (N America & C America)

1100-1240 ⒮ M-F *9765* (C America), M-F *15170* (W North Am)

1200-1240 ⒮ M-F *11815* (C America & S America)

1200-1400 ⒮ Su *9765* (C America), *11910* (SE Asia)

1200-1500 ⒲ Su *5970* (C America), Su *15170* (W North Am & C America), Sa/Su 21700 (C America & S America)

1200-1600 ⒮ Su *11815* & ⒲ Su *15125* (C America & S America)

1240-1255 ⒲ 13720 (W Europe), ⒲ M-F *15170* (W North Am), ⒮ Sa/Su 15585 & ⒲ 15585 (Europe), ⒮ Sa/Su 21540 & ⒲ 21540 (C Africa & S Africa), ⒮ Sa/Su 21570 & ⒲ 21570 (S America),

⒮ Sa/Su 21610 & ⒲ 21610 (Mideast)

1240-1300 ⒮ Sa/Su 13720 (W Europe)

1255-1340 M-F *15170* (W North Am), 15585 (Europe), 21540 (C Africa & S Africa), 21570 (S America), 21610 (Mideast)

1255-1400 ⒮ M-F *9765* (C America)

1300-1340 ⒲ M-F 17595 (N America)

1300-1400 Sa/Su 13720 (W Europe)

1300-1500 ⒮ 17595 (N America)

1340-1355 ⒮ M-F *15170* (W North Am), ⒮ 15585 & ⒲ Sa/Su 15585 (Europe), ⒮ 21540 & ⒲ Sa/Su 21540 (C Africa & S Africa), ⒮ 21570 & ⒲ Sa/Su 21570 (S America), ⒮ 21610 & ⒲ Sa/Su 21610 (Mideast)

1355-1500 M-F 17595 (N America), 21610 (Mideast)

1355-1700 15585 (Europe), 21570 (S America)

1400-1500 ⒮ Sa 15385 (W Africa & C Africa), ⒮ 17755 & ⒲ 21540 (C Africa & S Africa)

1500-1600 Su *9765* (C America), Su *17850* (W North Am)

1500-1700 M-Sa 15385 (W Africa & C Africa), 21610 (Mideast)

1500-1800 21700 (C America & S America)

1500-1900 17755 (C Africa & S Africa)

1600-1800 Sa/Su *9765* (C America), ⒮ Sa/Su *11815* & ⒲ Sa/Su *15125* (C America & S America), Sa/Su *17850* (W North Am)

1700-1900 17715 (S America)

1700-2000 Sa/Su 9665 (Europe)

1700-2300 7275 (Europe)

1800-2000 *9765* (C America), ⒮ *11815* & ⒲ *15125* (C America & S America), *17850* (W North Am)

1800-2100 Sa/Su 21700 (C America & S America)

1800-2230 M-F 21700 (Irr) (C America & S America)

1900-2100 Su 17755 (C Africa & S Africa)

1900-2300	15110 (N America & C America)
2000-2100	◼ Sa 9665 & ◼ Sa/Su 9665 (Europe)
2000-2230	M-F *9765* (Irr) (C America), ◼ M-F *11815* (Irr) & ◼ M-F *15125* (Irr) (C America & S America), M-F *17850* (Irr) (W North Am)
2000-2300	Sa/Su *9765* (C America), ◼ Sa/Su *11815* & ◼ Sa/Su *15125* (C America & S America), Sa/Su *17850* (W North Am)
2100-2200	◼ Sa 9665 (Europe), ◼ M-F 11625 (C Africa)
2100-2300	◼ Sa/Su 21700 (C America & S America)
2200-2300	7270 (N Africa & W Africa), ◼ Sa 11625 (C Africa)
2300-2400	◼ 6125 (S America), 9535 (N America & C America), 9620, ◼ 11680 & ◼ 11945 (S America), ◼ Su *15125* (Irr) & 15160 (C America & S America), Su *17850* (Irr) (W North Am)

SWEDEN—Swedish

RADIO SWEDEN

0000-0030	*9490* (S America)
0030-0100	◼ *6100* (E North Am & C America)
0200-0230 ◼	*6010* (E North Am)
0200-0230	◼ *11550* & ◼ *11675* (S Asia)
0300-0330 ◼	*6010* (W North Am)
0300-0330	◼ *9490* (S America)
0400-0500	◼ M-F 11650 (Mideast & E Africa)
0500-0600	◼ M-F 9490 (Mideast & E Africa)
0500-0700 ◼	M-F 6065 (Europe & N Africa)
0700-0800	◼ M-F 6065 (Europe & N Africa)
0730-0900 ◼	Sa 9490 (Europe & N Africa)
0800-1000 ◼	Su 9490 (Europe & N Africa)
1200-1215	◼ 7420 (E Asia)
1200-1230	◼ 15240 (E North Am & C America)
1215-1230	◼ Sa/Su 7420 (E Asia), ◼ M-F 11550 & ◼ M-F 15735 (E Asia & Australasia)
1300-1315	◼ 11640 & ◼ 15735 (SE Asia & Australasia)
1300-1330	◼ *11670* (N America)
1315-1330	◼ M-F 7420 (E Asia), ◼ Sa/Su 11640 & ◼ Sa/Su 15735 (SE Asia & Australasia)
1400-1430	◼ 11550 (SE Asia), ◼ 11820 (W Asia & S Asia), ◼ 15735 (SE Asia & Australasia)
1500-1530 ◼	15240 (W North Am)
1500-1530	◼ Sa/Su 7440 (Mideast)
1545-1700 ◼	6065 (Europe)
1700-1715 ◼	M-F 6065 (Europe)
1700-1730	◼ 5840 (E Europe), ◼ 7420 (Mideast)
1715-1730 ◼	M-Sa 6065 (Europe)
1800-1830 ◼	Su 6065 (Europe)
1800-1830	◼ 13710 (W Africa)
1900-1930 ◼	6065 (Europe)
1900-1930	◼ 7465 (W Europe & W Africa)
2000-2030 ◼	Su 6065 (Europe)
2000-2030 ◼	*7420* (SE Asia & Australasia)
2100-2130	*7120* (C Africa)
2100-2200	◼ 5840 (W Europe & W Africa)
2100-2230 ◼	6065 (Europe)

SYRIA—Arabic

RADIO DAMASCUS—(S America)

2330-0030	9330/13610 & 12085

THAILAND—Thai

RADIO THAILAND

0100-0200	*5890*/12095 (E North Am)
0230-0330	15275 (W North Am)
1000-1100	◼ 6185 & ◼ 11870 (SE Asia)
1330-1400	◼ 7160 & ◼ 11685 (E Asia)
1800-1900	◼ 9680 & ◼ 11855 (Mideast)
2045-2115	◼ 9535 & ◼ 9680 (Europe)

TUNISIA—Arabic

RTV TUNISIENNE
0200-0500 ☐ 9720 & 12005 (N Africa & Mideast)
0400-0630 ☐ 7275 (W Europe)
0400-0800 ☐ 7190 (N Africa)
1600-1900 ☐ 12005 (N Africa & Mideast)
1600-2100 ☐ 9720 (N Africa & Mideast)
1700-2110 ☐ 7225 (W Europe)
1700-2310 ☐ 7190 (N Africa)

TURKEY—Turkish

VOICE OF TURKEY
0200-0400 ☑ 7180 (C Asia)
0400-0700 ☒ 6040 (Mideast), ☒ 11980 (W Europe)
0500-0800 ☒ 9555 (Mideast), ☑ 9700 (W Europe)
0700-0900 ☒ 11750 (Mideast)
0700-1300 ☒ 15350 (Europe)
0800-1000 ☑ 11925 (Mideast)
0800-1400 ☐ 11955 (N Africa & Mideast)
0900-1300 ☒ 17645 (Australasia)
1000-1400 ☑ 15475 (Australasia)
1400-1630 ☑ 5980 (W Europe)
1530-2100 ☒ 5960 (Mideast), ☒ 9460 (Europe)
1630-2200 ☑ 5980 (W Europe & E North Am), ☑ 6080 & ☑ 6120 (Mideast), ☑ 9560 (Australasia)

UKRAINE—Ukrainian

RADIO UKRAINE INTERNATIONAL
0000-0100 ☐ 7440/5820 (E North Am)
0000-0500 ☒ 7530/5830 (W Asia)
0100-0600 ☑ 5830 (W Asia)
0200-0400 ☐ 7440/5820 (E North Am)
0600-0700 ☒ 9945/7420 (W Europe)
0700-0800 ☑ 7440 (W Europe)
0800-1100 ☒ 11550/9950 (W Europe)
0900-1200 ☑ 9925 (W Europe)
1200-1300 ☒ 11550/9950 (W Europe)
1300-1400 ☑ 9925 (W Europe)
1300-1700 ☒ 7530/5830 (W Asia)
1400-1800 ☑ 5830 (W Asia)
1800-2000 ☒ 7490/5830 (W Europe)
1900-2100 ☑ 5840 (W Europe)
2200-2300 ☒ 7510/5830 (W Europe)
2300-2400 ☑ 5840 (W Europe)

Trans World Radio's five-tower antenna array allows signals to be beamed to five different locations. TWR

VIETNAM—Vietnamese

VOICE OF VIETNAM
0000-0100 7285 (SE Asia)
0000-1600 5925, 5975, 7210, 9530
0130-0230 *6175* (E North Am & C America)
0150-1000 9875
0430-0530 *6175* (N America & C America)
1500-1600 7220 & 9550 (W Africa & C Africa)
1600-1700 F 5975, F 9530
1700-1800 7280 & 9730 (Europe)
1730-1830 ☒ *9725* (W Europe)
1830-1930 ☑ *5955* (W Europe)
1930-2030 ☒ *9725* (S Europe)
2030-2130 ☑ *5970* (S Europe)
2200-2400 5925, 5975, 7210, 9530

YEMEN—Arabic

REPUBLIC OF YEMEN RADIO—(Mideast)
0300-0650 9780
0300-1500 5950 & 6135
1700-1800 &
1900-2208 9780

Worldly Words

PASSPORT's Ultimate Glossary of World Band and Kindred Terms and Abbreviations

A variety of terms and abbreviations are used in world band parlance. Many are specialized and benefit from explanation; some are foreign words that need translation; while others are simply adaptations of everyday usage.

Here, then, is PASSPORT's A–Z guide to world band words and what they mean to your listening. For a thorough understanding of the specialized terms and lab tests used in evaluating world band radios, read the Radio Database International White Paper, *How to Interpret Receiver Lab Tests and Measurements*.

A

A. Summer schedule season for world band stations, typically valid from the last Sunday in March until the last Sunday in October. *See* ◨. *See* HFCC. *Cf.* B, ◪.

Absorption. Reduction in signal strength during bounces (refraction) off the earth's ionosphere (*see* Propagation) or the earth itself.

AC. Alternating ("household" or "mains") Current, 120V throughout North America, 100V in Japan and usually 220–240V elsewhere in the world.

AC Adaptor. Commonplace outboard device—"wall wart" or "pig in the anaconda"—that converts utility/mains current (*see* AC) to DC suitable for a given electronic or electrical device, such as a portable radio. AC input can be single-voltage, dual-voltage or automatic universal voltage; DC output needs to be of the correct voltage, center-tip polarity and minimum amperage to power the desired radio or other device. Finally, AC adaptors convert AC to DC using either a transformer or switching circuitry, but switching tends to cause RFI that can bother radio reception. Better AC adaptors 1) don't cause audible hum in the companion radio, 2) tend to be regulated, and 3) are UL and/or CE approved for fire safety.

Active Antenna. An antenna that electronically amplifies signals. Active, or amplified, antennas are typically mounted indoors, but some weatherproofed models can also be erected outdoors. Active antennas take up relatively little space, but their amplification circuits may introduce certain problems that can result in unwanted sounds being heard (*see* Dynamic Range). *Cf.* Passive Antenna. *See* Feedline.

Adjacent-Channel Interference. *See* Interference.

Adjacent-Channel Rejection. *See* Selectivity.

AGC. *See* Automatic Gain Control.

AGC Threshold. The threshold at which the automatic gain control (AGC, *see*) chooses to act relates to both listening pleasure and audible sensitivity. If the threshold is too low, the AGC will tend to act on internal receiver noise and minor static, desensitizing the receiver. However, if the threshold is too high, variations in loudness will be uncomfortable to the ear, forcing the listener to manually twiddle with the volume control to do, in effect, what the AGC should be doing automatically. Measured in μV (microvolts).

Alt. Freq. Alternative frequency or channel. Frequency or channel which may be used in place of that which is regularly scheduled.

Amateur Radio. *See* Hams.

AM Band. The 520–1705 kHz radio broadcast band that lies within the 0.3–3.0 MHz (300–3,000 kHz) mediumwave (MW) or Medium Frequency (MF) portion of the radio spectrum. Outside North America it is usually called the mediumwave (MW) band. However, in parts of Latin America it is sometimes called, by the general public and a few stations, *onda larga*—longwave band (*see*)—strictly speaking, a misnomer. In the United States, travelers information stations (TIS) and other public information services are sometimes also found on 1710 kHz, making 1715 kHz the *de facto* upper limit of the American AM band. *See* X-Band.

AM Equivalent (AME). *See* Single Sideband (third paragraph).

AM Mode. *See* Mode.

Amplified Antenna. *See* Active Antenna.

Analog Frequency Readout. This type of received-frequency indication is used on radios having needle-and-dial or "slide-rule" tuning. This is much less accurate and handy than digital frequency readout. *See* Synthesizer. *Cf.* Digital Frequency Display.

Antenna. *See* Active Antenna, Feedline, Passive Antenna.

Antennae. The accepted spelling for feelers protruding from insects. In electronics, the preferred plural for "antenna" is "antennas."

Antenna Polarization. *See* Polarization.

Arrestor. *See* MOV.

ATS. Automatic Tuning System; also, Auto Tuning Scan. Allows a receiver, while scanning up or down frequencies, to enter active frequencies into presets automatically, like when setting up a VCR or DVD recorder.

Attenuator. A circuit, typically switched with one or more levels, to desensitize a receiver by reducing the strength of incoming signals. *See* RF Gain.

Audio Quality. At PASSPORT, audio quality refers to what in computer testing is called "benchmark" quality. This means, primarily, the freedom from distortion of a signal fed through a receiver's entire circuitry—*not* just the audio stage—from the antenna input through to the speaker terminals. A lesser characteristic of audio quality is the audio bandwidth needed for pleasant world band reception of music. Also, *see* Enhanced Fidelity.

Automatic Gain Control (AGC). Smooths out fluctuations in signal strength brought about by fading (*see*), a regular occurrence with world band signals, so a receiver's audio level tends to stay relatively constant. This is accomplished by AGC attack, then AGC hang, and finally AGC decay. Each of these three actions involved in smoothing a fade has a micro-time preset at the factory for optimum performance. Top-end receivers often provide for user control of at least the decay timing—a few rarified models also allow for user control over one or both of the other two actions. *See* AGC Threshold.

Auto Tuning Scan. *See* ATS.

Automatic Tuning System. *See* ATS.

AV. A Voz—Portuguese for "The Voice." In PASSPORT, this term is also used to represent "The Voice of."

B

B. Winter schedule season for world band stations, typically valid from the last Sunday in October until the last Sunday in March. *See* ◪. *See* HFCC. *Cf.* A, ◨.

Balun. BALanced-to-UNbalanced device to match the two. Typically, a balun is placed between an unbalanced antenna feedline and a balanced antenna input, or *vice versa*.

Bands, Shortwave Broadcasting. *See* World Band Segments.

Bandwidth. A key variable that determines selectivity (*see*), bandwidth is the amount of radio signal, at –6 dB (–3 dB with *i.a.* professional gear), a radio's circuitry will let pass, and thus be heard. With world band channel spacing standardized at 5 kHz, the best single bandwidths are usually in the vicinity of 3 to 6 kHz. Better radios offer two or more selectable bandwidths: at least one of 5 to 9 kHz or so for when a station is in the clear, and one or more others between 2 to 6 kHz for when a station is hemmed in by other signals next to it; with synchronous selectable sideband (*see* Synchronous Detector), these bandwidths can safely be at the upper ends of these ranges to provide enhanced fidelity. Proper selectivity is a key determinant of the aural quality of what you hear, and some newer models of tabletop receivers have dozens of bandwidths.

Bandscanning. Hunting around for stations by continuously tuning up and/or down a given world band segment (*see*), such as in concert with PASSPORT's Blue Pages.

Baud. Measurement of the speed by which radioteletype (*see*), radiofax (*see*) and other digital data are transmitted. Baud is properly written entirely in lower case, and thus is abbreviated as b (baud), kb (kilobaud) or Mb (Megabaud). Baud rate standards are usually set by the international CCITT regulatory body.

BC. Broadcaster, Broadcasters, Broadcasting, Broadcasting Company, Broadcasting Corporation.

BCB (Broadcast Band). *See* AM Band.

Beverage Antenna. *See* Longwire Antenna.

Shutterstock/Anyka

BFO (beat-frequency oscillator). Carrier generated within a receiver. *Inter alia*, this replaces a received signal's full or vestigial transmitted carrier when a receiver is in the single-sideband mode *(see)* or synchronous selectable mode *(see)*.

Birdie. A silent spurious signal, similar to a station's open carrier, created by circuit interaction within a receiver. The fewer and weaker the birdies within a receiver's tuning range, the better, although in reality birdies rarely degrade reception.

Blocking. The ability of a receiver to avoid being desensitized by powerful adjacent signals or signals from other nearby frequencies. Measured in dB (decibels) at 100 kHz signal spacing.

BNC (British Naval Connector, Bayonet Nut Connector, Bayonet Neill Concelman). Reliable-performance, quick-connect/disconnect coaxial cable connector as defined by the IEC 169-8 standard. One of the three most common low-impedance (around 75 ohm) coax fittings used *i.a.* to connect world band and kindred outboard antenna lead-ins *(see)* to a receiver (typically tabletop or professional).

Boat Anchor. Radio slang for a classic or vintage tube-type communications receiver. These large, heavy biceps builders—Jackie Gleason called them "real radios"—were manufactured mainly from before World War II through the mid-1970s, although a few continued to be available up to a decade later. The definitive reference for collectors of elder receivers is *Shortwave Receivers Past & Present* by Universal Radio.

BPL. Broadband over Power Lines. Emerging technology to allow Internet and other digital communication via AC (mains) power grids. Thus far it has seen only limited use, offering throughput faster than that of dial-up but slower than that of broadband. A major side effect is noise *(see)* radiation, which seriously disrupts traditional and DRM *(see)* world band radio reception. From the perspective of enhanced government oversight this is a positive tradeoff, as it blots out relatively unfettered world band information and replaces it with controllable Internet links.

Broadcast. A radio or television transmission meant for the general public. *Cf.* Utility Stations, Hams.

BS. Broadcasting Station, Broadcasting Service.

Buzz. Noise typically generated by digital electronic circuitry. *See* Noise.

C

Can. Metal container for reel of tape or film. It continues to be used today in the expression, "It's in the can," meaning that a shooting, recording or other task has been completed.

Cans. Vintage slang for "headphones."

Carrier. *See* Mode.

Cd. Ciudad—Spanish for "City."

Cellular Telephone Bands. In the United States, the cellular telephone bands are 824–849 and 869–894 MHz. Years ago, when analog cell transmissions were the norm, a powerful senator was overheard engaged in an awkward conversation. Shortly thereafter, receivers which could tune cellular frequencies were made illegal in the United States. As a practical matter, eavesdropping on these bands yields nothing intelligible because of the encrypted nature of digital cellular transmissions that by now have all but replaced analog. Receivers tuning these "forbidden" ranges are readily acquired in Canada and nearly every other part of the world except North Korea.

Channel. An everyday term to indicate where a station is supposed to be located on the dial. World band channels are standardized at 5 kHz spacing. Stations operating outside this norm are "off-channel" (for these, PASSPORT provides resolution to better than 1 kHz to aid in station identification).

CINCH/AV. *See* RCA.

Chuffing, Chugging. The sound made by some synthesized tuning systems when the tuning knob is turned. Called "chugging" or "chuffing," as it is suggestive of the rhythmic "chuf, chuf" sound of steam locomotives or "chugalug" gulping of beverages.

Cl. Club, Clube.

Co-Channel Interference. *See* Interference.

CODEC (Compression, Decompression). A given proprietary or industry standard—there are many—that takes a native file or signal and converts (compresses) it into a smaller file or narrower signal without undue loss of quality.

Coordinated Universal Time. *See* UTC, World Time.

Cult. Cultura, Cultural.

Curtain Antennas. Often used for long-distance world band transmitting, these consist of horizontal dipole arrays interconnected and typically strung between a pair of masts or towers that are usually fixed, but which sometimes can be rotated. Curtains produce excellent forward gain, reasonable directivity and a low takeoff angle that is desirable for successful long-distance broadcasts. *See* Polarization.

CW. Continuous wave, or telegraph-type ("Morse code," etc.) communication by telegraph key that opens and closes an unmodulated signal to create variations of long and short bursts that on a radio with a BFO *(see)* sound like dih-dah "beeps." Used mainly by hams *(see)*, occasionally by utility stations *(see)*.

D

DAB. Digital audio broadcasting, typically referring to a digital system, not compatible with analog receivers, used for domestic broadcasting in Europe and various other parts of the world. *Cf.* Digital Radio Mondiale, HD Radio.

dBm. Logarithmic unit of power in decibels above the reference level of 1 milliwatt. An increase of 10 dBm represents a tenfold increase in power.

dB. *see* Decibel.

dBm. Logarithmic unit of power in decibels (dB) above the reference level of one milliwatt (mW). An increase of 10 dBm represents a tenfold increase in power.

DC. Direct current, such as emanates from batteries. *Cf.* AC.

DC-to-Daylight. Hyperbolic slang for an exceptionally wide frequency tuning range. For example, some wideband receivers will tune from under 10 kHz to over 3 GHz *(see)*. However, in the United States it is illegal to sell new radios to the public that tune the cellular telephone bands *(see)*.

Decibel (dB). Logarithmic measurement of the ratio between two quantities; *e.g.*, signal-to-noise ratio.

Default. The setting at which a control of a digitally operated electronic device, including many world band radios, normally operates, and to which it will eventually return (e.g., when the radio is next switched on).

Digital Frequency Display, Digital Frequency Readout. Indicates that a receiver displays the tuned frequency digitally, usually in kilohertz *(see)*. Because this is so much handier than an analog frequency readout, all models included in Passport Reports have digital frequency readout. Most models with digital frequency display are synthesizer *(see)* tuned, but some low-cost models are analog tuned.

Digital Radio Mondiale (DRM). International organization (www.drm.org) seeking to convert world band and other transmissions from traditional analog mode to DRM digital mode, which is now in limited regular use. DRM transmissions cannot be received on traditional analog receivers. Also, DRM transmissions—unlike the conventional analog variety—are easily jammed and otherwise disrupted by interference. *See* Mode, Interference. *Cf.* DAB, HD Radio.

Digital Signal Processing (DSP). Where digital circuitry and software are used to perform radio circuit functions traditionally done using analog circuits. Used on certain world band receivers; also, available as an add-on accessory for audio processing only.

Dipole. Center fed, usually passive *(see)*, antenna with two or more lengths of wire or other metal on either side of the feeder wire or cable. A simple dipole is half a wavelength, with limited effectiveness beyond a relatively narrow slice of frequencies as defined by doubling its half-wavelength. However, dipoles equipped with traps have a much broader range of covered frequencies. *See* Trap Dipole Antenna.

Distortion. *See* Overall Distortion.

Domestic Service. *See* DS.

Double Conversion a/k/a **Dual Conversion.** *See* IF.

DRM. *See* Digital Radio Mondiale.

DS. Domestic Service—Broadcasting intended primarily for audiences in the broadcaster's home country. However, some domestic programs are beamed on world band to expatriates and other kinfolk abroad, as well as to interested foreigners. *Cf.* ES.

DSP. *See* Digital Signal Processing.

Dual Conversion a/k/a/ **Double Conversion.** *See* IF.

DX, DXers, DXing. From an old telegraph abbreviation for distance (D) unknown (X); thus, to DX is to communicate over a great distance. DXers are those who specialize in finding distant or exotic stations that are considered to be rare catches. Few world band listeners are considered to be regular DXers, but many others seek out DX stations every now and then—usually by bandscanning, which is facilitated by Passport's Blue Pages.

DXpedition. Typically, a gathering of DXers who camp out in a remote location favorable to catching the toughest of stations. These DX bases are usually far away from electrically noisy AC power and cable TV lines.

Dynamic Range. The ability of, *i.a.*, a receiver or active antenna *(see)* to handle weak signals in the presence of strong competing signals within or near the same world band segment *(see* World Band Spectrum). Devices with inferior dynamic range sometimes "overload," especially with external antennas, causing a mishmash of false signals up and down—and even beyond—the segment being received. Dynamic range is closely related to the third-order intercept point, or IP3. Where possible, Passport measures dynamic range and IP3 at the traditional 20 kHz and more challenging 5 kHz signal-separation, or signal spacing, points.

E

Earliest Heard (or Latest Heard). See key at the bottom of each Blue Page. If the Passport monitoring team cannot establish the definite sign-on (or sign-off) time of a station, the earliest (or latest) time that the station could be traced is indicated by a left-facing or right-facing "arrowhead flag."

This means that the station almost certainly operates beyond the time shown by that "flag." It also means that, unless you live relatively close to the station, you're unlikely to be able to hear it beyond that "flagged" time.

EBS. Economic Broadcasting Station, a type of broadcast operation in China.

ECSS (Exalted-Carrier Selectable Sideband). Manual tuning of a conventional AM-mode signal, using a receiver's single-sideband circuitry to zero-beat *(see)* the receiver's BFO with the transmitted signal's carrier. The better-sounding of the signal's sidebands is then selected by the listener. As ECSS is manual, there is a degree, however slight, of phase mismatch between the fade-prone transmitted carrier and the stable synthetic replacement carrier generated within the receiver. *Cf.* Synchronous Selectable Sideband, Synchronous Detector.

Ed, Educ. Educational, Educação, Educadora.

Electrical Noise. *See* Noise.

Elevation Panel, Elevation Rod. Plastic panel or metal rod which flips out from a radio's back or bottom panel to place the radio at a comfortable operating angle.

Elevation Tab. Plastic tab, typically affixed to a portable radio's carrying strap, which when inserted into the radio's back panel places the radio at a comfortable operating angle.

Em. Emissora, Emisora, Emissor, Emetteur—in effect, "station" in various languages.

Enhanced Fidelity. Radios with good audio performance and certain types of high-tech circuitry can improve the fidelity of world band signals. Among the newer fidelity-enhancing techniques is synchronous detection *(see* Synchronous Detector), especially when coupled with selectable sideband. Another technological means to improve fidelity is digital world band transmission, which is currently being implemented *(see* Digital Radio Mondiale).

EP. Emissor Provincial—Portuguese for "Provincial Station."

ER. Emissor Regional—Portuguese for "Regional Station."

Ergonomics. How handy and comfortable—intuitive—a set is to operate, especially hour after hour.

ES. External Service—Broadcasting intended primarily for audiences abroad. *Cf.* DS.

Exalted-Carrier Selectable Sideband. *See* ECSS.

External Service. *See* ES.

F

F. Friday.

Fading. Signals which scatter off the ionosphere *(see* Propagation) are subject to some degree of phase mismatch as the scattered bits of signal arrive at a receiver at minutely varying times. This causes fading, where signal strength varies anywhere from a few times per minute to many times per second, the latter being known as "flutter fading" and often caused by disruption of the earth's geomagnetic field *(see* Great Circle Path). "Selective fading" is a special type that is audible on shortwave and mediumwave AM when a fade momentarily sweeps across a signal's three components (lower sideband, carrier, upper sideband), attenuating the carrier more than the sidebands; with the carrier thus attenuated, the result is "selective-fading distortion." *See* Automatic Gain Control, Propagation, Synchronous Detection.

Fax. *See* Radiofax.

Feeder, Shortwave. A utility *(see)* shortwave transmission from the broadcaster's home country to a shortwave or other relay site or local placement facility *(see)* some distance away. Although these specialized transmissions carry world band programs, they are not intended to be received by the general public. Many world band radios can process these quasi-broadcasts anyway. Shortwave feeders operate in lower sideband (LSB), upper sideband (USB) or independent sideband (termed ISL if heard on the lower side, ISU if heard on the upper side) modes. Feeders are now via satellites and Internet audio, but a few stations keep shortwave feeders in reserve should their satellite/Internet feeders fail. *See* Single Sideband, Utility Stations, NBFM.

Feedline. The wire or cable that runs between an antenna's receiving element(s) and a receiver. For sophisticated antennas, twin-lead ribbon feedlines are unusually efficient, and can reject much nearby electrical noise via phasing. However, coaxial cable feedlines are generally superior in high-local-electrical-noise environments. *See* Balun.

First IF Rejection. A relatively uncommon source of false signals occurs when powerful transmitters operate on the same frequency as a receiver's first intermediate frequency (IF). The ability of receiving circuitry to avoid such transmitters' causing reception problems is called "IF rejection."

Flutter Fading. *See* Fading.

FM. The FM broadcast band is now standardized at 87.5–108 MHz worldwide except in Japan (76–90 MHz) and parts of Eastern Europe (66–74 MHz). Also, for communications there is a special FM mode (*see* NBFM).

Frequency. The standard term to indicate where a station is located within the radio spectrum—regardless of whether it is "on-channel" or "off-channel" (*see* Channel). Below 30 MHz this is customarily expressed in kilohertz (kHz, *see*), but some receivers display in Megahertz (MHz, *see*). These differ only in the placement of a decimal; e.g., 5970 kHz is the same as 5.97 MHz. Either measurement is equally valid, but to minimize confusion PASSPORT and most stations designate frequencies only in kHz. *Cf.* Meters.

Frequency Synthesizer. *See* Synthesizer, Frequency.

Front-End Selectivity. The ability of the initial stage of receiving circuitry to admit only limited frequency ranges into succeeding stages of circuitry. Good front-end selectivity keeps signals from other, powerful bands or segments from being superimposed upon the frequency range you're tuning. For example, a receiver with good front-end selectivity will receive only shortwave signals at full strength within the range 3200–3400 kHz. However, a receiver with mediocre front-end selectivity might allow powerful local mediumwave AM stations from 520–1700 kHz to be heard "ghosting in" between 3200 and 3400 kHz, along with the desired shortwave signals. Obviously, mediumwave AM signals don't belong on shortwave. Receivers with inadequate front-end selectivity can benefit from the addition of a preselector (*see*) or a high-pass filter (*see*).

G

GHz. Gigahertz, equivalent to 1,000 MHz (*see*).

GMT. Greenwich Mean Time. *See* World Time.

Great Circle Path. The shortest route a signal takes to arrive at a receiving location, following the circumference of the earth. Normal printed maps are too distorted for this purpose, but an ideal solution is to take a globe and run a string from a station's transmitter site (*see* PASSPORT's Blue Pages) to your location. Among other things, the closer a signal's path is to the geomagnetic North Pole, the greater the chance of its being disrupted by flutter fading (*see* Fading) during geomagnetic propagational disturbances (*see* Propagation). An Internet search can turn up several software programs to generate great circle maps centered at your location, but for most a globe and string are more visually intuitive.

GUI. Graphical user interface for operating PCs and related hardware.

H

Hams. Government-licensed amateur radio hobbyists who *transmit* to each other by radio, often by voice using single sideband (*see*), within special amateur bands. Many of these

bands are within the shortwave spectrum (*see*). This spectrum is also used by world band radio, but world band radio and ham radio, which laymen sometimes confuse with each other, are two very separate entities. The easiest way is to think of hams as making something like phone calls, whereas world band stations are like long-distance versions of ordinary mediumwave AM stations.

Harmonic, Harmonic Radiation, Harmonic Signal. Usually, an unwanted weak spurious repeat of a signal in multiple(s) of the fundamental, or "real," frequency. Thus, the third harmonic of a mediumwave AM station on 1120 kHz might be heard faintly on 4480 kHz within the world band spectrum. Stations almost always try to minimize harmonic radiation, as it wastes energy and spectrum space. However, in rare cases stations have been known to amplify a harmonic signal so they can operate inexpensively on a second frequency. Also, *see* Subharmonic.

Hash. Electrical buzzing noise. *See* Noise.

HD Radio. Digital broadcasting system that is receivable with limited fidelity on traditional analog radios, and with full fidelity on HD receivers. Used primarily on AM/FM in the United States. *Cf.* DAB, Digital Radio Mondiale.

Hertz. *See* Hz.

Heterodyne. A whistle equal in pitch to the separation between two carriers. Thus, two world band stations 5 kHz apart will generate a 5000 Hz whistle unless receiver circuitry (e.g., *see* Notch Filter) keeps this from being audible.

High Fidelity. *See* Enhanced Fidelity.

High-Pass Filter. A filter which lets frequencies pass unattenuated only if they are above a designated frequency. For world band receivers and antennas, 2 MHz or thereabouts is the norm for high-pass filters, as this keeps out mediumwave AM and longwave signals.

HF (High Frequency). Shortwave. *See* Shortwave Spectrum.

HFCC (High Frequency Co-ordination Conference). Founded in 1990 and headquartered in Prague, the HFCC (www.hfcc.org) helps coordinate frequency usage by dozens of broadcasting organizations from numerous countries. These represent a solid majority of the global output for international shortwave broadcasting. Coordination meetings take place twice yearly: once for the "A" (summer) schedule season from the last Sunday in March until the last Sunday in October, another for "B" (winter), and these gatherings have been a great help in preventing frequency conflicts.

Hz. Hertz, a unit of frequency measurement formerly known as cycles per second (c/s). A thousand Hertz is equivalent to 1 kHz (*see*). Also, *see* Frequency, Meters, MHz.

I

IBS. International Broadcasting Services, Ltd., publishers of PASSPORT TO WORLD BAND RADIO.

IF (Intermediate Frequency). Virtually all world band receivers use the "superheterodyne" principle, where tuned radio frequencies are converted to a single intermediate frequency to facilitate reception, then amplified and detected to produce audio. In virtually all world band portables and most tabletop models, this frequency is either 455 kHz or 450 kHz. If this is not complemented by a second and higher intermediate frequency (double conversion), "images" readily occur at twice the IF; i.e., 910 kHz or 900 kHz. *See* Image.

IF Shift. *See* Passband Offset.

Image. A common type of spurious signal found on low-cost "single conversion" (single IF) radios where a strong signal appears at reduced strength, usually on a frequency 910 kHz or 900 kHz lower down. For example, the BBC on 5875 kHz might repeat on 4965 kHz, its "image frequency." Double-conversion (two IF) receivers have little problem with images, but the additional IF circuitry adds to manufacturing cost. *See* IF, Spurious-Signal Rejection.

Impedance. Opposition, expressed in ohms, to the flow of alternating current. Components work best when impedance is comparable from one to another; so, for example, a receiver with a 75-ohm antenna socket will work best with antennas having a similar feedline impedance. Antenna tuning units can resolve this, albeit at the cost of added operational complexity.

Independent Sideband. *See* Single Sideband.

Interference. Sounds from other signals, notably on the same frequency ("co-channel interference"), or on an adjacent or other nearby channel(s) ("adjacent-channel interference"), that disturb the station you are trying to hear; DRM *(see)* signals cause interference over a wider frequency range than do conventional analog signals. Worthy radios reduce interference by having good selectivity *(see)* and synchronous selectable sideband *(see* Synchronous Detector). Nearby television sets and cable television wiring may also generate a special type of radio interference called TVI, a "growl," typically from a television horizontal oscillator, heard every 15 kHz or so. Sometimes referred to as QRM, a term based on Morse-code shorthand.

Intermediate Frequency. *See* IF.

International Reply Coupon (IRC). Sold by selected post offices in most parts of the world, IRCs amount to official international "scrip" that may be exchanged for postage in most countries of the world. Because they amount to an international form of postage repayment, over many decades they have been handy for listeners trying to encourage foreign stations to write them back. However, IRCs are very costly for the amount in stamps that is provided in return. Too, an increasing number of countries are not forthcoming about "cashing in" IRCs, which are fading from general use. Specifics on this and related matters are provided in the Addresses PLUS section of this PASSPORT.

International Telecommunication Union (ITU). The regulatory body, headquartered in Geneva, for all international telecommunications, including world band radio. Sometimes incorrectly referred to as the "International Telecommunications Union." In recent years, the ITU has become increasingly ineffective as a regulatory body for world band radio, with much of its former role having been taken up by the HFCC *(see)*.

Internet Radio. *See* Web radio.

Inverted-L Antenna. *See* Passive Antenna.

Ionosphere. *See* Propagation.

IP3. Third-order intercept point. *See* Dynamic Range.

IRC. *See* International Reply Coupon.

Irr. Irregular operation or hours of operation; i.e., schedule tends to be unpredictable.

ISB. Independent sideband. *See* Single Sideband.

ISL. Independent sideband, lower. *See* Feeder.

ISO. International Organization for Standardization.

ISU. Independent sideband, upper. *See* Feeder.

ITU. *See* International Telecommunication Union.

J

Jack. Counterintuitive, perhaps, but a female connector.

Jamming. Deliberate interference to a transmission with the intent of discouraging listening. However, analog shortwave broadcasts, when properly transmitted, are uniquely resistant to jamming. This ability to avoid "gatekeeping" is a major reason why traditional shortwave continues to be the workhorse for international broadcasting. Jamming is practiced now much less than it was during the Cold War. The main exception is China, where superpower transmitters and rotatable curtain antennas from France are increasingly being used to disrupt world band broadcasts.

K

Keypad. On a world band radio, like a cell phone, a keypad can be used to control many variables. Radio keypads are used primarily so you can enter a station's frequency for reception, and the best keypads have real keys (not a membrane) in the standard telephone format of 3x4 with "zero" under the "8" key. Many keypads are also used for presets, but this means you have to remember code numbers for stations (e.g., BBC 5975 kHz is "07"); handier radios have separate keys for presets, while some others use LCD-displayed "pages" to access presets.

kHz. Kilohertz, the most common unit of frequency for measuring where a station is located on the world band dial if it is below 30,000 kHz. Formerly known as "kilocycles per second," or kc/s. 1,000 kilohertz equals one Megahertz. *See* Frequency. *Cf.* MHz, Meters.

kilohertz. *See* kHz. The "k" in "kilo" is not properly capitalized, although the computer modem industry got it wrong years back and most modem and kindred organizations have as yet to correct the error.

kilowatt. *See* kW.

kW. A kilowatt(s), the most common unit of measurement for transmitter power *(see* Power).

L

LCD. Liquid-crystal display. LCDs, if properly designed, are fairly easily seen in bright light, but require illumination under darker conditions. LCDs—typically monochrome and gray on gray—also tend to have mediocre contrast, and sometimes can be read from only a certain angle or angles, but they consume nearly no battery power.

Lead-in. Wire, twinlead or coaxial cable between an antenna's capture element (the "antenna" itself that catches signals from the air) and a receiver.

LED. Light-emitting diode. LEDs have a long life and are very easily read in the dark or in normal room light, but consume more battery power than LCDs and are hard to read in bright ambient light.

Lightning Arrestor. *See* MOV.

Line Output. Fixed-level audio output typically used to feed a recorder or outboard audio amplifier-speaker system.

Location. Physical location. In the case of a radio station, the transmitter location, which is what is cited in PASSPORT's Blue Pages, may be different from that of the studio location. Transmitter location is useful as a guide to reception quality. For example, if you're in eastern North America and wish to listen to the Voice of Russia, a transmitter located in St. Petersburg will almost certainly provide better reception than, say, one located in Siberia.

Longwave (LW) Band. The 148.5–283.5 kHz portion of the low-frequency (LF) radio spectrum used for domestic broadcasting in Europe, the Near East, North Africa, Russia and Mongolia. As a practical matter, these longwave signals, which have nothing to do with world band or other shortwave signals, are not readily audible in other parts of the world.

Longwire Antenna. A passive antenna *(see)* that is at least one wavelength at the lowest desired reception frequency. A variant is the Beverage antenna, preferably one-and-a-half to two wavelengths at the lowest desired reception frequency, mounted not far from the ground and with a terminating resistor at the far end.

Loop Antenna. Round (like a hula hoop) or square-ish antenna often used for reception of longwave, mediumwave AM and even shortwave signals. These can be highly directive below around 2 MHz, and can even show some directivity up to 5 MHz or 6 MHz. For this reason, most such antennas can be rotated and even tilted manually—or by an antenna

Prague monastery's library is a treat for the eyes.

Shutterstock/Filip Fuxa

rotor. "Barefoot" loops tend to have low gain, and thus need electrical amplification in order to reach their potential. When properly mounted, top-caliber amplified loops can produce superior signal-to-noise ratios that help with weak-signal (DX) reception.

☞ Strictly speaking, ferrite-rod antennas, found inside nearly every mediumwave AM radio as well as some specialty outboard antennas, are not loops. However, in everyday parlance these tiny antennas are often referred to as "loops" or "loopsticks."

Low-Pass Filter. A filter which lets frequencies pass unattenuated only if they are below a designated frequency. For world band receivers and antennas, 30 MHz or thereabouts is the norm for low-pass filters, as this keeps out VHF/UHF signals.

LSB. Lower Sideband. *See* Mode, Single Sideband, Feeder.

LV. La Voix, La Voz—French and Spanish for "The Voice." In PASSPORT, this term is also used to represent "The Voice of."

LW. *See* Longwave (LW) Band.

M

M. Monday.

Mains. *See* AC.

Manual Selectable Sideband. *See* ECSS.

Mediumwave Band, Mediumwave AM Band, Mediumwave Spectrum. *See* AM Band.

Megahertz. *See* MHz.

Memory, Memories. *See* Preset.

Meters (Wavelength). An elder unit of measurement used *i.a.* for individual world band segments of the shortwave spectrum. The frequency range covered by a given meters designation—also known as "wavelength"—can be gleaned from the following formula: *frequency (kHz) = 299,792 divided by meters*. Thus, 49 meters comes out to a frequency of 6118 kHz—well within the range of frequencies included in that segment (*see* World Band Spectrum). Inversely, wavelength in meters can be derived from the following: *wavelength (meters) = 299,792 divided by frequency (kHz)*.

☞ The figure 299,792 is based on the speed of light (299,792,458 m/s) as agreed upon by the International Committee on Weights and Measurements in 1983. However, in practice this fumbling figure is rounded to 300,000 for computational purposes. Thus, in everyday practice the two formulas are: *frequency (kHz) = 300,000 divided by meters*; *wavelength (meters) = 300,000 divided by frequency (kHz)*.

MHz. Megahertz, a common unit of frequency *(see)* to measure where a station is located on the dial, especially above 30 MHz, although in the purest sense all measurements above 3 MHz

are supposed to be in MHz. In earlier days of radio this was known as "Megacycles per second," or Mc/s. One Megahertz equals 1,000 kilohertz. *See* Frequency. *Cf.* kHz, Meters.

Mini-Plug (male), Mini-Jack (female). Low-impedance (around 50–75 ohm) 1/8-inch (3 mm) connector, usually for lightweight headphones or earpieces. These may be stereo or mono.

Mode. Method of transmission of radio signals. World band radio broadcasts are almost always in the analog AM (amplitude modulation) mode, the same mode used in the mediumwave AM band *(see)*. The AM mode consists of three components: two "sidebands," plus one "carrier" that resides between the two sidebands. Each sideband contains the same programming as the other, and the carrier carries no programming, so a few stations have experimented with the single-sideband (SSB, *see*) mode. SSB contains only one sideband, either the lower sideband (LSB) or upper sideband (USB), and a reduced carrier. It requires special radio circuitry to be demodulated, or made intelligible, which is the main reason SSB is unlikely to be widely adopted as a world band mode. However, major efforts are currently underway to implement digital-mode world band transmissions (*see* Digital Radio Mondiale).

☞ There are yet other modes used on shortwave, but not for world band. These include CW (Morse-type code, *see*), radiofax *(see)* and RTTY (radioteletype, *see*) used by utility *(see)* and ham *(see)* stations. A variant FM mode, narrow-band FM (NBFM, *see*), is also used by utility and ham operations; however, it is not for music or within the FM broadcast bands (*see* FM).

Modulation. The sounds contained within a radio signal.

MOV. Often used in power-line and antenna surge arrestors (a/k/a lightning arrestors) to shunt static and line-power surges to ground. MOVs perform well and are inexpensive, but tend to lose effectiveness with use; costlier alternatives are thus sometimes worth considering. On rare occasion they also appear to have been implicated in starting fires, so a UL or other recognized certification is helpful. For both these reasons MOV-based arrestors should be replaced at least once every decade that they are in service. *See* Surge Arrestor.

MW. Mediumwave AM band; *see* AM Band. Also, Megawatt, which equals 1,000 kW; *cf.* kilowatt; *see* Power.

N

N. New, Nueva, Nuevo, Nouvelle, Nacional, National, Nationale.

Nac. Nacional. Spanish and Portuguese for "National."

Narrow-band FM. *See* NBFM, Mode.

Nat, Natl, Nat'l. National, Nationale.

NB. *See* Noise Blanker.

NBFM. Narrow-band FM, used within the shortwave spectrum by some "utility" stations, including (between 25–30 MHz) point-to-point broadcast station remote links. *See* Mode.

NTSC (National Television Standards Committee). Traditional analog TV/video format with 525 lines per frame. This broadcast standard has long been used in United States, Canada, Japan and various other countries, but is being phased out in favor of digital HDTV. Once this phase-out is completed by decade's end, multiband radios that include "TV audio" will no longer perform this function. The same applies to such other analog video standards as PAL and SECAM.

Noise. Static, buzzes, pops and the like caused by the earth's atmosphere (typically lightning), and to a lesser extent by galactic noise. Also, electrical noise emanating from such man-made sources as electric blankets, fish-tank heaters, heating pads, electrical and gasoline motors, light dimmers, flickering light bulbs, non-incandescent lights, computers and computer peripherals, office machines, electric fences, electric utility wiring—especially with BPL (*see*)—and related components. Sometimes referred to as QRN, a term based on Morse-code shorthand.

Noise Blanker. Receiver circuit, often found on costly tabletop and professional models, that reduces the impact of pulse-type electrical noises (nearby light dimmers, etc.) or certain unusual types of pulse transmissions. In practice, these circuits use long-established designs which act only on pulses which are greater in strength than the received signal, although designs without this limitation exist on paper.

Noise Floor. *See* Sensitivity.

Notch Filter, Tunable. A feature found on some tabletop and professional receivers for reducing or rejecting annoying heterodyne *(see)* interference—the whistles, howls and squeals for which shortwave has traditionally been notorious. Some notch filters operate within the IF *(see)* stage, whereas others operate as audio filters. IF notch filters tend to respond exceptionally well where there is fading, whereas audio filters usually have more capacity to attack higher-pitched heterodynes.

O

Other. Programs are in a language other than one of the world's primary languages.

Overall Distortion. Nothing makes listening quite so tiring as distortion. PASSPORT has devised techniques to measure overall cumulative distortion from signal input through audio output—not just distortion within the audio stage. This level of distortion is thus equal to what is heard by the ear.

Overloading. *See* Dynamic Range.

P

Passband Offset. Continuously variable control that can be user-adjusted such that only the best-sounding portion of a given sideband is heard when the receiver is in either the single-sideband mode *(see)* or the synchronous selectable sideband mode *(see)*. This allows for a finer degree of control over adjacent-channel interference and tonal response than does a simple LSB or USB switch associated with a fixed BFO *(see)*. Also known as Passband Tuning, Passband Shift and IF Shift. The same nomenclature is sometimes used to describe variable-bandwidth circuitry.

Passband Shift. *See* Passband Offset.

Passband Tuning. *See* Passband Offset.

Passive Antenna. Not electronically amplified. Typically, such antennas are mounted outdoors, although the "tape-measure" type that comes as an accessory with some portables is usually strung indoors. For world band reception, virtually all outboard models for consumers are made from wire, rather than rods or tubular elements. The two most common designs are the inverted-L (so-called "longwire") and trapped dipole (mounted either horizontally or as a "sloper"). These antennas are usually preferable to active antennas (*cf.*), and are reviewed at length, along with construction and erection instructions, in the Radio Database International White Paper, PASSPORT *Evaluation of Popular Outdoor Antennas (Unamplified)*. *See* Feedline.

PBS. In China, People's Broadcasting Station.

Phase Cancellation. In synchronous selectable sideband *(see)*, two identical wave patterns (lower and upper sidebands) are brought together 180 degrees out of phase so as to cancel out the unwanted sideband. This is a less costly way of sideband attenuation than through the use of discrete IF filtering.

Phase Noise. Synthesizers and other circuits can create a "rushing" noise that is usually noticed only when the receiver is tuned alongside the edge of a powerful broadcast or other carrier. In effect, the signal becomes "modulated" by the noise. Phase noise is a useful measurement if you tune weak signals alongside powerful signals. Measured in dBc (decibels below carrier).

Phone Plug (male), Phone Connector (male), Phone Jack (female). Low-impedance (around 50–75 ohm) 1/4-inch (6 mm) connector, usually for full-sized headphones. These may be mono or stereo.

Phono Plug (male), Phono Connector (male), Phono Jack (female). *See* RCA.

Pirate. Illegal radio station operated by enthusiast(s) with little if any political purpose other than to defy radio laws. Programs typically consist of music, satire or comments relevant to pirate colleagues.

Placement Facility. Typically a local FM or mediumwave AM station which leases airtime for one or more programs or program segments from an international broadcaster. These programs are usually supplied by satellite feed, although some placement facilities pick up programs via regular world band radio.

PLL (Phase-Locked Loop). With world band receivers, a PLL circuit means that the radio can be tuned digitally, often using a number of handy tuning techniques, such as a keypad *(see)* and presets *(see)*.

Plug. Male connector.

Polarization. Radio and other over-the-air signals tend to be either horizontally or vertically polarized. Unsurprisingly, stations which transmit using vertical antennas produce vertically polarized signals, and so on. Long-haul world band transmissions are almost always horizontally polarized (*see* Curtain Antennas), so most outdoor receiving antennas are also horizontal. However, the scattering effects of the ionosphere turn the single horizontal transmitted signal, like a bread slicer, into numerous bits (*see* Fading). Some continue on as horizontal while others morph into vertical, but most fall somewhere in between. As a result, the angle of receiving antenna elements tends to be noncritical for reception of long-distance shortwave signals.

Power. Transmitter power *before* antenna gain, expressed in kilowatts (kW). The present range of world band powers is virtually always 0.01 to 1,000 kW.

Power Lock. *See* Travel Power Lock.

PR. People's Republic.

Preamplifier. An inboard or outboard broadband amplifier to increase the strength of signals fed into a receiver's circuitry. Active antennas *(see)* incorporate a preamplifier or an amplified preselector *(see)*.

Preselector. A circuit—outboard as an accessory, or inboard as part of the receiver—that effectively limits the range of frequencies which can enter a receiver's circuitry or the circuitry of an active antenna *(see)* at full strength; that is, which improves front-end selectivity *(see)*. For example, a preselector may let in the range 15000–16000 kHz unattenuated, thus helping ensure that your receiver or active antenna will not encounter problems within that range caused by signals from, say, 5730–6250 kHz or local mediumwave AM signals (520–1705 kHz). This range usually can be varied, manually or automatically, according to the frequency to which the receiver is being tuned. A preselector may be passive (unamplified) or active (amplified).

Preset. Allows you to select a station pre-stored in a radio's memory. The handiest presets require only one push of a button, as on a car radio.

Propagation. World band signals travel, like a basketball, up and down from the station to your radio. The "floor" below is the earth's surface, whereas the "player's hand" on high is the *ionosphere*, a gaseous layer that envelops the planet. While the earth's surface remains pretty much the same from day to day, the ionosphere—nature's own passive "satellite"—varies in how it propagates radio signals, depending on how much sunlight hits the "bounce points."

Thus, some world band segments do well mainly by day, whereas others are best by night. During winter there's less sunlight, so the "night bands" become unusually active, whereas the "day bands" become correspondingly less useful (see World Band Spectrum). Day-to-day changes in the sun's weather also cause short-term changes in world band radio reception; this explains why some days you can hear rare signals.

Additionally, the 11-year sunspot cycle has a long term effect on propagation, with sunspot maximum greatly enhancing reception on higher world band segments. The last maximum was in late 2000 with the next forecast to be around 2012. The next minimum is occurring now but is expected to end sometime in 2008.

These bounce, or refraction, points are not absolutely efficient. Some loss comes about from absorption (see), and signal scattering brings about fading (see). Too, some bounce points for a signal may be in sunlight (favoring higher frequencies), whereas others aren't (favoring lower frequencies), thus compromising propagation efficiency.

Propagation, like the weather, varies considerably, which adds to the intrigue of world band radio. The accepted standard for propagation prediction is WWV (and sometimes WWVH) on 2500, 5000, 10000, 15000 and 20000 kHz. An explanation of prediction measurements is at www.boulder.nist.gov/timefreq/stations/iform.html#geo. Also, view www.sunspotcycle.com.

PS. Provincial Station, Pangsong.
Pto. Puerto, Porto.

Q

QRM. See Interference.
QRN. See Noise.
QSL. See Verification.

R

R. Radio, Radiodiffusion, Radiodifusora, Radiodifusão, Radiophonikos, Radiostantsiya, Radyo, Radyosu, and so forth.
Radiofax, Radio Facsimile. Like ordinary telefax (facsimile by telephone lines), but by radio.
Radioteletype (RTTY). Characters, but not illustrations, transmitted by radio. See Baud.
RCA Plug (male), RCA Connector (male), RCA Jack (female). Low-impedance (around 50–75 ohm) coaxial cable connector. Simple, inexpensive and ubiquitous in audio systems, but flawed because 1) it is prone to discontinuity from everyday atmospheric corrosion; 2) male and female connectors must fit exactly but often don't; and 3) the positive ("hot") lead connects before the ground/negative lead. Sometimes also used as an antenna connector. Also known, instead of "RCA," as "phono" and CINCH/AV.
RDI®. Radio Database International®, a registered trademark of International Broadcasting Services, Ltd.
Receiver. Synonym for "radio," but sometimes—especially when called a "communications receiver"—implying a radio with superior tough-signal or utility-signal performance.
Reception Report. See Verification.
Reduced Carrier. See Single Sideband.
Reg. Regional.
Relay. A retransmission facility, often highlighted in "Worldwide Broadcasts in English" and "Voices from Home" in Passport's WorldScan® section. Relay facilities are generally considered to be located outside the broadcaster's country. Being closer to the target audience, they usually provide superior reception. See Feeder.
Rep. Republic, République, República.
RF Gain. A variable control to reduce the gain of a receiver's earliest amplification, in the RF stage. However, modern receivers often function better without an RF stage, in which case an RF gain control usually acts simply as a variable attenuator (see).
RN. See R and N.
RS. Radio Station, Radiostantsiya, Radiostudiya, Radiophonikos Stathmos.
RT, RTV. Radiodiffusion Télévision, Radio Télévision, and so forth.
RTTY. See Radioteletype.
[S] Transmission aired summer (midyear) only, typically from the last Sunday in March until the last Sunday in October; see "HFCC." Cf. **W**

S

S. San, Santa, Santo, São, Saint, Sainte. Also, South.
Sa. Saturday.
SASE. Self-addressed, stamped envelope. See introduction to Addresses PLUS in this PASSPORT.
Scan, Scanning. Circuitry within a radio that allows it to bandscan or memory scan automatically.
Season, Schedule Season. See HFCC.
Segments. See Shortwave Spectrum.
Selectivity. The ability of a radio to reject interference (see) from signals on adjacent channels. Thus, also known as adjacent-channel rejection, a key variable in radio quality. See Bandwidth. See Shape Factor. See Ultimate Rejection. See Synchronous Detector.
Sensitivity. The ability of a radio to receive weak signals; thus, also known as weak-signal sensitivity. Of special importance if you are listening during the day or tuning domestic tropical band broadcasts—or if you are located in such parts of the world as Western North America, Hawaii or Australasia, where signals tend to be relatively weak. The best measurement of sensitivity is the noise floor.
Shape Factor. Skirt selectivity helps reduce interference and increase audio fidelity. It is important if you will be tuning stations that are weaker than adjacent-channel signals. Skirt selectivity is measured by the shape factor, the ratio between the bandwidth at –6 dB (adjacent signal at about the same strength as the received station) and –60 dB (adjacent signal relatively much stronger), although with some professional receivers and in certain labs –3 dB is used in lieu of –6 dB. A good shape factor provides the best defense against adjacent powerful signals' muscling their way in to disturb reception of the desired signal.
SHF. Super high frequency, 3–30 GHz.
Shortwave Spectrum. The shortwave spectrum—also known as the High Frequency (HF) spectrum—is that portion of the radio spectrum from 3 MHz through 30 MHz (3,000–30,000 kHz). The shortwave spectrum is occupied not only by world band radio (see World Band Segments), but also hams (see) and utility stations (see).
Sideband. See Mode.
Signal Polarization. See Polarization.
Signal Separation, Signal Separation Points. See Dynamic Range.
Signal Spacing. See Dynamic Range.
Signal-to-Noise Ratio. A common form of noise comes from a radio's (and/or active antenna's) electronic circuitry and usually sounds like "hiss." Depending upon its antenna's location, a receiver may also pick up and reproduce noise (see) from nearby electrical and electronic sources, such as power and cable TV lines, light dimmers and digital electronic products. A third type of noise, galactic, is rarely a problem, and even then can be heard only above 20 MHz. Thus, a key part of enjoyable radio reception is to have a worthy signal-to-noise ratio; that is, where the received radio signal is strong enough relative to the various noises that it drowns out those noises.

SINAD. Signal plus noise plus distortion to noise plus distortion ratio.

Single Sideband, Independent Sideband. Spectrum- and power-conserving modes of transmission commonly used by utility stations *(see)* and hams *(see)*. Single-sideband transmitted signals usually consist of one full sideband (lower sideband, LSB; or, more typically, upper sideband, USB) and a reduced or suppressed carrier, but no second sideband. Very few broadcasters (e.g., the popular American AFRTS) use, or are expected ever to use, the single-sideband mode. Many world band radios are already capable of demodulating single-sideband transmissions, and some can even process independent-sideband signals.

Independent-sideband (ISB) signals are like single-sideband signals, but with both sidebands. Content is usually different in the two sidebands—for stereo, as in the original Kahn AM-stereo system where the left channel can be LSB, right channel USB. More typically, entirely different programming may be carried by each sideband, such as in a shortwave feed to a relay facility that retransmits two entirely different programs. *See* Feeder, Mode.

Certain world band broadcasters and time-standard stations emit single-sideband transmissions which have virtually no carrier reduction, or a minimum of reduction; say, 3 or 6 dB. These "AM equivalent" (AME) signals can be listened to, with slightly added distortion, on ordinary radios not equipped to demodulate pure single sideband signals. Properly designed synchronous detectors *(see)* help reduce distortion with AME transmissions. A variety of AME signals, called "compatible AM," include a minor FM component to help improve reception fidelity. This concept was experimented with decades ago by inventor Leonard Kahn and the VOA, but was not found to offer any meaningful improvement over ordinary AME transmission.

Site. *See* Location.

Skirt Selectivity. *See* Shape Factor.

Skyhook. Outdoor antenna, typically wire.

Slew Controls. Up/down controls, usually buttons, to tune a radio. On many radios with synthesized tuning, slewing is used in lieu of tuning by knob. Better is when slew controls are complemented by a genuine tuning knob, which is more versatile for bandscanning.

Sloper Antenna. *See* Passive Antenna.

Socket. Female connector.

Solar Cycle. Synonym for "sunspot cycle." *See* Propagation.

SPR. Spurious (false) extra signal from a transmitter actually operating on another frequency. One such type is harmonic *(see)*.

Spur. *See* SPR.

Spurious Signal. *See* SPR.

Spurious-Signal Rejection. The ability of a radio receiver to avoid producing false signals, such as images *(see)* and birdies *(see)*, that might otherwise interfere with the clarity of the station you're trying to hear.

Squelch. A circuit which mutes a receiver until the received signal's strength exceeds a specified threshold, which is usually user-adjustable.

SSB. *See* Single Sideband.

St, Sta, Sto. Abbreviations for words that mean "Saint."

Stability. The ability of a receiver to rest exactly the tuned frequency without drifting.

Static. *See* Noise.

Static Arrestor. *See* Surge Arrestor.

Su. Sunday.

Subharmonic. A harmonic heard at 1.5 or 0.5 times the operating frequency. This anomaly is caused by the way signals are generated within vintage-model transmitters, and thus cannot take place with modern transmitters. For example, the subharmonic of a station on 3360 kHz might be heard faintly on 5040 or 1680 kHz. Also, *see* Harmonic.

Shutterstock/Falko Matte

Sunspot Cycle. *See* Propagation.

Superheterodyne. *See* IF.

Surge Arrestor. Protective device to eliminate the harmful impact of voltage spikes, which enter electronic equipment via AC (mains) power lines, telephone lines and radio/TV antennas. *See* MOV, although some premium arrestors (e.g., ZeroSurge) use non-MOV technologies.

SW. *See* Shortwave Spectrum.

SWL. Shortwave listener. The overwhelming preponderance of shortwave listening is to world band stations, but some radio enthusiasts also enjoy eavesdropping on utility stations *(see)* and hams *(see)*.

Synchronous Detector, Synchronous Detection. Some world band radios are equipped with this high-tech circuit that greatly reduces fading distortion; unlike ECSS *(see)* it automatically steers clear of received *vs.* internally generated carrier phase mismatch. Better synchronous detectors also allow for synchronous selectable sideband *(see)*; that is, the ability to select the less-interfered of the two sidebands of a world band or other AM-mode signal. *See* Mode, Phase Cancellation.

Synchronous Selectable Sideband. Derived from synchronous detection *(see)* circuitry, this function greatly reduces the impact of adjacent-channel interference *(see)* on listening.

Synthesizer, Frequency. Better world band receivers utilize a digital frequency synthesizer to tune signals. Among other things, such synthesizers allow for pushbutton tuning and presets, and display the exact frequency digitally—pluses that make tuning to the world considerably easier. Virtually a "must" feature. *See* Analog Frequency Readout, Digital Frequency Display.

T

Target. The part of the world where a transmission is beamed, a/k/a target zone.

Th. Thursday.

THD. Total harmonic distortion.

Third Order Intercept Point. *See* Dynamic Range.

Travel Power Lock. Control which disables the on/off switch to prevent a radio from switching on accidentally.

Transmitter Power. *See* Power.

Trap Dipole Antenna, Trapped Dipole Antenna. Dipole *(see)* antenna with several coil "traps" that allow for optimum reception on several world band or other segments or bands. See Passive Antenna.

Tropical Band Segments. *See* World Band Segments.

Tu. Tuesday.

Twinlead, Twin Lead. Ribbon wire or "zip cord" *(see)* typically used as an antenna lead-in *(see)*. Impedance may be high (300 ohms) or low (around 50–75 ohms).

U

UHF. Ultra High Frequency, 300 MHz through 3 GHz.

UHF Connector. One of the three most common coax fittings (a/k/a PL-259, SO-239) used *i.a.* to connect world band and kindred outboard antenna lead-ins *(see)* to a receiver (typically tabletop or professional). Robust, but because it screws on it takes more time to connect/disconnect than most alternatives. Impedance varies, but typically is low (50–75 ohms).

Ultimate Rejection, Ultimate Selectivity. The point at which a receiver is no longer able to reject adjacent-channel interference. Ultimate rejection is important if you listen to signals that are markedly weaker than are adjacent signals. See Selectivity.

Universal Day. *See* World Time.

Universal Time. *See* World Time.

URL. Universal Resource Locator; i.e., the Internet address for a given webpage.

USB. Upper Sideband. See Mode, Single Sideband, Feeder.

UTC. Coordinated Universal Time. The occasional variation "Universal Time Coordinated" is not correct, although for everyday use it's okay to refer simply to "Universal Time." See World Time.

Utility Stations. Most signals within the shortwave spectrum are not world band stations. Rather, they are utility stations—radio telephones, ships at sea, aircraft, ionospheric sounders, over-the-horizon radar and the like—that transmit strange sounds (growls, gurgles, dih-dah sounds, etc.). Although these can be picked up on many receivers, they are rarely intended to be utilized by the general public. *Cf.* Broadcast, Feeders, Hams and Mode.

V

v. Variable frequency; i.e., one that is unstable or drifting because of a transmitter malfunction or, less often, to avoid jamming or other interference.

Variable-Rate Incremental Slewing (VRIS). Slewing button or other on/off bandscanning control where the tuning rate increases the longer the control is held down or otherwise kept on.

Variable-Rate Incremental Tuning (VRIT). Tuning knob or similar bandscanning control where the tuning rate increases the faster the control is turned. So, the faster the control is turned, the faster the *rate* in which frequencies zip by.

Verification. A "QSL" card or letter from a station verifying that a listener indeed heard that particular station. In order to stand a chance of qualifying for a verification card or letter, you should respond with a reception report shortly after having heard the transmission. You need to provide the station heard with, at a minimum, the following information in a three-number "SIO" code, in which "SIO 555" is best and "SIO 111" is worst:

• **S**ignal strength, with 5 being of excellent quality, comparable to that of a local mediumwave AM station, and 1 being inaudible or at least so weak as to be virtually unintelligible, 2 (faint, but somewhat intelligible), 3 (moderate strength) and 4 (good strength) represent the signal-strength levels usually encountered with world band stations.

• Interference from other stations, with 5 indicating no interference whatsoever, and 1 indicating such extreme interference that the desired signal is virtually drowned out. Ratings of 2 (heavy interference), 3 (moderate interference) and 4 (slight interference) represent the differing degrees of interference more typically encountered with world band signals. If possible, indicate the names of the interfering station(s) and the channel(s) they are on. Otherwise, at least describe what the interference sounds like.

• **O**verall quality of the signal, with 5 being best, 1 worst.

• In addition to providing SIO findings, you should indicate which programs you've heard, as well as comments on how you liked or disliked those programs. Refer to the Addresses PLUS section of this edition for information on where and to whom your report should be sent, and whether return postage should be included.

• Expanded versions of the SIO reporting code are the SINPO and SINFO codes, where "N" refers to atmospheric noise, "F" to fading and "P" to propagation conditions on the same 1–5 scale. As atmospheric noise is rarely audible below 20 MHz and propagation conditions are highly subjective, SIO tends to provide more accurate feedback. Fading, however, is not hard for an experienced monitor to rate, but the SIFO code has never caught on.

• Few stations wish to receive unsolicited recordings of their transmissions. However, a few stations' websites actively seek MP3, RealAudio or other Internet-sent files or mailed CD recordings of certain transmissions.

VHF. Very high frequency spectrum, 30–300 MHz, which starts just above the shortwave spectrum *(see)* and ends at the UHF spectrum. See FM, which operates within the VHF spectrum. Somewhat confusingly, in German VHF is known as UKW (Ultra Short Wave), which is different from UHF (Ultra High Frequency).

VHF Connector. *See* UHF Connector.

Vo. Voice of.

VRIS. *See* Variable-Rate Incremental Slewing.

VRIT. *See* Variable-Rate Incremental Tuning.

W

🅦 Transmission aired winter only, typically from the last Sunday in October until the last Sunday in March; see HFCC. *Cf.* 🅢

W. Wednesday.

Wavelength. *See* Meters.

Weak-Signal Sensitivity. *See* Sensitivity.

Webcasting. *See* Web Radio.

Web Radio, Webcasts. Broadcasts aired over the Internet. These thousands of stations worldwide include simulcast FM, mediumwave AM and world band stations, as well as Internet-only stations. Although webcasting was originally unfettered, it has increasingly been subjected to official gatekeeping (censorship), as well as uniquely steep copyright and union royalties and rules that have hobbled web simulcasting by AM/FM stations in the United States. This PASSPORT lists URL information for all world band stations which webcast live or on-demand.

World Band Radio. Broadcasts (news, music, sports and the like) transmitted within and just below the shortwave spectrum *(see)*. Virtually all are found within 14 discrete world band segments *(see)*. These broadcasting stations are similar to regular mediumwave AM band and FM band broadcasters, except that world band stations can be heard over enormous distances. As a result, they often carry programs created especially for audiences abroad. Traditional analog world band transmissions—with properly located, configured and operated facilities—are also uniquely difficult to "jam" (see Jamming), making world band the most effective vehicle for outflanking official censorship. Some world band stations have regular audiences in the tens of millions, and even over 100 million, including many who listen for extended periods. Although world band lacks the glamour of new broadcasting technologies, making it an easy target for tech-hungry officials, around 600 million people worldwide continue to listen.

World Band Segments. Fourteen slices—13 within the shortwave spectrum *(see)*, one toward the upper reaches of the mediumwave spectrum *(see* AM Band)—that are used almost exclusively for world band broadcasts. Those below 5.1 MHz are called "Tropical Band Segments" or simply "Tropical Bands." *See* "Best Times and Frequencies" sidebar elsewhere within this PASSPORT.

World Band Spectrum. *See* World Band Segments.

World Day. *See* World Time.

World Time. Also known as Coordinated Universal Time (UTC), Greenwich Mean Time (GMT), Zulu time (Z) and "military time." With over 150 countries on world band radio, if each announced its own local time you would need a calculator to figure it all out. To get around this, a single international time—World Time—is used. The differences between World Time and local time are detailed in the Addresses PLUS and Setting Your World Time Clock sections of this edition. World Time can also be determined simply by listening to time announcements given on the hour by world band stations—or minute by minute by WWV in the United States on 2500, 5000, 10000, 15000 and 20000 kHz; WWVH in Hawaii on 2500, 5000, 10000 and 15000 kHz; and CHU in Canada on 3330, 7335 and 14670 kHz. A 24-hour clock format is used, so "1800 World Time" means 6:00 PM World Time. If you're in, say, North America, Eastern Time is five hours behind World Time winters and four hours behind World Time summers, so 1800 World Time would be 1:00 PM EST or 2:00 PM EDT. The easiest solution is to use a 24-hour digital clock set to World Time. Many radios already have these built in, and World Time clocks are also available as accessories. World Time also applies to the days of the week. So if it's 9:00 PM (21:00) Wednesday in New York during the winter, it's 0200 *Thursday* World Time.

WS. World Service.

X-Band. The mediumwave AM band segment from 1605–1705 kHz in the Western Hemisphere, Australia and selected other areas. In the United States, travelers information stations (TIS) and other public information services are sometimes also found on 1710 kHz. *See* AM Band.

Yagi. Pioneering directional beam antenna invented by Japanese engineer Hidetsugu Yagi. Pickup elements are usually of aluminum tubing and include one or more of each of these three elements: dipole, slightly longer reflector and slightly shorter director. Size, cost and erection challenges make yagis impractical for nighttime world band listening. However, they are commonly used for VHF/UHF reception, as well as amateur radio shortwave transceiving down to 14 MHz/20 meters and occasionally 7 MHz/40 meters.

Zero beat. When tuning a world band or other AM-mode signal in the single-sideband mode, there is a whistle, or "beat," whose pitch is the result of the difference in frequency between the receiver's internally generated carrier (BFO, or beat-frequency oscillator) and the station's transmitted carrier. By tuning carefully, the listener can reduce the difference between these two carriers to the point where the whistle is deeper and deeper, to the point where it no longer audible. This silent sweet spot is known as "zero beat." *See* ECSS.

Zip Cord. Conventional twin-lead wire used to connect ordinary household appliances and lights to mains/wall-socket AC outlets. Sometimes used as low-cost antenna twinlead *(see)*.

Zulu Time. *See* World Time.

PASSPORT's Blue Pages

Frequency Guide to World Band Schedules

If you scan the world band airwaves, you'll even find stations that aren't aimed your way. That's because shortwave signals are scattered by the heavens, allowing broadcasts not targeted to your area to be heard.

Blue Pages Identify Stations

Yet, bandscanning can be frustrating if you don't have a "map"—PASSPORT's Blue Pages. Let's say you've stumbled across something Asian-sounding on 7410 kHz at 2035 World Time. The Blue Pages show All India Radio beamed to Western Europe, with 250 kW of power from Delhi. These suggest this is probably what you're hearing, even if you're not in Europe. You can also see that English from India will begin on that same channel in about ten minutes.

Signals targeted your way usually come in best, but those aimed elsewhere may also be heard—especially when they're beamed to nearby regions.

Schedules for Entire Year

Times and days of the week are in World Time, explained in "Setting Your World Time Clock" and "Worldly Words"; for local times in each country, see "Addresses PLUS." Midyear, some stations are an hour earlier (▱) or later (▰) because of Daylight Saving/Summer Time. Frequencies used only seasonally are labeled **S** for summer (midyear) and **W** for winter. Stations may also extend hours of transmission, or air special programs, for national holidays, emergencies or sports events.

To be as useful as possible over the months to come, PASSPORT's schedules consist not just of observed activity, but also that which we have creatively opined will take place during the forthcoming year. This predictive material is based on decades of experience and is original from us. Although inherently not as exact as real-time data, over the years it has been of tangible value to PASSPORT readers.

Guide to Blue Pages Format

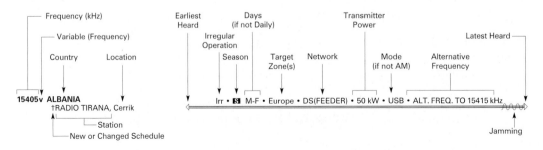

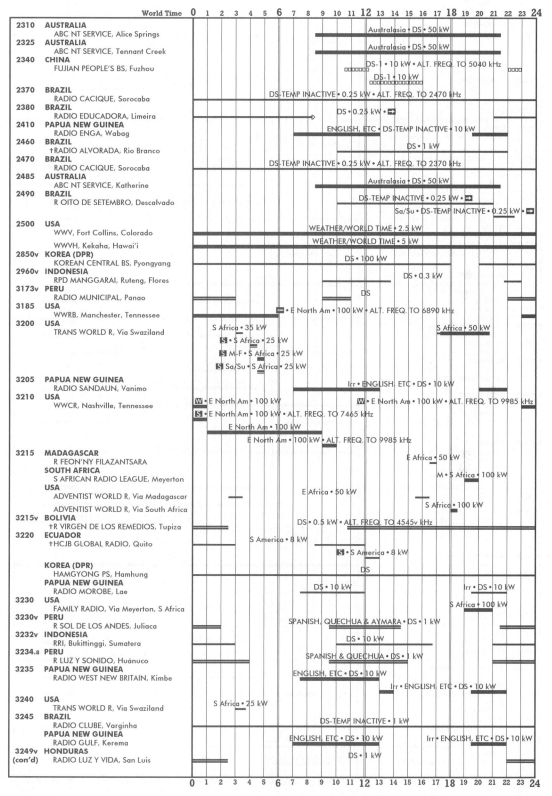

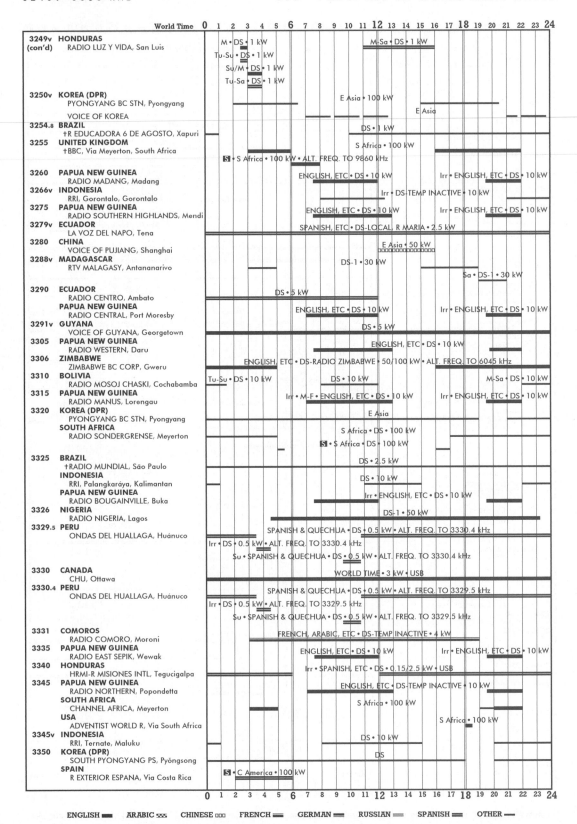

World Time 0 1 2 3 4 5 6 7 8 9 10 11 12 13 14 15 16 17 18 19 20 21 22 23 24

3249v HONDURAS
(con'd)   RADIO LUZ Y VIDA, San Luis
- M • DS • 1 kW
- Tu-Su • DS • 1 kW
- Su/M • DS • 1 kW
- Tu-Sa • DS • 1 kW

3250v KOREA (DPR)
    PYONGYANG BC STN, Pyongyang — E Asia • 100 kW
    VOICE OF KOREA — E Asia

3254.8 BRAZIL
    †R EDUCADORA 6 DE AGOSTO, Xapuri — DS • 1 kW

3255 UNITED KINGDOM
    †BBC, Via Meyerton, South Africa — S Africa • 100 kW
    ⑤ • S Africa • 100 kW • ALT. FREQ. TO 9860 kHz

3260 PAPUA NEW GUINEA
    RADIO MADANG, Madang — ENGLISH, ETC • DS • 10 kW   Irr • ENGLISH, ETC • DS • 10 kW

3266v INDONESIA
    RRI, Gorontalo, Gorontalo — Irr • DS-TEMP INACTIVE • 10 kW

3275 PAPUA NEW GUINEA
    RADIO SOUTHERN HIGHLANDS, Mendi — ENGLISH, ETC • DS • 10 kW   Irr • ENGLISH, ETC • DS • 10 kW

3279v ECUADOR
    LA VOZ DEL NAPO, Tena — SPANISH, ETC • DS-LOCAL, R MARIA • 2.5 kW

3280 CHINA
    VOICE OF PUJIANG, Shanghai — E Asia • 50 kW

3288v MADAGASCAR
    RTV MALAGASY, Antananarivo — DS-1 • 30 kW   Sa • DS-1 • 30 kW

3290 ECUADOR
    RADIO CENTRO, Ambato — DS • 5 kW
PAPUA NEW GUINEA
    RADIO CENTRAL, Port Moresby — ENGLISH, ETC • DS • 10 kW   Irr • ENGLISH, ETC • DS • 10 kW

3291v GUYANA
    VOICE OF GUYANA, Georgetown — DS • 5 kW

3305 PAPUA NEW GUINEA
    RADIO WESTERN, Daru — ENGLISH, ETC • DS • 10 kW

3306 ZIMBABWE
    ZIMBABWE BC CORP, Gweru — ENGLISH, ETC • DS-RADIO ZIMBABWE • 50/100 kW • ALT. FREQ. TO 6045 kHz

3310 BOLIVIA
    RADIO MOSOJ CHASKI, Cochabamba — Tu-Su • DS • 10 kW   DS • 10 kW   M-Sa • DS • 10 kW

3315 PAPUA NEW GUINEA
    RADIO MANUS, Lorengau — Irr • M-F • ENGLISH, ETC • DS • 10 kW   Irr • ENGLISH, ETC • DS • 10 kW

3320 KOREA (DPR)
    PYONGYANG BC STN, Pyongyang — E Asia
SOUTH AFRICA
    RADIO SONDERGRENSE, Meyerton — S Africa • DS • 100 kW
    ⑤ • S Africa • DS • 100 kW

3325 BRAZIL
    †RADIO MUNDIAL, São Paulo — DS • 2.5 kW
INDONESIA
    RRI, Palangkaráya, Kalimantan — DS • 10 kW
PAPUA NEW GUINEA
    RADIO BOUGAINVILLE, Buka — Irr • ENGLISH, ETC • DS • 10 kW

3326 NIGERIA
    RADIO NIGERIA, Lagos — DS-1 • 50 kW

3329.5 PERU
    ONDAS DEL HUALLAGA, Huánuco — SPANISH & QUECHUA • DS • 0.5 kW • ALT. FREQ. TO 3330.4 kHz
    Irr • DS • 0.5 kW • ALT. FREQ. TO 3330.4 kHz
    Su • SPANISH & QUECHUA • DS • 0.5 kW • ALT. FREQ. TO 3330.4 kHz

3330 CANADA
    CHU, Ottawa — WORLD TIME • 3 kW • USB

3330.4 PERU
    ONDAS DEL HUALLAGA, Huánuco — SPANISH & QUECHUA • DS • 0.5 kW • ALT. FREQ. TO 3329.5 kHz
    Irr • DS • 0.5 kW • ALT. FREQ. TO 3329.5 kHz
    Su • SPANISH & QUECHUA • DS • 0.5 kW • ALT. FREQ. TO 3329.5 kHz

3331 COMOROS
    RADIO COMORO, Moroni — FRENCH, ARABIC, ETC • DS-TEMP INACTIVE • 4 kW

3335 PAPUA NEW GUINEA
    RADIO EAST SEPIK, Wewak — ENGLISH, ETC • DS • 10 kW   Irr • ENGLISH, ETC • DS • 10 kW

3340 HONDURAS
    HRMI-R MISIONES INTL, Tegucigalpa — Irr • SPANISH, ETC • DS • 0.15/2.5 kW • USB

3345 PAPUA NEW GUINEA
    RADIO NORTHERN, Popondetta — ENGLISH, ETC • DS-TEMP INACTIVE • 10 kW
SOUTH AFRICA
    CHANNEL AFRICA, Meyerton — S Africa • 100 kW
USA
    ADVENTIST WORLD R, Via South Africa — S Africa • 100 kW

3345v INDONESIA
    RRI, Ternate, Maluku — DS • 10 kW

3350 KOREA (DPR)
    SOUTH PYONGYANG PS, Pyŏngsong — DS
SPAIN
    R EXTERIOR ESPANA, Via Costa Rica — ⑤ • C America • 100 kW

0 1 2 3 4 5 6 7 8 9 10 11 12 13 14 15 16 17 18 19 20 21 22 23 24

ENGLISH ▬   ARABIC ≋   CHINESE ▫▫▫   FRENCH ▬   GERMAN ▬   RUSSIAN ═   SPANISH ▬   OTHER ▬

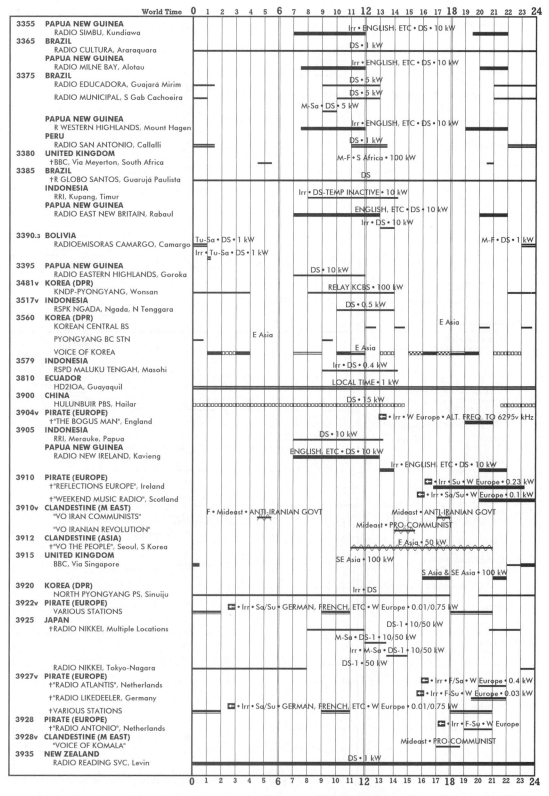

		World Time
3355	**PAPUA NEW GUINEA** RADIO SIMBU, Kundiawa	Irr • ENGLISH, ETC • DS • 10 kW
3365	**BRAZIL** RADIO CULTURA, Araraquara	DS • 1 kW
	PAPUA NEW GUINEA RADIO MILNE BAY, Alotau	Irr • ENGLISH, ETC • DS • 10 kW
3375	**BRAZIL** RADIO EDUCADORA, Guajará Mirim	DS • 5 kW
	RADIO MUNICIPAL, S Gab Cachoeira	DS • 5 kW
		M-Sa • DS • 5 kW
	PAPUA NEW GUINEA R WESTERN HIGHLANDS, Mount Hagen	Irr • ENGLISH, ETC • DS • 10 kW
	PERU RADIO SAN ANTONIO, Callalli	DS • 1 kW
3380	**UNITED KINGDOM** †BBC, Via Meyerton, South Africa	M-F • S Africa • 100 kW
3385	**BRAZIL** †R GLOBO SANTOS, Guarujá Paulista	DS
	INDONESIA RRI, Kupang, Timur	Irr • DS-TEMP INACTIVE • 10 kW
	PAPUA NEW GUINEA RADIO EAST NEW BRITAIN, Rabaul	ENGLISH, ETC • DS • 10 kW
		Irr • DS • 10 kW
3390.3	**BOLIVIA** RADIOEMISORAS CAMARGO, Camargo	Tu-Sa • DS • 1 kW M-F • DS • 1 kW
		Irr • Tu-Sa • DS • 1 kW
3395	**PAPUA NEW GUINEA** RADIO EASTERN HIGHLANDS, Goroka	DS • 10 kW
3481v	**KOREA (DPR)** KNDP-PYONGYANG, Wonsan	RELAY KCBS • 100 kW
3517v	**INDONESIA** RSPK NGADA, Ngada, N Tenggara	DS • 0.5 kW
3560	**KOREA (DPR)** KOREAN CENTRAL BS	E Asia
	PYONGYANG BC STN	E Asia
	VOICE OF KOREA	E Asia
3579	**INDONESIA** RSPD MALUKU TENGAH, Masohi	Irr • DS • 0.4 kW
3810	**ECUADOR** HD2IOA, Guayaquil	LOCAL TIME • 1 kW
3900	**CHINA** HULUNBUIR PBS, Hailar	DS • 15 kW
3904v	**PIRATE (EUROPE)** †"THE BOGUS MAN", England	⬅ • Irr • W Europe • ALT. FREQ. TO 6295v kHz
3905	**INDONESIA** RRI, Merauke, Papua	DS • 10 kW
	PAPUA NEW GUINEA RADIO NEW IRELAND, Kavieng	ENGLISH, ETC • DS • 10 kW
		Irr • ENGLISH, ETC • DS • 10 kW
3910	**PIRATE (EUROPE)** †"REFLECTIONS EUROPE", Ireland	⬅ • Irr • Su • W Europe • 0.23 kW
	†"WEEKEND MUSIC RADIO", Scotland	⬅ • Irr • Sa/Su • W Europe • 0.1 kW
3910v	**CLANDESTINE (M EAST)** "VO IRAN COMMUNISTS"	F • Mideast • ANTI-IRANIAN GOVT Mideast • ANTI-IRANIAN GOVT
	"VO IRANIAN REVOLUTION"	Mideast • PRO-COMMUNIST
3912	**CLANDESTINE (ASIA)** †"VO THE PEOPLE", Seoul, S Korea	E Asia • 50 kW
3915	**UNITED KINGDOM** BBC, Via Singapore	SE Asia • 100 kW
		S Asia & SE Asia • 100 kW
3920	**KOREA (DPR)** NORTH PYONGYANG PS, Sinuiju	Irr • DS
3922v	**PIRATE (EUROPE)** VARIOUS STATIONS	⬅ • Irr • Sa/Su • GERMAN, FRENCH, ETC • W Europe • 0.01/0.75 kW
3925	**JAPAN** †RADIO NIKKEI, Multiple Locations	DS-1 • 10/50 kW
		M-Sa • DS-1 • 10/50 kW
		Irr • M-Sa • DS-1 • 10/50 kW
	RADIO NIKKEI, Tokyo-Nagara	DS-1 • 50 kW
3927v	**PIRATE (EUROPE)** †"RADIO ATLANTIS", Netherlands	⬅ • Irr • F/Sa • W Europe • 0.4 kW
	†"RADIO LIKEDEELER", Germany	⬅ • Irr • F-Su • W Europe • 0.03 kW
	†VARIOUS STATIONS	⬅ • Irr • Sa/Su • GERMAN, FRENCH, ETC • W Europe • 0.01/0.75 kW
3928	**PIRATE (EUROPE)** †"RADIO ANTONIO", Netherlands	⬅ • Irr • F-Su • W Europe
3928v	**CLANDESTINE (M EAST)** "VOICE OF KOMALA"	Mideast • PRO-COMMUNIST
3935	**NEW ZEALAND** RADIO READING SVC, Levin	DS • 1 kW

SEASONAL Ⓢ OR Ⓦ   1-HR TIMESHIFT MIDYEAR ⬅ OR ➡   JAMMING / OR ∧   EARLIEST HEARD ◁   LATEST HEARD ▷   NEW FOR 2008 †

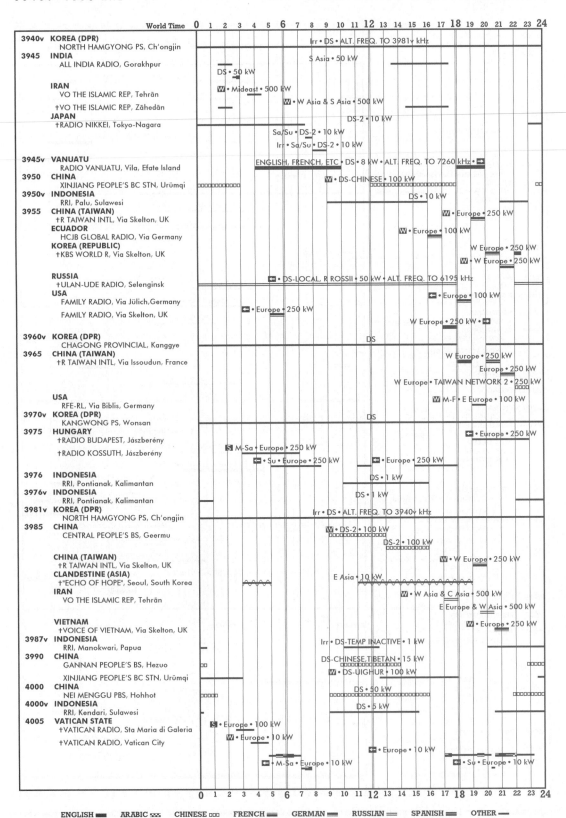

World Time

3940v	**KOREA (DPR)**
	NORTH HAMGYONG PS, Ch'ongjin
3945	**INDIA**
	ALL INDIA RADIO, Gorakhpur
	IRAN
	VO THE ISLAMIC REP, Tehrān
	†VO THE ISLAMIC REP, Zāhedān
	JAPAN
	†RADIO NIKKEI, Tokyo-Nagara
3945v	**VANUATU**
	RADIO VANUATU, Vila, Efate Island
3950	**CHINA**
	XINJIANG PEOPLE'S BC STN, Urümqi
3950v	**INDONESIA**
	RRI, Palu, Sulawesi
3955	**CHINA (TAIWAN)**
	†R TAIWAN INTL, Via Skelton, UK
	ECUADOR
	HCJB GLOBAL RADIO, Via Germany
	KOREA (REPUBLIC)
	†KBS WORLD R, Via Skelton, UK
	RUSSIA
	†ULAN-UDE RADIO, Selenginsk
	USA
	FAMILY RADIO, Via Jülich, Germany
	FAMILY RADIO, Via Skelton, UK
3960v	**KOREA (DPR)**
	CHAGONG PROVINCIAL, Kanggye
3965	**CHINA (TAIWAN)**
	†R TAIWAN INTL, Via Issoudun, France
	USA
	RFE-RL, Via Biblis, Germany
3970v	**KOREA (DPR)**
	KANGWONG PS, Wonsan
3975	**HUNGARY**
	†RADIO BUDAPEST, Jászberény
	†RADIO KOSSUTH, Jászberény
3976	**INDONESIA**
	RRI, Pontianak, Kalimantan
3976v	**INDONESIA**
	RRI, Pontianak, Kalimantan
3981v	**KOREA (DPR)**
	NORTH HAMGYONG PS, Ch'ongjin
3985	**CHINA**
	CENTRAL PEOPLE'S BS, Geermu
	CHINA (TAIWAN)
	†R TAIWAN INTL, Via Skelton, UK
	CLANDESTINE (ASIA)
	†"ECHO OF HOPE", Seoul, South Korea
	IRAN
	VO THE ISLAMIC REP, Tehrān
	VIETNAM
	†VOICE OF VIETNAM, Via Skelton, UK
3987v	**INDONESIA**
	RRI, Manokwari, Papua
3990	**CHINA**
	GANNAN PEOPLE'S BS, Hezuo
	XINJIANG PEOPLE'S BC STN, Urümqi
4000	**CHINA**
	NEI MENGGU PBS, Hohhot
4000v	**INDONESIA**
	RRI, Kendari, Sulawesi
4005	**VATICAN STATE**
	†VATICAN RADIO, Sta Maria di Galeria
	†VATICAN RADIO, Vatican City

Irr • DS • ALT. FREQ. TO 3981v kHz

S Asia • 50 kW

DS • 50 kW

W • Mideast • 500 kW

W • W Asia & S Asia • 500 kW

DS-2 • 10 kW

Sa/Su • DS-2 • 10 kW

Irr • Sa/Su • DS-2 • 10 kW

ENGLISH, FRENCH, ETC • DS • 8 kW • ALT. FREQ. TO 7260 kHz •

W • DS-CHINESE • 100 kW

DS • 10 kW

W • Europe • 250 kW

W • Europe • 100 kW

W Europe • 250 kW

W • W Europe • 250 kW

DS-LOCAL, R ROSSII • 50 kW • ALT. FREQ. TO 6195 kHz

• Europe • 100 kW

• Europe • 250 kW

W Europe • 250 kW •

DS

W Europe • 250 kW

Europe • 250 kW

W Europe • TAIWAN NETWORK 2 • 250 kW

W • M-F • E Europe • 100 kW

DS

• Europe • 250 kW

M-Sa • Europe • 250 kW

Su • Europe • 250 kW

• Europe • 250 kW

DS • 1 kW

DS • 1 kW

Irr • DS • ALT. FREQ. TO 3940v kHz

W • DS-2 • 100 kW

DS-2 • 100 kW

W • W Europe • 250 kW

E Asia • 10 kW

W • W Asia & C Asia • 500 kW

E Europe & W Asia • 500 kW

W • Europe • 250 kW

Irr • DS-TEMP INACTIVE • 1 kW

DS-CHINESE,TIBETAN • 15 kW

W • DS-UIGHUR • 100 kW

DS • 50 kW

DS • 5 kW

S • Europe • 100 kW

W • Europe • 10 kW

• Europe • 10 kW

• M-Sa • Europe • 10 kW

• Su • Europe • 10 kW

0 1 2 3 4 5 6 7 8 9 10 11 12 13 14 15 16 17 18 19 20 21 22 23 24

ENGLISH ▬ ARABIC ⧓ CHINESE ▭▭▭ FRENCH ▬ GERMAN ▬ RUSSIAN ═ SPANISH ▬ OTHER ▬

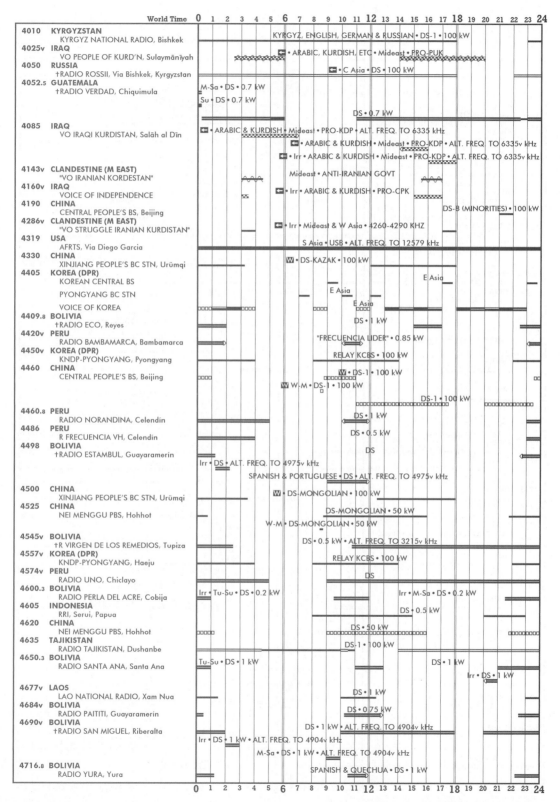

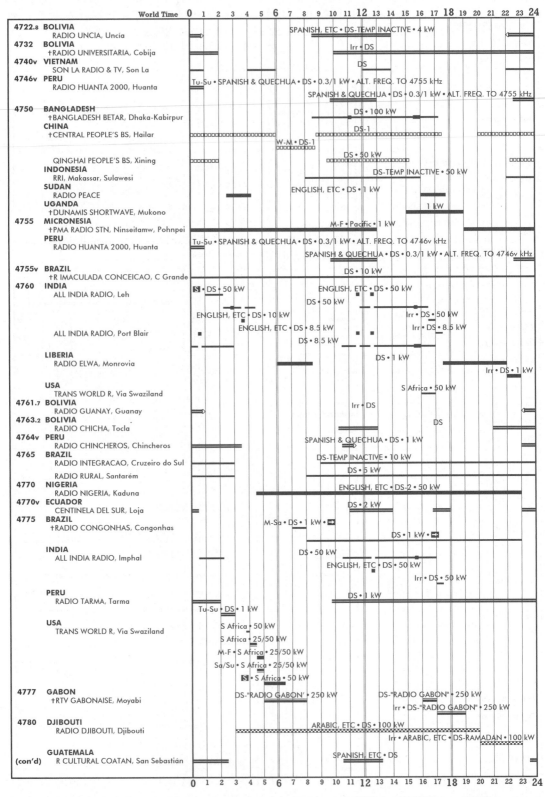

World Time 0 1 2 3 4 5 6 7 8 9 10 11 12 13 14 15 16 17 18 19 20 21 22 23 24

4722.8 BOLIVIA
RADIO UNCIA, Uncia — SPANISH, ETC • DS-TEMP INACTIVE • 4 kW

4732 BOLIVIA
†RADIO UNIVERSITARIA, Cobija — Irr • DS

4740v VIETNAM
SON LA RADIO & TV, Son La — DS

4746v PERU
RADIO HUANTA 2000, Huanta — Tu-Su • SPANISH & QUECHUA • DS • 0.3/1 kW • ALT. FREQ. TO 4755 kHz
SPANISH & QUECHUA • DS • 0.3/1 kW • ALT. FREQ. TO 4755 kHz

4750 BANGLADESH
†BANGLADESH BETAR, Dhaka-Kabirpur — DS • 100 kW

CHINA
†CENTRAL PEOPLE'S BS, Hailar — DS-1
W-M • DS-1

QINGHAI PEOPLE'S BS, Xining — DS • 50 kW

INDONESIA
RRI, Makassar, Sulawesi — DS-TEMP INACTIVE • 50 kW

SUDAN
RADIO PEACE — ENGLISH, ETC • DS • 1 kW

UGANDA
†DUNAMIS SHORTWAVE, Mukono — 1 kW

4755 MICRONESIA
†PMA RADIO STN, Ninseitamw, Pohnpei — M-F • Pacific • 1 kW

PERU
RADIO HUANTA 2000, Huanta — Tu-Su • SPANISH & QUECHUA • DS • 0.3/1 kW • ALT. FREQ. TO 4746v kHz
SPANISH & QUECHUA • DS • 0.3/1 kW • ALT. FREQ. TO 4746v kHz

4755v BRAZIL
†R IMACULADA CONCEICAO, C Grande — DS • 10 kW

4760 INDIA
ALL INDIA RADIO, Leh — S • DS • 50 kW ENGLISH, ETC • DS • 50 kW
DS • 50 kW
ENGLISH, ETC • DS • 10 kW Irr • DS • 50 kW

ALL INDIA RADIO, Port Blair — ENGLISH, ETC • DS • 8.5 kW Irr • DS • 8.5 kW
DS • 8.5 kW

LIBERIA
RADIO ELWA, Monrovia — DS • 1 kW
Irr • DS • 1 kW

USA
TRANS WORLD R, Via Swaziland — S Africa • 50 kW

4761.7 BOLIVIA
RADIO GUANAY, Guanay — Irr • DS

4763.2 BOLIVIA
RADIO CHICHA, Tocla — DS

4764v PERU
RADIO CHINCHEROS, Chincheros — SPANISH & QUECHUA • DS • 1 kW

4765 BRAZIL
RADIO INTEGRACAO, Cruzeiro do Sul — DS-TEMP INACTIVE • 10 kW

RADIO RURAL, Santarém — DS • 5 kW

4770 NIGERIA
RADIO NIGERIA, Kaduna — ENGLISH, ETC • DS-2 • 50 kW

4770v ECUADOR
CENTINELA DEL SUR, Loja — DS • 2 kW

4775 BRAZIL
†RADIO CONGONHAS, Congonhas — M-Sa • DS • 1 kW •
DS • 1 kW •

INDIA
ALL INDIA RADIO, Imphal — DS • 50 kW
ENGLISH, ETC • DS • 50 kW
Irr • DS • 50 kW

PERU
RADIO TARMA, Tarma — DS • 1 kW

USA
TRANS WORLD R, Via Swaziland — Tu-Su • DS • 1 kW
S Africa • 50 kW
S Africa • 25/50 kW
M-F • S Africa • 25/50 kW
Sa/Su • S Africa • 25/50 kW
S • S Africa • 50 kW

4777 GABON
†RTV GABONAISE, Moyabi — DS-"RADIO GABON" • 250 kW DS-"RADIO GABON" • 250 kW
Irr • DS-"RADIO GABON" • 250 kW

4780 DJIBOUTI
RADIO DJIBOUTI, Djibouti — ARABIC, ETC • DS • 100 kW
Irr • ARABIC, ETC • DS-RAMADAN • 100 kW

GUATEMALA
(con'd) R CULTURAL COATAN, San Sebastián — SPANISH, ETC • DS

0 1 2 3 4 5 6 7 8 9 10 11 12 13 14 15 16 17 18 19 20 21 22 23 24

ENGLISH ▬ ARABIC ▨ CHINESE ▫▫▫ FRENCH ▬ GERMAN ▬ RUSSIAN ═ SPANISH ▬ OTHER ▬

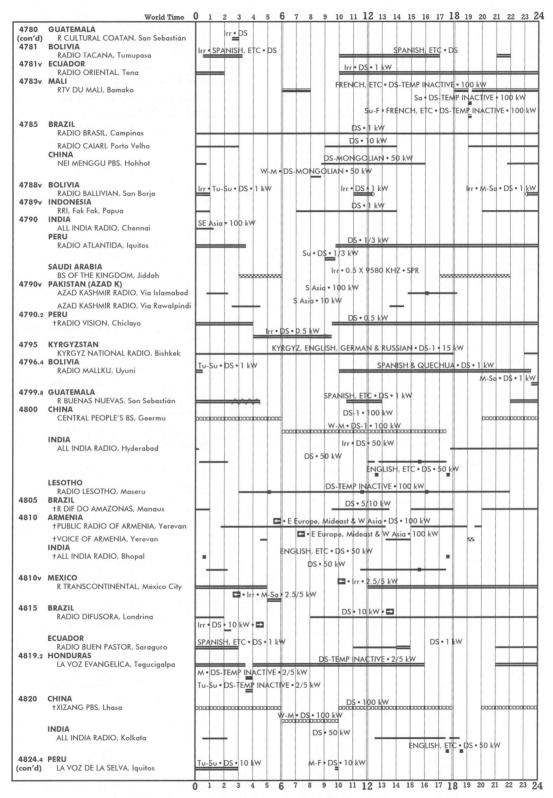

World Time: 0 1 2 3 4 5 6 7 8 9 10 11 12 13 14 15 16 17 18 19 20 21 22 23 24

4780 GUATEMALA
(con'd) R CULTURAL COATAN, San Sebastián — Irr • DS

4781 BOLIVIA
RADIO TACANA, Tumupasa — Irr • SPANISH, ETC • DS / SPANISH, ETC • DS

4781v ECUADOR
RADIO ORIENTAL, Tena — Irr • DS • 1 kW

4783v MALI
RTV DU MALI, Bamako — FRENCH, ETC • DS-TEMP INACTIVE • 100 kW / Sa • DS-TEMP INACTIVE • 100 kW / Su-F • FRENCH, ETC • DS-TEMP INACTIVE • 100 kW

4785 BRAZIL
RADIO BRASIL, Campinas — DS • 1 kW
RADIO CAIARI, Porto Velho — DS • 10 kW

CHINA
NEI MENGGU PBS, Hohhot — DS-MONGOLIAN • 50 kW / W-M • DS-MONGOLIAN • 50 kW

4788v BOLIVIA
RADIO BALLIVIAN, San Borja — Irr • Tu-Su • DS • 1 kW / Irr • DS • 1 kW / Irr • M-Sa • DS • 1 kW

4789v INDONESIA
RRI, Fak Fak, Papua — DS • 1 kW

4790 INDIA
ALL INDIA RADIO, Chennai — SE Asia • 100 kW

PERU
RADIO ATLANTIDA, Iquitos — DS • 1/3 kW / Su • DS • 1/3 kW

SAUDI ARABIA
BS OF THE KINGDOM, Jiddah — Irr • 0.5 X 9580 KHZ • SPR

4790v PAKISTAN (AZAD K)
AZAD KASHMIR RADIO, Via Islamabad — S Asia • 100 kW
AZAD KASHMIR RADIO, Via Rawalpindi — S Asia • 10 kW

4790.2 PERU
†RADIO VISION, Chiclayo — DS • 0.5 kW / Irr • DS • 0.5 kW

4795 KYRGYZSTAN
KYRGYZ NATIONAL RADIO, Bishkek — KYRGYZ, ENGLISH, GERMAN & RUSSIAN • DS-1 • 15 kW

4796.4 BOLIVIA
RADIO MALLKU, Uyuni — Tu-Su • DS • 1 kW / SPANISH & QUECHUA • DS • 1 kW / M-Sa • DS • 1 kW

4799.8 GUATEMALA
R BUENAS NUEVAS, San Sebastián — SPANISH, ETC • DS • 1 kW

4800 CHINA
CENTRAL PEOPLE'S BS, Geermu — DS-1 • 100 kW / W-M • DS-1 • 100 kW

INDIA
ALL INDIA RADIO, Hyderabad — Irr • DS • 50 kW / DS • 50 kW / ENGLISH, ETC • DS • 50 kW

LESOTHO
RADIO LESOTHO, Maseru — DS-TEMP INACTIVE • 100 kW

4805 BRAZIL
†R DIF DO AMAZONAS, Manaus — DS • 5/10 kW

4810 ARMENIA
†PUBLIC RADIO OF ARMENIA, Yerevan — • E Europe, Mideast & W Asia • DS • 100 kW
†VOICE OF ARMENIA, Yerevan — • E Europe, Mideast & W Asia • 100 kW

INDIA
†ALL INDIA RADIO, Bhopal — ENGLISH, ETC • DS • 50 kW / DS • 50 kW

4810v MEXICO
R TRANSCONTINENTAL, México City — • Irr • 2.5/5 kW / • Irr • M-Sa • 2.5/5 kW

4815 BRAZIL
RADIO DIFUSORA, Londrina — DS • 10 kW • / Irr • DS • 10 kW •

ECUADOR
RADIO BUEN PASTOR, Saraguro — SPANISH, ETC • DS • 1 kW / DS • 1 kW

4819.2 HONDURAS
LA VOZ EVANGELICA, Tegucigalpa — DS-TEMP INACTIVE • 2/5 kW / M • DS-TEMP INACTIVE • 2/5 kW / Tu-Su • DS-TEMP INACTIVE • 2/5 kW

4820 CHINA
†XIZANG PBS, Lhasa — DS • 100 kW / W-M • DS • 100 kW

INDIA
ALL INDIA RADIO, Kolkata — DS • 50 kW / ENGLISH, ETC • DS • 50 kW

4824.4 PERU
(con'd) LA VOZ DE LA SELVA, Iquitos — Tu-Su • DS • 10 kW / M-F • DS • 10 kW

0 1 2 3 4 5 6 7 8 9 10 11 12 13 14 15 16 17 18 19 20 21 22 23 24

SEASONAL S OR W   1-HR TIMESHIFT MIDYEAR ⇐ OR ⇒   JAMMING / OR /\   EARLIEST HEARD ◁   LATEST HEARD ▷   NEW FOR 2008 †

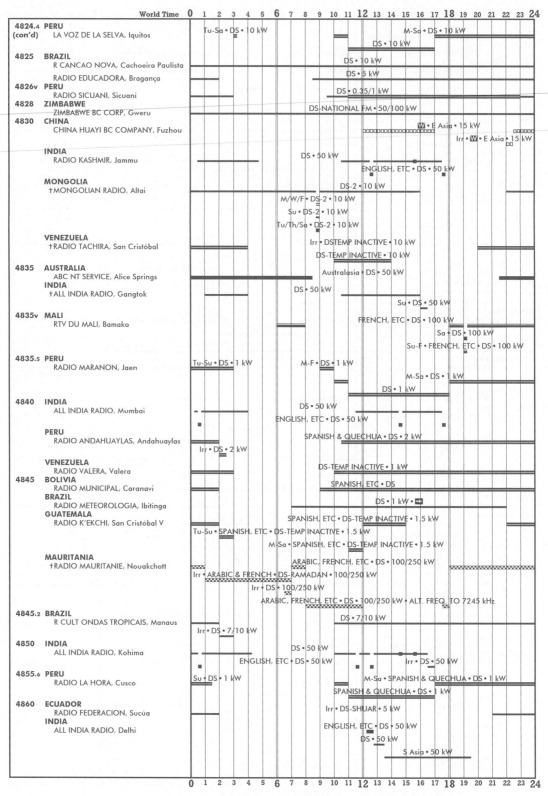

World Time

4824.4 PERU
(con'd)   LA VOZ DE LA SELVA, Iquitos

4825 BRAZIL
         R CANCAO NOVA, Cachoeira Paulista
         RADIO EDUCADORA, Bragança
4826v PERU
         RADIO SICUANI, Sicuani
4828 ZIMBABWE
         ZIMBABWE BC CORP, Gweru
4830 CHINA
         CHINA HUAYI BC COMPANY, Fuzhou

         INDIA
         RADIO KASHMIR, Jammu

         MONGOLIA
         †MONGOLIAN RADIO, Altai

         VENEZUELA
         †RADIO TACHIRA, San Cristóbal

4835 AUSTRALIA
         ABC NT SERVICE, Alice Springs
         INDIA
         †ALL INDIA RADIO, Gangtok

4835v MALI
         RTV DU MALI, Bamako

4835.5 PERU
         RADIO MARANON, Jaen

4840 INDIA
         ALL INDIA RADIO, Mumbai

         PERU
         RADIO ANDAHUAYLAS, Andahuaylas

         VENEZUELA
         RADIO VALERA, Valera
4845 BOLIVIA
         RADIO MUNICIPAL, Caranavi
         BRAZIL
         RADIO METEOROLOGIA, Ibitinga
         GUATEMALA
         RADIO K'EKCHI, San Cristóbal V

         MAURITANIA
         †RADIO MAURITANIE, Nouakchott

4845.2 BRAZIL
         R CULT ONDAS TROPICAIS, Manaus

4850 INDIA
         ALL INDIA RADIO, Kohima

4855.6 PERU
         RADIO LA HORA, Cusco

4860 ECUADOR
         RADIO FEDERACION, Sucúa
         INDIA
         ALL INDIA RADIO, Delhi

ENGLISH ▬ ARABIC ▨ CHINESE ▫▫▫ FRENCH ▬ GERMAN ▬ RUSSIAN ═ SPANISH ▬ OTHER ▬

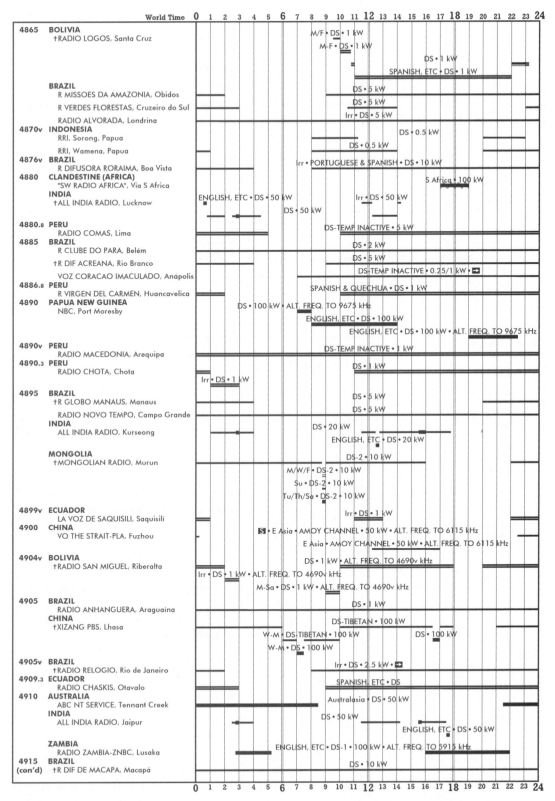

World Time 0 1 2 3 4 5 6 7 8 9 10 11 12 13 14 15 16 17 18 19 20 21 22 23 24

4865 BOLIVIA
†RADIO LOGOS, Santa Cruz
- M/F • DS • 1 kW
- M-F • DS • 1 kW
- DS • 1 kW
- SPANISH, ETC • DS • 1 kW

BRAZIL
R MISSOES DA AMAZONIA, Obidos — DS • 5 kW
R VERDES FLORESTAS, Cruzeiro do Sul — DS • 5 kW
RADIO ALVORADA, Londrina — Irr • DS • 5 kW

4870v INDONESIA
RRI, Sorong, Papua — DS • 0.5 kW
RRI, Wamena, Papua — DS • 0.5 kW

4876v BRAZIL
R DIFUSORA RORAIMA, Boa Vista — Irr • PORTUGUESE & SPANISH • DS • 10 kW

4880 CLANDESTINE (AFRICA)
"SW RADIO AFRICA", Via S Africa — S Africa • 100 kW

INDIA
†ALL INDIA RADIO, Lucknow
- ENGLISH, ETC • DS • 50 kW
- Irr • DS • 50 kW
- DS • 50 kW

4880.8 PERU
RADIO COMAS, Lima — DS-TEMP INACTIVE • 5 kW

4885 BRAZIL
R CLUBE DO PARA, Belém — DS • 2 kW
†R DIF ACREANA, Rio Branco — DS • 5 kW
VOZ CORACAO IMACULADO, Anápolis — DS-TEMP INACTIVE • 0.25/1 kW • ⟶

4886.8 PERU
R VIRGEN DEL CARMEN, Huancavelica — SPANISH & QUECHUA • DS • 1 kW

4890 PAPUA NEW GUINEA
NBC, Port Moresby
- DS • 100 kW • ALT. FREQ. TO 9675 kHz
- ENGLISH, ETC • DS • 100 kW
- ENGLISH, ETC • DS • 100 kW • ALT. FREQ. TO 9675 kHz

4890v PERU
RADIO MACEDONIA, Arequipa — DS-TEMP INACTIVE • 1 kW

4890.3 PERU
RADIO CHOTA, Chota
- DS • 1 kW
- Irr • DS • 1 kW

4895 BRAZIL
†R GLOBO MANAUS, Manaus — DS • 5 kW
RADIO NOVO TEMPO, Campo Grande — DS • 5 kW

INDIA
ALL INDIA RADIO, Kurseong
- DS • 20 kW
- ENGLISH, ETC • DS • 20 kW

MONGOLIA
†MONGOLIAN RADIO, Murun
- DS-2 • 10 kW
- M/W/F • DS-2 • 10 kW
- Su • DS-2 • 10 kW
- Tu/Th/Sa • DS-2 • 10 kW

4899v ECUADOR
LA VOZ DE SAQUISILI, Saquisili — Irr • DS • 1 kW

4900 CHINA
VO THE STRAIT-PLA, Fuzhou
- ⑤ E Asia • AMOY CHANNEL • 50 kW • ALT. FREQ. TO 6115 kHz
- E Asia • AMOY CHANNEL • 50 kW • ALT. FREQ. TO 6115 kHz

4904v BOLIVIA
†RADIO SAN MIGUEL, Riberalta
- DS • 1 kW • ALT. FREQ. TO 4690v kHz
- Irr • DS • 1 kW • ALT. FREQ. TO 4690v kHz
- M-Sa • DS • 1 kW • ALT. FREQ. TO 4690v kHz

4905 BRAZIL
RADIO ANHANGUERA, Araguaina — DS • 1 kW

CHINA
†XIZANG PBS, Lhasa
- DS-TIBETAN • 100 kW
- W-M • DS-TIBETAN • 100 kW
- DS • 100 kW
- W-M • DS • 100 kW

4905v BRAZIL
†RADIO RELOGIO, Rio de Janeiro — Irr • DS • 2.5 kW • ⟶

4909.3 ECUADOR
RADIO CHASKIS, Otavalo — SPANISH, ETC • DS

4910 AUSTRALIA
ABC NT SERVICE, Tennant Creek — Australasia • DS • 50 kW

INDIA
ALL INDIA RADIO, Jaipur
- DS • 50 kW
- ENGLISH, ETC • DS • 50 kW

ZAMBIA
RADIO ZAMBIA-ZNBC, Lusaka — ENGLISH, ETC • DS-1 • 100 kW • ALT. FREQ. TO 5915 kHz

4915 BRAZIL
(con'd) †R DIF DE MACAPA, Macapá — DS • 10 kW

0 1 2 3 4 5 6 7 8 9 10 11 12 13 14 15 16 17 18 19 20 21 22 23 24

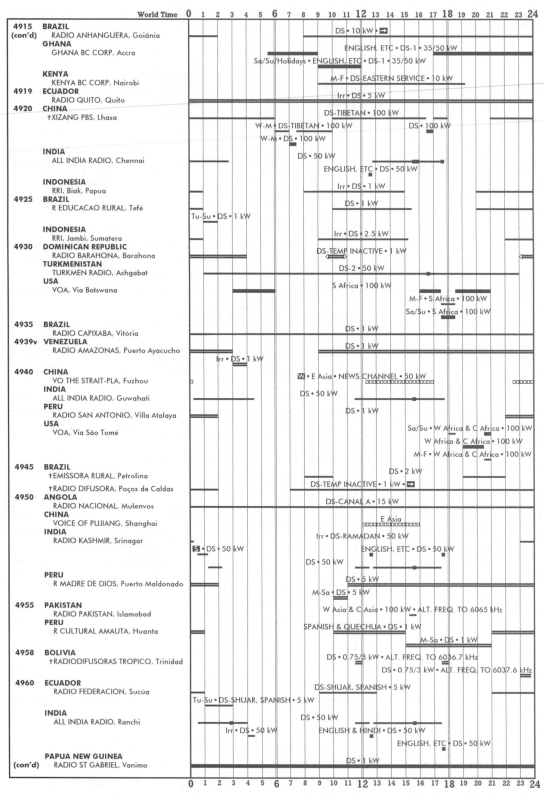

World Time 0 1 2 3 4 5 6 7 8 9 10 11 12 13 14 15 16 17 18 19 20 21 22 23 24

4915 **BRAZIL**
(con'd)   RADIO ANHANGUERA, Goiânia — DS • 10 kW •
GHANA
   GHANA BC CORP, Accra — ENGLISH, ETC • DS-1 • 35/50 kW
   Sa/Su/Holidays • ENGLISH, ETC • DS-1 • 35/50 kW
KENYA
   KENYA BC CORP, Nairobi — M-F • DS-EASTERN SERVICE • 10 kW
4919 **ECUADOR**
   RADIO QUITO, Quito — Irr • DS • 5 kW
4920 **CHINA**
   †XIZANG PBS, Lhasa — DS-TIBETAN • 100 kW
   W-M • DS-TIBETAN • 100 kW   DS • 100 kW
   W-M • DS • 100 kW
INDIA
   ALL INDIA RADIO, Chennai — DS • 50 kW
   ENGLISH, ETC • DS • 50 kW
INDONESIA
   RRI, Biak, Papua — Irr • DS • 1 kW
4925 **BRAZIL**
   R EDUCACAO RURAL, Tefé — DS • 1 kW
   Tu-Su • DS • 1 kW
INDONESIA
   RRI, Jambi, Sumatera — Irr • DS • 2.5 kW
4930 **DOMINICAN REPUBLIC**
   RADIO BARAHONA, Barahona — DS-TEMP INACTIVE • 1 kW
TURKMENISTAN
   TURKMEN RADIO, Ashgabat — DS-2 • 50 kW
USA
   VOA, Via Botswana — S Africa • 100 kW
   M-F • S Africa • 100 kW
   Sa/Su • S Africa • 100 kW
4935 **BRAZIL**
   RADIO CAPIXABA, Vitória — DS • 1 kW
4939v **VENEZUELA**
   RADIO AMAZONAS, Puerto Ayacucho — DS • 1 kW
   Irr • DS • 1 kW
4940 **CHINA**
   VO THE STRAIT-PLA, Fuzhou — W • E Asia • NEWS CHANNEL • 50 kW
INDIA
   ALL INDIA RADIO, Guwahati — DS • 50 kW
PERU
   RADIO SAN ANTONIO, Villa Atalaya — DS • 1 kW
USA
   VOA, Via São Tomé — Sa/Su • W Africa & C Africa • 100 kW
   W Africa & C Africa • 100 kW
   M-F • W Africa & C Africa • 100 kW
4945 **BRAZIL**
   †EMISSORA RURAL, Petrolina — DS • 2 kW
   †RADIO DIFUSORA, Poços de Caldas — DS-TEMP INACTIVE • 1 kW •
4950 **ANGOLA**
   RADIO NACIONAL, Mulenvos — DS-CANAL A • 15 kW
CHINA
   VOICE OF PUJIANG, Shanghai — E Asia
INDIA
   RADIO KASHMIR, Srinagar — Irr • DS-RAMADAN • 50 kW
   DS • 50 kW
   ENGLISH, ETC • DS • 50 kW
   DS • 50 kW
PERU
   R MADRE DE DIOS, Puerto Maldonado — DS • 5 kW
   M-Sa • DS • 5 kW
4955 **PAKISTAN**
   RADIO PAKISTAN, Islamabad — W Asia & C Asia • 100 kW • ALT. FREQ. TO 6065 kHz
PERU
   R CULTURAL AMAUTA, Huanta — SPANISH & QUECHUA • DS • 1 kW
   M-Sa • DS • 1 kW
4958 **BOLIVIA**
   †RADIODIFUSORAS TROPICO, Trinidad — DS • 0.75/3 kW • ALT. FREQ. TO 6036.7 kHz
   DS • 0.75/3 kW • ALT. FREQ. TO 6037.6 kHz
4960 **ECUADOR**
   RADIO FEDERACION, Sucúa — DS-SHUAR, SPANISH • 5 kW
   Tu-Su • DS-SHUAR, SPANISH • 5 kW
INDIA
   ALL INDIA RADIO, Ranchi — DS • 50 kW
   Irr • DS • 50 kW
   ENGLISH & HINDI • DS • 50 kW
   ENGLISH, ETC • DS • 50 kW
PAPUA NEW GUINEA
(con'd)   RADIO ST GABRIEL, Vanimo — DS • 1 kW

0 1 2 3 4 5 6 7 8 9 10 11 12 13 14 15 16 17 18 19 20 21 22 23 24

ENGLISH ▬   ARABIC ≋   CHINESE ▫▫▫   FRENCH ▬   GERMAN ▬   RUSSIAN ═   SPANISH ▬   OTHER ▬

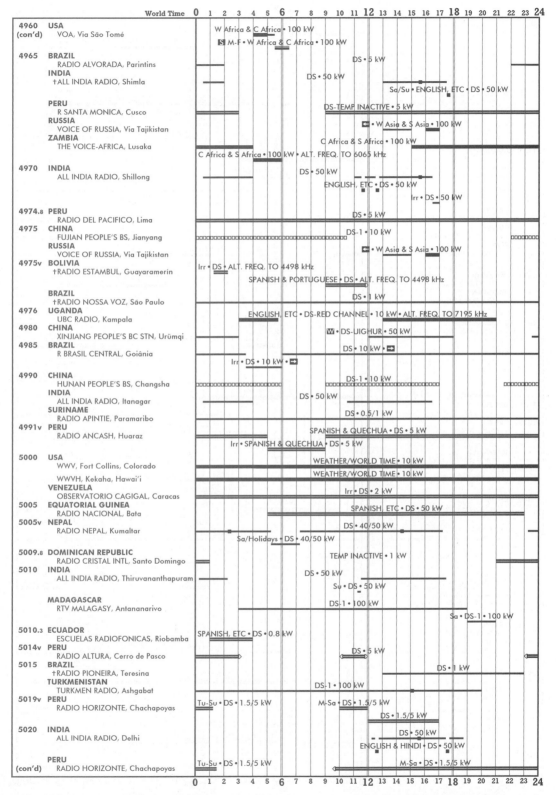

| | | World Time | 0 | 1 | 2 | 3 | 4 | 5 | 6 | 7 | 8 | 9 | 10 | 11 | 12 | 13 | 14 | 15 | 16 | 17 | 18 | 19 | 20 | 21 | 22 | 23 | 24 |

4960 USA
(con'd)   VOA, Via São Tomé — W Africa & C Africa • 100 kW
  🅂 M-F • W Africa & C Africa • 100 kW

4965 BRAZIL
  RADIO ALVORADA, Parintins — DS • 5 kW
  INDIA
  †ALL INDIA RADIO, Shimla — DS • 50 kW
  Sa/Su • ENGLISH, ETC • DS • 50 kW

  PERU
  R SANTA MONICA, Cusco — DS-TEMP INACTIVE • 5 kW
  RUSSIA
  VOICE OF RUSSIA, Via Tajikistan — W Asia & S Asia • 100 kW
  ZAMBIA
  THE VOICE-AFRICA, Lusaka — C Africa & S Africa • 100 kW
  C Africa & S Africa • 100 kW • ALT. FREQ. TO 6065 kHz

4970 INDIA
  ALL INDIA RADIO, Shillong — DS • 50 kW
  ENGLISH, ETC • DS • 50 kW
  Irr • DS • 50 kW

4974.8 PERU
  RADIO DEL PACIFICO, Lima — DS • 5 kW
4975 CHINA
  FUJIAN PEOPLE'S BS, Jianyang — DS-1 • 10 kW
  RUSSIA
  VOICE OF RUSSIA, Via Tajikistan — W Asia & S Asia • 100 kW
4975v BOLIVIA
  †RADIO ESTAMBUL, Guayaramerín — Irr • DS • ALT. FREQ. TO 4498 kHz
  SPANISH & PORTUGUESE • DS • ALT. FREQ. TO 4498 kHz

  BRAZIL
  †RADIO NOSSA VOZ, São Paulo — DS • 1 kW
4976 UGANDA
  UBC RADIO, Kampala — ENGLISH, ETC • DS-RED CHANNEL • 10 kW • ALT. FREQ. TO 7195 kHz
4980 CHINA
  XINJIANG PEOPLE'S BC STN, Urümqi — W • DS-UIGHUR • 50 kW
4985 BRAZIL
  R BRASIL CENTRAL, Goiânia — DS • 10 kW •
  Irr • DS • 10 kW •

4990 CHINA
  HUNAN PEOPLE'S BS, Changsha — DS-1 • 10 kW
  INDIA
  ALL INDIA RADIO, Itanagar — DS • 50 kW
  SURINAME
  RADIO APINTIE, Paramaribo — DS • 0.5/1 kW
4991v PERU
  RADIO ANCASH, Huaraz — SPANISH & QUECHUA • DS • 5 kW
  Irr • SPANISH & QUECHUA • DS • 5 kW

5000 USA
  WWV, Fort Collins, Colorado — WEATHER/WORLD TIME • 10 kW
  WWVH, Kekaha, Hawai'i — WEATHER/WORLD TIME • 10 kW
  VENEZUELA
  OBSERVATORIO CAGIGAL, Caracas — Irr • DS • 2 kW
5005 EQUATORIAL GUINEA
  RADIO NACIONAL, Bata — SPANISH, ETC • DS • 50 kW
5005v NEPAL
  RADIO NEPAL, Kumaltar — DS • 40/50 kW
  Sa/Holidays • DS • 40/50 kW

5009.8 DOMINICAN REPUBLIC
  RADIO CRISTAL INTL, Santo Domingo — TEMP INACTIVE • 1 kW
5010 INDIA
  ALL INDIA RADIO, Thiruvananthapuram — DS • 50 kW
  Su • DS • 50 kW

  MADAGASCAR
  RTV MALAGASY, Antananarivo — DS-1 • 100 kW
  Sa • DS-1 • 100 kW

5010.3 ECUADOR
  ESCUELAS RADIOFONICAS, Riobamba — SPANISH, ETC • DS • 0.8 kW
5014v PERU
  RADIO ALTURA, Cerro de Pasco — DS • 5 kW
5015 BRAZIL
  †RADIO PIONEIRA, Teresina — DS • 1 kW
  TURKMENISTAN
  TURKMEN RADIO, Ashgabat — DS-1 • 100 kW
5019v PERU
  RADIO HORIZONTE, Chachapoyas — Tu-Su • DS • 1.5/5 kW   M-Sa • DS • 1.5/5 kW
  DS • 1.5/5 kW

5020 INDIA
  ALL INDIA RADIO, Delhi — DS • 50 kW
  ENGLISH & HINDI • DS • 50 kW

  PERU
(con'd)   RADIO HORIZONTE, Chachapoyas — Tu-Su • DS • 1.5/5 kW   M-Sa • DS • 1.5/5 kW

SEASONAL 🅂 OR 🅆   1-HR TIMESHIFT MIDYEAR ⇦ OR ⇨   JAMMING / OR /\   EARLIEST HEARD ◁   LATEST HEARD ▷   NEW FOR 2008 †

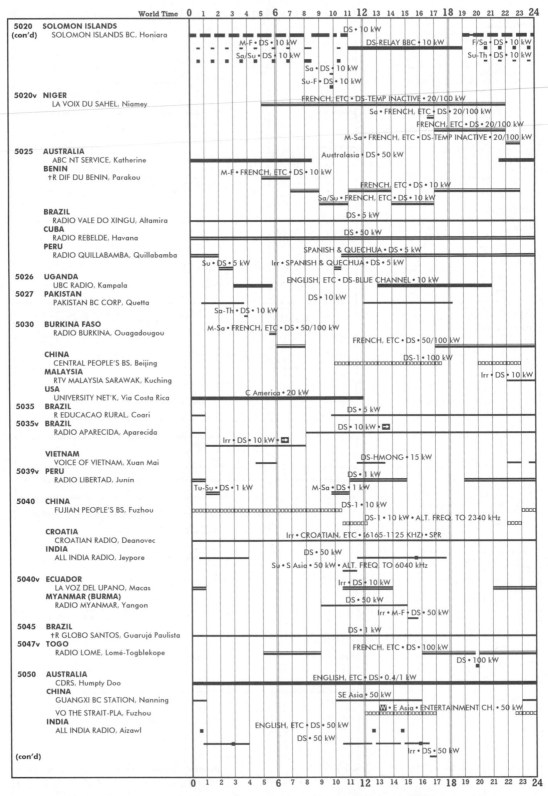

| | World Time | 0 | 1 | 2 | 3 | 4 | 5 | 6 | 7 | 8 | 9 | 10 | 11 | 12 | 13 | 14 | 15 | 16 | 17 | 18 | 19 | 20 | 21 | 22 | 23 | 24 |

5020 SOLOMON ISLANDS
(con'd) SOLOMON ISLANDS BC, Honiara — DS • 10 kW
M-F • DS • 10 kW   DS-RELAY BBC • 10 kW   F/Sa • DS • 10 kW
Sa/Su • DS • 10 kW   Su-Th • DS • 10 kW
Sa • DS • 10 kW
Su-F • DS • 10 kW

5020v NIGER
LA VOIX DU SAHEL, Niamey — FRENCH, ETC • DS-TEMP INACTIVE • 20/100 kW
Sa • FRENCH, ETC • DS • 20/100 kW
FRENCH, ETC • DS • 20/100 kW
M-Sa • FRENCH, ETC • DS-TEMP INACTIVE • 20/100 kW

5025 AUSTRALIA
ABC NT SERVICE, Katherine — Australasia • DS • 50 kW
BENIN
†R DIF DU BENIN, Parakou — M-F • FRENCH, ETC • DS • 10 kW
FRENCH, ETC • DS • 10 kW
Sa/Su • FRENCH, ETC • DS • 10 kW
BRAZIL
RADIO VALE DO XINGU, Altamira — DS • 5 kW
CUBA
RADIO REBELDE, Havana — DS • 50 kW
PERU
RADIO QUILLABAMBA, Quillabamba — SPANISH & QUECHUA • DS • 5 kW
Su • DS • 5 kW   Irr • SPANISH & QUECHUA • DS • 5 kW

5026 UGANDA
UBC RADIO, Kampala — ENGLISH, ETC • DS-BLUE CHANNEL • 10 kW
5027 PAKISTAN
PAKISTAN BC CORP, Quetta — DS • 10 kW
Sa-Th • DS • 10 kW

5030 BURKINA FASO
RADIO BURKINA, Ouagadougou — M-Sa • FRENCH, ETC • DS • 50/100 kW
FRENCH, ETC • DS • 50/100 kW
CHINA
CENTRAL PEOPLE'S BS, Beijing — DS-1 • 100 kW
MALAYSIA
RTV MALAYSIA SARAWAK, Kuching — Irr • DS • 10 kW
USA
UNIVERSITY NET'K, Via Costa Rica — C America • 20 kW
5035 BRAZIL
R EDUCACAO RURAL, Coari — DS • 5 kW
5035v BRAZIL
RADIO APARECIDA, Aparecida — DS • 10 kW •
Irr • DS • 10 kW •
VIETNAM
VOICE OF VIETNAM, Xuan Mai — DS-HMONG • 15 kW
5039v PERU
RADIO LIBERTAD, Junin — DS • 1 kW
Tu-Su • DS • 1 kW   M-Sa • DS • 1 kW
5040 CHINA
FUJIAN PEOPLE'S BS, Fuzhou — DS-1 • 10 kW
DS-1 • 10 kW • ALT. FREQ. TO 2340 kHz
CROATIA
CROATIAN RADIO, Deanovec — Irr • CROATIAN, ETC • (6165-1125 KHZ) • SPR
INDIA
ALL INDIA RADIO, Jeypore — DS • 50 kW
Su • S Asia • 50 kW • ALT. FREQ. TO 6040 kHz
5040v ECUADOR
LA VOZ DEL UPANO, Macas — Irr • DS • 10 kW
MYANMAR (BURMA)
RADIO MYANMAR, Yangon — DS • 50 kW
Irr • M-F • DS • 50 kW
5045 BRAZIL
†R GLOBO SANTOS, Guarujá Paulista — DS • 1 kW
5047v TOGO
RADIO LOME, Lomé-Togblekope — FRENCH, ETC • DS • 100 kW
DS • 100 kW
5050 AUSTRALIA
CDRS, Humpty Doo — ENGLISH, ETC • DS • 0.4/1 kW
CHINA
GUANGXI BC STATION, Nanning — SE Asia • 50 kW
VO THE STRAIT-PLA, Fuzhou — W • E Asia • ENTERTAINMENT CH. • 50 kW
INDIA
ALL INDIA RADIO, Aizawl — ENGLISH, ETC • DS • 50 kW
DS • 50 kW
Irr • DS • 50 kW

(con'd)

| | 0 | 1 | 2 | 3 | 4 | 5 | 6 | 7 | 8 | 9 | 10 | 11 | 12 | 13 | 14 | 15 | 16 | 17 | 18 | 19 | 20 | 21 | 22 | 23 | 24 |

ENGLISH ▬   ARABIC ⧓⧓⧓   CHINESE □□□   FRENCH ▬   GERMAN ▬   RUSSIAN ═══   SPANISH ▬   OTHER ▬

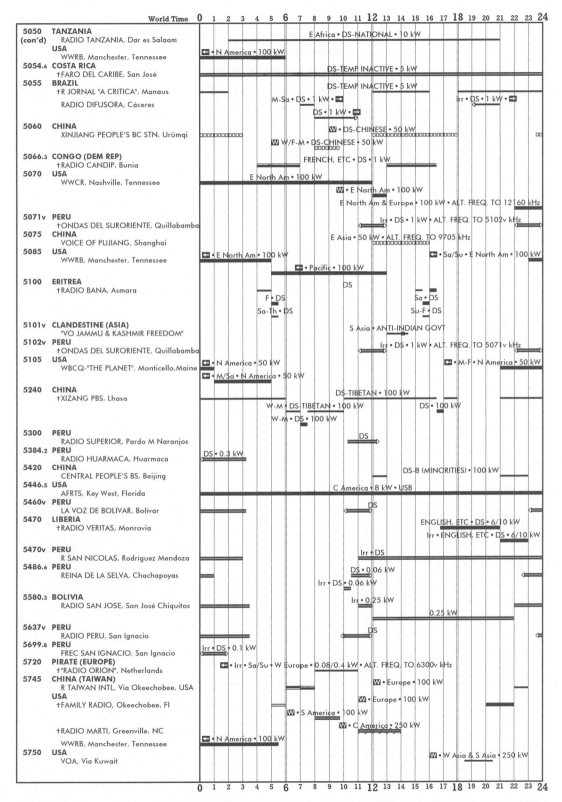

World Time 0 1 2 3 4 5 6 7 8 9 10 11 12 13 14 15 16 17 18 19 20 21 22 23 24

5050	TANZANIA
(con'd)	RADIO TANZANIA, Dar es Salaam	E Africa • DS-NATIONAL • 10 kW
	USA	
	WWRB, Manchester, Tennessee	◄⊒ • N America • 100 kW
5054.6	COSTA RICA	DS-TEMP INACTIVE • 5 kW
	†FARO DEL CARIBE, San José	
5055	BRAZIL	DS-TEMP INACTIVE • 5 kW
	†R JORNAL "A CRITICA", Manaus	M-Sa • DS • 1 kW • ⊒▶ Irr • DS • 1 kW • ⊒▶
	RADIO DIFUSORA, Cáceres	DS • 1 kW • ⊒▶
5060	CHINA	W • DS-CHINESE • 50 kW
	XINJIANG PEOPLE'S BC STN, Urümqi	▯▯▯▯▯▯▯▯▯▯▯ ▯▯▯▯▯▯▯▯▯▯▯▯▯▯▯▯▯▯
		W W/F-M • DS-CHINESE • 50 kW
		▯▯▯▯▯▯▯▯
5066.3	CONGO (DEM REP)	FRENCH, ETC • DS • 1 kW
	†RADIO CANDIP, Bunia	
5070	USA	E North Am • 100 kW
	WWCR, Nashville, Tennessee	W • E North Am • 100 kW
		E North Am & Europe • 100 kW • ALT. FREQ. TO 12160 kHz
5071v	PERU	Irr • DS • 1 kW • ALT. FREQ. TO 5102v kHz
	†ONDAS DEL SURORIENTE, Quillabamba	
5075	CHINA	E Asia • 50 kW • ALT. FREQ. TO 9705 kHz
	VOICE OF PUJIANG, Shanghai	▯▯▯▯▯▯▯▯▯▯▯▯▯
5085	USA	◄⊒ • E North Am • 100 kW ⊒► • Sa/Su • E North Am • 100 kW
	WWRB, Manchester, Tennessee	⊒► • Pacific • 100 kW
5100	ERITREA	DS
	†RADIO BANA, Asmara	F • DS Sa • DS
		Sa-Th • DS Su-F • DS
5101v	CLANDESTINE (ASIA)	S Asia • ANTI-INDIAN GOVT
	"VO JAMMU & KASHMIR FREEDOM"	
5102v	PERU	Irr • DS • 1 kW • ALT. FREQ. TO 5071v kHz
	†ONDAS DEL SURORIENTE, Quillabamba	
5105	USA	◄⊒ • N America • 50 kW ⊒► • M-F • N America • 50 kW
	WBCQ-"THE PLANET", Monticello, Maine	◄⊒ • M/Sa • N America • 50 kW
5240	CHINA	DS-TIBETAN • 100 kW
	†XIZANG PBS, Lhasa	W-M • DS-TIBETAN • 100 kW DS • 100 kW
		W-M • DS • 100 kW
5300	PERU	DS
	RADIO SUPERIOR, Pardo M Naranjos	
5384.2	PERU	DS • 0.3 kW
	RADIO HUARMACA, Huarmaca	
5420	CHINA	DS-8 (MINORITIES) • 100 kW
	CENTRAL PEOPLE'S BS, Beijing	
5446.5	USA	C America • 8 kW • USB
	AFRTS, Key West, Florida	
5460v	PERU	DS
	LA VOZ DE BOLIVAR, Bolivar	
5470	LIBERIA	ENGLISH, ETC • DS • 6/10 kW
	†RADIO VERITAS, Monrovia	Irr • ENGLISH, ETC • DS • 6/10 kW
5470v	PERU	Irr • DS
	R SAN NICOLAS, Rodríguez Mendoza	
5486.6	PERU	DS • 0.06 kW
	REINA DE LA SELVA, Chachapoyas	Irr • DS • 0.06 kW
5580.3	BOLIVIA	Irr • 0.25 kW
	RADIO SAN JOSE, San José Chiquitos	0.25 kW
5637v	PERU	DS
	RADIO PERU, San Ignacio	
5699.8	PERU	Irr • DS • 0.1 kW
	FREC SAN IGNACIO, San Ignacio	
5720	PIRATE (EUROPE)	⊒► • Irr • Sa/Su • W Europe • 0.08/0.4 kW • ALT. FREQ. TO 6300v kHz
	†"RADIO ORION", Netherlands	
5745	CHINA (TAIWAN)	W • Europe • 100 kW
	R TAIWAN INTL, Via Okeechobee, USA	
	USA	W • Europe • 100 kW
	†FAMILY RADIO, Okeechobee, Fl	W • S America • 100 kW
	†RADIO MARTI, Greenville, NC	W • C America • 250 kW
	WWRB, Manchester, Tennessee	◄⊒ • N America • 100 kW
5750	USA	W • W Asia & S Asia • 250 kW
	VOA, Via Kuwait	

0 1 2 3 4 5 6 7 8 9 10 11 12 13 14 15 16 17 18 19 20 21 22 23 24

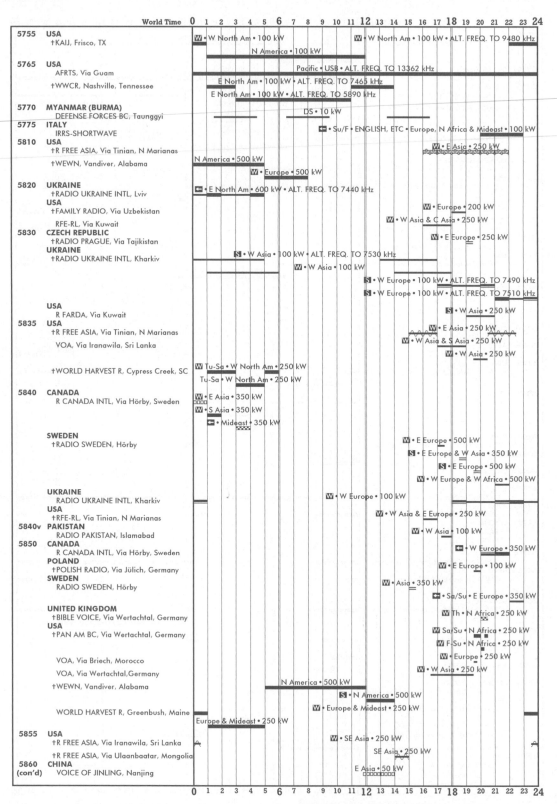

World Time 0 1 2 3 4 5 6 7 8 9 10 11 12 13 14 15 16 17 18 19 20 21 22 23 24

Freq	Country / Station
5755	**USA** — †KAIJ, Frisco, TX
5765	**USA** — AFRTS, Via Guam
	†WWCR, Nashville, Tennessee
5770	**MYANMAR (BURMA)** — DEFENSE FORCES BC, Taunggyi
5775	**ITALY** — IRRS-SHORTWAVE
5810	**USA** — †R FREE ASIA, Via Tinian, N Marianas
	†WEWN, Vandiver, Alabama
5820	**UKRAINE** — †RADIO UKRAINE INTL, Lviv
	USA — †FAMILY RADIO, Via Uzbekistan
	RFE-RL, Via Kuwait
5830	**CZECH REPUBLIC** — †RADIO PRAGUE, Via Tajikistan
	UKRAINE — †RADIO UKRAINE INTL, Kharkiv
	USA — R FARDA, Via Kuwait
5835	**USA** — †R FREE ASIA, Via Tinian, N Marianas
	VOA, Via Iranawila, Sri Lanka
	†WORLD HARVEST R, Cypress Creek, SC
5840	**CANADA** — R CANADA INTL, Via Hörby, Sweden
	SWEDEN — †RADIO SWEDEN, Hörby
	UKRAINE — RADIO UKRAINE INTL, Kharkiv
	USA — †RFE-RL, Via Tinian, N Marianas
5840v	**PAKISTAN** — RADIO PAKISTAN, Islamabad
5850	**CANADA** — R CANADA INTL, Via Hörby, Sweden
	POLAND — †POLISH RADIO, Via Jülich, Germany
	SWEDEN — RADIO SWEDEN, Hörby
	UNITED KINGDOM — †BIBLE VOICE, Via Wertachtal, Germany
	USA — †PAN AM BC, Via Wertachtal, Germany
	VOA, Via Briech, Morocco
	VOA, Via Wertachtal, Germany
	†WEWN, Vandiver, Alabama
	WORLD HARVEST R, Greenbush, Maine
5855	**USA** — †R FREE ASIA, Via Iranawila, Sri Lanka
	†R FREE ASIA, Via Ulaanbaatar, Mongolia
5860 (con'd)	**CHINA** — VOICE OF JINLING, Nanjing

Programme schedule bar notes:

5755 USA †KAIJ, Frisco, TX — W • W North Am • 100 kW; N America • 100 kW; W • W North Am • 100 kW • ALT. FREQ. TO 9480 kHz

5765 USA AFRTS, Via Guam — Pacific • USB • ALT. FREQ. TO 13362 kHz

†WWCR, Nashville, Tennessee — E North Am • 100 kW • ALT. FREQ. TO 7465 kHz; E North Am • 100 kW • ALT. FREQ. TO 5890 kHz

5770 MYANMAR (BURMA) DEFENSE FORCES BC, Taunggyi — DS • 10 kW

5775 ITALY IRRS-SHORTWAVE — • Su/F • ENGLISH, ETC • Europe, N Africa & Mideast • 100 kW

5810 USA †R FREE ASIA, Via Tinian, N Marianas — W • E Asia • 250 kW

†WEWN, Vandiver, Alabama — N America • 500 kW; W • Europe • 500 kW

5820 UKRAINE †RADIO UKRAINE INTL, Lviv — • E North Am • 600 kW • ALT. FREQ. TO 7440 kHz

USA †FAMILY RADIO, Via Uzbekistan — W • Europe • 200 kW

RFE-RL, Via Kuwait — W • W Asia & C Asia • 250 kW

5830 CZECH REPUBLIC †RADIO PRAGUE, Via Tajikistan — W • E Europe • 250 kW

UKRAINE †RADIO UKRAINE INTL, Kharkiv — S • W Asia • 100 kW • ALT. FREQ. TO 7530 kHz; W • W Asia • 100 kW; S • W Europe • 100 kW • ALT. FREQ. TO 7490 kHz; S • W Europe • 100 kW • ALT. FREQ. TO 7510 kHz

USA R FARDA, Via Kuwait — S • W Asia • 250 kW

5835 USA †R FREE ASIA, Via Tinian, N Marianas — W • E Asia • 250 kW

VOA, Via Iranawila, Sri Lanka — W • W Asia & S Asia • 250 kW; W • W Asia • 250 kW

†WORLD HARVEST R, Cypress Creek, SC — W Tu-Sa • W North Am • 250 kW; Tu-Sa • W North Am • 250 kW

5840 CANADA R CANADA INTL, Via Hörby, Sweden — W • E Asia • 350 kW; W • S Asia • 350 kW; • Mideast • 350 kW

SWEDEN †RADIO SWEDEN, Hörby — W • E Europe • 500 kW; S • E Europe & W Asia • 350 kW; S • E Europe • 500 kW; W • W Europe & W Africa • 500 kW

UKRAINE RADIO UKRAINE INTL, Kharkiv — W • W Europe • 100 kW

USA †RFE-RL, Via Tinian, N Marianas — W • W Asia & E Europe • 250 kW

5840v PAKISTAN RADIO PAKISTAN, Islamabad — W • W Asia • 100 kW

5850 CANADA R CANADA INTL, Via Hörby, Sweden — • W Europe • 350 kW

POLAND †POLISH RADIO, Via Jülich, Germany — W • E Europe • 100 kW

SWEDEN RADIO SWEDEN, Hörby — W • Asia • 350 kW; • Sa/Su • E Europe • 350 kW

UNITED KINGDOM †BIBLE VOICE, Via Wertachtal, Germany — W Th • N Africa • 250 kW

USA †PAN AM BC, Via Wertachtal, Germany — W Sa/Su • N Africa • 250 kW; W F-Su • N Africa • 250 kW

VOA, Via Briech, Morocco — W • Europe • 250 kW

VOA, Via Wertachtal, Germany — W • W Asia • 250 kW

†WEWN, Vandiver, Alabama — N America • 500 kW; S • N America • 500 kW; W • Europe & Mideast • 250 kW

WORLD HARVEST R, Greenbush, Maine — Europe & Mideast • 250 kW

5855 USA †R FREE ASIA, Via Iranawila, Sri Lanka — W • SE Asia • 250 kW

†R FREE ASIA, Via Ulaanbaatar, Mongolia — SE Asia • 250 kW

5860 CHINA VOICE OF JINLING, Nanjing — E Asia • 50 kW

0 1 2 3 4 5 6 7 8 9 10 11 12 13 14 15 16 17 18 19 20 21 22 23 24

ENGLISH ▬   **ARABIC** ⌇⌇⌇   **CHINESE** □□□   **FRENCH** ═══   **GERMAN** ▬▬   **RUSSIAN** ══   **SPANISH** ▭▭   **OTHER** ▭

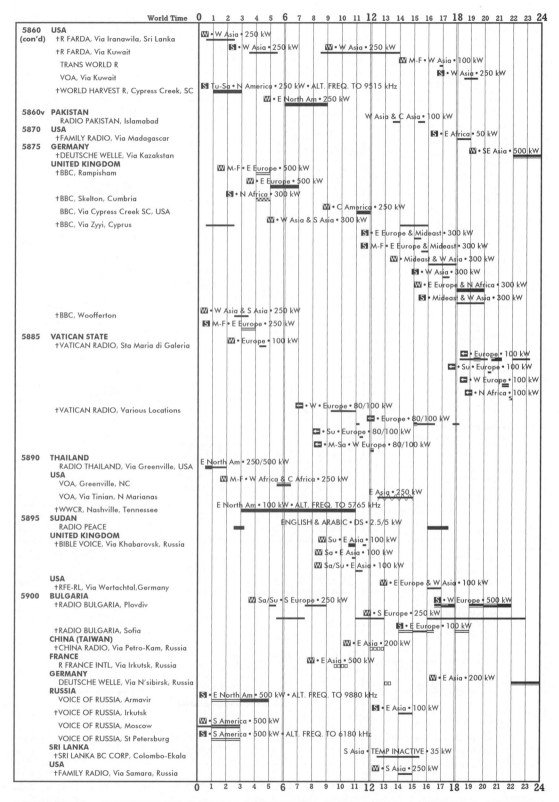

World Time

| | 0 1 2 3 4 5 6 7 8 9 10 11 12 13 14 15 16 17 18 19 20 21 22 23 24 |

5860 USA
(con'd) †R FARDA, Via Iranawila, Sri Lanka — W • W Asia • 250 kW
†R FARDA, Via Kuwait — S • W Asia • 250 kW / W • W Asia • 250 kW
TRANS WORLD R — W M-F • W Asia • 100 kW
VOA, Via Kuwait — S • W Asia • 250 kW
†WORLD HARVEST R, Cypress Creek, SC — S Tu-Sa • N America • 250 kW • ALT. FREQ. TO 9515 kHz
— W • E North Am • 250 kW

5860v PAKISTAN
RADIO PAKISTAN, Islamabad — W Asia & C Asia • 100 kW
5870 USA
†FAMILY RADIO, Via Madagascar — S • E Africa • 50 kW
5875 GERMANY
†DEUTSCHE WELLE, Via Kazakstan — W • SE Asia • 500 kW
UNITED KINGDOM
†BBC, Rampisham — W M-F • E Europe • 500 kW
— W • E Europe • 500 kW
— S • N Africa • 300 kW
†BBC, Skelton, Cumbria — W • C America • 250 kW
BBC, Via Cypress Creek SC, USA — W • W Asia & S Asia • 300 kW
†BBC, Via Zyyi, Cyprus — S • E Europe & Mideast • 300 kW
— S M-F • E Europe & Mideast • 300 kW
— W • Mideast & W Asia • 300 kW
— S • W Asia • 300 kW
— W • E Europe & N Africa • 300 kW
— S • Mideast & W Asia • 300 kW
†BBC, Woofferton — W • W Asia & S Asia • 250 kW
— S M-F • E Europe • 250 kW

5885 VATICAN STATE
†VATICAN RADIO, Sta Maria di Galeria — W • Europe • 100 kW
— ⇄ • Europe • 100 kW
— ⇄ • Su • Europe • 100 kW
— ⇄ • W Europe • 100 kW
— ⇄ • N Africa • 100 kW
†VATICAN RADIO, Various Locations — ⇄ • W • Europe • 80/100 kW
— ⇄ • Europe • 80/100 kW
— ⇄ • Su • Europe • 80/100 kW
— ⇄ • M-Sa • W Europe • 80/100 kW

5890 THAILAND
RADIO THAILAND, Via Greenville, USA — E North Am • 250/500 kW
USA
VOA, Greenville, NC — W M-F • W Africa & C Africa • 250 kW
VOA, Via Tinian, N Marianas — E Asia • 250 kW
†WWCR, Nashville, Tennessee — E North Am • 100 kW • ALT. FREQ. TO 5765 kHz
5895 SUDAN
RADIO PEACE — ENGLISH & ARABIC • DS • 2.5/5 kW
UNITED KINGDOM
†BIBLE VOICE, Via Khabarovsk, Russia — W Su • E Asia • 100 kW
— W Sa • E Asia • 100 kW
— W Sa/Su • E Asia • 100 kW
USA
†RFE-RL, Via Wertachtal, Germany — W • E Europe & W Asia • 100 kW
5900 BULGARIA
†RADIO BULGARIA, Plovdiv — W Sa/Su • S Europe • 250 kW
— S • W Europe • 500 kW
— W • S Europe • 250 kW
†RADIO BULGARIA, Sofia — S • E Europe • 100 kW
CHINA (TAIWAN)
†CHINA RADIO, Via Petro-Kam, Russia — W • E Asia • 200 kW
FRANCE
R FRANCE INTL, Via Irkutsk, Russia — W • E Asia • 500 kW
GERMANY
DEUTSCHE WELLE, Via N'sibirsk, Russia — W • E Asia • 200 kW
RUSSIA
VOICE OF RUSSIA, Armavir — S • E North Am • 500 kW • ALT. FREQ. TO 9880 kHz
— S • E Asia • 100 kW
†VOICE OF RUSSIA, Irkutsk
VOICE OF RUSSIA, Moscow — W • S America • 500 kW
VOICE OF RUSSIA, St Petersburg — S • S America • 500 kW • ALT. FREQ. TO 6180 kHz
SRI LANKA
†SRI LANKA BC CORP, Colombo-Ekala — S Asia • TEMP INACTIVE • 35 kW
USA
†FAMILY RADIO, Via Samara, Russia — W • S Asia • 250 kW

| | 0 1 2 3 4 5 6 7 8 9 10 11 12 13 14 15 16 17 18 19 20 21 22 23 24 |

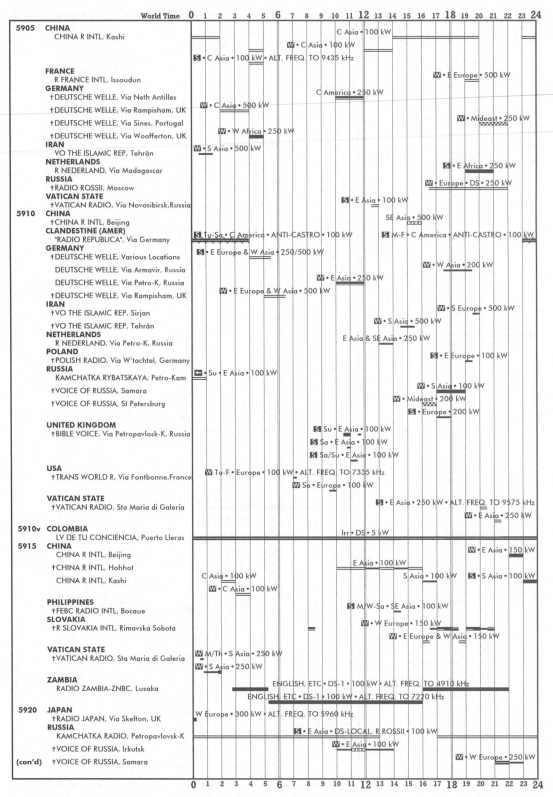

		World Time	0 1 2 3 4 5 6 7 8 9 10 11 12 13 14 15 16 17 18 19 20 21 22 23 24

5905 CHINA
CHINA R INTL, Kashi — C Asia • 100 kW · W • C Asia • 100 kW · S • C Asia • 100 kW • ALT. FREQ. TO 9435 kHz

FRANCE
R FRANCE INTL, Issoudun — W • E Europe • 500 kW
GERMANY
†DEUTSCHE WELLE, Via Neth Antilles — C America • 250 kW
†DEUTSCHE WELLE, Via Rampisham, UK — W • C Asia • 500 kW
†DEUTSCHE WELLE, Via Sines, Portugal — W • Mideast • 250 kW
†DEUTSCHE WELLE, Via Woofferton, UK — W • W Africa • 250 kW
IRAN
VO THE ISLAMIC REP, Tehrän — W • S Asia • 500 kW
NETHERLANDS
R NEDERLAND, Via Madagascar — S • E Africa • 250 kW
RUSSIA
†RADIO ROSSII, Moscow — W • Europe • DS • 250 kW
VATICAN STATE
†VATICAN RADIO, Via Novosibirsk,Russia — S • E Asia • 100 kW

5910 CHINA
†CHINA R INTL, Beijing — SE Asia • 500 kW
CLANDESTINE (AMER)
"RADIO REPUBLICA", Via Germany — S Tu-Sa • C America • ANTI-CASTRO • 100 kW · S M-F • C America • ANTI-CASTRO • 100 kW
GERMANY
†DEUTSCHE WELLE, Various Locations — S • E Europe & W Asia • 250/500 kW
DEUTSCHE WELLE, Via Armavir, Russia — W • W Asia • 200 kW
DEUTSCHE WELLE, Via Petro-K, Russia — W • E Asia • 250 kW
†DEUTSCHE WELLE, Via Rampisham, UK — W • E Europe & W Asia • 500 kW
IRAN
†VO THE ISLAMIC REP, Sirjan — W • S Europe • 500 kW
†VO THE ISLAMIC REP, Tehrän — W • S Asia • 500 kW
NETHERLANDS
R NEDERLAND, Via Petro-K, Russia — E Asia & SE Asia • 250 kW
POLAND
†POLISH RADIO, Via W'tachtal, Germany — S • E Europe • 100 kW
RUSSIA
KAMCHATKA RYBATSKAYA, Petro-Kam — S • Su • E Asia • 100 kW
†VOICE OF RUSSIA, Samara — W • S Asia • 100 kW
†VOICE OF RUSSIA, St Petersburg — W • Mideast • 200 kW · S • Europe • 200 kW
UNITED KINGDOM
†BIBLE VOICE, Via Petropavlosk-K, Russia — S Su • E Asia • 100 kW · S Sa • E Asia • 100 kW · S Sa/Su • E Asia • 100 kW
USA
†TRANS WORLD R, Via Fontbonne,France — W Tu-F • Europe • 100 kW • ALT. FREQ. TO 7335 kHz · W Sa • Europe • 100 kW
VATICAN STATE
†VATICAN RADIO, Sta Maria di Galeria — S • E Asia • 250 kW • ALT. FREQ. TO 9575 kHz · W • E Asia • 250 kW

5910v COLOMBIA
LV DE TU CONCIENCIA, Puerto Lleras — Irr • DS • 5 kW

5915 CHINA
CHINA R INTL, Beijing — W • E Asia • 150 kW
†CHINA R INTL, Hohhot — E Asia • 100 kW
CHINA R INTL, Kashi — C Asia • 100 kW · W • C Asia • 100 kW · S Asia • 100 kW · S • S Asia • 100 kW
PHILIPPINES
†FEBC RADIO INTL, Bocaue — S M/W-Sa • SE Asia • 100 kW
SLOVAKIA
†R SLOVAKIA INTL, Rimavská Sobota — W • W Europe • 150 kW · W • E Europe & W Asia • 150 kW
VATICAN STATE
†VATICAN RADIO, Sta Maria di Galeria — W M/Th • S Asia • 250 kW · W • S Asia • 250 kW
ZAMBIA
RADIO ZAMBIA-ZNBC, Lusaka — ENGLISH, ETC • DS-1 • 100 kW • ALT. FREQ. TO 4910 kHz · ENGLISH, ETC • DS-1 • 100 kW • ALT. FREQ. TO 7220 kHz

5920 JAPAN
†RADIO JAPAN, Via Skelton, UK — W Europe • 300 kW • ALT. FREQ. TO 5960 kHz
RUSSIA
KAMCHATKA RADIO, Petropavlovsk-K — S • E Asia • DS-LOCAL, R ROSSII • 100 kW
†VOICE OF RUSSIA, Irkutsk — W • E Asia • 100 kW
(con'd) †VOICE OF RUSSIA, Samara — W • W Europe • 250 kW

	0 1 2 3 4 5 6 7 8 9 10 11 12 13 14 15 16 17 18 19 20 21 22 23 24

ENGLISH ▬ ARABIC ⁂ CHINESE □□□ FRENCH ▬ GERMAN ▬ RUSSIAN ═ SPANISH ▬ OTHER ▬

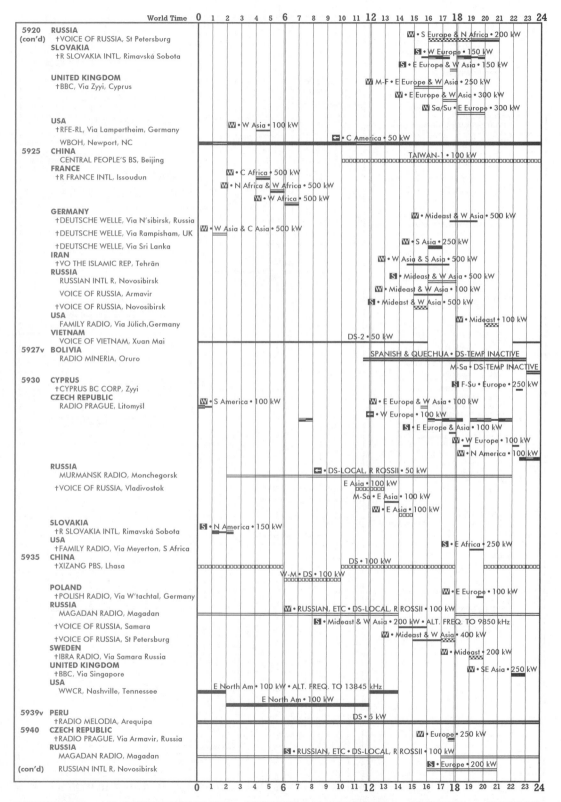

World Time	0 1 2 3 4 5 6 7 8 9 10 11 12 13 14 15 16 17 18 19 20 21 22 23 24

5920 **RUSSIA**
(con'd) †VOICE OF RUSSIA, St Petersburg — W•S Europe & N Africa•200 kW
SLOVAKIA
†R SLOVAKIA INTL, Rimavská Sobota — S•W Europe•150 kW
— S•E Europe & W Asia•150 kW

UNITED KINGDOM
†BBC, Via Zyyi, Cyprus — W M-F•E Europe & W Asia•250 kW
— W•E Europe & W Asia•300 kW
— W Sa/Su•E Europe•300 kW

USA
†RFE-RL, Via Lampertheim, Germany — W•W Asia•100 kW
WBOH, Newport, NC — C America•50 kW

5925 **CHINA**
CENTRAL PEOPLE'S BS, Beijing — TAIWAN-1•100 kW
FRANCE
†R FRANCE INTL, Issoudun — W•C Africa•500 kW
— W•N Africa & W Africa•500 kW
— W•W Africa•500 kW

GERMANY
†DEUTSCHE WELLE, Via N'sibirsk, Russia — W•Mideast & W Asia•500 kW
†DEUTSCHE WELLE, Via Rampisham, UK — W•W Asia & C Asia•500 kW
†DEUTSCHE WELLE, Via Sri Lanka — W•S Asia•250 kW
IRAN
†VO THE ISLAMIC REP, Tehrān — W•W Asia & S Asia•500 kW
RUSSIA
RUSSIAN INTL R, Novosibirsk — S•Mideast & W Asia•500 kW
VOICE OF RUSSIA, Armavir — W•Mideast & W Asia•100 kW
†VOICE OF RUSSIA, Novosibirsk — S•Mideast & W Asia•500 kW
USA
FAMILY RADIO, Via Jülich,Germany — W•Mideast•100 kW
VIETNAM
VOICE OF VIETNAM, Xuan Mai — DS-2•50 kW

5927v **BOLIVIA**
RADIO MINERIA, Oruro — SPANISH & QUECHUA•DS-TEMP INACTIVE
— M-Sa•DS-TEMP INACTIVE

5930 **CYPRUS**
†CYPRUS BC CORP, Zyyi — S F-Su•Europe•250 kW
CZECH REPUBLIC
RADIO PRAGUE, Litomyšl — W•S America•100 kW
— W•E Europe & W Asia•100 kW
— W•W Europe•100 kW
— S•E Europe & Asia•100 kW
— W•W Europe•100 kW
— W•N America•100 kW

RUSSIA
MURMANSK RADIO, Monchegorsk — DS-LOCAL, R ROSSII•50 kW
†VOICE OF RUSSIA, Vladivostok — E Asia•100 kW
— M-Sa•E Asia•100 kW
— W•E Asia•100 kW

SLOVAKIA
†R SLOVAKIA INTL, Rimavská Sobota — S•N America•150 kW
USA
†FAMILY RADIO, Via Meyerton, S Africa — S•E Africa•250 kW

5935 **CHINA**
†XIZANG PBS, Lhasa — DS•100 kW
— W-M•DS•100 kW

POLAND
†POLISH RADIO, Via W'tachtal, Germany — W•E Europe•100 kW
RUSSIA
MAGADAN RADIO, Magadan — W•RUSSIAN, ETC•DS-LOCAL, R ROSSII•100 kW
†VOICE OF RUSSIA, Samara — S•Mideast & W Asia•200 kW•ALT. FREQ. TO 9850 kHz
†VOICE OF RUSSIA, St Petersburg — W•Mideast & W Asia•400 kW
SWEDEN
†IBRA RADIO, Via Samara Russia — W•Mideast•200 kW
UNITED KINGDOM
†BBC, Via Singapore — W•SE Asia•250 kW
USA
WWCR, Nashville, Tennessee — E North Am•100 kW•ALT. FREQ. TO 13845 kHz
— E North Am•100 kW

5939v **PERU**
†RADIO MELODIA, Arequipa — DS•5 kW
5940 **CZECH REPUBLIC**
†RADIO PRAGUE, Via Armavir, Russia — W•Europe•250 kW
RUSSIA
MAGADAN RADIO, Magadan — S•RUSSIAN, ETC•DS-LOCAL, R ROSSII•100 kW
(con'd) RUSSIAN INTL R, Novosibirsk — S•Europe•200 kW

	0 1 2 3 4 5 6 7 8 9 10 11 12 13 14 15 16 17 18 19 20 21 22 23 24

SEASONAL S OR W   1-HR TIMESHIFT MIDYEAR ⬅ OR ➡   JAMMING / OR /\   EARLIEST HEARD ◁   LATEST HEARD ▷   NEW FOR 2008 †

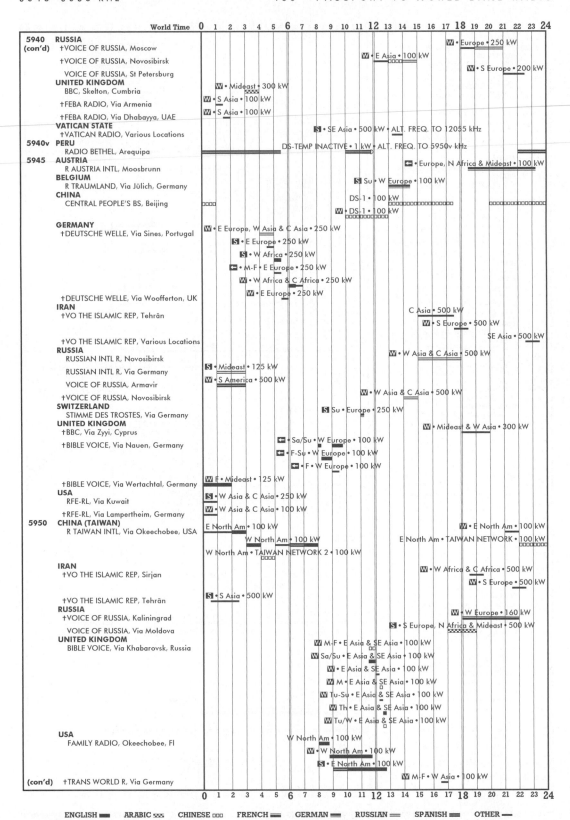

World Time 0 1 2 3 4 5 6 7 8 9 10 11 12 13 14 15 16 17 18 19 20 21 22 23 24

5940 RUSSIA
(con'd) †VOICE OF RUSSIA, Moscow — W • Europe • 250 kW
  †VOICE OF RUSSIA, Novosibirsk — W • E Asia • 100 kW
  VOICE OF RUSSIA, St Petersburg — W • S Europe • 200 kW
UNITED KINGDOM
  BBC, Skelton, Cumbria — W • Mideast • 300 kW
  †FEBA RADIO, Via Armenia — W • S Asia • 100 kW
  †FEBA RADIO, Via Dhabayya, UAE — W • S Asia • 100 kW
VATICAN STATE
  †VATICAN RADIO, Various Locations — S • SE Asia • 500 kW • ALT. FREQ. TO 12055 kHz
5940v PERU
  RADIO BETHEL, Arequipa — DS–TEMP INACTIVE • 1 kW • ALT. FREQ. TO 5950v kHz
5945 AUSTRIA
  R AUSTRIA INTL, Moosbrunn — ⊡ • Europe, N Africa & Mideast • 100 kW
BELGIUM
  R TRAUMLAND, Via Jülich, Germany — S • Su • W Europe • 100 kW
CHINA
  CENTRAL PEOPLE'S BS, Beijing — DS–1 • 100 kW / W • DS–1 • 100 kW
GERMANY
  †DEUTSCHE WELLE, Via Sines, Portugal — W • E Europe, W Asia & C Asia • 250 kW
  — S • E Europe • 250 kW
  — S • W Africa • 250 kW
  — ⊡ • M–F • E Europe • 250 kW
  — W • W Africa & C Africa • 250 kW
  — W • E Europe • 250 kW
  †DEUTSCHE WELLE, Via Woofferton, UK
IRAN
  †VO THE ISLAMIC REP, Tehrān — C Asia • 500 kW
  — W • S Europe • 500 kW
  — SE Asia • 500 kW
  †VO THE ISLAMIC REP, Various Locations
RUSSIA
  RUSSIAN INTL R, Novosibirsk — W • W Asia & C Asia • 500 kW
  RUSSIAN INTL R, Via Germany — S • Mideast • 125 kW
  VOICE OF RUSSIA, Armavir — W • S America • 500 kW
  †VOICE OF RUSSIA, Novosibirsk — W • W Asia & C Asia • 500 kW
SWITZERLAND
  STIMME DES TROSTES, Via Germany — S • Su • Europe • 250 kW
UNITED KINGDOM
  †BBC, Via Zyyi, Cyprus — W • Mideast & W Asia • 300 kW
  †BIBLE VOICE, Via Nauen, Germany — ⊡ • Sa/Su • W Europe • 100 kW
  — ⊡ • F–Su • W Europe • 100 kW
  — ⊡ • F • W Europe • 100 kW
  †BIBLE VOICE, Via Wertachtal, Germany — W • F • Mideast • 125 kW
USA
  RFE–RL, Via Kuwait — S • W Asia & C Asia • 250 kW
  †RFE–RL, Via Lampertheim, Germany — W • W Asia & C Asia • 100 kW
5950 CHINA (TAIWAN)
  R TAIWAN INTL, Via Okeechobee, USA — E North Am • 100 kW / W • E North Am • 100 kW
  — W North Am • 100 kW / E North Am • TAIWAN NETWORK • 100 kW
  — W North Am • TAIWAN NETWORK 2 • 100 kW
IRAN
  †VO THE ISLAMIC REP, Sirjan — W • W Africa & C Africa • 500 kW
  — W • S Europe • 500 kW
  †VO THE ISLAMIC REP, Tehrān — S • S Asia • 500 kW
RUSSIA
  †VOICE OF RUSSIA, Kaliningrad — W • W Europe • 160 kW
  VOICE OF RUSSIA, Via Moldova — S • S Europe, N Africa & Mideast • 500 kW
UNITED KINGDOM
  BIBLE VOICE, Via Khabarovsk, Russia — W • M–F • E Asia & SE Asia • 100 kW
  — W • Sa/Su • E Asia & SE Asia • 100 kW
  — W • E Asia & SE Asia • 100 kW
  — W • M • E Asia & SE Asia • 100 kW
  — W • Tu–Su • E Asia & SE Asia • 100 kW
  — W • Th • E Asia & SE Asia • 100 kW
  — W • Tu/W • E Asia & SE Asia • 100 kW
USA
  FAMILY RADIO, Okeechobee, Fl — W North Am • 100 kW
  — W • W North Am • 100 kW
  — S • E North Am • 100 kW
(con'd) †TRANS WORLD R, Via Germany — W • M–F • W Asia • 100 kW

0 1 2 3 4 5 6 7 8 9 10 11 12 13 14 15 16 17 18 19 20 21 22 23 24

ENGLISH ▬   ARABIC ≋   CHINESE ▫▫▫   FRENCH ▬   GERMAN ▬   RUSSIAN ═   SPANISH ▬   OTHER ▬

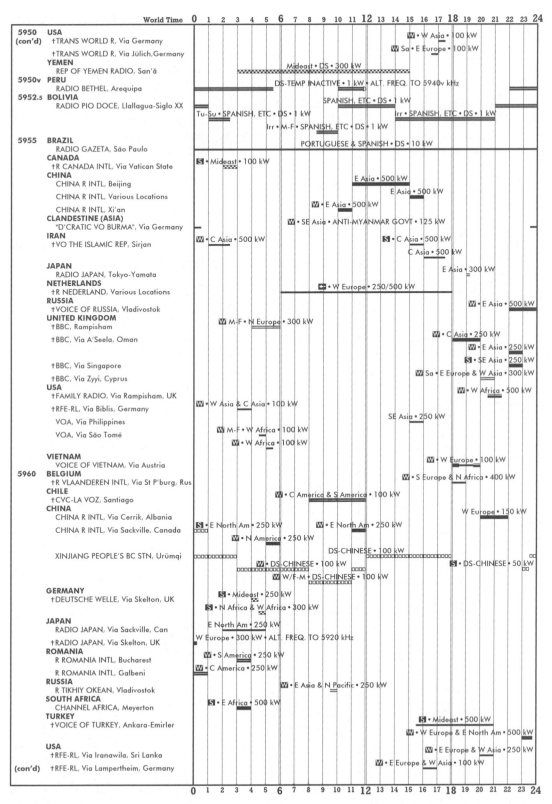

World Time

5950	**USA**			
(con'd)	†TRANS WORLD R, Via Germany		W • W Asia • 100 kW	
			W Sa • E Europe • 100 kW	
	YEMEN			
	REP OF YEMEN RADIO, San'ā	Mideast • DS • 300 kW		
5950v	**PERU**			
	RADIO BETHEL, Arequipa	DS-TEMP INACTIVE • 1 kW • ALT. FREQ. TO 5940v kHz		
5952.5	**BOLIVIA**			
	RADIO PIO DOCE, Llallagua-Siglo XX	SPANISH, ETC • DS • 1 kW		
		Tu-Su • SPANISH, ETC • DS • 1 kW	Irr • SPANISH, ETC • DS • 1 kW	
		Irr • M-F • SPANISH, ETC • DS • 1 kW		
5955	**BRAZIL**			
	RADIO GAZETA, São Paulo	PORTUGUESE & SPANISH • DS • 10 kW		
	CANADA			
	†R CANADA INTL, Via Vatican State	S • Mideast • 100 kW		
	CHINA			
	CHINA R INTL, Beijing	E Asia • 500 kW		
	CHINA R INTL, Various Locations	E Asia • 500 kW		
	CHINA R INTL, Xi'an	W • E Asia • 500 kW		
	CLANDESTINE (ASIA)			
	"D'CRATIC VO BURMA", Via Germany	W • SE Asia • ANTI-MYANMAR GOVT • 125 kW		
	IRAN			
	†VO THE ISLAMIC REP, Sirjan	W • C Asia • 500 kW	S • C Asia • 500 kW	
			C Asia • 500 kW	
	JAPAN			
	RADIO JAPAN, Tokyo-Yamata		E Asia • 300 kW	
	NETHERLANDS			
	†R NEDERLAND, Various Locations	⇆ • W Europe • 250/500 kW		
	RUSSIA			
	†VOICE OF RUSSIA, Vladivostok		W • E Asia • 500 kW	
	UNITED KINGDOM			
	†BBC, Rampisham	W M-F • N Europe • 300 kW		
	†BBC, Via A'Seela, Oman		W • C Asia • 250 kW	
	†BBC, Via Singapore		W • E Asia • 250 kW	
			S • SE Asia • 250 kW	
	†BBC, Via Zyyi, Cyprus		W Sa • E Europe & W Asia • 300 kW	
	USA			
	†FAMILY RADIO, Via Rampisham, UK		W • W Africa • 500 kW	
	†RFE-RL, Via Biblis, Germany	W • W Asia & C Asia • 100 kW		
	VOA, Via Philippines		SE Asia • 250 kW	
	VOA, Via São Tomé	W M-F • W Africa • 100 kW		
		W • W Africa • 100 kW		
	VIETNAM			
	VOICE OF VIETNAM, Via Austria		W • W Europe • 100 kW	
5960	**BELGIUM**			
	†R VLAANDEREN INTL, Via St P'burg, Rus		W • S Europe & N Africa • 400 kW	
	CHILE			
	†CVC-LA VOZ, Santiago	W • C America & S America • 100 kW		
	CHINA			
	CHINA R INTL, Via Cerrik, Albania		W Europe • 150 kW	
	CHINA R INTL, Via Sackville, Canada	S • E North Am • 250 kW	W • E North Am • 250 kW	
		W • N America • 250 kW		
	XINJIANG PEOPLE'S BC STN, Ürümqi	DS-CHINESE • 100 kW		
		W • DS-CHINESE • 100 kW	S • DS-CHINESE • 50 kW	
		W/F-M • DS-CHINESE • 100 kW		
	GERMANY			
	†DEUTSCHE WELLE, Via Skelton, UK	S • Mideast • 250 kW		
		S • N Africa & W Africa • 300 kW		
	JAPAN			
	RADIO JAPAN, Via Sackville, Can	E North Am • 250 kW		
	†RADIO JAPAN, Via Skelton, UK	W Europe • 300 kW • ALT. FREQ. TO 5920 kHz		
	ROMANIA			
	R ROMANIA INTL, Bucharest	W • S America • 250 kW		
	R ROMANIA INTL, Galbeni	W • C America • 250 kW		
	RUSSIA			
	R TIKHIY OKEAN, Vladivostok	W • E Asia & N Pacific • 250 kW		
	SOUTH AFRICA			
	CHANNEL AFRICA, Meyerton	S • E Africa • 500 kW		
	TURKEY			
	†VOICE OF TURKEY, Ankara-Emirler	S • Mideast • 500 kW		
			W • W Europe & E North Am • 500 kW	
	USA			
	†RFE-RL, Via Iranawila, Sri Lanka		W • E Europe & W Asia • 250 kW	
(con'd)	†RFE-RL, Via Lampertheim, Germany	W • E Europe & W Asia • 100 kW		

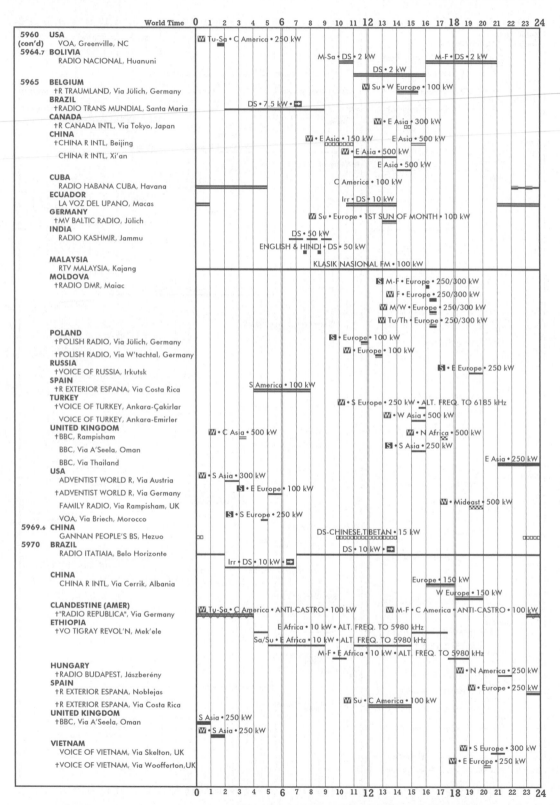

		World Time	0 1 2 3 4 5 6 7 8 9 10 11 12 13 14 15 16 17 18 19 20 21 22 23 24

5960 **USA**
(con'd)   VOA, Greenville, NC — W Tu-Sa • C America • 250 kW
5964.7 BOLIVIA
     RADIO NACIONAL, Huanuni — M-Sa • DS • 2 kW / M-F • DS • 2 kW / DS • 2 kW

5965 **BELGIUM**
     †R TRAUMLAND, Via Jülich, Germany — W Su • W Europe • 100 kW
     BRAZIL
     †RADIO TRANS MUNDIAL, Santa Maria — DS • 7.5 kW •
     CANADA
     †R CANADA INTL, Via Tokyo, Japan — W • E Asia • 300 kW
     CHINA
     †CHINA R INTL, Beijing — W • E Asia • 150 kW   E Asia • 500 kW
     CHINA R INTL, Xi'an — W • E Asia • 500 kW
                                              E Asia • 500 kW
     CUBA
     RADIO HABANA CUBA, Havana — C America • 100 kW
     ECUADOR
     LA VOZ DEL UPANO, Macas — Irr • DS • 10 kW
     GERMANY
     †MV BALTIC RADIO, Jülich — W Su • Europe • 1ST SUN OF MONTH • 100 kW
     INDIA
     RADIO KASHMIR, Jammu — DS • 50 kW
                            ENGLISH & HINDI • DS • 50 kW

     MALAYSIA
     RTV MALAYSIA, Kajang — KLASIK NASIONAL FM • 100 kW
     MOLDOVA
     †RADIO DMR, Maiac — S M-F • Europe • 250/300 kW
                          W F • Europe • 250/300 kW
                          W M/W • Europe • 250/300 kW
                          W Tu/Th • Europe • 250/300 kW

     POLAND
     †POLISH RADIO, Via Jülich, Germany — S • Europe • 100 kW
     †POLISH RADIO, Via W'tachtal, Germany — W • Europe • 100 kW
     RUSSIA
     †VOICE OF RUSSIA, Irkutsk — S • E Europe • 250 kW
     SPAIN
     †R EXTERIOR ESPANA, Via Costa Rica — S America • 100 kW
     TURKEY
     †VOICE OF TURKEY, Ankara-Çakirlar — W • S Europe • 250 kW • ALT. FREQ. TO 6185 kHz
     VOICE OF TURKEY, Ankara-Emirler — W • W Asia • 500 kW
     UNITED KINGDOM
     †BBC, Rampisham — W • C Asia • 500 kW   W • N Africa • 500 kW
     BBC, Via A'Seela, Oman — S • S Asia • 250 kW
     BBC, Via Thailand — E Asia • 250 kW
     USA
     ADVENTIST WORLD R, Via Austria — W • S Asia • 300 kW
     †ADVENTIST WORLD R, Via Germany — S • E Europe • 100 kW
     FAMILY RADIO, Via Rampisham, UK — W • Mideast • 500 kW
     VOA, Via Briech, Morocco — S • S Europe • 250 kW
5969.6 CHINA
     GANNAN PEOPLE'S BS, Hezuo — DS-CHINESE,TIBETAN • 15 kW
5970 **BRAZIL**
     RADIO ITATIAIA, Belo Horizonte — DS • 10 kW •
                                        Irr • DS • 10 kW •

     CHINA
     CHINA R INTL, Via Cerrik, Albania — Europe • 150 kW
                                          W Europe • 150 kW
     CLANDESTINE (AMER)
     †"RADIO REPUBLICA", Via Germany — W Tu-Sa • C America • ANTI-CASTRO • 100 kW   W M-F • C America • ANTI-CASTRO • 100 kW
     ETHIOPIA
     †VO TIGRAY REVOL'N, Mek'ele — E Africa • 10 kW • ALT. FREQ. TO 5980 kHz
                                    Sa/Su • E Africa • 10 kW • ALT. FREQ. TO 5980 kHz
                                    M-F • E Africa • 10 kW • ALT. FREQ. TO 5980 kHz

     HUNGARY
     †RADIO BUDAPEST, Jászberény — W • N America • 250 kW
     SPAIN
     †R EXTERIOR ESPANA, Noblejas — W • Europe • 250 kW
     †R EXTERIOR ESPANA, Via Costa Rica — W Su • C America • 100 kW
     UNITED KINGDOM
     †BBC, Via A'Seela, Oman — S Asia • 250 kW
                                W • S Asia • 250 kW

     VIETNAM
     VOICE OF VIETNAM, Via Skelton, UK — W • S Europe • 300 kW
     †VOICE OF VIETNAM, Via Woofferton,UK — W • E Europe • 250 kW

	0 1 2 3 4 5 6 7 8 9 10 11 12 13 14 15 16 17 18 19 20 21 22 23 24

ENGLISH ▬   ARABIC ⌇⌇⌇   CHINESE ▫▫▫   FRENCH ▬   GERMAN ▬   RUSSIAN ═   SPANISH ▬   OTHER ▬

World Time 0 1 2 3 4 5 6 7 8 9 10 11 12 13 14 15 16 17 18 19 20 21 22 23 24

5975 CHINA
CHINA R INTL, Kashi — Mideast • 500 kW
JAPAN
†RADIO JAPAN, Via Rampisham,UK — W Europe • 500 kW
NETHERLANDS
R NEDERLAND, Via Neth Antilles — C America • 250 kW
POLAND
†POLISH RADIO, Via Nauen, Germany — W • N Europe • 100 kW
†POLISH RADIO, Via W'tachtal, Germany — ⇦ • Europe • 100 kW
— S • W Europe • 100 kW
RUSSIA
RUSSIAN INTL R, Via Jülich, Germany — W • Mideast • 100 kW
†VOICE OF RUSSIA, Armavir — S • S America • 500 kW • ALT. FREQ. TO 9830 kHz
†VOICE OF RUSSIA, Kaliningrad — W • S Europe • 250 kW
TURKEY
VOICE OF TURKEY, Ankara-Emirler — S • Europe & N America • 500 kW
UNITED KINGDOM
†BBC, Skelton, Cumbria — W • W Africa & C Africa • 300 kW
†BBC, Various Locations — S Asia • 250 kW
BBC, Via Montsinéry, French Guiana — C America • 250 kW
†BBC, Via Thailand — W • E Asia • 250 kW
— S Asia • 250 kW
— S • S Asia • 250 kW
VIETNAM
VOICE OF VIETNAM, Hanoi — DS-1 • 50 kW
— F • DS-1 • 50 kW

5980 BRAZIL
RADIO GUARUJA, Florianópolis — DS-TEMP INACTIVE • 10 kW • ⇨
CHINA
CHINA R INTL, Beijing — W • E Asia • 500 kW
CLANDESTINE (AFRICA)
†"VO PEACE & DEMOCRACY", Ethiopia — E Africa • ANTI-ERITREA GOVT • 10 kW
ECUADOR
RADIO FEDERACION, Sucúa — Irr • Tu-Su • DS-SHUAR • 5 kW
— DS-SHUAR • 5 kW
ETHIOPIA
†VO TIGRAY REVOL'N, Mek'ele — E Africa • 10 kW • ALT. FREQ. TO 5970 kHz
— Sa/Su • E Africa • 10 kW • ALT. FREQ. TO 5970 kHz
— M-F • E Africa • 10 kW • ALT. FREQ. TO 5970 kHz
GERMANY
†DEUTSCHE WELLE, Via Dhabayya, UAE — W • E Europe & W Asia • 250 kW
HUNGARY
†RADIO BUDAPEST, Jászberény — W • N America • 250 kW
— W • Europe • 250 kW
MOROCCO
RTV MAROCAINE, Briech — W • N Africa & Mideast • 250 kW
TURKEY
†VOICE OF TURKEY, Ankara-Çakirlar — S • S Europe • 250 kW
†VOICE OF TURKEY, Ankara-Emirler — W • W Europe • 500 kW
— W • W Europe & E North Am • 500 kW
— S • Europe • 500 kW
UNITED KINGDOM
†BBC, Via Thailand — S • E Asia • 250 kW
USA
†RADIO MARTI, Greenville, NC — Tu-Su • C America • 250 kW
— S • C America • 250 kW
— W Tu-Su • C America • 250 kW
— C America • 250 kW
— W • C America • 250 kW

5985 CHINA
†CHINA R INTL, Beijing — E Africa • 500 kW
— C Africa & S Africa • 500 kW
CHINA R INTL, Via Cerrik, Albania — W • N Africa • 150 kW
CHINA R INTL, Xi'an — W • E Asia • 500 kW
CONGO (REPUBLIC)
RTV CONGOLAISE, Brazzaville — FRENCH, ETC • DS • 50/100 kW
— DS • 50/100 kW
INDIA
ALL INDIA RADIO, Ranchi — DS • 50 kW
— ENGLISH, ETC • DS • 50 kW
RUSSIA
RUSSIAN INTL R, Moscow — W • Mideast • 250 kW
RUSSIAN INTL R, Via Jülich, Germany — S • Mideast & W Asia • 100 kW
(con'd) †VOICE OF RUSSIA, Moscow — W • Mideast • 250 kW

SEASONAL S OR W   1-HR TIMESHIFT MIDYEAR ⇦ OR ⇨   JAMMING / OR /\   EARLIEST HEARD ◁   LATEST HEARD ▷   NEW FOR 2008 †

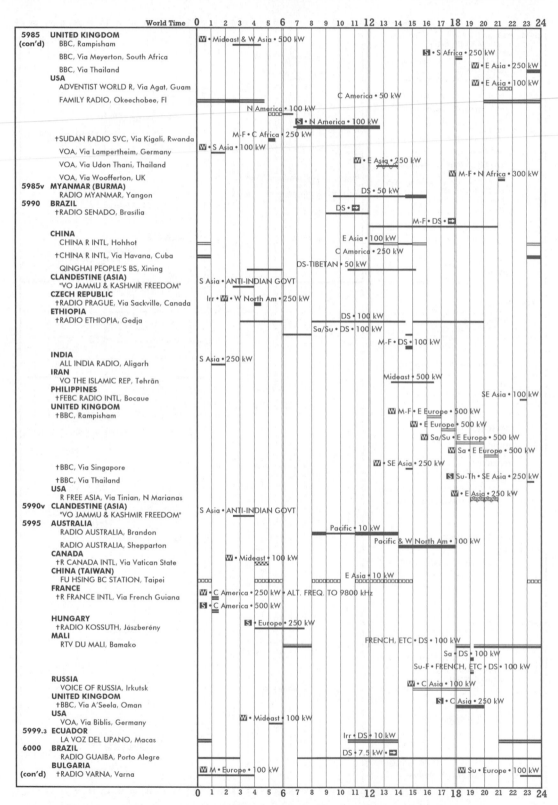

World Time 0 1 2 3 4 5 6 7 8 9 10 11 12 13 14 15 16 17 18 19 20 21 22 23 24

5985 **UNITED KINGDOM**
(con'd)   BBC, Rampisham — W • Mideast & W Asia • 500 kW
          BBC, Via Meyerton, South Africa — S • S Africa • 250 kW
          BBC, Via Thailand — W • E Asia • 250 kW
USA
          ADVENTIST WORLD R, Via Agat, Guam — W • E Asia • 100 kW
          FAMILY RADIO, Okeechobee, Fl — C America • 50 kW

          N America • 100 kW
          S • N America • 100 kW
          †SUDAN RADIO SVC, Via Kigali, Rwanda — M-F • C Africa • 250 kW
          VOA, Via Lampertheim, Germany — W • S Asia • 100 kW
          VOA, Via Udon Thani, Thailand — W • E Asia • 250 kW
          VOA, Via Woofferton, UK — M-F • N Africa • 300 kW
5985v **MYANMAR (BURMA)**
          RADIO MYANMAR, Yangon — DS • 50 kW
5990 **BRAZIL**
          †RADIO SENADO, Brasilia — DS • ▭
          M-F • DS • ▭
          CHINA
          CHINA R INTL, Hohhot — E Asia • 100 kW
          †CHINA R INTL, Via Havana, Cuba — C America • 250 kW
          QINGHAI PEOPLE'S BS, Xining — DS-TIBETAN • 50 kW
CLANDESTINE (ASIA)
          "VO JAMMU & KASHMIR FREEDOM" — S Asia • ANTI-INDIAN GOVT
CZECH REPUBLIC
          †RADIO PRAGUE, Via Sackville, Canada — Irr • W • W North Am • 250 kW
ETHIOPIA
          †RADIO ETHIOPIA, Gedja — DS • 100 kW
          Sa/Su • DS • 100 kW
          M-F • DS • 100 kW
          INDIA
          ALL INDIA RADIO, Aligarh — S Asia • 250 kW
IRAN
          VO THE ISLAMIC REP, Tehrän — Mideast • 500 kW
PHILIPPINES
          †FEBC RADIO INTL, Bocaue — SE Asia • 100 kW
UNITED KINGDOM
          †BBC, Rampisham — W • M-F • E Europe • 500 kW
          W • E Europe • 500 kW
          W • Sa/Su • E Europe • 500 kW
          W • Sa • E Europe • 500 kW
          †BBC, Via Singapore — W • SE Asia • 250 kW
          †BBC, Via Thailand — S • Su-Th • SE Asia • 250 kW
USA
          R FREE ASIA, Via Tinian, N Marianas — W • E Asia • 250 kW
5990v **CLANDESTINE (ASIA)**
          "VO JAMMU & KASHMIR FREEDOM" — S Asia • ANTI-INDIAN GOVT
5995 **AUSTRALIA**
          RADIO AUSTRALIA, Brandon — Pacific • 10 kW
          RADIO AUSTRALIA, Shepparton — Pacific & W North Am • 100 kW
CANADA
          †R CANADA INTL, Via Vatican State — W • Mideast • 100 kW
CHINA (TAIWAN)
          FU HSING BC STATION, Taipei — E Asia • 10 kW
FRANCE
          †R FRANCE INTL, Via French Guiana — W • C America • 250 kW • ALT. FREQ. TO 9800 kHz
          S • C America • 500 kW
HUNGARY
          †RADIO KOSSUTH, Jászberény — S • Europe • 250 kW
MALI
          RTV DU MALI, Bamako — FRENCH, ETC • DS • 100 kW
          Sa • DS • 100 kW
          Su-F • FRENCH, ETC • DS • 100 kW
          RUSSIA
          VOICE OF RUSSIA, Irkutsk — W • C Asia • 100 kW
UNITED KINGDOM
          †BBC, Via A'Seela, Oman — S • C Asia • 250 kW
USA
          VOA, Via Biblis, Germany — W • Mideast • 100 kW
5999.3 **ECUADOR**
          LA VOZ DEL UPANO, Macas — Irr • DS • 10 kW
6000 **BRAZIL**
          RADIO GUAIBA, Porto Alegre — DS • 7.5 kW • ▭
BULGARIA
(con'd)   †RADIO VARNA, Varna — W • M • Europe • 100 kW   W • Su • Europe • 100 kW

0 1 2 3 4 5 6 7 8 9 10 11 12 13 14 15 16 17 18 19 20 21 22 23 24

ENGLISH ▬ ARABIC ⁘ CHINESE □□□ FRENCH ▬ GERMAN ▬ RUSSIAN ═ SPANISH ▬ OTHER ▬

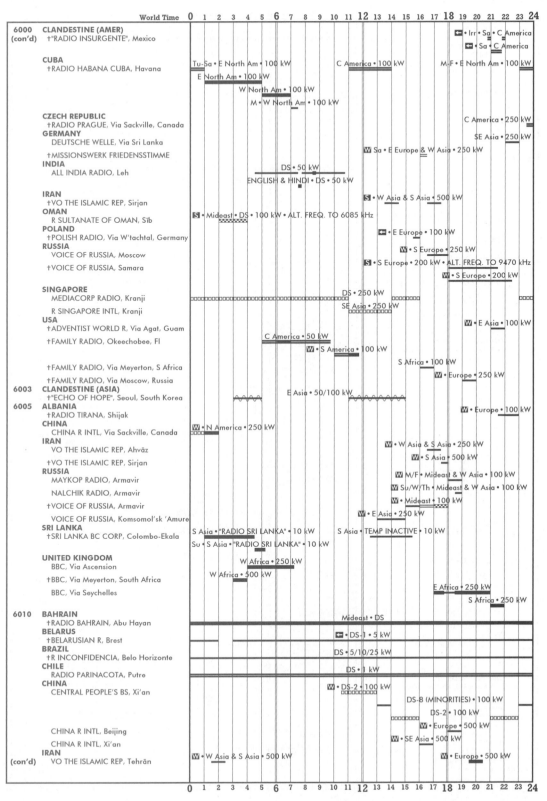

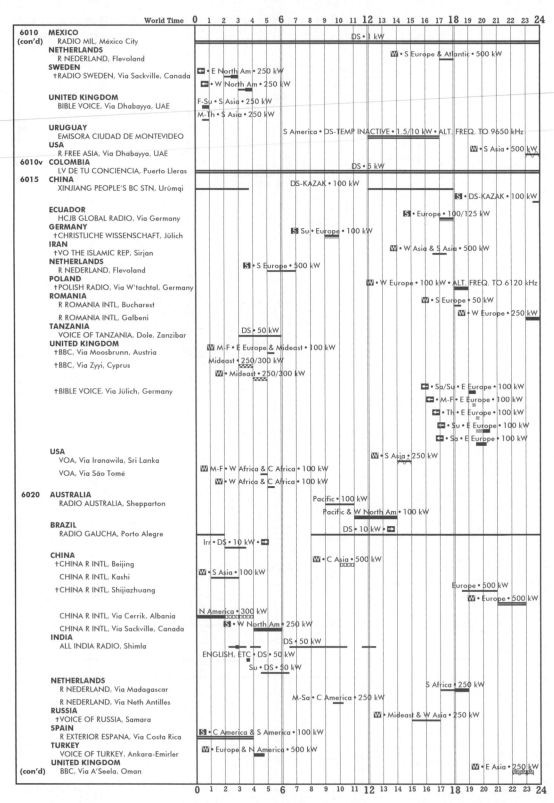

World Time 0 1 2 3 4 5 6 7 8 9 10 11 12 13 14 15 16 17 18 19 20 21 22 23 24

6010 MEXICO
(con'd) RADIO MIL, México City — DS • 1 kW
NETHERLANDS
R NEDERLAND, Flevoland — W • S Europe & Atlantic • 500 kW
SWEDEN
†RADIO SWEDEN, Via Sackville, Canada — • E North Am • 250 kW
— • W North Am • 250 kW
UNITED KINGDOM
BIBLE VOICE, Via Dhabayya, UAE — F-Su • S Asia • 250 kW
M-Th • S Asia • 250 kW
URUGUAY
EMISORA CIUDAD DE MONTEVIDEO — S America • DS-TEMP INACTIVE • 1.5/10 kW • ALT. FREQ. TO 9650 kHz
USA
R FREE ASIA, Via Dhabayya, UAE — W • S Asia • 500 kW
6010v COLOMBIA
LV DE TU CONCIENCIA, Puerto Lleras — DS • 5 kW
6015 CHINA
XINJIANG PEOPLE'S BC STN, Urümqi — DS-KAZAK • 100 kW
S • DS-KAZAK • 100 kW
ECUADOR
HCJB GLOBAL RADIO, Via Germany — S • Europe • 100/125 kW
GERMANY
†CHRISTLICHE WISSENSCHAFT, Jülich — S Su • Europe • 100 kW
IRAN
†VO THE ISLAMIC REP, Sirjan — W • W Asia & S Asia • 500 kW
NETHERLANDS
R NEDERLAND, Flevoland — S • S Europe • 500 kW
POLAND
†POLISH RADIO, Via W'tachtal, Germany — W • W Europe • 100 kW • ALT. FREQ. TO 6120 kHz
ROMANIA
R ROMANIA INTL, Bucharest — W • S Europe • 50 kW
R ROMANIA INTL, Galbeni — W • W Europe • 250 kW
TANZANIA
VOICE OF TANZANIA, Dole, Zanzibar — DS • 50 kW
UNITED KINGDOM
†BBC, Via Moosbrunn, Austria — W M-F • E Europe & Mideast • 100 kW
†BBC, Via Zyyi, Cyprus — Mideast • 250/300 kW
W • Mideast • 250/300 kW
†BIBLE VOICE, Via Jülich, Germany — • Sa/Su • E Europe • 100 kW
• M-F • E Europe • 100 kW
• Th • E Europe • 100 kW
• Su • E Europe • 100 kW
• Sa • E Europe • 100 kW
USA
VOA, Via Iranawila, Sri Lanka — W • S Asia • 250 kW
VOA, Via São Tomé — W M-F • W Africa & C Africa • 100 kW
W • W Africa & C Africa • 100 kW
6020 AUSTRALIA
RADIO AUSTRALIA, Shepparton — Pacific • 100 kW
Pacific & W North Am • 100 kW
BRAZIL
RADIO GAUCHA, Porto Alegre — DS • 10 kW • →
Irr • DS • 10 kW • →
CHINA
†CHINA R INTL, Beijing — W • C Asia • 500 kW
†CHINA R INTL, Kashi — W • S Asia • 100 kW
†CHINA R INTL, Shijiazhuang — Europe • 500 kW
W • Europe • 500 kW
CHINA R INTL, Via Cerrik, Albania — N America • 300 kW
CHINA R INTL, Via Sackville, Canada — S • W North Am • 250 kW
INDIA
ALL INDIA RADIO, Shimla — DS • 50 kW
ENGLISH, ETC • DS • 50 kW
Su • DS • 50 kW
NETHERLANDS
R NEDERLAND, Via Madagascar — S Africa • 250 kW
R NEDERLAND, Via Neth Antilles — M-Sa • C America • 250 kW
RUSSIA
†VOICE OF RUSSIA, Samara — W • Mideast & W Asia • 250 kW
SPAIN
R EXTERIOR ESPANA, Via Costa Rica — S • C America & S America • 100 kW
TURKEY
VOICE OF TURKEY, Ankara-Emirler — W • Europe & N America • 500 kW
UNITED KINGDOM
(con'd) BBC, Via A'Seela, Oman — W • E Asia • 250 kW

0 1 2 3 4 5 6 7 8 9 10 11 12 13 14 15 16 17 18 19 20 21 22 23 24

ENGLISH ▬ ARABIC ⌇ CHINESE ▢▢▢ FRENCH ▬ GERMAN ═ RUSSIAN = SPANISH = OTHER ▬

World Time

6020 (con'd)	**UNITED KINGDOM** BIBLE VOICE, Via Dhabayya, UAE	W • S Asia • 250 kW W Sa • S Asia • 250 kW
	USA FAMILY RADIO, Via Madagascar	E Africa • 50 kW
	VATICAN STATE VATICAN RADIO, Via Philippines	E Asia • 250 kW
	VIETNAM VOICE OF VIETNAM, Da Lai	DS • 50 kW
6020v	**PERU** RADIO VICTORIA, Lima	SPANISH & PORTUGUESE • DS • 5 kW
6025	**ALGERIA** †R ALGERIENNE, Via Woofferton, UK	W • N Africa • DS • 300 kW
	BOLIVIA †RADIO ILLIMANI, La Paz	SPANISH, AYMARA & QUECHUA • DS • 10 kW Tu-Su • DS • 10 kW
	CANADA †R CANADA INTL, Via Vatican State	W • Mideast • 100 kW
	CHINA CHINA R INTL, Xi'an	W • W Asia & C Asia • 250 kW
	DOMINICAN REPUBLIC R AMANECER INTL, Sto Domingo	DS • 1/5 kW Tu-Sa • DS • 1/5 kW
	HUNGARY †RADIO BUDAPEST, Jászberény	⬅ • Europe • 100 kW ⬅ • Sa/Su • Europe • 100 kW
	†RADIO KOSSUTH, Jászberény	⬅ • Europe • 100 kW
6030	**BRAZIL** RADIO GLOBO, Rio de Janeiro	DS • TEMP INACTIVE • 10 kW • ➡
	CANADA CFVP-CKMX, Calgary, Alberta	W North Am • DS • 0.1 kW
	CENTRAL AFRICAN REPUBLIC †RADIO ICDI, Baoli	FRENCH, ETC • C Africa • 1 kW
	CHINA CENTRAL PEOPLE'S BS, Beijing	DS-1 • 50 kW ▯▯▯▯▯▯▯▯▯▯▯▯▯▯▯▯▯▯▯▯▯▯ W-M • DS-1 • 50 kW
	CLANDESTINE (ASIA) †"MINGHUI RADIO", Via Taiwan	E Asia
	INDIA ALL INDIA RADIO, Delhi	DS • 50 kW
	KYRGYZSTAN RADIO MARANATHA, Bishkek	W Asia & C Asia • 100 kW
	RUSSIA †VOICE OF RUSSIA, St Petersburg	W • S Europe • 200 kW
	THAILAND RADIO THAILAND, Udon Thani	S • SE Asia • 250 kW
	TURKEY †VOICE OF TURKEY, Ankara-Emirler	W • S Europe • 500 kW
	UNITED KINGDOM †BBC, Via A'Seela, Oman	S • Mideast • 250 kW Mideast • 250 kW
	†BBC, Via Ascension	S • S Africa • 250 kW
	†BBC, Via Seychelles	E Africa • 250 kW
	†BBC, Via Zyyi, Cyprus	W • Mideast • 300 kW Mideast • 300 kW
	USA †RADIO MARTI, Greenville, NC	C America • 250 kW W • C America • 250 kW S • C America • 250 kW S Tu-Su • C America • 250 kW Tu-Su • C America • 250 kW W Tu-Su • C America • 250 kW
	VOA, Via Udon Thani, Thailand	S • S Asia • 250 kW
6035	**ALBANIA** †RADIO TIRANA, Shijak	S M-Sa • Europe • 100 kW ⬅ • M-Sa • Europe • 100 kW
	BHUTAN †BHUTAN BC SERVICE, Thimbu	DS • 100 kW
	CHINA †YUNNAN PEOPLE'S BS, Kunming	Irr • DS-"NEWS RADIO" • 50 kW DS-"NEWS RADIO" • 50 kW
	COLOMBIA LV DEL GUAVIARE, San José Guaviare	DS-RCN • 5 kW
	GERMANY †DEUTSCHE WELLE, Via Rampisham, UK	W • N Africa & Mideast • 500 kW
	†DEUTSCHE WELLE, Via Woofferton, UK	W • N Africa & Mideast • 300 kW
	IRAN VO THE ISLAMIC REP, Sirjan	W • W Asia • 500 kW
	JAPAN (con'd) †RADIO JAPAN, Tokyo-Yamata	E Asia • 300 kW

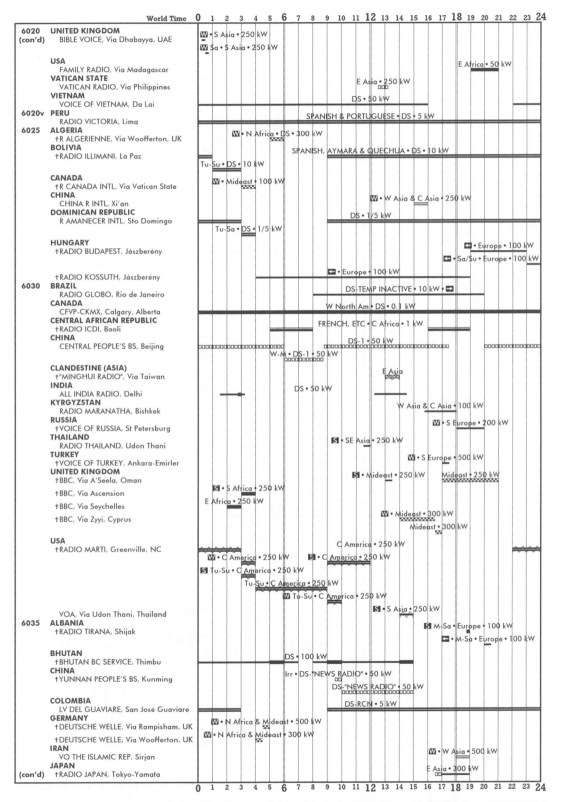

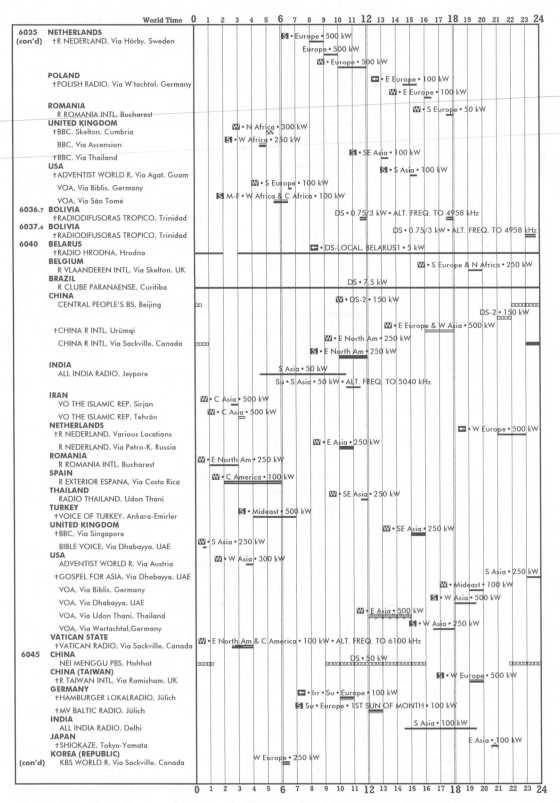

| World Time | 0 1 2 3 4 5 6 7 8 9 10 11 12 13 14 15 16 17 18 19 20 21 22 23 24 |

6035 **NETHERLANDS**
(con'd) †R NEDERLAND, Via Hörby, Sweden
- S • Europe • 500 kW
- Europe • 500 kW
- W • Europe • 500 kW

POLAND
†POLISH RADIO, Via W'tachtal, Germany
- E Europe • 100 kW
- W • E Europe • 100 kW

ROMANIA
R ROMANIA INTL, Bucharest
- W • S Europe • 50 kW

UNITED KINGDOM
†BBC, Skelton, Cumbria
- W • N Africa • 300 kW

BBC, Via Ascension
- S • W Africa • 250 kW

†BBC, Via Thailand
- S • SE Asia • 100 kW

USA
†ADVENTIST WORLD R, Via Agat, Guam
- S • S Asia • 100 kW

VOA, Via Biblis, Germany
- W • S Europe • 100 kW

VOA, Via São Tomé
- M-F • W Africa & C Africa • 100 kW

6036.7 BOLIVIA
†RADIODIFUSORAS TROPICO, Trinidad
- DS • 0.75/3 kW • ALT. FREQ. TO 4958 kHz

6037.6 BOLIVIA
†RADIODIFUSORAS TROPICO, Trinidad
- DS • 0.75/3 kW • ALT. FREQ. TO 4958 kHz

6040 BELARUS
†RADIO HRODNA, Hrodna
- DS-LOCAL, BELARUS1 • 5 kW

BELGIUM
R VLAANDEREN INTL, Via Skelton, UK
- W • S Europe & N Africa • 250 kW

BRAZIL
R CLUBE PARANAENSE, Curitiba
- DS • 7.5 kW

CHINA
CENTRAL PEOPLE'S BS, Beijing
- W • DS-2 • 150 kW
- DS-2 • 150 kW

†CHINA R INTL, Urümqi
- W • E Europe & W Asia • 500 kW

CHINA R INTL, Via Sackville, Canada
- W • E North Am • 250 kW
- S • E North Am • 250 kW

INDIA
ALL INDIA RADIO, Jeypore
- S Asia • 50 kW
- Su • S Asia • 50 kW • ALT. FREQ. TO 5040 kHz

IRAN
VO THE ISLAMIC REP, Sirjan
- W • C Asia • 500 kW

VO THE ISLAMIC REP, Tehrān
- W • C Asia • 500 kW

NETHERLANDS
†R NEDERLAND, Various Locations
- W Europe • 500 kW

R NEDERLAND, Via Petro-K, Russia
- W • E Asia • 250 kW

ROMANIA
R ROMANIA INTL, Bucharest
- W • E North Am • 250 kW

SPAIN
R EXTERIOR ESPANA, Via Costa Rica
- W • C America • 100 kW

THAILAND
RADIO THAILAND, Udon Thani
- W • SE Asia • 250 kW

TURKEY
†VOICE OF TURKEY, Ankara-Emirler
- S • Mideast • 500 kW

UNITED KINGDOM
†BBC, Via Singapore
- W • SE Asia • 250 kW

BIBLE VOICE, Via Dhabayya, UAE
- W • S Asia • 250 kW

USA
ADVENTIST WORLD R, Via Austria
- W • W Asia • 300 kW

†GOSPEL FOR ASIA, Via Dhabayya, UAE
- S Asia • 250 kW

VOA, Via Biblis, Germany
- W • Mideast • 100 kW

VOA, Via Dhabayya, UAE
- S • W Asia • 500 kW

VOA, Via Udon Thani, Thailand
- W • E Asia • 500 kW

VOA, Via Wertachtal, Germany
- S • W Asia • 250 kW

VATICAN STATE
†VATICAN RADIO, Via Sackville, Canada
- W • E North Am & C America • 100 kW • ALT. FREQ. TO 6100 kHz

6045 CHINA
NEI MENGGU PBS, Hohhot
- DS • 50 kW

CHINA (TAIWAN)
†R TAIWAN INTL, Via Ramisham, UK
- S • W Europe • 500 kW

GERMANY
†HAMBURGER LOKALRADIO, Jülich
- Irr • Su • Europe • 100 kW

†MV BALTIC RADIO, Jülich
- S Su • Europe • 1ST SUN OF MONTH • 100 kW

INDIA
ALL INDIA RADIO, Delhi
- S Asia • 100 kW

JAPAN
†SHIOKAZE, Tokyo-Yamata
- E Asia • 100 kW

KOREA (REPUBLIC)
(con'd) KBS WORLD R, Via Sackville, Canada
- W Europe • 250 kW

| | 0 1 2 3 4 5 6 7 8 9 10 11 12 13 14 15 16 17 18 19 20 21 22 23 24 |

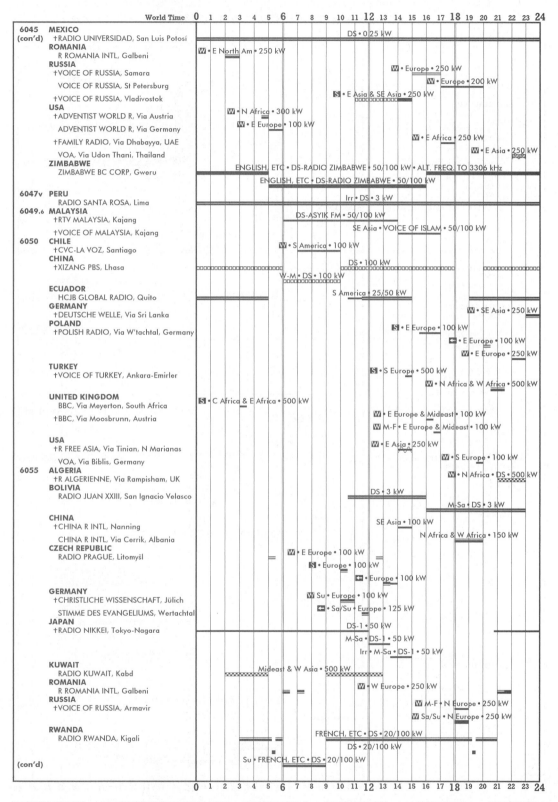

World Time

| | 0 | 1 | 2 | 3 | 4 | 5 | 6 | 7 | 8 | 9 | 10 | 11 | 12 | 13 | 14 | 15 | 16 | 17 | 18 | 19 | 20 | 21 | 22 | 23 | 24 |

6045 **MEXICO**
(con'd) †RADIO UNIVERSIDAD, San Luis Potosí — D$ • 0.25 kW
ROMANIA
R ROMANIA INTL, Galbeni — W • E North Am • 250 kW
RUSSIA
†VOICE OF RUSSIA, Samara — W • Europe • 250 kW
VOICE OF RUSSIA, St Petersburg — W • Europe • 200 kW
†VOICE OF RUSSIA, Vladivostok — S • E Asia & SE Asia • 250 kW
USA
†ADVENTIST WORLD R, Via Austria — W • N Africa • 300 kW
ADVENTIST WORLD R, Via Germany — W • E Europe • 100 kW
†FAMILY RADIO, Via Dhabayya, UAE — W • E Africa • 250 kW
VOA, Via Udon Thani, Thailand — W • E Asia • 250 kW
ZIMBABWE
ZIMBABWE BC CORP, Gweru — ENGLISH, ETC • DS-RADIO ZIMBABWE • 50/100 kW • ALT. FREQ. TO 3306 kHz
ENGLISH, ETC • DS-RADIO ZIMBABWE • 50/100 kW

6047v **PERU**
RADIO SANTA ROSA, Lima — Irr • DS • 3 kW
6049.6 **MALAYSIA**
†RTV MALAYSIA, Kajang — DS-ASYIK FM • 50/100 kW
†VOICE OF MALAYSIA, Kajang — SE Asia • VOICE OF ISLAM • 50/100 kW
6050 **CHILE**
†CVC-LA VOZ, Santiago — W • S America • 100 kW
CHINA
†XIZANG PBS, Lhasa — DS • 100 kW
W-M • DS • 100 kW
ECUADOR
HCJB GLOBAL RADIO, Quito — S America • 25/50 kW
GERMANY
†DEUTSCHE WELLE, Via Sri Lanka — W • SE Asia • 250 kW
POLAND
†POLISH RADIO, Via W'tachtal, Germany — S • E Europe • 100 kW
⇔ • E Europe • 100 kW
W • E Europe • 250 kW
TURKEY
†VOICE OF TURKEY, Ankara-Emirler — S • S Europe • 500 kW
W • N Africa & W Africa • 500 kW
UNITED KINGDOM
BBC, Via Meyerton, South Africa — S • C Africa & E Africa • 500 kW
†BBC, Via Moosbrunn, Austria — W • E Europe & Mideast • 100 kW
W M-F • E Europe & Mideast • 100 kW
USA
†R FREE ASIA, Via Tinian, N Marianas — W • E Asia • 250 kW
VOA, Via Biblis, Germany — W • S Europe • 100 kW
6055 **ALGERIA**
†R ALGERIENNE, Via Rampisham, UK — W • N Africa • DS • 500 kW
BOLIVIA
RADIO JUAN XXIII, San Ignacio Velasco — DS • 3 kW
M-Sa • DS • 3 kW
CHINA
†CHINA R INTL, Nanning — SE Asia • 100 kW
CHINA R INTL, Via Cerrik, Albania — N Africa & W Africa • 150 kW
CZECH REPUBLIC
RADIO PRAGUE, Litomyšl — W • E Europe • 100 kW
S • Europe • 100 kW
⇔ • Europe • 100 kW
GERMANY
†CHRISTLICHE WISSENSCHAFT, Jülich — W Su • Europe • 100 kW
STIMME DES EVANGELIUMS, Wertachtal — ⇔ • Sa/Su • Europe • 125 kW
JAPAN
†RADIO NIKKEI, Tokyo-Nagara — DS-1 • 50 kW
M-Sa • DS-1 • 50 kW
Irr • M-Sa • DS-1 • 50 kW
KUWAIT
RADIO KUWAIT, Kabd — Mideast & W Asia • 500 kW
ROMANIA
R ROMANIA INTL, Galbeni — W • W Europe • 250 kW
RUSSIA
†VOICE OF RUSSIA, Armavir — W M-F • N Europe • 250 kW
W Sa/Su • N Europe • 250 kW
RWANDA
RADIO RWANDA, Kigali — FRENCH, ETC • DS • 20/100 kW
DS • 20/100 kW
(con'd) — Su • FRENCH, ETC • DS • 20/100 kW

| | 0 | 1 | 2 | 3 | 4 | 5 | 6 | 7 | 8 | 9 | 10 | 11 | 12 | 13 | 14 | 15 | 16 | 17 | 18 | 19 | 20 | 21 | 22 | 23 | 24 |

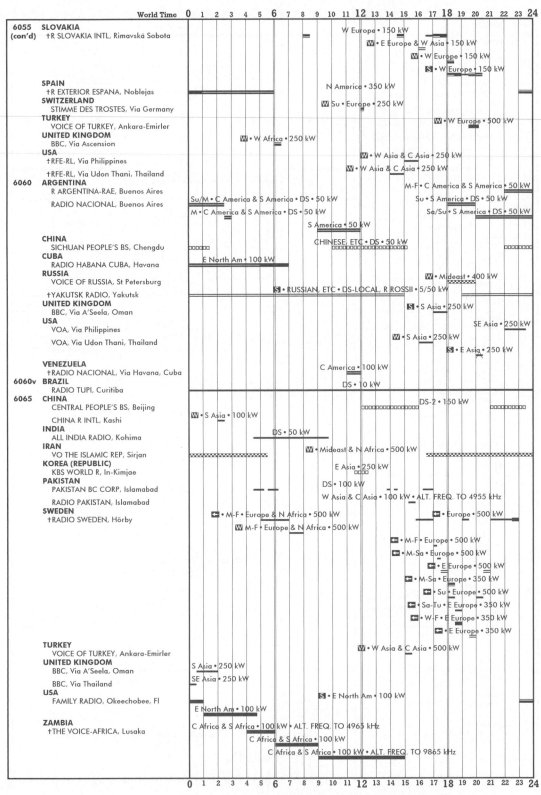

World Time 0 1 2 3 4 5 6 7 8 9 10 11 12 13 14 15 16 17 18 19 20 21 22 23 24

6055 SLOVAKIA
(con'd) †R SLOVAKIA INTL, Rimavská Sobota
- W Europe • 150 kW
- W • E Europe & W Asia • 150 kW
- W • W Europe • 150 kW
- S • W Europe • 150 kW

SPAIN
†R EXTERIOR ESPANA, Noblejas
- N America • 350 kW

SWITZERLAND
STIMME DES TROSTES, Via Germany
- W Su • Europe • 250 kW

TURKEY
VOICE OF TURKEY, Ankara-Emirler
- W • W Europe • 500 kW

UNITED KINGDOM
BBC, Via Ascension
- W • W Africa • 250 kW

USA
†RFE-RL, Via Philippines
- W • W Asia & C Asia • 250 kW

†RFE-RL, Via Udon Thani, Thailand
- W • W Asia & C Asia • 250 kW

6060 ARGENTINA
R ARGENTINA-RAE, Buenos Aires
- M-F • C America & S America • 50 kW

RADIO NACIONAL, Buenos Aires
- Su/M • C America & S America • DS • 50 kW
- Su • S America • DS • 50 kW
- M • C America & S America • DS • 50 kW
- Sa/Su • S America • DS • 50 kW
- S America • 50 kW

CHINA
SICHUAN PEOPLE'S BS, Chengdu
- CHINESE, ETC • DS • 50 kW

CUBA
RADIO HABANA CUBA, Havana
- E North Am • 100 kW

RUSSIA
VOICE OF RUSSIA, St Petersburg
- W • Mideast • 400 kW

†YAKUTSK RADIO, Yakutsk
- S • RUSSIAN, ETC • DS-LOCAL, R ROSSII • 5/50 kW

UNITED KINGDOM
BBC, Via A'Seela, Oman
- S • S Asia • 250 kW

USA
VOA, Via Philippines
- SE Asia • 250 kW
- W • S Asia • 250 kW

VOA, Via Udon Thani, Thailand
- S • E Asia • 250 kW

VENEZUELA
†RADIO NACIONAL, Via Havana, Cuba
- C America • 100 kW

6060v BRAZIL
RADIO TUPI, Curitiba
- DS • 10 kW

6065 CHINA
CENTRAL PEOPLE'S BS, Beijing
- DS-2 • 150 kW

CHINA R INTL, Kashi
- W • S Asia • 100 kW

INDIA
ALL INDIA RADIO, Kohima
- DS • 50 kW

IRAN
VO THE ISLAMIC REP, Sirjan
- W • Mideast & N Africa • 500 kW

KOREA (REPUBLIC)
KBS WORLD R, In-Kimjae
- E Asia • 250 kW

PAKISTAN
PAKISTAN BC CORP, Islamabad
- DS • 100 kW

RADIO PAKISTAN, Islamabad
- W Asia & C Asia • 100 kW • ALT. FREQ. TO 4955 kHz

SWEDEN
†RADIO SWEDEN, Hörby
- ← • M-F • Europe & N Africa • 500 kW
- ← • Europe • 500 kW
- W M-F • Europe & N Africa • 500 kW
- ← • M-F • Europe • 500 kW
- ← • M-Sa • Europe • 500 kW
- ← • E Europe • 500 kW
- ← • M-Sa • Europe • 350 kW
- ← • Su • Europe • 500 kW
- ← • Sa-Tu • E Europe • 350 kW
- ← • W-F • E Europe • 350 kW
- ← • E Europe • 350 kW

TURKEY
VOICE OF TURKEY, Ankara-Emirler
- W • W Asia & C Asia • 500 kW

UNITED KINGDOM
BBC, Via A'Seela, Oman
- S Asia • 250 kW

BBC, Via Thailand
- SE Asia • 250 kW

USA
FAMILY RADIO, Okeechobee, Fl
- S • E North Am • 100 kW
- E North Am • 100 kW

ZAMBIA
†THE VOICE-AFRICA, Lusaka
- C Africa & S Africa • 100 kW • ALT. FREQ. TO 4965 kHz
- C Africa & S Africa • 100 kW
- C Africa & S Africa • 100 kW • ALT. FREQ. TO 9865 kHz

0 1 2 3 4 5 6 7 8 9 10 11 12 13 14 15 16 17 18 19 20 21 22 23 24

ENGLISH ▬   ARABIC ⌇⌇⌇   CHINESE ▯▯▯   FRENCH ▬   GERMAN ▬   RUSSIAN ═   SPANISH ▬   OTHER ▬

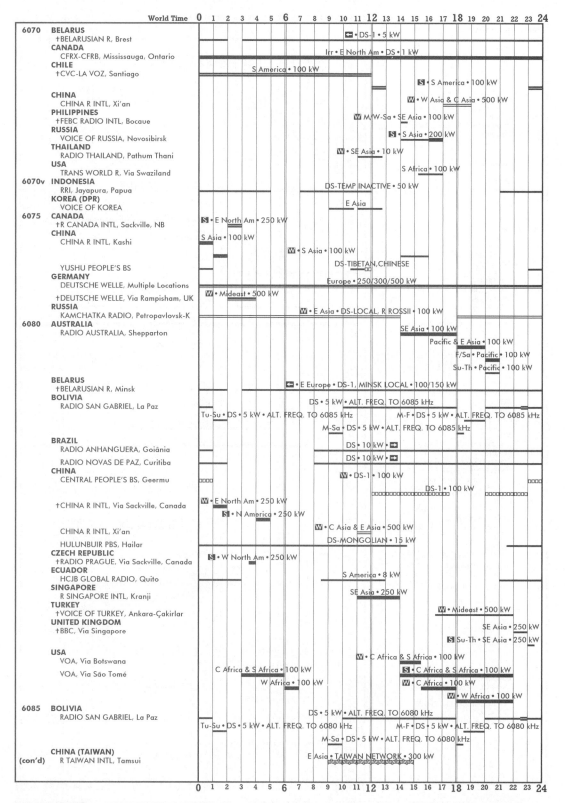

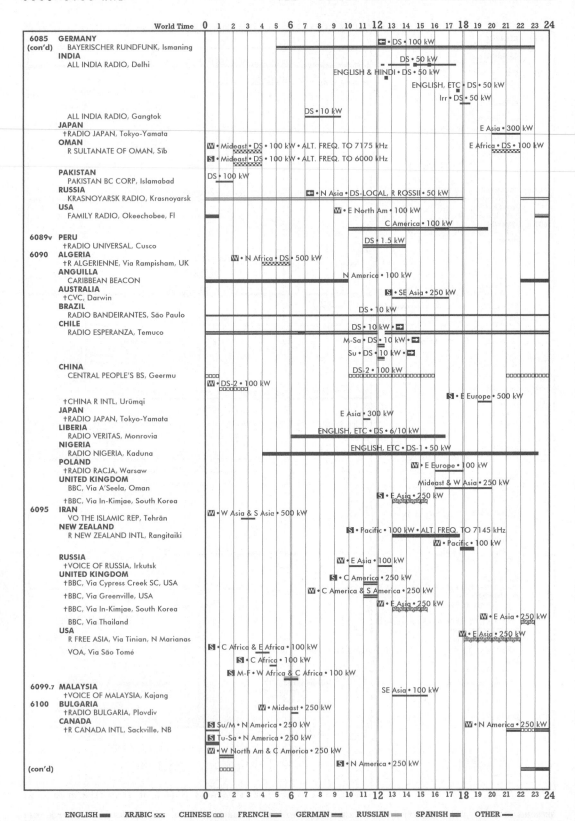

6085	GERMANY	
(con'd)	BAYERISCHER RUNDFUNK, Ismaning	▣ • DS • 100 kW
	INDIA	
	ALL INDIA RADIO, Delhi	DS • 50 kW
		ENGLISH & HINDI • DS • 50 kW
		ENGLISH, ETC • DS • 50 kW
		Irr • DS • 50 kW
	ALL INDIA RADIO, Gangtok	DS • 10 kW
	JAPAN	
	†RADIO JAPAN, Tokyo-Yamata	E Asia • 300 kW
	OMAN	
	R SULTANATE OF OMAN, Sīb	W • Mideast • DS • 100 kW • ALT. FREQ. TO 7175 kHz E Africa • DS • 100 kW
		S • Mideast • DS • 100 kW • ALT. FREQ. TO 6000 kHz
	PAKISTAN	
	PAKISTAN BC CORP, Islamabad	DS • 100 kW
	RUSSIA	
	KRASNOYARSK RADIO, Krasnoyarsk	▣ • N Asia • DS-LOCAL, R ROSSII • 50 kW
	USA	
	FAMILY RADIO, Okeechobee, Fl	W • E North Am • 100 kW
		C America • 100 kW
6089v	PERU	
	†RADIO UNIVERSAL, Cusco	DS • 1.5 kW
6090	ALGERIA	
	†R ALGERIENNE, Via Rampisham, UK	W • N Africa • DS • 500 kW
	ANGUILLA	
	CARIBBEAN BEACON	N America • 100 kW
	AUSTRALIA	
	†CVC, Darwin	S • SE Asia • 250 kW
	BRAZIL	
	RADIO BANDEIRANTES, São Paulo	DS • 10 kW
	CHILE	
	RADIO ESPERANZA, Temuco	DS • 10 kW • ▣
		M-Sa • DS • 10 kW • ▣
		Su • DS • 10 kW • ▣
	CHINA	
	CENTRAL PEOPLE'S BS, Geermu	DS-2 • 100 kW
		W • DS-2 • 100 kW
	†CHINA R INTL, Urümqi	S • E Europe • 500 kW
	JAPAN	
	†RADIO JAPAN, Tokyo-Yamata	E Asia • 300 kW
	LIBERIA	
	RADIO VERITAS, Monrovia	ENGLISH, ETC • DS • 6/10 kW
	NIGERIA	
	RADIO NIGERIA, Kaduna	ENGLISH, ETC • DS-1 • 50 kW
	POLAND	
	†RADIO RACJA, Warsaw	W • E Europe • 100 kW
	UNITED KINGDOM	
	BBC, Via A'Seela, Oman	Mideast & W Asia • 250 kW
	†BBC, Via In-Kimjae, South Korea	S • E Asia • 250 kW
6095	IRAN	
	VO THE ISLAMIC REP, Tehrān	W • W Asia & S Asia • 500 kW
	NEW ZEALAND	
	R NEW ZEALAND INTL, Rangitaiki	S • Pacific • 100 kW • ALT. FREQ. TO 7145 kHz
		W • Pacific • 100 kW
	RUSSIA	
	†VOICE OF RUSSIA, Irkutsk	W • E Asia • 100 kW
	UNITED KINGDOM	
	†BBC, Via Cypress Creek SC, USA	S • C America • 250 kW
	†BBC, Via Greenville, USA	W • C America & S America • 250 kW
	†BBC, Via In-Kimjae, South Korea	W • E Asia • 250 kW
	BBC, Via Thailand	W • E Asia • 250 kW
	USA	
	R FREE ASIA, Via Tinian, N Marianas	W • E Asia • 250 kW
	VOA, Via São Tomé	S • C Africa & E Africa • 100 kW
		S • C Africa • 100 kW
		S • M-F • W Africa & C Africa • 100 kW
6099.7	MALAYSIA	
	†VOICE OF MALAYSIA, Kajang	SE Asia • 100 kW
6100	BULGARIA	
	†RADIO BULGARIA, Plovdiv	W • Mideast • 250 kW
	CANADA	
	†R CANADA INTL, Sackville, NB	S Su/M • N America • 250 kW W • N America • 250 kW
		S Tu-Sa • N America • 250 kW
		W • W North Am & C America • 250 kW
(con'd)		S • N America • 250 kW

ENGLISH ▬   ARABIC ⧄⧄   CHINESE ▫▫▫   FRENCH ▭   GERMAN ▬   RUSSIAN ═   SPANISH ▬   OTHER ▬

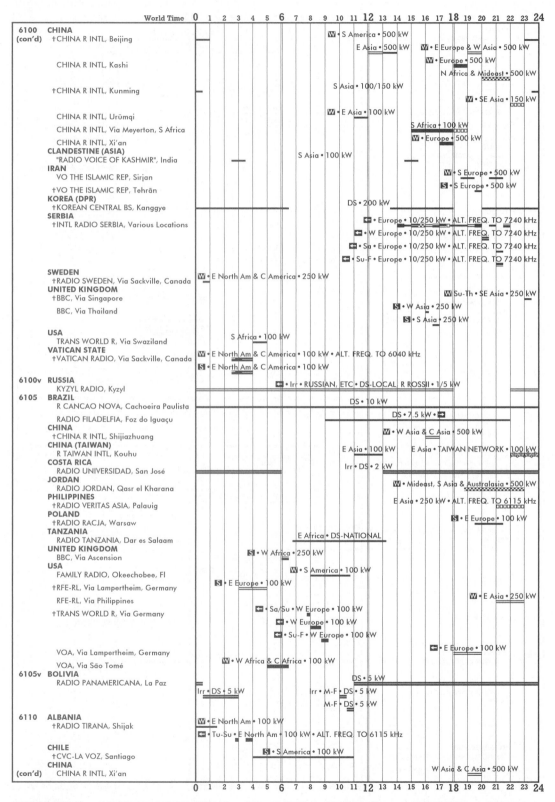

6100 (con'd)	**CHINA**
	†CHINA R INTL, Beijing
	W • S America • 500 kW
	E Asia • 500 kW
	W • E Europe & W Asia • 500 kW
	CHINA R INTL, Kashi
	W • Europe • 500 kW
	N Africa & Mideast • 500 kW
	†CHINA R INTL, Kunming
	S Asia • 100/150 kW
	W • SE Asia • 150 kW
	CHINA R INTL, Urümqi
	W • E Asia • 100 kW
	CHINA R INTL, Via Meyerton, S Africa
	S Africa • 100 kW
	CHINA R INTL, Xi'an
	W • Europe • 500 kW
	CLANDESTINE (ASIA)
	"RADIO VOICE OF KASHMIR", India
	S Asia • 100 kW
	IRAN
	VO THE ISLAMIC REP, Sirjan
	W • S Europe • 500 kW
	†VO THE ISLAMIC REP, Tehrān
	S • S Europe • 500 kW
	KOREA (DPR)
	†KOREAN CENTRAL BS, Kanggye
	DS • 200 kW
	SERBIA
	†INTL RADIO SERBIA, Various Locations
	• Europe • 10/250 kW • ALT. FREQ. TO 7240 kHz
	• W Europe • 10/250 kW • ALT. FREQ. TO 7240 kHz
	• Sa • Europe • 10/250 kW • ALT. FREQ. TO 7240 kHz
	• Su-F • Europe • 10/250 kW • ALT. FREQ. TO 7240 kHz
	SWEDEN
	†RADIO SWEDEN, Via Sackville, Canada
	W • E North Am & C America • 250 kW
	UNITED KINGDOM
	†BBC, Via Singapore
	W Su-Th • SE Asia • 250 kW
	BBC, Via Thailand
	S • W Asia • 250 kW
	S • S Asia • 250 kW
	USA
	TRANS WORLD R, Via Swaziland
	S Africa • 100 kW
	VATICAN STATE
	†VATICAN RADIO, Via Sackville, Canada
	W • E North Am & C America • 100 kW • ALT. FREQ. TO 6040 kHz
	S • E North Am & C America • 100 kW
6100v	**RUSSIA**
	KYZYL RADIO, Kyzyl
	• Irr • RUSSIAN, ETC • DS-LOCAL • R ROSSII • 1/5 kW
6105	**BRAZIL**
	R CANCAO NOVA, Cachoeira Paulista
	DS • 10 kW
	RADIO FILADELFIA, Foz do Iguaçu
	DS • 7.5 kW •
	CHINA
	†CHINA R INTL, Shijiazhuang
	W • W Asia & C Asia • 500 kW
	CHINA (TAIWAN)
	R TAIWAN INTL, Kouhu
	E Asia • 100 kW E Asia • TAIWAN NETWORK • 100 kW
	COSTA RICA
	RADIO UNIVERSIDAD, San José
	Irr • DS • 2 kW
	JORDAN
	RADIO JORDAN, Qasr el Kharana
	W • Mideast, S Asia & Australasia • 500 kW
	PHILIPPINES
	†RADIO VERITAS ASIA, Palauig
	E Asia • 250 kW • ALT. FREQ. TO 6115 kHz
	POLAND
	†RADIO RACJA, Warsaw
	S • E Europe • 100 kW
	TANZANIA
	RADIO TANZANIA, Dar es Salaam
	E Africa • DS-NATIONAL
	UNITED KINGDOM
	BBC, Via Ascension
	S • W Africa • 250 kW
	USA
	FAMILY RADIO, Okeechobee, Fl
	W • S America • 100 kW
	†RFE-RL, Via Lampertheim, Germany
	S • E Europe • 100 kW
	RFE-RL, Via Philippines
	W • E Asia • 250 kW
	†TRANS WORLD R, Via Germany
	• Sa/Su • W Europe • 100 kW
	• W Europe • 100 kW
	• Su-F • W Europe • 100 kW
	VOA, Via Lampertheim, Germany
	• E Europe • 100 kW
	VOA, Via São Tomé
	W • W Africa & C Africa • 100 kW
6105v	**BOLIVIA**
	RADIO PANAMERICANA, La Paz
	DS • 5 kW
	Irr • DS • 5 kW Irr • M-F • DS • 5 kW
	M-F • DS • 5 kW
6110	**ALBANIA**
	†RADIO TIRANA, Shijak
	W • E North Am • 100 kW
	• Tu-Su • E North Am • 100 kW • ALT. FREQ. TO 6115 kHz
	CHILE
	†CVC-LA VOZ, Santiago
	S • S America • 100 kW
	CHINA
(con'd)	CHINA R INTL, Xi'an
	W Asia & C Asia • 500 kW

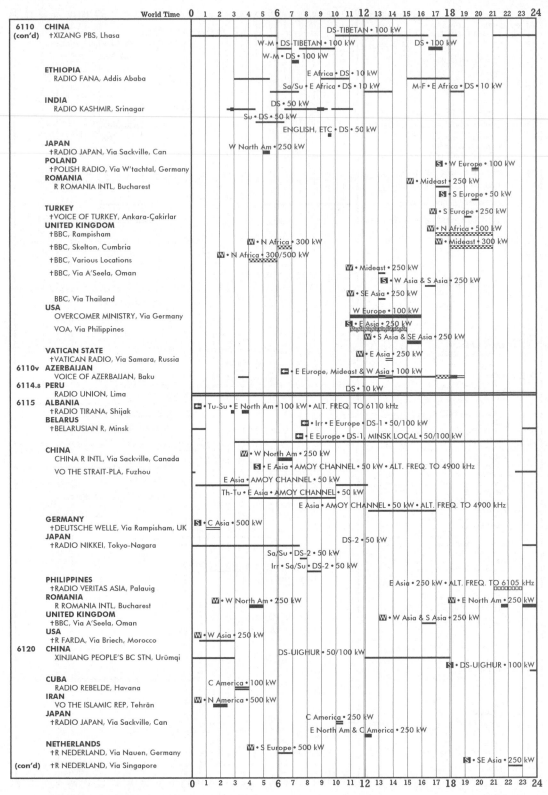

World Time 0 1 2 3 4 5 6 7 8 9 10 11 12 13 14 15 16 17 18 19 20 21 22 23 24

6110 CHINA
(con'd) †XIZANG PBS, Lhasa
    DS-TIBETAN • 100 kW
    W-M • DS-TIBETAN • 100 kW
    DS • 100 kW
    W-M • DS • 100 kW

ETHIOPIA
  RADIO FANA, Addis Ababa
    E Africa • DS • 10 kW
    Sa/Su • E Africa • DS • 10 kW
    M-F • E Africa • DS • 10 kW

INDIA
  RADIO KASHMIR, Srinagar
    DS • 50 kW
    Su • DS • 50 kW
    ENGLISH, ETC • DS • 50 kW

JAPAN
  †RADIO JAPAN, Via Sackville, Can
    W North Am • 250 kW
POLAND
  †POLISH RADIO, Via W'tachtal, Germany
    S • W Europe • 100 kW
ROMANIA
  R ROMANIA INTL, Bucharest
    W • Mideast • 250 kW
    S • S Europe • 50 kW
TURKEY
  †VOICE OF TURKEY, Ankara-Çakirlar
    W • S Europe • 250 kW
UNITED KINGDOM
  †BBC, Rampisham
    W • N Africa • 500 kW
    W • Mideast • 300 kW
  †BBC, Skelton, Cumbria
    W • N Africa • 300 kW
    W • N Africa • 300/500 kW
  †BBC, Via A'Seela, Oman
    W • Mideast • 250 kW
    S • W Asia & S Asia • 250 kW
    W • SE Asia • 250 kW
  BBC, Via Thailand
USA
  OVERCOMER MINISTRY, Via Germany
    W Europe • 100 kW
  VOA, Via Philippines
    S • E Asia • 250 kW
    W • S Asia & SE Asia • 250 kW
VATICAN STATE
  †VATICAN RADIO, Via Samara, Russia
    W • E Asia • 250 kW
6110v AZERBAIJAN
  VOICE OF AZERBAIJAN, Baku
    E Europe, Mideast & W Asia • 100 kW
6114.8 PERU
  RADIO UNION, Lima
    DS • 10 kW
6115 ALBANIA
  †RADIO TIRANA, Shijak
    Tu-Su • E North Am • 100 kW • ALT. FREQ. TO 6110 kHz
BELARUS
  †BELARUSIAN R, Minsk
    Irr • E Europe • DS-1 • 50/100 kW
    E Europe • DS-1, MINSK LOCAL • 50/100 kW
CHINA
  CHINA R INTL, Via Sackville, Canada
    W • W North Am • 250 kW
  VO THE STRAIT-PLA, Fuzhou
    S • E Asia • AMOY CHANNEL • 50 kW • ALT. FREQ. TO 4900 kHz
    E Asia • AMOY CHANNEL • 50 kW
    Th-Tu • E Asia • AMOY CHANNEL • 50 kW
    E Asia • AMOY CHANNEL • 50 kW • ALT. FREQ. TO 4900 kHz
GERMANY
  †DEUTSCHE WELLE, Via Rampisham, UK
    S • C Asia • 500 kW
JAPAN
  †RADIO NIKKEI, Tokyo-Nagara
    DS-2 • 50 kW
    Sa/Su • DS-2 • 50 kW
    Irr • Sa/Su • DS-2 • 50 kW
PHILIPPINES
  †RADIO VERITAS ASIA, Palauig
    E Asia • 250 kW • ALT. FREQ. TO 6105 kHz
ROMANIA
  R ROMANIA INTL, Bucharest
    W • W North Am • 250 kW
    W • E North Am • 250 kW
UNITED KINGDOM
  †BBC, Via A'Seela, Oman
    W • W Asia & S Asia • 250 kW
USA
  †R FARDA, Via Briech, Morocco
    W • W Asia • 250 kW
6120 CHINA
  XINJIANG PEOPLE'S BC STN, Urümqi
    DS-UIGHUR • 50/100 kW
    S • DS-UIGHUR • 100 kW
CUBA
  RADIO REBELDE, Havana
    C America • 100 kW
IRAN
  VO THE ISLAMIC REP, Tehrān
    W • N America • 500 kW
JAPAN
  †RADIO JAPAN, Via Sackville, Can
    C America • 250 kW
    E North Am & C America • 250 kW
NETHERLANDS
  †R NEDERLAND, Via Nauen, Germany
    W • S Europe • 500 kW
(con'd) †R NEDERLAND, Via Singapore
    S • SE Asia • 250 kW

0 1 2 3 4 5 6 7 8 9 10 11 12 13 14 15 16 17 18 19 20 21 22 23 24

ENGLISH ▬ ARABIC ▩ CHINESE ▢▢▢ FRENCH ▭ GERMAN ▬ RUSSIAN ═ SPANISH ▬ OTHER ▬

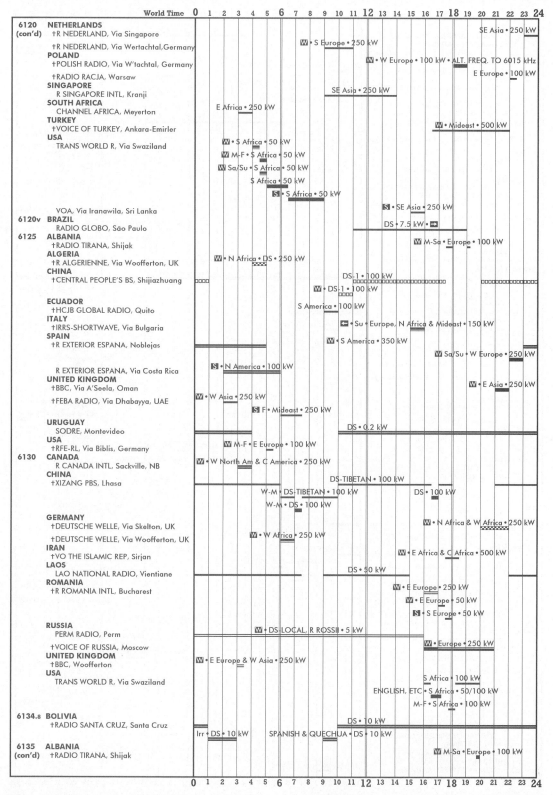

World Time | 0 1 2 3 4 5 6 7 8 9 10 11 12 13 14 15 16 17 18 19 20 21 22 23 24

6120 NETHERLANDS
(con'd)   †R NEDERLAND, Via Singapore — SE Asia • 250 kW

†R NEDERLAND, Via Wertachtal, Germany — W • S Europe • 250 kW
POLAND
†POLISH RADIO, Via W'tachtal, Germany — W • W Europe • 100 kW • ALT. FREQ. TO 6015 kHz

†RADIO RACJA, Warsaw — E Europe • 100 kW
SINGAPORE
R SINGAPORE INTL, Kranji — SE Asia • 250 kW
SOUTH AFRICA
CHANNEL AFRICA, Meyerton — E Africa • 250 kW
TURKEY
†VOICE OF TURKEY, Ankara-Emirler — W • Mideast • 500 kW
USA
TRANS WORLD R, Via Swaziland — W • S Africa • 50 kW
W M-F • S Africa • 50 kW
W Sa/Su • S Africa • 50 kW
S Africa • 50 kW
S • S Africa • 50 kW

VOA, Via Iranawila, Sri Lanka — S • SE Asia • 250 kW
6120v BRAZIL
RADIO GLOBO, São Paulo — DS • 7.5 kW • ➡
6125 ALBANIA
†RADIO TIRANA, Shijak — W M-Sa • Europe • 100 kW
ALGERIA
†R ALGERIENNE, Via Woofferton, UK — W • N Africa • DS • 250 kW
CHINA
†CENTRAL PEOPLE'S BS, Shijiazhuang — DS-1 • 100 kW
W • DS-1 • 100 kW

ECUADOR
†HCJB GLOBAL RADIO, Quito — S America • 100 kW
ITALY
†IRRS-SHORTWAVE, Via Bulgaria — ⬅ • Su • Europe, N Africa & Mideast • 150 kW
SPAIN
†R EXTERIOR ESPANA, Noblejas — W • S America • 350 kW

W Sa/Su • W Europe • 250 kW

R EXTERIOR ESPANA, Via Costa Rica — S • N America • 100 kW
UNITED KINGDOM
†BBC, Via A'Seela, Oman — W • E Asia • 250 kW

†FEBA RADIO, Via Dhabayya, UAE — W • W Asia • 250 kW
S • F • Mideast • 250 kW

URUGUAY
SODRE, Montevideo — DS • 0.2 kW
USA
†RFE-RL, Via Biblis, Germany — W M-F • E Europe • 100 kW
6130 CANADA
R CANADA INTL, Sackville, NB — W • W North Am & C America • 250 kW
CHINA
†XIZANG PBS, Lhasa — DS-TIBETAN • 100 kW
W-M • DS-TIBETAN • 100 kW — DS • 100 kW
W-M • DS • 100 kW

GERMANY
†DEUTSCHE WELLE, Via Skelton, UK — W • N Africa & W Africa • 250 kW

†DEUTSCHE WELLE, Via Woofferton, UK — W • W Africa • 250 kW
IRAN
†VO THE ISLAMIC REP, Sirjan — W • E Africa & C Africa • 500 kW
LAOS
LAO NATIONAL RADIO, Vientiane — DS • 50 kW
ROMANIA
†R ROMANIA INTL, Bucharest — W • E Europe • 250 kW
W • E Europe • 50 kW
S • S Europe • 50 kW

RUSSIA
PERM RADIO, Perm — W • DS-LOCAL, R ROSSII • 5 kW

†VOICE OF RUSSIA, Moscow — W • Europe • 250 kW
UNITED KINGDOM
†BBC, Woofferton — W • E Europe & W Asia • 250 kW
USA
TRANS WORLD R, Via Swaziland — S Africa • 100 kW
ENGLISH, ETC • S Africa • 50/100 kW
M-F • S Africa • 100 kW

6134.8 BOLIVIA
†RADIO SANTA CRUZ, Santa Cruz — DS • 10 kW
Irr • DS • 10 kW — SPANISH & QUECHUA • DS • 10 kW

6135 ALBANIA
(con'd)   †RADIO TIRANA, Shijak — W M-Sa • Europe • 100 kW

0 1 2 3 4 5 6 7 8 9 10 11 12 13 14 15 16 17 18 19 20 21 22 23 24

SEASONAL **S** OR **W**   1-HR TIMESHIFT MIDYEAR **⬅** OR **➡**   JAMMING / OR ∧   EARLIEST HEARD ◁   LATEST HEARD ▷   NEW FOR 2008 †

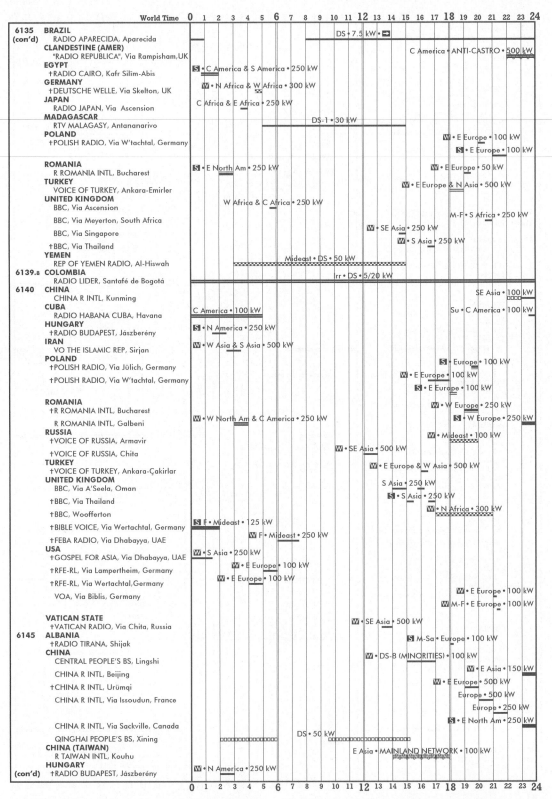

| | | World Time | 0 | 1 | 2 | 3 | 4 | 5 | 6 | 7 | 8 | 9 | 10 | 11 | 12 | 13 | 14 | 15 | 16 | 17 | 18 | 19 | 20 | 21 | 22 | 23 | 24 |

6135 BRAZIL
(con'd)   RADIO APARECIDA, Aparecida — DS • 7.5 kW •
CLANDESTINE (AMER)
  "RADIO REPUBLICA", Via Rampisham, UK — C America • ANTI-CASTRO • 500 kW
EGYPT
  †RADIO CAIRO, Kafr Silim-Abis — S • C America & S America • 250 kW
GERMANY
  †DEUTSCHE WELLE, Via Skelton, UK — W • N Africa & W Africa • 300 kW
JAPAN
  RADIO JAPAN, Via Ascension — C Africa & E Africa • 250 kW
MADAGASCAR
  RTV MALAGASY, Antananarivo — DS-1 • 30 kW
POLAND
  †POLISH RADIO, Via W'tachtal, Germany — W • E Europe • 100 kW / S • E Europe • 100 kW

ROMANIA
  R ROMANIA INTL, Bucharest — S • E North Am • 250 kW / W • E Europe • 50 kW
TURKEY
  VOICE OF TURKEY, Ankara-Emirler — W • E Europe & N Asia • 500 kW
UNITED KINGDOM
  BBC, Via Ascension — W Africa & C Africa • 250 kW
  BBC, Via Meyerton, South Africa — M-F • S Africa • 250 kW
  BBC, Via Singapore — W • SE Asia • 250 kW
  †BBC, Via Thailand — W • S Asia • 250 kW
YEMEN
  REP OF YEMEN RADIO, Al-Hiswah — Mideast • DS • 50 kW
6139.8 COLOMBIA
  RADIO LIDER, Santafé de Bogotá — Irr • DS • 5/20 kW

6140 CHINA
  CHINA R INTL, Kunming — SE Asia • 100 kW
CUBA
  RADIO HABANA CUBA, Havana — C America • 100 kW / Su • C America • 100 kW
HUNGARY
  †RADIO BUDAPEST, Jászberény — S • N America • 250 kW
IRAN
  VO THE ISLAMIC REP, Sirjan — W • W Asia & S Asia • 500 kW
POLAND
  †POLISH RADIO, Via Jülich, Germany — S • Europe • 100 kW
  †POLISH RADIO, Via W'tachtal, Germany — W • E Europe • 100 kW / S • E Europe • 100 kW

ROMANIA
  †R ROMANIA INTL, Bucharest — W • W Europe • 250 kW
  R ROMANIA INTL, Galbeni — W • W North Am & C America • 250 kW / S • W Europe • 250 kW
RUSSIA
  †VOICE OF RUSSIA, Armavir — W • Mideast • 100 kW
  †VOICE OF RUSSIA, Chita — W • SE Asia • 500 kW
TURKEY
  †VOICE OF TURKEY, Ankara-Çakirlar — W • E Europe & W Asia • 500 kW
UNITED KINGDOM
  BBC, Via A'Seela, Oman — S Asia • 250 kW
  †BBC, Via Thailand — S • S Asia • 250 kW
  †BBC, Woofferton — W • N Africa • 300 kW
  †BIBLE VOICE, Via Wertachtal, Germany — S F • Mideast • 125 kW
  †FEBA RADIO, Via Dhabayya, UAE — W F • Mideast • 250 kW
USA
  †GOSPEL FOR ASIA, Via Dhabayya, UAE — W • S Asia • 250 kW
  †RFE-RL, Via Lampertheim, Germany — W • E Europe • 100 kW
  †RFE-RL, Via Wertachtal, Germany — W • E Europe • 100 kW
  VOA, Via Biblis, Germany — W • E Europe • 100 kW / W M-F • E Europe • 100 kW

VATICAN STATE
  †VATICAN RADIO, Via Chita, Russia — W • SE Asia • 500 kW
6145 ALBANIA
  †RADIO TIRANA, Shijak — S M-Sa • Europe • 100 kW
CHINA
  CENTRAL PEOPLE'S BS, Lingshi — W • DS-8 (MINORITIES) • 100 kW
  CHINA R INTL, Beijing — W • E Asia • 150 kW
  †CHINA R INTL, Urümqi — W • E Europe • 500 kW
  CHINA R INTL, Via Issoudun, France — Europe • 500 kW / Europe • 250 kW
  CHINA R INTL, Via Sackville, Canada — S • E North Am • 250 kW
  QINGHAI PEOPLE'S BS, Xining — DS • 50 kW
CHINA (TAIWAN)
  R TAIWAN INTL, Kouhu — E Asia • MAINLAND NETWORK • 100 kW
HUNGARY
(con'd) †RADIO BUDAPEST, Jászberény — W • N America • 250 kW

| | World Time | 0 | 1 | 2 | 3 | 4 | 5 | 6 | 7 | 8 | 9 | 10 | 11 | 12 | 13 | 14 | 15 | 16 | 17 | 18 | 19 | 20 | 21 | 22 | 23 | 24 |

ENGLISH ▬   ARABIC ⌇⌇⌇   CHINESE ▫▫▫   FRENCH ▭   GERMAN ▬   RUSSIAN ═   SPANISH ▬   OTHER —

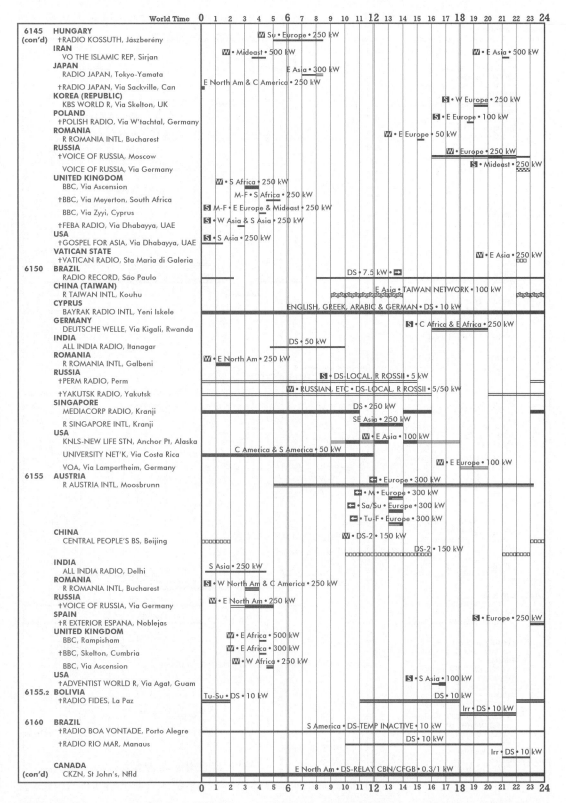

World Time

	0 1 2 3 4 5 6 7 8 9 10 11 12 13 14 15 16 17 18 19 20 21 22 23 24

6145 **HUNGARY**
(con'd) †RADIO KOSSUTH, Jászberény — W • Su • Europe • 250 kW
IRAN
VO THE ISLAMIC REP, Sirjan — W • Mideast • 500 kW / W • E Asia • 500 kW
JAPAN
RADIO JAPAN, Tokyo-Yamata — E Asia • 300 kW
†RADIO JAPAN, Via Sackville, Can — E North Am & C America • 250 kW
KOREA (REPUBLIC)
KBS WORLD R, Via Skelton, UK — S • W Europe • 250 kW
POLAND
†POLISH RADIO, Via W'tachtal, Germany — S • E Europe • 100 kW
ROMANIA
R ROMANIA INTL, Bucharest — W • E Europe • 50 kW
RUSSIA
†VOICE OF RUSSIA, Moscow — W • Europe • 250 kW
VOICE OF RUSSIA, Via Germany — S • Mideast • 250 kW
UNITED KINGDOM
BBC, Via Ascension — W • S Africa • 250 kW
†BBC, Via Meyerton, South Africa — M-F • S Africa • 250 kW
BBC, Via Zyyi, Cyprus — S M-F • E Europe & Mideast • 250 kW
†FEBA RADIO, Via Dhabayya, UAE — S • W Asia & S Asia • 250 kW
USA
†GOSPEL FOR ASIA, Via Dhabayya, UAE — S • S Asia • 250 kW
VATICAN STATE
†VATICAN RADIO, Sta Maria di Galeria — W • E Asia • 250 kW

6150 **BRAZIL**
RADIO RECORD, São Paulo — DS • 7.5 kW • →
CHINA (TAIWAN)
R TAIWAN INTL, Kouhu — E Asia • TAIWAN NETWORK • 100 kW
CYPRUS
BAYRAK RADIO INTL, Yeni Iskele — ENGLISH, GREEK, ARABIC & GERMAN • DS • 10 kW
GERMANY
DEUTSCHE WELLE, Via Kigali, Rwanda — S • C Africa & E Africa • 250 kW
INDIA
ALL INDIA RADIO, Itanagar — DS • 50 kW
ROMANIA
R ROMANIA INTL, Galbeni — W • E North Am • 250 kW
RUSSIA
†PERM RADIO, Perm — S • DS-LOCAL, R ROSSII • 5 kW
†YAKUTSK RADIO, Yakutsk — W • RUSSIAN, ETC • DS-LOCAL, R ROSSII • 5/50 kW
SINGAPORE
MEDIACORP RADIO, Kranji — DS • 250 kW
R SINGAPORE INTL, Kranji — SE Asia • 250 kW
USA
KNLS-NEW LIFE STN, Anchor Pt, Alaska — W • E Asia • 100 kW
UNIVERSITY NET'K, Via Costa Rica — C America & S America • 50 kW
VOA, Via Lampertheim, Germany — W • E Europe • 100 kW

6155 **AUSTRIA**
R AUSTRIA INTL, Moosbrunn — ⇆ • Europe • 300 kW
— ⇆ • M • Europe • 300 kW
— ⇆ • Sa/Su • Europe • 300 kW
— ⇆ • Tu-F • Europe • 300 kW
CHINA
CENTRAL PEOPLE'S BS, Beijing — W • DS-2 • 150 kW
— DS-2 • 150 kW
INDIA
ALL INDIA RADIO, Delhi — S Asia • 250 kW
ROMANIA
R ROMANIA INTL, Bucharest — S • W North Am & C America • 250 kW
RUSSIA
†VOICE OF RUSSIA, Via Germany — W • E North Am • 250 kW
SPAIN
†R EXTERIOR ESPANA, Noblejas — S • Europe • 250 kW
UNITED KINGDOM
BBC, Rampisham — W • E Africa • 500 kW
†BBC, Skelton, Cumbria — W • E Africa • 300 kW
BBC, Via Ascension — W • W Africa • 250 kW
USA
†ADVENTIST WORLD R, Via Agat, Guam — S • S Asia • 100 kW

6155.2 **BOLIVIA**
†RADIO FIDES, La Paz — Tu-Su • DS • 10 kW / DS • 10 kW
— Irr • DS • 10 kW

6160 **BRAZIL**
†RADIO BOA VONTADE, Porto Alegre — S America • DS-TEMP INACTIVE • 10 kW
†RADIO RIO MAR, Manaus — DS • 10 kW
— Irr • DS • 10 kW
CANADA
(con'd) CKZN, St John's, Nfld — E North Am • DS-RELAY CBN/CFGB • 0.3/1 kW

	0 1 2 3 4 5 6 7 8 9 10 11 12 13 14 15 16 17 18 19 20 21 22 23 24

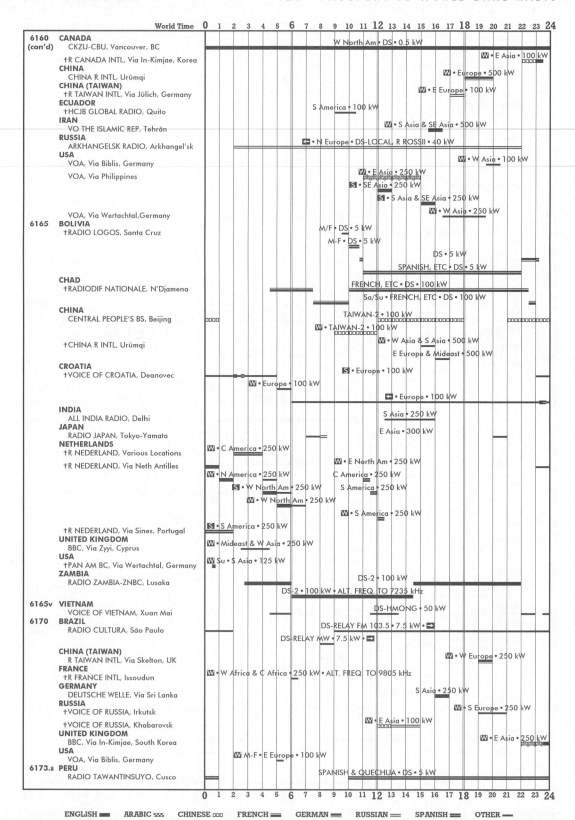

6160	**CANADA**
(con'd)	CKZU-CBU, Vancouver, BC
	†R CANADA INTL, Via In-Kimjae, Korea
	CHINA
	CHINA R INTL, Urümqi
	CHINA (TAIWAN)
	†R TAIWAN INTL, Via Jülich, Germany
	ECUADOR
	†HCJB GLOBAL RADIO, Quito
	IRAN
	VO THE ISLAMIC REP, Tehrān
	RUSSIA
	ARKHANGELSK RADIO, Arkhangel'sk
	USA
	VOA, Via Biblis, Germany
	VOA, Via Philippines
	VOA, Via Wertachtal, Germany
6165	**BOLIVIA**
	†RADIO LOGOS, Santa Cruz
	CHAD
	†RADIODIF NATIONALE, N'Djamena
	CHINA
	CENTRAL PEOPLE'S BS, Beijing
	†CHINA R INTL, Urümqi
	CROATIA
	†VOICE OF CROATIA, Deanovec
	INDIA
	ALL INDIA RADIO, Delhi
	JAPAN
	RADIO JAPAN, Tokyo-Yamata
	NETHERLANDS
	†R NEDERLAND, Various Locations
	†R NEDERLAND, Via Neth Antilles
	†R NEDERLAND, Via Sines, Portugal
	UNITED KINGDOM
	BBC, Via Zyyi, Cyprus
	USA
	†PAN AM BC, Via Wertachtal, Germany
	ZAMBIA
	RADIO ZAMBIA-ZNBC, Lusaka
6165v	**VIETNAM**
	VOICE OF VIETNAM, Xuan Mai
6170	**BRAZIL**
	RADIO CULTURA, São Paulo
	CHINA (TAIWAN)
	R TAIWAN INTL, Via Skelton, UK
	FRANCE
	†R FRANCE INTL, Issoudun
	GERMANY
	DEUTSCHE WELLE, Via Sri Lanka
	RUSSIA
	†VOICE OF RUSSIA, Irkutsk
	†VOICE OF RUSSIA, Khabarovsk
	UNITED KINGDOM
	BBC, Via In-Kimjae, South Korea
	USA
	VOA, Via Biblis, Germany
6173.8	**PERU**
	RADIO TAWANTINSUYO, Cusco

Annotations (left to right within chart):

- CKZU-CBU: W North Am • DS • 0.5 kW
- R CANADA INTL: W • E Asia • 100 kW
- CHINA R INTL: W • Europe • 500 kW
- R TAIWAN INTL, Jülich: W • E Europe • 100 kW
- HCJB GLOBAL RADIO: S America • 100 kW
- VO THE ISLAMIC REP: W • S Asia & SE Asia • 500 kW
- ARKHANGELSK RADIO: N Europe • DS-LOCAL, R ROSSII • 40 kW
- VOA, Biblis: W • W Asia • 100 kW
- VOA, Philippines: W • E Asia • 250 kW; S • SE Asia • 250 kW; S • S Asia & SE Asia • 250 kW
- VOA, Wertachtal: W • W Asia • 250 kW
- RADIO LOGOS: M/F • DS • 5 kW; M-F • DS • 5 kW; DS • 5 kW; SPANISH, ETC • DS • 5 kW
- RADIODIF NATIONALE: FRENCH, ETC • DS • 100 kW; Sa/Su • FRENCH, ETC • DS • 100 kW
- CENTRAL PEOPLE'S BS: TAIWAN-2 • 100 kW; W • TAIWAN-2 • 100 kW
- CHINA R INTL, Urümqi: W • W Asia & S Asia • 500 kW; E Europe & Mideast • 500 kW
- VOICE OF CROATIA: S • Europe • 100 kW; W • Europe • 100 kW; • Europe • 100 kW
- ALL INDIA RADIO: S Asia • 250 kW
- RADIO JAPAN: E Asia • 300 kW
- R NEDERLAND, Various: W • C America • 250 kW; W • E North Am • 250 kW
- R NEDERLAND, Neth Antilles: W • N America • 250 kW; C America • 250 kW; S • W North Am • 250 kW; S America • 250 kW; W • W North Am • 250 kW; W • S America • 250 kW
- R NEDERLAND, Sines: S • S America • 250 kW
- BBC, Zyyi: W • Mideast & W Asia • 250 kW
- PAN AM BC: W • Su • S Asia • 125 kW
- RADIO ZAMBIA-ZNBC: DS-2 • 100 kW; DS-2 • 100 kW • ALT. FREQ. TO 7235 kHz
- VOICE OF VIETNAM: DS-HMONG • 50 kW
- RADIO CULTURA: DS-RELAY FM 103.5 • 7.5 kW •; DS-RELAY MW • 7.5 kW •
- R TAIWAN INTL, Skelton: W • W Europe • 250 kW
- R FRANCE INTL: W • W Africa & C Africa • 250 kW • ALT. FREQ. TO 9805 kHz
- DEUTSCHE WELLE: S Asia • 250 kW
- VOICE OF RUSSIA, Irkutsk: W • S Europe • 250 kW
- VOICE OF RUSSIA, Khabarovsk: W • E Asia • 100 kW
- BBC, In-Kimjae: W • E Asia • 250 kW
- VOA, Biblis: W • M-F • E Europe • 100 kW
- RADIO TAWANTINSUYO: SPANISH & QUECHUA • DS • 5 kW

World Time scale: 0 1 2 3 4 5 6 7 8 9 10 11 12 13 14 15 16 17 18 19 20 21 22 23 24

ENGLISH ▬   ARABIC ∿∿   CHINESE ▫▫▫   FRENCH ▬   GERMAN ▬   RUSSIAN ═   SPANISH ▬   OTHER ▬

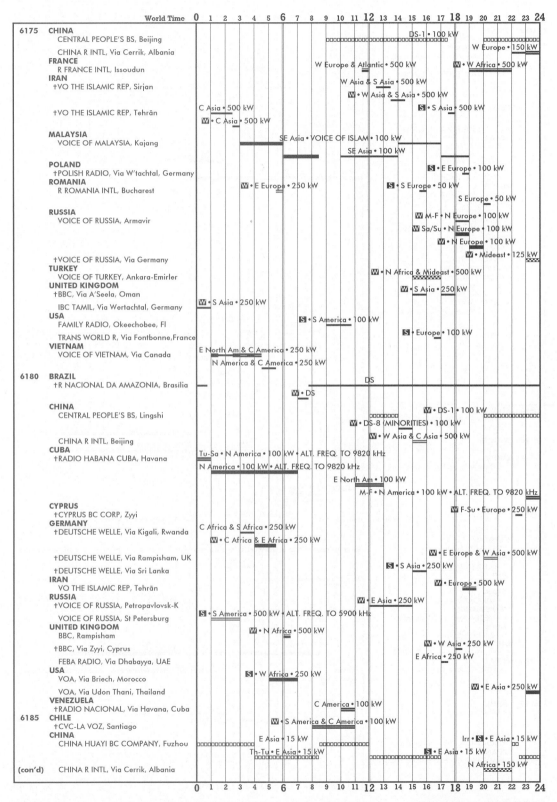

6175 CHINA
CENTRAL PEOPLE'S BS, Beijing — DS-1 • 100 kW

CHINA R INTL, Via Cerrik, Albania — W Europe • 150 kW
FRANCE
R FRANCE INTL, Issoudun — W Europe & Atlantic • 500 kW · W • W Africa • 500 kW
IRAN
†VO THE ISLAMIC REP, Sirjan — W Asia & S Asia • 500 kW · W • W Asia & S Asia • 500 kW · S • S Asia • 500 kW

†VO THE ISLAMIC REP, Tehrān — C Asia • 500 kW · W • C Asia • 500 kW
MALAYSIA
VOICE OF MALAYSIA, Kajang — SE Asia • VOICE OF ISLAM • 100 kW · SE Asia • 100 kW
POLAND
†POLISH RADIO, Via W'tachtal, Germany — S • E Europe • 100 kW
ROMANIA
R ROMANIA INTL, Bucharest — W • E Europe • 250 kW · S • S Europe • 50 kW · S Europe • 50 kW
RUSSIA
VOICE OF RUSSIA, Armavir — W • M-F • N Europe • 100 kW · W • Sa/Su • N Europe • 100 kW · W • N Europe • 100 kW

†VOICE OF RUSSIA, Via Germany — W • Mideast • 125 kW
TURKEY
VOICE OF TURKEY, Ankara-Emirler — W • N Africa & Mideast • 500 kW
UNITED KINGDOM
†BBC, Via A'Seela, Oman — W • S Asia • 250 kW

IBC TAMIL, Via Wertachtal, Germany — W • S Asia • 250 kW
USA
FAMILY RADIO, Okeechobee, Fl — S • S America • 100 kW

TRANS WORLD R, Via Fontbonne, France — S • Europe • 100 kW
VIETNAM
VOICE OF VIETNAM, Via Canada — E North Am & C America • 250 kW · N America & C America • 250 kW

6180 BRAZIL
†R NACIONAL DA AMAZONIA, Brasilia — DS · W • DS

CHINA
CENTRAL PEOPLE'S BS, Lingshi — W • DS-1 • 100 kW · W • DS-8 (MINORITIES) • 100 kW · W • W Asia & C Asia • 500 kW

CHINA R INTL, Beijing
CUBA
†RADIO HABANA CUBA, Havana — Tu-Sa • N America • 100 kW • ALT. FREQ. TO 9820 kHz · N America • 100 kW • ALT. FREQ. TO 9820 kHz · E North Am • 100 kW · M-F • N America • 100 kW • ALT. FREQ. TO 9820 kHz

CYPRUS
†CYPRUS BC CORP, Zyyi — W F-Su • Europe • 250 kW
GERMANY
†DEUTSCHE WELLE, Via Kigali, Rwanda — C Africa & S Africa • 250 kW · W • C Africa & E Africa • 250 kW

†DEUTSCHE WELLE, Via Rampisham, UK — W • E Europe & W Asia • 500 kW

†DEUTSCHE WELLE, Via Sri Lanka — S • S Asia • 250 kW
IRAN
VO THE ISLAMIC REP, Tehrān — W • Europe • 500 kW
RUSSIA
†VOICE OF RUSSIA, Petropavlovsk-K — W • E Asia • 250 kW

VOICE OF RUSSIA, St Petersburg — S • S America • 500 kW • ALT. FREQ. TO 5900 kHz
UNITED KINGDOM
BBC, Rampisham — W • N Africa • 500 kW

†BBC, Via Zyyi, Cyprus — W • W Asia • 250 kW

FEBA RADIO, Via Dhabayya, UAE — E Africa • 250 kW
USA
VOA, Via Briech, Morocco — S • W Africa • 250 kW

VOA, Via Udon Thani, Thailand — W • E Asia • 250 kW
VENEZUELA
†RADIO NACIONAL, Via Havana, Cuba — C America • 100 kW
6185 CHILE
†CVC-LA VOZ, Santiago — W • S America & C America • 100 kW
CHINA
CHINA HUAYI BC COMPANY, Fuzhou — E Asia • 15 kW · Irr • S • E Asia • 15 kW · Th-Tu • E Asia • 15 kW · S • E Asia • 15 kW · N Africa • 150 kW

(con'd) CHINA R INTL, Via Cerrik, Albania

SEASONAL S OR W   1-HR TIMESHIFT MIDYEAR ⇐ OR ⇒   JAMMING / OR ∧   EARLIEST HEARD ◁   LATEST HEARD ▷   NEW FOR 2008 †

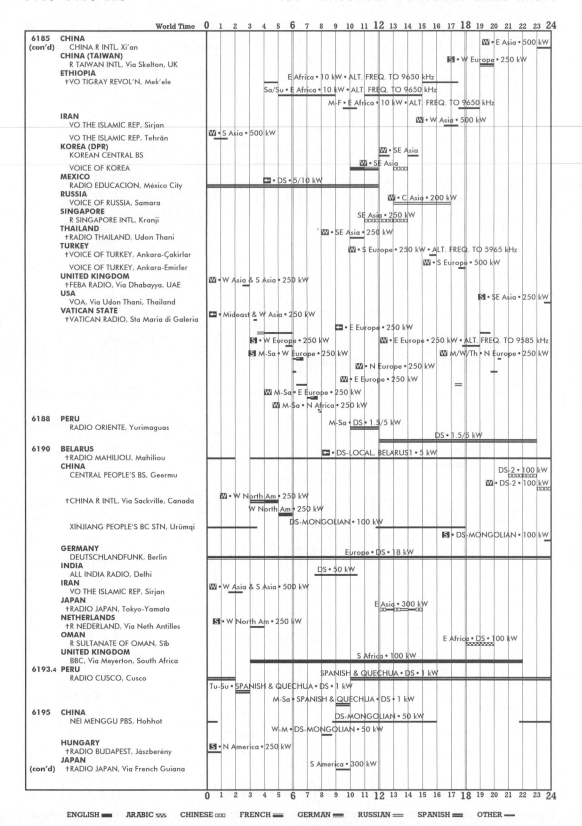

World Time

6185 **CHINA**
(con'd)   CHINA R INTL, Xi'an — W • E Asia • 500 kW
           CHINA (TAIWAN)
              R TAIWAN INTL, Via Skelton, UK — S • W Europe • 250 kW
           ETHIOPIA
              †VO TIGRAY REVOL'N, Mek'ele — E Africa • 10 kW • ALT. FREQ. TO 9650 kHz
                 Sa/Su • E Africa • 10 kW • ALT. FREQ. TO 9650 kHz
                 M-F • E Africa • 10 kW • ALT. FREQ. TO 9650 kHz
           IRAN
              VO THE ISLAMIC REP, Sirjan — W • W Asia • 500 kW
              VO THE ISLAMIC REP, Tehrān — W • S Asia • 500 kW
           KOREA (DPR)
              KOREAN CENTRAL BS — W • SE Asia
              VOICE OF KOREA — W • SE Asia
           MEXICO
              RADIO EDUCACION, México City — DS • 5/10 kW
           RUSSIA
              VOICE OF RUSSIA, Samara — W • C Asia • 200 kW
           SINGAPORE
              R SINGAPORE INTL, Kranji — SE Asia • 250 kW
           THAILAND
              †RADIO THAILAND, Udon Thani — W • SE Asia • 250 kW
           TURKEY
              †VOICE OF TURKEY, Ankara-Çakirlar — W • S Europe • 250 kW • ALT. FREQ. TO 5965 kHz
              VOICE OF TURKEY, Ankara-Emirler — W • S Europe • 500 kW
           UNITED KINGDOM
              †FEBA RADIO, Via Dhabayya, UAE — W • W Asia & S Asia • 250 kW
           USA
              VOA, Via Udon Thani, Thailand — S • SE Asia • 250 kW
           VATICAN STATE
              †VATICAN RADIO, Sta Maria di Galeria — • Mideast & W Asia • 250 kW
                 • E Europe • 250 kW
                 S • W Europe • 250 kW   W • E Europe • 250 kW • ALT. FREQ. TO 9585 kHz
                 S M-Sa • W Europe • 250 kW   W/M/W/Th • N Europe • 250 kW
                 W • N Europe • 250 kW
                 W • E Europe • 250 kW
                 W M-Sa • E Europe • 250 kW
                 W M-Sa • N Africa • 250 kW

6188 **PERU**
              RADIO ORIENTE, Yurimaguas — M-Sa • DS • 1.5/5 kW
                 DS • 1.5/5 kW

6190 **BELARUS**
              †RADIO MAHILIOU, Mahiliou — • DS-LOCAL, BELARUS1 • 5 kW
           CHINA
              CENTRAL PEOPLE'S BS, Geermu — DS-2 • 100 kW
                 W • DS-2 • 100 kW
              †CHINA R INTL, Via Sackville, Canada — W • W North Am • 250 kW
                 W North Am • 250 kW
              XINJIANG PEOPLE'S BC STN, Urümqi — DS-MONGOLIAN • 100 kW
                 S • DS-MONGOLIAN • 100 kW
           GERMANY
              DEUTSCHLANDFUNK, Berlin — Europe • DS • 18 kW
           INDIA
              ALL INDIA RADIO, Delhi — DS • 50 kW
           IRAN
              VO THE ISLAMIC REP, Sirjan — W • W Asia & S Asia • 500 kW
           JAPAN
              †RADIO JAPAN, Tokyo-Yamata — E Asia • 300 kW
           NETHERLANDS
              †R NEDERLAND, Via Neth Antilles — S • W North Am • 250 kW
           OMAN
              R SULTANATE OF OMAN, Sīb — E Africa • DS • 100 kW
           UNITED KINGDOM
              BBC, Via Meyerton, South Africa — S Africa • 100 kW
6193.4 **PERU**
              RADIO CUSCO, Cusco — SPANISH & QUECHUA • DS • 1 kW
                 Tu-Su • SPANISH & QUECHUA • DS • 1 kW
                 M-Sa • SPANISH & QUECHUA • DS • 1 kW

6195 **CHINA**
              NEI MENGGU PBS, Hohhot — DS-MONGOLIAN • 50 kW
                 W-M • DS-MONGOLIAN • 50 kW
           HUNGARY
              †RADIO BUDAPEST, Jászberény — S • N America • 250 kW
           JAPAN
(con'd)   †RADIO JAPAN, Via French Guiana — S America • 300 kW

ENGLISH ▬   ARABIC ⌇⌇⌇   CHINESE ▢▢▢   FRENCH ▬   GERMAN ▬   RUSSIAN ═   SPANISH ▬   OTHER ▬

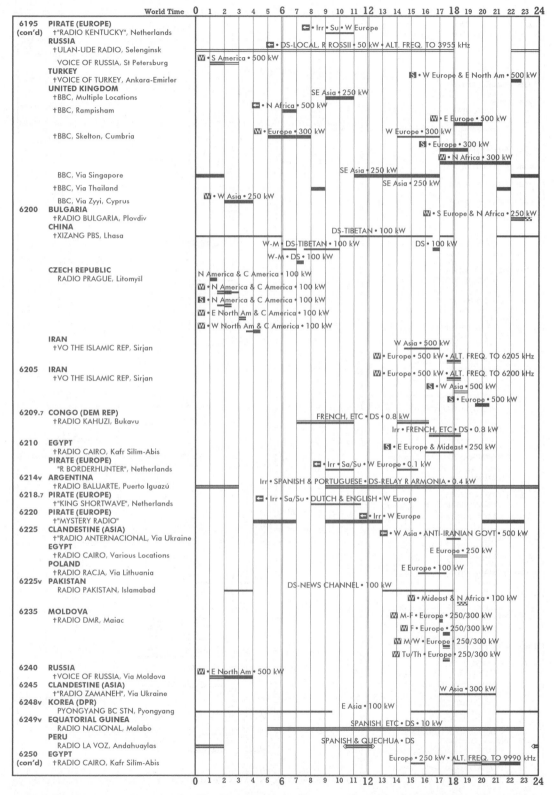

World Time 0 1 2 3 4 5 6 7 8 9 10 11 12 13 14 15 16 17 18 19 20 21 22 23 24

Freq	Station	Details
6195 (con'd)	**PIRATE (EUROPE)**	
	†"RADIO KENTUCKY", Netherlands	⬅ Irr • Su • W Europe
	RUSSIA	
	†ULAN-UDE RADIO, Selenginsk	⬅ • DS-LOCAL, R ROSSII • 50 kW • ALT. FREQ. TO 3955 kHz
	VOICE OF RUSSIA, St Petersburg	W • S America • 500 kW
	TURKEY	
	†VOICE OF TURKEY, Ankara-Emirler	S • W Europe & E North Am • 500 kW
	UNITED KINGDOM	
	†BBC, Multiple Locations	SE Asia • 250 kW
	†BBC, Rampisham	⬅ • N Africa • 500 kW
		W • E Europe • 500 kW
	†BBC, Skelton, Cumbria	W • Europe • 300 kW W Europe • 300 kW
		S • Europe • 300 kW
		W • N Africa • 300 kW
	BBC, Via Singapore	SE Asia • 250 kW
	†BBC, Via Thailand	SE Asia • 250 kW
	BBC, Via Zyyi, Cyprus	W • W Asia • 250 kW
6200	**BULGARIA**	W • S Europe & N Africa • 250 kW
	†RADIO BULGARIA, Plovdiv	
	CHINA	DS-TIBETAN • 100 kW
	†XIZANG PBS, Lhasa	W-M • DS-TIBETAN • 100 kW DS • 100 kW
		W-M • DS • 100 kW
	CZECH REPUBLIC	
	RADIO PRAGUE, Litomyšl	N America & C America • 100 kW
		W • N America & C America • 100 kW
		S • N America & C America • 100 kW
		W • E North Am & C America • 100 kW
		W • W North Am & C America • 100 kW
	IRAN	
	†VO THE ISLAMIC REP, Sirjan	W Asia • 500 kW
		W • Europe • 500 kW • ALT. FREQ. TO 6205 kHz
6205	**IRAN**	
	†VO THE ISLAMIC REP, Sirjan	W • Europe • 500 kW • ALT. FREQ. TO 6200 kHz
		S • W Asia • 500 kW
		S • Europe • 500 kW
6209.7	**CONGO (DEM REP)**	
	†RADIO KAHUZI, Bukavu	FRENCH, ETC • DS • 0.8 kW
		Irr • FRENCH, ETC • DS • 0.8 kW
6210	**EGYPT**	
	†RADIO CAIRO, Kafr Silim-Abis	S • E Europe & Mideast • 250 kW
	PIRATE (EUROPE)	
	"R BORDERHUNTER", Netherlands	⬅ • Irr • Sa/Su • W Europe • 0.1 kW
6214v	**ARGENTINA**	
	†RADIO BALUARTE, Puerto Iguazú	Irr • SPANISH & PORTUGUESE • DS-RELAY R ARMONIA • 0.4 kW
6218.7	**PIRATE (EUROPE)**	
	†"KING SHORTWAVE", Netherlands	⬅ • Irr • Sa/Su • DUTCH & ENGLISH • W Europe
6220	**PIRATE (EUROPE)**	
	†"MYSTERY RADIO"	⬅ • Irr • W Europe
6225	**CLANDESTINE (ASIA)**	
	†RADIO ANTERNACIONAL, Via Ukraine	⬅ • W Asia • ANTI-IRANIAN GOVT • 500 kW
	EGYPT	
	†RADIO CAIRO, Various Locations	E Europe • 250 kW
	POLAND	
	†RADIO RACJA, Via Lithuania	E Europe • 100 kW
6225v	**PAKISTAN**	
	RADIO PAKISTAN, Islamabad	DS-NEWS CHANNEL • 100 kW
		W • Mideast & N Africa • 100 kW
6235	**MOLDOVA**	
	†RADIO DMR, Maiac	W M-F • Europe • 250/300 kW
		W F • Europe • 250/300 kW
		W M/W • Europe • 250/300 kW
		W Tu/Th • Europe • 250/300 kW
6240	**RUSSIA**	
	†VOICE OF RUSSIA, Via Moldova	W • E North Am • 500 kW
6245	**CLANDESTINE (ASIA)**	
	†"RADIO ZAMANEH", Via Ukraine	W Asia • 300 kW
6248v	**KOREA (DPR)**	
	PYONGYANG BC STN, Pyongyang	E Asia • 100 kW
6249v	**EQUATORIAL GUINEA**	
	RADIO NACIONAL, Malabo	SPANISH, ETC • DS • 10 kW
	PERU	
	RADIO LA VOZ, Andahuaylas	SPANISH & QUECHUA • DS
6250 (con'd)	**EGYPT**	
	†RADIO CAIRO, Kafr Silim-Abis	Europe • 250 kW • ALT. FREQ. TO 9990 kHz

0 1 2 3 4 5 6 7 8 9 10 11 12 13 14 15 16 17 18 19 20 21 22 23 24

SEASONAL S OR W   1-HR TIMESHIFT MIDYEAR ⬅ OR ➡   JAMMING / OR ∧   EARLIEST HEARD ◁   LATEST HEARD ▷   NEW FOR 2008 †

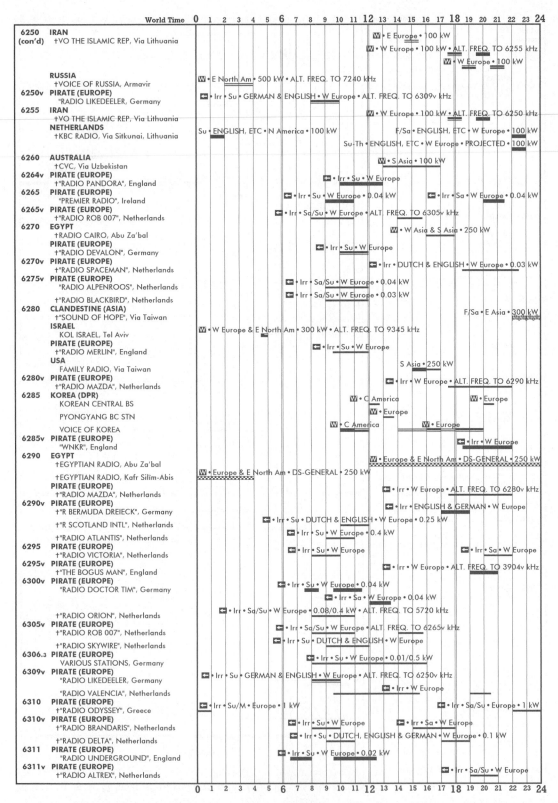

| World Time | 0 | 1 | 2 | 3 | 4 | 5 | 6 | 7 | 8 | 9 | 10 | 11 | 12 | 13 | 14 | 15 | 16 | 17 | 18 | 19 | 20 | 21 | 22 | 23 | 24 |

6250 IRAN
(con'd)   †VO THE ISLAMIC REP, Via Lithuania
W • E Europe • 100 kW
W • W Europe • 100 kW • ALT. FREQ. TO 6255 kHz
W • W Europe • 100 kW

RUSSIA
†VOICE OF RUSSIA, Armavir
W • E North Am • 500 kW • ALT. FREQ. TO 7240 kHz
6250v PIRATE (EUROPE)
"RADIO LIKEDEELER, Germany
• Irr • Su • GERMAN & ENGLISH • W Europe • ALT. FREQ. TO 6309v kHz

6255 IRAN
†VO THE ISLAMIC REP, Via Lithuania
W • W Europe • 100 kW • ALT. FREQ. TO 6250 kHz
NETHERLANDS
†KBC RADIO, Via Sitkunai, Lithuania
Su • ENGLISH, ETC • N America • 100 kW
F/Sa • ENGLISH, ETC • W Europe • 100 kW
Su-Th • ENGLISH, ETC • W Europe • PROJECTED • 100 kW

6260 AUSTRALIA
†CVC, Via Uzbekistan
W • S Asia • 100 kW
6264v PIRATE (EUROPE)
†"RADIO PANDORA", England
• Irr • Su • W Europe

6265 PIRATE (EUROPE)
"PREMIER RADIO", Ireland
• Irr • Su • W Europe • 0.04 kW
• Irr • Sa • W Europe • 0.04 kW
6265v PIRATE (EUROPE)
†"RADIO ROB 007", Netherlands
• Irr • Sa/Su • W Europe • ALT. FREQ. TO 6305v kHz

6270 EGYPT
†RADIO CAIRO, Abu Za'bal
W • W Asia & S Asia • 250 kW
PIRATE (EUROPE)
†"RADIO DEVALON", Germany
• Irr • Su • W Europe
6270v PIRATE (EUROPE)
†"RADIO SPACEMAN", Netherlands
• Irr • DUTCH & ENGLISH • W Europe • 0.03 kW
6275v PIRATE (EUROPE)
†"RADIO ALPENROOS", Netherlands
• Irr • Sa/Su • W Europe • 0.04 kW

†"RADIO BLACKBIRD", Netherlands
• Irr • Sa/Su • W Europe • 0.03 kW
6280 CLANDESTINE (ASIA)
†"SOUND OF HOPE", Via Taiwan
F/Sa • E Asia • 300 kW
ISRAEL
KOL ISRAEL, Tel Aviv
W • W Europe & E North Am • 300 kW • ALT. FREQ. TO 9345 kHz
PIRATE (EUROPE)
†"RADIO MERLIN", England
• Irr • Su • W Europe
USA
FAMILY RADIO, Via Taiwan
S Asia • 250 kW
6280v PIRATE (EUROPE)
†"RADIO MAZDA", Netherlands
• Irr • W Europe • ALT. FREQ. TO 6290 kHz
6285 KOREA (DPR)
KOREAN CENTRAL BS
W • C America
W • Europe

PYONGYANG BC STN
W • Europe

VOICE OF KOREA
W • C America
W • Europe
6285v PIRATE (EUROPE)
"WNKR", England
• Irr • W Europe
6290 EGYPT
†EGYPTIAN RADIO, Abu Za'bal
W • Europe & E North Am • DS-GENERAL • 250 kW

†EGYPTIAN RADIO, Kafr Silim-Abis
W • Europe & E North Am • DS-GENERAL • 250 kW
PIRATE (EUROPE)
†"RADIO MAZDA", Netherlands
• Irr • W Europe • ALT. FREQ. TO 6280v kHz
6290v PIRATE (EUROPE)
†"R BERMUDA DREIECK", Germany
• Irr • ENGLISH & GERMAN • W Europe

†"R SCOTLAND INTL", Netherlands
• Irr • Su • DUTCH & ENGLISH • W Europe • 0.25 kW

†"RADIO ATLANTIS", Netherlands
• Irr • Su • W Europe • 0.4 kW
6295 PIRATE (EUROPE)
†"RADIO VICTORIA", Netherlands
• Irr • Su • W Europe
• Irr • Sa • W Europe
6295v PIRATE (EUROPE)
†"THE BOGUS MAN", England
• Irr • W Europe • ALT. FREQ. TO 3904v kHz
6300v PIRATE (EUROPE)
"RADIO DOCTOR TIM", Germany
• Irr • Su • W Europe • 0.04 kW
• Irr • Sa • W Europe • 0.04 kW

†"RADIO ORION", Netherlands
• Irr • Sa/Su • W Europe • 0.08/0.4 kW • ALT. FREQ. TO 5720 kHz
6305v PIRATE (EUROPE)
†"RADIO ROB 007", Netherlands
• Irr • Sa/Su • W Europe • ALT. FREQ. TO 6265v kHz

†"RADIO SKYWIRE", Netherlands
• Irr • Su • DUTCH & ENGLISH • W Europe
6306.3 PIRATE (EUROPE)
VARIOUS STATIONS, Germany
• Irr • Su • W Europe • 0.01/0.5 kW
6309v PIRATE (EUROPE)
†"RADIO LIKEDEELER, Germany
• Irr • Su • GERMAN & ENGLISH • W Europe • ALT. FREQ. TO 6250v kHz

†"RADIO VALENCIA", Netherlands
• Irr • W Europe
6310 PIRATE (EUROPE)
†"RADIO ODYSSEY", Greece
• Irr • Su/M • Europe • 1 kW
• Irr • Sa/Su • Europe • 1 kW
6310v PIRATE (EUROPE)
†"RADIO BRANDARIS", Netherlands
• Irr • Su • W Europe
• Irr • Sa • W Europe

†"RADIO DELTA", Netherlands
• Irr • Su • DUTCH, ENGLISH & GERMAN • W Europe • 0.1 kW
6311 PIRATE (EUROPE)
†"RADIO UNDERGROUND", England
• Irr • Su • W Europe • 0.02 kW
6311v PIRATE (EUROPE)
†"RADIO ALTREX", Netherlands
• Irr • Sa/Su • W Europe

| 0 | 1 | 2 | 3 | 4 | 5 | 6 | 7 | 8 | 9 | 10 | 11 | 12 | 13 | 14 | 15 | 16 | 17 | 18 | 19 | 20 | 21 | 22 | 23 | 24 |

ENGLISH ▬▬   ARABIC ▨▨   CHINESE □□□   FRENCH ▬▬   GERMAN ▬▬   RUSSIAN ══   SPANISH ▬▬   OTHER ▬▬

World Time 0 1 2 3 4 5 6 7 8 9 10 11 12 13 14 15 16 17 18 19 20 21 22 23 24

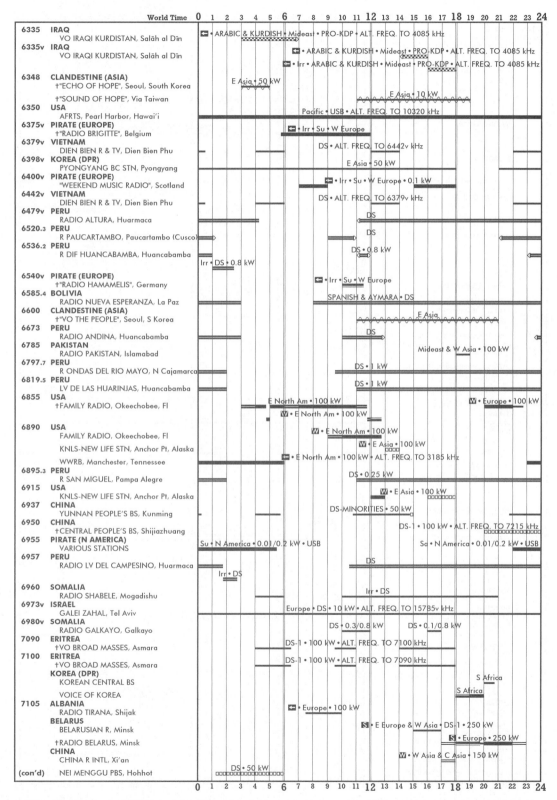

Freq	Country / Station	Details
6335	**IRAQ** — VO IRAQI KURDISTAN, Salāh al Dīn	ARABIC & KURDISH • Mideast • PRO-KDP • ALT. FREQ. TO 4085 kHz
6335v	**IRAQ** — VO IRAQI KURDISTAN, Salāh al Dīn	ARABIC & KURDISH • Mideast • PRO-KDP • ALT. FREQ. TO 4085 kHz / Irr • ARABIC & KURDISH • Mideast • PRO-KDP • ALT. FREQ. TO 4085 kHz
6348	**CLANDESTINE (ASIA)** — †"ECHO OF HOPE", Seoul, South Korea	E Asia • 50 kW
	†"SOUND OF HOPE", Via Taiwan	E Asia • 10 kW
6350	**USA** — AFRTS, Pearl Harbor, Hawai'i	Pacific • USB • ALT. FREQ. TO 10320 kHz
6375v	**PIRATE (EUROPE)** — †"RADIO BRIGITTE", Belgium	Irr • Su • W Europe
6379v	**VIETNAM** — DIEN BIEN R & TV, Dien Bien Phu	DS • ALT. FREQ. TO 6442v kHz
6398v	**KOREA (DPR)** — PYONGYANG BC STN, Pyongyang	E Asia • 50 kW
6400v	**PIRATE (EUROPE)** — "WEEKEND MUSIC RADIO", Scotland	Irr • Su • W Europe • 0.1 kW
6442v	**VIETNAM** — DIEN BIEN R & TV, Dien Bien Phu	DS • ALT. FREQ. TO 6379v kHz
6479v	**PERU** — RADIO ALTURA, Huarmaca	DS
6520.3	**PERU** — R PAUCARTAMBO, Paucartambo (Cusco)	DS
6536.2	**PERU** — R DIF HUANCABAMBA, Huancabamba	DS • 0.8 kW / Irr • DS • 0.8 kW
6540v	**PIRATE (EUROPE)** — †"RADIO HAMAMELIS", Germany	Irr • Su • W Europe
6585.4	**BOLIVIA** — RADIO NUEVA ESPERANZA, La Paz	SPANISH & AYMARA • DS
6600	**CLANDESTINE (ASIA)** — †"VO THE PEOPLE", Seoul, S Korea	E Asia
6673	**PERU** — RADIO ANDINA, Huancabamba	DS
6785	**PAKISTAN** — RADIO PAKISTAN, Islamabad	Mideast & W Asia • 100 kW
6797.7	**PERU** — R ONDAS DEL RIO MAYO, N Cajamarca	DS • 1 kW
6819.5	**PERU** — LV DE LAS HUARINJAS, Huancabamba	DS • 1 kW
6855	**USA** — †FAMILY RADIO, Okeechobee, Fl	E North Am • 100 kW / W • Europe • 100 kW / W • E North Am • 100 kW
6890	**USA** — FAMILY RADIO, Okeechobee, Fl	W • E North Am • 100 kW
	KNLS-NEW LIFE STN, Anchor Pt, Alaska	W • E Asia • 100 kW
	WWRB, Manchester, Tennessee	E North Am • 100 kW • ALT. FREQ. TO 3185 kHz
6895.3	**PERU** — R SAN MIGUEL, Pampa Alegre	DS • 0.25 kW
6915	**USA** — KNLS-NEW LIFE STN, Anchor Pt, Alaska	W • E Asia • 100 kW
6937	**CHINA** — YUNNAN PEOPLE'S BS, Kunming	DS-MINORITIES • 50 kW
6950	**CHINA** — †CENTRAL PEOPLE'S BS, Shijiazhuang	DS-1 • 100 kW • ALT. FREQ. TO 7215 kHz
6955	**PIRATE (N AMERICA)** — VARIOUS STATIONS	Su • N America • 0.01/0.2 kW • USB / Sa • N America • 0.01/0.2 kW • USB
6957	**PERU** — RADIO LV DEL CAMPESINO, Huarmaca	DS / Irr • DS
6960	**SOMALIA** — RADIO SHABELE, Mogadishu	Irr • DS
6973v	**ISRAEL** — GALEI ZAHAL, Tel Aviv	Europe • DS • 10 kW • ALT. FREQ. TO 15785v kHz
6980v	**SOMALIA** — RADIO GALKAYO, Galkayo	DS • 0.3/0.8 kW / DS • 0.1/0.8 kW
7090	**ERITREA** — †VO BROAD MASSES, Asmara	DS-1 • 100 kW • ALT. FREQ. TO 7100 kHz
7100	**ERITREA** — †VO BROAD MASSES, Asmara	DS-1 • 100 kW • ALT. FREQ. TO 7090 kHz
	KOREA (DPR) — KOREAN CENTRAL BS / VOICE OF KOREA	S Africa
7105	**ALBANIA** — RADIO TIRANA, Shijak	Europe • 100 kW
	BELARUS — BELARUSIAN R, Minsk	S • E Europe & W Asia • DS-1 • 250 kW
	†RADIO BELARUS, Minsk	S • Europe • 250 kW
	CHINA — CHINA R INTL, Xi'an	W • W Asia & C Asia • 150 kW
(con'd)	NEI MENGGU PBS, Hohhot	DS • 50 kW

0 1 2 3 4 5 6 7 8 9 10 11 12 13 14 15 16 17 18 19 20 21 22 23 24

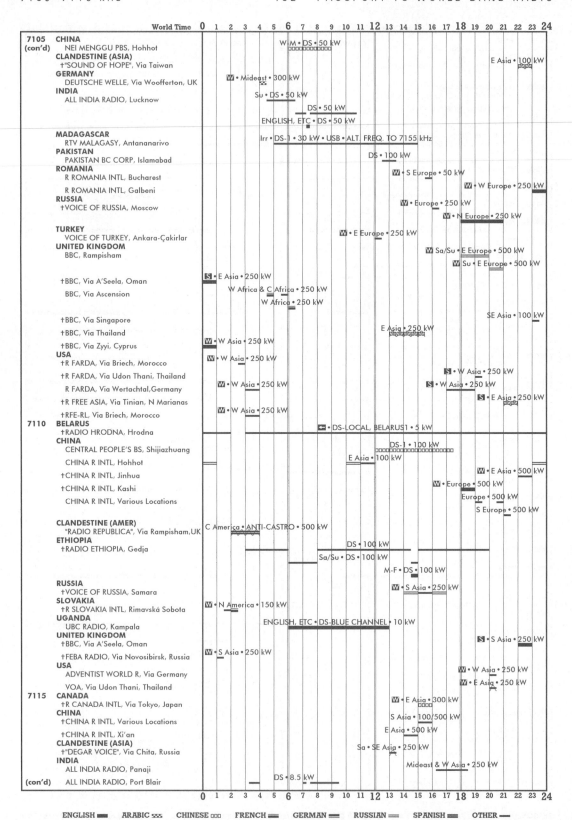

World Time 0 1 2 3 4 5 6 7 8 9 10 11 12 13 14 15 16 17 18 19 20 21 22 23 24

7105	**CHINA**
(con'd)	NEI MENGGU PBS, Hohhot — W-M • DS • 50 kW
	CLANDESTINE (ASIA)
	†"SOUND OF HOPE", Via Taiwan — E Asia • 100 kW
	GERMANY
	DEUTSCHE WELLE, Via Woofferton, UK — W • Mideast • 300 kW
	INDIA
	ALL INDIA RADIO, Lucknow — Su • DS • 50 kW / DS • 50 kW / ENGLISH, ETC • DS • 50 kW
	MADAGASCAR
	RTV MALAGASY, Antananarivo — Irr • DS-1 • 30 kW • USB • ALT. FREQ. TO 7155 kHz
	PAKISTAN
	PAKISTAN BC CORP, Islamabad — DS • 100 kW
	ROMANIA
	R ROMANIA INTL, Bucharest — W • S Europe • 50 kW
	R ROMANIA INTL, Galbeni — W • W Europe • 250 kW
	RUSSIA
	†VOICE OF RUSSIA, Moscow — W • Europe • 250 kW / W • N Europe • 250 kW
	TURKEY
	VOICE OF TURKEY, Ankara-Çakirlar — W • E Europe • 250 kW
	UNITED KINGDOM
	BBC, Rampisham — W Sa/Su • E Europe • 500 kW / W Su • E Europe • 500 kW
	†BBC, Via A'Seela, Oman — S • E Asia • 250 kW
	BBC, Via Ascension — W Africa & C Africa • 250 kW / W Africa • 250 kW
	†BBC, Via Singapore — SE Asia • 100 kW
	†BBC, Via Thailand — E Asia • 250 kW
	†BBC, Via Zyyi, Cyprus — W • W Asia • 250 kW
	USA
	†R FARDA, Via Briech, Morocco — W • W Asia • 250 kW
	†R FARDA, Via Udon Thani, Thailand — S • W Asia • 250 kW
	R FARDA, Via Wertachtal, Germany — W • W Asia • 250 kW / S • W Asia • 250 kW
	†R FREE ASIA, Via Tinian, N Marianas — S • E Asia • 250 kW
	†RFE-RL, Via Briech, Morocco — W • W Asia • 250 kW
7110	**BELARUS**
	†RADIO HRODNA, Hrodna — DS-LOCAL, BELARUS1 • 5 kW
	CHINA
	CENTRAL PEOPLE'S BS, Shijiazhuang — DS-1 • 100 kW
	CHINA R INTL, Hohhot — E Asia • 100 kW
	†CHINA R INTL, Jinhua — W • E Asia • 500 kW
	†CHINA R INTL, Kashi — W • Europe • 500 kW / Europe • 500 kW
	CHINA R INTL, Various Locations — S Europe • 500 kW
	CLANDESTINE (AMER)
	"RADIO REPUBLICA", Via Rampisham, UK — C America • ANTI-CASTRO • 500 kW
	ETHIOPIA
	†RADIO ETHIOPIA, Gedja — DS • 100 kW / Sa/Su • DS • 100 kW / M-F • DS • 100 kW
	RUSSIA
	†VOICE OF RUSSIA, Samara — W • S Asia • 250 kW
	SLOVAKIA
	†R SLOVAKIA INTL, Rimavská Sobota — W • N America • 150 kW
	UGANDA
	UBC RADIO, Kampala — ENGLISH, ETC • DS-BLUE CHANNEL • 10 kW
	UNITED KINGDOM
	†BBC, Via A'Seela, Oman — S • S Asia • 250 kW
	†FEBA RADIO, Via Novosibirsk, Russia — W • S Asia • 250 kW
	USA
	ADVENTIST WORLD R, Via Germany — W • W Asia • 250 kW
	VOA, Via Udon Thani, Thailand — W • E Asia • 250 kW
7115	**CANADA**
	†R CANADA INTL, Via Tokyo, Japan — W • E Asia • 300 kW
	CHINA
	†CHINA R INTL, Various Locations — S Asia • 100/500 kW
	†CHINA R INTL, Xi'an — E Asia • 500 kW
	CLANDESTINE (ASIA)
	†"DEGAR VOICE", Via Chita, Russia — Sa • SE Asia • 250 kW
	INDIA
	ALL INDIA RADIO, Panaji — Mideast & W Asia • 250 kW
(con'd)	ALL INDIA RADIO, Port Blair — DS • 8.5 kW

0 1 2 3 4 5 6 7 8 9 10 11 12 13 14 15 16 17 18 19 20 21 22 23 24

ENGLISH ▬ ARABIC ﹌ CHINESE ▫▫▫ FRENCH ▭ GERMAN ▬ RUSSIAN ═ SPANISH ▬ OTHER ▬

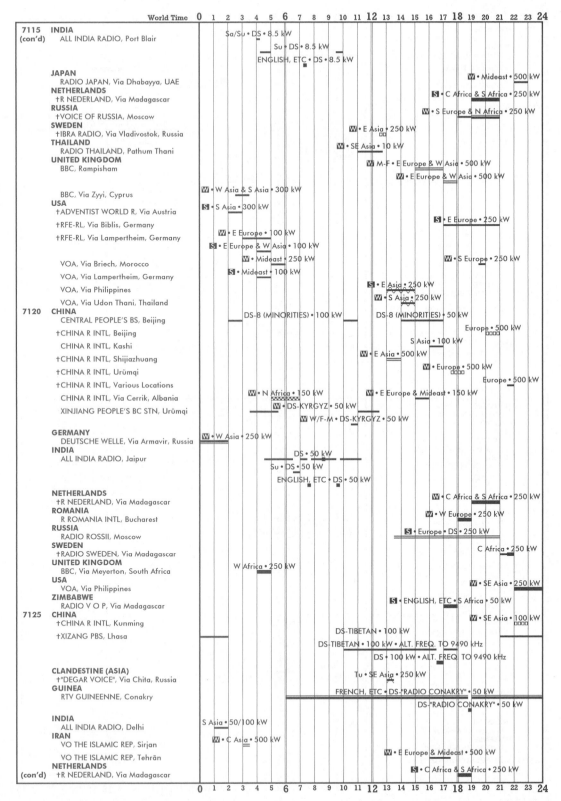

World Time 0 1 2 3 4 5 6 7 8 9 10 11 12 13 14 15 16 17 18 19 20 21 22 23 24

7115 INDIA
(con'd) ALL INDIA RADIO, Port Blair
- Sa/Su • DS • 8.5 kW
- Su • DS • 8.5 kW
- ENGLISH, ETC • DS • 8.5 kW

JAPAN
RADIO JAPAN, Via Dhabayya, UAE — W • Mideast • 500 kW
NETHERLANDS
†R NEDERLAND, Via Madagascar — S • C Africa & S Africa • 250 kW
RUSSIA
†VOICE OF RUSSIA, Moscow — W • S Europe & N Africa • 250 kW
SWEDEN
†IBRA RADIO, Via Vladivostok, Russia — W • E Asia • 250 kW
THAILAND
RADIO THAILAND, Pathum Thani — W • SE Asia • 10 kW
UNITED KINGDOM
BBC, Rampisham — W • M-F • E Europe & W Asia • 500 kW / W • E Europe & W Asia • 500 kW

BBC, Via Zyyi, Cyprus — W • W Asia & S Asia • 300 kW
USA
†ADVENTIST WORLD R, Via Austria — S • S Asia • 300 kW
†RFE-RL, Via Biblis, Germany — S • E Europe • 250 kW
†RFE-RL, Via Lampertheim, Germany — W • E Europe • 100 kW / S • E Europe & W Asia • 100 kW

VOA, Via Briech, Morocco — W • Mideast • 250 kW / W • S Europe • 250 kW
VOA, Via Lampertheim, Germany — S • Mideast • 100 kW
VOA, Via Philippines — S • E Asia • 250 kW
VOA, Via Udon Thani, Thailand — W • S Asia • 250 kW

7120 CHINA
CENTRAL PEOPLE'S BS, Beijing — DS-8 (MINORITIES) • 100 kW / DS-8 (MINORITIES) • 50 kW
†CHINA R INTL, Beijing — Europe • 500 kW
CHINA R INTL, Kashi — S Asia • 100 kW
†CHINA R INTL, Shijiazhuang — W • E Asia • 500 kW
†CHINA R INTL, Urümqi — W • Europe • 500 kW / Europe • 500 kW
†CHINA R INTL, Various Locations
CHINA R INTL, Via Cerrik, Albania — W • N Africa • 150 kW / W • E Europe & Mideast • 150 kW
XINJIANG PEOPLE'S BC STN, Urümqi — W • DS-KYRGYZ • 50 kW / W/F-M • DS-KYRGYZ • 50 kW

GERMANY
DEUTSCHE WELLE, Via Armavir, Russia — W • W Asia • 250 kW
INDIA
ALL INDIA RADIO, Jaipur — DS • 50 kW / Su • DS • 50 kW / ENGLISH, ETC • DS • 50 kW

NETHERLANDS
†R NEDERLAND, Via Madagascar — W • C Africa & S Africa • 250 kW
ROMANIA
R ROMANIA INTL, Bucharest — W • W Europe • 250 kW
RUSSIA
RADIO ROSSII, Moscow — S • Europe • DS • 250 kW
SWEDEN
†RADIO SWEDEN, Via Madagascar — C Africa • 250 kW
UNITED KINGDOM
BBC, Via Meyerton, South Africa — W Africa • 250 kW
USA
VOA, Via Philippines — W • SE Asia • 250 kW
ZIMBABWE
RADIO V O P, Via Madagascar — S • ENGLISH, ETC • S Africa • 50 kW

7125 CHINA
†CHINA R INTL, Kunming — W • SE Asia • 100 kW
†XIZANG PBS, Lhasa — DS-TIBETAN • 100 kW / DS-TIBETAN • 100 kW • ALT. FREQ. TO 9490 kHz / DS • 100 kW • ALT. FREQ. TO 9490 kHz

CLANDESTINE (ASIA)
†"DEGAR VOICE", Via Chita, Russia — Tu • SE Asia • 250 kW
GUINEA
RTV GUINEENNE, Conakry — FRENCH, ETC • DS-"RADIO CONAKRY" • 50 kW / DS-"RADIO CONAKRY" • 50 kW

INDIA
ALL INDIA RADIO, Delhi — S Asia • 50/100 kW
IRAN
VO THE ISLAMIC REP, Sirjan — W • C Asia • 500 kW
VO THE ISLAMIC REP, Tehrān — W • E Europe & Mideast • 500 kW
NETHERLANDS
(con'd) †R NEDERLAND, Via Madagascar — S • C Africa & S Africa • 250 kW

0 1 2 3 4 5 6 7 8 9 10 11 12 13 14 15 16 17 18 19 20 21 22 23 24

SEASONAL S OR W   1-HR TIMESHIFT MIDYEAR ⇐ OR ⇒   JAMMING / OR ∧   EARLIEST HEARD ◁   LATEST HEARD ▷   NEW FOR 2008 †

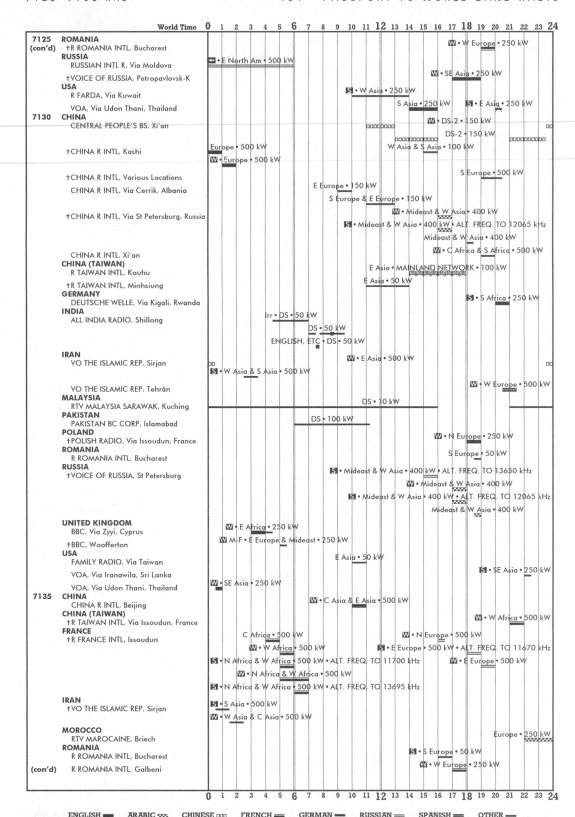

World Time

7125 **ROMANIA**
(con'd) †R ROMANIA INTL, Bucharest — W • W Europe • 250 kW
RUSSIA
RUSSIAN INTL R, Via Moldova — E North Am • 500 kW

†VOICE OF RUSSIA, Petropavlovsk-K — W • SE Asia • 250 kW
USA
R FARDA, Via Kuwait — S • W Asia • 250 kW

VOA, Via Udon Thani, Thailand — S Asia • 250 kW — S • E Asia • 250 kW
7130 **CHINA**
CENTRAL PEOPLE'S BS, Xi'an — W • DS-2 • 150 kW / DS-2 • 150 kW

†CHINA R INTL, Kashi — Europe • 500 kW / W Asia & S Asia • 100 kW / W • Europe • 500 kW / S Europe • 500 kW

†CHINA R INTL, Various Locations — E Europe • 150 kW
CHINA R INTL, Via Cerrik, Albania — S Europe & E Europe • 150 kW

†CHINA R INTL, Via St Petersburg, Russia — W • Mideast & W Asia • 400 kW / S • Mideast & W Asia • 400 kW • ALT. FREQ. TO 12065 kHz / Mideast & W Asia • 400 kW

CHINA R INTL, Xi'an — W • C Africa & S Africa • 500 kW
CHINA (TAIWAN)
R TAIWAN INTL, Kouhu — E Asia • MAINLAND NETWORK • 100 kW

†R TAIWAN INTL, Minhsiung — E Asia • 50 kW
GERMANY
DEUTSCHE WELLE, Via Kigali, Rwanda — S • S Africa • 250 kW
INDIA
ALL INDIA RADIO, Shillong — Irr • DS • 50 kW / DS • 50 kW / ENGLISH, ETC • DS • 50 kW

IRAN
VO THE ISLAMIC REP, Sirjan — W • E Asia • 500 kW / S • W Asia & S Asia • 500 kW

VO THE ISLAMIC REP, Tehrān — W • W Europe • 500 kW
MALAYSIA
RTV MALAYSIA SARAWAK, Kuching — DS • 10 kW
PAKISTAN
PAKISTAN BC CORP, Islamabad — DS • 100 kW
POLAND
†POLISH RADIO, Via Issoudun, France — W • N Europe • 250 kW
ROMANIA
R ROMANIA INTL, Bucharest — S Europe • 50 kW
RUSSIA
†VOICE OF RUSSIA, St Petersburg — S • Mideast & W Asia • 400 kW • ALT. FREQ. TO 13650 kHz / W • Mideast & W Asia • 400 kW / S • Mideast & W Asia • 400 kW • ALT. FREQ. TO 12065 kHz / Mideast & W Asia • 400 kW

UNITED KINGDOM
BBC, Via Zyyi, Cyprus — W • E Africa • 250 kW
†BBC, Woofferton — W M-F • E Europe & Mideast • 250 kW
USA
FAMILY RADIO, Via Taiwan — E Asia • 50 kW

VOA, Via Iranawila, Sri Lanka — S • SE Asia • 250 kW

VOA, Via Udon Thani, Thailand — W • SE Asia • 250 kW
7135 **CHINA**
CHINA R INTL, Beijing — W • C Asia & E Asia • 500 kW
CHINA (TAIWAN)
†R TAIWAN INTL, Via Issoudun, France — W • W Africa • 500 kW
FRANCE
†R FRANCE INTL, Issoudun — C Africa • 500 kW / W • N Europe • 500 kW / W • W Africa • 500 kW / S • E Europe • 500 kW • ALT. FREQ. TO 11670 kHz / S • N Africa & W Africa • 500 kW • ALT. FREQ. TO 11700 kHz / W • E Europe • 500 kW / W • N Africa & W Africa • 500 kW / S • N Africa & W Africa • 500 kW • ALT. FREQ. TO 13695 kHz

IRAN
†VO THE ISLAMIC REP, Sirjan — S • S Asia • 500 kW / W • W Asia & C Asia • 500 kW

MOROCCO
RTV MAROCAINE, Briech — Europe • 250 kW
ROMANIA
R ROMANIA INTL, Bucharest — S • S Europe • 50 kW
(con'd) R ROMANIA INTL, Galbeni — W • W Europe • 250 kW

ENGLISH ▬ ARABIC ▨ CHINESE ▯▯▯ FRENCH ▬ GERMAN ▬ RUSSIAN ══ SPANISH ▬ OTHER ▬

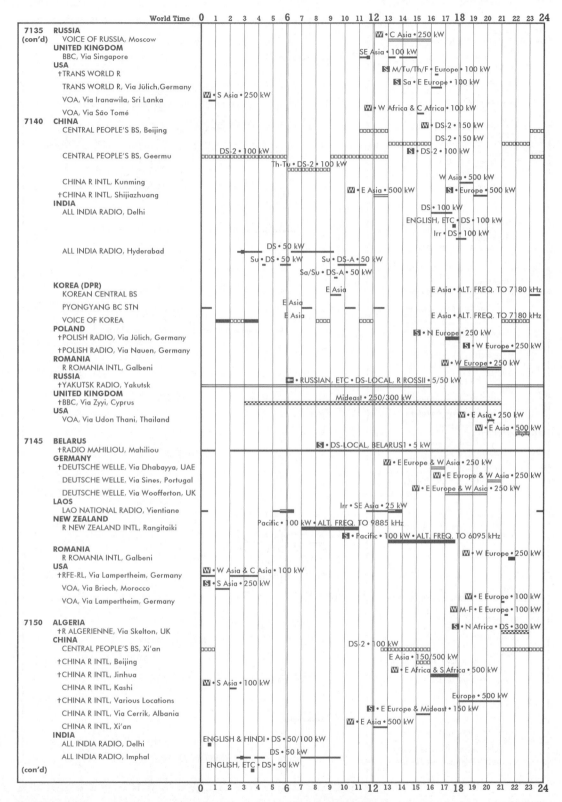

7135	**RUSSIA**	
(con'd)	VOICE OF RUSSIA, Moscow	W • C Asia • 250 kW
	UNITED KINGDOM	
	BBC, Via Singapore	SE Asia • 100 kW
	USA	
	†TRANS WORLD R	S M/Tu/Th/F • Europe • 100 kW
		S Sa • E Europe • 100 kW
	TRANS WORLD R, Via Jülich, Germany	
	VOA, Via Iranawila, Sri Lanka	W • S Asia • 250 kW
	VOA, Via São Tomé	W • W Africa & C Africa • 100 kW
7140	**CHINA**	
	CENTRAL PEOPLE'S BS, Beijing	W • DS-2 • 150 kW
		DS-2 • 150 kW
	CENTRAL PEOPLE'S BS, Geermu	DS-2 • 100 kW S • DS-2 • 100 kW
		Th-Tu • DS-2 • 100 kW
	CHINA R INTL, Kunming	W Asia • 500 kW
	†CHINA R INTL, Shijiazhuang	W • E Asia • 500 kW S • Europe • 500 kW
	INDIA	
	ALL INDIA RADIO, Delhi	DS • 100 kW
		ENGLISH, ETC • DS • 100 kW
		Irr • DS • 100 kW
	ALL INDIA RADIO, Hyderabad	DS • 50 kW
		Su • DS • 50 kW Su • DS-A • 50 kW
		Sa/Su • DS-A • 50 kW
	KOREA (DPR)	
	KOREAN CENTRAL BS	E Asia E Asia • ALT. FREQ. TO 7180 kHz
	PYONGYANG BC STN	E Asia
	VOICE OF KOREA	E Asia E Asia • ALT. FREQ. TO 7180 kHz
	POLAND	
	†POLISH RADIO, Via Jülich, Germany	S • N Europe • 250 kW
	†POLISH RADIO, Via Nauen, Germany	S • W Europe • 250 kW
	ROMANIA	
	R ROMANIA INTL, Galbeni	W • W Europe • 250 kW
	RUSSIA	
	†YAKUTSK RADIO, Yakutsk	⇄ • RUSSIAN, ETC • DS-LOCAL, R ROSSII • 5/50 kW
	UNITED KINGDOM	
	†BBC, Via Zyyi, Cyprus	Mideast • 250/300 kW
	USA	
	VOA, Via Udon Thani, Thailand	W • E Asia • 250 kW
		W • E Asia • 500 kW
7145	**BELARUS**	
	†RADIO MAHILIOU, Mahiliou	S • DS-LOCAL, BELARUS1 • 5 kW
	GERMANY	
	†DEUTSCHE WELLE, Via Dhabayya, UAE	W • E Europe & W Asia • 250 kW
	DEUTSCHE WELLE, Via Sines, Portugal	W • E Europe & W Asia • 250 kW
	DEUTSCHE WELLE, Via Woofferton, UK	W • E Europe & W Asia • 250 kW
	LAOS	
	LAO NATIONAL RADIO, Vientiane	Irr • SE Asia • 25 kW
	NEW ZEALAND	
	R NEW ZEALAND INTL, Rangitaiki	Pacific • 100 kW • ALT. FREQ. TO 9885 kHz
		S • Pacific • 100 kW • ALT. FREQ. TO 6095 kHz
	ROMANIA	
	R ROMANIA INTL, Galbeni	W • W Europe • 250 kW
	USA	
	†RFE-RL, Via Lampertheim, Germany	W • W Asia & C Asia • 100 kW
	VOA, Via Briech, Morocco	S • S Asia • 250 kW
	VOA, Via Lampertheim, Germany	W • E Europe • 100 kW
		W M-F • E Europe • 100 kW
7150	**ALGERIA**	
	†R ALGERIENNE, Via Skelton, UK	S • N Africa • DS • 300 kW
	CHINA	
	CENTRAL PEOPLE'S BS, Xi'an	DS-2 • 100 kW
	†CHINA R INTL, Beijing	E Asia • 150/500 kW
	†CHINA R INTL, Jinhua	W • E Africa & S Africa • 500 kW
	CHINA R INTL, Kashi	W • S Asia • 100 kW
	†CHINA R INTL, Various Locations	Europe • 500 kW
	CHINA R INTL, Via Cerrik, Albania	S • E Europe & Mideast • 150 kW
	CHINA R INTL, Xi'an	W • E Asia • 500 kW
	INDIA	
	ALL INDIA RADIO, Delhi	ENGLISH & HINDI • DS • 50/100 kW
	ALL INDIA RADIO, Imphal	DS • 50 kW
(con'd)		ENGLISH, ETC • DS • 50 kW

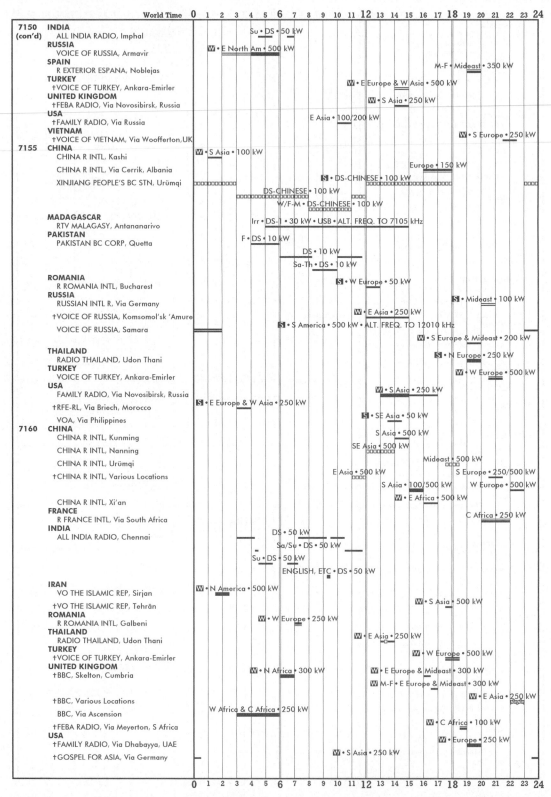

World Time 0 1 2 3 4 5 6 7 8 9 10 11 12 13 14 15 16 17 18 19 20 21 22 23 24

7150 **INDIA**
(con'd)   ALL INDIA RADIO, Imphal — Su • DS • 50 kW
 RUSSIA
   VOICE OF RUSSIA, Armavir — W • E North Am • 500 kW
 SPAIN
   R EXTERIOR ESPANA, Noblejas — M-F • Mideast • 350 kW
 TURKEY
   †VOICE OF TURKEY, Ankara-Emirler — W • E Europe & W Asia • 500 kW
 UNITED KINGDOM
   †FEBA RADIO, Via Novosibirsk, Russia — W • S Asia • 250 kW
 USA
   †FAMILY RADIO, Via Russia — E Asia • 100/200 kW
 VIETNAM
   †VOICE OF VIETNAM, Via Woofferton, UK — W • S Europe • 250 kW
7155 **CHINA**
   CHINA R INTL, Kashi — W • S Asia • 100 kW
   CHINA R INTL, Via Cerrik, Albania — Europe • 150 kW
   XINJIANG PEOPLE'S BC STN, Urümqi — S • DS-CHINESE • 100 kW
          DS-CHINESE • 100 kW
          W/F-M • DS-CHINESE • 100 kW
 MADAGASCAR
   RTV MALAGASY, Antananarivo — Irr • DS-1 • 30 kW • USB • ALT. FREQ. TO 7105 kHz
 PAKISTAN
   PAKISTAN BC CORP, Quetta — F • DS • 10 kW
          DS • 10 kW
          Sa-Th • DS • 10 kW
 ROMANIA
   R ROMANIA INTL, Bucharest — S • W Europe • 50 kW
 RUSSIA
   RUSSIAN INTL R, Via Germany — S • Mideast • 100 kW
   †VOICE OF RUSSIA, Komsomol'sk 'Amure — W • E Asia • 250 kW
   VOICE OF RUSSIA, Samara — S • S America • 500 kW • ALT. FREQ. TO 12010 kHz
          W • S Europe & Mideast • 200 kW
 THAILAND
   RADIO THAILAND, Udon Thani — S • N Europe • 250 kW
 TURKEY
   VOICE OF TURKEY, Ankara-Emirler — W • W Europe • 500 kW
 USA
   FAMILY RADIO, Via Novosibirsk, Russia — W • S Asia • 250 kW
   †RFE-RL, Via Briech, Morocco — S • E Europe & W Asia • 250 kW
   VOA, Via Philippines — S • SE Asia • 50 kW
7160 **CHINA**
   CHINA R INTL, Kunming — S Asia • 500 kW
   CHINA R INTL, Nanning — SE Asia • 500 kW
   CHINA R INTL, Urümqi — Mideast • 500 kW
   †CHINA R INTL, Various Locations — E Asia • 500 kW / S Europe • 250/500 kW
          S Asia • 100/500 kW / W Europe • 500 kW
   CHINA R INTL, Xi'an — W • E Africa • 500 kW
 FRANCE
   R FRANCE INTL, Via South Africa — C Africa • 250 kW
 INDIA
   ALL INDIA RADIO, Chennai — DS • 50 kW
          Sa/Su • DS • 50 kW
          Su • DS • 50 kW
          ENGLISH, ETC • DS • 50 kW
 IRAN
   VO THE ISLAMIC REP, Sirjan — W • N America • 500 kW
   †VO THE ISLAMIC REP, Tehrān — W • S Asia • 500 kW
 ROMANIA
   R ROMANIA INTL, Galbeni — W • W Europe • 250 kW
 THAILAND
   RADIO THAILAND, Udon Thani — W • E Asia • 250 kW
 TURKEY
   †VOICE OF TURKEY, Ankara-Emirler — W • W Europe • 500 kW
 UNITED KINGDOM
   †BBC, Skelton, Cumbria — W • N Africa • 300 kW
          W • E Europe & Mideast • 300 kW
          W M-F • E Europe & Mideast • 300 kW
   †BBC, Various Locations — W • E Asia • 250 kW
   BBC, Via Ascension — W Africa & C Africa • 250 kW
   †FEBA RADIO, Via Meyerton, S Africa — W • C Africa • 100 kW
 USA
   †FAMILY RADIO, Via Dhabayya, UAE — W • Europe • 250 kW
   †GOSPEL FOR ASIA, Via Germany — W • S Asia • 250 kW

0 1 2 3 4 5 6 7 8 9 10 11 12 13 14 15 16 17 18 19 20 21 22 23 24

ENGLISH ▬▬   ARABIC ⁓⁓⁓   CHINESE □□□   FRENCH ══   GERMAN ▭▭   RUSSIAN ══   SPANISH ══   OTHER ──

World Time 0 1 2 3 4 5 6 7 8 9 10 11 12 13 14 15 16 17 18 19 20 21 22 23 24

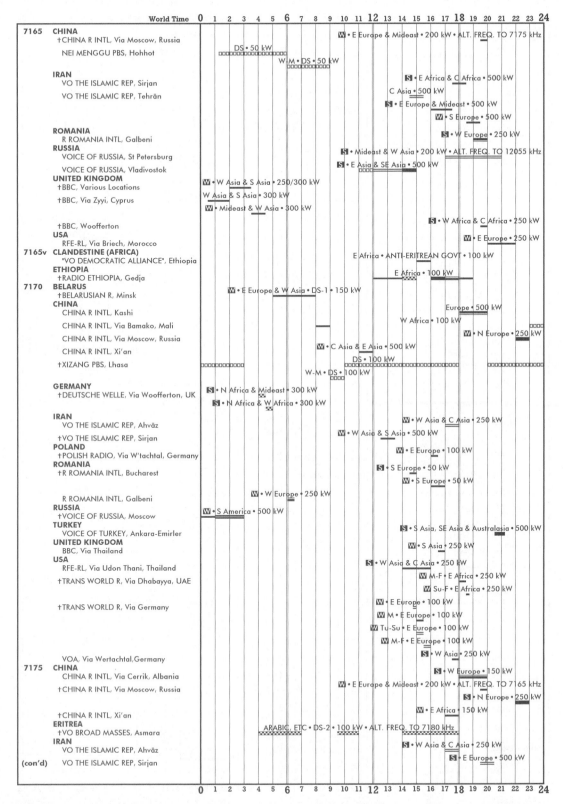

7165 CHINA
†CHINA R INTL, Via Moscow, Russia — W • E Europe & Mideast • 200 kW • ALT. FREQ. TO 7175 kHz
NEI MENGGU PBS, Hohhot — DS • 50 kW ; W-M • DS • 50 kW

IRAN
VO THE ISLAMIC REP, Sirjan — S • E Africa & C Africa • 500 kW
VO THE ISLAMIC REP, Tehrān — C Asia • 500 kW ; S • E Europe & Mideast • 500 kW ; W • S Europe • 500 kW

ROMANIA
R ROMANIA INTL, Galbeni — S • W Europe • 250 kW
RUSSIA
VOICE OF RUSSIA, St Petersburg — S • Mideast & W Asia • 200 kW • ALT. FREQ. TO 12055 kHz
VOICE OF RUSSIA, Vladivostok — S • E Asia & SE Asia • 500 kW
UNITED KINGDOM
†BBC, Various Locations — W • W Asia & S Asia • 250/300 kW
†BBC, Via Zyyi, Cyprus — W Asia & S Asia • 300 kW ; W • Mideast & W Asia • 300 kW
†BBC, Woofferton — S • W Africa & C Africa • 250 kW
USA
RFE-RL, Via Briech, Morocco — W • E Europe • 250 kW
7165v CLANDESTINE (AFRICA)
"VO DEMOCRATIC ALLIANCE", Ethiopia — E Africa • ANTI-ERITREAN GOVT • 100 kW
ETHIOPIA
†RADIO ETHIOPIA, Gedja — E Africa • 100 kW
7170 BELARUS
†BELARUSIAN R, Minsk — W • E Europe & W Asia • DS-1 • 150 kW
CHINA
CHINA R INTL, Kashi — Europe • 500 kW
CHINA R INTL, Via Bamako, Mali — W Africa • 100 kW
CHINA R INTL, Via Moscow, Russia — W • N Europe • 250 kW
CHINA R INTL, Xi'an — W • C Asia & E Asia • 500 kW
†XIZANG PBS, Lhasa — DS • 100 kW ; W-M • DS • 100 kW

GERMANY
†DEUTSCHE WELLE, Via Woofferton, UK — S • N Africa & Mideast • 300 kW ; S • N Africa & W Africa • 300 kW

IRAN
VO THE ISLAMIC REP, Ahvāz — W • W Asia & C Asia • 250 kW
†VO THE ISLAMIC REP, Sirjan — W • W Asia & S Asia • 500 kW
POLAND
†POLISH RADIO, Via W'tachtal, Germany — W • E Europe • 100 kW
ROMANIA
†R ROMANIA INTL, Bucharest — S • S Europe • 50 kW ; W • S Europe • 50 kW
R ROMANIA INTL, Galbeni — W • W Europe • 250 kW
RUSSIA
†VOICE OF RUSSIA, Moscow — W • S America • 500 kW
TURKEY
VOICE OF TURKEY, Ankara-Emirler — S • S Asia, SE Asia & Australasia • 500 kW
UNITED KINGDOM
BBC, Via Thailand — W • S Asia • 250 kW
USA
RFE-RL, Via Udon Thani, Thailand — S • W Asia & C Asia • 250 kW
†TRANS WORLD R, Via Dhabayya, UAE — W M-F • E Africa • 250 kW ; W Su-F • E Africa • 250 kW
†TRANS WORLD R, Via Germany — W • E Europe • 100 kW ; W M • E Europe • 100 kW ; W Tu-Su • E Europe • 100 kW ; W M-F • E Europe • 100 kW
VOA, Via Wertachtal, Germany — S • W Asia • 250 kW
7175 CHINA
CHINA R INTL, Via Cerrik, Albania — S • W Europe • 150 kW
†CHINA R INTL, Via Moscow, Russia — W • E Europe & Mideast • 200 kW • ALT. FREQ. TO 7165 kHz ; S • N Europe • 250 kW
†CHINA R INTL, Xi'an — W • E Africa • 150 kW
ERITREA
†VO BROAD MASSES, Asmara — ARABIC, ETC • DS-2 • 100 kW • ALT. FREQ. TO 7180 kHz
IRAN
VO THE ISLAMIC REP, Ahvāz — S • W Asia & C Asia • 250 kW
(con'd) VO THE ISLAMIC REP, Sirjan — S • E Europe • 500 kW

0 1 2 3 4 5 6 7 8 9 10 11 12 13 14 15 16 17 18 19 20 21 22 23 24

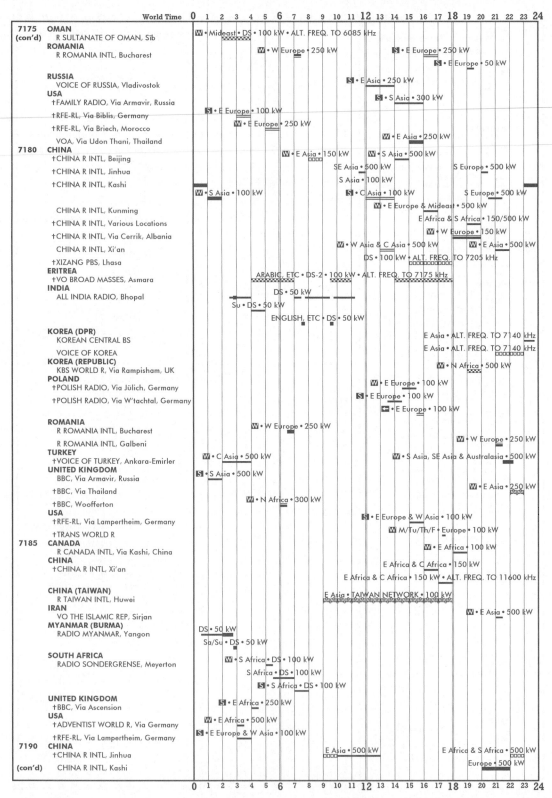

	World Time	0 1 2 3 4 5 6 7 8 9 10 11 12 13 14 15 16 17 18 19 20 21 22 23 24
7175 (con'd)	**OMAN** R SULTANATE OF OMAN, Sīb	W • Mideast • DS • 100 kW • ALT. FREQ. TO 6085 kHz
	ROMANIA R ROMANIA INTL, Bucharest	W • W Europe • 250 kW S • E Europe • 250 kW S • E Europe • 50 kW
	RUSSIA VOICE OF RUSSIA, Vladivostok	S • E Asia • 250 kW
	USA †FAMILY RADIO, Via Armavir, Russia	S • S Asia • 300 kW
	†RFE-RL, Via Biblis, Germany	S • E Europe • 100 kW
	†RFE-RL, Via Briech, Morocco	W • E Europe • 250 kW
	VOA, Via Udon Thani, Thailand	W • E Asia • 250 kW
7180	**CHINA** †CHINA R INTL, Beijing	W • E Asia • 150 kW W • S Asia • 500 kW
	†CHINA R INTL, Jinhua	SE Asia • 500 kW S Europe • 500 kW
	†CHINA R INTL, Kashi	S Asia • 100 kW
		W • S Asia • 100 kW S • C Asia • 100 kW S Europe • 500 kW
	CHINA R INTL, Kunming	W • E Europe & Mideast • 500 kW
	†CHINA R INTL, Various Locations	E Africa & S Africa • 150/500 kW
	†CHINA R INTL, Via Cerrik, Albania	W • W Europe • 150 kW
	CHINA R INTL, Xi'an	W • W Asia & C Asia • 500 kW W • E Asia • 500 kW
		DS • 100 kW • ALT. FREQ. TO 7205 kHz
	†XIZANG PBS, Lhasa	
	ERITREA †VO BROAD MASSES, Asmara	ARABIC, ETC • DS-2 • 100 kW • ALT. FREQ. TO 7175 kHz
	INDIA ALL INDIA RADIO, Bhopal	DS • 50 kW
		Su • DS • 50 kW
		ENGLISH, ETC • DS • 50 kW
	KOREA (DPR) KOREAN CENTRAL BS	E Asia • ALT. FREQ. TO 7140 kHz
	VOICE OF KOREA	E Asia • ALT. FREQ. TO 7140 kHz
	KOREA (REPUBLIC) KBS WORLD R, Via Rampisham, UK	W • N Africa • 500 kW
	POLAND †POLISH RADIO, Via Jülich, Germany	W • E Europe • 100 kW
	†POLISH RADIO, Via W'tachtal, Germany	S • E Europe • 100 kW
		◁ • E Europe • 100 kW
	ROMANIA R ROMANIA INTL, Bucharest	W • W Europe • 250 kW
	R ROMANIA INTL, Galbeni	W • W Europe • 250 kW
	TURKEY †VOICE OF TURKEY, Ankara-Emirler	W • C Asia • 500 kW W • S Asia, SE Asia & Australasia • 500 kW
	UNITED KINGDOM BBC, Via Armavir, Russia	S • S Asia • 500 kW
	†BBC, Via Thailand	W • E Asia • 250 kW
	†BBC, Woofferton	W • N Africa • 300 kW
	USA †RFE-RL, Via Lampertheim, Germany	S • E Europe & W Asia • 100 kW
	†TRANS WORLD R	W • M/Tu/Th/F • Europe • 100 kW
7185	**CANADA** R CANADA INTL, Via Kashi, China	W • E Africa • 100 kW
	CHINA †CHINA R INTL, Xi'an	E Africa & C Africa • 150 kW
		E Africa & C Africa • 150 kW • ALT. FREQ. TO 11600 kHz
	CHINA (TAIWAN) R TAIWAN INTL, Huwei	E Asia • TAIWAN NETWORK • 100 kW
	IRAN VO THE ISLAMIC REP, Sirjan	W • E Asia • 500 kW
	MYANMAR (BURMA) RADIO MYANMAR, Yangon	DS • 50 kW
		Sa/Su • DS • 50 kW
	SOUTH AFRICA RADIO SONDERGRENSE, Meyerton	W • S Africa • DS • 100 kW
		S Africa • DS • 100 kW
		S • S Africa • DS • 100 kW
	UNITED KINGDOM †BBC, Via Ascension	S • E Africa • 250 kW
	USA †ADVENTIST WORLD R, Via Germany	W • E Africa • 500 kW
	†RFE-RL, Via Lampertheim, Germany	S • E Europe & W Asia • 100 kW
7190	**CHINA** †CHINA R INTL, Jinhua	E Asia • 500 kW E Africa & S Africa • 500 kW
(con'd)	CHINA R INTL, Kashi	Europe • 500 kW

World Time	0 1 2 3 4 5 6 7 8 9 10 11 12 13 14 15 16 17 18 19 20 21 22 23 24

ENGLISH ▬   ARABIC ░░░   CHINESE □□□   FRENCH ▬   GERMAN ▬   RUSSIAN ═   SPANISH ▬   OTHER ▬

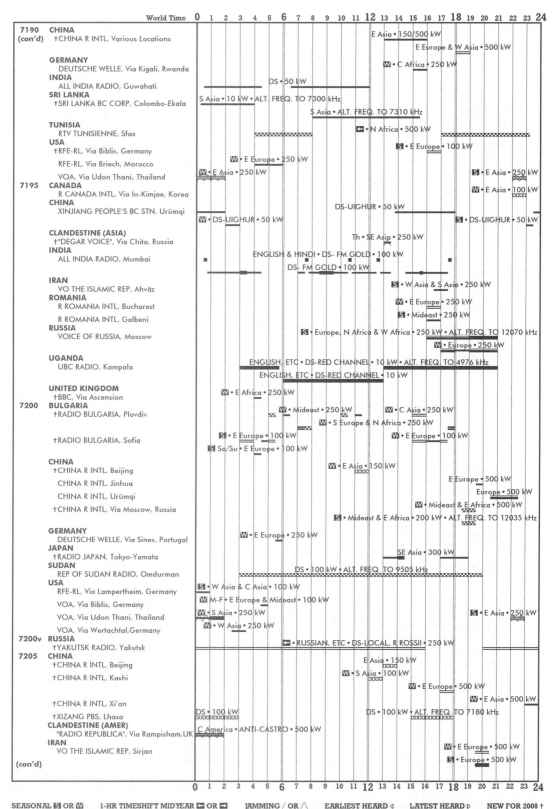

World Time	CHINA	
7190 (con'd)	CHINA	†CHINA R INTL, Various Locations • E Asia • 150/500 kW • E Europe & W Asia • 500 kW
	GERMANY	DEUTSCHE WELLE, Via Kigali, Rwanda • W • C Africa • 250 kW
	INDIA	ALL INDIA RADIO, Guwahati • DS • 50 kW
	SRI LANKA	†SRI LANKA BC CORP, Colombo-Ekala • S Asia • 10 kW • ALT. FREQ. TO 7300 kHz — S Asia • ALT. FREQ. TO 7310 kHz
	TUNISIA	RTV TUNISIENNE, Sfax • N Africa • 500 kW
	USA	†RFE-RL, Via Biblis, Germany • S • E Europe • 100 kW
		†RFE-RL, Via Briech, Morocco • W • E Europe • 250 kW
		VOA, Via Udon Thani, Thailand • W • E Asia • 250 kW • S • E Asia • 250 kW
7195	CANADA	R CANADA INTL, Via In-Kimjae, Korea • W • E Asia • 100 kW
	CHINA	XINJIANG PEOPLE'S BC STN, Urümqi • DS-UIGHUR • 50 kW • W • DS-UIGHUR • 50 kW • S • DS-UIGHUR • 50 kW
	CLANDESTINE (ASIA)	†"DEGAR VOICE", Via Chita, Russia • Th • SE Asia • 250 kW
	INDIA	ALL INDIA RADIO, Mumbai • ENGLISH & HINDI • DS- FM GOLD • 100 kW — DS- FM GOLD • 100 kW
	IRAN	VO THE ISLAMIC REP, Ahvāz • S • W Asia & S Asia • 250 kW
	ROMANIA	R ROMANIA INTL, Bucharest • W • E Europe • 250 kW
		R ROMANIA INTL, Galbeni • S • Mideast • 250 kW
	RUSSIA	VOICE OF RUSSIA, Moscow • S • Europe, N Africa & W Africa • 250 kW • ALT. FREQ. TO 12070 kHz • W • Europe • 250 kW
	UGANDA	UBC RADIO, Kampala • ENGLISH, ETC • DS-RED CHANNEL • 10 kW • ALT. FREQ. TO 4976 kHz — ENGLISH, ETC • DS-RED CHANNEL • 10 kW
	UNITED KINGDOM	†BBC, Via Ascension • W • E Africa • 250 kW
7200	BULGARIA	†RADIO BULGARIA, Plovdiv • W • Mideast • 250 kW • W • C Asia • 250 kW • W • S Europe & N Africa • 250 kW
		†RADIO BULGARIA, Sofia • S • E Europe • 100 kW • W • E Europe • 100 kW — S Sa/Su • E Europe • 100 kW
	CHINA	†CHINA R INTL, Beijing • W • E Asia • 150 kW
		CHINA R INTL, Jinhua • E Europe • 500 kW
		CHINA R INTL, Urümqi • Europe • 500 kW
		†CHINA R INTL, Via Moscow, Russia • W • Mideast & E Africa • 500 kW • S • Mideast & E Africa • 200 kW • ALT. FREQ. TO 12035 kHz
	GERMANY	DEUTSCHE WELLE, Via Sines, Portugal • W • E Europe • 250 kW
	JAPAN	†RADIO JAPAN, Tokyo-Yamata • SE Asia • 300 kW
	SUDAN	REP OF SUDAN RADIO, Omdurman • DS • 100 kW • ALT. FREQ. TO 9505 kHz
	USA	RFE-RL, Via Lampertheim, Germany • S • W Asia & C Asia • 100 kW
		VOA, Via Biblis, Germany • W • M-F • E Europe & Mideast • 100 kW
		VOA, Via Udon Thani, Thailand • W • S Asia • 250 kW • S • E Asia • 250 kW
		VOA, Via Wertachtal, Germany • W • W Asia • 250 kW
7200v	RUSSIA	†YAKUTSK RADIO, Yakutsk • RUSSIAN, ETC • DS-LOCAL, R ROSSII • 250 kW
7205	CHINA	†CHINA R INTL, Beijing • E Asia • 150 kW
		†CHINA R INTL, Kashi • W • S Asia • 100 kW • W • E Europe • 500 kW • W • E Asia • 500 kW
		†CHINA R INTL, Xi'an • DS • 100 kW • ALT. FREQ. TO 7180 kHz
		†XIZANG PBS, Lhasa • DS • 100 kW
	CLANDESTINE (AMER)	"RADIO REPUBLICA", Via Rampisham, UK • C America • ANTI-CASTRO • 500 kW
	IRAN	VO THE ISLAMIC REP, Sirjan • W • E Europe • 500 kW • S • Europe • 500 kW
(con'd)		

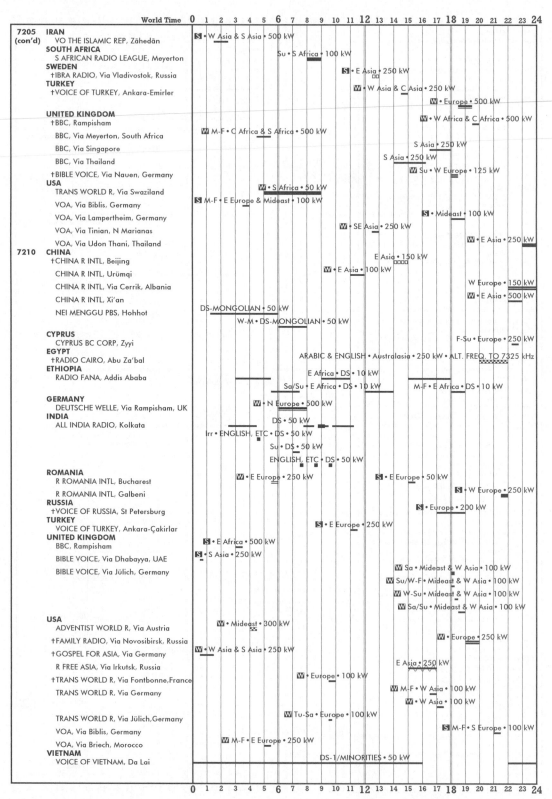

World Time　0　1　2　3　4　5　6　7　8　9　10　11　12　13　14　15　16　17　18　19　20　21　22　23　24

7205 **IRAN**
(con'd) VO THE ISLAMIC REP, Zāhedān — S • W Asia & S Asia • 500 kW
SOUTH AFRICA
S AFRICAN RADIO LEAGUE, Meyerton — Su • S Africa • 100 kW
SWEDEN
†IBRA RADIO, Via Vladivostok, Russia — S • E Asia • 250 kW
TURKEY
†VOICE OF TURKEY, Ankara-Emirler — W • W Asia & C Asia • 250 kW
W • Europe • 500 kW

UNITED KINGDOM
†BBC, Rampisham — W • W Africa & C Africa • 500 kW
BBC, Via Meyerton, South Africa — W M-F • C Africa & S Africa • 500 kW
BBC, Via Singapore — S Asia • 250 kW
BBC, Via Thailand — S Asia • 250 kW
†BIBLE VOICE, Via Nauen, Germany — W Su • W Europe • 125 kW
USA
TRANS WORLD R, Via Swaziland — W • S Africa • 50 kW
VOA, Via Biblis, Germany — S M-F • E Europe & Mideast • 100 kW
VOA, Via Lampertheim, Germany — S • Mideast • 100 kW
VOA, Via Tinian, N Marianas — W • SE Asia • 250 kW
VOA, Via Udon Thani, Thailand — W • E Asia • 250 kW

7210 **CHINA**
†CHINA R INTL, Beijing — E Asia • 150 kW
CHINA R INTL, Urümqi — W • E Asia • 100 kW
CHINA R INTL, Via Cerrik, Albania — W Europe • 150 kW
CHINA R INTL, Xi'an — W • E Asia • 500 kW
NEI MENGGU PBS, Hohhot — DS-MONGOLIAN • 50 kW
W-M • DS-MONGOLIAN • 50 kW

CYPRUS
CYPRUS BC CORP, Zyyi — F-Su • Europe • 250 kW
EGYPT
†RADIO CAIRO, Abu Za'bal — ARABIC & ENGLISH • Australasia • 250 kW • ALT. FREQ. TO 7325 kHz
ETHIOPIA
RADIO FANA, Addis Ababa — E Africa • DS • 10 kW
Sa/Su • E Africa • DS • 10 kW　　M-F • E Africa • DS • 10 kW
GERMANY
DEUTSCHE WELLE, Via Rampisham, UK — W • N Europe • 500 kW
INDIA
ALL INDIA RADIO, Kolkata — DS • 50 kW
Irr • ENGLISH, ETC • DS • 50 kW
Su • DS • 50 kW
ENGLISH, ETC • DS • 50 kW

ROMANIA
R ROMANIA INTL, Bucharest — W • E Europe • 250 kW
S • E Europe • 50 kW
R ROMANIA INTL, Galbeni — S • W Europe • 250 kW
RUSSIA
†VOICE OF RUSSIA, St Petersburg — S • Europe • 200 kW
TURKEY
VOICE OF TURKEY, Ankara-Çakirlar — S • E Europe • 250 kW
UNITED KINGDOM
BBC, Rampisham — S • E Africa • 500 kW
S • S Asia • 250 kW
BIBLE VOICE, Via Dhabayya, UAE — W Sa • Mideast & W Asia • 100 kW
BIBLE VOICE, Via Jülich, Germany — W Su/W-F • Mideast & W Asia • 100 kW
W W-Su • Mideast & W Asia • 100 kW
W Sa/Su • Mideast & W Asia • 100 kW

USA
ADVENTIST WORLD R, Via Austria — W • Mideast • 300 kW
W • Europe • 250 kW
†FAMILY RADIO, Via Novosibirsk, Russia
†GOSPEL FOR ASIA, Via Germany — W • W Asia & S Asia • 250 kW
R FREE ASIA, Via Irkutsk, Russia — E Asia • 250 kW
†TRANS WORLD R, Via Fontbonne, France — W • Europe • 100 kW
TRANS WORLD R, Via Germany — W M-F • W Asia • 100 kW
W • W Asia • 100 kW
TRANS WORLD R, Via Jülich, Germany — W Tu-Sa • Europe • 100 kW
VOA, Via Biblis, Germany — S M-F • S Europe • 100 kW
VOA, Via Briech, Morocco — W M-F • E Europe • 250 kW
VIETNAM
VOICE OF VIETNAM, Da Lai — DS-1/MINORITIES • 50 kW

0　1　2　3　4　5　6　7　8　9　10　11　12　13　14　15　16　17　18　19　20　21　22　23　24

ENGLISH ▬　ARABIC ※※　CHINESE □□□　FRENCH ▬　GERMAN ▬　RUSSIAN ══　SPANISH ▬　OTHER ▬

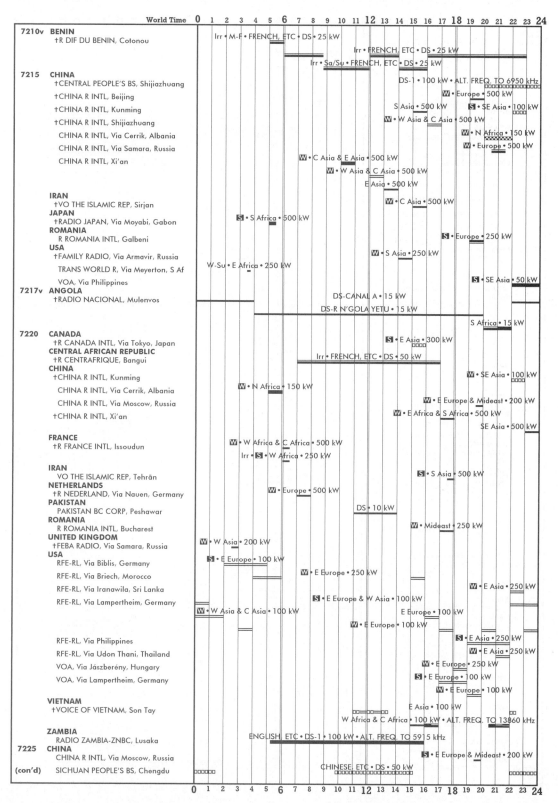

World Time 0 1 2 3 4 5 6 7 8 9 10 11 12 13 14 15 16 17 18 19 20 21 22 23 24

7210v BENIN
†R DIF DU BENIN, Cotonou
Irr • M-F • FRENCH, ETC • DS • 25 kW
Irr • FRENCH, ETC • DS • 25 kW
Irr • Sa/Su • FRENCH, ETC • DS • 25 kW

7215 CHINA
†CENTRAL PEOPLE'S BS, Shijiazhuang — DS-1 • 100 kW • ALT. FREQ. TO 6950 kHz
†CHINA R INTL, Beijing — W • Europe • 500 kW
†CHINA R INTL, Kunming — S Asia • 500 kW / S • SE Asia • 100 kW
†CHINA R INTL, Shijiazhuang — W • W Asia & C Asia • 500 kW
CHINA R INTL, Via Cerrik, Albania — W • N Africa • 150 kW
CHINA R INTL, Via Samara, Russia — W • Europe • 500 kW
CHINA R INTL, Xi'an — W • C Asia & E Asia • 500 kW
W • W Asia & C Asia • 500 kW
E Asia • 500 kW

IRAN
†VO THE ISLAMIC REP, Sirjan — W • C Asia • 500 kW
JAPAN
†RADIO JAPAN, Via Moyabi, Gabon — S • S Africa • 500 kW
ROMANIA
R ROMANIA INTL, Galbeni — S • Europe • 250 kW
USA
†FAMILY RADIO, Via Armavir, Russia — W • S Asia • 250 kW
TRANS WORLD R, Via Meyerton, S Af — W-Su • E Africa • 250 kW
VOA, Via Philippines — S • SE Asia • 50 kW

7217v ANGOLA
†RADIO NACIONAL, Mulenvos — DS-CANAL A • 15 kW
DS-R N'GOLA YETU • 15 kW
S Africa • 15 kW

7220 CANADA
†R CANADA INTL, Via Tokyo, Japan — S • E Asia • 300 kW
CENTRAL AFRICAN REPUBLIC
†R CENTRAFRIQUE, Bangui — Irr • FRENCH, ETC • DS • 50 kW
CHINA
†CHINA R INTL, Kunming — W • SE Asia • 100 kW
CHINA R INTL, Via Cerrik, Albania — W • N Africa • 150 kW
CHINA R INTL, Via Moscow, Russia — W • E Europe & Mideast • 200 kW
†CHINA R INTL, Xi'an — W • E Africa & S Africa • 500 kW
SE Asia • 500 kW

FRANCE
†R FRANCE INTL, Issoudun — W • W Africa & C Africa • 500 kW
Irr • S • W Africa • 250 kW

IRAN
VO THE ISLAMIC REP, Tehrān — S • S Asia • 500 kW
NETHERLANDS
†R NEDERLAND, Via Nauen, Germany — W • Europe • 500 kW
PAKISTAN
PAKISTAN BC CORP, Peshawar — DS • 10 kW
ROMANIA
R ROMANIA INTL, Bucharest — W • Mideast • 250 kW
UNITED KINGDOM
†FEBA RADIO, Via Samara, Russia — W • W Asia • 200 kW
USA
RFE-RL, Via Biblis, Germany — S • E Europe • 100 kW
RFE-RL, Via Briech, Morocco — W • E Europe • 250 kW
RFE-RL, Via Iranawila, Sri Lanka — W • E Asia • 250 kW
RFE-RL, Via Lampertheim, Germany — S • E Europe & W Asia • 100 kW
E Europe • 100 kW
W • W Asia & C Asia • 100 kW
W • E Europe • 100 kW
RFE-RL, Via Philippines — S • E Asia • 250 kW
RFE-RL, Via Udon Thani, Thailand — W • E Asia • 250 kW
VOA, Via Jászberény, Hungary — W • E Europe • 250 kW
VOA, Via Lampertheim, Germany — S • E Europe • 100 kW
W • E Europe • 100 kW

VIETNAM
†VOICE OF VIETNAM, Son Tay — E Asia • 100 kW
W Africa & C Africa • 100 kW • ALT. FREQ. TO 13860 kHz

ZAMBIA
RADIO ZAMBIA-ZNBC, Lusaka — ENGLISH, ETC • DS-1 • 100 kW • ALT. FREQ. TO 5915 kHz
7225 CHINA
CHINA R INTL, Via Moscow, Russia — S • E Europe & Mideast • 200 kW
(con'd) SICHUAN PEOPLE'S BS, Chengdu — CHINESE, ETC • DS • 50 kW

0 1 2 3 4 5 6 7 8 9 10 11 12 13 14 15 16 17 18 19 20 21 22 23 24

SEASONAL S OR W 1-HR TIMESHIFT MIDYEAR ⇐ OR ⇒ JAMMING / OR /\ EARLIEST HEARD ◁ LATEST HEARD ▷ NEW FOR 2008 †

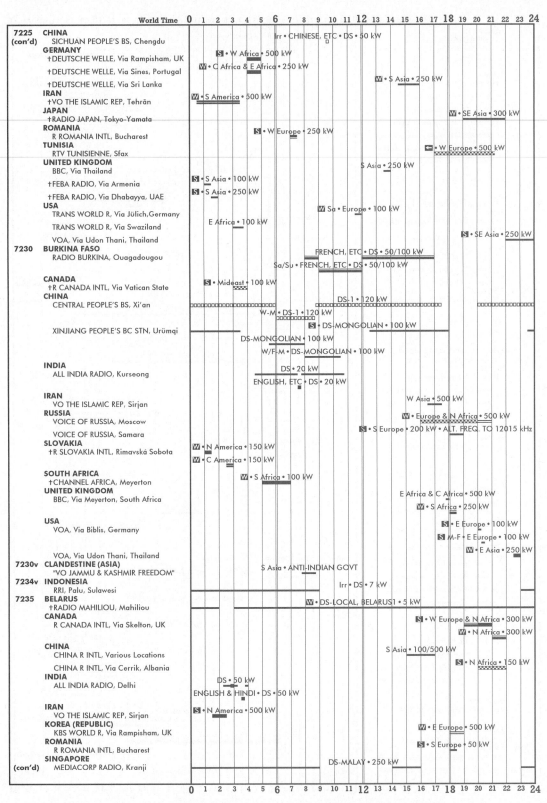

World Time 0 1 2 3 4 5 6 7 8 9 10 11 12 13 14 15 16 17 18 19 20 21 22 23 24

7225 (con'd)	CHINA
	SICHUAN PEOPLE'S BS, Chengdu — Irr • CHINESE, ETC • DS • 50 kW
	GERMANY
	†DEUTSCHE WELLE, Via Rampisham, UK — S • W Africa • 500 kW
	†DEUTSCHE WELLE, Via Sines, Portugal — W • C Africa & E Africa • 250 kW
	†DEUTSCHE WELLE, Via Sri Lanka — W • S Asia • 250 kW
	IRAN
	†VO THE ISLAMIC REP, Tehrān — W • S America • 500 kW
	JAPAN
	†RADIO JAPAN, Tokyo-Yamata — W • SE Asia • 300 kW
	ROMANIA
	R ROMANIA INTL, Bucharest — S • W Europe • 250 kW
	TUNISIA
	RTV TUNISIENNE, Sfax — • W Europe • 500 kW
	UNITED KINGDOM
	BBC, Via Thailand — S Asia • 250 kW
	†FEBA RADIO, Via Armenia — S • S Asia • 100 kW
	†FEBA RADIO, Via Dhabayya, UAE — S • S Asia • 250 kW
	USA
	TRANS WORLD R, Via Jülich, Germany — W • Sa • Europe • 100 kW
	TRANS WORLD R, Via Swaziland — E Africa • 100 kW
	VOA, Via Udon Thani, Thailand — S • SE Asia • 250 kW
7230	BURKINA FASO
	RADIO BURKINA, Ouagadougou — FRENCH, ETC • DS • 50/100 kW / Sa/Su • FRENCH, ETC • DS • 50/100 kW
	CANADA
	†R CANADA INTL, Via Vatican State — S • Mideast • 100 kW
	CHINA
	CENTRAL PEOPLE'S BS, Xi'an — DS-1 • 120 kW / W-M • DS-1 • 120 kW
	XINJIANG PEOPLE'S BC STN, Urümqi — DS-MONGOLIAN • 100 kW / DS-MONGOLIAN • 100 kW / W/F-M • DS-MONGOLIAN • 100 kW
	INDIA
	ALL INDIA RADIO, Kurseong — DS • 20 kW / ENGLISH, ETC • DS • 20 kW
	IRAN
	VO THE ISLAMIC REP, Sirjan — W Asia • 500 kW
	RUSSIA
	VOICE OF RUSSIA, Moscow — W • Europe & N Africa • 500 kW
	VOICE OF RUSSIA, Samara — S • S Europe • 200 kW • ALT. FREQ. TO 12015 kHz
	SLOVAKIA
	†R SLOVAKIA INTL, Rimavská Sobota — W • N America • 150 kW / W • C America • 150 kW
	SOUTH AFRICA
	†CHANNEL AFRICA, Meyerton — W • S Africa • 100 kW
	UNITED KINGDOM
	BBC, Via Meyerton, South Africa — E Africa & C Africa • 500 kW / W • S Africa • 250 kW
	USA
	VOA, Via Biblis, Germany — S • E Europe • 100 kW / S M-F • E Europe • 100 kW
	VOA, Via Udon Thani, Thailand — W • E Asia • 250 kW
7230v	CLANDESTINE (ASIA)
	"VO JAMMU & KASHMIR FREEDOM" — S Asia • ANTI-INDIAN GOVT
7234v	INDONESIA
	RRI, Palu, Sulawesi — Irr • DS • 7 kW
7235	BELARUS
	†RADIO MAHILIOU, Mahiliou — W • DS-LOCAL, BELARUS1 • 5 kW
	CANADA
	R CANADA INTL, Via Skelton, UK — S • W Europe & N Africa • 300 kW / W • N Africa • 300 kW
	CHINA
	CHINA R INTL, Various Locations — S Asia • 100/500 kW
	CHINA R INTL, Via Cerrik, Albania — S • N Africa • 150 kW
	INDIA
	ALL INDIA RADIO, Delhi — DS • 50 kW / ENGLISH & HINDI • DS • 50 kW
	IRAN
	VO THE ISLAMIC REP, Sirjan — S • N America • 500 kW
	KOREA (REPUBLIC)
	KBS WORLD R, Via Rampisham, UK — W • E Europe • 500 kW
	ROMANIA
	R ROMANIA INTL, Bucharest — S • S Europe • 50 kW
	SINGAPORE
(con'd)	MEDIACORP RADIO, Kranji — DS-MALAY • 250 kW

0 1 2 3 4 5 6 7 8 9 10 11 12 13 14 15 16 17 18 19 20 21 22 23 24

ENGLISH ▬▬ ARABIC ⌇⌇⌇ CHINESE □□□ FRENCH ▬▬ GERMAN ▭▭ RUSSIAN ═══ SPANISH ▭▭ OTHER ——

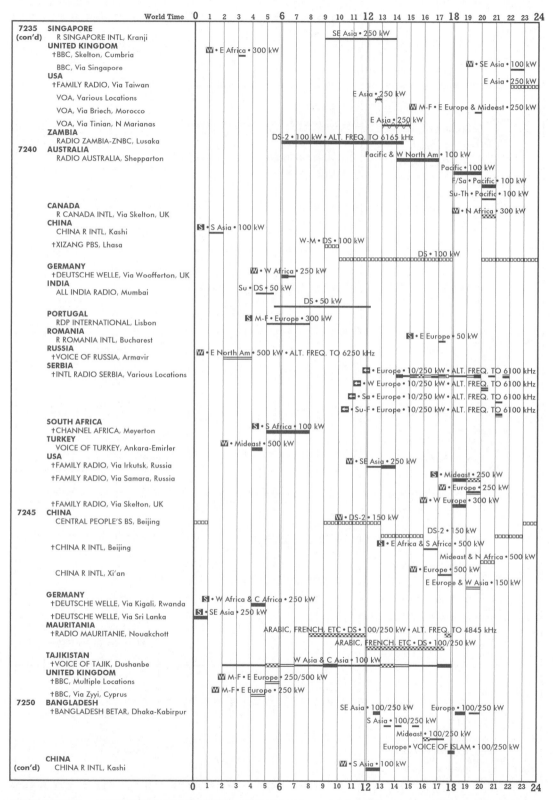

World Time 0 1 2 3 4 5 6 7 8 9 10 11 12 13 14 15 16 17 18 19 20 21 22 23 24

7235
(con'd)   SINGAPORE
    R SINGAPORE INTL, Kranji   SE Asia • 250 kW
   UNITED KINGDOM
    †BBC, Skelton, Cumbria   W • E Africa • 300 kW
    BBC, Via Singapore   W • SE Asia • 100 kW
   USA
    †FAMILY RADIO, Via Taiwan   E Asia • 250 kW
    VOA, Various Locations   E Asia • 250 kW
    VOA, Via Briech, Morocco   W M-F • E Europe & Mideast • 250 kW
    VOA, Via Tinian, N Marianas   E Asia • 250 kW
   ZAMBIA
    RADIO ZAMBIA-ZNBC, Lusaka   DS-2 • 100 kW • ALT. FREQ. TO 6165 kHz

7240   AUSTRALIA
    RADIO AUSTRALIA, Shepparton   Pacific & W North Am • 100 kW
    Pacific • 100 kW
    F/Sa • Pacific • 100 kW
    Su-Th • Pacific • 100 kW
   CANADA
    R CANADA INTL, Via Skelton, UK   W • N Africa • 300 kW
   CHINA
    CHINA R INTL, Kashi   S • S Asia • 100 kW
    †XIZANG PBS, Lhasa   W-M • DS • 100 kW
    DS • 100 kW
   GERMANY
    †DEUTSCHE WELLE, Via Woofferton, UK   W • W Africa • 250 kW
   INDIA
    ALL INDIA RADIO, Mumbai   Su • DS • 50 kW
    DS • 50 kW
   PORTUGAL
    RDP INTERNATIONAL, Lisbon   S M-F • Europe • 300 kW
   ROMANIA
    R ROMANIA INTL, Bucharest   S • E Europe • 50 kW
   RUSSIA
    †VOICE OF RUSSIA, Armavir   W • E North Am • 500 kW • ALT. FREQ. TO 6250 kHz
   SERBIA
    †INTL RADIO SERBIA, Various Locations   ⇆ • Europe • 10/250 kW • ALT. FREQ. TO 6100 kHz
    ⇆ • W Europe • 10/250 kW • ALT. FREQ. TO 6100 kHz
    ⇆ • Sa • Europe • 10/250 kW • ALT. FREQ. TO 6100 kHz
    ⇆ • Su-F • Europe • 10/250 kW • ALT. FREQ. TO 6100 kHz
   SOUTH AFRICA
    †CHANNEL AFRICA, Meyerton   S • S Africa • 100 kW
   TURKEY
    VOICE OF TURKEY, Ankara-Emirler   W • Mideast • 500 kW
   USA
    †FAMILY RADIO, Via Irkutsk, Russia   W • SE Asia • 250 kW
    †FAMILY RADIO, Via Samara, Russia   S • Mideast • 250 kW
    W • Europe • 250 kW
    †FAMILY RADIO, Via Skelton, UK   W • W Europe • 300 kW

7245   CHINA
    CENTRAL PEOPLE'S BS, Beijing   W • DS-2 • 150 kW
    DS-2 • 150 kW
    †CHINA R INTL, Beijing   S • E Africa & S Africa • 500 kW
    Mideast & N Africa • 500 kW
    CHINA R INTL, Xi'an   W • Europe • 500 kW
    E Europe & W Asia • 150 kW
   GERMANY
    †DEUTSCHE WELLE, Via Kigali, Rwanda   S • W Africa & C Africa • 250 kW
    †DEUTSCHE WELLE, Via Sri Lanka   S • SE Asia • 250 kW
   MAURITANIA
    †RADIO MAURITANIE, Nouakchott   ARABIC, FRENCH, ETC • DS • 100/250 kW • ALT. FREQ. TO 4845 kHz
    ARABIC, FRENCH, ETC • DS • 100/250 kW
   TAJIKISTAN
    †VOICE OF TAJIK, Dushanbe   W Asia & C Asia • 100 kW
   UNITED KINGDOM
    †BBC, Multiple Locations   W M-F • E Europe • 250/500 kW
    †BBC, Via Zyyi, Cyprus   W M-F • E Europe • 250 kW

7250   BANGLADESH
    †BANGLADESH BETAR, Dhaka-Kabirpur   SE Asia • 100/250 kW   Europe • 100/250 kW
    S Asia • 100/250 kW
    Mideast • 100/250 kW
    Europe • VOICE OF ISLAM • 100/250 kW
   CHINA
(con'd)   CHINA R INTL, Kashi   W • S Asia • 100 kW

0 1 2 3 4 5 6 7 8 9 10 11 12 13 14 15 16 17 18 19 20 21 22 23 24

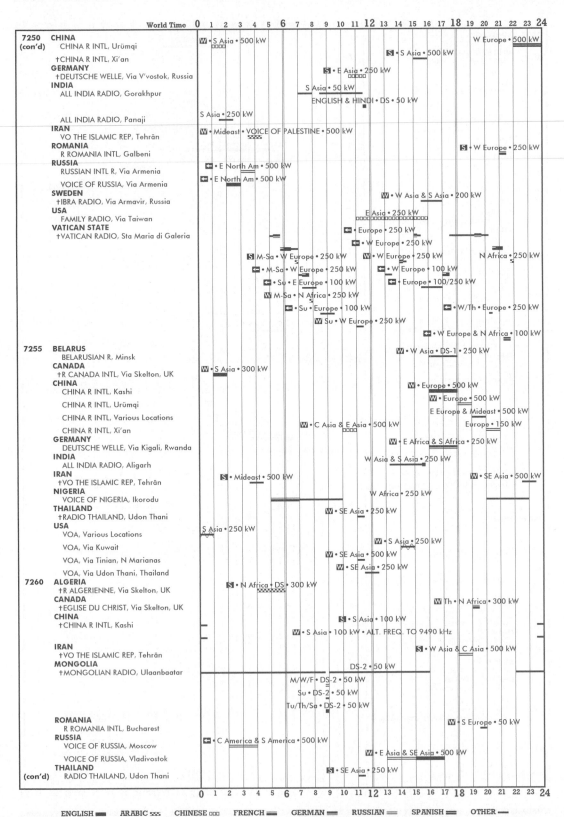

World Time   0 1 2 3 4 5 6 7 8 9 10 11 12 13 14 15 16 17 18 19 20 21 22 23 24

7250 **CHINA**
(con'd)   CHINA R INTL, Urümqi

          †CHINA R INTL, Xi'an
     GERMANY
          †DEUTSCHE WELLE, Via V'vostok, Russia
     INDIA
          ALL INDIA RADIO, Gorakhpur

          ALL INDIA RADIO, Panaji
     IRAN
          VO THE ISLAMIC REP, Tehrān
     ROMANIA
          R ROMANIA INTL, Galbeni
     RUSSIA
          RUSSIAN INTL R, Via Armenia

          VOICE OF RUSSIA, Via Armenia
     SWEDEN
          †IBRA RADIO, Via Armavir, Russia
     USA
          FAMILY RADIO, Via Taiwan
     VATICAN STATE
          †VATICAN RADIO, Sta Maria di Galeria

7255 **BELARUS**
          BELARUSIAN R, Minsk
     CANADA
          †R CANADA INTL, Via Skelton, UK
     CHINA
          CHINA R INTL, Kashi

          CHINA R INTL, Urümqi

          CHINA R INTL, Various Locations

          CHINA R INTL, Xi'an
     GERMANY
          DEUTSCHE WELLE, Via Kigali, Rwanda
     INDIA
          ALL INDIA RADIO, Aligarh
     IRAN
          †VO THE ISLAMIC REP, Tehrān
     NIGERIA
          VOICE OF NIGERIA, Ikorodu
     THAILAND
          †RADIO THAILAND, Udon Thani
     USA
          VOA, Various Locations

          VOA, Via Kuwait

          VOA, Via Tinian, N Marianas

          VOA, Via Udon Thani, Thailand
7260 **ALGERIA**
          †R ALGERIENNE, Via Skelton, UK
     CANADA
          †EGLISE DU CHRIST, Via Skelton, UK
     CHINA
          †CHINA R INTL, Kashi

     IRAN
          †VO THE ISLAMIC REP, Tehrān
     MONGOLIA
          †MONGOLIAN RADIO, Ulaanbaatar

     ROMANIA
          R ROMANIA INTL, Bucharest
     RUSSIA
          VOICE OF RUSSIA, Moscow

          VOICE OF RUSSIA, Vladivostok
     THAILAND
(con'd)   RADIO THAILAND, Udon Thani

     0 1 2 3 4 5 6 7 8 9 10 11 12 13 14 15 16 17 18 19 20 21 22 23 24

ENGLISH ▬   ARABIC ▨   CHINESE ⬚⬚⬚   FRENCH ▭   GERMAN ▬   RUSSIAN ═   SPANISH ▬   OTHER ▬

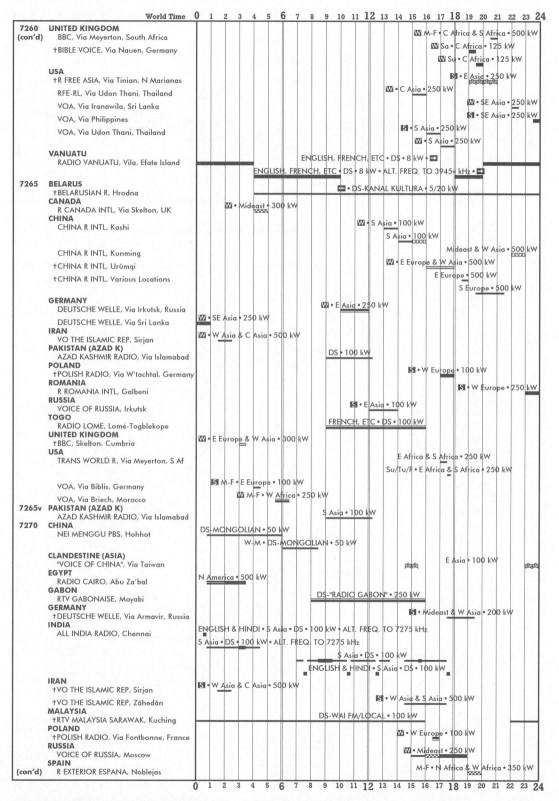

7260	**UNITED KINGDOM**	
(con'd)	BBC, Via Meyerton, South Africa	ⓦ M-F • C Africa & S Africa • 500 kW
	†BIBLE VOICE, Via Nauen, Germany	ⓦ Sa • C Africa • 125 kW
		ⓦ Su • C Africa • 125 kW
	USA	
	†R FREE ASIA, Via Tinian, N Marianas	ⓢ • E Asia • 250 kW
	RFE-RL, Via Udon Thani, Thailand	ⓦ • C Asia • 250 kW
	VOA, Via Iranawila, Sri Lanka	ⓦ • SE Asia • 250 kW
	VOA, Via Philippines	ⓦ • SE Asia • 250 kW
	VOA, Via Udon Thani, Thailand	ⓢ • S Asia • 250 kW
		• S Asia • 250 kW
	VANUATU	
	RADIO VANUATU, Vila, Efate Island	ENGLISH, FRENCH, ETC • DS • 8 kW ▣➡
		ENGLISH, FRENCH, ETC • DS • 8 kW • ALT. FREQ. TO 3945v kHz • ▣
7265	**BELARUS**	
	†BELARUSIAN R, Hrodna	▣ • DS-KANAL KULTURA • 5/20 kW
	CANADA	
	R CANADA INTL, Via Skelton, UK	ⓦ • Mideast • 300 kW
	CHINA	
	CHINA R INTL, Kashi	ⓦ • S Asia • 100 kW
		S Asia • 100 kW
	CHINA R INTL, Kunming	Mideast & W Asia • 500 kW
	†CHINA R INTL, Urümqi	ⓦ • E Europe & W Asia • 500 kW
	†CHINA R INTL, Various Locations	E Europe • 500 kW
		S Europe • 500 kW
	GERMANY	
	DEUTSCHE WELLE, Via Irkutsk, Russia	ⓦ • E Asia • 250 kW
	DEUTSCHE WELLE, Via Sri Lanka	ⓦ • SE Asia • 250 kW
	IRAN	
	VO THE ISLAMIC REP, Sirjan	ⓦ • W Asia & C Asia • 500 kW
	PAKISTAN (AZAD K)	
	AZAD KASHMIR RADIO, Via Islamabad	DS • 100 kW
	POLAND	
	†POLISH RADIO, Via W'tachtal, Germany	ⓢ • W Europe • 100 kW
	ROMANIA	
	R ROMANIA INTL, Galbeni	ⓢ • W Europe • 250 kW
	RUSSIA	
	VOICE OF RUSSIA, Irkutsk	ⓢ • E Asia • 100 kW
	TOGO	
	RADIO LOME, Lomé-Togblekope	FRENCH, ETC • DS • 100 kW
	UNITED KINGDOM	
	†BBC, Skelton, Cumbria	ⓦ • E Europe & W Asia • 300 kW
	USA	
	TRANS WORLD R, Via Meyerton, S Af	E Africa & S Africa • 250 kW
		Su/Tu/F • E Africa & S Africa • 250 kW
	VOA, Via Biblis, Germany	ⓢ M-F • E Europe • 100 kW
	VOA, Via Briech, Morocco	ⓦ M-F • W Africa • 250 kW
7265v	**PAKISTAN (AZAD K)**	
	AZAD KASHMIR RADIO, Via Islamabad	S Asia • 100 kW
7270	**CHINA**	
	NEI MENGGU PBS, Hohhot	DS-MONGOLIAN • 50 kW
		W-M • DS-MONGOLIAN • 50 kW
	CLANDESTINE (ASIA)	
	"VOICE OF CHINA", Via Taiwan	E Asia • 100 kW
	EGYPT	
	RADIO CAIRO, Abu Za'bal	N America • 500 kW
	GABON	
	RTV GABONAISE, Moyabi	DS-"RADIO GABON" • 250 kW
	GERMANY	
	†DEUTSCHE WELLE, Via Armavir, Russia	ⓢ • Mideast & W Asia • 200 kW
	INDIA	
	ALL INDIA RADIO, Chennai	ENGLISH & HINDI • S Asia • DS • 100 kW • ALT. FREQ. TO 7275 kHz
		S Asia • DS • 100 kW • ALT. FREQ. TO 7275 kHz
		S Asia • DS • 100 kW
		ENGLISH & HINDI • S Asia • DS • 100 kW
	IRAN	
	†VO THE ISLAMIC REP, Sirjan	ⓢ • W Asia & C Asia • 500 kW
	†VO THE ISLAMIC REP, Zāhedān	ⓢ • W Asia & S Asia • 500 kW
	MALAYSIA	
	†RTV MALAYSIA SARAWAK, Kuching	DS-WAI FM/LOCAL • 100 kW
	POLAND	
	†POLISH RADIO, Via Fontbonne, France	ⓦ • W Europe • 100 kW
	RUSSIA	
	VOICE OF RUSSIA, Moscow	ⓦ • Mideast • 250 kW
	SPAIN	
(con'd)	R EXTERIOR ESPANA, Noblejas	M-F • N Africa & W Africa • 350 kW

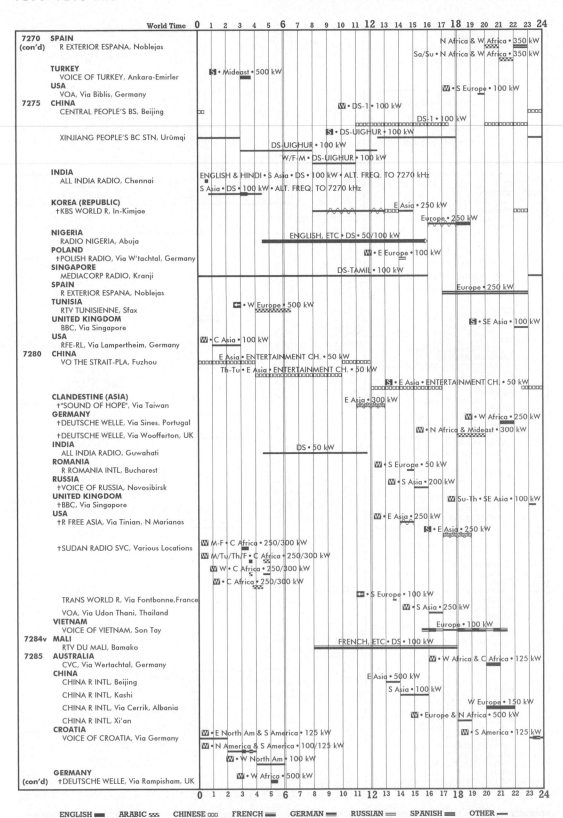

World Time

7270	**SPAIN**
(con'd)	R EXTERIOR ESPANA, Noblejas
	N Africa & W Africa • 350 kW
	Sa/Su • N Africa & W Africa • 350 kW
	TURKEY
	VOICE OF TURKEY, Ankara-Emirler
	S • Mideast • 500 kW
	USA
	VOA, Via Biblis, Germany
	W • S Europe • 100 kW
7275	**CHINA**
	CENTRAL PEOPLE'S BS, Beijing
	W • DS-1 • 100 kW
	DS-1 • 100 kW
	XINJIANG PEOPLE'S BC STN, Urümqi
	S • DS-UIGHUR • 100 kW
	DS-UIGHUR • 100 kW
	W/F-M • DS-UIGHUR • 100 kW
	INDIA
	ALL INDIA RADIO, Chennai
	ENGLISH & HINDI • S Asia • DS • 100 kW • ALT. FREQ. TO 7270 kHz
	S Asia • DS • 100 kW • ALT. FREQ. TO 7270 kHz
	KOREA (REPUBLIC)
	†KBS WORLD R, In-Kimjae
	E Asia • 250 kW
	Europe • 250 kW
	NIGERIA
	RADIO NIGERIA, Abuja
	ENGLISH, ETC • DS • 50/100 kW
	POLAND
	†POLISH RADIO, Via W'tachtal, Germany
	W • E Europe • 100 kW
	SINGAPORE
	MEDIACORP RADIO, Kranji
	DS-TAMIL • 100 kW
	SPAIN
	R EXTERIOR ESPANA, Noblejas
	Europe • 250 kW
	TUNISIA
	RTV TUNISIENNE, Sfax
	• W Europe • 500 kW
	UNITED KINGDOM
	BBC, Via Singapore
	S • SE Asia • 100 kW
	USA
	RFE-RL, Via Lampertheim, Germany
	W • C Asia • 100 kW
7280	**CHINA**
	VO THE STRAIT-PLA, Fuzhou
	E Asia • ENTERTAINMENT CH. • 50 kW
	Th-Tu • E Asia • ENTERTAINMENT CH. • 50 kW
	S • E Asia • ENTERTAINMENT CH. • 50 kW
	CLANDESTINE (ASIA)
	†"SOUND OF HOPE", Via Taiwan
	E Asia • 300 kW
	GERMANY
	†DEUTSCHE WELLE, Via Sines, Portugal
	W • W Africa • 250 kW
	†DEUTSCHE WELLE, Via Woofferton, UK
	W • N Africa & Mideast • 300 kW
	INDIA
	ALL INDIA RADIO, Guwahati
	DS • 50 kW
	ROMANIA
	R ROMANIA INTL, Bucharest
	W • S Europe • 50 kW
	RUSSIA
	†VOICE OF RUSSIA, Novosibirsk
	W • S Asia • 200 kW
	UNITED KINGDOM
	†BBC, Via Singapore
	W • Su-Th • SE Asia • 100 kW
	USA
	†R FREE ASIA, Via Tinian, N Marianas
	W • E Asia • 250 kW
	S • E Asia • 250 kW
	†SUDAN RADIO SVC, Various Locations
	W • M-F • C Africa • 250/300 kW
	W • M/Tu/Th/F • C Africa • 250/300 kW
	W • W • C Africa • 250/300 kW
	W • C Africa • 250/300 kW
	TRANS WORLD R, Via Fontbonne, France
	• S Europe • 100 kW
	VOA, Via Udon Thani, Thailand
	W • S Asia • 250 kW
	VIETNAM
	VOICE OF VIETNAM, Son Tay
	Europe • 100 kW
7284v	**MALI**
	RTV DU MALI, Bamako
	FRENCH, ETC • DS • 100 kW
7285	**AUSTRALIA**
	CVC, Via Wertachtal, Germany
	W • W Africa & C Africa • 125 kW
	CHINA
	CHINA R INTL, Beijing
	E Asia • 500 kW
	CHINA R INTL, Kashi
	S Asia • 100 kW
	CHINA R INTL, Via Cerrik, Albania
	W Europe • 150 kW
	CHINA R INTL, Xi'an
	W • Europe & N Africa • 500 kW
	CROATIA
	VOICE OF CROATIA, Via Germany
	W • E North Am & S America • 125 kW
	S • S America • 125 kW
	W • N America & S America • 100/125 kW
	W • W North Am • 100 kW
	GERMANY
(con'd)	†DEUTSCHE WELLE, Via Rampisham, UK
	W • W Africa • 500 kW

ENGLISH ▬   ARABIC ⌇⌇   CHINESE ▯▯▯   FRENCH ▬   GERMAN ▭   RUSSIAN ═   SPANISH ▬   OTHER ▬

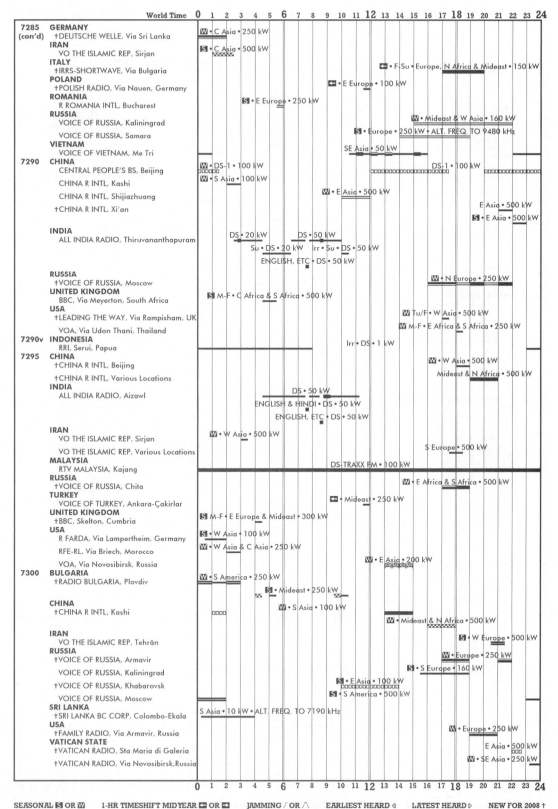

World Time	0 1 2 3 4 5 6 7 8 9 10 11 12 13 14 15 16 17 18 19 20 21 22 23 24

7285 (con'd) **GERMANY**
 †DEUTSCHE WELLE, Via Sri Lanka — W • C Asia • 250 kW
IRAN
 VO THE ISLAMIC REP, Sirjan — S • C Asia • 500 kW
ITALY
 †IRRS-SHORTWAVE, Via Bulgaria — F-Su • Europe, N Africa & Mideast • 150 kW
POLAND
 †POLISH RADIO, Via Nauen, Germany — E Europe • 100 kW
ROMANIA
 R ROMANIA INTL, Bucharest — S • E Europe • 250 kW
RUSSIA
 VOICE OF RUSSIA, Kaliningrad — W • Mideast & W Asia • 160 kW
 VOICE OF RUSSIA, Samara — S • Europe • 250 kW • ALT. FREQ. TO 9480 kHz
VIETNAM
 VOICE OF VIETNAM, Me Tri — SE Asia • 50 kW

7290 CHINA
 CENTRAL PEOPLE'S BS, Beijing — W • DS-1 • 100 kW   DS-1 • 100 kW
 CHINA R INTL, Kashi — W • S Asia • 100 kW
 CHINA R INTL, Shijiazhuang — W • E Asia • 500 kW
 †CHINA R INTL, Xi'an — E Asia • 500 kW
    S • E Asia • 500 kW
INDIA
 ALL INDIA RADIO, Thiruvananthapuram — DS • 20 kW   DS • 50 kW
    Su • DS • 20 kW Irr • Su • DS • 50 kW
    ENGLISH, ETC • DS • 50 kW
RUSSIA
 †VOICE OF RUSSIA, Moscow — W • N Europe • 250 kW
UNITED KINGDOM
 BBC, Via Meyerton, South Africa — S • M-F • C Africa & S Africa • 500 kW
USA
 †LEADING THE WAY, Via Rampisham, UK — W • Tu/F • W Asia • 500 kW
 VOA, Via Udon Thani, Thailand — W • M-F • E Africa & S Africa • 250 kW

7290v INDONESIA
 RRI, Serui, Papua — Irr • DS • 1 kW
7295 CHINA
 †CHINA R INTL, Beijing — W • W Asia • 500 kW
 †CHINA R INTL, Various Locations — Mideast & N Africa • 500 kW
INDIA
 ALL INDIA RADIO, Aizawl — DS • 50 kW
    ENGLISH & HINDI • DS • 50 kW
    ENGLISH, ETC • DS • 50 kW
IRAN
 VO THE ISLAMIC REP, Sirjan — W • W Asia • 500 kW
 VO THE ISLAMIC REP, Various Locations — S Europe • 500 kW
MALAYSIA
 RTV MALAYSIA, Kajang — DS-TRAXX FM • 100 kW
RUSSIA
 †VOICE OF RUSSIA, Chita — W • E Africa & S Africa • 500 kW
TURKEY
 VOICE OF TURKEY, Ankara-Çakirlar — † Mideast • 250 kW
UNITED KINGDOM
 †BBC, Skelton, Cumbria — S • M-F • E Europe & Mideast • 300 kW
USA
 R FARDA, Via Lampertheim, Germany — S • W Asia • 100 kW
 RFE-RL, Via Briech, Morocco — W • W Asia & C Asia • 250 kW
 VOA, Via Novosibirsk, Russia — W • E Asia • 200 kW

7300 BULGARIA
 †RADIO BULGARIA, Plovdiv — W • S America • 250 kW
    S • Mideast • 250 kW
CHINA
 †CHINA R INTL, Kashi — W • S Asia • 100 kW
    W • Mideast & N Africa • 500 kW
IRAN
 VO THE ISLAMIC REP, Tehrān — S • W Europe • 500 kW
RUSSIA
 †VOICE OF RUSSIA, Armavir — W • Europe • 250 kW
 VOICE OF RUSSIA, Kaliningrad — S • S Europe • 160 kW
 †VOICE OF RUSSIA, Khabarovsk — S • E Asia • 100 kW
 VOICE OF RUSSIA, Moscow — S • S America • 500 kW
SRI LANKA
 †SRI LANKA BC CORP, Colombo-Ekala — S Asia • 10 kW • ALT. FREQ. TO 7190 kHz
USA
 †FAMILY RADIO, Via Armavir, Russia — W • Europe • 250 kW
VATICAN STATE
 †VATICAN RADIO, Sta Maria di Galeria — E Asia • 500 kW
 †VATICAN RADIO, Via Novosibirsk, Russia — W • SE Asia • 250 kW

	0 1 2 3 4 5 6 7 8 9 10 11 12 13 14 15 16 17 18 19 20 21 22 23 24

SEASONAL Ⓢ OR Ⓦ   1-HR TIMESHIFT MIDYEAR ⬅ OR ➡   JAMMING / OR ⋀   EARLIEST HEARD ◁   LATEST HEARD ▷   NEW FOR 2008 †

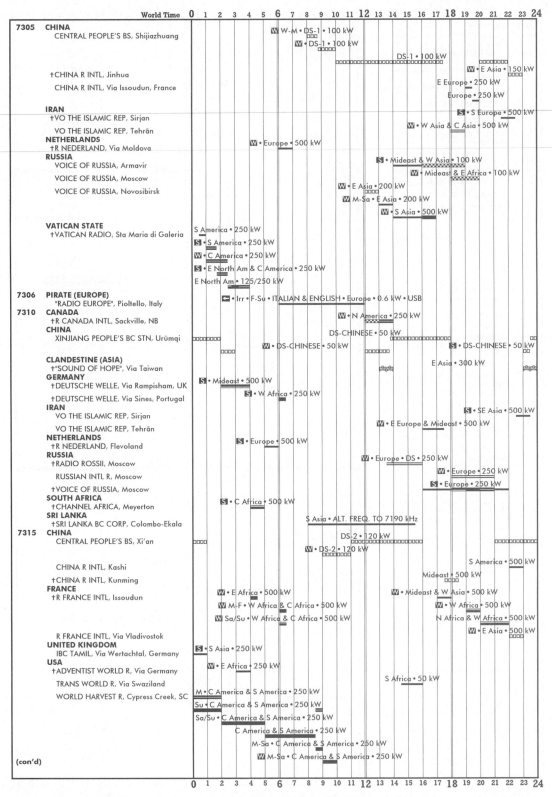

World Time	0 1 2 3 4 5 6 7 8 9 10 11 12 13 14 15 16 17 18 19 20 21 22 23 24
7305 CHINA	
CENTRAL PEOPLE'S BS, Shijiazhuang	W•W-M•DS-1•100 kW
	W•DS-1•100 kW
	DS-1•100 kW
	W•E Asia•150 kW
†CHINA R INTL, Jinhua	E Europe•250 kW
CHINA R INTL, Via Issoudun, France	Europe•250 kW
IRAN	
†VO THE ISLAMIC REP, Sirjan	S•S Europe•500 kW
VO THE ISLAMIC REP, Tehrān	W•W Asia & C Asia•500 kW
NETHERLANDS	
†R NEDERLAND, Via Moldova	W•Europe•500 kW
RUSSIA	
VOICE OF RUSSIA, Armavir	S•Mideast & W Asia•100 kW
VOICE OF RUSSIA, Moscow	W•Mideast & E Africa•100 kW
VOICE OF RUSSIA, Novosibirsk	W•E Asia•200 kW
	W•M-Sa•E Asia•200 kW
	W•S Asia•500 kW
VATICAN STATE	
†VATICAN RADIO, Sta Maria di Galeria	S America•250 kW
	S•S America•250 kW
	W•C America•250 kW
	S•E North Am & C America•250 kW
	E North Am•125/250 kW
7306 PIRATE (EUROPE)	
"RADIO EUROPE", Pioltello, Italy	◄►•Irr•F-Su•ITALIAN & ENGLISH•Europe•0.6 kW•USB
7310 CANADA	
†R CANADA INTL, Sackville, NB	W•N America•250 kW
CHINA	
XINJIANG PEOPLE'S BC STN, Urümqi	DS-CHINESE•50 kW
	W•DS-CHINESE•50 kW S•DS-CHINESE•50 kW
CLANDESTINE (ASIA)	
†"SOUND OF HOPE", Via Taiwan	E Asia•300 kW
GERMANY	
†DEUTSCHE WELLE, Via Rampisham, UK	S•Mideast•500 kW
†DEUTSCHE WELLE, Via Sines, Portugal	S•W Africa•250 kW
IRAN	
VO THE ISLAMIC REP, Sirjan	S•SE Asia•500 kW
VO THE ISLAMIC REP, Tehrān	W•E Europe & Mideast•500 kW
NETHERLANDS	
†R NEDERLAND, Flevoland	S•Europe•500 kW
RUSSIA	
†RADIO ROSSII, Moscow	W•Europe•DS•250 kW
RUSSIAN INTL R, Moscow	W•Europe•250 kW
†VOICE OF RUSSIA, Moscow	S•Europe•250 kW
SOUTH AFRICA	
†CHANNEL AFRICA, Meyerton	S•C Africa•500 kW
SRI LANKA	
†SRI LANKA BC CORP, Colombo-Ekala	S Asia•ALT. FREQ. TO 7190 kHz
7315 CHINA	
CENTRAL PEOPLE'S BS, Xi'an	DS-2•120 kW
	W•DS-2•120 kW
	S America•500 kW
CHINA R INTL, Kashi	Mideast•500 kW
†CHINA R INTL, Kunming	
FRANCE	
†R FRANCE INTL, Issoudun	W•E Africa•500 kW W•Mideast & W Asia•500 kW
	W•M-F•W Africa & C Africa•500 kW W•W Africa•500 kW
	W•Sa/Su•W Africa & C Africa•500 kW N Africa & W Africa•500 kW
	W•E Asia•500 kW
R FRANCE INTL, Via Vladivostok	
UNITED KINGDOM	
IBC TAMIL, Via Wertachtal, Germany	S•S Asia•250 kW
USA	
†ADVENTIST WORLD R, Via Germany	W•E Africa•250 kW
TRANS WORLD R, Via Swaziland	S Africa•50 kW
WORLD HARVEST R, Cypress Creek, SC	M•C America & S America•250 kW
	Su•C America & S America•250 kW
	Sa/Su•C America & S America•250 kW
	C America & S America•250 kW
	M-Sa•C America & S America•250 kW
	W•M-Sa•C America & S America•250 kW
(con'd)	

0 1 2 3 4 5 6 7 8 9 10 11 12 13 14 15 16 17 18 19 20 21 22 23 24

ENGLISH ▬   ARABIC ∼∼∼   CHINESE □□□   FRENCH ▬   GERMAN ═   RUSSIAN ═   SPANISH ▬   OTHER ▬

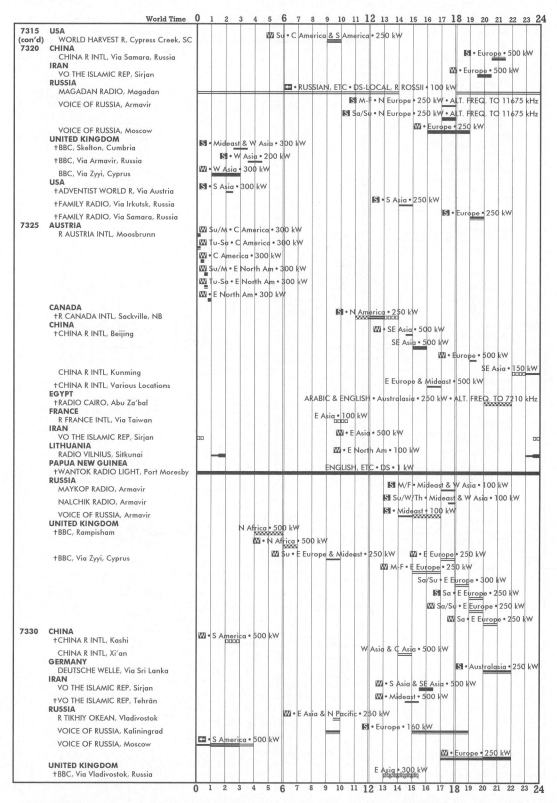

World Time scale: 0 1 2 3 4 5 6 7 8 9 10 11 12 13 14 15 16 17 18 19 20 21 22 23 24

7315
(con'd)
USA
WORLD HARVEST R, Cypress Creek, SC — W • Su • C America & S America • 250 kW

7320
CHINA
CHINA R INTL, Via Samara, Russia — S • Europe • 500 kW
IRAN
VO THE ISLAMIC REP, Sirjan — W • Europe • 500 kW
RUSSIA
MAGADAN RADIO, Magadan — RUSSIAN, ETC • DS-LOCAL, R ROSSII • 100 kW
VOICE OF RUSSIA, Armavir — S • M-F • N Europe • 250 kW • ALT. FREQ. TO 11675 kHz
— S • Sa/Su • N Europe • 250 kW • ALT. FREQ. TO 11675 kHz
VOICE OF RUSSIA, Moscow — W • Europe • 250 kW
UNITED KINGDOM
†BBC, Skelton, Cumbria — S • Mideast & W Asia • 300 kW
†BBC, Via Armavir, Russia — S • W Asia • 200 kW
BBC, Via Zyyi, Cyprus — W • W Asia • 300 kW
USA
†ADVENTIST WORLD R, Via Austria — S • S Asia • 300 kW
†FAMILY RADIO, Via Irkutsk, Russia — S • S Asia • 250 kW
†FAMILY RADIO, Via Samara, Russia — S • Europe • 250 kW

7325
AUSTRIA
R AUSTRIA INTL, Moosbrunn — W • Su/M • C America • 300 kW
— W • Tu-Sa • C America • 300 kW
— W • C America • 300 kW
— W • Su/M • E North Am • 300 kW
— W • Tu-Sa • E North Am • 300 kW
— W • E North Am • 300 kW
CANADA
†R CANADA INTL, Sackville, NB — S • N America • 250 kW
CHINA
†CHINA R INTL, Beijing — W • SE Asia • 500 kW
— SE Asia • 500 kW
— W • Europe • 500 kW
CHINA R INTL, Kunming — SE Asia • 150 kW
†CHINA R INTL, Various Locations — E Europe & Mideast • 500 kW
EGYPT
†RADIO CAIRO, Abu Za'bal — ARABIC & ENGLISH • Australasia • 250 kW • ALT. FREQ. TO 7210 kHz
FRANCE
R FRANCE INTL, Via Taiwan — E Asia • 100 kW
IRAN
VO THE ISLAMIC REP, Sirjan — W • E Asia • 500 kW
LITHUANIA
RADIO VILNIUS, Sitkunai — W • E North Am • 100 kW
PAPUA NEW GUINEA
†WANTOK RADIO LIGHT, Port Moresby — ENGLISH, ETC • DS • 1 kW
RUSSIA
MAYKOP RADIO, Armavir — S • M/F • Mideast & W Asia • 100 kW
NALCHIK RADIO, Armavir — S • Su/W/Th • Mideast & W Asia • 100 kW
VOICE OF RUSSIA, Armavir — S • Mideast • 100 kW
UNITED KINGDOM
†BBC, Rampisham — N Africa • 500 kW
— W • N Africa • 500 kW
†BBC, Via Zyyi, Cyprus — W • Su • E Europe & Mideast • 250 kW
— W • M-F • E Europe • 250 kW
— Sa/Su • E Europe • 300 kW
— S • Sa • E Europe • 250 kW
— W • Sa/Su • E Europe • 250 kW
— S • Sa • E Europe • 250 kW

7330
CHINA
†CHINA R INTL, Kashi — W • S America • 500 kW
CHINA R INTL, Xi'an — W Asia & C Asia • 500 kW
GERMANY
DEUTSCHE WELLE, Via Sri Lanka — S • Australasia • 250 kW
IRAN
VO THE ISLAMIC REP, Sirjan — W • S Asia & SE Asia • 500 kW
†VO THE ISLAMIC REP, Tehrān — W • Mideast • 500 kW
RUSSIA
R TIKHIY OKEAN, Vladivostok — W • E Asia & N Pacific • 250 kW
VOICE OF RUSSIA, Kaliningrad — S • Europe • 160 kW
VOICE OF RUSSIA, Moscow — S America • 500 kW
— W • Europe • 250 kW
UNITED KINGDOM
†BBC, Via Vladivostok, Russia — E Asia • 300 kW

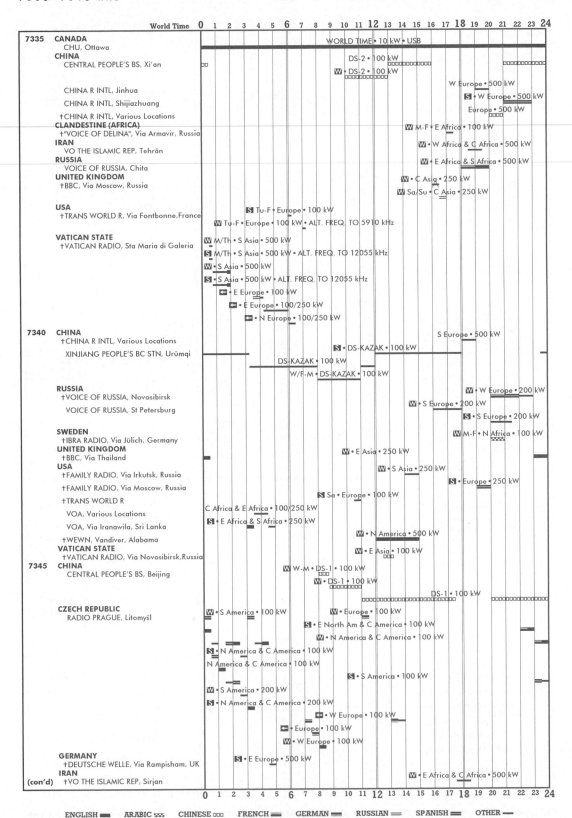

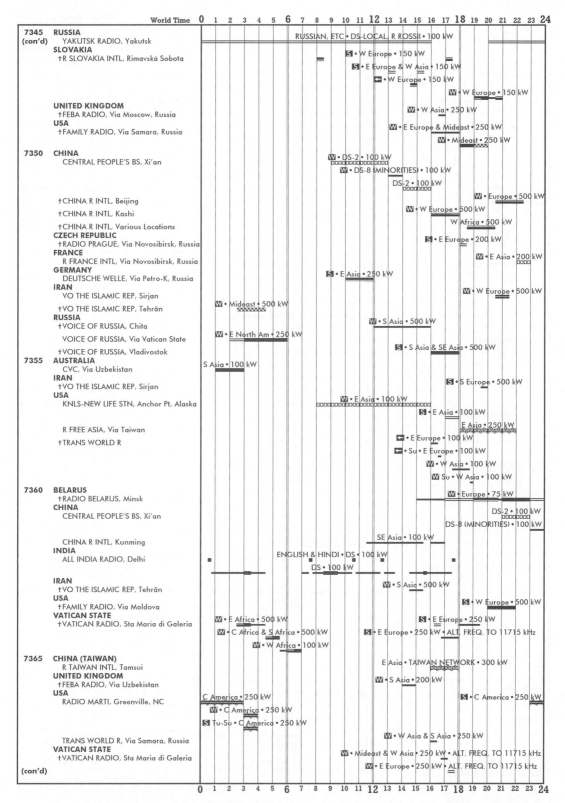

World Time 0 1 2 3 4 5 6 7 8 9 10 11 12 13 14 15 16 17 18 19 20 21 22 23 24

7345 **RUSSIA**
(con'd) YAKUTSK RADIO, Yakutsk — RUSSIAN, ETC • DS-LOCAL, R ROSSII • 100 kW
SLOVAKIA
†R SLOVAKIA INTL, Rimavská Sobota — S • W Europe • 150 kW
— S • E Europe & W Asia • 150 kW
— W Europe • 150 kW
— W • W Europe • 150 kW
UNITED KINGDOM
†FEBA RADIO, Via Moscow, Russia — W • W Asia • 250 kW
USA
†FAMILY RADIO, Via Samara, Russia — W • E Europe & Mideast • 250 kW
— W • Mideast • 250 kW

7350 **CHINA**
CENTRAL PEOPLE'S BS, Xi'an — W • DS-2 • 100 kW
— W • DS-8 (MINORITIES) • 100 kW
— DS-2 • 100 kW
†CHINA R INTL, Beijing — W • Europe • 500 kW
†CHINA R INTL, Kashi — W • W Europe • 500 kW
†CHINA R INTL, Various Locations — W Africa • 500 kW
CZECH REPUBLIC
†RADIO PRAGUE, Via Novosibirsk, Russia — S • E Europe • 200 kW
FRANCE
R FRANCE INTL, Via Novosibirsk, Russia — W • E Asia • 200 kW
GERMANY
DEUTSCHE WELLE, Via Petro-K, Russia — S • E Asia • 250 kW
IRAN
VO THE ISLAMIC REP, Sirjan — W • W Europe • 500 kW
†VO THE ISLAMIC REP, Tehrān — W • Mideast • 500 kW
RUSSIA
†VOICE OF RUSSIA, Chita — W • S Asia • 500 kW
VOICE OF RUSSIA, Via Vatican State — W • E North Am • 250 kW
†VOICE OF RUSSIA, Vladivostok — S • S Asia & SE Asia • 500 kW

7355 **AUSTRALIA**
CVC, Via Uzbekistan — S Asia • 100 kW
IRAN
†VO THE ISLAMIC REP, Sirjan — S • S Europe • 500 kW
USA
KNLS-NEW LIFE STN, Anchor Pt, Alaska — W • E Asia • 100 kW
— S • E Asia • 100 kW
— E Asia • 250 kW
R FREE ASIA, Via Taiwan — ⊏ • E Europe • 100 kW
†TRANS WORLD R — ⊏ • Su • E Europe • 100 kW
— W • W Asia • 100 kW
— W Su • W Asia • 100 kW

7360 **BELARUS**
†RADIO BELARUS, Minsk — W • Europe • 75 kW
CHINA
CENTRAL PEOPLE'S BS, Xi'an — DS-2 • 100 kW
— DS-8 (MINORITIES) • 100 kW
CHINA R INTL, Kunming — SE Asia • 100 kW
INDIA
ALL INDIA RADIO, Delhi — ENGLISH & HINDI • DS • 100 kW
— DS • 100 kW
IRAN
†VO THE ISLAMIC REP, Tehrān — W • S Asia • 500 kW
USA
†FAMILY RADIO, Via Moldova — S • W Europe • 500 kW
VATICAN STATE
†VATICAN RADIO, Sta Maria di Galeria — W • E Africa • 500 kW — S • E Europe • 250 kW
— W • C Africa & S Africa • 500 kW — S • E Europe • 250 kW • ALT. FREQ. TO 11715 kHz
— W • W Africa • 100 kW

7365 **CHINA (TAIWAN)**
R TAIWAN INTL, Tamsui — E Asia • TAIWAN NETWORK • 300 kW
UNITED KINGDOM
†FEBA RADIO, Via Uzbekistan — W • S Asia • 200 kW
USA
RADIO MARTI, Greenville, NC — C America • 250 kW — S • C America • 250 kW
— W • C America • 250 kW
— S Tu-Su • C America • 250 kW
— W • W Asia & S Asia • 250 kW
TRANS WORLD R, Via Samara, Russia
VATICAN STATE
†VATICAN RADIO, Sta Maria di Galeria — W • Mideast & W Asia • 250 kW • ALT. FREQ. TO 11715 kHz
— W • E Europe • 250 kW • ALT. FREQ. TO 11715 kHz
(con'd)

0 1 2 3 4 5 6 7 8 9 10 11 12 13 14 15 16 17 18 19 20 21 22 23 24

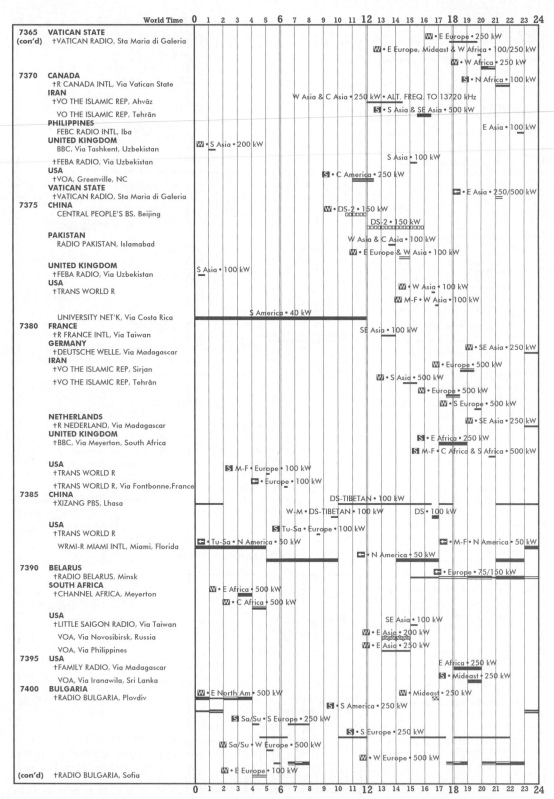

World Time

| 7365 | VATICAN STATE |
| (con'd) | †VATICAN RADIO, Sta Maria di Galeria |

W • E Europe • 250 kW
W • E Europe, Mideast & W Africa • 100/250 kW
W • W Africa • 250 kW

7370	CANADA
	†R CANADA INTL, Via Vatican State
	IRAN
	†VO THE ISLAMIC REP, Ahvāz
	VO THE ISLAMIC REP, Tehrān
	PHILIPPINES
	FEBC RADIO INTL, Iba
	UNITED KINGDOM
	BBC, Via Tashkent, Uzbekistan
	†FEBA RADIO, Via Uzbekistan
	USA
	†VOA, Greenville, NC
	VATICAN STATE
	†VATICAN RADIO, Sta Maria di Galeria

S • N Africa • 100 kW
W Asia & C Asia • 250 kW • ALT. FREQ. TO 13720 kHz
S • S Asia & SE Asia • 500 kW
E Asia • 100 kW
W • S Asia • 200 kW
S Asia • 100 kW
S • C America • 250 kW
E Asia • 250/500 kW

7375	CHINA
	CENTRAL PEOPLE'S BS, Beijing
	PAKISTAN
	RADIO PAKISTAN, Islamabad
	UNITED KINGDOM
	†FEBA RADIO, Via Uzbekistan
	USA
	†TRANS WORLD R
	UNIVERSITY NET'K, Via Costa Rica

W • DS-2 • 150 kW
DS-2 • 150 kW
W Asia & C Asia • 100 kW
W • E Europe & W Asia • 100 kW
S Asia • 100 kW
W • W Asia • 100 kW
W M-F • W Asia • 100 kW
S America • 40 kW

7380	FRANCE
	†R FRANCE INTL, Via Taiwan
	GERMANY
	†DEUTSCHE WELLE, Via Madagascar
	IRAN
	†VO THE ISLAMIC REP, Sirjan
	†VO THE ISLAMIC REP, Tehrān
	NETHERLANDS
	†R NEDERLAND, Via Madagascar
	UNITED KINGDOM
	†BBC, Via Meyerton, South Africa
	USA
	†TRANS WORLD R
	†TRANS WORLD R, Via Fontbonne, France

SE Asia • 100 kW
W • SE Asia • 250 kW
W • Europe • 500 kW
W • S Asia • 500 kW
W • Europe • 500 kW
W • S Europe • 500 kW
W • SE Asia • 250 kW
S • E Africa • 250 kW
S M-F • C Africa & S Africa • 500 kW
S M-F • Europe • 100 kW
• Europe • 100 kW

7385	CHINA
	†XIZANG PBS, Lhasa
	USA
	†TRANS WORLD R
	WRMI-R MIAMI INTL, Miami, Florida

DS-TIBETAN • 100 kW
W-M • DS-TIBETAN • 100 kW
DS • 100 kW
S Tu-Sa • Europe • 100 kW
Tu-Sa • N America • 50 kW
M-F • N America • 50 kW
N America • 50 kW

7390	BELARUS
	†RADIO BELARUS, Minsk
	SOUTH AFRICA
	†CHANNEL AFRICA, Meyerton
	USA
	†LITTLE SAIGON RADIO, Via Taiwan
	VOA, Via Novosibirsk, Russia
	VOA, Via Philippines

• Europe • 75/150 kW
W • E Africa • 500 kW
W • C Africa • 500 kW
SE Asia • 100 kW
W • E Asia • 200 kW
W • E Asia • 250 kW

7395	USA
	†FAMILY RADIO, Via Madagascar
	VOA, Via Iranawila, Sri Lanka
7400	BULGARIA
	†RADIO BULGARIA, Plovdiv

E Africa • 250 kW
S • Mideast • 250 kW
W • Mideast • 250 kW
W • E North Am • 500 kW
S • S America • 250 kW
S Sa/Su • S Europe • 250 kW
S • S Europe • 250 kW
W Sa/Su • W Europe • 500 kW
W • W Europe • 500 kW
W • E Europe • 100 kW

| (con'd) | †RADIO BULGARIA, Sofia |

ENGLISH ▬   ARABIC ░   CHINESE ▭▭▭   FRENCH ▬   GERMAN ▬   RUSSIAN ══   SPANISH ▬   OTHER ▬

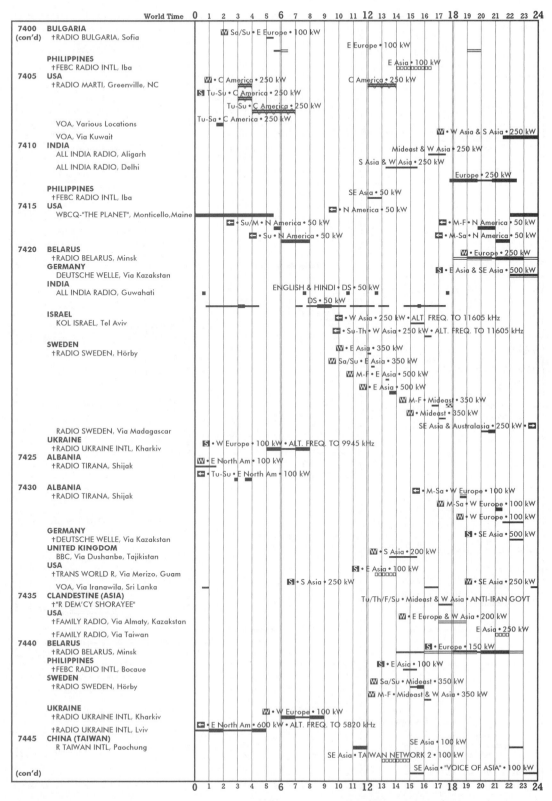

World Time		
7400 (con'd)	**BULGARIA** †RADIO BULGARIA, Sofia	W Sa/Su • E Europe • 100 kW; E Europe • 100 kW
	PHILIPPINES †FEBC RADIO INTL, Iba	E Asia • 100 kW
7405	**USA** †RADIO MARTI, Greenville, NC	W • C America • 250 kW; C America • 250 kW; S Tu-Su • C America • 250 kW; Tu-Su • C America • 250 kW; Tu-Sa • C America • 250 kW
	VOA, Various Locations	
	VOA, Via Kuwait	W • W Asia & S Asia • 250 kW
7410	**INDIA** ALL INDIA RADIO, Aligarh	Mideast & W Asia • 250 kW
	ALL INDIA RADIO, Delhi	S Asia & W Asia • 250 kW; Europe • 250 kW
	PHILIPPINES †FEBC RADIO INTL, Iba	SE Asia • 50 kW
7415	**USA** WBCQ-"THE PLANET", Monticello, Maine	◻ • N America • 50 kW; ◻ • Su/M • N America • 50 kW; ◻ • M-F • N America • 50 kW; ◻ • Su • N America • 50 kW; ◻ • M-Sa • N America • 50 kW
7420	**BELARUS** †RADIO BELARUS, Minsk	W • Europe • 250 kW
	GERMANY DEUTSCHE WELLE, Via Kazakstan	S • E Asia & SE Asia • 500 kW
	INDIA ALL INDIA RADIO, Guwahati	ENGLISH & HINDI • DS • 50 kW; DS • 50 kW
	ISRAEL KOL ISRAEL, Tel Aviv	◻ • W Asia • 250 kW • ALT. FREQ. TO 11605 kHz; ◻ • Su-Th • W Asia • 250 kW • ALT. FREQ. TO 11605 kHz
	SWEDEN †RADIO SWEDEN, Hörby	W • E Asia • 350 kW; W Sa/Su • E Asia • 350 kW; W M-F • E Asia • 500 kW; W • E Asia • 500 kW; W M-F • Mideast • 350 kW; W • Mideast • 350 kW
	RADIO SWEDEN, Via Madagascar	SE Asia & Australasia • 250 kW • ⇨
	UKRAINE †RADIO UKRAINE INTL, Kharkiv	S • W Europe • 100 kW • ALT. FREQ. TO 9945 kHz
7425	**ALBANIA** †RADIO TIRANA, Shijak	W • E North Am • 100 kW; ◻ • Tu-Su • E North Am • 100 kW
7430	**ALBANIA** †RADIO TIRANA, Shijak	◻ • M-Sa • W Europe • 100 kW; W M-Sa • W Europe • 100 kW; W • W Europe • 100 kW
	GERMANY †DEUTSCHE WELLE, Via Kazakstan	S • SE Asia • 500 kW
	UNITED KINGDOM BBC, Via Dushanbe, Tajikistan	W • S Asia • 200 kW
	USA †TRANS WORLD R, Via Merizo, Guam	S • E Asia • 100 kW
	VOA, Via Iranawila, Sri Lanka	S • S Asia • 250 kW; W • SE Asia • 250 kW
7435	**CLANDESTINE (ASIA)** †"R DEM'CY SHORAYEE"	Tu/Th/F/Su • Mideast & W Asia • ANTI-IRAN GOVT
	USA †FAMILY RADIO, Via Almaty, Kazakstan	W • E Europe & W Asia • 200 kW
	†FAMILY RADIO, Via Taiwan	E Asia • 250 kW
7440	**BELARUS** †RADIO BELARUS, Minsk	S • Europe • 150 kW
	PHILIPPINES †FEBC RADIO INTL, Bocaue	S • E Asia • 100 kW
	SWEDEN †RADIO SWEDEN, Hörby	W Sa/Su • Mideast • 350 kW; W M-F • Mideast & W Asia • 350 kW
	UKRAINE †RADIO UKRAINE INTL, Kharkiv	W • W Europe • 100 kW
	†RADIO UKRAINE INTL, Lviv	◻ • E North Am • 600 kW • ALT. FREQ. TO 5820 kHz
7445	**CHINA (TAIWAN)** R TAIWAN INTL, Paochung	SE Asia • 100 kW; SE Asia • TAIWAN NETWORK 2 • 100 kW; SE Asia • "VOICE OF ASIA" • 100 kW
(con'd)		

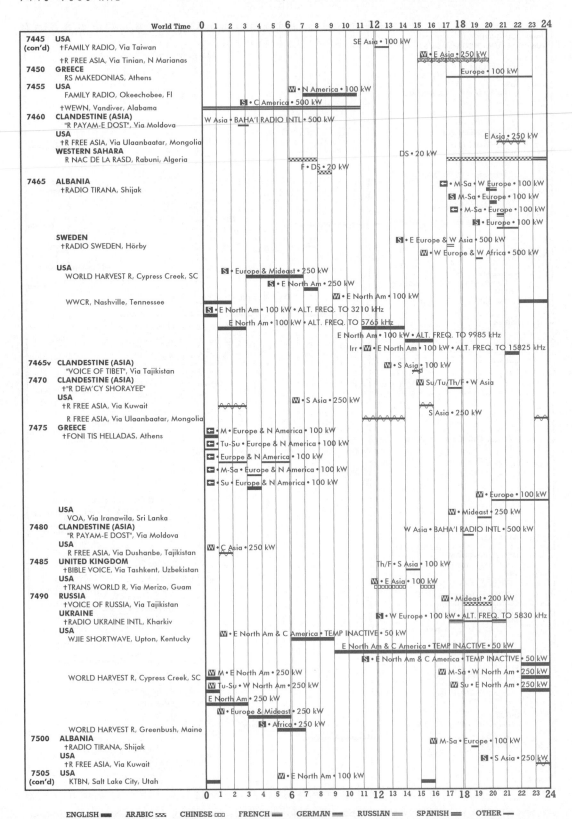

World Time 0 1 2 3 4 5 6 7 8 9 10 11 12 13 14 15 16 17 18 19 20 21 22 23 24

Freq	Station
7445 (con'd)	USA †FAMILY RADIO, Via Taiwan
	†R FREE ASIA, Via Tinian, N Marianas
7450	GREECE RS MAKEDONIAS, Athens
7455	USA FAMILY RADIO, Okeechobee, Fl
	†WEWN, Vandiver, Alabama
7460	CLANDESTINE (ASIA) "R PAYAM-E DOST", Via Moldova
	USA †R FREE ASIA, Via Ulaanbaatar, Mongolia
	WESTERN SAHARA R NAC DE LA RASD, Rabuni, Algeria
7465	ALBANIA †RADIO TIRANA, Shijak
	SWEDEN †RADIO SWEDEN, Hörby
	USA WORLD HARVEST R, Cypress Creek, SC
	WWCR, Nashville, Tennessee
7465v	CLANDESTINE (ASIA) "VOICE OF TIBET", Via Tajikistan
7470	CLANDESTINE (ASIA) †"R DEM'CY SHORAYEE"
	USA †R FREE ASIA, Via Kuwait
	R FREE ASIA, Via Ulaanbaatar, Mongolia
7475	GREECE †FONI TIS HELLADAS, Athens
	USA VOA, Via Iranawila, Sri Lanka
7480	CLANDESTINE (ASIA) "R PAYAM-E DOST", Via Moldova
	USA R FREE ASIA, Via Dushanbe, Tajikistan
7485	UNITED KINGDOM †BIBLE VOICE, Via Tashkent, Uzbekistan
	USA †TRANS WORLD R, Via Merizo, Guam
7490	RUSSIA †VOICE OF RUSSIA, Via Tajikistan
	UKRAINE †RADIO UKRAINE INTL, Kharkiv
	USA WJIE SHORTWAVE, Upton, Kentucky
	WORLD HARVEST R, Cypress Creek, SC
	WORLD HARVEST R, Greenbush, Maine
7500	ALBANIA †RADIO TIRANA, Shijak
	USA †R FREE ASIA, Via Kuwait
7505 (con'd)	USA KTBN, Salt Lake City, Utah

Data labels appearing in chart:
- SE Asia • 100 kW
- W • E Asia • 250 kW
- Europe • 100 kW
- W • N America • 100 kW
- S • C America • 500 kW
- W Asia • BAHA'I RADIO INTL • 500 kW
- E Asia • 250 kW
- DS • 20 kW
- F • DS • 20 kW
- M-Sa • W Europe • 100 kW
- S M-Sa • Europe • 100 kW
- M-Sa • Europe • 100 kW
- S • Europe • 100 kW
- S • E Europe & W Asia • 500 kW
- W • W Europe & W Africa • 500 kW
- S • Europe & Mideast • 250 kW
- S • E North Am • 250 kW
- W • E North Am • 100 kW
- S • E North Am • 100 kW • ALT. FREQ. TO 3210 kHz
- E North Am • 100 kW • ALT. FREQ. TO 5765 kHz
- E North Am • 100 kW • ALT. FREQ. TO 9985 kHz
- Irr • W • E North Am • 100 kW • ALT. FREQ. TO 15825 kHz
- W • S Asia • 100 kW
- W Su/Tu/Th/F • W Asia
- W • S Asia • 250 kW
- S Asia • 250 kW
- M • Europe & N America • 100 kW
- Tu-Su • Europe & N America • 100 kW
- Europe & N America • 100 kW
- M-Sa • Europe & N America • 100 kW
- Su • Europe & N America • 100 kW
- W • Europe • 100 kW
- W • Mideast • 250 kW
- W Asia • BAHA'I RADIO INTL • 500 kW
- W • C Asia • 250 kW
- Th/F • S Asia • 100 kW
- W • E Asia • 100 kW
- W • Mideast • 200 kW
- S • W Europe • 100 kW • ALT. FREQ. TO 5830 kHz
- W • E North Am & C America • TEMP INACTIVE • 50 kW
- E North Am & C America • TEMP INACTIVE • 50 kW
- S • E North Am & C America • TEMP INACTIVE • 50 kW
- W M • E North Am • 250 kW
- W Tu-Su • W North Am • 250 kW
- E North Am • 250 kW
- W • Europe & Mideast • 250 kW
- S • Africa • 250 kW
- W M-Sa • W North Am • 250 kW
- W Su • E North Am • 250 kW
- M-Sa • Europe • 100 kW
- S • S Asia • 250 kW
- W • E North Am • 100 kW

0 1 2 3 4 5 6 7 8 9 10 11 12 13 14 15 16 17 18 19 20 21 22 23 24

ENGLISH ▬   ARABIC ⋙   CHINESE ▫▫▫   FRENCH ▭   GERMAN ▬   RUSSIAN ═   SPANISH ▬   OTHER ▬

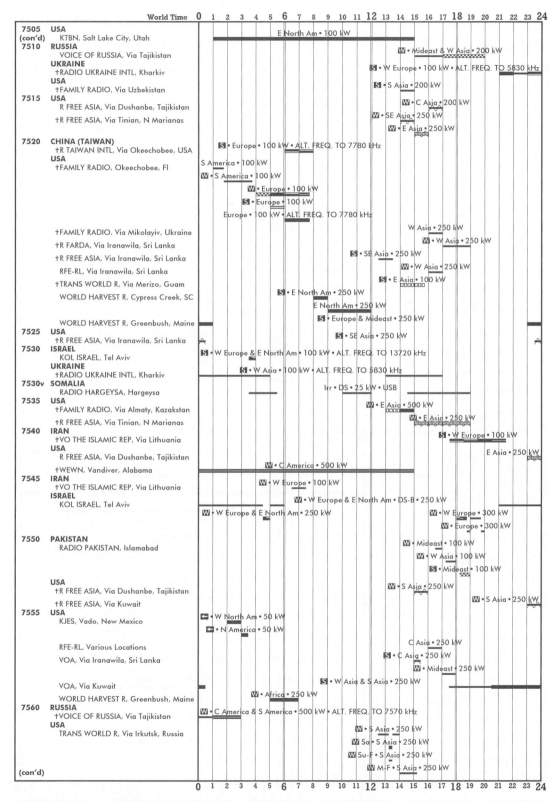

World Time

Freq	Station	Schedule
7505 (con'd)	**USA** KTBN, Salt Lake City, Utah	E North Am • 100 kW
7510	**RUSSIA** VOICE OF RUSSIA, Via Tajikistan	W • Mideast & W Asia • 200 kW
	UKRAINE †RADIO UKRAINE INTL, Kharkiv	S • W Europe • 100 kW • ALT. FREQ. TO 5830 kHz
	USA †FAMILY RADIO, Via Uzbekistan	S • S Asia • 200 kW
7515	**USA** R FREE ASIA, Via Dushanbe, Tajikistan	W • C Asia • 200 kW
	†R FREE ASIA, Via Tinian, N Marianas	W • SE Asia • 250 kW / W • E Asia • 250 kW
7520	**CHINA (TAIWAN)** †R TAIWAN INTL, Via Okeechobee, USA	S • Europe • 100 kW • ALT. FREQ. TO 7780 kHz
	USA †FAMILY RADIO, Okeechobee, Fl	S America • 100 kW / W • S America • 100 kW / W • Europe • 100 kW / S • Europe • 100 kW / Europe • 100 kW • ALT. FREQ. TO 7780 kHz
	†FAMILY RADIO, Via Mikolayiv, Ukraine	W Asia • 250 kW
	†R FARDA, Via Iranawila, Sri Lanka	W • W Asia • 250 kW
	†R FREE ASIA, Via Iranawila, Sri Lanka	S • SE Asia • 250 kW
	RFE-RL, Via Iranawila, Sri Lanka	W • W Asia • 250 kW
	†TRANS WORLD R, Via Merizo, Guam	S • E Asia • 100 kW
	WORLD HARVEST R, Cypress Creek, SC	S • E North Am • 250 kW / E North Am • 250 kW
	WORLD HARVEST R, Greenbush, Maine	S • Europe & Mideast • 250 kW
7525	**USA** †R FREE ASIA, Via Iranawila, Sri Lanka	S • SE Asia • 250 kW
7530	**ISRAEL** KOL ISRAEL, Tel Aviv	S • W Europe & E North Am • 100 kW • ALT. FREQ. TO 13720 kHz
	UKRAINE †RADIO UKRAINE INTL, Kharkiv	S • W Asia • 100 kW • ALT. FREQ. TO 5830 kHz
7530v	**SOMALIA** RADIO HARGEYSA, Hargeysa	Irr • DS • 25 kW • USB
7535	**USA** †FAMILY RADIO, Via Almaty, Kazakstan	W • E Asia • 500 kW
	†R FREE ASIA, Via Tinian, N Marianas	W • E Asia • 250 kW
7540	**IRAN** †VO THE ISLAMIC REP, Via Lithuania	S • W Europe • 100 kW
	USA R FREE ASIA, Via Dushanbe, Tajikistan	E Asia • 250 kW
	†WEWN, Vandiver, Alabama	W • C America • 500 kW
7545	**IRAN** †VO THE ISLAMIC REP, Via Lithuania	W • W Europe • 100 kW
	ISRAEL KOL ISRAEL, Tel Aviv	W • W Europe & E North Am • DS-B • 250 kW / W • W Europe & E North Am • 250 kW / W • W Europe • 300 kW / W • Europe • 300 kW
7550	**PAKISTAN** RADIO PAKISTAN, Islamabad	W • Mideast • 100 kW / W • W Asia • 100 kW / S • Mideast • 100 kW
	USA †R FREE ASIA, Via Dushanbe, Tajikistan	W • S Asia • 250 kW
	†R FREE ASIA, Via Kuwait	W • S Asia • 250 kW
7555	**USA** KJES, Vado, New Mexico	← • W North Am • 50 kW / ← • N America • 50 kW
	RFE-RL, Various Locations	C Asia • 250 kW
	VOA, Via Iranawila, Sri Lanka	S • C Asia • 250 kW / W • Mideast • 250 kW
	VOA, Via Kuwait	S • W Asia & S Asia • 250 kW
	WORLD HARVEST R, Greenbush, Maine	W • Africa • 250 kW
7560	**RUSSIA** †VOICE OF RUSSIA, Via Tajikistan	W • C America & S America • 500 kW • ALT. FREQ. TO 7570 kHz
	USA TRANS WORLD R, Via Irkutsk, Russia	W • S Asia • 250 kW / W Sa • S Asia • 250 kW / W Su-F • S Asia • 250 kW / W M-F • S Asia • 250 kW
(con'd)		

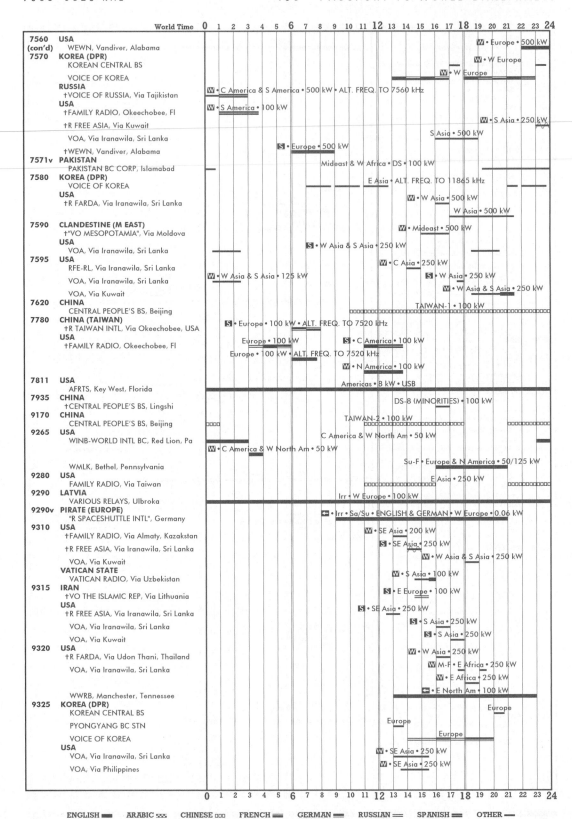

Freq	Country / Station	
7560 (con'd)	**USA** WEWN, Vandiver, Alabama	
7570	**KOREA (DPR)** KOREAN CENTRAL BS	
	VOICE OF KOREA	
	RUSSIA †VOICE OF RUSSIA, Via Tajikistan	
	USA †FAMILY RADIO, Okeechobee, Fl	
	†R FREE ASIA, Via Kuwait	
	VOA, Via Iranawila, Sri Lanka	
	†WEWN, Vandiver, Alabama	
7571v	**PAKISTAN** PAKISTAN BC CORP, Islamabad	
7580	**KOREA (DPR)** VOICE OF KOREA	
	USA †R FARDA, Via Iranawila, Sri Lanka	
7590	**CLANDESTINE (M EAST)** †"VO MESOPOTAMIA", Via Moldova	
	USA VOA, Via Iranawila, Sri Lanka	
7595	**USA** RFE-RL, Via Iranawila, Sri Lanka	
	VOA, Via Iranawila, Sri Lanka	
	VOA, Via Kuwait	
7620	**CHINA** CENTRAL PEOPLE'S BS, Beijing	
7780	**CHINA (TAIWAN)** †R TAIWAN INTL, Via Okeechobee, USA	
	USA †FAMILY RADIO, Okeechobee, Fl	
7811	**USA** AFRTS, Key West, Florida	
7935	**CHINA** †CENTRAL PEOPLE'S BS, Lingshi	
9170	**CHINA** CENTRAL PEOPLE'S BS, Beijing	
9265	**USA** WINB-WORLD INTL BC, Red Lion, Pa	
	WMLK, Bethel, Pennsylvania	
9280	**USA** FAMILY RADIO, Via Taiwan	
9290	**LATVIA** VARIOUS RELAYS, Ulbroka	
9290v	**PIRATE (EUROPE)** "R SPACESHUTTLE INTL", Germany	
9310	**USA** †FAMILY RADIO, Via Almaty, Kazakstan	
	†R FREE ASIA, Via Iranawila, Sri Lanka	
	VOA, Via Kuwait	
	VATICAN STATE VATICAN RADIO, Via Uzbekistan	
9315	**IRAN** †VO THE ISLAMIC REP, Via Lithuania	
	USA †R FREE ASIA, Via Iranawila, Sri Lanka	
	VOA, Via Iranawila, Sri Lanka	
	VOA, Via Kuwait	
9320	**USA** †R FARDA, Via Udon Thani, Thailand	
	VOA, Via Iranawila, Sri Lanka	
	WWRB, Manchester, Tennessee	
9325	**KOREA (DPR)** KOREAN CENTRAL BS	
	PYONGYANG BC STN	
	VOICE OF KOREA	
	USA VOA, Via Iranawila, Sri Lanka	
	VOA, Via Philippines	

ENGLISH ▬   ARABIC ⁓⁓⁓   CHINESE ▫▫▫   FRENCH ▬   GERMAN ▬   RUSSIAN ═   SPANISH ▬   OTHER ▬

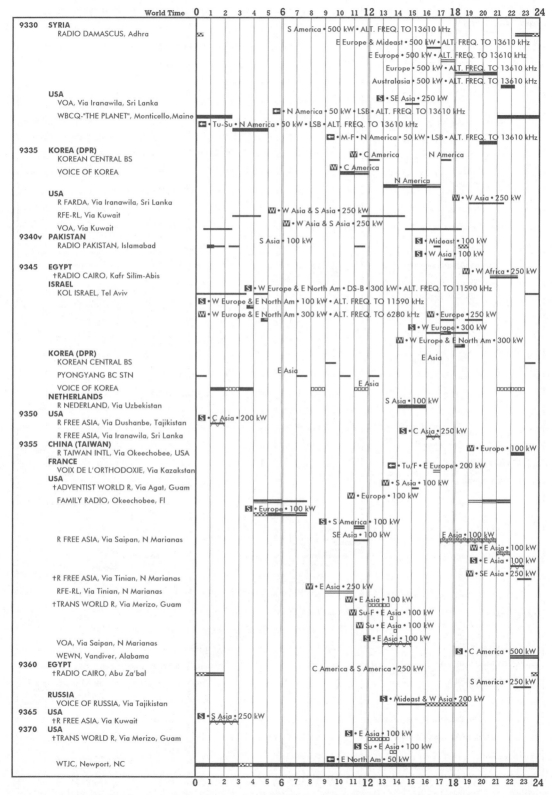

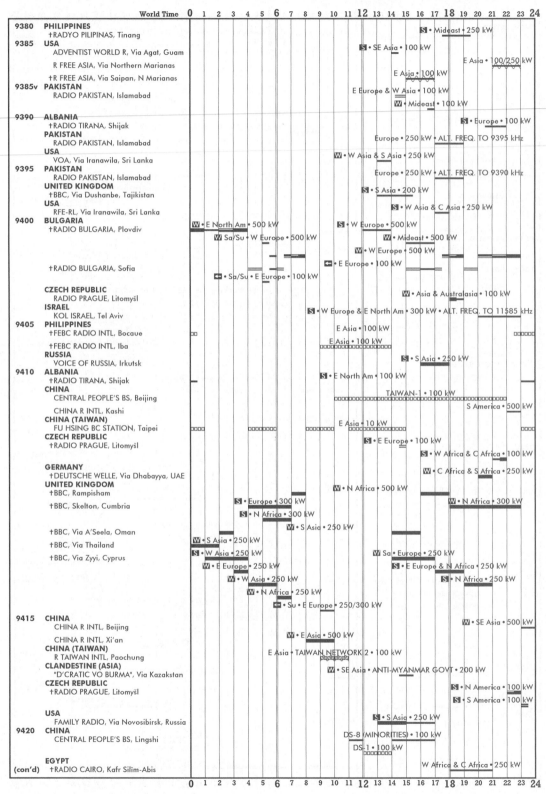

World Time 0 1 2 3 4 5 6 7 8 9 10 11 12 13 14 15 16 17 18 19 20 21 22 23 24

9380 PHILIPPINES
†RADYO PILIPINAS, Tinang — S • Mideast • 250 kW

9385 USA
ADVENTIST WORLD R, Via Agat, Guam — S • SE Asia • 100 kW
R FREE ASIA, Via Northern Marianas — E Asia • 100/250 kW
†R FREE ASIA, Via Saipan, N Marianas — E Asia • 100 kW

9385v PAKISTAN
RADIO PAKISTAN, Islamabad — E Europe & W Asia • 100 kW
W • Mideast • 100 kW

9390 ALBANIA
†RADIO TIRANA, Shijak — S • Europe • 100 kW
PAKISTAN
RADIO PAKISTAN, Islamabad — Europe • 250 kW • ALT. FREQ. TO 9395 kHz
USA
VOA, Via Iranawila, Sri Lanka — W • W Asia & S Asia • 250 kW

9395 PAKISTAN
RADIO PAKISTAN, Islamabad — Europe • 250 kW • ALT. FREQ. TO 9390 kHz
UNITED KINGDOM
†BBC, Via Dushanbe, Tajikistan — S • S Asia • 200 kW
USA
RFE-RL, Via Iranawila, Sri Lanka — S • W Asia & C Asia • 250 kW

9400 BULGARIA
†RADIO BULGARIA, Plovdiv — W • E North Am • 500 kW / S • W Europe • 500 kW
W Sa/Su • W Europe • 500 kW / W • Mideast • 500 kW
W • W Europe • 500 kW
†RADIO BULGARIA, Sofia — E Europe • 100 kW
Sa/Su • E Europe • 100 kW

CZECH REPUBLIC
RADIO PRAGUE, Litomyšl — W • Asia & Australasia • 100 kW
ISRAEL
KOL ISRAEL, Tel Aviv — S • W Europe & E North Am • 300 kW • ALT. FREQ. TO 11585 kHz

9405 PHILIPPINES
†FEBC RADIO INTL, Bocaue — E Asia • 100 kW
†FEBC RADIO INTL, Iba — E Asia • 100 kW
RUSSIA
VOICE OF RUSSIA, Irkutsk — S • S Asia • 250 kW

9410 ALBANIA
†RADIO TIRANA, Shijak — S • E North Am • 100 kW
CHINA
CENTRAL PEOPLE'S BS, Beijing — TAIWAN-1 • 100 kW
CHINA R INTL, Kashi — S America • 500 kW
CHINA (TAIWAN)
FU HSING BC STATION, Taipei — E Asia • 10 kW
CZECH REPUBLIC
†RADIO PRAGUE, Litomyšl — S • E Europe • 100 kW
S • W Africa & C Africa • 100 kW

GERMANY
†DEUTSCHE WELLE, Via Dhabayya, UAE — W • C Africa & S Africa • 250 kW
UNITED KINGDOM
†BBC, Rampisham — W • N Africa • 500 kW
†BBC, Skelton, Cumbria — S • Europe • 300 kW / W • N Africa • 300 kW
S • N Africa • 300 kW
†BBC, Via A'Seela, Oman — W • S Asia • 250 kW
†BBC, Via Thailand — W • S Asia • 250 kW
†BBC, Via Zyyi, Cyprus — S • W Asia • 250 kW / W Sa • Europe • 250 kW
W • E Europe • 250 kW / S • E Europe & N Africa • 250 kW
W • W Asia • 250 kW / S • N Africa • 250 kW
W • N Africa • 250 kW
Su • E Europe • 250/300 kW

9415 CHINA
CHINA R INTL, Beijing — W • SE Asia • 500 kW
CHINA R INTL, Xi'an — W • E Asia • 500 kW
CHINA (TAIWAN)
R TAIWAN INTL, Paochung — E Asia • TAIWAN NETWORK 2 • 100 kW
CLANDESTINE (ASIA)
"D'CRATIC VO BURMA", Via Kazakstan — W • SE Asia • ANTI-MYANMAR GOVT • 200 kW
CZECH REPUBLIC
†RADIO PRAGUE, Litomyšl — S • N America • 100 kW
S • S America • 100 kW
USA
FAMILY RADIO, Via Novosibirsk, Russia — S • S Asia • 250 kW

9420 CHINA
CENTRAL PEOPLE'S BS, Lingshi — DS-8 (MINORITIES) • 100 kW
DS-1 • 100 kW

EGYPT
(con'd) †RADIO CAIRO, Kafr Silim-Abis — W Africa & C Africa • 250 kW

0 1 2 3 4 5 6 7 8 9 10 11 12 13 14 15 16 17 18 19 20 21 22 23 24

ENGLISH ▬   ARABIC ▨   CHINESE ▦   FRENCH ▬   GERMAN ▬   RUSSIAN ═   SPANISH ▬   OTHER ─

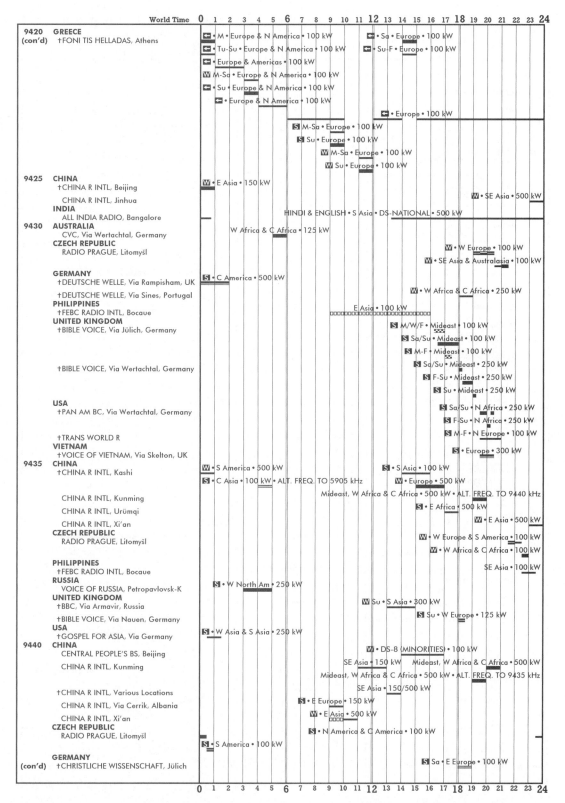

World Time 0 1 2 3 4 5 6 7 8 9 10 11 12 13 14 15 16 17 18 19 20 21 22 23 24

9420 GREECE
(con'd) †FONI TIS HELLADAS, Athens

- M • Europe & N America • 100 kW
- Sa • Europe • 100 kW
- Tu-Su • Europe & N America • 100 kW
- Su-F • Europe • 100 kW
- Europe & Americas • 100 kW
- W M-Sa • Europe & N America • 100 kW
- Su • Europe & N America • 100 kW
- Europe & N America • 100 kW
- Europe • 100 kW
- S M-Sa • Europe • 100 kW
- S Su • Europe • 100 kW
- W M-Sa • Europe • 100 kW
- W Su • Europe • 100 kW

9425 CHINA
†CHINA R INTL, Beijing — W • E Asia • 150 kW
CHINA R INTL, Jinhua — W • SE Asia • 500 kW
INDIA
ALL INDIA RADIO, Bangalore — HINDI & ENGLISH • S Asia • DS-NATIONAL • 500 kW

9430 AUSTRALIA
CVC, Via Wertachtal, Germany — W Africa & C Africa • 125 kW
CZECH REPUBLIC
RADIO PRAGUE, Litomyšl — W • W Europe • 100 kW / W • SE Asia & Australasia • 100 kW
GERMANY
†DEUTSCHE WELLE, Via Rampisham, UK — S • C America • 500 kW
†DEUTSCHE WELLE, Via Sines, Portugal — W • W Africa & C Africa • 250 kW
PHILIPPINES
†FEBC RADIO INTL, Bocaue — E Asia • 100 kW
UNITED KINGDOM
†BIBLE VOICE, Via Jülich, Germany — S M/W/F • Mideast • 100 kW / S Sa/Su • Mideast • 100 kW / S M-F • Mideast • 100 kW
†BIBLE VOICE, Via Wertachtal, Germany — S Sa/Su • Mideast • 250 kW / S F-Su • Mideast • 250 kW / S Su • Mideast • 250 kW
USA
†PAN AM BC, Via Wertachtal, Germany — S Sa/Su • N Africa • 250 kW / S F-Su • N Africa • 250 kW
†TRANS WORLD R — S M-F • N Europe • 100 kW
VIETNAM
†VOICE OF VIETNAM, Via Skelton, UK — S • Europe • 300 kW

9435 CHINA
†CHINA R INTL, Kashi — W • S America • 500 kW / S • S Asia • 100 kW
— S • C Asia • 100 kW • ALT. FREQ. TO 5905 kHz / W • Europe • 500 kW
CHINA R INTL, Kunming — Mideast, W Africa & C Africa • 500 kW • ALT. FREQ. TO 9440 kHz
CHINA R INTL, Urümqi — S • E Africa • 500 kW
CHINA R INTL, Xi'an — W • E Asia • 500 kW
CZECH REPUBLIC
RADIO PRAGUE, Litomyšl — W • W Europe & S America • 100 kW / W • W Africa & C Africa • 100 kW
PHILIPPINES
†FEBC RADIO INTL, Bocaue — SE Asia • 100 kW
RUSSIA
VOICE OF RUSSIA, Petropavlovsk-K — S • W North Am • 250 kW
UNITED KINGDOM
†BBC, Via Armavir, Russia — W Su • S Asia • 300 kW
†BIBLE VOICE, Via Nauen, Germany — S Su • W Europe • 125 kW
USA
†GOSPEL FOR ASIA, Via Germany — S • W Asia & S Asia • 250 kW

9440 CHINA
CENTRAL PEOPLE'S BS, Beijing — W • DS-8 (MINORITIES) • 100 kW
CHINA R INTL, Kunming — SE Asia • 150 kW / Mideast, W Africa & C Africa • 500 kW
— Mideast, W Africa & C Africa • 500 kW • ALT. FREQ. TO 9435 kHz
†CHINA R INTL, Various Locations — SE Asia • 150/500 kW
CHINA R INTL, Via Cerrik, Albania — S • E Europe • 150 kW
CHINA R INTL, Xi'an — W • E Asia • 500 kW
CZECH REPUBLIC
RADIO PRAGUE, Litomyšl — S • N America & C America • 100 kW
— S • S America • 100 kW
GERMANY
(con'd) †CHRISTLICHE WISSENSCHAFT, Jülich — S Sa • E Europe • 100 kW

0 1 2 3 4 5 6 7 8 9 10 11 12 13 14 15 16 17 18 19 20 21 22 23 24

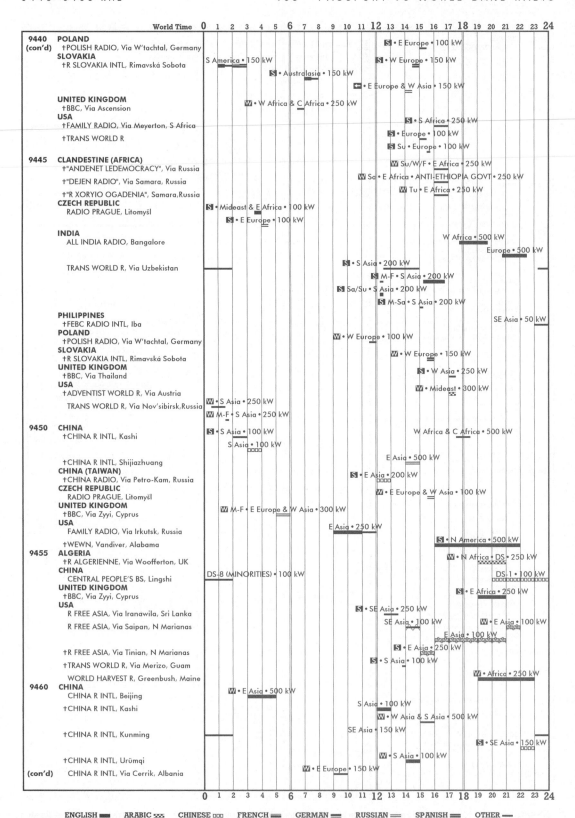

World Time 0 1 2 3 4 5 6 7 8 9 10 11 12 13 14 15 16 17 18 19 20 21 22 23 24

9440 POLAND
(con'd) †POLISH RADIO, Via W'tachtal, Germany · S · E Europe · 100 kW
SLOVAKIA
  †R SLOVAKIA INTL, Rimavská Sobota · S America · 150 kW · S · W Europe · 150 kW
  S · Australasia · 150 kW
  · E Europe & W Asia · 150 kW
UNITED KINGDOM
  †BBC, Via Ascension · W · W Africa & C Africa · 250 kW
USA
  †FAMILY RADIO, Via Meyerton, S Africa · S · S Africa · 250 kW
  †TRANS WORLD R · S · Europe · 100 kW
  · Su · Europe · 100 kW

9445 CLANDESTINE (AFRICA)
  †"ANDENET LEDEMOCRACY", Via Russia · W Su/W/F · E Africa · 250 kW
  †"DEJEN RADIO", Via Samara, Russia · W Sa · E Africa · ANTI-ETHIOPIA GOVT · 250 kW
  †"R XORYIO OGADENIA", Samara, Russia · W Tu · E Africa · 250 kW
CZECH REPUBLIC
  RADIO PRAGUE, Litomyšl · S · Mideast & E Africa · 100 kW
  · S · E Europe · 100 kW
INDIA
  ALL INDIA RADIO, Bangalore · W Africa · 500 kW
  · Europe · 500 kW
  TRANS WORLD R, Via Uzbekistan · S · S Asia · 200 kW
  · S M-F · S Asia · 200 kW
  · S Sa/Su · S Asia · 200 kW
  · S M-Sa · S Asia · 200 kW
PHILIPPINES
  †FEBC RADIO INTL, Iba · SE Asia · 50 kW
POLAND
  †POLISH RADIO, Via W'tachtal, Germany · W · W Europe · 100 kW
SLOVAKIA
  †R SLOVAKIA INTL, Rimavská Sobota · W · W Europe · 150 kW
UNITED KINGDOM
  †BBC, Via Thailand · S · W Asia · 250 kW
USA
  †ADVENTIST WORLD R, Via Austria · W · Mideast · 300 kW
  TRANS WORLD R, Via Nov'sibirsk, Russia · W · S Asia · 250 kW
  · W M-F · S Asia · 250 kW

9450 CHINA
  †CHINA R INTL, Kashi · S · S Asia · 100 kW
  · S Asia · 100 kW
  · W Africa & C Africa · 500 kW
  †CHINA R INTL, Shijiazhuang · E Asia · 500 kW
CHINA (TAIWAN)
  †CHINA RADIO, Via Petro-Kam, Russia · S · E Asia · 200 kW
CZECH REPUBLIC
  RADIO PRAGUE, Litomyšl · W · E Europe & W Asia · 100 kW
UNITED KINGDOM
  †BBC, Via Zyyi, Cyprus · W M-F · E Europe & W Asia · 300 kW
USA
  FAMILY RADIO, Via Irkutsk, Russia · E Asia · 250 kW
  †WEWN, Vandiver, Alabama · S · N America · 500 kW

9455 ALGERIA
  †R ALGERIENNE, Via Woofferton, UK · W · N Africa · DS · 250 kW
CHINA
  CENTRAL PEOPLE'S BS, Lingshi · DS-8 (MINORITIES) · 100 kW · DS-1 · 100 kW
UNITED KINGDOM
  †BBC, Via Zyyi, Cyprus · S · E Africa · 250 kW
USA
  R FREE ASIA, Via Iranawila, Sri Lanka · S · SE Asia · 250 kW
  R FREE ASIA, Via Saipan, N Marianas · SE Asia · 100 kW · W · E Asia · 100 kW
  · E Asia · 100 kW
  †R FREE ASIA, Via Tinian, N Marianas · S · E Asia · 250 kW
  †TRANS WORLD R, Via Merizo, Guam · S · S Asia · 100 kW
  WORLD HARVEST R, Greenbush, Maine · W · Africa · 250 kW

9460 CHINA
  CHINA R INTL, Beijing · W · E Asia · 500 kW
  †CHINA R INTL, Kashi · S Asia · 100 kW
  · W · W Asia & S Asia · 500 kW
  †CHINA R INTL, Kunming · SE Asia · 150 kW
  · S · SE Asia · 150 kW
  †CHINA R INTL, Urümqi · W · S Asia · 100 kW
(con'd) CHINA R INTL, Via Cerrik, Albania · W · E Europe · 150 kW

0 1 2 3 4 5 6 7 8 9 10 11 12 13 14 15 16 17 18 19 20 21 22 23 24

ENGLISH ▬▬   ARABIC ⁓⁓⁓   CHINESE □□□   FRENCH ▬▬   GERMAN ▬▬   RUSSIAN ══   SPANISH ══   OTHER ▬▬

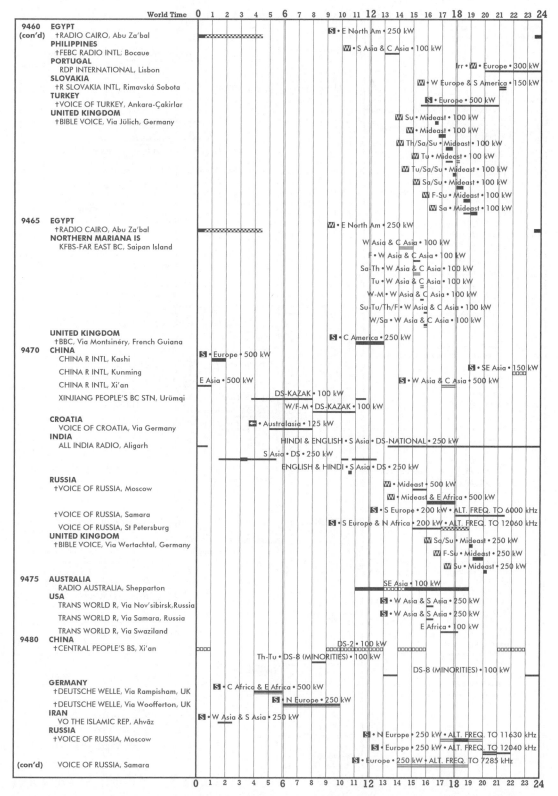

| | World Time | 0 | 1 | 2 | 3 | 4 | 5 | 6 | 7 | 8 | 9 | 10 | 11 | 12 | 13 | 14 | 15 | 16 | 17 | 18 | 19 | 20 | 21 | 22 | 23 | 24 |

9460 EGYPT
(con'd) †RADIO CAIRO, Abu Za'bal — S • E North Am • 250 kW
PHILIPPINES
  †FEBC RADIO INTL, Bocaue — W • S Asia & C Asia • 100 kW
PORTUGAL
  RDP INTERNATIONAL, Lisbon — Irr • W • Europe • 300 kW
SLOVAKIA
  †R SLOVAKIA INTL, Rimavská Sobota — W • W Europe & S America • 150 kW
TURKEY
  †VOICE OF TURKEY, Ankara-Çakirlar — S • Europe • 500 kW
UNITED KINGDOM
  †BIBLE VOICE, Via Jülich, Germany
    W • Su • Mideast • 100 kW
    W • Mideast • 100 kW
    W • Th/Sa/Su • Mideast • 100 kW
    W • Tu • Mideast • 100 kW
    W • Tu/Sa/Su • Mideast • 100 kW
    W • Sa/Su • Mideast • 100 kW
    W • F-Su • Mideast • 100 kW
    W • Sa • Mideast • 100 kW

9465 EGYPT
  †RADIO CAIRO, Abu Za'bal — W • E North Am • 250 kW
NORTHERN MARIANA IS
  KFBS-FAR EAST BC, Saipan Island
    W Asia & C Asia • 100 kW
    F • W Asia & C Asia • 100 kW
    Sa-Th • W Asia & C Asia • 100 kW
    Tu • W Asia & C Asia • 100 kW
    W-M • W Asia & C Asia • 100 kW
    Su-Tu/Th/F • W Asia & C Asia • 100 kW
    W/Sa • W Asia & C Asia • 100 kW

UNITED KINGDOM
  †BBC, Via Montsinéry, French Guiana — S • C America • 250 kW
9470 CHINA
  CHINA R INTL, Kashi — S • Europe • 500 kW
  CHINA R INTL, Kunming — S • SE Asia • 150 kW
  CHINA R INTL, Xi'an — E Asia • 500 kW — S • W Asia & C Asia • 500 kW
  XINJIANG PEOPLE'S BC STN, Urümqi — DS-KAZAK • 100 kW
    W/F-M • DS-KAZAK • 100 kW
CROATIA
  VOICE OF CROATIA, Via Germany — • Australasia • 125 kW
INDIA
  ALL INDIA RADIO, Aligarh
    HINDI & ENGLISH • S Asia • DS-NATIONAL • 250 kW
    S Asia • DS • 250 kW
    ENGLISH & HINDI • S Asia • DS • 250 kW

RUSSIA
  †VOICE OF RUSSIA, Moscow
    W • Mideast • 500 kW
    W • Mideast & E Africa • 500 kW
  †VOICE OF RUSSIA, Samara — S • S Europe • 200 kW • ALT. FREQ. TO 6000 kHz
  VOICE OF RUSSIA, St Petersburg — S • S Europe & N Africa • 200 kW • ALT. FREQ. TO 12060 kHz
UNITED KINGDOM
  †BIBLE VOICE, Via Wertachtal, Germany
    W • Sa/Su • Mideast • 250 kW
    W • F-Su • Mideast • 250 kW
    W • Su • Mideast • 250 kW

9475 AUSTRALIA
  RADIO AUSTRALIA, Shepparton — SE Asia • 100 kW
USA
  TRANS WORLD R, Via Nov'sibirsk, Russia — S • W Asia & S Asia • 250 kW
  TRANS WORLD R, Via Samara, Russia — S • W Asia & S Asia • 250 kW
  TRANS WORLD R, Via Swaziland — E Africa • 100 kW
9480 CHINA
  †CENTRAL PEOPLE'S BS, Xi'an — DS-2 • 100 kW
    Th-Tu • DS-8 (MINORITIES) • 100 kW
    DS-8 (MINORITIES) • 100 kW

GERMANY
  †DEUTSCHE WELLE, Via Rampisham, UK — S • C Africa & E Africa • 500 kW
  †DEUTSCHE WELLE, Via Woofferton, UK — S • N Europe • 250 kW
IRAN
  VO THE ISLAMIC REP, Ahvāz — S • W Asia & S Asia • 250 kW
RUSSIA
  †VOICE OF RUSSIA, Moscow — S • N Europe • 250 kW • ALT. FREQ. TO 11630 kHz
    S • Europe • 250 kW • ALT. FREQ. TO 12040 kHz
(con'd) VOICE OF RUSSIA, Samara — S • Europe • 250 kW • ALT. FREQ. TO 7285 kHz

| | 0 | 1 | 2 | 3 | 4 | 5 | 6 | 7 | 8 | 9 | 10 | 11 | 12 | 13 | 14 | 15 | 16 | 17 | 18 | 19 | 20 | 21 | 22 | 23 | 24 |

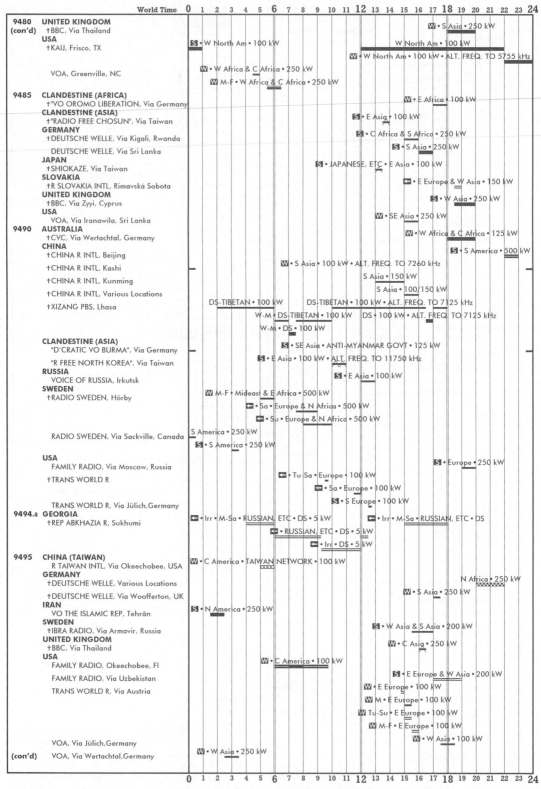

World Time 0 1 2 3 4 5 6 7 8 9 10 11 12 13 14 15 16 17 18 19 20 21 22 23 24

9480 UNITED KINGDOM
(con'd) †BBC, Via Thailand
USA
†KAIJ, Frisco, TX

VOA, Greenville, NC

9485 CLANDESTINE (AFRICA)
†"VO OROMO LIBERATION, Via Germany
CLANDESTINE (ASIA)
†"RADIO FREE CHOSUN", Via Taiwan
GERMANY
†DEUTSCHE WELLE, Via Kigali, Rwanda

DEUTSCHE WELLE, Via Sri Lanka
JAPAN
†SHIOKAZE, Via Taiwan
SLOVAKIA
†R SLOVAKIA INTL, Rimavská Sobota
UNITED KINGDOM
†BBC, Via Zyyi, Cyprus
USA
VOA, Via Iranawila, Sri Lanka
9490 AUSTRALIA
†CVC, Via Wertachtal, Germany
CHINA
†CHINA R INTL, Beijing

†CHINA R INTL, Kashi

†CHINA R INTL, Kunming

†CHINA R INTL, Various Locations

†XIZANG PBS, Lhasa

CLANDESTINE (ASIA)
"D'CRATIC VO BURMA", Via Germany

"R FREE NORTH KOREA", Via Taiwan
RUSSIA
VOICE OF RUSSIA, Irkutsk
SWEDEN
†RADIO SWEDEN, Hörby

RADIO SWEDEN, Via Sackville, Canada

USA
FAMILY RADIO, Via Moscow, Russia

†TRANS WORLD R

TRANS WORLD R, Via Jülich,Germany
9494.8 GEORGIA
†REP ABKHAZIA R, Sukhumi

9495 CHINA (TAIWAN)
R TAIWAN INTL, Via Okeechobee, USA
GERMANY
†DEUTSCHE WELLE, Various Locations

†DEUTSCHE WELLE, Via Woofferton, UK
IRAN
VO THE ISLAMIC REP, Tehrān
SWEDEN
†IBRA RADIO, Via Armavir, Russia
UNITED KINGDOM
†BBC, Via Thailand
USA
FAMILY RADIO, Okeechobee, Fl

FAMILY RADIO, Via Uzbekistan

TRANS WORLD R, Via Austria

VOA, Via Jülich,Germany
(con'd) VOA, Via Wertachtal,Germany

0 1 2 3 4 5 6 7 8 9 10 11 12 13 14 15 16 17 18 19 20 21 22 23 24

ENGLISH ▬ ARABIC ▨ CHINESE ▫▫▫ FRENCH ▬ GERMAN ▬ RUSSIAN ═ SPANISH ▬ OTHER ▬

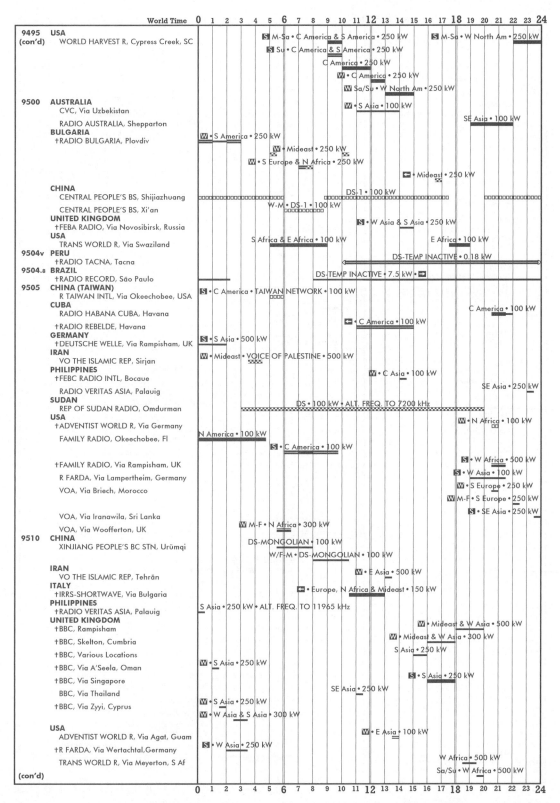

World Time	0 1 2 3 4 5 6 7 8 9 10 11 12 13 14 15 16 17 18 19 20 21 22 23 24
9495 USA (con'd) WORLD HARVEST R, Cypress Creek, SC	S • M-Sa • C America & S America • 250 kW S • M-Sa • W North Am • 250 kW
	S • Su • C America & S America • 250 kW
	C America • 250 kW
	W • C America • 250 kW
	W • Sa/Su • W North Am • 250 kW
9500 AUSTRALIA CVC, Via Uzbekistan	W • S Asia • 100 kW
RADIO AUSTRALIA, Shepparton	SE Asia • 100 kW
BULGARIA †RADIO BULGARIA, Plovdiv	W • S America • 250 kW
	W • Mideast • 250 kW
	W • S Europe & N Africa • 250 kW
	⇦ • Mideast • 250 kW
CHINA CENTRAL PEOPLE'S BS, Shijiazhuang	DS-1 • 100 kW
CENTRAL PEOPLE'S BS, Xi'an	W-M • DS-1 • 100 kW
UNITED KINGDOM †FEBA RADIO, Via Novosibirsk, Russia	S • W Asia & S Asia • 250 kW
USA TRANS WORLD R, Via Swaziland	S Africa & E Africa • 100 kW E Africa • 100 kW
9504v PERU †RADIO TACNA, Tacna	DS-TEMP INACTIVE • 0.18 kW
9504.8 BRAZIL †RADIO RECORD, São Paulo	DS-TEMP INACTIVE • 7.5 kW • ⇨
9505 CHINA (TAIWAN) R TAIWAN INTL, Via Okeechobee, USA	S • C America • TAIWAN NETWORK • 100 kW
CUBA RADIO HABANA CUBA, Havana	C America • 100 kW
†RADIO REBELDE, Havana	⇦ • C America • 100 kW
GERMANY †DEUTSCHE WELLE, Via Rampisham, UK	S • S Asia • 500 kW
IRAN VO THE ISLAMIC REP, Sirjan	W • Mideast • VOICE OF PALESTINE • 500 kW
PHILIPPINES †FEBC RADIO INTL, Bocaue	W • C Asia • 100 kW
RADIO VERITAS ASIA, Palauig	SE Asia • 250 kW
SUDAN REP OF SUDAN RADIO, Omdurman	DS • 100 kW • ALT. FREQ. TO 7200 kHz
USA †ADVENTIST WORLD R, Via Germany	W • N Africa • 100 kW
FAMILY RADIO, Okeechobee, Fl	N America • 100 kW
	S • C America • 100 kW
†FAMILY RADIO, Via Rampisham, UK	S • W Africa • 500 kW
R FARDA, Via Lampertheim, Germany	S • W Asia • 100 kW
VOA, Via Briech, Morocco	W • S Europe • 250 kW
	W • M-F • S Europe • 250 kW
VOA, Via Iranawila, Sri Lanka	S • SE Asia • 250 kW
VOA, Via Woofferton, UK	W • M-F • N Africa • 300 kW
9510 CHINA XINJIANG PEOPLE'S BC STN, Urümqi	DS-MONGOLIAN • 100 kW
	W/F-M • DS-MONGOLIAN • 100 kW
IRAN VO THE ISLAMIC REP, Tehrān	W • E Asia • 500 kW
ITALY †IRRS-SHORTWAVE, Via Bulgaria	⇦ • Europe, N Africa & Mideast • 150 kW
PHILIPPINES †RADIO VERITAS ASIA, Palauig	S Asia • 250 kW • ALT. FREQ. TO 11965 kHz
UNITED KINGDOM †BBC, Rampisham	W • Mideast & W Asia • 500 kW
†BBC, Skelton, Cumbria	W • Mideast & W Asia • 300 kW
†BBC, Various Locations	S Asia • 250 kW
†BBC, Via A'Seela, Oman	W • S Asia • 250 kW
†BBC, Via Singapore	S • S Asia • 250 kW
BBC, Via Thailand	SE Asia • 250 kW
†BBC, Via Zyyi, Cyprus	W • S Asia • 250 kW
	W • W Asia & S Asia • 300 kW
USA ADVENTIST WORLD R, Via Agat, Guam	W • E Asia • 100 kW
†R FARDA, Via Wertachtal, Germany	S • W Asia • 250 kW
TRANS WORLD R, Via Meyerton, S Af	W Africa • 500 kW
(con'd)	Sa/Su • W Africa • 500 kW

	0 1 2 3 4 5 6 7 8 9 10 11 12 13 14 15 16 17 18 19 20 21 22 23 24

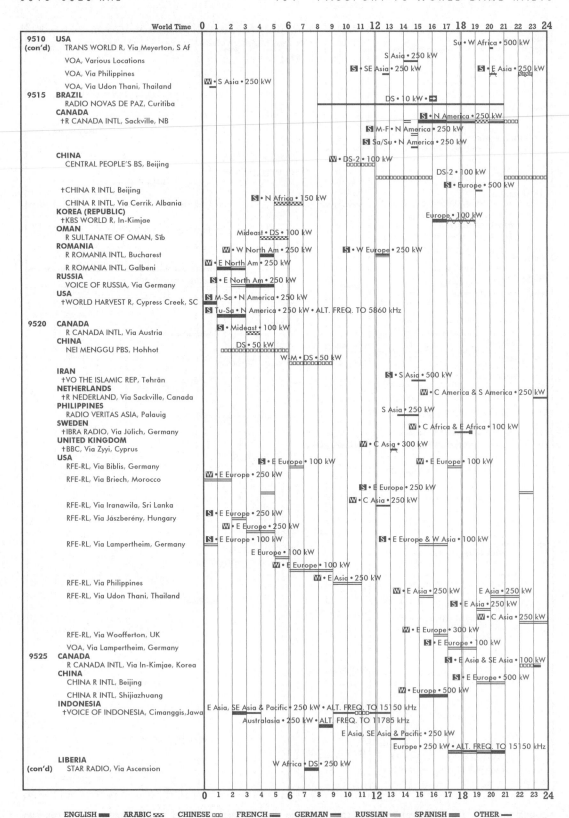

World Time 0 1 2 3 4 5 6 7 8 9 10 11 12 13 14 15 16 17 18 19 20 21 22 23 24

9510 USA
(con'd)　TRANS WORLD R, Via Meyerton, S Af
　　　VOA, Various Locations
　　　VOA, Via Philippines
　　　VOA, Via Udon Thani, Thailand

9515 BRAZIL
　　　RADIO NOVAS DE PAZ, Curitiba
CANADA
　　　†R CANADA INTL, Sackville, NB

CHINA
　　　CENTRAL PEOPLE'S BS, Beijing

　　　†CHINA R INTL, Beijing
　　　CHINA R INTL, Via Cerrik, Albania
KOREA (REPUBLIC)
　　　†KBS WORLD R, In-Kimjae
OMAN
　　　R SULTANATE OF OMAN, Sīb
ROMANIA
　　　R ROMANIA INTL, Bucharest
　　　R ROMANIA INTL, Galbeni
RUSSIA
　　　VOICE OF RUSSIA, Via Germany
USA
　　　†WORLD HARVEST R, Cypress Creek, SC

9520 CANADA
　　　R CANADA INTL, Via Austria
CHINA
　　　NEI MENGGU PBS, Hohhot

IRAN
　　　†VO THE ISLAMIC REP, Tehrān
NETHERLANDS
　　　†R NEDERLAND, Via Sackville, Canada
PHILIPPINES
　　　RADIO VERITAS ASIA, Palauig
SWEDEN
　　　†IBRA RADIO, Via Jülich, Germany
UNITED KINGDOM
　　　†BBC, Via Zyyi, Cyprus
USA
　　　RFE-RL, Via Biblis, Germany
　　　RFE-RL, Via Briech, Morocco

　　　RFE-RL, Via Iranawila, Sri Lanka
　　　RFE-RL, Via Jászberény, Hungary

　　　RFE-RL, Via Lampertheim, Germany

　　　RFE-RL, Via Philippines
　　　RFE-RL, Via Udon Thani, Thailand

　　　RFE-RL, Via Woofferton, UK
　　　VOA, Via Lampertheim, Germany
9525 CANADA
　　　R CANADA INTL, Via In-Kimjae, Korea
CHINA
　　　CHINA R INTL, Beijing
　　　CHINA R INTL, Shijiazhuang
INDONESIA
　　　†VOICE OF INDONESIA, Cimanggis, Jawa

LIBERIA
(con'd)　STAR RADIO, Via Ascension

Data labels within the chart:
- Su • W Africa • 500 kW
- S Asia • 250 kW
- S • SE Asia • 250 kW
- S • E Asia • 250 kW
- W • S Asia • 250 kW
- DS • 10 kW
- S • N America • 250 kW
- S • M-F • N America • 250 kW
- S • Sa/Su • N America • 250 kW
- W • DS-2 • 100 kW
- DS-2 • 100 kW
- S • Europe • 500 kW
- S • N Africa • 150 kW
- Europe • 100 kW
- Mideast • DS • 100 kW
- W • W North Am • 250 kW
- S • W Europe • 250 kW
- W • E North Am • 250 kW
- S • E North Am • 250 kW
- S • M-Sa • N America • 250 kW
- S • Tu-Sa • N America • 250 kW • ALT. FREQ. TO 5860 kHz
- S • Mideast • 100 kW
- DS • 50 kW
- W • M • DS • 50 kW
- S • S Asia • 500 kW
- W • C America & S America • 250 kW
- S Asia • 250 kW
- W • C Africa & E Africa • 100 kW
- W • C Asia • 300 kW
- S • E Europe • 100 kW
- W • E Europe • 100 kW
- W • E Europe • 250 kW
- S • E Europe • 250 kW
- W • C Asia • 250 kW
- S • E Europe • 250 kW
- W • E Europe • 250 kW
- S • E Europe • 100 kW
- S • E Europe & W Asia • 100 kW
- E Europe • 100 kW
- W • E Europe • 100 kW
- W • E Asia • 250 kW
- W • E Asia • 250 kW
- E Asia • 250 kW
- S • E Asia • 250 kW
- W • C Asia • 250 kW
- W • E Europe • 300 kW
- S • E Europe • 100 kW
- S • E Asia & SE Asia • 100 kW
- S • E Europe • 500 kW
- W • Europe • 500 kW
- E Asia, SE Asia & Pacific • 250 kW • ALT. FREQ. TO 15150 kHz
- Australasia • 250 kW • ALT. FREQ. TO 11785 kHz
- E Asia, SE Asia & Pacific • 250 kW
- Europe • 250 kW • ALT. FREQ. TO 15150 kHz
- W Africa • DS • 250 kW

0 1 2 3 4 5 6 7 8 9 10 11 12 13 14 15 16 17 18 19 20 21 22 23 24

ENGLISH ▬　ARABIC ▨　CHINESE ▭▭▭　FRENCH ▬▬　GERMAN ▬▬　RUSSIAN ══　SPANISH ▬▬　OTHER ——

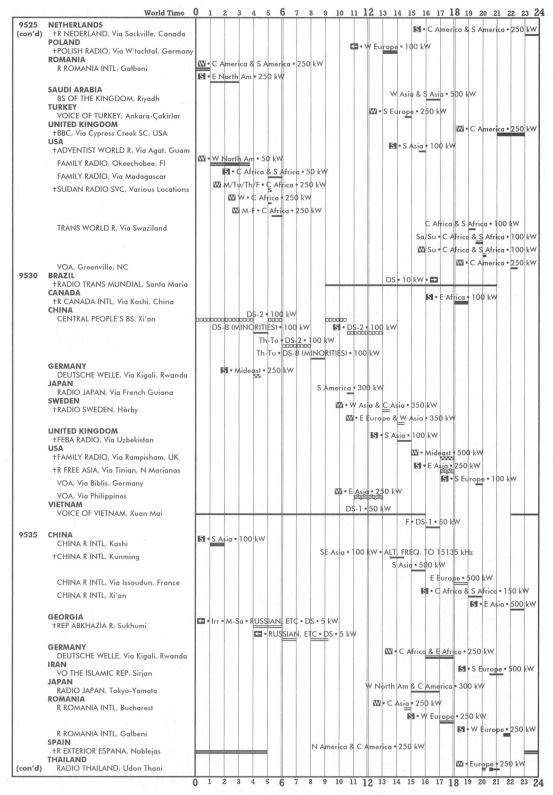

World Time

9525 NETHERLANDS
(con'd) †R NEDERLAND, Via Sackville, Canada — S • C America & S America • 250 kW

POLAND
†POLISH RADIO, Via W'tachtal, Germany — W Europe • 100 kW

ROMANIA
R ROMANIA INTL, Galbeni — W • C America & S America • 250 kW
S • E North Am • 250 kW

SAUDI ARABIA
BS OF THE KINGDOM, Riyadh — W Asia & S Asia • 500 kW

TURKEY
VOICE OF TURKEY, Ankara-Çakirlar — W • S Europe • 250 kW

UNITED KINGDOM
†BBC, Via Cypress Creek SC, USA — W • C America • 250 kW

USA
†ADVENTIST WORLD R, Via Agat, Guam — S • S Asia • 100 kW

FAMILY RADIO, Okeechobee, Fl — W • W North Am • 50 kW

FAMILY RADIO, Via Madagascar — S • C Africa & S Africa • 50 kW

†SUDAN RADIO SVC, Various Locations — W M/Tu/Th/F • C Africa • 250 kW
W • C Africa • 250 kW
W M-F • C Africa • 250 kW

TRANS WORLD R, Via Swaziland — C Africa & S Africa • 100 kW
Sa/Su • C Africa & S Africa • 100 kW
W Su • C Africa & S Africa • 100 kW
W • C America • 250 kW

VOA, Greenville, NC

9530 BRAZIL
†RADIO TRANS MUNDIAL, Santa Maria — DS • 10 kW

CANADA
†R CANADA INTL, Via Kashi, China — S • E Africa • 100 kW

CHINA
CENTRAL PEOPLE'S BS, Xi'an — DS-2 • 100 kW
DS-8 (MINORITIES) • 100 kW   S • DS-2 • 100 kW
Th-Tu • DS-2 • 100 kW
Th-Tu • DS-8 (MINORITIES) • 100 kW

GERMANY
DEUTSCHE WELLE, Via Kigali, Rwanda — S • Mideast • 250 kW

JAPAN
RADIO JAPAN, Via French Guiana — S America • 300 kW

SWEDEN
†RADIO SWEDEN, Hörby — W • W Asia & C Asia • 350 kW
W • E Europe & W Asia • 350 kW

UNITED KINGDOM
†FEBA RADIO, Via Uzbekistan — S • S Asia • 100 kW

USA
†FAMILY RADIO, Via Rampisham, UK — W • Mideast • 500 kW

†R FREE ASIA, Via Tinian, N Marianas — S • E Asia • 250 kW

VOA, Via Biblis, Germany — S • S Europe • 100 kW

VOA, Via Philippines — W • E Asia • 250 kW

VIETNAM
VOICE OF VIETNAM, Xuan Mai — DS-1 • 50 kW
F • DS-1 • 50 kW

9535 CHINA
CHINA R INTL, Kashi — S • S Asia • 100 kW

†CHINA R INTL, Kunming — SE Asia • 100 kW • ALT. FREQ. TO 15135 kHz
S Asia • 500 kW

CHINA R INTL, Via Issoudun, France — E Europe • 500 kW

CHINA R INTL, Xi'an — S • C Africa & S Africa • 150 kW
S • E Asia • 500 kW

GEORGIA
†REP ABKHAZIA R, Sukhumi — Irr • M-Sa • RUSSIAN, ETC • DS • 5 kW
RUSSIAN, ETC • DS • 5 kW

GERMANY
DEUTSCHE WELLE, Via Kigali, Rwanda — W • C Africa & E Africa • 250 kW

IRAN
VO THE ISLAMIC REP, Sirjan — S • S Europe • 500 kW

JAPAN
RADIO JAPAN, Tokyo-Yamata — W North Am & C America • 300 kW

ROMANIA
R ROMANIA INTL, Bucharest — W • C Asia • 250 kW
S • W Europe • 250 kW

R ROMANIA INTL, Galbeni — S • W Europe • 250 kW

SPAIN
†R EXTERIOR ESPANA, Noblejas — N America & C America • 250 kW

THAILAND
(con'd) RADIO THAILAND, Udon Thani — W • Europe • 250 kW

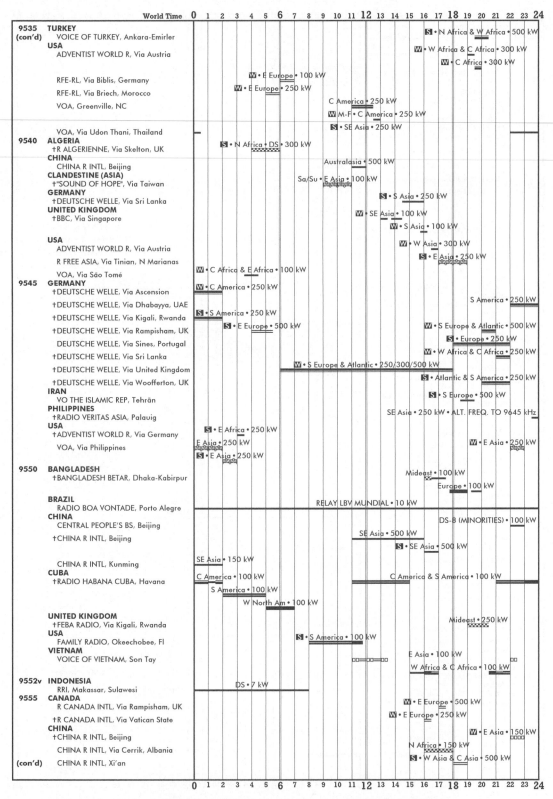

| World Time | 0 | 1 | 2 | 3 | 4 | 5 | 6 | 7 | 8 | 9 | 10 | 11 | 12 | 13 | 14 | 15 | 16 | 17 | 18 | 19 | 20 | 21 | 22 | 23 | 24 |

9535 TURKEY
(con'd)   VOICE OF TURKEY, Ankara-Emirler — S • N Africa & W Africa • 500 kW
USA
   ADVENTIST WORLD R, Via Austria — W • W Africa & C Africa • 300 kW; W • C Africa • 300 kW

   RFE-RL, Via Biblis, Germany — W • E Europe • 100 kW
   RFE-RL, Via Briech, Morocco — W • E Europe • 250 kW
   VOA, Greenville, NC — C America • 250 kW; W • M-F • C America • 250 kW

   VOA, Via Udon Thani, Thailand — S • SE Asia • 250 kW

9540 ALGERIA
   †R ALGERIENNE, Via Skelton, UK — S • N Africa • DS • 300 kW
CHINA
   CHINA R INTL, Beijing — Australasia • 500 kW
CLANDESTINE (ASIA)
   †"SOUND OF HOPE", Via Taiwan — Sa/Su • E Asia • 100 kW
GERMANY
   †DEUTSCHE WELLE, Via Sri Lanka — S • S Asia • 250 kW
UNITED KINGDOM
   †BBC, Via Singapore — W • SE Asia • 100 kW; W • S Asia • 100 kW

USA
   ADVENTIST WORLD R, Via Austria — W • W Asia • 300 kW
   R FREE ASIA, Via Tinian, N Marianas — S • E Asia • 250 kW
   VOA, Via São Tomé — W • C Africa & E Africa • 100 kW
9545 GERMANY
   †DEUTSCHE WELLE, Via Ascension — W • C America • 250 kW; S America • 250 kW
   †DEUTSCHE WELLE, Via Dhabayya, UAE — S • S America • 250 kW
   †DEUTSCHE WELLE, Via Kigali, Rwanda — S • E Europe • 500 kW; W • S Europe & Atlantic • 500 kW
   †DEUTSCHE WELLE, Via Rampisham, UK — S • Europe • 250 kW
   DEUTSCHE WELLE, Via Sines, Portugal — W • W Africa & C Africa • 250 kW
   †DEUTSCHE WELLE, Via Sri Lanka
   †DEUTSCHE WELLE, Via United Kingdom — W • S Europe & Atlantic • 250/300/500 kW
   †DEUTSCHE WELLE, Via Woofferton, UK — S • Atlantic & S America • 250 kW
IRAN
   VO THE ISLAMIC REP, Tehrān — S • S Europe • 500 kW
PHILIPPINES
   †RADIO VERITAS ASIA, Palauig — SE Asia • 250 kW • ALT. FREQ. TO 9645 kHz
USA
   †ADVENTIST WORLD R, Via Germany — S • E Africa • 250 kW; W • E Asia • 250 kW
   VOA, Via Philippines — E Asia • 250 kW; S • E Asia • 250 kW

9550 BANGLADESH
   †BANGLADESH BETAR, Dhaka-Kabirpur — Mideast • 100 kW; Europe • 100 kW

BRAZIL
   RADIO BOA VONTADE, Porto Alegre — RELAY LBV MUNDIAL • 10 kW
CHINA
   CENTRAL PEOPLE'S BS, Beijing — DS-8 (MINORITIES) • 100 kW
   †CHINA R INTL, Beijing — SE Asia • 500 kW; S • SE Asia • 500 kW

   CHINA R INTL, Kunming — SE Asia • 150 kW
CUBA
   †RADIO HABANA CUBA, Havana — C America • 100 kW; C America & S America • 100 kW; S America • 100 kW; W North Am • 100 kW

UNITED KINGDOM
   †FEBA RADIO, Via Kigali, Rwanda — Mideast • 250 kW
USA
   FAMILY RADIO, Okeechobee, Fl — S • S America • 100 kW
VIETNAM
   VOICE OF VIETNAM, Son Tay — E Asia • 100 kW; W Africa & C Africa • 100 kW

9552v INDONESIA
   RRI, Makassar, Sulawesi — DS • 7 kW
9555 CANADA
   R CANADA INTL, Via Rampisham, UK — W • E Europe • 500 kW
   †R CANADA INTL, Via Vatican State — W • E Europe • 250 kW
CHINA
   †CHINA R INTL, Beijing — W • E Asia • 150 kW

   CHINA R INTL, Via Cerrik, Albania — N Africa • 150 kW
(con'd)   CHINA R INTL, Xi'an — S • W Asia & C Asia • 500 kW

| 0 | 1 | 2 | 3 | 4 | 5 | 6 | 7 | 8 | 9 | 10 | 11 | 12 | 13 | 14 | 15 | 16 | 17 | 18 | 19 | 20 | 21 | 22 | 23 | 24 |

ENGLISH ▬   ARABIC ⋙   CHINESE ▫▫▫   FRENCH ▭▭   GERMAN ▬   RUSSIAN ═══   SPANISH ▬   OTHER ▬

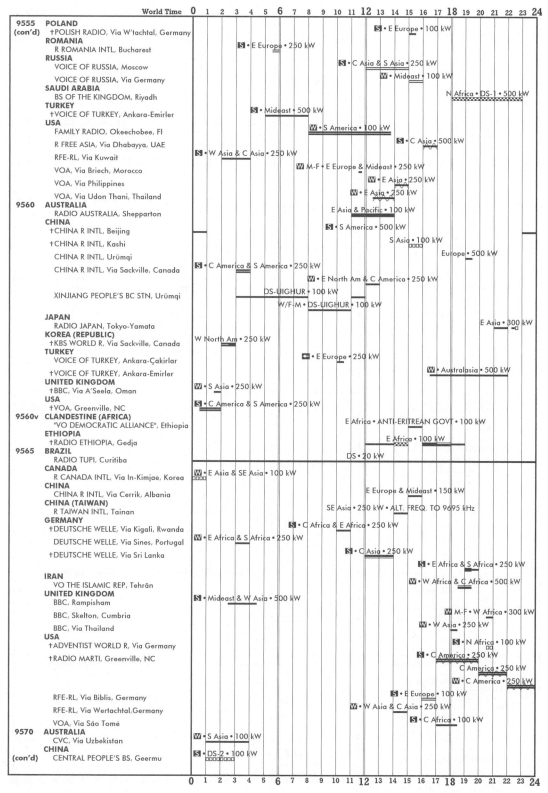

World Time

Frequency	Station	Schedule
9555 (con'd)	**POLAND**	
	†POLISH RADIO, Via W'tachtal, Germany	S • E Europe • 100 kW
	ROMANIA	
	R ROMANIA INTL, Bucharest	S • E Europe • 250 kW
	RUSSIA	
	VOICE OF RUSSIA, Moscow	S • C Asia & S Asia • 250 kW
	VOICE OF RUSSIA, Via Germany	W • Mideast • 100 kW
	SAUDI ARABIA	
	BS OF THE KINGDOM, Riyadh	N Africa • DS-1 • 500 kW
	TURKEY	
	†VOICE OF TURKEY, Ankara-Emirler	S • Mideast • 500 kW
	USA	
	FAMILY RADIO, Okeechobee, Fl	W • S America • 100 kW
	R FREE ASIA, Via Dhabayya, UAE	S • C Asia • 500 kW
	RFE-RL, Via Kuwait	S • W Asia & C Asia • 250 kW
	VOA, Via Briech, Morocco	W M-F • E Europe & Mideast • 250 kW
	VOA, Via Philippines	W • E Asia • 250 kW
	VOA, Via Udon Thani, Thailand	W • E Asia • 250 kW
9560	**AUSTRALIA**	
	RADIO AUSTRALIA, Shepparton	E Asia & Pacific • 100 kW
	CHINA	
	†CHINA R INTL, Beijing	S • S America • 500 kW
	†CHINA R INTL, Kashi	S Asia • 100 kW
	CHINA R INTL, Urümqi	Europe • 500 kW
	CHINA R INTL, Via Sackville, Canada	S • C America & S America • 250 kW
		W • E North Am & C America • 250 kW
	XINJIANG PEOPLE'S BC STN, Urümqi	DS-UIGHUR • 100 kW
		W/F-M • DS-UIGHUR • 100 kW
	JAPAN	
	RADIO JAPAN, Tokyo-Yamata	E Asia • 300 kW
	KOREA (REPUBLIC)	
	†KBS WORLD R, Via Sackville, Canada	W North Am • 250 kW
	TURKEY	
	VOICE OF TURKEY, Ankara-Çakirlar	⇆ • E Europe • 250 kW
	†VOICE OF TURKEY, Ankara-Emirler	W • Australasia • 500 kW
	UNITED KINGDOM	
	†BBC, Via A'Seela, Oman	W • S Asia • 250 kW
	USA	
	†VOA, Greenville, NC	S • C America & S America • 250 kW
9560v	**CLANDESTINE (AFRICA)**	
	"VO DEMOCRATIC ALLIANCE", Ethiopia	E Africa • ANTI-ERITREAN GOVT • 100 kW
	ETHIOPIA	
	†RADIO ETHIOPIA, Gedja	E Africa • 100 kW
9565	**BRAZIL**	
	RADIO TUPI, Curitiba	DS • 20 kW
	CANADA	
	R CANADA INTL, Via In-Kimjae, Korea	W • E Asia & SE Asia • 100 kW
	CHINA	
	CHINA R INTL, Via Cerrik, Albania	E Europe & Mideast • 150 kW
	CHINA (TAIWAN)	
	R TAIWAN INTL, Tainan	SE Asia • 250 kW • ALT. FREQ. TO 9695 kHz
	GERMANY	
	†DEUTSCHE WELLE, Via Kigali, Rwanda	S • C Africa & E Africa • 250 kW
	DEUTSCHE WELLE, Via Sines, Portugal	W • E Africa & S Africa • 250 kW
	†DEUTSCHE WELLE, Via Sri Lanka	S • C Asia • 250 kW
		S • E Africa & S Africa • 250 kW
	IRAN	
	VO THE ISLAMIC REP, Tehrān	W • W Africa & C Africa • 500 kW
	UNITED KINGDOM	
	BBC, Rampisham	S • Mideast & W Asia • 500 kW
	BBC, Skelton, Cumbria	W M-F • W Africa • 300 kW
	BBC, Via Thailand	W • W Asia • 250 kW
	USA	
	†ADVENTIST WORLD R, Via Germany	S • N Africa • 100 kW
	†RADIO MARTI, Greenville, NC	S • C America • 250 kW
		C America • 250 kW
		W • C America • 250 kW
	RFE-RL, Via Biblis, Germany	S • E Europe • 100 kW
	RFE-RL, Via Wertachtal, Germany	W • W Asia & C Asia • 250 kW
	VOA, Via São Tomé	S • C Africa • 100 kW
9570	**AUSTRALIA**	
	CVC, Via Uzbekistan	W • S Asia • 100 kW
	CHINA	
(con'd)	CENTRAL PEOPLE'S BS, Geermu	S • DS-2 • 100 kW

SEASONAL S OR W   1-HR TIMESHIFT MIDYEAR ⇆ OR ⇄   JAMMING / OR ∧   EARLIEST HEARD ◁   LATEST HEARD ▷   NEW FOR 2008 †

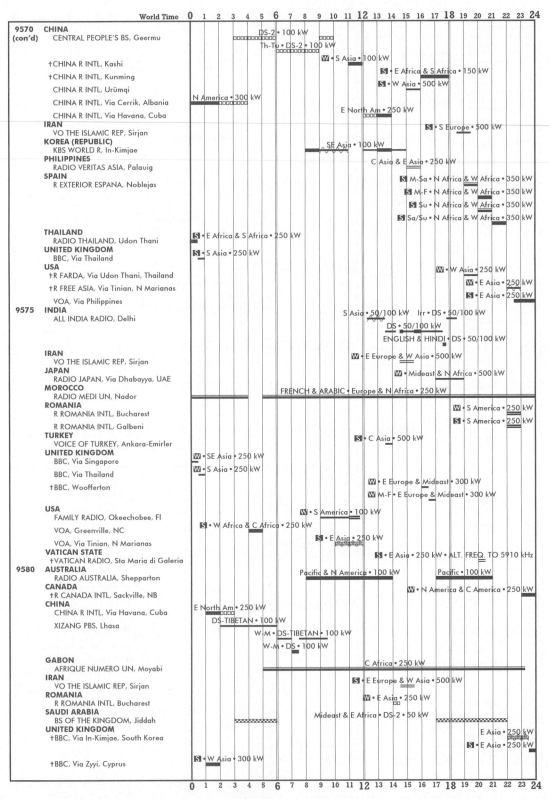

		World Time	0 1 2 3 4 5 6 7 8 9 10 11 12 13 14 15 16 17 18 19 20 21 22 23 24

9570 CHINA
(con'd)   CENTRAL PEOPLE'S BS, Geermu — DS-2 • 100 kW / Th-Tu • DS-2 • 100 kW

†CHINA R INTL, Kashi — W • S Asia • 100 kW
†CHINA R INTL, Kunming — S • E Africa & S Africa • 150 kW
CHINA R INTL, Urümqi — S • W Asia • 500 kW
CHINA R INTL, Via Cerrik, Albania — N America • 300 kW
CHINA R INTL, Via Havana, Cuba — E North Am • 250 kW

IRAN
VO THE ISLAMIC REP, Sirjan — S • S Europe • 500 kW

KOREA (REPUBLIC)
KBS WORLD R, In-Kimjae — SE Asia • 100 kW

PHILIPPINES
RADIO VERITAS ASIA, Palauig — C Asia & E Asia • 250 kW

SPAIN
R EXTERIOR ESPANA, Noblejas — S M-Sa • N Africa & W Africa • 350 kW / S M-F • N Africa & W Africa • 350 kW / S Su • N Africa & W Africa • 350 kW / S Sa/Su • N Africa & W Africa • 350 kW

THAILAND
RADIO THAILAND, Udon Thani — S • E Africa & S Africa • 250 kW

UNITED KINGDOM
BBC, Via Thailand — S • S Asia • 250 kW

USA
†R FARDA, Via Udon Thani, Thailand — W • W Asia • 250 kW
†R FREE ASIA, Via Tinian, N Marianas — W • E Asia • 250 kW
VOA, Via Philippines — S • E Asia • 250 kW

9575 INDIA
ALL INDIA RADIO, Delhi — S Asia • 50/100 kW • Irr • DS • 50/100 kW / DS • 50/100 kW / ENGLISH & HINDI • DS • 50/100 kW

IRAN
VO THE ISLAMIC REP, Sirjan — W • E Europe & W Asia • 500 kW

JAPAN
RADIO JAPAN, Via Dhabayya, UAE — W • Mideast & N Africa • 500 kW

MOROCCO
RADIO MEDI UN, Nador — FRENCH & ARABIC • Europe & N Africa • 250 kW

ROMANIA
R ROMANIA INTL, Bucharest — W • S America • 250 kW
R ROMANIA INTL, Galbeni — S • S America • 250 kW

TURKEY
VOICE OF TURKEY, Ankara-Emirler — S • C Asia • 500 kW

UNITED KINGDOM
BBC, Via Singapore — W • SE Asia • 250 kW
BBC, Via Thailand — W • S Asia • 250 kW
†BBC, Woofferton — W • E Europe & Mideast • 300 kW / W M-F • E Europe & Mideast • 300 kW

USA
FAMILY RADIO, Okeechobee, Fl — W • S America • 100 kW
VOA, Greenville, NC — S • W Africa & C Africa • 250 kW
VOA, Via Tinian, N Marianas — S • E Asia • 250 kW

VATICAN STATE
†VATICAN RADIO, Sta Maria di Galeria — S • E Asia • 250 kW • ALT. FREQ. TO 5910 kHz

9580 AUSTRALIA
RADIO AUSTRALIA, Shepparton — Pacific & N America • 100 kW / Pacific • 100 kW

CANADA
†R CANADA INTL, Sackville, NB — W • N America & C America • 250 kW

CHINA
CHINA R INTL, Via Havana, Cuba — E North Am • 250 kW
XIZANG PBS, Lhasa — DS-TIBETAN • 100 kW / W-M • DS-TIBETAN • 100 kW / W-M • DS • 100 kW

GABON
AFRIQUE NUMERO UN, Moyabi — C Africa • 250 kW

IRAN
VO THE ISLAMIC REP, Sirjan — S • E Europe & W Asia • 500 kW

ROMANIA
R ROMANIA INTL, Bucharest — W • E Asia • 250 kW

SAUDI ARABIA
BS OF THE KINGDOM, Jiddah — Mideast & E Africa • DS-2 • 50 kW

UNITED KINGDOM
†BBC, Via In-Kimjae, South Korea — E Asia • 250 kW / S • E Asia • 250 kW
†BBC, Via Zyyi, Cyprus — S • W Asia • 300 kW

	0 1 2 3 4 5 6 7 8 9 10 11 12 13 14 15 16 17 18 19 20 21 22 23 24

ENGLISH ▬   ARABIC ⌇⌇   CHINESE ▫▫▫   FRENCH ▭   GERMAN ▬   RUSSIAN ═   SPANISH ▬   OTHER ▬

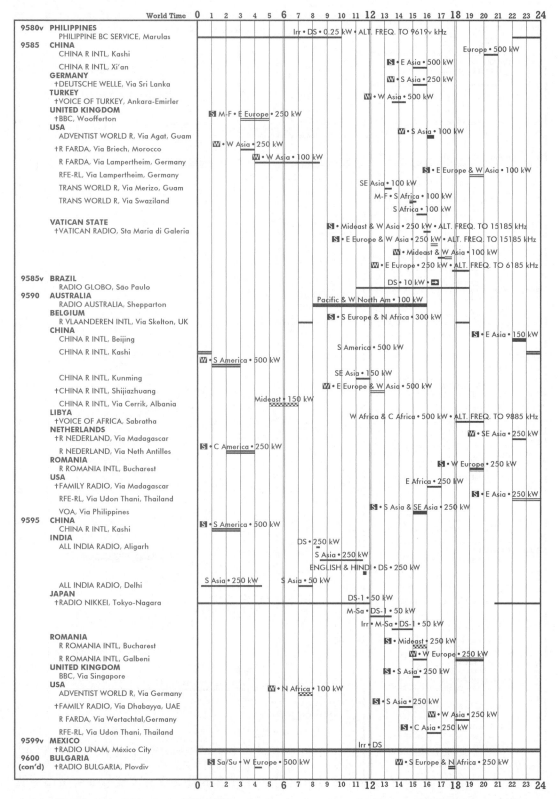

World Time   0 1 2 3 4 5 6 7 8 9 10 11 12 13 14 15 16 17 18 19 20 21 22 23 24

9580v PHILIPPINES	
PHILIPPINE BC SERVICE, Marulas	Irr • DS • 0.25 kW • ALT. FREQ. TO 9619v kHz
9585 CHINA	
CHINA R INTL, Kashi	Europe • 500 kW
CHINA R INTL, Xi'an	S • E Asia • 500 kW
GERMANY	
†DEUTSCHE WELLE, Via Sri Lanka	W • S Asia • 250 kW
TURKEY	
†VOICE OF TURKEY, Ankara-Emirler	W • W Asia • 500 kW
UNITED KINGDOM	
†BBC, Woofferton	S M-F • E Europe • 250 kW
USA	
ADVENTIST WORLD R, Via Agat, Guam	W • W Asia • 250 kW W • S Asia • 100 kW
†R FARDA, Via Briech, Morocco	
R FARDA, Via Lampertheim, Germany	W • W Asia • 100 kW
RFE-RL, Via Lampertheim, Germany	S • E Europe & W Asia • 100 kW
TRANS WORLD R, Via Merizo, Guam	SE Asia • 100 kW
TRANS WORLD R, Via Swaziland	M-F • S Africa • 100 kW
	S Africa • 100 kW
VATICAN STATE	
†VATICAN RADIO, Sta Maria di Galeria	S • Mideast & W Asia • 250 kW • ALT. FREQ. TO 15185 kHz
	S • E Europe & W Asia • 250 kW • ALT. FREQ. TO 15185 kHz
	W • Mideast & W Asia • 100 kW
	W • E Europe • 250 kW • ALT. FREQ. TO 6185 kHz
9585v BRAZIL	
RADIO GLOBO, São Paulo	DS • 10 kW • ⇒
9590 AUSTRALIA	
RADIO AUSTRALIA, Shepparton	Pacific & W North Am • 100 kW
BELGIUM	
R VLAANDEREN INTL, Via Skelton, UK	S • S Europe & N Africa • 300 kW
CHINA	
CHINA R INTL, Beijing	S • E Asia • 150 kW
CHINA R INTL, Kashi	S America • 500 kW
	W • S America • 500 kW
CHINA R INTL, Kunming	SE Asia • 150 kW
†CHINA R INTL, Shijiazhuang	W • E Europe & W Asia • 500 kW
CHINA R INTL, Via Cerrik, Albania	Mideast • 150 kW
LIBYA	
†VOICE OF AFRICA, Sabratha	W Africa & C Africa • 500 kW • ALT. FREQ. TO 9885 kHz
NETHERLANDS	
†R NEDERLAND, Via Madagascar	W • SE Asia • 250 kW
R NEDERLAND, Via Neth Antilles	S • C America • 250 kW
ROMANIA	
R ROMANIA INTL, Bucharest	S • W Europe • 250 kW
USA	
†FAMILY RADIO, Via Madagascar	E Africa • 250 kW
RFE-RL, Via Udon Thani, Thailand	S • E Asia • 250 kW
VOA, Via Philippines	S • S Asia & SE Asia • 250 kW
9595 CHINA	
CHINA R INTL, Kashi	S • S America • 500 kW
INDIA	
ALL INDIA RADIO, Aligarh	DS • 250 kW
	S Asia • 250 kW
	ENGLISH & HINDI • DS • 250 kW
ALL INDIA RADIO, Delhi	S Asia • 250 kW S Asia • 50 kW
JAPAN	
†RADIO NIKKEI, Tokyo-Nagara	DS-1 • 50 kW
	M-Sa • DS-1 • 50 kW
	Irr • M-Sa • DS-1 • 50 kW
ROMANIA	
R ROMANIA INTL, Bucharest	S • Mideast • 250 kW
R ROMANIA INTL, Galbeni	W • W Europe • 250 kW
UNITED KINGDOM	
BBC, Via Singapore	S • S Asia • 250 kW
USA	
ADVENTIST WORLD R, Via Germany	W • N Africa • 100 kW
†FAMILY RADIO, Via Dhabayya, UAE	S • S Asia • 250 kW
R FARDA, Via Wertachtal, Germany	W • W Asia • 250 kW
RFE-RL, Via Udon Thani, Thailand	S • C Asia • 250 kW
9599v MEXICO	
†RADIO UNAM, México City	Irr • DS
9600 BULGARIA	
(con'd) †RADIO BULGARIA, Plovdiv	S Sa/Su • W Europe • 500 kW W • S Europe & N Africa • 250 kW

0 1 2 3 4 5 6 7 8 9 10 11 12 13 14 15 16 17 18 19 20 21 22 23 24

SEASONAL S OR W   1-HR TIMESHIFT MIDYEAR ⇐ OR ⇒   JAMMING / OR /\   EARLIEST HEARD ◁   LATEST HEARD ▷   NEW FOR 2008 †

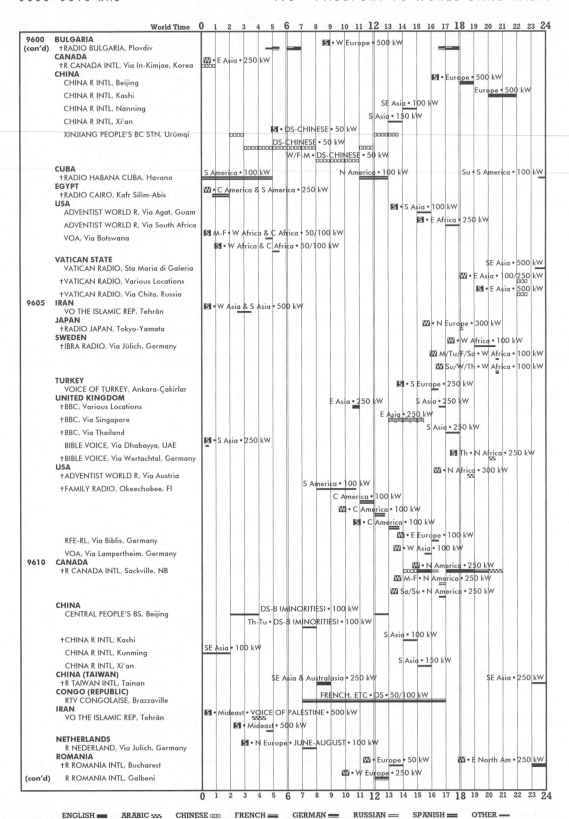

9600
(con'd)

BULGARIA		
†RADIO BULGARIA, Plovdiv	S • W Europe • 500 kW	
CANADA		
†R CANADA INTL, Via In-Kimjae, Korea	W • E Asia • 250 kW	
CHINA		
CHINA R INTL, Beijing	S • Europe • 500 kW	
CHINA R INTL, Kashi	Europe • 500 kW	
CHINA R INTL, Nanning	SE Asia • 100 kW	
CHINA R INTL, Xi'an	S Asia • 150 kW	
XINJIANG PEOPLE'S BC STN, Urümqi	S • DS-CHINESE • 50 kW	
	DS-CHINESE • 50 kW	
	W/F-M • DS-CHINESE • 50 kW	
CUBA		
†RADIO HABANA CUBA, Havana	S America • 100 kW N America • 100 kW Su • S America • 100 kW	
EGYPT		
†RADIO CAIRO, Kafr Silim-Abis	W • C America & S America • 250 kW	
USA		
ADVENTIST WORLD R, Via Agat, Guam	S • S Asia • 100 kW	
ADVENTIST WORLD R, Via South Africa	S • E Africa • 250 kW	
VOA, Via Botswana	S M-F • W Africa & C Africa • 50/100 kW	
	S • W Africa & C Africa • 50/100 kW	
VATICAN STATE		
VATICAN RADIO, Sta Maria di Galeria	SE Asia • 500 kW	
†VATICAN RADIO, Various Locations	W • E Asia • 100/250 kW	
†VATICAN RADIO, Via Chita, Russia	S • E Asia • 500 kW	

9605

IRAN		
VO THE ISLAMIC REP, Tehrān	S • W Asia & S Asia • 500 kW	
JAPAN		
†RADIO JAPAN, Tokyo-Yamata	W • N Europe • 300 kW	
SWEDEN		
†IBRA RADIO, Via Jülich, Germany	W • W Africa • 100 kW	
	W M/Tu/F/Sa • W Africa • 100 kW	
	W Su/W/Th • W Africa • 100 kW	
TURKEY		
VOICE OF TURKEY, Ankara-Çakirlar	S • S Europe • 250 kW	
UNITED KINGDOM		
†BBC, Various Locations	E Asia • 250 kW S Asia • 250 kW	
†BBC, Via Singapore	E Asia • 250 kW	
†BBC, Via Thailand	S Asia • 250 kW	
BIBLE VOICE, Via Dhabayya, UAE	S • S Asia • 250 kW	
†BIBLE VOICE, Via Wertachtal, Germany	S Th • N Africa • 250 kW	
USA		
†ADVENTIST WORLD R, Via Austria	W • N Africa • 300 kW	
†FAMILY RADIO, Okeechobee, Fl	S America • 100 kW	
	C America • 100 kW	
	W • C America • 100 kW	
	S • C America • 100 kW	
	W • E Europe • 100 kW	
RFE-RL, Via Biblis, Germany	W • W Asia • 100 kW	
VOA, Via Lampertheim, Germany		

9610

CANADA		
†R CANADA INTL, Sackville, NB	W • N America • 250 kW	
	W M-F • N America • 250 kW	
	W Sa/Su • N America • 250 kW	
CHINA		
CENTRAL PEOPLE'S BS, Beijing	DS-8 (MINORITIES) • 100 kW	
	Th-Tu • DS-8 (MINORITIES) • 100 kW	
†CHINA R INTL, Kashi	S Asia • 100 kW	
CHINA R INTL, Kunming	SE Asia • 100 kW	
CHINA R INTL, Xi'an	S Asia • 150 kW	
CHINA (TAIWAN)		
†R TAIWAN INTL, Tainan	SE Asia & Australasia • 250 kW SE Asia • 250 kW	
CONGO (REPUBLIC)		
RTV CONGOLAISE, Brazzaville	FRENCH, ETC • DS 50/100 kW	
IRAN		
VO THE ISLAMIC REP, Tehrān	S • Mideast • VOICE OF PALESTINE • 500 kW	
	S • Mideast • 500 kW	
NETHERLANDS		
R NEDERLAND, Via Julich, Germany	S • N Europe • JUNE-AUGUST • 100 kW	
ROMANIA		
†R ROMANIA INTL, Bucharest	W • Europe • 50 kW W • E North Am • 250 kW	

(con'd)   R ROMANIA INTL, Galbeni   W • W Europe • 250 kW

ENGLISH ■■ ARABIC ░░░ CHINESE □□□ FRENCH ▬▬ GERMAN ▬▬ RUSSIAN ══ SPANISH ══ OTHER ──

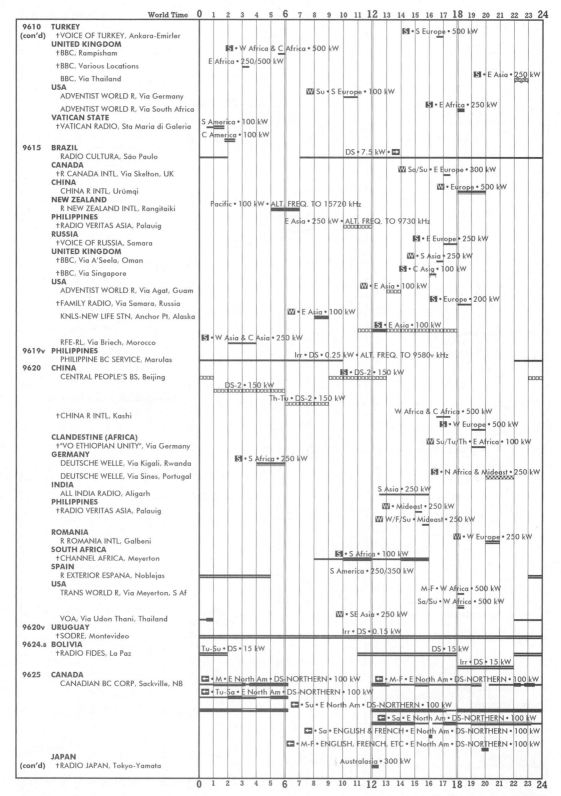

| | | World Time | 0 | 1 | 2 | 3 | 4 | 5 | 6 | 7 | 8 | 9 | 10 | 11 | 12 | 13 | 14 | 15 | 16 | 17 | 18 | 19 | 20 | 21 | 22 | 23 | 24 |

9610 (con'd) **TURKEY**
†VOICE OF TURKEY, Ankara-Emirler — S • S Europe • 500 kW
UNITED KINGDOM
†BBC, Rampisham — S • W Africa & C Africa • 500 kW
†BBC, Various Locations — E Africa • 250/500 kW
BBC, Via Thailand — S • E Asia • 250 kW
USA
ADVENTIST WORLD R, Via Germany — W Su • S Europe • 100 kW
ADVENTIST WORLD R, Via South Africa — S • E Africa • 250 kW
VATICAN STATE
†VATICAN RADIO, Sta Maria di Galeria — S America • 100 kW / C America • 100 kW

9615 **BRAZIL**
RADIO CULTURA, São Paulo — DS • 7.5 kW
CANADA
†R CANADA INTL, Via Skelton, UK — W Sa/Su • E Europe • 300 kW
CHINA
CHINA R INTL, Urümqi — W • Europe • 500 kW
NEW ZEALAND
R NEW ZEALAND INTL, Rangitaiki — Pacific • 100 kW • ALT. FREQ. TO 15720 kHz
PHILIPPINES
†RADIO VERITAS ASIA, Palauig — E Asia • 250 kW • ALT. FREQ. TO 9730 kHz
RUSSIA
†VOICE OF RUSSIA, Samara — S • E Europe • 250 kW
UNITED KINGDOM
†BBC, Via A'Seela, Oman — W • S Asia • 250 kW
†BBC, Via Singapore — S • C Asia • 100 kW
USA
ADVENTIST WORLD R, Via Agat, Guam — W • E Asia • 100 kW
†FAMILY RADIO, Via Samara, Russia — S • Europe • 200 kW
KNLS-NEW LIFE STN, Anchor Pt, Alaska — W • E Asia • 100 kW / S • E Asia • 100 kW
RFE-RL, Via Briech, Morocco — S • W Asia & C Asia • 250 kW

9619v **PHILIPPINES**
PHILIPPINE BC SERVICE, Marulas — Irr • DS • 0.25 kW • ALT. FREQ. TO 9580v kHz

9620 **CHINA**
CENTRAL PEOPLE'S BS, Beijing — S • DS-2 • 150 kW / DS-2 • 150 kW / Th-Tu • DS-2 • 150 kW
†CHINA R INTL, Kashi — W Africa & C Africa • 500 kW
— S • W Europe • 500 kW
CLANDESTINE (AFRICA)
†"VO ETHIOPIAN UNITY", Via Germany — W Su/Tu/Th • E Africa • 100 kW
GERMANY
DEUTSCHE WELLE, Via Kigali, Rwanda — S • S Africa • 250 kW
DEUTSCHE WELLE, Via Sines, Portugal — S • N Africa & Mideast • 250 kW
INDIA
ALL INDIA RADIO, Aligarh — S Asia • 250 kW
PHILIPPINES
†RADIO VERITAS ASIA, Palauig — W • Mideast • 250 kW / W W/F/Su • Mideast • 250 kW
ROMANIA
R ROMANIA INTL, Galbeni — W • W Europe • 250 kW
SOUTH AFRICA
†CHANNEL AFRICA, Meyerton — S • S Africa • 100 kW
SPAIN
R EXTERIOR ESPANA, Noblejas — S America • 250/350 kW
USA
TRANS WORLD R, Via Meyerton, S Af — M-F • W Africa • 500 kW / Sa/Su • W Africa • 500 kW
VOA, Via Udon Thani, Thailand — W • SE Asia • 250 kW

9620v **URUGUAY**
†SODRE, Montevideo — Irr • DS • 0.15 kW

9624.8 **BOLIVIA**
†RADIO FIDES, La Paz — Tu-Su • DS • 15 kW / DS • 15 kW / Irr • DS • 15 kW

9625 **CANADA**
CANADIAN BC CORP, Sackville, NB — M • E North Am • DS-NORTHERN • 100 kW / M-F • E North Am • DS-NORTHERN • 100 kW
— Tu-Sa • E North Am • DS-NORTHERN • 100 kW
— Su • E North Am • DS-NORTHERN • 100 kW
— Sa • E North Am • DS-NORTHERN • 100 kW
— Sa • ENGLISH & FRENCH • E North Am • DS-NORTHERN • 100 kW
— M-F • ENGLISH, FRENCH, ETC • E North Am • DS-NORTHERN • 100 kW
JAPAN
(con'd) †RADIO JAPAN, Tokyo-Yamata — Australasia • 300 kW

| | | | 0 | 1 | 2 | 3 | 4 | 5 | 6 | 7 | 8 | 9 | 10 | 11 | 12 | 13 | 14 | 15 | 16 | 17 | 18 | 19 | 20 | 21 | 22 | 23 | 24 |

SEASONAL ⑤ OR Ⓦ   1-HR TIMESHIFT MIDYEAR ⬅ OR ➡   JAMMING / OR ∧   EARLIEST HEARD ◁   LATEST HEARD ▷   NEW FOR 2008 †

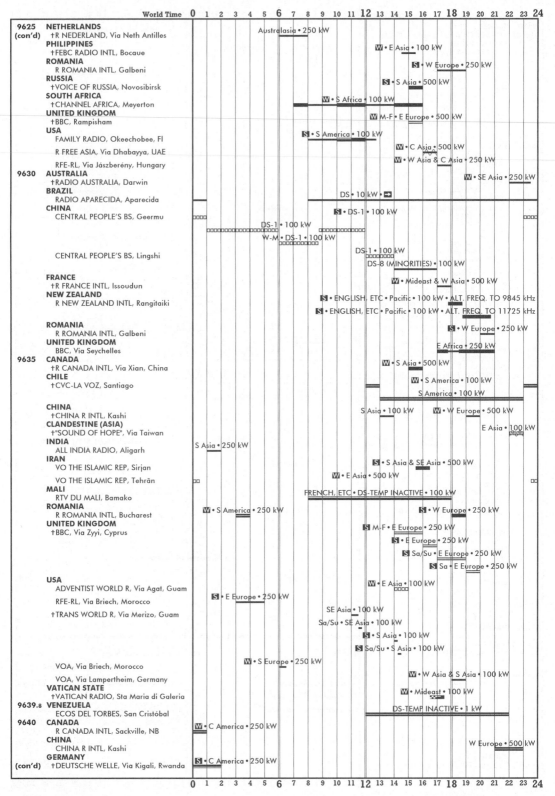

ENGLISH ▬   ARABIC ⬚⬚   CHINESE ▫▫▫   FRENCH ▬▬   GERMAN ▬   RUSSIAN ═   SPANISH ▬   OTHER ▬

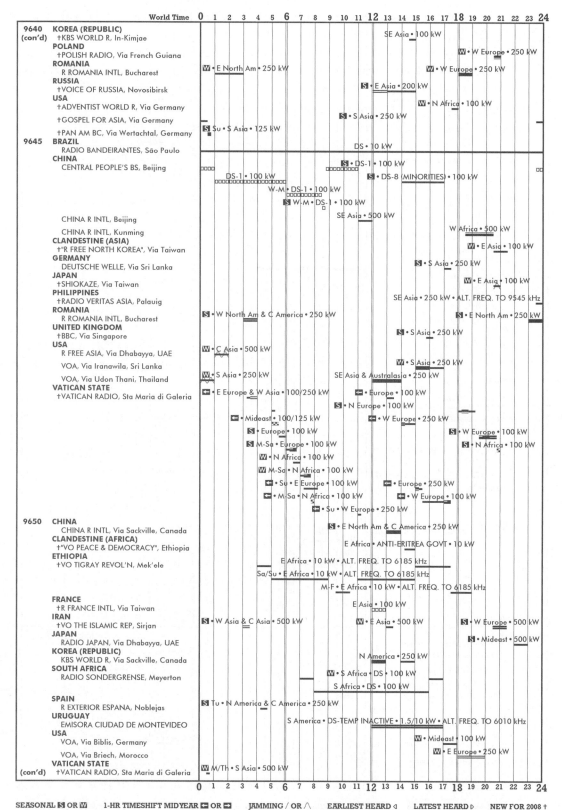

9640 (con'd) KOREA (REPUBLIC)
†KBS WORLD R, In-Kimjae — SE Asia • 100 kW

POLAND
†POLISH RADIO, Via French Guiana — W • W Europe • 250 kW

ROMANIA
R ROMANIA INTL, Bucharest — W • E North Am • 250 kW / W • W Europe • 250 kW

RUSSIA
†VOICE OF RUSSIA, Novosibirsk — S • E Asia • 200 kW

USA
†ADVENTIST WORLD R, Via Germany — W • N Africa • 100 kW
†GOSPEL FOR ASIA, Via Germany — S • S Asia • 250 kW
†PAN AM BC, Via Wertachtal, Germany — S • Su • S Asia • 125 kW

9645 BRAZIL
RADIO BANDEIRANTES, São Paulo — DS • 10 kW

CHINA
CENTRAL PEOPLE'S BS, Beijing — DS-1 • 100 kW / S • DS-1 • 100 kW / S • DS-8 (MINORITIES) • 100 kW / W-M • DS-1 • 100 kW / S W-M • DS-1 • 100 kW
CHINA R INTL, Beijing — SE Asia • 500 kW
CHINA R INTL, Kunming — W Africa • 500 kW / W • E Asia • 100 kW

CLANDESTINE (ASIA)
†"R FREE NORTH KOREA", Via Taiwan

GERMANY
DEUTSCHE WELLE, Via Sri Lanka — S • S Asia • 250 kW

JAPAN
†SHIOKAZE, Via Taiwan — W • E Asia • 100 kW

PHILIPPINES
†RADIO VERITAS ASIA, Palauig — SE Asia • 250 kW • ALT. FREQ. TO 9545 kHz

ROMANIA
R ROMANIA INTL, Bucharest — S • W North Am & C America • 250 kW / S • E North Am • 250 kW

UNITED KINGDOM
†BBC, Via Singapore — S • S Asia • 250 kW

USA
R FREE ASIA, Via Dhabayya, UAE — W • C Asia • 500 kW
VOA, Via Iranawila, Sri Lanka — W • S Asia • 250 kW
VOA, Via Udon Thani, Thailand — W • S Asia • 250 kW / SE Asia & Australasia • 250 kW

VATICAN STATE
†VATICAN RADIO, Sta Maria di Galeria — E Europe & W Asia • 100/250 kW / Europe • 100 kW / S • N Europe • 100 kW / Mideast • 100/125 kW / W Europe • 250 kW / S • Europe • 100 kW / S • W Europe • 100 kW / S M-Sa • Europe • 100 kW / S • N Africa • 100 kW / W • N Africa • 100 kW / W M-Sa • N Africa • 100 kW / Su • E Europe • 100 kW / Europe • 250 kW / M-Sa • N Africa • 100 kW / W Europe • 100 kW / Su • W Europe • 250 kW

9650 CHINA
CHINA R INTL, Via Sackville, Canada — S • E North Am & C America • 250 kW

CLANDESTINE (AFRICA)
†"VO PEACE & DEMOCRACY", Ethiopia — E Africa • ANTI-ERITREA GOVT • 10 kW

ETHIOPIA
†VO TIGRAY REVOL'N, Mek'ele — E Africa • 10 kW • ALT. FREQ. TO 6185 kHz / Sa/Su • E Africa • 10 kW • ALT. FREQ. TO 6185 kHz / M-F • E Africa • 10 kW • ALT. FREQ. TO 6185 kHz

FRANCE
†R FRANCE INTL, Via Taiwan — E Asia • 100 kW

IRAN
†VO THE ISLAMIC REP, Sirjan — S • W Asia & C Asia • 500 kW / W • E Asia • 500 kW / S • W Europe • 500 kW / S • Mideast • 500 kW

JAPAN
RADIO JAPAN, Via Dhabayya, UAE

KOREA (REPUBLIC)
KBS WORLD R, Via Sackville, Canada — N America • 250 kW

SOUTH AFRICA
RADIO SONDERGRENSE, Meyerton — W • S Africa • DS • 100 kW / S Africa • DS • 100 kW

SPAIN
R EXTERIOR ESPANA, Noblejas — S Tu • N America & C America • 250 kW

URUGUAY
EMISORA CIUDAD DE MONTEVIDEO — S America • DS-TEMP INACTIVE • 1.5/10 kW • ALT. FREQ. TO 6010 kHz

USA
VOA, Via Biblis, Germany — W • Mideast • 100 kW
VOA, Via Briech, Morocco — W • E Europe • 250 kW

VATICAN STATE
(con'd) †VATICAN RADIO, Sta Maria di Galeria — W M/TH • S Asia • 500 kW

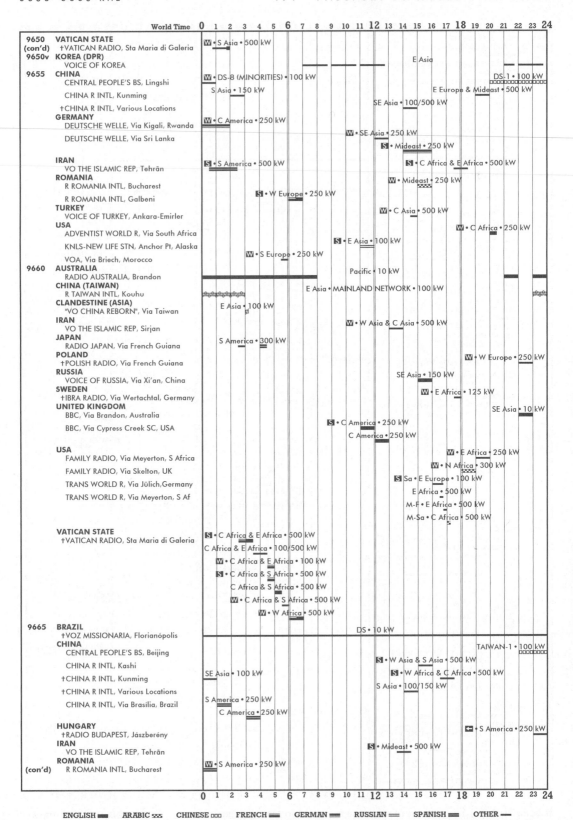

	World Time	0 1 2 3 4 5 6 7 8 9 10 11 12 13 14 15 16 17 18 19 20 21 22 23 24
9650 (con'd)	**VATICAN STATE** †VATICAN RADIO, Sta Maria di Galeria	**W** • S Asia • 500 kW
9650v	**KOREA (DPR)** VOICE OF KOREA	E Asia
9655	**CHINA** CENTRAL PEOPLE'S BS, Lingshi	**W** • DS-8 (MINORITIES) • 100 kW DS-1 • 100 kW
	CHINA R INTL, Kunming	S Asia • 150 kW E Europe & Mideast • 500 kW
	†CHINA R INTL, Various Locations	SE Asia • 100/500 kW
	GERMANY DEUTSCHE WELLE, Via Kigali, Rwanda	**W** • C America • 250 kW
	DEUTSCHE WELLE, Via Sri Lanka	**W** • SE Asia • 250 kW
		S • Mideast • 250 kW
	IRAN VO THE ISLAMIC REP, Tehrān	**S** • S America • 500 kW **S** • C Africa & E Africa • 500 kW
	ROMANIA R ROMANIA INTL, Bucharest	**W** • Mideast • 250 kW
	R ROMANIA INTL, Galbeni	**S** • W Europe • 250 kW
	TURKEY VOICE OF TURKEY, Ankara-Emirler	**W** • C Asia • 500 kW
	USA ADVENTIST WORLD R, Via South Africa	**W** • C Africa • 250 kW
	KNLS-NEW LIFE STN, Anchor Pt, Alaska	**S** • E Asia • 100 kW
	VOA, Via Briech, Morocco	**W** • S Europe • 250 kW
9660	**AUSTRALIA** RADIO AUSTRALIA, Brandon	Pacific • 10 kW
	CHINA (TAIWAN) R TAIWAN INTL, Kouhu	E Asia • MAINLAND NETWORK • 100 kW
	CLANDESTINE (ASIA) "VO CHINA REBORN", Via Taiwan	E Asia • 100 kW
	IRAN VO THE ISLAMIC REP, Sirjan	**W** • W Asia & C Asia • 500 kW
	JAPAN RADIO JAPAN, Via French Guiana	S America • 300 kW
	POLAND †POLISH RADIO, Via French Guiana	**W** • W Europe • 250 kW
	RUSSIA VOICE OF RUSSIA, Via Xi'an, China	SE Asia • 150 kW
	SWEDEN †IBRA RADIO, Via Wertachtal, Germany	**W** • E Africa • 125 kW
	UNITED KINGDOM BBC, Via Brandon, Australia	SE Asia • 10 kW
	BBC, Via Cypress Creek SC, USA	**S** • C America • 250 kW C America • 250 kW
	USA FAMILY RADIO, Via Meyerton, S Africa	**W** • E Africa • 250 kW
	FAMILY RADIO, Via Skelton, UK	**W** • N Africa • 300 kW
	TRANS WORLD R, Via Jülich, Germany	**S** Sa • E Europe • 100 kW
	TRANS WORLD R, Via Meyerton, S Af	E Africa • 500 kW M-F • E Africa • 500 kW M-Sa • C Africa • 500 kW
	VATICAN STATE †VATICAN RADIO, Sta Maria di Galeria	**S** • C Africa & E Africa • 500 kW C Africa & E Africa • 100/500 kW **W** • C Africa & E Africa • 100 kW **S** • C Africa & S Africa • 500 kW C Africa & S Africa • 500 kW **W** • C Africa & S Africa • 500 kW **W** • W Africa • 500 kW
9665	**BRAZIL** †VOZ MISSIONARIA, Florianópolis	DS • 10 kW
	CHINA CENTRAL PEOPLE'S BS, Beijing	TAIWAN-1 • 100 kW
	CHINA R INTL, Kashi	**S** • W Asia & S Asia • 500 kW
	†CHINA R INTL, Kunming	SE Asia • 100 kW **S** • W Africa & C Africa • 500 kW
	†CHINA R INTL, Various Locations	S Asia • 100/150 kW
	CHINA R INTL, Via Brasilia, Brazil	S America • 250 kW C America • 250 kW
	HUNGARY †RADIO BUDAPEST, Jászberény	◄► • S America • 250 kW
	IRAN VO THE ISLAMIC REP, Tehrān	**S** • Mideast • 500 kW
(con'd)	**ROMANIA** R ROMANIA INTL, Bucharest	**W** • S America • 250 kW
		0 1 2 3 4 5 6 7 8 9 10 11 12 13 14 15 16 17 18 19 20 21 22 23 24

ENGLISH ▬ ARABIC ▩ CHINESE ▭▭▭ FRENCH ▬▬ GERMAN ▬ RUSSIAN ═══ SPANISH ▬▬ OTHER ──

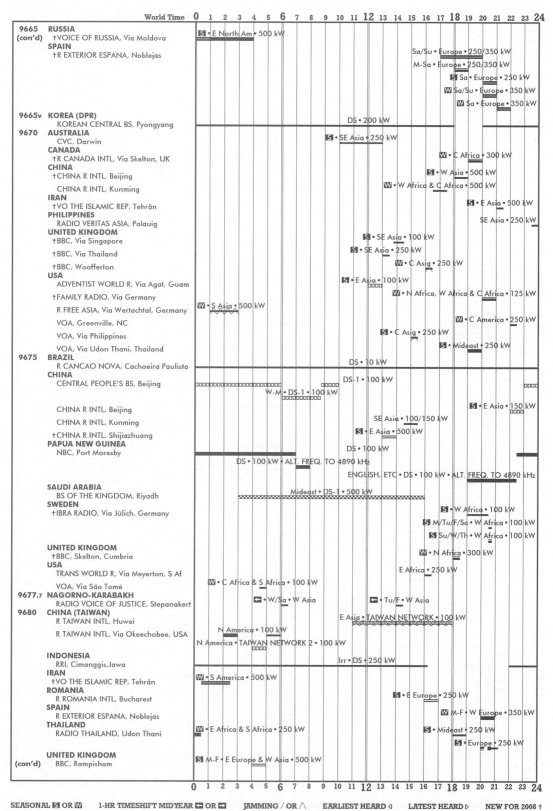

		World Time	0 1 2 3 4 5 6 7 8 9 10 11 12 13 14 15 16 17 18 19 20 21 22 23 24

9665 **RUSSIA**
(con'd) †VOICE OF RUSSIA, Via Moldova — S • E North Am • 500 kW
SPAIN
†R EXTERIOR ESPANA, Noblejas — Sa/Su • Europe • 250/350 kW
M-Sa • Europe • 250/350 kW
S Sa • Europe • 250 kW
W Sa/Su • Europe • 350 kW
W Sa • Europe • 350 kW

9665v **KOREA (DPR)**
KOREAN CENTRAL BS, Pyongyang — DS • 200 kW
9670 **AUSTRALIA**
CVC, Darwin — S • SE Asia • 250 kW
CANADA
†R CANADA INTL, Via Skelton, UK — W • C Africa • 300 kW
CHINA
†CHINA R INTL, Beijing — S • W Asia • 500 kW
CHINA R INTL, Kunming — W • W Africa & C Africa • 500 kW
IRAN
†VO THE ISLAMIC REP, Tehrān — W • E Asia • 500 kW
PHILIPPINES
RADIO VERITAS ASIA, Palauig — SE Asia • 250 kW
UNITED KINGDOM
†BBC, Via Singapore — S • SE Asia • 100 kW
†BBC, Via Thailand — S • SE Asia • 250 kW
†BBC, Woofferton — W • C Asia • 250 kW
USA
ADVENTIST WORLD R, Via Agat, Guam — S • E Asia • 100 kW
†FAMILY RADIO, Via Germany — W • N Africa, W Africa & C Africa • 125 kW
R FREE ASIA, Via Wertachtal, Germany — W • S Asia • 500 kW
VOA, Greenville, NC — W • C America • 250 kW
VOA, Via Philippines — S • C Asia • 250 kW
VOA, Via Udon Thani, Thailand — S • Mideast • 250 kW
9675 **BRAZIL**
R CANCAO NOVA, Cachoeira Paulista — DS • 10 kW
CHINA
CENTRAL PEOPLE'S BS, Beijing — DS-1 • 100 kW
W-M • DS-1 • 100 kW
CHINA R INTL, Beijing — S • E Asia • 150 kW
CHINA R INTL, Kunming — SE Asia • 100/150 kW
†CHINA R INTL, Shijiazhuang — S • E Asia • 500 kW
PAPUA NEW GUINEA
NBC, Port Moresby — DS • 100 kW
DS • 100 kW • ALT. FREQ. TO 4890 kHz
ENGLISH, ETC • DS • 100 kW • ALT. FREQ. TO 4890 kHz
SAUDI ARABIA
BS OF THE KINGDOM, Riyadh — Mideast • DS-1 • 500 kW
SWEDEN
†IBRA RADIO, Via Jülich, Germany — S • W Africa • 100 kW
S M/Tu/F/Sa • W Africa • 100 kW
S Su/W/Th • W Africa • 100 kW
UNITED KINGDOM
†BBC, Skelton, Cumbria — W • N Africa • 300 kW
USA
TRANS WORLD R, Via Meyerton, S Af — E Africa • 250 kW
VOA, Via São Tomé — W • C Africa & S Africa • 100 kW
9677.7 **NAGORNO-KARABAKH**
RADIO VOICE OF JUSTICE, Stepanakert — W/Sa • W Asia — Tu/F • W Asia
9680 **CHINA (TAIWAN)**
R TAIWAN INTL, Huwei — E Asia • TAIWAN NETWORK • 100 kW
R TAIWAN INTL, Via Okeechobee, USA — N America • 100 kW
N America • TAIWAN NETWORK 2 • 100 kW
INDONESIA
RRI, Cimanggis, Jawa — Irr • DS • 250 kW
IRAN
†VO THE ISLAMIC REP, Tehrān — W • S America • 500 kW
ROMANIA
R ROMANIA INTL, Bucharest — S • E Europe • 250 kW
SPAIN
R EXTERIOR ESPANA, Noblejas — W M-F • W Europe • 350 kW
THAILAND
RADIO THAILAND, Udon Thani — W • E Africa & S Africa • 250 kW
S • Mideast • 250 kW
S • Europe • 250 kW
UNITED KINGDOM
(con'd) BBC, Rampisham — S M-F • E Europe & W Asia • 500 kW

0 1 2 3 4 5 6 7 8 9 10 11 12 13 14 15 16 17 18 19 20 21 22 23 24

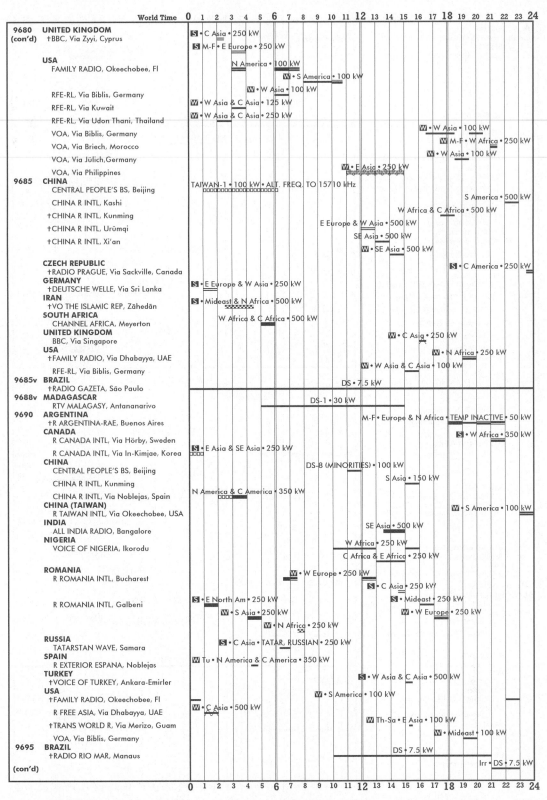

World Time 0 1 2 3 4 5 6 7 8 9 10 11 12 13 14 15 16 17 18 19 20 21 22 23 24

Frequency	Station	
9680 (con'd)	UNITED KINGDOM	
	†BBC, Via Zyyi, Cyprus	S • C Asia • 250 kW
		S M-F • E Europe • 250 kW
	USA	
	FAMILY RADIO, Okeechobee, Fl	N America • 100 kW
		W • S America • 100 kW
		W • W Asia • 100 kW
	RFE-RL, Via Biblis, Germany	W • W Asia & C Asia • 125 kW
	RFE-RL, Via Kuwait	W • W Asia & C Asia • 250 kW
	RFE-RL, Via Udon Thani, Thailand	W • W Asia • 100 kW
	VOA, Via Biblis, Germany	W M-F • W Africa • 250 kW
	VOA, Via Briech, Morocco	W • W Asia • 100 kW
	VOA, Via Jülich, Germany	W • W Asia • 100 kW
	VOA, Via Philippines	W • E Asia • 250 kW
9685	CHINA	
	CENTRAL PEOPLE'S BS, Beijing	TAIWAN-1 • 100 kW • ALT. FREQ. TO 15710 kHz
	CHINA R INTL, Kashi	S America • 500 kW
	†CHINA R INTL, Kunming	W Africa & C Africa • 500 kW
	†CHINA R INTL, Urümqi	E Europe & W Asia • 500 kW
	†CHINA R INTL, Xi'an	SE Asia • 500 kW
		W • SE Asia • 500 kW
	CZECH REPUBLIC	
	†RADIO PRAGUE, Via Sackville, Canada	S • C America • 250 kW
	GERMANY	
	†DEUTSCHE WELLE, Via Sri Lanka	S • E Europe & W Asia • 250 kW
	IRAN	
	†VO THE ISLAMIC REP, Zāhedān	S • Mideast & N Africa • 500 kW
	SOUTH AFRICA	
	CHANNEL AFRICA, Meyerton	W Africa & C Africa • 500 kW
	UNITED KINGDOM	
	BBC, Via Singapore	W • C Asia • 250 kW
	USA	
	†FAMILY RADIO, Via Dhabayya, UAE	W • N Africa • 250 kW
	RFE-RL, Via Biblis, Germany	W • W Asia & C Asia • 100 kW
9685v	BRAZIL	
	†RADIO GAZETA, São Paulo	DS • 7.5 kW
9688v	MADAGASCAR	
	RTV MALAGASY, Antananarivo	DS-1 • 30 kW
9690	ARGENTINA	
	†R ARGENTINA-RAE, Buenos Aires	M-F • Europe & N Africa • TEMP INACTIVE • 50 kW
	CANADA	
	R CANADA INTL, Via Hörby, Sweden	S • W Africa • 350 kW
	R CANADA INTL, Via In-Kimjae, Korea	S • E Asia & SE Asia • 250 kW
	CHINA	
	CENTRAL PEOPLE'S BS, Beijing	DS-8 (MINORITIES) • 100 kW
	CHINA R INTL, Kunming	S Asia • 150 kW
	CHINA R INTL, Via Noblejas, Spain	N America & C America • 350 kW
	CHINA (TAIWAN)	
	R TAIWAN INTL, Via Okeechobee, USA	W • S America • 100 kW
	INDIA	
	ALL INDIA RADIO, Bangalore	SE Asia • 500 kW
	NIGERIA	
	VOICE OF NIGERIA, Ikorodu	W Africa • 250 kW
		C Africa & E Africa • 250 kW
	ROMANIA	
	R ROMANIA INTL, Bucharest	W • W Europe • 250 kW
		S • C Asia • 250 kW
	R ROMANIA INTL, Galbeni	S • E North Am • 250 kW
		S • Mideast • 250 kW
		W • S Asia • 250 kW
		W • W Europe • 250 kW
		W • N Africa • 250 kW
	RUSSIA	
	TATARSTAN WAVE, Samara	S • C Asia • TATAR, RUSSIAN • 250 kW
	SPAIN	
	R EXTERIOR ESPANA, Noblejas	W Tu • N America & C America • 350 kW
	TURKEY	
	†VOICE OF TURKEY, Ankara-Emirler	S • W Asia & C Asia • 500 kW
	USA	
	†FAMILY RADIO, Okeechobee, Fl	W • S America • 100 kW
	R FREE ASIA, Via Dhabayya, UAE	W • C Asia • 500 kW
	†TRANS WORLD R, Via Merizo, Guam	W Th-Sa • E Asia • 100 kW
	VOA, Via Biblis, Germany	W • Mideast • 100 kW
9695	BRAZIL	
	†RADIO RIO MAR, Manaus	DS • 7.5 kW
(con'd)		Irr • DS • 7.5 kW

0 1 2 3 4 5 6 7 8 9 10 11 12 13 14 15 16 17 18 19 20 21 22 23 24

ENGLISH ▬ ARABIC ≈≈≈ CHINESE □□□ FRENCH ▭▭ GERMAN ══ RUSSIAN ══ SPANISH ══ OTHER ▬

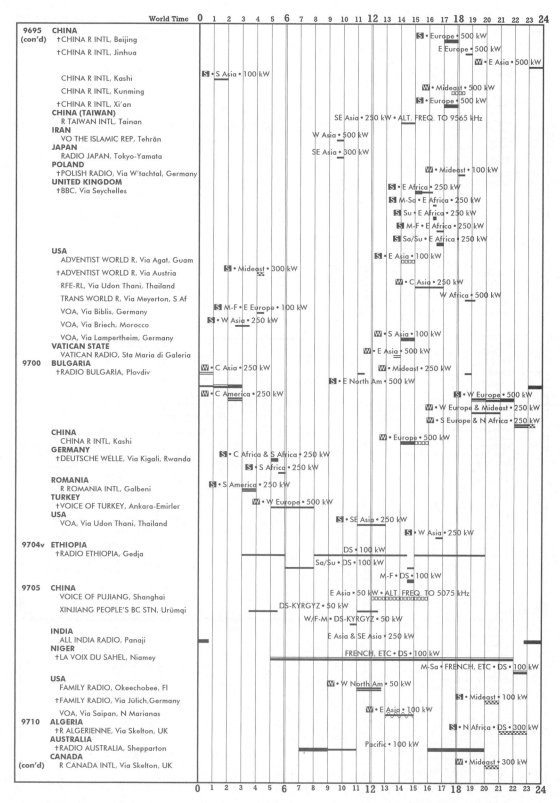

		World Time		
9695	**CHINA**			
(con'd)	†CHINA R INTL, Beijing	S • Europe • 500 kW
	†CHINA R INTL, Jinhua	E Europe • 500 kW
		W • E Asia • 500 kW
	CHINA R INTL, Kashi	S • S Asia • 100 kW
	CHINA R INTL, Kunming	W • Mideast • 500 kW
	†CHINA R INTL, Xi'an	S • Europe • 500 kW
	CHINA (TAIWAN)	
	R TAIWAN INTL, Tainan	SE Asia • 250 kW • ALT. FREQ. TO 9565 kHz
	IRAN	
	VO THE ISLAMIC REP, Tehrān	W Asia • 500 kW
	JAPAN	
	RADIO JAPAN, Tokyo-Yamata	SE Asia • 300 kW
	POLAND	
	†POLISH RADIO, Via W'tachtal, Germany	W • Mideast • 100 kW
	UNITED KINGDOM	
	†BBC, Via Seychelles	S • E Africa • 250 kW
		S M-Sa • E Africa • 250 kW
		S Su • E Africa • 250 kW
		S M-F • E Africa • 250 kW
		S Sa/Su • E Africa • 250 kW
	USA	
	ADVENTIST WORLD R, Via Agat, Guam	S • E Asia • 100 kW
	†ADVENTIST WORLD R, Via Austria	S • Mideast • 300 kW
	RFE-RL, Via Udon Thani, Thailand	W • C Asia • 250 kW
	TRANS WORLD R, Via Meyerton, S Af	W Africa • 500 kW
	VOA, Via Biblis, Germany	S M-F • E Europe • 100 kW
	VOA, Via Briech, Morocco	S • W Asia • 250 kW
	VOA, Via Lampertheim, Germany	W • S Asia • 100 kW
	VATICAN STATE	
	VATICAN RADIO, Sta Maria di Galeria	W • E Asia • 500 kW
9700	**BULGARIA**	
	†RADIO BULGARIA, Plovdiv	W • C Asia • 250 kW
		W • Mideast • 250 kW
		S • E North Am • 500 kW
		W • C America • 250 kW
		S • W Europe • 500 kW
		W • W Europe & Mideast • 250 kW
		W • S Europe & N Africa • 250 kW
	CHINA	
	CHINA R INTL, Kashi	W • Europe • 500 kW
	GERMANY	
	†DEUTSCHE WELLE, Via Kigali, Rwanda	S • C Africa & S Africa • 250 kW
		S • S Africa • 250 kW
	ROMANIA	
	R ROMANIA INTL, Galbeni	S • S America • 250 kW
	TURKEY	
	†VOICE OF TURKEY, Ankara-Emirler	W • W Europe • 500 kW
	USA	
	VOA, Via Udon Thani, Thailand	S • SE Asia • 250 kW
		S • W Asia • 250 kW
9704v	**ETHIOPIA**	
	†RADIO ETHIOPIA, Gedja	DS • 100 kW
		Sa/Su • DS • 100 kW
		M-F • DS • 100 kW
9705	**CHINA**	
	VOICE OF PUJIANG, Shanghai	E Asia • 50 kW • ALT. FREQ. TO 5075 kHz
	XINJIANG PEOPLE'S BC STN, Urümqi	DS-KYRGYZ • 50 kW
		W/F-M • DS-KYRGYZ • 50 kW
	INDIA	
	ALL INDIA RADIO, Panaji	E Asia & SE Asia • 250 kW
	NIGER	
	†LA VOIX DU SAHEL, Niamey	FRENCH, ETC • DS • 100 kW
		M-Sa • FRENCH, ETC • DS • 100 kW
	USA	
	FAMILY RADIO, Okeechobee, Fl	W • W North Am • 50 kW
	†FAMILY RADIO, Via Jülich, Germany	S • Mideast • 100 kW
	VOA, Via Saipan, N Marianas	W • E Asia • 100 kW
9710	**ALGERIA**	
	†R ALGERIENNE, Via Skelton, UK	S • N Africa • DS • 300 kW
	AUSTRALIA	
	†RADIO AUSTRALIA, Shepparton	Pacific • 100 kW
	CANADA	
(con'd)	R CANADA INTL, Via Skelton, UK	W • Mideast • 300 kW

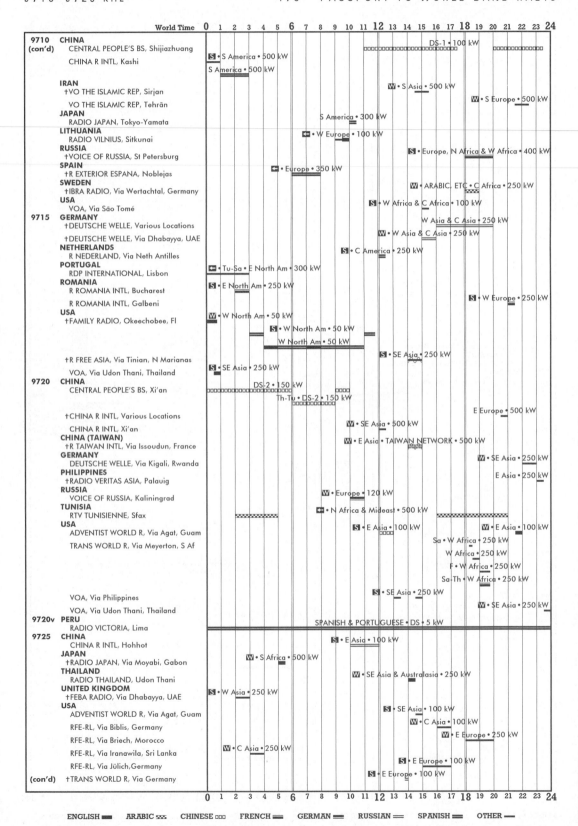

| | World Time | 0 | 1 | 2 | 3 | 4 | 5 | 6 | 7 | 8 | 9 | 10 | 11 | 12 | 13 | 14 | 15 | 16 | 17 | 18 | 19 | 20 | 21 | 22 | 23 | 24 |

9710 CHINA
(con'd)
- CENTRAL PEOPLE'S BS, Shijiazhuang — DS-1 • 100 kW; S • S America • 500 kW
- CHINA R INTL, Kashi — S America • 500 kW

IRAN
- †VO THE ISLAMIC REP, Sirjan — W • S Asia • 500 kW; W • S Europe • 500 kW
- VO THE ISLAMIC REP, Tehrān

JAPAN
- RADIO JAPAN, Tokyo-Yamata — S America • 300 kW

LITHUANIA
- RADIO VILNIUS, Sitkunai — W Europe • 100 kW

RUSSIA
- †VOICE OF RUSSIA, St Petersburg — S • Europe, N Africa & W Africa • 400 kW

SPAIN
- †R EXTERIOR ESPANA, Noblejas — Europe • 350 kW

SWEDEN
- †IBRA RADIO, Via Wertachtal, Germany — W • ARABIC, ETC • C Africa • 250 kW

USA
- VOA, Via São Tomé — S • W Africa & C Africa • 100 kW

9715 GERMANY
- †DEUTSCHE WELLE, Various Locations — W Asia & C Asia • 250 kW
- †DEUTSCHE WELLE, Via Dhabayya, UAE — W • W Asia & C Asia • 250 kW

NETHERLANDS
- R NEDERLAND, Via Neth Antilles — S • C America • 250 kW

PORTUGAL
- RDP INTERNATIONAL, Lisbon — Tu-Sa • E North Am • 300 kW

ROMANIA
- R ROMANIA INTL, Bucharest — S • E North Am • 250 kW
- R ROMANIA INTL, Galbeni — S • W Europe • 250 kW

USA
- †FAMILY RADIO, Okeechobee, Fl — W • W North Am • 50 kW; S • W North Am • 50 kW; W North Am • 50 kW

- †R FREE ASIA, Via Tinian, N Marianas — S • SE Asia • 250 kW
- VOA, Via Udon Thani, Thailand — S • SE Asia • 250 kW

9720 CHINA
- CENTRAL PEOPLE'S BS, Xi'an — DS-2 • 150 kW; Th-Tu • DS-2 • 150 kW

- †CHINA R INTL, Various Locations — E Europe • 500 kW
- CHINA R INTL, Xi'an — W • SE Asia • 500 kW

CHINA (TAIWAN)
- †R TAIWAN INTL, Via Issoudun, France — W • E Asia • TAIWAN NETWORK • 500 kW

GERMANY
- DEUTSCHE WELLE, Via Kigali, Rwanda — W • SE Asia • 250 kW

PHILIPPINES
- †RADIO VERITAS ASIA, Palauig — E Asia • 250 kW

RUSSIA
- VOICE OF RUSSIA, Kaliningrad — W • Europe • 120 kW

TUNISIA
- RTV TUNISIENNE, Sfax — N Africa & Mideast • 500 kW

USA
- ADVENTIST WORLD R, Via Agat, Guam — S • E Asia • 100 kW; W • E Asia • 100 kW
- TRANS WORLD R, Via Meyerton, S Af — Sa • W Africa • 250 kW; W Africa • 250 kW; F • W Africa • 250 kW; Sa-Th • W Africa • 250 kW

- VOA, Via Philippines — S • SE Asia • 250 kW
- VOA, Via Udon Thani, Thailand — W • SE Asia • 250 kW

9720v PERU
- RADIO VICTORIA, Lima — SPANISH & PORTUGUESE • DS • 5 kW

9725 CHINA
- CHINA R INTL, Hohhot — S • E Asia • 100 kW

JAPAN
- †RADIO JAPAN, Via Moyabi, Gabon — W • S Africa • 500 kW

THAILAND
- RADIO THAILAND, Udon Thani — W • SE Asia & Australasia • 250 kW

UNITED KINGDOM
- †FEBA RADIO, Via Dhabayya, UAE — S • W Asia • 250 kW

USA
- ADVENTIST WORLD R, Via Agat, Guam — S • SE Asia • 100 kW
- RFE-RL, Via Biblis, Germany — W • C Asia • 100 kW
- RFE-RL, Via Briech, Morocco — W • E Europe • 250 kW
- RFE-RL, Via Iranawila, Sri Lanka — W • C Asia • 250 kW
- RFE-RL, Via Jülich, Germany — S • E Europe • 100 kW
(con'd) †TRANS WORLD R, Via Germany — S • E Europe • 100 kW

| | 0 | 1 | 2 | 3 | 4 | 5 | 6 | 7 | 8 | 9 | 10 | 11 | 12 | 13 | 14 | 15 | 16 | 17 | 18 | 19 | 20 | 21 | 22 | 23 | 24 |

ENGLISH ▬   ARABIC ≈≈   CHINESE □□□   FRENCH ▬   GERMAN ▬   RUSSIAN ═   SPANISH ▬   OTHER ▬

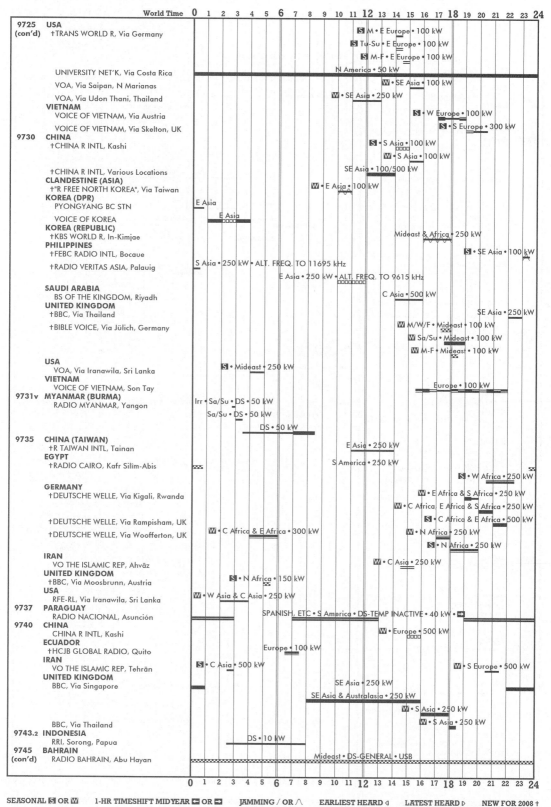

World Time	Station details		
9725 (con'd)	USA †TRANS WORLD R, Via Germany		S • M • E Europe • 100 kW / S • Tu-Su • E Europe • 100 kW / S • M-F • E Europe • 100 kW
	UNIVERSITY NET'K, Via Costa Rica		N America • 50 kW
	VOA, Via Saipan, N Marianas		W • SE Asia • 100 kW
	VOA, Via Udon Thani, Thailand		W • SE Asia • 250 kW
	VIETNAM VOICE OF VIETNAM, Via Austria		S • W Europe • 100 kW
	VOICE OF VIETNAM, Via Skelton, UK		S • S Europe • 300 kW
9730	CHINA †CHINA R INTL, Kashi		S • S Asia • 100 kW / W • S Asia • 100 kW
	†CHINA R INTL, Various Locations		SE Asia • 100/500 kW
	CLANDESTINE (ASIA) †"R FREE NORTH KOREA", Via Taiwan		W • E Asia • 100 kW
	KOREA (DPR) PYONGYANG BC STN	E Asia	
	VOICE OF KOREA	E Asia	
	KOREA (REPUBLIC) †KBS WORLD R, In-Kimjae		Mideast & Africa • 250 kW
	PHILIPPINES †FEBC RADIO INTL, Bocaue		S • SE Asia • 100 kW
	†RADIO VERITAS ASIA, Palauig	S Asia • 250 kW • ALT. FREQ. TO 11695 kHz		
		E Asia • 250 kW • ALT. FREQ. TO 9615 kHz	
	SAUDI ARABIA BS OF THE KINGDOM, Riyadh		C Asia • 500 kW
	UNITED KINGDOM †BBC, Via Thailand		SE Asia • 250 kW
	†BIBLE VOICE, Via Jülich, Germany		W • M/W/F • Mideast • 100 kW / W • Sa/Su • Mideast • 100 kW / W • M-F • Mideast • 100 kW
	USA VOA, Via Iranawila, Sri Lanka		S • Mideast • 250 kW
	VIETNAM VOICE OF VIETNAM, Son Tay		Europe • 100 kW
9731v	MYANMAR (BURMA) RADIO MYANMAR, Yangon	Irr • Sa/Su • DS • 50 kW / Sa/Su • DS • 50 kW / DS • 50 kW	
9735	CHINA (TAIWAN) †R TAIWAN INTL, Tainan		E Asia • 250 kW
	EGYPT †RADIO CAIRO, Kafr Silîm-Abis	S America • 250 kW	
	GERMANY †DEUTSCHE WELLE, Via Kigali, Rwanda		S • W Africa • 250 kW / W • E Africa & S Africa • 250 kW
	†DEUTSCHE WELLE, Via Rampisham, UK		W • C Africa, E Africa & S Africa • 250 kW / S • C Africa & E Africa • 500 kW
	†DEUTSCHE WELLE, Via Woofferton, UK	W • C Africa & E Africa • 300 kW		W • N Africa • 250 kW / S • N Africa • 250 kW
	IRAN VO THE ISLAMIC REP, Ahvãz		W • C Asia • 250 kW
	UNITED KINGDOM †BBC, Via Moosbrunn, Austria	S • N Africa • 150 kW	
	USA RFE-RL, Via Iranawila, Sri Lanka	W • W Asia & C Asia • 250 kW	
9737	PARAGUAY RADIO NACIONAL, Asunción	SPANISH, ETC • S America • DS-TEMP INACTIVE • 40 kW •	
9740	CHINA CHINA R INTL, Kashi		W • Europe • 500 kW
	ECUADOR †HCJB GLOBAL RADIO, Quito	Europe • 100 kW	
	IRAN VO THE ISLAMIC REP, Tehrãn	S • C Asia • 500 kW		W • S Europe • 500 kW
	UNITED KINGDOM BBC, Via Singapore		SE Asia • 250 kW
		SE Asia & Australasia • 250 kW	
			W • S Asia • 250 kW / W • S Asia • 250 kW
	BBC, Via Thailand		
9743.2	INDONESIA RRI, Sorong, Papua	DS • 10 kW	
9745 (con'd)	BAHRAIN RADIO BAHRAIN, Abu Hayan	Mideast • DS-GENERAL • USB	

SEASONAL S OR W   1-HR TIMESHIFT MIDYEAR ⬅ OR ➡   JAMMING / OR ∧   EARLIEST HEARD ◁   LATEST HEARD ▷   NEW FOR 2008 †

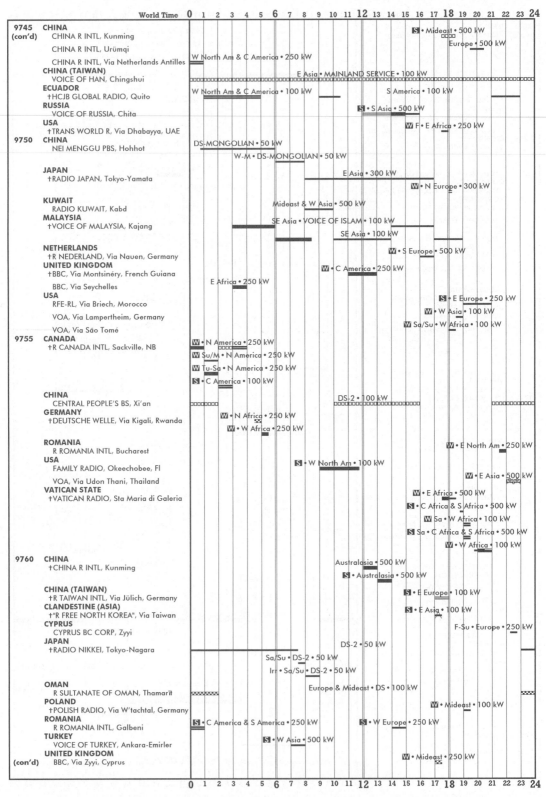

World Time 0 1 2 3 4 5 6 7 8 9 10 11 12 13 14 15 16 17 18 19 20 21 22 23 24

9745 CHINA
(con'd) CHINA R INTL, Kunming — S • Mideast • 500 kW
CHINA R INTL, Urümqi — Europe • 500 kW
CHINA R INTL, Via Netherlands Antilles — W North Am & C America • 250 kW
CHINA (TAIWAN) — E Asia • MAINLAND SERVICE • 100 kW
VOICE OF HAN, Chingshui
ECUADOR — W North Am & C America • 100 kW — S America • 100 kW
†HCJB GLOBAL RADIO, Quito
RUSSIA — S • S Asia • 500 kW
VOICE OF RUSSIA, Chita
USA — W F • E Africa • 250 kW
†TRANS WORLD R, Via Dhabayya, UAE

9750 CHINA — DS-MONGOLIAN • 50 kW
NEI MENGGU PBS, Hohhot
— W-M • DS-MONGOLIAN • 50 kW
JAPAN — E Asia • 300 kW
†RADIO JAPAN, Tokyo-Yamata
— W • N Europe • 300 kW
KUWAIT — Mideast & W Asia • 500 kW
RADIO KUWAIT, Kabd
MALAYSIA — SE Asia • VOICE OF ISLAM • 100 kW
†VOICE OF MALAYSIA, Kajang
— SE Asia • 100 kW
NETHERLANDS — W • S Europe • 500 kW
†R NEDERLAND, Via Nauen, Germany
UNITED KINGDOM — W • C America • 250 kW
†BBC, Via Montsinéry, French Guiana
BBC, Via Seychelles — E Africa • 250 kW
USA — S • E Europe • 250 kW
RFE-RL, Via Briech, Morocco
VOA, Via Lampertheim, Germany — W • W Asia • 100 kW
VOA, Via São Tomé — W Sa/Su • W Africa • 100 kW

9755 CANADA — W • N America • 250 kW
†R CANADA INTL, Sackville, NB
— W Su/M • N America • 250 kW
— W Tu-Sa • N America • 250 kW
— S • C America • 100 kW
CHINA — DS-2 • 100 kW
CENTRAL PEOPLE'S BS, Xi'an
GERMANY — W • N Africa • 250 kW
†DEUTSCHE WELLE, Via Kigali, Rwanda
— W • W Africa • 250 kW
ROMANIA — W • E North Am • 250 kW
R ROMANIA INTL, Bucharest
USA — S • W North Am • 100 kW
FAMILY RADIO, Okeechobee, Fl
VOA, Via Udon Thani, Thailand — W • E Asia • 500 kW
VATICAN STATE — W • E Africa • 500 kW
†VATICAN RADIO, Sta Maria di Galeria
— S • C Africa & S Africa • 500 kW
— W Sa • W Africa • 100 kW
— S Sa • C Africa & S Africa • 500 kW
— W • W Africa • 100 kW

9760 CHINA — Australasia • 500 kW
†CHINA R INTL, Kunming
— S • Australasia • 500 kW
CHINA (TAIWAN) — S • E Europe • 100 kW
†R TAIWAN INTL, Via Jülich, Germany
CLANDESTINE (ASIA) — S • E Asia • 100 kW
†"R FREE NORTH KOREA", Via Taiwan
CYPRUS — F-Su • Europe • 250 kW
CYPRUS BC CORP, Zyyi
JAPAN — DS-2 • 50 kW
†RADIO NIKKEI, Tokyo-Nagara
— Sa/Su • DS-2 • 50 kW
— Irr • Sa/Su • DS-2 • 50 kW
OMAN — Europe & Mideast • DS • 100 kW
R SULTANATE OF OMAN, Thamarīt
POLAND — W • Mideast • 100 kW
†POLISH RADIO, Via W'tachtal, Germany
ROMANIA — S • C America & S America • 250 kW — S • W Europe • 250 kW
R ROMANIA INTL, Galbeni
TURKEY — S • W Asia • 500 kW
VOICE OF TURKEY, Ankara-Emirler
UNITED KINGDOM — W • Mideast • 250 kW
(con'd) BBC, Via Zyyi, Cyprus

0 1 2 3 4 5 6 7 8 9 10 11 12 13 14 15 16 17 18 19 20 21 22 23 24

ENGLISH ▪▪ ARABIC ≋ CHINESE ▫▫▫ FRENCH ▬ GERMAN ▬ RUSSIAN ═ SPANISH ▬ OTHER ▬

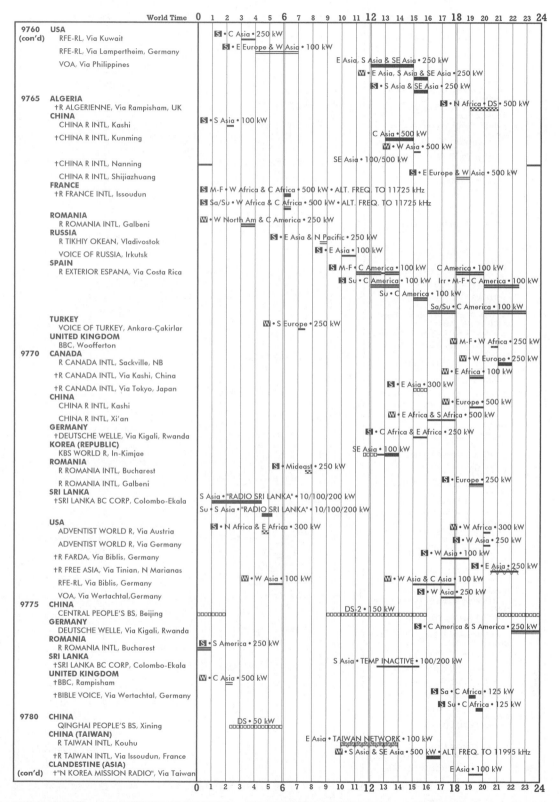

		World Time	0 1 2 3 4 5 6 7 8 9 10 11 12 13 14 15 16 17 18 19 20 21 22 23 24

9760 USA
(con'd)
- RFE-RL, Via Kuwait — S • C Asia • 250 kW
- RFE-RL, Via Lampertheim, Germany — S • E Europe & W Asia • 100 kW
- VOA, Via Philippines — E Asia, S Asia & SE Asia • 250 kW / W • E Asia, S Asia & SE Asia • 250 kW / S • S Asia & SE Asia • 250 kW

9765 ALGERIA
- †R ALGERIENNE, Via Rampisham, UK — S • N Africa • DS • 500 kW

CHINA
- CHINA R INTL, Kashi — S • S Asia • 100 kW
- †CHINA R INTL, Kunming — C Asia • 500 kW / W • W Asia • 500 kW
- †CHINA R INTL, Nanning — SE Asia • 100/500 kW
- CHINA R INTL, Shijiazhuang — S • E Europe & W Asia • 500 kW

FRANCE
- †R FRANCE INTL, Issoudun — S M-F • W Africa & C Africa • 500 kW • ALT. FREQ. TO 11725 kHz / S Sa/Su • W Africa & C Africa • 500 kW • ALT. FREQ. TO 11725 kHz

ROMANIA
- R ROMANIA INTL, Galbeni — W • W North Am & C America • 250 kW

RUSSIA
- R TIKHIY OKEAN, Vladivostok — S • E Asia & N Pacific • 250 kW
- VOICE OF RUSSIA, Irkutsk — S • E Asia • 100 kW

SPAIN
- R EXTERIOR ESPANA, Via Costa Rica — S M-F • C America • 100 kW   C America • 100 kW / S Su • C America • 100 kW   Irr • M-F • C America • 100 kW / Su • C America • 100 kW / Sa/Su • C America • 100 kW

TURKEY
- VOICE OF TURKEY, Ankara-Çakirlar — W • S Europe • 250 kW

UNITED KINGDOM
- BBC, Woofferton — W M-F • W Africa • 250 kW

9770 CANADA
- R CANADA INTL, Sackville, NB — W • W Europe • 250 kW / W • E Africa • 100 kW
- †R CANADA INTL, Via Kashi, China — S • E Asia • 300 kW
- †R CANADA INTL, Via Tokyo, Japan — W • Europe • 500 kW

CHINA
- CHINA R INTL, Kashi — W • E Africa & S Africa • 500 kW
- CHINA R INTL, Xi'an — S • C Africa & E Africa • 250 kW

GERMANY
- †DEUTSCHE WELLE, Via Kigali, Rwanda

KOREA (REPUBLIC)
- KBS WORLD R, In-Kimjae — SE Asia • 100 kW

ROMANIA
- R ROMANIA INTL, Bucharest — S • Mideast • 250 kW
- R ROMANIA INTL, Galbeni — S • Europe • 250 kW

SRI LANKA
- †SRI LANKA BC CORP, Colombo-Ekala — S Asia • "RADIO SRI LANKA" • 10/100/200 kW / Su • S Asia • "RADIO SRI LANKA" • 10/100/200 kW

USA
- ADVENTIST WORLD R, Via Austria — S • N Africa & E Africa • 300 kW
- ADVENTIST WORLD R, Via Germany — W • W Africa • 300 kW / S • W Asia • 250 kW
- †R FARDA, Via Biblis, Germany — S • W Asia • 100 kW
- †R FREE ASIA, Via Tinian, N Marianas — S • E Asia • 250 kW
- RFE-RL, Via Biblis, Germany — W • W Asia • 100 kW / W • W Asia & C Asia • 100 kW
- VOA, Via Wertachtal, Germany — S • W Asia • 250 kW

9775 CHINA
- CENTRAL PEOPLE'S BS, Beijing — DS-2 • 150 kW

GERMANY
- DEUTSCHE WELLE, Via Kigali, Rwanda — S • C America & S America • 250 kW

ROMANIA
- R ROMANIA INTL, Bucharest — S • S America • 250 kW

SRI LANKA
- †SRI LANKA BC CORP, Colombo-Ekala — S Asia • TEMP INACTIVE • 100/200 kW

UNITED KINGDOM
- †BBC, Rampisham — W • C Asia • 500 kW
- †BIBLE VOICE, Via Wertachtal, Germany — S Sa • C Africa • 125 kW / S Su • C Africa • 125 kW

9780 CHINA
- QINGHAI PEOPLE'S BS, Xining — DS • 50 kW

CHINA (TAIWAN)
- R TAIWAN INTL, Kouhu — E Asia • TAIWAN NETWORK • 100 kW
- †R TAIWAN INTL, Via Issoudun, France — W • S Asia & SE Asia • 500 kW • ALT. FREQ. TO 11995 kHz

CLANDESTINE (ASIA)
(con'd)
- †"N KOREA MISSION RADIO", Via Taiwan — E Asia • 100 kW

	0 1 2 3 4 5 6 7 8 9 10 11 12 13 14 15 16 17 18 19 20 21 22 23 24

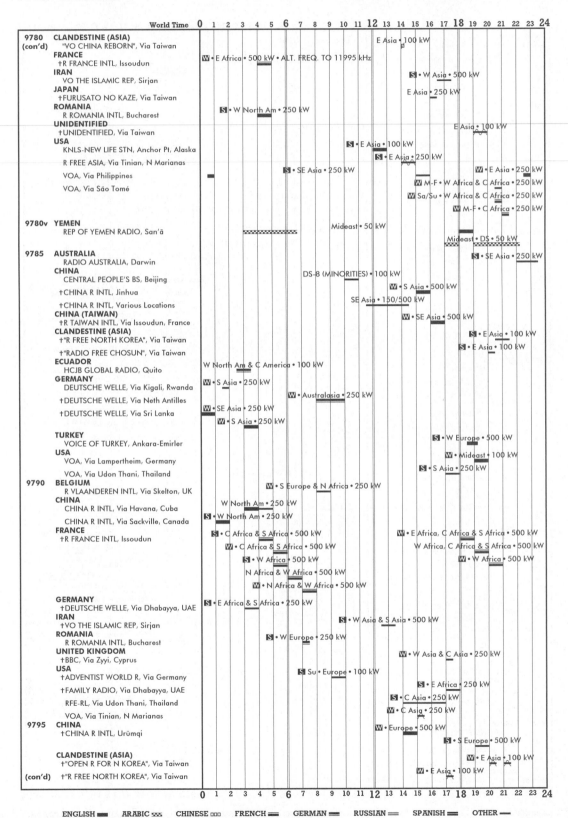

World Time 0 1 2 3 4 5 6 7 8 9 10 11 12 13 14 15 16 17 18 19 20 21 22 23 24

9780 CLANDESTINE (ASIA)
(con'd)   "VO CHINA REBORN", Via Taiwan — E Asia • 100 kW
        FRANCE
          †R FRANCE INTL, Issoudun — **W** • E Africa • 500 kW • ALT. FREQ. TO 11995 kHz
        IRAN
          VO THE ISLAMIC REP, Sirjan — **S** • W Asia • 500 kW
        JAPAN
          †FURUSATO NO KAZE, Via Taiwan — E Asia • 250 kW
        ROMANIA
          R ROMANIA INTL, Bucharest — **S** • W North Am • 250 kW
        UNIDENTIFIED
          †UNIDENTIFIED, Via Taiwan — E Asia • 100 kW
        USA
          KNLS-NEW LIFE STN, Anchor Pt, Alaska — **S** • E Asia • 100 kW
          R FREE ASIA, Via Tinian, N Marianas — **S** • E Asia • 250 kW
          VOA, Via Philippines — **S** • SE Asia • 250 kW / **W** • E Asia • 250 kW
          VOA, Via São Tomé — **W** • M-F • W Africa & C Africa • 250 kW / **W** Sa/Su • W Africa & C Africa • 250 kW / **W** • M-F • C Africa • 250 kW

9780v YEMEN
          REP OF YEMEN RADIO, San'ã — Mideast • 50 kW / Mideast • D**S** • 50 kW

9785 AUSTRALIA
          RADIO AUSTRALIA, Darwin — **S** • SE Asia • 250 kW
        CHINA
          CENTRAL PEOPLE'S BS, Beijing — DS-8 (MINORITIES) • 100 kW
          †CHINA R INTL, Jinhua — **W** • S Asia • 500 kW
          †CHINA R INTL, Various Locations — SE Asia • 150/500 kW
        CHINA (TAIWAN)
          †R TAIWAN INTL, Via Issoudun, France — **W** • SE Asia • 500 kW
        CLANDESTINE (ASIA)
          †"R FREE NORTH KOREA", Via Taiwan — **S** • E Asia • 100 kW
          †"RADIO FREE CHOSUN", Via Taiwan — **S** • E Asia • 100 kW
        ECUADOR
          HCJB GLOBAL RADIO, Quito — W North Am & C America • 100 kW
        GERMANY
          DEUTSCHE WELLE, Via Kigali, Rwanda — **W** • S Asia • 250 kW
          †DEUTSCHE WELLE, Via Neth Antilles — **W** • Australasia • 250 kW
          †DEUTSCHE WELLE, Via Sri Lanka — **W** • SE Asia • 250 kW / **W** • S Asia • 250 kW
        TURKEY
          VOICE OF TURKEY, Ankara-Emirler — **S** • W Europe • 500 kW
        USA
          VOA, Via Lampertheim, Germany — **W** • Mideast • 100 kW
          VOA, Via Udon Thani, Thailand — **S** • S Asia • 250 kW

9790 BELGIUM
          R VLAANDEREN INTL, Via Skelton, UK — **W** • S Europe & N Africa • 250 kW
        CHINA
          CHINA R INTL, Via Havana, Cuba — W North Am • 250 kW
          CHINA R INTL, Via Sackville, Canada — **S** • W North Am • 250 kW
        FRANCE
          †R FRANCE INTL, Issoudun — **S** • C Africa & S Africa • 500 kW / **W** • E Africa, C Africa & S Africa • 500 kW
            W • C Africa & S Africa • 500 kW / W Africa, C Africa & S Africa • 500 kW
            S • W Africa • 500 kW / **W** • W Africa • 500 kW
            N Africa & W Africa • 500 kW
            W • N Africa & W Africa • 500 kW
        GERMANY
          †DEUTSCHE WELLE, Via Dhabayya, UAE — **S** • E Africa & S Africa • 250 kW
        IRAN
          †VO THE ISLAMIC REP, Sirjan — **S** • W Asia & S Asia • 500 kW
        ROMANIA
          R ROMANIA INTL, Bucharest — **S** • W Europe • 250 kW
        UNITED KINGDOM
          †BBC, Via Zyyi, Cyprus — **W** • W Asia & C Asia • 250 kW
        USA
          †ADVENTIST WORLD R, Via Germany — **S** Su • Europe • 100 kW
          †FAMILY RADIO, Via Dhabayya, UAE — **S** • E Africa • 250 kW
          RFE-RL, Via Udon Thani, Thailand — **S** • C Asia • 250 kW
          VOA, Via Tinian, N Marianas — **W** • C Asia • 250 kW

9795 CHINA
          †CHINA R INTL, Urümqi — **W** • Europe • 500 kW / **S** • S Europe • 500 kW
        CLANDESTINE (ASIA)
          †"OPEN R FOR N KOREA", Via Taiwan — **W** • E Asia • 100 kW
(con'd)   †"R FREE NORTH KOREA", Via Taiwan — **W** • E Asia • 100 kW

0 1 2 3 4 5 6 7 8 9 10 11 12 13 14 15 16 17 18 19 20 21 22 23 24

ENGLISH ■■ ARABIC ⋙ CHINESE □□□ FRENCH ══ GERMAN ══ RUSSIAN ══ SPANISH ══ OTHER ──

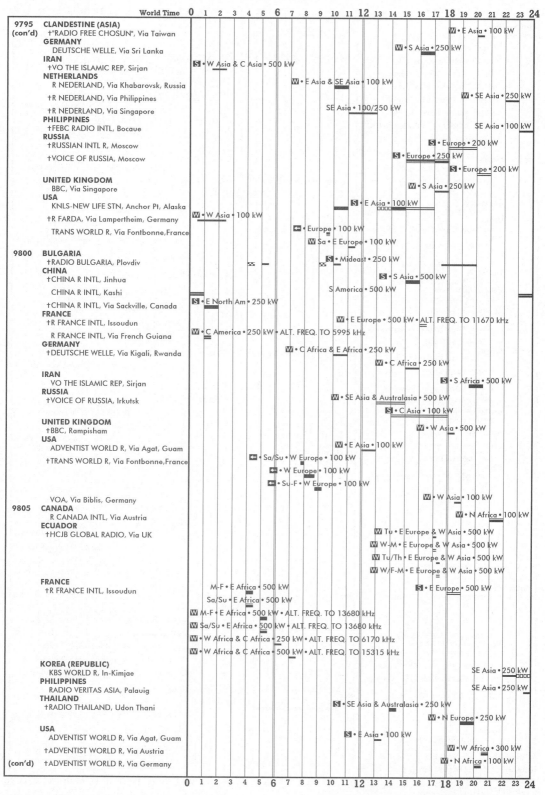

	World Time	0	1	2	3	4	5	6	7	8	9	10	11	12	13	14	15	16	17	18	19	20	21	22	23	24

9795 CLANDESTINE (ASIA)
(con'd) †"RADIO FREE CHOSUN", Via Taiwan — W • E Asia • 100 kW
GERMANY
DEUTSCHE WELLE, Via Sri Lanka — W • S Asia • 250 kW
IRAN
†VO THE ISLAMIC REP, Sirjan — S • W Asia & C Asia • 500 kW
NETHERLANDS
R NEDERLAND, Via Khabarovsk, Russia — W • E Asia & SE Asia • 100 kW
†R NEDERLAND, Via Philippines — W • SE Asia • 250 kW
†R NEDERLAND, Via Singapore — SE Asia • 100/250 kW
PHILIPPINES
†FEBC RADIO INTL, Bocaue — SE Asia • 100 kW
RUSSIA
†RUSSIAN INTL R, Moscow — S • Europe • 200 kW
†VOICE OF RUSSIA, Moscow — S • Europe • 250 kW / S • Europe • 200 kW
UNITED KINGDOM
BBC, Via Singapore — W • S Asia • 250 kW
USA
KNLS-NEW LIFE STN, Anchor Pt, Alaska — S • E Asia • 100 kW
†R FARDA, Via Lampertheim, Germany — W • W Asia • 100 kW
TRANS WORLD R, Via Fontbonne, France — ⬅ • Europe • 100 kW
— W Sa • E Europe • 100 kW

9800 BULGARIA
†RADIO BULGARIA, Plovdiv — S • Mideast • 250 kW
CHINA
†CHINA R INTL, Jinhua — S • S Asia • 500 kW
CHINA R INTL, Kashi — S America • 500 kW
†CHINA R INTL, Via Sackville, Canada — S • E North Am • 250 kW
FRANCE
†R FRANCE INTL, Issoudun — W • E Europe • 500 kW • ALT. FREQ. TO 11670 kHz
R FRANCE INTL, Via French Guiana — W • C America • 250 kW • ALT. FREQ. TO 5995 kHz
GERMANY
†DEUTSCHE WELLE, Via Kigali, Rwanda — W • C Africa & E Africa • 250 kW
— W • C Africa • 250 kW
IRAN
VO THE ISLAMIC REP, Sirjan — S • S Africa • 500 kW
RUSSIA
†VOICE OF RUSSIA, Irkutsk — W • SE Asia & Australasia • 500 kW
— S • C Asia • 100 kW
UNITED KINGDOM
†BBC, Rampisham — W • W Asia • 500 kW
USA
ADVENTIST WORLD R, Via Agat, Guam — W • E Asia • 100 kW
†TRANS WORLD R, Via Fontbonne, France — ⬅ • Sa/Su • W Europe • 100 kW
— ⬅ • W Europe • 100 kW
— ⬅ • Su-F • W Europe • 100 kW
VOA, Via Biblis, Germany — W • W Asia • 100 kW

9805 CANADA
R CANADA INTL, Via Austria — W • N Africa • 100 kW
ECUADOR
†HCJB GLOBAL RADIO, Via UK — W Tu • E Europe & W Asia • 500 kW
— W W-M • E Europe & W Asia • 500 kW
— W Tu/Th • E Europe & W Asia • 500 kW
— W W/F-M • E Europe & W Asia • 500 kW
FRANCE
†R FRANCE INTL, Issoudun — M-F • E Africa • 500 kW
— Sa/Su • E Africa • 500 kW
— W M-F • E Africa • 500 kW • ALT. FREQ. TO 13680 kHz
— W Sa/Su • E Africa • 500 kW • ALT. FREQ. TO 13680 kHz
— W • W Africa & C Africa • 250 kW • ALT. FREQ. TO 6170 kHz
— W • W Africa & C Africa • 500 kW • ALT. FREQ. TO 15315 kHz
— S • E Europe • 500 kW
KOREA (REPUBLIC)
KBS WORLD R, In-Kimjae — SE Asia • 250 kW
PHILIPPINES
RADIO VERITAS ASIA, Palauig — SE Asia • 250 kW
THAILAND
†RADIO THAILAND, Udon Thani — S • SE Asia & Australasia • 250 kW
— W • N Europe • 250 kW
USA
ADVENTIST WORLD R, Via Agat, Guam — S • E Asia • 100 kW
†ADVENTIST WORLD R, Via Austria — W • W Africa • 300 kW
(con'd) †ADVENTIST WORLD R, Via Germany — W • N Africa • 100 kW

	0	1	2	3	4	5	6	7	8	9	10	11	12	13	14	15	16	17	18	19	20	21	22	23	24

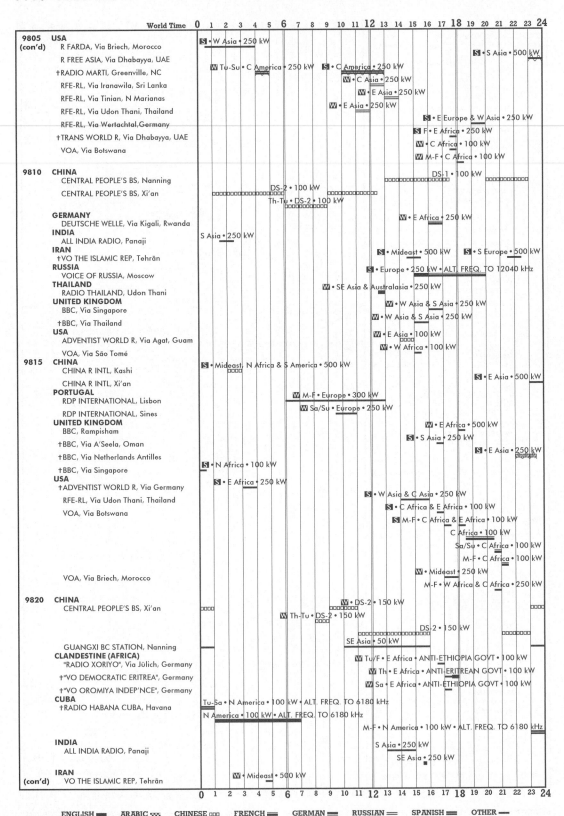

9805	**USA**	
(con'd)	R FARDA, Via Briech, Morocco	S • W Asia • 250 kW ... S • S Asia • 500 kW
	R FREE ASIA, Via Dhabayya, UAE	
	†RADIO MARTI, Greenville, NC	W • Tu-Su • C America • 250 kW S • C America • 250 kW
	RFE-RL, Via Iranawila, Sri Lanka	W • C Asia • 250 kW
	RFE-RL, Via Tinian, N Marianas	W • E Asia • 250 kW
	RFE-RL, Via Udon Thani, Thailand	W • E Asia • 250 kW
	RFE-RL, Via Wertachtal, Germany	S • E Europe & W Asia • 250 kW
	†TRANS WORLD R, Via Dhabayya, UAE	S F • E Africa • 250 kW
	VOA, Via Botswana	W • C Africa • 100 kW
		W M-F • C Africa • 100 kW

9810	**CHINA**	
	CENTRAL PEOPLE'S BS, Nanning	DS-1 • 100 kW
	CENTRAL PEOPLE'S BS, Xi'an	DS-2 • 100 kW Th-Tu • DS-2 • 100 kW
	GERMANY	
	DEUTSCHE WELLE, Via Kigali, Rwanda	W • E Africa • 250 kW
	INDIA	
	ALL INDIA RADIO, Panaji	S Asia • 250 kW
	IRAN	
	†VO THE ISLAMIC REP, Tehrān	S • Mideast • 500 kW S • S Europe • 500 kW
	RUSSIA	
	VOICE OF RUSSIA, Moscow	S • Europe • 250 kW • ALT. FREQ. TO 12040 kHz
	THAILAND	
	RADIO THAILAND, Udon Thani	W • SE Asia & Australasia • 250 kW
	UNITED KINGDOM	
	BBC, Via Singapore	W • W Asia & S Asia • 250 kW
	†BBC, Via Thailand	W • W Asia & S Asia • 250 kW
	USA	
	ADVENTIST WORLD R, Via Agat, Guam	W • E Asia • 100 kW
	VOA, Via São Tomé	W • W Africa • 100 kW

9815	**CHINA**	
	CHINA R INTL, Kashi	S • Mideast, N Africa & S America • 500 kW
	CHINA R INTL, Xi'an	S • E Asia • 500 kW
	PORTUGAL	
	RDP INTERNATIONAL, Lisbon	W M-F • Europe • 300 kW
	RDP INTERNATIONAL, Sines	W Sa/Su • Europe • 250 kW
	UNITED KINGDOM	
	BBC, Rampisham	W • E Africa • 500 kW
	†BBC, Via A'Seela, Oman	S • S Asia • 250 kW
	†BBC, Via Netherlands Antilles	S • E Asia • 250 kW
	†BBC, Via Singapore	S • N Africa • 100 kW
	USA	
	†ADVENTIST WORLD R, Via Germany	S • E Africa • 250 kW
	RFE-RL, Via Udon Thani, Thailand	S • W Asia & C Asia • 250 kW
	VOA, Via Botswana	S • C Africa & E Africa • 100 kW
		S M-F • C Africa & E Africa • 100 kW
		C Africa • 100 kW
		Sa/Su • C Africa • 100 kW
		M-F • C Africa • 100 kW
	VOA, Via Briech, Morocco	W • Mideast • 250 kW
		M-F • W Africa & C Africa • 250 kW

9820	**CHINA**	
	CENTRAL PEOPLE'S BS, Xi'an	W • DS-2 • 150 kW
		W Th-Tu • DS-2 • 150 kW
		DS-2 • 150 kW
		SE Asia • 50 kW
	GUANGXI BC STATION, Nanning	
	CLANDESTINE (AFRICA)	
	"RADIO XORIYO", Via Jülich, Germany	W Tu/F • E Africa • ANTI-ETHIOPIA GOVT • 100 kW
	†"VO DEMOCRATIC ERITREA", Germany	W Th • E Africa • ANTI-ERITREAN GOVT • 100 kW
	†"VO OROMIYA INDEP'NCE", Germany	W Sa • E Africa • ANTI-ETHIOPIA GOVT • 100 kW
	CUBA	
	†RADIO HABANA CUBA, Havana	Tu-Sa • N America • 100 kW • ALT. FREQ. TO 6180 kHz
		N America • 100 kW • ALT. FREQ. TO 6180 kHz
		M-F • N America • 100 kW • ALT. FREQ. TO 6180 kHz
	INDIA	
	ALL INDIA RADIO, Panaji	S Asia • 250 kW
		SE Asia • 250 kW
	IRAN	
(con'd)	VO THE ISLAMIC REP, Tehrān	W • Mideast • 500 kW

ENGLISH ▬   ARABIC ⧓⧓⧓   CHINESE □□□   FRENCH ▬   GERMAN ▬   RUSSIAN ═══   SPANISH ▬   OTHER ──

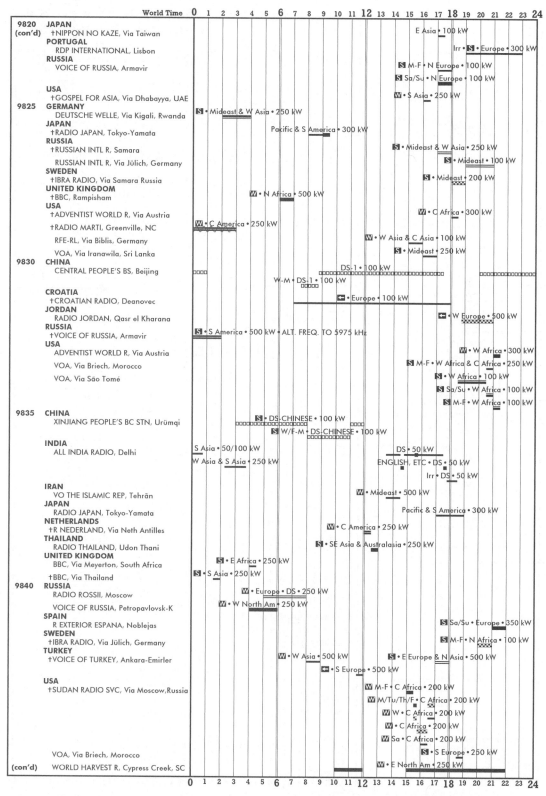

9820 (con'd)	**JAPAN**
	†NIPPON NO KAZE, Via Taiwan
	PORTUGAL
	RDP INTERNATIONAL, Lisbon
	RUSSIA
	VOICE OF RUSSIA, Armavir
	USA
	†GOSPEL FOR ASIA, Via Dhabayya, UAE
9825	**GERMANY**
	DEUTSCHE WELLE, Via Kigali, Rwanda
	JAPAN
	†RADIO JAPAN, Tokyo-Yamata
	RUSSIA
	†RUSSIAN INTL R, Samara
	RUSSIAN INTL R, Via Jülich, Germany
	SWEDEN
	†IBRA RADIO, Via Samara Russia
	UNITED KINGDOM
	†BBC, Rampisham
	USA
	†ADVENTIST WORLD R, Via Austria
	†RADIO MARTI, Greenville, NC
	RFE-RL, Via Biblis, Germany
	VOA, Via Iranawila, Sri Lanka
9830	**CHINA**
	CENTRAL PEOPLE'S BS, Beijing
	CROATIA
	†CROATIAN RADIO, Deanovec
	JORDAN
	RADIO JORDAN, Qasr el Kharana
	RUSSIA
	†VOICE OF RUSSIA, Armavir
	USA
	ADVENTIST WORLD R, Via Austria
	VOA, Via Briech, Morocco
	VOA, Via São Tomé
9835	**CHINA**
	XINJIANG PEOPLE'S BC STN, Urümqi
	INDIA
	ALL INDIA RADIO, Delhi
	IRAN
	VO THE ISLAMIC REP, Tehrān
	JAPAN
	RADIO JAPAN, Tokyo-Yamata
	NETHERLANDS
	†R NEDERLAND, Via Neth Antilles
	THAILAND
	RADIO THAILAND, Udon Thani
	UNITED KINGDOM
	BBC, Via Meyerton, South Africa
	†BBC, Via Thailand
9840	**RUSSIA**
	RADIO ROSSII, Moscow
	VOICE OF RUSSIA, Petropavlovsk-K
	SPAIN
	R EXTERIOR ESPANA, Noblejas
	SWEDEN
	†IBRA RADIO, Via Jülich, Germany
	TURKEY
	†VOICE OF TURKEY, Ankara-Emirler
	USA
	†SUDAN RADIO SVC, Via Moscow, Russia
	VOA, Via Briech, Morocco
(con'd)	WORLD HARVEST R, Cypress Creek, SC

SEASONAL Ⓢ OR Ⓦ   1-HR TIMESHIFT MIDYEAR ⬅ OR ➡   JAMMING / OR ∧   EARLIEST HEARD ◁   LATEST HEARD ▷   NEW FOR 2008 †

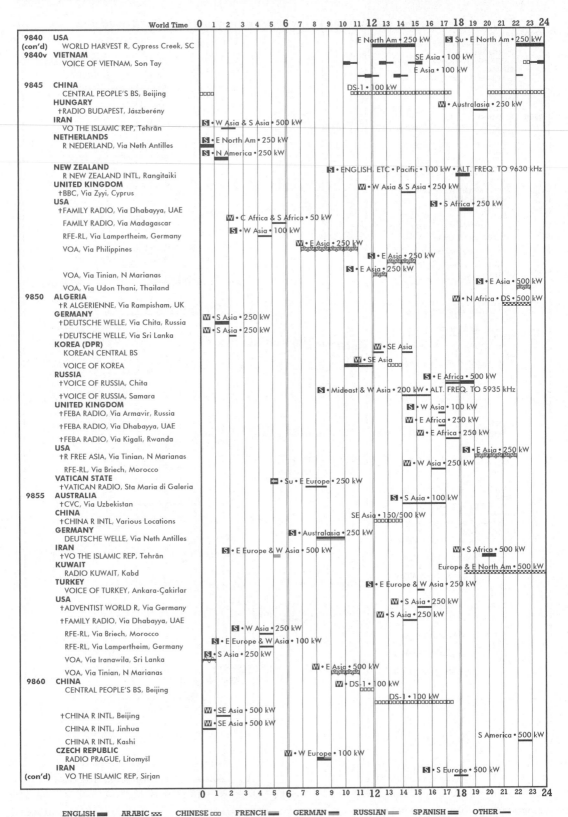

World Time	0 1 2 3 4 5 6 7 8 9 10 11 12 13 14 15 16 17 18 19 20 21 22 23 24
9840 (con'd) **USA**	
WORLD HARVEST R, Cypress Creek, SC	E North Am • 250 kW S • Su • E North Am • 250 kW
9840v VIETNAM	
VOICE OF VIETNAM, Son Tay	SE Asia • 100 kW
	E Asia • 100 kW
9845 CHINA	
CENTRAL PEOPLE'S BS, Beijing	DS-1 • 100 kW
HUNGARY	
†RADIO BUDAPEST, Jászberény	W • Australasia • 250 kW
IRAN	
VO THE ISLAMIC REP, Tehrān	S • W Asia & S Asia • 500 kW
NETHERLANDS	
R NEDERLAND, Via Neth Antilles	S • E North Am • 250 kW
	S • N America • 250 kW
NEW ZEALAND	
R NEW ZEALAND INTL, Rangitaiki	S • ENGLISH, ETC • Pacific • 100 kW • ALT. FREQ. TO 9630 kHz
UNITED KINGDOM	
†BBC, Via Zyyi, Cyprus	W • W Asia & S Asia • 250 kW
USA	
†FAMILY RADIO, Via Dhabayya, UAE	S • S Africa • 250 kW
FAMILY RADIO, Via Madagascar	W • C Africa & S Africa • 50 kW
RFE-RL, Via Lampertheim, Germany	S • W Asia • 100 kW
VOA, Via Philippines	W • E Asia • 250 kW
	S • E Asia • 250 kW
	S • E Asia • 250 kW
VOA, Via Tinian, N Marianas	S • E Asia • 500 kW
VOA, Via Udon Thani, Thailand	
9850 ALGERIA	
†R ALGERIENNE, Via Rampisham, UK	W • N Africa • DS • 500 kW
GERMANY	
†DEUTSCHE WELLE, Via Chita, Russia	W • S Asia • 250 kW
†DEUTSCHE WELLE, Via Sri Lanka	W • S Asia • 250 kW
KOREA (DPR)	
KOREAN CENTRAL BS	W • SE Asia
VOICE OF KOREA	W • SE Asia
RUSSIA	
†VOICE OF RUSSIA, Chita	S • E Africa • 500 kW
†VOICE OF RUSSIA, Samara	S • Mideast & W Asia • 200 kW • ALT. FREQ. TO 5935 kHz
UNITED KINGDOM	
†FEBA RADIO, Via Armavir, Russia	S • W Asia • 100 kW
†FEBA RADIO, Via Dhabayya, UAE	W • E Africa • 250 kW
†FEBA RADIO, Via Kigali, Rwanda	W • E Africa • 250 kW
USA	
†R FREE ASIA, Via Tinian, N Marianas	S • E Asia • 250 kW
RFE-RL, Via Briech, Morocco	W • W Asia • 250 kW
VATICAN STATE	
†VATICAN RADIO, Sta Maria di Galeria	• Su • E Europe • 250 kW
9855 AUSTRALIA	
†CVC, Via Uzbekistan	S • S Asia • 100 kW
CHINA	
†CHINA R INTL, Various Locations	SE Asia • 150/500 kW
GERMANY	
DEUTSCHE WELLE, Via Neth Antilles	S • Australasia • 250 kW
IRAN	
†VO THE ISLAMIC REP, Tehrān	W • S Africa • 500 kW
KUWAIT	
RADIO KUWAIT, Kabd	S • E Europe & W Asia • 500 kW
	Europe & E North Am • 500 kW
TURKEY	
VOICE OF TURKEY, Ankara-Çakirlar	S • E Europe & W Asia • 250 kW
USA	
†ADVENTIST WORLD R, Via Germany	W • S Asia • 250 kW
†FAMILY RADIO, Via Dhabayya, UAE	W • S Asia • 250 kW
RFE-RL, Via Briech, Morocco	S • W Asia • 250 kW
RFE-RL, Via Lampertheim, Germany	S • E Europe & W Asia • 100 kW
VOA, Via Iranawila, Sri Lanka	S • S Asia • 250 kW
VOA, Via Tinian, N Marianas	W • E Asia • 500 kW
9860 CHINA	
CENTRAL PEOPLE'S BS, Beijing	W • DS-1 • 100 kW
	DS-1 • 100 kW
†CHINA R INTL, Beijing	W • SE Asia • 500 kW
CHINA R INTL, Jinhua	W • SE Asia • 500 kW
CHINA R INTL, Kashi	S America • 500 kW
CZECH REPUBLIC	
RADIO PRAGUE, Litomyšl	W • W Europe • 100 kW
IRAN	
(con'd) VO THE ISLAMIC REP, Sirjan	S • S Europe • 500 kW

World Time	0 1 2 3 4 5 6 7 8 9 10 11 12 13 14 15 16 17 18 19 20 21 22 23 24

ENGLISH ▬   ARABIC ▨▨▨   CHINESE □□□   FRENCH ▬   GERMAN ▬   RUSSIAN ═   SPANISH ▬   OTHER ▬

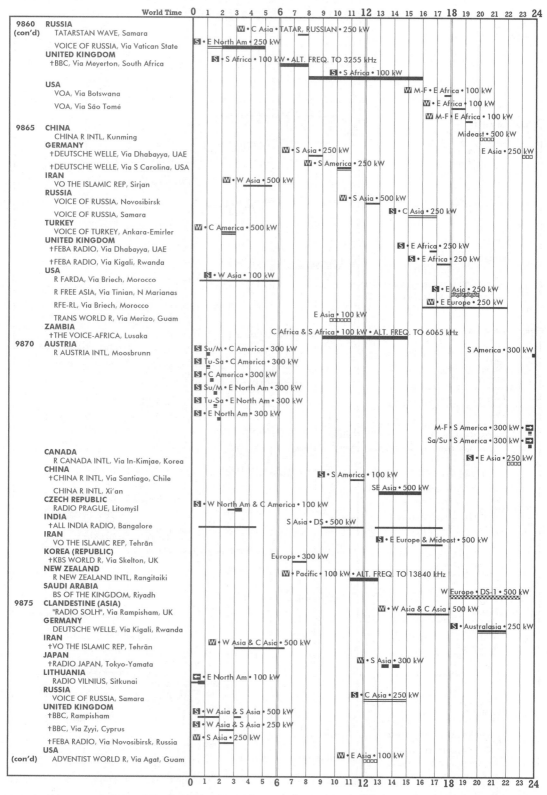

	World Time	0 1 2 3 4 5 6 7 8 9 10 11 12 13 14 15 16 17 18 19 20 21 22 23 24
9860 (con'd)	**RUSSIA**	
	TATARSTAN WAVE, Samara	W • C Asia • TATAR, RUSSIAN • 250 kW
	VOICE OF RUSSIA, Via Vatican State	S • E North Am • 250 kW
	UNITED KINGDOM	
	†BBC, Via Meyerton, South Africa	S • S Africa • 100 kW • ALT. FREQ. TO 3255 kHz
		S • S Africa • 100 kW
	USA	
	VOA, Via Botswana	W M-F • E Africa • 100 kW
	VOA, Via São Tomé	W • E Africa • 100 kW
		W M-F • E Africa • 100 kW
9865	**CHINA**	
	CHINA R INTL, Kunming	Mideast • 500 kW
	GERMANY	
	†DEUTSCHE WELLE, Via Dhabayya, UAE	W • S Asia • 250 kW
		E Asia • 250 kW
	†DEUTSCHE WELLE, Via S Carolina, USA	W • S America • 250 kW
	IRAN	
	VO THE ISLAMIC REP, Sirjan	W • W Asia • 500 kW
	RUSSIA	
	VOICE OF RUSSIA, Novosibirsk	W • S Asia • 500 kW
	VOICE OF RUSSIA, Samara	S • C Asia • 250 kW
	TURKEY	
	VOICE OF TURKEY, Ankara-Emirler	W • C America • 500 kW
	UNITED KINGDOM	
	†FEBA RADIO, Via Dhabayya, UAE	S • E Africa • 250 kW
	†FEBA RADIO, Via Kigali, Rwanda	S • E Africa • 250 kW
	USA	
	R FARDA, Via Briech, Morocco	S • W Asia • 100 kW
	R FREE ASIA, Via Tinian, N Marianas	S • E Asia • 250 kW
	RFE-RL, Via Briech, Morocco	W • E Europe • 250 kW
	TRANS WORLD R, Via Merizo, Guam	E Asia • 100 kW
	ZAMBIA	
	†THE VOICE-AFRICA, Lusaka	C Africa & S Africa • 100 kW • ALT. FREQ. TO 6065 kHz
9870	**AUSTRIA**	
	R AUSTRIA INTL, Moosbrunn	S Su/M • C America • 300 kW
		S Tu-Sa • C America • 300 kW
		S • C America • 300 kW
		S Su/M • E North Am • 300 kW
		S Tu-Sa • E North Am • 300 kW
		S • E North Am • 300 kW
		S America • 300 kW
		M-F • S America • 300 kW
		Sa/Su • S America • 300 kW
	CANADA	
	R CANADA INTL, Via In-Kimjae, Korea	S • E Asia • 250 kW
	CHINA	
	†CHINA R INTL, Via Santiago, Chile	S • S America • 100 kW
	CHINA R INTL, Xi'an	SE Asia • 500 kW
	CZECH REPUBLIC	
	RADIO PRAGUE, Litomyšl	S • W North Am & C America • 100 kW
	INDIA	
	†ALL INDIA RADIO, Bangalore	S Asia • DS • 500 kW
	IRAN	
	VO THE ISLAMIC REP, Tehrān	S • E Europe & Mideast • 500 kW
	KOREA (REPUBLIC)	
	†KBS WORLD R, Via Skelton, UK	Europe • 300 kW
	NEW ZEALAND	
	R NEW ZEALAND INTL, Rangitaiki	W • Pacific • 100 kW • ALT. FREQ. TO 13840 kHz
	SAUDI ARABIA	
	BS OF THE KINGDOM, Riyadh	W Europe • DS-1 • 500 kW
9875	**CLANDESTINE (ASIA)**	
	"RADIO SOLH", Via Rampisham, UK	W • W Asia & C Asia • 500 kW
	GERMANY	
	DEUTSCHE WELLE, Via Kigali, Rwanda	S • Australasia • 250 kW
	IRAN	
	†VO THE ISLAMIC REP, Tehrān	W • W Asia & C Asia • 500 kW
	JAPAN	
	†RADIO JAPAN, Tokyo-Yamata	W • S Asia • 300 kW
	LITHUANIA	
	RADIO VILNIUS, Sitkunai	• E North Am • 100 kW
	RUSSIA	
	VOICE OF RUSSIA, Samara	S • C Asia • 250 kW
	UNITED KINGDOM	
	†BBC, Rampisham	S • W Asia & S Asia • 500 kW
	†BBC, Via Zyyi, Cyprus	S • W Asia & S Asia • 250 kW
	†FEBA RADIO, Via Novosibirsk, Russia	W • S Asia • 250 kW
	USA	
(con'd)	ADVENTIST WORLD R, Via Agat, Guam	W • E Asia • 100 kW

	0 1 2 3 4 5 6 7 8 9 10 11 12 13 14 15 16 17 18 19 20 21 22 23 24

SEASONAL S OR W   1-HR TIMESHIFT MIDYEAR ⇐ OR ⇒   JAMMING / OR ∧   EARLIEST HEARD ◁   LATEST HEARD ▷   NEW FOR 2008 †

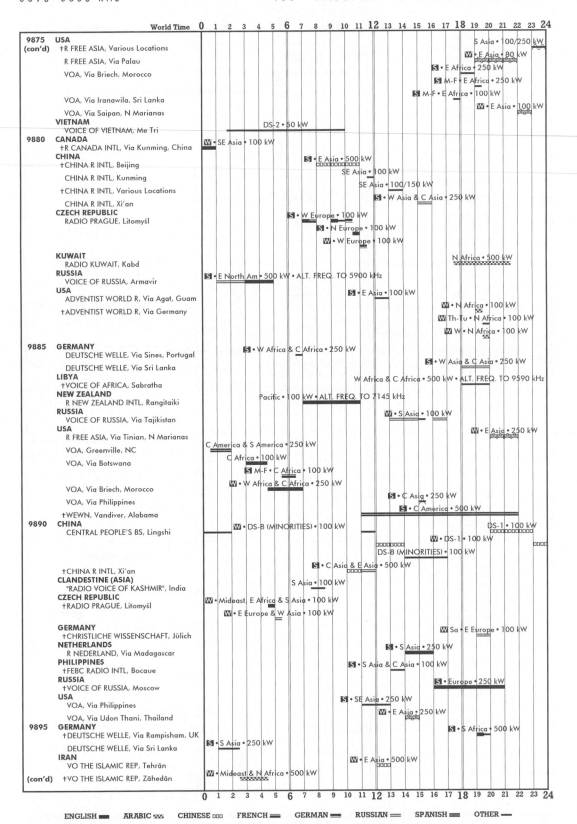

World Time	0 1 2 3 4 5 6 7 8 9 10 11 12 13 14 15 16 17 18 19 20 21 22 23 24
9875 **USA**	
(con'd) †R FREE ASIA, Various Locations	S Asia • 100/250 kW
R FREE ASIA, Via Palau	W • E Asia • 80 kW
VOA, Via Briech, Morocco	S • E Africa • 250 kW
	S M-F • E Africa • 250 kW
VOA, Via Iranawila, Sri Lanka	S M-F • E Africa • 100 kW
VOA, Via Saipan, N Marianas	W • E Asia • 100 kW
VIETNAM	
VOICE OF VIETNAM, Me Tri	DS-2 • 50 kW
9880 **CANADA**	
†R CANADA INTL, Via Kunming, China	W • SE Asia • 100 kW
CHINA	
†CHINA R INTL, Beijing	S • E Asia • 500 kW
CHINA R INTL, Kunming	SE Asia • 100 kW
†CHINA R INTL, Various Locations	SE Asia • 100/150 kW
CHINA R INTL, Xi'an	S • W Asia & C Asia • 250 kW
CZECH REPUBLIC	
RADIO PRAGUE, Litomyšl	S • W Europe • 100 kW
	S • N Europe • 100 kW
	W • W Europe • 100 kW
KUWAIT	
RADIO KUWAIT, Kabd	N Africa • 500 kW
RUSSIA	
VOICE OF RUSSIA, Armavir	S • E North Am • 500 kW • ALT. FREQ. TO 5900 kHz
USA	
ADVENTIST WORLD R, Via Agat, Guam	S • E Asia • 100 kW
†ADVENTIST WORLD R, Via Germany	W • N Africa • 100 kW
	W Th-Tu • N Africa • 100 kW
	W W • N Africa • 100 kW
9885 **GERMANY**	
DEUTSCHE WELLE, Via Sines, Portugal	S • W Africa & C Africa • 250 kW
DEUTSCHE WELLE, Via Sri Lanka	S • W Asia & C Asia • 250 kW
LIBYA	
†VOICE OF AFRICA, Sabratha	W Africa & C Africa • 500 kW • ALT. FREQ. TO 9590 kHz
NEW ZEALAND	
R NEW ZEALAND INTL, Rangitaiki	Pacific • 100 kW • ALT. FREQ. TO 7145 kHz
RUSSIA	
VOICE OF RUSSIA, Via Tajikistan	W • S Asia • 100 kW
USA	
R FREE ASIA, Via Tinian, N Marianas	W • E Asia • 250 kW
VOA, Greenville, NC	C America & S America • 250 kW
VOA, Via Botswana	C Africa • 100 kW
	S M-F • C Africa • 100 kW
VOA, Via Briech, Morocco	W • W Africa & C Africa • 250 kW
VOA, Via Philippines	S • C Asia • 250 kW
†WEWN, Vandiver, Alabama	S • C America • 500 kW
9890 **CHINA**	
CENTRAL PEOPLE'S BS, Lingshi	W • DS-B (MINORITIES) • 100 kW DS-1 • 100 kW
	W • DS-1 • 100 kW
	DS-8 (MINORITIES) • 100 kW
†CHINA R INTL, Xi'an	S • C Asia & E Asia • 500 kW
CLANDESTINE (ASIA)	
"RADIO VOICE OF KASHMIR", India	S Asia • 100 kW
CZECH REPUBLIC	
†RADIO PRAGUE, Litomyšl	W • Mideast, E Africa & S Asia • 100 kW
	W • E Europe & W Asia • 100 kW
GERMANY	
†CHRISTLICHE WISSENSCHAFT, Jülich	W Sa • E Europe • 100 kW
NETHERLANDS	
R NEDERLAND, Via Madagascar	S • S Asia • 250 kW
PHILIPPINES	
†FEBC RADIO INTL, Bocaue	S • S Asia & C Asia • 100 kW
RUSSIA	
†VOICE OF RUSSIA, Moscow	S • Europe • 250 kW
USA	
VOA, Via Philippines	S • SE Asia • 250 kW
VOA, Via Udon Thani, Thailand	W • E Asia • 250 kW
9895 **GERMANY**	
†DEUTSCHE WELLE, Via Rampisham, UK	S • S Africa • 500 kW
DEUTSCHE WELLE, Via Sri Lanka	S • S Asia • 250 kW
IRAN	
VO THE ISLAMIC REP, Tehrān	W • E Asia • 500 kW
(con'd) †VO THE ISLAMIC REP, Zāhedān	W • Mideast & N Africa • 500 kW
	0 1 2 3 4 5 6 7 8 9 10 11 12 13 14 15 16 17 18 19 20 21 22 23 24

ENGLISH ▬▬   ARABIC ⬚⬚⬚   CHINESE ▫▫▫   FRENCH ▬▬   GERMAN ▬▬   RUSSIAN ══   SPANISH ▬▬   OTHER ▬

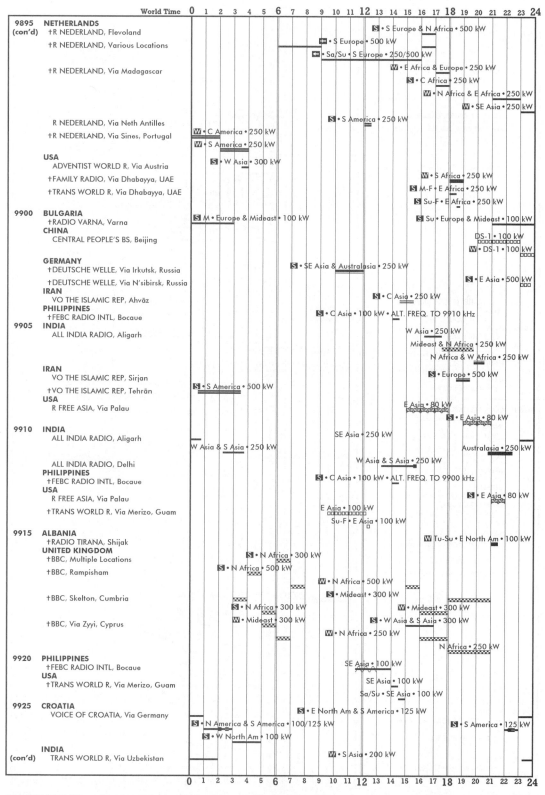

World Time

Freq	Station
9895 (con'd)	**NETHERLANDS**
	†R NEDERLAND, Flevoland — S • S Europe & N Africa • 500 kW
	†R NEDERLAND, Various Locations — • S Europe • 500 kW
	• Sa/Su • S Europe • 250/500 kW
	†R NEDERLAND, Via Madagascar — W • E Africa & Europe • 250 kW
	S • C Africa • 250 kW
	W • N Africa & E Africa • 250 kW
	W • SE Asia • 250 kW
	R NEDERLAND, Via Neth Antilles — S • S America • 250 kW
	†R NEDERLAND, Via Sines, Portugal — W • C America • 250 kW
	W • S America • 250 kW
	USA
	ADVENTIST WORLD R, Via Austria — S • W Asia • 300 kW
	†FAMILY RADIO, Via Dhabayya, UAE — W • S Africa • 250 kW
	†TRANS WORLD R, Via Dhabayya, UAE — S M-F • E Africa • 250 kW
	S Su-F • E Africa • 250 kW
9900	**BULGARIA**
	†RADIO VARNA, Varna — S M • Europe & Mideast • 100 kW S Su • Europe & Mideast • 100 kW
	CHINA
	CENTRAL PEOPLE'S BS, Beijing — DS-1 • 100 kW W • DS-1 • 100 kW
	GERMANY
	†DEUTSCHE WELLE, Via Irkutsk, Russia — S • SE Asia & Australasia • 250 kW
	†DEUTSCHE WELLE, Via N'sibirsk, Russia — S • E Asia • 500 kW
	IRAN
	VO THE ISLAMIC REP, Ahvāz — S • C Asia • 250 kW
	PHILIPPINES
	†FEBC RADIO INTL, Bocaue — S • C Asia • 100 kW • ALT. FREQ. TO 9910 kHz
9905	**INDIA**
	ALL INDIA RADIO, Aligarh — W Asia • 250 kW
	Mideast & N Africa • 250 kW
	N Africa & W Africa • 250 kW
	IRAN
	VO THE ISLAMIC REP, Sirjan — S • Europe • 500 kW
	†VO THE ISLAMIC REP, Tehrān — S • S America • 500 kW
	USA
	R FREE ASIA, Via Palau — E Asia • 80 kW
	S • E Asia • 80 kW
9910	**INDIA**
	ALL INDIA RADIO, Aligarh — SE Asia • 250 kW
	W Asia & S Asia • 250 kW Australasia • 250 kW
	ALL INDIA RADIO, Delhi — W Asia & S Asia • 250 kW
	PHILIPPINES
	†FEBC RADIO INTL, Bocaue — S • C Asia • 100 kW • ALT. FREQ. TO 9900 kHz
	USA
	R FREE ASIA, Via Palau — S • E Asia • 80 kW
	†TRANS WORLD R, Via Merizo, Guam — E Asia • 100 kW
	Su-F • E Asia • 100 kW
9915	**ALBANIA**
	†RADIO TIRANA, Shijak — W Tu-Su • E North Am • 100 kW
	UNITED KINGDOM
	†BBC, Multiple Locations — S • N Africa • 300 kW
	†BBC, Rampisham — S • N Africa • 500 kW
	W • N Africa • 500 kW
	S • Mideast • 300 kW
	†BBC, Skelton, Cumbria — S • N Africa • 300 kW W • Mideast • 300 kW
	†BBC, Via Zyyi, Cyprus — W • Mideast • 300 kW S • W Asia & S Asia • 300 kW
	W • N Africa • 250 kW
	N Africa • 250 kW
9920	**PHILIPPINES**
	†FEBC RADIO INTL, Bocaue — SE Asia • 100 kW
	USA
	†TRANS WORLD R, Via Merizo, Guam — SE Asia • 100 kW
	Sa/Su • SE Asia • 100 kW
9925	**CROATIA**
	VOICE OF CROATIA, Via Germany — S • E North Am & S America • 125 kW
	S • N America & S America • 100/125 kW S • S America • 125 kW
	S • W North Am • 100 kW
	INDIA (con'd)
	TRANS WORLD R, Via Uzbekistan — W • S Asia • 200 kW

World Time

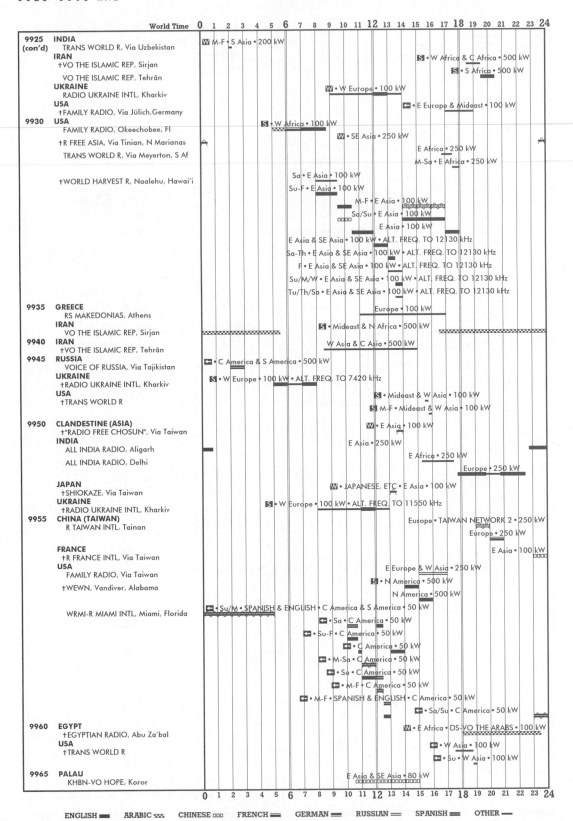

9925 (con'd)	**INDIA** TRANS WORLD R, Via Uzbekistan	W · M-F · S Asia · 200 kW
	IRAN †VO THE ISLAMIC REP, Sirjan	S · W Africa & C Africa · 500 kW
	VO THE ISLAMIC REP, Tehrān	S · S Africa · 500 kW
	UKRAINE RADIO UKRAINE INTL, Kharkiv	W · W Europe · 100 kW
	USA †FAMILY RADIO, Via Jülich, Germany	← E Europe & Mideast · 100 kW
9930	**USA** FAMILY RADIO, Okeechobee, Fl	S · W Africa · 100 kW
	†R FREE ASIA, Via Tinian, N Marianas	W · SE Asia · 250 kW
	TRANS WORLD R, Via Meyerton, S Af	E Africa · 250 kW · M-Sa · E Africa · 250 kW
	†WORLD HARVEST R, Naalehu, Hawai'i	Sa · E Asia · 100 kW · Su-F · E Asia · 100 kW · M-F · E Asia · 100 kW · Sa/Su · E Asia · 100 kW · E Asia · 100 kW · E Asia & SE Asia · 100 kW · ALT. FREQ. TO 12130 kHz · Sa-Th · E Asia & SE Asia · 100 kW · ALT. FREQ. TO 12130 kHz · F · E Asia & SE Asia · 100 kW · ALT. FREQ. TO 12130 kHz · Su/M/W · E Asia & SE Asia · 100 kW · ALT. FREQ. TO 12130 kHz · Tu/Th/Sa · E Asia & SE Asia · 100 kW · ALT. FREQ. TO 12130 kHz
9935	**GREECE** RS MAKEDONIAS, Athens	Europe · 100 kW
	IRAN VO THE ISLAMIC REP, Sirjan	S · Mideast & N Africa · 500 kW
9940	**IRAN** †VO THE ISLAMIC REP, Tehrān	W Asia & C Asia · 500 kW
9945	**RUSSIA** VOICE OF RUSSIA, Via Tajikistan	← · C America & S America · 500 kW
	UKRAINE †RADIO UKRAINE INTL, Kharkiv	S · W Europe · 100 kW · ALT. FREQ. TO 7420 kHz
	USA †TRANS WORLD R	S · Mideast & W Asia · 100 kW · S · M-F · Mideast & W Asia · 100 kW
9950	**CLANDESTINE (ASIA)** †"RADIO FREE CHOSUN", Via Taiwan	W · E Asia · 100 kW
	INDIA ALL INDIA RADIO, Aligarh	E Asia · 250 kW
	ALL INDIA RADIO, Delhi	E Africa · 250 kW · Europe · 250 kW
	JAPAN †SHIOKAZE, Via Taiwan	W · JAPANESE, ETC · E Asia · 100 kW
	UKRAINE †RADIO UKRAINE INTL, Kharkiv	S · W Europe · 100 kW · ALT. FREQ. TO 11550 kHz
9955	**CHINA (TAIWAN)** R TAIWAN INTL, Tainan	Europe · TAIWAN NETWORK 2 · 250 kW · Europe · 250 kW · E Asia · 100 kW
	FRANCE †R FRANCE INTL, Via Taiwan	E Europe & W Asia · 250 kW
	USA FAMILY RADIO, Via Taiwan	S · N America · 500 kW
	†WEWN, Vandiver, Alabama	N America · 500 kW
	WRMI-R MIAMI INTL, Miami, Florida	← · Su/M · SPANISH & ENGLISH · C America & S America · 50 kW · ← · Sa · C America · 50 kW · ← · Su-F · C America · 50 kW · ← · C America · 50 kW · ← · M-Sa · C America · 50 kW · ← · Su · C America · 50 kW · ← · M-F · C America · 50 kW · ← · M-F · SPANISH & ENGLISH · C America · 50 kW · ← · Sa/Su · C America · 50 kW
9960	**EGYPT** †EGYPTIAN RADIO, Abu Za'bal	W · E Africa · DS-VO THE ARABS · 100 kW
	USA †TRANS WORLD R	← · W Asia · 100 kW · ← · Su · W Asia · 100 kW
9965	**PALAU** KHBN-VO HOPE, Koror	E Asia & SE Asia · 80 kW

ENGLISH ▬   ARABIC ▨   CHINESE ▫▫▫   FRENCH ▬   GERMAN ▬   RUSSIAN ═   SPANISH ▬   OTHER ▬

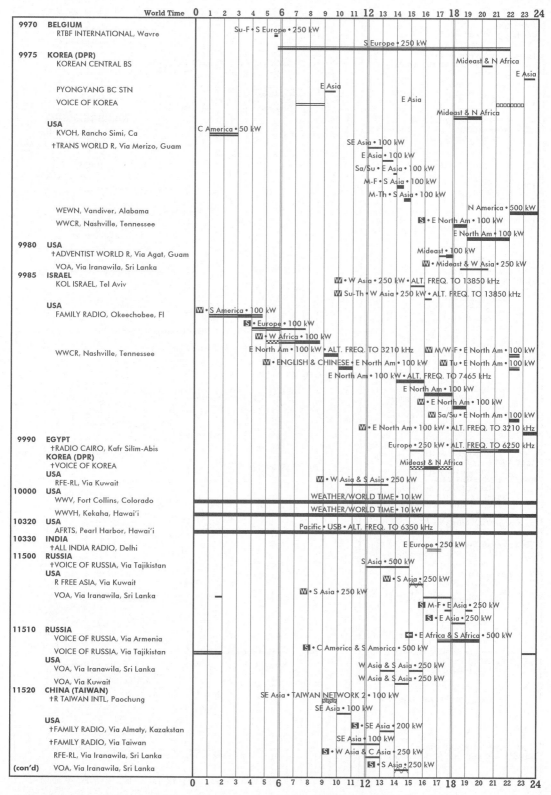

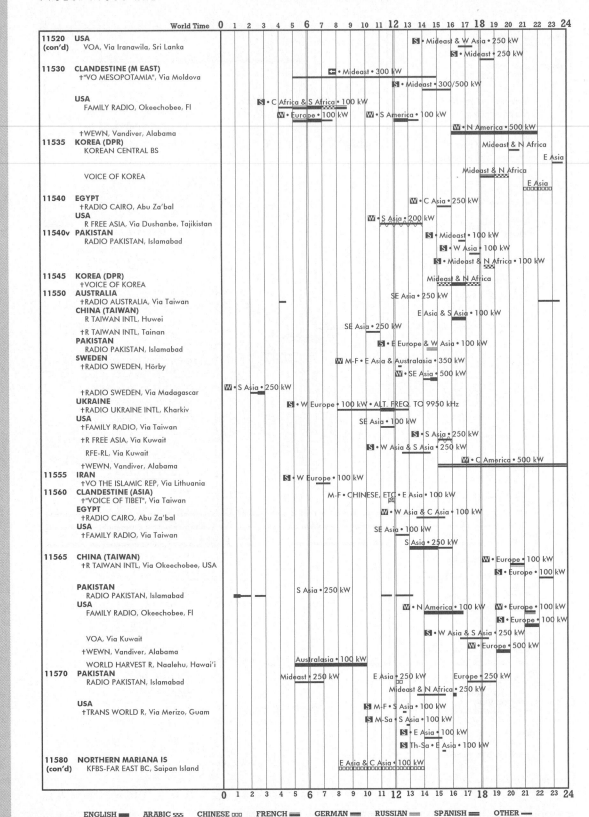

11520 (con'd)	**USA** VOA, Via Iranawila, Sri Lanka		S • Mideast & W Asia • 250 kW / S • Mideast • 250 kW
11530	**CLANDESTINE (M EAST)** †"VO MESOPOTAMIA", Via Moldova		← Mideast • 300 kW / S • Mideast • 300/500 kW
	USA FAMILY RADIO, Okeechobee, Fl		S • C Africa & S Africa • 100 kW / W • Europe • 100 kW / W • S America • 100 kW
	†WEWN, Vandiver, Alabama		W • N America • 500 kW
11535	**KOREA (DPR)** KOREAN CENTRAL BS		Mideast & N Africa / E Asia
	VOICE OF KOREA		Mideast & N Africa / E Asia
11540	**EGYPT** †RADIO CAIRO, Abu Za'bal		W • C Asia • 250 kW
	USA R FREE ASIA, Via Dushanbe, Tajikistan		W • S Asia • 200 kW
11540v	**PAKISTAN** RADIO PAKISTAN, Islamabad		S • Mideast • 100 kW / S • W Asia • 100 kW / S • Mideast & N Africa • 100 kW
11545	**KOREA (DPR)** †VOICE OF KOREA		Mideast & N Africa
11550	**AUSTRALIA** †RADIO AUSTRALIA, Via Taiwan		SE Asia • 250 kW
	CHINA (TAIWAN) R TAIWAN INTL, Huwei		E Asia & S Asia • 100 kW
	†R TAIWAN INTL, Tainan		SE Asia • 250 kW
	PAKISTAN RADIO PAKISTAN, Islamabad		S • E Europe & W Asia • 100 kW
	SWEDEN †RADIO SWEDEN, Hörby		W M-F • E Asia & Australasia • 350 kW / W • SE Asia • 500 kW
	†RADIO SWEDEN, Via Madagascar		W • S Asia • 250 kW
	UKRAINE †RADIO UKRAINE INTL, Kharkiv		S • W Europe • 100 kW • ALT. FREQ. TO 9950 kHz
	USA †FAMILY RADIO, Via Taiwan		SE Asia • 100 kW
	†R FREE ASIA, Via Kuwait		S • S Asia • 250 kW
	RFE-RL, Via Kuwait		S • W Asia & S Asia • 250 kW
	†WEWN, Vandiver, Alabama		W • C America • 500 kW
11555	**IRAN** †VO THE ISLAMIC REP, Via Lithuania		S • W Europe • 100 kW
11560	**CLANDESTINE (ASIA)** †"VOICE OF TIBET", Via Taiwan		M-F • CHINESE, ETC • E Asia • 100 kW
	EGYPT †RADIO CAIRO, Abu Za'bal		W • W Asia & C Asia • 100 kW
	USA †FAMILY RADIO, Via Taiwan		SE Asia • 100 kW / S Asia • 250 kW
11565	**CHINA (TAIWAN)** †R TAIWAN INTL, Via Okeechobee, USA		W • Europe • 100 kW / S • Europe • 100 kW
	PAKISTAN RADIO PAKISTAN, Islamabad		S Asia • 250 kW
	USA FAMILY RADIO, Okeechobee, Fl		W • N America • 100 kW / W • Europe • 100 kW / S • Europe • 100 kW
	VOA, Via Kuwait		S • W Asia & S Asia • 250 kW
	†WEWN, Vandiver, Alabama		W • Europe • 500 kW
	WORLD HARVEST R, Naalehu, Hawai'i		Australasia • 100 kW
11570	**PAKISTAN** RADIO PAKISTAN, Islamabad		Mideast • 250 kW / E Asia • 250 kW / Europe • 250 kW / Mideast & N Africa • 250 kW
	USA †TRANS WORLD R, Via Merizo, Guam		S M-F • S Asia • 100 kW / S M-Sa • S Asia • 100 kW / S • E Asia • 100 kW / S Th-Sa • E Asia • 100 kW
11580 (con'd)	**NORTHERN MARIANA IS** KFBS-FAR EAST BC, Saipan Island		E Asia & C Asia • 100 kW

ENGLISH ▬ ARABIC ▧ CHINESE ▫▫▫ FRENCH ▬ GERMAN ▬ RUSSIAN ═ SPANISH ▬ OTHER ▬

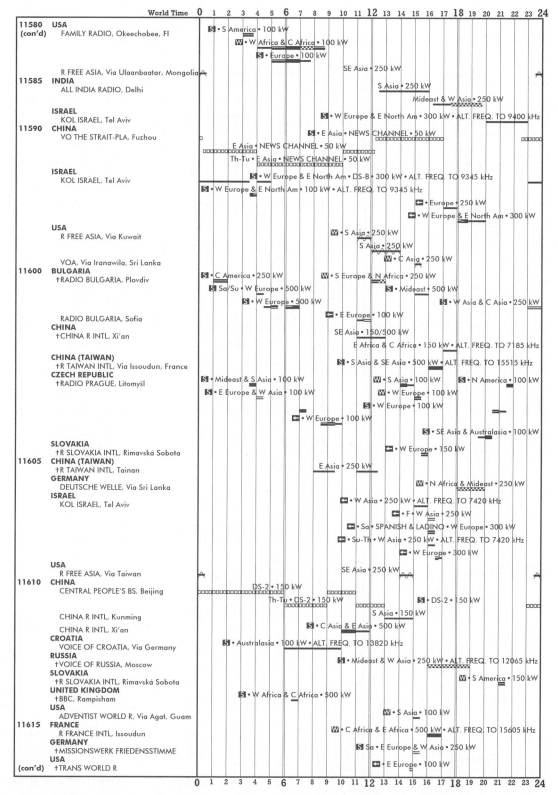

World Time

11580 (con'd)	USA
	FAMILY RADIO, Okeechobee, Fl
	S • S America • 100 kW
	W • W Africa & C Africa • 100 kW
	S • Europe • 100 kW
	R FREE ASIA, Via Ulaanbaatar, Mongolia • SE Asia • 250 kW
11585	INDIA
	ALL INDIA RADIO, Delhi • S Asia • 250 kW
	Mideast & W Asia • 250 kW
	ISRAEL
	KOL ISRAEL, Tel Aviv • S • W Europe & E North Am • 300 kW • ALT. FREQ. TO 9400 kHz
11590	CHINA
	VO THE STRAIT-PLA, Fuzhou • S • E Asia • NEWS CHANNEL • 50 kW
	E Asia • NEWS CHANNEL • 50 kW
	Th-Tu • E Asia • NEWS CHANNEL • 50 kW
	ISRAEL
	KOL ISRAEL, Tel Aviv • S • W Europe & E North Am • DS-B • 300 kW • ALT. FREQ. TO 9345 kHz
	S • W Europe & E North Am • 100 kW • ALT. FREQ. TO 9345 kHz
	⇦ • Europe • 250 kW
	⇦ • W Europe & E North Am • 300 kW
	USA
	R FREE ASIA, Via Kuwait • W • S Asia • 250 kW
	S Asia • 250 kW
	VOA, Via Iranawila, Sri Lanka • W • C Asia • 250 kW
11600	BULGARIA
	†RADIO BULGARIA, Plovdiv • S • C America • 250 kW
	W • S Europe & N Africa • 250 kW
	S • Sa/Su • W Europe • 500 kW
	S • Mideast • 500 kW
	S • W Europe • 500 kW
	S • W Asia & C Asia • 250 kW
	RADIO BULGARIA, Sofia
	CHINA
	†CHINA R INTL, Xi'an • ⇦ • E Europe • 100 kW
	SE Asia • 150/500 kW
	E Africa & C Africa • 150 kW • ALT. FREQ. TO 7185 kHz
	CHINA (TAIWAN)
	†R TAIWAN INTL, Via Issoudun, France • S • S Asia & SE Asia • 500 kW • ALT. FREQ. TO 15515 kHz
	CZECH REPUBLIC
	†RADIO PRAGUE, Litomyšl • S • Mideast & S Asia • 100 kW
	W • S Asia • 100 kW
	S • N America • 100 kW
	S • E Europe & W Asia • 100 kW
	W • W Europe • 100 kW
	S • W Europe • 100 kW
	⇦ • W Europe • 100 kW
	S • SE Asia & Australasia • 100 kW
	SLOVAKIA
	†R SLOVAKIA INTL, Rimavská Sobota • ⇦ • W Europe • 150 kW
11605	CHINA (TAIWAN)
	†R TAIWAN INTL, Tainan • E Asia • 250 kW
	GERMANY
	DEUTSCHE WELLE, Via Sri Lanka • W • N Africa & Mideast • 250 kW
	ISRAEL
	KOL ISRAEL, Tel Aviv • ⇦ • W Asia • 250 kW • ALT. FREQ. TO 7420 kHz
	⇦ • F • W Asia • 250 kW
	⇦ • Sa • SPANISH & LADINO • W Europe • 300 kW
	⇦ • Su-Th • W Asia • 250 kW • ALT. FREQ. TO 7420 kHz
	⇦ • W Europe • 300 kW
	USA
	R FREE ASIA, Via Taiwan • SE Asia • 250 kW
11610	CHINA
	CENTRAL PEOPLE'S BS, Beijing • DS-2 • 150 kW
	Th-Tu • DS-2 • 150 kW
	S • DS-2 • 150 kW
	CHINA R INTL, Kunming • S Asia • 150 kW
	CHINA R INTL, Xi'an • S • C Asia & E Asia • 500 kW
	CROATIA
	VOICE OF CROATIA, Via Germany • S • Australasia • 100 kW • ALT. FREQ. TO 13820 kHz
	RUSSIA
	†VOICE OF RUSSIA, Moscow • S • Mideast & W Asia • 250 kW • ALT. FREQ. TO 12065 kHz
	SLOVAKIA
	†R SLOVAKIA INTL, Rimavská Sobota • W • S America • 150 kW
	UNITED KINGDOM
	†BBC, Rampisham • S • W Africa & C Africa • 500 kW
	USA
	ADVENTIST WORLD R, Via Agat, Guam • W • S Asia • 100 kW
11615	FRANCE
	R FRANCE INTL, Issoudun • W • C Africa & E Africa • 500 kW • ALT. FREQ. TO 15605 kHz
	GERMANY
	†MISSIONSWERK FRIEDENSSTIMME • S • Sa • E Europe & W Asia • 250 kW
	USA
(con'd)	†TRANS WORLD R • ⇦ • E Europe • 100 kW

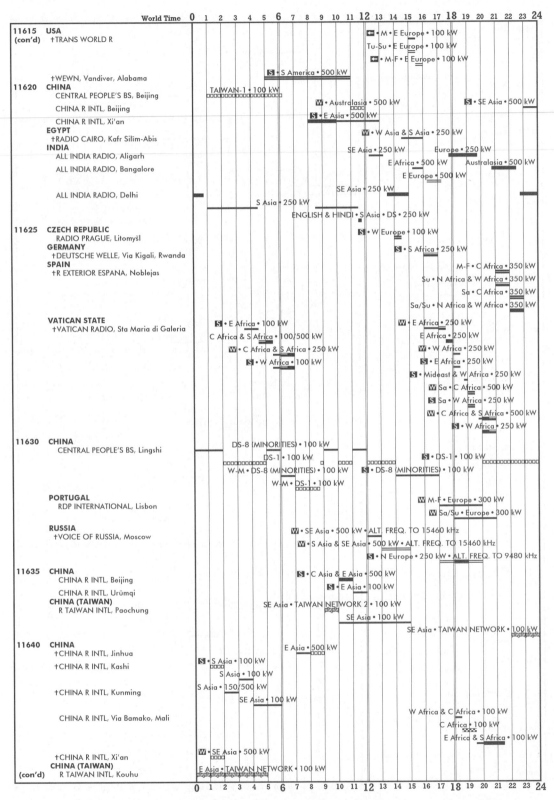

World Time   0 1 2 3 4 5 6 7 8 9 10 11 12 13 14 15 16 17 18 19 20 21 22 23 24

11615 USA
(con'd) †TRANS WORLD R
       • M • E Europe • 100 kW
       Tu-Su • E Europe • 100 kW
       • M-F • E Europe • 100 kW
       †WEWN, Vandiver, Alabama   S • S America • 500 kW
11620 CHINA
       CENTRAL PEOPLE'S BS, Beijing   TAIWAN-1 • 100 kW
       CHINA R INTL, Beijing   W • Australasia • 500 kW   S • SE Asia • 500 kW
       CHINA R INTL, Xi'an   S • E Asia • 500 kW
EGYPT
       †RADIO CAIRO, Kafr Silīm-Abis   W • W Asia & S Asia • 250 kW
INDIA
       ALL INDIA RADIO, Aligarh   SE Asia • 250 kW   Europe • 250 kW
       ALL INDIA RADIO, Bangalore   E Africa • 500 kW   Australasia • 500 kW
                                    E Europe • 500 kW
       ALL INDIA RADIO, Delhi   SE Asia • 250 kW
                                S Asia • 250 kW
                                ENGLISH & HINDI • S Asia • DS • 250 kW
11625 CZECH REPUBLIC
       RADIO PRAGUE, Litomyšl   S • W Europe • 100 kW
GERMANY
       †DEUTSCHE WELLE, Via Kigali, Rwanda   S • S Africa • 250 kW
SPAIN
       †R EXTERIOR ESPAÑA, Noblejas   M-F • C Africa • 350 kW
                                    Su • N Africa & W Africa • 350 kW
                                    Sa • C Africa • 350 kW
                                    Sa/Su • N Africa & W Africa • 350 kW
VATICAN STATE
       †VATICAN RADIO, Sta Maria di Galeria   S • E Africa • 100 kW   W • E Africa • 250 kW
                                    C Africa & S Africa • 100/500 kW   E Africa • 250 kW
                                    W • C Africa & S Africa • 250 kW   W • W Africa • 250 kW
                                    S • W Africa • 100 kW   S • E Africa • 250 kW
                                    S • Mideast & W Africa • 250 kW
                                    W Sa • C Africa • 500 kW
                                    S Sa • W Africa • 250 kW
                                    W • C Africa & S Africa • 500 kW
                                    S • W Africa • 250 kW
11630 CHINA
       CENTRAL PEOPLE'S BS, Lingshi   DS-8 (MINORITIES) • 100 kW
                                    DS-1 • 100 kW   S • DS-1 • 100 kW
                                    W-M • DS-8 (MINORITIES) • 100 kW   S • DS-8 (MINORITIES) • 100 kW
                                    W-M • DS-1 • 100 kW
PORTUGAL
       RDP INTERNATIONAL, Lisbon   W M-F • Europe • 300 kW
                                    W Sa/Su • Europe • 300 kW
RUSSIA
       †VOICE OF RUSSIA, Moscow   W • SE Asia • 500 kW • ALT. FREQ. TO 15460 kHz
                                    W • S Asia & SE Asia • 500 kW • ALT. FREQ. TO 15460 kHz
                                    S • N Europe • 250 kW • ALT. FREQ. TO 9480 kHz
11635 CHINA
       CHINA R INTL, Beijing   S • C Asia & E Asia • 500 kW
       CHINA R INTL, Urümqi   S • E Asia • 100 kW
CHINA (TAIWAN)
       R TAIWAN INTL, Paochung   SE Asia • TAIWAN NETWORK 2 • 100 kW
                                    SE Asia • 100 kW
                                    SE Asia • TAIWAN NETWORK • 100 kW
11640 CHINA
       †CHINA R INTL, Jinhua   E Asia • 500 kW
       †CHINA R INTL, Kashi   S • S Asia • 100 kW
                                S Asia • 100 kW
       †CHINA R INTL, Kunming   S Asia • 150/500 kW
                                SE Asia • 100 kW
       CHINA R INTL, Via Bamako, Mali   W Africa & C Africa • 100 kW
                                    C Africa • 100 kW
                                    E Africa & S Africa • 100 kW
       †CHINA R INTL, Xi'an   W • SE Asia • 500 kW
CHINA (TAIWAN)
(con'd) R TAIWAN INTL, Kouhu   E Asia • TAIWAN NETWORK • 100 kW

   0 1 2 3 4 5 6 7 8 9 10 11 12 13 14 15 16 17 18 19 20 21 22 23 24

ENGLISH ▬   ARABIC ▒   CHINESE ▫▫▫   FRENCH ▬   GERMAN ▬   RUSSIAN ═   SPANISH ▬   OTHER ▬

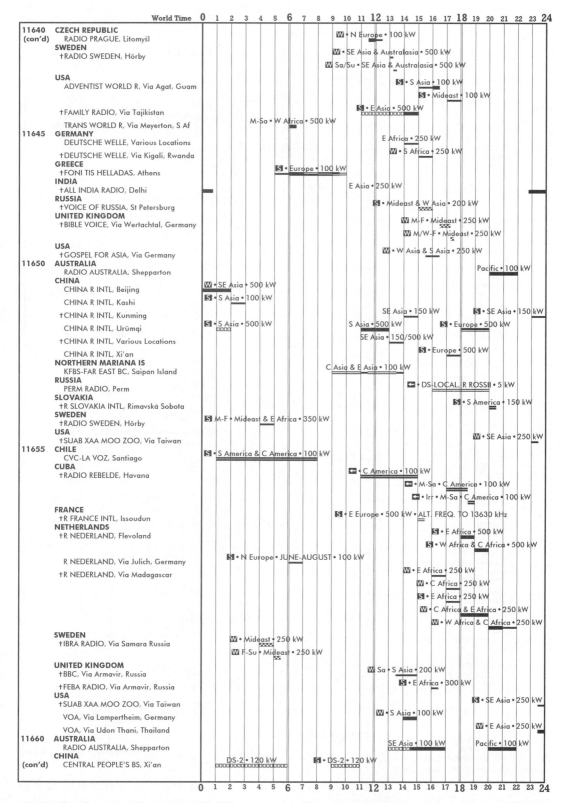

World Time		0 1 2 3 4 5 6 7 8 9 10 11 12 13 14 15 16 17 18 19 20 21 22 23 24
11640 (con'd)	**CZECH REPUBLIC**	
	RADIO PRAGUE, Litomyšl	W • N Europe • 100 kW
	SWEDEN	
	†RADIO SWEDEN, Hörby	W • SE Asia & Australasia • 500 kW
		W Sa/Su • SE Asia & Australasia • 500 kW
	USA	
	ADVENTIST WORLD R, Via Agat, Guam	S • S Asia • 100 kW
		S • Mideast • 100 kW
	†FAMILY RADIO, Via Tajikistan	S • E Asia • 500 kW
	TRANS WORLD R, Via Meyerton, S Af	M-Sa • W Africa • 500 kW
11645	**GERMANY**	
	DEUTSCHE WELLE, Various Locations	E Africa • 250 kW
	†DEUTSCHE WELLE, Via Kigali, Rwanda	W • S Africa • 250 kW
	GREECE	
	†FONI TIS HELLADAS, Athens	S • Europe • 100 kW
	INDIA	
	†ALL INDIA RADIO, Delhi	E Asia • 250 kW
	RUSSIA	
	†VOICE OF RUSSIA, St Petersburg	S • Mideast & W Asia • 200 kW
	UNITED KINGDOM	
	†BIBLE VOICE, Via Wertachtal, Germany	W M-F • Mideast • 250 kW
		W M/W-F • Mideast • 250 kW
	USA	
	†GOSPEL FOR ASIA, Via Germany	W • W Asia & S Asia • 250 kW
11650	**AUSTRALIA**	
	RADIO AUSTRALIA, Shepparton	Pacific • 100 kW
	CHINA	
	CHINA R INTL, Beijing	W • SE Asia • 500 kW
	CHINA R INTL, Kashi	S • S Asia • 100 kW
	†CHINA R INTL, Kunming	SE Asia • 150 kW S • SE Asia • 150 kW
	CHINA R INTL, Urümqi	S • S Asia • 500 kW S Asia • 500 kW S • Europe • 500 kW
	†CHINA R INTL, Various Locations	SE Asia • 150/500 kW
	CHINA R INTL, Xi'an	S • Europe • 500 kW
	NORTHERN MARIANA IS	
	KFBS-FAR EAST BC, Saipan Island	C Asia & E Asia • 100 kW
	RUSSIA	
	PERM RADIO, Perm	DS-LOCAL, R ROSSII • 5 kW
	SLOVAKIA	
	†R SLOVAKIA INTL, Rimavská Sobota	S • S America • 150 kW
	SWEDEN	
	†RADIO SWEDEN, Hörby	S M-F • Mideast & E Africa • 350 kW
	USA	
	†SUAB XAA MOO ZOO, Via Taiwan	W • SE Asia • 250 kW
11655	**CHILE**	
	CVC-LA VOZ, Santiago	S • S America & C America • 100 kW
	CUBA	
	†RADIO REBELDE, Havana	C America • 100 kW
		M-Sa • C America • 100 kW
		Irr • M-Sa • C America • 100 kW
	FRANCE	
	†R FRANCE INTL, Issoudun	S • E Europe • 500 kW • ALT. FREQ. TO 13630 kHz
	NETHERLANDS	
	†R NEDERLAND, Flevoland	S • E Africa • 500 kW
		S • W Africa & C Africa • 500 kW
	R NEDERLAND, Via Julich, Germany	S • N Europe • JUNE-AUGUST • 100 kW
	†R NEDERLAND, Via Madagascar	W • E Africa • 250 kW
		W • C Africa • 250 kW
		S • E Africa • 250 kW
		W • C Africa & E Africa • 250 kW
		W • W Africa & C Africa • 250 kW
	SWEDEN	
	†IBRA RADIO, Via Samara Russia	W • Mideast • 250 kW
		W F-Su • Mideast • 250 kW
	UNITED KINGDOM	
	†BBC, Via Armavir, Russia	W Sa • S Asia • 200 kW
	†FEBA RADIO, Via Armavir, Russia	S • E Africa • 300 kW
	USA	
	†SUAB XAA MOO ZOO, Via Taiwan	S • SE Asia • 250 kW
	VOA, Via Lampertheim, Germany	W • S Asia • 100 kW
	VOA, Via Udon Thani, Thailand	W • E Asia • 250 kW
11660	**AUSTRALIA**	
	RADIO AUSTRALIA, Shepparton	SE Asia • 100 kW Pacific • 100 kW
(con'd)	**CHINA**	
	CENTRAL PEOPLE'S BS, Xi'an	DS-2 • 120 kW S • DS-2 • 120 kW

SEASONAL S OR W   1-HR TIMESHIFT MIDYEAR ◱ OR ◰   JAMMING / OR ∧   EARLIEST HEARD ◁   LATEST HEARD ▷   NEW FOR 2008 †

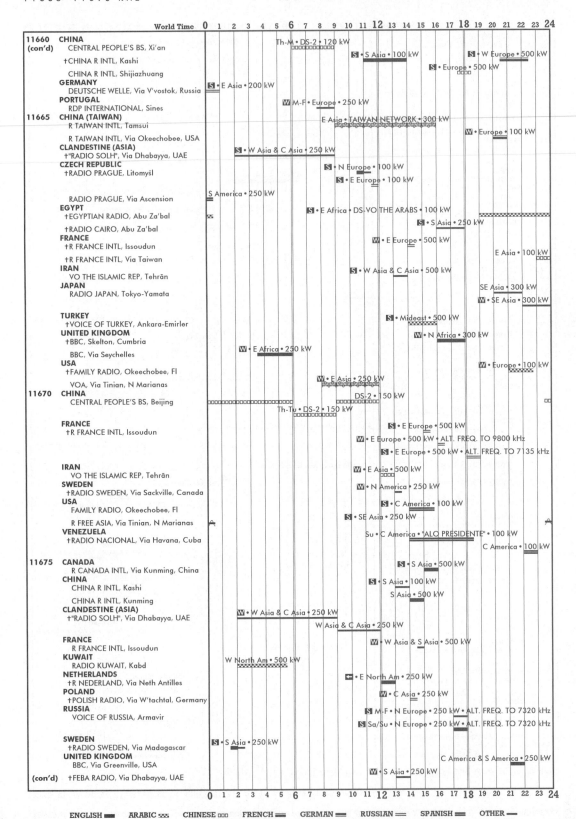

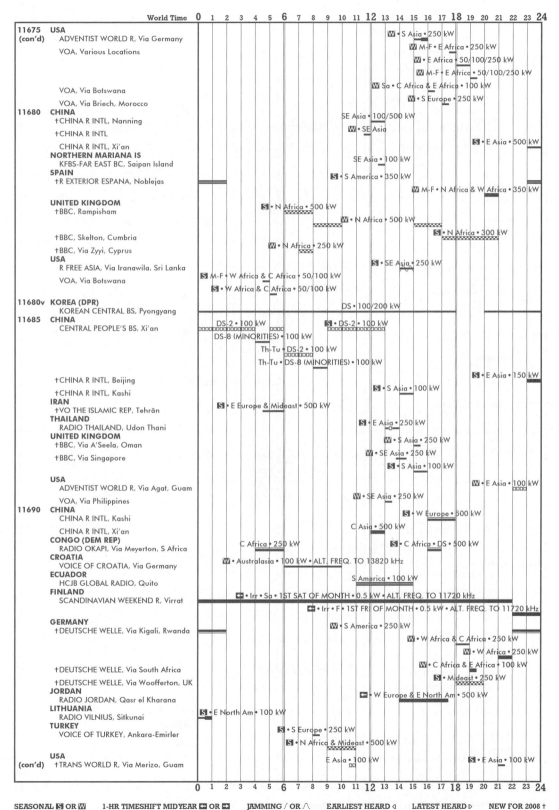

World Time 0 1 2 3 4 5 6 7 8 9 10 11 12 13 14 15 16 17 18 19 20 21 22 23 24

11675 **USA**
(con'd)   ADVENTIST WORLD R, Via Germany — W • S Asia • 250 kW
          VOA, Various Locations — W M-F • E Africa • 250 kW
                                    W • E Africa • 50/100/250 kW
                                    W M-F • E Africa • 50/100/250 kW
          VOA, Via Botswana — W Sa • C Africa & E Africa • 100 kW
          VOA, Via Briech, Morocco — W • S Europe • 250 kW

11680 **CHINA**
          †CHINA R INTL, Nanning — SE Asia • 100/500 kW
          †CHINA R INTL — W • SE Asia
          CHINA R INTL, Xi'an — S • E Asia • 500 kW
          NORTHERN MARIANA IS
          KFBS-FAR EAST BC, Saipan Island — SE Asia • 100 kW
          SPAIN
          †R EXTERIOR ESPANA, Noblejas — S • S America • 350 kW
                                          W M-F • N Africa & W Africa • 350 kW
          UNITED KINGDOM
          †BBC, Rampisham — S • N Africa • 500 kW
                             W • N Africa • 500 kW
          †BBC, Skelton, Cumbria — S • N Africa • 300 kW
          †BBC, Via Zyyi, Cyprus — W • N Africa • 250 kW
          USA
          R FREE ASIA, Via Iranawila, Sri Lanka — S • SE Asia • 250 kW
          VOA, Via Botswana — S M-F • W Africa & C Africa • 50/100 kW
                               S • W Africa & C Africa • 50/100 kW

11680v **KOREA (DPR)**
          KOREAN CENTRAL BS, Pyongyang — DS • 100/200 kW

11685 **CHINA**
          CENTRAL PEOPLE'S BS, Xi'an — DS-2 • 100 kW   S • DS-2 • 100 kW
                                       DS-8 (MINORITIES) • 100 kW
                                       Th-Tu • DS-2 • 100 kW
                                       Th-Tu • DS-8 (MINORITIES) • 100 kW
                                       S • E Asia • 150 kW
          †CHINA R INTL, Beijing — S • S Asia • 100 kW
          †CHINA R INTL, Kashi
          IRAN
          †VO THE ISLAMIC REP, Tehrān — S • E Europe & Mideast • 500 kW
          THAILAND
          RADIO THAILAND, Udon Thani — S • E Asia • 250 kW
          UNITED KINGDOM
          †BBC, Via A'Seela, Oman — W • S Asia • 250 kW
          †BBC, Via Singapore — W • SE Asia • 250 kW
                                 S • S Asia • 100 kW
          USA
          ADVENTIST WORLD R, Via Agat, Guam — W • E Asia • 100 kW
          VOA, Via Philippines — W • SE Asia • 250 kW

11690 **CHINA**
          CHINA R INTL, Kashi — S • W Europe • 500 kW
          CHINA R INTL, Xi'an — C Asia • 500 kW
          CONGO (DEM REP)
          RADIO OKAPI, Via Meyerton, S Africa — C Africa • 250 kW   S • C Africa • DS • 500 kW
          CROATIA
          VOICE OF CROATIA, Via Germany — W • Australasia • 100 kW • ALT. FREQ. TO 13820 kHz
          ECUADOR
          HCJB GLOBAL RADIO, Quito — S America • 100 kW
          FINLAND
          SCANDINAVIAN WEEKEND R, Virrat — ⇄ • Irr • Sa • 1ST SAT OF MONTH • 0.5 kW • ALT. FREQ. TO 11720 kHz
                                            ⇄ • Irr • F • 1ST FRI OF MONTH • 0.5 kW • ALT. FREQ. TO 11720 kHz
          GERMANY
          †DEUTSCHE WELLE, Via Kigali, Rwanda — W • S America • 250 kW
                                                W • W Africa & C Africa • 250 kW
                                                W • W Africa • 250 kW
          †DEUTSCHE WELLE, Via South Africa — W • C Africa & E Africa • 100 kW
          †DEUTSCHE WELLE, Via Woofferton, UK — S • Mideast • 250 kW
          JORDAN
          RADIO JORDAN, Qasr el Kharana — ⇄ • W Europe & E North Am • 500 kW
          LITHUANIA
          RADIO VILNIUS, Sitkunai — S • E North Am • 100 kW
          TURKEY
          VOICE OF TURKEY, Ankara-Emirler — S • S Europe • 250 kW
                                            S • N Africa & Mideast • 500 kW
          USA
(con'd)   †TRANS WORLD R, Via Merizo, Guam — E Asia • 100 kW   S • E Asia • 100 kW

0 1 2 3 4 5 6 7 8 9 10 11 12 13 14 15 16 17 18 19 20 21 22 23 24

SEASONAL S OR W   1-HR TIMESHIFT MIDYEAR ⇄ OR ⇄   JAMMING / OR ∧   EARLIEST HEARD ◁   LATEST HEARD ▷   NEW FOR 2008 †

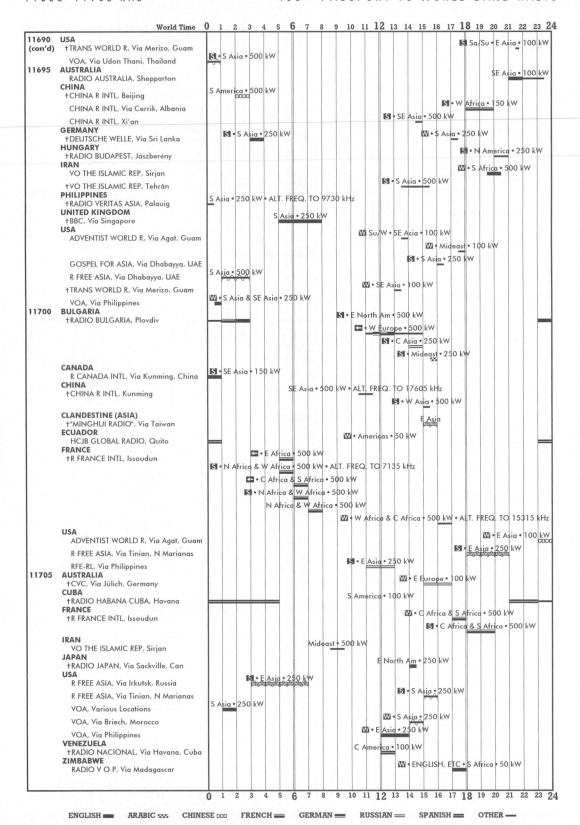

ENGLISH ▬   ARABIC ⌇⌇⌇   CHINESE ▫▫▫   FRENCH ▭   GERMAN ▬   RUSSIAN ═   SPANISH ▬   OTHER ▬

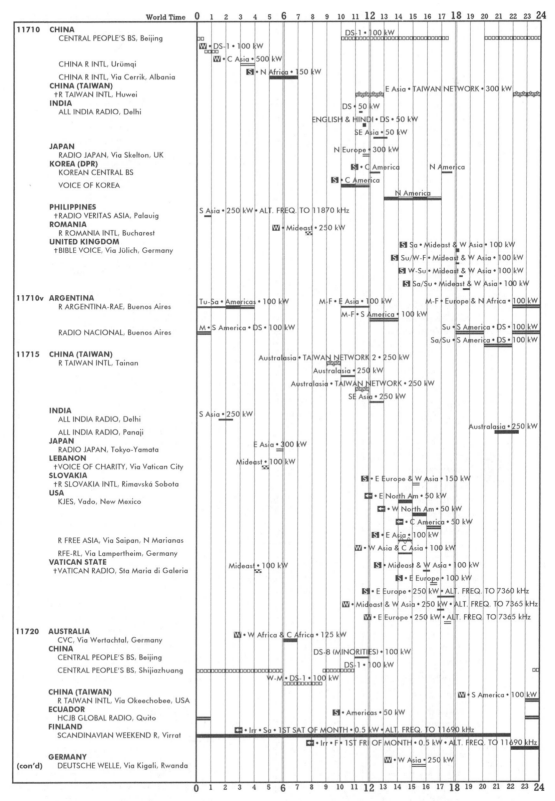

World Time 0 1 2 3 4 5 6 7 8 9 10 11 12 13 14 15 16 17 18 19 20 21 22 23 24

11710 CHINA
CENTRAL PEOPLE'S BS, Beijing
W • DS-1 • 100 kW
DS-1 • 100 kW

CHINA R INTL, Urümqi
W • C Asia • 500 kW

CHINA R INTL, Via Cerrik, Albania
S • N Africa • 150 kW

CHINA (TAIWAN)
†R TAIWAN INTL, Huwei
E Asia • TAIWAN NETWORK • 300 kW

INDIA
ALL INDIA RADIO, Delhi
DS • 50 kW
ENGLISH & HINDI • DS • 50 kW
SE Asia • 50 kW

JAPAN
RADIO JAPAN, Via Skelton, UK
N Europe • 300 kW

KOREA (DPR)
KOREAN CENTRAL BS
S • C America   N America

VOICE OF KOREA
S • C America
N America

PHILIPPINES
†RADIO VERITAS ASIA, Palauig
S Asia • 250 kW • ALT. FREQ. TO 11870 kHz

ROMANIA
R ROMANIA INTL, Bucharest
W • Mideast • 250 kW

UNITED KINGDOM
†BIBLE VOICE, Via Jülich, Germany
S Sa • Mideast & W Asia • 100 kW
S Su/W-F • Mideast & W Asia • 100 kW
S W-Su • Mideast & W Asia • 100 kW
S Sa/Su • Mideast & W Asia • 100 kW

11710v ARGENTINA
R ARGENTINA-RAE, Buenos Aires
Tu-Sa • Americas • 100 kW   M-F • E Asia • 100 kW   M-F • Europe & N Africa • 100 kW
M-F • S America • 100 kW

RADIO NACIONAL, Buenos Aires
M • S America • DS • 100 kW
Su • S America • DS • 100 kW
Sa/Su • S America • DS • 100 kW

11715 CHINA (TAIWAN)
R TAIWAN INTL, Tainan
Australasia • TAIWAN NETWORK 2 • 250 kW
Australasia • 250 kW
Australasia • TAIWAN NETWORK • 250 kW
SE Asia • 250 kW

INDIA
ALL INDIA RADIO, Delhi
S Asia • 250 kW

ALL INDIA RADIO, Panaji
Australasia • 250 kW

JAPAN
RADIO JAPAN, Tokyo-Yamata
E Asia • 300 kW

LEBANON
†VOICE OF CHARITY, Via Vatican City
Mideast • 100 kW

SLOVAKIA
†R SLOVAKIA INTL, Rimavská Sobota
S • E Europe & W Asia • 150 kW

USA
KJES, Vado, New Mexico
⇄ • E North Am • 50 kW
⇄ • W North Am • 50 kW
⇄ • C America • 50 kW

R FREE ASIA, Via Saipan, N Marianas
S • E Asia • 100 kW

RFE-RL, Via Lampertheim, Germany
W • W Asia & C Asia • 100 kW

VATICAN STATE
†VATICAN RADIO, Sta Maria di Galeria
Mideast • 100 kW
S • Mideast & W Asia • 100 kW
S • E Europe • 100 kW
S • E Europe • 250 kW • ALT. FREQ. TO 7360 kHz
W • Mideast & W Asia • 250 kW • ALT. FREQ. TO 7365 kHz
W • E Europe • 250 kW • ALT. FREQ. TO 7365 kHz

11720 AUSTRALIA
CVC, Via Wertachtal, Germany
W • W Africa & C Africa • 125 kW

CHINA
CENTRAL PEOPLE'S BS, Beijing
DS-8 (MINORITIES) • 100 kW

CENTRAL PEOPLE'S BS, Shijiazhuang
DS-1 • 100 kW
W-M • DS-1 • 100 kW

CHINA (TAIWAN)
R TAIWAN INTL, Via Okeechobee, USA
W • S America • 100 kW

ECUADOR
HCJB GLOBAL RADIO, Quito
S • Americas • 50 kW

FINLAND
SCANDINAVIAN WEEKEND R, Virrat
⇄ • Irr • Sa • 1ST SAT OF MONTH • 0.5 kW • ALT. FREQ. TO 11690 kHz
⇄ • Irr • F • 1ST FRI OF MONTH • 0.5 kW • ALT. FREQ. TO 11690 kHz

GERMANY
(con'd) DEUTSCHE WELLE, Via Kigali, Rwanda
W • W Asia • 250 kW

0 1 2 3 4 5 6 7 8 9 10 11 12 13 14 15 16 17 18 19 20 21 22 23 24

SEASONAL S OR W   1-HR TIMESHIFT MIDYEAR ⇄ OR ⇄   JAMMING / OR ∧   EARLIEST HEARD ◁   LATEST HEARD ▷   NEW FOR 2008 †

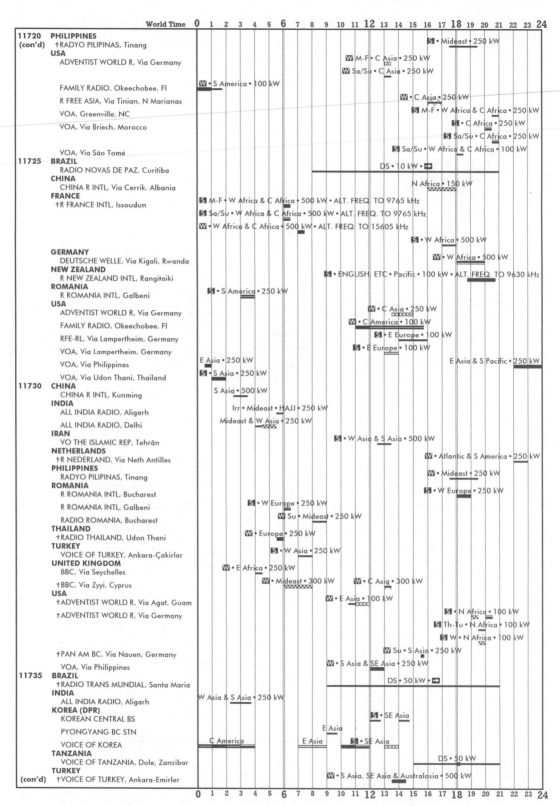

World Time 0 1 2 3 4 5 6 7 8 9 10 11 12 13 14 15 16 17 18 19 20 21 22 23 24

11720
(con'd) **PHILIPPINES**
   †RADYO PILIPINAS, Tinang — **S** • Mideast • 250 kW
USA
   ADVENTIST WORLD R, Via Germany — **W** M-F • C Asia • 250 kW
                              W Sa/Su • C Asia • 250 kW
   FAMILY RADIO, Okeechobee, Fl — **W** • S America • 100 kW
   R FREE ASIA, Via Tinian, N Marianas — **W** • C Asia • 250 kW
   VOA, Greenville, NC — **S** M-F • W Africa & C Africa • 250 kW
   VOA, Via Briech, Morocco — **S** • C Africa • 250 kW
                             S Sa/Su • C Africa • 250 kW
   VOA, Via São Tomé — **S** Sa/Su • W Africa & C Africa • 100 kW
11725 **BRAZIL**
   RADIO NOVAS DE PAZ, Curitiba — DS • 10 kW • →
CHINA
   CHINA R INTL, Via Cerrik, Albania — N Africa • 150 kW
FRANCE
   †R FRANCE INTL, Issoudun — **S** M-F • W Africa & C Africa • 500 kW • ALT. FREQ. TO 9765 kHz
            S Sa/Su • W Africa & C Africa • 500 kW • ALT. FREQ. TO 9765 kHz
            W • W Africa & C Africa • 500 kW • ALT. FREQ. TO 15605 kHz
            S • W Africa • 500 kW
GERMANY
   DEUTSCHE WELLE, Via Kigali, Rwanda — **W** • W Africa • 500 kW
NEW ZEALAND
   R NEW ZEALAND INTL, Rangitaiki — **S** • ENGLISH, ETC • Pacific • 100 kW • ALT. FREQ. TO 9630 kHz
ROMANIA
   R ROMANIA INTL, Galbeni — **S** • S America • 250 kW
USA
   ADVENTIST WORLD R, Via Germany — **W** • C Asia • 250 kW
   FAMILY RADIO, Okeechobee, Fl — **W** • C America • 100 kW
   RFE-RL, Via Lampertheim, Germany — **S** • E Europe • 100 kW
   VOA, Via Lampertheim, Germany — **S** • E Europe • 100 kW
   VOA, Via Philippines — E Asia • 250 kW   E Asia & S Pacific • 250 kW
   VOA, Via Udon Thani, Thailand — **S** • S Asia • 250 kW
11730 **CHINA**
   CHINA R INTL, Kunming — S Asia • 500 kW
INDIA
   ALL INDIA RADIO, Aligarh — Irr • Mideast • HAJJ • 250 kW
   ALL INDIA RADIO, Delhi — Mideast & W Asia • 250 kW
IRAN
   VO THE ISLAMIC REP, Tehrān — **S** • W Asia & S Asia • 500 kW
NETHERLANDS
   †R NEDERLAND, Via Neth Antilles — **W** • Atlantic & S America • 250 kW
PHILIPPINES
   RADYO PILIPINAS, Tinang — **W** • Mideast • 250 kW
ROMANIA
   R ROMANIA INTL, Bucharest — **S** • W Europe • 250 kW
   R ROMANIA INTL, Galbeni — **S** • W Europe • 250 kW
   RADIO ROMANIA, Bucharest — **W** Su • Mideast • 250 kW
THAILAND
   †RADIO THAILAND, Udon Thani — **W** • Europe • 250 kW
TURKEY
   VOICE OF TURKEY, Ankara-Çakirlar — **S** • W Asia • 250 kW
UNITED KINGDOM
   BBC, Via Seychelles — **W** • E Africa • 250 kW
   †BBC, Via Zyyi, Cyprus — **W** • Mideast • 300 kW   **W** • C Asia • 300 kW
USA
   †ADVENTIST WORLD R, Via Agat, Guam — **W** • E Asia • 100 kW
   †ADVENTIST WORLD R, Via Germany — **S** • N Africa • 100 kW
                       S Th-Tu • N Africa • 100 kW
                       S W • N Africa • 100 kW
   †PAN AM BC, Via Nauen, Germany — **W** Su • S Asia • 250 kW
   VOA, Via Philippines — **W** • S Asia & SE Asia • 250 kW
11735 **BRAZIL**
   †RADIO TRANS MUNDIAL, Santa Maria — DS • 50 kW • →
INDIA
   ALL INDIA RADIO, Aligarh — W Asia & S Asia • 250 kW
KOREA (DPR)
   KOREAN CENTRAL BS — **S** • SE Asia
   PYONGYANG BC STN — E Asia
   VOICE OF KOREA — C America   E Asia   **S** • SE Asia
TANZANIA
   VOICE OF TANZANIA, Dole, Zanzibar — DS • 50 kW
TURKEY
(con'd) †VOICE OF TURKEY, Ankara-Emirler — **W** • S Asia, SE Asia & Australasia • 500 kW

0 1 2 3 4 5 6 7 8 9 10 11 12 13 14 15 16 17 18 19 20 21 22 23 24

ENGLISH ▬ ARABIC ⋙ CHINESE □□□ FRENCH ▬ GERMAN ▬ RUSSIAN ═ SPANISH ▬ OTHER ▬

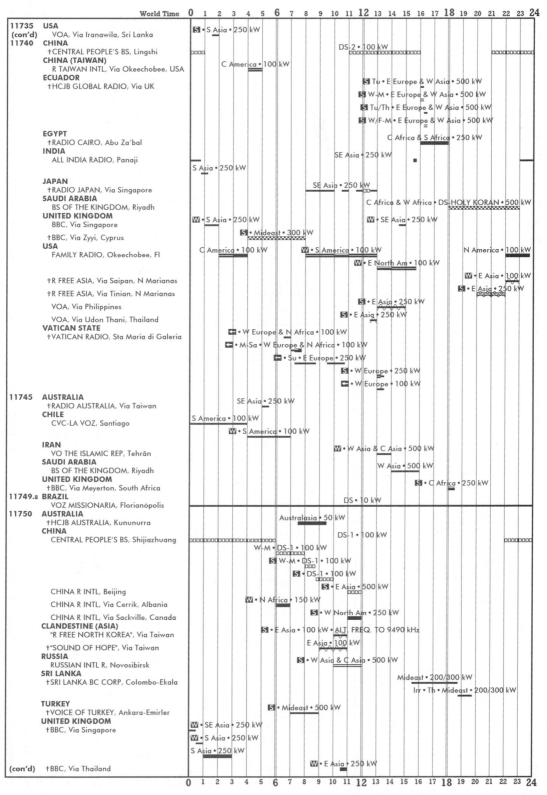

World Time scale: 0 1 2 3 4 5 6 7 8 9 10 11 12 13 14 15 16 17 18 19 20 21 22 23 24

11735 USA
(con'd) VOA, Via Iranawila, Sri Lanka — S•S Asia•250 kW

11740 CHINA
†CENTRAL PEOPLE'S BS, Lingshi — DS-2•100 kW

CHINA (TAIWAN)
R TAIWAN INTL, Via Okeechobee, USA — C America•100 kW

ECUADOR
†HCJB GLOBAL RADIO, Via UK — S•Tu•E Europe & W Asia•500 kW
— S•W-M•E Europe & W Asia•500 kW
— S•Tu/Th•E Europe & W Asia•500 kW
— S•W/F-M•E Europe & W Asia•500 kW

EGYPT
†RADIO CAIRO, Abu Za'bal — C Africa & S Africa•250 kW

INDIA
ALL INDIA RADIO, Panaji — SE Asia•250 kW
— S Asia•250 kW

JAPAN
†RADIO JAPAN, Via Singapore — SE Asia•250 kW

SAUDI ARABIA
BS OF THE KINGDOM, Riyadh — C Africa & W Africa•DS-HOLY KORAN•500 kW

UNITED KINGDOM
BBC, Via Singapore — W•S Asia•250 kW
— W•SE Asia•250 kW

†BBC, Via Zyyi, Cyprus — S•Mideast•300 kW

USA
FAMILY RADIO, Okeechobee, Fl — C America•100 kW
— W•S America•100 kW
— N America•100 kW
— W•E North Am•100 kW

†R FREE ASIA, Via Saipan, N Marianas — W•E Asia•100 kW

†R FREE ASIA, Via Tinian, N Marianas — S•E Asia•250 kW

VOA, Via Philippines — S•E Asia•250 kW

VOA, Via Udon Thani, Thailand — S•E Asia•250 kW

VATICAN STATE
†VATICAN RADIO, Sta Maria di Galeria — ⇨•W Europe & N Africa•100 kW
— ⇦•M-Sa•W Europe & N Africa•100 kW
— ⇦•Su•E Europe•250 kW
— S•W Europe•250 kW
— ⇦•W Europe•100 kW

11745 AUSTRALIA
†RADIO AUSTRALIA, Via Taiwan — SE Asia•250 kW

CHILE
CVC-LA VOZ, Santiago — S America•100 kW
— W•S America•100 kW

IRAN
VO THE ISLAMIC REP, Tehrān — W•W Asia & C Asia•500 kW

SAUDI ARABIA
BS OF THE KINGDOM, Riyadh — W Asia•500 kW

UNITED KINGDOM
†BBC, Via Meyerton, South Africa — S•C Africa•250 kW

11749.8 BRAZIL
VOZ MISSIONARIA, Florianópolis — DS•10 kW

11750 AUSTRALIA
†HCJB AUSTRALIA, Kununurra — Australasia•50 kW

CHINA
CENTRAL PEOPLE'S BS, Shijiazhuang — DS-1•100 kW
— W-M•DS-1•100 kW
— S•W-M•DS-1•100 kW
— S•DS-1•100 kW

CHINA R INTL, Beijing — S•E Asia•500 kW

CHINA R INTL, Via Cerrik, Albania — W•N Africa•150 kW

CHINA R INTL, Via Sackville, Canada — S•W North Am•250 kW

CLANDESTINE (ASIA)
"R FREE NORTH KOREA", Via Taiwan — S•E Asia•100 kW•ALT. FREQ. TO 9490 kHz

†"SOUND OF HOPE", Via Taiwan — E Asia•100 kW

RUSSIA
RUSSIAN INTL R, Novosibirsk — S•W Asia & C Asia•500 kW

SRI LANKA
†SRI LANKA BC CORP, Colombo-Ekala — Mideast•200/300 kW
— Irr•Th•Mideast•200/300 kW

TURKEY
†VOICE OF TURKEY, Ankara-Emirler — S•Mideast•500 kW

UNITED KINGDOM
†BBC, Via Singapore — W•SE Asia•250 kW
— W•S Asia•250 kW
— S Asia•250 kW

(con'd) †BBC, Via Thailand — W•E Asia•250 kW

World Time scale: 0 1 2 3 4 5 6 7 8 9 10 11 12 13 14 15 16 17 18 19 20 21 22 23 24

SEASONAL S OR W   1-HR TIMESHIFT MIDYEAR ⇦ OR ⇨   JAMMING / OR ∧   EARLIEST HEARD ◁   LATEST HEARD ▷   NEW FOR 2008 †

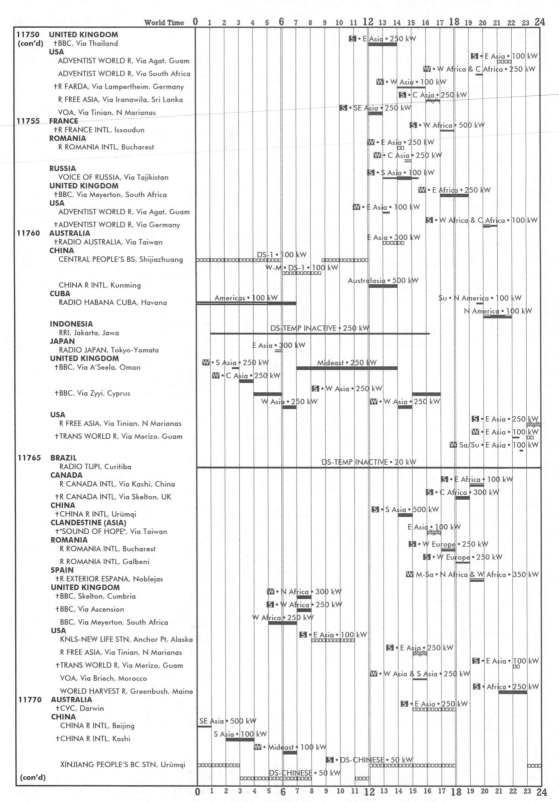

World Time																								

11750 UNITED KINGDOM (con'd)
†BBC, Via Thailand — ⑤ • E Asia • 250 kW
USA
ADVENTIST WORLD R, Via Agat, Guam — ⑤ • E Asia • 100 kW
ADVENTIST WORLD R, Via South Africa — Ⓦ • W Africa & C Africa • 250 kW
†R FARDA, Via Lampertheim, Germany — Ⓦ • W Asia • 100 kW
R FREE ASIA, Via Iranawila, Sri Lanka — ⑤ • C Asia • 250 kW
VOA, Via Tinian, N Marianas — ⑤ • SE Asia • 250 kW

11755 FRANCE
†R FRANCE INTL, Issoudun — ⑤ • W Africa • 500 kW
ROMANIA
R ROMANIA INTL, Bucharest — Ⓦ • E Asia • 250 kW
— Ⓦ • C Asia • 250 kW
RUSSIA
VOICE OF RUSSIA, Via Tajikistan — ⑤ • S Asia • 100 kW
UNITED KINGDOM
†BBC, Via Meyerton, South Africa — Ⓦ • E Africa • 250 kW
USA
ADVENTIST WORLD R, Via Agat, Guam — Ⓦ • E Asia • 100 kW
†ADVENTIST WORLD R, Via Germany — ⑤ • W Africa & C Africa • 100 kW

11760 AUSTRALIA
†RADIO AUSTRALIA, Via Taiwan — E Asia • 300 kW
CHINA
CENTRAL PEOPLE'S BS, Shijiazhuang — DS-1 • 100 kW
— Ⓦ-M • DS-1 • 100 kW
CHINA R INTL, Kunming — Australasia • 500 kW
CUBA
RADIO HABANA CUBA, Havana — Americas • 100 kW
— Su • N America • 100 kW
— N America • 100 kW
INDONESIA
RRI, Jakarta, Jawa — DS-TEMP INACTIVE • 250 kW
JAPAN
RADIO JAPAN, Tokyo-Yamata — E Asia • 300 kW
UNITED KINGDOM
†BBC, Via A'Seela, Oman — Ⓦ • S Asia • 250 kW
— Mideast • 250 kW
— Ⓦ • C Asia • 250 kW
— ⑤ • W Asia • 250 kW
†BBC, Via Zyyi, Cyprus — W Asia • 250 kW
— Ⓦ • W Asia • 250 kW
USA
R FREE ASIA, Via Tinian, N Marianas — ⑤ • E Asia • 250 kW
†TRANS WORLD R, Via Merizo, Guam — Ⓦ • E Asia • 100 kW
— Ⓦ Sa/Su • E Asia • 100 kW

11765 BRAZIL
RADIO TUPI, Curitiba — DS-TEMP INACTIVE • 20 kW
CANADA
R CANADA INTL, Via Kashi, China — ⑤ • E Africa • 100 kW
†R CANADA INTL, Via Skelton, UK — ⑤ • C Africa • 300 kW
CHINA
†CHINA R INTL, Urümqi — ⑤ • S Asia • 500 kW
CLANDESTINE (ASIA)
†"SOUND OF HOPE", Via Taiwan — E Asia • 100 kW
ROMANIA
R ROMANIA INTL, Bucharest — ⑤ • W Europe • 250 kW
R ROMANIA INTL, Galbeni — ⑤ • W Europe • 250 kW
SPAIN
†R EXTERIOR ESPANA, Noblejas — Ⓦ M-Sa • N Africa & W Africa • 350 kW
UNITED KINGDOM
†BBC, Skelton, Cumbria — Ⓦ • N Africa • 300 kW
†BBC, Via Ascension — ⑤ • W Africa • 250 kW
BBC, Via Meyerton, South Africa — W Africa • 250 kW
USA
KNLS-NEW LIFE STN, Anchor Pt, Alaska — ⑤ • E Asia • 100 kW
R FREE ASIA, Via Tinian, N Marianas — ⑤ • E Asia • 250 kW
†TRANS WORLD R, Via Merizo, Guam — ⑤ • E Asia • 100 kW
VOA, Via Briech, Morocco — Ⓦ • W Asia & S Asia • 250 kW
WORLD HARVEST R, Greenbush, Maine — ⑤ • Africa • 250 kW

11770 AUSTRALIA
†CVC, Darwin — ⑤ • E Asia • 250 kW
CHINA
CHINA R INTL, Beijing — SE Asia • 500 kW
†CHINA R INTL, Kashi — S Asia • 100 kW
— Ⓦ • Mideast • 100 kW
XINJIANG PEOPLE'S BC STN, Urümqi — ⑤ • DS-CHINESE • 50 kW
— DS-CHINESE • 50 kW
(con'd)

ENGLISH ▬ ARABIC ⌇⌇⌇ CHINESE ▫▫▫ FRENCH ▭▭▭ GERMAN ▬▬ RUSSIAN ═══ SPANISH ▬▬ OTHER ▬

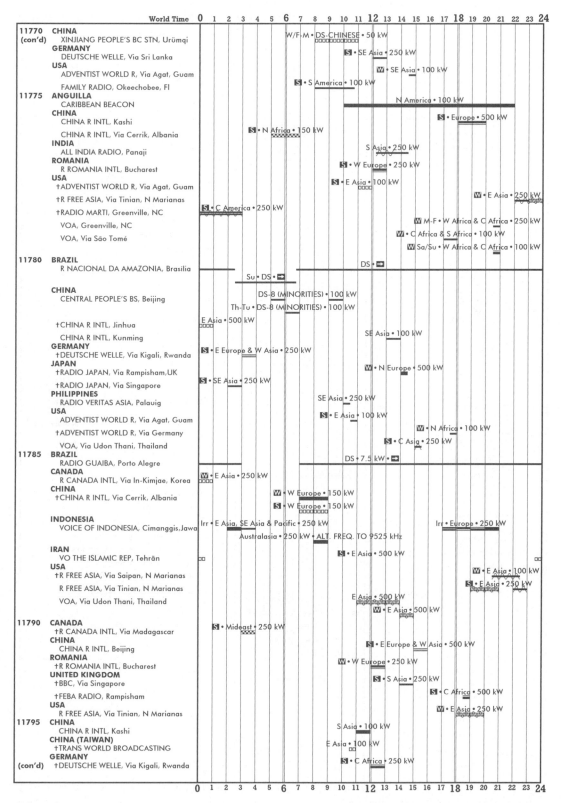

World Time	0 1 2 3 4 5 6 7 8 9 10 11 12 13 14 15 16 17 18 19 20 21 22 23 24
11770 **CHINA**	
(con'd) XINJIANG PEOPLE'S BC STN, Urümqi	W/F-M • DS-CHINESE • 50 kW
GERMANY	
DEUTSCHE WELLE, Via Sri Lanka	S • SE Asia • 250 kW
USA	
ADVENTIST WORLD R, Via Agat, Guam	W • SE Asia • 100 kW
FAMILY RADIO, Okeechobee, Fl	S • S America • 100 kW
11775 **ANGUILLA**	
CARIBBEAN BEACON	N America • 100 kW
CHINA	
CHINA R INTL, Kashi	S • Europe • 500 kW
CHINA R INTL, Via Cerrik, Albania	S • N Africa • 150 kW
INDIA	
ALL INDIA RADIO, Panaji	S Asia • 250 kW
ROMANIA	
R ROMANIA INTL, Bucharest	S • W Europe • 250 kW
USA	
†ADVENTIST WORLD R, Via Agat, Guam	S • E Asia • 100 kW
†R FREE ASIA, Via Tinian, N Marianas	W • E Asia • 250 kW
†RADIO MARTI, Greenville, NC	S • C America • 250 kW
VOA, Greenville, NC	W M-F • W Africa & C Africa • 250 kW
VOA, Via São Tomé	W • C Africa & S Africa • 100 kW
	W Sa/Su • W Africa & C Africa • 100 kW
11780 **BRAZIL**	
R NACIONAL DA AMAZONIA, Brasilia	DS • ⇨
	Su • DS • ⇨
CHINA	
CENTRAL PEOPLE'S BS, Beijing	DS-8 (MINORITIES) • 100 kW
	Th-Tu • DS-8 (MINORITIES) • 100 kW
†CHINA R INTL, Jinhua	E Asia • 500 kW
CHINA R INTL, Kunming	SE Asia • 100 kW
GERMANY	
†DEUTSCHE WELLE, Via Kigali, Rwanda	S • E Europe & W Asia • 250 kW
JAPAN	
†RADIO JAPAN, Via Rampisham,UK	W • N Europe • 500 kW
†RADIO JAPAN, Via Singapore	S • SE Asia • 250 kW
PHILIPPINES	
RADIO VERITAS ASIA, Palauig	SE Asia • 250 kW
USA	
ADVENTIST WORLD R, Via Agat, Guam	S • E Asia • 100 kW
†ADVENTIST WORLD R, Via Germany	W • N Africa • 100 kW
VOA, Via Udon Thani, Thailand	S • C Asia • 250 kW
11785 **BRAZIL**	
RADIO GUAIBA, Porto Alegre	DS • 7.5 kW • ⇨
CANADA	
R CANADA INTL, Via In-Kimjae, Korea	W • E Asia • 250 kW
CHINA	
†CHINA R INTL, Via Cerrik, Albania	W • W Europe • 150 kW
	S • W Europe • 150 kW
INDONESIA	
VOICE OF INDONESIA, Cimanggis,Jawa	Irr • E Asia, SE Asia & Pacific • 250 kW Irr • Europe • 250 kW
	Australasia • 250 kW • ALT. FREQ. TO 9525 kHz
IRAN	
VO THE ISLAMIC REP, Tehrān	S • E Asia • 500 kW
USA	
†R FREE ASIA, Via Saipan, N Marianas	W • E Asia • 100 kW
R FREE ASIA, Via Tinian, N Marianas	S • E Asia • 250 kW
VOA, Via Udon Thani, Thailand	E Asia • 500 kW
	W • E Asia • 500 kW
11790 **CANADA**	
†R CANADA INTL, Via Madagascar	S • Mideast • 250 kW
CHINA	
CHINA R INTL, Beijing	S • E Europe & W Asia • 500 kW
ROMANIA	
†R ROMANIA INTL, Bucharest	W • W Europe • 250 kW
UNITED KINGDOM	
†BBC, Via Singapore	S • S Asia • 250 kW
†FEBA RADIO, Rampisham	S • C Africa • 500 kW
USA	
R FREE ASIA, Via Tinian, N Marianas	W • E Asia • 250 kW
11795 **CHINA**	
CHINA R INTL, Kashi	S Asia • 100 kW
CHINA (TAIWAN)	
†TRANS WORLD BROADCASTING	E Asia • 100 kW
GERMANY	
(con'd) †DEUTSCHE WELLE, Via Kigali, Rwanda	S • C Africa • 250 kW

World Time	0 1 2 3 4 5 6 7 8 9 10 11 12 13 14 15 16 17 18 19 20 21 22 23 24

SEASONAL **S** OR **W**   1-HR TIMESHIFT MIDYEAR **⇦** OR **⇨**   JAMMING / OR ∧   EARLIEST HEARD ◁   LATEST HEARD ▷   NEW FOR 2008 †

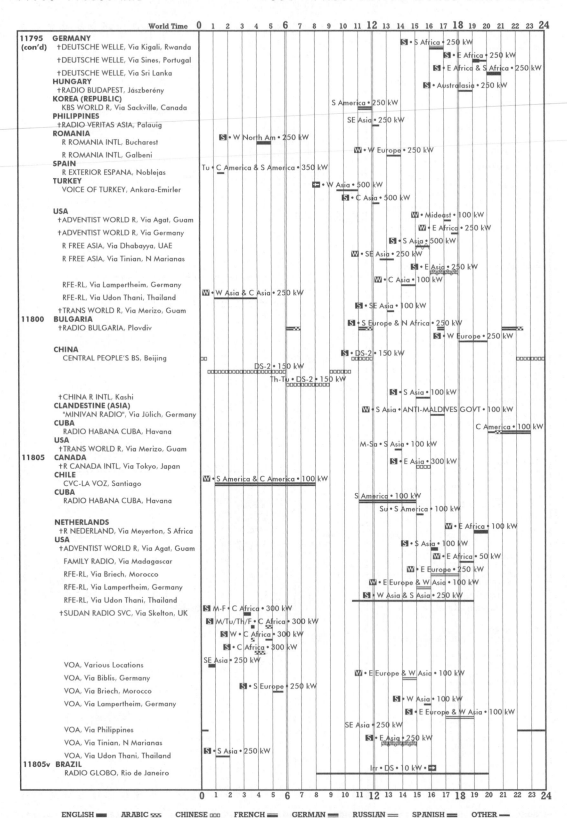

Frequency / Country / Station	Target / Power
11795 GERMANY	
(con'd) †DEUTSCHE WELLE, Via Kigali, Rwanda	S • S Africa • 250 kW
†DEUTSCHE WELLE, Via Sines, Portugal	S • E Africa • 250 kW
†DEUTSCHE WELLE, Via Sri Lanka	S • E Africa & S Africa • 250 kW
HUNGARY	
†RADIO BUDAPEST, Jászberény	S • Australasia • 250 kW
KOREA (REPUBLIC)	
KBS WORLD R, Via Sackville, Canada	S America • 250 kW
PHILIPPINES	
†RADIO VERITAS ASIA, Palauig	SE Asia • 250 kW
ROMANIA	
R ROMANIA INTL, Bucharest	S • W North Am • 250 kW
R ROMANIA INTL, Galbeni	W • W Europe • 250 kW
SPAIN	
R EXTERIOR ESPANA, Noblejas	Tu • C America & S America • 350 kW
TURKEY	
VOICE OF TURKEY, Ankara-Emirler	• W Asia • 500 kW
	S • C Asia • 500 kW
USA	
†ADVENTIST WORLD R, Via Agat, Guam	W • Mideast • 100 kW
†ADVENTIST WORLD R, Via Germany	W • E Africa • 250 kW
R FREE ASIA, Via Dhabayya, UAE	S • S Asia • 500 kW
R FREE ASIA, Via Tinian, N Marianas	W • SE Asia • 250 kW
	S • E Asia • 250 kW
RFE-RL, Via Lampertheim, Germany	W • C Asia • 100 kW
RFE-RL, Via Udon Thani, Thailand	W • W Asia & C Asia • 250 kW
†TRANS WORLD R, Via Merizo, Guam	S • SE Asia • 100 kW
11800 BULGARIA	
†RADIO BULGARIA, Plovdiv	S • S Europe & N Africa • 250 kW
	S • W Europe • 250 kW
CHINA	
CENTRAL PEOPLE'S BS, Beijing	S • DS-2 • 150 kW
	DS-2 • 150 kW
	Th-Tu • DS-2 • 150 kW
†CHINA R INTL, Kashi	S • S Asia • 100 kW
CLANDESTINE (ASIA)	
"MINIVAN RADIO", Via Jülich, Germany	W • S Asia • ANTI-MALDIVES GOVT • 100 kW
CUBA	
RADIO HABANA CUBA, Havana	C America • 100 kW
USA	
†TRANS WORLD R, Via Merizo, Guam	M-Sa • S Asia • 100 kW
11805 CANADA	
†R CANADA INTL, Via Tokyo, Japan	S • E Asia • 300 kW
CHILE	
CVC-LA VOZ, Santiago	W • S America & C America • 100 kW
CUBA	
RADIO HABANA CUBA, Havana	S America • 100 kW
	Su • S America • 100 kW
NETHERLANDS	
†R NEDERLAND, Via Meyerton, S Africa	W • E Africa • 100 kW
USA	
†ADVENTIST WORLD R, Via Agat, Guam	S • S Asia • 100 kW
FAMILY RADIO, Via Madagascar	W • E Africa • 50 kW
RFE-RL, Via Briech, Morocco	W • E Europe • 250 kW
RFE-RL, Via Lampertheim, Germany	W • E Europe & W Asia • 100 kW
RFE-RL, Via Udon Thani, Thailand	S • W Asia & S Asia • 250 kW
†SUDAN RADIO SVC, Via Skelton, UK	S • M-F • C Africa • 300 kW
	S • M/Tu/Th/F • C Africa • 300 kW
	S • W • C Africa • 300 kW
	S • C Africa • 300 kW
VOA, Various Locations	SE Asia • 250 kW
VOA, Via Biblis, Germany	W • E Europe & W Asia • 100 kW
VOA, Via Briech, Morocco	S • S Europe • 250 kW
VOA, Via Lampertheim, Germany	S • W Asia • 100 kW
	S • E Europe & W Asia • 100 kW
VOA, Via Philippines	SE Asia • 250 kW
VOA, Via Tinian, N Marianas	S • E Asia • 250 kW
VOA, Via Udon Thani, Thailand	S • S Asia • 250 kW
11805v BRAZIL	
RADIO GLOBO, Rio de Janeiro	Irr • DS • 10 kW

ENGLISH ▬   ARABIC ⌇⌇⌇   CHINESE ▢▢▢   FRENCH ▬▬   GERMAN ▬   RUSSIAN ═══   SPANISH ▬   OTHER ▬

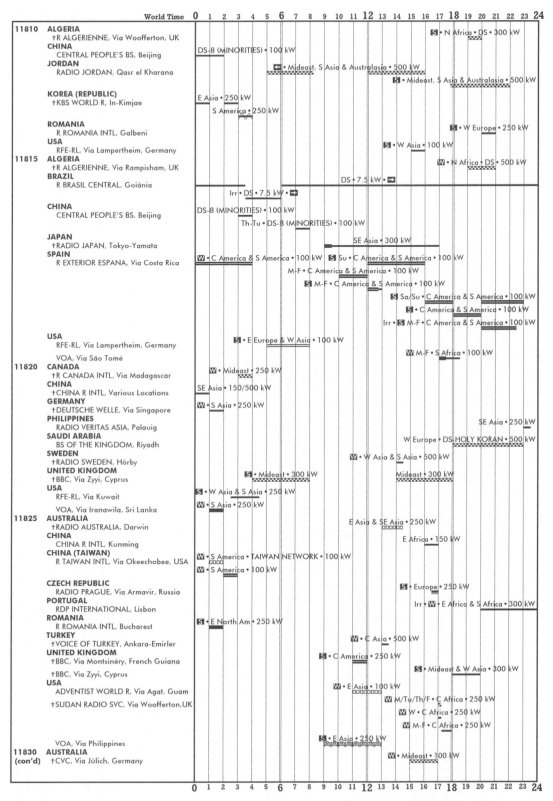

World Time 0 1 2 3 4 5 6 7 8 9 10 11 12 13 14 15 16 17 18 19 20 21 22 23 24

11810 ALGERIA
†R ALGERIENNE, Via Woofferton, UK — S • N Africa • DS • 300 kW
CHINA
CENTRAL PEOPLE'S BS, Beijing — DS-8 (MINORITIES) • 100 kW
JORDAN
RADIO JORDAN, Qasr el Kharana — Mideast, S Asia & Australasia • 500 kW; S • Mideast, S Asia & Australasia • 500 kW

KOREA (REPUBLIC)
†KBS WORLD R, In-Kimjae — E Asia • 250 kW; S America • 250 kW

ROMANIA
R ROMANIA INTL, Galbeni — S • W Europe • 250 kW
USA
RFE-RL, Via Lampertheim, Germany — S • W Asia • 100 kW
11815 ALGERIA
†R ALGERIENNE, Via Rampisham, UK — W • N Africa • DS • 500 kW
BRAZIL
R BRASIL CENTRAL, Goiânia — DS • 7.5 kW; Irr • DS • 7.5 kW

CHINA
CENTRAL PEOPLE'S BS, Beijing — DS-8 (MINORITIES) • 100 kW; Th-Tu • DS-8 (MINORITIES) • 100 kW

JAPAN
†RADIO JAPAN, Tokyo-Yamata — SE Asia • 300 kW
SPAIN
R EXTERIOR ESPANA, Via Costa Rica — W • C America & S America • 100 kW; S Su • C America & S America • 100 kW; M-F • C America & S America • 100 kW; S M-F • C America & S America • 100 kW; S Sa/Su • C America & S America • 100 kW; S • C America & S America • 100 kW; Irr • S M-F • C America & S America • 100 kW

USA
RFE-RL, Via Lampertheim, Germany — S • E Europe & W Asia • 100 kW
VOA, Via São Tomé — W M-F • S Africa • 100 kW
11820 CANADA
†R CANADA INTL, Via Madagascar — W • Mideast • 250 kW
CHINA
†CHINA R INTL, Various Locations — SE Asia • 150/500 kW
GERMANY
†DEUTSCHE WELLE, Via Singapore — W • S Asia • 250 kW; SE Asia • 250 kW
PHILIPPINES
RADIO VERITAS ASIA, Palauig
SAUDI ARABIA
BS OF THE KINGDOM, Riyadh — W Europe • DS-HOLY KORAN • 500 kW
SWEDEN
†RADIO SWEDEN, Hörby — W • W Asia & S Asia • 500 kW
UNITED KINGDOM
†BBC, Via Zyyi, Cyprus — S • Mideast • 300 kW; Mideast • 300 kW
USA
RFE-RL, Via Kuwait — S • W Asia & S Asia • 250 kW
VOA, Via Iranawila, Sri Lanka — W • S Asia • 250 kW
11825 AUSTRALIA
†RADIO AUSTRALIA, Darwin — E Asia & SE Asia • 250 kW
CHINA
CHINA R INTL, Kunming — E Africa • 150 kW
CHINA (TAIWAN)
R TAIWAN INTL, Via Okeechobee, USA — W • S America • TAIWAN NETWORK • 100 kW; W • S America • 100 kW

CZECH REPUBLIC
RADIO PRAGUE, Via Armavir, Russia — S • Europe • 250 kW
PORTUGAL
RDP INTERNATIONAL, Lisbon — Irr • W • E Africa & S Africa • 300 kW
ROMANIA
R ROMANIA INTL, Bucharest — S • E North Am • 250 kW
TURKEY
†VOICE OF TURKEY, Ankara-Emirler — W • C Asia • 500 kW
UNITED KINGDOM
†BBC, Via Montsinéry, French Guiana — S • C America • 250 kW
†BBC, Via Zyyi, Cyprus — S • Mideast & W Asia • 300 kW
USA
ADVENTIST WORLD R, Via Agat, Guam — W • E Asia • 100 kW
†SUDAN RADIO SVC, Via Woofferton, UK — W M/Tu/Th/F • C Africa • 250 kW; W W • C Africa • 250 kW; W M-F • C Africa • 250 kW

VOA, Via Philippines — S • E Asia • 250 kW
11830 AUSTRALIA
(con'd) †CVC, Via Jülich, Germany — W • Mideast • 100 kW

0 1 2 3 4 5 6 7 8 9 10 11 12 13 14 15 16 17 18 19 20 21 22 23 24

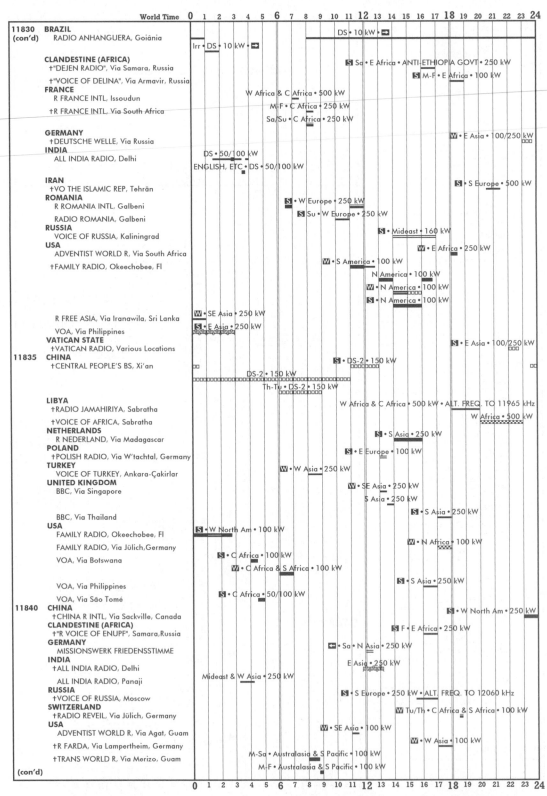

World Time 0 1 2 3 4 5 6 7 8 9 10 11 12 13 14 15 16 17 18 19 20 21 22 23 24

11830
(con'd) **BRAZIL**
RADIO ANHANGUERA, Goiânia — DS • 10 kW •
Irr • DS • 10 kW •

CLANDESTINE (AFRICA)
†"DEJEN RADIO", Via Samara, Russia — Sa • E Africa • ANTI-ETHIOPIA GOVT • 250 kW
†"VOICE OF DELINA", Via Armavir, Russia — M-F • E Africa • 100 kW
FRANCE
R FRANCE INTL, Issoudun — W Africa & C Africa • 500 kW
†R FRANCE INTL, Via South Africa — M-F • C Africa • 250 kW
Sa/Su • C Africa • 250 kW

GERMANY
†DEUTSCHE WELLE, Via Russia — W • E Asia • 100/250 kW
INDIA
ALL INDIA RADIO, Delhi — DS • 50/100 kW
ENGLISH, ETC • DS • 50/100 kW

IRAN
†VO THE ISLAMIC REP, Tehrān — S • S Europe • 500 kW
ROMANIA
R ROMANIA INTL, Galbeni — S • W Europe • 250 kW
RADIO ROMANIA, Galbeni — S • Su • W Europe • 250 kW
RUSSIA
VOICE OF RUSSIA, Kaliningrad — S • Mideast • 160 kW
USA
ADVENTIST WORLD R, Via South Africa — W • E Africa • 250 kW
†FAMILY RADIO, Okeechobee, Fl — W • S America • 100 kW
N America • 100 kW
W • N America • 100 kW
S • N America • 100 kW

R FREE ASIA, Via Iranawila, Sri Lanka — W • SE Asia • 250 kW
VOA, Via Philippines — S • E Asia • 250 kW
VATICAN STATE
†VATICAN RADIO, Various Locations — S • E Asia • 100/250 kW
11835 **CHINA**
†CENTRAL PEOPLE'S BS, Xi'an — S • DS-2 • 150 kW
DS-2 • 150 kW
Th-Tu • DS-2 • 150 kW

LIBYA
†RADIO JAMAHIRIYA, Sabratha — W Africa & C Africa • 500 kW • ALT. FREQ. TO 11965 kHz
†VOICE OF AFRICA, Sabratha — W Africa • 500 kW
NETHERLANDS
R NEDERLAND, Via Madagascar — S • S Asia • 250 kW
POLAND
†POLISH RADIO, Via W'tachtal, Germany — S • E Europe • 100 kW
TURKEY
VOICE OF TURKEY, Ankara-Çakirlar — W • W Asia • 250 kW
UNITED KINGDOM
BBC, Via Singapore — W • SE Asia • 250 kW
S Asia • 250 kW

BBC, Via Thailand — S • S Asia • 250 kW
USA
FAMILY RADIO, Okeechobee, Fl — S • W North Am • 100 kW
FAMILY RADIO, Via Jülich, Germany — W • N Africa • 100 kW
VOA, Via Botswana — S • C Africa • 100 kW
W • C Africa & S Africa • 100 kW

VOA, Via Philippines — S • S Asia • 250 kW
VOA, Via São Tomé — S • C Africa • 50/100 kW
11840 **CHINA**
†CHINA R INTL, Via Sackville, Canada — S • W North Am • 250 kW
CLANDESTINE (AFRICA)
†"R VOICE OF ENUPF", Samara, Russia — S • F • E Africa • 250 kW
GERMANY
MISSIONSWERK FRIEDENSSTIMME — • Sa • N Asia • 250 kW
INDIA
†ALL INDIA RADIO, Delhi — E Asia • 250 kW
ALL INDIA RADIO, Panaji — Mideast & W Asia • 250 kW
RUSSIA
†VOICE OF RUSSIA, Moscow — S • S Europe • 250 kW • ALT. FREQ. TO 12060 kHz
SWITZERLAND
†RADIO REVEIL, Via Jülich, Germany — W Tu/Th • C Africa & S Africa • 100 kW
USA
ADVENTIST WORLD R, Via Agat, Guam — W • SE Asia • 100 kW
†R FARDA, Via Lampertheim, Germany — W • W Asia • 100 kW
†TRANS WORLD R, Via Merizo, Guam — M-Sa • Australasia & S Pacific • 100 kW
M-F • Australasia & S Pacific • 100 kW
(con'd)

0 1 2 3 4 5 6 7 8 9 10 11 12 13 14 15 16 17 18 19 20 21 22 23 24

ENGLISH ▬   ARABIC ▨   CHINESE □□□   FRENCH ▬   GERMAN ▬   RUSSIAN ═   SPANISH ▬   OTHER ▬

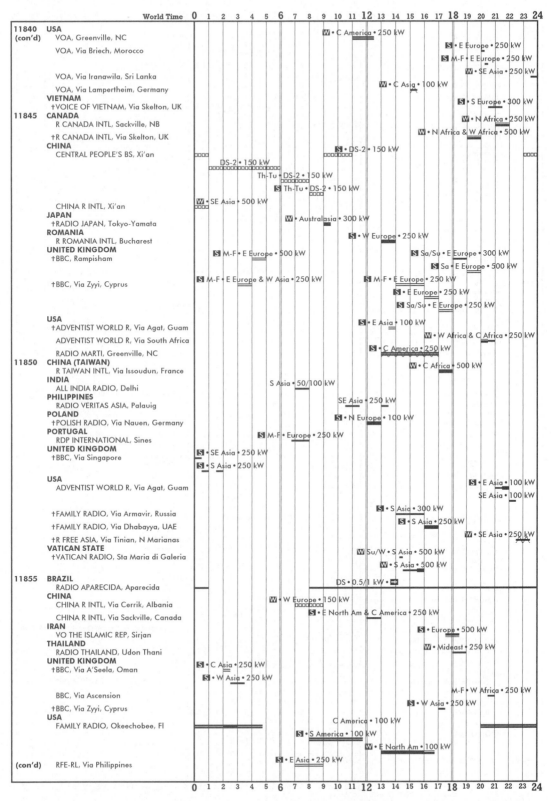

| | World Time | 0 | 1 | 2 | 3 | 4 | 5 | 6 | 7 | 8 | 9 | 10 | 11 | 12 | 13 | 14 | 15 | 16 | 17 | 18 | 19 | 20 | 21 | 22 | 23 | 24 |

11840 (con'd) **USA**
  VOA, Greenville, NC — W • C America • 250 kW
  VOA, Via Briech, Morocco — S • E Europe • 250 kW / S M-F • E Europe • 250 kW / W • SE Asia • 250 kW
  VOA, Via Iranawila, Sri Lanka
  VOA, Via Lampertheim, Germany — W • C Asia • 100 kW
VIETNAM
  †VOICE OF VIETNAM, Via Skelton, UK — S • S Europe • 300 kW
11845 CANADA
  R CANADA INTL, Sackville, NB — W • N Africa • 250 kW
  †R CANADA INTL, Via Skelton, UK — W • N Africa & W Africa • 500 kW
CHINA
  CENTRAL PEOPLE'S BS, Xi'an — DS-2 • 150 kW / S • DS-2 • 150 kW / Th-Tu • DS-2 • 150 kW / S Th-Tu • DS-2 • 150 kW
  CHINA R INTL, Xi'an — W • SE Asia • 500 kW
JAPAN
  †RADIO JAPAN, Tokyo-Yamata — W • Australasia • 300 kW
ROMANIA
  R ROMANIA INTL, Bucharest — S • W Europe • 250 kW
UNITED KINGDOM
  †BBC, Rampisham — S M-F • E Europe • 500 kW / S Sa/Su • E Europe • 300 kW / S Sa • E Europe • 500 kW
  †BBC, Via Zyyi, Cyprus — S M-F • E Europe & W Asia • 250 kW / S M-F • E Europe • 250 kW / S • E Europe • 250 kW / S Sa/Su • E Europe • 250 kW
USA
  †ADVENTIST WORLD R, Via Agat, Guam — S • E Asia • 100 kW
  ADVENTIST WORLD R, Via South Africa — W • W Africa & C Africa • 250 kW
  RADIO MARTI, Greenville, NC — S • C America • 250 kW
11850 CHINA (TAIWAN)
  R TAIWAN INTL, Via Issoudun, France — W • C Africa • 500 kW
INDIA
  ALL INDIA RADIO, Delhi — S Asia • 50/100 kW
PHILIPPINES
  RADIO VERITAS ASIA, Palauig — SE Asia • 250 kW
POLAND
  †POLISH RADIO, Via Nauen, Germany — S • N Europe • 100 kW
PORTUGAL
  RDP INTERNATIONAL, Sines — S M-F • Europe • 250 kW
UNITED KINGDOM
  †BBC, Via Singapore — S • SE Asia • 250 kW / S • S Asia • 250 kW
USA
  ADVENTIST WORLD R, Via Agat, Guam — S • E Asia • 100 kW / SE Asia • 100 kW
  †FAMILY RADIO, Via Armavir, Russia — S • S Asia • 300 kW
  †FAMILY RADIO, Via Dhabayya, UAE — S • S Asia • 250 kW
  †R FREE ASIA, Via Tinian, N Marianas — W • SE Asia • 250 kW
VATICAN STATE
  †VATICAN RADIO, Sta Maria di Galeria — W Su/W • S Asia • 500 kW / W • S Asia • 500 kW
11855 BRAZIL
  RADIO APARECIDA, Aparecida — DS • 0.5/1 kW •
CHINA
  CHINA R INTL, Via Cerrik, Albania — W • W Europe • 150 kW
  CHINA R INTL, Via Sackville, Canada — S • E North Am & C America • 250 kW
IRAN
  VO THE ISLAMIC REP, Sirjan — S • Europe • 500 kW
THAILAND
  RADIO THAILAND, Udon Thani — W • Mideast • 250 kW
UNITED KINGDOM
  †BBC, Via A'Seela, Oman — S • C Asia • 250 kW / S • W Asia • 250 kW
  BBC, Via Ascension — M-F • W Africa • 250 kW
  †BBC, Via Zyyi, Cyprus — S • W Asia • 250 kW
USA
  FAMILY RADIO, Okeechobee, Fl — C America • 100 kW / S • S America • 100 kW / W • E North Am • 100 kW
(con'd) RFE-RL, Via Philippines — S • E Asia • 250 kW

| | World Time | 0 | 1 | 2 | 3 | 4 | 5 | 6 | 7 | 8 | 9 | 10 | 11 | 12 | 13 | 14 | 15 | 16 | 17 | 18 | 19 | 20 | 21 | 22 | 23 | 24 |

SEASONAL S OR W   1-HR TIMESHIFT MIDYEAR ⇦ OR ⇨   JAMMING / OR /\   EARLIEST HEARD ◁   LATEST HEARD ▷   NEW FOR 2008 †

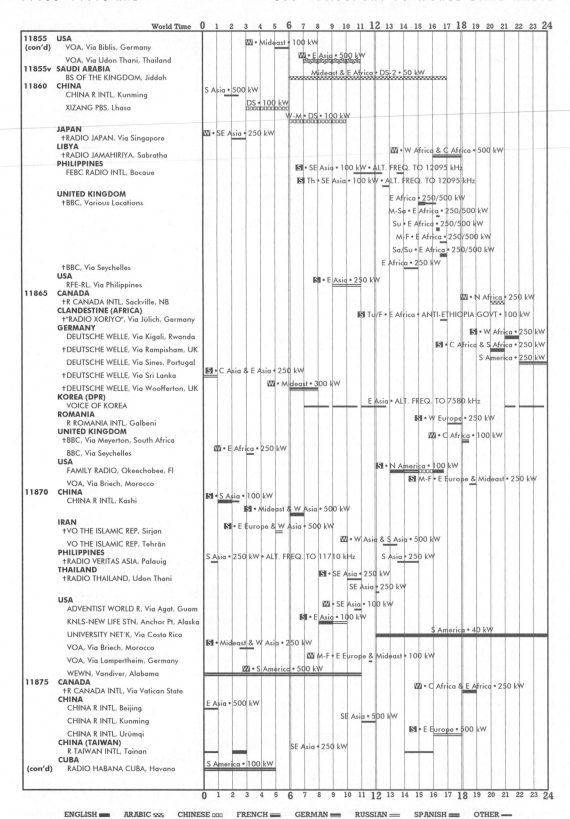

World Time 0 1 2 3 4 5 6 7 8 9 10 11 12 13 14 15 16 17 18 19 20 21 22 23 24

11855 **USA**
(con'd)   VOA, Via Biblis, Germany — W • Mideast • 100 kW
          VOA, Via Udon Thani, Thailand — W • E Asia • 500 kW
11855v **SAUDI ARABIA**
          BS OF THE KINGDOM, Jiddah — Mideast & E Africa • DS-2 • 50 kW
11860 **CHINA**
          CHINA R INTL, Kunming — S Asia • 500 kW
          XIZANG PBS, Lhasa — DS • 100 kW / W-M • DS • 100 kW

          JAPAN
          †RADIO JAPAN, Via Singapore — W • SE Asia • 250 kW
          LIBYA
          †RADIO JAMAHIRIYA, Sabratha — W • W Africa & C Africa • 500 kW
          PHILIPPINES
          FEBC RADIO INTL, Bocaue — S • SE Asia • 100 kW • ALT. FREQ. TO 12095 kHz / S Th • SE Asia • 100 kW • ALT. FREQ. TO 12095 kHz

          UNITED KINGDOM
          †BBC, Various Locations — E Africa • 250/500 kW / M-Sa • E Africa • 250/500 kW / Su • E Africa • 250/500 kW / M-F • E Africa • 250/500 kW / Sa/Su • E Africa • 250/500 kW

          †BBC, Via Seychelles — E Africa • 250 kW
          USA
          RFE-RL, Via Philippines — S • E Asia • 250 kW
11865 **CANADA**
          †R CANADA INTL, Sackville, NB — W • N Africa • 250 kW
          CLANDESTINE (AFRICA)
          †"RADIO XORIYO", Via Jülich, Germany — S Tu/F • E Africa • ANTI-ETHIOPIA GOVT • 100 kW
          GERMANY
          DEUTSCHE WELLE, Via Kigali, Rwanda — S • W Africa • 250 kW
          †DEUTSCHE WELLE, Via Rampisham, UK — S • C Africa & S Africa • 250 kW
          DEUTSCHE WELLE, Via Sines, Portugal — S America • 250 kW
          †DEUTSCHE WELLE, Via Sri Lanka — S • C Asia & E Asia • 250 kW
          †DEUTSCHE WELLE, Via Woofferton, UK — W • Mideast • 300 kW
          KOREA (DPR)
          VOICE OF KOREA — E Asia • ALT. FREQ. TO 7580 kHz
          ROMANIA
          R ROMANIA INTL, Galbeni — S • W Europe • 250 kW
          UNITED KINGDOM
          †BBC, Via Meyerton, South Africa — W • C Africa • 100 kW
          BBC, Via Seychelles — W • E Africa • 250 kW
          USA
          FAMILY RADIO, Okeechobee, Fl — S • N America • 100 kW
          VOA, Via Briech, Morocco — S M-F • E Europe & Mideast • 250 kW
11870 **CHINA**
          CHINA R INTL, Kashi — S • S Asia • 100 kW / S • Mideast & W Asia • 500 kW
          IRAN
          †VO THE ISLAMIC REP, Sirjan — S • E Europe & W Asia • 500 kW
          VO THE ISLAMIC REP, Tehrān — W • W Asia & S Asia • 500 kW
          PHILIPPINES
          †RADIO VERITAS ASIA, Palauig — S Asia • 250 kW • ALT. FREQ. TO 11710 kHz / S Asia • 250 kW
          THAILAND
          †RADIO THAILAND, Udon Thani — S • SE Asia • 250 kW / SE Asia • 250 kW
          USA
          ADVENTIST WORLD R, Via Agat, Guam — W • SE Asia • 100 kW
          KNLS-NEW LIFE STN, Anchor Pt, Alaska — S • E Asia • 100 kW
          UNIVERSITY NET'K, Via Costa Rica — S America • 40 kW
          VOA, Via Briech, Morocco — S • Mideast & W Asia • 250 kW
          VOA, Via Lampertheim, Germany — W M-F • E Europe & Mideast • 100 kW
          WEWN, Vandiver, Alabama — W • S America • 500 kW
11875 **CANADA**
          †R CANADA INTL, Via Vatican State — W • C Africa & E Africa • 250 kW
          CHINA
          CHINA R INTL, Beijing — E Asia • 500 kW
          CHINA R INTL, Kunming — SE Asia • 500 kW
          CHINA R INTL, Urümqi — S • E Europe • 500 kW
          CHINA (TAIWAN)
          R TAIWAN INTL, Tainan — SE Asia • 250 kW
          CUBA
(con'd)   RADIO HABANA CUBA, Havana — S America • 100 kW

0 1 2 3 4 5 6 7 8 9 10 11 12 13 14 15 16 17 18 19 20 21 22 23 24

ENGLISH ▬ ARABIC ▨ CHINESE ⬚ FRENCH ▬ GERMAN ▬ RUSSIAN ═ SPANISH ▬ OTHER —

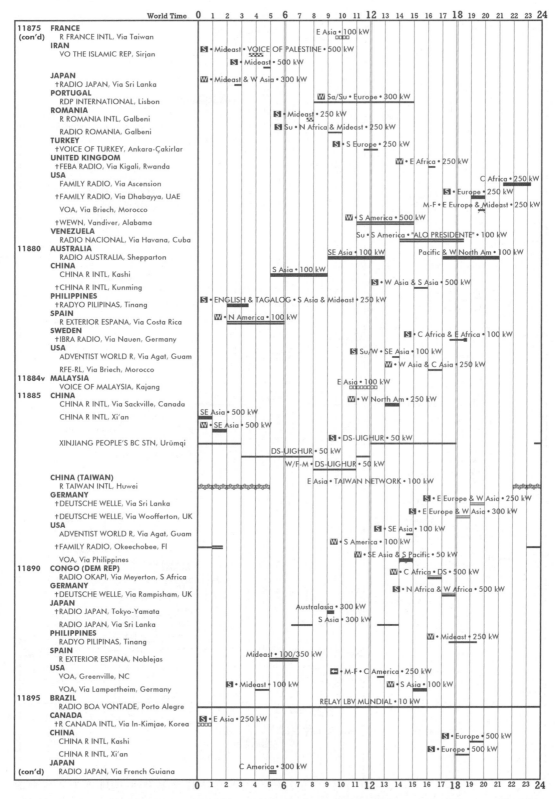

World Time

11875 **FRANCE**	
(con'd) R FRANCE INTL, Via Taiwan	E Asia • 100 kW
IRAN	
VO THE ISLAMIC REP, Sirjan	S • Mideast • VOICE OF PALESTINE • 500 kW
	S • Mideast • 500 kW
JAPAN	
†RADIO JAPAN, Via Sri Lanka	W • Mideast & W Asia • 300 kW
PORTUGAL	
RDP INTERNATIONAL, Lisbon	W • Sa/Su • Europe • 300 kW
ROMANIA	
R ROMANIA INTL, Galbeni	S • Mideast • 250 kW
RADIO ROMANIA, Galbeni	S • Su • N Africa & Mideast • 250 kW
TURKEY	
†VOICE OF TURKEY, Ankara-Çakirlar	S • S Europe • 250 kW
UNITED KINGDOM	
†FEBA RADIO, Via Kigali, Rwanda	W • E Africa • 250 kW
USA	
FAMILY RADIO, Via Ascension	C Africa • 250 kW
†FAMILY RADIO, Via Dhabayya, UAE	S • Europe • 250 kW
VOA, Via Briech, Morocco	M-F • E Europe & Mideast • 250 kW
†WEWN, Vandiver, Alabama	W • S America • 500 kW
VENEZUELA	
RADIO NACIONAL, Via Havana, Cuba	Su • S America • "ALO PRESIDENTE" • 100 kW
11880 **AUSTRALIA**	
RADIO AUSTRALIA, Shepparton	SE Asia • 100 kW Pacific & W North Am • 100 kW
CHINA	
CHINA R INTL, Kashi	S Asia • 100 kW
†CHINA R INTL, Kunming	W • W Asia & S Asia • 500 kW
PHILIPPINES	
†RADYO PILIPINAS, Tinang	S • ENGLISH & TAGALOG • S Asia & Mideast • 250 kW
SPAIN	
R EXTERIOR ESPANA, Via Costa Rica	W • N America • 100 kW
SWEDEN	
†IBRA RADIO, Via Nauen, Germany	S • C Africa & E Africa • 100 kW
USA	
ADVENTIST WORLD R, Via Agat, Guam	S • Su/W • SE Asia • 100 kW
RFE-RL, Via Briech, Morocco	W • W Asia & C Asia • 250 kW
11884v **MALAYSIA**	
VOICE OF MALAYSIA, Kajang	E Asia • 100 kW
11885 **CHINA**	
CHINA R INTL, Via Sackville, Canada	W • W North Am • 250 kW
CHINA R INTL, Xi'an	SE Asia • 500 kW
	W • SE Asia • 500 kW
XINJIANG PEOPLE'S BC STN, Urümqi	S • DS-UIGHUR • 50 kW
	DS-UIGHUR • 50 kW
	W/F-M • DS-UIGHUR • 50 kW
CHINA (TAIWAN)	
R TAIWAN INTL, Huwei	E Asia • TAIWAN NETWORK • 100 kW
GERMANY	
†DEUTSCHE WELLE, Via Sri Lanka	S • E Europe & W Asia • 250 kW
†DEUTSCHE WELLE, Via Woofferton, UK	S • E Europe & W Asia • 300 kW
USA	
ADVENTIST WORLD R, Via Agat, Guam	S • SE Asia • 100 kW
†FAMILY RADIO, Okeechobee, Fl	W • S America • 100 kW
VOA, Via Philippines	W • SE Asia & S Pacific • 50 kW
11890 **CONGO (DEM REP)**	
RADIO OKAPI, Via Meyerton, S Africa	W • C Africa • DS • 500 kW
GERMANY	
†DEUTSCHE WELLE, Via Rampisham, UK	S • N Africa & W Africa • 500 kW
JAPAN	
†RADIO JAPAN, Tokyo-Yamata	Australasia • 300 kW
RADIO JAPAN, Via Sri Lanka	S Asia • 300 kW
PHILIPPINES	
RADYO PILIPINAS, Tinang	W • Mideast • 250 kW
SPAIN	
R EXTERIOR ESPANA, Noblejas	Mideast • 100/350 kW
USA	
VOA, Greenville, NC	⟷ • M-F • C America • 250 kW
VOA, Via Lampertheim, Germany	S • Mideast • 100 kW W • S Asia • 100 kW
11895 **BRAZIL**	
RADIO BOA VONTADE, Porto Alegre	RELAY LBV MUNDIAL • 10 kW
CANADA	
†R CANADA INTL, Via In-Kimjae, Korea	S • E Asia • 250 kW
CHINA	
CHINA R INTL, Kashi	S • Europe • 500 kW
CHINA R INTL, Xi'an	S • Europe • 500 kW
JAPAN	
(con'd) RADIO JAPAN, Via French Guiana	C America • 300 kW

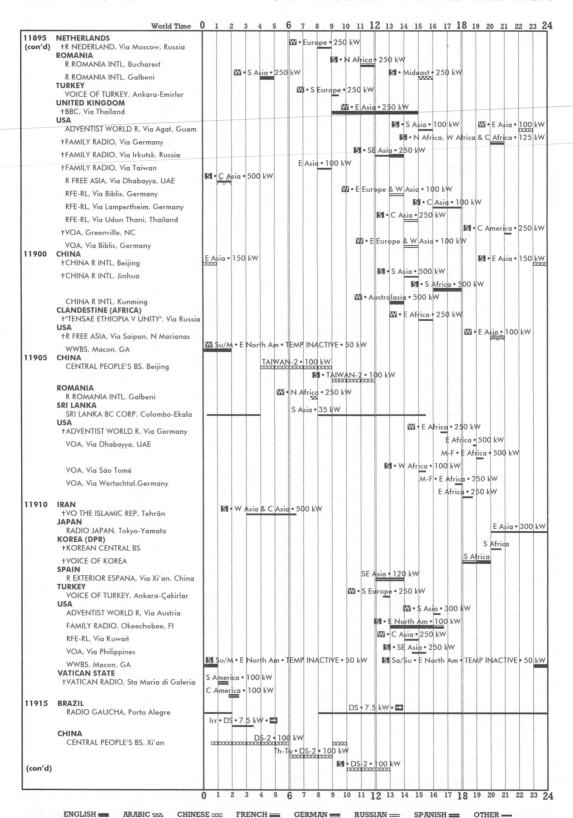

World Time 0 1 2 3 4 5 6 7 8 9 10 11 12 13 14 15 16 17 18 19 20 21 22 23 24

11895 NETHERLANDS
(con'd) †R NEDERLAND, Via Moscow, Russia — W • Europe • 250 kW
ROMANIA
  R ROMANIA INTL, Bucharest — S • N Africa • 250 kW
  R ROMANIA INTL, Galbeni — W • S Asia • 250 kW / S • Mideast • 250 kW
TURKEY
  VOICE OF TURKEY, Ankara-Emirler — W • S Europe • 250 kW
UNITED KINGDOM
  †BBC, Via Thailand — W • E Asia • 250 kW
USA
  ADVENTIST WORLD R, Via Agat, Guam — S • S Asia • 100 kW / W • E Asia • 100 kW
  †FAMILY RADIO, Via Germany — S • N Africa, W Africa & C Africa • 125 kW
  †FAMILY RADIO, Via Irkutsk, Russia — S • SE Asia • 250 kW
  †FAMILY RADIO, Via Taiwan — E Asia • 100 kW
  R FREE ASIA, Via Dhabayya, UAE — S • C Asia • 500 kW
  RFE-RL, Via Biblis, Germany — W • E Europe & W Asia • 100 kW
  RFE-RL, Via Lampertheim, Germany — S • C Asia • 100 kW
  RFE-RL, Via Udon Thani, Thailand — S • C Asia • 250 kW
  †VOA, Greenville, NC — S • C America • 250 kW
  VOA, Via Biblis, Germany — W • E Europe & W Asia • 100 kW
11900 CHINA
  †CHINA R INTL, Beijing — E Asia • 150 kW / S • E Asia • 150 kW
  †CHINA R INTL, Jinhua — S • S Asia • 500 kW
  CHINA R INTL, Kunming — S • S Africa • 500 kW / W • Australasia • 500 kW
CLANDESTINE (AFRICA)
  †"TENSAE ETHIOPIA V UNITY", Via Russia — W • E Africa • 250 kW
USA
  †R FREE ASIA, Via Saipan, N Marianas — W • E Asia • 100 kW
  WWBS, Macon, GA — W Su/M • E North Am • TEMP INACTIVE • 50 kW
11905 CHINA
  CENTRAL PEOPLE'S BS, Beijing — TAIWAN-2 • 100 kW / S • TAIWAN-2 • 100 kW
ROMANIA
  R ROMANIA INTL, Galbeni — W • N Africa • 250 kW
SRI LANKA
  SRI LANKA BC CORP, Colombo-Ekala — S Asia • 35 kW
USA
  †ADVENTIST WORLD R, Via Germany — W • E Africa • 250 kW
  VOA, Via Dhabayya, UAE — E Africa • 500 kW / M-F • E Africa • 500 kW
  VOA, Via São Tomé — S • W Africa • 100 kW
  VOA, Via Wertachtal, Germany — M-F • E Africa • 250 kW / E Africa • 250 kW
11910 IRAN
  †VO THE ISLAMIC REP, Tehrān — S • W Asia & C Asia • 500 kW
JAPAN
  RADIO JAPAN, Tokyo-Yamata — E Asia • 300 kW
KOREA (DPR)
  †KOREAN CENTRAL BS — S Africa
  †VOICE OF KOREA — S Africa
SPAIN
  R EXTERIOR ESPANA, Via Xi'an, China — SE Asia • 120 kW
TURKEY
  VOICE OF TURKEY, Ankara-Çakirlar — W • S Europe • 250 kW
USA
  ADVENTIST WORLD R, Via Austria — W • S Asia • 300 kW
  FAMILY RADIO, Okeechobee, Fl — S • E North Am • 100 kW
  RFE-RL, Via Kuwait — W • C Asia • 250 kW
  VOA, Via Philippines — S • SE Asia • 250 kW
  WWBS, Macon, GA — S Su/M • E North Am • TEMP INACTIVE • 50 kW / S Sa/Su • E North Am • TEMP INACTIVE • 50 kW
VATICAN STATE
  †VATICAN RADIO, Sta Maria di Galeria — S America • 100 kW / C America • 100 kW
11915 BRAZIL
  RADIO GAUCHA, Porto Alegre — DS • 7.5 kW • → / Irr • DS • 7.5 kW • →
CHINA
  CENTRAL PEOPLE'S BS, Xi'an — DS-2 • 100 kW / Th-Tu • DS-2 • 100 kW / S • DS-2 • 100 kW

(con'd)

World Time 0 1 2 3 4 5 6 7 8 9 10 11 12 13 14 15 16 17 18 19 20 21 22 23 24

ENGLISH ▬   ARABIC ⩘⩘   CHINESE ☐☐☐   FRENCH ▭   GERMAN ▬   RUSSIAN ═   SPANISH ▬   OTHER ▬

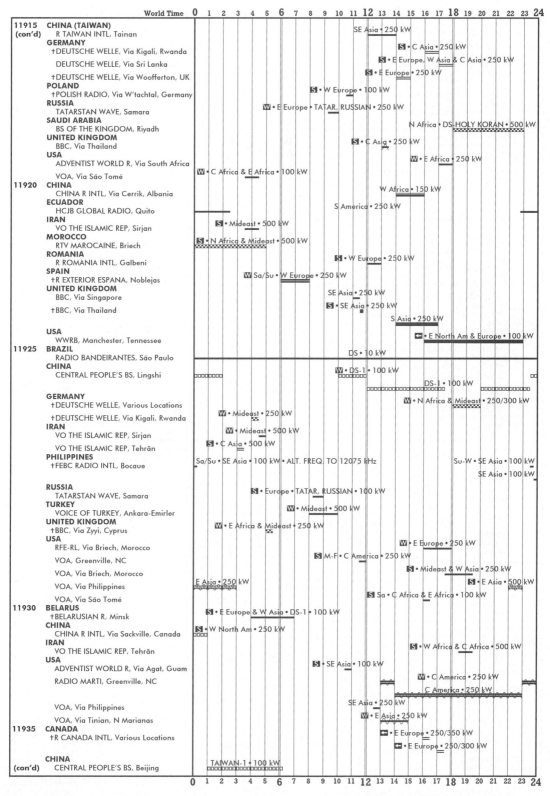

World Time

Freq	Station	Details
11915 (con'd)	**CHINA (TAIWAN)** R TAIWAN INTL, Tainan	SE Asia • 250 kW
	GERMANY †DEUTSCHE WELLE, Via Kigali, Rwanda	S • C Asia • 250 kW
	DEUTSCHE WELLE, Via Sri Lanka	S • E Europe, W Asia & C Asia • 250 kW
	†DEUTSCHE WELLE, Via Woofferton, UK	S • E Europe • 250 kW
	POLAND †POLISH RADIO, Via W'tachtal, Germany	S • W Europe • 100 kW
	RUSSIA TATARSTAN WAVE, Samara	W • E Europe • TATAR, RUSSIAN • 250 kW
	SAUDI ARABIA BS OF THE KINGDOM, Riyadh	N Africa • DS-HOLY KORAN • 500 kW
	UNITED KINGDOM BBC, Via Thailand	S • C Asia • 250 kW
	USA ADVENTIST WORLD R, Via South Africa	W • E Africa • 250 kW
	VOA, Via São Tomé	W • C Africa & E Africa • 100 kW
11920	**CHINA** CHINA R INTL, Via Cerrik, Albania	W Africa • 150 kW
	ECUADOR HCJB GLOBAL RADIO, Quito	S America • 250 kW
	IRAN VO THE ISLAMIC REP, Sirjan	S • Mideast • 500 kW
	MOROCCO RTV MAROCAINE, Briech	S • N Africa & Mideast • 500 kW
	ROMANIA R ROMANIA INTL, Galbeni	S • W Europe • 250 kW
	SPAIN †R EXTERIOR ESPANA, Noblejas	W Sa/Su • W Europe • 250 kW
	UNITED KINGDOM BBC, Via Singapore	SE Asia • 250 kW
	†BBC, Via Thailand	S • SE Asia • 250 kW
		S Asia • 250 kW
	USA WWRB, Manchester, Tennessee	⇆ • E North Am & Europe • 100 kW
11925	**BRAZIL** RADIO BANDEIRANTES, São Paulo	DS • 10 kW
	CHINA CENTRAL PEOPLE'S BS, Lingshi	W • DS-1 • 100 kW / DS-1 • 100 kW
	GERMANY †DEUTSCHE WELLE, Various Locations	W • N Africa & Mideast • 250/300 kW
	†DEUTSCHE WELLE, Via Kigali, Rwanda	W • Mideast • 250 kW
	IRAN VO THE ISLAMIC REP, Sirjan	W • Mideast • 500 kW
	VO THE ISLAMIC REP, Tehrān	S • C Asia • 500 kW
	PHILIPPINES †FEBC RADIO INTL, Bocaue	Sa/Su • SE Asia • 100 kW • ALT. FREQ. TO 12075 kHz Su-W • SE Asia • 100 kW SE Asia • 100 kW
	RUSSIA TATARSTAN WAVE, Samara	S • Europe • TATAR, RUSSIAN • 100 kW
	TURKEY VOICE OF TURKEY, Ankara-Emirler	W • Mideast • 500 kW
	UNITED KINGDOM †BBC, Via Zyyi, Cyprus	W • E Africa & Mideast • 250 kW
	USA RFE-RL, Via Briech, Morocco	W • E Europe • 250 kW
	VOA, Greenville, NC	S M-F • C America • 250 kW
	VOA, Via Briech, Morocco	S • Mideast & W Asia • 250 kW
	VOA, Via Philippines	E Asia • 250 kW S • E Asia • 500 kW
	VOA, Via São Tomé	S Sa • C Africa & E Africa • 100 kW
11930	**BELARUS** †BELARUSIAN R, Minsk	S • E Europe & W Asia • DS-1 • 100 kW
	CHINA CHINA R INTL, Via Sackville, Canada	S • W North Am • 250 kW
	IRAN VO THE ISLAMIC REP, Tehrān	S • W Africa & C Africa • 500 kW
	USA ADVENTIST WORLD R, Via Agat, Guam	S • SE Asia • 100 kW
	RADIO MARTI, Greenville, NC	W • C America • 250 kW C America • 250 kW
	VOA, Via Philippines	SE Asia • 250 kW
	VOA, Via Tinian, N Marianas	W • E Asia • 250 kW
11935	**CANADA** †R CANADA INTL, Various Locations	⇆ • E Europe • 250/350 kW ⇆ • E Europe • 250/300 kW
	CHINA (con'd) CENTRAL PEOPLE'S BS, Beijing	TAIWAN-1 • 100 kW

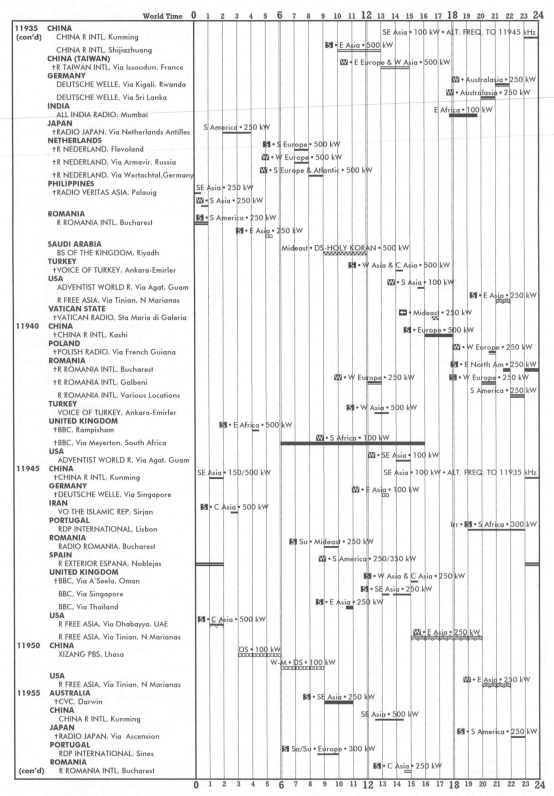

World Time

11935
(con'd)
CHINA
  CHINA R INTL, Kunming — SE Asia • 100 kW • ALT. FREQ. TO 11945 kHz

  CHINA R INTL, Shijiazhuang — S • E Asia • 500 kW
CHINA (TAIWAN)
  †R TAIWAN INTL, Via Issoudun, France — W • E Europe & W Asia • 500 kW
GERMANY
  DEUTSCHE WELLE, Via Kigali, Rwanda — W • Australasia • 250 kW

  DEUTSCHE WELLE, Via Sri Lanka — W • Australasia • 250 kW
INDIA
  ALL INDIA RADIO, Mumbai — E Africa • 100 kW
JAPAN
  †RADIO JAPAN, Via Netherlands Antilles — S America • 250 kW
NETHERLANDS
  †R NEDERLAND, Flevoland — S • S Europe • 500 kW

  †R NEDERLAND, Via Armavir, Russia — W • W Europe • 500 kW

  †R NEDERLAND, Via Wertachtal, Germany — W • S Europe & Atlantic • 500 kW
PHILIPPINES
  †RADIO VERITAS ASIA, Palauig — SE Asia • 250 kW

  W • S Asia • 250 kW
ROMANIA
  R ROMANIA INTL, Bucharest — S • S America • 250 kW

  S • E Asia • 250 kW
SAUDI ARABIA
  BS OF THE KINGDOM, Riyadh — Mideast • DS-HOLY KORAN • 500 kW
TURKEY
  †VOICE OF TURKEY, Ankara-Emirler — S • W Asia & C Asia • 500 kW
USA
  ADVENTIST WORLD R, Via Agat, Guam — W • S Asia • 100 kW

  R FREE ASIA, Via Tinian, N Marianas — S • E Asia • 250 kW
VATICAN STATE
  †VATICAN RADIO, Sta Maria di Galeria — ← • Mideast • 250 kW

11940
CHINA
  †CHINA R INTL, Kashi — S • Europe • 500 kW
POLAND
  †POLISH RADIO, Via French Guiana — W • W Europe • 250 kW
ROMANIA
  †R ROMANIA INTL, Bucharest — S • E North Am • 250 kW

  †R ROMANIA INTL, Galbeni — W • W Europe • 250 kW

  R ROMANIA INTL, Various Locations — W • W Europe • 250 kW
                                      — S America • 250 kW
TURKEY
  VOICE OF TURKEY, Ankara-Emirler — S • W Asia • 500 kW
UNITED KINGDOM
  †BBC, Rampisham — S • E Africa • 500 kW

  †BBC, Via Meyerton, South Africa — W • S Africa • 100 kW
USA
  ADVENTIST WORLD R, Via Agat, Guam — W • SE Asia • 100 kW

11945
CHINA
  †CHINA R INTL, Kunming — SE Asia • 150/500 kW — SE Asia • 100 kW • ALT. FREQ. TO 11935 kHz
GERMANY
  †DEUTSCHE WELLE, Via Singapore — W • E Asia • 100 kW
IRAN
  VO THE ISLAMIC REP, Sirjan — S • C Asia • 500 kW
PORTUGAL
  RDP INTERNATIONAL, Lisbon — Irr • S • S Africa • 300 kW
ROMANIA
  RADIO ROMANIA, Bucharest — S • Su • Mideast • 250 kW
SPAIN
  R EXTERIOR ESPANA, Noblejas — W • S America • 250/350 kW
UNITED KINGDOM
  †BBC, Via A'Seela, Oman — S • W Asia & C Asia • 250 kW

  BBC, Via Singapore — S • SE Asia • 250 kW

  BBC, Via Thailand — S • E Asia • 250 kW
USA
  R FREE ASIA, Via Dhabayya, UAE — S • C Asia • 500 kW

  R FREE ASIA, Via Tinian, N Marianas — W • E Asia • 250 kW

11950
CHINA
  XIZANG PBS, Lhasa — DS • 100 kW
                    — W-M • DS • 100 kW
USA
  R FREE ASIA, Via Tinian, N Marianas — W • E Asia • 250 kW

11955
AUSTRALIA
  †CVC, Darwin — S • SE Asia • 250 kW
CHINA
  CHINA R INTL, Kunming — SE Asia • 500 kW
JAPAN
  †RADIO JAPAN, Via Ascension — S • S America • 250 kW
PORTUGAL
  RDP INTERNATIONAL, Sines — S • Sa/Su • Europe • 300 kW
ROMANIA
(con'd)
  R ROMANIA INTL, Bucharest — S • C Asia • 250 kW

ENGLISH ▬   ARABIC ░░░   CHINESE ▢▢▢   FRENCH ▬▬   GERMAN ▬▬   RUSSIAN ═══   SPANISH ▬▬   OTHER ▬

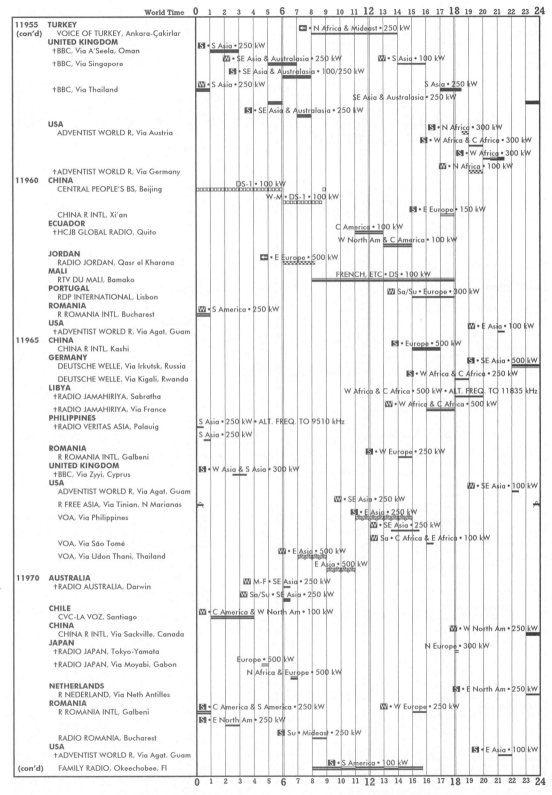

World Time

11955
(con'd) **TURKEY**
VOICE OF TURKEY, Ankara-Çakirlar — N Africa & Mideast • 250 kW
UNITED KINGDOM
†BBC, Via A'Seela, Oman — S • S Asia • 250 kW
†BBC, Via Singapore — W • SE Asia & Australasia • 250 kW — W • S Asia • 100 kW
S • SE Asia & Australasia • 100/250 kW
†BBC, Via Thailand — W • S Asia • 250 kW — S Asia • 250 kW
SE Asia & Australasia • 250 kW
S • SE Asia & Australasia • 250 kW

USA
ADVENTIST WORLD R, Via Austria — S • N Africa • 300 kW
S • W Africa & C Africa • 300 kW
• W Africa • 300 kW
†ADVENTIST WORLD R, Via Germany — W • N Africa • 100 kW

11960 **CHINA**
CENTRAL PEOPLE'S BS, Beijing — DS-1 • 100 kW
W-M • DS-1 • 100 kW
CHINA R INTL, Xi'an — S • E Europe • 150 kW
ECUADOR
†HCJB GLOBAL RADIO, Quito — C America • 100 kW
W North Am & C America • 100 kW

JORDAN
RADIO JORDAN, Qasr el Kharana — • E Europe • 500 kW
MALI
RTV DU MALI, Bamako — FRENCH, ETC • DS • 100 kW
PORTUGAL
RDP INTERNATIONAL, Lisbon — W Sa/Su • Europe • 300 kW
ROMANIA
R ROMANIA INTL, Bucharest — W • S America • 250 kW
USA
†ADVENTIST WORLD R, Via Agat, Guam — W • E Asia • 100 kW

11965 **CHINA**
CHINA R INTL, Kashi — S • Europe • 500 kW
GERMANY
DEUTSCHE WELLE, Via Irkutsk, Russia — S • SE Asia • 500 kW
DEUTSCHE WELLE, Via Kigali, Rwanda — S • W Africa & C Africa • 250 kW
LIBYA
†RADIO JAMAHIRIYA, Sabratha — W Africa & C Africa • 500 kW • ALT. FREQ. TO 11835 kHz
†RADIO JAMAHIRIYA, Via France — W • W Africa & C Africa • 500 kW
PHILIPPINES
†RADIO VERITAS ASIA, Palauig — S Asia • 250 kW • ALT. FREQ. TO 9510 kHz
S Asia • 250 kW

ROMANIA
R ROMANIA INTL, Galbeni — S • W Europe • 250 kW
UNITED KINGDOM
†BBC, Via Zyyi, Cyprus — S • W Asia & S Asia • 300 kW
USA
ADVENTIST WORLD R, Via Agat, Guam — W • SE Asia • 100 kW
R FREE ASIA, Via Tinian, N Marianas — W • SE Asia • 250 kW
VOA, Via Philippines — S • E Asia • 250 kW
W • SE Asia • 250 kW
VOA, Via São Tomé — W Sa • C Africa & E Africa • 100 kW
VOA, Via Udon Thani, Thailand — W • E Asia • 500 kW
E Asia • 500 kW

11970 **AUSTRALIA**
†RADIO AUSTRALIA, Darwin — W M-F • SE Asia • 250 kW
W Sa/Su • SE Asia • 250 kW
CHILE
CVC-LA VOZ, Santiago — W • C America & W North Am • 100 kW
CHINA
CHINA R INTL, Via Sackville, Canada — W • W North Am • 250 kW
JAPAN
†RADIO JAPAN, Tokyo-Yamata — N Europe • 300 kW
†RADIO JAPAN, Via Moyabi, Gabon — Europe • 500 kW
N Africa & Europe • 500 kW
NETHERLANDS
R NEDERLAND, Via Neth Antilles — S • E North Am • 250 kW
ROMANIA
R ROMANIA INTL, Galbeni — S • C America & S America • 250 kW — W • W Europe • 250 kW
S • E North Am • 250 kW
RADIO ROMANIA, Bucharest — S Su • Mideast • 250 kW
USA
†ADVENTIST WORLD R, Via Agat, Guam — S • E Asia • 100 kW
(con'd) FAMILY RADIO, Okeechobee, Fl — S • S America • 100 kW

SEASONAL S OR W   1-HR TIMESHIFT MIDYEAR ⇐ OR ⇒   JAMMING / OR ⋀   EARLIEST HEARD ◁   LATEST HEARD ▷   NEW FOR 2008 †

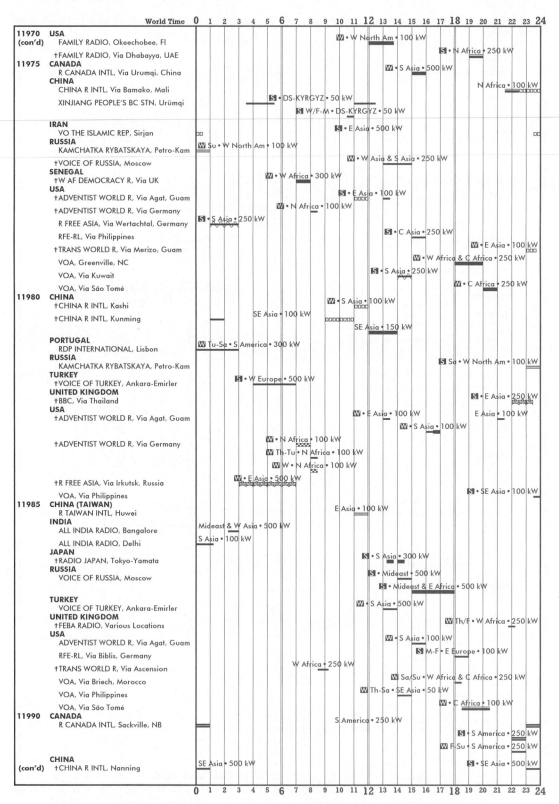

World Time	0 1 2 3 4 5 6 7 8 9 10 11 12 13 14 15 16 17 18 19 20 21 22 23 24
11970 USA	
(con'd) FAMILY RADIO, Okeechobee, Fl	**W** • W North Am • 100 kW
†FAMILY RADIO, Via Dhabayya, UAE	**S** • N Africa • 250 kW
11975 CANADA	
R CANADA INTL, Via Urumqi, China	**W** • S Asia • 500 kW
CHINA	
CHINA R INTL, Via Bamako, Mali	N Africa • 100 kW
XINJIANG PEOPLE'S BC STN, Urümqi	**S** • DS-KYRGYZ • 50 kW
	S W/F-M • DS-KYRGYZ • 50 kW
IRAN	
VO THE ISLAMIC REP, Sirjan	**S** • E Asia • 500 kW
RUSSIA	
KAMCHATKA RYBATSKAYA, Petro-Kam	**W** Su • W North Am • 100 kW
†VOICE OF RUSSIA, Moscow	**W** • W Asia & S Asia • 250 kW
SENEGAL	
†W AF DEMOCRACY R, Via UK	**W** • W Africa • 300 kW
USA	
†ADVENTIST WORLD R, Via Agat, Guam	**S** • E Asia • 100 kW
†ADVENTIST WORLD R, Via Germany	**W** • N Africa • 100 kW
R FREE ASIA, Via Wertachtal, Germany	**S** • S Asia • 250 kW
RFE-RL, Via Philippines	**S** • C Asia • 250 kW
†TRANS WORLD R, Via Merizo, Guam	**W** • E Asia • 100 kW
VOA, Greenville, NC	**W** • W Africa & C Africa • 250 kW
VOA, Via Kuwait	**S** • S Asia • 250 kW
VOA, Via São Tomé	**W** • C Africa • 250 kW
11980 CHINA	
†CHINA R INTL, Kashi	**W** • S Asia • 100 kW
†CHINA R INTL, Kunming	SE Asia • 100 kW
	SE Asia • 150 kW
PORTUGAL	
RDP INTERNATIONAL, Lisbon	**W** Tu-Sa • S America • 300 kW
RUSSIA	
KAMCHATKA RYBATSKAYA, Petro-Kam	**S** Sa • W North Am • 100 kW
TURKEY	
†VOICE OF TURKEY, Ankara-Emirler	**S** • W Europe • 500 kW
UNITED KINGDOM	
†BBC, Via Thailand	**S** • E Asia • 250 kW
USA	
†ADVENTIST WORLD R, Via Agat, Guam	**W** • E Asia • 100 kW E Asia • 100 kW
	W • S Asia • 100 kW
†ADVENTIST WORLD R, Via Germany	**W** • N Africa • 100 kW
	W Th-Tu • N Africa • 100 kW
	W • N Africa • 100 kW
†R FREE ASIA, Via Irkutsk, Russia	**W** • E Asia • 500 kW
VOA, Via Philippines	**S** • SE Asia • 100 kW
11985 CHINA (TAIWAN)	
R TAIWAN INTL, Huwei	E Asia • 100 kW
INDIA	
ALL INDIA RADIO, Bangalore	Mideast & W Asia • 500 kW
ALL INDIA RADIO, Delhi	S Asia • 100 kW
JAPAN	
†RADIO JAPAN, Tokyo-Yamata	**S** • S Asia • 300 kW
RUSSIA	
VOICE OF RUSSIA, Moscow	**S** • Mideast • 500 kW
	S • Mideast & E Africa • 500 kW
TURKEY	
VOICE OF TURKEY, Ankara-Emirler	**W** • S Asia • 500 kW
UNITED KINGDOM	
†FEBA RADIO, Various Locations	**W** Th/F • W Africa • 250 kW
USA	
ADVENTIST WORLD R, Via Agat, Guam	**W** • S Asia • 100 kW
RFE-RL, Via Biblis, Germany	**S** M-F • E Europe • 100 kW
†TRANS WORLD R, Via Ascension	W Africa • 250 kW
VOA, Via Briech, Morocco	**W** Sa/Su • W Africa & C Africa • 250 kW
VOA, Via Philippines	**W** Th-Sa • SE Asia • 50 kW
VOA, Via São Tomé	**W** • C Africa • 100 kW
11990 CANADA	
R CANADA INTL, Sackville, NB	S America • 250 kW
	S • S America • 250 kW
	W F-Su • S America • 250 kW
CHINA	
(con'd) †CHINA R INTL, Nanning	SE Asia • 500 kW **S** • SE Asia • 500 kW

ENGLISH ▬   ARABIC ⌇⌇⌇   CHINESE ⣀⣀⣀   FRENCH ▭▭   GERMAN ▬▬   RUSSIAN ═══   SPANISH ══   OTHER ▬

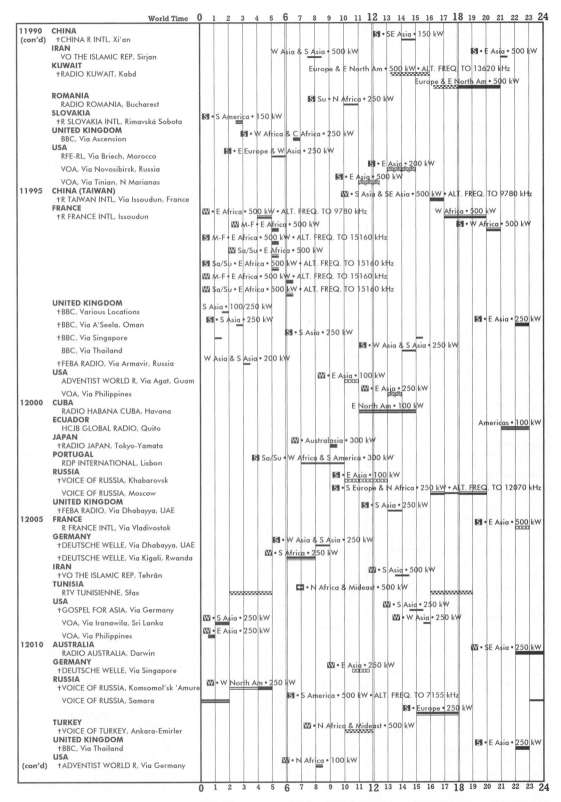

World Time

11990 CHINA
(con'd) †CHINA R INTL, Xi'an — Ⓢ • SE Asia • 150 kW
IRAN
VO THE ISLAMIC REP, Sirjan — W Asia & S Asia • 500 kW / Ⓢ • E Asia • 500 kW
KUWAIT
†RADIO KUWAIT, Kabd — Europe & E North Am • 500 kW • ALT. FREQ. TO 13620 kHz / Europe & E North Am • 500 kW

ROMANIA
RADIO ROMANIA, Bucharest — Ⓢ Su • N Africa • 250 kW
SLOVAKIA
†R SLOVAKIA INTL, Rimavská Sobota — Ⓢ • S America • 150 kW
UNITED KINGDOM
BBC, Via Ascension — Ⓢ • W Africa & C Africa • 250 kW
USA
RFE-RL, Via Briech, Morocco — Ⓢ • E Europe & W Asia • 250 kW
VOA, Via Novosibirsk, Russia — Ⓢ • E Asia • 200 kW
VOA, Via Tinian, N Marianas — Ⓢ • E Asia • 500 kW

11995 CHINA (TAIWAN)
†R TAIWAN INTL, Via Issoudun, France — Ⓦ • S Asia & SE Asia • 500 kW • ALT. FREQ. TO 9780 kHz
FRANCE
†R FRANCE INTL, Issoudun — Ⓦ • E Africa • 500 kW • ALT. FREQ. TO 9780 kHz / W Africa • 500 kW
Ⓦ M-F • E Africa • 500 kW
Ⓢ • W Africa • 500 kW
Ⓢ M-F • E Africa • 500 kW • ALT. FREQ. TO 15160 kHz
Ⓦ Sa/Su • E Africa • 500 kW
Ⓢ Sa/Su • E Africa • 500 kW • ALT. FREQ. TO 15160 kHz
Ⓦ M-F • E Africa • 500 kW • ALT. FREQ. TO 15160 kHz
Ⓦ Sa/Su • E Africa • 500 kW • ALT. FREQ. TO 15160 kHz

UNITED KINGDOM
†BBC, Various Locations — S Asia • 100/250 kW
†BBC, Via A'Seela, Oman — Ⓢ • S Asia • 250 kW / Ⓢ • E Asia • 250 kW
†BBC, Via Singapore — Ⓢ • S Asia • 250 kW
BBC, Via Thailand — Ⓢ • W Asia & S Asia • 250 kW
†FEBA RADIO, Via Armavir, Russia — W Asia & S Asia • 200 kW
USA
ADVENTIST WORLD R, Via Agat, Guam — Ⓦ • E Asia • 100 kW
VOA, Via Philippines — Ⓦ • E Asia • 250 kW
12000 CUBA
RADIO HABANA CUBA, Havana — E North Am • 100 kW
ECUADOR
HCJB GLOBAL RADIO, Quito — Americas • 100 kW
JAPAN
†RADIO JAPAN, Tokyo-Yamata — Ⓦ • Australasia • 300 kW
PORTUGAL
RDP INTERNATIONAL, Lisbon — Ⓢ Sa/Su • W Africa & S America • 300 kW
RUSSIA
†VOICE OF RUSSIA, Khabarovsk — Ⓢ • E Asia • 100 kW
VOICE OF RUSSIA, Moscow — Ⓢ • S Europe & N Africa • 250 kW • ALT. FREQ. TO 12070 kHz
UNITED KINGDOM
†FEBA RADIO, Via Dhabayya, UAE — Ⓢ • S Asia • 250 kW
12005 FRANCE
R FRANCE INTL, Via Vladivostok — Ⓢ • E Asia • 500 kW
GERMANY
†DEUTSCHE WELLE, Via Dhabayya, UAE — Ⓢ • W Asia & S Asia • 250 kW
†DEUTSCHE WELLE, Via Kigali, Rwanda — Ⓦ • S Africa • 250 kW
IRAN
†VO THE ISLAMIC REP, Tehrān — Ⓦ • S Asia • 500 kW
TUNISIA
RTV TUNISIENNE, Sfax — ⬄ • N Africa & Mideast • 500 kW
USA
†GOSPEL FOR ASIA, Via Germany — Ⓦ • S Asia • 250 kW
VOA, Via Iranawila, Sri Lanka — Ⓦ • S Asia • 250 kW / Ⓦ • W Asia • 250 kW
VOA, Via Philippines — Ⓦ • E Asia • 250 kW
12010 AUSTRALIA
RADIO AUSTRALIA, Darwin — Ⓦ • SE Asia • 250 kW
GERMANY
†DEUTSCHE WELLE, Via Singapore — Ⓦ • E Asia • 250 kW
RUSSIA
†VOICE OF RUSSIA, Komsomol'sk 'Amure — Ⓦ • W North Am • 250 kW
VOICE OF RUSSIA, Samara — Ⓢ • S America • 500 kW • ALT. FREQ. TO 7155 kHz / Ⓢ • Europe • 250 kW

TURKEY
†VOICE OF TURKEY, Ankara-Emirler — Ⓦ • N Africa & Mideast • 500 kW
UNITED KINGDOM
†BBC, Via Thailand — Ⓢ • E Asia • 250 kW
USA
(con'd) †ADVENTIST WORLD R, Via Germany — Ⓦ • N Africa • 100 kW

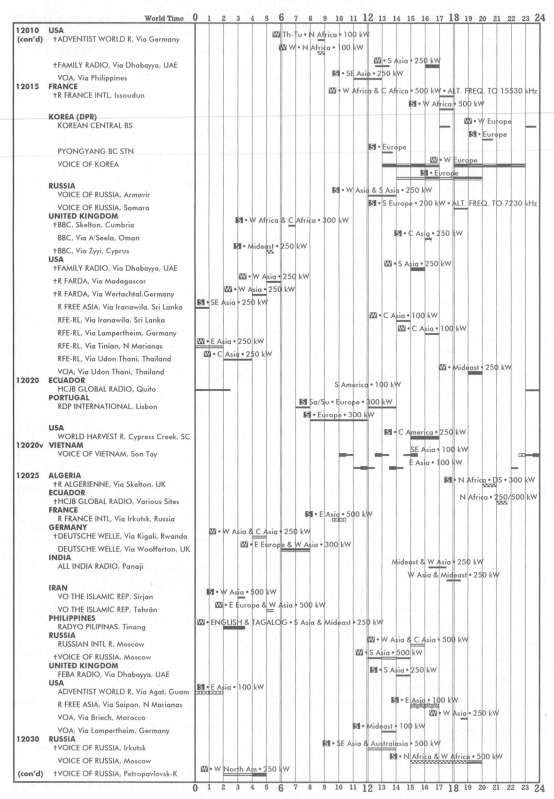

12010	**USA**	
(con'd)	†ADVENTIST WORLD R, Via Germany	W • Th-Tu • N Africa • 100 kW
		W • W • N Africa • 100 kW
	†FAMILY RADIO, Via Dhabayya, UAE	W • S Asia • 250 kW
	VOA, Via Philippines	S • SE Asia • 250 kW
12015	**FRANCE**	
	†R FRANCE INTL, Issoudun	W • W Africa & C Africa • 500 kW • ALT. FREQ. TO 15530 kHz
		S • W Africa • 500 kW
	KOREA (DPR)	
	KOREAN CENTRAL BS	W • W Europe
		S • Europe
	PYONGYANG BC STN	S • Europe
	VOICE OF KOREA	W • W Europe
		S • Europe
	RUSSIA	
	VOICE OF RUSSIA, Armavir	S • W Asia & S Asia • 250 kW
	VOICE OF RUSSIA, Samara	S • S Europe • 200 kW • ALT. FREQ. TO 7230 kHz
	UNITED KINGDOM	
	†BBC, Skelton, Cumbria	S • W Africa & C Africa • 300 kW
	BBC, Via A'Seela, Oman	S • C Asia • 250 kW
	†BBC, Via Zyyi, Cyprus	S • Mideast • 250 kW
	USA	
	†FAMILY RADIO, Via Dhabayya, UAE	W • S Asia • 250 kW
	†R FARDA, Via Madagascar	W • W Asia • 250 kW
	†R FARDA, Via Wertachtal, Germany	W • W Asia • 250 kW
	R FREE ASIA, Via Iranawila, Sri Lanka	S • SE Asia • 250 kW
	RFE-RL, Via Iranawila, Sri Lanka	W • C Asia • 100 kW
	RFE-RL, Via Lampertheim, Germany	W • C Asia • 100 kW
	RFE-RL, Via Tinian, N Marianas	W • E Asia • 250 kW
	RFE-RL, Via Udon Thani, Thailand	W • C Asia • 250 kW
	VOA, Via Udon Thani, Thailand	W • Mideast • 250 kW
12020	**ECUADOR**	
	HCJB GLOBAL RADIO, Quito	S America • 100 kW
	PORTUGAL	
	RDP INTERNATIONAL, Lisbon	S • Sa/Su • Europe • 300 kW
		S • Europe • 300 kW
	USA	
	WORLD HARVEST R, Cypress Creek, SC	S • C America • 250 kW
12020v	**VIETNAM**	
	VOICE OF VIETNAM, Son Tay	SE Asia • 100 kW
		E Asia • 100 kW
12025	**ALGERIA**	
	†R ALGERIENNE, Via Skelton, UK	S • N Africa • DS • 300 kW
	ECUADOR	
	†HCJB GLOBAL RADIO, Various Sites	N Africa • 250/500 kW
	FRANCE	
	R FRANCE INTL, Via Irkutsk, Russia	S • E Asia • 500 kW
	GERMANY	
	†DEUTSCHE WELLE, Via Kigali, Rwanda	W • W Asia & C Asia • 250 kW
	DEUTSCHE WELLE, Via Woofferton, UK	W • E Europe & W Asia • 300 kW
	INDIA	
	ALL INDIA RADIO, Panaji	Mideast & W Asia • 250 kW
		W Asia & Mideast • 250 kW
	IRAN	
	VO THE ISLAMIC REP, Sirjan	S • W Asia • 500 kW
	VO THE ISLAMIC REP, Tehrān	W • E Europe & W Asia • 500 kW
	PHILIPPINES	
	RADYO PILIPINAS, Tinang	W • ENGLISH & TAGALOG • S Asia & Mideast • 250 kW
	RUSSIA	
	RUSSIAN INTL R, Moscow	W • W Asia & C Asia • 500 kW
	†VOICE OF RUSSIA, Moscow	W • S Asia • 500 kW
	UNITED KINGDOM	
	FEBA RADIO, Via Dhabayya, UAE	S • S Asia • 250 kW
	USA	
	ADVENTIST WORLD R, Via Agat, Guam	S • E Asia • 100 kW
	R FREE ASIA, Via Saipan, N Marianas	S • E Asia • 100 kW
	VOA, Via Briech, Morocco	W • W Asia • 250 kW
	VOA, Via Lampertheim, Germany	S • Mideast • 100 kW
12030	**RUSSIA**	
	†VOICE OF RUSSIA, Irkutsk	S • SE Asia & Australasia • 500 kW
	VOICE OF RUSSIA, Moscow	S • N Africa & W Africa • 500 kW
(con'd)	†VOICE OF RUSSIA, Petropavlovsk-K	W • W North Am • 250 kW

ENGLISH ▬▬   ARABIC ▨▨   CHINESE ▢▢▢   FRENCH ▬▬   GERMAN ▬▬   RUSSIAN ══   SPANISH ▬▬   OTHER ▬▬

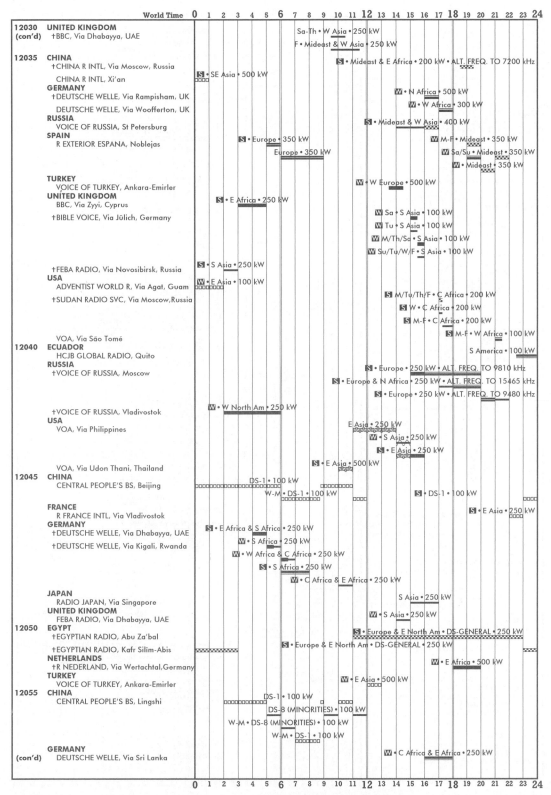

World Time	0 1 2 3 4 5 6 7 8 9 10 11 12 13 14 15 16 17 18 19 20 21 22 23 24
12030 UNITED KINGDOM	
(con'd) †BBC, Via Dhabayya, UAE	Sa-Th • W Asia • 250 kW / F • Mideast & W Asia • 250 kW
12035 CHINA	
†CHINA R INTL, Via Moscow, Russia	S • Mideast & E Africa • 200 kW • ALT. FREQ. TO 7200 kHz
CHINA R INTL, Xi'an	S • SE Asia • 500 kW
GERMANY	
†DEUTSCHE WELLE, Via Rampisham, UK	W • N Africa • 500 kW
DEUTSCHE WELLE, Via Woofferton, UK	W • W Africa • 300 kW
RUSSIA	
VOICE OF RUSSIA, St Petersburg	S • Mideast & W Asia • 400 kW
SPAIN	
R EXTERIOR ESPANA, Noblejas	S • Europe • 350 kW W • M-F • Mideast • 350 kW
	Europe • 350 kW W • Sa/Su • Mideast • 350 kW
	W • Mideast • 350 kW
TURKEY	
VOICE OF TURKEY, Ankara-Emirler	W • W Europe • 500 kW
UNITED KINGDOM	
BBC, Via Zyyi, Cyprus	S • E Africa • 250 kW
†BIBLE VOICE, Via Jülich, Germany	W • Sa • S Asia • 100 kW
	W • Tu • S Asia • 100 kW
	W • M/Th/Sa • S Asia • 100 kW
	W • Su/Tu/W/F • S Asia • 100 kW
†FEBA RADIO, Via Novosibirsk, Russia	S • S Asia • 250 kW
USA	W • E Asia • 100 kW
ADVENTIST WORLD R, Via Agat, Guam	
†SUDAN RADIO SVC, Via Moscow, Russia	S • M/Tu/Th/F • C Africa • 200 kW
	S • W • C Africa • 200 kW
	S • M-F • C Africa • 200 kW
VOA, Via São Tomé	S • M-F • W Africa • 100 kW
12040 ECUADOR	S America • 100 kW
HCJB GLOBAL RADIO, Quito	
RUSSIA	S • Europe • 250 kW • ALT. FREQ. TO 9810 kHz
†VOICE OF RUSSIA, Moscow	S • Europe & N Africa • 250 kW • ALT. FREQ. TO 15465 kHz
	S • Europe • 250 kW • ALT. FREQ. TO 9480 kHz
†VOICE OF RUSSIA, Vladivostok	W • W North Am • 250 kW
USA	E Asia • 250 kW
VOA, Via Philippines	W • S Asia • 250 kW
	S • E Asia • 250 kW
VOA, Via Udon Thani, Thailand	S • E Asia • 500 kW
12045 CHINA	
CENTRAL PEOPLE'S BS, Beijing	DS-1 • 100 kW
	W-M • DS-1 • 100 kW S • DS-1 • 100 kW
FRANCE	
R FRANCE INTL, Via Vladivostok	S • E Asia • 250 kW
GERMANY	
†DEUTSCHE WELLE, Via Dhabayya, UAE	S • E Africa & S Africa • 250 kW
†DEUTSCHE WELLE, Via Kigali, Rwanda	W • S Africa • 250 kW
	W • W Africa & C Africa • 250 kW
	S • S Africa • 250 kW
	W • C Africa & E Africa • 250 kW
JAPAN	
RADIO JAPAN, Via Singapore	S Asia • 250 kW
UNITED KINGDOM	
FEBA RADIO, Via Dhabayya, UAE	W • S Asia • 250 kW
12050 EGYPT	
†EGYPTIAN RADIO, Abu Za'bal	S • Europe & E North Am • DS-GENERAL • 250 kW
†EGYPTIAN RADIO, Kafr Silim-Abis	S • Europe & E North Am • DS-GENERAL • 250 kW
NETHERLANDS	
†R NEDERLAND, Via Wertachtal, Germany	W • E Africa • 500 kW
TURKEY	
VOICE OF TURKEY, Ankara-Emirler	W • E Asia • 500 kW
12055 CHINA	
CENTRAL PEOPLE'S BS, Lingshi	DS-1 • 100 kW
	DS-8 (MINORITIES) • 100 kW
	W-M • DS-8 (MINORITIES) • 100 kW
	W-M • DS-1 • 100 kW
GERMANY	
(con'd) DEUTSCHE WELLE, Via Sri Lanka	W • C Africa & E Africa • 250 kW

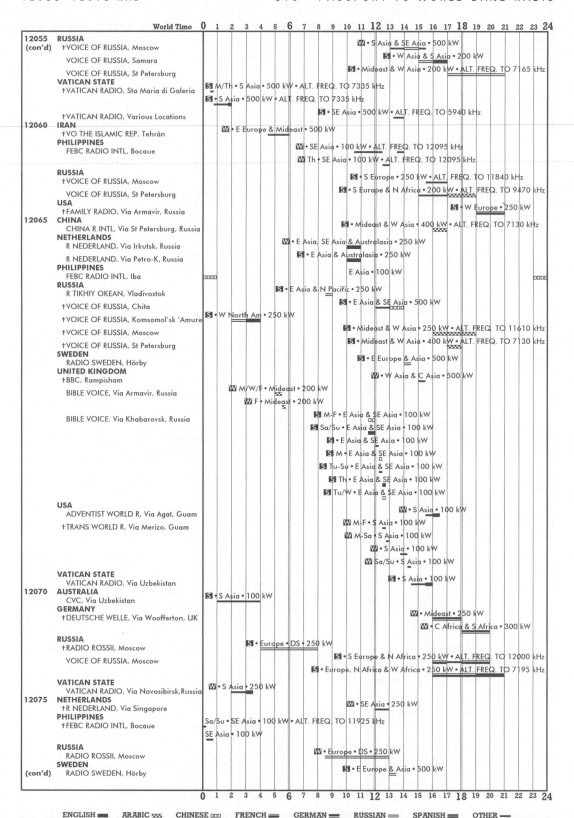

World Time 0 1 2 3 4 5 6 7 8 9 10 11 12 13 14 15 16 17 18 19 20 21 22 23 24

12055 **RUSSIA**
(con'd) †VOICE OF RUSSIA, Moscow — W • S Asia & SE Asia • 500 kW
 VOICE OF RUSSIA, Samara — W Asia & S Asia • 200 kW
 VOICE OF RUSSIA, St Petersburg — S • Mideast & W Asia • 200 kW • ALT. FREQ. TO 7165 kHz
VATICAN STATE
 †VATICAN RADIO, Sta Maria di Galeria — S M/Th • S Asia • 500 kW • ALT. FREQ. TO 7335 kHz
 S • S Asia • 500 kW • ALT. FREQ. TO 7335 kHz
 †VATICAN RADIO, Various Locations — S • SE Asia • 500 kW • ALT. FREQ. TO 5940 kHz
12060 **IRAN**
 †VO THE ISLAMIC REP, Tehrān — W • E Europe & Mideast • 500 kW
PHILIPPINES
 FEBC RADIO INTL, Bocaue — W • SE Asia • 100 kW • ALT. FREQ. TO 12095 kHz
 W Th • SE Asia • 100 kW • ALT. FREQ. TO 12095 kHz
RUSSIA
 †VOICE OF RUSSIA, Moscow — S • S Europe • 250 kW • ALT. FREQ. TO 11840 kHz
 VOICE OF RUSSIA, St Petersburg — S • S Europe & N Africa • 200 kW • ALT. FREQ. TO 9470 kHz
USA
 †FAMILY RADIO, Via Armavir, Russia — S • W Europe • 250 kW
12065 **CHINA**
 CHINA R INTL, Via St Petersburg, Russia — S • Mideast & W Asia • 400 kW • ALT. FREQ. TO 7130 kHz
NETHERLANDS
 R NEDERLAND, Via Irkutsk, Russia — W • E Asia, SE Asia & Australasia • 250 kW
 R NEDERLAND, Via Petro-K, Russia — S • E Asia & Australasia • 250 kW
PHILIPPINES
 FEBC RADIO INTL, Iba — E Asia • 100 kW
RUSSIA
 R TIKHIY OKEAN, Vladivostok — S • E Asia & N Pacific • 250 kW
 †VOICE OF RUSSIA, Chita — S • E Asia & SE Asia • 500 kW
 †VOICE OF RUSSIA, Komsomol'sk 'Amure — S • W North Am • 250 kW
 †VOICE OF RUSSIA, Moscow — S • Mideast & W Asia • 250 kW • ALT. FREQ. TO 11610 kHz
 †VOICE OF RUSSIA, St Petersburg — S • Mideast & W Asia • 400 kW • ALT. FREQ. TO 7130 kHz
SWEDEN
 RADIO SWEDEN, Hörby — S • E Europe & Asia • 500 kW
UNITED KINGDOM
 †BBC, Rampisham — W • W Asia & C Asia • 500 kW
 BIBLE VOICE, Via Armavir, Russia — W M/W/F • Mideast • 200 kW
 W F • Mideast • 200 kW
 BIBLE VOICE, Via Khabarovsk, Russia — S M-F • E Asia & SE Asia • 100 kW
 S Sa/Su • E Asia & SE Asia • 100 kW
 S • E Asia & SE Asia • 100 kW
 S M • E Asia & SE Asia • 100 kW
 S Tu-Su • E Asia & SE Asia • 100 kW
 S Th • E Asia & SE Asia • 100 kW
 S Tu/W • E Asia & SE Asia • 100 kW
USA
 ADVENTIST WORLD R, Via Agat, Guam — W • S Asia • 100 kW
 †TRANS WORLD R, Via Merizo, Guam — W M-F • S Asia • 100 kW
 W M-Sa • S Asia • 100 kW
 W • S Asia • 100 kW
 W Sa/Su • S Asia • 100 kW
VATICAN STATE
 VATICAN RADIO, Via Uzbekistan — S • S Asia • 100 kW
12070 **AUSTRALIA**
 CVC, Via Uzbekistan — S • S Asia • 100 kW
GERMANY
 †DEUTSCHE WELLE, Via Woofferton, UK — W • Mideast • 250 kW
 W • C Africa & S Africa • 300 kW
RUSSIA
 †RADIO ROSSII, Moscow — S • Europe • DS • 250 kW
 VOICE OF RUSSIA, Moscow — S • S Europe & N Africa • 250 kW • ALT. FREQ. TO 12000 kHz
 S • Europe, N Africa & W Africa • 250 kW • ALT. FREQ. TO 7195 kHz
VATICAN STATE
 VATICAN RADIO, Via Novosibirsk, Russia — W • S Asia • 250 kW
12075 **NETHERLANDS**
 †R NEDERLAND, Via Singapore — W • SE Asia • 250 kW
PHILIPPINES
 †FEBC RADIO INTL, Bocaue — Sa/Su • SE Asia • 100 kW • ALT. FREQ. TO 11925 kHz
 SE Asia • 100 kW
RUSSIA
 RADIO ROSSII, Moscow — W • Europe • DS • 250 kW
SWEDEN
(con'd) RADIO SWEDEN, Hörby — S • E Europe & Asia • 500 kW

0 1 2 3 4 5 6 7 8 9 10 11 12 13 14 15 16 17 18 19 20 21 22 23 24

ENGLISH ▬ ARABIC ⋙ CHINESE □□□ FRENCH ▬ GERMAN ▬ RUSSIAN ═ SPANISH ▬ OTHER ▬

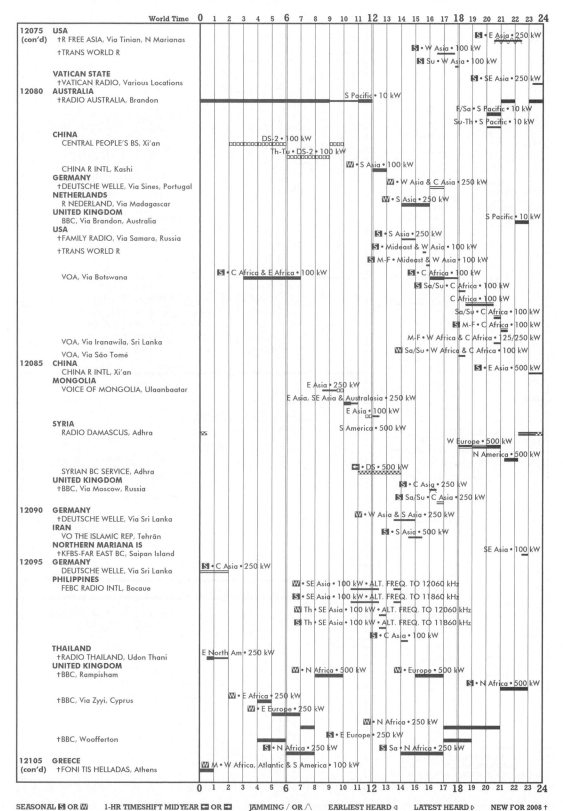

12075 (con'd)	USA	†R FREE ASIA, Via Tinian, N Marianas
		†TRANS WORLD R
	VATICAN STATE	†VATICAN RADIO, Various Locations
12080	AUSTRALIA	†RADIO AUSTRALIA, Brandon
	CHINA	CENTRAL PEOPLE'S BS, Xi'an
		CHINA R INTL, Kashi
	GERMANY	†DEUTSCHE WELLE, Via Sines, Portugal
	NETHERLANDS	R NEDERLAND, Via Madagascar
	UNITED KINGDOM	BBC, Via Brandon, Australia
	USA	†FAMILY RADIO, Via Samara, Russia
		†TRANS WORLD R
		VOA, Via Botswana
		VOA, Via Iranawila, Sri Lanka
		VOA, Via São Tomé
12085	CHINA	CHINA R INTL, Xi'an
	MONGOLIA	VOICE OF MONGOLIA, Ulaanbaatar
	SYRIA	RADIO DAMASCUS, Adhra
		SYRIAN BC SERVICE, Adhra
	UNITED KINGDOM	†BBC, Via Moscow, Russia
12090	GERMANY	†DEUTSCHE WELLE, Via Sri Lanka
	IRAN	VO THE ISLAMIC REP, Tehrān
	NORTHERN MARIANA IS	†KFBS-FAR EAST BC, Saipan Island
12095	GERMANY	DEUTSCHE WELLE, Via Sri Lanka
	PHILIPPINES	FEBC RADIO INTL, Bocaue
	THAILAND	†RADIO THAILAND, Udon Thani
	UNITED KINGDOM	†BBC, Rampisham
		†BBC, Via Zyyi, Cyprus
		†BBC, Woofferton
12105 (con'd)	GREECE	†FONI TIS HELLADAS, Athens

SEASONAL ⒮ OR ⒲   1-HR TIMESHIFT MIDYEAR ⬅ OR ➡   JAMMING / OR /\   EARLIEST HEARD ◁   LATEST HEARD ▷   NEW FOR 2008 †

World Time 0 1 2 3 4 5 6 7 8 9 10 11 12 13 14 15 16 17 18 19 20 21 22 23 24

12105	GREECE
(con'd)	†FONI TIS HELLADAS, Athens

W • Tu-Su • W Africa, Atlantic & S America • 100 kW
W • W Africa, Atlantic & S America • 100 kW
W • M-Sa • W Africa, Atlantic & S America • 100 kW
W • Su • W Africa, Atlantic & S America • 100 kW
W • W Africa • 100 kW

USA
ADVENTIST WORLD R, Via Agat, Guam
S • E Asia • 100 kW

R FREE ASIA, Via Iranawila, Sri Lanka
W • S Asia • 100 kW
W • SE Asia • 250 kW

12110	CHINA
	CHINA R INTL, Kunming

SE Asia • 100 kW

USA
RFE-RL, Via Iranawila, Sri Lanka
C Asia • 250 kW

VOA, Via Jülich, Germany
W • W Asia • 100 kW

12115	RUSSIA
	VOICE OF RUSSIA, Via Tajikistan

S • S Asia • 100 kW

12120	NORTHERN MARIANA IS
	KFBS-FAR EAST BC, Saipan Island

SE Asia • 100 kW

USA
ADVENTIST WORLD R, Via Agat, Guam
W • E Asia • 100 kW   **S** • E Asia • 100 kW

VOA, Via Tinian, N Marianas
S • SE Asia • 250 kW

12130	USA
	†ADVENTIST WORLD R, Via Agat, Guam

S • S Asia • 100 kW

†TRANS WORLD R, Via Merizo, Guam
⬅ • F/Sa • E Asia • 100 kW

E Asia • 100 kW

†WORLD HARVEST R, Naalehu, Hawai'i
E Asia & SE Asia • 100 kW • ALT. FREQ. TO 9930 kHz
Sa-Th • E Asia & SE Asia • 100 kW • ALT. FREQ. TO 9930 kHz
F • E Asia & SE Asia • 100 kW • ALT. FREQ. TO 9930 kHz
Su/M/W • E Asia & SE Asia • 100 kW • ALT. FREQ. TO 9930 kHz
Tu/Th/Sa • E Asia & SE Asia • 100 kW • ALT. FREQ. TO 9930 kHz

12133.5	USA
	AFRTS, Key West, Florida

Americas • 8 kW • USB

12135	USA
	†R FREE ASIA, Via Iranawila, Sri Lanka

W • SE Asia • 250 kW

12140	USA
	RFE-RL, Via Kuwait

W Asia & S Asia • 250 kW
W • W Asia & S Asia • 250 kW
S • W Asia & S Asia • 250 kW

VOA, Via Kuwait

12150	USA
	†FAMILY RADIO, Via Almaty, Kazakstan

W • E Asia • 500 kW

RFE-RL, Via Kuwait
S • C Asia • 250 kW

VOA, Via Iranawila, Sri Lanka
W • S Asia • 250 kW
W • E Asia & SE Asia • 250 kW
S • S Asia • 250 kW

12160	USA
	WWCR, Nashville, Tennessee

Irr • E North Am & Europe • 100 kW
E North Am & Europe • 100 kW
E North Am & Europe • 100 kW • ALT. FREQ. TO 5070 kHz

12257	PIRATE (EUROPE)
	"WREKIN RADIO INTL", England

⬅ • Irr • Su • W Europe • 0.03 kW

12579	USA
	AFRTS, Via Diego Garcia

S Asia • USB • ALT. FREQ. TO 4319 kHz

13362	USA
	AFRTS, Via Guam

Pacific • USB • ALT. FREQ. TO 5765 kHz

13570	USA
	WINB-WORLD INTL BC, Red Lion, Pa

C America & W North Am • 50 kW
W • C America & W North Am • 50 kW

13580	CHINA
	†CHINA R INTL, Beijing

SE Asia • 500 kW

CHINA R INTL, Kunming
Australasia • 500 kW

	CZECH REPUBLIC
	†RADIO PRAGUE, Litomyšl

S • W Europe • 100 kW
S • C Africa & S Africa • 100 kW
W • N America • 100 kW
S • E Europe & W Asia • 100 kW
⬅ • W Europe • 100 kW
S • S Europe & N Africa • 100 kW

	SWEDEN
	RADIO SWEDEN, Hörby

S • E Asia & Australasia • 500 kW

	UNITED KINGDOM
(con'd)	†BIBLE VOICE, Via Wertachtal, Germany

S • M-F • Mideast • 250 kW

0 1 2 3 4 5 6 7 8 9 10 11 12 13 14 15 16 17 18 19 20 21 22 23 24

ENGLISH ▬ ARABIC ▨ CHINESE ▫▫▫ FRENCH ▬▬ GERMAN ▬▬ RUSSIAN ═══ SPANISH ▬▬ OTHER ▬

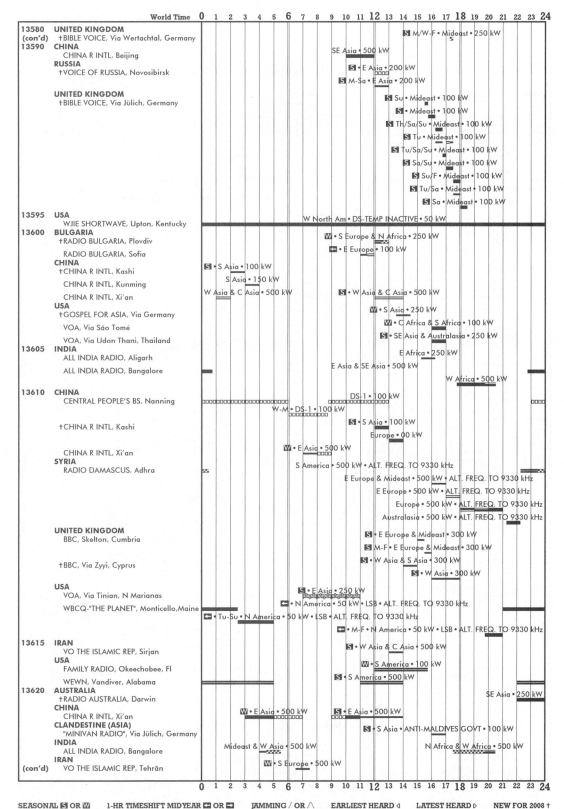

World Time 0 1 2 3 4 5 6 7 8 9 10 11 12 13 14 15 16 17 18 19 20 21 22 23 24

13580 **UNITED KINGDOM**
(con'd) †BIBLE VOICE, Via Wertachtal, Germany
S • M/W-F • Mideast • 250 kW

13590 **CHINA**
CHINA R INTL, Beijing
SE Asia • 500 kW

RUSSIA
†VOICE OF RUSSIA, Novosibirsk
S • E Asia • 200 kW
S • M-Sa • E Asia • 200 kW

UNITED KINGDOM
†BIBLE VOICE, Via Jülich, Germany
S • Su • Mideast • 100 kW
S • Mideast • 100 kW
S • Th/Sa/Su • Mideast • 100 kW
S • Tu • Mideast • 100 kW
S • Tu/Sa/Su • Mideast • 100 kW
S • Sa/Su • Mideast • 100 kW
S • Su/F • Mideast • 100 kW
S • Tu/Sa • Mideast • 100 kW
S • Sa • Mideast • 100 kW

13595 **USA**
WJIE SHORTWAVE, Upton, Kentucky
W North Am • DS-TEMP INACTIVE • 50 kW

13600 **BULGARIA**
†RADIO BULGARIA, Plovdiv
W • S Europe & N Africa • 250 kW

RADIO BULGARIA, Sofia
→ • E Europe • 100 kW

CHINA
†CHINA R INTL, Kashi
S • S Asia • 100 kW

CHINA R INTL, Kunming
S Asia • 150 kW

CHINA R INTL, Xi'an
W Asia & C Asia • 500 kW
S • W Asia & C Asia • 500 kW

USA
†GOSPEL FOR ASIA, Via Germany
W • S Asia • 250 kW

VOA, Via São Tomé
W • C Africa & S Africa • 100 kW

VOA, Via Udon Thani, Thailand
S • SE Asia & Australasia • 250 kW

13605 **INDIA**
ALL INDIA RADIO, Aligarh
E Africa • 250 kW

ALL INDIA RADIO, Bangalore
E Asia & SE Asia • 500 kW
W Africa • 500 kW

13610 **CHINA**
CENTRAL PEOPLE'S BS, Nanning
DS-1 • 100 kW
W-M • DS-1 • 100 kW

†CHINA R INTL, Kashi
S • S Asia • 100 kW
Europe • 00 kW

CHINA R INTL, Xi'an
W • E Asia • 500 kW

SYRIA
RADIO DAMASCUS, Adhra
S America • 500 kW • ALT. FREQ. TO 9330 kHz
E Europe & Mideast • 500 kW • ALT. FREQ. TO 9330 kHz
E Europe • 500 kW • ALT. FREQ. TO 9330 kHz
Europe • 500 kW • ALT. FREQ. TO 9330 kHz
Australasia • 500 kW • ALT. FREQ. TO 9330 kHz

UNITED KINGDOM
BBC, Skelton, Cumbria
S • E Europe & Mideast • 300 kW
S • M-F • E Europe & Mideast • 300 kW

†BBC, Via Zyyi, Cyprus
S • W Asia & S Asia • 300 kW
S • W Asia • 300 kW

USA
VOA, Via Tinian, N Marianas
S • E Asia • 250 kW

WBCQ-"THE PLANET", Monticello, Maine
← • N America • 50 kW • LSB • ALT. FREQ. TO 9330 kHz
← • Tu-Su • N America • 50 kW • LSB • ALT. FREQ. TO 9330 kHz
← • M-F • N America • 50 kW • LSB • ALT. FREQ. TO 9330 kHz

13615 **IRAN**
VO THE ISLAMIC REP, Sirjan
S • W Asia & C Asia • 500 kW

USA
FAMILY RADIO, Okeechobee, Fl
W • S America • 100 kW

WEWN, Vandiver, Alabama
S • S America • 500 kW

13620 **AUSTRALIA**
†RADIO AUSTRALIA, Darwin
SE Asia • 250 kW

CHINA
CHINA R INTL, Xi'an
W • E Asia • 500 kW
S • E Asia • 500 kW

CLANDESTINE (ASIA)
"MINIVAN RADIO", Via Jülich, Germany
S • S Asia • ANTI-MALDIVES GOVT • 100 kW

INDIA
ALL INDIA RADIO, Bangalore
Mideast & W Asia • 500 kW
N Africa & W Africa • 500 kW

IRAN
(con'd) VO THE ISLAMIC REP, Tehrān
W • S Europe • 500 kW

0 1 2 3 4 5 6 7 8 9 10 11 12 13 14 15 16 17 18 19 20 21 22 23 24

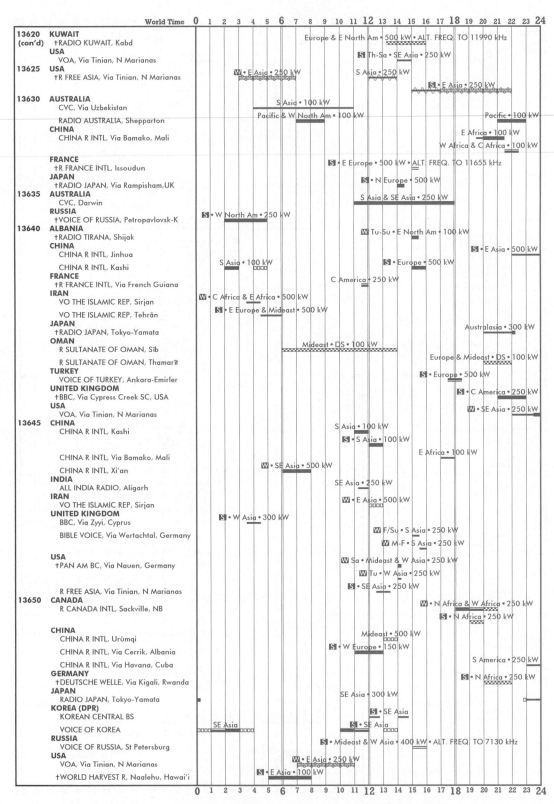

13620 (con'd)	KUWAIT †RADIO KUWAIT, Kabd	Europe & E North Am • 500 kW • ALT. FREQ. TO 11990 kHz
	USA VOA, Via Tinian, N Marianas	ⓈTh-Sa • SE Asia • 250 kW
13625	USA †R FREE ASIA, Via Tinian, N Marianas	Ⓦ • E Asia • 250 kW S Asia • 250 kW Ⓢ • E Asia • 250 kW
13630	AUSTRALIA CVC, Via Uzbekistan	S Asia • 100 kW
	RADIO AUSTRALIA, Shepparton	Pacific & W North Am • 100 kW Pacific • 100 kW
	CHINA CHINA R INTL, Via Bamako, Mali	E Africa • 100 kW W Africa & C Africa • 100 kW
	FRANCE †R FRANCE INTL, Issoudun	Ⓢ • E Europe • 500 kW • ALT. FREQ. TO 11655 kHz
	JAPAN †RADIO JAPAN, Via Rampisham, UK	Ⓢ • N Europe • 500 kW
13635	AUSTRALIA CVC, Darwin	S Asia & SE Asia • 250 kW
	RUSSIA †VOICE OF RUSSIA, Petropavlovsk-K	Ⓢ • W North Am • 250 kW
13640	ALBANIA †RADIO TIRANA, Shijak	Ⓦ Tu-Su • E North Am • 100 kW
	CHINA CHINA R INTL, Jinhua	Ⓢ • E Asia • 500 kW
	CHINA R INTL, Kashi	S Asia • 100 kW Ⓢ • Europe • 500 kW
	FRANCE †R FRANCE INTL, Via French Guiana	C America • 250 kW
	IRAN VO THE ISLAMIC REP, Sirjan	Ⓦ • C Africa & E Africa • 500 kW
	VO THE ISLAMIC REP, Tehrān	Ⓢ • E Europe & Mideast • 500 kW
	JAPAN †RADIO JAPAN, Tokyo-Yamata	Australasia • 300 kW
	OMAN R SULTANATE OF OMAN, Sīb	Mideast • DS • 100 kW
	R SULTANATE OF OMAN, Thamarīt	Europe & Mideast • DS • 100 kW
	TURKEY VOICE OF TURKEY, Ankara-Emirler	Ⓢ • Europe • 500 kW
	UNITED KINGDOM †BBC, Via Cypress Creek SC, USA	Ⓢ • C America • 250 kW
	USA VOA, Via Tinian, N Marianas	Ⓦ • SE Asia • 250 kW
13645	CHINA CHINA R INTL, Kashi	S Asia • 100 kW
		Ⓢ • S Asia • 100 kW
	CHINA R INTL, Via Bamako, Mali	E Africa • 100 kW
	CHINA R INTL, Xi'an	Ⓦ • SE Asia • 500 kW
	INDIA ALL INDIA RADIO, Aligarh	SE Asia • 250 kW
	IRAN VO THE ISLAMIC REP, Sirjan	Ⓦ • E Asia • 500 kW
	UNITED KINGDOM BBC, Via Zyyi, Cyprus	Ⓢ • W Asia • 300 kW
	BIBLE VOICE, Via Wertachtal, Germany	Ⓦ F/Su • S Asia • 250 kW Ⓦ M-F • S Asia • 250 kW
	USA †PAN AM BC, Via Nauen, Germany	Ⓦ Sa • Mideast & W Asia • 250 kW Ⓦ Tu • W Asia • 250 kW
	R FREE ASIA, Via Tinian, N Marianas	Ⓢ • SE Asia • 250 kW
13650	CANADA R CANADA INTL, Sackville, NB	Ⓦ • N Africa & W Africa • 250 kW Ⓢ • N Africa • 250 kW
	CHINA CHINA R INTL, Urümqi	Mideast • 500 kW
	CHINA R INTL, Via Cerrik, Albania	Ⓢ • W Europe • 150 kW
	CHINA R INTL, Via Havana, Cuba	S America • 250 kW
	GERMANY †DEUTSCHE WELLE, Via Kigali, Rwanda	Ⓢ • N Africa • 250 kW
	JAPAN RADIO JAPAN, Tokyo-Yamata	SE Asia • 300 kW
	KOREA (DPR) KOREAN CENTRAL BS	Ⓢ • SE Asia
	VOICE OF KOREA	SE Asia Ⓢ • SE Asia
	RUSSIA VOICE OF RUSSIA, St Petersburg	Ⓢ • Mideast & W Asia • 400 kW • ALT. FREQ. TO 7130 kHz
	USA VOA, Via Tinian, N Marianas	Ⓦ • E Asia • 250 kW
	†WORLD HARVEST R, Naalehu, Hawai'i	Ⓢ • E Asia • 100 kW

ENGLISH ▬▬ ARABIC ∿∿∿ CHINESE □□□ FRENCH ▬▬ GERMAN ▬▬ RUSSIAN ══ SPANISH ▬▬ OTHER ──

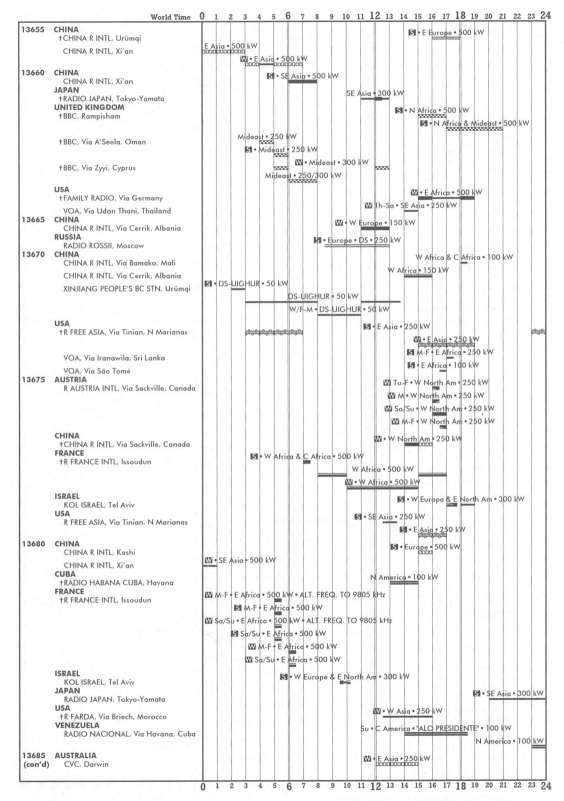

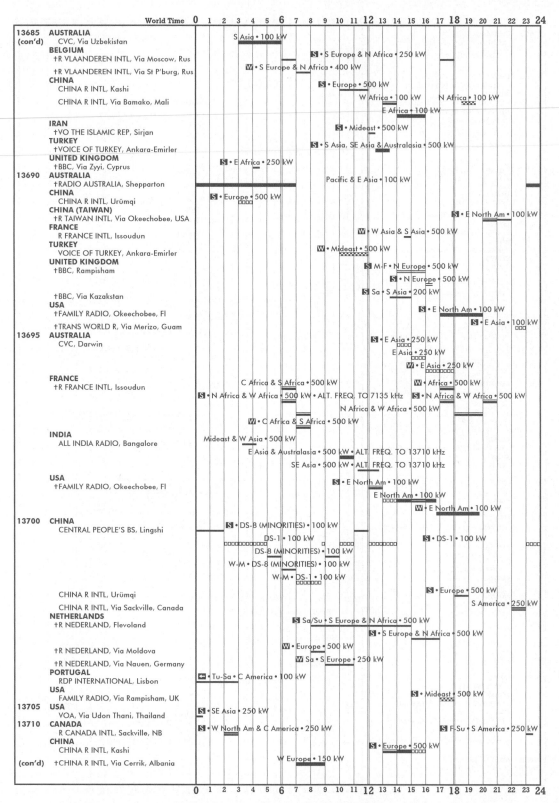

13685	**AUSTRALIA**	
(con'd)	CVC, Via Uzbekistan	S Asia • 100 kW
	BELGIUM	
	†R VLAANDEREN INTL, Via Moscow, Rus	S • S Europe & N Africa • 250 kW
	†R VLAANDEREN INTL, Via St P'burg, Rus	W • S Europe & N Africa • 400 kW
	CHINA	
	CHINA R INTL, Kashi	S • Europe • 500 kW
	CHINA R INTL, Via Bamako, Mali	W Africa • 100 kW N Africa • 100 kW
		E Africa • 100 kW
	IRAN	
	†VO THE ISLAMIC REP, Sirjan	S • Mideast • 500 kW
	TURKEY	
	†VOICE OF TURKEY, Ankara-Emirler	S • S Asia, SE Asia & Australasia • 500 kW
	UNITED KINGDOM	
	†BBC, Via Zyyi, Cyprus	S • E Africa • 250 kW
13690	**AUSTRALIA**	
	†RADIO AUSTRALIA, Shepparton	Pacific & E Asia • 100 kW
	CHINA	
	CHINA R INTL, Urümqi	S • Europe • 500 kW
	CHINA (TAIWAN)	
	†R TAIWAN INTL, Via Okeechobee, USA	S • E North Am • 100 kW
	FRANCE	
	R FRANCE INTL, Issoudun	W • W Asia & S Asia • 500 kW
	TURKEY	
	VOICE OF TURKEY, Ankara-Emirler	W • Mideast • 500 kW
	UNITED KINGDOM	
	†BBC, Rampisham	S • M-F • N Europe • 500 kW
		S • N Europe • 500 kW
	†BBC, Via Kazakstan	S • Sa • S Asia • 200 kW
	USA	
	†FAMILY RADIO, Okeechobee, Fl	S • E North Am • 100 kW
	†TRANS WORLD R, Via Merizo, Guam	S • E Asia • 100 kW
13695	**AUSTRALIA**	
	CVC, Darwin	S • E Asia • 250 kW
		E Asia • 250 kW
		W • E Asia • 250 kW
	FRANCE	
	†R FRANCE INTL, Issoudun	C Africa & S Africa • 500 kW W • Africa • 500 kW
		S • N Africa & W Africa • 500 kW • ALT. FREQ. TO 7135 kHz S • N Africa & W Africa • 500 kW
		N Africa & W Africa • 500 kW
		W • C Africa & S Africa • 500 kW
	INDIA	
	ALL INDIA RADIO, Bangalore	Mideast & W Asia • 500 kW
		E Asia & Australasia • 500 kW • ALT. FREQ. TO 13710 kHz
		SE Asia • 500 kW • ALT. FREQ. TO 13710 kHz
	USA	
	†FAMILY RADIO, Okeechobee, Fl	S • E North Am • 100 kW
		E North Am • 100 kW
		W • E North Am • 100 kW
13700	**CHINA**	
	CENTRAL PEOPLE'S BS, Lingshi	S • DS-8 (MINORITIES) • 100 kW
		DS-1 • 100 kW S • DS-1 • 100 kW
		DS-8 (MINORITIES) • 100 kW
		W-M • DS-8 (MINORITIES) • 100 kW
		W-M • DS-1 • 100 kW
	CHINA R INTL, Urümqi	S • Europe • 500 kW
	CHINA R INTL, Via Sackville, Canada	S America • 250 kW
	NETHERLANDS	
	†R NEDERLAND, Flevoland	S • Sa/Su • S Europe & N Africa • 500 kW
		S • S Europe & N Africa • 500 kW
	†R NEDERLAND, Via Moldova	W • Europe • 500 kW
	†R NEDERLAND, Via Nauen, Germany	W • Sa • S Europe • 250 kW
	PORTUGAL	
	RDP INTERNATIONAL, Lisbon	• Tu-Sa • C America • 100 kW
	USA	
	FAMILY RADIO, Via Rampisham, UK	S • Mideast • 500 kW
13705	**USA**	
	VOA, Via Udon Thani, Thailand	S • SE Asia • 250 kW
13710	**CANADA**	
	R CANADA INTL, Sackville, NB	S • W North Am & C America • 250 kW S • F-Su • S America • 250 kW
	CHINA	
	CHINA R INTL, Kashi	S • Europe • 500 kW
(con'd)	†CHINA R INTL, Via Cerrik, Albania	W Europe • 150 kW

ENGLISH ▬   ARABIC ▨▨▨   CHINESE ▫▫▫   FRENCH ═   GERMAN ▭▭   RUSSIAN ═   SPANISH ▬   OTHER ▬

World Time 0 1 2 3 4 5 6 7 8 9 10 11 12 13 14 15 16 17 18 19 20 21 22 23 24

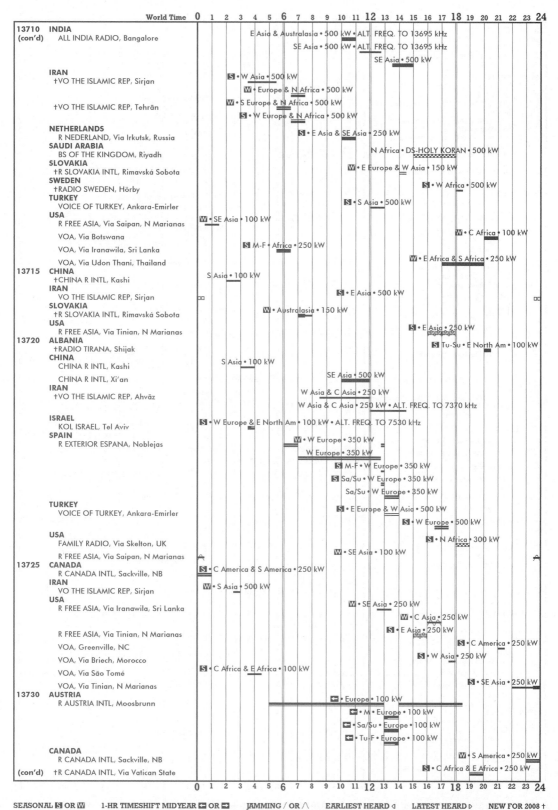

13710 INDIA
(con'd) ALL INDIA RADIO, Bangalore — E Asia & Australasia • 500 kW • ALT. FREQ. TO 13695 kHz
— SE Asia • 500 kW • ALT. FREQ. TO 13695 kHz
— SE Asia • 500 kW

IRAN
†VO THE ISLAMIC REP, Sirjan — S • W Asia • 500 kW
— W • Europe & N Africa • 500 kW
†VO THE ISLAMIC REP, Tehrān — W • S Europe & N Africa • 500 kW
— S • W Europe & N Africa • 500 kW

NETHERLANDS
R NEDERLAND, Via Irkutsk, Russia — S • E Asia & SE Asia • 250 kW
SAUDI ARABIA
BS OF THE KINGDOM, Riyadh — N Africa • DS-HOLY KORAN • 500 kW
SLOVAKIA
†R SLOVAKIA INTL, Rimavská Sobota — W • E Europe & W Asia • 150 kW
SWEDEN
†RADIO SWEDEN, Hörby — S • W Africa • 500 kW
TURKEY
VOICE OF TURKEY, Ankara-Emirler — S • S Asia • 500 kW
USA
R FREE ASIA, Via Saipan, N Marianas — W • SE Asia • 100 kW
VOA, Via Botswana — W • C Africa • 100 kW
VOA, Via Iranawila, Sri Lanka — S • M-F • Africa • 250 kW
VOA, Via Udon Thani, Thailand — W • E Africa & S Africa • 250 kW

13715 CHINA
†CHINA R INTL, Kashi — S Asia • 100 kW
IRAN
VO THE ISLAMIC REP, Sirjan — S • E Asia • 500 kW
SLOVAKIA
†R SLOVAKIA INTL, Rimavská Sobota — W • Australasia • 150 kW
USA
R FREE ASIA, Via Tinian, N Marianas — S • E Asia • 250 kW

13720 ALBANIA
†RADIO TIRANA, Shijak — S • Tu-Su • E North Am • 100 kW
CHINA
CHINA R INTL, Kashi — S Asia • 100 kW
CHINA R INTL, Xi'an — SE Asia • 500 kW
IRAN
†VO THE ISLAMIC REP, Ahvāz — W Asia & C Asia • 250 kW
— W Asia & C Asia • 250 kW • ALT. FREQ. TO 7370 kHz
ISRAEL
KOL ISRAEL, Tel Aviv — S • W Europe & E North Am • 100 kW • ALT. FREQ. TO 7530 kHz
SPAIN
R EXTERIOR ESPANA, Noblejas — W • W Europe • 350 kW
— W Europe • 350 kW
— S • M-F • W Europe • 350 kW
— S • Sa/Su • W Europe • 350 kW
— Sa/Su • W Europe • 350 kW
TURKEY
VOICE OF TURKEY, Ankara-Emirler — S • E Europe & W Asia • 500 kW
— S • W Europe • 500 kW
USA
FAMILY RADIO, Via Skelton, UK — S • N Africa • 300 kW
R FREE ASIA, Via Saipan, N Marianas — W • SE Asia • 100 kW

13725 CANADA
R CANADA INTL, Sackville, NB — S • C America & S America • 250 kW
IRAN
VO THE ISLAMIC REP, Sirjan — W • S Asia • 500 kW
USA
R FREE ASIA, Via Iranawila, Sri Lanka — W • SE Asia • 250 kW
— W • C Asia • 250 kW
R FREE ASIA, Via Tinian, N Marianas — S • E Asia • 250 kW
VOA, Greenville, NC — S • C America • 250 kW
VOA, Via Briech, Morocco — S • W Asia • 250 kW
VOA, Via São Tomé — S • C Africa & E Africa • 100 kW
VOA, Via Tinian, N Marianas — S • SE Asia • 250 kW

13730 AUSTRIA
R AUSTRIA INTL, Moosbrunn — ⮂ • Europe • 100 kW
— ⮂ • M • Europe • 100 kW
— ⮂ • Sa/Su • Europe • 100 kW
— ⮂ • Tu-F • Europe • 100 kW
CANADA
R CANADA INTL, Sackville, NB — W • S America • 250 kW
(con'd) †R CANADA INTL, Via Vatican State — S • C Africa & E Africa • 250 kW

0 1 2 3 4 5 6 7 8 9 10 11 12 13 14 15 16 17 18 19 20 21 22 23 24

SEASONAL S OR W 1-HR TIMESHIFT MIDYEAR ⮂ OR ⮀ JAMMING / OR /\ EARLIEST HEARD ◁ LATEST HEARD ▷ NEW FOR 2008 †

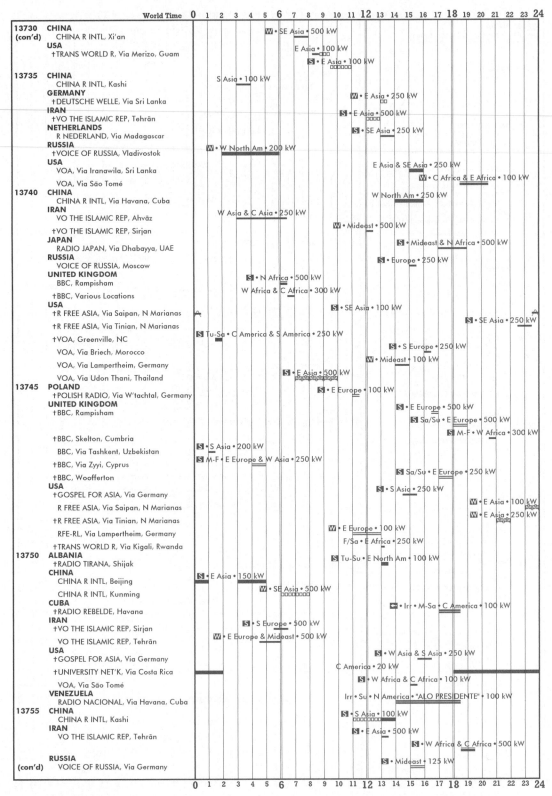

World Time 0 1 2 3 4 5 6 7 8 9 10 11 12 13 14 15 16 17 18 19 20 21 22 23 24

13730 **CHINA**
(con'd)   CHINA R INTL, Xi'an — W • SE Asia • 500 kW
          USA
          †TRANS WORLD R, Via Merizo, Guam — E Asia • 100 kW
                                            S • E Asia • 100 kW

13735 **CHINA**
          CHINA R INTL, Kashi — S Asia • 100 kW
          GERMANY
          †DEUTSCHE WELLE, Via Sri Lanka — W • E Asia • 250 kW
          IRAN
          †VO THE ISLAMIC REP, Tehrān — S • E Asia • 500 kW
          NETHERLANDS
          R NEDERLAND, Via Madagascar — S • SE Asia • 250 kW
          RUSSIA
          †VOICE OF RUSSIA, Vladivostok — W • W North Am • 200 kW
          USA
          VOA, Via Iranawila, Sri Lanka — E Asia & SE Asia • 250 kW
          VOA, Via São Tomé — W • C Africa & E Africa • 100 kW

13740 **CHINA**
          CHINA R INTL, Via Havana, Cuba — W North Am • 250 kW
          IRAN
          VO THE ISLAMIC REP, Ahvāz — W Asia & C Asia • 250 kW
          †VO THE ISLAMIC REP, Sirjan — W • Mideast • 500 kW
          JAPAN
          RADIO JAPAN, Via Dhabayya, UAE — S • Mideast & N Africa • 500 kW
          RUSSIA
          VOICE OF RUSSIA, Moscow — S • Europe • 250 kW
          UNITED KINGDOM
          BBC, Rampisham — S • N Africa • 500 kW
                           W Africa & C Africa • 300 kW
          †BBC, Various Locations
          USA
          †R FREE ASIA, Via Saipan, N Marianas — S • SE Asia • 100 kW
          †R FREE ASIA, Via Tinian, N Marianas — S • SE Asia • 250 kW
          †VOA, Greenville, NC — S Tu-Sa • C America & S America • 250 kW
          VOA, Via Briech, Morocco — S • S Europe • 250 kW
          VOA, Via Lampertheim, Germany — W • Mideast • 100 kW
          VOA, Via Udon Thani, Thailand — S • E Asia • 500 kW

13745 **POLAND**
          †POLISH RADIO, Via W'tachtal, Germany — S • E Europe • 100 kW
          UNITED KINGDOM
          †BBC, Rampisham — S • E Europe • 500 kW
                            S Sa/Su • E Europe • 500 kW
                            W M-F • W Africa • 300 kW
          †BBC, Skelton, Cumbria — S • S Asia • 200 kW
          BBC, Via Tashkent, Uzbekistan — S M-F • E Europe & W Asia • 250 kW
          †BBC, Via Zyyi, Cyprus — S Sa/Su • E Europe • 250 kW
          †BBC, Woofferton — S • S Asia • 250 kW
          USA
          †GOSPEL FOR ASIA, Via Germany — W • E Asia • 100 kW
          R FREE ASIA, Via Saipan, N Marianas — W • E Asia • 250 kW
          †R FREE ASIA, Via Tinian, N Marianas
          RFE-RL, Via Lampertheim, Germany — W • E Europe • 100 kW
                                             F/Sa • E Africa • 250 kW
          †TRANS WORLD R, Via Kigali, Rwanda

13750 **ALBANIA**
          †RADIO TIRANA, Shijak — S Tu-Su • E North Am • 100 kW
          CHINA
          CHINA R INTL, Beijing — S • E Asia • 150 kW
          CHINA R INTL, Kunming — W • SE Asia • 500 kW
          CUBA
          †RADIO REBELDE, Havana — Irr • M-Sa • C America • 100 kW
          IRAN
          †VO THE ISLAMIC REP, Sirjan — S • S Europe • 500 kW
          VO THE ISLAMIC REP, Tehrān — W • E Europe & Mideast • 500 kW
          USA
          †GOSPEL FOR ASIA, Via Germany — S • W Asia & S Asia • 250 kW
          †UNIVERSITY NET'K, Via Costa Rica — C America • 20 kW
          VOA, Via São Tomé — S • W Africa & C Africa • 100 kW
          VENEZUELA
          RADIO NACIONAL, Via Havana, Cuba — Irr • Su • N America • "ALO PRESIDENTE" • 100 kW

13755 **CHINA**
          CHINA R INTL, Kashi — S • S Asia • 100 kW
          IRAN
          VO THE ISLAMIC REP, Tehrān — S • E Asia • 500 kW
                                       W Africa & C Africa • 500 kW
          RUSSIA
(con'd)   VOICE OF RUSSIA, Via Germany — S • Mideast • 125 kW

0 1 2 3 4 5 6 7 8 9 10 11 12 13 14 15 16 17 18 19 20 21 22 23 24

ENGLISH ▬ ARABIC ▦ CHINESE ▭▭▭ FRENCH ═ GERMAN ▬▬ RUSSIAN ══ SPANISH ▬▬ OTHER ▬

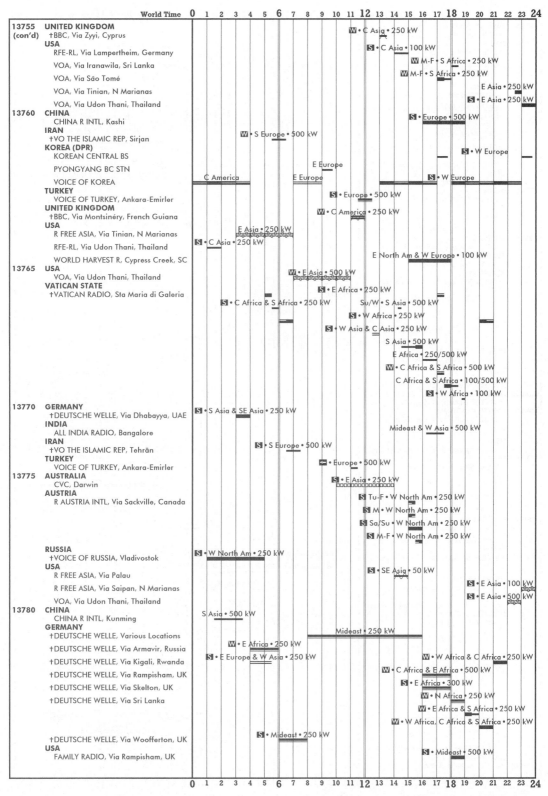

| World Time | 0 | 1 | 2 | 3 | 4 | 5 | 6 | 7 | 8 | 9 | 10 | 11 | 12 | 13 | 14 | 15 | 16 | 17 | 18 | 19 | 20 | 21 | 22 | 23 | 24 |

13755 UNITED KINGDOM
(con'd) †BBC, Via Zyyi, Cyprus — W • C Asia • 250 kW
USA
  RFE-RL, Via Lampertheim, Germany — S • C Asia • 100 kW
  VOA, Via Iranawila, Sri Lanka — W M-F • S Africa • 250 kW
  VOA, Via São Tomé — W M-F • S Africa • 250 kW
  VOA, Via Tinian, N Marianas — E Asia • 250 kW
  VOA, Via Udon Thani, Thailand — S • E Asia • 250 kW
13760 CHINA
  CHINA R INTL, Kashi — S • Europe • 500 kW
IRAN
  †VO THE ISLAMIC REP, Sirjan — W • S Europe • 500 kW
KOREA (DPR)
  KOREAN CENTRAL BS — S • W Europe
  PYONGYANG BC STN — E Europe
  VOICE OF KOREA — C America / E Europe / S • W Europe
TURKEY
  VOICE OF TURKEY, Ankara-Emirler — S • Europe • 500 kW
UNITED KINGDOM
  †BBC, Via Montsinéry, French Guiana — W • C America • 250 kW
USA
  R FREE ASIA, Via Tinian, N Marianas — E Asia • 250 kW
  RFE-RL, Via Udon Thani, Thailand — S • C Asia • 250 kW
  WORLD HARVEST R, Cypress Creek, SC — E North Am & W Europe • 100 kW
13765 USA
  VOA, Via Udon Thani, Thailand — W • E Asia • 500 kW
VATICAN STATE
  †VATICAN RADIO, Sta Maria di Galeria — S • E Africa • 250 kW
  S • C Africa & S Africa • 250 kW
  Su/W • S Asia • 500 kW
  S • W Africa • 250 kW
  S • W Asia & C Asia • 250 kW
  S Asia • 500 kW
  E Africa • 250/500 kW
  W • C Africa & S Africa • 500 kW
  C Africa & S Africa • 100/500 kW
  S • W Africa • 100 kW
13770 GERMANY
  †DEUTSCHE WELLE, Via Dhabayya, UAE — S • S Asia & SE Asia • 250 kW
INDIA
  ALL INDIA RADIO, Bangalore — Mideast & W Asia • 500 kW
IRAN
  †VO THE ISLAMIC REP, Tehrān — S • S Europe • 500 kW
TURKEY
  VOICE OF TURKEY, Ankara-Emirler — ⇐ • Europe • 500 kW
13775 AUSTRALIA
  CVC, Darwin — S • E Asia • 250 kW
AUSTRIA
  R AUSTRIA INTL, Via Sackville, Canada — S Tu-F • W North Am • 250 kW
  S M • W North Am • 250 kW
  S Sa/Su • W North Am • 250 kW
  S M-F • W North Am • 250 kW
RUSSIA
  †VOICE OF RUSSIA, Vladivostok — S • W North Am • 250 kW
USA
  R FREE ASIA, Via Palau — S • SE Asia • 50 kW
  R FREE ASIA, Via Saipan, N Marianas — S • E Asia • 100 kW
  VOA, Via Udon Thani, Thailand — S • E Asia • 500 kW
13780 CHINA
  CHINA R INTL, Kunming — S Asia • 500 kW
GERMANY
  †DEUTSCHE WELLE, Various Locations — Mideast • 250 kW
  †DEUTSCHE WELLE, Via Armavir, Russia — W • E Africa • 250 kW
  †DEUTSCHE WELLE, Via Kigali, Rwanda — S • E Europe & W Asia • 250 kW
  W • W Africa & C Africa • 250 kW
  †DEUTSCHE WELLE, Via Rampisham, UK — W • C Africa & E Africa • 500 kW
  †DEUTSCHE WELLE, Via Skelton, UK — S • E Africa • 300 kW
  †DEUTSCHE WELLE, Via Sri Lanka — W • N Africa • 250 kW
  W • E Africa & S Africa • 250 kW
  W • W Africa, C Africa & S Africa • 250 kW
  †DEUTSCHE WELLE, Via Woofferton, UK — S • Mideast • 250 kW
USA
  FAMILY RADIO, Via Rampisham, UK — S • Mideast • 500 kW

| | 0 | 1 | 2 | 3 | 4 | 5 | 6 | 7 | 8 | 9 | 10 | 11 | 12 | 13 | 14 | 15 | 16 | 17 | 18 | 19 | 20 | 21 | 22 | 23 | 24 |

SEASONAL ⑤ OR ⑩   1-HR TIMESHIFT MIDYEAR ⇐ OR ⇒   JAMMING / OR ∧   EARLIEST HEARD ◁   LATEST HEARD ▷   NEW FOR 2008 †

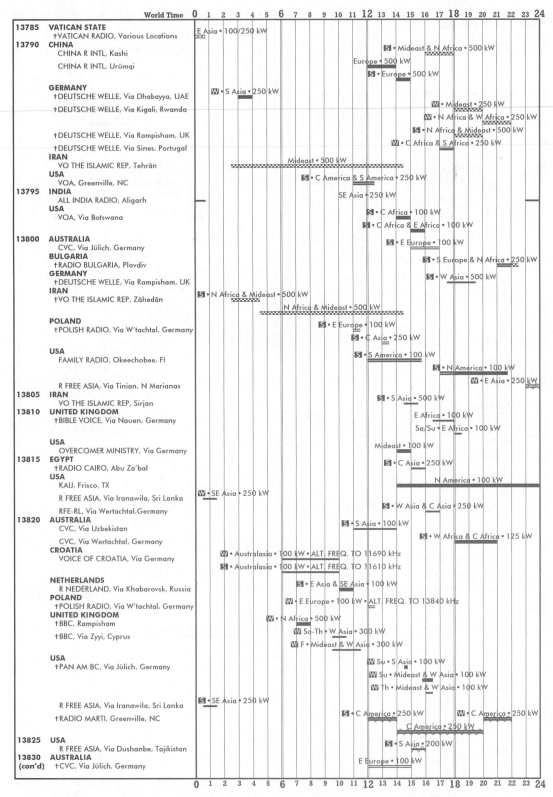

| | World Time | 0 | 1 | 2 | 3 | 4 | 5 | 6 | 7 | 8 | 9 | 10 | 11 | 12 | 13 | 14 | 15 | 16 | 17 | 18 | 19 | 20 | 21 | 22 | 23 | 24 |

13785 VATICAN STATE
†VATICAN RADIO, Various Locations — E Asia • 100/250 kW

13790 CHINA
CHINA R INTL, Kashi — S • Mideast & N Africa • 500 kW
CHINA R INTL, Urümqi — Europe • 500 kW
S • Europe • 500 kW

GERMANY
†DEUTSCHE WELLE, Via Dhabayya, UAE — W • S Asia • 250 kW
†DEUTSCHE WELLE, Via Kigali, Rwanda — W • Mideast • 250 kW
W • N Africa & W Africa • 250 kW
†DEUTSCHE WELLE, Via Rampisham, UK — S • N Africa & Mideast • 500 kW
†DEUTSCHE WELLE, Via Sines, Portugal — W • C Africa & S Africa • 250 kW

IRAN
VO THE ISLAMIC REP, Tehrān — Mideast • 500 kW

USA
VOA, Greenville, NC — S • C America & S America • 250 kW

13795 INDIA
ALL INDIA RADIO, Aligarh — SE Asia • 250 kW

USA
VOA, Via Botswana — S • C Africa • 100 kW
S • C Africa & E Africa • 100 kW

13800 AUSTRALIA
CVC, Via Jülich, Germany — S • E Europe • 100 kW

BULGARIA
†RADIO BULGARIA, Plovdiv — S • S Europe & N Africa • 250 kW

GERMANY
†DEUTSCHE WELLE, Via Rampisham, UK — S • W Asia • 500 kW

IRAN
†VO THE ISLAMIC REP, Zāhedān — S • N Africa & Mideast • 500 kW
N Africa & Mideast • 500 kW

POLAND
†POLISH RADIO, Via W'tachtal, Germany — S • E Europe • 100 kW
S • C Asia • 250 kW

USA
FAMILY RADIO, Okeechobee, Fl — S • S America • 100 kW
S • N America • 100 kW
W • E Asia • 250 kW

R FREE ASIA, Via Tinian, N Marianas

13805 IRAN
VO THE ISLAMIC REP, Sirjan — S • S Asia • 500 kW

13810 UNITED KINGDOM
†BIBLE VOICE, Via Nauen, Germany — E Africa • 100 kW
Sa/Su • E Africa • 100 kW

USA
OVERCOMER MINISTRY, Via Germany — Mideast • 100 kW

13815 EGYPT
†RADIO CAIRO, Abu Za'bal — S • C Asia • 250 kW

USA
KAIJ, Frisco, TX — N America • 100 kW
R FREE ASIA, Via Iranawila, Sri Lanka — W • SE Asia • 250 kW
RFE-RL, Via Wertachtal, Germany — S • W Asia & C Asia • 250 kW

13820 AUSTRALIA
CVC, Via Uzbekistan — S • S Asia • 100 kW
CVC, Via Wertachtal, Germany — S • W Africa & C Africa • 125 kW

CROATIA
VOICE OF CROATIA, Via Germany — W • Australasia • 100 kW • ALT. FREQ. TO 11690 kHz
S • Australasia • 100 kW • ALT. FREQ. TO 11610 kHz

NETHERLANDS
R NEDERLAND, Via Khabarovsk, Russia — S • E Asia & SE Asia • 100 kW

POLAND
†POLISH RADIO, Via W'tachtal, Germany — W • E Europe • 100 kW • ALT. FREQ. TO 13840 kHz

UNITED KINGDOM
†BBC, Rampisham — W • N Africa • 500 kW
†BBC, Via Zyyi, Cyprus — W Sa-Th • W Asia • 300 kW
W F • Mideast & W Asia • 300 kW

USA
†PAN AM BC, Via Jülich, Germany — W Su • S Asia • 100 kW
W Su • Mideast & W Asia • 100 kW
W Th • Mideast & W Asia • 100 kW

R FREE ASIA, Via Iranawila, Sri Lanka — S • SE Asia • 250 kW
†RADIO MARTI, Greenville, NC — S • C America • 250 kW
W • C America • 250 kW
C America • 250 kW

13825 USA
R FREE ASIA, Via Dushanbe, Tajikistan — S • S Asia • 200 kW

13830 AUSTRALIA
(con'd) †CVC, Via Jülich, Germany — E Europe • 100 kW

| 0 | 1 | 2 | 3 | 4 | 5 | 6 | 7 | 8 | 9 | 10 | 11 | 12 | 13 | 14 | 15 | 16 | 17 | 18 | 19 | 20 | 21 | 22 | 23 | 24 |

ENGLISH ▬ ARABIC ⧢ CHINESE ⬚⬚⬚ FRENCH ▭ GERMAN ▬ RUSSIAN ═ SPANISH ▬ OTHER ▬

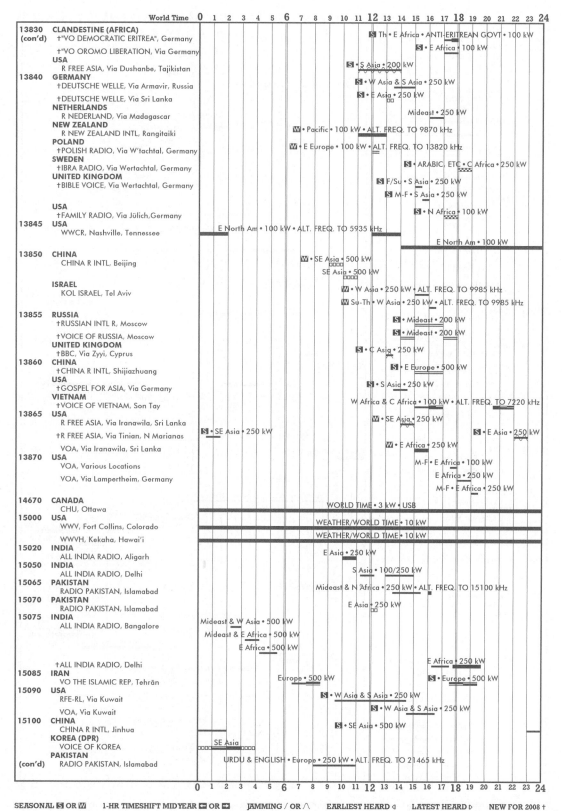

World Time 0 1 2 3 4 5 6 7 8 9 10 11 12 13 14 15 16 17 18 19 20 21 22 23 24

13830 **CLANDESTINE (AFRICA)**
(con'd) †"VO DEMOCRATIC ERITREA", Germany
S • Th • E Africa • ANTI-ERITREAN GOVT • 100 kW

†"VO OROMO LIBERATION, Via Germany
S • E Africa • 100 kW
USA
R FREE ASIA, Via Dushanbe, Tajikistan
S • S Asia • 200 kW
13840 **GERMANY**
†DEUTSCHE WELLE, Via Armavir, Russia
S • W Asia & S Asia • 250 kW

†DEUTSCHE WELLE, Via Sri Lanka
S • E Asia • 250 kW
NETHERLANDS
R NEDERLAND, Via Madagascar
Mideast • 250 kW
NEW ZEALAND
R NEW ZEALAND INTL, Rangitaiki
W • Pacific • 100 kW • ALT. FREQ. TO 9870 kHz
POLAND
†POLISH RADIO, Via W'tachtal, Germany
W • E Europe • 100 kW • ALT. FREQ. TO 13820 kHz
SWEDEN
†IBRA RADIO, Via Wertachtal, Germany
S • ARABIC, ETC • C Africa • 250 kW
UNITED KINGDOM
†BIBLE VOICE, Via Wertachtal, Germany
S • F/Su • S Asia • 250 kW
S • M-F • S Asia • 250 kW

USA
†FAMILY RADIO, Via Jülich, Germany
S • N Africa • 100 kW
13845 **USA**
WWCR, Nashville, Tennessee
E North Am • 100 kW • ALT. FREQ. TO 5935 kHz
E North Am • 100 kW

13850 **CHINA**
CHINA R INTL, Beijing
W • SE Asia • 500 kW
SE Asia • 500 kW

ISRAEL
KOL ISRAEL, Tel Aviv
W • W Asia • 250 kW • ALT. FREQ. TO 9985 kHz
W • Su-Th • W Asia • 250 kW • ALT. FREQ. TO 9985 kHz
13855 **RUSSIA**
†RUSSIAN INTL R, Moscow
S • Mideast • 200 kW

†VOICE OF RUSSIA, Moscow
S • Mideast • 200 kW
UNITED KINGDOM
†BBC, Via Zyyi, Cyprus
S • C Asia • 250 kW
13860 **CHINA**
†CHINA R INTL, Shijiazhuang
S • E Europe • 500 kW
USA
†GOSPEL FOR ASIA, Via Germany
S • S Asia • 250 kW
VIETNAM
†VOICE OF VIETNAM, Son Tay
W Africa & C Africa • 100 kW • ALT. FREQ. TO 7220 kHz
13865 **USA**
R FREE ASIA, Via Iranwila, Sri Lanka
W • SE Asia • 250 kW

†R FREE ASIA, Via Tinian, N Marianas
S • SE Asia • 250 kW
S • E Asia • 250 kW

VOA, Via Iranawila, Sri Lanka
W • E Africa • 250 kW
13870 **USA**
VOA, Various Locations
M-F • E Africa • 100 kW

VOA, Via Lampertheim, Germany
E Africa • 250 kW
M-F • E Africa • 250 kW

14670 **CANADA**
CHU, Ottawa
WORLD TIME • 3 kW • USB
15000 **USA**
WWV, Fort Collins, Colorado
WEATHER/WORLD TIME • 10 kW

WWVH, Kekaha, Hawai'i
WEATHER/WORLD TIME • 10 kW
15020 **INDIA**
ALL INDIA RADIO, Aligarh
E Asia • 250 kW
15050 **INDIA**
ALL INDIA RADIO, Delhi
S Asia • 100/250 kW
15065 **PAKISTAN**
RADIO PAKISTAN, Islamabad
Mideast & N Africa • 250 kW • ALT. FREQ. TO 15100 kHz
15070 **PAKISTAN**
RADIO PAKISTAN, Islamabad
E Asia • 250 kW
15075 **INDIA**
ALL INDIA RADIO, Bangalore
Mideast & W Asia • 500 kW
Mideast & E Africa • 500 kW
E Africa • 500 kW

†ALL INDIA RADIO, Delhi
E Africa • 250 kW
15085 **IRAN**
VO THE ISLAMIC REP, Tehrān
Europe • 500 kW
S • Europe • 500 kW
15090 **USA**
RFE-RL, Via Kuwait
S • W Asia & S Asia • 250 kW

VOA, Via Kuwait
S • W Asia & S Asia • 250 kW
15100 **CHINA**
CHINA R INTL, Jinhua
S • SE Asia • 500 kW
KOREA (DPR)
VOICE OF KOREA
SE Asia
PAKISTAN
(con'd) RADIO PAKISTAN, Islamabad
URDU & ENGLISH • Europe • 250 kW • ALT. FREQ. TO 21465 kHz

0 1 2 3 4 5 6 7 8 9 10 11 12 13 14 15 16 17 18 19 20 21 22 23 24

SEASONAL S OR W   1-HR TIMESHIFT MIDYEAR ⮀ OR ⮕   JAMMING / OR ⋀   EARLIEST HEARD ◁   LATEST HEARD ▷   NEW FOR 2008 †

World Time

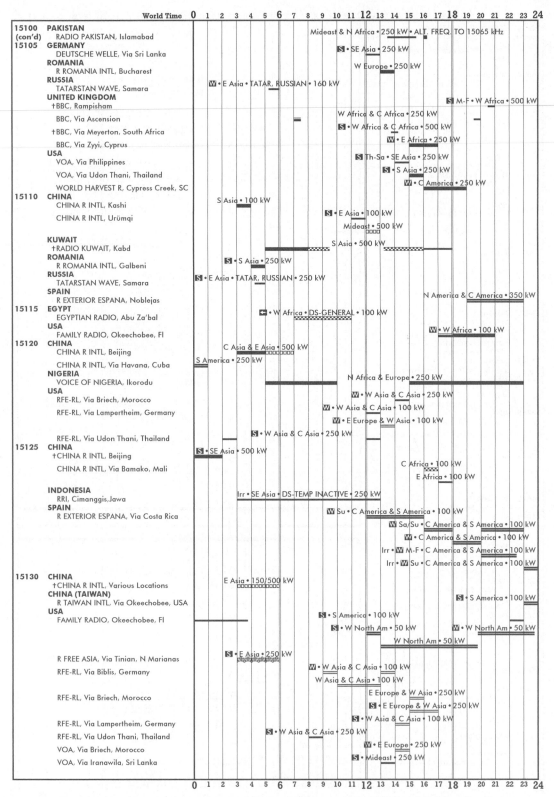

Frequency	Country / Station	Schedule
15100 (con'd)	**PAKISTAN** — RADIO PAKISTAN, Islamabad	Mideast & N Africa • 250 kW • ALT. FREQ. TO 15065 kHz
15105	**GERMANY** — DEUTSCHE WELLE, Via Sri Lanka	S • SE Asia • 250 kW
	ROMANIA — R ROMANIA INTL, Bucharest	W Europe • 250 kW
	RUSSIA — TATARSTAN WAVE, Samara	W • E Asia • TATAR, RUSSIAN • 160 kW
	UNITED KINGDOM — †BBC, Rampisham	S M-F • W Africa • 500 kW
	BBC, Via Ascension	W Africa & C Africa • 250 kW
	†BBC, Via Meyerton, South Africa	S • W Africa & C Africa • 500 kW
	BBC, Via Zyyi, Cyprus	W • E Africa • 250 kW
	USA — VOA, Via Philippines	S Th-Sa • SE Asia • 250 kW
	VOA, Via Udon Thani, Thailand	S • S Asia • 250 kW
	WORLD HARVEST R, Cypress Creek, SC	W • C America • 250 kW
15110	**CHINA** — CHINA R INTL, Kashi	S Asia • 100 kW
	CHINA R INTL, Urümqi	S • E Asia • 100 kW / Mideast • 500 kW
	KUWAIT — †RADIO KUWAIT, Kabd	S Asia • 500 kW
	ROMANIA — R ROMANIA INTL, Galbeni	S • S Asia • 250 kW
	RUSSIA — TATARSTAN WAVE, Samara	S • E Asia • TATAR, RUSSIAN • 250 kW
	SPAIN — R EXTERIOR ESPANA, Noblejas	N America & C America • 350 kW
15115	**EGYPT** — EGYPTIAN RADIO, Abu Za'bal	• W Africa • DS-GENERAL • 100 kW
	USA — FAMILY RADIO, Okeechobee, Fl	W • W Africa • 100 kW
15120	**CHINA** — CHINA R INTL, Beijing	C Asia & E Asia • 500 kW
	CHINA R INTL, Via Havana, Cuba	S America • 250 kW
	NIGERIA — VOICE OF NIGERIA, Ikorodu	N Africa & Europe • 250 kW
	USA — RFE-RL, Via Briech, Morocco	W • W Asia & C Asia • 250 kW
	RFE-RL, Via Lampertheim, Germany	W • W Asia & C Asia • 100 kW / W • E Europe & W Asia • 100 kW
	RFE-RL, Via Udon Thani, Thailand	S • W Asia & C Asia • 250 kW
15125	**CHINA** — †CHINA R INTL, Beijing	S • SE Asia • 500 kW
	CHINA R INTL, Via Bamako, Mali	C Africa • 100 kW / E Africa • 100 kW
	INDONESIA — RRI, Cimanggis, Jawa	Irr • SE Asia • DS-TEMP INACTIVE • 250 kW
	SPAIN — R EXTERIOR ESPANA, Via Costa Rica	W Su • C America & S America • 100 kW
		W Sa/Su • C America & S America • 100 kW
		W • C America & S America • 100 kW
		Irr • W M-F • C America & S America • 100 kW
		Irr • W Su • C America & S America • 100 kW
15130	**CHINA** — †CHINA R INTL, Various Locations	E Asia • 150/500 kW
	CHINA (TAIWAN) — R TAIWAN INTL, Via Okeechobee, USA	S • S America • 100 kW
	USA — FAMILY RADIO, Okeechobee, Fl	S • S America • 100 kW / S • W North Am • 50 kW / W • W North Am • 50 kW / W North Am • 50 kW
	R FREE ASIA, Via Tinian, N Marianas	S • E Asia • 250 kW
	RFE-RL, Via Biblis, Germany	W • W Asia & C Asia • 100 kW / W Asia & C Asia • 100 kW
	RFE-RL, Via Briech, Morocco	E Europe & W Asia • 250 kW / S • E Europe & W Asia • 250 kW
	RFE-RL, Via Lampertheim, Germany	S • W Asia & C Asia • 100 kW
	RFE-RL, Via Udon Thani, Thailand	S • W Asia & C Asia • 250 kW
	VOA, Via Briech, Morocco	W • E Europe • 250 kW
	VOA, Via Iranawila, Sri Lanka	S • Mideast • 250 kW

ENGLISH ▬   ARABIC ▨   CHINESE ▭▭▭   FRENCH ▬   GERMAN ▭▭   RUSSIAN ══   SPANISH ▬   OTHER ▬

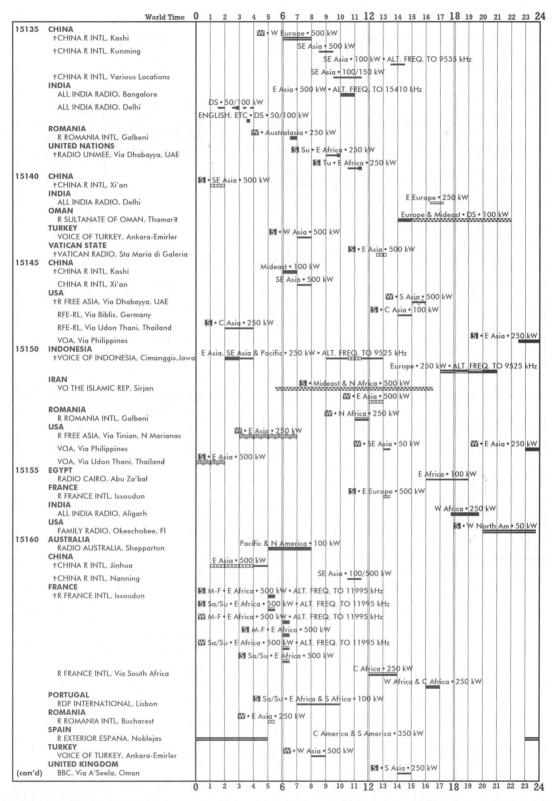

| | World Time | 0 | 1 | 2 | 3 | 4 | 5 | 6 | 7 | 8 | 9 | 10 | 11 | 12 | 13 | 14 | 15 | 16 | 17 | 18 | 19 | 20 | 21 | 22 | 23 | 24 |

15135 CHINA
- †CHINA R INTL, Kashi — W • W Europe • 500 kW
- †CHINA R INTL, Kunming — SE Asia • 500 kW / SE Asia • 100 kW • ALT. FREQ. TO 9535 kHz
- †CHINA R INTL, Various Locations — SE Asia • 100/150 kW

INDIA
- ALL INDIA RADIO, Bangalore — E Asia • 500 kW • ALT. FREQ. TO 15410 kHz
- ALL INDIA RADIO, Delhi — DS • 50/100 kW / ENGLISH, ETC • DS • 50/100 kW

ROMANIA
- R ROMANIA INTL, Galbeni — W • Australasia • 250 kW

UNITED NATIONS
- †RADIO UNMEE, Via Dhabayya, UAE — S • Su • E Africa • 250 kW / S • Tu • E Africa • 250 kW

15140 CHINA
- †CHINA R INTL, Xi'an — S • SE Asia • 500 kW

INDIA
- ALL INDIA RADIO, Delhi — E Europe • 250 kW

OMAN
- R SULTANATE OF OMAN, Thamarīt — Europe & Mideast • DS • 100 kW

TURKEY
- VOICE OF TURKEY, Ankara-Emirler — S • W Asia • 500 kW

VATICAN STATE
- †VATICAN RADIO, Sta Maria di Galeria — S • E Asia • 500 kW

15145 CHINA
- †CHINA R INTL, Kashi — Mideast • 100 kW
- CHINA R INTL, Xi'an — SE Asia • 500 kW

USA
- †R FREE ASIA, Via Dhabayya, UAE — W • S Asia • 500 kW
- RFE-RL, Via Biblis, Germany — S • C Asia • 100 kW
- RFE-RL, Via Udon Thani, Thailand — S • C Asia • 250 kW
- VOA, Via Philippines — S • E Asia • 250 kW

15150 INDONESIA
- †VOICE OF INDONESIA, Cimanggis, Jawa — E Asia, SE Asia & Pacific • 250 kW • ALT. FREQ. TO 9525 kHz / Europe • 250 kW • ALT. FREQ. TO 9525 kHz

IRAN
- VO THE ISLAMIC REP, Sirjan — S • Mideast & N Africa • 500 kW / W • E Asia • 500 kW

ROMANIA
- R ROMANIA INTL, Galbeni — W • N Africa • 250 kW

USA
- R FREE ASIA, Via Tinian, N Marianas — W • E Asia • 250 kW
- VOA, Via Philippines — W • SE Asia • 50 kW / W • E Asia • 250 kW
- VOA, Via Udon Thani, Thailand — S • E Asia • 500 kW

15155 EGYPT
- RADIO CAIRO, Abu Za'bal — E Africa • 100 kW

FRANCE
- R FRANCE INTL, Issoudun — S • E Europe • 500 kW

INDIA
- ALL INDIA RADIO, Aligarh — W Africa • 250 kW

USA
- FAMILY RADIO, Okeechobee, Fl — S • W North Am • 50 kW

15160 AUSTRALIA
- RADIO AUSTRALIA, Shepparton — Pacific & N America • 100 kW

CHINA
- †CHINA R INTL, Jinhua — E Asia • 500 kW
- †CHINA R INTL, Nanning — SE Asia • 100/500 kW

FRANCE
- †R FRANCE INTL, Issoudun — S M-F • E Africa • 500 kW • ALT. FREQ. TO 11995 kHz / S Sa/Su • E Africa • 500 kW • ALT. FREQ. TO 11995 kHz / W M-F • E Africa • 500 kW • ALT. FREQ. TO 11995 kHz / S M-F • E Africa • 500 kW / W Sa/Su • E Africa • 500 kW • ALT. FREQ. TO 11995 kHz / S Sa/Su • E Africa • 500 kW
- R FRANCE INTL, Via South Africa — C Africa • 250 kW / W Africa & C Africa • 250 kW

PORTUGAL
- RDP INTERNATIONAL, Lisbon — S Sa/Su • E Africa & S Africa • 100 kW

ROMANIA
- R ROMANIA INTL, Bucharest — W • E Asia • 250 kW

SPAIN
- R EXTERIOR ESPANA, Noblejas — C America & S America • 350 kW

TURKEY
- VOICE OF TURKEY, Ankara-Emirler — W • W Asia • 500 kW

UNITED KINGDOM
(con'd) — BBC, Via A'Seela, Oman — S • S Asia • 250 kW

| | 0 | 1 | 2 | 3 | 4 | 5 | 6 | 7 | 8 | 9 | 10 | 11 | 12 | 13 | 14 | 15 | 16 | 17 | 18 | 19 | 20 | 21 | 22 | 23 | 24 |

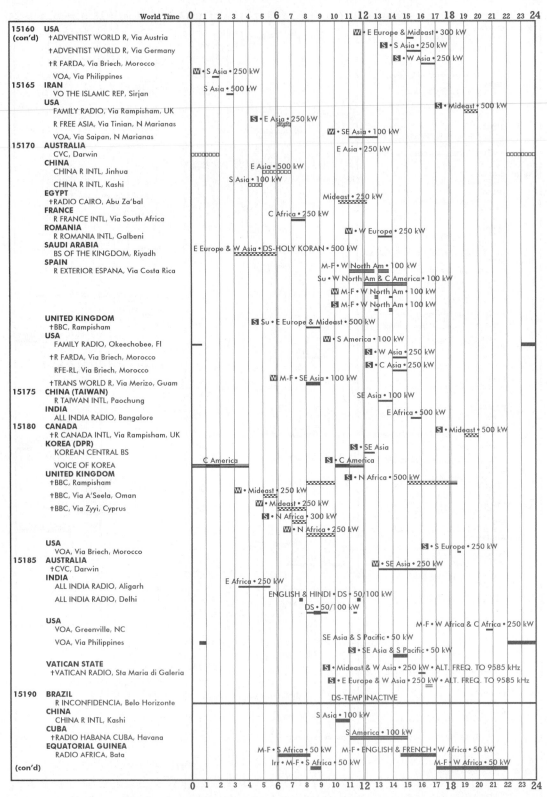

World Time 0 1 2 3 4 5 6 7 8 9 10 11 12 13 14 15 16 17 18 19 20 21 22 23 24

15160 USA
(con'd) †ADVENTIST WORLD R, Via Austria — W • E Europe & Mideast • 300 kW
         †ADVENTIST WORLD R, Via Germany — S • S Asia • 250 kW
         †R FARDA, Via Briech, Morocco — W • W Asia • 250 kW
         VOA, Via Philippines — W • S Asia • 250 kW

15165 IRAN
         VO THE ISLAMIC REP, Sirjan — S Asia • 500 kW
USA
         FAMILY RADIO, Via Rampisham, UK — S • Mideast • 500 kW
         R FREE ASIA, Via Tinian, N Marianas — S • E Asia • 250 kW
         VOA, Via Saipan, N Marianas — W • SE Asia • 100 kW

15170 AUSTRALIA
         CVC, Darwin — E Asia • 250 kW
CHINA
         CHINA R INTL, Jinhua — E Asia • 500 kW
         CHINA R INTL, Kashi — S Asia • 100 kW
EGYPT
         †RADIO CAIRO, Abu Za'bal — Mideast • 250 kW
FRANCE
         R FRANCE INTL, Via South Africa — C Africa • 250 kW
ROMANIA
         R ROMANIA INTL, Galbeni — W • W Europe • 250 kW
SAUDI ARABIA
         BS OF THE KINGDOM, Riyadh — E Europe & W Asia • DS-HOLY KORAN • 500 kW
SPAIN
         R EXTERIOR ESPANA, Via Costa Rica — M-F • W North Am • 100 kW
                                           — Su • W North Am & C America • 100 kW
                                           — W • M-F • W North Am • 100 kW
                                           — S • M-F • W North Am • 100 kW
UNITED KINGDOM
         †BBC, Rampisham — S • Su • E Europe & Mideast • 500 kW
USA
         FAMILY RADIO, Okeechobee, Fl — W • S America • 100 kW
         †R FARDA, Via Briech, Morocco — S • W Asia • 250 kW
         RFE-RL, Via Briech, Morocco — S • C Asia • 250 kW
         †TRANS WORLD R, Via Merizo, Guam — W • M-F • SE Asia • 100 kW

15175 CHINA (TAIWAN)
         R TAIWAN INTL, Paochung — SE Asia • 100 kW
INDIA
         ALL INDIA RADIO, Bangalore — E Africa • 500 kW

15180 CANADA
         †R CANADA INTL, Via Rampisham, UK — S • Mideast • 500 kW
KOREA (DPR)
         KOREAN CENTRAL BS — S • SE Asia
         VOICE OF KOREA — C America / S • C America
UNITED KINGDOM
         †BBC, Rampisham — S • N Africa • 500 kW
         †BBC, Via A'Seela, Oman — W • Mideast • 250 kW
         †BBC, Via Zyyi, Cyprus — W • Mideast • 250 kW
                               — S • N Africa • 250 kW
                               — W • N Africa • 250 kW
USA
         VOA, Via Briech, Morocco — S • S Europe • 250 kW

15185 AUSTRALIA
         †CVC, Darwin — W • SE Asia • 250 kW
INDIA
         ALL INDIA RADIO, Aligarh — E Africa • 250 kW
         ALL INDIA RADIO, Delhi — ENGLISH & HINDI • DS • 50/100 kW
                               — DS • 50/100 kW
USA
         VOA, Greenville, NC — M-F • W Africa & C Africa • 250 kW
         VOA, Via Philippines — SE Asia & S Pacific • 50 kW
                             — S • SE Asia & S Pacific • 50 kW
VATICAN STATE
         †VATICAN RADIO, Sta Maria di Galeria — S • Mideast & W Asia • 250 kW • ALT. FREQ. TO 9585 kHz
                                              — S • E Europe & W Asia • 250 kW • ALT. FREQ. TO 9585 kHz

15190 BRAZIL
         R INCONFIDENCIA, Belo Horizonte — DS-TEMP INACTIVE
CHINA
         CHINA R INTL, Kashi — S Asia • 100 kW
CUBA
         †RADIO HABANA CUBA, Havana — S America • 100 kW
EQUATORIAL GUINEA
         RADIO AFRICA, Bata — M-F • S Africa • 50 kW   M-F • ENGLISH & FRENCH • W Africa • 50 kW
                            — Irr • M-F • S Africa • 50 kW   M-F • W Africa • 50 kW
(con'd)

0 1 2 3 4 5 6 7 8 9 10 11 12 13 14 15 16 17 18 19 20 21 22 23 24

ENGLISH ▬▬   ARABIC ⸙⸙⸙   CHINESE □□□   FRENCH ▭▭   GERMAN ▭▭▭   RUSSIAN ═══   SPANISH ▬▬   OTHER ▬▬

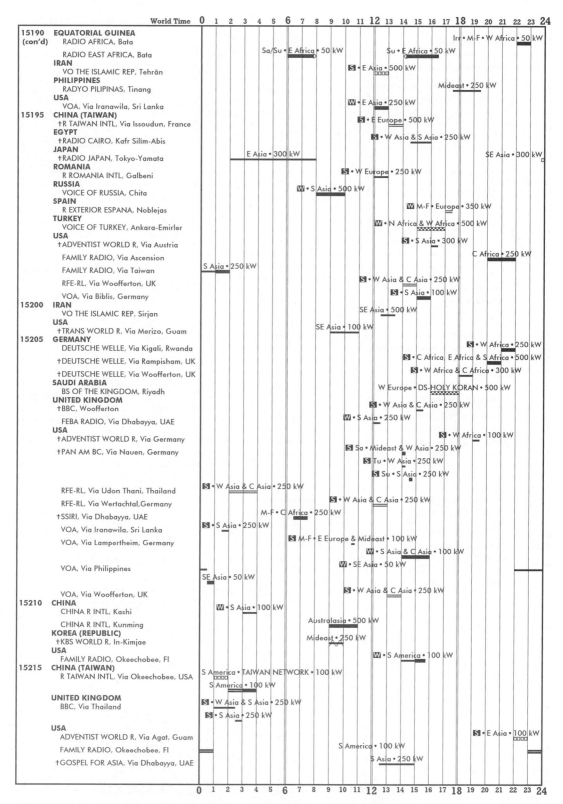

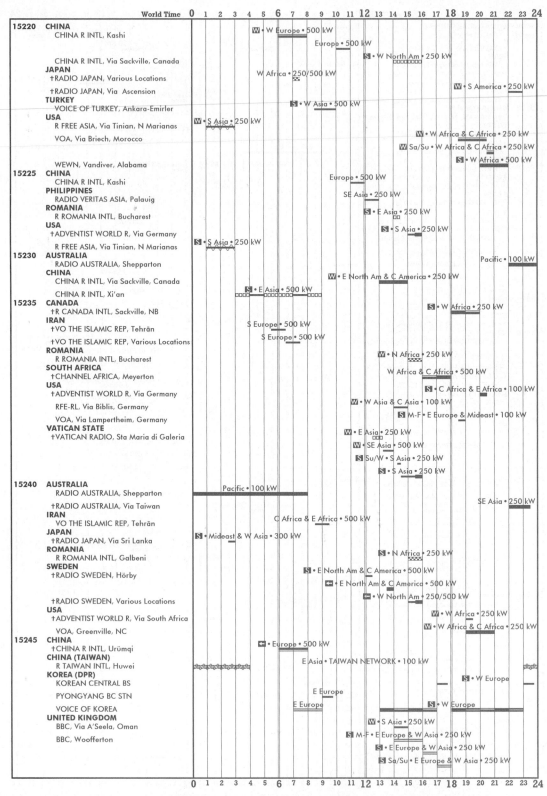

World Time 0 1 2 3 4 5 6 7 8 9 10 11 12 13 14 15 16 17 18 19 20 21 22 23 24

15220 CHINA
CHINA R INTL, Kashi — W • W Europe • 500 kW
— Europe • 500 kW
— S • W North Am • 250 kW
CHINA R INTL, Via Sackville, Canada
JAPAN
†RADIO JAPAN, Various Locations — W Africa • 250/500 kW
†RADIO JAPAN, Via Ascension — W • S America • 250 kW
TURKEY
VOICE OF TURKEY, Ankara-Emirler — S • W Asia • 500 kW
USA
R FREE ASIA, Via Tinian, N Marianas — W • S Asia • 250 kW
VOA, Via Briech, Morocco — W • W Africa & C Africa • 250 kW
— W Sa/Su • W Africa & C Africa • 250 kW
— S • W Africa • 500 kW
WEWN, Vandiver, Alabama

15225 CHINA
CHINA R INTL, Kashi — Europe • 500 kW
PHILIPPINES
RADIO VERITAS ASIA, Palauig — SE Asia • 250 kW
ROMANIA
R ROMANIA INTL, Bucharest — S • E Asia • 250 kW
USA
†ADVENTIST WORLD R, Via Germany — S • S Asia • 250 kW
R FREE ASIA, Via Tinian, N Marianas — S • S Asia • 250 kW

15230 AUSTRALIA
RADIO AUSTRALIA, Shepparton — Pacific • 100 kW
CHINA
CHINA R INTL, Via Sackville, Canada — W • E North Am & C America • 250 kW
CHINA R INTL, Xi'an — S • E Asia • 500 kW

15235 CANADA
†R CANADA INTL, Sackville, NB — S • W Africa • 250 kW
IRAN
†VO THE ISLAMIC REP, Tehrān — S Europe • 500 kW
†VO THE ISLAMIC REP, Various Locations — S Europe • 500 kW
ROMANIA
R ROMANIA INTL, Bucharest — W • N Africa • 250 kW
SOUTH AFRICA
†CHANNEL AFRICA, Meyerton — W Africa & C Africa • 500 kW
USA
†ADVENTIST WORLD R, Via Germany — S • C Africa & E Africa • 100 kW
RFE-RL, Via Biblis, Germany — W • W Asia & C Asia • 100 kW
VOA, Via Lampertheim, Germany — S M-F • E Europe & Mideast • 100 kW
VATICAN STATE
†VATICAN RADIO, Sta Maria di Galeria — W • E Asia • 250 kW
— W • SE Asia • 500 kW
— S Su/W • S Asia • 250 kW
— S • S Asia • 250 kW

15240 AUSTRALIA
RADIO AUSTRALIA, Shepparton — Pacific • 100 kW
†RADIO AUSTRALIA, Via Taiwan — SE Asia • 250 kW
IRAN
VO THE ISLAMIC REP, Tehrān — C Africa & E Africa • 500 kW
JAPAN
†RADIO JAPAN, Via Sri Lanka — S • Mideast & W Asia • 300 kW
ROMANIA
R ROMANIA INTL, Galbeni — S • N Africa • 250 kW
SWEDEN
†RADIO SWEDEN, Hörby — S • E North Am & C America • 500 kW
— E North Am & C America • 500 kW
†RADIO SWEDEN, Various Locations — W North Am • 250/500 kW
USA
†ADVENTIST WORLD R, Via South Africa — W • W Africa • 250 kW
VOA, Greenville, NC — W • W Africa & C Africa • 250 kW

15245 CHINA
†CHINA R INTL, Urümqi — Europe • 500 kW
CHINA (TAIWAN)
R TAIWAN INTL, Huwei — E Asia • TAIWAN NETWORK • 100 kW
KOREA (DPR)
KOREAN CENTRAL BS — S • W Europe
PYONGYANG BC STN — E Europe
VOICE OF KOREA — E Europe
— S • W Europe
UNITED KINGDOM
BBC, Via A'Seela, Oman — W • S Asia • 250 kW
BBC, Woofferton — S M-F • E Europe & W Asia • 250 kW
— S • E Europe & W Asia • 250 kW
— S Sa/Su • E Europe & W Asia • 250 kW

0 1 2 3 4 5 6 7 8 9 10 11 12 13 14 15 16 17 18 19 20 21 22 23 24

ENGLISH ▬   ARABIC ≋   CHINESE ▫▫▫   FRENCH ▬   GERMAN ▬   RUSSIAN ═   SPANISH ▬   OTHER ▬

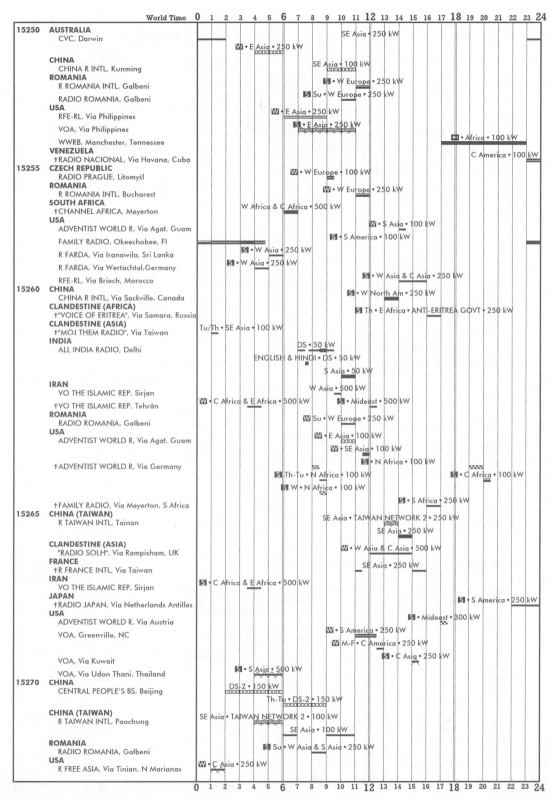

World Time 0 1 2 3 4 5 6 7 8 9 10 11 12 13 14 15 16 17 18 19 20 21 22 23 24

15250	AUSTRALIA	
	CVC, Darwin	SE Asia • 250 kW
		W • E Asia • 250 kW
	CHINA	
	CHINA R INTL, Kunming	SE Asia • 100 kW
	ROMANIA	
	R ROMANIA INTL, Galbeni	S • W Europe • 250 kW
	RADIO ROMANIA, Galbeni	S Su • W Europe • 250 kW
	USA	
	RFE-RL, Via Philippines	W • E Asia • 250 kW
	VOA, Via Philippines	S • E Asia • 250 kW
	WWRB, Manchester, Tennessee	⮂ • Africa • 100 kW
	VENEZUELA	
	†RADIO NACIONAL, Via Havana, Cuba	C America • 100 kW
15255	CZECH REPUBLIC	
	RADIO PRAGUE, Litomyšl	W • W Europe • 100 kW
	ROMANIA	
	R ROMANIA INTL, Bucharest	W • W Europe • 250 kW
	SOUTH AFRICA	
	†CHANNEL AFRICA, Meyerton	W Africa & C Africa • 500 kW
	USA	
	ADVENTIST WORLD R, Via Agat, Guam	W • S Asia • 100 kW
	FAMILY RADIO, Okeechobee, Fl	S • S America • 100 kW
	R FARDA, Via Iranawila, Sri Lanka	S • W Asia • 250 kW
	R FARDA, Via Wertachtal, Germany	S • W Asia • 250 kW
	RFE-RL, Via Briech, Morocco	S • W Asia & C Asia • 250 kW
15260	CHINA	
	CHINA R INTL, Via Sackville, Canada	S • W North Am • 250 kW
	CLANDESTINE (AFRICA)	
	†"VOICE OF ERITREA", Via Samara, Russia	S Th • E Africa • ANTI-ERITREA GOVT • 250 kW
	CLANDESTINE (ASIA)	
	†"MOJ THEM RADIO", Via Taiwan	Tu/Th • SE Asia • 100 kW
	INDIA	
	ALL INDIA RADIO, Delhi	DS • 50 kW
		ENGLISH & HINDI • DS • 50 kW
		S Asia • 50 kW
	IRAN	
	VO THE ISLAMIC REP, Sirjan	W Asia • 500 kW
	†VO THE ISLAMIC REP, Tehrān	W • C Africa & E Africa • 500 kW
		S • Mideast • 500 kW
	ROMANIA	
	RADIO ROMANIA, Galbeni	W Su • W Europe • 250 kW
	USA	
	ADVENTIST WORLD R, Via Agat, Guam	W • E Asia • 100 kW
		W • SE Asia • 100 kW
		S • N Africa • 100 kW
	†ADVENTIST WORLD R, Via Germany	S Th-Tu • N Africa • 100 kW
		S • C Africa • 100 kW
		S W • N Africa • 100 kW
	†FAMILY RADIO, Via Meyerton, S Africa	S • S Africa • 250 kW
15265	CHINA (TAIWAN)	
	R TAIWAN INTL, Tainan	SE Asia • TAIWAN NETWORK 2 • 250 kW
		SE Asia • 250 kW
	CLANDESTINE (ASIA)	
	"RADIO SOLH", Via Rampisham, UK	W • W Asia & C Asia • 500 kW
	FRANCE	
	†R FRANCE INTL, Via Taiwan	SE Asia • 250 kW
	IRAN	
	VO THE ISLAMIC REP, Sirjan	S • C Africa & E Africa • 500 kW
	JAPAN	
	†RADIO JAPAN, Via Netherlands Antilles	S • S America • 250 kW
	USA	
	ADVENTIST WORLD R, Via Austria	S • Mideast • 300 kW
	VOA, Greenville, NC	W • S America • 250 kW
		W M-F • C America • 250 kW
	VOA, Via Kuwait	S • C Asia • 250 kW
	VOA, Via Udon Thani, Thailand	S • S Asia • 500 kW
15270	CHINA	
	CENTRAL PEOPLE'S BS, Beijing	DS-2 • 150 kW
		Th-Tu • DS-2 • 150 kW
	CHINA (TAIWAN)	
	R TAIWAN INTL, Paochung	SE Asia • TAIWAN NETWORK 2 • 100 kW
		SE Asia • 100 kW
	ROMANIA	
	RADIO ROMANIA, Galbeni	S Su • W Asia & S Asia • 250 kW
	USA	
	R FREE ASIA, Via Tinian, N Marianas	W • C Asia • 250 kW

0 1 2 3 4 5 6 7 8 9 10 11 12 13 14 15 16 17 18 19 20 21 22 23 24

SEASONAL S OR W   1-HR TIMESHIFT MIDYEAR ⮂ OR ⮀   JAMMING / OR /\   EARLIEST HEARD ◁   LATEST HEARD ▷   NEW FOR 2008 †

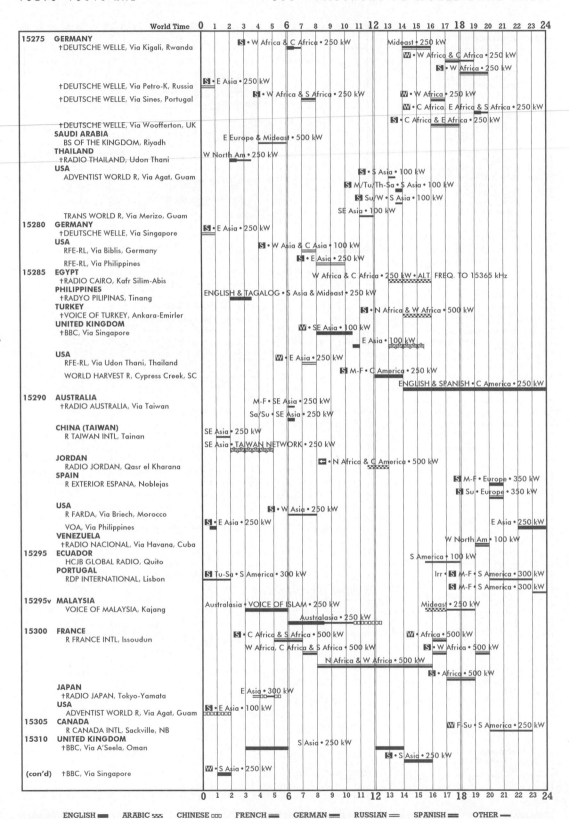

World Time 0 1 2 3 4 5 6 7 8 9 10 11 12 13 14 15 16 17 18 19 20 21 22 23 24

15275 GERMANY
†DEUTSCHE WELLE, Via Kigali, Rwanda — **S** • W Africa & C Africa • 250 kW / Mideast • 250 kW / **W** • W Africa & C Africa • 250 kW / **S** • W Africa • 250 kW

†DEUTSCHE WELLE, Via Petro-K, Russia — **S** • E Asia • 250 kW

†DEUTSCHE WELLE, Via Sines, Portugal — **S** • W Africa & S Africa • 250 kW / **W** • W Africa • 250 kW / **W** • C Africa, E Africa & S Africa • 250 kW

†DEUTSCHE WELLE, Via Woofferton, UK — **S** • C Africa & E Africa • 250 kW

SAUDI ARABIA
BS OF THE KINGDOM, Riyadh — E Europe & Mideast • 500 kW

THAILAND
†RADIO THAILAND, Udon Thani — W North Am • 250 kW

USA
ADVENTIST WORLD R, Via Agat, Guam — **S** • S Asia • 100 kW / **S** M/Tu/Th-Sa • S Asia • 100 kW / **S** Su/W • S Asia • 100 kW / SE Asia • 100 kW

TRANS WORLD R, Via Merizo, Guam

15280 GERMANY
†DEUTSCHE WELLE, Via Singapore — **S** • E Asia • 250 kW

USA
RFE-RL, Via Biblis, Germany — **S** • W Asia & C Asia • 100 kW

RFE-RL, Via Philippines — **S** • E Asia • 250 kW

15285 EGYPT
†RADIO CAIRO, Kafr Silim-Abis — W Africa & C Africa • 250 kW • ALT. FREQ. TO 15365 kHz

PHILIPPINES
†RADYO PILIPINAS, Tinang — ENGLISH & TAGALOG • S Asia & Mideast • 250 kW

TURKEY
†VOICE OF TURKEY, Ankara-Emirler — **S** • N Africa & W Africa • 500 kW

UNITED KINGDOM
†BBC, Via Singapore — **W** • SE Asia • 100 kW / E Asia • 100 kW

USA
RFE-RL, Via Udon Thani, Thailand — **W** • E Asia • 250 kW

WORLD HARVEST R, Cypress Creek, SC — **S** M-F • C America • 250 kW / ENGLISH & SPANISH • C America • 250 kW

15290 AUSTRALIA
†RADIO AUSTRALIA, Via Taiwan — M-F • SE Asia • 250 kW / Sa/Su • SE Asia • 250 kW

CHINA (TAIWAN)
R TAIWAN INTL, Tainan — SE Asia • 250 kW / SE Asia • TAIWAN NETWORK • 250 kW

JORDAN
RADIO JORDAN, Qasr el Kharana — • N Africa & C America • 500 kW

SPAIN
R EXTERIOR ESPANA, Noblejas — **S** M-F • Europe • 350 kW / **S** Su • Europe • 350 kW

USA
R FARDA, Via Briech, Morocco — **S** • W Asia • 250 kW

VOA, Via Philippines — **S** • E Asia • 250 kW / E Asia • 250 kW

VENEZUELA
†RADIO NACIONAL, Via Havana, Cuba — W North Am • 100 kW

15295 ECUADOR
HCJB GLOBAL RADIO, Quito — S America • 100 kW

PORTUGAL
RDP INTERNATIONAL, Lisbon — **S** Tu-Sa • S America • 300 kW / Irr • **S** M-F • S America • 300 kW / **S** M-F • S America • 300 kW

15295v MALAYSIA
VOICE OF MALAYSIA, Kajang — Australasia • VOICE OF ISLAM • 250 kW / Mideast • 250 kW / Australasia • 250 kW

15300 FRANCE
R FRANCE INTL, Issoudun — **S** • C Africa & S Africa • 500 kW / **W** • Africa • 500 kW / W Africa, C Africa & S Africa • 500 kW / **S** • W Africa • 500 kW / N Africa & W Africa • 500 kW / **S** • Africa • 500 kW

JAPAN
†RADIO JAPAN, Tokyo-Yamata — E Asia • 300 kW

USA
ADVENTIST WORLD R, Via Agat, Guam — **S** • E Asia • 100 kW

15305 CANADA
R CANADA INTL, Sackville, NB — **W** F-Su • S America • 250 kW

15310 UNITED KINGDOM
†BBC, Via A'Seela, Oman — S Asia • 250 kW / **S** • S Asia • 250 kW

(con'd) †BBC, Via Singapore — **W** • S Asia • 250 kW

0 1 2 3 4 5 6 7 8 9 10 11 12 13 14 15 16 17 18 19 20 21 22 23 24

ENGLISH ▬ ARABIC ⌇⌇⌇ CHINESE □□□ FRENCH ═ GERMAN ▬ RUSSIAN ═ SPANISH ═ OTHER —

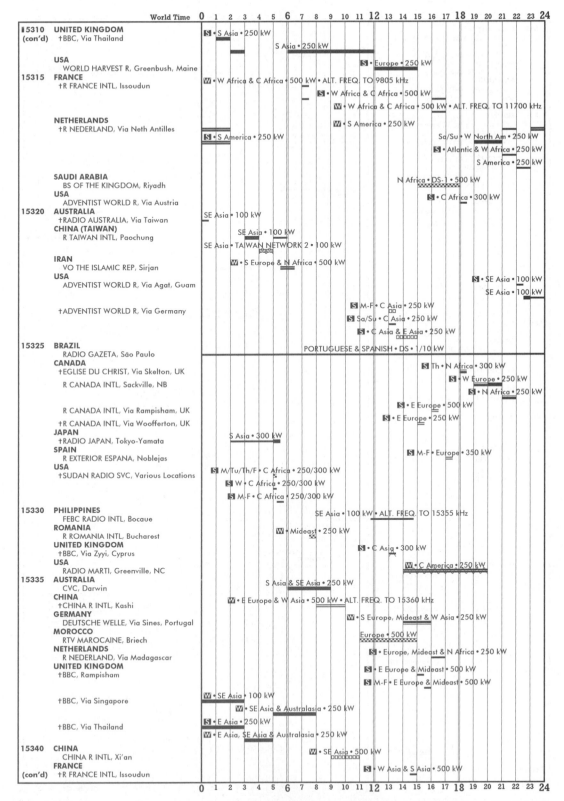

World Time

15310 (con'd)   **UNITED KINGDOM**   †BBC, Via Thailand
- S • S Asia • 250 kW
- S Asia • 250 kW

USA   WORLD HARVEST R, Greenbush, Maine
- S • Europe • 250 kW

15315   **FRANCE**   †R FRANCE INTL, Issoudun
- W • W Africa & C Africa • 500 kW • ALT. FREQ. TO 9805 kHz
- S • W Africa & C Africa • 500 kW
- W • W Africa & C Africa • 500 kW • ALT. FREQ. TO 11700 kHz

NETHERLANDS   †R NEDERLAND, Via Neth Antilles
- W • S America • 250 kW
- S • S America • 250 kW
- Sa/Su • W North Am • 250 kW
- S • Atlantic & W Africa • 250 kW
- S America • 250 kW

SAUDI ARABIA   BS OF THE KINGDOM, Riyadh
- N Africa • DS-1 • 500 kW

USA   ADVENTIST WORLD R, Via Austria
- S • C Africa • 300 kW

15320   **AUSTRALIA**   †RADIO AUSTRALIA, Via Taiwan
- SE Asia • 100 kW

CHINA (TAIWAN)   R TAIWAN INTL, Paochung
- SE Asia • 100 kW
- SE Asia • TAIWAN NETWORK 2 • 100 kW

IRAN   VO THE ISLAMIC REP, Sirjan
- W • S Europe & N Africa • 500 kW

USA   ADVENTIST WORLD R, Via Agat, Guam
- S • SE Asia • 100 kW
- SE Asia • 100 kW

†ADVENTIST WORLD R, Via Germany
- S • M-F • C Asia • 250 kW
- S • Sa/Su • C Asia • 250 kW
- S • C Asia & E Asia • 250 kW

15325   **BRAZIL**   RADIO GAZETA, São Paulo
- PORTUGUESE & SPANISH • DS • 1/10 kW

CANADA   †EGLISE DU CHRIST, Via Skelton, UK
- S • Th • N Africa • 300 kW

R CANADA INTL, Sackville, NB
- S • W Europe • 250 kW
- S • N Africa • 250 kW

R CANADA INTL, Via Rampisham, UK
- S • E Europe • 500 kW

†R CANADA INTL, Via Woofferton, UK
- S • E Europe • 250 kW

JAPAN   †RADIO JAPAN, Tokyo-Yamata
- S Asia • 300 kW

SPAIN   R EXTERIOR ESPANA, Noblejas
- S • M-F • Europe • 350 kW

USA   †SUDAN RADIO SVC, Various Locations
- S • M/Tu/Th/F • C Africa • 250/300 kW
- S • W • C Africa • 250/300 kW
- S • M-F • C Africa • 250/300 kW

15330   **PHILIPPINES**   FEBC RADIO INTL, Bocaue
- SE Asia • 100 kW • ALT. FREQ. TO 15355 kHz

ROMANIA   R ROMANIA INTL, Bucharest
- W • Mideast • 250 kW

UNITED KINGDOM   †BBC, Via Zyyi, Cyprus
- S • C Asia • 300 kW

USA   RADIO MARTI, Greenville, NC
- W • C America • 250 kW

15335   **AUSTRALIA**   CVC, Darwin
- S Asia & SE Asia • 250 kW

CHINA   †CHINA R INTL, Kashi
- W • E Europe & W Asia • 500 kW • ALT. FREQ. TO 15360 kHz

GERMANY   DEUTSCHE WELLE, Via Sines, Portugal
- W • S Europe, Mideast & W Asia • 250 kW

MOROCCO   RTV MAROCAINE, Briech
- Europe • 500 kW

NETHERLANDS   R NEDERLAND, Via Madagascar
- S • Europe, Mideast & N Africa • 250 kW

UNITED KINGDOM   †BBC, Rampisham
- S • E Europe & Mideast • 500 kW
- S • M-F • E Europe & Mideast • 500 kW

†BBC, Via Singapore
- W • SE Asia • 100 kW
- W • SE Asia & Australasia • 250 kW

†BBC, Via Thailand
- S • E Asia • 250 kW
- W • E Asia, SE Asia & Australasia • 250 kW

15340   **CHINA**   CHINA R INTL, Xi'an
- W • SE Asia • 500 kW

FRANCE (con'd)   †R FRANCE INTL, Issoudun
- S • W Asia & S Asia • 500 kW

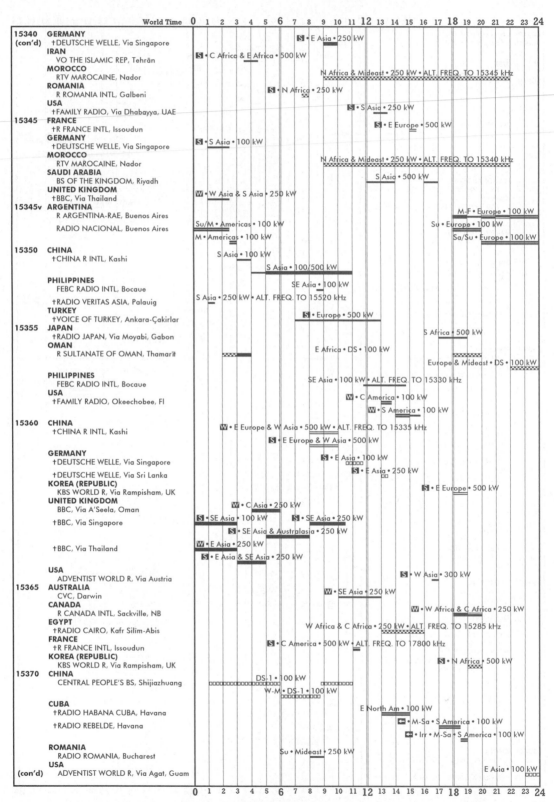

| | World Time | 0 | 1 | 2 | 3 | 4 | 5 | 6 | 7 | 8 | 9 | 10 | 11 | 12 | 13 | 14 | 15 | 16 | 17 | 18 | 19 | 20 | 21 | 22 | 23 | 24 |

15340 GERMANY
(con'd)   †DEUTSCHE WELLE, Via Singapore — S • E Asia • 250 kW
IRAN
VO THE ISLAMIC REP, Tehrän — S • C Africa & E Africa • 500 kW
MOROCCO
RTV MAROCAINE, Nador — N Africa & Mideast • 250 kW • ALT. FREQ. TO 15345 kHz
ROMANIA
R ROMANIA INTL, Galbeni — S • N Africa • 250 kW
USA
†FAMILY RADIO, Via Dhabayya, UAE — S • S Asia • 250 kW

15345 FRANCE
†R FRANCE INTL, Issoudun — S • E Europe • 500 kW
GERMANY
†DEUTSCHE WELLE, Via Singapore — S • S Asia • 100 kW
MOROCCO
RTV MAROCAINE, Nador — N Africa & Mideast • 250 kW • ALT. FREQ. TO 15340 kHz
SAUDI ARABIA
BS OF THE KINGDOM, Riyadh — S Asia • 500 kW
UNITED KINGDOM
†BBC, Via Thailand — W • W Asia & S Asia • 250 kW

15345v ARGENTINA
R ARGENTINA-RAE, Buenos Aires — M-F • Europe • 100 kW
RADIO NACIONAL, Buenos Aires — Su/M • Americas • 100 kW / Su • Europe • 100 kW
— M • Americas • 100 kW / Sa/Su • Europe • 100 kW

15350 CHINA
†CHINA R INTL, Kashi — S Asia • 100 kW / S Asia • 100/500 kW
PHILIPPINES
FEBC RADIO INTL, Bocaue — SE Asia • 100 kW
†RADIO VERITAS ASIA, Palauig — S Asia • 250 kW • ALT. FREQ. TO 15520 kHz
TURKEY
†VOICE OF TURKEY, Ankara-Çakirlar — S • Europe • 500 kW

15355 JAPAN
†RADIO JAPAN, Via Moyabi, Gabon — S Africa • 500 kW
OMAN
R SULTANATE OF OMAN, Thamarït — E Africa • DS • 100 kW / Europe & Mideast • DS • 100 kW
PHILIPPINES
FEBC RADIO INTL, Bocaue — SE Asia • 100 kW • ALT. FREQ. TO 15330 kHz
USA
†FAMILY RADIO, Okeechobee, Fl — W • C America • 100 kW / W • S America • 100 kW

15360 CHINA
†CHINA R INTL, Kashi — W • E Europe & W Asia • 500 kW • ALT. FREQ. TO 15335 kHz
— S • E Europe & W Asia • 500 kW
GERMANY
†DEUTSCHE WELLE, Via Singapore — S • E Asia • 100 kW
†DEUTSCHE WELLE, Via Sri Lanka — S • E Asia • 250 kW
KOREA (REPUBLIC)
KBS WORLD R, Via Rampisham, UK — S • E Europe • 500 kW
UNITED KINGDOM
BBC, Via A'Seela, Oman — W • C Asia • 250 kW
†BBC, Via Singapore — S • SE Asia • 100 kW / S • SE Asia • 250 kW
— S • SE Asia & Australasia • 250 kW
†BBC, Via Thailand — W • E Asia • 250 kW
— S • E Asia & SE Asia • 250 kW
USA
ADVENTIST WORLD R, Via Austria — S • W Asia • 300 kW

15365 AUSTRALIA
CVC, Darwin — W • SE Asia • 250 kW
CANADA
R CANADA INTL, Sackville, NB — W • W Africa & C Africa • 250 kW
EGYPT
†RADIO CAIRO, Kafr Silim-Abis — W Africa & C Africa • 250 kW • ALT. FREQ. TO 15285 kHz
FRANCE
†R FRANCE INTL, Issoudun — S • C America • 500 kW • ALT. FREQ. TO 17800 kHz
KOREA (REPUBLIC)
KBS WORLD R, Via Rampisham, UK — S • N Africa • 500 kW

15370 CHINA
CENTRAL PEOPLE'S BS, Shijiazhuang — DS-1 • 100 kW / W-M • DS-1 • 100 kW
CUBA
†RADIO HABANA CUBA, Havana — E North Am • 100 kW / M-Sa • S America • 100 kW
†RADIO REBELDE, Havana — Irr • M-Sa • S America • 100 kW
ROMANIA
RADIO ROMANIA, Bucharest — Su • Mideast • 250 kW
USA
(con'd)   ADVENTIST WORLD R, Via Agat, Guam — E Asia • 100 kW

| | 0 | 1 | 2 | 3 | 4 | 5 | 6 | 7 | 8 | 9 | 10 | 11 | 12 | 13 | 14 | 15 | 16 | 17 | 18 | 19 | 20 | 21 | 22 | 23 | 24 |

ENGLISH ▬   ARABIC ∿∿   CHINESE ▭▭▭   FRENCH ▬▬   GERMAN ▬▬   RUSSIAN ══   SPANISH ▬▬   OTHER ▬

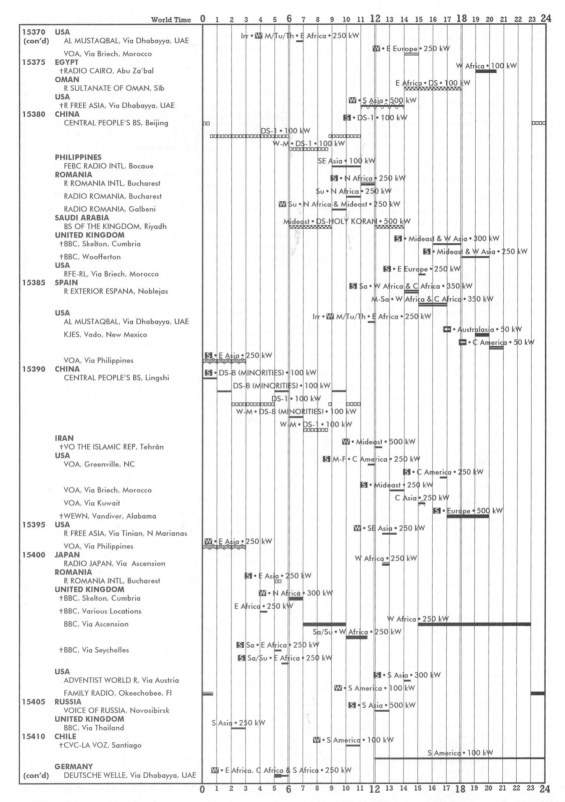

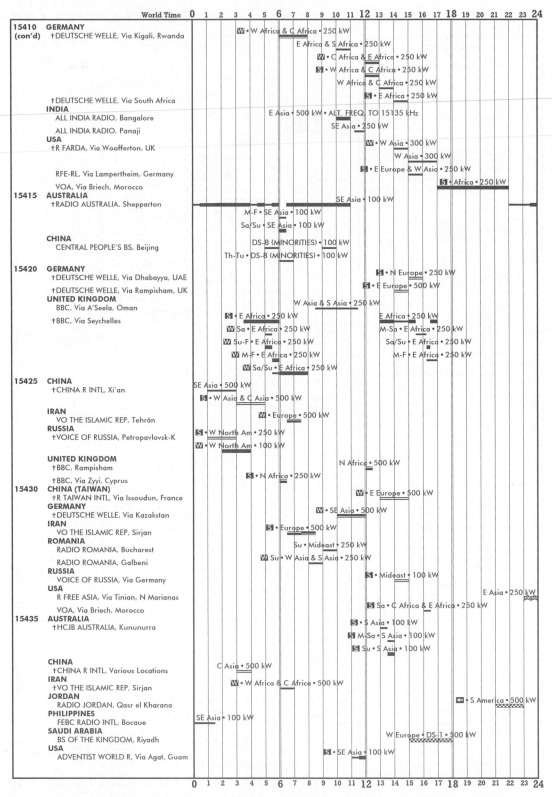

World Time 0 1 2 3 4 5 6 7 8 9 10 11 12 13 14 15 16 17 18 19 20 21 22 23 24

15410 GERMANY
(con'd) †DEUTSCHE WELLE, Via Kigali, Rwanda
 W • W Africa & C Africa • 250 kW
 E Africa & S Africa • 250 kW
 W • C Africa & E Africa • 250 kW
 S • W Africa & C Africa • 250 kW
 W Africa & C Africa • 250 kW
 S • E Africa • 250 kW

 †DEUTSCHE WELLE, Via South Africa
INDIA
 ALL INDIA RADIO, Bangalore
 E Asia • 500 kW • ALT. FREQ. TO 15135 kHz
 ALL INDIA RADIO, Panaji
 SE Asia • 250 kW
USA
 †R FARDA, Via Woofferton, UK
 W • W Asia • 300 kW
 W Asia • 300 kW

 RFE-RL, Via Lampertheim, Germany
 S • E Europe & W Asia • 250 kW
 VOA, Via Briech, Morocco
 S • Africa • 250 kW
15415 AUSTRALIA
 †RADIO AUSTRALIA, Shepparton
 SE Asia • 100 kW
 M-F • SE Asia • 100 kW
 Sa/Su • SE Asia • 100 kW

CHINA
 CENTRAL PEOPLE'S BS, Beijing
 DS-8 (MINORITIES) • 100 kW
 Th-Tu • DS-8 (MINORITIES) • 100 kW

15420 GERMANY
 †DEUTSCHE WELLE, Via Dhabayya, UAE
 S • N Europe • 250 kW
 †DEUTSCHE WELLE, Via Rampisham, UK
 S • E Europe • 500 kW
UNITED KINGDOM
 BBC, Via A'Seela, Oman
 W Asia & S Asia • 250 kW
 †BBC, Via Seychelles
 S • E Africa • 250 kW
 E Africa • 250 kW
 W • Sa • E Africa • 250 kW
 M-Sa • E Africa • 250 kW
 W • Su-F • E Africa • 250 kW
 Sa/Su • E Africa • 250 kW
 W • M-F • E Africa • 250 kW
 M-F • E Africa • 250 kW
 W • Sa/Su • E Africa • 250 kW

15425 CHINA
 †CHINA R INTL, Xi'an
 SE Asia • 500 kW
 S • W Asia & C Asia • 500 kW
IRAN
 VO THE ISLAMIC REP, Tehrān
 W • Europe • 500 kW
RUSSIA
 †VOICE OF RUSSIA, Petropavlovsk-K
 S • W North Am • 250 kW
 W • W North Am • 100 kW

UNITED KINGDOM
 †BBC, Rampisham
 N Africa • 500 kW
 †BBC, Via Zyyi, Cyprus
 S • N Africa • 250 kW
15430 CHINA (TAIWAN)
 †R TAIWAN INTL, Via Issoudun, France
 W • E Europe • 500 kW
GERMANY
 †DEUTSCHE WELLE, Via Kazakstan
 W • SE Asia • 500 kW
IRAN
 VO THE ISLAMIC REP, Sirjan
 S • Europe • 500 kW
ROMANIA
 RADIO ROMANIA, Bucharest
 Su • Mideast • 250 kW
 RADIO ROMANIA, Galbeni
 W Su • W Asia & S Asia • 250 kW
RUSSIA
 VOICE OF RUSSIA, Via Germany
 S • Mideast • 100 kW
USA
 R FREE ASIA, Via Tinian, N Marianas
 E Asia • 250 kW
 VOA, Via Briech, Morocco
 S • Sa • C Africa & E Africa • 250 kW
15435 AUSTRALIA
 †HCJB AUSTRALIA, Kununurra
 S • S Asia • 100 kW
 S • M-Sa • S Asia • 100 kW
 S • Su • S Asia • 100 kW

CHINA
 †CHINA R INTL, Various Locations
 C Asia • 500 kW
IRAN
 †VO THE ISLAMIC REP, Sirjan
 W • W Africa & C Africa • 500 kW
JORDAN
 RADIO JORDAN, Qasr el Kharana
 S America • 500 kW
PHILIPPINES
 FEBC RADIO INTL, Bocaue
 SE Asia • 100 kW
SAUDI ARABIA
 BS OF THE KINGDOM, Riyadh
 W Europe • DS-1 • 500 kW
USA
 ADVENTIST WORLD R, Via Agat, Guam
 S • SE Asia • 100 kW

0 1 2 3 4 5 6 7 8 9 10 11 12 13 14 15 16 17 18 19 20 21 22 23 24

ENGLISH ▬ ARABIC ▨ CHINESE □□□ FRENCH ▬ GERMAN ═ RUSSIAN ═ SPANISH ▬ OTHER ▬

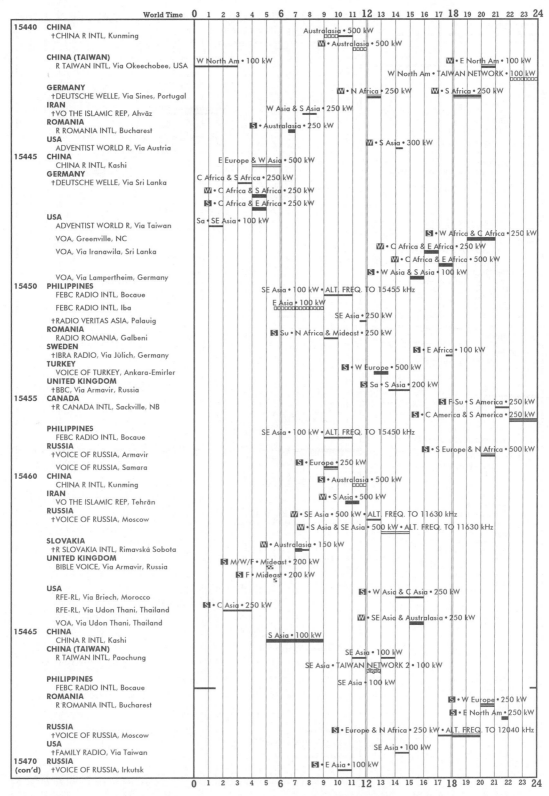

| World Time | 0 1 2 3 4 5 6 7 8 9 10 11 12 13 14 15 16 17 18 19 20 21 22 23 24 |

15440 CHINA
†CHINA R INTL, Kunming
— Australasia • 500 kW
— W • Australasia • 500 kW

CHINA (TAIWAN)
R TAIWAN INTL, Via Okeechobee, USA
— W North Am • 100 kW
— W • E North Am • 100 kW
— W North Am • TAIWAN NETWORK • 100 kW

GERMANY
†DEUTSCHE WELLE, Via Sines, Portugal
— W • N Africa • 250 kW
— W • S Africa • 250 kW

IRAN
†VO THE ISLAMIC REP, Ahvāz
— W Asia & S Asia • 250 kW

ROMANIA
R ROMANIA INTL, Bucharest
— S • Australasia • 250 kW

USA
ADVENTIST WORLD R, Via Austria
— W • S Asia • 300 kW

15445 CHINA
CHINA R INTL, Kashi
— E Europe & W Asia • 500 kW

GERMANY
†DEUTSCHE WELLE, Via Sri Lanka
— C Africa & S Africa • 250 kW
— W • C Africa & S Africa • 250 kW
— S • C Africa & E Africa • 250 kW

USA
ADVENTIST WORLD R, Via Taiwan
— Sa • SE Asia • 100 kW

VOA, Greenville, NC
— S • W Africa & C Africa • 250 kW

VOA, Via Iranawila, Sri Lanka
— W • C Africa & E Africa • 250 kW
— W • C Africa & E Africa • 500 kW

VOA, Via Lampertheim, Germany
— S • W Asia & S Asia • 100 kW

15450 PHILIPPINES
FEBC RADIO INTL, Bocaue
— SE Asia • 100 kW • ALT. FREQ. TO 15455 kHz

FEBC RADIO INTL, Iba
— E Asia • 100 kW

†RADIO VERITAS ASIA, Palauig
— SE Asia • 250 kW

ROMANIA
RADIO ROMANIA, Galbeni
— S Su • N Africa & Mideast • 250 kW

SWEDEN
†IBRA RADIO, Via Jülich, Germany
— S • E Africa • 100 kW

TURKEY
VOICE OF TURKEY, Ankara-Emirler
— S • W Europe • 500 kW

UNITED KINGDOM
†BBC, Via Armavir, Russia
— S Sa • S Asia • 200 kW

15455 CANADA
†R CANADA INTL, Sackville, NB
— S F-Su • S America • 250 kW
— S • C America & S America • 250 kW

PHILIPPINES
FEBC RADIO INTL, Bocaue
— SE Asia • 100 kW • ALT. FREQ. TO 15450 kHz

RUSSIA
†VOICE OF RUSSIA, Armavir
— S • S Europe & N Africa • 500 kW

VOICE OF RUSSIA, Samara
— S • Europe • 250 kW

15460 CHINA
CHINA R INTL, Kunming
— S • Australasia • 500 kW

IRAN
VO THE ISLAMIC REP, Tehrān
— W • S Asia • 500 kW

RUSSIA
†VOICE OF RUSSIA, Moscow
— W • SE Asia • 500 kW • ALT. FREQ. TO 11630 kHz
— W • S Asia & SE Asia • 500 kW • ALT. FREQ. TO 11630 kHz

SLOVAKIA
†R SLOVAKIA INTL, Rimavská Sobota
— W • Australasia • 150 kW

UNITED KINGDOM
BIBLE VOICE, Via Armavir, Russia
— S M/W/F • Mideast • 200 kW
— S F • Mideast • 200 kW

USA
RFE-RL, Via Briech, Morocco
— S • W Asia & C Asia • 250 kW

RFE-RL, Via Udon Thani, Thailand
— S • C Asia • 250 kW

VOA, Via Udon Thani, Thailand
— W • SE Asia & Australasia • 250 kW

15465 CHINA
CHINA R INTL, Kashi
— S Asia • 100 kW

CHINA (TAIWAN)
R TAIWAN INTL, Paochung
— SE Asia • 100 kW
— SE Asia • TAIWAN NETWORK 2 • 100 kW

PHILIPPINES
FEBC RADIO INTL, Bocaue
— SE Asia • 100 kW

ROMANIA
R ROMANIA INTL, Bucharest
— S • W Europe • 250 kW
— S • E North Am • 250 kW

RUSSIA
†VOICE OF RUSSIA, Moscow
— S • Europe & N Africa • 250 kW • ALT. FREQ. TO 12040 kHz

USA
†FAMILY RADIO, Via Taiwan
— SE Asia • 100 kW

15470 RUSSIA
(con'd) †VOICE OF RUSSIA, Irkutsk
— S • E Asia • 100 kW

| 0 1 2 3 4 5 6 7 8 9 10 11 12 13 14 15 16 17 18 19 20 21 22 23 24 |

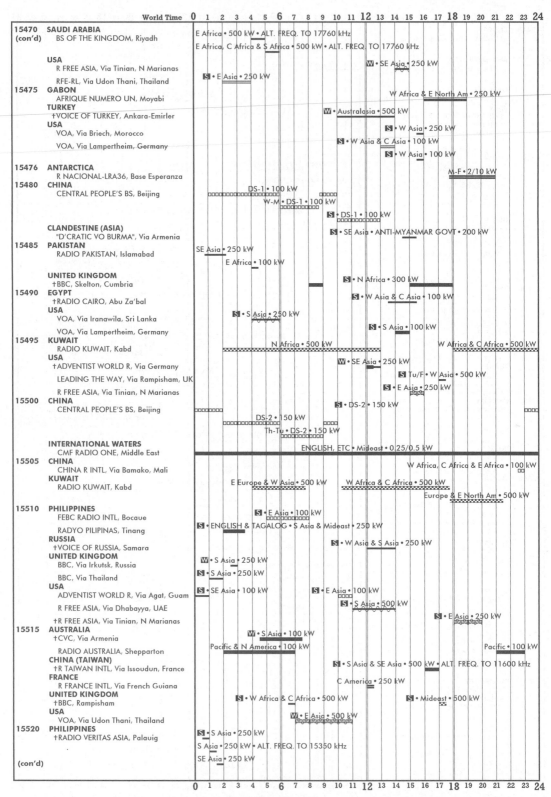

| World Time | 0 | 1 | 2 | 3 | 4 | 5 | 6 | 7 | 8 | 9 | 10 | 11 | 12 | 13 | 14 | 15 | 16 | 17 | 18 | 19 | 20 | 21 | 22 | 23 | 24 |

15470 **SAUDI ARABIA**
(con'd)   BS OF THE KINGDOM, Riyadh
  E Africa • 500 kW • ALT. FREQ. TO 17760 kHz
  E Africa, C Africa & S Africa • 500 kW • ALT. FREQ. TO 17760 kHz

USA
  R FREE ASIA, Via Tinian, N Marianas
  W • SE Asia • 250 kW
  RFE-RL, Via Udon Thani, Thailand
  S • E Asia • 250 kW
15475 **GABON**
  AFRIQUE NUMERO UN, Moyabi
  W Africa & E North Am • 250 kW
TURKEY
  †VOICE OF TURKEY, Ankara-Emirler
  W • Australasia • 500 kW
USA
  VOA, Via Briech, Morocco
  S • W Asia • 250 kW
  VOA, Via Lampertheim, Germany
  S • W Asia & C Asia • 100 kW
  S • W Asia • 100 kW

15476 **ANTARCTICA**
  R NACIONAL-LRA36, Base Esperanza
  M-F • 2/10 kW
15480 **CHINA**
  CENTRAL PEOPLE'S BS, Beijing
  DS-1 • 100 kW
  W-M • DS-1 • 100 kW
  S • DS-1 • 100 kW

CLANDESTINE (ASIA)
  "D'CRATIC VO BURMA", Via Armenia
  S • SE Asia • ANTI-MYANMAR GOVT • 200 kW
15485 **PAKISTAN**
  RADIO PAKISTAN, Islamabad
  SE Asia • 250 kW
  E Africa • 100 kW

UNITED KINGDOM
  †BBC, Skelton, Cumbria
  S • N Africa • 300 kW
15490 **EGYPT**
  †RADIO CAIRO, Abu Za'bal
  S • W Asia & C Asia • 100 kW
USA
  VOA, Via Iranawila, Sri Lanka
  S • S Asia • 250 kW
  VOA, Via Lampertheim, Germany
  S • S Asia • 100 kW
15495 **KUWAIT**
  RADIO KUWAIT, Kabd
  N Africa • 500 kW   W Africa & C Africa • 500 kW
USA
  †ADVENTIST WORLD R, Via Germany
  W • SE Asia • 250 kW
  LEADING THE WAY, Via Rampisham, UK
  S • Tu/F • W Asia • 500 kW
  R FREE ASIA, Via Tinian, N Marianas
  S • E Asia • 250 kW
15500 **CHINA**
  CENTRAL PEOPLE'S BS, Beijing
  S • DS-2 • 150 kW
  DS-2 • 150 kW
  Th-Tu • DS-2 • 150 kW

INTERNATIONAL WATERS
  CMF RADIO ONE, Middle East
  ENGLISH, ETC • Mideast • 0.25/0.5 kW
15505 **CHINA**
  CHINA R INTL, Via Bamako, Mali
  W Africa, C Africa & E Africa • 100 kW
KUWAIT
  RADIO KUWAIT, Kabd
  E Europe & W Asia • 500 kW   W Africa & C Africa • 500 kW
  Europe & E North Am • 500 kW
15510 **PHILIPPINES**
  FEBC RADIO INTL, Bocaue
  S • E Asia • 100 kW
  RADYO PILIPINAS, Tinang
  S • ENGLISH & TAGALOG • S Asia & Mideast • 250 kW
RUSSIA
  †VOICE OF RUSSIA, Samara
  S • W Asia & S Asia • 250 kW
UNITED KINGDOM
  BBC, Via Irkutsk, Russia
  W • S Asia • 250 kW
  BBC, Via Thailand
  S • S Asia • 250 kW
USA
  ADVENTIST WORLD R, Via Agat, Guam
  S • SE Asia • 100 kW   S • E Asia • 100 kW
  R FREE ASIA, Via Dhabayya, UAE
  S • S Asia • 500 kW
  †R FREE ASIA, Via Tinian, N Marianas
  S • E Asia • 250 kW
15515 **AUSTRALIA**
  †CVC, Via Armenia
  W • S Asia • 100 kW
  RADIO AUSTRALIA, Shepparton
  Pacific & N America • 100 kW   Pacific • 100 kW
CHINA (TAIWAN)
  †R TAIWAN INTL, Via Issoudun, France
  S • S Asia & SE Asia • 500 kW • ALT. FREQ. TO 11600 kHz
FRANCE
  R FRANCE INTL, Via French Guiana
  C America • 250 kW
UNITED KINGDOM
  †BBC, Rampisham
  S • W Africa & C Africa • 500 kW   S • Mideast • 500 kW
USA
  VOA, Via Udon Thani, Thailand
  W • E Asia • 500 kW
15520 **PHILIPPINES**
  †RADIO VERITAS ASIA, Palauig
  S • S Asia • 250 kW
  S Asia • 250 kW • ALT. FREQ. TO 15350 kHz
  SE Asia • 250 kW

(con'd)

| | 0 | 1 | 2 | 3 | 4 | 5 | 6 | 7 | 8 | 9 | 10 | 11 | 12 | 13 | 14 | 15 | 16 | 17 | 18 | 19 | 20 | 21 | 22 | 23 | 24 |

ENGLISH ▬   ARABIC ⌇⌇⌇   CHINESE □□□   FRENCH ▬▬   GERMAN ▬▬   RUSSIAN ═══   SPANISH ▬▬   OTHER ▬

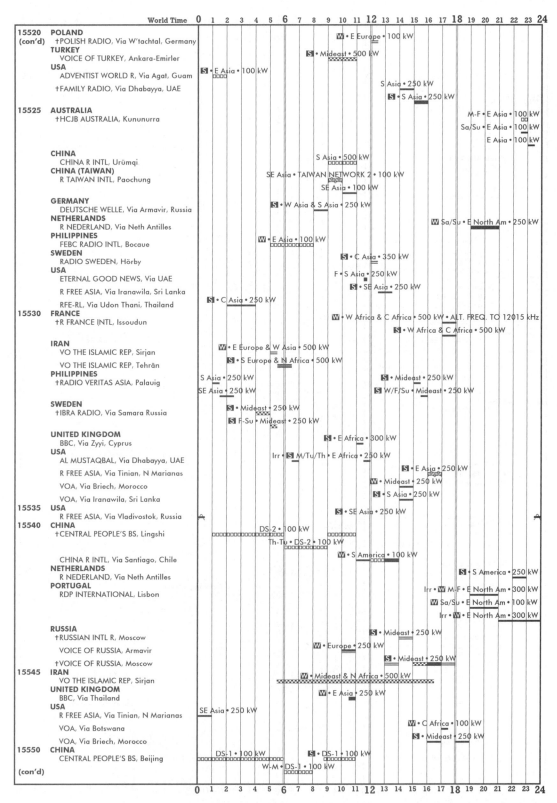

	World Time	0 1 2 3 4 5 6 7 8 9 10 11 12 13 14 15 16 17 18 19 20 21 22 23 24
15520 (con'd)	POLAND	
	†POLISH RADIO, Via W'tachtal, Germany	W • E Europe • 100 kW
	TURKEY	
	VOICE OF TURKEY, Ankara-Emirler	S • Mideast • 500 kW
	USA	
	ADVENTIST WORLD R, Via Agat, Guam	S • E Asia • 100 kW
	†FAMILY RADIO, Via Dhabayya, UAE	S Asia • 250 kW
		S • S Asia • 250 kW
15525	AUSTRALIA	
	†HCJB AUSTRALIA, Kununurra	M-F • E Asia • 100 kW
		Sa/Su • E Asia • 100 kW
		E Asia • 100 kW
	CHINA	
	CHINA R INTL, Urümqi	S Asia • 500 kW
	CHINA (TAIWAN)	
	R TAIWAN INTL, Paochung	SE Asia • TAIWAN NETWORK 2 • 100 kW
		SE Asia • 100 kW
	GERMANY	
	DEUTSCHE WELLE, Via Armavir, Russia	S • W Asia & S Asia • 250 kW
	NETHERLANDS	
	R NEDERLAND, Via Neth Antilles	W Sa/Su • E North Am • 250 kW
	PHILIPPINES	
	FEBC RADIO INTL, Bocaue	W • E Asia • 100 kW
	SWEDEN	
	RADIO SWEDEN, Hörby	S • C Asia • 350 kW
	USA	
	ETERNAL GOOD NEWS, Via UAE	F • S Asia • 250 kW
	R FREE ASIA, Via Iranawila, Sri Lanka	S • SE Asia • 250 kW
	RFE-RL, Via Udon Thani, Thailand	S • C Asia • 250 kW
15530	FRANCE	
	†R FRANCE INTL, Issoudun	W • W Africa & C Africa • 500 kW • ALT. FREQ. TO 12015 kHz
		S • W Africa & C Africa • 500 kW
	IRAN	
	VO THE ISLAMIC REP, Sirjan	W • E Europe & W Asia • 500 kW
	VO THE ISLAMIC REP, Tehrān	S • S Europe & N Africa • 500 kW
	PHILIPPINES	
	†RADIO VERITAS ASIA, Palauig	S Asia • 250 kW
		S • Mideast • 250 kW
		SE Asia • 250 kW
		W/F/Su • Mideast • 250 kW
	SWEDEN	
	†IBRA RADIO, Via Samara Russia	S • Mideast • 250 kW
		S F-Su • Mideast • 250 kW
	UNITED KINGDOM	
	BBC, Via Zyyi, Cyprus	S • E Africa • 300 kW
	USA	
	AL MUSTAQBAL, Via Dhabayya, UAE	Irr • S M/Tu/Th • E Africa • 250 kW
	R FREE ASIA, Via Tinian, N Marianas	S • E Asia • 250 kW
	VOA, Via Briech, Morocco	W • Mideast • 250 kW
	VOA, Via Iranawila, Sri Lanka	S • S Asia • 250 kW
15535	USA	
	R FREE ASIA, Via Vladivostok, Russia	S • SE Asia • 250 kW
15540	CHINA	
	†CENTRAL PEOPLE'S BS, Lingshi	DS-2 • 100 kW
		Th-Tu • DS-2 • 100 kW
	CHINA R INTL, Via Santiago, Chile	W • S America • 100 kW
	NETHERLANDS	
	R NEDERLAND, Via Neth Antilles	S • S America • 250 kW
	PORTUGAL	
	RDP INTERNATIONAL, Lisbon	Irr • W M-F • E North Am • 300 kW
		W Sa/Su • E North Am • 100 kW
		Irr • W • E North Am • 300 kW
	RUSSIA	
	†RUSSIAN INTL R, Moscow	S • Mideast • 250 kW
	VOICE OF RUSSIA, Armavir	W • Europe • 250 kW
	†VOICE OF RUSSIA, Moscow	S • Mideast • 250 kW
15545	IRAN	
	VO THE ISLAMIC REP, Sirjan	W • Mideast & N Africa • 500 kW
	UNITED KINGDOM	
	BBC, Via Thailand	W • E Asia • 250 kW
	USA	
	R FREE ASIA, Via Tinian, N Marianas	SE Asia • 250 kW
	VOA, Via Botswana	W • C Africa • 100 kW
	VOA, Via Briech, Morocco	S • Mideast • 250 kW
15550	CHINA	
	CENTRAL PEOPLE'S BS, Beijing	DS-1 • 100 kW
		S • DS-1 • 100 kW
		W-M • DS-1 • 100 kW
(con'd)		

0 1 2 3 4 5 6 7 8 9 10 11 12 13 14 15 16 17 18 19 20 21 22 23 24

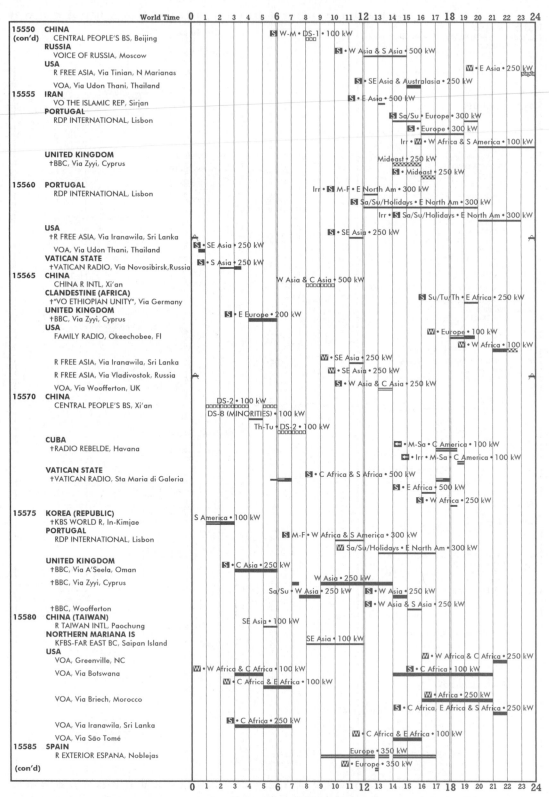

World Time 0 1 2 3 4 5 6 7 8 9 10 11 12 13 14 15 16 17 18 19 20 21 22 23 24

15550
(con'd)
CHINA
  CENTRAL PEOPLE'S BS, Beijing — S W-M • DS-1 • 100 kW
RUSSIA
  VOICE OF RUSSIA, Moscow — S • W Asia & S Asia • 500 kW
USA
  R FREE ASIA, Via Tinian, N Marianas — W • E Asia • 250 kW
  VOA, Via Udon Thani, Thailand — S • SE Asia & Australasia • 250 kW

15555
IRAN
  VO THE ISLAMIC REP, Sirjan — S • E Asia • 500 kW
PORTUGAL
  RDP INTERNATIONAL, Lisbon — S • Sa/Su • Europe • 300 kW
  — S • Europe • 300 kW
  — Irr • W • W Africa & S America • 100 kW

UNITED KINGDOM
  †BBC, Via Zyyi, Cyprus — Mideast • 250 kW
  — S • Mideast • 250 kW

15560
PORTUGAL
  RDP INTERNATIONAL, Lisbon — Irr • S • M-F • E North Am • 300 kW
  — S • Sa/Su/Holidays • E North Am • 300 kW
  — Irr • S • Sa/Su/Holidays • E North Am • 300 kW

USA
  †R FREE ASIA, Via Iranawila, Sri Lanka — S • SE Asia • 250 kW
  VOA, Via Udon Thani, Thailand — S • SE Asia • 250 kW
VATICAN STATE
  †VATICAN RADIO, Via Novosibirsk, Russia — S • S Asia • 250 kW
15565
CHINA
  CHINA R INTL, Xi'an — W Asia & C Asia • 500 kW
CLANDESTINE (AFRICA)
  †"VO ETHIOPIAN UNITY", Via Germany — S • Su/Tu/Th • E Africa • 250 kW
UNITED KINGDOM
  †BBC, Via Zyyi, Cyprus — S • E Europe • 200 kW
USA
  FAMILY RADIO, Okeechobee, Fl — W • Europe • 100 kW
  — W • W Africa • 100 kW

  R FREE ASIA, Via Iranawila, Sri Lanka — W • SE Asia • 250 kW
  R FREE ASIA, Via Vladivostok, Russia — W • SE Asia • 250 kW
  VOA, Via Woofferton, UK — S • W Asia & C Asia • 250 kW
15570
CHINA
  CENTRAL PEOPLE'S BS, Xi'an — DS-2 • 100 kW
  — DS-8 (MINORITIES) • 100 kW
  — Th-Tu • DS-2 • 100 kW

CUBA
  †RADIO REBELDE, Havana — • M-Sa • C America • 100 kW
  — • Irr • M-Sa • C America • 100 kW

VATICAN STATE
  †VATICAN RADIO, Sta Maria di Galeria — S • C Africa & S Africa • 500 kW
  — S • E Africa • 500 kW
  — S • W Africa • 250 kW

15575
KOREA (REPUBLIC)
  †KBS WORLD R, In-Kimjae — S America • 100 kW
PORTUGAL
  RDP INTERNATIONAL, Lisbon — S • M-F • W Africa & S America • 300 kW
  — W • Sa/Su/Holidays • E North Am • 300 kW

UNITED KINGDOM
  †BBC, Via A'Seela, Oman — S • C Asia • 250 kW
  †BBC, Via Zyyi, Cyprus — W Asia • 250 kW
  — Sa/Su • W Asia • 250 kW — S • W Asia • 250 kW

  †BBC, Woofferton — S • W Asia & S Asia • 250 kW
15580
CHINA (TAIWAN)
  R TAIWAN INTL, Paochung — SE Asia • 100 kW
NORTHERN MARIANA IS
  KFBS-FAR EAST BC, Saipan Island — SE Asia • 100 kW
USA
  VOA, Greenville, NC — W • W Africa & C Africa • 250 kW
  VOA, Via Botswana — W • W Africa & C Africa • 100 kW — S • C Africa • 100 kW
  — W • C Africa & E Africa • 100 kW

  VOA, Via Briech, Morocco — W • Africa • 250 kW
  — S • C Africa, E Africa & S America • 250 kW

  VOA, Via Iranawila, Sri Lanka — S • C Africa • 250 kW
  VOA, Via São Tomé — W • C Africa & E Africa • 100 kW
15585
SPAIN
  R EXTERIOR ESPANA, Noblejas — Europe • 350 kW
  — W • Europe • 350 kW
(con'd)

0 1 2 3 4 5 6 7 8 9 10 11 12 13 14 15 16 17 18 19 20 21 22 23 24

ENGLISH ▬   ARABIC ≈≈≈   CHINESE □□□   FRENCH ═══   GERMAN ▬▬   RUSSIAN ══   SPANISH ═══   OTHER ──

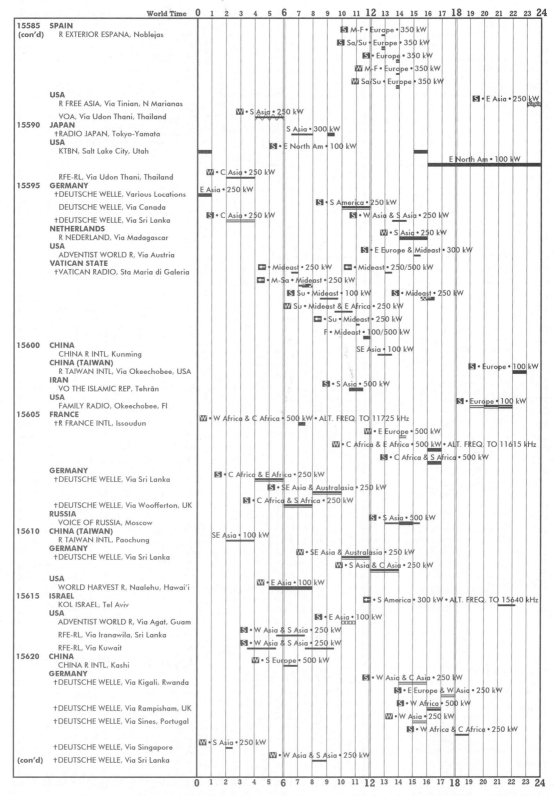

World Time	0 1 2 3 4 5 6 7 8 9 10 11 12 13 14 15 16 17 18 19 20 21 22 23 24
15585 SPAIN	
(con'd) R EXTERIOR ESPANA, Noblejas	S M-F • Europe • 350 kW
	S Sa/Su • Europe • 350 kW
	S • Europe • 350 kW
	W M-F • Europe • 350 kW
	W Sa/Su • Europe • 350 kW
USA	
R FREE ASIA, Via Tinian, N Marianas	S • E Asia • 250 kW
VOA, Via Udon Thani, Thailand	W • S Asia • 250 kW
15590 JAPAN	
†RADIO JAPAN, Tokyo-Yamata	S Asia • 300 kW
USA	
KTBN, Salt Lake City, Utah	S • E North Am • 100 kW
	E North Am • 100 kW
RFE-RL, Via Udon Thani, Thailand	W • C Asia • 250 kW
15595 GERMANY	E Asia • 250 kW
†DEUTSCHE WELLE, Various Locations	
DEUTSCHE WELLE, Via Canada	S • S America • 250 kW
†DEUTSCHE WELLE, Via Sri Lanka	S • C Asia • 250 kW / S • W Asia & S Asia • 250 kW
NETHERLANDS	
R NEDERLAND, Via Madagascar	W • S Asia • 250 kW
USA	
ADVENTIST WORLD R, Via Austria	S • E Europe & Mideast • 300 kW
VATICAN STATE	
†VATICAN RADIO, Sta Maria di Galeria	⇦ • Mideast • 250 kW / ⇦ • Mideast • 250/500 kW
	⇦ • M-Sa • Mideast • 250 kW
	S Su • Mideast • 100 kW / S • Mideast • 250 kW
	W Su • Mideast & E Africa • 250 kW
	⇦ • Su • Mideast • 250 kW
	F • Mideast • 100/500 kW
15600 CHINA	
CHINA R INTL, Kunming	SE Asia • 100 kW
CHINA (TAIWAN)	
R TAIWAN INTL, Via Okeechobee, USA	S • Europe • 100 kW
IRAN	
VO THE ISLAMIC REP, Tehrān	S • S Asia • 500 kW
USA	
FAMILY RADIO, Okeechobee, Fl	S • Europe • 100 kW
15605 FRANCE	
†R FRANCE INTL, Issoudun	W • W Africa & C Africa • 500 kW • ALT. FREQ. TO 11725 kHz
	W • E Europe • 500 kW
	W • C Africa & E Africa • 500 kW • ALT. FREQ. TO 11615 kHz
	S • C Africa & S Africa • 500 kW
GERMANY	
†DEUTSCHE WELLE, Via Sri Lanka	S • C Africa & E Africa • 250 kW
	S • SE Asia & Australasia • 250 kW
†DEUTSCHE WELLE, Via Woofferton, UK	S • C Africa & S Africa • 250 kW
RUSSIA	
VOICE OF RUSSIA, Moscow	S • S Asia • 500 kW
15610 CHINA (TAIWAN)	
R TAIWAN INTL, Paochung	SE Asia • 100 kW
GERMANY	
†DEUTSCHE WELLE, Via Sri Lanka	W • SE Asia & Australasia • 250 kW
	W • S Asia & C Asia • 250 kW
USA	
WORLD HARVEST R, Naalehu, Hawai'i	W • E Asia • 100 kW
15615 ISRAEL	
KOL ISRAEL, Tel Aviv	⇦ • S America • 300 kW • ALT. FREQ. TO 15640 kHz
USA	
ADVENTIST WORLD R, Via Agat, Guam	S • E Asia • 100 kW
RFE-RL, Via Iranawila, Sri Lanka	S • W Asia & S Asia • 250 kW
RFE-RL, Via Kuwait	S • W Asia & S Asia • 250 kW
15620 CHINA	
CHINA R INTL, Kashi	W • S Europe • 500 kW
GERMANY	
†DEUTSCHE WELLE, Via Kigali, Rwanda	S • W Asia & C Asia • 250 kW
	S • E Europe & W Asia • 250 kW
†DEUTSCHE WELLE, Via Rampisham, UK	S • W Africa • 500 kW
†DEUTSCHE WELLE, Via Sines, Portugal	W • W Asia • 250 kW
	S • W Africa & C Africa • 250 kW
†DEUTSCHE WELLE, Via Singapore	W • S Asia • 250 kW
(con'd) †DEUTSCHE WELLE, Via Sri Lanka	W • W Asia & S Asia • 250 kW

0 1 2 3 4 5 6 7 8 9 10 11 12 13 14 15 16 17 18 19 20 21 22 23 24

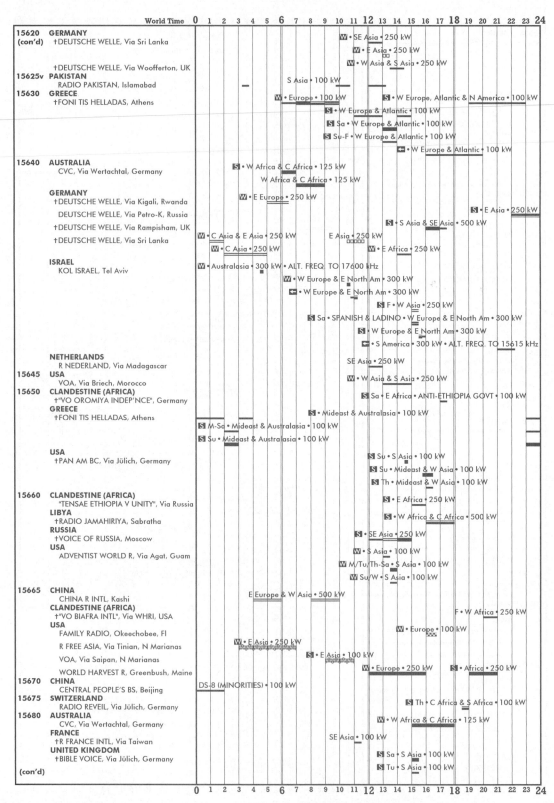

	World Time	
15620 (con'd)	**GERMANY** †DEUTSCHE WELLE, Via Sri Lanka	W•SE Asia•250 kW W•E Asia•250 kW W•W Asia & S Asia•250 kW
	†DEUTSCHE WELLE, Via Woofferton, UK	
15625v	**PAKISTAN** RADIO PAKISTAN, Islamabad	S Asia•100 kW
15630	**GREECE** †FONI TIS HELLADAS, Athens	W•Europe•100 kW S•W Europe, Atlantic & N America•100 kW S•W Europe & Atlantic•100 kW S Sa•W Europe & Atlantic•100 kW S Su-F•W Europe & Atlantic•100 kW ←•W Europe & Atlantic•100 kW
15640	**AUSTRALIA** CVC, Via Wertachtal, Germany	S•W Africa & C Africa•125 kW W Africa & C Africa•125 kW
	GERMANY †DEUTSCHE WELLE, Via Kigali, Rwanda	W•E Europe•250 kW
	DEUTSCHE WELLE, Via Petro-K, Russia	S•E Asia•250 kW
	†DEUTSCHE WELLE, Via Rampisham, UK	S•S Asia & SE Asia•500 kW
	†DEUTSCHE WELLE, Via Sri Lanka	W•C Asia & E Asia•250 kW E Asia•250 kW W•C Asia•250 kW W•E Africa•250 kW
	ISRAEL KOL ISRAEL, Tel Aviv	W•Australasia•300 kW•ALT. FREQ. TO 17600 kHz W•W Europe & E North Am•300 kW ←•W Europe & E North Am•300 kW S F•W Asia•250 kW S Sa•SPANISH & LADINO•W Europe & E North Am•300 kW S•W Europe & E North Am•300 kW ←•S America•300 kW•ALT. FREQ. TO 15615 kHz
	NETHERLANDS R NEDERLAND, Via Madagascar	SE Asia•250 kW
15645	**USA** VOA, Via Briech, Morocco	W•W Asia & S Asia•250 kW
15650	**CLANDESTINE (AFRICA)** †"VO OROMIYA INDEP'NCE", Germany	S Sa•E Africa•ANTI-ETHIOPIA GOVT•100 kW
	GREECE †FONI TIS HELLADAS, Athens	S•Mideast & Australasia•100 kW S M-Sa•Mideast & Australasia•100 kW S Su•Mideast & Australasia•100 kW
	USA †PAN AM BC, Via Jülich, Germany	S Su•S Asia•100 kW S Su•Mideast & W Asia•100 kW S Th•Mideast & W Asia•100 kW
15660	**CLANDESTINE (AFRICA)** "TENSAE ETHIOPIA V UNITY", Via Russia	S•E Africa•250 kW
	LIBYA †RADIO JAMAHIRIYA, Sabratha	S•W Africa & C Africa•500 kW
	RUSSIA †VOICE OF RUSSIA, Moscow	S•SE Asia•250 kW
	USA ADVENTIST WORLD R, Via Agat, Guam	W•S Asia•100 kW W M/Tu,Th-Sa•S Asia•100 kW W Su•W•S Asia•100 kW
15665	**CHINA** CHINA R INTL, Kashi	E Europe & W Asia•500 kW
	CLANDESTINE (AFRICA) †"VO BIAFRA INTL", Via WHRI, USA	F•W Africa•250 kW
	USA FAMILY RADIO, Okeechobee, Fl	W•Europe•100 kW
	R FREE ASIA, Via Tinian, N Marianas	W•E Asia•250 kW
	VOA, Via Saipan, N Marianas	S•E Asia•100 kW
	WORLD HARVEST R, Greenbush, Maine	W•Europe•250 kW S•Africa•250 kW
15670	**CHINA** CENTRAL PEOPLE'S BS, Beijing	DS-8 (MINORITIES)•100 kW
15675	**SWITZERLAND** RADIO REVEIL, Via Jülich, Germany	S Th•C Africa & S Africa•100 kW
15680	**AUSTRALIA** CVC, Via Wertachtal, Germany	W•W Africa & C Africa•125 kW
	FRANCE †R FRANCE INTL, Via Taiwan	SE Asia•100 kW
	UNITED KINGDOM †BIBLE VOICE, Via Jülich, Germany	S Sa•S Asia•100 kW S Tu•S Asia•100 kW
(con'd)		

ENGLISH ▬   ARABIC ⋙   CHINESE ▫▫▫   FRENCH ═   GERMAN ▬   RUSSIAN =   SPANISH ▬   OTHER —

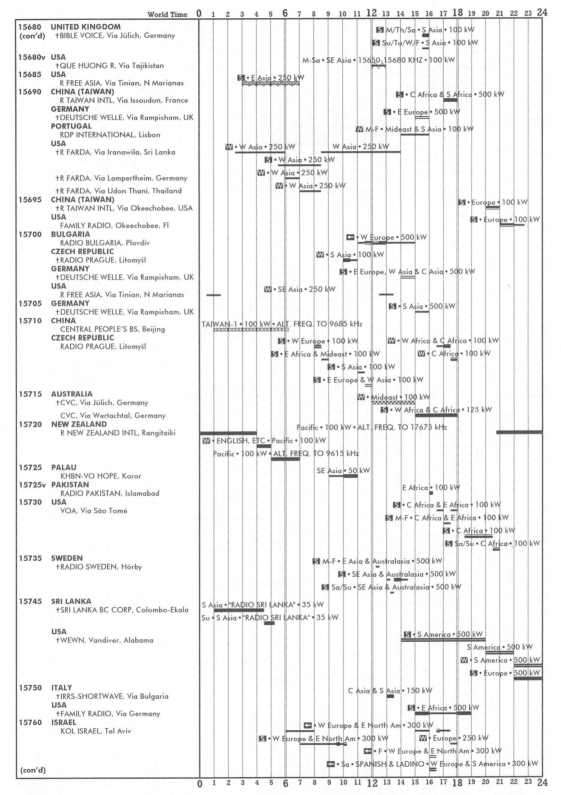

World Time

15680 (con'd)	**UNITED KINGDOM**
	†BIBLE VOICE, Via Jülich, Germany
15680v	**USA**
	†QUE HUONG R, Via Tajikistan
15685	**USA**
	R FREE ASIA, Via Tinian, N Marianas
15690	**CHINA (TAIWAN)**
	R TAIWAN INTL, Via Issoudun, France
	GERMANY
	†DEUTSCHE WELLE, Via Rampisham, UK
	PORTUGAL
	RDP INTERNATIONAL, Lisbon
	USA
	†R FARDA, Via Iranawila, Sri Lanka
	†R FARDA, Via Lampertheim, Germany
	†R FARDA, Via Udon Thani, Thailand
15695	**CHINA (TAIWAN)**
	†R TAIWAN INTL, Via Okeechobee, USA
	USA
	FAMILY RADIO, Okeechobee, Fl
15700	**BULGARIA**
	RADIO BULGARIA, Plovdiv
	CZECH REPUBLIC
	†RADIO PRAGUE, Litomyšl
	GERMANY
	†DEUTSCHE WELLE, Via Rampisham, UK
	USA
	R FREE ASIA, Via Tinian, N Marianas
15705	**GERMANY**
	†DEUTSCHE WELLE, Via Rampisham, UK
15710	**CHINA**
	CENTRAL PEOPLE'S BS, Beijing
	CZECH REPUBLIC
	RADIO PRAGUE, Litomyšl
15715	**AUSTRALIA**
	†CVC, Via Jülich, Germany
	CVC, Via Wertachtal, Germany
15720	**NEW ZEALAND**
	R NEW ZEALAND INTL, Rangitaiki
15725	**PALAU**
	KHBN-VO HOPE, Koror
15725v	**PAKISTAN**
	RADIO PAKISTAN, Islamabad
15730	**USA**
	VOA, Via São Tomé
15735	**SWEDEN**
	†RADIO SWEDEN, Hörby
15745	**SRI LANKA**
	†SRI LANKA BC CORP, Colombo-Ekala
	USA
	†WEWN, Vandiver, Alabama
15750	**ITALY**
	†IRRS-SHORTWAVE, Via Bulgaria
	USA
	†FAMILY RADIO, Via Germany
15760	**ISRAEL**
	KOL ISRAEL, Tel Aviv
(con'd)	

Program detail (read left-to-right across World Time 0–24):

- 15680 UNITED KINGDOM — †BIBLE VOICE: **S** M/Th/Sa • S Asia • 100 kW; **S** Su/Tu/W/F • S Asia • 100 kW
- 15680v USA — †QUE HUONG R: M-Sa • SE Asia • 15650-15680 KHZ • 100 kW
- 15685 USA — R FREE ASIA: **S** • E Asia • 250 kW
- 15690 CHINA (TAIWAN) — R TAIWAN INTL: **S** • C Africa & S Africa • 500 kW
- GERMANY — †DEUTSCHE WELLE: **S** • E Europe • 500 kW
- PORTUGAL — RDP INTERNATIONAL: **W** M-F • Mideast & S Asia • 100 kW
- USA — †R FARDA: **W** • W Asia • 250 kW; W Asia • 250 kW; **S** • W Asia • 250 kW
- †R FARDA, Via Lampertheim: **W** • W Asia • 250 kW
- †R FARDA, Via Udon Thani: **W** • W Asia • 250 kW
- 15695 CHINA (TAIWAN) — †R TAIWAN INTL: **S** • Europe • 100 kW
- USA — FAMILY RADIO: **S** • Europe • 100 kW
- 15700 BULGARIA — RADIO BULGARIA: ⇦ • W Europe • 500 kW
- CZECH REPUBLIC — †RADIO PRAGUE: **W** • S Asia • 100 kW
- GERMANY — †DEUTSCHE WELLE: **S** • E Europe, W Asia & C Asia • 500 kW
- USA — R FREE ASIA: **W** • SE Asia • 250 kW
- 15705 GERMANY — †DEUTSCHE WELLE: **S** • S Asia • 500 kW
- 15710 CHINA — CENTRAL PEOPLE'S BS: TAIWAN-1 • 100 kW • ALT. FREQ. TO 9685 kHz
- CZECH REPUBLIC — RADIO PRAGUE: **S** • W Europe • 100 kW; **W** • W Africa & C Africa • 100 kW; **S** • E Africa & Mideast • 100 kW; **W** • C Africa • 100 kW; **S** • S Asia • 100 kW; **S** • E Europe & W Asia • 100 kW
- 15715 AUSTRALIA — †CVC: **W** • Mideast • 100 kW; **S** • W Africa & C Africa • 125 kW
- 15720 NEW ZEALAND — R NEW ZEALAND INTL: Pacific • 100 kW • ALT. FREQ. TO 17675 kHz; **W** • ENGLISH, ETC • Pacific • 100 kW; Pacific • 100 kW • ALT. FREQ. TO 9615 kHz
- 15725 PALAU — KHBN-VO HOPE: SE Asia • 50 kW
- 15725v PAKISTAN — RADIO PAKISTAN: E Africa • 100 kW
- 15730 USA — VOA: **S** • C Africa & E Africa • 100 kW; **S** M-F • C Africa & E Africa • 100 kW; **S** • C Africa • 100 kW; **S** Sa/Su • C Africa • 100 kW
- 15735 SWEDEN — †RADIO SWEDEN: **S** M-F • E Asia & Australasia • 500 kW; **S** • SE Asia & Australasia • 500 kW; **S** Sa/Su • SE Asia & Australasia • 500 kW
- 15745 SRI LANKA — †SRI LANKA BC CORP: S Asia • "RADIO SRI LANKA" • 35 kW; Su • S Asia • "RADIO SRI LANKA" • 35 kW
- USA — †WEWN: **S** • S America • 500 kW; S America • 500 kW; **W** • S America • 500 kW; **S** • Europe • 500 kW
- 15750 ITALY — †IRRS-SHORTWAVE: C Asia & S Asia • 150 kW
- USA — †FAMILY RADIO: **S** • E Africa • 500 kW
- 15760 ISRAEL — KOL ISRAEL: ⇦ • W Europe & E North Am • 300 kW; **S** • W Europe & E North Am • 300 kW; **W** • Europe • 250 kW; ⇦ • F • W Europe & E North Am • 300 kW; ⇦ • Sa • SPANISH & LADINO • W Europe & S America • 300 kW

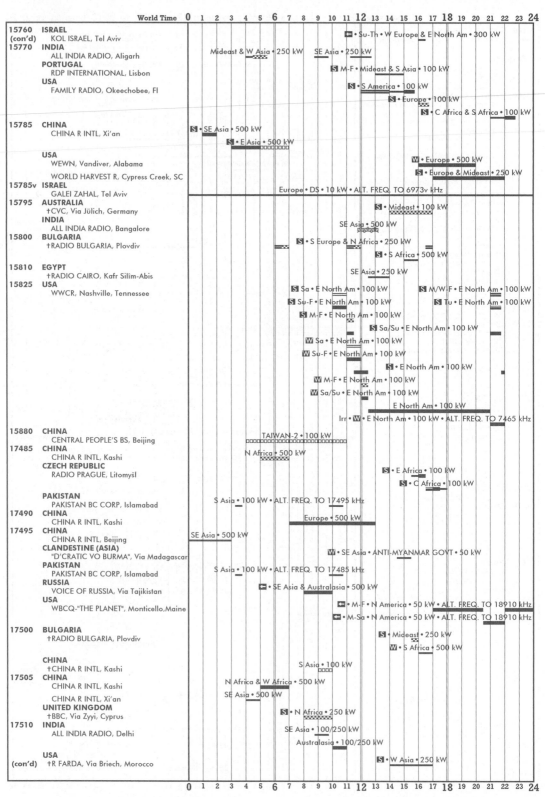

World Time	0 1 2 3 4 5 6 7 8 9 10 11 12 13 14 15 16 17 18 19 20 21 22 23 24
15760 (con'd) **ISRAEL** KOL ISRAEL, Tel Aviv	• Su-Th • W Europe & E North Am • 300 kW
15770 INDIA ALL INDIA RADIO, Aligarh	Mideast & W Asia • 250 kW SE Asia • 250 kW
PORTUGAL RDP INTERNATIONAL, Lisbon	• M-F • Mideast & S Asia • 100 kW
USA FAMILY RADIO, Okeechobee, Fl	• S America • 100 kW
	• Europe • 100 kW
	• C Africa & S Africa • 100 kW
15785 CHINA CHINA R INTL, Xi'an	• SE Asia • 500 kW
	• E Asia • 500 kW
USA WEWN, Vandiver, Alabama	• Europe • 500 kW
WORLD HARVEST R, Cypress Creek, SC	• Europe & Mideast • 250 kW
15785v ISRAEL GALEI ZAHAL, Tel Aviv	Europe • DS • 10 kW • ALT. FREQ. TO 6973v kHz
15795 AUSTRALIA †CVC, Via Jülich, Germany	• Mideast • 100 kW
INDIA ALL INDIA RADIO, Bangalore	SE Asia • 500 kW
15800 BULGARIA †RADIO BULGARIA, Plovdiv	• S Europe & N Africa • 250 kW
	• S Africa • 500 kW
15810 EGYPT †RADIO CAIRO, Kafr Silim-Abis	SE Asia • 250 kW
15825 USA WWCR, Nashville, Tennessee	Sa • E North Am • 100 kW M/W-F • E North Am • 100 kW
	Su-F • E North Am • 100 kW Tu • E North Am • 100 kW
	M-F • E North Am • 100 kW
	Sa/Su • E North Am • 100 kW
	Sa • E North Am • 100 kW
	Su-F • E North Am • 100 kW
	• E North Am • 100 kW
	M-F • E North Am • 100 kW
	Sa/Su • E North Am • 100 kW
	E North Am • 100 kW
	Irr • E North Am • 100 kW • ALT. FREQ. TO 7465 kHz
15880 CHINA CENTRAL PEOPLE'S BS, Beijing	TAIWAN-2 • 100 kW
17485 CHINA CHINA R INTL, Kashi	N Africa • 500 kW
CZECH REPUBLIC RADIO PRAGUE, Litomyšl	• E Africa • 100 kW
	• C Africa • 100 kW
PAKISTAN PAKISTAN BC CORP, Islamabad	S Asia • 100 kW • ALT. FREQ. TO 17495 kHz
17490 CHINA CHINA R INTL, Kashi	Europe • 500 kW
17495 CHINA CHINA R INTL, Beijing	SE Asia • 500 kW
CLANDESTINE (ASIA) "D'CRATIC VO BURMA", Via Madagascar	• SE Asia • ANTI-MYANMAR GOVT • 50 kW
PAKISTAN PAKISTAN BC CORP, Islamabad	S Asia • 100 kW • ALT. FREQ. TO 17485 kHz
RUSSIA VOICE OF RUSSIA, Via Tajikistan	• SE Asia & Australasia • 500 kW
USA WBCQ-"THE PLANET", Monticello, Maine	• M-F • N America • 50 kW • ALT. FREQ. TO 18910 kHz
	• M-Sa • N America • 50 kW • ALT. FREQ. TO 18910 kHz
17500 BULGARIA †RADIO BULGARIA, Plovdiv	• Mideast • 250 kW
	• S Africa • 500 kW
CHINA †CHINA R INTL, Kashi	S Asia • 100 kW
17505 CHINA CHINA R INTL, Kashi	N Africa & W Africa • 500 kW
CHINA R INTL, Xi'an	SE Asia • 500 kW
UNITED KINGDOM †BBC, Via Zyyi, Cyprus	• N Africa • 250 kW
17510 INDIA ALL INDIA RADIO, Delhi	SE Asia • 100/250 kW
	Australasia • 100/250 kW
USA (con'd) †R FARDA, Via Briech, Morocco	• W Asia • 250 kW

0 1 2 3 4 5 6 7 8 9 10 11 12 13 14 15 16 17 18 19 20 21 22 23 24

ENGLISH ▬ ARABIC ≋ CHINESE ▫▫▫ FRENCH ▬ GERMAN ▬ RUSSIAN ═ SPANISH ▬ OTHER ▬

World Time 0 1 2 3 4 5 6 7 8 9 10 11 12 13 14 15 16 17 18 19 20 21 22 23 24

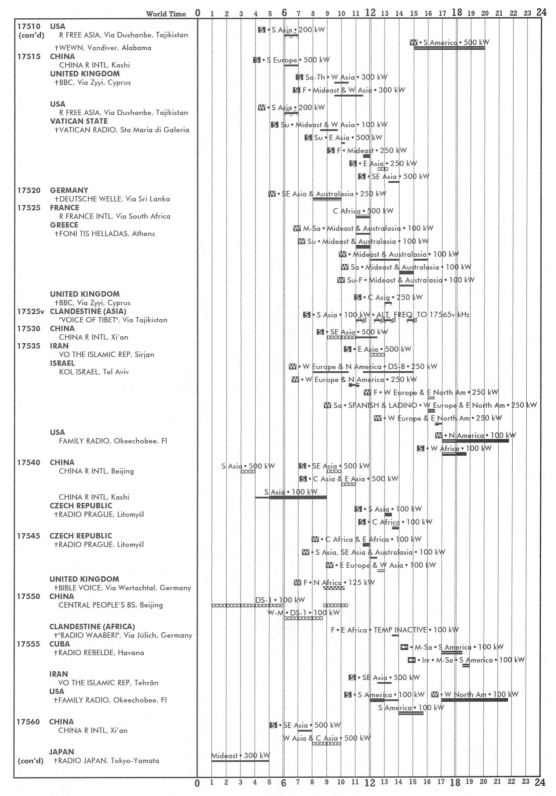

17510 (con'd)	**USA** R FREE ASIA, Via Dushanbe, Tajikistan	S • S Asia • 200 kW
	†WEWN, Vandiver, Alabama	W • S America • 500 kW
17515	**CHINA** CHINA R INTL, Kashi	S • S Europe • 500 kW
	UNITED KINGDOM †BBC, Via Zyyi, Cyprus	S • Sa-Th • W Asia • 300 kW
		S • F • Mideast & W Asia • 300 kW
	USA R FREE ASIA, Via Dushanbe, Tajikistan	W • S Asia • 200 kW
	VATICAN STATE †VATICAN RADIO, Sta Maria di Galeria	S • Su • Mideast & W Asia • 100 kW
		S • Su • E Asia • 500 kW
		S • F • Mideast • 250 kW
		S • E Asia • 250 kW
		S • SE Asia • 500 kW
17520	**GERMANY** †DEUTSCHE WELLE, Via Sri Lanka	W • SE Asia & Australasia • 250 kW
17525	**FRANCE** R FRANCE INTL, Via South Africa	C Africa • 500 kW
	GREECE †FONI TIS HELLADAS, Athens	W • M-Sa • Mideast & Australasia • 100 kW
		W • Su • Mideast & Australasia • 100 kW
		W • Mideast & Australasia • 100 kW
		W • Sa • Mideast & Australasia • 100 kW
		W • Su-F • Mideast & Australasia • 100 kW
	UNITED KINGDOM †BBC, Via Zyyi, Cyprus	S • C Asia • 250 kW
17525v	**CLANDESTINE (ASIA)** "VOICE OF TIBET", Via Tajikistan	S • S Asia • 100 kW • ALT. FREQ. TO 17565v kHz
17530	**CHINA** CHINA R INTL, Xi'an	S • SE Asia • 500 kW
17535	**IRAN** VO THE ISLAMIC REP, Sirjan	S • E Asia • 500 kW
	ISRAEL KOL ISRAEL, Tel Aviv	W • W Europe & N America • DS-B • 250 kW
		W • W Europe & N America • 250 kW
		W • F • W Europe & E North Am • 250 kW
		W • Sa • SPANISH & LADINO • W Europe & E North Am • 250 kW
		W • W Europe & E North Am • 250 kW
	USA FAMILY RADIO, Okeechobee, Fl	W • N America • 100 kW
		S • W Africa • 100 kW
17540	**CHINA** CHINA R INTL, Beijing	S Asia • 500 kW
		S • SE Asia • 500 kW
		S • C Asia & E Asia • 500 kW
	CHINA R INTL, Kashi	S Asia • 100 kW
	CZECH REPUBLIC †RADIO PRAGUE, Litomyšl	S • S Asia • 100 kW
		S • C Africa • 100 kW
17545	**CZECH REPUBLIC** †RADIO PRAGUE, Litomyšl	W • C Africa & E Africa • 100 kW
		W • S Asia, SE Asia & Australasia • 100 kW
		W • E Europe & W Asia • 100 kW
	UNITED KINGDOM †BIBLE VOICE, Via Wertachtal, Germany	W • F • N Africa • 125 kW
17550	**CHINA** CENTRAL PEOPLE'S BS, Beijing	DS-1 • 100 kW
		W-M • DS-1 • 100 kW
	CLANDESTINE (AFRICA) †"RADIO WAABERI", Via Jülich, Germany	F • E Africa • TEMP INACTIVE • 100 kW
17555	**CUBA** †RADIO REBELDE, Havana	M-Sa • S America • 100 kW
		Irr • M-Sa • S America • 100 kW
	IRAN VO THE ISLAMIC REP, Tehrān	S • SE Asia • 500 kW
	USA †FAMILY RADIO, Okeechobee, Fl	S • S America • 100 kW
		W • W North Am • 100 kW
		S America • 100 kW
17560	**CHINA** CHINA R INTL, Xi'an	S • SE Asia • 500 kW
		W Asia & C Asia • 500 kW
(con'd)	**JAPAN** †RADIO JAPAN, Tokyo-Yamata	Mideast • 300 kW

0 1 2 3 4 5 6 7 8 9 10 11 12 13 14 15 16 17 18 19 20 21 22 23 24

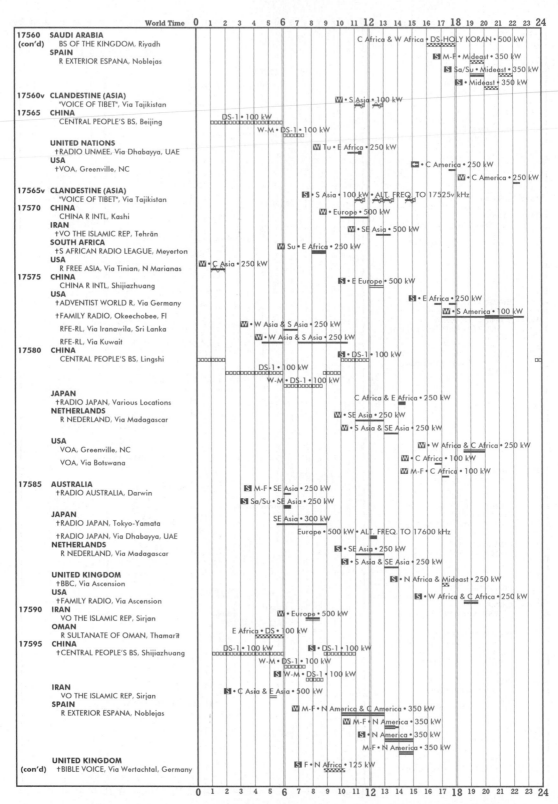

| World Time | 0 | 1 | 2 | 3 | 4 | 5 | 6 | 7 | 8 | 9 | 10 | 11 | 12 | 13 | 14 | 15 | 16 | 17 | 18 | 19 | 20 | 21 | 22 | 23 | 24 |

17560 SAUDI ARABIA
(con'd) BS OF THE KINGDOM, Riyadh — C Africa & W Africa • DS-HOLY KORAN • 500 kW

SPAIN
  R EXTERIOR ESPANA, Noblejas — S M-F • Mideast • 350 kW
  S Sa/Su • Mideast • 350 kW
  S • Mideast • 350 kW

17560v CLANDESTINE (ASIA)
  "VOICE OF TIBET", Via Tajikistan — W • S Asia • 100 kW

17565 CHINA
  CENTRAL PEOPLE'S BS, Beijing — DS-1 • 100 kW
  W-M • DS-1 • 100 kW

UNITED NATIONS
  †RADIO UNMEE, Via Dhabayya, UAE — W Tu • E Africa • 250 kW

USA
  †VOA, Greenville, NC — • C America • 250 kW
  W • C America • 250 kW

17565v CLANDESTINE (ASIA)
  "VOICE OF TIBET", Via Tajikistan — S • S Asia • 100 kW • ALT. FREQ. TO 17525v kHz

17570 CHINA
  CHINA R INTL, Kashi — W • Europe • 500 kW

IRAN
  †VO THE ISLAMIC REP, Tehrān — W • SE Asia • 500 kW

SOUTH AFRICA
  †S AFRICAN RADIO LEAGUE, Meyerton — W Su • E Africa • 250 kW

USA
  R FREE ASIA, Via Tinian, N Marianas — W • C Asia • 250 kW

17575 CHINA
  CHINA R INTL, Shijiazhuang — S • E Europe • 500 kW

USA
  †ADVENTIST WORLD R, Via Germany — S • E Africa • 250 kW
  †FAMILY RADIO, Okeechobee, Fl — W • S America • 100 kW
  RFE-RL, Via Iranawila, Sri Lanka — W • W Asia & S Asia • 250 kW
  RFE-RL, Via Kuwait — W • W Asia & S Asia • 250 kW

17580 CHINA
  CENTRAL PEOPLE'S BS, Lingshi — S • DS-1 • 100 kW
  DS-1 • 100 kW
  W-M • DS-1 • 100 kW

JAPAN
  †RADIO JAPAN, Various Locations — C Africa & E Africa • 250 kW

NETHERLANDS
  R NEDERLAND, Via Madagascar — W • SE Asia • 250 kW
  W • S Asia & SE Asia • 250 kW

USA
  VOA, Greenville, NC — W • W Africa & C Africa • 250 kW
  VOA, Via Botswana — W • C Africa • 100 kW
  W M-F • C Africa • 100 kW

17585 AUSTRALIA
  †RADIO AUSTRALIA, Darwin — S M-F • SE Asia • 250 kW
  S Sa/Su • SE Asia • 250 kW

JAPAN
  †RADIO JAPAN, Tokyo-Yamata — SE Asia • 300 kW
  †RADIO JAPAN, Via Dhabayya, UAE — Europe • 500 kW • ALT. FREQ. TO 17600 kHz

NETHERLANDS
  R NEDERLAND, Via Madagascar — S • SE Asia • 250 kW
  S • S Asia & SE Asia • 250 kW

UNITED KINGDOM
  †BBC, Via Ascension — S • N Africa & Mideast • 250 kW

USA
  †FAMILY RADIO, Via Ascension — S • W Africa & C Africa • 250 kW

17590 IRAN
  VO THE ISLAMIC REP, Sirjan — W • Europe • 500 kW

OMAN
  R SULTANATE OF OMAN, Thamarīt — E Africa • DS • 100 kW

17595 CHINA
  †CENTRAL PEOPLE'S BS, Shijiazhuang — DS-1 • 100 kW
  S • DS-1 • 100 kW
  W-M • DS-1 • 100 kW
  S W-M • DS-1 • 100 kW

IRAN
  VO THE ISLAMIC REP, Sirjan — S • C Asia & E Asia • 500 kW

SPAIN
  R EXTERIOR ESPANA, Noblejas — W M-F • N America & C America • 350 kW
  W M-F • N America • 350 kW
  S • N America • 350 kW
  M-F • N America • 350 kW

UNITED KINGDOM
(con'd) †BIBLE VOICE, Via Wertachtal, Germany — S F • N Africa • 125 kW

| | 0 | 1 | 2 | 3 | 4 | 5 | 6 | 7 | 8 | 9 | 10 | 11 | 12 | 13 | 14 | 15 | 16 | 17 | 18 | 19 | 20 | 21 | 22 | 23 | 24 |

ENGLISH ▪▪ ARABIC ⌇⌇ CHINESE □□□ FRENCH ▬▬ GERMAN ══ RUSSIAN ═══ SPANISH ▬▬ OTHER ──

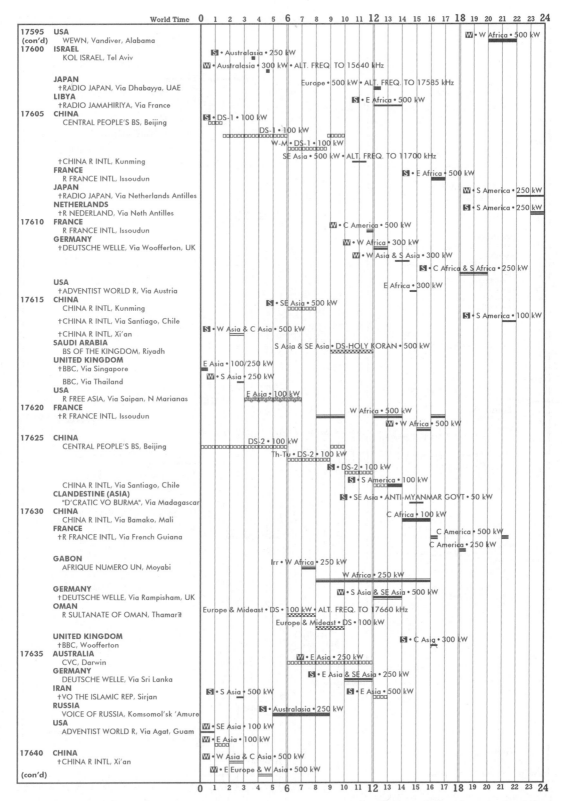

World Time 0 1 2 3 4 5 6 7 8 9 10 11 12 13 14 15 16 17 18 19 20 21 22 23 24

17595 **USA**
(con'd) WEWN, Vandiver, Alabama — W • W Africa • 500 kW
17600 **ISRAEL**
KOL ISRAEL, Tel Aviv — S • Australasia • 250 kW
— W • Australasia • 300 kW • ALT. FREQ. TO 15640 kHz

JAPAN
†RADIO JAPAN, Via Dhabayya, UAE — Europe • 500 kW • ALT. FREQ. TO 17585 kHz
LIBYA
†RADIO JAMAHIRIYA, Via France — S • E Africa • 500 kW
17605 **CHINA**
CENTRAL PEOPLE'S BS, Beijing — S • DS-1 • 100 kW
— DS-1 • 100 kW
— W-M • DS-1 • 100 kW
— SE Asia • 500 kW • ALT. FREQ. TO 11700 kHz

†CHINA R INTL, Kunming
FRANCE
R FRANCE INTL, Issoudun — S • E Africa • 500 kW
JAPAN
†RADIO JAPAN, Via Netherlands Antilles — W • S America • 250 kW
NETHERLANDS
†R NEDERLAND, Via Neth Antilles — S • S America • 250 kW
17610 **FRANCE**
R FRANCE INTL, Issoudun — W • C America • 500 kW
GERMANY
†DEUTSCHE WELLE, Via Woofferton, UK — W • W Africa • 300 kW
— W • W Asia & S Asia • 300 kW
— S • C Africa & S Africa • 250 kW

USA
†ADVENTIST WORLD R, Via Austria — E Africa • 300 kW
17615 **CHINA**
CHINA R INTL, Kunming — S • SE Asia • 500 kW

†CHINA R INTL, Via Santiago, Chile — S • S America • 100 kW

†CHINA R INTL, Xi'an — S • W Asia & C Asia • 500 kW
SAUDI ARABIA
BS OF THE KINGDOM, Riyadh — S Asia & SE Asia • DS-HOLY KORAN • 500 kW
UNITED KINGDOM
†BBC, Via Singapore — E Asia • 100/250 kW

BBC, Via Thailand — W • S Asia • 250 kW
USA
R FREE ASIA, Via Saipan, N Marianas — E Asia • 100 kW
17620 **FRANCE**
†R FRANCE INTL, Issoudun — W Africa • 500 kW
— W • W Africa • 500 kW
17625 **CHINA**
CENTRAL PEOPLE'S BS, Beijing — DS-2 • 100 kW
— Th-Tu • DS-2 • 100 kW
— S • DS-2 • 100 kW

CHINA R INTL, Via Santiago, Chile — S • S America • 100 kW
CLANDESTINE (ASIA)
"D'CRATIC VO BURMA", Via Madagascar — S • SE Asia • ANTI-MYANMAR GOVT • 50 kW
17630 **CHINA**
CHINA R INTL, Via Bamako, Mali — C Africa • 100 kW
FRANCE
†R FRANCE INTL, Via French Guiana — C America • 500 kW
— C America • 250 kW

GABON
AFRIQUE NUMERO UN, Moyabi — Irr • W Africa • 250 kW
— W Africa • 250 kW

GERMANY
†DEUTSCHE WELLE, Via Rampisham, UK — W • S Asia & SE Asia • 500 kW
OMAN
R SULTANATE OF OMAN, Thamarīt — Europe & Mideast • DS • 100 kW • ALT. FREQ. TO 17660 kHz
— Europe & Mideast • DS • 100 kW

UNITED KINGDOM
†BBC, Woofferton — S • C Asia • 300 kW
17635 **AUSTRALIA**
CVC, Darwin — W • E Asia • 250 kW
GERMANY
DEUTSCHE WELLE, Via Sri Lanka — S • E Asia & SE Asia • 250 kW
IRAN
†VO THE ISLAMIC REP, Sirjan — S • S Asia • 500 kW — S • E Asia • 500 kW
RUSSIA
VOICE OF RUSSIA, Komsomol'sk 'Amure — S • Australasia • 250 kW
USA
ADVENTIST WORLD R, Via Agat, Guam — W • SE Asia • 100 kW
— W • E Asia • 100 kW

17640 **CHINA**
†CHINA R INTL, Xi'an — W • W Asia & C Asia • 500 kW
(con'd) — W • E Europe & W Asia • 500 kW

0 1 2 3 4 5 6 7 8 9 10 11 12 13 14 15 16 17 18 19 20 21 22 23 24

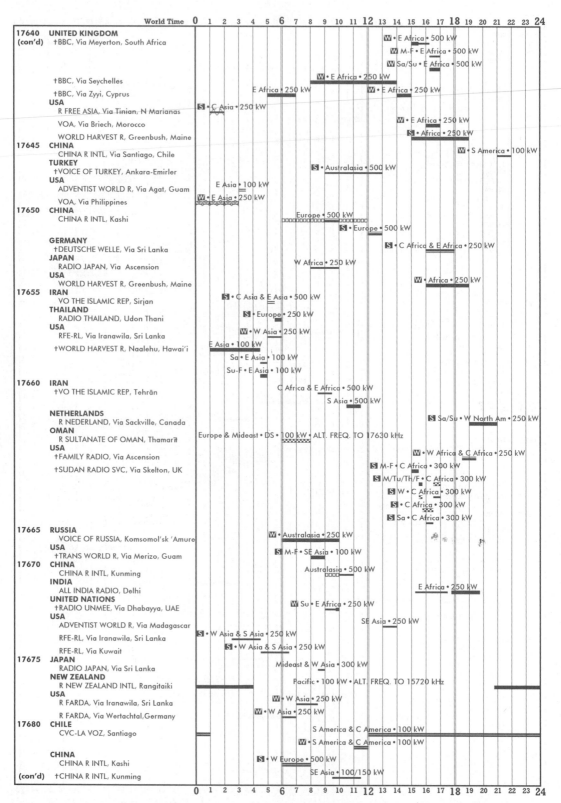

World Time	0 1 2 3 4 5 6 7 8 9 10 11 12 13 14 15 16 17 18 19 20 21 22 23 24
17640 **UNITED KINGDOM**	
(con'd) †BBC, Via Meyerton, South Africa	W • E Africa • 500 kW
	W M-F • E Africa • 500 kW
	W Sa/Su • E Africa • 500 kW
†BBC, Via Seychelles	W • E Africa • 250 kW
†BBC, Via Zyyi, Cyprus	E Africa • 250 kW W • E Africa • 250 kW
USA	
R FREE ASIA, Via Tinian, N Marianas	S • C Asia • 250 kW
VOA, Via Briech, Morocco	W • E Africa • 250 kW
WORLD HARVEST R, Greenbush, Maine	S • Africa • 250 kW
17645 **CHINA**	
CHINA R INTL, Via Santiago, Chile	W • S America • 100 kW
TURKEY	
†VOICE OF TURKEY, Ankara-Emirler	S • Australasia • 500 kW
USA	
ADVENTIST WORLD R, Via Agat, Guam	E Asia • 100 kW
VOA, Via Philippines	W • E Asia • 250 kW
17650 **CHINA**	
CHINA R INTL, Kashi	Europe • 500 kW
	S • Europe • 500 kW
GERMANY	
†DEUTSCHE WELLE, Via Sri Lanka	S • C Africa & E Africa • 250 kW
JAPAN	
RADIO JAPAN, Via Ascension	W Africa • 250 kW
USA	
WORLD HARVEST R, Greenbush, Maine	W • Africa • 250 kW
17655 **IRAN**	
VO THE ISLAMIC REP, Sirjan	S • C Asia & E Asia • 500 kW
THAILAND	
RADIO THAILAND, Udon Thani	S • Europe • 250 kW
USA	
RFE-RL, Via Iranawila, Sri Lanka	W • W Asia • 250 kW
†WORLD HARVEST R, Naalehu, Hawai'i	E Asia • 100 kW
	Sa • E Asia • 100 kW
	Su-F • E Asia • 100 kW
17660 **IRAN**	
†VO THE ISLAMIC REP, Tehrān	C Africa & E Africa • 500 kW
	S Asia • 500 kW
NETHERLANDS	
R NEDERLAND, Via Sackville, Canada	S Sa/Su • W North Am • 250 kW
OMAN	
R SULTANATE OF OMAN, Thamarīt	Europe & Mideast • DS • 100 kW • ALT. FREQ. TO 17630 kHz
USA	
†FAMILY RADIO, Via Ascension	W • W Africa & C Africa • 250 kW
†SUDAN RADIO SVC, Via Skelton, UK	S M-F • C Africa • 300 kW
	S M/Tu/Th/F • C Africa • 300 kW
	S W • C Africa • 300 kW
	S • C Africa • 300 kW
	S Sa • C Africa • 300 kW
17665 **RUSSIA**	
VOICE OF RUSSIA, Komsomol'sk 'Amure	W • Australasia • 250 kW
USA	
†TRANS WORLD R, Via Merizo, Guam	S M-F • SE Asia • 100 kW
17670 **CHINA**	
CHINA R INTL, Kunming	Australasia • 500 kW
INDIA	
ALL INDIA RADIO, Delhi	E Africa • 250 kW
UNITED NATIONS	
†RADIO UNMEE, Via Dhabayya, UAE	W Su • E Africa • 250 kW
USA	
ADVENTIST WORLD R, Via Madagascar	SE Asia • 250 kW
RFE-RL, Via Iranawila, Sri Lanka	S • W Asia & S Asia • 250 kW
RFE-RL, Via Kuwait	S • W Asia & S Asia • 250 kW
17675 **JAPAN**	
RADIO JAPAN, Via Sri Lanka	Mideast & W Asia • 300 kW
NEW ZEALAND	
R NEW ZEALAND INTL, Rangitaiki	Pacific • 100 kW • ALT. FREQ. TO 15720 kHz
USA	
R FARDA, Via Iranawila, Sri Lanka	W • W Asia • 250 kW
R FARDA, Via Wertachtal, Germany	W • W Asia • 250 kW
17680 **CHILE**	
CVC-LA VOZ, Santiago	S America & C America • 100 kW
	W • S America & C America • 100 kW
CHINA	
CHINA R INTL, Kashi	S • W Europe • 500 kW
(con'd) †CHINA R INTL, Kunming	SE Asia • 100/150 kW

0 1 2 3 4 5 6 7 8 9 10 11 12 13 14 15 16 17 18 19 20 21 22 23 24

ENGLISH ▬   ARABIC ⌇⌇⌇   CHINESE ▫▫▫   FRENCH ▬   GERMAN ▬   RUSSIAN ═   SPANISH ▬   OTHER ▬

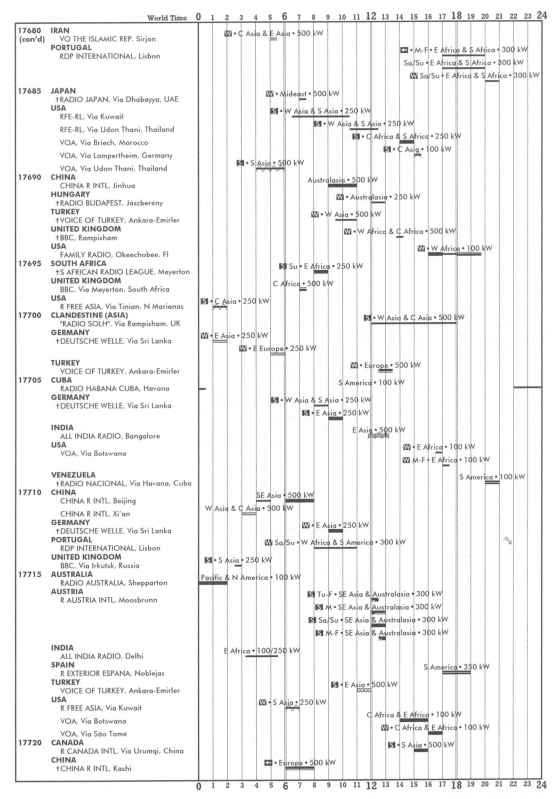

kHz	Station	
17680 (con'd)	IRAN	VO THE ISLAMIC REP, Sirjan — W • C Asia & E Asia • 500 kW
	PORTUGAL	RDP INTERNATIONAL, Lisbon — ⬅ • M-F • E Africa & S Africa • 300 kW; Sa/Su • E Africa & S Africa • 300 kW; W Sa/Su • E Africa & S Africa • 300 kW
17685	JAPAN	†RADIO JAPAN, Via Dhabayya, UAE — W • Mideast • 500 kW
	USA	RFE-RL, Via Kuwait — S • W Asia & S Asia • 250 kW
		RFE-RL, Via Udon Thani, Thailand — S • W Asia & S Asia • 250 kW
		VOA, Via Briech, Morocco — S • C Africa & S Africa • 250 kW
		VOA, Via Lampertheim, Germany — S • C Asia • 100 kW
		VOA, Via Udon Thani, Thailand — S • S Asia • 500 kW
17690	CHINA	CHINA R INTL, Jinhua — Australasia • 500 kW
	HUNGARY	†RADIO BUDAPEST, Jászberény — W • Australasia • 250 kW
	TURKEY	†VOICE OF TURKEY, Ankara-Emirler — W • W Asia • 500 kW
	UNITED KINGDOM	†BBC, Rampisham — W • W Africa & C Africa • 500 kW
	USA	FAMILY RADIO, Okeechobee, Fl — W • W Africa • 100 kW
17695	SOUTH AFRICA	†S AFRICAN RADIO LEAGUE, Meyerton — S Su • E Africa • 250 kW
	UNITED KINGDOM	BBC, Via Meyerton, South Africa — C Africa • 500 kW
	USA	R FREE ASIA, Via Tinian, N Marianas — S • C Asia • 250 kW
17700	CLANDESTINE (ASIA)	"RADIO SOLH", Via Rampisham, UK — S • W Asia & C Asia • 500 kW
	GERMANY	†DEUTSCHE WELLE, Via Sri Lanka — W • E Asia • 250 kW; W • E Europe • 250 kW
	TURKEY	VOICE OF TURKEY, Ankara-Emirler — W • Europe • 500 kW
17705	CUBA	RADIO HABANA CUBA, Havana — S America • 100 kW
	GERMANY	†DEUTSCHE WELLE, Via Sri Lanka — S • W Asia & S Asia • 250 kW; S • E Asia • 250 kW
	INDIA	ALL INDIA RADIO, Bangalore — E Asia • 500 kW
	USA	VOA, Via Botswana — W • E Africa • 100 kW; W M-F • E Africa • 100 kW
	VENEZUELA	†RADIO NACIONAL, Via Havana, Cuba — S America • 100 kW
17710	CHINA	CHINA R INTL, Beijing — SE Asia • 500 kW
		CHINA R INTL, Xi'an — W Asia & C Asia • 500 kW
	GERMANY	†DEUTSCHE WELLE, Via Sri Lanka — W • E Asia • 250 kW
	PORTUGAL	RDP INTERNATIONAL, Lisbon — W Sa/Su • W Africa & S America • 300 kW
	UNITED KINGDOM	BBC, Via Irkutsk, Russia — S • S Asia • 250 kW
17715	AUSTRALIA	RADIO AUSTRALIA, Shepparton — Pacific & N America • 100 kW
	AUSTRIA	R AUSTRIA INTL, Moosbrunn — S Tu-F • SE Asia & Australasia • 300 kW; S M • SE Asia & Australasia • 300 kW; S Sa/Su • SE Asia & Australasia • 300 kW; S M-F • SE Asia & Australasia • 300 kW
	INDIA	ALL INDIA RADIO, Delhi — E Africa • 100/250 kW
	SPAIN	R EXTERIOR ESPANA, Noblejas — S America • 350 kW
	TURKEY	VOICE OF TURKEY, Ankara-Emirler — S • E Asia • 500 kW
	USA	R FREE ASIA, Via Kuwait — W • S Asia • 250 kW
		VOA, Via Botswana — C Africa & E Africa • 100 kW
		VOA, Via São Tomé — W • C Africa & E Africa • 100 kW
17720	CANADA	R CANADA INTL, Via Urumqi, China — S • S Asia • 500 kW
	CHINA	†CHINA R INTL, Kashi — ⬅ • Europe • 500 kW

SEASONAL ⓢ OR ⓦ   1-HR TIMESHIFT MIDYEAR ⬅ OR ➡   JAMMING / OR ∧   EARLIEST HEARD ◁   LATEST HEARD ▷   NEW FOR 2008 †

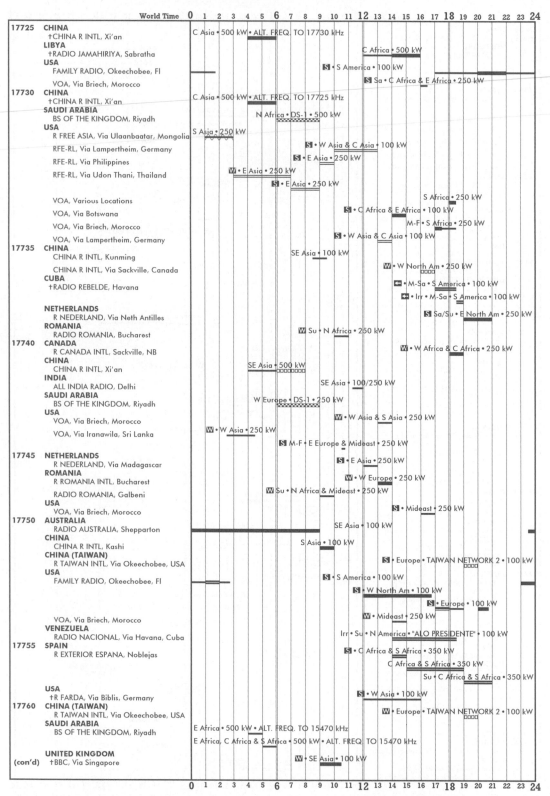

World Time							
17725	**CHINA** †CHINA R INTL, Xi'an	C Asia • 500 kW • ALT. FREQ. TO 17730 kHz					
	LIBYA †RADIO JAMAHIRIYA, Sabratha			C Africa • 500 kW			
	USA FAMILY RADIO, Okeechobee, Fl	S • S America • 100 kW					
	VOA, Via Briech, Morocco	Sa • C Africa & E Africa • 250 kW					
17730	**CHINA** †CHINA R INTL, Xi'an	C Asia • 500 kW • ALT. FREQ. TO 17725 kHz					
	SAUDI ARABIA BS OF THE KINGDOM, Riyadh	N Africa • DS-1 • 500 kW					
	USA R FREE ASIA, Via Ulaanbaatar, Mongolia	S Asia • 250 kW					
	RFE-RL, Via Lampertheim, Germany	S • W Asia & C Asia • 100 kW					
	RFE-RL, Via Philippines	S • E Asia • 250 kW					
	RFE-RL, Via Udon Thani, Thailand	W • E Asia • 250 kW					
		S • E Asia • 250 kW					
	VOA, Various Locations	S Africa • 250 kW					
	VOA, Via Botswana	S • C Africa & E Africa • 100 kW					
	VOA, Via Briech, Morocco	M-F • S Africa • 250 kW					
	VOA, Via Lampertheim, Germany	S • W Asia & C Asia • 100 kW					
17735	**CHINA** CHINA R INTL, Kunming	SE Asia • 100 kW					
	CHINA R INTL, Via Sackville, Canada	W • W North Am • 250 kW					
	CUBA †RADIO REBELDE, Havana	M-Sa • S America • 100 kW					
		Irr • M-Sa • S America • 100 kW					
	NETHERLANDS R NEDERLAND, Via Neth Antilles	S • Sa/Su • E North Am • 250 kW					
	ROMANIA RADIO ROMANIA, Bucharest	W • Su • N Africa • 250 kW					
17740	**CANADA** R CANADA INTL, Sackville, NB	W • W Africa & C Africa • 250 kW					
	CHINA CHINA R INTL, Xi'an	SE Asia • 500 kW					
	INDIA ALL INDIA RADIO, Delhi	SE Asia • 100/250 kW					
	SAUDI ARABIA BS OF THE KINGDOM, Riyadh	W Europe • DS-1 • 250 kW					
	USA VOA, Via Briech, Morocco	W • W Asia & S Asia • 250 kW					
	VOA, Via Iranawila, Sri Lanka	W • W Asia • 250 kW					
		S • M-F • E Europe & Mideast • 250 kW					
17745	**NETHERLANDS** R NEDERLAND, Via Madagascar	S • E Asia • 250 kW					
	ROMANIA R ROMANIA INTL, Bucharest	W • W Europe • 250 kW					
	RADIO ROMANIA, Galbeni	W • Su • N Africa & Mideast • 250 kW					
	USA VOA, Via Briech, Morocco	S • Mideast • 250 kW					
17750	**AUSTRALIA** RADIO AUSTRALIA, Shepparton	SE Asia • 100 kW					
	CHINA CHINA R INTL, Kashi	S Asia • 100 kW					
	CHINA (TAIWAN) R TAIWAN INTL, Via Okeechobee, USA	S • Europe • TAIWAN NETWORK 2 • 100 kW					
	USA FAMILY RADIO, Okeechobee, Fl	S • S America • 100 kW					
		S • W North Am • 100 kW					
		S • Europe • 100 kW					
	VOA, Via Briech, Morocco	W • Mideast • 250 kW					
	VENEZUELA RADIO NACIONAL, Via Havana, Cuba	Irr • Su • N America • "ALO PRESIDENTE" • 100 kW					
17755	**SPAIN** R EXTERIOR ESPANA, Noblejas	S • C Africa & S Africa • 350 kW					
		C Africa & S Africa • 350 kW					
		Su • C Africa & S Africa • 350 kW					
	USA †R FARDA, Via Biblis, Germany	S • W Asia • 100 kW					
17760	**CHINA (TAIWAN)** R TAIWAN INTL, Via Okeechobee, USA	W • Europe • TAIWAN NETWORK 2 • 100 kW					
	SAUDI ARABIA BS OF THE KINGDOM, Riyadh	E Africa • 500 kW • ALT. FREQ. TO 15470 kHz					
		E Africa, C Africa & S Africa • 500 kW • ALT. FREQ. TO 15470 kHz					
(con'd)	**UNITED KINGDOM** †BBC, Via Singapore	W • SE Asia • 100 kW					

ENGLISH ▬   ARABIC ∼∼∼   CHINESE □□□   FRENCH ▬▬   GERMAN ▬▬   RUSSIAN ══   SPANISH ▬▬   OTHER ▬

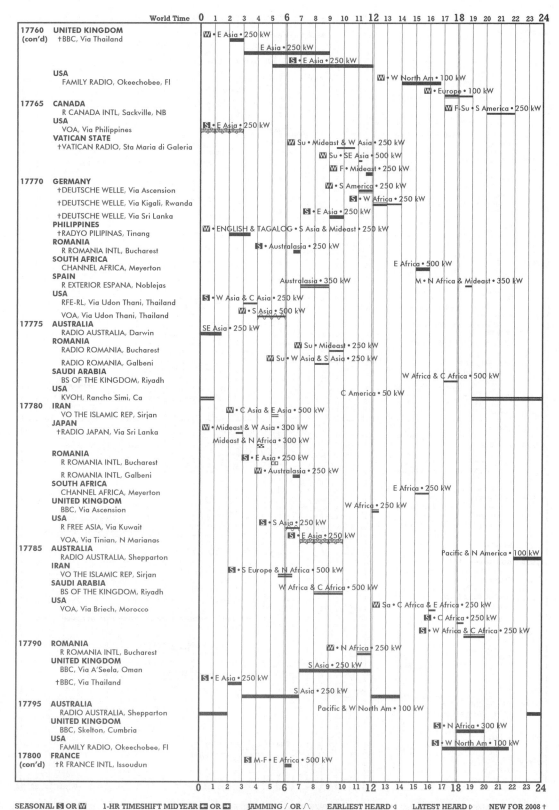

World Time	0 1 2 3 4 5 6 7 8 9 10 11 12 13 14 15 16 17 18 19 20 21 22 23 24

17760 UNITED KINGDOM
(con'd)　†BBC, Via Thailand
- W • E Asia • 250 kW
- E Asia • 250 kW
- S • E Asia • 250 kW

USA
　FAMILY RADIO, Okeechobee, Fl
- W • W North Am • 100 kW
- W • Europe • 100 kW

17765 CANADA
　R CANADA INTL, Sackville, NB
- W F-Su • S America • 250 kW

USA
　VOA, Via Philippines
- S • E Asia • 250 kW

VATICAN STATE
　†VATICAN RADIO, Sta Maria di Galeria
- W Su • Mideast & W Asia • 250 kW
- W Su • SE Asia • 500 kW
- W F • Mideast • 250 kW

17770 GERMANY
　†DEUTSCHE WELLE, Via Ascension
- W • S America • 250 kW

　†DEUTSCHE WELLE, Via Kigali, Rwanda
- S • W Africa • 250 kW

　†DEUTSCHE WELLE, Via Sri Lanka
- S • E Asia • 250 kW

PHILIPPINES
　†RADYO PILIPINAS, Tinang
- W • ENGLISH & TAGALOG • S Asia & Mideast • 250 kW

ROMANIA
　R ROMANIA INTL, Bucharest
- S • Australasia • 250 kW

SOUTH AFRICA
　CHANNEL AFRICA, Meyerton
- E Africa • 500 kW

SPAIN
　R EXTERIOR ESPANA, Noblejas
- Australasia • 350 kW
- M • N Africa & Mideast • 350 kW

USA
　RFE-RL, Via Udon Thani, Thailand
- S • W Asia & C Asia • 250 kW

　VOA, Via Udon Thani, Thailand
- W • S Asia • 500 kW

17775 AUSTRALIA
　RADIO AUSTRALIA, Darwin
- SE Asia • 250 kW

ROMANIA
　RADIO ROMANIA, Bucharest
- W Su • Mideast • 250 kW

　RADIO ROMANIA, Galbeni
- W Su • W Asia & S Asia • 250 kW

SAUDI ARABIA
　BS OF THE KINGDOM, Riyadh
- W Africa & C Africa • 500 kW

USA
　KVOH, Rancho Simi, Ca
- C America • 50 kW

17780 IRAN
　VO THE ISLAMIC REP, Sirjan
- W • C Asia & E Asia • 500 kW

JAPAN
　†RADIO JAPAN, Via Sri Lanka
- W • Mideast & W Asia • 300 kW
- Mideast & N Africa • 300 kW

ROMANIA
　R ROMANIA INTL, Bucharest
- S • E Asia • 250 kW

　R ROMANIA INTL, Galbeni
- W • Australasia • 250 kW

SOUTH AFRICA
　CHANNEL AFRICA, Meyerton
- E Africa • 250 kW

UNITED KINGDOM
　BBC, Via Ascension
- W Africa • 250 kW

USA
　R FREE ASIA, Via Kuwait
- S • S Asia • 250 kW

　VOA, Via Tinian, N Marianas
- S • E Asia • 250 kW

17785 AUSTRALIA
　RADIO AUSTRALIA, Shepparton
- Pacific & N America • 100 kW

IRAN
　VO THE ISLAMIC REP, Sirjan
- S • S Europe & N Africa • 500 kW

SAUDI ARABIA
　BS OF THE KINGDOM, Riyadh
- W Africa & C Africa • 500 kW

USA
　VOA, Via Briech, Morocco
- W Sa • C Africa & E Africa • 250 kW
- S • C Africa • 250 kW
- S • W Africa & C Africa • 250 kW

17790 ROMANIA
　R ROMANIA INTL, Bucharest
- W • N Africa • 250 kW

UNITED KINGDOM
　BBC, Via A'Seela, Oman
- S Asia • 250 kW

　†BBC, Via Thailand
- S • E Asia • 250 kW
- S Asia • 250 kW

17795 AUSTRALIA
　RADIO AUSTRALIA, Shepparton
- Pacific & W North Am • 100 kW

UNITED KINGDOM
　BBC, Skelton, Cumbria
- S • N Africa • 300 kW

USA
　FAMILY RADIO, Okeechobee, Fl
- S • W North Am • 100 kW

17800 FRANCE
(con'd)　†R FRANCE INTL, Issoudun
- S M-F • E Africa • 500 kW

	0 1 2 3 4 5 6 7 8 9 10 11 12 13 14 15 16 17 18 19 20 21 22 23 24

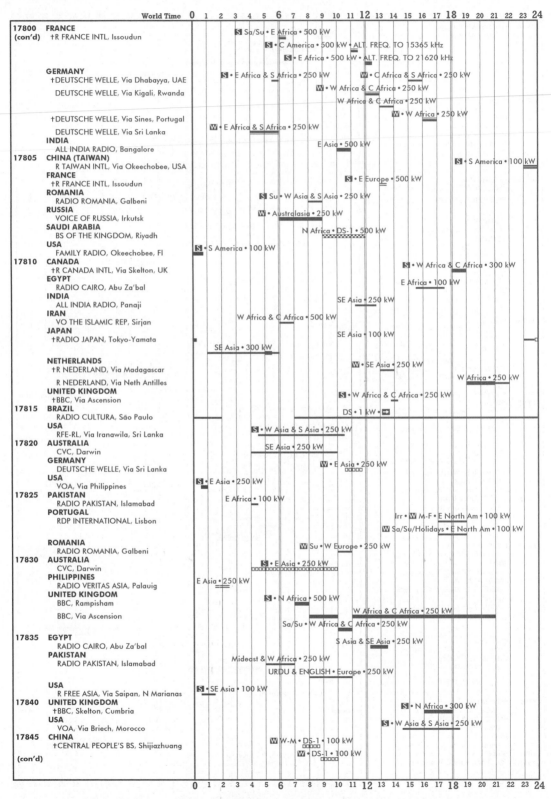

World Time 0 1 2 3 4 5 6 7 8 9 10 11 12 13 14 15 16 17 18 19 20 21 22 23 24

17800 FRANCE
(con'd) †R FRANCE INTL, Issoudun — S • Sa/Su • E Africa • 500 kW
— S • C America • 500 kW • ALT. FREQ. TO 15365 kHz
— S • E Africa • 500 kW • ALT. FREQ. TO 21620 kHz

GERMANY
†DEUTSCHE WELLE, Via Dhabayya, UAE — S • E Africa & S Africa • 250 kW — W • C Africa & S Africa • 250 kW
DEUTSCHE WELLE, Via Kigali, Rwanda — W • W Africa & C Africa • 250 kW
W Africa & C Africa • 250 kW

†DEUTSCHE WELLE, Via Sines, Portugal — W • W Africa • 250 kW
DEUTSCHE WELLE, Via Sri Lanka — W • E Africa & S Africa • 250 kW

INDIA
ALL INDIA RADIO, Bangalore — E Asia • 500 kW

17805 CHINA (TAIWAN)
R TAIWAN INTL, Via Okeechobee, USA — S • S America • 100 kW

FRANCE
†R FRANCE INTL, Issoudun — S • E Europe • 500 kW

ROMANIA
RADIO ROMANIA, Galbeni — S • Su • W Asia & S Asia • 250 kW

RUSSIA
VOICE OF RUSSIA, Irkutsk — W • Australasia • 250 kW

SAUDI ARABIA
BS OF THE KINGDOM, Riyadh — N Africa • DS-1 • 500 kW

USA
FAMILY RADIO, Okeechobee, Fl — S • S America • 100 kW

17810 CANADA
†R CANADA INTL, Via Skelton, UK — S • W Africa & C Africa • 300 kW

EGYPT
RADIO CAIRO, Abu Za'bal — E Africa • 100 kW

INDIA
ALL INDIA RADIO, Panaji — SE Asia • 250 kW

IRAN
VO THE ISLAMIC REP, Sirjan — W Africa & C Africa • 500 kW

JAPAN
†RADIO JAPAN, Tokyo-Yamata — SE Asia • 100 kW
— SE Asia • 300 kW

NETHERLANDS
†R NEDERLAND, Via Madagascar — W • SE Asia • 250 kW
R NEDERLAND, Via Neth Antilles — W Africa • 250 kW

UNITED KINGDOM
†BBC, Via Ascension — S • W Africa & C Africa • 250 kW

17815 BRAZIL
RADIO CULTURA, São Paulo — DS • 1 kW • →

USA
RFE-RL, Via Iranawila, Sri Lanka — S • W Asia & S Asia • 250 kW

17820 AUSTRALIA
CVC, Darwin — SE Asia • 250 kW

GERMANY
DEUTSCHE WELLE, Via Sri Lanka — W • E Asia • 250 kW

USA
VOA, Via Philippines — S • E Asia • 250 kW

17825 PAKISTAN
RADIO PAKISTAN, Islamabad — E Africa • 100 kW

PORTUGAL
RDP INTERNATIONAL, Lisbon — Irr • W • M-F • E North Am • 100 kW
— W • Sa/Su/Holidays • E North Am • 100 kW

ROMANIA
RADIO ROMANIA, Galbeni — W • Su • W Europe • 250 kW

17830 AUSTRALIA
CVC, Darwin — S • E Asia • 250 kW

PHILIPPINES
RADIO VERITAS ASIA, Palauig — E Asia • 250 kW

UNITED KINGDOM
BBC, Rampisham — S • N Africa • 500 kW
BBC, Via Ascension — W Africa & C Africa • 250 kW
— Sa/Su • W Africa & C Africa • 250 kW
— S Asia & SE Asia • 250 kW

17835 EGYPT
RADIO CAIRO, Abu Za'bal — Mideast & W Africa • 250 kW

PAKISTAN
RADIO PAKISTAN, Islamabad — URDU & ENGLISH • Europe • 250 kW

USA
R FREE ASIA, Via Saipan, N Marianas — S • SE Asia • 100 kW

17840 UNITED KINGDOM
†BBC, Skelton, Cumbria — S • N Africa • 300 kW

USA
VOA, Via Briech, Morocco — S • W Asia & S Asia • 250 kW

17845 CHINA
†CENTRAL PEOPLE'S BS, Shijiazhuang — W • W-M • DS-1 • 100 kW
— W • DS-1 • 100 kW

(con'd)

0 1 2 3 4 5 6 7 8 9 10 11 12 13 14 15 16 17 18 19 20 21 22 23 24

ENGLISH ■■ ARABIC ⸝⸝⸝ CHINESE □□□ FRENCH ▬▬ GERMAN ▬ ▬ RUSSIAN = = SPANISH ≡≡ OTHER —

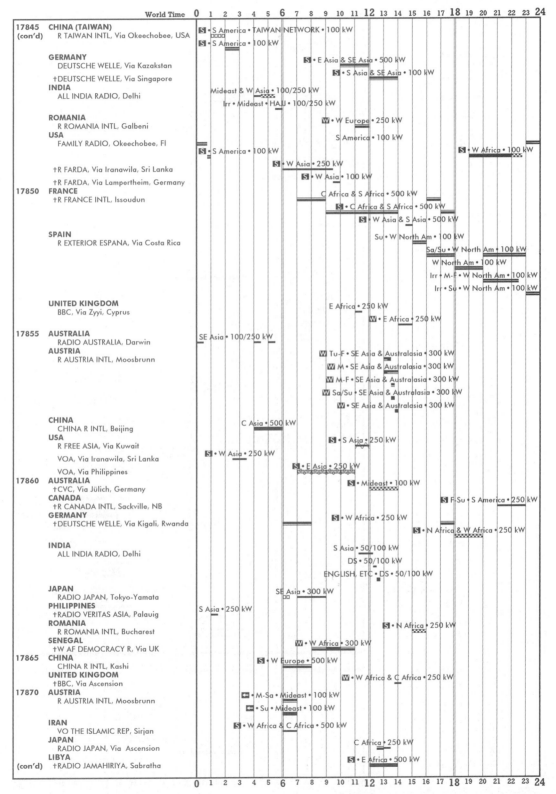

	World Time	0 1 2 3 4 5 6 7 8 9 10 11 12 13 14 15 16 17 18 19 20 21 22 23 24

17845 (con'd) CHINA (TAIWAN)
R TAIWAN INTL, Via Okeechobee, USA
- S • S America • TAIWAN NETWORK • 100 kW
- S • S America • 100 kW

GERMANY
DEUTSCHE WELLE, Via Kazakstan
- S • E Asia & SE Asia • 500 kW

†DEUTSCHE WELLE, Via Singapore
- S • S Asia & SE Asia • 100 kW

INDIA
ALL INDIA RADIO, Delhi
- Mideast & W Asia • 100/250 kW
- Irr • Mideast • HAJJ • 100/250 kW

ROMANIA
R ROMANIA INTL, Galbeni
- W • W Europe • 250 kW

USA
FAMILY RADIO, Okeechobee, Fl
- S America • 100 kW
- S • S America • 100 kW
- S • W Africa • 100 kW

†R FARDA, Via Iranawila, Sri Lanka
- S • W Asia • 250 kW

†R FARDA, Via Lampertheim, Germany
- S • W Asia • 100 kW

17850 FRANCE
†R FRANCE INTL, Issoudun
- C Africa & S Africa • 500 kW
- S • C Africa & S Africa • 500 kW
- S • W Asia & S Asia • 500 kW

SPAIN
R EXTERIOR ESPANA, Via Costa Rica
- Su • W North Am • 100 kW
- Sa/Su • W North Am • 100 kW
- W North Am • 100 kW
- Irr • M-F • W North Am • 100 kW
- Irr • Su • W North Am • 100 kW

UNITED KINGDOM
BBC, Via Zyyi, Cyprus
- E Africa • 250 kW
- W • E Africa • 250 kW

17855 AUSTRALIA
RADIO AUSTRALIA, Darwin
- SE Asia • 100/250 kW

AUSTRIA
R AUSTRIA INTL, Moosbrunn
- W Tu-F • SE Asia & Australasia • 300 kW
- W M • SE Asia & Australasia • 300 kW
- W M-F • SE Asia & Australasia • 300 kW
- W Sa/Su • SE Asia & Australasia • 300 kW
- W • SE Asia & Australasia • 300 kW

CHINA
CHINA R INTL, Beijing
- C Asia • 500 kW

USA
R FREE ASIA, Via Kuwait
- S • S Asia • 250 kW

VOA, Via Iranawila, Sri Lanka
- S • W Asia • 250 kW

VOA, Via Philippines
- S • E Asia • 250 kW

17860 AUSTRALIA
†CVC, Via Jülich, Germany
- S • Mideast • 100 kW

CANADA
†R CANADA INTL, Sackville, NB
- F-Su • S America • 250 kW

GERMANY
†DEUTSCHE WELLE, Via Kigali, Rwanda
- S • W Africa • 250 kW
- S • N Africa & W Africa • 250 kW

INDIA
ALL INDIA RADIO, Delhi
- S Asia • 50/100 kW
- DS • 50/100 kW
- ENGLISH, ETC • DS • 50/100 kW

JAPAN
RADIO JAPAN, Tokyo-Yamata
- SE Asia • 300 kW

PHILIPPINES
†RADIO VERITAS ASIA, Palauig
- S Asia • 250 kW

ROMANIA
R ROMANIA INTL, Bucharest
- S • N Africa • 250 kW

SENEGAL
†W AF DEMOCRACY R, Via UK
- W • W Africa • 300 kW

17865 CHINA
CHINA R INTL, Kashi
- S • W Europe • 500 kW

UNITED KINGDOM
†BBC, Via Ascension
- W • W Africa & C Africa • 250 kW

17870 AUSTRIA
R AUSTRIA INTL, Moosbrunn
- M-Sa • Mideast • 100 kW
- Su • Mideast • 100 kW

IRAN
VO THE ISLAMIC REP, Sirjan
- S • W Africa & C Africa • 500 kW

JAPAN
RADIO JAPAN, Via Ascension
- C Africa • 250 kW

LIBYA (con'd)
†RADIO JAMAHIRIYA, Sabratha
- S • E Africa • 500 kW

	0 1 2 3 4 5 6 7 8 9 10 11 12 13 14 15 16 17 18 19 20 21 22 23 24

SEASONAL S OR W   1-HR TIMESHIFT MIDYEAR ⇦ OR ⇨   JAMMING / OR ∧   EARLIEST HEARD ◁   LATEST HEARD ▷   NEW FOR 2008 †

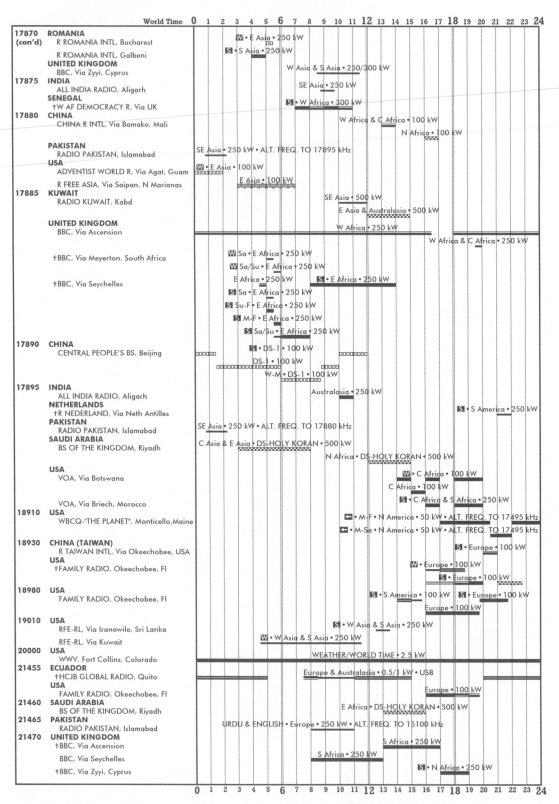

World Time	0 1 2 3 4 5 6 7 8 9 10 11 12 13 14 15 16 17 18 19 20 21 22 23 24

17870 ROMANIA
(con'd)   R ROMANIA INTL, Bucharest — W • E Asia • 250 kW
           R ROMANIA INTL, Galbeni — S • S Asia • 250 kW
       UNITED KINGDOM
           BBC, Via Zyyi, Cyprus — W Asia & S Asia • 250/300 kW
17875 INDIA
           ALL INDIA RADIO, Aligarh — SE Asia • 250 kW
       SENEGAL
           †W AF DEMOCRACY R, Via UK — S • W Africa • 300 kW
17880 CHINA
           CHINA R INTL, Via Bamako, Mali — W Africa & C Africa • 100 kW
                                          N Africa • 100 kW
       PAKISTAN
           RADIO PAKISTAN, Islamabad — SE Asia • 250 kW • ALT. FREQ. TO 17895 kHz
       USA
           ADVENTIST WORLD R, Via Agat, Guam — W • E Asia • 100 kW
           R FREE ASIA, Via Saipan, N Marianas — E Asia • 100 kW
17885 KUWAIT
           RADIO KUWAIT, Kabd — SE Asia • 500 kW
                              E Asia & Australasia • 500 kW
       UNITED KINGDOM
           BBC, Via Ascension — W Africa • 250 kW
                              W Africa & C Africa • 250 kW
           †BBC, Via Meyerton, South Africa — W Sa • E Africa • 250 kW
                                              W Sa/Su • E Africa • 250 kW
           †BBC, Via Seychelles — E Africa • 250 kW   S • E Africa • 250 kW
                                S Sa • E Africa • 250 kW
                                S Su-F • E Africa • 250 kW
                                S M-F • E Africa • 250 kW
                                S Sa/Su • E Africa • 250 kW
17890 CHINA
           CENTRAL PEOPLE'S BS, Beijing — S • DS-1 • 100 kW
                                          DS-1 • 100 kW
                                          W-M • DS-1 • 100 kW
17895 INDIA
           ALL INDIA RADIO, Aligarh — Australasia • 250 kW
       NETHERLANDS
           †R NEDERLAND, Via Neth Antilles — S • S America • 250 kW
       PAKISTAN
           RADIO PAKISTAN, Islamabad — SE Asia • 250 kW • ALT. FREQ. TO 17880 kHz
       SAUDI ARABIA
           BS OF THE KINGDOM, Riyadh — C Asia & E Asia • DS-HOLY KORAN • 500 kW
                                       N Africa • DS-HOLY KORAN • 500 kW
       USA
           VOA, Via Botswana — W • C Africa • 100 kW
                             C Africa • 100 kW
                             S • C Africa & S Africa • 250 kW
           VOA, Via Briech, Morocco
18910 USA
           WBCQ-"THE PLANET", Monticello, Maine — M-F • N America • 50 kW • ALT. FREQ. TO 17495 kHz
                                                  M-Sa • N America • 50 kW • ALT. FREQ. TO 17495 kHz
18930 CHINA (TAIWAN)
           R TAIWAN INTL, Via Okeechobee, USA — S • Europe • 100 kW
       USA
           †FAMILY RADIO, Okeechobee, Fl — W • Europe • 100 kW
                                          S • Europe • 100 kW
18980 USA
           FAMILY RADIO, Okeechobee, Fl — S • S America • 100 kW   S • Europe • 100 kW
                                          Europe • 100 kW
19010 USA
           RFE-RL, Via Iranawila, Sri Lanka — S • W Asia & S Asia • 250 kW
           RFE-RL, Via Kuwait — W • W Asia & S Asia • 250 kW
20000 USA
           WWV, Fort Collins, Colorado — WEATHER/WORLD TIME • 2.5 kW
21455 ECUADOR
           †HCJB GLOBAL RADIO, Quito — Europe & Australasia • 0.5/1 kW • USB
       USA
           FAMILY RADIO, Okeechobee, Fl — Europe • 100 kW
21460 SAUDI ARABIA
           BS OF THE KINGDOM, Riyadh — E Africa • DS-HOLY KORAN • 500 kW
21465 PAKISTAN
           RADIO PAKISTAN, Islamabad — URDU & ENGLISH • Europe • 250 kW • ALT. FREQ. TO 15100 kHz
21470 UNITED KINGDOM
           †BBC, Via Ascension — S Africa • 250 kW
           BBC, Via Seychelles — S Africa • 250 kW
           †BBC, Via Zyyi, Cyprus — S • N Africa • 250 kW

	0 1 2 3 4 5 6 7 8 9 10 11 12 13 14 15 16 17 18 19 20 21 22 23 24

ENGLISH ■■■   ARABIC ⬚⬚⬚   CHINESE ┅┅┅   FRENCH ▬▬   GERMAN ══   RUSSIAN ══   SPANISH ▬▬   OTHER ──

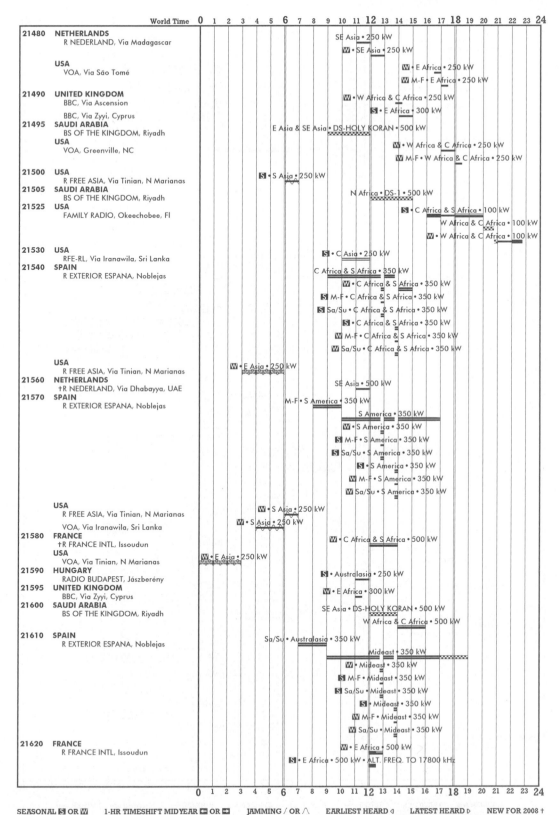

		World Time			
21480	**NETHERLANDS**	R NEDERLAND, Via Madagascar		SE Asia • 250 kW	
				W • SE Asia • 250 kW	
	USA	VOA, Via São Tomé		W • E Africa • 250 kW	
				W M-F • E Africa • 250 kW	
21490	**UNITED KINGDOM**	BBC, Via Ascension		W • W Africa & C Africa • 250 kW	
		BBC, Via Zyyi, Cyprus		S • E Africa • 300 kW	
21495	**SAUDI ARABIA**	BS OF THE KINGDOM, Riyadh	E Asia & SE Asia • DS-HOLY KORAN • 500 kW		
	USA	VOA, Greenville, NC		W • W Africa & C Africa • 250 kW	
				W M-F • W Africa & C Africa • 250 kW	
21500	**USA**	R FREE ASIA, Via Tinian, N Marianas	S • S Asia • 250 kW		
21505	**SAUDI ARABIA**	BS OF THE KINGDOM, Riyadh		N Africa • DS-1 • 500 kW	
21525	**USA**	FAMILY RADIO, Okeechobee, Fl		S • C Africa & S Africa • 100 kW	
				W Africa & C Africa • 100 kW	
				W • W Africa & C Africa • 100 kW	
21530	**USA**	RFE-RL, Via Iranawila, Sri Lanka	S • C Asia • 250 kW		
21540	**SPAIN**	R EXTERIOR ESPANA, Noblejas	C Africa & S Africa • 350 kW		
			W • C Africa & S Africa • 350 kW		
			S M-F • C Africa & S Africa • 350 kW		
			S Sa/Su • C Africa & S Africa • 350 kW		
			S • C Africa & S Africa • 350 kW		
			W M-F • C Africa & S Africa • 350 kW		
			W Sa/Su • C Africa & S Africa • 350 kW		
	USA	R FREE ASIA, Via Tinian, N Marianas	W • E Asia • 250 kW		
21560	**NETHERLANDS**	†R NEDERLAND, Via Dhabayya, UAE		SE Asia • 500 kW	
21570	**SPAIN**	R EXTERIOR ESPANA, Noblejas	M-F • S America • 350 kW		
				S America • 350 kW	
			W • S America • 350 kW		
			S M-F • S America • 350 kW		
			S Sa/Su • S America • 350 kW		
			S • S America • 350 kW		
			W M-F • S America • 350 kW		
			W Sa/Su • S America • 350 kW		
	USA	R FREE ASIA, Via Tinian, N Marianas	W • S Asia • 250 kW		
		VOA, Via Iranawila, Sri Lanka	W • S Asia • 250 kW		
21580	**FRANCE**	†R FRANCE INTL, Issoudun	W • C Africa & S Africa • 500 kW		
	USA	VOA, Via Tinian, N Marianas	W • E Asia • 250 kW		
21590	**HUNGARY**	RADIO BUDAPEST, Jászberény	S • Australasia • 250 kW		
21595	**UNITED KINGDOM**	BBC, Via Zyyi, Cyprus	W • E Africa • 300 kW		
21600	**SAUDI ARABIA**	BS OF THE KINGDOM, Riyadh	SE Asia • DS-HOLY KORAN • 500 kW		
			W Africa & C Africa • 500 kW		
21610	**SPAIN**	R EXTERIOR ESPANA, Noblejas	Sa/Su • Australasia • 350 kW		
				Mideast • 350 kW	
			W • Mideast • 350 kW		
			S M-F • Mideast • 350 kW		
			S Sa/Su • Mideast • 350 kW		
			S • Mideast • 350 kW		
			W M-F • Mideast • 350 kW		
			W Sa/Su • Mideast • 350 kW		
21620	**FRANCE**	R FRANCE INTL, Issoudun	W • E Africa • 500 kW		
			S • E Africa • 500 kW • ALT. FREQ. TO 17800 kHz		

SEASONAL **S** OR **W**   1-HR TIMESHIFT MIDYEAR ⊂ OR ⊃   JAMMING / OR /\   EARLIEST HEARD ◁   LATEST HEARD ▷   NEW FOR 2008 †

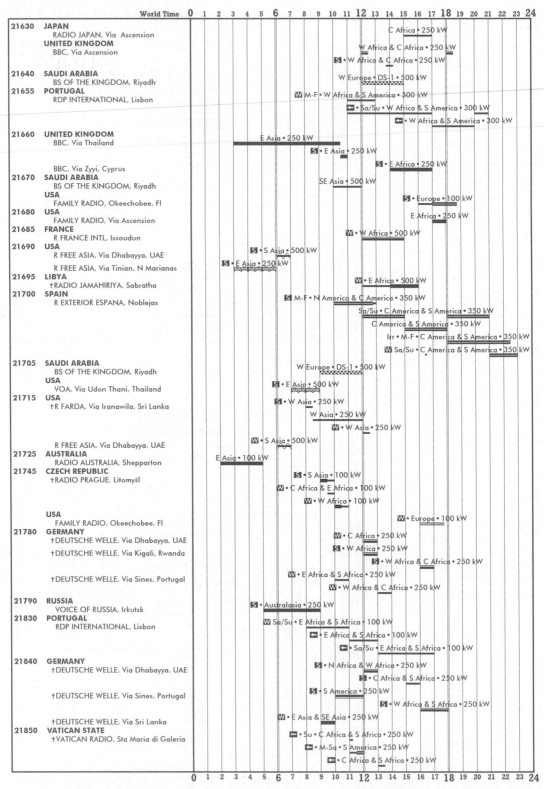

21630	**JAPAN** — RADIO JAPAN, Via Ascension — C Africa • 250 kW
	UNITED KINGDOM — BBC, Via Ascension — W Africa & C Africa • 250 kW / S • W Africa & C Africa • 250 kW
21640	**SAUDI ARABIA** — BS OF THE KINGDOM, Riyadh — W Europe • DS-1 • 500 kW
21655	**PORTUGAL** — RDP INTERNATIONAL, Lisbon — M-F • W Africa & S America • 300 kW / Sa/Su • W Africa & S America • 300 kW / W Africa & S America • 300 kW
21660	**UNITED KINGDOM** — BBC, Via Thailand — E Asia • 250 kW / S • E Asia • 250 kW / S • E Africa • 250 kW
	BBC, Via Zyyi, Cyprus
21670	**SAUDI ARABIA** — BS OF THE KINGDOM, Riyadh — SE Asia • 500 kW
	USA — FAMILY RADIO, Okeechobee, Fl — S • Europe • 100 kW
21680	**USA** — FAMILY RADIO, Via Ascension — E Africa • 250 kW
21685	**FRANCE** — R FRANCE INTL, Issoudun — W • W Africa • 500 kW
21690	**USA** — R FREE ASIA, Via Dhabayya, UAE — S • S Asia • 500 kW
	R FREE ASIA, Via Tinian, N Marianas — S • E Asia • 250 kW
21695	**LIBYA** — †RADIO JAMAHIRIYA, Sabratha — W • E Africa • 500 kW
21700	**SPAIN** — R EXTERIOR ESPANA, Noblejas — M-F • N America & C America • 350 kW / Sa/Su • C America & S America • 350 kW / C America & S America • 350 kW / Irr • M-F • C America & S America • 350 kW / W Sa/Su • C America & S America • 350 kW
21705	**SAUDI ARABIA** — BS OF THE KINGDOM, Riyadh — W Europe • DS-1 • 500 kW
	USA — VOA, Via Udon Thani, Thailand — S • E Asia • 500 kW
21715	**USA** — †R FARDA, Via Iranawila, Sri Lanka — S • W Asia • 250 kW / W Asia • 250 kW / W • W Asia • 250 kW
	R FREE ASIA, Via Dhabayya, UAE — W • S Asia • 500 kW
21725	**AUSTRALIA** — RADIO AUSTRALIA, Shepparton — E Asia • 100 kW
21745	**CZECH REPUBLIC** — †RADIO PRAGUE, Litomyšl — S • S Asia • 100 kW / W • C Africa & E Africa • 100 kW / W • W Africa • 100 kW
	USA — FAMILY RADIO, Okeechobee, Fl — W • Europe • 100 kW
21780	**GERMANY** — †DEUTSCHE WELLE, Via Dhabayya, UAE — W • C Africa • 250 kW
	†DEUTSCHE WELLE, Via Kigali, Rwanda — S • W Africa • 250 kW / S • W Africa & C Africa • 250 kW
	†DEUTSCHE WELLE, Via Sines, Portugal — W • E Africa & S Africa • 250 kW / W • W Africa & C Africa • 250 kW
21790	**RUSSIA** — VOICE OF RUSSIA, Irkutsk — S • Australasia • 250 kW
21830	**PORTUGAL** — RDP INTERNATIONAL, Lisbon — W Sa/Su • E Africa & S Africa • 100 kW / E Africa & S Africa • 100 kW / Sa/Su • E Africa & S Africa • 100 kW
21840	**GERMANY** — †DEUTSCHE WELLE, Via Dhabayya, UAE — S • N Africa & W Africa • 250 kW / S • C Africa & S Africa • 250 kW
	†DEUTSCHE WELLE, Via Sines, Portugal — S • S America • 250 kW / S • W Africa & S Africa • 250 kW
	†DEUTSCHE WELLE, Via Sri Lanka — W • E Asia & SE Asia • 250 kW
21850	**VATICAN STATE** — †VATICAN RADIO, Sta Maria di Galeria — Su • C Africa & S Africa • 250 kW / M-Sa • S America • 250 kW / C Africa & S Africa • 250 kW

ENGLISH ▬ ARABIC ▨ CHINESE ▫▫▫ FRENCH ▭ GERMAN ▭ RUSSIAN ═ SPANISH ▭ OTHER —